Strategic Human Resource Management

Fourth Edition

Strategic Human Resource Management

Jeffrey A. Mello

Fourth Edition

CENGAGE
Learning®

Australia • Brazil • Mexico • Singapore • United Kingdom • United States

Strategic Human Resource Management, Fourth Edition
Jeffrey A. Mello

Senior Vice President, Global Product Management: Jack W. Calhoun

Vice President, General Manager, Social Science & Qualitative Business: Erin Joyner

Product Director: Mike Schenk

Senior Product Manager: Michael Roche

Content Developer: Christopher Santos

Product Assistant: Megan Fischer

Brand Manager: Robin Lefevre

Market Development Manager: Emily Horowitz

Marketing Coordinator: Michael Saver

Art and Cover Direction, Production Management, and Composition: PreMediaGlobal

Senior Media Developer: John Rich

Rights Acquisition Director: Audrey Pettengill

Rights Acquisition Specialist, Text and Image: Amber Hosea

Manufacturing Planner: Ron Montgomery

Cover/Internal Image: Novastock/Age Fotostock/Getty Images

For product information and technology assistance, contact us at
Cengage Learning Customer & Sales Support, 1-800-354-9706

For permission to use material from this text or product, submit all requests online at **www.cengage.com/permissions**
Further permissions questions can be emailed to
permissionrequest@cengage.com

Library of Congress Control Number: 2013947154

ISBN-13: 978-1-285-42679-2

ISBN-10: 1-285-42679-7

Cengage Learning
200 First Stamford Place, 4th Floor
Stamford, CT 06902
USA

Cengage Learning is a leading provider of customized learning solutions with office locations around the globe, including Singapore, the United Kingdom, Australia, Mexico, Brazil, and Japan. Locate your local office at **www.cengage.com/global**

Cengage Learning products are represented in Canada by Nelson Education, Ltd.

To learn more about Cengage Learning Solutions, visit **www.cengage.com**

Purchase any of our products at your local college store or at our preferred online store **www.cengagebrain.com**

Printed in the United States of America
1 2 3 4 5 6 7 17 16 15 14 13

To my amazing daughter Logan
and my equally amazing parents,
Gabe and Lorraine

BRIEF CONTENTS

CONTENTS

Part two

Implementation of Strategic Human Resource Management

PREFACE

Since the publication of the third edition of this text, heightened attention continues to be shown and greater appreciation paid toward the value of strategic human resource management in organizations. Boards of Directors, business owners, stockholders and senior executives are gaining a greater understanding of the relationship between HR and organizational, market and financial performance as cutting-edge research illustrates the connection between HR practices and firm performance.

Scholarly HR-related publications continue to thrive, while practitioner-oriented management publications—traditionally dominated by articles focused on marketing and finance—are publishing an increasingly significant number of articles on human resource management, particularly strategic aspects of HR. Within the academy, there continues to be a significant increase in the number of HR-related articles in journals focused on general management and even those related to strategy. No longer is HR simply relegated to specialized journals that deal with HR. This significant movement toward the publication of more HR-focused articles in both the general management academic and practitioner literatures illustrates clearly that executives are realizing the role HR plays in an organization's success as well as the fact die HR is a general management responsibility and its effective practice a key to successful operating results.

Also since the publication of the third edition, the resources that are available to those of us who teach have greatly expanded. The Society for Human Resource Management, the world's largest HR professional association, has continued to develop programs and materials to support HR education which include 1) curriculum guidebooks and templates for both undergraduate and graduate programs; 2) dozens of cases and learning modules to assist with course design and delivery; and 3) a significant database of the latest research and position papers on critical issues in strategic HR, which allow instructors to remain very current on trends, best practices, and legislative and court activity. Much of this material is available to non-members at the SHRM website, www.shrm.org, under Resources for HR Educators, which is under the Education and Certification tab. In addition, the *Journal of Human Resources Education (JHRE),* continues to publish exciting original work which supports HR education.

Organization and Content

Strategic Human Resource Management, 4e is designed for: 1) graduate students enrolled in survey courses in human resource management who would benefit from a general management approach to strategic HR; 2) working professionals enrolled in specialized HR and executive programs as a capstone offering; and 3) undergraduate students enrolled in a capstone course in an HR degree program or those seeking an advanced level HR course to complement their strategy course.

The text is organized into two sections. The first section, Chapters 1-7, examines the context of strategic HR and develops a framework and conceptual model for the practice of strategic HR. The chapters in this section examine employees as "investments;" explore trends that affect human resource management practice; describe what strategic HR is, particularly in contrast to more traditional approaches to HR; and look at how both the design of work systems and relevant employment laws influence the practice of managing people in organizations. The second section, Chapters 8-14, examines the actual practice and implementation of strategic HR through a discussion of strategic issues that need to be addressed while developing specific programs and policies related to the traditional functional areas of HR. Covered within this section are strategic issues related to staffing, training, performance management, compensation, labor relations, employee separation, and managing a global workforce. Both the integrative framework that requires linkage between and consistency among these functional HR activities and the approach toward writing about these traditional functional areas from a strategic perspective distinguish the text from what is currently on the market.

Chapter Features

All chapters contain the following:

- an opening "in practice" vignette featuring a well-known organization to introduce the chapter topic as well as numerous additional vignettes within each chapter that illustrate pertinent chapter concepts
- carefully selected readings that are integrated within the text discussion
- end-of-chapter discussion questions and exercises designed to apply chapter content and facilitate discussion of issues

New to the Fourth Edition

As the field of strategic human resource management has evolved since the third edition, this text has similarly done so in response. More than 50 percent of the end-of chapter readings are new to this edition. The retained readings are those that have become "classics" and are presented alongside those that represent the latest in thinking and practice in human resource management. There are also numerous new original exhibits that explain chapter concepts; 22 new "in practice" vignettes that describe strategic HR practices in a wide variety of organizations; and 117 new references.

There is also significant new content in each of the 14 chapters. This includes, but is not limited to, new or greatly expanded coverage of the roles and uses of social networking and social media in strategic human resource management; legal and legislative updates with the latest court rulings on existing laws and coverage of the Dodd-Frank Act, Genetic Information Nondiscrimination Act, right-to-work legislation and same-sex marriage and their implications for human resource management; and competency models, CEO succession planning, sustainability, employment branding, customer relationship management, trust and engagement as components of job satisfaction, "hiring for fit" and alumni relations management.

Instructor's Resources

Also available are an Instructor's Manual and PowerPoint slides to accompany the book which were prepared by the author. They can be accessed visiting www.CengageBrain.com. The Instructor's Manual includes chapter outlines, answers to end-of-chapter content, and suggested topics for student papers, while the PowerPoint slides offers all main text concepts to encourage classroom discussion and classroom engagement.

Acknowledgments

Many individuals were instrumental in ensuring the success of the first three editions of this text as well as the development of this fourth edition. Professional staff members of Cengage, especially Charles McCormack, Joe Sabatino, Mardell Glinski-Shultz, Daniel Noguera, Michele Rhoades and Mike Roche have provided much-appreciated support for this project since its inception. Chris Santos has become a welcome and valued team member in assuming the developmental work for this edition.

I again owe a tremendous debt of gratitude to some close longtime personal friends who have careers in HR—both in academia and/or as senior executives—and have been generous with their time and expertise in allowing me to seek their advice on various ideas I have had for this project. Sincere thanks to Jan Aspelund, David Balkin, Brian Brown, John Cunningham, Jeff Friant and Harsh Luthar with an extra special thanks to Deb Cohen also wish to thank the following reviewers for the feedback and valuable recommendations they provided that greatly assisted me in the development of this edition: Yezdi Godiwalla, University of Wisconsin-Whitewater; Tracy Porter, Cleveland State University; William Kostner, Doane College; Wayne Davis, Webster University; Xuguang Guo, University of Wisconsin-Whitewater; Timothy Wiedman, Doane College; Linda Gibson, Pacific Lutheran University;Jim Maddox, Friends University; Julie Palmer-Schuyler, Webster University.

Finally, heartfelt thanks to my family for the unconditional love and support they provide.

Jeffrey A. Mello

ABOUT THE AUTHOR

Jeffrey A. Mello
Siena College

Jeffrey A. Mello is Dean of the School of Business and Professor of Business Law and Management at Siena College. He has held faculty and administrative positions at Barry University, Towson University, the George Washington University, the University of California at Berkeley, Golden Gate University and Northeastern University, from where he received his Ph.D. He has been a recipient of the David L. Bradford Outstanding Educator Award, presented by the Organizational Behavior Teaching Society, and has received international, national, and institutional awards for his research, teaching, and service. He has authored five books and published more than one hundred book chapters, journal articles, and conference papers in journals such as the JOURNAL OF BUSINESS ETHICS, BUSINESS HORIZONS, INTERNATIONAL JOURNAL OF PUBLIC ADMINISTRATION, BUSINESS & SOCIETY REVIEW, JOURNAL OF EMPLOYMENT DISCRIMINATION LAW, SETON HALL LEGISLATIVE JOURNAL, JOURNAL OF INDIVIDUAL EMPLOYMENT RIGHTS, PUBLIC PERSONNEL MANAGEMENT, EMPLOYEE RESPONSIBILITIES AND RIGHTS JOURNAL, LABOR LAW JOURNAL, JOURNAL OF LAW AND BUSINESS, and the JOURNAL OF MANAGEMENT EDUCATION. He has served as an editor for the JOURNAL OF MANAGEMENT EDUCATION, JOURNAL OF LEGAL STUDIES EDUCATION and EMPLOYEE RESPONSIBILITIES AND RIGHTS JOURNAL as well as on numerous editorial boards. He is a member of the Academy of Legal Studies in Business, Organizational Behavior Teaching Society, Society for Human Resource Management, and Academy of Management.

The Context of Strategic Human Resource Management

PART 1

CHAPTER 1

An Investment Perspective of Human Resource Management

LEARNING OBJECTIVES

- Understand the sources of employee value
- Gain an appreciation of the importance of human capital and how it can be measured
- Understand how competitive advantage can be achieved through investment in employees
- Gain an appreciation of metrics, their measures, and their usefulness
- Understand the obstacles that prevent organizations from investing in their employees

Human Resources at Nordstrom

How can a retailer gain a competitive advantage in a cut-throat marketplace? Middle- and high-end retailers generally locate in close proximity to each other and often carry similar—but not identical—merchandise. Consequently their sales and profit margins are usually in tandem. Nordstrom, however, has consistently produced above-industry-average profits and continues to be profitable when its competitors' profits are falling or flat.

The key to Nordstrom's success lies with the different way it manages its employees. Sales employees are known as "associates" and considered the organization's most valuable asset. The company's success is rooted in its strategy of providing superlative customer service. Associates are encouraged to act as entrepreneurs and build strong personal relationships with customers, or "clients." In fact, many clients shop only with a particular Nordstrom associate and call in advance to determine the associates' schedules or to make appointments.

Nordstrom's strategy involves a heavy investment in the organization's sales force. Nordstrom provides associates with extensive training on merchandising and product lines and offers high compensation. Its commitment to its employees is evident from the fact that the company's organization chart is depicted inverse from that of a traditional retailer. Associates are at the highest level on the chart, followed by department and merchandise managers and, finally, executives. This depiction cements the organization's philosophy that the customer is king. All efforts of senior-, middle-, and lower-level managers should support the efforts of the sales force.

Effective organizations are increasingly realizing that of the varied factors that contribute to performance, the human element is clearly the most critical. Regardless of the size or nature of an organization, the activities it undertakes, and the environment in which it operates, its success is determined by the decisions its employees make and the behaviors in which they engage. Managers at all levels in organizations are becoming increasingly aware that a critical source of competitive advantage often comes not from having the most ingenious product design or service, the best marketing strategy, state-of-the-art technology, or the most savvy financial management but from having the appropriate systems for attracting, motivating, and managing the organizations' human resources (HR).

Adopting a strategic view of HR, in large part, involves considering employees as human "assets" and developing appropriate policies and programs as investments in these assets to increase their value to the organization and the marketplace. The characterization of employees as human assets can have a chilling effect on those who find the term derogatory because of its connotation that employees are to be considered "properly." However, the characterization of employees as assets is fitting, considering what an asset actually is: something of value and worth. Effective organizations realize that their employees do have value, much as the organization's physical and capital assets have value. Exhibit 1.1 illustrates some of the value employees bring to an organization.

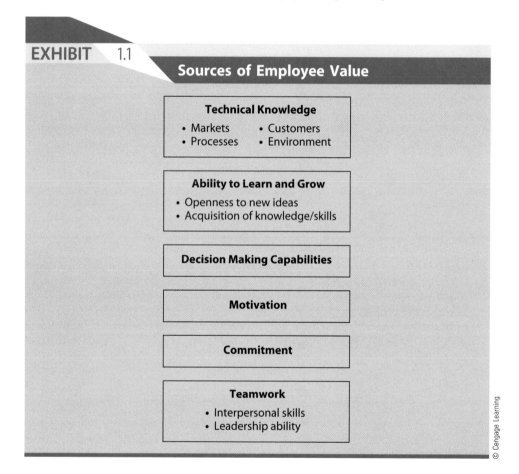

EXHIBIT   1.1

Sources of Employee Value

Technical Knowledge
- Markets
- Customers
- Processes
- Environment

Ability to Learn and Grow
- Openness to new ideas
- Acquisition of knowledge/skills

Decision Making Capabilities

Motivation

Commitment

Teamwork
- Interpersonal skills
- Leadership ability

© Cengage Learning

Adopting an Investment Perspective

The characterization of employees as human assets has important implications for the strategic management of HR in that it allows us to consider HR from an investment perspective. Physical and capital assets in organizations, such as plant, property, machinery, and technology, are acquired and subsequently managed most effectively by treating them as investments; the organization determines the optimal mix of high-performance, high-return assets to its strategic objectives. Analyses are made of the costs and benefits of certain expenditures, with judgments made concerning the riskiness and potential returns of such expenditures. Viewing HR from an investment perspective, much as physical assets are viewed, rather than as variable costs of production, allows an organization to determine how to best invest in its people. Furthermore, considering the risk and return on possible expenditures related to acquiring or developing human assets allows an organization to consider how current expenditures can be best allocated to meet long-term performance goals.

In considering whether to undertake the expense of a new training program, for example, an organization needs to consider not only the out-of-pocket costs for the training but also the related opportunity costs, such as lost time on the job, and weigh these costs against the potential benefits of the training, such as enhanced performance, potential increased loyalty, and motivation. The training also needs to be assessed relative to risk because the enhanced marketability of employees makes them more desirable to competitors. Similarly, in considering compensation programs as an investment, an organization needs to consider what it is "investing" in when it pays someone (knowledge, commitment, new ideas, retention of employees from competitors). The potential return on the organization's financial outlay in compensation will determine whether its compensation system is a viable investment strategy.

Taking an investment perspective toward HR/assets is critical considering that other physical assets, such as facilities, products and services, technologies, and markets, can be readily cloned or imitated by competitors.[1] Human assets cannot be duplicated and therefore become the *competitive advantage* that an organization enjoys in its market(s). This is becoming increasingly important as the skills required for most jobs become less manual and more cerebral and knowledge-based in nature.[2] Rapid and ongoing advances in technology have created a workplace where laborers are being replaced by knowledge workers. An organization's "technology" is becoming more invested in people than in capital. Thought and decision making processes as well as skills in analyzing complex data are not "owned" by an organization but by individual employees. This is in stark contrast to traditional manufacturing organizations where the employer usually owns or leases the machinery and production processes, and duplication of the organization's "capital" is restricted primarily by cost considerations.

Managing Employees at United Parcel Service

Although taking a strategic approach to HR management usually involves looking at employees as assets and considering them as investments, this does not always mean that an organization will adopt a "human relations" approach to HR. A few successful organizations still utilize principles of scientific management, where worker needs and interests are subordinate to efficiency. United Parcel Service (UPS) is a prime example of this. At UPS, all jobs from truck loaders to drivers to customer service representatives are designed around measures of efficiency. Wages are relatively high, but performance expectations are also high. This approach toward managing people is still "strategic" in nature because the systems for managing people are designed around the company's strategic objectives of efficiency. Consequently, all employee training, performance management, compensation, and work design systems are developed to promote this strategic objective of efficiency.

Managing an organization's employees as investments mandates the development of an appropriate and integrated approach to managing HR that is consistent with the organization's strategy. As an example, consider an organization whose primary strategic objective involves innovation. An organization pursuing an innovation strategy cannot afford high levels of turnover within its ranks. It needs to retain employees and transfer among employees the new knowledge being developed in-house. It cannot afford to have its employees develop innovative products, services, and processes and then take this knowledge to a competitor for implementation. The significant investment in research and development ends up having no return. Because the outcome of this expenditure (research and development) is knowledge that employees have developed, it is critical as part of the organization's overall strategy for the organization to devise strategies to retain its employees and their knowledge bases until the "new knowledge" becomes "owned" by the organization itself (through diffusion throughout the organization) rather than by the employee.

This leads to a dilemma involving investing in human assets. An organization that does not invest in its employees may be less attractive to prospective employees and may have a more difficult time retaining current employees; this causes inefficiency (downtime to recruit, hire, and train new employees) and a weakening of the organization's competitive position. However, an organization that does invest in its people needs to ensure that these investments are not lost. Well-trained employees, for example, become more attractive in the marketplace, particularly to competitors who may be able to pay the employee more because they have not had to invest in the training that the employee has already received. Although an organization's physical assets cannot "walk," its human assets can, making the latter a much more risky investment. An organization can certainly buy or sell its physical assets because it has "ownership" of them, but it does not own its human assets. Consequently, organizations need to develop strategies to ensure that employees stay on long enough for the organization to realize an acceptable return on its investment relative to the employees' acquired skills and knowledge, particularly when the organization has subsidized the acquisition. This requires the organization to determine the actual "value" of each employee. Valuation of human assets has implications for compensation, advancement opportunities, and retention strategies as well as how much should be invested in each area for each employee.

Valuation of Assets

Five major kinds of assets or capital that organizations can leverage to aid in performance and add value to operations are financial assets/capital, physical assets/capital, market assets/capital, operational assets/capital, and human assets/capital, as shown in Exhibit 1.2. Financial assets/capital include equity, securities and investments, and accounts receivable. Physical assets/capital include plant, land, equipment, and raw materials. Market assets/capital include goodwill, branding, customer loyalty, distribution networks, product lines and patents, trademarks, and copyrights. Operational assets/capital include management practices, the structure of work, and the use of technology. Human assets/capital include employee education levels, knowledge, skills, competencies, work habits and motivation, and relationships with coworkers, customers, suppliers, regulators, and lenders.

Financial and physical assets/capital are relatively easy to measure via accounting practices. Most of these assets are tangible and have some clear market value. Market and operational assets/capital are a bit more challenging to measure, but accounting practices have been developed that can place a general subjective value on such assets. Human assets/capital, however, are very difficult to measure; attempts to do so are at the forefront of current research being conducted in HR management.

A direct result of this difficulty in measuring human assets is that the valuation of current and future human assets is often ignored from consideration when organizations are facing economic and financial challenges. The media and financial markets usually respond favorably when decision makers announce restructurings or right-sizing initiatives, which reduce the size of the organization's work force, allowing it to reduce short-term costs. Such actions, however, involve the loss of human assets, which have value to the organization, often without consideration of the longer-term impact of such losses on the organization's ability to regain its position in the marketplace. Effective management recognizes that the organization's survival and renewal require the right size and mix of human capital and balances short-term needs to reduce or restructure costs with a clear strategy for the future. The key issue organizations face here is how to leverage the value of the organization's human assets for the good of the organization in the immediate, short, and long-term.

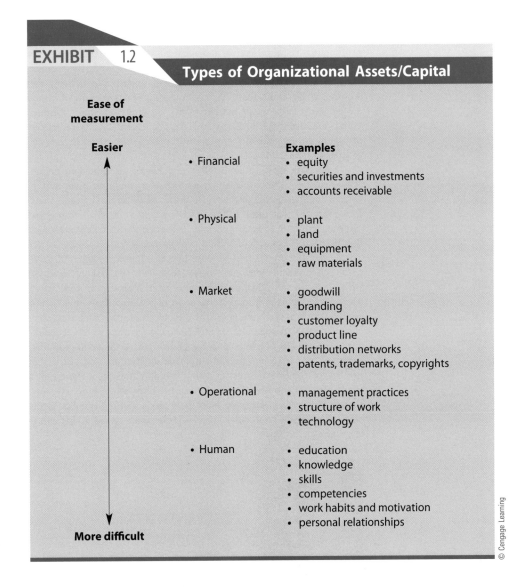

EXHIBIT 1.2   **Types of Organizational Assets/Capital**

Ease of measurement

Easier

- Financial

  Examples
  - equity
  - securities and investments
  - accounts receivable

- Physical
  - plant
  - land
  - equipment
  - raw materials

- Market
  - goodwill
  - branding
  - customer loyalty
  - product line
  - distribution networks
  - patents, trademarks, copyrights

- Operational
  - management practices
  - structure of work
  - technology

- Human
  - education
  - knowledge
  - skills
  - competencies
  - work habits and motivation
  - personal relationships

More difficult

© Cengage Learning

One model of employment that can provide valuable lessons in the valuation of and appreciation for human assets is that utilized in India. Reading 1.1, "The India Way: Lessons for the U.S.," illustrates how Indian organizations are able to integrate investing in their employees with their missions without compromising their commitment to either.

Understanding and Measuring Human Capital

Given that employees and their collective skills, knowledge, and abilities represent a significant asset for organizations, a critical issue for organizations becomes measuring this value as well as its contribution to the organization's bottom line. One of the first studies that successfully demonstrated this relationship was conducted by Huselid in the mid-1990s. This study identified what were called "high performance work systems" (HPWS) and demonstrated that integrated, strategically focused HR practices were directly related to profitability and market value.[3] A recent study by Watson Wyatt Worldwide found that the primary reason for organizational profitability is the effective management of human capital. This involves, in part, providing employees with rewards that are commensurate with their contributions and ensuring that investments in employees are not lost to competitors by actively managing employee retention.[4] Another study found that effective, integrated management of human capital can result in up to a 47 percent increase in market value.[5] A landmark study conducted by Becker, Huselid, and Ulrich that examined a variety of HR management quality indices found that the top 10 percent of organizations studied enjoyed a 391 percent return on investment (ROI) in the management of their human capital.[6]

Extending these findings, Dyer and Reeves attempted to define what can be called the HR "value chain."[7] They argued that performance could be measured via four different sets of outcomes: employee, organizational, financial and accounting, and market-based. More importantly, they proposed that these sets of outcomes had a sequential cause-and-effect relationship, as indicated in Exhibit 1.3. Each outcome fueled success in a subsequent outcome, establishing a causal link between HR practices and an organization's market value.

Given this proven link between integrated and strategic HR practices and bottom-line performance, HR practitioners have been faced with the task of developing appropriate HR metrics, which specifically illustrate the value of HR practices and activities, particularly relative to accounting profits and market valuation of the organization. This task has proven to be far more complex than anticipated, given the difficulties of measuring human assets/capital. One study concluded that 90 percent of *Fortune* 500 organizations in the United States, Canada, and Europe evaluate their HR operations on the basis of three rather limited metrics: employee retention and turnover, corporate morale and employee satisfaction, and HR expense as a percentage of operational expenses.[8] Such "staffing metrics" simply document the extent to which HR performs traditional job functions without necessarily illustrating how HR impacts company profits and shareholder value. Moreover, a focus on such staffing metrics involves a demonstration of how employees can be treated as expenses rather than as assets that can be managed, invested in, and leveraged for profit.

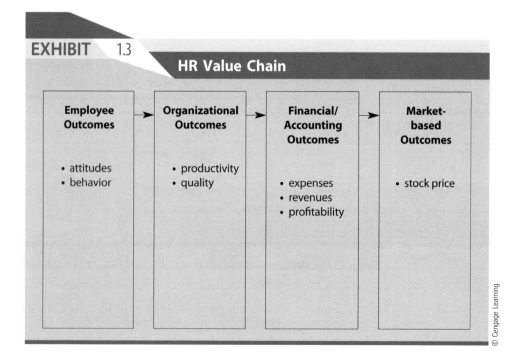

EXHIBIT 1.3   HR Value Chain

Employee Outcomes	Organizational Outcomes	Financial/ Accounting Outcomes	Market-based Outcomes
• attitudes • behavior	• productivity • quality	• expenses • revenues • profitability	• stock price

© Cengage Learning

Senior HR executives in these organizations stressed that they lacked accurate and meaningful methods that measured performance, despite the fact that human assets/capital can account for as much as 80 percent of the value of an organization.[9] One reason is that most accounting valuation methods stress the past and current value of assets. Much of the value of human assets/capital rests with the value of an organization and its ability to proactively meet challenges that lie ahead, relative to responsiveness to changing economic, political, and market conditions. As a result, valuation of human assets/capital and analysis of human capital investments can be value-laden, subjective, expensive—and, hence, ignored.

Measuring Human Assets/Capital at Dow Chemical

Dow Chemical has been a leader in forging the frontiers of measuring human capital. Dow has attempted to develop a reliable measure to help calculate each employee's current and anticipated future contribution to the financial goals of the business. A pilot project is currently being tested in a single business unit; it examines employee performance on project assignments by using two specific metrics: expected human capital return (EHCR) and actual human capital return (AHCR). EHCR involves a calculation of the break-even point of investment in an employee, above salary and additional outlays, such as recruiting and training expenses. AHCR involves a calculation of the "value created" by the employee based on the projects he or she was worked on. This metric considers the skills and knowledge of each employee relative to the net present value of a specific project. The desired outcomes of these measures are assisting managers with matching employee talents and project needs, identifying employee development opportunities, and creating a more efficient and effective means for project team staffing. Although the program is still in the pilot stage, with validation studies in progress, Dow anticipates rolling out the metrics to other business units in the very near future.[10]

Given the complex nature of measuring human assets/capital and return on such investments, where does an organization begin in assuming such an undertaking? One helpful model has been developed by Mercer, which can allow those concerned with measuring HR performance and documenting the value added by specific initiatives to demonstrate to senior management the value added and bottom-line impact.[11] This model involves six steps: (1) identify a specific business problem that HR can impact; (2) calculate the actual cost of the problem to the organization; (3) choose a HR solution that addresses all or part of the problem; (4) calculate the cost of the solution; (5) 6 to 24 months after implementation, calculate the value of the improvement for the organization; and (6) calculate the specific ROI metric.

One caveat should be obvious from not only Mercer's approach but also that currently being employed at Dow Chemical. Unlike the returns on other types of assets/capital, the ROI in human assets/capital are often not realized until some point in the future. Key decision makers need to be patient in waiting for these results, and HR also needs to subsequently take interim measures and provide status reports to senior management that illustrate preliminary beneficial results. HR needs to move away from mere data collection, however, and perform more comprehensive analysis of performance measures that relate to the critical metrics for which operating divisions are held accountable. Toward this end, HR needs to partner with chief financial officers to understand the language of investment and asset management. If HR continues to be seen as a cost center, it will be the primary target during cost-cutting operations, given that labor is the primary cost incurred in the service- and information-intensive sectors that are fueling the growth in our economy. One study places the relative expenses for human capital as high as 70 percent of overall expenditures.[12] Hence, the challenge for HR is to provide senior management with value-added human capital investments backed by solid and meaningful financial metrics.

Moneyball and the Oakland Athletics

The 2003 best-selling book, Moneyball, later made into a motion picture in 2011, chronicled the real-life application of HR metrics in major league baseball and their impact on performance. Starting with his appointment in 1998 as Oakland Athletics general manager, Billy Beane was forced to rethink how he selected players given the fact that his small-market team could not compete financially with big-market teams, such as those in New York and Boston, which consistently ended up signing the biggest name free agent players at hefty salaries. Beane looked beyond traditional statistical measures of player "value" such as batting average and home runs for position players and games won, earned run average and strikeouts for pitchers to seek out players that were generally undervalued. Beane and his statistician instead considered alternative metrics, such as on-base percentage and average number of pitches required to complete an at-bat, and discovered that such metrics had a higher correlation with games won by a team. Applying these new metrics as part of an ongoing staffing plan, Beane's cash-poor team qualified for the post-season from 2000 to 2003 with an average of 98 victories per season despite having one of the lowest payrolls in baseball. Soon, other teams were copying Beane's approach and the Athletics lost their competitive advantage. Beane's approach illustrates that the use of staffing metrics can translate into significant success for an organization. The key is selecting the appropriate metrics and analytical techniques, which may be different from those currently in use by the organization or standard within the industry.

HR Metrics

Many CEOs openly acknowledge the importance of effective and strategic HR management in their organization's success. Jack Welch noted in one of his last General Electric annual reports: "Developing and motivating people is the most important part of my job. I spent one-third of my time on people. We invest $1 billion annually in training to make them better. I spend most of my time on the top 600 leaders in the company. This is how you create a culture."[13] One recent study of *Fortune* 100 annual reports found that 14 percent of such reports contained at least one quantitative measure of HR management, such as turnover rate, investment in training, percentage of pay that is variable, or results from an employee attitude survey.[14] Despite this, Wall Street analysts still generally fail to acknowledge human capital in their assessment of the potential worth of a company's stock or the effects which human capital measures can have on a company's stock price.

Perhaps one reason for this lack of reporting of and respect for metrics related to human capital rests with the fact that there are no universally accepted metrics for the valuation of human capital or a standard format for measuring and reporting such data. Indeed, the Society for Human Resource Management has identified a number of common metrics for measuring the performance and value of human capital, a number of which are presented in Exhibit 1.4. These are measures that can easily be translated into bottom-line measures of performance as well as compared to industry benchmarks. Exhibit 1.5 provides examples of how five of these metrics that are often regarded as the most prominent measures of human capital management can be calculated and utilized. Nonetheless, stock analysts are more concerned with talking with operations, accounting, and finance heads rather than those in HR, as analysts usually have their training in, understand, and are most familiar and comfortable with these areas.

Labor Supply Chain Management at Valero Energy

San Antonio–based Valero Energy is a $70 billion energy-refining and marketing company that has reinvented its staffing function through the application of principles of supply chain management. Conceptualizing the acquisition and management of talent as a supply chain, Valero scrapped its traditional staffing processes by which managers would request specific numbers of employees from HR who, in turn, would solicit referrals from employees and contact recruiters. After an analysis of data related to hiring sources, how long new employees remained employed, performance and productivity of new hires, and "fit" with the company culture, Valero gained a sense of how to recruit the best talent at the lowest cost.

Valero's new staffing process involves forecasting three years in advance the demand for talent by both division and title. Five years of data were mined into a database, and a series of mathematical algorithms was developed for turnover trend analysis by location, position type, salary, tenure, and division. Another series of algorithms projected those trends forward for three years in line with anticipated workforce needs for future capital projects, updated systems, and anticipated new services. The result is the development of talent "pipelines," which address specific future talent needs relative to the organization's strategy and business model, allowing the development of related training and development programs and succession plans.[15]

EXHIBIT 1.4

Common HR Metrics

Absence Rate

Cost per Hire

Health Care Costs per Employee

HR Expense Factor

Human Capital Return on Investment (ROI)

Human Capital Value Added

Labor Costs as a Percentage of Sales or Revenues

Profit per Employee

Revenue per Employee

Time to Fill

Training Investment Factor

Training Return on Investment (ROI)

Turnover Costs

Turnover Rate (Monthly/Annually)

Vacancy Costs

Vacancy Rate

Workers' Compensation Cost per Employee

Workers' Compensation Incident Rate

Workers' Compensation Severity Rate

Yield Ratio

© Cengage Learning

There are no "perfect" metrics, however, as the appropriate human capital metrics would depend on the organization or business unit's strategy. Organizations concerned about minimizing costs might be most concerned with metrics related to turnover and revenue per employee. Organizations pursuing a strategy of aggressive growth might rely on metrics such as time to fill, while those concerned with innovation might closely monitor training costs per employee. Divisions or subsidiaries within the same organization might use totally different metrics, dependent on their unit's goals and strategies.

Calculation of Human Capital Measures

Measure	Formula	Value/Use
Human Capital ROI	Revenue − (operating expenses − compensation + benefits costs) / compensation + benefits costs	Allows determination of return on human investments relative to productivity and profitability; represents pre-tax profit for amounts invested in employee pay and benefits after removal of capital expenses
Profit per Employee	Revenue − operating expenses / number of full-time equivalent (FTE) employees	Illustrates the value created by employees; provides a means of productivity and expense analysis
HR Expense Factor	Total HR expense / total operating expenses	Illustrates the degree of leverage of human capital; provides a benchmark for overall expense analysis relative to targets or budgets
Human Capital Value Added	Revenue − (operating expenses − compensation + benefits costs) / total number of FTE employees	Shows the value of employee knowledge, skills, and performance and how human capital adds value to an organization
Turnover Rate	Number of employee separations (during a given time period) / number of employees	Provides a measure of workplace retention efforts, which can impact direct costs, stability, profitability morale, and productivity; can be used as a measure of success for retention and reward programs

Sources: For a more complete list of metrics, formulas, and uses, see Society for Human Resource Management, HR Metrics Toolkit, published Nov. 15, 2007. Available at *http://moss07.shrm.org/hrdisciplines/Pages/CMS_005910.aspx*

Factors Influencing How "Investment Oriented" an Organization Is

Not all organizations realize that human assets can be strategically managed from an investment perspective. As shown in Exhibit 1.6, five major factors affect how "investment oriented" a company is in its management of HR. The first of these is management values.[16] Management may or may not have an appreciation of the value of its human assets relative to other capital assets, such as brand names, distribution channels, real estate, facilities and equipment, and information systems. The extent to which an organization can be characterized as investment-oriented may be revealed through answers to the following questions:

- Does the organization see its people as being central to its mission/strategy?
- Do the company's mission statement and strategic objectives, both company-wide and within individual business units, espouse the value of or even mention human assets and their roles in achieving goals?
- More importantly, does the management philosophy of the organization encourage the development of any strategy to prevent the depreciation of its human assets or are they considered replicable and amortizable, like physical assets?

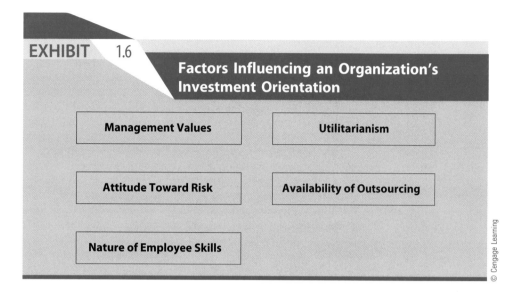

EXHIBIT 1.6 Factors Influencing an Organization's Investment Orientation

Management Values

Utilitarianism

Attitude Toward Risk

Availability of Outsourcing

Nature of Employee Skills

© Cengage Learning

Senior management values and actions determine organizational investment in assets. It is critical to understand how the organization's strategy mandates the investment in particular assets relative to others. Whether management values its people is a critical factor in its willingness to invest in them.

The second factor is attitude toward risk. The most fundamental lesson in financial management is that a trade-off exists between risk and return. Higher-risk investments are generally expected to have a greater potential return; lower-risk, safer investments are generally expected to have a more modest return. For example, in financial markets, bonds are considered less-risky investments than stocks but have a limited, fixed return. Stocks, on the other hand, are considered higher-risk investments but have no limit as to their potential return.

Both personal and institutional investment strategies can be highly conservative (risk averse) or pursue unlimited returns with reckless abandon. Investments in human assets are generally far more risky for an organization than investments in physical assets: Unlike physical assets, human assets are not *owned* by the organization. An organization with risk-averse management philosophies is far less likely to make significant investments in people. Other organizations see investments in employees as necessary for their success and develop strategies to minimize the potential risk of losing their investments. An organization can attempt to gain some "ownership" of employee services through long-term employment contracts or by offering employees financial incentives, such as stock-ownership programs, as well as additional professional development opportunities.

The third factor is the nature of the skills needed by employees. Certain organizations require employees to develop and utilize very specialized skills that might not be applicable in another organization; another employer might have employees utilize and develop skills that are highly marketable. For example, if an employer has a custom-made information system to handle administrative HR functions, employees using that system might not transfer those skills to another employer. However, if an employer uses a popular software program for which there is high demand for skilled employees among competitors, the investment in employees becomes more risky.

As a result, an organization that decides to provide its employees with specialized training in skills that can be utilized by others in the marketplace has a much stronger need to develop a strong retention strategy than an organization that teaches employees skills that are less marketable. Employees with skills demanded in the marketplace become more valuable and sought-after assets by companies that choose not to make expenditures or invest in training and skill development.

The fourth factor affecting the investment orientation is the "utilitarian" mentality of the organization. Organizations that take a utilitarian, or "bottom line," perspective evaluate investments by using utility analysis, also known as *cost-benefit analysis*. Here, the costs of any investment are weighted against its benefits to determine whether the prospective investment is either profitable or, more commonly, achieves the target rate of return the organization has set for its investments. A highly utilitarian approach attempts to quantify all costs and benefits. For example, rather than just considering direct cash expenditures, this approach would also consider the cost for the time involved to develop and administer an innovative performance measurement system (by considering how much people are being paid for the time involved in the process), the cost of having larger applicant pools (by considering how much longer it would take to screen applicants), and the cost of employing more extensive employee selection procedures (again, by considering time and its monetary value).

The distinct problem many utilitarian organizations run into regarding investments in people involves the fact that many benefits of HR programs and policies are extremely difficult to quantify. If these programs and policies can be assessed quantitatively, subjectivity as to the actual value of the benefit may make consensus on the overall value difficult. This is especially true for programs that attempt to enhance performance in service organizations. As an example, consider the customer service division of your local Internet service provider. Measures of effective service are not only difficult to assess objectively, but the organization may not be able to determine how much service is necessary to prevent customers from jumping to competitors and maintain their loyalty instead. Additional investments in service may not have any direct financial benefit.

Similarly, a government organization or public utility that attempts to develop a program to enhance efficiency may have a difficult time in finding the cost justifiable. Given that no market mechanisms exist for government agencies or legal monopolies, customers have no choice among competitors. Customers may complain to regulators or officials, but there may be no incentive or benefit for the organization to enhance its efficiency from an investment perspective. On a more basic level, a program that is designed to improve employee morale can have benefits that may be very difficult to measure and quantify. A utilitarian organization is likely to reject such "soft" programs that have no quantifiable return. Hence, the more utilitarian an organization, the more likely it is to see HR programs as investments, creating a challenge for those advocating for such HR programs to find a means to show their impact on the bottom line. Some very recent studies have begun to address this issue by attempting to establish a link between HR strategies and systems and an organization's financial performance. Initial results have shown a significant impact of HR systems on both market-based and accounting-based measures of performance.[17]

The final factor impacting an organization's willingness to invest in its people is the availability of cost-effective outsourcing. An investment-oriented approach to managing an organization will attempt to determine whether its investments produce a *sustainable* competitive advantage over time. When specialists who may perform certain functions much more efficiently exist outside an organization, any internal programs will be challenged and have to be evaluated relative to such a standard. This is true for virtually any organizational function, including customer service, accounting, manufacturing, and HR management functions.

The organization is further likely to invest its resources where key decision-makers perceive they will have the greatest potential return. This may result in few investments in people at the expense of investment in market and product development, physical expansion, or acquisition of new technology. As an example, employers in the fast-food industry, such as at McDonald's, invest little in their people; they require minimal experience, provide little training, pay low wages, and expect high turnover because the supply of workers is excessive relative to demand. Organizations in this industry tend to invest much more in new product development, physical expansion, and marketing through competitive advertising.

HR professionals can be strong catalysts in influencing the extent to which an organization's leaders truly understand the inherent value of its people. It has been argued that those in the HR profession have an ethical obligation and bear responsibility for leadership in this regard. Reading 1.2, "Strategic Human Resource Management as Ethical Stewardship," describes these responsibilities of the profession and outlines the benefits of strategic HR for employees, employers, and the larger society.

Conclusion

Developing an effective strategy to manage an organization's human assets requires considering employees as investments. Such an approach helps to ensure that HR practices and principles are clearly in sync with the organization's overall strategy, forces the organization to invest in its best opportunities, and ensures that performance standards are met. As an example, employee stock-ownership programs attempt to strategically invest in the organization and its people by making employees owners of the company. Instead of having a conflict as to how profits should be allocated (bonuses to employees or reinvested in the business), both can be achieved simultaneously. In turn, this has the goal of gaining more commitment from employees and encouraging them to adopt a long-term focus toward the organization; this is often a shortcoming or deficiency of American organizations that are concerned with short-run indicators of performance. Employees who now intend to stay with the organization longer, given their vested ownership rights, provide organizations with an incentive to incur the short-term costs involved with investing in human assets for the long-term financial gains that can result from such investments.

An investment perspective of HR is often not adopted because it involves making a longer-term commitment to employees. Because employees can "walk" and because American organizations are so infused with short-term measures of performance, investments in human assets, which tend to be longer-term investments, are often ignored. Organizations performing well financially may feel no need to change their investment strategies. Those not doing well usually need a quick fix to turn things around and therefore ignore longer-term investments in people.

However, while investments in HR are longer term, once an organization gains a competitive advantage through its employees, the outcomes associated with the strategy are likely to be enduring and difficult to duplicate by competitors as such programs and values become more firmly entrenched in the organization's culture. The commitment that an organization makes to its employees through its investments in them is often rewarded with the return of employees making a longer-term commitment to the organization. Although investments in human assets may be risky and the return may take a long time to materialize, investment in people continues to be the main source of sustainable competitive advantage for organizations.

Critical Thinking

1. Why do senior managers often fail to realize the value of human assets vis-à-vis other assets?

2. Why do line managers often fail to realize the value of human assets vis-à-vis other assets?

3. Why and how might a line or an operating manager value specific metrics related to the unit's employees?

4. What can HR do to make senior and line managers take more of an investment approach to human assets?

5. Why is a competitive advantage based on a heavy investment in human assets more sustainable than investments in other types of assets?

6. Why can some organizations that fail to invest heavily in human assets still be financially successful? Why can some organizations that do invest heavily in human assets still be financially unsuccessful?

7. What challenges exist relative to the valuation of human assets and measuring human capital?

Reading 1.1

8. Upon what cultural factors does the "Indian Way" depend upon for its success? To what extent can organizations from your country and culture adopt successful Indian practices, what obstacles exist to full implementation, which of these obstacles can be overcome, and specifically how can they be overcome?

Reading 1.2

9. Explain the ethical steward and transformative leader role as applied to HR professionals. Specifically how does each contribute to the practice of strategic HR management?

Exercises

1. Obtain the annual report for a *Fortune* 500 company of your choice. Review the material presented and the language used in the text. Write a one-page memo that assesses how investment-oriented the organization appears to be toward its human assets.

2. Arrange yourselves in small groups of four or five students and compare and contrast the similarities and differences among the organizations you investigated. Can you isolate any factors that appear to influence how an organization perceives the value of its employees?

3. How might different HR metrics be best employed in (1) a nonprofit organization, (2) a professional sports organization, (3) a healthcare facility, (4) a small technology-based startup, and (5) a large *Fortune* 500 company?

4. Consider your current or most recent employer. Does the organization employ any human capital metrics or key performance indicators? If so, which ones, how are they used, and are they appropriate given the organization's strategy? If not, suggest some appropriate human capital metrics or key performance indicators given the organization's strategy.

Chapter References

1. Quinn, J. B., Doorley, T. L. and Paquette, P. C. "Beyond Products: Services-Based Strategy," *Harvard Business Review*, 90, (2), pp. 59–67.

2. Lawler, E. III. *The Ultimate Advantage: Creating the High Involvement Organization*, San Francisco, CA: Jossey-Bass, 1992, p. 21.

3. Huselid, M. A. "The Impact of Human Resource Management Practices on Turnover, Productivity, Corporate Financial Performance," *Academy of Management Journal*, 38, (3), pp. 635–672.

4. Bates, S. "Study Links HR Practices with the Bottom Line," *HR Magazine*, December 2001, 46, (12), p. 14.

5. Gachman, I. and Luss, R. "Building the Business Case for HR in Today's Climate," *Strategic HR Review*, 1, (4), pp. 26–29.

6. Becker, B. E., Huselid, M. A. and Ulrich, D. *The HR Scorecard: Linking People, Strategy and Performance*. Boston, MA: Harvard Business School Press, 2001.

7. Dyer, L. and Reeves, T. "HR Strategies and Firm Performance: What Do We Know and Where Do We Need to Go?" *International Journal of Human Resource Management*, 6, (3), pp. 656–670.

8. Bates, S. "Executives Judge HR Based on Poor Metrics, Study Finds," *HR Magazine*, September 2003, 48, (9), p. 12.

9. Ibid.

10. Bates, S. "The Metrics Maze," *HR Magazine*, December 2003, pp. 51–60.

11. Mercer, M. *Turning Your Human Resources Department into a Profit Center*. New York: AMACOM, 1989.

12. Weatherly, L. A. "Human Capital—The Elusive Assets," Society for Human Resource Management, Research Quarterly, 2003.

13. General Electric Annual Report (2005).

14. Krell, E. "Notable By Its Absence," *HR Magazine*, December, 2006, pp. 51–56.

15. Schneider, C. "The New Human-Capital Metrics," *CFO Magazine*, February 15, 2006. Available at http://www.cro.com/printable/article.cfm/5491043

16. Greer, C. R. Strategy and Human Resources: A General Manager's Perspective, Englewood Cliffs, NJ: Prentice-Hall, 1995.

17. Becker, B. E. and Huselid, M. A. "High Performance Work Systems and Firm Performance: A Synthesis of Research and Managerial Implications," *Research in Personnel and Human Resource Management*, 16, 1998, pp. 53–101.

READING 1.1

The India Way: Lessons for the U.S.

Peter Cappelli, Harbir Singh, Jitendra Singh, and Michael Useem

Executive Overview

We describe a distinctive approach to business associated with the major corporations in India and contrast it with practices in the United States. Specifically, the Indian approach eschews the explicit pursuit of shareholder value in favor of goals associated with a social mission. These companies make extraordinary investments in their employees and empower them in decision making. These practices combine with a distinctively Indian approach to problem solving to create a competitive advantage that has led to spectacular business growth, not just within India but in international markets as well. A particularly important lesson for the United States is that the major Indian companies are not succeeding despite the fact that they are pursuing a social mission and investing in their employees. They are succeeding precisely because they do so.

The contemporary U.S. model for business is in trouble. That model asserts that maximizing shareholder value is the primary goal of business—indeed, some would say the only goal of contemporary business. This model is fairly recent, however. Until the early 1980s, the dominant model in the United States was the "stakeholder" model, which asserts that business has many groups with an interest or stake in its operations, and that the interests of these different stakeholders have to be balanced. This model was pushed aside by theoretical arguments emanating from the field of finance, which then played out in the sphere of public policy beginning in the 1980s (Epstein, 2005; Williamson, 1993).

With respect to management practices, we believe there are three additional elements at the heart of the contemporary U.S. model that are significantly different than practices elsewhere. The first concerns business strategy. The U.S.

approach focuses attention outside the firm in the search for opportunities and, to a lesser extent, in a related search for competencies through mergers and acquisitions and joint ventures. The second element focuses on restructuring: When markets or strategies change, U.S. companies lay off employees to cut costs and then hire new ones to redirect the business toward new markets or to meet new skill needs. The ability to restructure is seen as a key to competitiveness. Finally, in this model efforts to harness the motivation and abilities of employees tend to focus mainly at the top, with financial incentives (via equity) offered to executives and top managers. They, in turn, figure out how to motivate the rest of the workforce; the threat of job loss is typically an important part of the mix.

There are three recent and important challenges to these aspects of the U.S. model. The first is that it has not worked well for employees, perhaps not surprisingly given that employees are no longer seen as explicit stakeholders whose interests have to be balanced against those of shareholders. Except for a brief period of very tight labor markets at the end of the 1990s, employment outcomes have advanced little in a generation. Compared to previous decades, jobs are much less secure, wage growth is markedly lower, and at least by some measures, employee attitudes toward their jobs and their employers are worse. Specifically, evidence suggests that there has been a long-term trend toward greater insecurity across most occupations and groups (Kalle-berg, in press), that even before the 2008 recession outcomes for the "middle class" actually declined slightly during the economic expansion from 2001 through 2007 (Mishel, Bernstein, & Shierholz, 2009), and that outcomes and conditions worsened markedly for those at the bottom of the income and occupational distribution (Bertrand, Mehta, & Mullainathan, 2008). While interpreting longitudinal studies of employee attitudes is at best difficult, those that exist show a downward trend (Franco, Gibbons, & Barrington, 2010).

Second, U.S. corporate governance has been plagued in recent years by a sharp increase in malfeasance. There has been an unending (as of this date) stream of corporate financial scandals that began in the mid-1990s in which we saw executives manipulating finances to improve share prices and pad their own pockets. The most prominent of these were on such a monumental scale that they literally brought down companies—Enron, WorldCom, Adelphia, and Global Crossing (Markham, 2006). The list of companies where financial malfeasance was bad but not quite bad enough to force the failure of the company is much longer: Xerox, Sunbeam, Waste Management, Tyco, HealthSouth, and many more. An objective marker for financial irregularities is earnings restatements, serious accounting errors where companies are forced to revise earnings that had previously been presented as accurate. These restatements, once quite rare, grew by 145% from 1997 to 2001, and about 10% of all publicly traded companies restated earnings during that period (General Accounting Office, 2002). The fact that these scandals were so common in the United States and so much less so in other countries suggests that practices distinctive to the U.S. might be to blame (Coffee, 2005).

Then there is the 2007 financial meltdown, which started on Wall Street and led to a worldwide economic decline (see, e.g., Reinhardt & Rogoff, 2008) and then to profound concerns about U.S business practices. At the 2010 meeting of the World Economic Forum in Davos, Switzerland, for example, any whiff of American triumphalism from the previous decades had given way to U.S. contrition in the wake of the great financial crisis of 2008–2009. Capturing the essence of the mood, one of the event's leading figures put it bluntly: The calamity was caused by a "failure of leadership" in both financial services and government where the centers were the United States and to a lesser extent the United Kingdom (Useem, 2010).

Third, and for our purposes most important, there are now alternative business models that can lay claim to being more successful. Even putting aside the financial scandals, the overall U.S. economy and the corporate sector performed poorly this past decade, especially as compared to international standards. In absolute terms, the U.S. now ranks 14th in per capita gross domestic product (World Bank, 2009), with a growth rate over the 2000s of only about 1.2% per year (U.S. Bureau of Labor Statistics, 2009). Equity prices for U.S. firms, the main measure of success in the corporate world, lost 3.85% in nominal terms over the course of the decade, one of the worst performances in the industrialized world.

There are many alternatives to the U.S. model, but the one from which U.S. corporations could learn the most, in our view, comes from India, the country with the second-fastest growth rates in the world over the past decade. During much of the 2000s, India's GDP has risen by better than 9% per year—several times that of the U.S. and nearly that of China. Foreign institutional and direct investment has grown rapidly as well, rising by a factor of 13 from $4.9 billion in 1995–1996 to $63.7 billion in 2007–2008 (Reserve Bank of India, 2009b). A host of surveys have

confirmed that India has become one of the most favored destinations for direct investment, behind China but ahead of the U.S. (India Brand Equity Foundation, 2010). India's foreign exchange reserves rose from less than $1 billion at their bottom in 1991 to more than $300 billion at the peak in 2008, and the value of Indian exports increased by 2.5 times from 2004 to 2008 (Reserve Bank of India, 2009a). And all this occurred despite the fact that the infrastructure in India is by all accounts less developed than that in most Western nations (Hamm & Lakshman, 2007) and the challenges of doing business are great (see Figure 1).

Our interest in India is in the practices of its large corporations. Reliance, ICICI, Infosys, and hundreds of India's other top companies have been clambering on to the world stage to compete directly against Western multinationals in virtually all sectors, including those that had been seen as the future of the U.S. economy: high-human-capital service businesses such as information technology, healthcare, and business services.

And Indian companies have become international acquirers, able to compete with the best of enterprises and operating well beyond the boundaries of India. Tata Steel purchased the Anglo-Dutch Corus Steel in 2007 for $13.2 billion, and aluminum producer Hindalco bought the Canadian aluminum maker Novelis (with executive offices in Atlanta, Georgia) the same year for $6 billion (Economist.com, 2007). In collaboration with Steven Spielberg's Dreamworks, Reliance Entertainment in 2008 invested $1.2 billion in a new U.S. film company (Schuker, 2008), and Tata Motors acquired the marquee auto brands Jaguar and Land Rover from the American Ford Motor Company in 2008 for $2.3 billion (Spector & Bellman, 2008). When Indian companies took over publicly traded American firms, the acquired firms increased both their efficiency and profitability (Chari, Chen, & Dominguez, 2009). And Indian executives are increasingly on the short lists of corporate recruiters seeking talent for Western companies (Yee, 2007).

India shares a great many traits with the United States—including democratic principles and the associated arrangements of civil society such as a free press, a strong and independent judiciary, a highly diverse population, and open capital and labor markets—and Indian business leaders are well aware of the U.S. and other Western models. But they have blazed their own path in the area of business. For example, India was largely able to sidestep the 2007 financial crisis that brought most Western economies to their knees. Though rooted in the traditions and times of the subcontinent, the value of their distinctive path can, we believe, transcend the milieu from which it arose and offer lessons for companies elsewhere.

Our two-year study of Indian business involved interviews with the leaders of the 100 largest companies in India

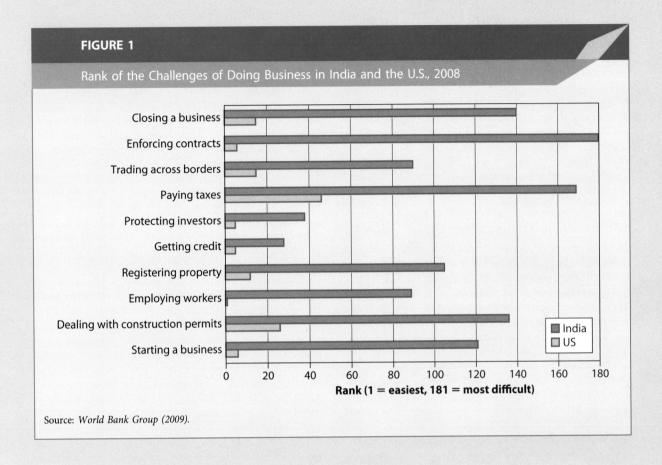

FIGURE 1

Rank of the Challenges of Doing Business in India and the U.S., 2008

Rank (1 = easiest, 181 = most difficult)

Source: *World Bank Group (2009).*

as well as other data from them.[1] We reached our conclusions about the attributes of the Indian approach through an inductive process that was aided by comparisons with U.S. practices and the extensive experience each author has with different aspects of management in the United States. "The India way," as we see it, is characterized by and distinct

from the U.S. business model in four fundamental ways (see also, Spencer, Rajah, Mohan, & Lahiri, 2008).

First, Indian companies see their most important goal as serving a social mission, not maximizing shareholder value, as is the case in the United States. An advantage of this approach for corporate performance is that it greatly enhances the ability to motivate and engage employees. As earlier work in job design established and more recent studies in positive psychology affirm, seeing meaning in work is a powerful motivator.

Second, Indian companies take the management of human capital seriously. They invest in the capabilities of their employees, promote internally rather than relying on outside hiring, and engage employees with empowerment and similar arrangements. An indication of the fact that they take these issues seriously is that they measure and manage almost every aspect of human resource practices and effectiveness carefully, more so than U.S. firms do.

Third, the persistence of engaged employees contributes to a uniquely Indian approach to problem solving that we describe with the Hindi term *jugaad*, banging away at hard problems with a trial-and-error approach that is deeply rooted in a culture of scarcity and constraints.

[1]Our project began with the National Human Resource Development Network, arguably the most influential business group in India. The network arranged interviews with the leaders of India's largest publicly listed companies by market capitalization. We conducted structured interviews with 105 leaders from 98 companies. Relatively few of these companies use the CEO model. At 71 of them, the top executive is called the "managing director." Leadership is shared at seven of them, so there we interviewed two leaders. We asked what qualities these executives saw as most vital to their success, how they worked with their boards, and where they perceived convergence and divergence with Western practices. We asked how they recruited talent and managed teams, and what legacies they hoped to leave behind. We also gathered survey data from the heads of HR at these companies. We compared the responses to those in a series of surveys of U.S. CEOs and HR executives. The most important data on U.S. CEOs come from a New York Stock Exchange survey, and most of the comparative data on HR practices come from surveys conducted by the Society for Human Resources Management. We supplemented these data with information from previous studies and descriptive information and case studies about the practices in these companies.

Fourth, these practices come together to create a unique approach to business strategy, one that is internal and rests on innovations in the companies' value chains. They are much less interested in acquiring competencies through mergers and acquisitions, joint ventures, or other externally oriented approaches as compared to U.S. firms. And they are much more likely to stick with traditional customers and search for better ways to meet their long-term needs, as opposed to relying on market research to find new opportunities.

We next delve deeper into each of these four aspects of the "India Way."

Social Mission Trumps Shareholder Value

Chief executives in publicly held American companies are expected to say that maximizing shareholder value is their most important priority. Indeed, everything they do is justified against that goal. When we asked Indian business leaders to rank their priorities (see list below), they placed maximizing shareholder value fourth, below the interests of employees. We also asked the top human resource executives in the same companies to answer the same question about their chief executives' priorities, and their ranking was virtually identical. No Indian business leaders in our conversations placed shareholder value as the top company priority or advanced the view that investors were the most important stakeholder, which is notable given that many executives were major holders of their company shares, and in some cases their companies are listed on U.S. stock exchanges.

Indian Business Leader Priorities

1. Chief input for business strategy
2. Keeper of organizational culture
3. Guide or teacher for employees
4. Representative of owner and investor interests
5. Representative of other stakeholders (e.g., employees and the community)
6. Civic leadership within the business community
7. Civic leadership outside the business community

Rank *ordering from the top executives of 98 companies.*

Corporate Governance

The single most distinctive feature of corporate governance across the Indian companies we studied was the determination to balance the interests of the firm's diverse stakeholders, all the groups that have a claim on what the company does. What was especially striking was the emphasis on the interests of the broader community, which extended from the immediate vicinity of the business out to encompass the entire nation (Singh, 2009), reminiscent of the pre-1980s stakeholder models from the United States.

Corporate governance in India differs substantially from that of the United States in the ownership structure of its firms, with many firms operating under the umbrella of business groups and a significant number of infrastructure firms owned by the government (Chakrabarti, Megginson, & Yadav, 2008). The firms we examined were publicly traded, but the ownership of many remained concentrated in the promoter family's holdings. The priority of interests noted in the list above did not vary noticeably with the ownership structure of the companies, however.

This is not to say that there are no problems with governance in Indian firms. The rights of minority shareholders have been a special concern, for example, in companies where concentrated majority ownership and holding company structures create incentives to shift assets inappropriately across companies, a process known as "tunneling" (Bertrand et al., 2002; Sarkar & Sarkar, 2000). Board structure also varies across companies (Tuteja, 2006), and larger boards in particular have been associated with lower performance (Ghosh, 2006). The independence of Indian boards has been questioned, but board quality rather than independence per se seems to be most correlated with corporate performance (Sarkar, Sarkar, & Sen, 2008).

No matter the ownership or board structure, Indian executives generally placed less weight on the board's monitoring function than was common in the West, at least in part because Indian firms and their directors faced a less active market for corporate control than did their U.S. counterparts (Morck & Steier, 2005; Reed & Mukherjee, 2004). Indian boards as a rule monitor finances less than American ones because financial performance is less a concern for these corporations. As B. Muthuraman, the managing director of Tata Steel, explained, "The Tata Group is less rules-based and more values-based. We have always believed you really cannot frame rules for corporate governance."[2] Nonexecutive directors in Indian boardrooms take more of a strategic partnership role with company executives, working with management to create and market new products and services, and comparatively less of a shareholder monitoring or rules-based role, as one would see with the American approach. Protecting shareholder value is not ignored, but Indian directors incorporate the concerns of a range of constituencies—just as Indian executives do—in reaching board decisions in partnership with management.

Mission-Driven

Central to the distinctiveness of the Indian model is the sense of mission, a social goal for the business that goes beyond making money and helps employees see a purpose in their work. Every company we saw articulated a clear social

---

[2] All quotes in the article unless indicated otherwise are from interviews with the authors. Details about the interviews are outlined in Appendix B of *The India Way.*

mission for their business. ITC, a leading conglomerate, echoed the views of the companies we interviewed in this statement describing the company's purpose: "Envisioning a larger societal purpose has always been a hallmark of ITC. The company sees no conflict between the twin goals of shareholder value enhancement and societal value creation" (ITC, 2010, p. 1).

U.S. companies talk about doing good in their communities, and many do. The difference is that Indian companies describe their social mission publicly as *the* purpose of the business, not just a separate act of charity. Typically, that sense of mission extends to helping India and its citizens. In that sense, they act quite differently from standard notions of corporate social responsibility as self-regulation and a concern about doing good while making money (see Williams and Aguilera, 2008, for a comparative discussion of corporate social responsibility). The social mission for Bharti Airtel, for example, was to get cell phones into the hands of the hundreds of millions of people in India who otherwise had no way to communicate with each other; the Tata Nano story had a similar goal with respect to providing low-cost transportation (see below). The social mission of the pharmaceutical and healthcare company Dr. Reddy's Labs is to address the unmet medical needs of the poor in India as well as around the world. Hindustan Unilever's Project Shakti uses microfinance principles to create a sales force in the poorest regions of the country. Some of these approaches build on the "fortune at the bottom of the pyramid" approach, which emphasizes business opportunities among the poor (Prahalad, 2004). But making money is never presented as the primary objective.

These companies also put their money where their mouth is with respect to mission. Two thirds of the profits of the Tata Group companies, for example, go to its charitable foundations and then back into Indian society. The Godrej Group has constructed schools, medical clinics, and living facilities for employees on a massive scale unknown among American companies, where directors and executives are far more likely to see employee welfare as a drag on shareholder value than an asset for company growth. Dr. Reddy's Labs guaranteed to meet the healthcare needs of 40,000 children. Infosys has built and staffed entire hospitals, rolled out a nationwide curriculum for school-age students in part to improve its future applicant pool, and engaged in hundreds of other projects, all in the same year. ITC developed a rural initiative, Mission Sunehra Kal (the Golden Tomorrow), that includes knowledge portals to advise farmers, help for them to band together to negotiate with suppliers, job opportunities for women, and expansion of education, involving five million people (Lakshman, 2009). Virtually every major company has similar efforts under way. The focus on mission cuts across companies that are family or "promoter" controlled, companies that operate in international markets and every other dimension we

examined. No doubt the social needs are greater in India than in most other countries, but the efforts of these companies to address them are nevertheless there for all to see.

The Motivation for Mission
The priority and value placed in India on service to others and the widely held belief that one's goal in life should extend beyond oneself, especially beyond one's material needs, is no doubt part of the driver for the sense of mission. The third of the four stages of Hindu life, the *vanaprastha ashrama,* focuses on the search for meaning, helping others, and a gradual withdrawal from the competitive business world, and it neatly coincides with the typical age (over 50) of senior business leaders. It is worth noting, however, that the concern about mission extends to companies run by non-Hindus as well. In comparative research on leadership, the Indian region scored the highest of any area in desiring leaders who were humane, compassionate, and generous (Javidan, Dorfman, De Luque, & House, 2006). That preference fit nicely with the aspect of national culture manifesting service to others as a source of motivation.

And some part of explanation for the mission fits this altruistic norm. Mallika Srinivasan, director of Tractors and Farm Equipment, told us that almost everywhere companies operate in India they are encircled by throngs of destitute people, needs are stark, and government intervention is inadequate. Like many other big companies, Tractors and Farm Equipment maintains a first-world, campus-like facility within sight of third-world slums. "Corporate social responsibility and good governance are related to the state of the development of the country," Srinivasan told us. "We are all seeing these islands of prosperity surrounded by so much poverty." Echoing a sentiment we heard from many executives, Srinivasan explained that her company feels duty bound to step forward. Some of the social engagement is also driven by necessity. The rapid growth of the Indian market and the inadequate scale of health and education systems have forced companies to develop healthcare and classes for their own talent.

But social investment pays off for these companies as well. For B. Muthuraman, the managing director of Tata Steel, efforts to aid the broader community create a reputational asset. "Our history in corporate social responsibility," he acknowledged, "has enhanced the group brand." That has proved invaluable for recruiting and retaining employees at Tata Steel. A recent study of employee turnover in India found, for example, that the perception of a company's social responsibility is one of the main factors in retaining talent (Grant, E., 2008). Acting responsibly may also pay off especially in dealing with regulators: Obtaining industrial licenses and environmental clearance in India can depend on being known for public responsibility.

Mission as a business goal also affects relationships with customers. Individuals have long memories, and doing good things for people when they have no money and are not customers can redound to a company's advantage when those individuals do have money and are in the market for your products. We also know that consumers care about the values of the companies with which they do business—witness the current rush of companies touting their "green" environmental practices. At least some substantial share of customers would rather do business with companies that do good things for the community (Lev, Petrovits, & Radhakrishnan, 2010). R. Gopalakrishnan, executive director of Tata Sons, said that he believed the Tata Group was *loved* by the people in India, not just by their employees, for the contributions their companies have made to Indian society. How many companies anywhere could make that claim?

Most important, using a social mission is a powerful way to motivate employees. We know from the original work on job design that the connection individuals see between the tasks they perform and the overall product or outcome of the organization is an important source of positive employee outcomes (Hackman & Oldham, 1975). More recent work shows that the effects of task significance on job performance are much more powerful when they contribute to helping others, and social impact more generally can lead to performance outcomes that are orders of magnitude greater (Grant, A. M., 2008). The focus on helping fellow Indians as the social mission makes this connection between the work one does and helping others very clear. There is every reason to believe it leads to the same increases in performance in these companies as research studies have documented elsewhere.

Social Mission Versus the U.S. Model

Contrast this Indian model, where a company's business goal is seen as bettering society, with the U.S. model, where we try to motivate employees around the corporate goal of making shareholders rich. The U.S. approach is at a sizable disadvantage because it is difficult for most people to see making money for shareholders as a goal that is personally meaningful. While it is possible to tie pay to shareholder value, it is extremely expensive to pay the average employee enough in share-based incentives to get him or her to focus on shareholder value.

The overwhelming focus on creating shareholder value in the United States has led executives to concentrate on the interests of their own enterprise and devote less attention to the welfare of the community or society. This could be seen in the recent U.S. financial crisis, where virtually no executives were willing to take measures beyond their own company's self-interest that might have helped avert the 2007 financial meltdown and subsequent recession. When Bear Stearns neared collapse in March 2008, one bank acquired the firm at the behest of the U.S. Treasury to avoid broader disruption to the economy, but when Lehman was on the verge of bankruptcy in September of the same year, no banks stepped forward to help resolve a far bigger threat to the system. With narrow self-interest prevailing, Lehman failed, the stock market plunged, financial institutions such as AIG and Merrill Lynch buckled, the economy went into reverse, and unemployment soared around the world (Paulson, 2010; Sorkin, 2009). Shareholder capitalism had predictably led most bankers to focus entirely on their own immediate welfare, even at a moment when their common interest would have pointed to collective intervention. The fact that Bill Gates and Warren Buffet stand out so prominently for their interest in improving society is because so few other American business leaders have comparably stood forward. Indian executives, by contrast, are willing not only to articulate societal interests but to act on them.

The focus on mission may also relate to differences in leadership style. We used the most widely used assessment of leadership in the United States, the Multifactor Leadership Questionnaire (MLQ), to examine the leadership styles of these Indian leaders (Antonakis, Avolio, & Sivasubramaniam, 2003; Bass & Avolio, 2004). We asked the heads of human resources at the companies whose executives we interviewed to assess the leadership style of their top bosses. Not surprisingly given the picture of Indian business leadership already described—actively engaged in building mission-driven organizations—the executives scored low on passive and avoidance practices. Nor were we surprised to see that Indian business leaders ranked highest in practices that fall generally under "transformational style": inspirational motivation, idealized influence, intellectual stimulation, and individual consideration. On the transactional side, Indian leaders, like their American counterparts, are quick to use contingent rewards—that is, rewards based on performance—but less prone to manage by exception or look for mistakes.

When we compared these results with those from a sample of 48 chief executives of U.S. Fortune 500 companies, however, we found that the American leaders were significantly more likely to use "transactional leadership" styles that tie performance to rewards than were our Indian executives. Comparisons with a different study of 56 American chief executives also suggested that Indian executives create a significantly greater sense of empowerment among employees, scoring higher, for instance, on the "intellectual stimulation" category (Waldman, Ramirez, House, & Puranam, 2001).

Taking Human Capital Seriously

Beyond the sense of mission lies the actual management of employees. Indian companies, we found, built employee commitment by creating a sense of reciprocity with the workforce, looking after their interests and those of their families and implicitly asking employees to look after the firm's interests in return. To translate commitment into action, the business leaders went to extraordinary lengths to empower employees in a way that often conflicted with historical and cultural norms, giving them the freedom to plunge into problems they encountered and create their own solutions. Then they devoted a great deal of executive attention and resources to the practices that support this approach, such as finding the right people to hire, developing them internally, and improving morale. Business leaders directed their attention to building organizational culture, their number-two priority, which shows employees how to behave, and to demonstrating the connection between employee competencies and business strategies.

Figure 2 compares the results of our survey of these top 100 Indian companies concerning their human resource practices to a similar survey of U.S. companies. The Indian firms were more likely to measure and track all human resource outcomes than were U.S. firms. Given that it is difficult to manage and take seriously issues that are not measured, these results are consistent with the notion that HR functions in India were at least taken more seriously and are arguably more sophisticated than those in the United States. Companies in the U.S. clearly know how to track these outcomes. They just choose not to.

FIGURE 2

Company Use of Human Resource Metrics

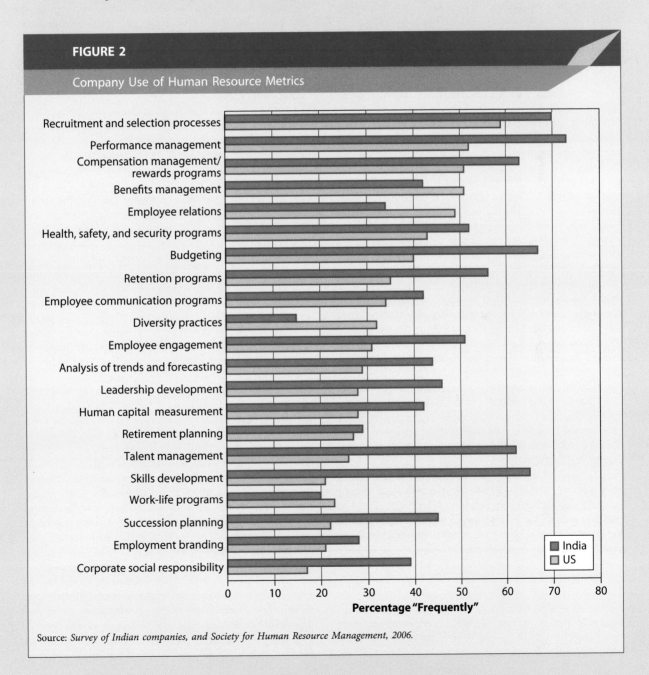

Source: *Survey of Indian companies, and Society for Human Resource Management, 2006.*

The biggest differences in measurement had to do with investments in the development of employees: 62% of the Indian firms frequently tracked progress in overall talent management, compared with only 26% in the U.S.; 65% frequently measured the development of skills of employees, versus only 21% in the U.S.; 45% frequently tracked the ability to promote from within through succession, versus 21% in the U.S.; and 46% frequently used metrics to assess the development of leaders, versus 28% in the U.S. Despite high turnover in the red-hot Indian labor market, these leading firms seem dedicated to policies of promotion from within (SHRM India, 2008).

Training

They are also investing heavily in their employees, especially their new hires. One study of practices in India found that the IT industry provides new hires with more than 60 days of formal training—about 12 weeks of classroom training, a massive investment given that employees are paid during that time. Some companies do even more: Tata Consultancy Services, for example, has a seven-month training program for science graduates being converted into business consultant roles, and everyone in the company gets 14 days of formal training each year. MindTree Consulting, another IT company, combines classroom training, mentoring, and peer-based learning communities. Even relatively low-skill industries such as business process outsourcing and call centers provide something like 30 days of training, and retail companies require about 20 days (Wadhwa, de Vitton, & Gereffi, 2008).

New recruits for clerks and other front-line jobs at Pantaloon, a leading retailer, receive six weeks of training, including five and a half days in residence at a company training center followed by five weeks of on-the-job training directed by local store managers. Kishore Biyani, Pantaloon's chief executive, explains that much of their training goes beyond practical job skills: "We run a program in the organization which everyone has to go through, called 'design management,' which basically trains people to use both sides of the brain," both "the visual and aesthetic side and the logical-rational." After that, store staff receive a week of new training each year (Wadhwa et al., 2008). Training is one way the company develops a shopping experience more suited to customers. Even experienced hires get training. Dr. Reddy's Laboratories puts all its outside hires, including those with substantial experience, through a *one-year* training program that includes ten weeks of assignments abroad as well as a culminating cross-functional project presented to the top executives. Again, these investments occur in the context of tight labor markets and high turnover, factors that are often used to explain the lack of training in the U.S.

Systematic data on training among U.S. companies is hard to come by, but the available statistics suggest that 23% of new hires received no training of any kind from their employer in the first two years of employment, while the average amount of training received for new hires—those with two years or less of tenure—was about 24 hours per year in those first two years (U.S. Bureau of Labor Statistics, 1995).

Employee Appreciation

A different measure of the priority that India Way companies place on their employees comes from what they tell shareholders and the broader community about their operations. An interesting study of the annual reports in the Indian information technology industry found that the most common mention of any human resource issue—so common, in fact, that it happened on average more than once in each report—was to thank employees for their contributions. The second most common HR mention was to highlight individual employees, typically for their special contributions or sometimes for their life experiences. That was followed in frequency by mentions of employee capabilities and efforts to train and develop employees. And the fourth most common mention was to discuss contributions employees were making to the broader community, outside of their work tasks (Murthy & Abey-sekera, 2007). By contrast, the annual reports of the leading U.S. information-technology companies contained nary a mention of the employees. This is the case for the 2007 annual reports for the five biggest IT employers in the U.S.: IBM, HP, Microsoft, Oracle, and Cisco. The closest statement to the India model is a reasonably generic sentence in Cisco's shareholder letter that says, "While we're proud of the financial results we delivered," we "are also very proud of our people, our culture, and the way Cisco operates as a company" (Chambers, 2007). (See Appendix A for a brief discussion of how Infosys trains its new recruits.)

The reason Indian companies invest in their employees is that they see employees as key to building the organizational capabilities that drive competitiveness. Four of five of the top Indian human resource executives reported that building capabilities for the organization was an important purpose for employee learning. A meager 4% of their American counterparts in training and learning roles said the same thing (see Figure 3). In fact, capability building ranked next to the bottom on the list of U.S. outcomes, a stunning difference. In general, the American executives rarely saw learning as serving strategic-level goals for the organization. The outcome American executives reported most frequently as the purpose of employee learning was to better execute existing strategies: "Learning" seemed more like training, designed to improve performance on existing tasks. Even then it was embraced by only 14% of respondents.

Much like Japanese companies, the Indian corporations also take pains to protect those investments in employees. Keshub Mahindra, chairman of the Mahindra Group, told us that they contemplated laying off workers in the recent downturn but decided against it in large measure because they knew that for every employee laid off, there were five family members who would suffer alongside. They could

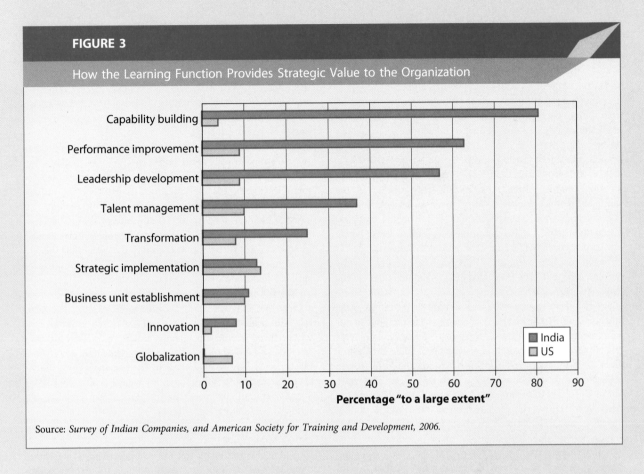

FIGURE 3

How the Learning Function Provides Strategic Value to the Organization

Source: *Survey of Indian Companies, and American Society for Training and Development, 2006.*

not in good conscience do this to their loyal employees. So they put their otherwise redundant employees to work in the company gardens. With some satisfaction, he added that the company now has some of the finest gardens in India!

Employee Empowerment and Transparency

Having motivated and skilled employees might not matter if they were not given the opportunity to use those skills. The software company Mind-Tree has adopted a host of innovative methods for fostering ideas and execution, beginning with an entire menu of ways for the employees to give feedback to executives. Among the arrangements: monthly updates called Snapshots that describe the competitive environment and the state of the company; All Minds Meet, a regular open house with the company's leadership where all questions are tackled on the spot; People Net intranet, where grievances are addressed; and Petals, a blogging site (Mind-Tree, 2010b). But the most unusual aspect of the MindTree approach, both in transparency and role modeling, can be found in the company's integrity policy. MindTree posts on its Web site accounts of ethical failures and violations of company policies, and the lessons the firm has learned from each (MindTree, 2010a).

The idea is that by acknowledging mistakes, especially those made by leaders, the company encourages others to admit theirs and to follow its lead in making changes.

The high-water mark for a culture of openness and flat hierarchy probably goes to the Sasken Corporation, which Rajiv Mody started in Silicon Valley and moved back to his home in Bangalore in 1991. The company's "single-status" policy means that all employees, from entry-level to Mody himself, are treated identically—same offices, same travel policies (coach class), same criteria for compensation (no separate executive compensation policies). While the company is known for being cheap in the area of compensation, it is otherwise extremely employee-friendly, with policies that include extensive programs for leaves, including a six-week sabbatical after four years of employment (Express Computer, 2007).

As an example of empowerment, Vineet Nayar, the CEO of HCL Technologies, has become well-known for his motto of "employee first, customer second." The point, Nayar said, is that "if you are willing to be accountable to your employees, then the way the employee behaves with the customer is with a high degree of ownership." At HCL, Nayar contended, "command and control" is giving way to "collaborative management." To that end, he has pushed for ever "smaller units of decision makers for faster speed and higher accuracy in decisions" to provide HCL's customers with more timely and customized service.

To make this happen, he spends as much as half his time in town hall meetings with the company's employees, communicating this vision for the company and managing the corporate culture. He makes it a personal goal to shake the hand of every employee every year, and when asked what he would like to be his greatest legacy to the company in five years, Nayar responded without missing a beat: "They would say that I have destroyed the office of the CEO." Pressed to explain, he said he sought so much "transparency" and "empowerment" in the company that "decisions would be made at the points where the decisions should be made"—that is, where the company meets the client. The "organization would be inverted, where the top is accountable to the bottom, and therefore the CEO's office will become irrelevant." His public blogs on the company website include a 2008 post titled "Destroying the office of the CEO" (Nayar, 2008).

HCL seeks to invert the organizational pyramid by making, as Vineet Nayar told us, "our managers accountable to our employees." One tactic for doing so is to encourage employees to submit electronic "tickets" on what needs to be changed or fixed, even the very personal, which have ranged from "I have a problem with my bonus" to "my boss sucks." An even more unusual tactic is to require 360-degree feedback reports on the 1,500 most senior company managers worldwide, including the chief executive himself. Employees have the option of evaluating not just their boss but also their boss's boss and three other managers. And the 360-degree feedback, including Nayar's own, is posted on an intranet site within several weeks for all employees to see—all of it, the good and the bad. As he told us, "our competitive differentiation should be the fact that we are more transparent than anybody else in our industry and therefore the customer likes us because of transparency; employees like us because there are no hidden secrets. So we built transparency." The idea of performance improvement has become more broadly acceptable, and the heightened personal transparency at the top serves to reduce the sense of vertical separation (Som, 2006).

Jugaad and Adaptability

The Hindi term *jugaad* describes the ability to improvise and find a way around problems, often using trial and error methods. The unique cultural context of learning to work in a tough, resource-constrained country where the ability to make do and improvise with what little was available created the necessity for *jugaad*. Keeping old equipment running with improvised spare parts is the classic example. In these modern corporations, though, the *jugaad* phenomenon plays out through motivated and committed employees hammering away at tough problems, persisting until they find creative solutions and workarounds. What makes them willing to do

that? Again, having a sense of mission and social goal for the organization helps employees see a purpose in their work that goes beyond their immediate self-interest, beyond the achievements of the firm and its owners. And empowerment provides the opportunity to make use of that motivation. When we combine *jugaad* with the unique Indian approach to strategy, we get a sense of how these firms are competing and winning on the international stage.

Creative adaptation, not weary resignation, is central to the Indian approach to management. Vijay Mahajan, chief executive of Basix, a micro-finance organization, argued for many in offering his explanation of the power of *jugaad,* an ability "to manage somehow, in spite of lack of resources." It constitutes a cornerstone of Indian enterprise, in his view, and the "spirit *of jugaad* has enabled the Indian businessman to survive and get by" in an economy that was until the late 1990s oppressed by controls and stymied by a lack of widespread purchasing power.

The English word *adjust* is also spoken in various local accents in India. It is used in a wide range of situations, usually with a plaintive smile. One can use it in a crowded bus, where three people are already seated on a seat for two, requesting them to "adjust" to accommodate a fourth person. Or, it is used by businessmen when they meet government officials, seeking to "adjust" various regulations, obviously for a consideration, to speed up the myriad permissions still required to do anything in India.

Doing More With Less, Strategically

Consider also the better known example of the Tata Nano, the pint-sized car built by Tata Motors, India's largest maker of automobiles and trucks. Conventional market strategy would have suggested staying away from the low end of the market, where Japanese quality and prices dominated. But realizing that India's mass market hungered for even lower cost transportation, Tata set out to engineer an automobile whose price would not just be marginally lower than the lowest end existing products but radically lower, 75% below the cheapest competitor. Here as well, the business goal involved a social mission: creating transportation for the poorest consumers. Meeting this extraordinary challenge for its traditional customers required an extensive application of *jugaad*.

Tata Motors knew that it would have to do the engineering largely on its own, without the benefit of the research and development that one might find in universities and government laboratories in other countries. It also knew that the Nano would have to be developed on a shorter cycle. "We can't have 48 or 36 months to bring out the new products," said Tata Motors executive director for finance Praveen Kadle; now it's just 24 or 18 months. With all that in mind, Tata Motors swiftly designed the Nano from a clean sheet of paper to meet what appeared to be an impossibly low price point: 100,000 rupees per car, about $2,500 at the time. That figure was not generated by market research. It came about as an off-the-cuff estimate by Ratan Tata, which generated huge attention, and so he decided to make it the target price point (ICFAI, 2008). Presented as the world's most inexpensive car when unveiled in January 2008, its sticker price was to be on par with the cost of a DVD-player option in luxury Western autos (Kurczewski, 2009). It achieved this price point not through technological innovation but by a completely new approach that closely resembles the *jugaad* concept: deep frugality, a willingness to challenge conventional wisdom, and a single-minded determination by Tata's top managers to work through the many constraints and challenges of operating in the Indian environment. They designed everything in the Nano from scratch, and they deleted features that were taken for granted by other carmakers, including air conditioning, power brakes, and radios.

The long-run plan for the Nano also includes an important innovation in the value chain: Kits of components are to be sold en masse for assembly and distribution by local entrepreneurs. Ratan Tata talked about "creating entrepreneurs across the country that would produce the car ..., my idea of dispersing wealth" (Surender & Bose, 2008, p. 1). Tata even anticipated providing the tools for local mechanics to assemble the car in existing auto shops or new garages created to cater to rural customers. Termed "open distribution innovation" by *Business Week,* the method could create not only the world's least expensive automobile but also its largest selling one. "Tata Motors has built up a position," said Gopalakrishnan, "where international car companies are not able to compete with us." And that, in essence, is a large part of what the India Way is all about: a strategy of focusing the energy and attention of company managers on the hard and persistent needs of their customers, achieving outcomes that break through traditional standards of products and services.

The hospital group Narayana Hrudayalaya offers a similar story of *jugaad* and strategy. It was founded by Devi Shetty to help the thousands of Indian children who need cardiac surgery and cannot afford it. The group discovered that the only way to provide quality operations cheap enough for the masses to afford (a challenge yet to be mastered in the West) was to standardize and effectively automate them. So it set about learning to perform them at scale, changing the way surgery is performed. It now performs more than twice as many cardiac surgeries as the biggest U.S. hospital, with outcomes as good and at about one-tenth the cost as the best U.S. provider. Its profit margins are slightly above those of its U.S. peers, and it is now planning hospitals outside India, including one not far from Miami, Florida (Narayana Hrudayalaya Hospitals, 2010).

ICICI Bank did something similar for rural banking. Whereas a typical savings account in the West might be $10,000, a typical one in urban India was apt to be no more than $1,000, and in rural India only a tenth of that. That meant operating expenses had to be pared down proportionately: Urban banking in India had to be conducted at one-tenth the cost of banking in the West, and rural banking at one-hundredth. "We need to be able to conceptualize how to deliver value to this market at an extremely low cost," ICICI chief executive K.V. Kamath said. "That's where the challenge is, as well as the opportunity and the excitement." A scaled-down urban branch model was still prohibitively expensive for rural banking, so Kamath and his team turned to alternative, far less costly avenues for reaching the poor, ranging from nonprofit microfinance groups to using local fertilizer distributors as agents.

Strategy From Within

None of the Indian business leaders we interviewed claimed that his company succeeded based on his own cleverness or even on the efforts of a top team. Almost without exception, Indian business leaders—and the industry analysts and business journalists who follow their companies—described the source of comparative advantage as coming from deep inside the company, from motivated employees, new and better ideas, and superior execution. And these outcomes, in turn, were traced to the positive attitudes and behaviors of employees. The obvious conclusion: Strategy in these companies comes from internal capabilities. The source of the distinctiveness of the India Way and the ability to focus the business on solving hard problems rests heavily on the management of people: They invest in them, use social mission to create motivation, empower them, and tap into the cultural aspect of *jugaad* to hammer away at hard problems until they break through.

As noted earlier, our interviewees saw being the "chief input to strategy" as their most important task. Strategy is often seen as a staff function in U.S. companies, and in that sense the fact that the number-one priority for the Indian CEOs was to be the main input into strategy may seem like a puzzle. But it makes perfect sense given that the sources of strategy among the Indian corporations we examined are deeply rooted within the firms, supported by a set of attributes such as organizational culture and practices around managing people that help drive their strategies. Building strategy means building these capabilities and stressing alignment within the organization, ensuring that many separate practices are consistent with one another and mutually reinforcing. In this context, being the "chief input into the strategy process" means that the CEOs monitor and maintain the infrastructure of their organizations, the firms' architecture and culture and systems for investing in and engaging their employees.

While most mainstream U.S. corporations are organized into strategic business units each responsible for its own strategy, in these Indian firms, the leaders own a significant part of the strategy function for the entire company, setting the agenda and taking a visible role in the strategies developed in various units. The focus for them is less on the analytics behind the strategies and more on creating the context: designing the incentive structures, managing the organizational culture, and in turn, shaping the strategies that managers then develop. Their view of strategy is therefore as a set of enduring principles, an approach to business that they can encode into the firms' responses to market opportunities. This approach to strategy allows for improvisation and flexibility in unit-level practices while incorporating interventions and inputs from the CEOs into the strategies of various businesses.

Other differences related to strategy concern the identification of opportunities in the market. U.S. companies are inclined to begin the strategy process with market research to identify new customers and opportunities that offer superior profit opportunities. The India Way companies, in contrast, are much more likely to stick with their traditional customers and take on the long-term, persistent challenges those customers face. Table 1 shows comparative data on how these top executives in India and their U.S. counterparts have changed their allocation of time in recent years, an indication of priorities. Indian leaders saw the biggest increases in strategy and in customer relationships. Customer relationships were the area of largest net decline for U.S. CEOs, and their increased focus was all on factors outside the firm. Indian leaders report the biggest declines in their time in the area of day-to-day management, giving more autonomy to lower management. (Careful readers will see that leaders in both countries paradoxically report they were devoting more time to just about every priority in the past three years.)

An even more telling discrepancy emerged in a 2007 Conference Board survey of chief executives worldwide. When asked to identify their most critical challenges from among several dozen, American executives ranked "consistent execution of strategy" considerably above "speed, flexibility, [and] adaptability to change" (Baranowska, 2007). Their Indian counterparts reversed the ranking. For them, speed, flexibility, and adaptability were at the heart of strategy and the greater priority.

We also asked Indian business leaders to identify the capacities that have been most critical to the leadership of the firm over the past five years. They placed their greatest stress on four capacities: visioning, architecture and culture of the firm, personal qualities, and human resource issues. This is consistent with the notion that developing enduring capabilities is the key to success.

Strategy in the Indian context, then, is about the CEO's involvement in setting the core business principles by which the firm or business group will compete in the marketplace. CEOs recognized the need for capability development as the market opened up postreform. Beyond setting the architecture of the firm, CEOs provide input into strategies developed in the units reporting to them to a far greater extent than we see in U.S. corporations, making sure those strategies remain consistent with the core business principles. Adaptation, improvisation (*jugaad*), and doing more with less characterize key elements of strategy. The Tata Nano example and others above illustrate this adaptability and creative extension and utilization of resources. There is always the risk that quality could be compromised in this search for ever more creative ways of competing. But a theme present

Table 1

How Indian and American Business Leaders Have Changed Their Allocation of Time Over the Past Three Years

Leadership Tasks	U.S.		India	
	% More Time	% Less Time	% More Time	% Less Time
1. **Regulatory/compliance issues**	**98**	2	41	24
2. **Reporting to the board**	**72**	1	41	17
3. **Shareholder relations**	**58**	4	41	31
4. **Setting strategy**	47	9	**93**	0
5. **Media relations**	31	11	31	17
6. **Day-to-day management**	28	27	24	**55**
7. **Fostering workplace diversity**	26	13	21	41
8. **Customer relations**	22	27	**62**	7

(Items in bold: More than half of the executives affirmed)

Source: *U.S. figures from N.Y. Stock Exchange (2006) survey. Omitted column is "no change."*

throughout is an emphasis on capability development and on resilience in a rapidly changing environment.

The process of driving strategy through core principles, especially social mission, also helps these companies find opportunities where no one else was looking. Hindustan Unilever's (HUL) development of a system for selling products through rural self-help groups illustrates how new structures made it possible to address a new market. HUL challenged head-on the assumption that standardized consumer products could not be sold to lower income consumers. Although a subsidiary of a multinational consumer products company, HUL was also very much an Indian company with many products unique to India. That helped it to look past Western business models that use standard marketing and supply-chain practices.

A persistent and previously unsolved problem for retail in India is that the rural market is scattered in some 600,000 villages, more than half of which were not effectively connected to urban centers by electronic media, newspapers, and rail. Project Shakti (meaning strength or empowerment), launched in 2000, was designed to address this gap. With rising competition from Procter and Gamble and local competitors in traditional markets, HUL realized that opening new markets was a way to create new opportunities. The project aimed at the most remote and lowest income consumers to extend the firm's reach beyond traditional marketing channels. They reached the new market through women's self-help groups. These groups, set up by non-governmental organizations, typically comprise 10 to 15 women from a single village. They operate as mutual thrift societies, combining small amounts of cash toward a common pool. Microcredit agencies then lend additional funds to finance approved microcommercial initiatives.

Shakti entrepreneurs borrow money from their self-help groups, apply it to the purchase of HUL products, and then resell them to their neighbors. As most of the women in the self-help groups have no prior sales or business experience, HUL hires rural-sales promoters to coach the nascent entrepreneurs. The self-help-group entrepreneurs work as social influencers, increasing local awareness and changing attitudes toward usage of various products, mostly those targeted at women. At the same time, Shakti creates jobs for the rural women. HUL has extended Shakti to 15 states, and by the end of 2010, the company plans to have more than 100,000 Shakti entrepreneurs covering 500,000 villages.

Roots of the India Way: Can It Translate?

Is the India Way so unique to the Indian context that it cannot apply elsewhere? It has aspects that are consistent with traditional Indian culture, especially Hindi culture, such as obligations to the community, but it is nothing like a simple application of Indian cultural norms or business practices to modern corporations. In fact, the model looks relatively little like the practices of companies before the 1990 economic reforms. The new generation of leaders who created the India Way for the most part did not

come from the executive ranks of the legacy companies. They were by and large entrepreneurs who started from scratch or, in the case of existing companies such as the Bank of Baroda, leaders with a mandate to reshape the drawing board. The India Way model they created responded to the remarkably different environment for business offered up by the economic reforms and more open markets after 1990.

The India Way is unique, but the set of practices that comprise it are not necessarily dependent on the Indian context. At least some of the practices, such as stakeholder-based governance and investments in employees, were part of the U.S. model in a previous generation. While it might be tempting to think that Indian practices might over time evolve into something closer to the current U.S. model, there are no apparent forces to drive such an evolution: The Indian firms are already exposed to the international investment industry—several are listed on U.S. stock markets—and they are succeeding mightily in international competition. It is more likely, we argue, that the India Way should serve as a model for other countries in part because it addresses the intense pressures for greater social responsibility but most importantly because it is succeeding in the competitive environment with a competitive advantage that appears to be sustainable in the long run. (See Appendix B about the accepted views on Indian culture as they relate to business.)

Conclusions

We understand that not all Indian business leaders are saints, not all Indian companies pursue the practices we describe here, and that even for these leading companies, we may be describing their best attributes. But the same can be said for accounts of companies in other contexts as well. Models are built on archetypes and the attributes that distinguish them from other models. While there are bits and pieces of the India Way in other contexts, the complete package of the India Way could be found nowhere else. Some parts of the system, like *jugaad*, seem unique; others, such as the dedication to a social mission, are practiced elsewhere but not at the level we see in India.

Clearly there are limits to the transferability of the India Way to other contexts. The fact that so many of the current business leaders in India were also founders of their companies gives them influence over organizational culture and company goals that professional executives of long-established firms do not have. The spectacular growth of Indian corporations may also make it easier to find resources for pursuing social missions, and the extraordinary problems of Indian society make the need for such missions much more urgent than in the West. And the fact that so many leading companies are all going down the path we describe creates normative comparisons that make it easier to keep going in that direction.

As concerns about current U.S. corporate practices mount, it is especially important to look at other models. The India Way offers a compelling example of a model that succeeds financially while succeeding socially. Indeed, we argue that its success is precisely because of its social mission. While the culture and context of India may seem quite foreign to the U.S., the practices that make up the India Way are easily recognizable to managers anywhere and indeed may not be all that different from what we might have seen in U.S. corporations a generation ago. It is time to take a closer look at those practices.

REFERENCES

Antonakis, J., Avolio, B. J., & Sivasubramaniam, N. (2003). Context and leadership: An examination of the nine-factor full-range leadership theory using the Multifactor Leadership Questionnaire. *The Leadership Quarterly*, 14(3), 261–295.

Baranowska, L. (2007, July). *Growing globally in an age of disruptions: How India's top companies are meeting the challenge* (Report A-0241-07-EA). New York: The Conference Board.

Bass, B. M., & Avolio, B. J. (2004). MLQ *manual & sampler set* (3rd ed.). Menlo Park, CA: Mind Garden, Inc.

Bertrand, M., Mehta, P., & Mullainathan, S. (2002). Ferreting out tunneling: An application to Indian business groups. *Quarterly Journal of Economics*, 117(1), 121–148.

Chakrabarti, R., Megginson, W., & Yadav, P. K. (2008). Corporate governance in India. *Journal of Applied Corporate Finance*, 20(1), 59–72.

Chambers, J. T. (2007). To our shareholders [Section: Corporate citizenship and social responsibility]. *Cisco annual report 2007*. Retrieved April 1, 2010, from http://www.cisco.com/web/about/ac49/ac20/ac19/ar2007/letter_to_shareholders/index.html.

Chari, A., Chen, W., & Dominguez, K. M. E. (2009, March). *Foreign ownership and firm performance: Emerging-market acquisitions in the United States* (Working Paper No. 14786). Cambridge, MA: National Bureau of Economic Research.

Coffee, J. C., Jr. (2005). A theory of corporate scandals: Why the USA and Europe differ. *Oxford Review of Economic Policy*, 21(2), 198–211.

Economist.com. (2007, March 29). India's acquisitive companies: Marauding maharajahs. Retrieved April 1, 2010, from http://www.economist.com/business-finance/displaystory.cfm?story_id=E1_RJPQGSN.

Epstein, G. A. (Ed.). (2005). *Financialization and the world economy*. Cheltenham, UK, and Northampton, MA: Edward Elgar.

Express Computer. (2007, July 23). Work culture: "Single status" for all. Retrieved April 1, 2010, from http://www.expresscomputeronline.com/20070723/technologylife04.shtml.

Franco, L., Gibbons, J., & Barrington, L. (2010). I *can't get no … job satisfaction, that is: America's unhappy workers* (No. R-1459-09-RR). New York: The Conference Board.

General Accounting Office. (2002). *Financial statement restatements: Trends, market impacts, regulatory responses, and remaining challenges*. GAO-03-138. Retrieved April 1, 2010, from http://www.gao.gov/new.items/d03138.pdf.

Ghosh, S. (2006). Do board characteristics affect corporate performance? Firm-level evidence for India. *Applied Economics Letters*, 13(7), 435–443.

Gopalan, S., & Rivera, J. B. (1997). Gaining a perspective on Indian value orientations: Implications for expatriate managers. *International Journal of Organizational Analysis*, 5(2), 156–179.

Grant, A. M. (2008). The significance of task significance: Job performance effects, relational mechanisms, and boundary conditions. *Journal of Applied Psychology*, 93(1), 108–124.

Grant, E. (2008). *How to retain talent in India.* [Synopsis of working paper, *How to manage talent in a fast-moving labor market: Some findings from India*, by J. Doh, S. Stumpf, W. Tymon, & M. Haid.] MIT *Sloan Management Review*, 50(1), 6–7.

Guha, R. (2007). *India after Gandhi: The history of the world's largest democracy*. New York: Ecco.

Hackman, J. R., & Oldham, G. R. (1975). Development of the job diagnostic survey. *Journal of Applied Psychology*, 60(2), 159–170.

Hamm, S., & Lakshman, N. (2007, March 19). The trouble with India: Crumbling roads, jammed airports, and power blackouts could hobble growth. *Business Week Online*. Retrieved April 1, 2010, from http://www.businessweek.com/magazine/content/07_12/b4026001.htm.

ICFAI Business School Case Development Centre (IBSCDC). (2008). *Tata Group's strategy: Ratan Tata's vision* (Case Study VMG0015C). Hyderabad, India: ICFAI Business School.

India Brand Equity Foundation. (2010). Foreign direct investment [Web Page]. Retrieved April 1, 2010, from http://www.ibef.org/economy/fdi.aspx.

ITC. (2010). A commitment beyond the market [Web Page]. Retrieved April 1, 2010, from http://www.itcportal.com/rural-development/home.htm.

Javidan, M., Dorfman, P. W., De Luque, M. S., & House, R. J. (2006). In the eye of the beholder: Cross-cultural lessons in leadership from Project GLOBE. *Academy of Management Perspectives*, 20(1), 67–90.

Kalleberg, A. L. (in press). Precarious work, insecure workers: Employment relations in transition. *American Sociological Review*.

Kurczewski, N. (2009, June 28). And now, for some serious belt-tightening. *New York Times*, p. 10.

Lakshman, C. (2009). Corporate social responsibility through knowledge leadership in India: ITC Ltd. and Y. C. Devesh-war. Asian *Business & Management* 8(2), 185–203.

Lazonick, W., & O'Sullivan, M. (2000). Maximizing share-holder value: A new ideology for corporate governance. *Economy & Society*, 29(1), 13–35.

Lev, B., Petrovits, C., & Radhakrishnan, S. (2010). Is doing good good for you? How corporate charitable contributions enhance revenue growth. *Strategic Management Journal*, 31(2), 182–200.

Markham, J. W. (2006). *Financial history of modern U.S. corporate scandals: From Enron to reform*. Armonk, NY: M. E. Sharpe.

MindTree. (2010a). Integrity policy [Web Page]. Retrieved April 1, 2010, from http://www.mindtree.com/aboutus /integrity_policy.html.

MindTree. (2010b). People focused innovation [Web Page].Retrieved April 1, 2010, from http://www.mindtree .com/aboutus/people_focused_innovation.html.

Mishel, L., Bernstein, J., & Shierholz, H. (2009). *The state of working America: 2008/2009*. Washington, DC: The Economic Policy Institute.

Morck, R. K., & Steier, L. (2005, January). *The global history of global governance: An introduction* (Working Paper No. 11062). Cambridge, MA: National Bureau of Economic Research.

Murthy, V., & Abeysekera, I. (2007). Human capital value creation practices of software and service exporter firms in India. *Journal of HRCA: Human Resource Costing & Accounting*, 11(2), 84–103.

Narayana Hrudayalaya Hospitals. (2010). Narayana Hru-dayalaya Hospitals [Web Page]. Retrieved April 1, 2010, from http://www.narayanahospitals.com/index.html.

Nayar, V. (2008, March 11). Destroying the office of the CEO [Blog]. Retrieved April 1, 2010, from http://www.vineetnayar .com/destroying-the-office-of-the-ceo/.

New York Stock Exchange. (2006, May). NYSE CEO *report 2007: Planning for growth, valuing people*. Princeton, NJ: Opinion Research Corporation.

Paulson, H. M. (2010). *On the brink: Inside the race to stop the collapse of the global financial system*. New York: Business Plus.

Prahalad, C. K. (2004). *The fortune at the bottom of the pyr-amid: Eradicating poverty through profits*. Upper Saddle River, NJ: Wharton School Publishing.

Rao, H., & Hoyt, D. (2007). *Infosys: Building a talent engine to sustain growth* (Case Study HR30). Palo Alto, CA: Stanford Graduate School of Business.

Reed, D., & Mukherjee, S. (Eds.). (2004). *Corporate gover-nance, economic reforms, and development: The Indian expe-rience*. New Delhi and New York: Oxford University Press.

Reinhardt, C. M., & Rogoff, K. S. (2008). Is the 2007 U.S. sub-prime financial crisis so different? An international his-torical comparison. *American Economic Review, American Economic Association*, 98(2), 339–344.

Reserve Bank of India. (2009a, January). *Monthly bulletin, Table 44: Foreign exchange reserves*. Retrieved April 1, 2010, from http://rbidocs.rbi.org.in/rdocs/Bulletin/PDFs/ 89874.pdf.

Reserve Bank of India. (2009b, January). *Monthly bulletin, Table 46: Foreign investment inflows*. Retrieved April 1, 2010, from http://rbidocs.rbi.org.in/rdocs/Bulletin/PDFs/ 89876.pdf.

Sarkar, J., & Sarkar, S. (2000). Large shareholder activism in corporate governance in developing countries: Evidence from India. *International Review of Finance*, 1(3), 161–194.

Sarkar, J., Sarkar, S., & Sen, K. (2008). Board of directors and opportunistic earnings management: Evidence from India. *Journal of Accounting, Auditing & Finance*, 23(4), 517–551.

Schuker, L. A. E. (2008, September 20). Spielberg, India's Reliance to form studio. *Wall Street Journal*, p. B7.

SHRM India. (2008, November). Corporate Indian companies: Forging new talent pipelines and creative career pathways. Retrieved April 1, 2010, from http://www.shrm.org/Research /SurveyFindings/Articles/Documents/09-0685_SHRM_India _Article_FNL.pdf.

Singh, M. (2009). Customer value via an intranet: A case application of B2E at HCL Technologies. *International Jour-nal of Information Management*, 29(6), 497–501.

Som, A. (2006). Bracing for MNC competition through innovative HRM practices: The way ahead for Indian firms. *Thunderbird International Business Review*, 48(2), 207–237.

Sorkin, A. R. (2009). Too *big to fail: The inside story of how Wall Street and Washington fought to save the financial sys-tem from crisis—and themselves*. New York: Viking.

Spector, M., & Bellman, E. (2008, March 27). Tata and Ford reach deal for Land Rover, Jaguar: Indian firm will pay about $2.3 billion. *Wall Street Journal*, p. B3.

Spencer, S. M., Rajah, T., Mohan, S., & Lahiri, G. (2008). *The Indian CEO—A portrait of excellence*. New Delhi: Response Books.

Surender, T., & Bose, J. (2008, January 11). I'm in a lonely phase of my life: Ratan Tata. *The Times of India*. Retrieved April 1, 2010, from http://timesofindia.indiatimes.com/biz

/india-business/Im-in-a-lonely-phase-of-my-life-Ratan-Tata/ articleshow/2690777.cms.

Tosi, H. L., Misangyi, V. F., Fanelli, A., Waldman, D. A., & Yammarino, F. J. (2004). CEO charisma, compensation, and firm performance. *Leadership Quarterly*, 15(3), 405–420.

Tuteja, S. K. (2006). Board structure in Indian companies. *Journal of Management Research*, 6(3), 145–156.

U.S. Bureau of Labor Statistics. (1995). 1995 *survey of employer provided training-employee results, Table 5: Percent of employees who received training by selected employment characteristics* .Retrieved April 1, 2010, from http://www.bls.gov/news.release/ sept.t05.htm.

U.S. Bureau of Labor Statistics. (2009, July 28). *International comparisons of* GDP *per capita and per employed person: 17 countries, 1960–2008.* Retrieved April 1, 2010, from http:// www.bls.gov/fls/flsgdp.pdf.

Useem, M. (2010). The Asia way: Market capitalism 2.0 in Davos. *Wharton Leadership Digest* [Web Page], *14(3–4)*. Retrieved April 1, 2010, from http://leadership.wharton .upenn.edu/digest/01-10. shtml.

Wadhwa, V., de Vitton, U. K., & Gereffi, G. (2008, July). *The disciple became a guru: Is it time for the U.S. to learn workforce development from former disciple India?* Retrieved April 1, 2010, from http://sites.kauffman.org/pdf /disciple_became_guru_72208.pdf.

Waldman, D. A., Ramirez, G. G., House, R. J., & Puranam, P. (2001). Does leadership matter? CEO leadership attributes and profitability under conditions of perceived environmental uncertainty. *Academy of Management Journal*, 44(1), 134–143.

Williams, C. A., & Aguilera, R. V. (2008). Corporate social responsibility in a comparative perspective. In A. Crane, A. McWilliams, D. Matten, J. Moon, & D. Siegel (Eds.), *The Oxford handbook of corporate social responsibility* (pp. 452–472). Oxford, UK: Oxford University Press.

Williamson, J. (1993). Democracy and the "Washington consensus." *World Development*, 21(8), 1329–1336.

World Bank. (2009, July 1). Gross national income per capita 2008, Atlas method and PPP. Retrieved April 1, 2010, from World Development Indicators Database: http://siteresources .worldbank.org/DATASTATISTICS/ Resources/GNIPC.pdf.

World Bank Group. (2009). *Doing business* (Annual report series by country). Washington, DC: World Bank and International Finance Corporation. Retrieved April 1, 2010, from http://www.doingbusiness.org.

Yee, A. (2007, June 30). Stars of India: Around the world, more and more companies are recruiting people from the subcontinent for top management positions. Amy Yee discovers why. *Financial Times Weekend Magazine*, p. 40.

Appendices

Appendix A: Training at Infosys

Once hired at Infosys, new recruits move to the largest corporate training facility in the world, just short of 300 acres outside of Mysore. The facility can handle 6,000 trainees at a time, with plans to quadruple in size. The training center was designed to feel like a college campus. When we visited, we were struck by how much the training-session rooms resembled typical college classrooms, a similarity that makes the transition from college to the company as smooth as possible. The 14-week training regimen includes regular exams and assessments that the new hires must pass to continue in the program. Candidates hired from outside India receive even longer training, six months, to help them adapt to the Indian and Infosys cultures. Company managers are assessed based on the percentage of new hires in their group who achieve an A grade on these tests, the number who achieve various competency certifications, and the percentage of outside or lateral hires who are rated as "good" in their first reviews. More senior managers are assessed based on the job satisfaction of their employees and the percentage of leadership positions that have an identified internal successor. Holding supervisors similarly responsible for the achievements of their subordinates was quite common in the U.S. before the mid-1980s but is now extremely rare (Rao & Hoyt, 2007).

Appendix B: Indian National Culture and Business

Suresh Gopalan and Joan Rivera (1997) summarized the accepted views about Indian national culture as they relate to business as follows: The Hindu religion's belief in predestination reduces personal ambition and persistence; the country's deep historical orientation leads to conformity with the past and resistance to change; a long tradition of hierarchical social relations make individual leaders more important than the goals they pursue. Others have made similar arguments, for example, that Indian salespersons perform better under more hierarchical authority arrangements than do their U.S. counterparts and that the greater power imbalance between superiors and subordinates in Indian society requires leadership styles that are much more task-oriented, leaving little room for individual autonomy. These views of Indian culture, however, are hard to reconcile with the fast-moving, innovative Indian business scene, empowered employees, and ambitious leaders who populate the India Way.

Source: Peter Cappelli, Harbir Singh, Jitendra Singh, and Michael Useem, Academy of Management Perspectives.

READING 1.2

Strategic Human Resource Management as Ethical Stewardship

Cam Caldwell, Do X. Truong, Pham T. Linh, and Anh Tuan

ABSTRACT. *The research about strategic human resource management (SHRM) has suggested that human resource professionals (HRPs) have the opportunity to play a greater role in contributing to organizational success if they are effective in developing systems and policies aligned with the organization's values, goals, and mission. We suggest that HRPs need to raise the standard of their performance and that the competitive demands of the modern economic environment create implicit ethical duties that HRPs owe to their organizations. We define ethical stewardship as a model of governance that honors obligations due to the many stakeholders and that maximizes long-term organizational wealth creation. We propose that if HRPs adopt an ethical stewardship framework and the qualities of transformative leaders, they will be more aware of their ethical duties to their organizations and more effective in helping their organizations to create increased wealth, achieve desired organizational outcomes, and establish work environments that are more satisfying to employees.*

Research about the strategic role of human resource management (HRM) has exponentially increased over the last decade (Hartel et al., 2007), with scholars and practitioners acknowledging the critical importance of ethical issues in HRM as key factors in aligning and guiding organizational success (Hernandez, 2008; Werhane et al. 2004). Scholars have also noted that the strategic focus of human resource systems is more effective when aligned with an organization's mission, purposes, values, and structure (Becker and Gerhart, 1996; Becker and Huselid, 2006; Huselid and Becker, 1997). This article examines the ethical duties associated with the implementation of HRM systems in helping organizations to achieve their potential (cf. Payne and Wayland, 1999) and identifies the leadership roles which make up an ethical stewardship approach to organizational systems.

We begin by citing the strategic human resource management (SHRM) literature to provide a contextual framework for examining the importance of the alignment and congruence of HRM systems (Becker and Huselid, 2006; Pfeffer, 1998) with the strategic goals of an organization (Becker et al., 2001). We then examine the nature and duties of ethical stewardship (Caldwell et al., 2008) related to the effective governance of organizations. Integrating the importance of SHRM with this framework of ethical stewardship, we identify important but sometimes implicit leadership roles that human resource professionals (HRPs) ought to contribute in optimizing the ability of their organizations to achieve that long-term wealth creation (Senge, 2006). We conclude by identifying the contributions of our article and offer comments about the importance of ethical leadership in creating the work systems, cultures, and the high level of employee commitment that are essential for organizations in today's global workplace (Pfeffer, 1998, 2007).

Strategic Human Resource Management

Understanding of the important role of SHRM in the modern organization provides an important context to understanding the ethical duties owed by HRPs. The most effective HRPs add value to their organization's effectiveness by linking people, strategy, values, and performance (Becker et al., 2001). This linking of an organization's overall strategy with aligned human resource systems is critical to the maximization of performance outcomes (Ulrich and Brockbank, 2005) in a world that is increasingly dependent upon the initiative, creativity, and commitment of employees to succeed (Covey, 2004; Senge, 2006). A growing body of empirical evidence has suggested that aligned systems in combination create superior organizational outcomes as compared to the implementation of individual human resource practices, although many scholars note that an incremental approach is more likely to occur (Pfeffer, 1998; Sun et al., 2007). However, the goals of effective organizations are not simply instrumental or outcome oriented. Great organizations are also normative, or value-based, and achieve their greatness because of their commitment to values and principles which guide employees (Collins, 2001; Collins and Porras, 2004) and which create strong and effective employee cultures (Schein, 2004).

Becker and Huselid (1999) noted that integrating key human resource functions to reframe an organization's internal environment results in significantly higher organizational outcomes and financial performance that is superior to what firms can attain by implementing individual human resource program elements piecemeal. The three key functions that Becker and Huselid (1999) cited as most important were (1) a management culture aligned with the corporate strategy; (2) operational and professional excellence in conducting key tasks; and (3) a human resource structure focusing on human resource managers as business partners to other departments. These three organizational factors are interrelated (Becker and Huselid, 1999; Paine, 2003) and organizational cultures can enrich human lives as well as increase profitability (Cameron, 2003; Senge, 2006).

Empirical evidence by an award-winning HRM study (Huselid, 1995) demonstrated that high performance HRM systems had a significant positive impact upon overall financial performance, productivity, and turnover. Pfeffer (1998) has provided a comprehensive body of business evidence citing studies that demonstrate that strategically crafted HRM systems can generate organizational wealth when effectively integrated with organizational goals. More importantly, Pfeffer's research and that of other scholars provides valuable insight about *how to implement* those systems. Pfeffer (1998, p. xv) noted that "enormous economic returns (can be) obtained through the implementation of what are variously called high involvement, high performance, or high commitment management practices."

Unfortunately, many HRPs and organizational leaders have consistently lacked the know-how to design and implement systems and policies that mesh with organizational goals. 2005). As Pfeffer (1998, p. 14) and Kouzes and Posner (2007, p. 75) have emphasized in their discussions of the roles of organizational leaders, the key to effective organizational change is execution. Becker and Huselid (2006, p. 99) called HR architecture, "the systems, practices, competencies, and employee performance behaviors" of SHRM a key element to "building sustainable competitive advantage and creating above-average financial performance." Ulrich and Beatty (2001, p. 293) have explained that the critical contribution made by human resources in accomplishing strategic goals required that they fill the roles of coach, architect, facilitator, conscience, and contributing leader—rising from the status of subservient "partners" to substantial "players." In order to achieve that higher level of status and impact, Beer (1997, pp. 49-51) noted that a successful transformation of the human resource function focused on three key change factors:

Focus on cost-effectiveness: *Reframing the human resource function to deliver services at a reduced cost made the HRM function more financially accountable.*

Merger of the HRM function with the strategic role: *Aligning core processes—the key tasks performed by organizations—so that when systems mesh rather than conflict the entire organization is able to utilize people efficiently and effectively.*

Development of new knowledge: *Empirical studies (e.g., Collins and Porras, 2004) confirmed that organizational culture, financial performance, and goal achievement were interdependent elements of successful organizations—and that valuing people and treating them well improved the bottom line.*

Successful SHRM "involves designing and implementing a set of internally consistent policies and practices that ensure that employees' collective knowledge, skills, and abilities contribute to the achievement of its business objectives" (Huselid et al., 1997, p. 172). If HRPs lack the knowledge and skill to craft these policies and practices and implement them in their organizations, then they fail to honor their professional duties and ethical obligations to the organizations they serve.

Historically, HRPs have traditionally played the role of internal service provider and deliverer of programs for operating departments (Beer, 1997; Lawler III, 2008). Organizational leaders and HRPs have apparently been slow to either understand the benefits of implementing high performance and high commitment systems, or they simply lack the skills required to implement such systems (Pfeffer, 1998). Pfeffer (1998, Part II) thoughtfully examines the consistent failure of HRPs and organizational leaders to apply the best thinking and empirical research that affirms proven principles of HRM, and clearly identifies the need for today's organizations to raise the standard of their performance in applying those principles. Yet the sub-optimization of organization performance persists and organization leaders miss opportunities to effectively serve their employees, shareholders, and society at large (Pfeffer, 1998, Chapter 1).

Increasingly, today's HRPs acknowledge that they can earn a place at their organization's strategic policy making table only if they understand how to measure the added value of employee contributions—the "decision science" of human resources—and help create organizational programs and systems that reinforce desired employee behaviors (Boud-reau and Ramstad, 2005, p. 17). Clardy (2008) has suggested that to manage the core competencies and human capital of the entire firm, HRPs must clearly understand the strategic goals of the firm and must then play a key leadership role in taking advantage of those competencies. Despite this obligation, HRPs are often unprepared to help their organizations to optimize the use of human capital and today's organizations fail to perform effectively (Lawler III, 2008). This inability to respond to the needs of the modern organization is an implicit but often unacknowledged and unintended violation of the responsibilities and duties owed to the organizations that those HRPs serve (Hosmer, 2007).

The HR Professional as Ethical Steward

The role of the leader as a steward in the governance of organizations has received increasing attention in the post-Enron era (Caldwell et al., 2008; Hernandez, 2008; Hosmer, 2007). In articulating the relationship that exists between organizations and their employees, Block (1993) described leaders as stewards who owed a complex set of duties to stakeholders. These duties achieve long-term wealth creation which ultimately benefits all stakeholders and honors the obligations owed by business to society (Caldwell and Karri, 2005; Solomon, 1992). DePree (2004, Ch. 1) and Pava (2003, Chapter 1) have described the duties of organizational leaders as "covenantal" in nature, suggesting that the relationship that organizations owed to employees was akin to both a contact and a sacred obligation.

Ethical stewardship has been defined as "the honoring of duties owed to employees, stakeholders, and society in the pursuit of long-term wealth creation" (Caldwell et al., 2008, p. 153). Ethical stewardship is a theory of organizational governance in which leaders seek the best interests of stakeholders by creating high trust cultures that honor a broad range of duties owed by organizations to followers (Caldwell and Karri, 2005; Pava, 2003). Covey (2004) has described the stewardship role as value-based, principle-centered, and committed to the welfare of all stakeholders. In pursuit of the best interests of each stakeholder, Covey has emphasized that the duty of leaders is to optimize outcomes, rather than settling for a compromise position that overlooks opportunities—a phrase Covey (2004, pp. 204–234) has described as "Win-Win or No Deal."

Both Block (1993) and DePree (2004) viewed the ethical obligations of organizations as neither idealistic nor soft. Block (1993, pp. 91–97) has argued that the responsibility of organizations was to fully disclose critical information and to clearly identify threats facing an organization as well as the accompanying implications of those threats upon employees. Block (1993, pp. 25–26) advocated treating employees as "owners and partners" in the governance process and emphasized that in the highly competitive global that relationship encompassed sharing honest and extensive communication. DePree (2004, p. 11) emphasized that "(t)he first task of the leader is to define reality"—a reality that included an obligation to tell all of the truth to employees, rather than withholding key information that might treat the employees as mere hirelings or the means by which the firm achieved its goals.

The moral position of ethical stewardship is that organizational leaders have the obligation to pursue long-term wealth creation by implementing systems that strengthen the organizational commitment of each stakeholder (Caldwell and Karri, 2005). Ethical stewards in HRM demonstrate the insights of great organizations that transform their companies into human and humane communities which emphasize inclusion, shared partnership, empowerment, and leadership trustworthiness (Kanter, 2008). This transforming culture occurs when followers believe that systems will enable employees to achieve desired outcomes and that social contracts will be honored (Caldwell and Karri, 2005; Caldwell et al., 2008). Such a culture is also achieved by treating employees as "yous" or as valued individuals and organizational partners, rather than as "its" or a mere organizational commodity with a human form (cf. Buber, 2008).

Grossman (2007) has noted that the HR professional must become a steward in framing an organization's culture and in facilitating change. Although some scholars have advocated that HRPs become ethical advocates (Payne and Wayland, 1999), the scope of that advocating role and the ethical values to be incorporated therein have been a source of debate (Guest, 2007; Legge, 2000; Palmer, 2007; Schultz and Brender-Ilan, 2004). Nonetheless, human resource managers have not typically reported performing a major role as ethical educators within their organizations nor have they been successful when they attempted to perform that role (Coltrin, 1991). HRPs would benefit to understand that organizations owe a complex set of duties to multiple stakeholders, and that they must be accountable to help organizations understand the ethical implications of their actions (Hosmer, 2007). In providing a glimpse into the ethics of management and the duties of organizations to society, Hosmer (2007) is just one of many ethics scholars who have addressed the responsibilities of organizational leaders to constantly examine the moral calculus of leadership in evaluating consequences of a firm's behaviors to diverse stakeholders.

If the HRP is to function as an ethical steward in the modern organization, she/he must combine a profound knowledge (Deming, 2000) of the operations of the firm, an understanding about how to implement systems by which organizations can maximize human performance (Becker and Huselid, 2006), an understanding of the empirical value and cost/benefit contribution of high performance systems (Pfeffer, 1998), and the ability to communicate effectively to top management and Boards of Directors in a convincing manner so that those policy makers will adopt policies and systems essential for creating integrated and effective HRM systems that support organizational goals (Lawler III, 2008).

HRPs and the Duties of Leadership

As organizational leaders HRPs have responsibilities that require insight, skills, wisdom, experience, and a profound knowledge of their organizations (Becker and Huselid, 1999). In this section of our article, we suggest that HRPs are "transformative leaders" (Bennis and Nanus, 2007) who honor a broad set of ethical duties in their role as ethical stewards.

The HRPs demonstrate principles of *transformational leadership* when they combine a commitment to helping both individuals and organizations to achieve unprecedented excellence (Kupers and Weibler, 2006). Dvir et al. (2002)

found that transformational leaders had a positive impact on followers' development and performance and the accomplishment of organizational priorities, affirming Bass and Avolio's (1990, p. 22) claim that transformational leaders "elevate the desires of followers for achievement and self-development while also promoting the development of groups and organizations." Citing the example of the U.S. Naval Academy graduate, Jim Schwappach, Kouzes and Posner (2007, pp. 118–119) describe Schwappach as a leader who was effective at listening deeply to others and involving others in developing solutions that empower employees while greatly increasing the effectiveness of an organization in accomplishing organizational goals. HRM practices that view employees as valued assets and contributors to the creation of strategic competitive advantage empower people to enhance their potential to contribute to the organization's success while simultaneously improving employees' skill sets along the way (Becker and Gerhart, 1996; DePree, 2004). Empowering employees maximizes commitment and enables employees to become a source of strategic competitive advantage that competitors rarely can duplicate (Becker et al., 2001).

Becker et al. (2001, p. 4) have noted that "(w)e're living in a time when a new economic paradigm—characterized by speed, innovation, short cycle times, quality, and customer satisfaction—is highlighting the importance of intangible assets." The intangible human assets essential for sustaining competitive advantage depend on whether a firm's leadership understands how to integrate people into the achievement of organizational goals (Becker and Huselid, 1998, 2006). The ability of transformational leadership to simultaneously pursue both individual needs and organizational goals has long been considered a critical element of organizational success (Barnard, 1938), and is widely regarded as an important characteristic of high performance organizations (Cameron, 2003).

The HRPs also honor their duties to others when they apply principles of charismatic leadership. *Charismatic* leaders are ethical stewards to the degree that they personally inspire others to achieve worthy goals (Caldwell et al., 2007). Charismatic leadership is "an attribution based on follower perceptions of their leader's behavior", and reflects the followers' "perception of their leader's extraordinary character" (Conger et al., 2000, p. 748). House (1977) described charismatic leadership as being characterized by high emotional expressiveness, self-confidence, self-determination, freedom from internal conflict, and a conviction of the correctness of the leader's own beliefs. Kouzes and Posner (2007, p. 133) emphasized that inspiring leaders appeal to common ideals and animate an organization's vision in a way that resonates deeply within the hearts of others.

Charismatic leaders recognize that it is in resonating with people at the emotional level that creates the greatest personal commitment (Boyatzis and McKee, 2005). While writing of effective human resource leadership, Pfeffer (1998, p. 125) cited the case of Elmar Toime of the New

Zealand Post who implemented high trust practices based upon close relationships with individual employees. Toime's style demonstrates the influence of charismatic leadership in implementing human resource practices which transformed the New Zealand Post "from a typical government bureaucracy to a profitable state-owned enterprise and the most efficient post office in the world" (Pfeffer, 1998, p. 125).

The HRPs, who demonstrate the ability to create a personal charismatic connection with organizational employees, and who maintain that connection by honoring commitments, honor the duties of ethical stewardship by encouraging the hearts of employees (Kouzes and Posner, 2007, Chapters 11 and 12). That ability to create high commitment and high trust is at the heart of high performing organizations (Senge, 2006) and is a key responsibility of effective leadership.

In honoring ethical duties, HRPs are also principle-centered. *Principle-centered* leadership incorporates foundations of ethical stewardship to the degree that it seeks to integrate the instrumental and normative objectives of an organization while being congruent with universal principles demonstrated by effective leaders. Covey (1992, 2004) argued that leadership is the most successful when it adheres to a patterned set of well-accepted principles of effectiveness and respected moral values. According to Covey (1992, p. 31), principle-centered leadership is practiced "from the inside out" at the personal, interpersonal, managerial, and organizational levels. Principle-centered leaders earn trust based upon their character and competence (Covey, 2004). Kouzes and Posner (2003b, 2007) have noted that great leaders sustain their credibility based upon their consistency in modeling correct principles and in honoring values that demonstrate personal integrity.

The principle-centered leader recognizes that virtuous outcomes supersede adherence to rules (Kohlberg, 1985) and that moral purposes complement best practices in achieving stewardship goals (Caldwell and Karri, 2005). Principle-centered leaders model organizational values (Kouzes and Posner, 2007) and recognize that effective leadership is ultimately the integration of both ends and means (cf. Burns, 1978). In their classic study of the most successful businesses of the past century, Collins and Porras (2004, pp. 131–135) noted the emphasis that Procter and Gamble placed on creating a strong principle-based culture based on core values and a core ideology.

The HRPs honor the obligations of ethical stewards when they develop a knowledge of guiding principles that characterize great organizations (Pfeffer, 1998), and when they help organizations to create aligned organizational cultures that match actual behaviors with espoused values (Schein, 2004). This commitment to values and principles of principle-centered leadership is a key element in establishing and implementing human resource systems that earn employee commitment and trust (Covey, 2004).

The HRPs that demonstrate principles of servant leadership build trust and inspire the confidence of others. *Servant leadership* is at the heart of ethical stewardship (Caldwell et al., 2007) and exemplifies its depth of commitment to serving the individual. DePree (2004, p. 11), one of the most highly regarded advocates of servant leadership, opined that organizational leaders had the ethical responsibility to be "a servant and a debtor" to employees by establishing policies that demonstrate the organization's commitment to the welfare of each employee. Hamilton and Nord (2005, p. 875) describe servant leadership as "valuing individuals and developing people, building community, practicing authenticity, and providing leadership that focuses on the good of those who are being led and those whom the organization serves."

Greenleaf (2004, p. 2) emphasized that the great leader is a servant first because that commitment to serving others is his identity "deep down inside." Servant leadership honors each individual as a valued end, rather than simply as a means to organizational outcomes (cf. Buber, 2008; Hosmer, 1995). The servant leader puts the needs, desires, interests, and welfare of others above his or her self-interest (Ludema and Cox, 2007, p. 343) while also honoring duties owed to the organization (DePree, 2004). Pfeffer (1998, pp. 91–92) noted that Herb Kelleher, the former CEO of Southwest Airlines, and Sam Walton, the founder of Wal-Mart, were both known for valuing employees as critical to the success of their organizations and for adopting a leadership philosophy incorporating principles of servant leadership. This valuing of employees at both Wal-Mart and at Southwest Airlines balanced a consideration for employees' welfare with a recognition that treating employees well increases their commitment in return.

The HRPs who demonstrate a commitment to the "welfare, growth, and wholeness" (Caldwell et al., 2002, p. 162) of stakeholders are servant leaders and ethical stewards. It is this commitment to stakeholder interests that makes leaders credible and trustworthy (Kouzes and Posner, 2003a). HRPs, who fail to create policies that demonstrate a commitment to serving employees, and who do not behave congruently with those values, undermine the trust of employees and inhibit the ability of organizations to maximize long-term wealth creation (Senge, 2006).

The HRPs are Level 5 leaders when they demonstrate their fierce commitment to the success of the organization while creating systems that recognize employee contributions and give credit to employees for achieving an organization's success. *Level* 5 leaders demonstrate a leadership insight that willingly shares both power and the credit for accomplishments while accepting personal responsibility for organizational failures (Collins, 2001). In his study of great corporations, Collins (2001, pp. 17–40) found that the leaders of the organizations that evolved "from good to great" were typified by high commitment coupled with great personal humility. In discussing these Level 5 leaders, Marcum and Smith (2007) explained that Level 5 leaders avoided the counterfeit leadership qualities of egoistic self-interest that typified high profile leaders in many organizations. Collins (2001, p. 27) emphasized that Level 5 leaders were not "I-centered" leaders who pursued self-serving goals or who viewed themselves as the upfront personification of their organization's success. Instead, they tended to be described by those who worked with or wrote about them as *"quiet, humble, modest, reserved, shy, gracious, mild-mannered, self-effacing, understated, did not believe his own clippings;* and so forth" [Italics in the original] (Collins, 2001, p. 27).

Collins (2001, p. 30) reported that Level 5 leaders also possessed a "ferocious resolve, an almost stoic determination to do whatever needs to be done" to serve the organization and to make it great. Werhane (2007, p. 433) also noted that the most successful leaders in her study of effective women leaders were Level 5 leaders who "seem to care more about the sustained success of their organization than their own legacy." Level 5 leaders are transformative in demonstrating humility about their own accomplishments, giving credit to others in their organization for success while accepting full responsibility for the errors made by an organization and working unceasingly to address those errors (Collins, 2001, 2005). Citing the case of AES Corporation's CEO, Dennis Bakke, Pfeffer (1998, pp. 99–103) emphasized that effective organizations do not achieve short-term profitability by short-changing employees. Working for the long-term success of an organization and creating policies and systems that reward employees for laying the foundation to achieve long-term growth rather than a short-term appearance of growth takes courage and integrity in the face of pressures to achieve short-term results in today's distorted business environment (Pfeffer, 1998).

Human resource professionals act as both ethical stewards and Level 5 leaders when they create human resource systems and processes that are fully aligned with the normative and instrumental goals of the organization while giving employees credit for their role in the accomplishment of those goals (Caldwell et al., 2007). These aligned and congruent systems and processes balance the needs of the organization with a commitment to the best interests of its stakeholders (Pauchant, 2005) and create reward systems that also reward employees for contributing to organizational success.

When HRPs model the behaviors of covenantal leadership, they help organizations create new knowledge which enables firms to create and maintain competitive advantage and constantly improve. *Covenantal* leadership integrates the roles of the leader as a servant, role model, a source of inspiration and as a creator of new insight and meaning (Caldwell et al., 2007; Pava, 2003). Covenantal leadership encompasses the pursuit of a noble purpose, often described as rising to the level of a contractual or even a sacred duty (Barnett and Schubert, 2002; DePree, 2004; Pava, 2003). Covenantal leaders seek not only to enhance the skills and abilities of those with whom they associate, but also to "unleash the great human potential which is often dormant and silent" in organizations (Pava, 2003, p. 26). Striving to serve both individuals and the organization, sharing knowledge, inspiring by personal example, and learning with others, covenantal leadership is attuned to the importance of continuous learning (Pava, 2003).

Covenantal leadership incorporates ethical stewardship's commitment to creating new solutions to problems, creating new wealth and value, and working for the welfare of stakeholders (Caldwell et al., 2006). It is in this ability to help people to discover new truths and achieve the best within themselves at both the individual and organizational levels, enabling organizations to optimize wealth creation (Senge, 2006) and honor their role as covenantal leaders and ethical stewards (Caldwell and Dixon, 2007; Caldwell et al., 2007). Kouzes and Posner (2007, p. 317) cited the example of Bob Branchi, the Managing Director of Western Australia's largest network of automobile dealerships, in teaching a delivery driver that his value as an individual and his role in the organization were also important to the organization's success—thereby helping that individual not only to share in the organization's accomplishments but also to redefine himself.

Sung-Choon et al. (2007) have emphasized the vital role of knowledge creation in firms as an important element of the human resource architecture and have advocated the importance of adopting a learning organization culture to create a sustainable competitive advantage. HRPs become covenantal leaders when they focus on individuals, empower them to increase their level of commitment to themselves and to the organization, and create opportunities for creating new knowledge and insight that benefits both the organization and the individual (cf. Pava, 2003; Senge, 2006).

As HRPs adopt the characteristics of ethical stewardship, they help their organizations add value to the lives of individuals and organizations. Solomon and Flores (2003, p. 6) have called leaders who demonstrate high commitment to others and to their organizations "authentic" and praise the trustworthiness and integrity of those who lead unselfishly and effectively. Kolp and Rea (2005, pp. 154–158) have also cited the character of such leaders and have described their accomplishments as balancing "value and virtue" in creating cultures where employees feel empowered to take risks and achieve unprecedented results. HRPs who adopt the leadership behaviors of ethical stewardship understand the value of the individual as well as the organization while holding both people and the organization in high regard.

By integrating the best elements of leadership, HRPs honor their role as ethical stewards and contribute to the capability of their organizations while profoundly benefiting the employees who work in those organizations. As contributors to the optimal strategic accomplishment of an organization's mission, HRPs who exhibit transformative leadership behaviors have the opportunity to serve the needs of a multiple set of stakeholders in honoring a broad range of ethical duties (Hosmer, 2007). HRPs can help organizations to build trust and commitment in the pursuit of long-term wealth creation (cf. Senge, 2006) as ethical stewards when they serve their organizations as transformative leaders.

Contributions of our article

Today's modern organizations desperately need leaders who they can trust if their organizations are to be successful in a highly competitive global market place (Cameron, 2003). Those leaders include highly competent, knowledgeable, and skilled HRPs who understand how to align HRM programs with corporate objectives and strategic plans (Becker et al., 2001). We argue that the leadership skills of these HRPs must encompass the moral perspectives of ethical stewardship and the unique contributions of transformative leadership.

We suggest that our article contributes to the SHRM literature in four significant ways.

1. *We affirm the importance of SHRM as a vital element of successful organizations when aligned with the overall goals, values, and priorities of that organization. We note, however, that many HRPs either fail to understand this strategic role of HRM or lack the abilities to align HRM systems to serve their firms.* Human resource management practices that are integrated in a manner that reinforces strategic objectives can play a major role in enabling organizations to utilize employees as the source of strategic competitive advantage (Hartel et al., 2007; Konzelmann et al., 2006). Although designing aligned human resource systems and framing a well-conceived strategy are important, it is in implementing these systems that a firm achieves desired organizational outcomes (Pfeffer, 1998; Sun et al., 2007). The failures of organizations to create aligned and congruent organizations with HR systems that mesh with strategic objectives are well documented by management scholars (Lawler III, 2008; Pfeffer, 1998, 2007).

2. *We describe and clarify the role of SHRM as it relates to the principles of ethical stewardship and emphasize the implicit ethical duties owed by HRPs to their organizations.* Ethical stewardship is a philosophy of leadership and governance that optimizes long-term wealth creation and that honors duties owed to all stakeholders (Caldwell and Karri, 2005; Pava, 2003). As a framework that integrates both normative and instrumental ethical values (cf. Paine, 2003), the principles of ethical stewardship build both the trust and the commitment of followers (Caldwell et al., 2008). HRPs owe their organizations a set of obligations and duties that include helping the top management team to contribute to the strategic effectiveness of the firm while simultaneously meeting the needs of organizational members (Barnard, 1938; Becker and Huselid, 1999). Rarely are organizations

able to earn the trust of employees if HRM systems and processes conflict with the strategic goals of the firm (Pfeffer, 1998). Congruent and effective leadership and consistent policies help organizations to obtain the commitment from employees which is the key to long-term wealth creation (Senge, 2006).

3. *We identify the importance of the ethical duties inherent in best leadership practices as essential elements of the HRPs' responsibilities in honoring their organizational roles.* The leadership obligations and responsibilities of HRPs incorporate the best elements of transformational leadership, charismatic leadership, servant leadership, Level 5 leadership, and covenantal leadership. Each of these six leadership perspectives of leadership is normatively and instrumentally consistent with the scope and duties of SHRM (Pfeffer, 1998, 2007) and facilitate both social and financial outcomes of organizations (cf. Collins, 2001; Hosmer, 2007; Paine, 2003). These ethical responsibilities demonstrate the importance of aligned and congruent organizational systems and are consistent with the empirical evidence that affirms the importance of high performing organizations in creating long-term wealth (Collins, 2001; Paine, 2003; Senge, 2006).

4. *We reinforce the importance of human resource professionals elevating their contribution to organizations professionally, ethically, and strategically.* HRPs have often been ineffective at contributing to the success of organizations because they have failed to demonstrate the requisite knowledge and skills to help organizations to achieve objectives that are vital to their role as business partners and major decision makers (Lawler and Mohrman, 2000). In today's highly competitive business environment, the role of employees has become increasingly important to achieving strategic competitive advantage, and the opportunity for organizations to create that advantage by unlocking employee potential is often the key difference for both competitive advantage and increased profitability (Pfeffer, 2007). HRPs who help create organizational cultures based on normatively virtuous principles can increase the ability of their companies to earn the high trust and employee commitment which leads to better quality, improved customer service, and increased profitability (Cameron, 2003). The roles of HRPs in organizations enable their companies to be more professional and more successful strategically while enabling the companies to honor the implicit ethical duties owed to employees.

The clear message of management scholars who study today's organizations is that "good" is not good enough and is, in fact, "the enemy of great" (Collins, 2001, p. 1). The challenge for today's leaders is to move from "effectiveness" to "greatness" (Covey, 2004, pp. 3–4) to optimize the potential of the modern organization.

Conclusion

Only when HRPs are perceived as competent and ethical will they be able to merit the trust of those organizational stakeholders with whom they work (Graham and Tarbell, 2006). Adopting the standards of ethical stewardship and the best practices of leadership may be a daunting challenge for HRPs. Nonetheless, this challenge is consistent with the needs of organizations that must compete in an increasingly competitive world that is heavily dependent on the skills and commitment of employees to create value and long-term wealth (Covey, 2004; Pfeffer, 2007).

Although the role of HRM has changed substantially over the past 20 years, HRPs continue to have opportunities to broaden and strengthen their role in helping organizations maximize productivity, govern more ethically, and compete more effectively (Pfeffer, 2007). In understanding their role as transformative organizational leaders, HRPs have the obligation to prepare themselves to accomplish the goals of their organizations by honing their expertise about organizational goals, developing the skills of organizational members, and creating aligned systems that are critical to the success of modern organizations (Hosmer, 2007; Werhane et al., 2004). Such preparation demands that HRPs also develop insights about ethical and moral issues and that they set the example as ethical leaders (Kouzes and Posner, 2007; Pinnington, et al., 2007).

The willingness of organizations to pursue systematically the twin goals of achieving organizational mission and assisting employees to achieve their personal goals is an implicit obligation of ethical stewardship and organizational leadership (Barnard and Andrews, 2007; Caldwell et al., 2008). The resource-based view of the firm emphasizes the importance of meeting the needs of employees to retain them as a resource-based source of competitive advantage (Barney and Wright, 1998). Scholarly research about successful organizations has increasingly suggested that the most successful companies are those that balance *instrumental* or outcome-based and *normative* or value-based objectives (Cameron, 2003; Collins, 2001; Pfeffer, 1998). Measuring results and maintaining a commitment to people are well-respected elements of high performance systems that balance the instrumental and normative priorities of organizations (Pfeffer, 1998, 2007).

Organizations that integrate principles of ethical leadership with a strategic approach to HRM optimize the maximization of values and outcomes and achieve results which pay off long-term (Collins and Clark, 2003; Paine, 2003). By honoring their duties as ethical stewards and incorporating principles of transformative leadership, HRPs can make a major contribution to their organization's financial success while helping their organizations honor the implicit duties owed to organization members (DePree, 2004; Paine, 2003).

Source: © Springer 2010.

REFERENCES

Barnard, C. I.: 1938, *Functions of the Executive* (Harvard Business School Press, Cambridge, MA).

Barnard, C. I. and K. R. Andrews: 2007, *Functions of the Executive: 30th Anniversary Edition* (Harvard University Press, Cambridge, MA).

Barnett, T. and E. Schubert: 2002, 'Perceptions of the Ethical Climate and Covenantal Relationships', *Journal of Business Ethics* 36(3), 279–290.

Barney, J. B. and P. M. Wright: 1998, 'On Becoming a Strategic Partner: The Role of Human Resources in Gaining Competitive Advantage', *Human Resource Management* 37(1), 31–46.

Bass, B. M. and B. J. Avolio: 1990, 'Developing Transformational Leadership: 1992 and Beyond', *Journal of European Industrial Training* 14(5), 21–27.

Becker, B. E. and M. A. Huselid: 1998, 'High Performance Work Systems and Firm Performance: A Synthesis of Research and Managerial Implications', in G. Ferris (ed.), *Research in Personnel and Human Resources Management*, Vol. 16 (JAI Press, Greenwich, CT), pp. 53–101.

Becker, B. E. and B. Gerhart: 1996, 'The Impact of Human Resource Management on Organizational Performance, Progress, and Prospects', *Academy of Management Journal* 39(4), 779–801.

Becker, B. E. and M. A. Huselid: 1999, 'Overview: Strategic Human Resource Management in Five Leading Firms', *Human Resource Management* 38(4), 287–301.

Becker, B. E. and M. A. Huselid: 2006, 'Strategic Human Resource Management: Where do we go from Here?', *Journal of Management* 32(6), 898–925.

Becker, B. E., M. A. Huselid and D. Ulrich: 2001, *The HR Scorecard: Linking People, Strategy, and Performance* (Harvard Business School Press, Boston, MA).

Beer, M.: 1997, 'The Transformation of the Human Resource Function: Resolving the Tension Between Traditional Administrative and a New Strategic Role', *Human Resource Management* 36(1), 49–56.

Bennis, W. G. and B. Nanus: 2007, *Leaders: Strategies for Taking Charge* (Harper, New York).

Block, P.: 1993, *Stewardship: Choosing Service over Self-Interest* (Jossey-Bass, San Francisco, CA).

Boudreau, J. W. and P. M. Ramstad: 2005, 'Talentship, Talent Segmentation, and Sustainability: A New HR Decision Science Paradigm for a New Strategy Definition', *Human Resource Management* 44(2), 129–136.

Boyatzis, R. and A. McKee: 2005, *Resonant Leadership: Renewing Yourself and Connecting with Others Through Mindfulness, Hope, and Compassion* (Harvard Business School Press, Boston, MA).

Buber, M.: 2008, *I and Thou* (Hesperides Press, New York).

Burns, J. M.: 1978, *Leadership* (Harper & Row, New York).

Caldwell, C., S.J. Bischoff and R. Karri: 2002, 'The Four Umpires: A Paradigm for Ethical Leadership', *Journal of Business Ethics* 36(1/2), 153–163.

Caldwell, C. and R. Dixon: 2007, Transformative Leadership—An Integrative Theory of Ethical Stewardship. Paper Presented at the Fourteenth Annual International Conference on Ethics in Business at DePaul University on November 1, 2007.

Caldwell, C., L. Hayes, P. Bernal and R. Karri: 2008, 'Ethical Stewardship: The Role of Leadership Behavior and Perceived Trustworthiness', *Journal of Business Ethics* 78(1/2), 153–164.

Caldwell, C. and R. J. Karri: 2005, 'Organizational Governance and Ethical Systems: A Covenantal Approach to Building Trust', *Journal of Business Ethics* 58(1), 249–259.

Caldwell, C., R. Karri and P. Vollmar: 2006, 'Principal Theory and Principle Theory: Ethical Governance from the Follower's Perspective', *Journal of Business Ethics* 66(2–3), 207–223.

Caldwell, C., C. Voelker, R. D. Dixon and A. LeJeune: 2007, *Transformative Leadership: An Ethical Stewardship Model for Healthcare* (Healthcare, Business, and Policy, Fall Edition, Organizational Ethics), pp. 126–134.

Cameron, K. S.: 2003, 'Ethics, Virtuousness, and Constant Change', in N. M. Tichy and A. R. McGill (eds.), *The Ethical Challenge: How to Lead with Unyielding Integrity* (Jossey-Bass, San Francisco, CA), pp. 185–194.

Clardy, A.: 2008, 'The Strategic Role of Human Resource Development in Managing Core Competencies', *Human Resource Development International* 11(2), 183–197.

Collins, J.: 2001, *Good to Great: Why Some Companies Make the Leap ... and Others don't* (Harper-Collins, New York).

Collins, J.: 2005, 'Level 5 Leadership: The Triumph of Humility and Fierce Resolve', *Harvard Business Review* 83(7/8), 136–146.

Collins, C. J. and K. D. Clark: 2003, 'Strategic Human Resource Practices, Top Management Team Social Networks, and Firm Performance: The Role of Human Resource Practices in Creating Organizational Competitive Advantage', *Academy of Management Journal* 46(6), 740–751.

Collins, J. and J. I. Porras: 2004, *Built to Last: Successful Habits of Visionary Companies*, 2nd Edition (HarperCollins, New York).

Coltrin, S. A.: 1991, 'Ethics—More than Legal Compliance', *Human Resource Management* 26, 1–12.

Conger, J. A., R. N. Kanungo and S. T. Menon: 2000, 'Charismatic Leadership and Follower Effects', *Journal of Organizational Behavior* 21(7), 747–767.

Covey, S. R.: 1992, *Principle Centered Leadership* (Simon & Schuster, New York).

Covey, S. R.: 2004, *The 8th Habit: From Effectiveness to Greatness* (Free Press, New York).

Deming, W. E.: 2000, *Out of the Crisis* (MIT Press, Cambridge, MA).

DePree, M.: 2004, *Leadership is an Art* (Doubleday, New York).

Dvir, T., D. Eden, B. J. Avolio and B. Shamir: 2002, 'Impact of Transformational Leadership on Follower Development and Performance: A Field Experiment', *Academy of Management Journal* 45(4), 735–744.

Graham, M. E. and L. M. Tarbell: 2006, 'The Importance of the Employee Perspective in the Competency Development of Human Resource Professionals', *Human Resource Management* 45(3), 337–355.

Greenleaf, R. K.: 2004, 'Who Is the Servant-Leader?', in L. C. Spears and M. Lawrence (eds.), *Practicing Servant Leadership: Succeeding Through Trust, Bravery, and Forgiveness* Jossey-Bass, San Francisco), pp. 1–7.

Grossman, R. J.: 2007, 'New Competencies for HR', *HR Magazine* 52(6), 58–62.

Guest, D. E.: 2007, 'HRM and Performance: Can Partnership Address the Ethical Dilemmas?', in A. Pinnington, R. Macklin and T. Campbell (eds.), *Human Resource Management: Ethics and Employment* (Oxford University Press, Oxford), pp. 52–65.

Hamilton, F. and W. R. Nord: 2005, 'Practicing Servant-Leadership: Succeeding Through Trust, Bravery, and Forgiveness', *Academy of Management Review* 30(4), 875–877.

Hartel, C., Y. Fujimoto, V. E. Strybosch and K. Fitzpatrick: 2007, *Human Resource Management: Transforming Theory into Innovative Practice* (Pearson Education, Australia).

Hernandez, M.: 2008, 'Promoting Stewardship Behavior in Organizations: A Leadership Model', *Journal of Business Ethics* 80(1), 121–128.

Hosmer, L. T.: 1995, 'Trust: The Connecting Link Between Organizational Theory and Behavior', *Academy of Management Review* 20, 379–404.

Hosmer, L. T.: 2007, *The Ethics of Management*, 6th Edition (McGraw-Hill, New York).

House, R. J.: 1977, 'A 1976 Theory of Charismatic Leadership', in J. G. Hunt and L. L. Larson (eds.), *Leadership: The Cutting Edge* (Southern Illinois University Press, Carbondale, IL), pp. 189–207.

Huselid, M. A.: 1995, 'The Impact of Human Resource Management Practices on Turnover, Productivity, and Corporate Financial Performance', *Academy of Management Journal* 38, 635–672.

Huselid, M. A. and B. E. Becker: 1997, The Impact of High Performance Work Systems, Implementation Effectiveness, and Alignment with Strategy on Shareholder Wealth. Academy of Management Proceedings.

Huselid, M. A., S. E. Jackson and R. S. Schuler: 1997, 'Technical and Strategic Human Resource Management Effectiveness as Determinants of Firm Performance', *Academy of Management Journal* 40(1), 171–188.

Kanter, R. M.: 2008, 'Transforming Giants', *Harvard Business Review* 86(1), 43–52.

Kohlberg, L.: 1985, 'The Just Community Approach to Moral Education in Theory and Practice', in M. W. Berkowitz and F. Oser (eds.), *Moral Education: Theory and Practice* (Erlbaum, Hillsdale, NY).

Kolp, A. and P. Rea: 2005, *Leading with Integrity: Character Based Leadership* (Atomic Dog Publishing, New York).

Konzelmann, S., N. Conway, L. Trenberth and F. Wilkinson: 2006, 'Corporate Governance and Human Resource Management', *British Journal of Industrial Relations* 44(3), 541–567.

Kouzes, J. M. and B. Z. Posner: 2003a, *Credibility: How Leaders Gain and Lose It, Why People Demand It*, 2nd Edition (Wiley & Sons, San Francisco, CA).

Kouzes, J. M. and B. Z. Posner: 2003b, *Encouraging the Heart: A Leader's Guide to Rewarding and Recognizing Others* (Jossey-Boss, San Francisco, CA).

Kouzes, J. M. and B. Z. Posner: 2007, *Leadership Challenge*, 4th Edition (Wiley & Sons, San Francisco, CA).

Kupers, W. and J. Weibler: 2006, 'How Emotional is Transformational Leadership Really? Some Suggestions for a Necessary Extension', *Leadership & Organizational Development Journal* 27(5), 368–385.

Lawler, E. E. III: 2008, 'The HR Department: Give It More Respect', *Wall Street Journal — Eastern Edition* 251(57), R8.

Lawler, E. E. III and S. A. Mohrman: 2000, 'Beyond the Vision: What Makes HR Effective?', *Human Resource Planning* 23(4), 10–20.

Legge, K.: 2000, 'The Ethical Context of HRM: The Ethical Organisation in the Boundaryless World', in D. Winstanley and J. Woodall (eds.), *Ethical Issues in Contemporary Human Resource Management* (MacMillan Press, London), pp. 23–40.

Ludema, J. D. and C. K. Cox: 2007, 'Leadership for World Benefit: New Horizons for Research and Practice', in S. K. Piderit, R. E. Fry and D. L. Coo-perrider (eds.), *Handbook of Transformative Cooperation: New Designs and Dynamics* (Stanford Business Books, Palo Alto, CA), pp. 333–373.

Marcum, D. and S. Smith: 2007, *egonomics: What Makes Ego Our Greatest Asset (or Most Expensive Liability)* (Fireside Publishing, Wichita, KS).

Paine, L. S.: 2003, *Value Shift: Why Companies must Merge Social and Financial Imperatives to Achieve Superior Performance* (McGraw-Hill, New York).

Palmer, G.: 2007, 'Socio-Political Theory and Ethics in HRM', in A. Pinnington, R. Macklin. T. Campbell (eds.), *Human Resource Management: Ethics and Employment* (Oxford University Press, Oxford), pp. 23–34.

Pauchant, T. C.: 2005, 'Integral Leadership: A Research Proposal', *Journal of Organizational Change Management* 18(3), 211–229.

Pava, M.: 2003, *Leading with Meaning: Using Covenantal Leadership to Build a Better Organization* (Palgrave MacMillan, New York).

Payne, S. L. and R. F. Wayland: 1999, 'Ethical Obligation and Diverse Value Assumptions in HRM', *International Journal of Manpower* 20(5/6), 297–308.

Pfeffer, J.: 1998, *The Human Equation: Building Profits by Putting People First* (Harvard Business School Press, Boston, MA).

Pfeffer, J.: 2007, 'Human Resources from an Organizational Behavior Perspective: Some Paradoxes Explained', *Journal of Economic Perspectives* 21(4), 115–134.

Pinnington, A., R. Macklin and T. Campbell: 2007, 'Introduction: Ethical Human Resource Management', in A. Pinnington, R. Macklin and T. Campbell (eds.), *Human Resource Management: Ethics and Employment* (Oxford University Press, Oxford), pp. 1–20.

Schein, E. H.: 2004, *Organizational Culture and Leadership* (Jossey-Bass, San Francisco, CA).

Schultz, T. and Y. Brender-Ilan: 2004, 'Beyond Justice: Introducing Personal Moral Philosophies to Ethical Evaluations of Human Resource Practices', *Business Ethics: A European Review* 13(4), 302–316.

Senge, P. M.: 2006, *The Fifth Discipline: The Art and Practice of the Learning Organization* (Doubleday, New York).

Solomon, R. C.: 1992, *Ethics and Excellence: Cooperation and Integrity in Business* (Oxford University Press, New York).

Solomon, R. C. and F. Flores: 2003, *Building Trust: In Business, Politics, Relationships, and Life* (Oxford University Press, New York).

Sun, L.-Y., S. Aryee and K. S. Law: 2007, 'High-Performance Human Resource Practices, Citizenship Behavior, and Organizational Performance: A Relational Perspective', *Academy of Management Journal* 50(3), 558–577.

Sung-Choon, K., S. S. Morris and S. A. Snell: 2007, 'Relational Archetypes, Organizational Learning and Value Creation: Extending the Human Resource Architecture', *Academy of Management Review* 32(1), 236–256.

Ulrich, D. and D. Beatty: 2001, 'From Partners to Players: Extending the HR Playing Field', *Human Resource Management* 40(4), 293–299.

Ulrich, D. and W. Brockbank: 2005, 'The Work of HR Part One: People and Performance', *Strategic HR Review* 4(5), 20–23.

Werhane, P. H.: 2007, 'Women Leaders in a Globalized World', *Journal of Business Ethics* 74(4), 425–435.

Werhane, P. H., T. J. Radin and N. E. Bowie: 2004, *Employment and Employee Rights* (Blackwell Publishing, Oxford).

Cam Caldwell
University of Georgia,
Athens, GA, U.S.A.
E-mail: cam.caldwell@gmail.com

Do X. Truong, Pham T. Linh and Anh Tuan
Vietnam National University,
Hanoi, Vietnam

CHAPTER 2

Social Responsibility and Human Resource Management

- Understand the challenges organizations face in managing diversity, strategies for doing so, and the critical role played by human resources
- Appreciate the importance of ethics awareness, training, and compliance and of the critical contributions human resources can make to an ethics program
- Gain an awareness of the movement toward corporate social responsibility/ sustainability as well as the contributions human resources can make toward sustainability initiatives

Developing Female Leaders at Safeway

Safeway is a Pleasanton, California-based Fortune 500 corporation that operates retail grocery stores around the country. In the early 2000s, Safeway realized that its competitive landscape had changed dramatically with the advent and rise of premium specialty grocers and, on the other end, from the expanded product lines of big-box hardline retailers such as Wal-Mart and Target. As a result, Safeway decided to try to position itself as an employer of choice. Realizing that 70 percent of its customer base was female and that male leadership was the norm in the retail grocery industry, Safeway decided to shift its culture and broaden its workforce in line with its customer base.

As part of its "Championing Change for Women" program, Safeway developed a Retail Leadership Development program, a formal full-time career development program that has groomed 90 percent of the company's 1,800 retail store managers. Many of these individuals started with the company as entry-level sales clerks or grocery baggers. Integral to this program, however, was the realization that women often need to coordinate their work hours with family responsibilities and that such responsibilities made frequent store relocations undesirable.

The program also involved the establishment of the Women's Leadership Network within the organizations, which provided mentoring and events, such as the Women's Road Show, which involved presentations by female executives at Safeway at locations throughout the country to facilitate learning, networking, and talent identification. Since the inception of the program, female store management has increased by 42 percent, with the number of white female store mangers increasing 31 percent and women of color in store management increasing by 92 percent. The Championing Change for Women program has been honored with the highly coveted Catalyst Award, which is presented to exemplary companies that promote the career development of women and minorities.[1]

In addition to the many challenges organizations face in abandoning traditional approaches to managing people as part of adopting an investment perspective to human resource (HR) management, they are also dealing with an increasingly diverse workforce and being increasingly called upon to be socially responsible in their operations and employment practices. This chapter examines some critical social issues—namely, diversity, ethics, and sustainability—that face organizations and the impact these issues have on HR management.

Workforce Demographic Changes and Diversity

Demographic changes in society and the composition of the workforce are also creating a number of challenges for management of HR. Diversity has become and continues to be one of the principal buzzwords for both public and private organizations, as recognizing and promoting diversity is seen as critical for organizational success. The motivation behind diversity initiatives can vary from organization to organization. Some employers have a commitment to understanding and appreciating diversity, whereas others implement diversity initiatives simply to ensure compliance with federal, state, and local employment laws.

Congress has passed numerous laws that prohibit discrimination in employment in both private and public sector organizations. Title VII of the Civil Rights Act of 1964 prohibits discrimination based on race, color, religion, gender, and national origin. Subsequently, numerous federal laws, such as the Pregnancy Discrimination Act, the Age Discrimination in Employment Act, and the Americans with Disabilities Act, have been passed to protect employees. Each of these federal laws is discussed in Chapter 7. In addition, many individual states and municipalities have passed additional laws that protect certain groups of employees. The processes and outcomes associated with diversity initiatives that are rooted in compliance differ greatly from those that truly embrace diversity. These differences are presented in Exhibit 2.1.

One of the biggest challenges organizations face in managing diversity is overcoming some of the deep-set stereotypes that individual employees hold about certain groups in society. These stereotypes are often ingrained into individuals at a very young age and reinforced by family members, religious and educational institutions, and a local society in general. Reading 2.1, "Stereotype Threat at Work," discusses some of the challenges posed by stereotyping and proposes a means by which the consequences of stereotyping can be managed effectively in organizations.

Organizations first started paying attention to diversity in the mid-1960s, largely as a result of civil rights unrest, and the resultant legislation that was passed prohibited discrimination in employment against a variety of groups. At that point, diversity was largely focused on compliance with the

EXHIBIT 2.1	**Differences Between Legal Compliance and Managing Diversity**	
	Compliance with EEO Laws	**Managing Diversity**
Impetus	Mandatory, forced, external	Voluntary, internal
Focus	Productivity, compliance	Understanding
Elements	Usually limited to race, gender, ethnicity	All elements of diversity
Company Culture	Fitting employees into existing culture	Creating a culture that is fluid, adaptive
Outcomes	Preferences, quotas	Equality
Time Frame	Short-term, one-shot	Continuous and ongoing
Scope	Independent of other HR activities and company strategy	Fully integrated with other HR activities and company strategy

© Cengage Learning

law and maintained that focus until the early 1980s. By the mid-1980s, however, the focus of diversity training had shifted to improving working conditions by minimizing conflict between and among workers. In the mid-1990s, the focus evolved to understanding, accepting, and leveraging diversity as a means of enhancing organizational performance and remains as such to this day.[2]

The history of diversity in organizations is rooted in social justice and civil rights, but its evolution into a strategic HR and business issue has resulted in diversity becoming somewhat of an amorphous concept. A recent survey conducted by the Society for Human Resource Management among HR executives revealed eight distinct definitions of diversity, with 71 percent of respondents indicating that their organizations did not have a formal definition of diversity.[3] Consequently, while many organizations embrace diversity in concept, they have not fully considered it as a strategic business issue relative to the mission and strategy of their organization. Indeed, the survey concluded with respondents identifying the needs to (1) more closely articulate the relationships between diversity initiatives and business results and (2) expand the focus away from diversity initiatives as a means of compliance with labor and employment laws.

At the other end of the spectrum are employers who have elevated diversity to the C-suite in the form of a chief diversity officer (CDO). Generally tasked with creating, maintaining, and developing a work environment and culture in which all employees can develop and reach their full potential, CDOs, or comparable executive level positions, are now found in about 60 percent of *Fortune 500* companies. They hail from a variety of backgrounds within the organization with 65 percent being female and 37 percent being African American.[4] However, only 25 percent report directly to their organization's CEO with others reporting to corporate HRs or another department or functional executive.

Diversity at Pricewaterhouse Coopers (PwC)

Global accounting and consulting firm PwC first established a CDO role in 2003. At that time, the position was contained within the HR function, reporting to the head of HR. The position now reports directly to the chairman of the board and senior partner, reflecting the increasing importance PwC has placed on diversity and the accomplishments realized by the CDO. The position is important enough to PwC that it rotates its own senior partners in and out of the role every two years. This stature of the position and rotation of senior partners not only allows more infusion of diversity into the organization's culture but also allows heightened accountability for results and credibility of diversity initiatives within the organization.[5]

Generational Diversity

Advances in healthcare are allowing us, as a society, to live longer, remain healthier longer, and remain in the workplace longer. Census data show that 13 percent of the U.S. population is aged 65 or older, with that percentage expected to grow to 20 percent, or 70 million individuals, by 2030.[6] As baby boomers continue to live longer and remain healthy, 80 percent of this group plan to continue working past the age of 65.[7] These "working retirements" suggest a very different type of employment relationship and a very different kind of lifestyle than that chosen by previous generations. A benefit to society is that these individuals' continued self-sufficiency may result in their being far less dependent on cash-strapped government pensions and healthcare programs. Organizations clearly benefit through the knowledge and contacts these individuals have developed through their years of professional experience.

This "graying of the workforce" can create a number of challenges, both real and perceived. Older workers are often perceived to be more resistant to change, particularly in implementing radically new programs and utilizing new technology that break from long-established ways of doing things. They may also have increased healthcare costs relative to their younger counterparts. As older workers remain in the workplace longer, fewer advancement opportunities are made available for younger workers, and in many instances, older workers command higher salaries despite the fact that they may have skills and training that are less current than those of younger workers, particularly relative to technology.

At the same time, it is important to remember that older workers can be as productive, if not more productive, than younger employees. The United States is a society that tends to devalue its older citizens, and such biases and predispositions are often found in organizational settings. However, older workers may have much more loyalty to their employers than their younger counterparts. They can also provide significant knowledge of the organization and industry as well as key contacts within their professional networks.

A number of employers have developed incentive programs for early retirement and then, in many cases, hired retirees back on a part-time basis or as consultants to take advantage of their knowledge and experience. Such programs need to be implemented carefully, however, as federal laws prohibit the setting of a mandatory retirement age in the overwhelming majority of occupations as well as using coercion to "encourage" older workers to retire.

Baby boomers—those born between 1945 and approximately 1962—are now in their mid-career years, and employers are finding that the supply of workers in this age bracket exceeds the demand for them in the middle- and senior-management-level ranks. As one moves up the management hierarchy, fewer and fewer positions are available, and the competition for senior management positions among boomers has become intense. Ironically, technology often plays a role here, as many middle- and senior-level-management positions have been eliminated because of flatter organizational structures and the increased use of information technology to perform functions previously done by middle managers. Many of these individuals will never progress beyond middle management. This can be greatly disconcerting for those who have been long-term employees of an organization and have seen their pre-boomer predecessors and coworkers rewarded and promoted for performance. Consequently, this creates a new HR challenge in managing these "plateaued" workers. Organizations need to find ways to retain them and keep them motivated despite the fact that they may have mastered their current responsibilities and aspire to advance in their careers. Slower and alternative career paths have become the norm for many of these workers. An increasing number are choosing to go out and start their own businesses.

Consequently, baby busters—those born during the declining birthrate years from approximately 1963 to the mid-1970s—also need to have lower expectations relative to the pace of their careers. The baby boomers of the previous generation have essentially created a bottleneck in the management hierarchy that baby busters find themselves behind. Until the baby boom generation has retired, there may be fewer opportunities in larger organizations for baby busters.

At the same time, this baby bust generation—which assumes low- and some mid-level-management positions—often receives higher wages than some of the baby boomers because of the forces of supply and demand. Far fewer individuals are in this lower age bracket, and in many industries, particularly rapidly growing ones—such as multimedia and the Internet—these workers have skills and training that the previous generation lacks, and they therefore command significant incomes in their early career years. In many organizations, workers in their 30s may be making as much as or more than coworkers 20 and 30 years their senior. The combination of limited supply of younger workers, high illiteracy among many new workforce entrants, and demand for skills fueled by technological change has resulted in a whole new workplace dynamic for this generation.

A different workplace dynamic is being created by what are known as Generation X employees. Generation X is those born from the mid-1960s to the late 1970s. Many of these individuals were raised in families of divorce and may have developed a tolerance for upheaval and readjustment. They witnessed firings and layoffs of family members, which may greatly influence their limited loyalty to an employer. They have also been using computers and other advanced technologies all their lives and have been exposed since birth to near-constant change in their everyday lives. More important, they bring attitudes and perceptions about work that differ significantly from those of preceding generations. These include an expectation of increased employee self-control; perceptions of themselves as independent contractors or consultants rather than as employees; less interest in job security; no expectations of long-term employment; and a demand for opportunities for personal growth and creativity.[8]

Generation Y employees, sometimes called the Baby Boom Echo, are those born after 1979. They are just beginning to enter the workforce and represent a cohort that is as large as the baby boom generation. Like the Generation X cohort, they have high comfort levels with technology but also tend to bring a more global and tolerant outlook on life to the workplace, having been raised in more culturally diverse environments and been exposed to cultural differences through the media. Twenty-five percent live in a single-parent household.[9] They are often very entrepreneurial in nature and, on average, have shorter attention spans. They also may fail to see the need to work from an office or for a particular employer, opting for more transient and variable project work.[10]

Generation Y employees are much more social and value collective action and teamwork. They tend to have a stronger sense of social responsibility than other generations and value authenticity and transparency. They eschew dictatorial leaders, rigid hierarchies and control systems and favor work environments in which their input is sought and they can make an active contribution.[11] Challenging work and the opportunity to grow and develop professionally are the main outcomes they seek from their employment with both being more important than salary.[12]

Generation Y and Diversity at Abercrombie and Fitch

Fashion retailer Abercrombie and Fitch employs a workplace that consists predominantly of members of Generation Y. To engage these workers, Abercrombie conducts an annual diversity champion competition in which 25 employees are cited for their efforts to break down barriers surrounding differences such as religion, race, and sexual orientation. Last year, the company received more than 600 employee submissions, which included essays, poems, art, and videos, which related the importance of inclusion and working together. The winning submissions are selected by peers, an important reference group for Generation Y employees. Abercrombie doesn't believe in employee resource groups, believing that they can be isolating, but rather opts to create "one big family," consistent with the values and attitudes of Generation Y employees. The company's Office of Diversity maintains its own Facebook page, which features open conversations with and among employees surrounding diversity issues.[13]

Generation Y, or millennials, have received a great deal of attention recently because of the fact that they are the current new entrants to the workforce, represent its growth and evolution, and have different needs than their predecessors. Exhibit 2.2 highlights some of the differences between the generations now part of the workforce.

EXHIBIT 2.2 Generations in the Workplace[14]

Generation	Percentage of Workforce	Contributions	Leadership Preferences	"Fit" Sought
Traditionalists (1922–1945)	8%	Diligent, stable, loyal, detail oriented, focused, emotionally mature	Fair, consistent, direct, respectful	Contribution (experience, balance, caring)
Baby Boomers (1946–1964)	44%	Team oriented, experienced, knowledgeable, loyal	Equality, democratic, personable, mission focused	Relationships (security, coworkers)
Generation X (1965–1980)	34%	Independent, adaptable, creative, nonconforming	Direct, competent, informal, flexible, supportive	Job (challenge, participation, outcomes)
Generation Y/Millennials (1981–2000)	14% (increasing)	Optimism, multitasking, socially responsible, diverse, tech-savvy	Positive, mentor, motivational, organized	Culture (progressive, autonomous, flexible, fast paced)

Given these differences, there is a question as to what extent these differences manifest themselves in the form of intergenerational conflict in the workplace. A recent study by the Society for Human Resource Management found that 25 percent of organizations reported substantial levels of intergenerational conflict in their workplaces. Older workers complained about the inappropriate dress and "poor work ethic" of younger employees while younger employees found their elders resistant to change, unwilling to recognize their efforts and micromanagers.[15]

Despite some of the acknowledged and pronounced disparity among them, different generations have been found to share some commonalities. First, they all value family and are willing to make compromises and sacrifices in support of their family members. Second, they all want respect, although different generations do not define it the same way. Older workers expect their opinions to be considered, while younger workers simply want the opportunity to be heard. Third, all generations look for trustworthiness in leaders. Fourth, all generations have some resistance to change, which has less to do with age and more to do with how an individual is personally affected by change. Fifth, all generations look for opportunities to learn, grow, and develop. And, finally, everyone in an organization, regardless of age, appreciates feedback on what they are doing and how they are performing.[16]

Sexual Orientation

Sexual orientation has been an area of diversity that increasingly has been embraced by both large and small and public and private employers. Nine of the 10 largest corporations in the United States, as well as nearly 400 of the *Fortune 500* employers, now prohibit discrimination on the basis of sexual orientation.[17] More than 200 of these employers offer full benefits for domestic partners of employees regardless of sexual orientation, although extension of benefits to domestic partners was prompted by demands from gay and lesbian employees for equality in benefits. Currently more than 25 of *Fortune 100* employers allow coverage for transgender-related medical treatment in their health insurance plans.

Sexual orientation has also provided some challenges to employers from a legal perspective beyond compliance with nondiscrimination statues. California, New Hampshire, New Jersey, Vermont, and Oregon all require employers to provide the equivalent of full spousal rights to employees who are part of a same-sex couple. The District of Columbia, Hawaii, Maine, and Washington each has laws that provide for some spousal rights for same-sex couples. As of June 2013, Massachusetts, Connecticut, Iowa, New Hampshire, New York, Vermont, Delaware, Maine, Maryland, Minnesota, Rhode Island, Washington, and the District of Columbia allow same-sex individuals to legally marry. As a result, employers need to carefully review mandates of these laws relative to the provision of employee benefits.

The provision of employee benefits for same-sex couples can create tremendous complexities for employers. Despite the fact that 58 percent of *Fortune 500* companies now provide equal benefits for same-sex partners and spouses, the tax treatment of such benefits is fraught with legal complications. Because same-sex unions are not recognized at the national level, same-sex benefits are treated as taxable income at the federal level, but not at the state level. As a result, in addition to more complex recordkeeping for employers, employees with same-sex partners pay significantly more in taxes than do their coworkers who have opposite-gender partners. To neutralize this effect, a number of private employers, including Credit Suisse, Facebook, Google, and the Kimpton Hotel and Restaurant Group, reimburse their employees receiving same-sex partner benefits to offset the higher taxes to which these employees are subjected.[18]

While no federal law exists that prohibits discrimination in employment based on sexual orientation, a number of states and municipalities have passed nondiscrimination laws and ordinances. Canadian organizations and employers that are members of European Union countries are prohibited by statute from discriminating in employment on the basis of sexual orientation. In addition to feelings about equality, some organizations are motivated to address sexual orientation issues because of the bottom line. Surveys have shown 70 percent of gay and lesbian consumers to be brand loyal to those companies that have progressive employment policies regarding sexual orientation. This gay and lesbian consumer market is estimated at $500 billion annually.[19]

Despite laws that prohibit discrimination based on sexual orientation and increasing social acceptance of sexual minorities, many gay and lesbian professional employees still fear disclosure of their sexual orientation in the workplace. A recent *Harvard Business Review* article noted that 48 percent of LGBT (lesbian, gay, bisexual, and transgendered) employees did not feel comfortable being public about their sexual orientation at work, and LGBT employees who remained "closeted" at work were 73 percent more likely to leave their companies within a three-year period.[20]

Individuals with Disabilities

Individuals with disabilities are protected from discrimination in employment under the Americans with Disabilities Act of 1990, as discussed in Chapter 7. Nonetheless, individuals with disabilities are often not included in diversity initiatives nor have they experienced full eradication of employment discrimination. There are 54 million Americans with disabilities; of those, nearly 70 percent who are capable of working are unemployed, making individuals with disabilities the demographic group with the highest rate of unemployment in the United States.[21] Many technological innovations are increasing the ability for individuals with severe disabilities to be employed, closing the gap between physical limitations and productivity. However, the lack of employment opportunities for individuals with disabilities has less to do with ability than with the fact that many supervisors do not understand the needs of employees with disabilities, and stereotypes about disabilities believed by supervisors and coworkers prevent individuals with disabilities from being fully integrated into the workplace.[22] Hence, diversity initiatives need to pay particular attention to misperceptions surrounding individuals with disabilities.

Employees with disabilities present organizations with a challenge uncommon to other dimensions of diversity. The disabled is one minority group that any individual can join at any time in the future and often sometimes unexpectedly. Because the physical and mental ability of any employee is a variable dimension of diversity, employers need to pay special attention to disability issues. As the average age of the workforce increases, and employees opt to stay employed for longer periods of time, disability issues will clearly escalate for most employers, particularly given the fact that many disabilities can develop later in life. Indeed, while 13 percent of the population aged 21–64 has a disability, 30 percent of those from 65 to 74 and 53 percent of those 75 and older have a documented disability.[23]

Employing Workers with Disabilities at Walgreens

While many employers have policies that encourage the recruiting and hiring of individuals with disabilities, few have gone as far as Walgreens, the national largest retail drugstore chain, to employ those with disabilities. In late 2007, Walgreens opened a brand new state-of-the-art distribution facility in Windsor, Connecticut, which was designed specifically to employ individuals with disabilities. This center was designed to be a model for future distribution centers, with a goal of having at least one-third of its jobs filled by individuals with disabilities. The Windsor location has exceeded that goal with 40 percent of its employees having a disclosed physical or cognitive disability. The facility has reported 20 percent increases in efficiency in its operations since process improvements were installed as accommodations as it expands to its full capacity of 800 employees.[24]

Diversity at Hasbro

Several years ago, Pawtucket, Rhode Island-based toy manufacturer Hasbro, Inc., rolled out a diversity initiative that was offered as a half-day workshop to all of its 8,000 employees. Called "D@H5p3," which stands for "diversity at Hasbro equals people, products and productivity," the program received an award from the Society for Human Resource Management. The program involves a series of three exercises related to diversity. The first, a variation of the game show Who Wants to Be a Millionaire, focuses on the benefits diversity can have for a business. The second, an adaptation of Hasbro's Pokeman trading card game, facilitates an understanding of how cultural and individual differences impact an organization. The third uses Hasbro-manufactured toys, such as Lincoln Logs, to illustrate community building and an individual's place as a responsible member of his or her community. The program was designed to allow participants to better understand diversity as a business and competitive issue for Hasbro, understand each individual's frame of reference relative to diversity, and identify opportunities for development and increased effectiveness that can be achieved through diversity. The response to the program was overwhelming, with individuals asking to be involved with future workshops about diversity.[25]

Diversity at Texas Instruments

In approaching diversity, Texas instruments (TI) eschewed the conventional strategy of bringing in external consultants for mandatory training and instead focused on an approach that attempted to embed the ideals of inclusion throughout the organization. This approach involved the establishment of "business resource groups," which include groups formed on the basis of religion, race, gender, sexual orientation, and single-parent status. These groups' distinctions relative to traditional "affinity groups" supported by other employers is that the primary function of business resource groups at TI is business rather than social. All business resource groups are open to all employees, regardless of background. The diversity within these groups helps to make them unique relative to those found in other organizations. Under the mentorship of an executive-level sponsor, the groups focus not only on career issues but also on business issues, as each group is required to contribute to the company's success in some measurable way.[26]

Other Dimensions of Diversity

One of the most notable consequences of these new workplace dynamics is that there is now an increased emphasis on the management of professionals. With fewer and fewer nonprofessional employees in organizations, situations often arise where a highly skilled or trained employee reports to a direct supervisor who is not familiar with the nature of the work being performed by subordinates. These technical workers need and want more autonomy in their responsibilities and seek greater input and participation in their work activities. In response to this, some organizations have established two separate career tracks: technical–professional and managerial–administrative. However, managers who have oversight of technical areas in which their skills are not as well developed as those of their subordinates require us to re-evaluate the nature of supervision and develop alternative strategies for managing employees.

The use of project teams helps to address this issue. Here, a technical employee often reporting to a technical supervisor is also assigned to a project team overseen by a project or engagement manager. This model, which has been used for many years in accounting, management consulting, and advertising, often involves technical workers being responsible to both the technical and project managers and can provide enhanced opportunities for employee skill and career development. However, this dual reporting relationship can be extremely frustrating for the technical employee who may receive conflicting requests from technical and project supervisors as well as for those supervisors who do not have full authority over their subordinates.

The employees of today, both younger workers and their older peers, have values and attitudes that stress less loyalty to the company and more loyalty to one's self and one's career than those exhibited by employees in the past. This is not surprising in light of the waves of corporate downsizing and layoffs and the manner in which they have eroded employee loyalty and commitment. Workers are generally staying with employers for far shorter periods than they did previously and are moving on to other opportunities, particularly those with smaller startup organizations in the same industry or with clients. Employees with higher levels of training, education, and skills demand more meaningful work and more involvement in organizational decisions that affect them. Employees are becoming much more proactive and taking their career management into their own hands rather than leaving this responsibility with their employer. Larger employers who wish to retain the experience and skills of their employees need to develop creative retention strategies to prevent the flight of employees who may be attractive to competitors. For example, both Charles Schwab and Solectron provide employees with stock options that vest only after the employee has been with the company for a given number of years. Both of these organizations have employees who have experiences that make them highly marketable. Requiring a certain length of service in order to receive full vesting benefits not only allows better retention but also facilitates HR planning efforts; both Schwab and Solectron can anticipate dates when key employees might be more likely to consider separation.

Personal and family life dynamics also continue to evolve and create challenges for organizations. The increased incidence of single-parent families and dual-career couples creates issues around child and elder care, relocation, and "parental stigma" where employees, particularly managerial employees, who devote significant time to family issues are seen as less promotable and less committed to their careers and employers. This stigma has presented particular challenges for women. Nontraditional family arrangements, where opposite or same-sex partners share their lives and living expenses, place increased pressure on organizations to offer domestic partner benefits to employees equal to those that the organization provides to employees with legal spouses. Although the provision of domestic partner benefits has increased dramatically in both large and small organizations, political and religious groups continue to lobby against and fight such efforts and to call for boycotts of companies that provide benefits to nonmarried couples.

The need for greater balance between employees' work and home lives has resulted in employee preferences and demands for policies that provide for a more optimal balance. The proliferation of dual-career households and school vacation schedules of children has resulted in difficulties in scheduling vacation time away from the office. Employees are now using paid time off in a more episodic fashion, opting for several days at a time rather than the traditional one or two weeks at a time.[27] Three- and four-day "long weekend" vacations allow more flexibility for family schedules and also provide the benefit of allowing a shorter possible period of "disengagement" from work. Few executives and even lower-level employees are willing to go a week or more without maintaining some contact from work, preventing them from full "separation" from their jobs and not allowing a true vacation. However, shorter vacation periods can allow employees the appropriate time to disengage from work and truly reap the benefits of their time away from work, benefiting both the employee and employer.

Work–life balance issues tend to affect women more disproportionately than men, given that women are often the primary caretakers for family members. While there are no easy solutions to such challenges, one model of career development for women, called the kaleidoscope, suggests that women be allowed to shift the patterns of their careers, rotating through stages where career and life issues take on different relative emphasis.[28] During the early career years, goal achievement and challenge are emphasized as a woman pursues her career interests. During the mid-career years, issues of balance and accommodation relative to family demands are the priority with the organization understanding and supporting this pursuit of balance. In late career, issues of balance have been resolved, but preferences may differ, and acknowledgement is made of an individual woman's choice as to how she wants to balance career and life at that point.

Fathers also have particular challenges in balancing work and family, as an increasing number of men desire to become more involved in the lives and upbringing of their children: 53 percent say that the benefit they most desire is a flexible work schedule, and 82 percent view employers in a more positive light if they offer a flextime benefit. However, while 58 percent of men took advantage of their employer's paternity leave option, 31 percent fear that taking time off to attend to family would hurt their careers.[29]

An increasing number of employees are opting for nontraditional work relationships, often in the form of part-time work, independent consulting, or contingent or temporary employment. Workers opting for such arrangements often seek to enjoy more flexibility in their lives as well as the opportunity to have time to pursue other endeavors. Organizations encourage these arrangements, which allow them to enjoy lower costs in employing these workers and the added ease of being able to expand or contract their workforce as necessary. These workers, however, generally receive few or no benefits and obviously have little job security. Consequently, they tend to be less loyal to their employers than permanent, full-time employees. There is a growing trend for organizations to outsource or contract certain functions or activities outside of the organization, which simultaneously creates numerous entrepreneurial opportunities for individuals. Many plateaued baby boomers have, in fact, left their organizations and then taken their former employers on as clients.

Given the changes that have been taking place in the composition of the workforce and employee values and attitudes, it is not surprising that in recent years, organizations have become much more concerned about managing diversity. Understanding and appreciating diversity is critical for organizations, as the increasing proportions of various ethnic and minority groups in the American consumer population make it imperative for organizations to understand the needs and wants of these groups if they hope to effectively market goods and services to them. Consider the following U.S. Census Bureau predictions:

- By 2050, close to 50 percent of the U.S. population will be non-Caucasian.
- By 2005, the ethnic minority share of the workforce will be 28 percent, up from 22 percent in 1990 and 18 percent in 1980.
- By 2025, African Americans will represent 14 percent of the population, up from 12 percent in 1994.
- By 2025, Hispanics will represent 17 percent of the population, up from 10 percent in 1994.
- By 2025, Asians and Pacific Islanders will represent 8 percent of the population, more than doubling from 3 percent in 1994.[30]

Diversity Initiatives at Intel

Intel, one of the world's leading manufacturers of computer chips, understands the importance of diversity in the workplace. In an industry where demand for trained professionals greatly exceeds supply, Intel has developed a creative program for recruiting and developing minority employees.

To assist with recruiting, Intel hired a leading consulting firm to assist it in identifying the ten colleges and universities with the highest minority enrollments in the field of circuitry design. Intel has also established an undergraduate minority scholarship fund that awards in excess of $1 million annually to undergraduate students. Although recipients are not required to work for Intel after graduation, a significant number of them opt to do so.

Intel has also established a college internship program whereby students are identified as high-potential employees as early as their sophomore year. Interns receive employment and are matched with mentors for their entire college careers. Those who choose to stay onboard after graduation are assigned to supervisors who provide specific training that will allow their protégés to develop a variety of skills that can be applied to different jobs within the organization and will willingly allow employees to transfer within the company in order to retain their services. As a result, Intel has seen the proportion of ethnic minorities in management positions jump from 13 to 17 percent in a four-year period, despite efforts by its competitors to recruit its talent away.[31]

There is probably no better way to understand and market to these groups than to have them represented as employees at all levels of the organization. In addition to this, diversity initiatives help to ensure that personal differences that have nothing to do with job performance are less likely to impact hiring, promotion, and retention decisions. Intense competition and tight labor market conditions make it imperative that such decisions result in the hiring and promotion of the most qualified individuals.

One popular strategy organizations are using for recruiting and retaining diverse talent is the support of employee network or affinity groups. Affinity groups can be formed around any commonality shared by employees, including ethnicity, age, disability, family status, religion, sexual orientation, and usually have some association with a culture or perspective that has faced challenges in either the society or the organization. Employee networks or affinity groups can provide the organization with a number of benefits, including: (1) aiding in the recruiting and retention of employees from the affinity group; (2) gaining broader perspectives on the organization's employment practices and business strategy; and (3) assisting an organization with its consumer awareness and reach in the marketplace. Affinity groups can provide the organizations with heightened insights into the culture, perceptions, and needs and wants of various consumer groups as well as bridge gaps between the organizations and various potential consumer groups worldwide. More so, affinity groups can benefit both the organization and individual employees through the opportunities for leadership development they offer. Many organizations have tapped the leaders of in-house affinity groups for broader leadership opportunities with the organization.[32]

Managing Diversity at PepsiCo

PepsiCo has been one of the corporate leaders in promoting diversity among its employees, and its commitment to diversity includes holding senior executives themselves personally accountable for diversity. Each of PepsiCo's CEO's direct reports has the responsibility of working with a specific group of employees in understanding the workplace issues each group—including white males, black employees, Latinos, gay and lesbian employees, and employees with disabilities—faces. However, each group's executive comes from outside the group being overseen and mentored. Executives identify high-performing, high-potential individuals within their groups, communicate the needs of each group to each other, and are held accountable for addressing the concerns of their assigned group. This level of executive commitment and accountability greatly distinguishes PepsiCo from its corporate peers relative to diversity.[33]

Affinity Groups at Frito-Lay and PepsiCo

The Frito-Lay snack food division of PepsiCo has enjoyed tremendous success as a result of the work of one of its affinity groups. The Latino Employee Network, known as Adelante, provided invaluable assistance during the development of Doritos' guacamole-flavored tortilla chips. Members of the group were actively involved in product development decisions related to taste and packaging to ensure that the product would be seen as authentic in the Latino community. The participation of Adelante in the development of guacamole-flavored Doritos resulted in one of the most successful new product launches in the company's history, with first-year sales in excess of $100 million.[34]

Corporate parent PepsiCo used an affinity group to push boundaries in creating awareness. During the 2008 Super Bowl telecast, PepsiCo purchased a multimillion-dollar advertising slot and aired an ad completely void of sound. The ad was created by and featured PepsiCo employees who are part of the employee group EnAble, which attempts to promote understanding and inclusion of individuals with disabilities. The ad featured two friends driving to the house of a third friend to watch a football game. Communicating only in American Sign Language, the two friends lamented the fact that they could not remember the house number of the third friend's home. They then proceed to drive slowly down the street, honking their horn repeatedly as lights flashed on in each house but one—the only one apparently undisturbed by the noise. The ad was designed not to sell a product but to create awareness with broad appeal and clearly displays PepsiCo's commitment to diversity.[35]

While affinity groups were traditionally found in only larger organizations, they are becoming increasingly popular in small- to medium-sized organizations, aided by the fact that they require little to no expense to start up and maintain.[36] They are best aided when the organization provides them with a structure, including a formal application process for recognition, complete with a mission, goals, and a leadership plan. They also tend to function best when encouraged to focus on solutions rather than problems.[37] However, employers have to be careful that affinity groups are not developed and allowed to exist in isolation. A number of organizations which encouraged affinity groups found that as numerous affinity groups proliferated within a company, the groups tended to evolve into silos rather than be fully integrated within the organization. Because affinity groups were conceptualized, developed, and implemented to promote inclusiveness of diverse employees, it is critical that they be actively managed as part of a broad diversity strategy to ensure that they do not produce consequences or outcomes that are opposite of those desired.[38]

As a result, diversity management programs have become quite popular. In fact, an entire industry has developed around helping organizations manage diversity. However, many diversity initiatives are ill-conceived, not integrated with the organization's mission and objectives, and can create additional challenges above those for which they were designed to respond. Key decision makers in organizations need to ask themselves what benefits diversity specifically provides their organization. There are numerous ways to implement diversity initiatives and different levels on which to understand diversity. There is no one best way to manage diversity in organizations; the optimal way is contingent on the organization, its people, its mission, and its culture. Diversity initiatives also have to make the critical decisions about where to draw the line, meaning which elements of diversity are incorporated into the initiative and which are excluded.

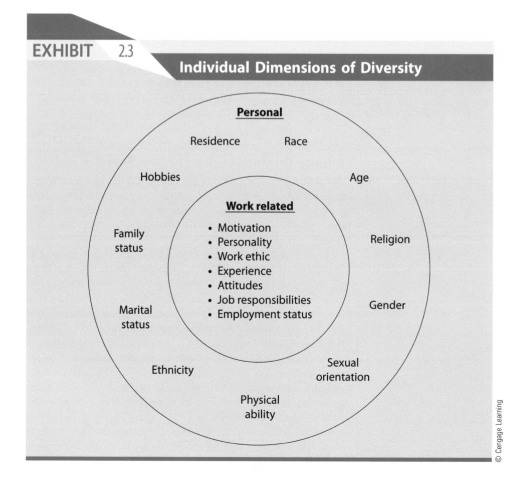

EXHIBIT 2.3   Individual Dimensions of Diversity

© Cengage Learning

EXHIBIT 2.4

The Strategic Management of Diversity

1. Determine why diversity is important for the organization.
2. Articulate how diversity relates to the mission and the strategic objectives of the organization.
3. Define diversity and determine how inclusive its efforts will be.
4. Make a decision as to whether special efforts should be extended to attract a diverse workforce.
5. Assess how existing employees, customers, and other constituencies feel about diversity.
6. Determine specific types of diversity initiatives that will be undertaken.

© Cengage Learning

Diversity initiatives can present organizations with a complicated mosaic. Exhibit 2.3 presents a model of some of the individual dimensions of diversity. Both work-related and personal sources of diversity are presented. While most diversity initiatives cover some combination of personal dimensions, managers must remain cognizant of the work-related dimensions of diversity in ensuring that workers are managed and given job assignments that allow for both maximum satisfaction and productivity.

An understanding of and appreciation for diversity is both necessary and desirable for all organizations. However, it is important that those responsible for diversity initiatives realize that diversity can be a double-edged sword. Prior to undertaking any diversity issues, an organization needs to strategize its approach in dealing with diversity. This involves consideration of six issues, as illustrated in Exhibit 2.4.

Ethical Behavior

The recent series of corporate bankruptcies, scandals, and business meltdowns has re-invigorated the discussion and debate about ethical behavior in organizations. Ethics, however, go far beyond issues related to financial reporting and disclosure. Many areas of operations, as well as aspects of how employees are treated, leave a tremendous amount of discretion for employers relative to their practices and policies. Many executives report that an organization's reputation is a paramount concern in deciding whether to accept an offer of employment. A recent survey found that 65 percent of executives reported that they would thoroughly investigate the culture and value system of any prospective employer.[39] This same survey found that 40 percent of executives had resigned from an organization at least once because of the employer's perceived unethical business practices. Of this group, 75 percent reported that they did not expose the behavior at the time but 33 percent stated that, given recent corporate scandals, they would disclose and report the behavior if faced with the situation again.

While many organizations have long had ethics and social responsibility as central components of their mission and operating standards, the first federal government action related to ethics in organizations was the Federal Sentencing Guidelines for Organizations (FSGO) of 1991. The FSGO set minimum voluntary standards for employers in the areas of implementation of a code of ethical conduct, ethics training for officers and employees, high-level internal oversight of ethics and periodic measurement of the effectiveness of ethics initiatives. Compliance with the FSGO would result in lesser penalties in the case of organizational misconduct. A 2004 amendment to the FSGO provides more specific and strict guidance for ethics training and also emphasizes the responsibility of the organization to create a company culture that embraces ethics, rather than just piecemeal compliance with FSGO guidelines.

There are numerous dimensions of the employment relationship where ethical decisions need to be made by senior management. The challenge faced by these individuals rests with the fact that ethics are not universally defined but rather subject to personal values and convictions. Ethical behavior is subjectively assessed as right or wrong, appropriate or inappropriate, and, in some cases, moral or immoral.

One area of ethical concern for HR is employee off-duty behavior. Winn-Dixie Stores, Inc., faced a very challenging situation when it terminated a truck driver with a 20-year history of exemplary service and performance when it was discovered he was a cross-dresser in his private life. The truck driver, dressed as a woman and assuming a female identity, accompanied his wife and family in public. Concerns about the company image caused Winn-Dixie to terminate his employment. He sued on the grounds that he was terminated for something that had nothing to do with his employment and job performance, but there is no law that universally protects employee's off-duty behavior. Winn-Dixie did win in court but may have lost significantly in the court of public opinion. The story generated tremendous media attention that provided a good deal of support for the driver, from both the general public and his Winn-Dixie coworkers.[40]

The Winn-Dixie's example pertains to only one area of off-duty conduct. Employers also face dilemmas about off-duty behavior involving tobacco, alcohol and drug use, political and religious activity, and prior arrests and/or convictions. The majority of jobs are considered to be "at-will," which will be discussed in depth in Chapter 7, and employees have very limited protection at the federal level from arbitrary dismissal from their jobs. However, there has been a movement toward providing greater protection for employees in regard to their off-duty behavior. At this juncture, four states—New York, California, North Dakota, and Colorado—protect all off-duty, legal activity of employees.

Another increasingly important area of ethical consideration for employers is ownership of work. Given that a good deal of employee work in a knowledge economy involves the application of knowledge and skills in the development of new and improved products, services, and processes, conflicts have arisen concerning intellectual property rights. Employers have used nondisclosure and noncompete agreements to ensure that the work developed by its employees stays with the employer when employees leave. This is serious business for large and small employers alike. It is estimated that *Fortune 1000* organizations incur losses exceeding $45 billion annually from trade-secret theft.[41] Technology has made it much easier for such confidential information to be transmitted. No longer are documents stored in locked file cabinets in secure rooms; now they are contained on hard drives and diskettes that can be accessed more easily.

A related ethical dilemma is the "fairness" of noncompete clauses, which may address the employee going to work for a competitor or starting her or his own business. When accountants, consultants, attorneys, physicians, or other trained professionals decide to start their own business, do they have a right to bring clients with them and/or actively recruit former clients? Noncompete agreements have received mixed reviews in the courts. Some courts have found them to be binding legal contracts and hold former employees to their obligations. Other courts have found them to be invalid and unnecessarily restrictive of free enterprise and the right to compete. The ethical concern involves balancing the rights of employers to "own" work that was done for compensation by employees versus the rights of individuals to work for whom they chose, including themselves.

Intrapreneurship at Intel

One very unique approach to balancing ownership rights has been developed by Intel. Given the demand for services and products provided in Intel's markets, many employees have opted to start their own businesses, which then have competed against Intel. In lieu of requiring that employees sign noncompete agreements, Intel created a New Business Initiative (NBI) division that actively solicits new business proposals from its employees. The NBI functions as a kind of internal venture capital operation. It operates autonomously: Its staff receives proposals from employees and makes recommendations for start-up funding for those ventures it deems worthy. NBI has proven to be a highly successful retention tool and has afforded Intel the opportunity to avoid the often antagonistic work environment that results from noncompete agreements.[42]

In response to the accounting scandals that rocked the U.S. economy in the early part of the decade, Congress passed the Sarbanes-Oxley Act of 2002. The act was passed to eliminate both deception in accounting and management practices by increasing government oversight of financial reporting and holding senior executives more directly responsible for violations. As a result, organizations need to respond seriously to, and investigate, employee complaints of possible wrongdoing or fraud. Much of the responsibility will fall with HR to create policies and procedures to communicate anonymous, confidential concerns and to establish a review mechanism for such reports.[43]

An important provision of Sarbanes-Oxley is the protection it provides to "whistle-blowers," employees who provide information and/or assistance to investigators, who assist in the review of potential violations of federal laws related to fraud against shareholders. Such whistle-blowers are protected only when information is provided to one of three sources: a federal regulatory or law enforcement agency, any member or committee of Congress, and a person with supervisory authority over the employee who has the authority to investigate such allegations.

Reporting such activity to the media or even an HR manager may fall outside of the protection offered by the act. In fact, the Ninth Circuit Court of Appeals issued a ruling, in *Tides v. Boeing*, which held that an employer did not violate the whistle-blower provision of the Sarbanes-Oxley Act when it terminated two employees who disclosed internal company information to the media. In this case, the court reasoned that Congress intended to protect whistle-blowing activity which was communicated to entities that have the capacity to act effectively on the information provided, notably the three sources noted previously. The court found that employees often have access to sensitive information, public disclosure of which could have devastating consequences for their employers through its adverse effect on a company's reputation and relations with customers, shareholders, government entities, and the general public. Consequently, disclosure of any such activity or information to the media is not protected activity under Sarbanes-Oxley. An employee is protected as long as he or she "reasonably believes" that the reported conduct is a violation, regardless of the outcome of any investigation. The Sarbanes-Oxley Act further mandates that all publically traded organizations disclose whether a code of ethics for senior officers has been adopted.

Given the increased concern for ethical behavior and accountability, it is clearly in an organization's best interest to establish some kind of code of ethics. Currently, more than 90 percent of *Forbes 500* organizations have such codes and more than 82 percent have recently revised them.[44] Exhibit 2.5 presents the Code of Ethical and Professional Standards in Human Resource Management developed by the Society for Human Resource Management for its members and profession. Such industry-specific standards can greatly assist executives in developing an in-house code, but an organization's formal code needs to address a variety of issues specific to the organization. Frank Ashen, executive vice president for Human Resources at the New York Stock Exchange, has developed some guidelines for an organization's Code of Ethics that are presented in Exhibit 2.6.[45]

History has shown that the majority of organizations that undertake ethic awareness and training initiatives do so as a means of complying with legal mandates in attempting to minimize potential liability.[46] However, there is increasing evidence that ethics training and the creation and maintenance of a culture that stresses ethics has a positive impact on employee recruitment, morale, and retention. One survey of employees conducted by Deloitte and Touche found that the indicators of ethics sought by applicants and employees were the behaviors of supervisors and officers relative to giving proper credit for work performed, honesty in dealing with employees and coworkers, and treating people in a fair and just manner without showing preferential treatment.[47]

Ethics training programs should not be developed in a piecemeal manner but rather tied in to, if not fully integrated with, the organization's mission and strategy. Only when this critical link has been established and communicated can an ethics training program be developed that truly has the potential to be effective. The ideal components of an ethics training program include (1) mandatory attendance for all employees, including senior managers and officers; (2) a strict code of ethics that sets standards for behavior in areas such as responsibility, respect, fairness, and

EXHIBIT 2.5

Society for Human Resource Management Code of Ethical and Professional Standards in Human Resource Management

Society for Human Resource Management
CODE PROVISIONS

Professional Responsibility

Core Principle

As HR professionals, we are responsible for adding value to the organizations we serve and contributing to the ethical success of those organizations. We accept professional responsibility for our individual decisions and actions. We are also advocates for the profession by engaging in activities that enhance its credibility and value.

Intent

- To build respect, credibility and strategic importance for the HR profession within our organizations, the business community, and the communities in which we work.
- To assist the organizations we serve in achieving their objectives and goals.
- To inform and educate current and future practitioners, the organizations we serve, and the general public about principles and practices that help the profession.
- To positively influence workplace and recruitment practices.
- To encourage professional decision making and responsibility.
- To encourage social responsibility.

Guidelines

1. Adhere to the highest standards of ethical and professional behavior.
2. Measure the effectiveness of HR in contributing to or achieving organizational goals.
3. Comply with the law.
4. Work consistent with the values of the profession.
5. Strive to achieve the highest levels of service, performance, and social responsibility.
6. Advocate for the appropriate use and appreciation of human beings as employees.
7. Advocate openly and within the established forums for debate in order to influence decision making and results.

PROFESSIONAL DEVELOPMENT

Core Principle

As professionals we must strive to meet the highest standards of competence and commit to strengthen our competencies on a continuous basis.

Intent

- To expand our knowledge of human resource management to further our understanding of how our organizations function.
- To advance our understanding of how organizations work ("the business of the business").

Guidelines

1. Pursue formal academic opportunities.
2. Commit to continuous learning, skills development, and application of new knowledge related to both human resource management and the organizations we serve.
3. Contribute to the body of knowledge, the evolution of the profession, and the growth of individuals through teaching, research, and dissemination of knowledge.
4. Pursue certification such as CCP, CEBS, PHR, SPHR, etc., where available, or comparable measures of competencies and knowledge.

ETHICAL LEADERSHIP

Core Principle

HR professionals are expected to exhibit individual leadership as a role model for maintaining the highest standards of ethical conduct.

Intent

- To set the standard and be an example for others.
- To earn individual respect and increase our credibility with those we serve.

Guidelines

1. Be ethical; act ethically in every professional interaction.
2. Question pending individual and group actions when necessary to ensure that decisions are ethical and are implemented in an ethical manner.
3. Seek expert guidance if ever in doubt about the ethical propriety of a situation.
4. Through teaching and mentoring, champion the development of others as ethical leaders in the profession and in organizations.

FAIRNESS AND JUSTICE

Core Principle

As human resource professionals, we are ethically responsible for promoting and fostering fairness and justice for all employees and their organizations.

Intent

To create and sustain an environment that encourages all individuals and the organization to reach their fullest potential in a positive and productive manner.

Guidelines

1. Respect the uniqueness and intrinsic worth of every individual.
2. Treat people with dignity, respect, and compassion to foster a trusting work environment free of harassment, intimidation, and unlawful discrimination.
3. Ensure that everyone has the opportunity to develop their skills and new competencies.
4. Assure an environment of inclusiveness and a commitment to diversity in the organizations we serve.
5. Develop, administer, and advocate policies and procedures that foster fair, consistent, and equitable treatment for all.
6. Regardless of personal interests, support decisions made by our organizations that are both ethical and legal.
7. Act in a responsible manner and practice sound management in the country(ies) in which the organizations we serve operate.

CONFLICTS OF INTEREST

Core Principle

As HR professionals, we must maintain a high level of trust with our stakeholders. We must protect the interests of our stakeholders as well as our professional integrity and should not engage in activities that create actual, apparent, or potential conflicts of interest.

Intent

To avoid activities that are in conflict or may appear to be in conflict with any of the provisions of this Code of Ethical and Professional Standards in Human Resource Management or with one's responsibilities and duties as a member of the human resource profession and/or as an employee of any organization.

Guidelines

1. Adhere to and advocate the use of published policies on conflicts of interest within your organization.
2. Refrain from using your position for personal, material, or financial gain or the appearance of such.
3. Refrain from giving or seeking preferential treatment in the human resource processes.

4. Prioritize your obligations to identify conflicts of interest or the appearance thereof; when conflicts arise, disclose them to relevant stakeholders.

USE OF INFORMATION

Core Principle

HR professionals consider and protect the rights of individuals, especially in the acquisition and dissemination of information while ensuring truthful communications and facilitating informed decision making.

Intent

To build trust among all organization constituents by maximizing the open exchange of information, while eliminating anxieties about inappropriate and/or inaccurate acquisition and sharing of information.

Guidelines

1. Acquire and disseminate information through ethical and responsible means.
2. Ensure only appropriate information is used in decisions affecting the employment relationship.
3. Investigate the accuracy and source of information before allowing it to be used in employment-related decisions.
4. Maintain current and accurate HR information.
5. Safeguard restricted or confidential information.
6. Take appropriate steps to ensure the accuracy and completeness of all communicated information about HR policies and practices.
7. Take appropriate steps to ensure the accuracy and completeness of all communicated information used in HR-related training.

honesty—at a minimum; (3) presentations of relevant laws related to the organization's business and operations; (4) decision making models that present questions employees can ask themselves when faced with ethical dilemmas (such as the possible repercussions of the decision); (5) in-house resources for questions related to ethics or for reporting perceived violations; and (6) role-playing scenarios that present possible ethical dilemmas an employee in an organization might face or a re-enactment of situations that have already taken place.[48]

The establishment of a code of ethics and ethics training program are critical components of an organization's ethics program, but unless there is ongoing communication concerning oversight of ethics initiatives, continued attention to and compliance with ethics becomes less likely. In response to this, an increasing number of organizations are creating the position of ethics officer. This role is sometimes contained within the HR function, with compliance responsibility ultimately resting with the head of HR. However, most organizations prefer to have an ethics officer who has an accounting and/or legal background, given the proliferation of regulations related to financial reporting and compliance.[49] Particularly since the passage of Sarbanes-Oxley, HR members usually do not have the specialized knowledge and technical skills to understand the intricacies of financial compliance.

Regardless of whether HR oversees the organization's ethics program, HR and its staff face their own ethical dilemmas on a regular basis in the conduct of their own work. Ensuring that immigrant workers have proper documentation; classifying employees appropriately under the Fair Labor Standards Act; ensuring that hiring, performance management, and compensation systems are free from bias; and investigating charges of discrimination and harassment are just a few of the areas in which HR functions as the organization's ethical "compass." An HR officer frequently finds him or herself in a situation in which he or she is at odds with his or her own ethical standards and/or the ethical standards of the profession and the expectations or demands of senior managers or owners of the business.[50] Reading 2.2, "The Ethics of Human Resource Management," explores many of the ethical dilemmas that HR professionals face on a continuous basis in carrying out their job responsibilities.

EXHIBIT 2.6

Guidelines for Developing a Code of Ethics/Conduct

- Need for Personal Integrity—a statement about dealing with individuals both inside and outside of the organization
- Compliance and Laws—addressing intolerance for violating employment, labor, or any other laws that affect the organization
- Political Contributions and Activity—a statement concerning the employer's policy in this domain, including solicitation of personal and/or financial support
- Confidential Information—a statement that identifies what is considered confidential and how such information should be treated, including a statement on employee expectations of privacy
- Conflicts of Interest—a statement that employees are expected to act in the employer's interests in carrying out their job duties along with disclosure requirements
- Books and Records—a statement stressing the practice of using accurate and accepted standards for financial reporting, as well as a prohibition against falsification
- Employment Policies—a general statement on how employees are to be treated, including issues of fairness, discrimination, and safety
- Securities Transactions—a statement on any restrictions that might exist relative to the purchase or sale of stock, as well as a statement and policy directed at insider trading
- Use of Company Assets—a statement that assets will be used only for business, rather than personal interests and needs
- Gifts, Gratuities, and Entertainment—a statement about such relationships and exchanges with clients, with further guidance provided for employees who deal with individuals from other countries where customs, laws, and business practices may differ from those domestically
- The Environment—a statement about the organization's relationship to its environment, if the area of business has an impact on the environment
- Compliance—a statement concerning how the Code of Ethics is to be communicated, certified, implemented, and enforced

Codes of ethics/conduct can be effective only if communicated to all employees and reinforced through the behaviors of senior managers and the organization's reward system. Codes that are developed, then exist, isolated from specific business practices and rewards are likely to have little impact on employees' behavior. Senior managers need to lead by example, modeling the kinds of behaviors expected of employees at all levels of the organization. Finally, such codes can succeed only if a mechanism exists to enforce compliance with their terms, including follow-up and corrective action.

© Cengage Learning

Corporate Social Responsibility/Sustainability

While ethics programs focus on behavior and decision making, corporate social responsibility (CSR) is more macro-focused and looks at how the organization's operations interface with and affect the larger society and world. The World Business Council for Sustainable Development defines CSR as "contributing to sustainable development by working to improve quality of life with employees, their families, the local community and stakeholders up and down the supply chain." CSR is often operationalized relative to what has been called the "triple bottom line," where considerations are paid simultaneously to profits (economic bottom line), people (social bottom line), and the planet (environmental bottom line). Organizations who successfully and simultaneously invest in all three areas vie for inclusion in the Dow Jones Sustainability World Index (DJSWI), which includes 250 worldwide organizations based on their successes relative to economic, environmental, and social performance. There is considerable debate as to whether the costs of being a socially responsible organization and employer exceed the benefits. However, since its inception, the DJSWI has outperformed the Standard & Poor 500 Index by 15 percent, according to Pricewaterhouse Coopers.[51]

The conventional wisdom surrounding environmental protection and responsibility is that it comes at a significant additional cost to an organization, which may erode efficiency and competitiveness. However, evidence exists that suggests that improving an organization's environmental performance can actually lead to improved financial performance rather than an escalation of costs and erosion of profits.

Such enhanced financial performance can be the result of (1) better access to certain markets, (2) differentiated products, (3) sale of pollution-control devices, (4) enhanced risk management and relations with external stakeholders, (5) decreased costs of material, energy, and services, (6) decreased costs of capital, and (7) decreased cost of labor.[52] Exhibit 2.7 illustrates the organizational circumstances that make each of these outcomes more likely and provides a specific organizational example of each type of success. It is critical to remember that environmental stewardship is not always associated with improved financial performance but is realistically possible in a variety of organizational scenarios, contrary to much popular belief.

A challenge many organizations face relative to the implementation of sustainability initiatives is embedding a sustainability mindset at the organization level. Reading 2.3, "How Do Corporations Embed Sustainability Across the Organization?" provides both guidelines as to how this can be accomplished as well as a case study example of these guidelines in practice.

From an HR perspective, CSR initiatives have been found to have a direct positive impact on enhanced recruitment, retention of top performers, and increased productivity.[53] A recent survey of North American business students revealed that 70 percent would not apply for a position with an employer they deemed to be socially irresponsible and 68 percent responded that salary was less important than working for a socially responsible employer. Another survey found that MBA graduates would sacrifice an average of $13,700 in annual salary to work for a socially responsible employer.[54] An additional survey found that 81 percent of employees prefer to work for a company that has a good reputation for social responsibility, 92 percent of students and entry-level hires would be more inclined to work for environmentally friendly employers, and 80 percent of young professionals seek employment with organizations that have a net positive impact on the environment.[55]

Sustainability at General Electric

GE CEO Jeffrey Immelt launched the multibillion-dollar Ecomagination initiative at GE in 2005 to enhance financial and environmental performance simultaneously in driving company growth. Consistent with the GE corporate citizenship philosophy—"make money, make it ethically, make a difference"—Ecomagination is designed to invest in clean technology research and development, introduce environmentally friendly products for consumers, and reduce GE's own gas emissions. Every dimension of the initiative, however, is driven by employees.

GE regularly sponsors employee contests to solicit ideas to reduce the use or waste of energy as well as engage employees in the design of environmentally friendly products and processes. To date, these have included energy-efficient appliances, compact fluorescent lighting, and wind turbine power. The company has developed an internal certification process that quantifies the environmental impacts and benefits of each new product or process on a scorecard, which are externally verified by an external source. The "bottom line" results are startling. From 2004 to 2009, GE's investment in "green" technologies doubled from $750 million to $1.5 billion. During the same period, its revenues from certified "green" technologies similarly doubled from $10 billion to $20 billion.[56]

EXHIBIT 2.7

Summary of Positive Links Between Environmental and Economic Performance

Opportunities for Increasing Revenues	Circumstances Making This Possibility More Likely	Examples
1. Better access to certain markets	More likely for firms selling to the public sector (construction, energy, transportation equipment, medical products, and office equipment) and to other businesses.	The Quebec government now cares about the environmental performance of all vehicles it buys, not only about the price.
2. Differentiating products	More likely when there is: a. Credible information about the environmental features of the product b. Willingness-to-pay by consumers c. Barrier to imitation. Wide range of possibilities	Toyota has announced that all its models will be available with hybrid engines in 2012.
3. Selling pollution-control technologies	More likely when firms already have R&D facilities.	Alcan has patented a process to recycle its own spent pot lining, and that of other companies.
Opportunities for Reducing Costs		
4. Risk management and relations with external stakeholders	More likely in industries that are highly regulated and scrutinized by the public, such as chemical, energy, pulp and paper, metallurgy, etc.	Statoil injects 1 million tons of CO_2 a year beneath the seabed of the North Sea, thus avoiding the Norway carbon tax.
5. Cost of materials, energy, and services	More likely when: a. Firms have a flexible production process b. Firms are in highly competitive industries where optimization of resources is important c. Firms are in industries where market-based environmental policies are implemented d. Firms already have R&D facilities	BP has reduced its emissions of GHGs 10% below their level in 1990 at no cost by implementing an internal tradable permit mechanism (see Reinhardt, 2001).
6. Cost of capital	More likely for firms with shares exchanged on stock markets.	The stock value of Exxon went down by $4.7 billion following the wreck of the Exxon Valdez.
7. Cost of labor	More likely for: a. Firms whose emissions may affect their workers' health b. Firms that seek to attract young, well-educated workers c. Firms located in areas where sensitivity to environmental concerns is important	A 2004 survey of Stanford MBAs found that 97% of them were willing to forgo 14% (on average) of their expected income to work for an organization with a better reputation for corporate social responsibility.

Source: "Does It Pay to be Green: A Systematic Overview" by Stefan Ambec and Paul Lanoie. *Academy of Management Perspectives*, 22, (4), 2008, 45–62.

Offshoring at Gap, Inc.

American apparel manufacturers have been subjected to great criticism in recent years over the offshoring of their manufacturing operations to less-developed countries and the corresponding deplorable working conditions and wages found in such "sweatshops." San Francisco-based Gap, Inc., was one of the first apparel manufacturers to take action in this area with the establishment of its Global Compliance program. Initially started in 1992, the program sets standards for labor, environmental, and health and safety standards for all of the organization's third-party manufacturers. The initial program has evolved into a full company function of more than 90 full-time employees, called vendor compliance officers, who work strictly on ensuring compliance with the standards. These employees are based globally and represent 25 different countries of origin, with most working in countries or communities to which they are native. They conduct inspections of all existing as well as prospective facilities that may enter into manufacturing contracts with Gap, Inc. Since 2003, Gap, Inc. has been publicly releasing a biannual Social Responsibility Report that outlines the company's efforts and successes in ethical outsourcing and labor relations and standards as well as its collaborative and partnership initiatives with all stakeholders. These include the development of an "integrated sourcing scorecard," which provides reports of each factory's compliance history and production standards relative to measures such as quality, innovation, cost, and speed to market.[57] Such transparency in the apparel manufacturing industry is unprecedented and sets the benchmark for others relative to both CSR and reporting of success and initiatives.

Organizational benefits of sustainability initiatives include improved public opinion and enhanced customer and government relations.[58]

HR usually plays a central role in any sustainability initiatives. While often strategic and operational in nature, they involve the need to communicate with and train employees as well as shape the organization's culture around issues of sustainability and CSR. Given the desire of many members of the workforce to be employed in socially responsible organizations, such initiatives may also form the basis for the employment branding of an organization. Indeed, of the 79 indicators of performance identified by the Amsterdam-based Global Reporting Initiative, which produces the generally accepted framework for corporate reporting on sustainability, 24 of these relate to HR management. Performance management and compensation systems, whose design and oversight is usually under the purview of HR, can be revamped to provide incentives for sustainability and CSR initiatives. These are presented in Exhibit 2.8.[59]

Much as many employers are designating chief ethics officers, many are similarly designating chief sustainability officers. This trend reflects the fact that sustainability has become a key business issue and a strategic focus for many organizations. It has been argued that we are fast approaching the day when an organization's "carbon statement" will be as prominent as its financial statements.[60] Indeed, pension funds, state controllers, institutional investors, and even investment bankers are already pressuring organizations to be responsive to environmental issues.[61] Despite a focus on environmental issues that began in the early 1990s, Mitsubishi International, Corp., did not designate a chief sustainability officer until early 2008. Mitsubishi's approach, however, is not piecemeal. The focus of its sustainability office is to look holistically at the effects of climate change, resource depletion, and energy uses and prices on the organization from a strategic planning standpoint rather than simply a compliance standpoint.

A 2012 study by the Boston Consulting Group in partnership with the Sloan School of Management found that from 2011 to 2012 the percentage of organizations that reported that sustainability initiatives are essential to remain competitive in the marketplace increased from 55 to 70 percent. However, of this group only 31 percent reported that their sustainability initiatives were having a positive impact on their financial position. These organizations reporting financial success with sustainability were organized to have a separate sustainability reporting function, a chief sustainability officer, and key operational performance indicators related to sustainability. However, these organizations noted the difficulty in measuring key performance metrics such as the impact on brand reputation and employee engagement, commitment, and productivity. The study found that energy/utilities, consumer

EXHIBIT   2.8

Global Reporting Initiatives That Pertain to Human Resource Management[62]

Labor and Decent Work

1. Total workforce by employment type, employment contract, and region.
2. Total number and rate of employee turnover by age group, gender, and region.
3. Benefits provided to full-time employees not provided to temporary or part-time employees.
4. Percentage of employees covered by collective-bargaining agreements.
5. Minimum notice periods regarding significant operational changes, including whether specified in collective agreements.
6. Percentage of total workforce represented in joint management/worker/health and safety committees that help monitor and advise on occupational health and safety programs.
7. Rates of injury, lost days, and absenteeism and the total number of work-related fatalities by region.
8. Education, training, counseling, prevention, and risk-control programs in place to assist workforce members, their families, or community members regarding serious diseases.
9. Health and safety topics covered in formal agreements with trade unions.
10. Average hours of training per year per employee.
11. Programs for skill management and lifelong learning that support the continued employability of employees and assist them in managing career endings.
12. Percentage of employees receiving regular performance and career development reviews.
13. Composition of governance bodies and breakdown of employees per category according to gender, age group, minority group membership, and other indicators of diversity.
14. Ratio of basic salary of men to women by employee category.

Human Rights

15. Total hours of employee training on policies and procedures concerning aspects of human rights relevant to operations.
16. Total number of incidents of discrimination and actions taken.
17. Operations identified in which the right to exercise freedom of association and collective bargaining may be at significant risk and actions taken to support these rights.
18. Operations identified as having significant risk for incidents of child labor and measures taken to contribute to the elimination of child labor.
19. Operations identified as having significant risk for incidents of forced or compulsory labor and measures to contribute to the elimination of forced or compulsory labor.
20. Total number of incidents of violations involving rights of indigenous people and actions taken.

Social

21. Nature, scope, and effectiveness of any programs and practices that assess and manage the impacts of operations on communities, including entering, operating, and exiting.

Economic

22. Coverage of the organization's defined benefit plan obligations.
23. Range of ratios of standard entry-level wage compared to local minimum wage at significant locations of operation.
24. Procedures for local hiring and proportion of senior management hired from the local community at significant locations of operation.

products, chemicals, and the automotive industries were the leaders in sustainability while service and technology organizations tended to be less involved with sustainability.[63]

The most critical factor that affected financial performance related to sustainability was motivation. Only 9 percent of organizations that adopted business practices related to sustainability as a means of government/regulatory compliance found their practices to be profitable, while 41 percent of those who did so due to market forces and customer demand and expectations found that their sustainability initiatives had a positive impact on the bottom line.

Conclusion

The contexts in which HR is managed in today's organizations are constantly changing. The larger environments in which organizations operate can be in a state of constant change. Nowhere is this more evident than in the areas of ethics and accountability, workforce composition, and corporate social responsibility. Organizations of the twenty-first century cannot expect to be successful without an understanding of and response to these trends and changes. No longer do organizations utilize one set of manufacturing processes, employ a homogeneous group of loyal employees for long periods of time, or develop one set way of structuring how work is done and supervisory responsibility is assigned. Constant, if not continuous, changes in who organizations employ and what these employees do require HR practices and systems that are well conceived and effectively implemented to ensure high performance and continued success.

More importantly, HR practices must constantly be reviewed and evaluated to allow an organization to respond to changes taking place in its environment. Nothing should be accepted as a "given." Failure to allow HR to assess and drive change initiatives can greatly compromise an organization's ability to remain competitive in an ever-changing marketplace and society.

Critical Thinking

1. What are the most important societal trends affecting HR today?

2. What are the most important workplace trends affecting HR today?

3. How well do you feel HR as a profession responds to these trends?

4. Predict societal changes that you believe might take place within the next 10 years. What challenges will these changes present to organizations?

5. Predict workplace changes that you believe might take place within the next 10 years. What challenges will these changes present to organizations?

6. How will HR be impacted by these changes? How can HR help organizations become more effective in meeting the challenges these changes present?

Reading 2.1

7. Should managers promote open discussion of stereotypes as part of a strategy for managing diversity?

What risks and potential advantages and disadvantages are inherent with such a strategy?

Reading 2.2

8. What involvement should HR have with organization-wide ethics initiatives? What organizational decisions or policies might challenge the professional ethics of an HR professional? What day-to-day challenges do line managers face relative to HR-related ethical issues?

Reading 2.3

9. Identify obstacles that may prohibit the potential "win-win" outcomes (the simultaneous pursuit of social and environmental goals and financial performance) associated with sustainability. How can HR be involved with sustainability issues? Identify the benefits, costs, and challenges associated with such involvement.

Exercises

1. In small groups, identify and discuss the significant trends related to diversity, ethics, and sustainability that impact your college, university, or employer. What challenges do these trends present? What initiatives have been established thus far to meet these challenges?

2. List various groups who are often stereotyped in society or school (i.e., members of religious and racial groups, individuals with disabilities, athletes, sexual minorities, etc.), the stereotypes associated with each group, and the basis for the formation of these stereotypes. For individuals who belong to one of these groups, share how it feels for you to be stereotyped and judged as such.

3. Visit the Web site of the U.S. Bureau of Labor Statistics (http://www.bls.gov). What trends do you see taking place in the data presented? What information at the site is most useful for organizations in assessing workforce trends?

4. Develop a code of ethics for students at your institution as well as one for your faculty. What institutional values are embedded in these codes? How can these codes by developed and implemented most effectively?

5. What are the main arguments against sustainability and corporate social responsibility initiatives? Is resistance to such activity more prevalent in certain sectors of the economy?

Chapter References

1. Pomeroy, A. "Cultivating Female Leaders," *HR Magazine*, 52, (4), April 2007, 44–50.

2. Anand, R. and Winters, M. "A Retrospective View of Corporate Diversity Training from 1964 to the Present," *Academy of Management Learning & Education*, 7, (3), 2008, 356–372.

3. Society for Human Resource Management. 2007 State of Workplace Diversity Management. Alexandria, VA: Society for Human Resource Management. 2008.

4. Kwoh, L. "Firms Hail New Chiefs (of Diversity)," *Wall Street Journal*, January 5, 2012, p. B10.

5. Ibid.

6. Society for Human Resource Management, *Workplace Visions*, No. 4, 2001.

7. Ibid.

8. Harvey, B. H. "Technology, Diversity and Work Culture—Key Trends in the Next Millennium," *HR Magazine*, 45, (7), July 2000, p. 59.

9. Society for Human Resource Management, *Workplace Visions*, No. 2, 2001.

10. Robinson, K. "Get Ready to Mediate among Generations, Speakers Advise," *HR News*, December 2002.

11. Hughes, K. "What Does Generation 'Why?' Really Want?" Society for Human Resource Management, February 9, 2011. Available at http://www.shrm.org/hrdisciplines/Diversity/Articles/Pages/WhatDoesGenerationWhyReallyWant.aspx

12. SHRM Online Staff. "Generation Y Goes Directly to Source in Job Hunt." Society for Human Resource Management, April 25, 2011. Available at http://www.shrm.org/Publications/HRNews/Pages/GenYGoesToSource.aspx

13. Babcock, P. "Collaboration in the Intergenerational Workplace." Society for Human Resource Management, August 2, 2011. Available at http://www.shrm.org/hrdisciplines/diversity/articles/pages/collaborationintheintergenerational.aspx

14. Compiled from AARP, Leading A Multigenerational Workforce. Washington, DC 2007; Sabatini, F., Hartmann, D. and McNally, K. "The Multigenerational Workforce: Management Implications and Strategies for Collaboration." Boston: Boston College Center for Work & Family, 2008; Tyler, K. The Tethered Generation. *HR Magazine*, May, 2007, 41–46; Zemke, R., Raines, C. and Filipczak, B. Generations At Work: Managing the Clash of Veterans, Boomers Xers and Nexters in Your Workplace. New York: American Management Association, 2000; Eisner, S. Managing Generation Y. *SAM Advanced Management Journal*, 70, (4), 4–15, Autumn 2005.

15. Society for Human Resource Management. "SHRM Poll Intergenerational Conflict in the Workplace." April 29, 2011.

16. Deal, J. *Retiring the Generation Gap: How Employees Young & Old Can Find Common Ground.* San Francisco: Jossey-Bass. 2006.

17. Human Rights Campaign Workplace Project, www.hrc.org

18. Heylum, S. R. "Equal Benefits Gain Ground," *HR Magazine,* 56, (6), June 2011, pp. 103–108.

19. Cadrain, D. "Equality's Last Frontier," *HR Magazine,* 48, (3), March 2003, pp. 64–68.

20. Hewlett, S. A. and Sumberg, K. "For LGBT Workers, Being "Out" Brings Advantages," *Harvard Business Review,* July/August, 2011. Available at http://hbr.org/2011/07/for-lgbt-workers-being-out-brings-advantages/ar/1

21. Cohen, S. "High-Tech Tools Lower Barriers for the Disabled," *HR Magazine,* October 2002, pp. 60–65.

22. Gray, C. "Employees A-Plenty: The Emerging Workforce of People with Disabilities," Society for Human Resource Management, *Mosaics,* 8, (1), 2002.

23. Wells, S. "Counting on Workers with Disability," *HR Magazine,* 53, (4), April 2008, 45–49.

24. Wells, S. "Counting on Workers with Disability," *HR Magazine,* 53, (4), April 2008, 45–49.

25. Leonard, B. "Reflecting the Wide World of HR," *HR Magazine,* July 2002, 50–56.

26. Frase-Blunt, M. "Thwarting the Diversity Backlash," *HR Magazine,* June 2003, 137–143.

27. Gurchiek, K. "Workers Opt for Long Weekends Over Big Vacations," *Society for Human Resource Management, article 021719,* published at www.shrm.org/hrnews_/published/articles/ CMS_021719.asp May 31, 2007.

28. Mainiero, L. and Sullivan, S. "Kaleidoscope Careers: An Alternate Explanation for the "Opt-Out Revolution," *Academy of Management Executive,* 19, (1), 2005, 106–123.

29. Gurchiek, K. "Providing Work/Life Benefits for Dads Can Give Employers an Edge," *Society for Human Resource Management, article 021880.* Published at www.shrm.org/hrnews_/published/articles/CMS_021880.asp June 15, 2007.

30. Minehan, M. "The Fastest Growing U.S. Ethnic Groups," *HR Magazine,* 42, (5), May 1997.

31. Adams, M. "Diversity: Building a Rainbow One Stripe at a Time," *HR Magazine,* 43, (8), August 1998.

32. Leonard, B. "Resurgent Employee Resource Groups Help Build Leaders." Society for Human Resource Management, October 20, 2011. Available at http://www.shrm.org/hrdisciplines/Diversity/Articles/Pages/ERGStrategy.aspx

33. Rodriguez, R. "Diversity Finds Its Place," *HR Magazine,* 51, (8), August 2006, 56–61.

34. Ibid.

35. Hastings, R. "Pepsi Listens to Employees, Airs 60 Seconds of Silence." *Society for Human Resource Management,* Article 24468, published at www.shrm.org/hrnews_/published/articles/CMS_24468.asp January 31, 2008.

36. Arnold, J. "Employee Networks," *HR Magazine,* 51, (6), June 2006, 145–152.

37. Ibid.

38. Leonard, op. cit.

39. Leonard, B. "Corporate Scandals Will Slow the Pace of Executive Recruitment," *HR Magazine,* October 2002, pp. 27–28.

40. Hirschman, C. "Off Duty, Out of Work," *HR Magazine,* February 2003, 51–56.

41. Society for Human Resource Management, *Workplace Visions,* No. 5, 2001, p. 4.

42. Ibid.

43. Fitzgerald, P. W., Warren, S., Bergman, J., Teeple, M. and Elrod, G. B. "Employment Law Implications of the Sarbanes-Oxley Act of 2002: What Should Human Resource Managers Do Now?" Paper presented at the Academy of Legal Studies in Business Annual Meeting. Nashville, TN, 2003.

44. Ashen, F. Z. "Corporate Ethics—Who Is Minding the Store?" *Society for Human Resource Management White Paper,* www.shrm.org/hrresources/whitepapers_published/CMS_00248.asp

45. Ibid.

46. Tyler, K. "Do the Right Thing." *HR Magazine,* 50, (2), February 2005, 99–102.

47. Gurchiek, K. "Report Lines Work/Life Balance to Ethical Behavior." *Society for Human Resource Management,* Article 021322, published at www.shrm.org/hrnews_/published/articles/CMS_023659.asp, accessed April 23, 2007

48. Tyler, K. "Do the Right Thing," *HR Magazine,* 50, (2), February, 2005, 99–102.

49. Buss, B. "Corporate Compass," *HR Magazine,* 49, (6), June 2004, 127–132.

50. Pomeroy, A. "The Ethics Squeeze," *HR Magazine,* 51, (3), March 2006, 48–55.

51. Fox, A. "Corporate Social Responsibility Pays Off," *HR Magazine,* 52, (8), August 2007, 43–48.

52. Ambec, S. and Lenoie, P. "Does It Pay to be Greet? A Systematic Overview," *Academy of Management Perspectives,* 22, (4), 2008, 45–62.

53. Willard, B. *The Sustainability Advantage: Seven Business Case Benefits of a Triple Bottom Line.* New Society Publishers, 2002.

54. Fox, A. "Corporate Social Responsibility Pays Off," *HR Magazine,* 52, (8), August 2007, 43–48.

55. Fox, A. "Getting in the Business of Being Green," *HR Magazine,* 53, (6), June 2008, 45–50.

56. Fox 2007, op. cit.

57. Ansett, S. "Labor Standards in the Supply Chain: The Steep Climb to Sustainability," *Perspectives on Work,* 9, (2), Winter 2006, 11–13.

58. Fox 2008, op. cit.

59. Fox 2008, op. cit.

60. Woodward, N. "New Breed of Human Resource Leader," *HR Magazine,* 53, (6), June 2008, 52–56.

61. Fox 2008, op. cit.

62. Fox, 2008, op. cit..

63. Ambec, S. and Lenoie, P. "Does It Pay to be Greet? A Systematic Overview," *Academy of Management Perspectives,* 22, (4), 2008, 45–62.

READING 2.1

Stereotype Threat at Work

Loriann Roberson and Carol T. Kulik

Executive Overview

Managing diversity in organizations requires creating an environment where all employees can succeed. This paper explains how understanding "stereotype threat"—the fear of being judged according to a negative stereotype—can help managers create positive environments for diverse employees. While stereotype threat has received a great deal of academic research attention, the issue is usually framed in the organizational literature as a problem affecting performance on tests used for admission and selection decisions. Further, articles discussing stereotype threat usually report the results of experimental studies and are targeted to an academic audience. We summarize 12 years of research findings on stereotype threat, address its commonplace occurrence in the workplace, and consider how interventions effective in laboratory settings for reducing stereotype threat might be implemented by managers in organizational contexts. We end the paper with a discussion of how attention to stereotype threat can improve the management of diversity in organizations.

Ongoing demographic trends (increasing percentages of African Americans, Hispanics, and Asians in the American workforce, an aging population, expanding female labor force participation) have made diversity a fact of organizational life. When these trends were first identified in the mid-1980s, they were heralded as an opportunity for organizations to become more creative, to reach previously untapped markets, and in general to achieve and maintain a competitive advantage (Cox, 1994; Robinson & Dechant, 1997; Thomas & Ely, 1996).

However, employee diversity does not *necessarily* boost creativity, market share, or competitive advantage. In fact, research suggests that left unmanaged, employee diversity is more likely to damage morale, increase turnover, and cause significant communication problems and conflict within the organization (Jackson et al., 1991; Jehn, Neale, & Northcraft, 1999; Tsui, Egan, & O'Reilly, 1992; Zenger & Lawrence, 1989). Thus, "managing diversity" has become a sought-after managerial skill, and concerns about effective diversity management have spawned an industry of diversity training

programs, diversity videos, and diversity consultants. But despite several decades of effort and millions of dollars invested, the evidence suggests that organizations continue to do a poor job of managing diversity. A recent comprehensive report concluded that organizations rarely are able to leverage diversity and capitalize on its potential benefits (Hansen, 2003; Kochan et al., 2003). What's the problem? Are we missing a key piece of the diversity management puzzle?

Most of the attention in the diversity management literature has been focused on the organizational decision maker—the manager who is prejudiced against certain groups and who allows these prejudices to influence how he or she treats employees. These individual-level prejudices become institutionalized—meaning, they become embodied in organizational policies and practices that systematically disadvantage some employees. In their efforts to reduce discrimination, organizations are increasingly concerned about hiring nonprejudiced managers, redesigning biased selection, appraisal, and promotion procedures, and generally eradicating stereotypes from managerial decision making (Greengard, 2003; Rice, 1996). If we eliminate stereotypes from organizational decision making, the logic goes, we'll create an organization where all employees can flourish and advance.

Unfortunately, even if an organization were successful in hiring only non-prejudiced managers and eliminating stereotypes from its formal decision making, stereotypes would still exist in broader society. As a result, every employee walking through the door of the organization knows the stereotypes that might be applied to him or her and wonders whether organizational decision makers and coworkers will endorse those stereotypes. Here, we discuss the effects of these stereotypes and highlight an important aspect of diversity management that has not received much attention by diversity or management scholars: stereotype threat, the fear of being judged and treated according to a negative stereotype about members of your group (Steele, Spencer, & Aronson, 2002). Research on stereotype threat has shown that societal stereotypes can have a negative effect on employee feelings and behavior, making it difficult for an employee to perform to his or her true potential. Research has also indicated that stereotype threat can result in employees working harder, but not better. When stereotype threat is present, performance declines. Therefore, a nonprejudiced manager who uses objective performance indicators as a basis for decision making risks underestimating the employee's true ability. When an organizational context contains the conditions that create stereotype threat, nontraditional employees experience additional barriers to success despite the good intentions of everyone involved. Therefore, stereotype threat places certain demands on the manager of diverse employees—demands to create conditions that minimize the occurrence of stereotype threat, so that all employees can perform effectively.

Stereotype threat has been discussed almost exclusively as an issue for high stakes testing, particularly in educational arenas. For example, we're all familiar with the opportunities that hang on scores from tests such as the Scholastic Aptitude Test (SAT), the Graduate Record Examination (6RE), and the Graduate Management Achievement Test (GMAT): without the "right" scores, a student won't be able to get into the best college for his or her chosen field. In 1999, PBS aired a documentary concluding that stereotype threat was suppressing the standardized test performance of African American students (Chandler, 1999). These effects on high stakes tests are important, but stereotype threat is not limited to African American students taking large-scale standardized academic tests. It is also present in the everyday routine situations that are a part of all jobs. Thus, knowledge of stereotype threat and its corrosive effects on performance is needed to understand the work experience of members of stereotyped groups and to manage diversity more effectively in the organization. In this article, we answer the following questions: What is stereotype threat and what are its effects? How can stereotype threat be reduced?

We begin with a short review of the concept and the research evidence. We then describe the conditions that increase the risk of stereotype threat. Because these conditions regularly occur in the workplace, stereotype threat is also likely to be a common part of many people's work experience. Finally, we present strategies for reducing stereotype threat from the academic research literature and consider if and how those strategies might be applied in organizations. We also discuss how attention to stereotype threat adds value to current organizational approaches to managing diversity.

Stereotype Threat at Work

Every job involves being judged by other people, whether you are giving a sales presentation to clients, representing your work team at a meeting, or showing your boss your work for some informal feedback. Being evaluated can raise anxieties for anyone. Apprehension in these kinds of situations is a common phenomenon, and in fact, a little anxiety can even boost performance (Cocchiara & Quick, 2004; Reio & Callahan, 2004; Yerkes & Dodson, 1908). But anxieties can be heightened for those employees who are members of a negatively stereotyped group, especially when they are performing a kind of task on which, according to the stereotype, members of their group do poorly. Consider these statements by people who are members of stereotyped groups:

> *From a marketing manager: "You can see in someone's eyes when you are first introduced that you're dead in the water just because you're seen as old." Many older workers refer to "the look" on someone's face as they are introduced. A 57 year old accounts supervisor recounted that on meeting someone face to face for the first time, she was told with a tone of disappointment, "Oh, you have such a young voice on the phone" (Blank & Shipp, 1994).*

> *From a White loan officer (concerned about being perceived as racist or sexist): "I'm always worried about how I was heard. How will I be interpreted? Did I say the wrong thing?" (Blank & Shipp, 1994).*

> *From a Black manager: "I felt Whites had a lot of negative ideas about Blacks. I felt evaluated when I asked questions. Asking questions became painful for me" (Dickins & Dickins, 1991).*

> *From an overweight worker: "... I work extra hard because I know the stereotype, and I feel I need to prove myself. I work harder than most of my coworkers who do the same job. Yet my (skinny, size-10) boss continually talks about me behind my back to my coworkers - she says that I'm lazy and that I don't take any initiative, and who knows what else. She sees me for maybe half an hour out of the work week, which is hardly enough time to judge me on my work ... It doesn't matter that I know the job inside-out, or that my customer-service skills are topnotch. It doesn't matter that I'm on time and do any stupid little task that I'm asked. All that matters is the width of my ass" (Personal blog, 2005).*

The individuals quoted here are members of different identity groups, but they all voice a common concern: the fear of being seen and judged according to a negative stereotype about their group, and the concern that they might do something that would inadvertently confirm the negative stereotype (Steele, 1997; Steele et al., 2002). These individuals are experiencing "stereotype threat."

Stereotype threat describes the psychological experience of a person who, while engaged in a task, is aware of a stereotype about his or her identity group, suggesting that he or she will not perform well on that task. For example, a woman taking a math test is familiar with the common stereotype that "girls aren't good at math." Or a Black faculty member preparing his case for promotion is aware that some people believe that Blacks are intellectually inferior. This awareness can have a disruptive effect on performance—ironically resulting in the individual confirming the very stereotype he or she wanted to disconfirm (Kray, Thompson, & Galinsky, 2001). Anyone can experience anxiety while performing a task with important implications (a test to get into graduate school or a presentation to a big client), but stereotype threat places an *additional* burden on members of stereotyped groups. They feel "in the spotlight," where their failure would reflect negatively not only on themselves as individuals, but on the larger group to which they belong. As singer and actress Beyonce Knowles said in an interview with *Newsweek* in 2003: "It's like you have something to prove, and you don't want to mess it up and be a negative reflection on black women" (quoted in Smith, 2004, p. 198).

In the first (and now classic) study on stereotype threat, Claude Steele and Joshua Aronson (1995) asked Black and White students to take a very difficult test. The test was composed of items from the verbal section of the Graduate Record Examination, and it was deliberately designed to tax students' ability. For some students, this test was described simply as a laboratory problem-solving task. However, for other students, the test was described as a "genuine test of your verbal abilities and limitations." The important difference between these two descriptions was that race stereotypes were irrelevant in the "laboratory task" version—there was no reason for a Black participant to expect race to impact his or her performance, or to think that other people might expect race to have an impact. However, in the scenario where the test was described as a genuine test of abilities and limitations (the stereotype threat condition), the racial stereotype (that Blacks lack intellectual ability) *was* relevant, and the researchers predicted that Black participants would be both aware of the stereotype and want to avoid confirming it.

When Steele and Aronson examined the results, they found that White students' performance was largely unaffected by the test instructions—the White students performed about equally well whether the test had been described as an ability test or as a laboratory problem-solving task. However, the instructions made a big difference in the performance of Black students. They performed less well in the ability test condition than in the problem-solving condition—even though the test was equally difficult in both conditions. In fact, after Steele and Aronson controlled for pre-study differences in ability (measured by the students' SAT scores), they found that Black and White students in the laboratory problem-solving condition performed about the same—but Black students underperformed relative to Whites in the ability test condition (Steele & Aronson, 1995).

This basic experimental design, in which researchers compare the performance of two groups (one group is negatively stereotyped, the other is not) in two task conditions (one condition presents the task as stereotype-relevant, the other does not), has been replicated many times over the last twelve years with consistent results. The negatively stereotyped group underperforms when the stereotype is seen as relevant to the task. This research is summarized in Table 1.

As the table shows, the stereotype threat phenomenon has been documented in a large number of groups, across a wide range of diversity dimensions, and in many different performance domains. In the top (unshaded) part of the Table, the "Who was affected?" column includes the people we generally think of as disadvantaged in the workplace due to negative stereotypes—racial and ethnic minorities, members of lower socio-economic classes, women, older people, gay and bisexual men, and people with disabilities. The academic literature sometimes describes members of these groups as "stigma conscious" (Aronson et al., 1999). That means that members of these groups can be very aware of the social stereotypes other people associate with their group. Since the relevant stereotype is very likely to come to mind, concerns about stereotype confirmation are easily aroused. As a result, very subtle contextual variations (a slight wording difference in the way a test is described, for example) may be enough to make the stereotype salient and disrupt performance.

But research has shown that this phenomenon does not apply only to people in disadvantaged groups. In fact, the bottom (shaded) part of Table 1 shows that even members of high status groups can experience stereotype threat. For example, we don't normally think of White men as being disadvantaged in the workplace. White men generally enjoy more hiring opportunities, higher salaries, and more organizational status than women or members of racial minority groups with comparable education and ability (Hite, 2004; Parks-Yancy, 2006). However, even high status groups have some negative stereotypes associated with them, and one of the stereotypes most strongly associated with the White group is the belief that Whites are racist (Frantz et al., 2004). The research suggests that many Whites are chronically concerned with not appearing racist (and inadvertently confirming the stereotype). Therefore, task situations that are described as dependent on racial attitudes can trigger stereotype threat in Whites (and result in participants looking more prejudiced than they might actually be) (Frantz et al., 2004).

Further, members of any group may experience stereotype threat when their identity group is negatively compared with another group. For example, comparative stereotypes suggest that Whites have less mathematical ability than Asians, men are less effective in processing affective (emotional) information than women, and White men have less athletic prowess than Black men. These negative comparisons can induce stereotype threat, and members of the target group demonstrate the short-term

Table 1

Examples of Stereotype Threat[a]

Who Was Affected?	How Did the Researchers Create Stereotype Threat?	What Stereotype Was Activated?	What Happened?
Black students	Told the students that they were about to take a very difficult test that was a "genuine test of your verbal abilities and limitations"	"Blacks lack intellectual ability"	The students performed less well on the test
Latino students	Told the students that they were about to take a very difficult mathematical and spatial ability test that would provide a "genuine test of your actual abilities and limitations"	"Latinos lack intellectual ability"	The students performed less well on the test
Low socioeconomic status (SES) students	Asked the students to provide background information including their parents' occupation and education, then told them they were about to take a difficult test that would "assess your intellectual ability for solving verbal problems"	"Low SES students lack intellectual ability"	The students attempted to solve fewer problems and had fewer correct answers on the test
Women	Reminded the women that "previous research has sometimes shown gender differences" in math ability, then asked them to take a test that "had shown gender differences in the past"	"Women have weak math ability"	The women performed more poorly on the math test
Older individuals (60 years and older)	Gave the older people a series of memory tests and presented them with a list of "senile" behaviors ("can't recall birthdate") too quickly for conscious awareness. Then researchers gave the older people the memory tests a second time	"Older people have bad memory"	The older people had a significant decline in memory performance from pretest to posttest
Gay and bisexual men	Asked the men to indicate their sexual orientation on a demographic survey, then videotaped the participants while they engaged in a "free play" activity with children	"Gay men are dangerous to young children"	Judges rated the men as more anxious and less suitable for a job at a daycare center
People with a head injury history	Told participants that a "growing number" of neuropsychological studies find that individuals with head injuries "show cognitive deficits on neuropsychological tests," then gave participants a series of tests assessing memory and attention	"Persons with a head injury history experience a loss of cognitive performance"	The participants performed worse on tests of general intellect, immediate memory, and delayed memory

Table 1

Examples of Stereotype Threat *(continued)*

Who Was Affected?	How Did the Researchers Create Stereotype Threat?	What Stereotype Was Activated?	What Happened?
Whites	Told participants that a "high proportion of Whites show a preference for White people" before asking them to complete the IAT (implicit attitude test) that would measure their "unconscious racial attitudes toward Blacks and Whites"	"Whites are racist"	The participants had a larger IAT effect (the difference in response time between incompatible and compatible trials), suggesting a preference for White faces
White students	Gave the students a packet of newspaper articles emphasizing a "growing gap in academic performance between Asian and White students" before asking them to take a very challenging math test	"White students have less mathematical ability than Asian students"	The students solved fewer problems on the math test
Men	Reminded participants that "it is a well-known fact that men are not as apt as women to deal with affect … and to process affective information as effectively" then asked them to indicate whether a series of words were "affective" or not	"Men are less capable than women in dealing with affective (emotional) information"	The men made more errors on the task
White men	Told the men that they would be engaged in a golf task that measured their "natural athletic ability." The men completed a demographic survey that included a question about their racial identity, then took the test	"White men have less athletic prowess than Black men"	The men made more strokes (performed worse) on the golf task

[a]The research summarized in this table include the following articles: Steele, C. M., & Aronson, J. (1995). *Stereotype threat and the intellectual test performance of African Americans. Journal of Personality and Social Psychology,* 69, 797–811; Gonzales, P. M., Blanton, H., & Williams, K. J. (2002). The effects of stereotype threat and double-minority status on the test performance of Latino women. *Personality and Social Psychology Bulletin,* 28, 659–670; Croize, J., & Claire, T. (1998). Extending the concept of stereotype threat to social class: The intellectual underperformance of students from low socioeconomic backgrounds. *Personality and Social Psychology Bulletin,* 24, 588–594; Spencer, S. J., Steele, C. M., & Quinn, D. M. (1999). Stereotype threat and women's math performance. *Journal of Experimental Social Psychology,* 35, 4–28; Bosson, J. K., Haymovitz, E. L., & Pinel, E. C. (2004). When saying and doing diverge: The effects of stereotype threat and self-reported versus non-verbal ability. *Journal of Experimental Social Psychology,* 40, 247–255; Suhr, J. A., & Gunstad, J. (2002). "Diagnosis threat": The effect of negative expectations on cognitive performance in head injury. *Journal of Clinical and Experimental Neuropsychology,* 24, 448–457; Frantz, C. M., Cuddy, A. J. C., Burnett, M., Ray, H., & Hart, A. (2004). A threat in the computer: The race implicit association test as a stereotype threat experience. *Personality and Social Psychology Bulletin,* 30, 1611–1624; Aronson, J., Lustina, M. J., Good, C., Keough, K., Steele, C. M., & Brown, J. (1999). When White men can't do math: Necessary and sufficient factors in stereotype threat. *Journal of Experimental Social Psychology,* 35, 29–46; Leyens, J., Desert, M., Croizet, J., & Darcis, C. (2000). Stereotype threat: Are lower status and history of stigmatization preconditions of stereotype threat? *Personality and Social Psychology Bulletin,* 26, 1189–1199; Stone, J., Lynch, C. I., Sjomeling, M., & Darley, J. M. (1999). Stereotype threat effects on Black and White athletic performance. *Journal of Personality and Social Psychology,* 77, 1213–1227.

performance detriments associated with stereotype threat, as the studies listed in the table have found. One conclusion that can be drawn from looking at the table is that stereotype threat can affect all of us because each of us is a member of at least one group about which stereotypes exist. If you think about the stereotypes that could be applied to your own social group, you might recall situations where you personally experienced stereotype threat. If you think about the stereotypes that could apply to your employees, you can also identify the situations where they might be vulnerable to stereotype threat.

The research referred to in the table has decisively shown that stereotype threat has a negative impact on short term performance. But an unresolved question is why does stereotype threat have this negative impact? Researchers have suggested several different answers to this question (the literature calls these answers "mediating" explanations), but there is no consensus on which is the "right" answer. The dominant explanation has to do with anxiety (Aronson, Quinn, & Spencer, 1998), but there is still some disagreement over how anxiety affects performance. One argument suggests that anxiety increases a person's motivation and effort. Stereotype threatened participants are very motivated to perform well, and sometimes they try too hard or are too cautious in performing (Cadinu et al., 2003). For example, Steele and Aronson (1995) found that the Black participants in their research spent too much time trying to answer a small number of problems. They worked too hard on getting the right answer, and they disadvantaged themselves by not answering enough questions. Another argument proposes the opposite—that anxiety decreases a person's motivation and effort (Cadinu et al., 2003). The explanation is that stereotype threatened participants lose confidence that they can perform well, and in a self-fulfilling way this undermines performance. Given that the evidence thus far is still mixed and unclear, we will have to wait for further research to provide a more definitive answer to the why question. However, research has clearly identified the conditions under which stereotype threat is more and less likely to occur. This brings us to the next section of our paper.

Conditions for Stereotype Threat

We've seen that the content of stereotypes about groups includes beliefs about the abilities of group members to perform certain kinds of tasks. Stereotype threat will only occur for those tasks associated with the stereotype. But simply being *asked* to perform a stereotype-relevant task is not enough to create stereotype threat. Research has identified two additional conditions needed for stereotype threat to emerge: task difficulty and personal task investment. In addition, the context can influence the perceived relevance of the stereotype for performance of the task or job. We have diagrammed these conditions, and the stereotype threat process, in Figure 1.

Stereotype Relevance of the Task: What Does it Take to Perform Well?

Stereotype threat is situation specific, felt in situations where one can be "judged by, treated and seen in terms of, or self-fulfill a negative stereotype about one's group" (Spencer, Steele, & Quinn, 1999, p. 6). These situations occur when doing well on the task requires an ability on which, according to the stereotype, the person performing the task has a deficit. In the studies we have reviewed, the stereotype relevance of the task has often been created by telling participants that the task is a direct "test" of the stereotyped ability. So, for example, math tests have been used to create a stereotype relevant task for women and verbal or cognitive ability tests used to create stereotype relevant tasks for African Americans and Hispanics. But stereotype relevance isn't limited to standardized tests. Laura Kray and her colleagues surveyed participants to show that negotiation tasks are stereotype relevant for women. The researchers found that people believed that good negotiators were "assertive and concerned with personal gain" and that "men are more likely to be assertive than women" (Kray, Galinsky, & Thompson, 2002). Therefore, it logically follows that "men are better negotiators than women."

Research has shown that in our society many people believe successful managers have attributes more similar to those of men and Whites than to those of women, Hispanics, or African Americans (Chung-Herrera & Lankau, 2005; Heilman, Block, Martell, & Simon, 1989; Tomkiewicz, Brenner, & Adeyemi-Bello, 1998). But beliefs about the traits necessary for jobs can also be organization specific. The potential for stereotype threat exists any time employees' beliefs about the particular traits needed for good job performance are linked to stereotypes about groups.

Task Difficulty: Why Is This So Hard?

Stereotype threat is most likely to influence performance on very difficult tasks—those that are at the limits of a person's abilities (Steele et al., 2002). On easier tasks, stereotype threat doesn't have much negative effect. According to psychologist Claude Steele, experiencing frustration with task accomplishment is an important trigger for stereotype threat (Steele et al., 2002). On a simple task there is little frustration—the person is doing well and knows it. But with a difficult task, progress is not so smooth. People who experience frustration with a task try to explain their difficulty to themselves: "Why is this so hard? Is this job just impossible? Am I not working hard enough? Am I having a bad day?" They also think about

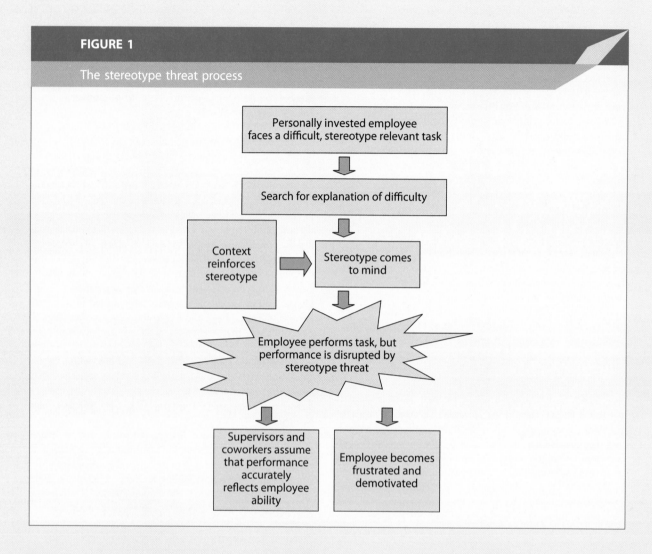

FIGURE 1

The stereotype threat process

how others (coworkers, supervisors) will explain their difficulty: "Will they think I'm not working hard enough?" But when the person is a member of a stereotyped group, the stereotype is also likely to come to mind as a potential explanation that others might use: "Will they think the stereotype is true? It's going to look like the stereotype is true."

A negative dynamic operates between task difficulty and stereotype threat. When a task is difficult, stereotype threat evokes concern over performance. But this concern also has a greater impact on the performance of difficult tasks. Difficult jobs require concentration and focus; all of one's cognitive/mental resources must be directed toward accomplishing the work. If some of those resources are diverted toward worrying about one's skills and how one will be viewed by others, performance decrements occur (Beilock & Carr, 2005; Verbeke & Bagozzi, 2000). Thus, difficult tasks trigger stereotype threat and also are most affected by it.

In work settings then, difficult, complex, and challenging tasks are where stereotype threat is most likely to occur. This creates a dilemma for managers. Task difficulty is not just a fact in many (especially professional) jobs, it is a desired condition. For years, job design experts have recommended that every job contain some challenging aspects to increase job involvement and avoid boredom and skill atrophy (Greenberg, 1996; Hackman & Oldham, 1980). In fact, giving demanding assignments to new hires is sometimes recommended as a good way to develop employees. Early demanding experiences predict later career success (Habermas & Bluck, 2000). In many organizations, "stretch" assignments (assignments for which an employee is not yet fully qualified, "stretching" the employee's skills and abilities) (McCauley, Eastman, & Ohlott, 1995) are used as developmental tools throughout a person's tenure (Noe, 1999). Stretch assignments are needed for skill development, but managers must be aware of the extra potential for stereotype threat these assignments might involve for stereotyped employees, and counteract this risk. (We discuss how managers might do this later in the paper.)

In addition, tasks that are new and unfamiliar to the person performing them may be more at risk for stereotype threat than routine, familiar ones. New employees in particular are likely to find task accomplishment challenging as they learn their responsibilities. Thus, managers also must be aware of the higher potential for stereotype threat for their new hires.

Personal Task Investment: How Important Is This to Who I Am?

Personal task investment refers to how important doing well on the task is to the individual's self-esteem and identity. Some employees strongly identify with a particular skill or competency as a part of who they are. We often hear people say, "I'm good with people," or "I'm a techie." For these people, the skill is a part of how they define themselves. For such invested people, doing well in that task domain is important for their self-esteem and for feeling good about themselves. Researchers have argued that people who are personally invested in the task would be most influenced by stereotype threat because they are the ones who really care about their performance (Steele, 1997; Steele et al., 2002). If you want your work performance to say something about you personally, then the prospect of being viewed in terms of a negative stereotype is most disturbing. Studies have consistently confirmed this. Those invested in the task are more negatively affected by stereotype threat than those without such personal task investment.

What does this mean, practically? People tend to be invested in tasks they are good at (Steele, 1997). So the heavy impact of stereotype threat on the personally invested means that "the most capable members of stereotyped groups tend to be the most adversely affected in their performance by stereotype threat" (Kray et al., 2002, p. 388). This carries an important reminder for managers: the employees who care about their work and really want to do well are generally the ones that a manager is least likely to worry about since they are the ones he or she thinks will succeed on their own, and thus don't need coaxing, coaching, or extra attention. Yet, these are the people most likely to be affected by stereotype threat, and therefore, most in need of a manager's efforts to address and reduce it. For example, a manager might think that because the talented Hispanic salesperson graduated at the top of his class, he's already proven that stereotypes don't apply to him and isn't bothered by them. Or that the efficient accountant who earned her CPA despite caring for four children no longer worries about not being taken seriously by male managers. But it's exactly these employees, the ones who have made a big investment in their work, who might be most likely to suffer the effects of stereotype threat.

The Context: Is this a Place Where Stereotypes Operate?

We've seen that the most important condition for stereotype threat is stereotype relevance: stereotype threat only occurs when the stereotype seems relevant to performing the task (Steele et al., 2002). In the academic research described earlier, stereotype relevance was created by the way the researchers described the tasks in a laboratory setting. In work settings, the relevance of the stereotype for performance can also be signaled and reinforced by the diversity (or the lack of diversity) of people who are currently performing the job. Rosabeth Moss Kanter used the term "token" to describe individuals who are different from others on a salient demographic dimension—race, sex, or age (Kanter, 1977). Kanter and others have shown that tokens feel very "visible"—that they stand out from the rest of the group. In addition, those in the majority are more likely to view tokens in terms of their distinguishing characteristic: as *the* woman or *the* Asian. Because everyone (the tokens and the tokens' colleagues) is more aware of group memberships under these conditions, associated stereotypes are more likely to come to mind (Niemann & Dovidio, 1998). In addition, the numerical differences reinforce the relevance of the stereotype for performance in the setting. Consider the solitary woman in a team of software engineers. Being the "only one" suggests that the stereotype about women lacking quantitative skills is true, and therefore sex is relevant to job performance. After all, the reasoning goes, if "those people" were good at this kind of job, wouldn't we see more of them performing it? Two studies have provided evidence of the link between token status and stereotype threat. In one, laboratory experimenters found that token women showed lower performance than non-tokens only on a math task (a stereotyped domain) and not on a verbal task (a non stereotyped domain) (Inzlicht & BenZeev, 2003). In the other, field researchers found that Black managers who were tokens in their work group reported higher levels of stereotype threat than non-tokens (Roberson, Deitch, Brief, & Block, 2003).

Thus, group representation can raise the relevance of the stereotype for performance. Work situations involving lone members of a social or demographic group are common. For example, in the field research described above, 18% of the Black managers were tokens in their work group (Roberson et al., 2003). Managers need to be aware of this effect of the environment and find ways to neutralize it.

In summary, these conditions make stereotype threat more likely for members of negatively stereotyped groups:

- The employee is invested in doing well, on:
- A difficult, stereotype relevant task, where:
- The context reinforces the stereotype

When stereotype threat occurs, performance is disrupted. But the effects of stereotype threat go beyond short-term performance decrements. The Black managers who experienced stereotype threat in the field research said that they spent more time monitoring their performance (for example, by comparing themselves to peers) and were more likely to discount performance feedback that they received from the organization (Roberson et al., 2003). So, for example, a Black employee who is regularly exposed to stereotype threat about his intellectual ability might dismiss performance feedback from his White manager that would have helped him to meet organizational performance expectations and get on the promotion "fast track."

But maybe these responses are functional. If your manager holds a negative stereotype about you, maybe you should discount feedback from that person (or at least, take it with a large grain of salt). If you can't trust your manager, monitoring the performance of your peers might yield more credible information with which to assess your performance. And if stereotype threat causes people to work harder, couldn't that be a positive benefit? Earlier, we quoted Beyonce Knowles as feeling like she had "something to prove." Beyonce has clearly been able to channel those feelings in a positive way in order to become a successful performer. Maybe a strong motivation to disprove a negative stereotype about your group can increase persistence and determination to succeed. Research on achievement goals has shown that a desire to prove one's ability can be a powerful form of motivation (Elliott & Harackiewicz, 1996), most effective in improving performance and persistence on simple tasks that are familiar to the performer (Steele-Johnson, Beauregard, Hoover, & Schmidt, 2000; Vandewalle, 2001). If you know *how* to perform a task, this kind of motivation can help you to perform better. But remember the Black students in Steele and Aronson's research—the ones who spent a lot of time answering very few questions? Those students were very motivated, but they were working on very complex, challenging problems and their efforts did not pay off. This kind of motivation often works for you, but it can work against you.

Questions about whether employee responses to stereotype threat can be functional or potentially beneficial indicate that we need to know a lot more about the long-term consequences of repeated exposure to stereotype threat. To answer these questions, research has to study stereotype threat over time in real-world organizational settings. So far, the research suggests that repeated exposure to stereotype threat may have serious, and primarily negative, side effects. Stereotype threat is accompanied by physiological reactions such as an increase in blood pressure, leading researchers to speculate that long-term exposure to stereotype threat conditions might contribute to chronic health problems such as hypertension (Blascovich, Spencer, Quinn, & Steele, 2001). Stereotype threat is also associated with lower job satisfaction (Niemann & Dovidio, 1998; Roberson et al.,

2003). Researchers have further suggested that repeated, regular exposure to stereotype threat may lead a person to disengage (or "disidentify") with the performance domain (Steele, 1997). That solo female in your engineering group may begin to think that an alternative career path might be preferable. This leads one to wonder whether long-term exposure to stereotype threat could be one cause of turnover for women and racial/ethnic minorities in professional and managerial jobs. Indeed, some studies have found that members of these groups leave jobs at a higher rate than White men (Horn, Roberson, & Ellis, 2007).

Fortunately, research on the conditions under which stereotype threat is most likely to occur also provides information about reducing the risk of stereotype threat. Recent studies have directly examined ways to reduce or eliminate stereotype threat by changing the conditions that produce the effect—in essence, interrupting the process. These studies are important because they point to some steps that can be taken by managers to lessen the possibility that stereotype threat operates for their employees. We now turn to specific strategies for reducing the likelihood of stereotype threat.

Interrupting the Stereotype Threat Process

Strategies for Reducing Stereotype Threat

We have mentioned that stereotype threat effects are strongest for people who are highly identified with the task domain. Researchers fear that over time, stereotyped people may find one way to reduce stereotype threat themselves—by disidentifying with the affected task domain. In other words, they break the psychological connection between their performance and their self-esteem so that doing well on that kind of task is less important. This is the only solution under the individual's control, but it is also perhaps the worst solution, costly for both the individual who gives up a valued part of the self, and for the organization that loses an engaged and motivated employee. Here we describe some alternatives to this worst case scenario—other strategies for reducing stereotype threat. These strategies, demonstrated to be effective in laboratory studies, all involve changing the conditions for stereotype threat. The strategies, and the points in the process at which they intervene, are shown in Figure 2.

Provide a Successful Task Strategy

We know that stereotype threat influences people only on very difficult tasks—those at the outer limits of ability and skill. Evidence suggests that stereotype threatened people seek to distance themselves from the stereotype by acting opposite to it (Aronson, 2002). They often put their noses to the grindstone, work harder and longer to prove the stereotype wrong-to show it does not apply to them. In the original study by Steele and Aronson, stereotype threatened Black students worked harder and more diligently at the task,

FIGURE 2

Interrupting the stereotype threat process

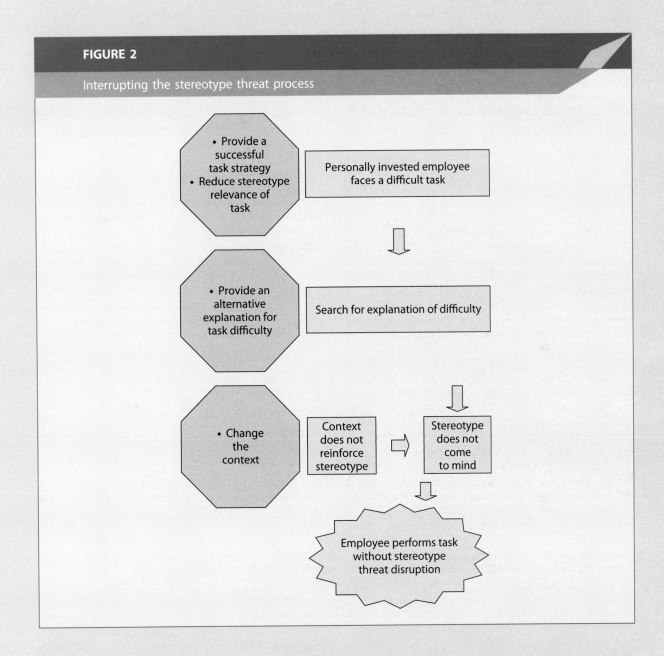

- Provide a successful task strategy
- Reduce stereotype relevance of task

Personally invested employee faces a difficult task

- Provide an alternative explanation for task difficulty

Search for explanation of difficulty

- Change the context

Context does not reinforce stereotype

Stereotype does not come to mind

Employee performs task without stereotype threat disruption

expending more effort than the unthreatened. Unfortunately, working harder and more carefully didn't increase performance. The task they were working on was extremely difficult, right at the outer limit of their abilities. Effort *alone* couldn't boost performance—what the students needed was an effective strategy for solving the problems.

A recent study provided stereotype threatened participants with a strategy to successfully counteract the stereotype. In a negotiation task, women were explicitly told about gender stereotypes, suggesting that women are less assertive than men and tend not to act in their own self-interest; these characteristics

reduce their effectiveness in negotiations. The women in the study were able to counteract the stereotype by acting particularly assertively when making opening offers to their partners, and this strategy improved their performance in the negotiation. However, the women acted this way only when they were *explicitly* told about gender's effect on negotiation. The women already knew how to act assertively—all they needed to perform successfully was a cue that this context was one in which acting assertively was a good strategy (Kray et al., 2001).

This research suggests that one way to reduce stereotype threat is to teach affected employees behavioral strategies for improving performance and counteracting negative stereotypes. This intervention addresses task difficulty—one of the conditions for stereotype threat. Having good strategies available to cope with challenges makes the task seem less difficult and less frustrating. This research suggests that when using stretch assignments, managers should set goals, and also help employees develop strategies toward attaining them. The "sink or swim" attitude toward stretch assignments common in many organizations can be particularly detrimental for stereotype threatened individuals. If managers discuss and suggest task strategies to employees, stereotype threat should be reduced.

Reduce the Stereotype Relevance of the Task

We also know that stereotype threat happens when the stereotype is relevant to the task; when performance on a task is believed to reflect an ability or trait that differentiates stereotyped and nonstereotyped groups (e.g., women and men; Blacks and Whites). Several studies have eliminated stereotype threat effects by refuting or diminishing the stereotype relevance of the task. In one study, researchers asked men and women to take a difficult math test composed of items from the GRE exam. All participants were told that they were taking the math test as part of an effort to develop new testing procedures for the university. Half of the participants were also informed that this particular test had been shown not to produce gender differences—that men and women performed equally well. The other half were not given any information about gender differences. The researchers predicted that stereotype threat would operate when there was no information given about gender differences, because when labeled simply as a "math test," the gender stereotype that "women can't do math" would be relevant. However, being told explicitly that there were no gender differences would reduce the relevance of the stereotype to the task, and hence reduce stereotype threat. By presenting the test as one with no gender differences, the stereotype would be irrelevant to interpreting performance on the test. These results were confirmed: women underperformed relative to men in the "no information" (stereotype relevant) condition, but performed equally to men in the "no gender difference" (stereotype irrelevant) condition (Spencer et al., 1999).

Another study reduced the stereotype relevance of the task in a slightly different way, by emphasizing characteristics shared by both groups. Male and female college students participated in a negotiation exercise. For half of the participants, researchers made gender stereotypes relevant by saying that the most effective negotiators are "rational and assertive" rather than "emotional and passive" (cueing gender stereotypes). For the other half, researchers eliminated the relevance of the gender stereotype for performance. They told this half of the participants that "rational and assertive"

people do better than "emotional and passive" individuals. But then they added, "people who are in competitive academic environments, like you, do exceptionally well in the negotiation. This is true for men and women alike." This description highlighted characteristics important for performance that are shared by both men and women, diminishing the stereotype relevance of the task. This strategy was also successful in decreasing stereotype threat and gender differences in performance (Kray et al., 2001).

These studies show that reducing the stereotype relevance of the task—one of the conditions for stereotype threat—is effective in removing stereotype threat. But is this a realistic strategy in organizations? In the laboratory, it is possible to label an unfamiliar task as one showing group differences or not. It is easy to manipulate participants' beliefs about whether a task reflects group differences when those participants have no prior experience with the task. The situation is different with real world tasks or jobs where employees and coworkers may have strong opinions about the types of people who do well in various jobs or roles. Consider technical or mathematical tasks. Belief in gender differences on such tasks is widespread (Brown & Josephs, 1999), so when faced with a technical or mathematical task, a woman may not believe a manager who says it does not reflect gender differences. It might be more effective for managers instead to use the strategy in the second experiment. For example, rather than try to discredit gender differences, one could make gender differences irrelevant by stressing *common* characteristics of employees that are relevant for performing the task. This could be done by identifying characteristics important for task success that are unlinked to group stereotypes. Perhaps a manager could inform all employees that they were hired precisely because they have the skills needed to do well. For example, "We have such good hiring procedures—the people who we bring in, both men and women, have the skills to perform well."

Provide an Alternative Explanation for Task Difficulty

Task difficulty is a trigger for stereotype threat because people try to explain their difficulty to themselves: on a stereotype relevant task, where the context reinforces the stereotype, they are more likely to think of the stereotype as a potential explanation. The resulting anxiety and distress then disrupts performance. Several studies have shown that by giving an explanation for task difficulty *besides* the stereotype, stereotype threat can be reduced.

In one study, men and women students who came to the laboratory were told they would take a math test being developed by the psychology department for placement purposes. Immediately after this general description, half of the students were asked to begin the test, and were given 20 minutes to complete 20 problems. The other half were told that there would be a practice session before the test, administered on a computer. The experimenter explained that this would help them to "warm up," allowing a better assessment of their true ability level on the actual test. However, when the experimenter turned on the computer, the screen was unreadable (the computer had been rigged). After fiddling with the knobs and controls to no avail, the experimenter then announced that the students would have to take the test without the benefit of warming up, and this extenuating circumstance would be noted on their answer sheets. The researchers designed this study because they reasoned that being denied the "warm up" opportunity would provide a viable alternative to the gender stereotype as an explanation for any experienced task difficulty, reducing stereotype threat effects for women. Results confirmed this: men's performance was not affected by the test conditions. However, the performance of women was greatly affected. Women performed better on the math test when they were denied their "warm up" opportunity (Brown & Josephs, 1999).

In another study, researchers induced stereotype threat for White men by heightening the salience of the stereotype that Whites have less natural athletic ability than Blacks. The researchers then informed half of these participants that the lab space where they would perform athletic tasks had recently been renovated, and that the lab administration wanted "to know if the new changes made research participants feel tense or uneasy." Because of this concern, the participants would be asked to rate the lab space and its effects on their emotions after the experiment (Stone, Lynch, Sjomeling, & Darley, 1999). This information provided participants with another explanation (the renovated lab space) for any anxiety they experienced during the task. White men who received this alternative explanation for poor performance performed better than those who did not.

Again, however effective these manipulations are in the laboratory, their feasibility for the work setting may be limited. Managers certainly shouldn't lie to their employees (as in the first study) to give them an excuse for task difficulty and poor performance. But managers could remind employees about real-life factors that might be constraining their performance (e.g., a difficult client, limited resources, or a tight deadline). Another feasible strategy for providing an alternative explanation comes from a third study. The experimenters induced stereotype threat for women using the usual setup—telling participants that they would be completing a standardized math test for a study of gender differences. One group received just these instructions. With another group, in addition to these instructions, the experimenters described the phenomenon of stereotype threat and said, "... if you are feeling anxious while taking this test, this anxiety could be the result of these negative [gender] stereotypes that are widely known in society and have nothing to do with your actual ability to do well" (Johns, Schmader, & Martens,

2005: 176). These instructions had a positive effect on test performance. Women underperformed on the math test relative to men when given only the "math test" description. When stereotype threat was explained and offered as a possible cause of their anxiety, the performance of men and women was similar.

Telling people who might be affected by stereotype threat about the phenomenon has some advantages. Stereotype threat is real, and its effects on performance are well-documented. You might think that explicitly raising the issue of stereotype threat with a potentially affected employee might make matters worse by drawing attention to the stereotype—better to keep quiet and act like it doesn't exist. But instead the opposite appears to be true. Telling employees that you know stereotype threat can happen, and that they should be aware of it, gives them a different attribution for their difficulty and anxiety (it's not the stereotype, it's the stereotype *threat*).

Change the Context

The context is another condition that can affect the likelihood of stereotype threat. We discussed how one aspect of the context—the diversity of people performing the job—can reinforce or diminish the relevance of stereotypes. The research showing that tokens are more likely to experience stereotype threat also suggests a way to reduce stereotype threat: change the context by removing people from token situations.

This strategy may work in the laboratory, but how can managers realistically achieve this goal? In organizations, the composition of work groups is already constrained by employee skills, task interdependence, and other factors. Managers can't shuffle employees around based on their demographics to avoid token situations. However, several studies have changed the context using another strategy that does not involve changing the demographic make-up of the work group: presenting a role model who contradicts the stereotype. In one study, participants were administered a difficult math test by either a male or female experimenter. The experimenters gave identical instructions designed to accomplish two goals: 1) induce stereotype threat in the women by presenting the test as diagnostic of ability; and 2) create perceptions of the experimenter's competence in math. Scores on the math test showed that women underperformed relative to men only when the test was administered by a male experimenter. A follow-up study revealed that it was not the physical presence of the female experimenter, but rather her perceived competence that protected the women from stereotype threat. Seeing a woman who was competent in the math domain boosted women's beliefs in their own mathematical abilities and maintained their performance (Marx & Roman, 2002).

Other researchers found similar results when role models were presented in a different way. One study asked participants to read and critique four biographical essays. Half of the participants read essays concerning successful women in a variety of fields such as medicine and law. The other half read essays concerning successful corporations. Then all the participants completed a math test administered by a male experimenter. Results indicated that the role model manipulation reduced stereotype threat: Women scored worse than men on the test when they had read about successful corporations, but women scored at the same level as men when they had read about successful women (McIntyre, Paulson, & Lord, 2003).

These studies suggest that managers may be able to change the context for stereotyped employees by boosting the salience and visibility of role models. Note that in the "essay" study, the physical presence of a role model was not necessary—what was important was that the competence of the role model was salient. This strategy could be feasibly implemented in organizations. Managers can increase access to role models by encouraging employee participation in mentoring programs, professional associations, and employee network groups (Friedman & Holtom, 2002; Friedman, Kane, & Cornfield, 1998). If managers maintain a diverse network of associates themselves, they can be more aware of potential role models for all of their employees, and attempt to connect people.

Implications for Diversity Management

Would a greater focus on reducing stereotype threat add anything new to diversity management? We think it would. Existing diversity management programs tend to have two major objectives (Kellough & Naff, 2004): One goal is to change managers' *attitudes*—to reduce negative attitudes, stereotypes, and prejudice against members of different groups. Much diversity training is geared toward this goal. A second related goal is to change managers' *behaviors-how* they select, appraise, and develop employees (Brief & Barsky, 2000). For example, managers are encouraged, and often required, to specify explicit behavioral and performance standards for promotion or advancement, and to adhere to these in making decisions. These are important objectives. However, these objectives ignore two realities. First, changing attitudes and reducing stereotypes is a long term endeavor. Stereotypes are embedded in the culture, and reinforced outside of the work setting (Brief, 1998). Until society changes, stereotypes about different groups will remain. Even if a particular manager is unprejudiced, others in the workgroup may not be, and employees may still feel stereotype threat. While we need to try to reduce stereotypes, in the foreseeable future we have to deal with existing attitudes, and try to reduce the *impact* of stereotypes on affected employees. Second, while increasing the objectivity of measurement and decisions is necessary, the presence of stereotype threat means that performance *itself* may convey biased information about a person's true ability. So the well-intentioned manager

who relies on objective performance data without understanding the impact of stereotype threat will still unfairly underestimate performance. Focusing on stereotype threat takes these realities into account and highlights two principles that are currently downplayed in most diversity management efforts:

1. Acknowledge stereotypes and address them directly. Unfortunately, the goal of eliminating stereotypes from organizational decision making sometimes leads organizational members to deny their existence. People sometimes confuse stereotype awareness with stereotype endorsement (Adler, 2002). Yet research has shown that even unprejudiced people are familiar with the content of common stereotypes and can easily describe what prejudiced people believe about members of certain groups (Devine, 1989). Putting our strategies into action means that a manager has to honestly acknowledge the stereotypes that exist. The manager who acknowledges the existence and potential impact of stereotypes does not have to endorse or support those stereotypes. Only a manager who acknowledges stereotypes can acknowledge the opportunity for stereotype threat and take corrective action.

The strategies for reducing stereotype threat further imply that managers should talk explicitly about stereotypes with their potentially threatened employees (Kray et al., 2001). Rarely are stereotypes directly named and described—particularly to the affected parties. Although many people (managers and subordinates alike) might see this as a risky step, explicit discussion about stereotypes can be useful in reducing their impact. If supervisors and subordinates trust one another, it can be a good strategy. David Thomas' comparison of successful and plateaued non-White executives demonstrated that successful executives found mentors early in their careers who were able to talk directly about race and the challenges it presented (Thomas, 2001; Thomas & Gabarro, 1999). Such openness about the existence of stereotypes and stereotype threat provides employees with alternative explanations for task difficulty and also may decrease concerns that they will be judged in light of the stereotype. Many managers would shy away from such a frank discussion, but the evidence says that evasion is not always helpful. Honest engagement of the problem and an exploration of action strategies to counteract perceptions can increase trust, reduce stereotype threat, and improve performance. How can managers be encouraged to take these risks? Perhaps diversity training should focus on providing managers with the skills and confidence to talk about stereotypes with their employees.

2. Shift the focus from the manager to the environment. Diversity management programs tend to focus on the manager as the target of change. Diversity training programs, for example, are designed to change managerial attitudes and behavior (Bendick, Egan, & Lofhjelm, 2001). In contrast, the strategies for reducing stereotype threat focus on the *environment* as the target of change. In other words, changing the conditions that lead to stereotype threat. Managers need to attend to managing the environment and reducing the cues that signal to employees that stereotypes are operating.

Effective diversity management has always meant creating an environment where all can succeed (Cox, 1994; Thomas, 1991). Knowledge of stereotype threat increases our understanding of what that really means. It is more than being personally nonprejudiced and unbiased. It means actively reducing cues that limit the contributions of *all* employees. Only in this way can the benefits of diversity be realized.

Source: Academy of Management Perspectives, 21, (2), 2007, 24–40.

REFERENCES

Adler, N. J. (2002). *International dimensions of organizational behavior.* Fourth Edition. Cincinnati OH: South-Western Publishing.

Aronson, J. (2002). Stereotype threat: Contending and coping with unnerving expectations. In J. Aronson (Ed.) *Improving academic achievement: Impact of psychological factors on education* (pp. 279–301). San Francisco: Elsevier.

Aronson, J., Lustina, M. J., Good, C., Keough, K., Steele, C. M., & Brown, J. (1999). When White men can't do math: Necessary and sufficient factors in stereotype threat. *Journal of Experimental Social Psychology*, 35, 29–46.

Aronson, J., Quinn, D. M., & Spencer, S. J. (1998). Stereotype threat and the academic underperformance of minorities and women. In Swim, J. K., & Stangor, C. (Eds.), *Prejudice: The target's perspective* (pp. 83–103). New York: Academic Press.

Beilock, S. L., & Carr, T. H. (2005). When high-powered people fail: Working memory and "choking under pressure" in math. *Psychological Science,* 76, 101–105.

Bendick, M., Egan, M. L., & Lofhjelm, S. M. (2001). Workforce diversity training: From anti-discrimination compliance to organizational development. *Human Resource Planning*, 24, 10–36.

Blank, R., & Shipp, S. (1994). *Voices of diversity: Real people talk about problems and solutions in a workplace where everyone is not alike.* New York: AMACOM.

Blascovich, J., Spencer, S. J., Quinn, D., & Steele, C. (2001). African Americans and high blood pressure: The role of stereotype threat. *Psychological Science*, 12, 225–229.

Brief, A. P. (1998). *Attitudes in and around organizations.* Thousand Oaks, CA: Sage.

Brief, A. P., & Barsky, A. (2000). Establishing a climate for diversity: The inhibition of prejudiced reactions in the workplace. *Research in Personnel and Human Resources Management*, 19, 91–129.

Brown, R. P., & Josephs, R. A. (1999). A burden of proof: Stereotype relevance and gender differences in math performance. *Journal of Personality and Social Psychology,* 76, 246–257.

Cadinu, M., Maass, A., Frigerio, S., Impagliazzo, L., & Latinotti, S. (2003). Stereotype threat: The effect of expectancy on performance. *European Journal of Social Psychology*, 33, 267–285.

Chandler, M. (1999, October 4). *Secrets of the SAT* (FRONTLINE, #1802). New York and Washington, D.C.: Public Broadcasting Service.

Chung-Herrera, B. 6, & Lankau, M. J. (2005). Are we there yet? An assessment of fit between stereotypes of minority managers and the successful-manager prototype. *Journal of Applied Social Psychology*, 35, 2029–2056.

Cocchiara, F. K., & Quick, J. C. (2004). The negative effects of positive stereotypes: Ethnicity-related stressors and implications on organizational health. *Journal of Organizational Behavior*, 25, 781–785.

Cox, T. H. Jr. (1994). *Cultural diversity in organizations: Theory, research, and practice.* San Francisco, CA: Berrett-Koehler.

Devine, P. 6. (1989). Stereotypes and prejudice: Their automatic and controlled components. *Journal of Personality and Social Psychology*, 56, 5–18.

Dickins, F., & Dickens, J. B. (1991). *The Black manager: Making it in the corporate world.* New York: AMACOM.

Elliott, A. J., &. Harackiewicz, J. M. (1996). Approach and avoidance achievement goals and intrinsic motivation: A mediational analysis. *Journal of Personality and Social Psychology*, 70, 461–475.

Frantz, C. M., Cuddy, A. J. C., Burnett, M., Ray, H., & Hart, A. (2004). A threat in the computer: The race implicit association test as a stereotype threat experience. *Personality and Social Psychology Bulletin*, 30, 1611–1614.

Friedman, R. A., & Holtom, B. (2002). The effects of network groups on minority employee turnover intentions. *Human Resource Management*, 47, 405–421.

Friedman, R. A., Kane, M., & Cornfield, D. B. (1998). Social support and career optimism: Examining the effectiveness of network groups among Black managers. *Human Relations,* 51, 1155–1177.

Greenberg, J. (1996). *Managing behavior in organizations: Science in service to practice.* Upper Saddle River, NJ: Prentice Hall.

Greengard, S. (2003). Gimme attitude. *Workforce*, 82, 56–60.

Habermas, T., & Bluck, S. (2000). Getting a life: The emergence of the life story in adolescence. *Psychological Bulletin*, 12, 748–769.

Hackman, J. R., & Oldham, G. R. (1980). *Work redesign*. Reading, MA: Addison-Wesley.

Hansen, F. (2003). Diversity's business case doesn't add up. *Workforce*, 82, 28–32.

Heilman, M. E., Block, C. J., Martell, R. F., & Simon, M. C. (1989). Has anything changed? Current characterizations of men, women, and managers. *Journal of Applied Psychology*, 74, 935–942.

Hite, L. M. (2004). Black and White women managers: Access to opportunity. *Human Resource Development Quarterly*, 15, 131–146.

Horn, P. W., Roberson, L., & Ellis, A. D. (2007). *Challenging conventional wisdom about who quits: Revelations from corporate America* Manuscript submitted for publication, Arizona State University.

Inzlicht, M., & Ben Zeev, T. (2003). Do high-achieving female students underperform in private? The implications of threatening environments on intellectual processing. *Journal of Educational Psychology* 95, 796–805.

Jackson, S. E., Brett, J. F., Sessa, V. I., Cooper, D. M., Julin, J. A., & Peyronnin, K. (1991). Some differences make a difference: Individual dissimilarity and group heterogeneity as correlates of recruitment, promotions, and turnover. *Journal of Applied Psychology*, 76, 675–689.

Jehn, K. A., Neale, M., & Northcraft, G. (1999). Why differences make a difference: A field study of diversity, conflict, and performance in workgroups. *Administrative Science Quarterly*, 44, 741–763.

Johns, M., Schmader, T., & Martens, A. (2005). Knowing is half the battle: Teaching stereotype threat as a means of improving women's math performance. *Psychological Science*, 16, 175–179.

Kanter, R. (1977). *Men and women of the organization*. New York: Basic Books.

Kellough, J. E., & Naff, K. C. (2004). Responding to a wake up call: An examination of Federal Agency Diversity Management Programs. *Administration & Society*, 36, 62–91.

Kochan, T., Bezrukova, K., Ely, R., Jackson, S., Joshi, A., Jehn, K., Leonare, J., Levine, D., & Thomas, D. (2003). The effects of diversity on business performance: Report of the diversity research network. *Human Resource Management*, 42, 3–21.

Kray, L J., Galinsky, A. D., & Thompson, L. (2002). Reversing the gender gap in negotiations: An exploration of stereotype

regeneration. *Organizational Behavior and Human Decision Processes*, 87, 386–409.

Kray, L. J., Thompson, L., &. Galinsky, A. (2001). Battle of the sexes: Gender stereotype confirmation and reactance in negotiations. *Journal of Personality and Social Psychology*, 80, 942–958.

Marx, D. M., & Roman, J. S. (2002). Female role models: Protecting women's math test performance. *Personality and Social Psychology Bulletin*, 28, 1183–1193.

McCauley, C., Eastman, L., & Ohlott, P. (1995). Linking management selection and development through stretch assignments. *Human Resource Management*, 34, 93–115.

McIntyre, R. B., Paulson, R. M., & Lord, C. G. (2003). Alleviating women's mathematics stereotype threat through salience of group achievements. *Journal of Experimental Social Psychology*, 39, 83–90.

Niemann, Y. F., & Dovidio, J. F. (1998). Relationship of solo status, academic rank, and perceived distinctiveness to job satisfaction of racial/ethnic minorities. *Journal of Applied Psychology*, 83, 55–71.

Noe, R. A. (1999). *Employee training and development*. Boston: Irwin McGraw-Hill.

Parks-Yancy, R. (2006). The effects of social group membership and social capital resources on career. *Journal of Black Studies*, 36, 515–545.

Personal blog. (2005, June 3). Available at: http://www.bigfatblog.com/archives/001607.php.

Reio, Jr., T. G., & Callahan, J. L. (2004). Affect, curiosity, and socialization-related learning: A path analysis of antecedents to job performance. *Journal of Business and Psychology*, 19, 3–22.

Rice, F. (1996). Denny's changes its spots. *Fortune*, 133, 133–138.

Roberson L., Deitch, E., Brief, A. P., & Block, C. J. (2003). Stereotype threat and feedback seeking in the workplace. *Journal of Vocational Behavior*, 62, 176–188.

Robinson, G., & Dechant, K. (1997). Building a business case for diversity. *Academy of Management Executive*, 11, 21–31.

Smith, J. L. (2004). Understanding the process of stereotype threat: A review of mediational variables and new performance goal directions. *Educational Psychology Review*, 16, 177–206.

Spencer, S. J., Steele, C. M., & Quinn, D. M. (1999). Stereotype threat and women's math performance. *Journal of Experimental Social Psychology*, 35, 4–28.

Steele, C. M. (1997). A threat in the air: How stereotypes shape intellectual identity and performance. *American Psychologist*, 52, 613–629.

Steele, C. M., & Aronson, J. (1995). Stereotype threat and the intellectual test performance of African Americans. *Journal of Personality and Social Psychology, 85,* 440–452.

Steele, C. M., Spencer, S. J., & Aronson, J. (2002). Contending with group image: The psychology of stereotype and social identity threat. *Advances in Experimental Social Psychology, 34,* 379–440.

Steele-Johnson, D., Beauregard, R. S., Hoover, P. B., & Schmidt, A. M. (2000). Goal orientation and task demand effects on motivation, affect, and performance. *Journal of Applied Psychology, 85,* 724–738.

Stone, J., Lynch, C. L., Sjomeling, M., & Darley, J. M. (1999). Stereotype threat effects on Black and White athletic performance. *Journal of Personality and Social Psychology, 77,* 1213–1227.

Thomas, D. A. (2001). The truth about mentoring minorities: Race matters. *Harvard Business Review, 79,* 98–107.

Thomas, D. A., & Ely, R. J. (1996). Making differences matter: A new paradigm for managing diversity. *Harvard Business Review, 74,* 79–91.

Thomas, D. A., & Gabarro, J. J. (1999). *Breaking through: The making of minority executives in corporate America.* Boston, MA: Harvard Business School Press.

Thomas, R. R. Jr. (1991). *Beyond race and gender: Unleashing the power of your total work force by managing diversity.* NY: AMACOM.

Tomkiewicz, J., Brenner, O. C., & Adeyemi-Bello, T. (1998). The impact of perceptions and stereotypes on the managerial mobility of African Americans. *Journal of Social Psychology, 138,* 88–92.

Tsui, A. Egan, T., & O'Reilly, C. (1992). Being different: Relational demography and organizational attachment. *Administrative Science Quarterly, 37,* 549–579.

Verbeke, W., & Bagozzi, R. (2000). Sales call anxiety: Exploring what it means when fear rules a sales encounter. *Journal of Marketing, 64,* 88–102.

Vandewalle, D. (2001). Goal orientation: Why wanting to look successful doesn't always lead to success. *Organizational Dynamics, 30,* 162–171.

Yerkes, R. M., & Dodson, J. D. (1908). The relation of strength of stimulus to rapidity of habit formation. *Journal of Comparative Neurology, 18,* 459–482.

Zenger, T., & Lawrence, B. (1989). Organizational demography: The differential effects of age and tenure distributions on technical communications. *Academy of Management Journal, 32,* 353–376.

The Ethics of Human Resource Management

Elizabeth D. Scott

In a time when most organizations claim that "our employees are our most important [most valuable, greatest] asset," the ethical challenge to human resource (HR) managers is clear: How do we avoid treating employees merely as *means?* The term "human resources" may be relatively new, but viewing employees as something to be used is as old as the Roman days, when the tools of production were classified as "dumb tools" (used of plows, shovels), "semi-speaking tools" (used of animals), and "speaking tools" (used of slaves). While many employees would prefer to be referred to as an asset rather than as an expense or liability, the phrase "human resources" still rankles among those who see it as evidence that employers have not changed over the millennia. Assuming, *arguendo,* that we are discussing HR managers who wish to be ethical, one of their main challenges is to belie their titles. That is, they must manage humans not as resources but as autonomous individuals with legitimate rights and interests.

Ethical Theories

Elsewhere in this volume, others describe ethical theories in depth. I will not repeat those theories, save to suggest that each has something to say about how HR managers do their jobs. HR managers face the Kantian ethical question of how to ensure that their treatment of employees, applicants, and former employees respects the autonomy of those constituents. Stakeholder ethics also requires that the HR manager consider the interests of employees, applicants, and former employees, at least if we are to accept Clarkson's definition that "stakeholders are persons or groups that have or claim ownership, rights, or interests in a corporation and its activities, past, present, or future" (1995:106). HR managers who judge ethics by fairness or justice must apply them to employees, applicants, and former employees, and they may even be required by Rawls's (1971) conception of justice to ensure that the least well off are not disadvantaged by the policies they implement and also have a voice in decision making processes.

Utilitarian HR managers must consider the outcomes of their decisions on everyone, including employees, applicants, and former employees. And virtue ethics would recommend developing habits that contribute to the flourishing of humans, as individuals and in community. While there might be special situations in which a particular ethical theory would prescribe behavior different from that prescribed by other theories, my interest is not in ferreting out those exceptions but in illustrating the claims these theories make on HR managers desiring to be ethical in performing their functions. Therefore, where I use such words as "fairness," "stakeholder," and "duty," I intend to invoke principles of ethics derived from the theories discussed elsewhere.

Types of Ethical Issues Addressed

Three different types of ethical problems face HR managers. The first type is the need for discernment—determining the right thing to do in very complex situations. The HR manager has both authority and the support of management to make and implement decisions, but he or she still must weigh options and make decisions with incomplete information. The second type of problem is a conflict between the HR manager's professional judgment of what is right and the responsibility as an agent of the employer to do what the employer asks. The third type of problem involves conflict of interest—or *appearance* of conflict of interest—when the HR manager's personal interest differs from the responsibility as an agent of the employer. The first type of problem has the potential to turn into the second or third type once the HR manager determines the appropriate course of action.

The common challenge with all three problems is recognizing them (Rest 1976). Often, in the day-to-day requirements of running a human resource operation, the manager does not have time to reflect on the ethical implications of an action (Moberg 2000). The more obviously "ethical" situations involve virtue or moral courage—the HR manager simply has to refuse to do that which is not right and choose to do what is. For example, an HR manager who looks the other way or even helps falsify the paperwork when a hiring manager uses slave labor is not facing an ethical issue but rather simply failing to do right. There are many cases, though, where HR managers do not know all of the facts, do not think about the implications of a decision, or do not see themselves as moral agents in the decision and thus do not recognize it as a moral issue.

One challenge, then, to HR managers who wish to behave ethically, is to find ways to increase their abilities to recognize moral issues. They can do this by setting time aside to reflect, by talking with other managers about issues, by reading journals and newspaper columns devoted to discussion of ethics, and by listening carefully to employees who voice concerns. The allocation of resources to this effort becomes an ethical issue in itself. How much time can an HR manager devote to better recognizing ethical issues before being guilty of neglecting other duties? Is once a year enough? Is every day too often? The more HR managers develop their moral sensitivities, though, the more difficult it may be to learn of ethical issues, because other employees in the organization may go out of their way to hide information. There may be a counterbalancing tendency of wronged individuals to seek out the HR manager known to be ethical (Trevino, Hartman, and Brown 2000), but since many of those wronged may be outside of the organization, they may never learn of the HR manager's reputation. HR managers wishing to behave ethically thus must also increase their abilities to discover hidden motives and activities.

Even after recognizing a moral issue, obtaining facts and determining right action is still difficult. Not all facts are available, and many that are cannot be obtained in a timely (or fiscally responsible) manner. Taking incomplete information, considering it, and making decisions are what managers do. Some decisions are just more difficult to make than others, especially when several different duties or interests are opposed and the information gap is large.

Problems related to fetal protection can fall in this category. While adults may be able to evaluate incomplete scientific data and determine whether the risks of working in a particular environment are worth the other benefits of engaging in that work, they may not be in a position to make those decisions for their future offspring. The HR manager must consider interests of both the firm and its stockholders and the firm's ability to mitigate potential harms, all in an environment where data are incomplete and the HR manager's power is limited. Knowing the history of industries where scientists withheld information about harm to consumers, such as the tobacco industry, the HR manager may be very skeptical of the scientific data that *are* available.

"Right action," once discerned by the HR manager, is sometimes translated into policy and procedure, to provide guidance to other managers and information to employees. Policies and procedures help HR managers ensure fairness by making the decision-making process more consistent and transparent. However, policies and procedures can also detract from HR managers' recognizing some ethical issues, because policy may be applied without regard for changes over time or for individual situations. One approach to that dilemma is to set up systems whereby employees review HR policies and practices regularly (Kochan 2002).

HR managers can also turn to their professional associations for guidance. Codes of ethics established by professional associations of human resource managers require certain levels of integrity, obedience to the letter and spirit of the law, contribution to the organization and the profession, loyalty, and confidentiality (Wiley 2000). A more skeptical view of these codes' usefulness has been expressed by Scoville (1993).

This chapter does not address the ethical issues faced by HR managers as managers dealing with their subordinates. Instead, it addresses their responsibilities with respect to the organization's policies and procedures and the special role of HR manager. This chapter also does not discuss the legal requirements affecting HR managers. It assumes that the HR manager has an obligation to obey the law unless the law itself is immoral. The chapter does address, however, ethical issues faced by HR managers when others violate laws, when laws are immoral, and when the letter and spirit of the law do not coincide.

Functions of an HR Manager

HR managers are taught that they have four basic functions with respect to employees: to recruit, to train, to motivate, and to retain. A fifth function, terminating, is also performed by HR managers, albeit usually after failing somehow at one of the other four functions. All of these functions are aimed at achieving the goals of the organization, and each has the potential for all three kinds of ethical issues. Some responsibilities (e.g., compensation, benefits, labor relations, record-keeping) cross several functions. For example, compensation is used to recruit applicants and to motivate and retain employees. Labor relations (addressed in another chapter) affect recruiting, training, motivating, retaining, and terminating employees. Practices in organizations vary widely, so not all of the descriptions of issues here will apply to every organization.

Recruitment

HR managers know all too well that, despite organizational rhetoric, they are not looking for *the* best qualified person for each job. They are looking for someone who can do the job well and, in some cases, for someone who shows promise for being promoted. To this end, HR managers are expected to outline minimum qualifications, set an entry salary range, advertise the position, refer applicants to hiring managers, and review selection decisions in a way that balances the organization's resources with the likelihood of finding a well-qualified person. The ethical challenge is to balance individuals' expectations of (and rights to) equal opportunities with the organization's obligation of resource stewardship.

Minimum Qualifications   To recruit employees, an HR manager needs a clear idea of qualifications needed to perform job duties. Before advertising a vacancy, the HR manager usually establishes the minimum knowledge, skills, and abilities a person must have to be considered for the position. Setting minimum qualifications is an ethical decision, but it is often approached as merely a strategic one. The strategic decision is certainly important. Setting the minimum qualifications too high will result in applicants unwilling to accept either the position or the salary offered. Setting the minimum qualifications too low will result, at best, in applications from so many people that extensive secondary screening procedures will be required and, at worst, in signaling to the most desirable applicants that they need not apply because they will be judged over-qualified.

In addition, however, the HR manager is often faced with special requests—such as ensuring that the qualifications don't exclude the hiring manager's preselected favorite candidate—that further complicate the process of determining what qualifications to require. Ever since the days of (*Griggs v. Duke Power* 1971:424), it has been evident that managers can use minimum qualifications to exclude people who are perfectly capable of doing a job. While the *Griggs* decision outlawed these exclusions where they distinguish on the basis of race, sex, or other legally defined classification, there is no similar protection when the minimum qualifications exclude individuals who cannot claim "adverse impact" under *Griggs*. However, ethical principles would still require fairness.

It is sometimes difficult for the HR manager to discern why a hiring manager insists on a particular qualification that does not seem necessary for performance of the job duties. Sometimes the HR manager does not fully understand the job duties, but other times the hiring manager wants to avoid having to consider a particular employee. The hiring manager may have good reason not to want this employee, but manipulating the minimum qualifications is not the way to achieve that end. The HR manager has an ethical obligation to try to eliminate such managerial behavior—both because it can be disastrous for the employer and because it singles out individuals for unfair treatment. A typical example occurs when a hiring manager prefers a relatively new employee over more senior candidates. Observing that the more senior candidates have no college degrees, the hiring manager requests that a degree be one of the minimum qualifications—erroneously believing that in the end this will appear to be an "objective" reason why the junior person obtained the job and thus head off internal bickering. Unfortunately for the manager, the other internal applicants are not usually so easily fooled. Depending on the HR manager's authority within the situation, he or she may be able to refuse the hiring manager's request outright or may have to pursue another avenue (e.g., internal whistleblowing) to eliminate this kind of behavior.

Entry Salary Range   HR managers must balance several consideration in setting appropriate salary ranges. First, there is the question of what the current labor market demands. This is mainly a practical consideration. If the labor market demands more than the employer is willing to pay, it may be foolish to spend resources to recruit applicants. However, there are also ethical considerations associated with internal equity. If the current labor market demands more than it once did, employers may find themselves paying new employees more than long-term employees doing the same job. This fact may not always be apparent to the existing employees, who may not realize that they could command higher salaries elsewhere and may not have direct contact with other employees doing the same work. The ethical consideration for the HR manager then becomes whether to take steps to increase the salaries of the existing employees or change the job classifications of the new employees. If there are real differences between the skills and abilities of those in the external labor market and the existing employees, changing the job classification of the vacant position may be the appropriate action. The change may take the form of a higher classification for people with greater skills and abilities or of a lower classification to attract trainees who do not yet have the skills and abilities necessary. If there are no real differences, the ethical HR manager will address the question of internal equity before advertising the job, developing a plan to ensure that existing employees are not penalized with lower salaries for failing to seek jobs elsewhere.

The second question regarding entry salary levels relates to what has been called "comparable worth." If applicants would be hireable at lower salaries due to generalized discrimination against members of the labor market, does the employer have an ethical obligation to pay on the basis of the contribution made to the organization? An HR manager with limited resources is unlikely to conduct studies assessing the "worth" of jobs, but failing to do so because one wants to avoid legal liability would be, in Kantian term, not produced by a "good will."

The third question is whether to advertise the salary range for the position and, if so what portion. Omitting a salary or salary range may simply be an effort to save on advertising costs. However, when it is done to enable employers to negotiate lower salaries for those most desperate for work, it violates the Rawlsian principle of setting up systems that protect the least advantaged. Similarly, advertising just the top of the salary range when most employees achieve only a small percentage of it is dishonest. When the vast majority of employees in a particular job make minimum wage, advertisements that claim employees can earn huge bonuses and commissions, even if true, mislead potential applicants to believe they *will* earn significantly more than is true.

Advertising   A position can be advertised very narrowly, such as by handing a vacancy announcement to one person, or very broadly, by putting a sign in the window, a link on a web page, an ad in the paper, or a commercial on television. The decision about how broadly to advertise has both strategic and ethical components. When the position would represent a promotion (or even a more desirable career path) for current employees, the strategic component involves considering the costs and benefits of going outside the organization. Possible costs include monetary expense for ads, lost productivity during the recruiting period, and turnover by disappointed employees. There also may be adverse effects caused by creating new vacancies and encouraging complacency by promoting from within. Organizations wishing to encourage employee loyalty often require posting positions internally first and going outside the organization only after all internal candidates have been rejected. Other organizations, hoping to encourage creativity and internal competition, routinely recruit outside. This assessment of costs and benefits remains in the strategic realm as long as the HR manager's concern is to maximize the welfare of the organization, but as the concern broadens to include maximizing the welfare of society, the analysis enters the realm of utilitarian ethics.

One of the ethical balancing acts an HR manager must perform regarding advertising is between fulfilling promises (or psychological contracts) regarding career advancement and providing legitimate opportunities for those outside the organization to obtain employment. Hiring managers sometimes request advertisements with no intention of considering anyone beyond a particular individual. Such pro forma advertisements waste applicants' time, energy, money, and hope, and they either encourage favored candidates to believe it is acceptable to mislead others or they cause favored candidates to feel insecure about jobs they have already been promised. Often the advertisement is placed at the behest of the HR manager, who insists that the position be advertised to provide equal employment opportunities. But since advertising does not ensure that the hiring manager will be any more open to considering all applicants, the HR manager's goal would be better served by establishing a procedure under which hiring managers can request exemption from any requirement to advertise vacancies by providing evidence that forgoing advertisement is appropriate in the particular case.

With a decision to advertise outside the organization made, the HR manager should consider the organization's stated values and choose methods that reflect them. Word-of-mouth advertising, for example, is most likely to generate applicants similar to current employees. If the organization claims to value diversity but is not already diverse, this form of recruitment would call into question the truth of the organization's claim. Similarly, website advertising may create a bias in favor of wealthier and younger applicants. If computer skills are not important to the job, such advertising diminishes the integrity of the process. The HR manager's job is to consider cost-effective outlets where qualified candidates are most likely to see or hear a vacancy announcement. In choosing among those outlets, the HR manager's ethical obligation is, foremost, not to bias the pool unfairly and, second, not to bias it in ways that conflict with the organization's stated values. (If the values themselves are unfair, the HR manager has no obligation to ensure that they are enacted in advertising positions.)

Adhering to the organization's stated values is, in ethical terms, promise keeping. If the organization promises in its stated values to promote from within, an initial advertisement beyond the bounds of the organization would violate that promise. The more difficult problem for the HR manager is determining when the inevitable bias caused by the choice of advertisements is significant enough to render the process unfair. One important consideration is the intentionality of the bias (Kant's notion of a "good will"). For example, it is impossible to ensure that no employee is on leave when a vacancy is announced, but if a hiring manager waits until a particular employee's vacation week to advertise a vacancy because the manager wants to avoid considering the person, that bias is unfair. A second important consideration is the potential effect of the choice of advertisement on society. Ethical theories put varying degrees of emphasis on the outcomes of an action, but they would suggest considering whether the bias caused by the advertising benefited those least well off in society, whether there was more good than harm done by the bias, and whether important stakeholders were considered in the decision. The advertisement of any particular vacancy is probably unlikely to affect society in an appreciable way, but a policy or practice of a large corporation to, for example, post all entry-level vacancies with the local employment service office or in shelters for battered women has the potential to affect local economies.

The HR manager sometimes faces the question of whether to recruit applicants from competitors, suppliers, customers, or regulators. HR managers should not encourage among potential or actual employees disloyalty, dishonesty, or violation of "noncompete" agreements that have been legitimately negotiated (i.e., by knowledgeable participants with relatively equal power). But they should also respect the autonomy of potential employees to choose to leave another employer. Whether an applicant has slighted, or even breached a duty to, a current employer is difficult for the HR manager to monitor, because such information is not always available. HR managers have a duty to scrutinize any decisions to hire people who have had prior dealings with the organization as employees of another organization, especially if the prior dealings resulted in unusually advantageous decisions for the hiring organization. And, since violations are so hard to find, those that are found should be punished sufficiently harshly to transmit the message that the behavior is contrary to any employer's values.

An issue currently in the forefront or business ethics is outsourcing. In order to determine the ethical stance in this discussion, an HR manager must clearly understand the anticipated outcomes regarding all of the stakeholders: employees, potential employees, local communities, external communities, and stockholders (Arnold and Bowie 2003). The manager also needs to clearly understand all of the contracts, both actual and psychological, surrounding the relationships with current employees.

Selection   The final step in the recruitment process is to select from among the applicants for a position. Selection is so important that it is sometimes listed as a separate function of HR managers. However, it is often performed by the hiring manager, after the HR department has collected applications and eliminated the people who clearly don't qualify. The HR manager establishes policies and procedures to be followed but may have little control over what occurs in the actual selection process.

Screening of applicants can be performed by HR staff. They may add a set of preferred qualifications that are more stringent than the minimum qualifications posted in the advertisement. They may use written or performance tests. In both of these cases, the HR manager has to worry not only about being fair but also about appearing fair. Tests or screening criteria that do not have face validity appear unfair to applicants, even when the employer knows that they are valid through extensive studies linking test scores with job success. One threat to test validity exists if applicants who take a test multiple times can do better on that specific test, but not necessarily on the job, just because they have practiced the test (Huasknecht, Trevor, and Farr 2002). If there are practice effects that are not related to on-the-job performance, to preserve fairness HR managers should consider whether to implement rules limiting the number of times an applicant can take the same test.

HR staff may conduct recruiting or screening interviews, and surely every HR manager has experienced having a CEO or other senior staff member send people to be interviewed "as a favor." In these cases, HR's role is to represent the organization well and to become familiar enough with the applicant's qualifications to help locate vacancies in the organization that might prove fruitful. The ethical HR representative must be careful not to overpromise to the applicant or to misread the degree of assistance promised by the senior staff member.

After the applicant pool is narrowed through evaluating preferred qualifications and testing, there is often a small set of applicants presented to the hiring manager for interviews and the selection decision. The HR manager bears some responsibility for training the hiring manager in interviewing technique and for reviewing the process to ensure that interviews are conducted and evaluated fairly. Many organizations are moving toward establishing work teams, with the team empowered to select its members. There is some evidence that teams are more likely to pick people like themselves,

demographically, and thus engage in unlawful discrimination as agents of the employer (Goins and Mannix 1999). The HR manager has an obligation to create mechanisms that reduce this tendency.

An ethical issue associated with the interviewing process is the amount of privacy protection due applicants. Depending on the applicant's power in the situation, various ethicists have recommended eliminating all questions aimed at determining attitudes, motivations, and beliefs, arguing that applicants have a right to keep this information to themselves. Others see this position as paternalistic (Nye 2002). The HR manager's job is to discern the appropriate amount of privacy protection due applicants and convey this to hiring managers.

As genetic screening tests become available, employers face the possibility of having information that could be relevant to long-term employment decisions. Knowing that a particular employee has a greater likelihood of developing a serious disease can tempt an employer to pass over that person for promotions or for training requiring long-term investment. HR managers have a responsibility to ensure that these records are not available to anyone but the employee and that such data are not collected without the employee's knowledge and consent.

Many HR managers in industries with very low-wage jobs find themselves in the position of not knowing whether their employees are legally allowed to work—for example, because they are aliens, because they are below a minimum age, or because they have not obtained required licenses. In some cases, line managers obtain forged supporting documents (birth certificates, passports, etc.) proving eligibility to work. While lack of participating in the forgery may exempt the HR manager from legal liability, he or she still has an ethical obligation to take reasonable steps to ensure that neither line managers nor new employees violate laws that are themselves ethical. Random checks of original documents may eliminate widespread violations, but there may be no way to thwart the determined violator. Internal whistleblowing by the HR manager may be necessary to bring violations to the attention of someone with the power to enact sanctions. Clear and relatively harsh consequences for employees who are complicit in hiring illegally may be the only way to convey the organization's lack of support for such behavior.

Violating hiring laws would generally fall in the area of unethical behavior. However, HR managers sometimes must discern whether the law, various regulations, or court decisions are ethical. For example, organizations considering employing persons with disabilities whose conditions pose a threat to their own health and safety on the job but not the health and safety of others faced conflicting Equal Employment Opportunity Commission (EEOC) regulations and court decisions. The EEOC allowed employers to refuse employment on this basis, but the 9th Circuit Court of

Appeals did not. While this controversy has been resolved by the U.S. Supreme Court, in favor of the EEOC regulations, it illustrates a case where the HR manager must balance concern for the health and welfare of the prospective employee against employees' rights to make decisions about their own health and welfare (Reed 2003). Similarly, HR managers of multinational corporations during apartheid in South Africa made decisions to violate local laws requiring separation of the races.

A common complaint from applicants is that they submitted applications and "never heard back" from the employer. This contributes to a perception of unfairness, and it may actually inhibit the freedom of an applicant who waits to hear about an employment application rather than go on vacation or accept other employment. At the conclusion of the selection process, the ethical HR manager will ensure that unsuccessful applicants are notified promptly and kindly of rejection decisions.

Successful Applicants Having identified successful applicants, HR managers face several ethical challenges. The HR manager must carefully explain the employment contract. Some ethicists argue that "at will" contracts are not morally permissible (Werhane 1983; Radin and Werhane 2003; McCall 2003), while others argue simply that the employer should not sugarcoat the nature of the relationship (Roehling 2003). If a union represents the prospective employee's position, the collective bargaining contract must be provided to the applicant. While there is pressure on the HR manager to "woo" successful applicants, the ethical manager will provide an accurate picture of the job and the organization. There may also be pressure to negotiate the lowest possible salary, but ethics require that the manager not take advantage of applicants' vulnerabilities (Brenkert 1998), and fairness requires equal pay for equal work.

Determining the point at which to check references requires balancing the need to protect applicants' privacy against the need to obtain relevant information. In many industries, employees are fired if their employers learn they are even applying for other jobs. Reference checking is especially important in jobs where the incumbent will have unsupervised responsibility for children or elderly persons or access to large quantities of cash. If the applicant is internal, the HR manager must decide what information gained from within is appropriate to transmit to the hiring manager and what information is irrelevant to the hiring decision. If the applicant is external, an HR manager often draws upon personal or professional contacts to obtain reference information about an applicant. In this case, the HR manager has an obligation to balance the discretion due the informant and the fair hearing due the applicant.

Conflict of Interest The recruitment function is not fraught with large conflicts of interest for HR managers. There may

be a temptation to use the power of the position to provide jobs to friends or relatives or to ensure that recruiting trips include the HR manager's alma mater, but since there is usually a separation between functions of the HR and the hiring managers, the HR manager may find efforts to place family and friends thwarted.

Training and Development

Typically, training is divided into two types: general training, which will make an employee more flexible and adaptable within the organization and more marketable outside it, and specific training, which is unique to the organization or even the position. Employee development involves examining an employee's career prospects and offering support in his or her career path. The ethical challenge to HR managers is to devise systems of providing training and development opportunities that are fair to all employees.

General Training Organizations are often reluctant to provide general training, because they see themselves as paying for training that an employee can then take to a competitor and use against them. There is no ethical obligation to promote general training programs, but doing so is one way to treat employees as more than a means to an end. One financial safeguard used by some employers is to require employees to sign agreements to repay the cost of their training if they leave within a certain period. The ethical issue facing the HR manager drafting such an agreement is to ensure that it is clearly explained and does not take unfair advantage of the employee.

Safety Training While HR managers may have no ethical obligation to provide general training, they are obliged to ensure that all employees are aware of any safety hazards associated with their jobs or their work environments. Beyond simply providing safety warnings, HR managers have an ethical obligation to ensure that the warnings are clearly understood by employees, particularly those who may not be able to read the language of the warning or who otherwise may not understand the danger being identified in the warning. Literacy training may be a necessary precursor to safety training.

A special case of safety training involves protection against potentially contagious diseases, such as AIDS and hepatitis. When possible, safety training should be designed to prevent or reduce transmission of disease, whether or not the infection status of a person is known. Gloving, hand washing, and proper instrument disposal are all techniques that can be taught to employees. However, employees understandably want to be informed whenever their risk level increases. They expect employers to provide them with the identities of infected co-workers, clients, or customers. The HR manager must balance the likelihood that an employee will become infected against the infected person's right to privacy. In this balancing, the HR manager must consider that knowing the identities of some but not all people who are infected may actually put employees at a higher risk, because it will give them a false sense of security with any others who are infected but not known to be.

A second special case of safety training is balancing an employee's right to make decisions about undertaking risk and the employer's responsibility to protect others from harm. When an employee's job involves risk to bystanders if done incorrectly, an employer cannot stop after providing training and assume that the employee will bear the ethical burden of keeping others safe. The employer has an obligation to ensure that the job is performed as taught and that the employee is not provided with incentives to take unnecessary risks. Again, while the burden of legal liability may be on someone else, an ethical HR manager will implement systems to monitor the transfer of the training to the workplace and will build incentive systems that encourage safety.

Values Training   Some employees resent being required to attend values training because they see it as an attempt to indoctrinate them into a particular religion or to brainwash them. The HR manager, who presumably shares the organization's values, should ensure clear consistency both between values addressed in training and those supported by the organization and between these values and the organization's reward and discipline systems. The training should also recognize that new employees may intend to be ethical but may be less sophisticated than experienced employees in evaluating the implications of various behaviors (Stevens 2001).

There should also be some provision for employees to opt out of training they consider morally objectionable. However, enough such requests should give the HR manager pause. It could be simply the method of training and not the core value that is in question, but it could also be time to reexamine the underlying values or the employee selection methods. Ever since Weber (1930) described how religious beliefs can fuel corporate profits, employers have sought to select employees with some set of religious or quasireligious beliefs or to create it in them. The Kantian idea of a categorical imperative can guide HR managers trying to ensure that all employees accept certain values. Some values, such as participative management, tolerance, and diversity, create internal inconsistencies when organizations attempt to require them as "rules for all." Requiring all managers to use participative management, for example, does not allow managers to participate in the decision to use it. Requiring tolerance of all employees is intolerant of those who are themselves intolerant. Embracing diversity means embracing even those who do not embrace diversity. Rules that the HR manager either does not want applied universally or cannot imagine applying universally should not be implemented. The HR manager

should periodically review values-training programs to ensure that they are consistent with all of the organization's values, not simply the one or ones being addressed in that particular session.

Employers have occasionally been required by law or court order to train employees in certain values, such as diversity. In these cases, the HR manager is faced with following the law, advocating for a change in the law, breaking the law, or resigning. Deciding among these options requires considering one's personal position and the organization's position. If they are not in concert, and neither party is convinced by the other to change, an ethical HR manager will resign. This is because ethical HR managers cannot abrogate their responsibilities to their employers by acting on behalf of an employer to violate a law the employer would have them follow or to follow a law the employer would have them violate. However, ethical HR managers also cannot abrogate responsibility to themselves by following a law they believe to be immoral or violating one they believe to be moral. If the HR manager and the organization are in concert, they can devise an approach together. Where the organization, the HR manager, and the law are all in concert, the decision-making process is relatively simple: the law is followed. Decision making becomes complex where the law differs from what the HR manager and organization believe. An organization should not take lightly the decision to violate a law or court order. Avenues of appeal and legislative influence should be exhausted first, but where the law is immoral (not simply inconvenient or costly for the employer to implement), the organization can ethically engage in civil disobedience. Laws or court orders that require employers to trample on employees' freedoms should give HR managers great pause. Some managers who have been too quick to follow such laws or too enthusiastic in sanctioning employees who object to the training have found that courts subsequently overturned the laws in question.

Conflict of Interest   Building a training staff large enough to provide any kind of training for the organization can contribute to the HR manager's personal influence and even compensation level. Being able to select from among consultants can give HR managers opportunities to assist friends or family in the consulting firm or to receive gifts or favors from the consultants. Both situations represent conflicts of interest that the ethical HR manager will avoid. Decisions should be made on the basis of the HR manager's professional judgment, not personal interests.

Career Development   Many organizations use mentoring programs to foster career development, pairing new (or at least junior) employees one-on-one with employees with significant experience. What was once an informal practice has become much more formal in many organizations. Mentors can take advantage of their positions of power with respect to the employees they are mentoring, so the HR manager's ethical responsibility is to ensure that abuses of power are minimized (Moberg and Velasquez 2004).

A typical career development program includes succession planning, in which the organization identifies employees who are prepared (or have the potential to be prepared) to step into vacancies as key staff retire, are promoted, or otherwise leave their positions. The organization provides training to prepare the designated employees for eventual vacancies and does not provide such training to those deemed not promotable. To ensure that such planning does not treat employees unfairly, HR managers should develop procedures that, at a very minimum, allow employees to indicate their interests in being promoted and notify those deemed not promotable of the decision. Employees remain with organizations with the belief that they will have a chance to compete for future vacancies on a level playing field. If a determination is made to give the inside track to certain employees, in terms of both training offered and preference for assignments, then the employees deemed not promotable should not be deceived into thinking that, if they are loyal employees, their tenure will be rewarded with promotions. They should be provided with clear feedback that enables them to consider whether they want to remain with the current organization without being promoted or to try their chances at another. If current trends continue, such that employees have reduced expectations that they will remain with the same employer for life, this may become less of an ethical issue (Cappelli 1999).

Motivation
In designing motivation systems, HR managers seek to align employees' goals with those of the organization. This can be done coercively or by convincing employees of the worthiness of the organization's goals and the value of employee contributions to them. Designing effective motivation systems is difficult; ensuring that they have no coercive element is almost impossible. The HR manager's ethical challenge is to consider the amount of coercion used and discern whether it is reasonably balanced against the employee's power in the situation and whether it serves the goals and values articulated by the employee. Taking the car keys away from a drunk would-be driver is coercive, but it properly considers other stakeholders as well as the values the driver has when sober. Similarly, docking the salary of an employee who fails to follow safety regulations is a coercive way to change behavior, but it can also be an ethical way to motivate a recalcitrant employee. On the other hand, offering huge sums of money to employees to work in dangerous environments may be an unethical form of coercion, especially if the technology exists to make the environment less dangerous. The problem of discernment for an HR manager wishing to behave ethically is determining the point at which "hazardous duty pay" stops being a reasonable recognition of risk freely

undertaken by an employee and becomes an offer the employee truly *couldn't* refuse. Coercion removes the employee's freedom to choose, thus abridging the right to liberty (Greenwood 2002).

Systems to motivate employees are developed both by HR managers and by direct supervisors. While supervisory intervention may have the most significant effect on employee motivation, tools that the HR manager provides can make supervisors more effective. These tools can include compensation systems, performance appraisal systems, employee monitoring systems, organizational climate, charitable contribution campaigns, job design, work teams, progressive disciplinary systems, and others. Line supervisors can use the tools ethically or unethically; the HR manager's ethical responsibility is to design tools that are not easily used unethically and to develop procedures to monitor their use.

Compensation   Though compensation systems are designed to align the interests of employee and employer, they can also create conflicts of interest. Commission compensation systems can provide incentives to salespeople to disregard the interests of customers in order to obtain the highest commission (Robertson and Anderson 1993; Kurland 1999). Insurance agents, stock brokers, and real estate buyers' agents, for example, may urge clients to purchase a more expensive product to increase commissions. Supervisors who receive bonuses for number of days without a lost-time accident may pressure employees not to seek treatment for injuries. Managers whose performance is measured by staff productivity may require subordinate employees to work "off the clock" or to skip their breaks. In each of these cases, the organization motivates employees to perform well using some proxy (seniority, supervisor's assessment, hours worked, quantity of output) to estimate the value of the employee's contribution. There is nothing inherently unethical about any of these compensation systems, but other parts of the organization must be operated ethically in order for the compensation systems not to create conflicts of interest. Using seniority as a method of determining pay, for example, is often criticized as unfair. However, this criticism may arise because seniority no longer operates as a proxy for performance on the job. This could occur for one or a number of reasons: because employees who should have been fired were not, because technology has changed and long-term employees were not trained, because the selection system used in the past was faulty, because the cumulative effect of a number of years of working for the employer decreases employees' abilities. The HR manager has the responsibility to ensure that every compensation system contains effective mechanisms to reduce conflicts of interest.

HR managers face a personal conflict of interest in implementing and administering compensation systems. They might be tempted to implement systems that benefit them financially. For example, if the system establishes pay caps for jobs based on market analysis, the manager may be tempted to recommend eliminating caps as he or she approaches the limit, based on the desire to earn more money rather than professional judgment about the caps. The ethical obligation is to ignore such temptation and instead continue to develop a system that is best for the employer, administer it impartially, and build in checks and balances.

HR managers' problem of discernment requires determining a compensation system that is fair and just, and this may differ within and between organizations. Issues include the appropriate difference between pay for the CEO and for rank-and-file employees, systems for paying line versus staff employees, comparable worth, merit-based pay, team-based pay, power differences in salary negotiations, coercively high pay, unpaid work, paid breaks, travel pay, overtime pay, vacation pay, holiday pay, and sick pay, among many others. In some jurisdictions, local and national laws govern the treatment of some of these issues, and the problem becomes more complex in multistate and multinational organizations (Graham and Trevor 2000; Donaldson 2001).

Much of the current controversy regarding compensation addresses executive compensation, especially for CEOs in publicly held firms (Hannafey 2003). Decisions on executive compensation are almost always outside of the HR manager's job, though the manager may be able to use informal influence and earned authority to affect these decisions. In cases where the HR manager cannot create a fair compensation system because of decisions made by senior managers or the board of directors, the only ethical recourse may be to resign.

Performance Appraisal Systems   Performance appraisals are almost universally dreaded. Despite this, HR managers argue, at least publicly, that appraisals are valuable because they know that feedback is important to smooth organizational functioning and that informal feedback, while essential, is not remembered the same by both parties. At their best, performance appraisals motivate employees to continue the things they are doing well, to improve at things they are doing poorly, and to cease things they should not be doing at all. At their worst, they are used to attack or protect employees based on managers' likes and dislikes. Ethics dictate that the HR manager not create a system so complex, cumbersome, or unmonitored that supervisors ignore it or use it improperly.

Employee Monitoring   Many employers have systems of monitoring employees—to measure productivity, to prevent theft, or to protect others (Hoffman and Hartman 2003)—through videotaping, capturing keystrokes, reviewing e-mail, tapping telephones, collecting specimens for drug testing, or tracking locations (Mishra 1998). In all cases, the HR manager must weigh the employee's right to privacy against the

reason for the monitoring. Some ethicists argue that monitoring systems offend against employees' freedoms and that the legitimate ends of monitoring can be achieved in less intrusive ways (Mishra 1998).

Climate and Culture   There is evidence that the organizational climate and subunit climate can motivate employees to engage in ethical or unethical behavior (VanSandt 2003; Weber, Kurke, and Pentico 2003). Insofar as the HR manager has control over climate, there is an ethical obligation to ensure that it is ethical. However, even when the HR manager cannot control climate, especially in subunits, he or she may set up systems to monitor climate and provide training or advice to managers on how to improve it.

Charitable Contribution Campaigns   Many employers seek to motivate employees by projecting an image as a caring, socially responsible organization. Some sponsor campaigns to encourage employees to contribute to charitable organizations, including, in the cases of qualified organizations, the employer itself. This practice, when carried out without coercion, can contribute to employees' sense that their employer does good, especially when the employer matches employee contributions. However, some employers pressure employees for contributions, eliminating the strategic purpose of motivation and reducing the overall good done by the organization. HR managers are usually removed from the solicitation activity, giving them freedom to lessen pressure on employees by reminding both solicitors and those solicited that contributions are truly voluntary. They should remind management, in particular, to discourage campaigns seeking 100% participation and to recognize employee charitable activities not connected with the organization's campaign.

Job Design   The HR literature argues that jobs need to be intrinsically rewarding to be motivating. Hackman and Oldham's classic set of factors is still used today (Hackman, Oldham, Janson, and Purdy 1975). Jobs must have skill variety, task identity, task significance, autonomy, and feedback to have the potential to be motivating. Some ethicists suggest that employers have an obligation to ensure that jobs are intrinsically rewarding. Others suggest that it is an obligation to design jobs in a way that makes them more accessible to people with disabilities. HR managers should consider such arguments in writing job descriptions. Similarly, there is considerable debate over the number of hours a week a person is expected to work. Flexibility in hours worked makes jobs more accessible to people with lower levels of stamina, with competing home responsibilities, or with restrictions on the income they can earn. Determining that a job is "part-time" has significant implications for most benefits contracts. Many organizations provide reduced or no benefits to people in part-time positions.

Teams and Quality Circles Teams can make employees happier with their jobs and more likely to stay (Hunter, Macduffie, and Doucet 2002), and they have been used to motivate employees by giving them more control over their jobs. However, teams have also been shown to be related to increases in injuries (Brenner and Fairris 2004). HR managers have an ethical obligation to monitor the behavior of teams to ensure that the increased motivation is not misdirected toward activities that endanger team members.

Progressive Discipline HR policies usually include a range of disciplinary actions that can be taken to motivate employees when more positive reinforcement fails, including such things as warnings, reprimands, docking pay, demotion, suspension, and firing. The HR manager's ethical challenge is to ensure internal equity in the selection of appropriate disciplinary action and to ensure that the person disciplined is treated with respect. For example, the Minnesota Department of Corrections failed to ensure internal equity when it reprimanded some employees for reading religious texts during training but did not reprimand others for reading magazines, doing paperwork, or sleeping (*Altman & Minnesota Department of Corrections* 2001).

Disciplinary action is often taken without consultation with the HR manager. An ethical manager will use mechanisms such as employee handbooks, training, and newsletters to provide notice of policies and performance requirements. It is especially important to provide such notice when it is not obvious that a behavior is proscribed. An HR manager need not provide notice to employees regarding the employer's objection to punching a supervisor, but organizations with rules against accepting tips or holding secondary employment have an obligation to put employees on notice. Consequently, much of the mechanism to ensure fairness must be incorporated in policy and supervisory training. If disciplinary actions are regularly overturned by arbitration panels or courts, HR managers should take steps to correct problems quickly. Otherwise, some actions warranting discipline may go unchecked because a supervisor does not want to go through the process of a disciplinary action only to be overturned. This would result in inequities in implementing discipline (and therefore even more decisions overturned) and might also result in employees suffering harassment or other abuse at the hands of co-workers because supervisors believe it is impossible to discipline anyone successfully. Some supervisors are very concerned about the effects of their actions on subordinates and their families, to the point where HR managers should be alert to instances where employees without families receive harsher discipline than those with families (Butterfield, Trevino, and Ball 1996).

Retention

The origin of many HR departments can be traced to Henry Ford's efforts to maintain a stable, trained workforce. He paid employees more money and offered them long-term benefits, such as retirement, that made it very difficult for them to quit. The first ethical challenge for HR managers is to examine the measures used to retain employees and to ensure that they do not make it so difficult to quit that employees will not leave or confront the organization even when put in untenable ethical positions. Do the on-site child care, company-subsidized mortgage, stock-option incentive pay, and family-friendly health plan tie employees so closely to the company that they are afraid to quit or to report irregularities? Even if the HR manager determines that the benefits offered have enough portability not to bind employees too closely, there are ethical issues surrounding the specific programs implemented and the amount of choice given employees.

Benefits The negotiating power that a large employer has in providing benefits for employees helps drive the costs lower than they would be if they were purchased individually by the employees. However, HR managers must consider the ethical implications of reducing costs for their own full-time employees while increasing them for their part-time employees, the unemployed, and persons employed in the secondary labor market. This is probably irrelevant for some of the more trendy benefits, such as on-site dry cleaning and fitness centers, but for retirement and health insurance, the reflective HR manager whose ethical concern goes beyond the organization's boundaries must consider these implications. I do not mean to suggest that any individual HR manager has the power to reverse the dominant U.S. model for providing health benefits to employees. In fact, were any organization to cut its benefits significantly, it might be violating its duty to keep promises to employees unless it made arrangements for the same benefits to be provided through another source. HR managers in multinational firms, however, would do well to consider whether adding U.S.-style benefits might begin a trend to undermine functioning national systems.

The most common method of providing benefits to employees of large organizations is to offer them an array from which they can choose. In some cases, employees are given a fixed sum of benefit dollars to spend; in others, they are given the option to use part of their salary to purchase the benefit. Many benefits are available through salary reduction, which shields part of the employee's salary from income taxes.

Even where there is a choice in benefits, the HR manager must decide which benefits will be included and, usually, which carrier will provide them. An ethical issue facing HR managers in this arena is the potential for conflict of interest. It can take two forms. First, the HR manager, as an employee, can be tempted to select programs for the benefit smorgasbord that are personally appealing. Second, since large revenues hinge upon these decisions, insurance carriers can be tempted to offer kickbacks or other incentives for the HR manager to select them. In both cases, the HR manager has a clear ethical obligation not to allow personal considerations to affect professional choices.

HR managers also have to balance the welfare of employees against the cost of benefit plans, and they have to make decisions about the amount of choice employees can reasonably be given. Obviously, companies could go bankrupt offering employee benefits. The strategy of offering benefits thus must take into account the likelihood that offering a particular benefit will help the employer attract better employees, retain desirable employees at lower overall cost, and motivate employees to devote more hours to productive work. The strategic question is not easily answered by a formula. Some benefits have a very short half-life on the employee-motivation scale, after which they become minimum requirements. By offering "cafeteria" plans of benefit choice, employers reduce the need to up the benefit ante every year, but they also increase administrative costs and decrease their purchasing power. So even within their obligation to be good stewards of employer resources, HR managers have real choices to make that have ethical implications.

Over the past half century, the costs of benefits have skyrocketed, with health insurance costs accounting for a large portion of the increase. The introduction of health maintenance organizations (HMOs) and preferred provider organizations (PPOs) to the Mix slowed the rise for some time, but some of the limitations imposed by these plans created very real problems for employees. HR managers were faced with angry employees, who felt that their psychological contract with the employer had been violated (Lucero and Allen 1994). As demand for lifting the restrictions increased, so did costs. In response, some companies are cutting benefits or increasing the portion of the costs paid by employees. The ethical implications of cutting benefits or increasing co-payments mean that even when employers offer benefits, many lower-paid employees (Rawls's "least advantaged") are unable to purchase them.

The amount of choice provided to employees can be overwhelming. HR managers can provide a real service by examining plans carefully and providing information to employees making choices. The problem of discernment the HR manager faces is determining when the restriction of choice infringes on employee freedoms.

Balance   There is considerable current research on the effects on workers of trying to balance work with "family" or "life" or "nonwork" activities. Organizations seeking to retain employees have instituted "work-family" benefits, including such things as on-site day care, work-family training, day-care referral programs, elder care assistance, and flexible schedules (Osterman 1995). These programs have generally been hailed by the business ethics literature as virtuous (Marchese, Bassham, and Ryan 2002), but the HR manager

must address the issue of fairness, as employees with fewer dependents may begin to complain that they are shouldering more than their share of the work or receiving disproportionately fewer benefits.

Compensation Systems   Compensation systems are also important to retention (Gerhart and Trevor 1996). HR managers must ensure that employees perceive their jobs as being worth at least as much as any alternative employment available to them. Some ethicists suggest that employers who receive higher-than-average profits in an industry have a moral obligation to pay their employees higher-than-average wages for that industry (Koys 2001). Turnover is related not only to the amount of compensation but also to the growth of compensation over time (Trevor, Gerhart, and Boudreau 1997). Certain compensation systems are designed as "golden handcuffs" that force employees to stay even when they wish to leave. Stock options that don't mature for years, longevity salary increases, and other devices intended to link the long-term interests of the organization with the employee's interests can become coercive if they represent a sufficient percentage of the employee's compensation.

Employee Complaint Mechanisms   Hirschman (1970) suggests that people given the opportunity to voice complaints will be less likely to choose "exit" as their strategy. Many organizations have employee complaint procedures, administered through the HR department. Typically, they allow an employee to bring a formal complaint first to the supervisor or manager accused of wrongdoing, then to successively higher levels of management. One of the challenges facing HR managers is to ensure that the power differential between managers and employees does not quash complaints that should be heard. Unfortunately, one of the few ways to ensure this is to allow the expression of complaints that shouldn't be heard, taking up valuable staff time. An independent complaint investigator may lend credibility to the procedure. There is some evidence that having decision makers who are not part of management increases the number of grievances (Colvin 2003). However, even if the typical system is used, it is important for managers to receive training that enables them to see the employees' side of issues (Moberg 2003). An ethical HR manager will encourage legitimate grievances, will have them heard in a just platform, and will seek meaningful resolutions.

Termination

Not mentioned in the core responsibilities of HR managers but still a very real part of their jobs are employee dismissals, layoffs, resignations, and retirements. Employees who violate the organization's rules or fail to meet the standards established for their employment are dismissed. Those whose jobs are no longer needed, due to changes in organizational structure, goals, or finances, are laid off, The main difference between the two is that dismissal is person specific while lay-off is job specific. In either case, the person affected is often devastated, and the HR manager has the ability to make the process less distressing. While the law in some places allows an employer to fire an employee for "a good reason, a bad reason, or no reason at all," Kant ([1785] 1981) would suggest that only actions done for good reasons can be good.

Dismissal Dismissals for rule violations are different from dismissals for poor performance: the first is willful, while the second may not be. The distinction has implications for how an HR manager addresses dismissals. "Fault" and "blame" should not be ascribed to people who are unable to achieve the standards of the organization, especially if they have been able to achieve those standards for years or are new employees. In the first case, it is likely declining capabilities that cause the inability to meet standards, and blaming a person for a natural process is cruel. In the second case, the HR manager is perhaps more blameworthy, having assessed the person's qualifications and determined that he or she could perform the job duties. However, in cases where the employee has chosen not to meet standards or has intentionally violated a rule, the HR manager may take pains to explain that the dismissal was within the employee's control.

HR managers have an obligation to make sure that systems of dismissing employees for rule violations are fairly designed and administered and clearly articulated. While employees whose productivity is high may be given special dispensation to violate rules (for example, to come to work late), it is important for HR managers to ascertain that all similarly situated employees receive the same dispensation. It is easy to look at an individual's record and say, "Of course that person deserves to be fired," but fairness cannot be determined until the HR manager has compared that record to the records of those who are not being considered for firing. The manner in which the employee is informed of the dismissal, as well as treatment after the notice has been provided, must respect the dignity of the employee and the safety of co-workers. Cases where disgruntled people take up arms and attack former supervisors or coworkers are rare enough to make front-page news, but the HR manager's ethical responsibility is to take steps to make sure they stay rare.

Layoffs When there are insufficient funds or orders to justify the size of the workforce, workers are laid off, either temporarily (until business picks up) or permanently. Layoffs are sometimes conducted under very strict rules, requiring people to be dismissed in reverse order from their hiring and providing "bumping rights" to people to return to previously held positions, forcing the incumbents to be laid off instead. The first job of the ethical HR manager is to provide alternatives to layoffs, outsourcing, or downsizing to the other managers considering the action. This requires clearly understanding the anticipated outcomes in terms of what might happen to all of the stakeholders: employees, potential employees, local communities, external communities, and stockholders (Arnold and Bowie 2003). The HR manager must also clearly understand all of the contracts, both actual and psychological, surrounding the relationships with current employees.

Assuming that a layoff does occur, the second job of the ethical HR manager is to provide notice, placement assistance, and recommendations for those being laid off. The specifics for each of these depend on the situation. The ethical HR manager should focus on looking out for those least advantaged by the decision. The third job is to provide for the emotional reactions of the "survivors," both rank-and-file co-workers and managers in the affected unit (Dewitt, Trevino, and Mollica 2003).

Resignation Employees who quit their jobs sometimes leave because they haven't found an outlet where they can voice their complaints. One way an HR manager can help these employees is to provide exit interviews, which, though not completely satisfying, may at least help the employees to feel as if their departure could help those left behind. Assuming the HR manager investigates and acts on complaints voiced in these interviews, other employees can be helped by subsequent reforms. One practice prevalent in some industries is to process all resignations immediately, despite any employee attempts to give notice. Unless there is a compelling reason to do otherwise, HR managers should encourage practices that reward giving notice rather than punish it.

Death Employees who die while employed leave family members in vulnerable positions with respect to the employer. The ethical HR manager can smooth the way for survivors by providing prompt and clear information on final paychecks, life insurance, continuation of health coverage and other benefits that might be useful. Similarly, the HR manager can provide support for co-workers, including notices of the death and funeral arrangements and time off to attend the funeral, and can work with the direct supervisor to ensure smooth transitions.

Conclusion

Having been an HR practitioner for more than a decade, I have special sympathy for the pressures HR managers live under. It is rare that they can sit back and reflect on the many ethical issues involved in every decision they make. It is even rarer that they find other managers in the organization who are attuned to HR issues from an ethical perspective. While it may be easy for those removed from the situation to point to all of the ethical lapses of HR managers. I would hope that industrial relations and HR faculty would recognize their great potential to assist current practitioners and influence the behavior of future practitioners.

Teaching faculty can stress strategic or ethical considerations in their HR courses. Stressing ethical considerations would be one way to help develop an ethical sense among future practitioners. Faculty can make a course in ethics a prerequisite for their own HR courses and then address ethics regularly in relation to the topics they cover. They can invite ethicists to give guest lectures and local HR managers to talk about ethical issues they face. A few of the available HR textbooks address ethics in almost every chapter—choosing those over textbooks that ignore ethics or relegate it to a paragraph or two would be one way to underscore that students should consider ethics in all that they do. In "HR for the non-HR manager" courses, faculty can give other managers an appreciation for the multiplicity of ethical issues involved in their interactions with employees and with the HR department.

Research faculty have the opportunity to do considerably more work in the area of HR ethics. They have examined HR practices alone and in "bundles" to determine whether there are any that characterize more productive organizations. The consensus seems to be that there are "bundles" of best practices, but they are industry- or organization-specific (Macduffie 1995; Hunter 2000). That is, HR practices must work together toward the achievement of the organizational goal. How the ethics of human resources fits into this picture is not clearly understood. Researchers have yet to add what they know about ethics to what they know about bundles of practices. Similarly, researchers could examine the human costs of various HR practices.

In the end, though, the burden is on each individual HR manager to be reflective, always alert to the potential that what appears to be a routine decision may actually be a chance to do right.

Source: In The Ethics of Human Resources and Industrial Relations. Budd, J. and Scoville, J. (eds.) Labor and Employment Relations Association (2005), 173–201. Reprinted by permission.

REFERENCES

Altman v Minnesota Department of Corrections, 251 F.3d 1199 (8th Or, 2001).

Arnold, Denis 6, and Norman E. Bowie. 2003. "Sweatshops and Respect for Persons." *Business Ethics Quarterly,* Vol. 13, no. 2 (April), pp. 221–43.

Brenkert, George 6. 1998. "Marketing and the Vulnerable," *Business Ethics Quarterly, The Ruffin Series [Special issue],* No. 1, pp. 7–20.

Brenner Mark, and David Fairris. 2004. "Flexible Work Practices and Occupational Safety and Health: Exploring the Relationship Between Cumulative Trauma Disorders and Workplace Transformation." *Industrial Relations,* Vol. 43, no. 1 (January), pp. 242–67.

Butterfield, Kenneth D., Linda Klebe Trevino, and Gail A. Ball. 1996. "Punishment from the Manager's Perspective: A Grounded Investigation and Inductive Model." *Academy of Management Journal,* Vol. 39, no. 6 (December), pp. 1479–1512.

Cappelli, Peter. 1999. "Career Jobs Are Dead." *California Management Review,* Vol. 42, no. 1 (Fall), pp. 146–67.

Clarkson, Max E. 1995. "A Stakeholder Framework for Analyzing and Evaluating Corporate Social Performance." *Academy of Management Review,* Vol. 20, no. 1 (January), pp. 92–118.

Colvin, Alexander J. S. 2003. "The Dual Transformation of Workplace Dispute Resolution." *Industrial Relations,* Vol. 42, no. 4 (October), pp. 712–36.

Dewitt, Rocki-Lee, Linda Klebe Trevino, and Kelly A. Mollica. 2003. "Stuck in the Middle: A Control-Based Model of Managers' Reactions to Their Subordinates' Layoffs." *Journal of Managerial Issues,* Vol. 15, no. 1 (Spring), pp. 32–49.

Donaldson, John, 2001. "Multinational Enterprises, Employment Relations, and Ethics," *Employee Relations,* Vol. 23. no. 6 (November), pp. 627–42.

Gerhart, Barry, and Charlie O. Trevor. 1996. "Employment Variability Under Different Managerial Compensation Systems." *Academy of Management Journal,* Vol. 39, no. 6 (December), pp. 1692–712.

Goins, Sheila, and Elizabeth A. Mannix. 1999. "Self-Selection and Its Impact on Team Diversity and Performance." *Performance Improvement Quarterly,* Vol. 12, no. 1, pp. 127–47.

Graham, Mary E., and Charlie O. Trevor. 2000. "Managing New Pay Program Introductions to Enhance the Competitiveness of Multinational Corporations." *Competitiveness Review,* Vol. 10, no. 1, pp. 136–54.

Greenwood, Michelle R. 2002. "Ethics and HRM: A Review and Conceptual Analysis." *Journal of Business Ethics,* Vol. 3, no. 3 (March), pp. 261–78.

Griggs v. Duke Power 401 U.S. 424 (1971).

Hackman, J. Richard, Greg Oldham, Robert Janson, and Kenneth Purdy. 1975. "A New Strategy for Job Enrichment." *California Management Review,* Vol. 17, no. 4 (Summer), pp. 57–71.

Hannafey, Francis T. 2003. "Economic and Moral Criteria of Executive Compensation." *Business and Society Review,* Vol. 108, no. 3 (Fall), pp. 405–15.

Hirschman, Albert O. 1970, *Exit, Voice, and Loyalty : Responses to Decline in Firms, Organizations, and States.* Cambridge, MA: Harvard University Press.

Hoffman, W Michael, and Laura P. Hartman. 2003. "You've Got Mail … and the Boss Knows: A Survey by the Center for Business Ethics of Companies' Email and Internet Monitoring." *Business and Society Review,* Vol. 108, no. 3 (Fall), pp. 285–307.

Huasknecht, John P., Charlie O. Trevor, and James L Farr. 2002. "Retaking Ability Tests in a Selection Setting: Implications for Practice Effects, Training Performance, and Turnover." *Journal of Applied Psychology,* Vol. 87, no. 2 (April), pp. 243–54.

Hunter, Larry W. 2000. "The Adoption of Innovative Work Practices in Service Environments." *International Journal of Human Resource Management,* Vol. 11, no. 3 (June), pp. 477–97.

Hunter, Larry W., John Paul MacDuffie, and Lorna Doucet. 2002. "What Makes Teams Take? Employee Reactions to Work Reforms." *Industrial and Labor Relations Review,* Vol. 55, no. 3 (April), pp. 448–73.

Kant, Immanuel. [1785]. 1981. *Groundings for the Metaphysics of Morals.* Indianapolis: Hackett.

Kochan, Thomas A. 2002. "Addressing the Crisis in Confidence in Corporations: Root Causes. Victims, and Strategies for Reform." *Academy of Management Executive,* Vol. 16. no. 3 (August), pp. 139–42.

Koys, Daniel J. 2001. "Integrating Religious Principles and Human Resource Management Activities," *Teaching Business Ethics,* Vol. 5. no. 2 (May), pp. 121–39.

Kurland, Nancy. 1999. "Ethics and Commission." *Business and Society Review,* Vol. 104, no. 1 (Spring), pp. 29–33.

Lucero, Margaret A., and Robert E. Allen 1994. "Employee Benefits: A Growing Source of Psychological Contract Violations." *Human Resource Management,* Vol. 33, no. 3 (Fall), pp. 425–46.

MacDuffie, John Paul. 1995. "Human Resource Bundles and Manufacturing Performance: Organizational Logic and Flexible Production Systems in the Automobile Industry." *Industrial and Labor Relations Review,* Vol. 48, no. 2 (January), pp. 197–222.

Marchese, Marc C., Gregory Bassham, and Jack Ryan. 2002. " Work-Family Conflict: A Virtue Ethics Analysis." *Journal of Business Ethics,* Vol. 40, no. 2 (October), pp. 145–54.

McCall, John J. 2003. "A Defense of Just Cause Dismissal Rules." *Business Ethics Quarterly,* Vol. 13, no. 2 (April), pp. 151–76.

Mishra, Jitendra M. 1998. "Employee Monitoring: Privacy in the Workplace?" *S.A.M. Advanced Management Journal,* Vol. 63. no. 3 (Summer), pp. 4–15.

Moberg, Dennis J. 2000. "Time Pressure and Ethical Decision Making The Case for Moral Readiness." *Business and Professional Ethics Journal,* Vol, 19, no. 2 (Summer), pp. 41–67.

_____. 2003. "Managers as Judges in Employee Disputes: An Occasion for Moral Imagination." *Business Ethics Quarterly,* Vol. 13, no. 4 (October), pp. 453–78.

Moberg, Dennis, and Manuel Velasquez. 2004. "The Ethics of Mentoring." *Business Ethics Quarterly,* Vol. 14. no. 1 (January), pp. 95–133.

Nye, David. 2002. "The Privacy in Employment Critique: A Consideration of Some of the Arguments for Ethical HRM Professional Practice." *Business Ethics: A European Review,* Vol. 11, no. 3 (July), pp. 224–33.

Osterman, Paul. 1995. "Work/Family Programs and the Employment Relationship." *Administrative Science Quarterly,* Vol. 40, no. 4 (December), pp. 681–701.

Radin, Tara J., and Patricia H. Werhane. 2003. " Employment-at-Will, Employee Rights, and Future Directions for Employment." *Business Ethics Quarterly,* Vol. 13. no. 2 (April), pp. 113–30.

Rawls, John. 1971.4 *Theory of Justice.* Cambridge, MA: Belknap Press.

Reed, Lisa J. 2003. "Paternalism May Excuse Disability Discrimination When May an Employer Refuse to Employ a Disabled Individual Due to Concerns for the Individual's Safety?" *Business and Society Review,* Vol. 108, no. 3 (Fall), pp. 417–24.

Rest, James R. 1976. "New Approaches in the Assessment of Moral Judgment." In Thomas Lickona, ed. *Moral Development and Behavior Theory, Research, and Social Issues.* New York: Holt, Rinehart and Winston, pp. 198–218.

Robertson, Diana C., and Erin Anderson, 1993. "Control Systems and Task Environment Effects on Ethical Judgment: An Exploratory Study of Industrial Salespeople." *Organization Science,* Vol. 4, no. 4 (November), pp. 617–44.

Roehling, Mark V. 2003. "The Employment-at-Will Doctrine: Second Level Ethical Issues said Analysis." *Journal of Business Ethics,* Vol. 47, no. 2 (October), pp. 115–25.

Scoville, James G. 1993. "The Past and Present of Ethics in Industrial Relations." *Proceedings of the Forty-Fifth Annual Meeting* (Anaheim, CA, January 5–8, 1993). Madison, WI: Industrial Relations Research Association, pp. 198–206.

Stevens, Betsy. 2001. "Hospitality Ethics: Responses from Human Resource Directors and Students to Seven Ethical Scenarios." *Journal of Business Ethics,* Vol. 30, no. 3 (April), pp. 233–42.

Trevino, Linda Klebe, Laura Pincus Hartman, and Michael Brown. 2000. "Moral Person and Moral Manager: How Executives Develop a Reputation for Ethical Leadership." *California Management Review,* Vol. 42, no. 4 (Summer), pp. 128–42.

Trevor, Charlie O., Barry Gerhart, and John W Boudreau. 1997. "Voluntary Turnover and Job Performance: Curvilinearity and the Moderating Influences of Salary Growth and Promotions." *Journal of Applied Psychology,* Vol. 82, no. 1 (February), pp. 44–61.

VanSandt, Craig V. 2003. "The Relationship Between Ethical Work Climate and Moral Awareness." *Business and Society,* Vol. 42, no. 1 (March), pp. 144–52.

Weber, James, Lance B. Kurke, and David W. Pentico. 2003. 'Why Do Employees Steal?" *Business and Society,* Vol. 42, no. 3 (September), pp. 359–80.

Weber, Max. 1930. *The Protestant Ethic and the Spirit of Capitalism.* London: Allen & Unwin.

Werhane, Patricia. 1983. "Individual Rights in Business." In Tom Regan, ed., *Just Business.* Philadelphia, PA: Temple University Press, pp. 100–29.

Wiley, Carolyn. 2000. "Ethical Standards for Human Resource Management Professionals: A Comparative Analysis of Five Major Codes." *Journal of Business Ethics,* Vol. 25, no. 2 (May), pp. 93–114.

READING 2.3

How Do Corporations Embed Sustainability Across the Organization?

Helen M. Haugh and Alka Talwar

Company action to implement sustainable management solutions implicitly assumes that managers and employees are aware of and implement corporate sustainability policies and procedures. However this assumption can be a leap of faith—many employees may be unaware of sustainability issues beyond their immediate work responsibilities. We explore how technical, action, and social learning are used by large corporations to embed sustainability across the organization. We illustrate eight training and development tools with examples drawn from global companies and complement these with deeper insights from companies within the Indian business conglomerate, Tata Group.

There is a growing belief that corporations can, and indeed should, pursue more active strategies to achieve sustainable solutions to social and environmental problems (UN, 2005; de Bettignies & Lépineux, 2009). The resources and power of multinational corporations (MNCs) give them the potential to make a major contribution to development, and people increasingly expect corporations to take account of their impact on society and the environment in the ways that they do business (WBCSD, 2000). Typical MNC action to address the importance of sustainability ranges from ethical sourcing initiatives (Fung, O'Rourke, & Sabel, 2001; Frenkel & Scott, 2002; Perez-Aleman & Sandilands, 2008); environmentally sensitive facilities; product design and production methods that reduce energy consumption and control emissions (Shrivastava, 1995; Bansal & Roth, 2000; Christmann, 2004), and active participation in social and humanitarian projects (Hess, Rogovsky, & Dunfee, 2002; Selsky & Parker, 2005). Corporate changes to implement sustainable management solutions implicitly assume that managers and employees are aware of and implement such

We would like to thank the guest coeditor, Professor Mark Starik, and two anonymous reviewers for their valuable feedback that greatly improved our paper.

policies and procedures. However this assumption can be a leap of faith—many employees may be unaware of sustainability issues beyond their immediate work responsibilities. We explore how eight methods have been used by MNCs to integrate sustainability into employee training and development programs. We illustrate the methods with examples drawn from global companies and complement these with deeper insights from companies within the Indian business conglomerate, Tata Group. Although an enormous amount of literature describes the corporate social responsibility (CSR) activities of corporations, our aim here is to explore the practical methods used by organizations to raise employee awareness about sustainability. The question is, "How do corporations enable employees to learn about sustainability?"

Our findings lead us to four recommendations. First, learning about sustainability is a company-wide necessity that should not be restricted to the discourse of leaders and senior managers; second, collaborative approaches to raising awareness need to be cross-functional and spread across the full range of business functions; third, as opportunities for employees to gain practical experience of sustainability initiatives substantially increases not just their knowledge but also their interest in and commitment to sustainability, embedding sustainability should include technical and action-learning opportunities; finally, to integrate sustainability into the long-term learning strategy of the organization the learning cycle should include opportunities for social learning and expansion of company knowledge systems.

Sustainability

Sustainability is a broad and evolving construct that defies a universally agreed definition. Most definitions of *sustainability* draw on the principles of the Brundtland Commission: "Meeting the needs of the present without compromising the ability of future generations to meet their own needs" (WCED, 1987: 8). An emerging consensus is that there are three pillars of sustainability; namely, economic, social, and environmental (Elkington, 1998; Schmidheiny, 1992;

Rondinelli & Berry, 2000; Bansal, 2005). *Economic sustainability* is fundamental to corporate financial success—in the long run the corporation simply cannot survive if expenditure exceeds income. *Social sustainability* embodies the humanitarian context of business and relates to issues of poverty and income inequality; disease, especially HIV/AIDS and malaria; access to health care, clean water, and sanitation; education, especially for females; and broader problems associated with the impact of globalization on economic development. Third, *environmental sustainability* considers the impact of business on the quality and quantity of natural resources, the environment, global warming, ecological concerns, waste management, reductions in energy and resource use, alternative energy production, and improved pollution and emissions management (Townsend, 2008). The threat of climate change resulting from human activity (IPCC, 2007) shows that the three pillars of sustainability are closely related, and their impacts deeply interconnected (Stern, Young, & Druckman, 1992; Gladwin, Krause, & Kenelly, 1995; Scaltegger & Synnestvedt, 2002; Townsend, 2008). Collectively, the need to address the three pillars is encompassed in the Millennium Development Goals of the United Nations (UN, 2006).

Few would disagree that social and environmental problems require attention—but the question remains as to whether their resolution is the responsibility of corporations (Bansal, 2002). Investing in sustainability has potential benefits for the corporation, as it signals to stakeholders that it is committed to social and environmental goals, and this has been linked to positive corporate performance (Podsakoff & MacKenzie, 1997; Waddock & Graves, 1997; Orlitsky, Schmidt, & Rynes, 2003); competitive advantage (Cordano, 1993; Porter & van der Linde, 1995; Porter & Kramer, 2006); customer loyalty (Ellen, Mohr, & Webb, 2000); enhanced company image and goodwill (Fombrun & Shanley, 1990; Hart, 1995; Russo & Fouts, 1997; Mc-Williams & Siegel, 2001; Peterson, 2004); legitimacy (Suchman, 1995; Brønn & Vidaver-Cohen, 2009); and improvements in employee recruitment and retention (Aguilera, Rupp, Williams, & Ganapathi, 2007; Turban & Greening, 1997). However, investing in sustainability can incur costs (Jaffe, Peterson, Portney, & Stavins, 1995) that corporations have a fiduciary obligation to evaluate to ensure this expenditure is in line with shareholders' interests.

The relationships between organizations, society, and the environment are complex and characterized by the dialectic between the responsibility of business to maximize returns to shareholders (Friedman, 1970) and benefits to a wider range of stakeholders, including the natural environment (Freeman, 1984; Starik, 1995). By embedding sustainability across business functions, organizations can address some of the negative impacts of globalization and contribute to economic development, poverty alleviation, and environmental protection. Integrating sustainability into the

repertoire of organizational responsibilities is not yet mandatory, but internal and external pressures urge organizations to confront these issues. Pressure has come from three general sources: internal stakeholders, external stakeholders, and institutional forces (Bansal & Roth, 2000; Waddock, Bodwell, & Graves, 2002). Internally, pressure from investors, employees, customers, and suppliers has pushed sustainability up the corporate agenda. Externally, legislation, regulations, and voluntary codes of practice, such as the United Nations Global Compact (UNGC; UN, 2007) have added to the pressure for corporations to be seen to act in a sustainable way. Institutional forces in the shape of norms and expectations have also required corporations to acknowledge the importance of sustainability (WBCSD, 2000). Corporations can address sustainability through internal voluntary initiatives as well as externally through partnerships and collaborations (Fren-kel & Scott, 2002; Selsky & Parker, 2005). As societal awareness of and interest in sustainability increases, and pressure group activity in this domain becomes more visible, senior managers have made greater efforts to integrate these issues into the responsibilities of their organizations (Spar & LaMure, 2003).

Learning About Sustainability

Corporations that aim to integrate sustainability into their facilities, processes, and products are likely to face significant challenges to adapt, and in some cases, completely redesign their businesses (Siebenhüner & Arnold, 2007). Radically changing the orientation of the organization to focus on sustainability will mean "a shift in managerial mindset on the role, purpose and impact of the MNC on society" (Waddock & McIntosh, 2009: 298) and will need more than the dissemination of leaflets and reports and a few training days for selected employees requiring double-loop learning (Argyris & Schön, 1996), in which there is change in the fundamental value system of the firm (Cramer, 2005); the incorporation of changing business practices (Perez-Aleman & Sandilands, 2008); dialogue and interaction with internal and external stakeholders (Polonsky & Ottman, 1998; Stace & Dunphy, 1998; Sharma & Henriques, 2005); and the implementation of new and sustainable business strategies (Shrivastava & Hart, 1995; Ricart, Enright, Ghemawat, Hart, & Khanna, 2004; Hart, 2005).

These challenges demand new knowledge (Siebenhüner & Arnold, 2007) and mean that learning lies at the heart of such organizational transformations. Changing employee attitudes to appreciate that sustainability is a key driver of the organization, not an optional add-on (UN, 2008a), will require investment to enable employees to learn about the relationships between sustainability and their employing organization. Although comprehensive in its coverage of technology, innovation, creativity, and change (Loveridge & Pitt, 1990; Dodgson, 1991; Nonaka & Takeuchi, 1995), the learning literature concerning sustainability is as yet small (Cramer, 2005; Siebenhüner & Arnold, 2007). When sustainability is the basis of the competitive advantage of the firm, then learning about sustainability becomes a fundamental core competency (Gladwin et al., 1995) that impacts the long-term success of the organization (Dodgson, 1993; Collis, 1994; Grant, 1996).

Our framework for employee learning about sustainability is based on technical and action learning and links social learning to embedding sustainability in organizational learning. Although individual learning and organizational learning are frequently used interchangeably, individual learning is the foundation of, and ultimately contributes to, organizational learning. From a cognitive perspective, learning involves the transmission of knowledge from one context, to another, (e.g., from the training room to the learner) in a process in which the individual's mental models and maps (Argyris & Schön, 1996) are reshaped and reorganized to take account of new information. Knowledge comes from "formal teaching and from personal experience" (Penrose, 1959: 53) and can be either codified, for example, in sustainability codes of conduct, impact measures, and company policies, or held tacitly by employees (Polanyi, 1966). When information is explicit and in the public domain, learning is fundamentally a technical process concerned with the effective processing, interpretation of, and response to information (Easterby-Smith & Araujo, 1999). Tacit knowledge, however, is knowledge that individuals do not know that they have and is difficult to articulate, and therefore, is inferred from action (Morgan, 1986). Information about technical standards and procedures that are stored in words, images, codes, and principles of the organization can be relatively easy for employees to learn (Cramer, 2005), and we would expect to find organizations using methods to relay this type of information about sustainability to employees.

Action learning (Argyris, 1993), in which employees become active participants in their own learning rather than passive listeners, acknowledges that we also learn from practical experience. Although traditional methods, such as formal courses, are perceived to be the most effective methods for employee learning (Armstrong & Sadler-Smith, 2008), the role of experience in learning (Kolb, 1984) has been found to lead to more useful and better outcomes (Waddock & McIntosh, 2009). Teaching employees about formal technical standards can be helpful; however, action learning, in which employees have the opportunity to participate in practical sustainability projects, makes learning both interesting and worthwhile for employees and also contributes to genuine advances in economic development, poverty alleviation, and environmental sustainability (Aragón-Correa & Sharma, 2003; Hillman & Keim, 2001). Work placements, internships, and volunteering have also been found to impact on moral development (Boss, 1994); increase awareness of social issues

(Kolenko, Porter, Wheatley, & Colby, 1996); tolerance of diversity (Dumas, 2002); and encouragement of social responsibility (Gabelnick, 1997; Lester, Tomkovick, Wells, Flunker, & Kickul, 2005). Opportunities to learn about sustainability from company visits and active involvement in social and environmental projects, therefore, have the potential to yield valuable and additional benefits for the individual and the MNC.

Learning also emerges from everyday experiences and social interactions in the workplace, and in this way, can be conceived of as spread across organizational practices and rooted in an organization's culture (Lave & Wenger, 1991). Social learning posits that learning occurs through observation, participation, and interaction in social processes, so that to become fully integrated into the organization, employees must learn how to align their behavior with what is important to other members of the organization. When at work, employees interact with others, the organization, and its artifacts, and learning is unavoidable in this situated context. For example, the shared value of sustainability can be made explicit in a facility's design that embodies environmental sensitivity, energy efficiency, and recycling across all business functions. An employee would observe this context daily and learn about the importance of sustainability for their employer. Sustainability thus becomes part of identity development, as the organization gives an account of what it does and adjusts to what needs to be done to achieve its goals. In this way organizational adjustment illustrates that the organization, as well as individuals, is capable of learning.

Organizational learning defines the "ways firms build, supplement and organize knowledge and routines around their activities and within their cultures" (Dodgson, 1993: 377). This supports the view that organizations are cultural entities that can learn on a collective basis; that is, they are more than a collection of individuals. Learning is achieved when there is a change in the knowledge base of the organization (Argyris & Schön, 1996) and when the organization changes its behavior as a consequence of new knowledge (Huber, 1991). The creation of structures and opportunities for technical, action, and social learning thus has the potential to transform individual learning about sustainability into organizational learning.

The voluntary nature of sustainability principles means that implementation is open to individual adaptation and practice at the company level. There is as yet no blueprint or stereotype, and hence, we can learn from examples of the tools that have been employed by corporations around the world. Internalizing sustainability within an organization is a double-edged sword, providing both opportunities and risk. Because sustainability is focused on the long term, examining social concerns and environmental issues helps an organization to keep reinventing itself and its products and services. However, there is always the risk of not being able to bring in the required balance between the short term and the long term, especially when encountering barriers to learning. In the next section we present illustrative examples of methods used by MNCs to teach employees about sustainability. The examples have been drawn from the United Nations, a leader in raising awareness about the impact of globalization on sustainability. We selected corporations that have implemented activities oriented toward awareness, knowledge, and skills in sustainability. This is followed by deeper insights into employee learning about sustainability at Tata Group, provided by the head of community development, Tata Chemicals (India).

How Do Corporations Enable Employees to Learn About Sustainability?

Learning about sustainability can draw on a range of tools and techniques. If the corporation does not have the necessary knowledge and skills in its workforce, these can be imported by employing specialist consultants. When implementing sustainable management solutions, corporations can work independently or in partnership with other organizations. Government agencies, nonprofit organizations, and nongovernmental organizations (NGOs) have commitments to sustainable development (Perez-Aleman & Sandilands, 2008), and through partnerships with them and with membership of sustainability networks, corporations can raise employee awareness and knowledge about sustainability. Volkswagen (VW) employed teams of consultants, factory inspectors, and planners to address health and safety issues in its supply chain. The project began in 2004 and was designed to enable VW to work with suppliers in Mexico, South Africa, and Brazil. In association with the International Labor Organization (ILO) and the German Corporation for Technical Cooperation (GTZ), VW produced a replicable model to disseminate best practice in supply chain management to other organizations and suppliers by way of a network of consultants (UN, 2007).

Codes of Conduct

Voluntary codes of conduct range from vague to substantive declarations of intent to guide corporate action and can be used to enable employees to learn about sustainability (Rowledge, Barton, & Brady, 1999). Codes specify minimum acceptable standards in corporate processes and procedures; for them to be successfully implemented, employees need to be both aware of the standards and committed to achieving them. Indeed successful implementation has been found to be positively associated with active stakeholder involvement in the design of corporate codes of conduct (van Tulder, van Wijk, & Kolk, 2009). Codes of conduct range from international framework agreements and industry and professional association codes to company-specific codes. When used proactively, they can change mind-sets about sustainability and value creation (Engen & DiPiazza, 2005). Perhaps the

best-known international codes of conduct relating to labor and social issues are the European Convention on Human Rights (1950), UN Code of Conduct on Transnational Corporations (1972), OECD Guidelines for Multinational Enterprises (1976), the ILO Tripartite Declaration of Principles Concerning Multinational Enterprises and Social Policy (1977), and the UNGC (2000). The earliest environmental reporting and management scheme was introduced by CERES in 1989 after the Exxon Valdez oil spill in Alaska. The CERES code of 10 environmental principles establishes "an environmental ethic with criteria by which investors and others can assess the environmental performance of companies" (CERES, 2002: 31). In 1999 CERES partnered with the United Nations Environmental Programme to develop the Global Reporting Initiative (GRI; GRI, 2000). The children's toy manufacturer Lego employs approximately 7,400 people, making it one of the largest toy manufacturers in the world. Their commitment to sustainability is inscribed in the Lego Group Code of Conduct introduced in 1997, which requires suppliers to observe, at a minimum, the ILO conventions on labor rights, the OECD guidelines, and the Universal Declaration of Human Rights as well as local legislation. When preparing their Code of Conduct, the company consulted with different stakeholder groups in order to define its core business ethics to ensure that employees bought into the code (UN, 2005).

Impact Measures

Organizational performance has traditionally been measured in terms of financial metrics, and only recently have social and environmental impact assessment tools been adopted and become widespread. Societal demands for greater accountability and transparency have brought about innovations in measuring and communicating the broader impact of corporations on different stakeholder groups. Social and environmental accounting tools, (e.g., the GRI; GRI, 2000), and environmental impact measures (e.g., ISO 14001), are part of a gradual movement toward designing standardized methods to calculate social and environmental impact (Lehman, 1999). The process of measuring performance and tracking changes over time can lead to significant learning within the corporation (O'Rourke, 2004). For example, in 2004 Novozymes initiated a process of devising business integrity measures to combat bribery, facilitation payments, money laundering, protection money, gifts, and political and charitable contributions. The launch of the integrity measures was accompanied by a companywide awareness-raising campaign for all employees and business partners. One of the first groups to be involved in the training workshops was the purchasing and supply chain executives, followed by sales and marketing personnel located in countries classified as the most corrupt (UN, 2007).

Company Structure and Policies

Sustainability can be implemented through designing company structures and policies that embody the principles of economic, social, and environmental sustainability (Bansal, 2002). Integrating sustainability principles into an organization requires decisions concerning with whom, where, and how this responsibility will be managed. Previous studies have examined the integration of sustainability principles into corporate governance structures (Ricart, Rodriguez, & Sanchez, 2005; Mackenzie, 2007) and decision-making policies (deWit, Wade, & Schouten, 2006). We give two examples of how this has been achieved. Prior to 2004, the reputation of the South African bank, Ned-bank Group Limited, had been tarnished by falling revenue and corporate governance scandals. In 2004 Nedbank established an Enterprise Governance and Compliance division to proactively detect and eliminate unethical action, especially fraud, and to create and strengthen a culture resistant and intolerant to fraud (UN, 2007, 2008b).

The Danish health care company, Novo Nordisk, delivers diabetes care, haemostasis management, growth hormone therapy, and hormone replacement therapy products to more than 179 countries. The company employs approximately 20,700 employees in 69 countries. To comply with the UNGC, in 1999 the company undertook a human rights review of its activities. In 2002 a project was launched to systematically embed equality and diversity across the corporation. The company introduced a raft of new policies anchored on the principle that central and local initiatives complement each other (UN, 2005).

Purchasing and Supply Chain Initiatives

The low cost of production coupled with less stringent regulation and control of pollution makes developing countries an economically attractive production and manufacturing base (Bansal, 2002). To address these inequalities corporations can initiate dialogue with suppliers on the importance of sustainability in the supply chain. In South Africa the electricity utility corporation, ESKOM, introduced employment equity policies, performance indicators, and reward systems to ensure that its values represent those of its host country. Targets and performance indicators are set for affirmative action, gender equity, rights of people with disabilities, and procurement practices that proactively support Black economic empowerment (BEE), in particular, Black women-owned business and small- and medium-sized enterprises (UN, 2007).

Communications and Dialogue

Corporate publications such as annual reports, booklets, and guides are major tools to communicate the importance of sustainability both internally across the organization and externally to stakeholders (Rowledge et al., 1999). Sustainability reports backed by global or national framework certification are useful for measuring action and for enabling stakeholders to assess company performance. Stock market indices such as the Dow Jones Sustainability Index and the FTSE4Good also communicate sustainability performance to

stakeholders. The Kjaer Group has 240 employees and provides transportation services to individual and corporate clients. In recognition of the fact that the majority of its employees in Africa are local and live in countries where HIV/AIDS is a major issue and that 95% of all people with HIV/AIDS belong to the active workforce, the Kjaer Group developed a handbook on HIV/AIDS for employees. In addition consultants were employed to deliver training on HIV/AIDS. In the spirit of strengthening the UNGC principles that were already embedded in their corporate values, Kjaer Group also invited employees and agents from all over the world to participate in workshops on the 10 principles. Participants were also required to keep a diary so they could share their experiences with friends (UN, 2005).

More recent advances in communications technology using social media and the Internet offer novel tools for sharing knowledge. Future employees born after the millennium have grown up with Web 2.0 technology and social media tools that have the potential to increase awareness of sustainability in new audiences (Fieseler, Fleck, & Meckel, 2010). Electronic learning tools have been found to be effective in formal learning situations (Brower, 2003), and they also have potential for assisting social learning from continuous listening to naturally occurring conversations on blogs, Facebook, and Twitter. The UN blog (http://unworks.blogspot.com) has feeds into Twitter and posts daily updates on its involvement in humanitarian and environmental projects.

Employee Training and Workshops

Employee training courses and workshops are effective teaching methods (Armstrong & Sadler-Smith, 2008), and we would expect most organizations to use them to deliver technical information about sustainability to employees. To teach employees about sustainability, Hartman, a global company that specializes in manufacturing molded-fiber packaging based on recycled paper, developed a 5-stage STEP model. The model consists of six activity areas: networks, systematic management, proactive actions, life-cycle management, communications, and employee development. Employees learn about the model in an internal training program. The implementation of the model has led to continuous implementation of management systems across health and safety, social responsibility, and environmental management, and to closer cooperation with stakeholders. Measurable outputs include working with a recycling cooperative in Brazil, supporting a humanitarian organization in Croatia, and food distribution to low-income families in Israel (UN, 2005).

Company Visits

Company visits enable employees to interact with and learn from other organizations that have successfully implemented sustainability initiatives. Mozambique International Port Services (MIPS) has the capacity for more than 100,000 containers and has developed an environmental policy, an environmental management system, and a company code of conduct. The policy, system, and code are designed to manage environmental impact, especially in terms of waste management, hazardous cargo, grease and spills. To share knowledge, the local network of the UNGC organized a visit to MIPS to help other network members learn more about their sustainability commitments (UN, 2008).

Employee Volunteering Opportunities

Practical experiences in the context of work are a primary learning opportunity for managers and employees (Dragoni, Tesluk, Russell, & Oh, 2009). Opportunities to volunteer are often arranged in association with an NGO partner (Hess et al., 2002) and enable employees to contribute their knowledge and skills to social and environmental projects. Through these activities, employees can enhance their knowledge and skills, expand their networks, gain recognition in the managerial hierarchy, learn something different, and try something novel (Peloza, Hudson, & Hassay, 2009). The professional services company, Deloitte, delivers audit, tax, consulting and advisory services through 3,600 personnel, including 250 partners, and directors in 16 offices in Southern Africa. Project Siyakula is run by trainee accountants employed by Deloitte across South Africa to help disadvantaged pupils from townships to learn skills in accounting and mathematics. By 2008 the project had assisted more than 1,000 students in grades 11 and 12 (UN, 2008). As well as sharing knowledge about sustainability, different types of work experience, such as taking on a new assignment, implementing change, and overcoming obstacles have also been found to develop motivation as well as promote learning (Tesluk & Jacobs, 1998). Volunteering opportunities and internships offer novel experiences and enhance not just knowledge, but employee ability to learn, flexibility and adaptation, as well ethical and moral education.

The technical and action-learning tools presented show how MNCs are actively designing and implementing employee-learning activities that create opportunities for social learning to embed sustainability across the organizations. In the next section we focus more deeply on one MNC to illustrate how cross-organizational teaching and learning ensures that sustainability is at the core of the corporation.

Learning About Sustainability at Tata Group

Tata Group is India's largest private sector employer. Established in 1868 by Jamsetji Tata, the group consists of more than 90 companies, employs more than 350,000 people worldwide, and produced total revenue of $70.8 billion in 2008–2009. Fundamental to the organization's value system is a stewardship philosophy that marries operational performance with social and community impact. This philosophy has been maintained throughout the corporation's history "... *corporate enterprises must be managed not merely in the interests of their owners, but equally in those of their employees, of the customers of their products, of the local community*

and finally of the country as a whole" (J. R. D. Tata). This value system is communicated and shared with Tata employees throughout all company policies, processes, and action. Each Tata company operates independently and has its own board of directors and shareholders. Two thirds of the equity of Tata Sons, the promoter company with shareholdings in various Tata companies, is held by the Sir Dorabji Tata and Sir Ratan Tata philanthropic trusts that together fund research, education, and community development.

Sustainable development practices vary within and among national jurisdictions because of differences in economic, social, political, and technological contexts (Bansal, 2005). Awareness of the need for sustainability has grown (Waddock & McIntosh, 2009); however, in India, in common with other developing countries, the basic human needs of millions of people have remained unmet. Consumer purchasing power is low and inadequate for basic food, shelter, and health needs (Prahalad & Hammond, 2002; Banerjee & Duflo, 2007). MNCs thus have the potential to make vital contributions to raising awareness about economic, social, and environmental sustainability by implementing strategies that deliver triple bottom-line outcomes.

Codes of Conduct

The Tata business excellence model (TBEM) was introduced by Ratan Tata in 1994 and formally records the values of the Tata Group. Facilitated by the Tata Quality Management System (TQMS), TBEM is a tool to embed performance excellence in the organization and focus on stakeholder engagement and sustainability. Organizations undertake an annual assessment using the TBEM model that helps them assess performance against different stakeholder expectations and to develop short- and long-term plans for corporate sustainability. Tata's policy on ethics goes beyond financial issues and is documented in the Tata Code of Conduct that lays out guidelines on ethics that are formally compiled and shared by all Tata companies. To address climate change and environmental degradation, Tata Group is reducing greenhouse gas emissions in the top five Tata companies to bring them in line with global benchmarks.

Impact Measures

In 2003 the Tata Index for Sustainable Human Development was introduced to assess the social responsibility activities of Tata companies. The Index is in partnership with TQMS and is deployed annually to assess performance and encourage continuous improvement across the corporation (Branzei & Nadkarni, 2008). To better reflect the focus on sustainability, the Index was revised and renamed the Corporate Sustainability Protocol Index in 2009. The Index measures processes and outcomes at three levels of sustainability: systems (leadership, networking, strategy, and accountability); people (recruitment, training, empowering, and relationships); and programs (risk management, opportunities, community and livelihoods, and entrepreneurship and self-employment). In addition, the Tata Group recommends ISO 14000 certification, GRI reporting, and the integration of environmental measures into impact assessment at company level.

Company Structure and Policies

The Tata Council for Community Initiatives (TCCI) is the central agency for supporting and managing sustainability across Tata companies. It brings together CEOs from Tata companies and more than 200 facilitators and 11,500 volunteers. The TCCI charter embraces social development, environmental management, biodiversity restoration, and employee volunteering. The guidelines for implementing TCCI include a flow chart of activities that incorporates the training and learning activities already discussed. Some Tata companies have an in-house organization to implement and manage community development projects (e.g., Tata Chemicals Society for Rural Development; TCSRD, and Tata Steel Rural Development Society; TSRDS); whereas many others channel this activity through their human resources function. Currently in development at Tata is a Climate Change Cell, which hopes *"to be the thought and action partner of Tata companies in mitigating climate change."* This has already been added to TQMS.

Purchasing and Supply Chain Initiatives

Except for the mention in the Tata Code of Conduct, there is no formal structure to drive purchasing and supply chain initiatives in the way that there is for community initiatives, climate change, codes of conduct, and so forth. However, there are individual examples of Tata companies who have adopted innovative methods, such as Tata Tea's initiative of establishing the Kanan Devan Hill Plantation Division where tea plantations are now owned and managed by workers themselves, and the Titan Industries Management of Enterprise & Development of Women (MEADOW) program to train and develop traditional artisans and women self-help group members to become key suppliers of services and products, as well as a community development policy to provide opportunities for disabled people in functions including packing, polishing, assembling, and sorting.

Communications and Dialogue

Booklets detailing the TBEM and Code of Conduct are given to all new employees, suppliers, and agents. Group Corporate Affairs and Media at Tata put together case studies of initiatives across the Tata companies for internal communication. The TCCI annual meeting is the forum for networking and communication when companies share their best practices and evolve strategies for further integrating sustainability within their respective organizations. Internal communication is also undertaken through various means, for example, employee events and activities such as games, quizzes, and competitions. Information about TCCI initiatives is available on-line where case studies, reports, and interviews can be downloaded (www.Tata.com). Information about humanitarian projects with Tata Companies (e.g, Tata Steel Community Initiatives

in Orissa) has been posted on YouTube. The corporate blog of Tata Interactive Systems posts information about learning, and in 2009 the Tata Interactive Learning Forum was established to provide a platform to share knowledge, innovations, and achievements. In addition the Tata Interactive Disability Forum pools knowledge from Tata volunteers to create software to help children with learning disabilities.

Employee Training and Workshops

New employees are introduced to the Tata values during their corporate induction. Tata Steel recruits spend 2 days in the neighboring rural communities, and management trainees at Tata Chemicals spend up to 8 weeks learning about sustainability as part of their induction program. Tata Administrative Services officers, recruited from the leading business schools in India to be the future leadership of the group companies, undergo a 7-week rural/community stint with live projects, either with Tata companies or with the various projects supported by the Tata Trusts.

Company Visits

The large scale and wide range of activities of Tata group companies are used as a resource for employee learning about sustainability. Senior managers can participate in company visits, and employees also have opportunities for internal company transfer. Visits to other companies are less common, and in the long term this could constrain learning opportunities for employees by restricting the flow of new knowledge into the organization.

Employee Volunteering Opportunities

Participation in Tata volunteering opportunities is high, and rates vary (10–25%) across Tata companies. Tata Steel's employee volunteer program is innovative and offers a new type of volunteer opportunity that is embedded in the strategy and culture of the organization. At Tata Chemicals, volunteers can either contribute to ongoing programs or elect to work on their own programs; for example, at the Okha-mandal site of Tata Chemicals in the Gujarat, volunteers from the company established a biodiversity reserve plantation project and seed bank to protect endangered species. This has led to reforestation of 90 acres and the protection of 12 native species. In 2009 a whale shark (*Rhinocodon Typus*) conservation program was established, and plans include supporting ecotourism ventures in the state. Senior leaders in the organization also mentor and give advice to significant projects. Through TCCI, individual companies are also part of regional groups where they can undertake volunteer projects together. The feedback from Tata volunteers with TCSRD (see Exhibit 1) provides support for claims concerning the impact of volunteering on individual and organizational learning.

The examples presented show that MNCs employ technical and action-learning methods as well as create opportunities for social learning to enable employees to learn about sustainability. The cumulative effect of the these modes of

EXHIBIT 1

Reflections on Volunteering From Tata Employees

"My time with TCSRD was a very memorable one and it gave me immense learning in a very short period of time. I have been to villages all my life, but have never worked with villagers or spoken to them at length so this was a fresh perspective. While working with the rural people, I came to know of their lifestyle, their concerns and grievances, mind-sets and the way in which they carry out their farming activities. I felt that these were people who were toiling to make our economy run, yet there is so little being done to make their lives easier. Another learning was that it is very natural for people of different origins to dislike each other as we are uncomfortable with differences. The challenge for me is to be comfortable with differences and accept people as they are and not pass opinions on them. Without this knowledge and sensitivity I would be unable to take the right decisions when in a position to do so. There is a great difference between just hearing a story and living through it." (Volunteer, TCSRD).

"The most important learning is to realize firsthand the rural realities of which I had a limited exposure. It is a first-hand experience of these realities that drive in the need to contribute to development of those who are not so privileged. The underdevelopment is due to sheer lack of access to avenues where skills can be learnt. In the long term a business can sustain itself if it is in sync with the community around it. The leaders and the founders of the Tata group have built businesses with the philosophy that the community is the very purpose of the existence of the business. To understand this group philosophy and to play a key role in the group in the future it is essential that one understands these motivations. The future markets in the country are in the rural areas—the sheer size and the untapped potential of these customers, the challenges of cost and service delivery here, is a strong reason to study them. Lastly, and most importantly, it is thrilling to get in touch with ground realities—something one needs to reconnect to every now and then." (Volunteer, Pragati Poultry project).

"For me the community development assignment has been a very enriching experience in getting a glimpse of real India and also being part of it. It has been my only connection with one piece of 70% of India's population—and hence a very valuable one. It has been an amalgam of two basic exercises/objectives: one, to connect with the people of the villages at an emotional level; and two, to make business sense an absolutely different and challenging environment. The real learning was in bringing together both these objectives to coherence in order that the company and the beneficiaries of the company can mutually benefit each other." (Volunteer, GOAL project).

learning is to extend learning about sustainability from practical methods at the surface artefact level of the organization (Schein, 2004) to embedding sustainability deeper in knowledge management systems (Preuss & Cordóba-Pachon, 2009) and the cultural values of the organization (Roome, 1994). This can be beneficial to MNCs, as developing a culture of learning has been found to produce improvements in returns to shareholders, innovation, customer loyalty, and employee recruitment and retention (Di Bella, 2001). In addition significant attention to sustainability has the potential to drive social change (Aguilera et al., 2007). In this way Tata Group's reputation for taking human capital development seriously by investing in training has contributed to motivating and engaging employees and to benefiting the entire nation (Cappelli, Singh, Singh, & Useem, 2010).

Challenges to Teaching Employees About Sustainability

Although the two preceding sections have presented practical examples of how MNCs can successfully embed sustainability across the organization, we have identified five challenges

that may hinder the achievement of this goal. First, company resources are finite, and the range of issues associated with economic, social, and environmental performance means that choices concerning the issues to address are unavoidable. Inevitably some issues will take priority over others, and this may conflict with the expectations of different stakeholder groups. Environmental concerns are not as high on government agendas when a large part of the population lives in poverty, lacks housing, and faces life-threatening diseases, and hence, MNCs can be instrumental in raising employee awareness of social and environmental sustainability. Second, raising employee awareness about sustainability issues may simultaneously increase expectations about the extent of the contribution that the MNC can make to their resolution. The expectation–performance gap will need to be acknowledged and addressed in corporate communications, and the skills gap can be overcome by working in partnership with specialist organizations. Third, the solutions to sustainability problems may be beyond the remit of the MNC. The knowledge and skills required to teach employees about sustainability, in social and community development projects, for example, will require professionally qualified employees.

Unless a strong business case for sustainability can be made, these costs may be perceived by some stakeholders as nonessential to achieving the goals of the MNC. Fourth, to successfully embed sustainability across the organization, corporate investment in teaching and learning opportunities will need to be aligned with employee enthusiasm, interest, and motivation to learn. Employees may be neither willing to commit to double-loop learning and critical reflection in order to learn about new policies, processes, and procedures, nor willing to implement them by changing their usual patterns of behavior. Novel learning tools that use Web 2.0 technology and social media could be used strategically to stimulate employee interest in sustainability. Finally, it is inevitable that there will be differences in the rates of changes in the external environment of the MNC, the pace of employee learning, and the impact of corporate action to address sustainability. Tensions arising from these differences will need to be managed to ensure that the MNC is both responsive and effective in its actions. The current economic downturn may cause MNCs to reduce their investment in sustainability initiatives at a time when social and environmental problems appear to be escalating inexorably. The balance between what is achievable and what is manageable will need to be continually monitored.

Conclusion

In presenting our perspective of how organizations can address sustainability issues, we have drawn on practical examples from MNCs around the world. Our focus has been on large organizations with access to resources and commitments in developed and developing countries. In smaller firms, although the operating context may be less diverse and access to resources may be more constrained, sustainability is just as important. With fewer employees, internal communication is likely to be facilitated, and motivating employees to learn easier to initiate and sustain. Similarly, we have used examples from a range of industries and sectors to illustrate the diversity of initiatives. Inevitably, different industries will face specific challenges that will need to be addressed in the sustainability strategy planning process. Although we can learn from examples of good practice, tailored solutions are preferable to off the peg solutions that are unlikely to yield maximum benefits for employees and stakeholders.

We have shown that the dissemination of information about sustainability should be company-wide and not restricted to small groups of selected employees. Action that is not companywide tends to address operational issues, such as purchasing and supply chain, and is less likely to change the collectively held shared values of the organization than companywide programs. Hence, it is likely that results will be tactical and short term. Sustainability is a long-term goal and should be embedded as an integral part of being a responsible corporation. Sustainability cuts across business functions from production, manufacturing, supply chains and distribution, marketing and selling to finance and management control. As such, collaborative approaches to sustainability training ought to include employees from across the range of business functions so that sustainability can be embedded in the shared cultural values of the organization. Learning about sustainability requires employees to acquire new knowledge and change the way they work. Organizational change is rarely smooth. Employee training and development should, therefore, be part of a long-term learning strategy that includes reflection about, feedback into, and expansion of company knowledge systems. Building time and resources into employee sustainability training in order to embed new knowledge in the corporation has the potential to enhance the learning capacity of the organization and strengthen its ability to continue to learn. The corporation thus develops the capacity to change and commitment to continuous improvement. As the construct of sustainability continues to evolve to reflect how different stakeholders interpret its meaning, the ability to learn becomes fundamental to organizational and employee development. Finally, opportunities for employees to gain practical experience of supporting or working with sustainability initiatives substantially increases their knowledge, interest, and commitment to sustainability. Hence to ensure the development of a culture of sustainability, they should be integral to employee training and development programs. We offer these recommendations to educators and practitioners in the hope that they can be incorporated in teaching and learning activities oriented to increase awareness, knowledge, and skills in sustainability management.

REFERENCES

Aguilera, R. V., Rupp, D. E., Williams, C. A., & Ganapathi, J. 2007. Putting the S back into corporate social responsibility: A multilevel theory of social change in organizations. *Academy of Management Review,* 32(3): 836–863.

Aragón-Correa, J., & Sharma, S. 2003. A contingent resource-based view of proactive corporate environmental strategy. *Academy of Management Review,* 28(1): 71–88.

Argyris, C. 1993. *Knowledge for action: A guide to overcoming barriers to organizational change.* San Francisco: Jossey Bass.

Argyris, C., & Schön, D. A. 1996. *Organizational learning II. Theory, method and practice.* Reading, MA: Addison-Wesley.

Armstrong, S. J., & Sadler-Smith, E. 2008. Learning on demand, at your own pace, in rapid bite-sized chunks: The future shape of management development? *Academy of Management Learning & Education,* 7(4): 571–586.

Banerjee, A., & Duflo, E. 2007. The economic lives of the poor. *Journal of Economic Perspectives,* 21(1): 141–167.

Bansal, P. 2002. The corporate challenges of sustainable development. *Academy of Management Executive,* 16(2): 122–131.

Bansal, P. 2005. Evolving sustainably: A longitudinal study of corporate sustainable development. *Strategic Management Journal,* 26(3): 197–218.

Bansal, P., & Roth, K. 2000. Why companies go green: A model of ecological responsiveness. *Academy of Management Review,* 43(4): 717–736.

Boss, J. A. 1994. The effect of community service work on the moral development of college ethics students. *Journal of Moral Education,* 23: 183–198.

Branzei, O., & Nadkarni, A. G. 2008. The Tata way: Evolving and executing sustainable business strategies. *Ivey Business Journal,* March/April.

Brønn, P. S., & Vidaver-Cohen, D. 2009. Corporate motives for social initiatives: Legitimacy, sustainability or the bottom-line?*Journal of Business Ethics,* 45(3): 78–97.

Brower, H. H. 2003. On emulating classroom discussion in a distance-delivered OBHR course. Creating an on-line community. *Academy of Management Learning and Education,* 2(1): 22–36.

Cappelli, P., Singh, H., Singh, J., & Useem, M. 2010. The India way: Lesson for the U.S. *Academy of Management Perspectives,* 24(2): 6–24.

CERES 2002. *Life in the edge environment.* 2001 Annual Report. Boston: CERES.

Christmann, P. 2004. Multinational companies and the natural environment: Determinants of global environmental policy standardization. *Academy of Management Journal,* 45(5): 747–760.

Collis, D. J. 1994. Research note. How valuable are organizational capabilities? *Strategic Management Journal,* 15: 143–152.

Cordano, M. 1993. Making the natural connection: Justifying investment in environmental innovation. *Proceedings of the International Association for Business and Society:* 530–537.

Cramer, J. 2005. Company learning about corporate social responsibility. *Business Strategy and the Environment,* 14: 255–266.

DeBettignies, H.-C., & Lepineux, F. 2009. Can multinational corporations afford to ignore the global common good? *Business & Society Review,* 114(2): 153–182.

De Wit, M., Wade, M. R., & Schouten, E. 2006. Hardwiring and soft wiring corporate social responsibility: A vital combination. *Corporate Governance,* 2(1): 151–60.

DiBella, A. J. 2001. Learning practices: Assessment and action for organizational improvement. Upper Saddle River, NJ: Prentice Hall.

Dodgson, M. 1991. *The management of technological learning.* Berlin: De Gruyter.

Dodgson, M. 1993. Organizational learning: A review of some literatures. *Organization Studies,* 14(3): 375–394.

Dragoni, L., Tesluk, P. E., Russell, J. A., & Oh, I.-S. 2009. Understanding managerial development: Integrating developmental assignments, learning orientation, and access to developmental opportunities in predicting managerial competencies. *Academy of Management Journal,* 52(4): 731–743.

Dumas, C. 2002. Community-based service-learning: Does it have a role in management education? *International Journal of Value-Based Management,* 15: 249–264.

Easterby-Smith, M., & Araujo, L. 1999. Organizational learning: Current debates and opportunities. In M. Easterby-Smith, J. Burgoyne, & L. Araujo (Eds.), *Organizational learning and the learning organization. Developments in theory and practice:* 23–44. London: Sage.

Elkington, J. 1998. *Cannibals with forks: The triple bottom line of sustainability.* Gabriola Island, BC: New Society Publishers.

Ellen, P., Mohr, L., & Webb, D. 2000. Charitable programs and the retailer: Do they mix? *Journal of Retailing,* 76: 393–406.

Engen, T., & DiPiazza, S. 2005. *Beyond reporting: Creating business value and accountability.* Switzerland: World Business Council for Sustainable Development.

Fieseler, C., Fleck, M., & Meckel, M. 2010. Corporate social responsibility in the blogosphere. *Journal of Business Ethics,* 91(4): 599–614.

Freeman, R. E. 1984. *Strategic management: A stakeholder approach.* Boston: Pitman Publishing.

Frenkel, S. J., & Scott, D. 2002. Compliance, collaboration and codes of labor practice: The Adidas connection. *California Management Review,* 45(1): 29–49.

Friedman, M. 1970. The social responsibility of business is to increase its profits. *New York Times Magazine,* September 13.

Fombrun, C., & Shanley, M. 1990. What's in a name? Reputation building and corporate strategy. *Academy of Management Journal,* 33(2): 233–258.

Fung, A., O'Rourke, D., & Sabel, C. 2001. *Can we put an end to sweatshops?* Boston: Beacon Press.

Gabelnick, F. 1997. Educating a committed citizenry. *Change,* 29(1): 30–35.

Gladwin, P. C., Krause, T., & Kenelly, J. J. 1995. Beyond eco-efficiency: Towards socially sustainable business. *Sustainable Development,* 3(1): 35–43.

Grant, R. M. 1996. Prospering in dynamically-competitive environments–organizational capability as knowledge generation. *Organization Science,* 2(1): 375–387.

GRI, 2000. *Sustainability reporting guidelines.* Global Reporting Initiative: Amsterdam.

Hart, S. L. 1995. A natural resource-based view of the firm. *Academy of Management Journal,* 37(2): 986–1014.

Hart, S. 2005. *Capitalism at the crossroads: The unlimited business opportunities in solving the world's most difficult problems.* Upper Saddle River, NJ: Wharton School of Publishing.

Hess, D., Rogovsky, N., & Dunfee, T. W. 2002. The next wave of corporate involvement: Corporate social initiatives. *California Management Review,* 44(2): 110–125.

Hillman, A. J., & Keim, G. D. 2001. Shareholder value, stakeholder management and social issues. What's the bottom line? *Strategic Management Journal,* 22: 125–139.

Huber, G. P. 1991. Organizational learning: The contributing processes and the literatures. *Organization Science,* 2(1): 88–115.

IPCC, 2007. *Fourth assessment report. Climate change 2007. Synthesis Report.* Intergovernmental Panel on Climate Change.

Jaffe, A., Peterson, S., Portney, P., & Stavins, R. 1995. Environmental regulation and the competitiveness of U. S. manufacturing: What does the evidence tell us? *Journal of Economic Literature,* 33(1): 132–163.

Kolb, D. A. 1984. *Experiential learning: Experience as the source of learning and development.* Englewood Cliffs, NJ: Prentice-Hall.

Kolenko, T. A., Porter, G., Wheatley, W., & Colby, M. 1996. A critique of service learning projects in management education: Pedagogical foundations, barriers, and guidelines. *Journal of Business Ethics,* 15: 133–142.

Lave, J., & Wenger, E. 1991. *Situated learning: Legitimate peripheral participation.* Cambridge, UK: Cambridge University Press.

Lehman, G. 1999. Disclosing new worlds: A role for social and environmental accounting. *Accounting, Organizations and Society,* 24(3): 217–241.

Lester, S. W., Tomkovick, C., Wells, T., Flunker, L., & Kickul, J. 2005. Does service-learning add value? Examining the perspectives of multiple stakeholders. *Academy of Management Education & Learning,* 4: 278–294.

Loveridge, R., & Pitt, M. 1990. *The strategic management of technological innovation.* Chichester: Wiley.

Mackenzie, C. 2007. Boards, incentives and corporate social responsibility: The case for a change of emphasis. *Corporate Governance: An International Review,* 15(5): 935–943.

McWilliams, A., & Siegel, D. 2001. Corporate social responsibility: A theory of the firm perspective. *Academy of Management Review,* 26(1): 117–127.

Morgan, G. 1986. *Images of organizations.* Newbury Park, CA: Sage.

Nonaka, I. H., & Takeuchi, H. 1995. *The knowledge-creating company: How Japanese companies create the dynamics of innovation.* Oxford, UK: Oxford University Press.

Orlitsky, M., Schmidt, F. L., & Rynes, L. 2003. Corporate social and financial performance: A meta-analysis. *Organization Studies,* 24(3): 493–441.

O'Rourke, D. 2004. *Opportunities and obstacles for corporate social responsibility reporting in developing countries.* Washington, DC: World Bank Group.

Peloza, J., Hudson, S., & Hassay, D. N. 2009. The marketing of employee volunteerism. *Journal of Business Ethics,* 85: 371–386.

Penrose, E. T. 1959. *The theory of the growth of the firm.* Oxford: Blackwell.

Perez-Aleman, P., & Sandilands, M. 2008. Building value at the top and bottom of the global supply chain: MNC-NGO partnerships. *California Management Review,* 51(1): 24–49.

Peterson, D. K. 2004. Benefits of participation in corporate volunteer programs: Employee perceptions. *Personnel Review,* 33(6): 615–627.

Podsakoff, P. M., & MacKenzie, S. B. 1997. Impact of organizational citizenship behaviour on organizational performance: A review and suggestions for future research. *Human Performance,* 10(2): 133–151.

Polanyi, M. 1966. *The tacit dimension.* London: Routledge & Kegan Paul, Ltd.

Polonsky, M. J., & Ottman, J. 1998. Stakeholders' contribution to the green new product development process. *Journal of Marketing Management,* 14(6): 533–557.

Porter, M. E., & Kramer, M. R. 2006. Strategy and society: The link between competitive advantage and corporate social responsibility. *Harvard Business Review,* 84(12): 78–92.

Porter, M. E., & van der Linde, C. 1995. Toward a new conception of environment-competitiveness relationship. *Journal of Economic Perspectives,* 9(4): 97–118.

Prahalad, C. K., & Hammond, A. 2002. Serving the world's poor, profitably. *Harvard Business Review,* 80(9): 48–57.

Preuss, L., & Cordõba-Pachon, J.-R. 2009. A knowledge management perspective of corporate social responsibility. *Corporate Governance,* 9(4): 517–527.

Ricart, J. E., Enright, M. J., Ghemawat, P., Hart, S., & Khanna, T. 2004. New frontiers in international strategy. *Journal of International Business Strategy,* 35(5): 175–200.

Ricart, J. E., Rodriguez, M. A., & Sanchez, P. 2005. Sustainability in the boardroom: An empirical investigation of Dow Jones Sustainability World Index leaders. *Corporate Governance,* 5(3): 24–41.

Rondinelli, D. A., & Berry, M. A. 2000. Environmental citizenship in multinational corporations: Social responsibility and sustainable development. *European Management Journal,* 18(1): 70–85.

Roome, N. 1994. *Environmental responsibility: An agenda for further and higher education—management and business.* London: Pluto.

Rowledge, L. R., Barton, R. S., & Brady, K. S. 1999. *Mapping the journey, case studies in strategy and action toward sustainable development.* Sheffield: Greenleaf.

Russo, M. V., & Fouts, P. A. 1997. A resource-based perspective on corporate environmental performance and profitability. *Academy of Management Journal,* 40(3): 534–559.

Scaltegger, S., & Synnestvedt, T. 2002. The link between 'green' and economic success: Environmental management as the crucial trigger between environmental and economic performance. *Journal of Environmental Management,* 65: 339–346.

Schein, E. 2004. *Organizational culture and leadership.* San Francisco: Jossey Bass.

Schmidheiny, S. 1992. The business logic of sustainable development. *Columbia Journal of World Business,* 27(3/4): 19–24.

Selsky, J. W., & Parker, B. 2005. Cross-sector partnerships to address social issues: Challenges to theory and practice. *Journal of Management,* 31(6): 849–873.

Sharma, S., & Henriques, I. 2005. Stakeholder influences on sustainability practices in the Canadian forest products industry. *Strategic Management Journal,* 26(2): 159–180.

Shrivastava, P. 1995. The role of corporations in achieving ecological sustainability. *Academy of Management Review,* 20(4): 936–960.

Shrivastava, P., & Hart, S. 1995. Creating sustainable corporations. *Business Strategy and the Environment,* 4(3): 154–165.

Siebenhüner, B., & Arnold, M. 2007. Organizational learning to manage sustainable development. *Business Strategy and the Environment,* 16: 339–353.

Spar, D., & LaMure, L. 2003. The power of activism: Assessing the impact of NGOs on global business. *California Management Review,* 45(3): 78–97.

Stace, D., & Dunphy, D. 1998. *Beyond the boundaries: Leading and recreating the successful enterprise.* New York: McGraw Hill.

Starik, M. 1995. Should trees have managerial standing? Toward a stakeholder status for non-human nature. *Journal of Business Ethics,* 14(3): 207–218.

Stern, P. C., Young, O. R., & Druckman, D., (Eds.). 1992. *Global environmental change: Understanding the human dimensions.* Washington, DC: National Academy Press.

Suchman, M. C. 1995. Managing legitimacy: Strategic and institutional approaches. *Academy of Management Review,* 20(3): 571–560.

Tesluk, P. E., & Jacobs, R. R. 1998. *Toward an integrated model of work experience. Personnel Psychology,* 51: 321–355.

Townsend, C. R. 2008. *Ecological applications: Towards a sustainable world.* Oxford: Blackwell.

Turban, D., & Greening, D. 1997. Corporate social performance and organizational attractiveness to prospective employees. *Academy of Management Journal,* 40(3): 658–672.

UN, 2005. *Implementing the UN Global Compact. A booklet for inspiration.* United Nations.

UN, 2006. *Millennium development goals.* United Nations.

UN, 2007. *UN Global compact annual review. 2007 leaders summit.* United Nations.

UN, 2008a. *Toward global corporate citizenship.* United Nations global compact leading companies retreat. Summary report. Boston College Center for Corporate Citizenship.

UN, 2008b. *An inspirational guide to implementing the United Nations global compact.* United Nations.

van Tulder, R., van Wijk, J., & Kolk, A. 2009. From chain liability to chain responsibility. *Journal of Business Ethics,* 85: 399–412.

Waddock, S. A., Bodwell, C., & Graves, S. B. 2002. Responsibility: The new business imperative. *Academy of Management Executive,* 16(2): 132–148.

Waddock, S. A., & Graves, S. B. 1997. The corporate social performance-financial performance link. *Strategic Management Journal,* 18(4): 303–319.

Waddock, S. A., & McIntosh, M. 2009. Beyond corporate responsibility: Implications for management development. *Business and Society Review,* 114(3): 295–325.

WBCSD, 2000. *Meeting changing expectations.* Corporate Social Responsibility Study. http://sustainable-finance.org. Accessed August 2009.

WCED, 1987. *Our common future. Report of the World Commission on Environment and Development.* G. H. Brundtland, (Ed.). Oxford: Oxford University Press. You Tube. Tata Steel Community Initiatives in Orissa-1. Accessed 7 March, 2010. http://www.tata.com/article.aspx?artid=lV/ tF5W9eeQ. Accessed 7 March, 2010.

CHAPTER 3

Strategic Management

- Understand the differences between the two traditional models of strategy and the strengths and weaknesses of each
- Explain the steps in the strategic management process and the interrelatedness of its sequence of steps
- Appreciate the different corporate and business unit strategies and the human resource challenges inherent with each
- Understand the different human–resource related challenges in private and publicly held organizations

Strategic Management at Costco

Costco is an international chain of membership retail warehouse stores that offers brand-name merchandise at prices lower than those of other retailers. Costco has effectively utilized a strategy that has allowed it to produce stellar financial results relative to competitors. Although Sam's Club, another warehouse retailer and chief competitor, has 42 percent more members and 70 percent more stores, Costco's annual sales exceed those at Sam's by $1 billion. This is particularly impressive, given that Sam's is affiliated with Walmart stores.

Costco's strategy involves having a lower overhead by utilizing warehouse space and buying in bulk, both of which drive their costs down. Perhaps more important, Costco only carries approximately 4,000 SKUs (stock-keeping units) of inventory as opposed to the typical supermarket, which carries about 30,000 SKUs, or the typical discount retailer, which carriers about 40,000 SKUs. Consequently, the consumer is not overwhelmed at Costco, as the organization does the comparison shopping for its customers through its buying process and selection of merchandise. Costco also employs very limited staff outside of the functions of buying and merchandising products, further eliminating unnecessary overhead.

Costco realizes a need among busy consumers who not only want value but also want convenience. Costco's streamlined operations and willingness to accept lower profit margins on merchandise than its competitors allow them to offer goods at very competitive prices. Costco also offers convenience to time-sensitive customers by offering a variety of products, including electronics, clothing, food, furniture, jewelry, and appliances, under one roof. Clearly, Costco knows its customers' needs, and its strategy is effective, as it is been rewarded with increased sales and customer loyalty, reflected in its 97percent member renewal rate.[1]

The central idea behind strategic human resource (HR) management is that all initiatives involving how people are managed need to be aligned with and in support of the organization's overall strategy. No organization can expect to be successful if it has people management systems that are at odds with its vision and mission. Many organizations suffer from the syndrome of seeking certain types of behaviors and performance from employees but have HR management programs, particularly those related to performance feedback and compensation, that reward the opposite behaviors.[2] As a prerequisite for understanding how to strategically manage HR, it is necessary to understand the process of strategic management.

Strategic management is the process by which organizations attempt to determine what needs to be done to achieve corporate objectives and, more important, *how* these objectives are to be met. Ideally, it is a process by which senior management examines the organization and the environment in which it operates and attempts to establish an appropriate and optimal "fit" between the two to ensure the organization's success. Strategic planning is usually done over three- to five-year time horizons by senior management, with a major review of the strategic plan on an annual basis or when some significant change impacts the organization, such as a merger or acquisition, or its environment.

Models of Strategy

Two major models outline the process of what strategy is and how it should be developed. The first is the industrial organization (I/O) model. This "traditional" model formed the basis of strategic management through the 1980s.[3] The I/O model argues that the primary determinant of an organization's strategy should be the external environment in which the organization operates and that such considerations have a greater influence on performance than internal decisions made by managers.[4] The I/O model assumes that the environment presents threats and opportunities to organizations, that organizations within an industry control or have equal access to resources, and that these resources are highly mobile between firms.[5] The I/O model argues that organizations should choose to locate themselves in industries that present the greatest opportunities and learn to utilize their resources to suit the needs of the environment.[6] The model further suggests that an organization can be most successful by offering goods and services at a lower cost than its competitors or by differentiating its products from those of competitors such that consumers are willing to pay a premium price.

The second major model is the resource-based model, sometimes referred to as the resource-based view (RBV) of the firm. The resource-based model argues that the organization's resources and capabilities, rather than environmental conditions, should be the basis for organizational decisions.[7] Included among these resources are an organization's HR.[8] Organizations hence gain competitive advantage through the acquisition and value of their resources. This approach is consistent with the investment perspective of HR management. It has been argued that the RBV of the firm has formed the foundation for strategic HR management as an understanding of its theoretical foundation is indispensable when attempting to implement the concepts of strategic HR management in the workplace.[9]

The RBV challenges the assumptions of the I/O model and assumes that an organization will identify and locate key valuable resources and, over time, acquire them.[10] Hence, under this model, resources may not be highly mobile across organizations because once they are acquired by a particular organization, that organization will attempt to retain those resources that are of value.[11] However, resources are only of value to an organization when they are costly to imitate and nonsubstitutable.[12]

In contrasting the two approaches, the I/O model suggests that an organization's strategy is driven by external considerations; the RBV argues that strategy should be driven by internal considerations. The I/O model argues that strategy will drive resource acquisition; the RBV argues that strategy is determined by resources. Interestingly enough, research has provided support for both positions.[13]

Sarasota Memorial Hospital

Why would a nurse pass up a job paying $2 more per hour than her current position with an employer whose facility she drives past on her way to work? For nurses at Florida's Sarasota Hospital, the answer is simple. Sarasota Hospital's strategic plan centers around a "pillars of excellence" concept, adopted after a benchmarking study that included hospitals from across the United States. Sarasota developed its five pillars of excellence—service, people, quality, finance, and growth—then did all strategic planning around them. A performance management system was designed to support the pillars; HR was given the directive to establish a strategic plan under the "people" pillar. It created a set of cross-functional team leadership development; service recovery; measurement; reward and recognition; inpatient, outpatient, and ER patient satisfaction; and physician satisfaction. Each team engaged in process mapping and eliminated duplicated steps. Next to be cut were steps that did not add value, followed by nonessential, "sacred cow" steps. The outcome? Both customer and employee satisfaction have increased dramatically, and operations have become far more efficient. Customer satisfaction rose from the 43rd to the 97th percentile in one year. During this time, staff turnover decreased from 24 percent to 16 percent, with the current rate this year further reduced to 9 percent. The culture of the organization—and the ability of each employee to see her or his contribution to it—helps explain why employees are willing to drive further to work for lower pay at Sarasota Memorial.[14]

While the I/O and RBV models present contrasting philosophies as to whether strategy should be developed from internal or external perspectives, they are not the only perspectives on strategy. Indeed, both perspectives have found support in both research and practice, but more important is the fact that strategy is a dynamic field of study with new theories, models, and perspectives constantly being advanced. Strategy itself has become somewhat ill-defined and a catch-all term for a variety of organizational activities. Reading 3.1, "Are You Sure You Have a Strategy?" presents an alternative framework for the design of strategy by considering strategy as an overarching integrative concept with five distinct components.

The Process of Strategic Management

Our examination of strategy, for the purposes of understanding the relationship between HR and strategy, will consider the premises of both the I/O and RBV models. In line with this, the process of strategic management is presented as a series of five distinct steps, as outlined in Exhibit 3.1.

I: Mission Statement

The first stage of strategic management is for the organization to establish or examine, if it currently has one, its mission statement. Virtually all organizations have a mission statement that explains in very simple terms the organization's purpose and reason for existence. Mission statements are usually very broad and generally limited to no more than a couple of sentences. Although the statement appears to be simple, it is often very difficult to construct because it serves as the foundation for everything that the organization does. It requires those formulating it to have a clear and articulated understanding and vision of the organization and to be in consensus on what the organization is all about and why it exists in the first place.

Exhibit 3.2 presents the mission statement for Solectron. Established in 1977, Solectron is the world's largest electronics manufacturing services organization, offering supply-chain management systems for many of the world's leading electronics equipment manufacturers. Solectron has

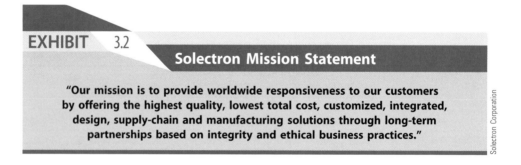

EXHIBIT 3.1

The Process of Strategic Management

Mission Statement

Environmental Analysis
- Competition/ Industry Structure
- Regulations
- Technology
- Market Trends
- Economic Trends

Organization Self-Assessment

Resources
- Financial
- Physical
- Human
- Technological
- Capital

Management Systems
- Culture
- Structure
- Power Dynamics/Politics
- Decision Making Processes
- Past Strategy and Performance
- Work Systems

Goals and Objectives

Strategy

Identify Assumptions

© Cengage Learning

EXHIBIT 3.2

Solectron Mission Statement

"Our mission is to provide worldwide responsiveness to our customers by offering the highest quality, lowest total cost, customized, integrated, design, supply-chain and manufacturing solutions through long-term partnerships based on integrity and ethical business practices."

Solectron Corporation

received more than 200 quality and service awards and was the first company to win the Malcolm Baldrige National Quality Award twice.[15]

Some organizations develop mission statements which are far more complex and lengthy, extended beyond a single sentence and unifying idea. Exhibit 3.3 presents the mission statement for Microsoft Corporation. Noteworthy about Microsoft's mission statement is an explicit presentation of the kinds of employees it seeks and needs to deliver its mission as well as the tenets or values which support this mission.

EXHIBIT 3.3

Who We Are/Mission & Values Delivering on our Mission

To enable people and businesses throughout the world to realize their full potential.

Delivering on this mission requires a clearly defined set of values and tenets. Our company values are not new, but have recently been articulated to reinforce our new mission.

Great people with great values	• Achieving our mission requires great people who are bright, creative, and energetic, and who possess the following values: • Integrity and honesty • Passion for customers, partners, and technology • Open and respectful with others and dedicated to making them better • Willingness to take on big challenges and see them through • Self-critical, questioning and committed to personal excellence and self-improvement • Accountable for commitments, results, and quality to customers, shareholders, partners and employees.
Tenets that propel our mission	*The tenets central to accomplishing our mission include:* **Customer trust.** This means earning customer trust through the quality of our products and our responsiveness and accountability to customers and partners. **Broad customer connection.** This means connecting broadly with customers, understanding their needs and uses of technology, and providing support when they have questions or concerns. **Innovative, evolving, and responsible platform leadership.** This means expanding platform innovation, benefits, and opportunities for customers and partners, openness in discussing our future directions, getting feedback, and working with others to ensure that their products and our platforms work well together. **Enabling people to do new things.** This means broadening choices for customers by identifying new areas of business, incubating new products, integrating new customer scenarios into existing businesses, exploring acquisition of key talent and experience, and integrating more deeply with new and existing partners. **A global inclusive commitment.** This means thinking and acting globally, employing a multicultural workforce that generates innovative decision making for a diverse universe of customers and partners, innovating to lower the costs of technology, and showing leadership in supporting the communities in which we work and live. **Excellence.** This means excellence in everything we do to deliver on our mission.

At Microsoft, we're committed to our mission: improving the potential of our customers, and the world.

Source: *Microsoft, http://members.microsoft.com/careers/mslife/whoweare/mission.mspx*

II: Analysis of Environment

Upon establishing a mission statement, the next step is to analyze the external environment in which the organization operates consistent with the I/O model of strategic management. Decision makers need to analyze a variety of different components of the external organization, identify key "players" within those domains, and be very cognizant of both threats and opportunities within the environment. Among the critical components of the external environment are competition and industry structure, government regulations, technology, market trends, and economic trends as indicated in Exhibit 3.1.[16]

In examining competition and industry structure, critical issues that need to be identified include who the chief competitors are, the means by which they compete, where "power" lies within the industry, barriers to entry, opportunities to acquire and merge with other organizations, critical success factors within the industry, and industry "maturity level." In addition, consideration must be paid to industries that produce complementary or substitute goods or services that may impact the demand for the organization's output.

In examining government regulation, critical issues that need to be identified include the scope of laws and regulations that may impact what the organization does. This involves everything from federal laws regulating the industry and the employment relationship to local zoning ordinances that may affect the size, scope, and location of operations. A significant number of strategic HR management decisions that must be made have to be done within the context of federal, state, and local labor laws. Similarly, organizations need to establish beneficial relationships with agencies that enforce these laws and legislators who propose, pass, amend, and repeal such laws.

The technological sector of the environment involves looking at automation processes, new materials and techniques for producing goods and services, and improved products and special features. It also involves an assessment of how to obtain new technology and the decision as to whether the organization wants to pioneer new technology or allow others to do so and then attempt to copy it.

Analyzing market trends involves examining who existing customers are, their needs and wants, and how well satisfied they are. It also involves looking at potential customers who do not utilize the product or service and determining how existing products and services can be adopted or modified to address the needs of different target groups of consumers and developing strategies to increase the rate or level of usage by current customers. It also involves examining demographic, psychographic, and lifestyle issues among consumers, such as family status, age, interests, residence, education, and income level and determining shifts that are taking place in society relative to these areas.

Analyzing economic trends involves forecasting the condition and direction of the national and local economy. Although it is critical to remember that any kind of forecasting isn't an exact science and that no one can accurately predict the future, organizations need to plan for what may happen in the economy that can have a significant impact on operations. Interest rates, levels of inflation and unemployment, international exchange rates, fiscal and monetary policy, and levels of gross national product (GNP) and economic growth will impact what an organization can accomplish; these need to be factored in to any assessment of future direction of the firm.

The analysis of an organization's environment can be a complex undertaking. Some organizations operate in a highly complex environment where a large number of often interrelated factors impact the organization. Some organizations also operate in volatile environments where the elements that impact the organization are dynamic and often in a state of near-constant change.

Southwest Airlines and Its Environment

When it was founded in 1967, Southwest Airlines was an anomaly in its industry. As the original discount carrier, Southwest developed a successful strategy and business model which resonated with leisure/vacation travelers and distinguished it from its competitors by offering lower fares and utilizing short-haul flights, often to secondary than major cities. However, the competitive environment in which Southwest operates has changed dramatically over the past decade. Large "legacy" carriers, such as United, Delta, Northwest, Continental, US Airways, and American, have filed for bankruptcy and emerged with new cost structures which allow them to compete more effectively with Southwest. Subsequent to these filings, the six large carriers have entered into merger agreements together, providing greater operating economies of scale and more far-reaching, seamless, global transportation networks, while Southwest has remained a domestic carrier. In addition, Southwest's business model and strategy have been successfully copied by other low-cost carriers, such as JetBlue and Spirit. Southwest no longer enjoys the significantly lower cost structure than those of the legacy carriers or the distinctive strategy of being the only low-cost operator. The dramatic change in its competitive environment mandates that Southwest re-examine its strategy.[17]

III: Organization Self-Assessment

Once an organization has scanned and assessed its external environment and identified any threats and opportunities, it then turns to the third stage of strategic management: assessing the internal environment of the organization. In this stage, the key outcome is for decision makers to identify the organization's primary strengths and weaknesses and find ways to capitalize on the strengths and improve or minimize the weaknesses, as espoused by the RBV of strategic management. This requires the organization to examine both its resources and its internal management systems as indicated in Exhibit 3.1.

Resources

Financial resources can significantly affect an organization's competitive advantage. An organization that has the ability to generate internal funds and/or borrow significant sums is able to convert these funds into other assets. Virtually all components of an organization's business can be purchased, so the presence or absence of financial resources can have a significant impact on an organization's performance.

Physical resources include the actual equipment and machinery owned or leased as well as the location of the business and its proximity to customers, labor, raw materials, and transportation. Physical location is clearly a more important resource in some industries than others. A large manufacturing facility has far different choices and considerations with its physical resources than does a small electronic-commerce business.

HR includes not only the sum of technical knowledge of employees but also their personal traits, including commitment, loyalty, judgment, and motivation. An organization is only as strong or as weak as its employees, and the skills, backgrounds, and motivation these employees bring to their jobs will therefore be a key factor in the organization's overall performance. The organization also needs to consider the kinds of obligations it has to employees in the form of contracts or agreements to continue to employ them and the extent that it wishes to enter into such agreements in the future.

Technological resources include the processes by which the organization produces its goods and services. The technology used by an organization can be a major influence on its cost structures and measures of efficiency. A large number of organizations leverage this resource to their advantage by obtaining patents, trademarks, or copyrights. The extent to which an organization is able to safeguard its production processes can be a tremendous resource.

Capital resources include all other items of value, including brand names, reputations with customers, relationships with key constituents in the environment, and goodwill. Many items that can be grouped here are intangibles that do not show up on an organization's financial statements. It has been argued that the more unobservable or intangible a resource is, the more sustainable an advantage it might supply.[18]

Management Systems

In assessing culture, an organization needs to understand the core values and philosophies that guide its day-to-day activities. Many aspects of culture are covert and not clearly articulated but are rather assumptions that individuals in the organization make about the company. As part of the strategic planning process, it is critical that elements of culture be identified and that an understanding be achieved about how these elements of culture influence behavior and impact overall performance.

No standard type of organization structure or way to draw up an organization chart exists. However, certain types of structural configurations may be more suited to certain types of conditions than others.[19] Organization structure has a significant impact on how work is carried out, how groups and departments interact with each other, and where accountability for performance lies. Certain types of structures are also most conducive to certain strategic objectives. Essentially, an organization's structure can act as a catalyst for achieving certain strategic objectives or as an impediment to performance.

Assessing power dynamics and politics allows an organization to see who *really* controls what happens in an organization. Power is not necessarily related to hierarchical position; those in low-level positions can often obtain significant amounts of power and influence the behaviors and activities of others in organizations. Politics is a process by which people utilize the power they have in order to influence outcomes in a manner that they desire. How power and politics are utilized in an organization can allow it to achieve its objectives or be self-serving obstacles to success.

Decision making processes can be a competitive advantage to an organization or a weight that inhibits timely, effective action. In assessing decision making, one needs to look at whether decisions are made by individuals or groups; who gets involved in decision making; how information is collected, distributed, and made available to which individuals in the organization; how long it takes for decisions to be made; and the information criteria that are employed in reaching decisions. These assessments can allow the organization to see whether its decision making processes promote or inhibit effective performance as defined by the organization's strategic objectives.

An examination of the organization's past strategy and performance is critical to understanding its internal environment. By looking at past strategic initiatives and measuring the organization's success in meeting them, an organization can attempt to determine how and why it was or was not successful in the past, re-examine the processes that facilitated or hindered its success, and take action that attempts to capitalize on its successes and remedy its shortcomings.

Finally, it is critical to examine the organization's work systems. Work systems involve the design of jobs and allocation of responsibilities to assist an organization in meeting its objectives. Considerations that need to be addressed include the "fit" between job requirements and employee skills and the extent to which changes in how work is done can be met by either providing current employees with further training or seeking applicants from outside the organization. The organization needs to ensure that it has designed work systems in an optimal manner to allow it to pursue its current and future objectives.

Best Buy's Turnaround Strategy

In early 2012, retailer Best Buy found itself at a critical juncture with its stock price having declined by 50% over the previous five years. With the 2009 failure of its one-time rival Circuit City in the big box consumer retail market and the 2012 failure of Borders Books, senior executive at Best Buy realized that a change was needed in how it conducted its business. Best Buy's traditional strategy, large megastores, at up to 58,000 square feet, stocked with deep and wide selections of discounted movies and music discs lured customers into stores who then shopped for (and purchased) higher-priced, higher-margin items such as flat-screen televisions and stereo equipment.

Four significant threats faced Best Buy as it attempted to stay in business. The first is showrooming, whereby customers browse and see merchandise in Best Buy stores then purchase the merchandise elsewhere, online. The second was deep discounting being done by online retailers who didn't have to assume the costs of running physical locations and were able to sell to customers without having to collect sales tax. The third was the retail operations of consumer electronics titan Apple, which contrasted to Best Buy, by offering an experience that provided a highly trained, technologically savvy sales force in an environment that encourages customers to browse and use Apple products. Finally, there was little incentive to build relationships with customers, encouraging loyalty and repeat business.

Best Buy's turnaround strategy involved a response to each of these four challenges. In response to showrooming, Best Buy plans to increase the training and customer service skills of its sales force and offer incentives to close sales while customers browse. In response to deep discounting, Best Buy plans to close 50 stores, lay off 400 corporate staff and reduce costs by $800 million, allowing it to pass these savings on to consumers. In response to Apple, Best Buy plans to remodel its existing stores and offer a broader array of the most in-demand products, such as tablet computer and smart phones, de-emphasizing the larger bulky electronics and appliances. In response to its customers, Best Buy plans to expand its existing loyalty program with free shipping and a 60-day price match guarantee.[20]

IV: Establishing Goals and Objectives

Once the organization has established and articulated its mission, assessed its external environment, and identified internal resources and management systems that affect its performance, it is then ready to establish its goals and objectives for the next time period. Goals should be specific and measurable; in fact, at the same time they are established, decision makers should also identify *how* performance toward these goals will be measured and evaluated. In the planning process, measurement of goals is often overlooked. It serves little purpose to set goals and subsequently have no means to measure performance toward them.

Goals also need to be flexible. Because the whole process of setting goals involves dealing with the future and anticipating what might or might not happen, realistic goals should *not* be "carved in stone." What will actually happen in the external environment may likely be different from that which was assumed or anticipated when the goals were set. To maintain goals that were set under assumed conditions that have not materialized is unrealistic and impractical. Goals can be adjusted upward as well as downward in response to how events in the environment have unfolded. For this reason, some organizations, particularly those that operate in highly volatile environments, rely more on a strategic vision for the organization over the longer term. Visions are generally less detailed and formal than strategic plans but can still guide managers at all levels in their day-to-day decision making.

V: Setting Strategy

Once goals have been defined, an organization is then ready to determine its strategy. Strategy, very simply, is *how* the organization intends to achieve its goals. The means it will use, the courses of action it will take, and how it will generally operate and compete constitute the organization's strategy. The close involvement of the HR function through all stages of strategic management is essential for the success of both planning and implementation efforts. The value of and unique contributions which the HR function makes to strategic decision is outlined in Reading 3.2, "Bringing Human Resources Back into Strategic Planning."

The strategic choices an organization makes then need to be incorporated into a general HR strategy, which will be discussed in subsequent chapters. Ideally, this HR strategy will serve as a framework by which the organization can develop a consistent and aligned set of practices, policies, and programs that will allow employees to achieve the organization's objectives. Ideally, HR strategy will serve to ensure a "fit" between corporate strategy and individual HR programs and policies. It is important to remember that there is no one "model" way to manage HR strategically because every organization is different. One organization should not necessarily copy the management systems of another organization—even a successful organization that operates in the same industry. Every organization is unique, and any "best practices" that are considered or even adopted should be evaluated within the context of the specific organization in which they are being implemented.

First Tennessee National Corp.

Eyebrows were raised when First Tennessee National, a bank holding company and financial service organization, hired an executive who had a background in finance to head its HR function. HR was given the directive to not only maximize financial performance but to also demonstrate to shareholders the value-added benefits of HR programs and policies. This decision resulted in a strategic partnership between HR and finance that has greatly aided the profitability of First Tennessee. Studies were undertaken that aligned the organization's reward system with business strategy. Several years of data were mined that related HR activities to employee performance, retention, market share, profitability, customer value, and loyalty. Relationships between tenure, retention, and team performance were established. As a result, more visible career paths for high-potential and high-performing employees were established to aid in retention and, ultimately, profitability.[21]

Corporate Strategies

Different types of organization strategies require different types of HR programs. In essence, there are three different generic organization strategies,[22] and each would require a significantly different approach to managing people.

The first strategy is growth. Growth can allow an organization to reap the benefits of economies of scale, to enhance its position in the industry vis-à-vis its competitors, and to provide more opportunities for professional development and advancement to its employees. Growth can be pursued internally or externally. Growth can be achieved internally by further penetrating existing markets, developing new markets, or developing new products or services to sell in existing and/or new markets. Chief strategic HR issues associated with a growth strategy involve adequate planning to ensure that new employees are hired and trained in a timely manner to handle market demand, alerting current employees about promotion and development opportunities, and ensuring that quality and performance standards are maintained during periods of rapid growth.

External growth comes from acquiring other organizations. This is commonly done with competitors or with other organizations that might supply raw materials or be part of the organization's distribution chain (called *vertical integration*). There are two key strategic HR issues associated with external growth. The first involves merging dissimilar HR systems from different organizations. It is probable that two different systems existed for staffing, compensation, performance management, and employee relations, and the appropriate new system may or may not be one of the previous systems or even a hybrid of such. The process may involve starting from scratch and establishing an entirely new HR strategy for the "new" organization. The key factor to be considered here is whether the organization's overall strategy has changed as a result of the merger or acquisition and how this strategy changes.

The second strategic HR issue involves the fact that mergers and acquisitions usually result in the dismissal of employees. Critical decisions will need to be made concerning who is retained and who is let go, and a well-developed retention program should be developed that is cognizant of all legal obligations to employees that the organization might have.

The second organizational strategy involves stability or simply "maintaining the status quo." An organization pursuing this strategy may see very limited opportunities in its environment and decide to continue operations as is. The critical strategic HR issue for this type of organization would be the fact that an organization that is not growing will also be limited in the opportunities it is able to offer to its employees. There may be fewer opportunities for upward mobility, and employees may decide to leave and pursue opportunities with other employers. Hence, it is critical for the employer to identify key employees and develop a specific retention strategy to assist in keeping them.

The third type of overall strategy is a turnaround or retrenchment strategy. Here, the organization decides to downsize or streamline its operations in an attempt to fortify its basic competency. Often, a large organization will grow to the point where it becomes inefficient, particularly relative to smaller competitors, and finds itself unable to respond quickly to changes in the marketplace. Decision makers may see the environment as offering far more threats than opportunities and the organization's weaknesses as exceeding its strengths. Therefore, the organization tries to retool itself to capitalize on its existing strengths and remain solvent. In a retrenchment strategy, a key issue that needs to be addressed is cost-cutting; in many organizations, particularly service organizations, payroll is the chief expense. As with an acquisition strategy, the organization must be careful to adhere to all laws that regulate the employment relationship in selecting individuals to be terminated.

At the same time, the organization also needs to develop a strategy to manage the "survivors." This is, without question, one of the most neglected aspects of downsizing in organizations. It is often assumed by managers that those whose jobs are spared will be relieved that their employment is maintained and will consequently be grateful and return to their jobs motivated and productive. However, the opposite is often true. Many organizations announce the intention to lay off employees well in advance of the actual notification of individually affected employees. As a result, many of these "survivors" may have been working for several months in fear that their employment was in jeopardy. When their jobs are retained, they then find many friends and coworkers, with whom they may have worked alongside for many years, gone. They are often asked to assume additional job responsibilities of those who have departed, generally without any additional compensation. Furthermore, they may feel that during any subsequent layoffs, they may not be as "fortunate" and lose their jobs. Boosting the morale of these employees is a significant HR challenge. Many are demoralized, depressed, significantly stressed, and less loyal to their employer. However, the organization now depends on these employees for high performance more than it ever did. Consequently, these individuals will directly affect whether the organization stays in business.

Business Unit Strategies

There is a significant and growing trend for larger organizations to break their operations into smaller, more manageable, and more responsive units. Subdivisions are often established by product or service, customer group, or geographic region. In addition to the general, corporate-level strategies explained earlier, many individual business units or product, service, or customer divisions develop a more specific strategy to fit the circumstances of their marketplace and competitive environment. Consequently, there are three different business unit strategies that require correspondingly different strategic approaches to HR.[23]

The first of these business unit strategies is cost leadership. An organization pursuing this strategy attempts to increase its efficiency, cut costs, and pass the savings on to the consumer. It assumes that the price elasticity of demand for its products is high—or, in other words, that a small change in price will significantly affect customer demand. It also assumes that consumers are more price sensitive than brand loyal—or, in other words, they see the product or service of each organization as being nondistinguishable. Suave has successfully utilized this strategy in the shampoo market. Knowing that a large segment of consumers are price sensitive in shampoo purchase decisions has allowed Suave to compete quite successfully in a very competitive industry.

This type of organization would center its HR strategy around short-term, rather than long-term, performance measures that focused on *results*. Because efficiency is the norm, job assignments would be more specialized, but employees might be cross-trained during slack or downtime periods. Cost-cutting measures might also result in developing incentives for employees to leave the organization, particularly higher salaried managerial employees.

The second business unit strategy is differentiation. An organization pursuing this strategy distinguishes its product or service from those of competitors or, at least, attempts to make consumers *perceive* that there are differences. This allows the organization to demand a premium price over the price charged by competitors and attempts to gain the loyalty of consumers toward a particular brand. Nike has successfully utilized this strategy to gain tremendous loyalty among its customers. Whether there are actual or perceived performance benefits for athletes or some status identification with the brand name, many consumers will not wear any other brand of athletic footwear.

With this type of strategy, creativity and innovation in product design or service delivery are important in developing such a distinction. Consequently, this type of strategy would involve the organization offering incentives and compensation for creativity. Measures for performance might be more long term in establishing and building brand names. Staffing may focus more on external hiring and recruiting individuals who bring a fresh, unique, outside perspective to the organization rather than being bound by existing ways of doing things.

The third business unit strategy is a focus strategy. An organization pursuing this strategy realizes that different segments of the market have different needs and attempts to satisfy one particular group. For example, this might involve a restaurant that targets families, a clothing store that targets larger individuals, or a retail business that targets a particular ethnic group. Big 'N' Tall clothing stores for men and Dress Barn for women have successfully used this strategy to gain a loyal following among an often-neglected group of consumers.

The key strategic HR issue here is ensuring that employees are very aware of what makes the particular market unique. Training and ensuring customer satisfaction are critical factors in this strategy. An organization often attempts to hire employees who are part of the target market and therefore are able to empathize with customers. A large woman would probably be more comfortable dealing with a salesperson in a clothing store who was also large than one who was slim and svelte.

Another framework developed for examining business unit strategy depicts strategies by "logics of control" and identifies three separate strategies: an investment logic, an inducement logic, and an involvement logic.[24] An investment logic is adopted by organizations concerned with adaptability to changing market conditions. Consistent with the I/O model, it bases strategic decisions on external considerations and utilizes very loose control of day-to-day operations. A minimum of formal rules and procedures facilitates adaptability and change in response to the organization's environment. Jobs and responsibilities are broadly defined, and compensation programs encourage and reward initiative and creativity.

An inducement logic is adopted by organizations concerned largely with cost containment and efficiency. Day-to-day management decisions are governed by tight control mechanisms in the form of budgets and special reports. Job responsibilities are narrowly defined to promote maximum efficiency in operations. Loyalty and commitment are rewarded to discourage excessive amounts of turnover.

An involvement logic is adopted by organizations that have a dual strategy of cost containment and innovation. This type of organization tends to adopt management practices that have some consistency with both the investment and inducement logics, as illustrated in Exhibit 3.4. Some systems are consistent with those of the investment logic, while others are consistent with those of the inducement logic.

Innovation and Creativity as Components of Strategy

One theme that often cuts across many of the strategies noted above is innovation. Indeed, innovation is one of the drivers of growth and can even be a critical component of a turnaround or retrenchment strategy as the organization attempts to find new ways of conducting its business in order to survive. Cost leadership, differentiation, and focus are all strategies that can involve if not mandate innovation. Innovation is often referred to as a strategy itself, yet it tends to be more of a driver or means of carrying out one of the previously mentioned strategies. Indeed, Procter & Gamble, which is known for producing a large number of innovations in its various businesses, considers innovation to be a competency that it seeks and attempts to measure among its new employee recruits.[25] One leading management consultant has argued that in the future, "no company is going to be able to opt out of business innovation," given the pace of change in our world.[26]

EXHIBIT 3.4	Dyer and Holder's Typology of Strategies		

Logics

Goals	Investment	Inducement	Involvement
Contribution	High initiative and creativity; high performance expectations; some flexibility	Some initiative and creativity; very high performance standards; modest flexibility	Very high initiative and creativity; very high performance expectations; high flexibility; self-managed
Composition	Comfortable head count (core and buffer); high skill mix; moderate staff	Lean head count (core and buffer); low skill mix; minimal staff	Comfortable head count; protected core; high skill mix; minimal staff
Competence	High	Adequate	Very high
Commitment	High; identification with company	High; instrumental	Very high; strong identification with work, team, and company

Practices

	Investment	Inducement	Involvement
Staffing	Careful selection, extensive career development; some flexibility; minimal layoffs	Careful selection; few career options, use of temps; minimal layoffs	Very careful selection; some career development; extreme flexibility; minimal (or no) layoffs
Development	Extensive; continuous learning	Minimal	Extensive, continuous learning
Rewards	Tall structure; competitive, fixed, job-based, merit, many benefits	Flat structure; high, variable, piece rate; profit sharing; minimal benefits	Flat structure, high, partially variable, skill- and competency-based; gain sharing; flexible benefits
Work systems	Broad jobs; employee initiative; some groups	Narrow jobs; employee paced; individualized	Enriched jobs; self-managed work teams
Supervision	Extensive, supportive	Minimal, directive	Minimal, facilitative
Employee relations	Much communication; high voice; high due process; high employee assistance	Some communication; some voice; egalitarian	Open and extensive communication; high voice; some due process; egalitarian, some employee assistance
Labor relations	Nonissue	Union avoidance or conflict	Union avoidance and/or cooperation
Government relations	Overcompliance	Compliance	Compliance

Source: *Dyer and Holder (1988, pp. 1–21).*

Innovation at Whirlpool

Whirlpool Corp, the Michigan-based industry leader in the home appliance industry, has always embraced risk taking and innovation as a means of maintaining its dominant position in the marketplace. Employee teams—consisting of engineers, industrial designers, and marketers—conduct field research by going into homes and observing how consumers live and use their products. These observations have resulted in numerous product innovations with greatly reduced development time. Because innovation is a core competency for Whirlpool, all company employees are required to be trained and company-certified at an appropriate proficiency level in innovation. The level depends on the individual employee job. HR is centrally involved in developing training and proficiency measures for certification as well as developing a compensation program that reflects the organization's commitment to innovation. The organization maintains an intranet to view all ideas currently in the "idea pipeline" at any given moment so employees can contribute to development.[27]

A critical question related to innovation is how it can be promoted and nurtured within an organization. Clearly, an organization's culture and reward system can either encourage or discourage creativity and risk taking. One of the world's most successful creative organizations has developed a blueprint for encouraging creativity among its workers, which can be applied to any organization.

Creativity at Cirque du Soleil

Cirque du Soleil, the world-renowned troupe of performance artists, began in 1984 as a small group of street performers in Montreal. Using a circus tent provided by the Quebec government, the group began performing in Quebec and Ontario. In 1987, they began touring the United States and secured a permanent performance space in Las Vegas in 1992. Cirque du Soleil has produced more than a dozen full-length feature shows and currently employs more than 4,000 employees.[28] To entice creativity within the organization, the company employs seven different tools, which it calls "doors": (1) setting expectations that tap into the creativity that everyone has within them; (2) encouraging employees to trust their senses and intuitions; (3) seeking open-minded risk takers who feel no boundaries or constraints in their lives; (4) creating and maintaining a nurturing environment to encourage productivity, creativity, personal growth, and teamwork; (5) acknowledging constraints and using such constraints to fuel further resourcefulness and creativity; (6) enhancing risk tasking through acknowledging employee credibility gained through learning from mistakes; and (7) encouraging continuous feedback through the value of shared creativity.[29]

The Privatization Decision as Part of Strategy

Although not a strategy, one critical strategic business decision that many organizations are currently facing is the decision whether to remain a publicly held company or revert to private ownership. This question actually reverses the typical evolution of the majority of for-profit organizations. Starting out as privately held entrepreneurial endeavors, successful organizations usually reach a critical point in their development when they decide to provide an initial public offering (IPO) of stock for sale. At this point, the owners seek a significant infusion of outside ownership capital to fuel the continued growth of the organization. IPOs are often greatly anticipated and significant newsworthy events for both the financial community and the general public.

More recently, there has been a pronounced trend in reversing this process whereby publicly held and traded organizations are taken private. There are a number of reasons for this. In some instances, executives and board members tire of attempting to gain the support and goodwill of Wall Street analysts and feel that reports on the organization's stock have it undervalued. Second, the significantly increased costs of compliance associated with the Sarbanes-Oxley Act (discussed in Chapter 2) have lessened the desirability of maintaining public status. One estimate puts the cost of post Sarbanes-Oxley compliance at double that incurred prior to its passage and implementation, with the greatest costs increases incurred from director and officer liability insurance.[30]

Third, corporate governance and disclosure requirements for publicly traded companies can be significant and provide information that the organization would prefer to keep from its competitors. Finally, long-term strategic initiatives can be pursued more easily in a privately held organization that is not under pressure for short-term quarterly results sought by Wall Street and the investment community. This latter issue was a key factor in the decision to privatize Dole Food, Co., the world's largest producer of fruits and vegetables, in 2003.

HR plays a critical role in the success or failure of any decision to take a publicly traded company private. From the perspective of recruiting, prospective employees might be less attracted to an employer whose stock is not publically traded on a stock exchange because of lessened perceptions of the prestige of the organization. On the other hand, a privately held company may be less susceptible to a buyout or takeover, which could result in layoffs. Compensation issues can be affected dramatically in a decision to take an organization private. Without the performance-based incentives of stock grants or options, employers need to devise a way to allow employees to fully share in the financial success of the organization once it becomes privately held. This is particularly true when the employer previously offered those forms of compensation that were lost with the decision to go private. Many younger workers still dream of initially working for a small, private startup with a low salary but generous stock options that could make them wealthy in the event of an initial public offering. In addition, stock options are a relatively low-cost form of compensation, so any substitute form of performance-based compensation is likely to be more costly because of direct out-of-pocket expenses for employers. In attempting to address these issues in retaining top performers during a privatization decision, HR has at least as critical a role in the success of the initiative as any other department or function within the organization.

Conclusion

Many organizations have difficulty achieving their strategic objectives because employees don't really understand what these are or how their jobs contribute to overall organizational effectiveness. Less than 50 percent of employees understand their organization's strategy and the steps that are being taken toward fulfilling the organization's mission. Furthermore, only 35 percent see the connection between their job performance and their compensation. Effective strategic management requires not only that the organization's strategic objectives be communicated to employees but that there be a link between employee productivity—relative to these objectives—and the organization's reward system, as is discussed in Chapter 10. Organizations that communicate their objectives to employees and tie in rewards with objectives-driven performance have much higher shareholder rates of return than organizations that do not.[31]

A critical lesson to be learned is that the development of an organization's strategy is a process unique to every individual organization. The factors identified in Exhibit 3.1 can vary dramatically from one organization to another. Even organizations in the same industry can have radically different strategies.

The process of setting an organization's strategy should be the driving force in the establishment of all HR policies, programs, and practices. A strategic approach to HR provides an organization with three critical benefits: (1) It facilitates the development of a high-quality workforce through its focus on the types of people and skills needed; (2) it facilitates cost-effective utilization of labor, particularly in service industries where labor is generally the greatest cost; and (3) it facilitates planning and assessment of environmental uncertainty and adaptation to the forces that impact the organization, as is further discussed in Chapter 4.

Critical Thinking

1. Compare and contrast the premises and assumptions of the I/O and resource-based models of strategic planning. What benefits does each model offer that aid in strategic planning?

2. Identify the HR challenges associated with each of the three major corporate strategies.

3. Identify the HR challenges associated with each of the three major business unit strategies.

4. Critique the model presented in Exhibit 3.1. What benefits can be gained from this process? What shortcomings exist within the model?

5. Examine your current organization's process of strategic management. How effective is this process relative to the organization's performance? What factors contribute to its effectiveness or ineffectiveness?

Reading 3.1

6. Explain how the five elements of strategy portrayed in the reading relate to either the I/O or RBV traditional models of strategy.

Reading 3.2

7. What role does the HR function play with the strategic planning process? What unique value and perspectives does the HR function bring to strategic planning?

Exercises

1. Obtain a copy of a publicly held organization's most recent annual report. To what is its performance for the past year attributed? What strategy does it seem to be following and how integrated with this strategy do the operating units appear to be?

2. Select an organization of your choice and apply the five major elements of strategy from the Hambrick reading to explain its success, failure, or stagnation.

3. Apply the I/O and RBV models of planning to your college or university. What are the key factors in the environment that impact the school's performance? What are its key resources, and how can they best be deployed?

4. Select a particular industry (i.e., pharmaceuticals, shipping, auto, or manufacturing) and identify at least three major competitors in that industry. Visit their Web sites and identify key strategic issues within the industry as well as key strategic issues for the individual firms.

Chapter References

1. Hitt, M. A., Ireland, R. D. and Hoskisson, R. E. "Costco Companies, Inc.: The Retail Warehouse Store Revolution," in *Strategic Management: Competitiveness and Globalization,* 3rd ed., Cincinnati, OH: South-Western College Publishing, 1999.

2. For a discussion of this, see Kerr, S. "On the Folly of Rewarding A, While Hoping for B," *Academy of Management Journal,* 18, 1975, pp. 769–783.

3. Barney, J. B. "Firm Resources and Sustained Competitive Advantage," *Journal of Management,* 17, 1991, pp. 99–120.

4. Schendel, D. "Introduction to Competitive Organizational Behavior: Toward an Organizationally Based Theory of Competitive Advantage," *Strategic Management Journal,* 15(2), Special Winter Issue, 1994.

5. Seth, A. and Thomas, H. "Theories of the Firm: Implications for Strategy Research," *Journal of Management Studies,* 31, 1994, pp. 165–191.

6. Hitt, M. A., Ireland, R. D. and Hoskisson, R. E. *Strategic Management: Competitiveness and Globalization,* 3rd ed., Cincinnati: Southwestern College Publishing, 1998, p. 19.

7. Cool, K. and Dierckz, I. "Commentary: Investments in Strategic Assets; Industry and Firm-Level Perspectives," in Shrivastava, P., Huff, A. and Dutton, J. (eds.), *Advances in Strategic Management* 10A, Greenwich, CT: JAI Press, 1994, pp. 35–44.

8. Barney, op. cit; Hitt et al., op. cit, pp. 1–41.

9. Wright, P. M., Dunford, B. B. and Snell, S. A. "Human Resources and the Resource-Based View of the Firm," *Journal of Management*, 27, 2001, pp. 701–721.

10. Barney, op. cit, pp. 113–115.

11. Hitt et al., op. cit, p. 21.

12. Barney, op. cit

13. McGahan, A. M. and Porter, M. E. "How Much Does Industry Matter, Really?" *Strategic Management Journal*, 18, 1997, Special Summer Issue, pp. 15–30; Henderson, R. and Mitchell, W. "The Interactions of Organizational and Competitive Influences on Strategy and Performance," *Strategic Management Journal*, 18, Special Summer Issue, 1997, pp. 5–14.

14. Heuring, L H. "Patients First," *HR Magazine,* July 2003, pp. 65–69.

15. Taken from http://www.solectron.com.

16. For an excellent discussion of the components of an organization's external environment, see Hitt et al., op. cit, Chapter 2, pp. 42–81.

17. Carey, S. and Nicas, J. "Rivals Invade Southwest's Air Space," *Wall Street Journal*, December 16, 2011, p. B8.

18. Godfrey, P. C. and Hill, C. W. L "The Problem of Unobservables in Strategic Management Research," *Strategic Management Journal*, 16, 1995, pp. 519–533.

19. For a complete discussion of the different forms of organization structure and their appropriateness, see Daft, R. L. *Organization Theory*, 6th ed., Cincinnati, OH: South-Western College Publishing, 1998, pp. 200–233.

20. Bustillo, M. "Best Buy Forced to Rethink Big Box," *Wall Street Journal*, March 30, 2012. p. B1

21. Bates, S. "First Tennessee–Talking to the People," *HR Magazine,* 48, (9), September 2003, p. 48.

22. This typology was developed by Michael E. Porter. *Competitive Strategy,* New York: Free Press, 1980.

23. This typology was developed by William F. Glueck. *Business Policy: Strategy Formulation and Management Action,* New York: McGraw-Hill, 1976.

24. Dyer, L. and Holder, G. W. "A Strategic Perspective of Human Resources Management," in Dyer, L. and Holder, G. W. (eds.), *Human Resources Management: Evolving Roles and Responsibilities,* Washington, DC: American Society for Personnel Administration, 1988, pp. 1–45.

25. Pomeroy, A. "Cooking Up Innovation," *HR Magazine,* 49, (11), November 2004, pp. 46–53.

26. Hamel, G. "Leading the Revolution," *How to Thrive in Turbulent Times by Making Innovation a Way of Life,* New York: Plume Books, 2002.

27. Pomeroy, A. "Cooking Up Innovation" *HR Magazine,* 49, (11), November, 2004, pp. 46–53.

28. Smith, J. "Promoting Creativity Is Cirque du Soleil's Business Strategy" Society for Human Resource Management, Article 025197, published at www.shrm.org/hrnews_/published/articles/CMS_025197.asp April 3, 2008.

29. Bacon, J. *Cirque du Soleil: The Spark—Igniting the Creative Fire that Lives within Us All.* Toronto, ON: Doubleday, 2006.

30. Ladika, S. "Going Private" *HR Magazine,* 49, (12), December 2004, pp. 50–54.

31. Bates, S. "Murky Corporate Goals Can Undermine Recovery," *HR Magazine,* November 2002, p. 14.

READING 3.1

Are You Sure You Have a Strategy?

Donald C. Hambrick and James W. Fredrickson

Executive Overview

After more than 30 years of hard thinking about strategy, consultants and scholars have provided an abundance of frameworks for analyzing strategic situations. Missing, however, has been any guidance as to what the product of these tools should be—or what actually constitutes a strategy. Strategy has become a catchall term used to mean whatever one wants it to mean. Executives now talk about their "service strategy," their "branding strategy," their "acquisition strategy," or whatever kind of strategy that is on their mind at a particular moment. But strategists—whether they are CEOs of established firms, division presidents, or entrepreneurs—must have a strategy, an integrated, overarching concept of how the business will achieve its objectives. If a business must have a single, unified strategy, then it must necessarily have parts. What are those parts? We present a framework for strategy design, arguing that a strategy has five elements, providing answers to five questions—arenas: where will we be active? vehicles: how will we get there? differentiators: how will we win in the marketplace? staging: what will be our speed and sequence of moves? economic logic: how will we obtain our returns? Our article develops and illustrates these domains of choice, particularly emphasizing how essential it is that they form a unified whole.

Consider these statements of strategy drawn from actual documents and announcements of several companies:

> *"Our strategy is to be the low-cost provider."*

> *"We're pursuing a global strategy."*

> *"The company's strategy is to integrate a set of regional acquisitions."*

> *"Our strategy is to provide unrivaled customer service."*

> *"Our strategic intent is to always be the first-mover."*

> *"Our strategy is to move from defense to industrial applications."*

What do these grand declarations have in common? Only that none of them is a strategy. They are strategic threads, mere elements of strategies. But they are no more

strategies than Dell Computer's strategy can be summed up as selling direct to customers, or than Hannibal's strategy was to use elephants to cross the Alps. And their use reflects an increasingly common syndrome—the catchall fragmentation of strategy.

After more than 30 years of hard thinking about strategy, consultants and scholars have provided executives with an abundance of frameworks for analyzing strategic situations. We now have five-forces analysis, core competencies, hypercompetition, the resource-based view of the firm, value chains, and a host of other helpful, often powerful, analytic tools.[1] Missing, however, has been any guidance as to what the product of these tools should be—or what actually constitutes a strategy. Indeed, the use of specific strategic tools tends to draw the strategist toward narrow, piecemeal conceptions of strategy that match the narrow scope of the tools themselves. For example, strategists who are drawn to Porter's five-forces analysis tend to think of strategy as a matter of selecting industries and segments within them. Executives who dwell on "co-opetition" or other game-theoretic frameworks see their world as a set of choices about dealing with adversaries and allies.

This problem of strategic fragmentation has worsened in recent years, as narrowly specialized academics and consultants have started plying their tools in the name of strategy. But strategy is not pricing. It is not capacity decisions. It is not setting R&D budgets. These are pieces of strategies, and they cannot be decided—or even considered—in isolation.

Imagine an aspiring painter who has been taught that colors and hues determine the beauty of a picture. But what can really be done with such advice? After all, magnificent pictures require far more than choosing colors: attention to shapes and figures, brush technique, and finishing processes. Most importantly, great paintings depend on artful combinations of *all* these elements. Some combinations are classic, tried-and-true; some are inventive and fresh; and many combinations—even for avant-garde art—spell trouble.

Strategy has become a catchall term used to mean whatever one wants it to mean. Business magazines now have regular sections devoted to strategy, typically discussing how featured firms are dealing with distinct issues, such as customer service, joint ventures, branding, or e-commerce. In turn, executives talk about their "service strategy," their "joint venture strategy," their "branding strategy," or whatever kind of strategy is on their minds at a particular moment.

Executives then communicate these strategic threads to their organizations in the mistaken belief that doing so will help managers make tough choices. But how does knowing that their firm is pursuing an "acquisition strategy" or a "first-mover strategy" help the vast majority of managers do their jobs or set priorities? How helpful is it to have new initiatives announced periodically with the word strategy tacked on? When executives call everything strategy, and end up with a collection of strategies, they create confusion and undermine their own credibility. They especially reveal that they don't really have an integrated conception of the business.

Many readers of works on the topic know that strategy is derived from the Greek *strategos,* or "the art of the general." But few have thought much about this important origin. For example, what is special about the general's job, compared with that of a field commander? The general is responsible for multiple units on multiple fronts and multiple battles over time. The general's challenge—and the value-added of generalship—is in orchestration and comprehensiveness. Great generals think about the whole. They have a strategy; it has pieces, or elements, but they form a coherent whole, Business generals, whether they are CEOs of established firms, division presidents, or entrepreneurs, must also have a strategy—a central, integrated, externally oriented concept of how the business will achieve its objectives. Without a strategy, time and resources are easily wasted on piecemeal, disparate activities; mid-level managers will fill the void with their own, often parochial, interpretations of what the business should be doing; and the result will be a potpourri of disjointed, feeble initiatives.

Examples abound of firms that have suffered because they lacked a coherent strategy. Once a towering force in retailing, Sears spent 10 sad years vacillating between an emphasis on hard goods and soft goods, venturing in and out of ill-chosen businesses, failing to differentiate itself in any of them, and never building a compelling economic logic. Similarly, the once-unassailable Xerox is engaged in an attempt to revive itself, amid criticism from its own executives that the company lacks a strategy. Says one: "I hear about asset sales, about refinancing, but I don't hear anyone saying convincingly, 'Here is your future.'"[2]

A strategy consists of an integrated set of choices, but it isn't a catchall for every important choice an executive faces. As Figure 1 portrays, the company's mission and objectives, for example, stand apart from, and guide, strategy. Thus we would not speak of the commitment of the *New York Times* to be America's newspaper of record as part of its strategy. GE's objective of being number one or number two in all its markets drives its strategy, but is not strategy itself. Nor

would an objective of reaching a particular revenue or earnings target be part of a strategy.

Similarly, because strategy addresses how the business intends to engage its environment, choices about internal organizational arrangements are not part of strategy. So we should not speak of compensation policies, information systems, or training programs as being strategy. These are critically important choices, which should reinforce and support strategy; but they do not make up the strategy itself.[3] If everything important is thrown into the strategy bucket, then this essential concept quickly comes to mean nothing.

We do not mean to portray strategy development as a simple, linear process. Figure 1 leaves out feedback arrows and other indications that great strategists are iterative, loop thinkers.[4] The key is not in following a sequential process, but rather in achieving a robust, reinforced consistency among the elements of the strategy itself.

The Elements of Strategy

If a business must have a strategy, then the strategy must necessarily have parts. What are those parts? As Figure 2 portrays, a strategy has five elements, providing answers to five questions:

- Arenas: where will we be active?
- Vehicles: how will we get there?
- Differentiators: how will we win in the marketplace?
- Staging: what will be our speed and sequence of moves?
- Economic logic: how will we obtain our returns?

This article develops and illustrates these domains of choice, emphasizing how essential it is that they form a unified whole. Where others focus on the inputs to strategic thinking (the top box in Figure 1), we focus on the output—the composition and design of the strategy itself.

Arenas

The most fundamental choices strategists make are those of where, or in what arenas, the business will be active. This is akin to the question Peter Drucker posed decades ago: "What business will we be in?"[5] The answer, however, should not be one of broad generalities. For instance, "We will be the leader in information technology consulting" is more a vision or objective than part of a strategy. In articulating arenas, it is important to be as specific as possible about the product categories, market segments, geographic areas, and core technologies, as well as the value-adding stages (e.g., product design, manufacturing, selling, servicing, distribution) the business intends to take on.

For example, as a result of an in-depth analysis, a biotechnology company specified its arenas: the company intended to use T-cell receptor technology to develop both

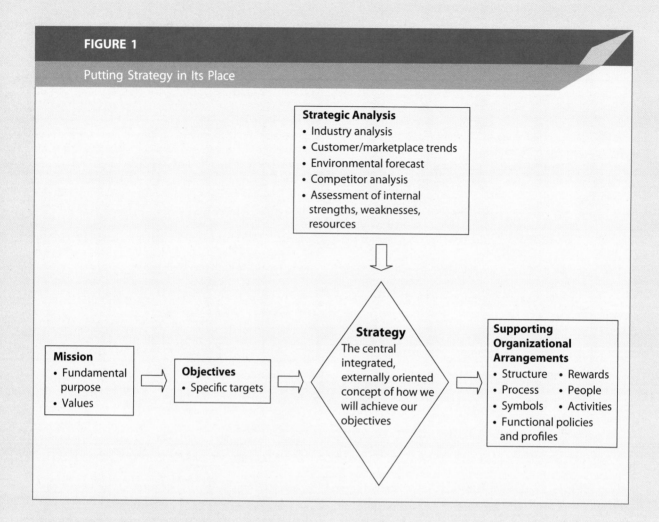

FIGURE 1

Putting Strategy in Its Place

Strategic Analysis
- Industry analysis
- Customer/marketplace trends
- Environmental forecast
- Competitor analysis
- Assessment of internal strengths, weaknesses, resources

Mission
- Fundamental purpose
- Values

Objectives
- Specific targets

Strategy
The central integrated, externally oriented concept of how we will achieve our objectives

Supporting Organizational Arrangements
- Structure
- Process
- Symbols
- Functional policies and profiles
- Rewards
- People
- Activities

diagnostic and therapeutic products for battling a certain class of cancers; it chose to keep control of all research and product development activity, but to outsource manufacturing and a major part of the clinical testing process required for regulatory approvals. The company targeted the U.S. and major European markets as its geographic scope. The company's chosen arenas were highly specific, with products and markets even targeted by name. In other instances, especially in businesses with a wider array of products, market segments, or geographic scope, the strategy may instead reasonably specify the classes of, or criteria for, selected arenas—e.g., women's high-end fashion accessories, or countries with per-capita GDP over $5,000. But in all cases, the challenge is to be as specific as possible.

In choosing arenas, the strategist needs to indicate not only where the business will be active, but also how much emphasis will be placed on each. Some market segments, for instance, might be identified as centrally important, while others are deemed secondary. A strategy might reasonably be centered on one product category, with others—while necessary for defensive purposes or for offering customers a full line—being of distinctly less importance.

Vehicles

Beyond deciding on the arenas in which the business will be active, the strategist also needs to decide how to get there. Specifically, the means for attaining the needed presence in a particular product category, market segment, geographic area, or value-creation stage should be the result of deliberate strategic choice. If we have decided to expand our product range, are we going to accomplish that by relying on organic, internal product development, or are there other vehicles—such as joint ventures or acquisitions—that offer a better means for achieving our broadened scope? If we are committed to international expansion, what should be our primary modes, or vehicles—green-field startups, local acquisitions, licensing, or joint ventures? The executives of

FIGURE 2

The Five Major Elements of Strategy

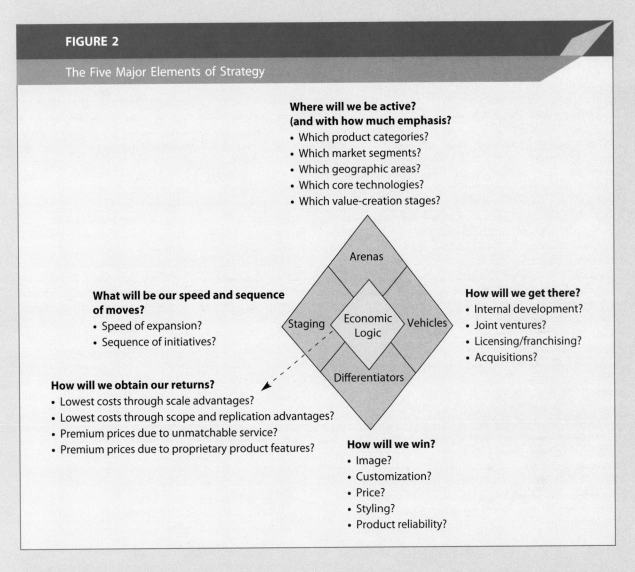

**Where will we be active?
(and with how much emphasis?)**
- Which product categories?
- Which market segments?
- Which geographic areas?
- Which core technologies?
- Which value-creation stages?

**What will be our speed and sequence
of moves?**
- Speed of expansion?
- Sequence of initiatives?

How will we get there?
- Internal development?
- Joint ventures?
- Licensing/franchising?
- Acquisitions?

How will we obtain our returns?
- Lowest costs through scale advantages?
- Lowest costs through scope and replication advantages?
- Premium prices due to unmatchable service?
- Premium prices due to proprietary product features?

How will we win?
- Image?
- Customization?
- Price?
- Styling?
- Product reliability?

(Diamond labels: Arenas, Staging, Economic Logic, Vehicles, Differentiators)

the biotechnology company noted earlier decided to rely on joint ventures to achieve their new presence in Europe, while committing to a series of tactical acquisitions for adding certain therapeutic products to complement their existing line of diagnostic products.

The means by which arenas are entered matters greatly. Therefore, selection of vehicles should not be an afterthought or viewed as a mere implementation detail. A decision to enter new product categories is rife with uncertainty. But that uncertainty may vary immensely depending on whether the entry is attempted by licensing other companies' technologies, where perhaps the firm has prior experience, or by acquisitions, where the company is a novice. Failure to explicitly consider and articulate the intended expansion vehicles can result in the hoped-for entry's being seriously delayed, unnecessarily costly, or totally stalled.

There are steep learning curves associated with the use of alternative expansion modes. Research has found, for instance, that companies can develop highly advantageous, well-honed capabilities in making acquisitions or in managing joint ventures.[6] The company that uses various vehicles on an ad hoc or patchwork basis, without an overarching logic and programmatic approach, will be at a severe disadvantage compared with companies that have such coherence.

Differentiators

A strategy should specify not only where a firm will be active (arenas) and how it will get there (vehicles), but also how the firm will win in the marketplace—how it will get customers to come its way. In a competitive world, winning is the result of differentiators, and such edges don't just happen. Rather, they require executives to make upfront, conscious choices about which weapons will be assembled, honed, and deployed to beat competitors in the fight for customers, revenues, and profits. For example, Gillette uses its proprietary product and process technology to develop superior razor products, which the company further differentiates through a distinctive, aggressively advertised brand image. Goldman Sachs, the investment bank, provides customers unparalleled service by maintaining close relationships with client executives and coordinating the array of services it offers to each client. Southwest Airlines attracts and retains customers by offering the lowest possible fares and extraordinary on-time reliability.

Achieving a compelling marketplace advantage does not necessarily mean that the company has to be at the extreme on one differentiating dimension; rather, sometimes having the best combination of differentiators confers a tremendous marketplace advantage. This is the philosophy of Honda in automobiles. There are better cars than Hondas, and there are less expensive cars than Hondas; but many car buyers believe that there is no better value—quality for the price— than a Honda, a strategic position the company has worked hard to establish and reinforce.

Regardless of the intended differentiators—image, customization, price, product styling, after-sale services, or others—the critical issue for strategists is to make up-front, deliberate choices. Without that, two unfortunate outcomes loom. One is that, if top management doesn't attempt to create unique differentiation, none will occur. Again, differentiators don't just materialize; they are very hard to achieve. And firms without them lose.

The other negative outcome is that, without up-front, careful choices about differentiators, top management may seek to offer customers across-the-board superiority, trying simultaneously to outdistance competitors on too broad an array of differentiators—lower price, better service, superior styling, and so on. Such attempts are doomed, however, because of their inherent inconsistencies and extraordinary resource demands. In selecting differentiators, strategists should give explicit preference to those few forms of superiority that are mutually reinforcing (e.g., image and product styling), consistent with the firm's resources and capabilities, and, of course, highly valued in the arenas the company has targeted.

Staging

Choices of arenas, vehicles, and differentiators constitute what might be called the substance of a strategy—what executives plan to do. But this substance cries out for decisions on a fourth element—staging, or the speed and sequence of major moves to take in order to heighten the likelihood of success.[7] Most strategies do not call for equal, balanced initiatives on all fronts at all times. Instead, usually some initiatives must come

first, followed only then by others, and then still others. In erecting a great building, foundations must be laid, followed by walls, and only then the roof.

Of course, in business strategy there is no universally superior sequence. Rather the strategist's judgment is required. Consider a printing equipment company that committed itself to broadening its product line and expanding internationally. The executives decided that the new products should be added first, in stage one, because the elite sales agents they planned to use for international expansion would not be able or willing to represent a narrow product line effectively. Even though the executives were anxious to expand geographically, if they had tried to do so without the more complete line in place, they would have wasted a great deal of time and money. The left half of Figure 3 shows their two-stage logic.

The executives of a regional title insurance company, as part of their new strategy, were committed to becoming national in scope through a series of acquisitions. For their differentiators, they planned to establish a prestigious brand backed by aggressive advertising and superb customer service. But the executives faced a chicken-and-egg problem: they couldn't make the acquisitions on favorable terms without the brand image in place; but with only their current limited geographic scope, they couldn't afford the quantity or quality of advertising needed to establish the brand. They decided on a three-stage plan (shown in the right half of Figure 3): 1) make selected acquisitions in adjacent regions, hence becoming a super-regional in size and scale; 2) invest moderately heavily in advertising and brand-building; 3) make acquisitions in additional regions on more favorable terms (because of the enhanced brand, a record of growth, and, they hoped, an appreciated stock price) while simultaneously continuing to push further in building the brand.

Decisions about staging can be driven by a number of factors. One, of course, is resources. Funding and staffing every envisioned initiative, at the needed levels, is generally not possible at the outset of a new strategic campaign. Urgency is a second factor affecting staging; some elements of a strategy may face brief windows of opportunity, requiring that they be pursued first and aggressively. A third factor is the achievement of credibility. Attaining certain thresholds—in specific arenas, differentiators, or vehicles— can be critically valuable for attracting resources and stakeholders that are needed for other parts of the strategy. A fourth factor is the pursuit of early wins. It may be far wiser to successfully tackle a part of the strategy that is relatively doable before attempting more challenging or unfamiliar initiatives. These are only some of the factors that might go into decisions about the speed and sequence of strategic initiatives. However, since the concept of staging has gone largely unexplored in the strategy literature, it is often given far too little attention by strategists themselves.

FIGURE 3

Examples of Strategic Staging

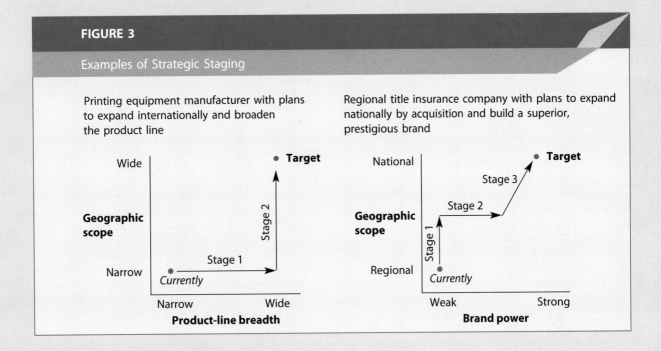

Printing equipment manufacturer with plans to expand internationally and broaden the product line

Regional title insurance company with plans to expand nationally by acquisition and build a superior, prestigious brand

Economic Logic

At the heart of a business strategy must be a clear idea of how profits will be generated—not just some profits, but profits above the firm's cost of capital.[8] It is not enough to vaguely count on having revenues that are above costs. Unless there's a compelling basis for it, customers and competitors won't let that happen. And it's not enough to generate a long list of reasons why customers will be eager to pay high prices for your products, along with a long list of reasons why your costs will be lower than your competitors'. That's a sure-fire route to strategic schizophrenia and mediocrity.

The most successful strategies have a central economic logic that serves as the fulcrum for profit creation. In some cases, the economic key may be to obtain premium prices by offering customers a difficult-to-match product. For instance, the *New York Times* is able to charge readers a very high price (and strike highly favorable licensing arrangements with on-line information distributors) because of its exceptional journalistic quality; in addition, the *Times* is able to charge advertisers high prices because it delivers a large number of dedicated, affluent readers. ARAMARK, the highly profitable international food-service company, is able to obtain premium prices from corporate and institutional clients by offering a level of customized service and responsiveness that competitors cannot match. The company seeks out only those clients that want superior food service and are willing to pay for it. For example, once domestic airlines became less interested in distinguishing themselves through their in-flight meals, ARAMARK dropped that segment.

In some instances, the economic logic might reside on the cost side of the profit equation. ARAMARK—adding to its pricing leverage—uses its huge scale of operations and presence in multiple market segments (business, educational, healthcare, and correctional-system food service) to achieve a sizeable cost advantage in food purchases—an advantage that competitors cannot duplicate. 6KN Sinter Metals, which has grown by acquisition to become the world's major powdered-metals company, benefits greatly from its scale in obtaining raw materials and in exploiting, in country after country, its leading-edge capabilities in metal-forming processes.

In these examples the economic logics are not fleeting or transitory. They are rooted in the firms' fundamental and relatively enduring capabilities. ARAMARK and the *New York Times* can charge premium prices because their offerings are superior in the eyes of their targeted customers, customers highly value that superiority, and competitors can't readily imitate the offerings. ARAMARK and 6KN Sinter Metals have lower costs than their competitors because of systemic advantages of scale, experience, and know-how sharing. Granted, these leads may not last forever or be completely unassailable, but the economic logics that are at work at these companies account for their abilities to deliver strong year-in, year-out profits.

The Imperative of Strategic Comprehensiveness

By this point, it should be clear why a strategy needs to encompass all five elements—arenas, vehicles, differentiators, staging, and economic logic. First, all five are important enough to require intentionality. Surprisingly, most strategic plans emphasize one or two of the elements without giving any consideration to the others. Yet to develop a strategy without attention to all five leaves critical omissions.

Second, the five elements call not only for choice, but also for preparation and investment. All five require certain capabilities that cannot be generated spontaneously.

Third, all five elements must align with and support each other. When executives and academics think about alignment, they typically have in mind that internal organizational arrangements need to align with strategy (in tribute to the maxim that "structure follows strategy"[9]), but few pay much attention to the consistencies required among the elements of the strategy itself.

Finally, it is only after the specification of all five strategic elements that the strategist is in the best position to turn to designing all the other supporting activities—functional policies, organizational arrangements, operating programs, and processes—that are needed to reinforce the strategy. The five elements of the strategy diamond can be considered the hub or central nodes for designing a comprehensive, integrated activity system.[10]

Comprehensive Strategies at IKEA and Brake Products International
IKEA: Revolutionizing an Industry

So far we have identified and discussed the five elements that make up a strategy and form our strategy diamond. But a strategy is more than simply choices on these five fronts: it is an integrated, mutually reinforcing set of choices—choices that form a coherent whole. To illustrate the importance of this coherence we will now discuss two examples of fully elaborated strategy diamonds. As a first illustration, consider the strategic intent of IKEA, the remarkably successful global furniture retailer. IKEA's strategy over the past 25 years has been highly coherent, with all five elements reinforcing each other.

The arenas in which IKEA operates are well defined: the company sells relatively inexpensive, contemporary, Scandinavian-style furniture and home furnishings. IKEA's target market is young, primarily white-collar customers. The geographic scope is worldwide, or at least all countries where socioeconomic and infrastructure conditions support the concept. IKEA is not only a retailer, but also maintains control of product design to ensure the integrity of its unique image and to accumulate unrivaled expertise in designing for efficient manufacturing. The company, however, does not manufacture, relying instead on a host of long-term suppliers who ensure efficient, geographically dispersed production.

As its primary vehicle for getting to its chosen arenas, IKEA engages in organic expansion, building its own wholly owned stores. IKEA has chosen not to make acquisitions of existing retailers, and it engages in very few joint ventures. This reflects top management's belief that the company needs to fully control local execution of its highly innovative retailing concept.

IKEA attracts customers and beats competitors by offering several important differentiators. First, its products are of very reliable quality but are low in price (generally 20 to 30 percent below the competition for comparable quality goods). Second, in contrast to the stressful, intimidating feeling that shoppers often encounter in conventional furniture stores, IKEA customers are treated to a fun, non-threatening experience, where they are allowed to wander through a visually exciting store with only the help they request. And third, the company strives to make customer fulfillment immediate. Specifically, IKEA carries an extensive inventory at each store, which allows a customer to take the item home or have it delivered the same day. In contrast, conventional furniture retailers show floor models, but then require a 6- to 10-week wait for the delivery of each special-order item.

As for staging, or IKEA's speed and sequence of moves, once management realized that its approach would work in a variety of countries and cultures, the company committed itself to rapid international expansion, but only one region at a time. In general, the company's approach has been to use its limited resources to establish an early foothold by opening a single store in each targeted country. Each such entry is supported with aggressive public relations and advertising, in order to lay claim to the radically new retailing concept in that market. Later, IKEA comes back into each country and fills in with more stores.

The economic logic of IKEA rests primarily on scale economies and efficiencies of replication. Although the company doesn't sell absolutely identical products in all its geographic markets, IKEA has enough standardization that it can take great advantage of being the world's largest furniture retailer. Its costs from long-term suppliers are exceedingly low, and made even lower by IKEA's proprietary, easy-to-manufacture product designs. In each region, IKEA has enough scale to achieve substantial distribution and promotional efficiencies. And each individual store is set up as a high-volume operation, allowing further economies in inventories, advertising, and staffing. IKEA's phased international expansion has allowed executives to benefit, in country after country, from what they have learned about site selection, store design, store openings, and ongoing operations. They are vigilant, astute learners, and they put that learning to great economic use.

Note how all of IKEA's actions (shown in Figure 4) fit together. For example, consider the strong alignment between its targeted arenas and its competitive differentiators. An emphasis on low price, fun, contemporary styling, and instant fulfillment is well suited to the company's focus on young, first-time furniture buyers. Or consider the logical

FIGURE 4

IKEA's Strategy

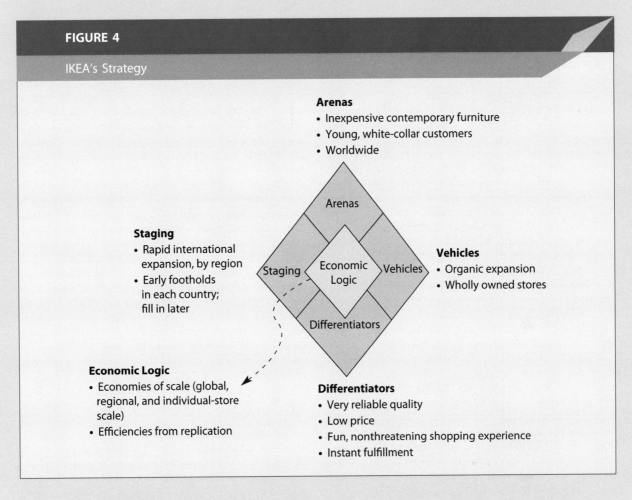

Arenas
- Inexpensive contemporary furniture
- Young, white-collar customers
- Worldwide

Staging
- Rapid international expansion, by region
- Early footholds in each country; fill in later

Vehicles
- Organic expansion
- Wholly owned stores

Economic Logic
- Economies of scale (global, regional, and individual-store scale)
- Efficiencies from replication

Differentiators
- Very reliable quality
- Low price
- Fun, nonthreatening shopping experience
- Instant fulfillment

fit between the company's differentiators and vehicles—providing a fun shopping experience and instant fulfillment requires very intricate local execution, which can be achieved far better through wholly owned stores than by using acquisitions, joint ventures, or franchises. These alignments, along with others, help account for IKEA's long string of years with double-digit sales growth, and current revenues of $8 billion.

The IKEA example allows us to illustrate the strategy diamond with a widely familiar business story. That example, however, is admittedly retrospective, looking backward to interpret the company's strategy according to the framework. But the real power and role of strategy, of course, is in looking forward. Based on a careful and complete analysis of a company's environment, marketplace, competitors, and internal capabilities, senior managers need to craft a strategic intent for their firm. The diamond is a useful framework for doing just that, as we will now illustrate with a business whose top executives set out to develop a new strategy that would allow them to break free from a spiral of mediocre profits and stagnant sales.

Brake Products International: Charting a New Direction

The strategy diamond proved very useful when it was applied by the new executive team of Brake Products International (BPI), a disguised manufacturer of components used in braking and suspension systems for passenger cars and light trucks. In recent years, BPI had struggled as the worldwide auto industry consolidated. Its reaction had been a combination of disparate, half-hearted diversification initiatives, alternating with across-the-board expense cuts. The net result, predictably, was not good, and a new management team was brought in to try to revive performance. As part of this turnaround effort, BPI's new executives developed a new strategic intent by making critical decisions for each of the five elements—arenas, vehicles, differentiators, staging, and economic logic. We will not attempt to convey the analysis that gave rise to their choices, but rather (as with the IKEA example) will use BPI to illustrate the articulation of a comprehensive strategy.

For their targeted arenas, BPI executives committed to expanding beyond their current market scope of North American and European car plants by adding Asia, where global carmakers were rapidly expanding. They considered widening their product range to include additional auto components, but concluded that their unique design and manufacturing expertise was limited to brake and suspension components. They did decide, however, that they should apply their advanced capability in antilock-braking and electronic traction-control systems to develop braking products for off-road vehicles, including construction and farm equipment. As an additional commitment, executives decided to add a new service, systems integration, that would involve bundling BPI products with other related components, from other manufacturers, that form a complete suspension system, and then providing the carmakers with easy-to-handle, preassembled systems modules. This initiative would allow the carmakers to reduce assembly costs significantly, as well as to deal with a single suspension-system supplier, with substantial logistics and inventory savings.

The management team identified three major vehicles for achieving BPI's presence in their selected arenas. First, they were committed to organic internal development of new generations of leading-edge braking systems, including those for off-road vehicles. To become the preferred suspension-system integrator for the major auto manufacturers, executives decided to enter into strategic alliances with the leading producers of other key suspension components. Finally, to serve carmakers that were expanding their operations in Asia, BPI planned to initiate equity joint ventures with brake companies in China, Korea, and Singapore. BPI would provide the technology and oversee the manufacturing of leading-edge, high-quality antilock brakes; the Asian partners would take the lead in marketing and government relations.

BPI's executives also committed to achieving and exploiting a small set of differentiators. The company was already a technology leader, particularly in antilock-braking systems and electronic traction-control systems. These proprietary technologies were seen as centrally important and would be further nurtured. Executives also believed they could establish a preeminent position as a systems integrator of entire suspension assemblies. However, achieving this advantage would require new types of manufacturing and logistics capabilities, as well as new skills in managing relationships with other component companies. This would include an extensive e-business capability that linked BPI with its suppliers and customers. And finally, as one of the few brakes/suspension companies with a manufacturing presence in North America and Europe—and now in Asia—BPI executives concluded that they had a potential advantage—what they referred to as "global reach"—that was well suited to the global consolidation of the automobile industry. If BPI did a better job of coordinating activities among its geographically dispersed operations, it could provide the one-stop, low-cost global purchasing that the industry giants increasingly sought.

BPI's executives approached decisions about staging very deliberately. They felt urgency on various fronts, but also realized that, after several years of lackluster performance, the firm lacked the resources and credibility to do everything all at once. As is often the case, decisions about staging were most important for those initiatives where the gaps between the status quo and the strategic intent were the greatest. For example, executives decided that, in order to provide a clear, early sign of continued commitment to the major global auto manufacturers, a critical first step was to establish the joint ventures with brake manufacturers in Asia. They felt just as much urgency to gain a first-mover advantage as a suspension-system integrator. Therefore, management committed to promptly establish alliances with a select group of manufacturers of other suspension components, and to experiment with one pilot customer. These two sets of initiatives constituted stage one of BPI's strategic intent. For stage two, the executives planned to launch the full versions of the systems-integration and global-reach concepts, complete with aggressive marketing. Also in this second stage, expansion into the off-road vehicle market would commence.

BPI's economic logic hinged on securing premium prices from its customers, by offering them at least three valuable, difficult-to-imitate benefits. First, BPI was the worldwide technology leader in braking systems; car companies would pay to get access to these products for their new high-end models. Second, BPI would allow global customers an economical single source for braking products; this would save customers considerable contract administration and quality-assurance costs—savings that they would be willing to share. And third, through its alliances with major suspension-component manufacturers, BPI would be able to deliver integrated-suspension-system kits to customers—again saving customers in purchasing costs, inventory costs, and even assembly costs, for which they would pay a premium.

BPI's turnaround was highly successful. The substance of the company's strategy (shown in Figure 5) was critically important in the turnaround, as was the concise strategy statement that was communicated throughout the firm. As the CEO stated:

We've finally identified what we want to be, and what's important to us. Just as importantly, we've decided what we don't want to be, and have stopped wasting time and effort. Since we started talking about BPI in terms of arenas, vehicles, differentiators, staging, and economic logic, we have been able to get our top team on the same page. A whole host of decisions have logically fallen into place in support of our comprehensive strategic agenda,

---

FIGURE 5

BPI's Strategy

Arenas
- North American, European, and Asian passenger-car and light-truck makers
- Brakes and suspension-system components
- Suspension-system integration
- Braking systems for off-road vehicles

Staging
- Stage 1: Asian JVs and alliances with suspension-component companies
- Stage 2: Aggressively design and market systems-integration offering; commence off-road vehicle market

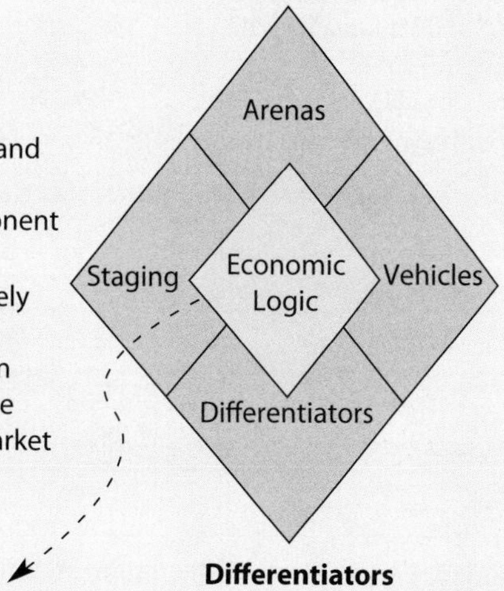

Vehicles
- Internal development of new, leading-edge braking products
- Strategic alliances with suspension-component manufacturers
- Joint ventures with brake companies in Asia

[Diamond diagram with: Arenas (top), Staging (left), Vehicles (right), Differentiators (bottom), Economic Logic (center)]

Economic Logic
- Preferred supplier status and premium pricing, due to leading-edge technology
- Preferred supplier status and premium pricing, by providing customers global solutions
- Premium pricing by providing customers integrated kits

Differentiators
- ABS design technology
- Electronic traction control technology
- Systems integration capability
- E-business capability with suppliers and customers
- Global reach

Of Strategy, Better Strategy, and No Strategy

Our purpose in this article has been elemental—to identify what constitutes a strategy. This basic agenda is worthwhile because executives and scholars have lost track of what it means to engage in the art of the general. We particularly hope to counter the recent catchall fragmentation of the strategy concept, and to remind strategists that orchestrated holism is their charge.

But we do not want to be mistaken. We don't believe that it is sufficient to simply make these five sets of choices. No—a business needs not just a strategy, but a *sound* strategy. Some strategies are clearly far better than others.

Fortunately, this is where the wealth of strategic-analysis tools that have been developed in the last 30 years becomes valuable. Such tools as industry analysis, technology cycles, value chains, and core competencies, among others, are very helpful for improving the soundness of strategies. When we compare these tools and extract their most powerful central messages, several key criteria emerge to help executives test the quality of a proposed strategy. These criteria are presented in Table 1.[11] We strongly encourage executives to apply these tests throughout the strategy-design process and especially when a proposed strategy emerges.

There might be those who wonder whether strategy isn't a concept of yesteryear, whose time has come and gone. In an era of rapid, discontinuous environmental shifts, isn't the company that attempts to specify its future just flirting with disaster? Isn't it better to be flexible, fast-on-the-feet, ready to grab opportunities when the right ones come along?

Some of the skepticism about strategy stems from basic misconceptions. First, a strategy need not be static: it can evolve and be adjusted on an ongoing basis. Unexpected opportunities need not be ignored because they are outside the strategy. Second, a strategy doesn't require a business to become rigid. Some of the best strategies for today's turbulent environment keep multiple options open and build in desirable flexibility—through alliances, outsourcing, leased assets, toehold investments in promising technologies, and numerous other means. A strategy can help to intentionally build in many forms of flexibility—if that's what is called for. Third, a strategy doesn't deal only with an unknowable, distant future.

The appropriate lifespans of business strategies have become shorter in recent years. Strategy used to be equated with 5- or 10-year horizons, but today a horizon of two to three years is often more fitting. In any event, strategy does not deal as much with preordaining the future as it does with assessing current conditions and future likelihoods, then making the best decisions possible today.

Strategy is not primarily about planning. It is about intentional, informed, and integrated choices. The noted strategic thinkers Gary Hamel and C. K. Prahalad said: "[A company's] leadership cannot be planned for, but neither can it happen without a grand and well-considered aspiration."[12] We offer the strategy diamond as a way to craft and articulate a business aspiration.

Source: D. Hambrick and W. Fredrickson, "Are You Sure You Have a Strategy?" Academy of Management Executive, 2005, Vol. 19, No. 4, © 2001, p. 51. Reprinted by permission.

Table 1

Testing the Quality of Your Strategy

Key Evaluation Criteria

1. **Does your strategy fit with what's going on in the environment?**

   Is there healthy profit potential where you're headed? Does your strategy align with the key success factors of your chosen environment?

2. **Does your strategy exploit your key resources?**

   With your particular mix of resources, does this strategy give you a good head start on competitors? Can you pursue this strategy more economically than competitors?

3. **Will your envisioned differentiators be sustainable?**

   Will competitors have difficulty matching you? If not, does your strategy explicitly include a ceaseless regimen of innovation and opportunity creation?

4. **Are the elements of your strategy internally consistent?**

   Have you made choices of arenas, vehicles, differentiators, and staging, and economic logic? Do they all fit and mutually reinforce each other?

5. **Do you have enough resources to pursue this strategy?**

   Do you have the money, managerial time, and talent, and other capabilities to do all you envision? Are you sure you're not spreading your resources too thinly, only to be left with a collection of feeble positions?

6. **Is your strategy implementable?**

   Will your key constituencies allow you to pursue this strategy? Can your organization make it through the transition? Are you and your management team able and willing to lead the required changes?

Acknowledgments

We thank the following people for helpful suggestions: Ralph Biggadike, Warren Boeker, Kathy Harrigan, Paul Ingram, Xavier Martin, Atul Nerkar, and Jaeyong Song.

ENDNOTES

1. Porter, M. E. 1980. *Competitive strategy.* New York: The Free Press, provides an in-depth discussion of the five-forces model. Hypercompetition is addressed in D'Aveni, R. A. 1994. *Hypercompetition.* New York: The Free Press. The resource-based view of the firm is discussed in Barney, J. 1991. Firm resources and sustained competitive advantage. *Journal of Management* 17: 99–120. See Brandenburger, M., & Nalebuff, R.J. 1995. The right game: Use game theory to shape strategy. *Harvard Business Review,* July-August: 57–71, for a discussion of co-opetition.

2. Bianco, A., & Moore, P. L 2001. Downfall: The inside story of the management fiasco at Xerox. *Business-Week,* 5 March 2001.

3. A widely applicable framework for strategy implementation is discussed in Galbraith, J. R., & Kazanjian, R. K. 1986. *Strategy implementation: Structure, systems and process,* 2nd ed. St. Paul West Publishing. A similar tool is offered in Hambrick, D. C., & Cannella, A. 1989. Strategy implementation as substance and selling. *The Academy of Management Executive,* 3(4): 278–285.

4. This observation has been made for years by many contributors, including Quinn, J. B. 1980. *Strategies for change: Logical incrementalism.* Homewood, IL: Richard D. Irwin Publishing: and Mintzberg, H. 1973. Strategy making in three modes. *California Management Review,* 15: 44–53.

5. Drucker, P. 1954. *The practice of management.* New York: Harper & Row.

6. Haleblian, J., & Finkelstein, S. 1999. The influence of organizational acquisition experience on acquisition performance: A behavioral learning perspective. *Administrative Science Quarterly* 44: 29–56.

7. Eisenhardt, K. M., & Brown, S. L 1998. Time pacing: Competing in markets that won't stand still. *Harvard Business Review,* March-April: 59–69, discusses "time pacing" as a component of a process of contending with rapidly changing environments.

8. The collapse of stock market valuations for Internet companies lacking in profits—or any prospect of profits—marked a return to economic reality. Profits above the firm's cost of capital are required in order to yield sustained or longer-term shareholder returns.

9. Galbraith & Kazanjian, op. cit, and Hambrick & Cannella, op. cit

10. Porter, M. E. 1996. What is strategy? *Harvard Business Review,* November-December: 61–78.

11. See Tilles, S. 1963. How to evaluate strategy. *Harvard Business Review,* July–August: 112–121, for a classic, but more limited, set of evaluative tests.

12. See Hamel, G., & Prahalad, C. K. 1993. Strategy as stretch and leverage. *Harvard Business Review,* March-April: 84–91.

READING 3.2

Bringing Human Resources Back into Strategic Planning

Robert A. Simpkins

When was the last time that you can recall senior leadership in your organization asking for the HR department's help in creating an organization's strategic plan? For that matter, when was the last time that the HR organization even knew that a new or revised strategic plan was being created?

If your HR organization is like most others, informative consultation takes place only after the plan is constructed to ensure that HR will be able to provide the right number of people, in the right place, with the right training. At this point, the contribution of the HR department will be too little, too late—too little because you lack adequate information about why personnel with specific or generalized capabilities are required and too late to meet the requirements in the necessitated time frame. Unfortunately, this sequence of events has become commonplace in too many organizations. Why is this trend occurring, why does it need to be reversed, and what can HR executives do to make sure it is reversed in their organizations?

In today's increasingly fast-paced and competitive environment, a troubling mindset has begun to unfold among senior leadership. It doesn't matter whether we are focusing on private enterprise, not-for-profit, government, or military organizations; leaders are becoming, either by choice or through carelessness, more and more isolated from the daily operational realities of the very entities they are charged with guiding. There has never been a time like the present when those given the top responsibility in organizations actually know so little about what is happening operationally on a day-by-day basis in their own organizations.

There are two primary reasons for this challenging occurrence. First, if your leaders are developed from talent within the organization and internally promoted up the ranks, it is very likely that remarkable changes have occurred since they last performed the frontline functions themselves. In other words, when they performed the operational jobs,

© 2008 Wiley Periodicals, Inc.
Published online in Wiley InterScience (www.interscience.wiley.com). DOI 10.1002/ert.20212

the world was a very different place. Technology and processes have undoubtedly changed many times, and the way that employees interact with the newer technologies has also changed. What customers value and why they prefer one organization's products or services over another organization's are also in constant shift. The competition's market position and capabilities probably changed frequently. And something in the general operational environment (global, regulatory, economic, psychological, and demographic issues, etc.) changed in a dynamic way every day. Most importantly, and something that is critical to all HR professionals, organizational associates' attitudes and opinions change more often than in the past as to whom they wish to work for and why they wish to perform a particular job.

The second reason for this senior-management disconnect occurs when leaders are brought in from outside the organization. The result is a deficiency of contextual understanding. They often lack an appreciation of what is actually taking place in the new organization and what it will take to move it toward renewed, improved, or sustained success. Don't get me wrong—organizations need an occasional infusion of new thinking from intelligent leaders who have a successful track record, albeit sometimes in very different organizations. Over and over again, however, organizations have paid huge sums of money to successful leaders who have achieved great results in other organizations, industries, or environments only to watch them become incapable of leading the new organization. This is most often due to their lack of operational familiarity and initial ignorance of the indigenous and deeply ingrained thought process behind problem solving in their new organization.

When these imported leaders realize their deficiencies, they frequently ask operational heads to provide them with archival *activity-based counts*. In other words, they want to know how many times something has been, or is being, done so they can benchmark it against some other more familiar organization's best practices, even when the bench-marked organization is in a completely different environment. The result is that these new leaders, in very short order, become overwhelmed with information when, in fact, what they really need is *performance-based measurements* that determine where the organization currently is and how fast it is moving toward a specific goal. More activity-based counting leads to more confusion. More confusion leads to more activity-based counting. In no time at all, the employees of the organization will find themselves spending a larger percentage of their time filling out count sheets than they do on the functional role for which they were hired. This is not an effective foundation for creating an actionable strategic plan.

It's time for HR, with its knowledge of which employees possess operational expertise, to take back the role as primary process managers to any strategic planning initiative. To put it in a more straightforward way, the HR department must become an organization's visibly recognized authority about the strategic-planning process and its experts in overcoming the obstacles that often prevent planning success. This does not mean the HR department should do the strategic planning for an organization; rather, it should be the conduit for subject-matter contribution and the linchpin that sustains and holds the process together.

Stepping back for a moment, let's take a look at a sadly typical strategic planning sequence of events. In most cases, an organization has an ill-defined process that cycles something like this: (1) excitement for a hot new-fad planning model; (2) deployment of a fluffy, imprecise, and foundationless strategy; (3) frustration with the slow pace and poor quality of implementation resulting from varying levels of resistance; (4) disillusionment with the whole effort; and (5) abandonment in favor of the next fad planning model. If a final strategic plan is ever rolled out, the employees often express amusement because, based on past experience:

- They don't believe the organization really means it because they've seen far too many previous examples of a lack of sustained leadership commitment.
- They know the organization doesn't have a chance of achieving it because they know the realities of the operational environment and availability of resources (people, time, tools, and money).
- They don't see how it relates to their functional work because the plan is too high level and neglects to make a connection to each person's accountability for the success of the plan.

Steps To Creating A Strategic Plan

To build their own expertise, HR leaders must be knowledgeable about the primary and elemental steps to creating a *successful, actionable, and measurable* strategic plan, not just another pretty binder that collects dust on a workplace shelf until the outer shell is needed for some other project. Successful and valued strategic planning consists of specific steps or stages. These are outlined below with a description of how HR can contribute toward

ensuring the success of any planning effort. We also take a look at real-life organizations who probably fell short in integrating HR into a specific stage, as well as look at some of the *very few* (sadly) who have recognized and integrated the strength of the HR department into their planning process.

Understand the Planning Legacy

First, there is a need to review and understand the historical *legacy* of strategies and strategic planning in an organization (even newly merged ones). Answers to the following questions can help in getting a picture of the type of planning that has been undertaken previously:

- What's been done before?
- What was the result of any previous work?
- Where were the successes and failures?
- How have employees been affected?
- What is the organizational attitude, at all levels, toward the strategic planning process and the resulting plans?

Without this knowledge, strategic planning teams will often repeat the same mistakes of their predecessors. Human resources departments have the ability to conduct this type of research at all levels of the organization. HR must proactively assure that they have access to key senior leaders, middle management, and operational personnel and be recognized by various vertical and horizontal departments as an entity that can effectively and efficiently gather pertinent information. In other words, HR must gain knowledge of, and become skilled at, strategic planning's best practices and drive the acceptance of their knowledge across the organization—not when senior leaders decide to create a new strategy, but prior to any initiative.

Going back a few years, consider the merger (or acquisition) of America Online and Time Warner. AOL was created during the earliest upswing in the new world of the Internet. Dynamic and innovative, they represented the extremely rapid growth in the need for information management and manipulation. Their employees were young, flexible, and had a whole lot of new ideas about a newly emerging marketplace. Time Warner, itself a product of many, many mergers and acquisitions, represented the old-line diversified media powerhouse. Bureaucratic and rigidly structured, their growth was starting to slow down as they searched for new markets. Their employees were more middle and older age, conservative, and searching for new ideas. Although it would be easy to blame one or the other for the lack of the initial harmonious integration, I suspect the fault lies with both. In AOL's case, the planning environment was populated with individuals who had no experience with setbacks and challenges and knew only rapid growth with no end in sight. In Time Warner's case, strategic planning was done by a high-level team reporting to senior leadership. Do you think the legacy of strategic planning would be very different in each firm? A proactive, combined HR team could have evaluated and adjusted for these legacy differences.

Create a Diverse Planning Team

Next is *team formation*—the formation of an intelligent strategic-planning team. This includes two critical issues: diversity of thought and diversity of skills. Diversity should encompass, as any HR manager knows, more than just gender and race. Although these two areas are very important, diversity regarding age, experience, knowledge, skills, regionalism, culture, education, and personality should also be valued. Each of these categories, with all their subsets, brings varying perceptions and understanding of realities and events to the planning table. If an organization doesn't recognize the value of diversity, and incorporate it into the strategic planning team, there is little likelihood of success. Skill requirements are also critically important to planning success. In addition to having knowledge about a particular organizational process or function, a team must be formed with a variety of strategic-planning-required skills that include, but should not be limited to, team management, project management, interviewing, critical analysis, collaboration, negotiations, time management, scenario or simulation planning, trend analysis, market analysis, perspective analysis, supply-chain analysis, research, value-proposition analysis, competitive analysis, finance and accounting, regulatory research and compliance, and communications (oral and written). It's not that everyone on the team must possess all these skills, but the capability must be present somewhere on the strategic planning team. Note that if you are a global or globalizing organization you should include team members who have a strong understanding of civilizations, values, and cultures.

It would be wrong to assemble a strategic planning team from only one hierarchal level in your organization. In my most recent book, *Not Another Pretty Binder: Strategic Planning That Actually Works* (HRD Press, 2008), I described three typical scenarios often found in team formation:

1. *The overpowered team.* This consists only of senior leaders and is often found assembling a plan behind some secretive closed doors. The plan won't work because it is, typically, too vague and rests heavily on only long-term visionary thinking.
2. *The underpowered team.* Here, the team consists of only middle or lower management. The plan will come out too tactical and short-term in its perspective, and so it will likely meet with resistance from senior leaders.
3. *The tow-truck team.* In this case, the charter to develop a strategic plan is given to individuals who don't have a lot to do because they are nearing retirement or in transition between assignments. The resulting strategic plan will never work because the developers of the plan have little or no vested interest in its outcome because they won't be around to see the consequences of its full deployment.

Here again, the HR department is the key to a successful strategic-planning process. HR is not only the "owner" of the physical bodies within the organization, but also the coordinator of intellectual details that knows exactly where a specific knowledge or functional expertise resides. Proper selection and usage of these aptitudes in the planning process can best be managed by personnel professionals. HR knows each employee's capabilities at the point of being hired, what new skills the employee acquired through training and practice, and his or her success at applying the skills while on the job.

During the next steps in the strategic-planning process, operational expertise will be required to interpret and clarify data from *all* parts of the organization. Members from the law department can provide critical information about legal, regulatory, and contractual issues. Production personnel can provide knowledge about the realities of the daily operational requirements. Marketing can provide intelligence about changes in the targeted markets and competition. Sales and the customer service representatives can provide intimate knowledge about customer values. Members of the finance department can provide important details about cash flow and availability. Quality staff and research can also bring great expertise to the planning process. There is no part of your organization that can't provide some intelligence to a strategic plan. Remember, though, as you select contributors to the planning team, they must have enthusiasm, time, and knowledge to be a part of any strategic planning effort.

A great example of this step would be Southwest Airlines, probably the only airline making a profit during these difficult times. Of course, as all its publicity correctly states, Southwest likes to make sure its employees have fun at work. But, when it comes to planning, Southwest's approach can best be summed up by Colleen C. Barret, retiring president of the airline and the one primarily responsible for employee and customer satisfaction over her rise from secretary to head of the airline. A close partner to Southwest's legendary founder, Herb Kelleher, she once said "When it comes to getting things done, we need fewer architects and more bricklayers."

Align Planning with Leadership Goals

The next step in strategic planning is leadership *alignment*. What is the direction of the organization, as envisioned by the organization's highest-level leadership, and what are their personally important issues? In this stage, a comprehensive examination must be made of leadership's vision and mission statements, plus any other visionary thoughts they might have. If the eventual strategic plan does not integrate and support their directional perceptions, the plan will be treated as a failure and tossed aside.

HR, once again, must set the stage for access to the senior leaders and help facilitate effective and well-structured interviewing sessions that will uncover their thinking. It should be noted, though, that HR should not be the only department responsible for actually conducting the interviews with senior leaders. Additional selected team members, with their specific operational expertise, should be in on the interviews to help bring clarity to statements and dialogues.

I have had the privilege of working for several years with the U.S. Army National Guard in almost every state and territory. The deliverable was to create a strategic plan. Sadly, in most states and territories, there was an absence of visionary communications from the Office of The Adjutant General (TAG; the top person in each state and territory). The greatest successes, though, came from those where the TAG was willing (and able) to convey a clear understanding to the team about the short, intermediate, and long-term vision of the specific Guard. The incentive for doing so was always based on the HR officer clearly conveying the rationale and benefits for doing so to the most senior leadership.

Analyze Current Realities

Moving on through the strategic planning process, it would now be time to *analyze the organizational realities*. The planning team is in possession of the legacy experiences to know what has and hasn't worked in the past, a full and diverse team, and an understanding of the senior leader's perceptions. The planning team must compare the organization's history with its current status and determine the aspects of the organization and its environment that can be leveraged to move it forward and support the visionary and mission direction, as well as identify the aspects that will present obstacles and pitfalls to moving forward. This is typically done with the SWOT process (which analyzes strengths, weaknesses, opportunities, and threats). This is a great tool for planning teams, where every relevant piece of information (hard and soft) is categorized into one of four boxes. Identifying the organization's internal strengths and weaknesses will determine the organization's ability to achieve its shorter-term purpose and mission. Determining the organization's future external opportunities and threats will clarify the thinking behind the longer-term vision and suggest what could prevent the company from achieving it. To complete a SWOT analysis with any degree of accuracy, specific functional expertise must come from those who know what the organizational reality is at the current time, where it's been, and what is the trend.

The HR department is very essential to this stage. HR managers help select the subject-matter experts who can best determine the realities. Although they may not have enterprisewide knowledge of the organization, they know their specific operation or processes better than others. Also, HR helps coordinate with the managers of the experts the time

necessary to participate on the planning, conduct the research, and make a successful contribution to the initiative, avoiding departmental distractions that can undermine team efforts. In addition, by being part of the team, HR professionals can provide expertise about laws and regulations affecting existing and potential employees, plus any information gleaned from employee surveys. Finally, HR professionals can help structure, coordinate, align, and distribute any and all communications about the strategic plan (with senior leadership approval, of course) before initiative development, during plan creation, and after the rollout.

If you want to emulate an organization, look to Nordstrom, the high-end department store. When its HR leader was asked how the company trained employees to be so good, he said it didn't train them. Nordstrom hired the best people and let them develop their own ideas about providing the best customer service.

Develop Alternative Performance Options

Once the realities of the organization are clear, to the point, and measurable, the planning team must work on *alternative development options*—to determine how to fix current performance-improvement problems and address future transformational issues. Any good strategy planning team knows that there is always more than one way to fix a problem, so they evaluate multiple solutions. They do this by determining where the organization needs to be changed, the priorities of change, and what requirements are needed to achieve the desired change. Weighing these options will establish prioritized action plans.

This may be, in addition to the team-building activity, one of the most important stages for HR involvement. Human resources is the *only* department that can determine, with any degree of accuracy, what resources (people, time, tools, and money) realistically exist in the current organization, which ones can be acquired from outside the organization, and which ones can be redistributed around the organization to achieve any alternative options. Until this knowledge is applied to the strategic planning process, alternative solutions have a potential for being meaningless.

It always amazes me when I hear that an organization has lost its direction because of changes in reality. I was once with a group from NASA, the famed governmental space organization, and asked them how their customers (the U.S. taxpayers) viewed NASA's value. They told me "wonderful—they think we are one of America's greatest assets." I asked them how they knew that, and they answered that they had conducted a survey and that was the answer that those over 40 years of age gave. I asked them about the responses from those under 40, and they told me that they generally considered NASA to be inconsequential. I asked them whether that answer bothered them, and they said it didn't "because

NASA's budget came from Congress and they were all over 40!" These were rocket scientists, and yet they couldn't see the need for assessing alternative realities that would inevitably arrive down the road when those under 40 grow older and become the budget makers for Congress.

Measure Progress

The next stage of strategic planning is to construct a *scorecard* that clearly identifies specific improvement actions that are being taken to measure progress and communicate success. There's been a lot of talk in the popular media about a balanced scorecard, but, if the previous stage was done correctly, organizational priorities will actually be given different weights from less important activities.

The reality is that strategic plans will end up unbalanced, and that's OK. Any organization will always be constrained by availability of resources, and therefore the deployment of these resources will, by necessity, be in areas that will achieve the greatest organizational improvement.

The recommendation for HR's involvement in this stage is, first, to make sure that the scorecard language and the associated measurements are clear and understandable to all personnel in all departments at all levels. If this doesn't occur and individuals in the organization don't recognize the language or how it addresses their specific needs, the plan will be written off as "fluff." Also, HR, once again, needs to make sure there are the necessary human resources to complete whatever actions have been designed.

Over and over again, I've been called into an organization because the senior leadership can't figure out why their strategic plan is not being implemented well or not at all. Upon an exhaustive analysis, it becomes clear the vision is bigger than the realities. Think of it like this: have you ever tried to carry more bags of groceries than your arms could hold? The result is disaster.

Once the strategic planning team has a solid scorecard based on the comparative analysis between the vision/mission/purpose and the organizational realities, it will be able to measure near-term and long-term performance. The scorecard will prescribe some immediate performance-improvement activities, as well as long-term transformational activities.

It is also important at this juncture to assign a person to be accountable for each planned action, including assuring that the action is being performed and progress toward a goal is being measured, recognizing any deviations from the plan, and reporting progress back to the planning team. HR departments help facilitate this aspect of planning by assuring that those individuals selected to manage the action actually understand their *accountability* and have the capability to sustain and complete the actions. HR can also help by making sure that all the strategic-initiative timelines are realistic, considering the requirements of the regular production schedule.

Perhaps an example, and one that was very close to me personally, was when the original AT&T bought NCR in a very hostile takeover. The visionary rationale for the acquisition was sound—NCR had an international presence and AT&T did not. If AT&T was to globalize, something they'd been wanting to do since the spin-off of ITT in 1958, then they needed someone with experience and infrastructure. There were so many things that went wrong with this acquisition that it's hard to know where to start. But one of the most visible was that no existing strategic business unit's president had the slightest idea of how to integrate NCR into a complementary operational model. No one knew what their accountability was for making the merger work.

Deploy the Strategic Plan

One of the final steps in strategic planning is to *deploy*, or roll out, the new or revised strategy. Although there are several components to this activity, perhaps the most important is to develop effective communication models that make sure enthusiasm and positive attitudes are maintained. Nothing succeeds like success, and it's important that the team demonstrate, as quickly as possible, improvement, even if it is only for a small component of the plan.

HR, once again, must play a visible role in the creation and distribution of all communications related to a strategic plan. The HR team must prepare an information-sharing plan that recognizes the variations in the informational needs of different departments and how best to deliver information to them. Once a unique model is in place, HR must assure clarity by testing the understanding of the communicated message and make proper and continuous adjustments to improve it. Remember, it's not what's said but what people hear that drives employee opinion.

Think about how often you have heard a senior leader in business or government say he or she had been misquoted. Organizations abhor an absence of communications. If real knowledge isn't available, rumors will quickly fill in the empty spaces. When Airbus, a major competitor to Boeing, began to have some problems with development of new planes, the communications became a catastrophe. Unions, suppliers, financial partners, investment analysts, and customers began to question their strategic plan. Only after a change of leadership resulting in improved communications did the organization get back to doing what it does so well—producing aircraft.

Develop Contingency Plans

Although we consider this the final step, the reality is that strategic planning is a continuous process. *Contingency plans* help sustain the process. It's very easy for a strategic plan to melt away when the urgent replaces the important. Remember the old, but true, saying: "What can go wrong will go wrong." For every short- and long-term improvement action shown on the strategy scorecard, a team must work proactively to develop a contingency plan—alternative approaches to achieving the goal if realities change and the developed action is no longer feasible. If team members wait for the engine to derail before they consider how to get the train back on the track, precious time will be lost that will, most likely, negatively affect the perception and results of the strategy.

Human resource team members must make a major contribution to this stage by assuring that a contingency plan is created for every action, by helping determine the true cause-and-effect relationship for any deviations or anomalies in the measured progress or results, and by preparing team members to approach any problems with critical-thinking capabilities.

This past summer, as the home-mortgage crisis reached a critical point, the White House stated that it had gathered a group of financial minds together to come up with a contingency plan for the mortgage-landing institutions of Fannie Mae and Freddie Mac if they failed. Having worked several years ago with both of these fine institutions, I know how valuable they are to our country. The only problem was that the White House team was not working on a contingency plan, but a disaster-recovery plan. Contingency plans must be done during the development of a strategic plan and not "when the train falls off the track." I know a lot of people at the two firms, and I know they know the difference!

As this strategic-planning process demonstrates, HR can, and must, play a proactive and premeditated role in the development of the planning process. From the legacy to the contingency, HR professionals are uniquely vital to the success of each stage, as well as the overall strategy attainment. If an organization needs outside assistance, it should be from those who recognize the intricacies of strategic planning and the role that HR can play in it. Educate your senior leadership early about your contributing value and become the driver of strategic change in your organization.

Source: Robert A. Simpkins, © 2008 Wiley Periodicals, Inc.

CHAPTER 4

The Evolving/Strategic Role of Human Resource Management

LEARNING OBJECTIVES

- Understand the fundamental differences between traditional and strategic human resource
- Explain why some organizations still fail to deliver human resource strategically
- Describe the outcomes and benefits of strategic human resource
- Understand how different company strategies might result in the need for human resource to assume different primary roles

Strategic HR at Netflix

Online movie rental subscription service Netflix utilizes a very nontraditional approach to human resource (HR) management. During the early years of its launch, senior management at Netflix realized that the talent they sought had a multitude of employment opportunities and that Netflix had to offer something distinctive to its recruits and employees if the company were to prosper. Hence, they sought to develop a company culture that attracted individuals who identified with and understood the business, sought a flexible working environment, and wanted to work with other high-performing peers.

Netflix headquarters, unlike that of other technology companies, requires no employee identification badges, has no security checkpoints, and encourages employees to come and go as they please. Participation in meetings is often virtual, at the discretion of the employee, from employee homes, coffee shops, or even employee cars. The CEO himself has no office at headquarters. Netflix has no policy regarding vacation or means by which vacation is "counted"; rather, employees decide how much vacation or other leave to take and when it will be taken. This is a reflection of the company philosophy of focusing on what people get done rather than the amount of time spent working and that creativity, which benefits the employer, is often stimulated outside of the workplace and regular work hours. Similarly, employees have no limits on expense accounts related to travel or entertainment but rather use their own judgment as part of "acting in Netflix's best interests."

The type of creative employee Netflix seeks thrives on freedom and is guided by Netflix's definition of success: continued growth in revenue, profits, and reputation. Netflix provides no formal training to employees and encourages employees to self-manage their own career development. Similarly, the company provides no annual bonuses or long-term incentives but pays highly competitive salaries, which are adjusted annually on an individual basis. Salary may be taken in cash or a combination of cash and company stock options, which vest immediately. Evidence of whether or not this approach works for Netflix is reflected in the fact that from 2009 to 2011 both subscriptions and revenues doubled to 26 million and $3.2 billion, respectively.[1]

The role of HR management in organizations has been evolving dramatically in recent years. The days of HR as the "personnel department"—performing recordkeeping, paper pushing, file maintenance, and other largely clerical functions—are over. Any organization that continues to utilize its HR function solely to perform these administrative duties does not understand the contributions that HR can make to an organization's performance. In the most financially successful organizations, HR is increasingly being seen as a critical strategic partner and assuming far-reaching and transformational roles and responsibilities.

Taking a strategic approach to HR management involves abandoning the mindset and practices of "personnel management" and focusing more on strategic issues than operational issues. Strategic HR management involves making the function of managing people the most important priority in the organization and integrating all HR programs and policies within the framework of a company's strategy. Strategic HR management realizes that people make or break an organization because all decisions made regarding finance, marketing, operations, or technology are made by an organization's people.

Strategic HR management involves the *development of a consistent, aligned collection of practices, programs, and policies to facilitate the achievement of the organization's strategic objectives*. It considers the implications of corporate strategy for all HR systems within an organization by translating company objectives into specific people management systems. The specific approach and process utilized will vary from organization to organization, but the key concept is consistent; essentially all HR programs and policies are integrated within a larger framework facilitating, in general, the organization's mission and, specifically, its objectives.

Probably, the single-most important caveat of strategic HR management is that there is no one best way to manage people in any given organization. Even within a given industry, HR practices can vary extensively from one organization to another, as seen in Reading 4.1, "Distinctive Human Resources Are Firms' Core Competencies," and in any organization, a critical prerequisite for success is people management systems that clearly support the organization's mission and strategy.

Establishing a strong HR strategy that is clearly linked to the organization's strategy is not enough. HR strategy needs to be communicated, practiced, and—perhaps most important—spelled out and written down. A recent study by global consulting firm Pricewaterhouse Coopers found that those organizations with a written HR strategy tend to be more profitable than those without one.[2] It appears that writing down an organization's HR strategy facilitates the process of involvement and buy-in on the parts of both senior executives and other employees. The study found that organizations with a specific written HR strategy had revenues per employee that are 35 percent higher than organizations without a written strategy and that those organizations with a written strategy had 12 percent less employee absenteeism and lower turnover.[3]

Strategic HR at General Electric

With revenues exceeding $100 billion annually, General Electric (GE) operates in more than 100 countries, employing more than 290,000 people, including 155,000 in the United States. A key component to GE's success is the belief that the HR function is a critical factor in driving its performance, worldwide. The importance of GE's people to the attainment of its corporate objectives is echoed at even the highest levels of the organization. Former GE CEO Jack Welch, in his annual letter to shareholders, refers to GE as "evolving to a company of A' products and A' services delivered by A' players."

Susan Peters, vice president of HR at GE Appliances, has noted that at GE, the HR function is "truly a value-added business partner who is a fully participating member of the business decision making team." At GE, HR executives are expected to have a keen understanding of the factors that are critical to the success of the business, including finance, marketing, and operations issues. Top management feels that it would otherwise not be possible to develop HR programs and policies that support business goals.

To support this need, newly hired HR professionals attend a comprehensive Human Resources Leadership Program (HRLP), designed to allow them to assume this critical role as a strategic partner. Those who enroll in the HRLP commit to an extensive period of training, conducted over a two-year period. During this time, they develop skills through a combination of hands-on rotational assignments and training seminars. These assignments include working both in HR as well as in non-HR operating divisions to allow enrollees to develop an understanding of the numerous factors that impact the success of the individual business units. In addition to recruiting talent from top business schools across the country, GE also recruits internally from other functions within GE. These individuals receive specialized training in HR that augments the operating experience they have within GE. In both cases, GE ensures that its HR professionals have technical HR knowledge as well as a keen understanding of the business in which they work to allow them to meet expectations and fully contribute to their business as a true strategic partner?[4]

Strategic HR Versus Traditional HR

Strategic HR can be contrasted to the more traditional administrative focus of HR through an examination of four different roles that HR can play in an organization. Ulrich developed a framework, presented in Exhibit 4.1, which proposes an entirely new role and agenda for HR that focuses less on traditional functional activities, such as compensation and staffing, and more on outcomes.[5] In this scenario, HR would be defined not by what it does but rather by what it delivers. Ideally, HR should deliver results that enrich the organization's value to its customers, its investors, and its employees. This can be accomplished through four roles: by HR becoming (1) a partner with senior and line managers in strategy execution; (2) an expert in the way that work is organized and executed; (3) a champion for employees, working to increase employee contribution and commitment to the organization; and (4) an agent of continuous transformation who shapes processes and culture to improve an organization's capacity for change.

EXHIBIT 4.1

Possible Roles Assumed by the HR Function

Strategic Focus

Strategic Partner   Change Agent

Systems   People

Administrative Expert   Employee Champion

Operational Focus

© Cengage Learning

The first role involves becoming a partner in strategy execution. Here, HR is held responsible for the organizational architecture or structure. HR would then conduct an organizational audit to help managers identify those components that need to be changed to facilitate strategy execution. HR should then identify methods for renovating the parts of the organizational architecture that need it. Finally, HR would take stock of its own work and set clear priorities to ensure delivery of results. These activities require HR executives to acquire new skills and capabilities to allow HR to add value for the executive team with confidence.

For decades, HR professionals have fulfilled an administrative function within their organizations. In the administrative expert role, these individuals should shed their image of rule-making police while ensuring that the required routine work still gets done effectively and efficiently. This requires improving or "rethinking" a number of traditional HR functions, such as benefits and selection, which now can be automated by using technology and therefore be more cost-efficient. Such streamlining of functions would help HR professionals become strategic partners in their organizations and enhance their credibility.

An organization cannot thrive unless its employees are committed to and fully engaged in the organization and their jobs. In the new role of employee champion, HR professionals are held accountable for ensuring that employees are fully engaged in and committed to the organization. This involves, in part, partnering with line management to enhance employee morale and training line managers to recognize—and avoid—the causes of low morale, such as unclear goals, unfocused priorities, and ambiguous performance management. It also involves acting as an advocate for employees, representing them and being their voice with senior management, particularly on decisions that impact them directly.

The pace of change experienced by organizations today can be dizzying. As a change agent, HR has to be able to build the organization's capacity to embrace and capitalize on new situations, ensuring that change initiatives are defined, developed, and delivered in a timely manner. HR also needs to help the organization plan for and overcome any resistance to change that might present itself. Particularly challenging are any efforts to alter the organization's culture.

HR Roles at Mercantile Bank

One organization that has effectively redesigned its HR function to assume all four roles is Mercantile Bank. Headquartered in St. Louis, Missouri, Mercantile Bank is a multibank holding company, with $131 billion in assets and more than 10,000 employees. The bank strategically redesigned its HR function during the 1990s, when it went through more than 39 mergers and acquisitions. As part of this process, Mercantile's HR function moved beyond traditional recordkeeping and compliance to become more strategic in nature. This transformation happened through streamlining work processes, eliminating unnecessary activities, reevaluating technology, and outsourcing nonstrategic functions. Furthermore, some retained HR functions remain centralized at headquarters; others are deployed to operating divisions. Consequently, Mercantile's HR function is able to assume the roles of strategic partner, change agent, administrative expert, and employee champion simultaneously.[6]

A number of other models have been developed relative to the portfolio of roles that HR can and/or should play in becoming a strategic partner in the knowledge-based economy. Lengnick-Hall and Lengnick-Hall found that for HR to build strategic credibility, new roles needed to be assumed that expanded both the methods and processes traditionally used in HR.[7] These roles include human capital steward, knowledge facilitator, relationship builder, and rapid deployment specialist, as illustrated in Exhibit 4.2.

The human capital steward role involves the creation of an environment and culture in which employees voluntarily want to contribute their skills, ideas, and energy. This is based on the premise that unlike raw materials, plant, and equipment, human capital is not "owned" by the organization; it can move freely from organization to organization at the employee's whim.

EXHIBIT   4.2

HR Roles in a Knowledge-Based Economy

- Human capital steward
- Knowledge facilitator
- Relationship builder
- Rapid deployment specialist

© Cengage Learning

A competitive advantage can be maintained only when the best employees are recruited, duly motivated, and retained.

The knowledge facilitator role involves the procurement of the necessary employee knowledge and skill sets that allow information to be acquired, developed, and disseminated, providing a competitive advantage. This process can succeed only as part of a strategically designed employee development plan, whereby employees teach and learn from each other and sharing knowledge is valued and rewarded.

The relationship builder role involves the development of structure, work practices, and organizational culture that allow individuals to work together, across departments and functions. To ensure competitiveness, networks need to be developed that focus on the strategic objectives of the organization and how synergies and teamwork that lead to outstanding performance are valued and rewarded.

The rapid deployment specialist role involves the creation of an organization structure and HR systems that are fluid and adaptable to rapid change in response to external opportunities and threats. The global, knowledge-based economy changes quickly and frequently, and success in such an environment mandates flexibility and a culture that embraces change.

In addition to these models, a study sponsored by the Society for Human Resource Management (SHRM) and the Global Consulting Alliance found that HR's success as a true strategic business partner was dependent on five specific competencies being displayed by HR,[8] as illustrated in Exhibit 4.3. These competencies are radically different from those required in the past, when HR played a more administrative role. The first—strategic contribution—requires the development of strategy, connecting organizations to external constituents, and implementing systems that align employee performance with company strategy. The second—business knowledge—involves understanding the nuts and bolts of the organization's operations and leveraging this knowledge into results. The third—personal credibility—requires that measurable value be demonstrated in programs and policies implemented. The fourth—HR delivery—involves serving internal customers through effective and efficient

EXHIBIT   4.3

SHRM Critical HR Competencies

- Strategic contribution
- Business knowledge
- Personal credibility
- HR delivery
- HR technology

© Cengage Learning

programs related to staffing, performance management, and employee development. The fifth—HR technology—involves using technology to improve the organization's management of its people.

Although the SHRM study identifies a set of competencies that all HR executives will need, others conclude that HR roles may need to become more highly specialized. One set of roles identifies five competencies that might easily become areas of specialization.[8] The first role is "chief financial officer" for HR, an individual who is an expert at metrics and financial analysis and can argue the cost-effectiveness of various HR programs. The second role is "internal consultant," an individual who trains and empowers line managers to assume much of the day-to-day responsibility for managing employees and understanding the legal aspects of the employment relationship. The third role is "talent manager," an individual who focuses on finding, developing, and retaining the optimal mix of employees to facilitate the organization's strategic objectives. The fourth role is "vendor manager," an individual who determines which functions can be better handled internally or externally and assumes the responsibility for sourcing and selecting vendors as well as managing vendor relations. The fifth role is "self-service manager," an individual who oversees the technology applications of HR management, including all aspects of e-HR.

Strategic HR at Google

Internet products and services provider Google has developed its HR function, known as "People Operations" around a "three-thirds" model whereby three different complimentary teams work to staff the rapidly growing organization, which competes for talent in a very competitive environment. Approximately one-third of the People Operations team have backgrounds in HR, including specialized expertise in employment law and compensation and benefits. This group identifies trends and issues regarding HR, allowing Google to respond in a proactive manner.

Another third have little to no HR background and were recruited from strategic consulting firms or from Google operating divisions, such as engineering and sales. This group is embedded within business units and contributes knowledge and problem-solving skills regarding the macro perspective of the organization which are incorporated into HR-related programs and solutions. The final third is a workforce analytics team that consists of individuals who hold advanced degrees in statistics, finance, and organizational psychology. They determine appropriate metrics to allow Google to remain competitive in its search for talent, including appropriate compensation, interview processes, and factors that relate to employee retention.

Google's rapid growth rate requires an accelerated rate of professional staff development, and most of its People Operations staff participate in a yearlong "base camp" training that combines HR specialist training with an MBA-like program in which participants work on Internet consulting projects aimed at solving business problems.[9]

So far, our discussion has focused on roles that HR needs to assume and competencies that need to be demonstrated to ensure that HR be seen as a true strategic partner as well as to facilitate high performance. This discussion has ignored the fact that different organizations engage in different types of employment in pursuing their strategies. To better understand these employment models, a system was developed by Lepak and Snell that identifies four different employment models and examines the types of HR systems required by each.[10]

Lepak and Snell first analyzed the characteristics of human capital by using two dimensions. The first is its *strategic value,* or the extent of its potential to improve efficiency and effectiveness, exploit market opportunities, and/or neutralize potential threats. The authors found that as the strategic value of human capital increased, the greater the likelihood that the organization would employ it internally rather than externally. The second is its *uniqueness,* or the degree to which it is specialized and not widely available. The authors found that the more unique an organization's human capital, the greater potential source of competitive advantage it would provide. These two dimensions form the matrix, presented in Exhibit 4.4, which identifies the four types of employment modes.

Quadrant 1 illustrates knowledge-based employment, human capital that is unique and has high strategic value to the organization. This type of employment requires *commitment-based* HR management. Commitment-based HR involves heavy investment in training and development, employee autonomy and participation, employment security, and compensation systems that are long term (i.e., stock options) and knowledge based.

Quadrant 2 illustrates job-based employment, human capital that has limited uniqueness but is of high strategic value to the organization. This type of employment requires *productivity-based* HR management. Less investment will be made in employees, and the organization will seek to acquire individuals with the requisite skills rather than provide training in skills that are generic. Shorter time frames will be established for performance and rewards, and jobs will be more standardized.

Quadrant 3 illustrates contractual employment, human capital that is neither unique nor of strategic value to the organization. This type of employment requires *compliance-based* HR management. Structure and direction would be provided for employees and systems established to ensure that employees comply with rules, regulations, and procedures. Workers would receive little discretion, and any training, performance management, and compensation would be based on ensuring compliance with the set work structures.

Quadrant 4 illustrates alliance/partnership employment, human capital that is unique but of limited strategic value to the organization. This type of employment requires *collaborative-based* HR management. Much of the work would be outsourced to an outside vendor based on the sharing of information and establishment of trust. The organization would select alliance partners who are committed to the relationship as well as the organization's success. Performance standards and incentives would be established that mutually benefit both partners.

EXHIBIT 4.4

Lepak and Snell's Employment Models

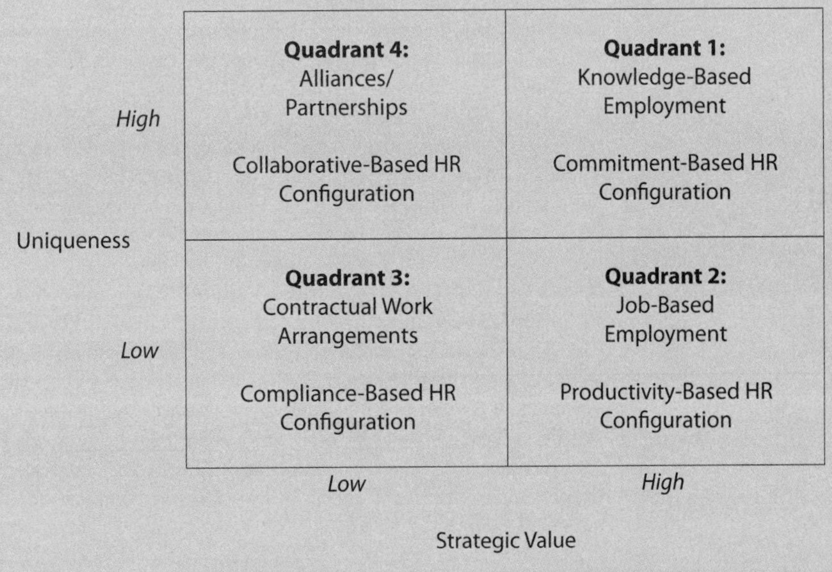

Uniqueness		
High	**Quadrant 4:** Alliances/ Partnerships Collaborative-Based HR Configuration	**Quadrant 1:** Knowledge-Based Employment Commitment-Based HR Configuration
Low	**Quadrant 3:** Contractual Work Arrangements Compliance-Based HR Configuration	**Quadrant 2:** Job-Based Employment Productivity-Based HR Configuration
	Low	*High*

Strategic Value

© Cengage Learning

Strategic HR Management at Southwest Airlines

Southwest Airlines (SWA) was one of the most successful airline companies in the 1990s. Throughout the decade, it was the only major domestic airline to turn a profit, and it consistently outperformed its competitors in customer service. A key factor in the success of SWA has been its unique corporate culture and the HR management practices that have been developed as part of this culture. These practices are integrated with each other and directly developed under founding CEO Herb Kelliher and maintained as part of Southwest's competitive strategy of delivering both low costs and superior service. These HR practices create shareholder value through employees via low turnover and high productivity and allow employees to experience significant job satisfaction.

Southwest's success centers around a "value cycle": Southwest first creates value through its HR practices for employees; this value is then converted, in part, to customer value via the design of specific operating processes and then captured through the provision of low costs and superior service relative to competitors. This cycle of creating, converting, and capturing value is unique among not only airlines but labor-intensive organizations in general. Other airlines have traditionally competed by creating barriers to entry via the development of hub-and-spoke networks and by sophisticated customer segmentation and information processing via computer reservation systems.

Southwest sees its competition not as other airlines but rather the automobile. Most of its flights are "short-haul" (less than 90 minutes) and involve quick turnaround of planes at the gate and the use of less-congested airports. The company also restricts its growth relative to the rate at which it can hire and train new employees who fit with the company culture.

Southwest practices an alternative strategy called value analysis. Here, a value chain is created for the buyer, firm, and supplier. SWA does this by increasing its passengers' willingness to pay, decreasing the price passengers are charged, decreasing its own costs, and reducing employees' opportunity cost. SWA increases its passengers' willingness to pay by providing a higher level of service than its competitors, offering more frequent departures, and amusing its passengers, which makes the end of a long workday more entertaining. SWA also attempts to offer the lowest airline fare in a specific market. This allows SWA to differentiate itself from competitors that offer a relatively generic service.

Personnel is one of the most significant costs an airline incurs. At SWA, however, employees are more productive than at other major airlines. Most SWA employees are directly involved in moving passengers from departure to destination as gate agents, ramp agents, baggage handlers, flight attendants, or pilots. The result? An average airplane takes 45 minutes to turnaround: SWA averages only 17 minutes.

SWA can turn around its aircraft in 17 minutes for three reasons. First, it uses standardized aircraft—737s only. Second, no meals are provided on flights, enhancing efficiency and reducing costs. Finally, the airline has designed its work systems to allow cross-functional coordination by all its employees. From the moment an SWA flight touches down until the minute it clears the gate, every member of the flight and ground crews does everything necessary to get the next flight segment out on time.

Southwest has a culture that stresses "LUV" and "FUN." "LUV" refers to one of the company's core values, involving respect for individuality and a genuine concern for others. "FUN" refers to the company's philosophy of employees enjoying themselves at work and creating an atmosphere that allows customers to also have fun. FUN and LUV are critical elements of SWA's culture and are embedded in the hiring process, with prospective employees being asked to describe their most embarrassing moment. FUN and LUV are also critical components of SWA's compensation system. Actual salaries are at the industry average, but most employees consider SWA's work environment to be a form of nonmonetary compensation.

SWA uses a variety of HR practices to create its unique labor force. Starting with a rigorous selection process, employees are paid an average compensation, combined with significant nonmonetary awards. Employees treat one another well, and there is a focus on ongoing training and development. Employees' are also constantly solicited. The nurturing, ongoing development of the organizational culture is critical to Southwest's competitive advantage.[11]

Strategic HR differs radically from traditional HR in a number of ways, as illustrated in Exhibit 4.5. In a traditional approach to HR, the main responsibility for people management programs rests with staff specialists in the corporate HR division. A strategic approach places the responsibility for managing people with the individuals most in contact with them: their respective line managers. In essence, strategic HR would argue that any individual in an organization who has responsibility for people is an HR manager, regardless of the technical area in which he or she works.

Traditional HR focuses its activities on employee relations, ensuring that employees are motivated and productive and that the organization is in compliance with all necessary employment laws, as illustrated in the operational quadrants in Exhibit 4.1 on page 151. A strategic approach shifts the focus to partnerships with internal and external constituent groups. Employees are only one constituency that needs to be considered. The focus on managing people is more systemic, with an understanding of the myriad factors that impact employees and the organization and how to manage multiple relationships to ensure satisfaction at all levels of the organization. Critical partners in the process include employees, customers, stockholders/owners, regulatory agencies, and public interest groups.

Traditional HR assumes a role of handling transactions as they arise. These may involve compliance with changing laws, rectifying problems between supervisors and subordinates, recruiting and screening applicants for current needs, and basically responding to events after they happen. Strategic HR is much more transformational and realizes that the success of any initiatives for growth, adaptation, or change within the organization depend on the employees who utilize any changes in technology or produce any changes in the organization's product or service. HR therefore plays more of a transformational role in assisting the organization in identifying and meeting

EXHIBIT 4.5

Traditional HR Versus Strategic HR

	Traditional HR	**Strategic HR**
Responsibility for HR	Staff specialists	Line managers
Focus	Employee relations	Partnerships with internal and external customers
Role of HR	Transactional change follower and respondent	Transformational change leader and initiator
Initiatives	Slow, reactive, fragmented	Fast, proactive, integrated
Time horizon	Short term	Short, medium, long (as necessary)
Control	Bureaucratic—roles, policies, procedures	Organic—flexible, whatever is necessary to succeed
Job design	Tight division of labor, independence, specialization	Broad, flexible, cross-training, teams
Key investments	Capital, products	People, knowledge
Accountability	Cost center	Investment center

© Cengage Learning

the larger challenges it faces in its external environment by ensuring that the internal mechanisms that facilitate change are in place.

Similarly, any initiatives for change coming from traditional HR are usually slow and fragmented, piecemeal, and not integrated with larger concerns. Strategic HR is more proactive and systemic in change initiatives. Rectifying a specific employee discipline problem or moving to a new sales commission system are examples of the former approach. Strategic HR is flexible enough to consider the various time frames (short, medium, and/or long-run) as necessary to facilitate the development of programs and policies that address the critical strategic challenges being faced by the organization. At the same time, these strategically conceived initiatives must be developed and implemented in concert with other HR systems.

As an example, the HR systems at Mercantile Bank were not developed independent of each other. As the HR function evolved with subsequent mergers and acquisitions, HR initiatives were developed in tandem with other HR programs and policies. For example, job analysis procedures developed competencies that formed the basis for recruiting, testing, performance feedback, and compensation programs. The performance feedback program was developed in tandem with a succession planning program and incentive programs for high performers. These types of integrated initiatives are one of the principal differences between traditional and strategic HR management.

The traditional approach to HR manifests itself in bureaucratic control through rules, procedures, and policies that ensure fair treatment of employees and predictability in operations. Indeed, Exhibit 4.1 notes the role of HR as administrative expert in developing and enforcing rules and standards of behavior for employees. Strategic HR, on the other hand, realizes that such an approach limits an organization's ability to grow and respond to a rapidly changing environment. Strategic HR utilizes control that is much more "organic," or loose and free-flowing, with as few restrictions on employee actions and behaviors as possible. Flexibility in work processes and job responsibilities are common and is discussed in Chapter 6. Rather than being bound by excessive rules and regulations, operations are controlled by whatever is necessary to succeed, and control systems are modified as needed to meet changing conditions.

Traditional HR grew out of principles of scientific management and job specialization to increase employee efficiency. A tight division of labor with independent tasks allowed employees to develop specific skills and maintain a focus on their specific job responsibilities. A strategic approach to HR allows a very broad job design, emphasizing flexibility and a need to respond as change takes place in the external environment. Specialization is replaced by cross-training, and independent tasks are replaced by teams and groups—some of which are permanent, some of which are temporary, and many of which are managed autonomously by the workers themselves.

The traditional approach to HR sees an organization's key investments as its capital, products, brand name, technology, and investment strategy. Strategic HR sees the organization's key investment as its people and their knowledge and abilities. This approach realizes that competitive advantage is enjoyed by an organization that can attract and retain "knowledge workers" who can optimally utilize and manage the organization's capital resources. In the long run, people are an organization's only sustainable competitive advantage.[12]

Finally, accountability for HR activities in the traditional approach considers functions, including HR, as cost centers, with an emphasis on monitoring expenditures and charging overhead to fiscal units. An investment approach considers returns as well as expenditures, with attention paid toward the "value added" by HR activities.

As the above discussion illustrates, traditional HR is largely focused on administrative oversight and process. Strategic HR, on the other hand, focuses on deliverables, quantifiable results, and value creation. One conceptualization of strategic HR sees HR adding value with the effective management of four "flows": (1) the flow of people; (2) the flow of performance; (3) the flow of information; and (4) the flow of work.[13] The flow of people considers how employees enter, move through, and eventually leave the organization. The flow of performance considers the development of standards and rewards that are consistent with the interests of stakeholders. The flow of information considers how employees are made aware of priorities and activities and provided feedback. The flow of work considers the processes in which employees engage and the appropriate responsibility for these processes.

As noted in Chapter 1, organizations are increasingly utilizing metrics to illustrate the value of HR activities and processes and their resultant impact on organizational performance. However, such an approach is of value to small organizations as well as larger ones. One recent study of HR practices in small businesses found a direct correlation between three key HR strategies and organizational performance.[14] The first strategy is ensuring that selection strategies for the organization focus on person–organization fit rather than person–job fit. Hiring to ensure a fit with company culture is far more critical than ensuring that an individual has the necessary experience and skills to do a job. The second strategy is allowing employee autonomy, providing workers with discretion to decide how to schedule and complete their work rather than constantly monitoring employee activities. This allows employees to be more involved in decision making, suggest new and better ways to complete their jobs, and become more involved with the work of their team. The third strategy is motivating and rewarding employees through a family-like atmosphere rather than individualized monetary rewards. Employers who create a social dimension to the job provide employees with a kind of compensation that is difficult for competitors to replicate. While other employers can match and even exceed levels of pay and benefits, each organization can create a unique culture that might make employees less likely to leave. The study found that employers who utilized all three strategies experienced 22 percent higher sales growth, 23 percent higher profits, and 67 percent less attrition than those who did not. Even employers who implemented only one of the three strategies still saw significant improvements in their financial performance.

The question remains, though, as to how to create a culture that promotes employee engagement to ensure that the organization benefits from improved sales and profitability and lower attrition. A variety of specific HR programs can be developed around an overall HR strategy that attempts to increase employee engagement and commitment, as discussed in Reading 4.2, "Employee Engagement and Commitment: A Guide to Understanding, Measuring and Increasing Engagement in Your Organization."

Employee Engagement at Aetna Corp.

Hartford, Connecticut-based Aetna found itself in serious trouble at the turn of the millennium. Despite more than 150 years in business, the company found itself performing poorly as its diversified multinational multibusiness strategy had the company on the verge of bankruptcy. The decision to downsize and focus solely on Aetna's core businesses of health insurance and employee benefit products wasn't enough, as even the downsized organization was still losing more than $1 million per day. However, by 2007, Aetna had completed one of the most lauded turnarounds in American corporate history, turning a $2.5 billion annual loss into a $1.7 billion profit and increasing market valuation from $3.3 billion to $29 billion in just six years.

The journey began with the new CEO asking all employees to provide input as to what they wanted the organization to be. This yielded a company values statement of integrity, quality service, excellence and accountability, and employee engagement. Every year, employees complete a 70-question online "climate survey," which provides feedback about employee beliefs concerning values and vision. Employee engagement is assessed via four questions: (1) I would recommend Aetna as a good place to work; (2) I rarely think about looking for a new job with another company; (3) I am proud I work for Aetna; and (4) Overall, I am extremely satisfied with Aetna as a place to work. HR facilitates much of this engagement through a succession planning program where top executives identify the "top 200" employees who are being groomed for future leadership. This process is facilitated by a $50 million automated system called Talent Manager, which contains data about Aetna's 34,000 employees. The system contains information about jobs held and correlated skills and competencies. Employees and supervisors access and update records where both parties provide performance feedback and ratings. Solid performers, at-risk employees, and "mismatches" are identified through this system to assist with planning and engagement. The system has not only improved financial performance, but since its implementation, employee retention has held steady at 90 percent annually.[15]

Employee engagement is directly related to increased performance, increased innovation, increased commitment, and lower attrition. However, job satisfaction and trust are critical factors in creating and maintaining a sense of engagement among employees, as illustrated in Exhibit 4.6.

Individuals who enjoy their work but don't trust their supervisors will be less engaged and less likely to be innovative and assume risks.[16] Trust relationships are built over time as individuals spend more time together and get to know each other. One model of trust portrays it as having two dimensions; head trust and heart trust. Head trust relates to the competence of the individual and heart trust relates to the belief that the individual will "do the right thing" with no resulting harm.[17] Employees who trust their managers and superiors are more likely to be engaged at work than those who do not. Exhibit 4.7 lists some of the major dimensions of trust, which have been identified by various researchers.

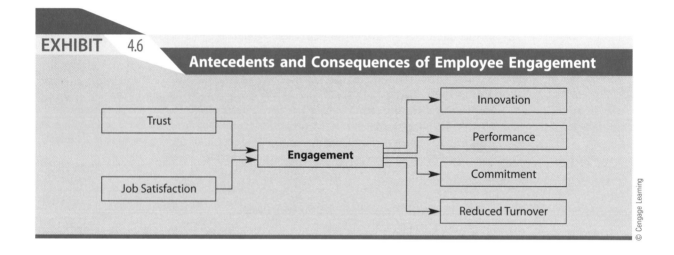

EXHIBIT   4.6

Antecedents and Consequences of Employee Engagement

© Cengage Learning

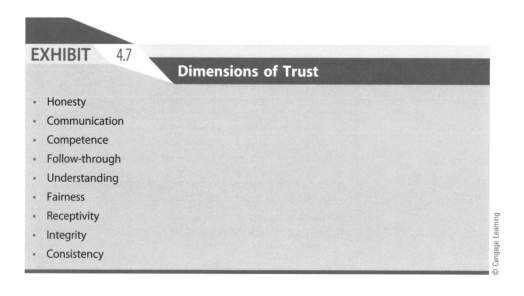

EXHIBIT   4.7

Dimensions of Trust

- Honesty
- Communication
- Competence
- Follow-through
- Understanding
- Fairness
- Receptivity
- Integrity
- Consistency

© Cengage Learning

Trust and Engagement at 3M Company

3M is a St. Paul, Minnesota-based technology company with a diversified portfolio of businesses in a variety of industries. Senior executives realized that enhanced employee engagement was necessary to continue to drive innovation within the company. With more than 75,000 employees across 35 divisions and operations in more than 200 countries, the company needed a very comprehensive and strategized approach to engagement. The organization first conducted an employee survey and found that how supervisors treat employees, the nature of the work being done, and the fairness of recognition and rewards were critical to the engagement of 3M employees. After developing and delivering a comprehensive training program for managers on how to develop trust and engagement, employees and supervisors engaged in employee-centered discussions related to the employee's view of his or her current job/position, desired development opportunities, compensation and benefits, and the work environment. In tandem with these meetings, HR professionals analyzed compensation and benefits plans to more directly link pay with performance and trained supervisors to understand and explain to their direct reports exactly how compensation was determined. This transparency helped to develop a stronger level of trust of supervisors among subordinates and increase engagement.[18]

Job satisfaction will be discussed in greater depth in Chapter 6, but it is critical for a better understanding of employee engagement and to know the factors that contribute to job satisfaction. Exhibit 4.8 presents the results of a recent survey conducted by the SHRM, which investigated the factors that were most related to job satisfaction.

While the above results are important in understanding general job satisfaction, it is critical to remain cognizant of the fact that the factors that contribute to job satisfaction can vary across age and demographic groups as well as within demographic groups on an individual basis. One recent survey found that for employees between the ages of 35 and 44 work–life balance was the greatest contributor to job satisfaction, while among 18- to 34-year olds, opportunities to learn and grow was the most important factor. Hence, employers need to understand their own employees' needs and motivations and measure job satisfaction accordingly.[19]

Barriers to Strategic HR

Although the concept of strategic HR may make sense logically and intuitively, many organizations have a difficult time taking a strategic approach to HR. A number of reasons contribute to this. The first is that most organizations adopt a short-term mentality and focus on current performance. Performance evaluations and compensation throughout organizations tend to be based on current performance. This is not surprising given the emphasis by most shareholders and Wall Street on short-term organizational performance in terms of quarterly measures of profitability and return on investments. CEOs need to focus on short-term quarterly financial performance in order to retain their jobs. Several consecutive "down" quarters will often result in dismissal. This philosophy then trickles throughout the organization. Rewards are not provided for laying plans that may (or may not) provide significant gain three or five years in the future. Most owners and investors do not take a long-term view of their investments; they expect to see quarterly progress in wealth building. There are few, if any, clear incentives for managers to think long term in making their decisions. Consequently, although many organizations desire management decisions that will benefit the organization in the long run, rewards are based on short-term performance.[20]

A second barrier to strategic HR is the fact that many HR managers do not think strategically, given their segmented understanding of the entire business. HR management is a complex and ever-changing function, requiring a tremendous amount of technical knowledge. HR managers often have insufficient general management training to understand the entire organization and the issues and challenges being experienced in the finance, operations, and marketing departments. Consequently, their ability to think strategically may be impaired, and their ability to

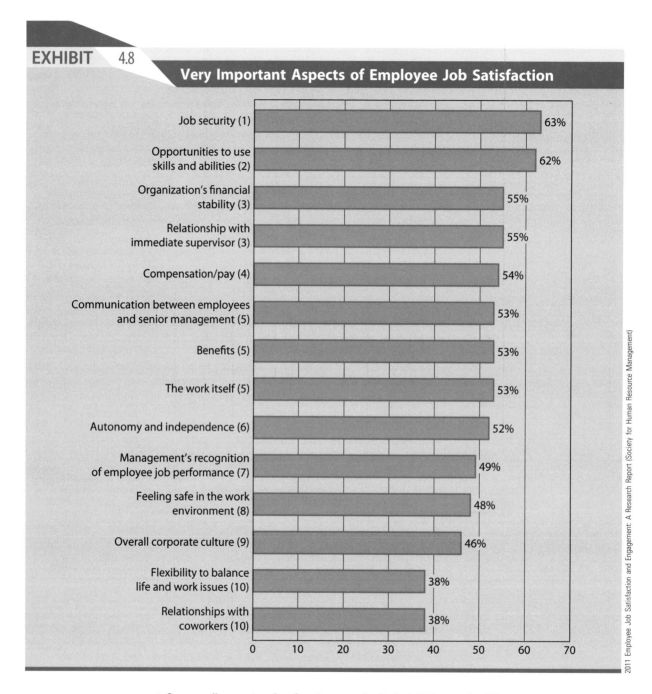

EXHIBIT 4.8

Very Important Aspects of Employee Job Satisfaction

Aspect	Percentage
Job security (1)	63%
Opportunities to use skills and abilities (2)	62%
Organization's financial stability (3)	55%
Relationship with immediate supervisor (3)	55%
Compensation/pay (4)	54%
Communication between employees and senior management (5)	53%
Benefits (5)	53%
The work itself (5)	53%
Autonomy and independence (6)	52%
Management's recognition of employee job performance (7)	49%
Feeling safe in the work environment (8)	48%
Overall corporate culture (9)	46%
Flexibility to balance life and work issues (10)	38%
Relationships with coworkers (10)	38%

2011 Employee Job Satisfaction and Engagement: A Research Report (Society for Human Resource Management)

influence colleagues in other functions may be limited. Unless senior HR managers can appreciate these functional issues and speak the language of these disciplines, they cannot fully contribute to the organization in a strategic manner nor gain the support of managers in these areas.

A third barrier is that most senior managers lack appreciation for the value of HR and its ability to contribute to the organization from a strategic perspective. Many simply understand the traditional or operational function of HR and fail to realize the contributions HR can make as a strategic partner. Managers throughout the organization often see the HR function as providing unnecessary bureaucracy to their work and being more of an adversary than an ally. Their perception of HR is that it is inflexible and rules oriented—"You can't do this. You have to do that."—and that it delays their ability to do their jobs (taking time to get job descriptions written and approved, postings, delays, procedures). Although a key function of HR is ensuring compliance with laws that regulate the employment relationship, many managers see the HR function as detracting from their ability to do their jobs because of the perceived added administrative work required by HR.

A fourth barrier is that few functional managers see *themselves* as HR managers and are concerned more with the technical aspects of their areas of responsibility than the human aspects. Regardless of the function or technical specialty of a manager, any individual who has responsibility for people is an HR manager. Although a controller, chief financial officer, or information technology manager might not consider him or herself to be an HR manager, any individual responsible for the performance of other employees is, in fact, an HR manager. The role of HR as a strategic partner involves line managers assuming more responsibility for day-to-day operational issues, with HR providing internal support or assistance for employee relations rather than assuming full and sole responsibility for it.

A fifth barrier to strategic HR is the difficulty in quantifying many of the outcomes and benefits of HR programs. With competitive pressures making organizations more bottom–line oriented, programs that may not have any direct quantifiable benefit—such as team building—may be disregarded or shelved. Senior HR managers consistently find resistance toward resources being allocated to programs that have less tangible, measurable benefits than those that do.

Another barrier to strategic HR is the fact that human assets are not owned by organizations and, therefore, are perceived as a higher risk investment than capital assets. Particularly in highly competitive industries where key executives may be recruited from competitors, there is an incentive to invest less on employees than on technology and information, which are more proprietary. Organizations adopting this mindset fail to realize that it is the people who utilize the technology and information that provide an organization with stellar performance and a competitive advantage; investments in these individuals can be more critical than corresponding investments in technology and information. Although technology and information constantly need to be replaced because of depreciation in their value, an organization's HR hold their value and can have this value enhanced by minimal investments in them.

Finally, strategic HR may be resisted because of the incentives for change that might arise. Taking a strategic approach to HR may mean making drastic changes in how work is organized; how employees are hired, trained, and developed; how performance is measured; how employees are compensated; standards of performance; and relations between employees and supervisors and among employees themselves. Because people tend to be creatures of habit and enjoy maintaining the status quo—particularly older workers and those with less training and skills—organizations often find resistance to any change initiatives. Such significant changes can be very risky for those responsible for implementation if such efforts fail. An organization that "punishes" those responsible for unsuccessful change efforts, instead of looking at such endeavors as learning experiences, provides disincentives for change. Exhibit 4.9 summarizes these barriers to change.

EXHIBIT 4.9   Barriers to Strategic HR

- Short-term mentality/focus on current performance
- Inability of HR to think strategically
- Lack of appreciation of what HR can contribute
- Failure to understand general manager's role as an HR manager
- Difficulty in quantifying many HR outcomes
- Perception of human assets as higher-risk investments
- Incentives for change that might arise

Most of these barriers are rooted in the culture of an organization. As noted, the organization's history, values, and management practices can act as disincentives for any change initiative. The question remains concerning if and how an organization's HR systems can promote or encourage change initiatives.

Outsourcing and Revamping HR

One critical strategic decision that many organizations are facing relative to their HR operations is whether to outsource some components or all of it. A strategic approach to HR moves the HR function and staff away from administrative "transactional" kinds of responsibilities toward those that create value and provide a clear return. However, those administrative functions—including enrolling employees for benefits, managing payroll, counseling employees, testing and background checks for applicants, and creating and maintaining a database—still need to be performed. The past two decades have seen proliferation of entrants into the HR services industry, where organizations provide specialized or packaged HR services administration for employers.

The benefits of outsourcing include (1) allowing the organization to reduce its HR staff (and possibly save money); (2) enhancing the quality of HR services provided; (3) freeing up HR staff to focus on more strategic, value-added activities; and (4) frequent reduction in the costs of outsourced services through economies of scale "bundling" of services with other employers. It involves a shift in the culture of the organization relative to the roles and expectations for in-house HR professionals and certainly allows HR to display its understanding of the needs of the organization and how it can deliver value from a strategic perspective.

Rather than outsource some or all of the HR function, an organization may decide that it needs to totally reinvent its HR programs and systems in response to a change in strategy and/or the environment in which the organization operates. The decision to centralize the HR function at headquarters provides economies of scale but not responsiveness to individual business needs and locations. Decentralized HR provides responsiveness relative to the needs and differences of different operational locations but often produces duplication of effort and inefficiencies.

Remodeling the HR Function at Home Depot

In 2008, Home Depot eliminated more than 1,200 positions in HR throughout the organization by eliminating individual HR managers in its stores who had worked as business partners with store general managers. Chronic ongoing problems with retention, skills deficiencies, and poor customer service had plagued the organization, and the restructuring of the HR function was designed to free up salaries of laid-off employees and to address these issues.

Traditionally, store managers enjoyed tremendous autonomy and did their own HR work, relying on district HR managers for outside counsel; however, district HR managers were assigned as many as 30 stores. A new senior management team re-engineered HR to create a full-time exempt HR presence in each store along with a variety of HR metrics to which stores were held accountable.

The housing crisis and faltering economy started to take its toll on Home Depot as the decade worked on and as customer service scores continued to slide to the bottom of its industry. The in-store HR managers experienced the stress of a dual-reporting relationship, taxing workloads, excessive paperwork, and demand for employees which greatly exceeded the supply of those with requisite skills.

Under the reorganization, 230 district HR teams each oversees 6–10 stores. Each district manager has three generalists as direct reports; one for staffing and development, one for employee relations, and one for performance management. Routine transactions have moved to a centralized service center.[21] The move has resulted in significant cost savings for Home Depot relative to the elimination of unnecessary positions.[22]

Conclusion

Recognizing that a strategic approach to HR management needs to be undertaken within the context of a specific organization is paramount to successful implementation: What works for one organization will not necessarily work for another. This point is well illustrated by looking at how two large organizations revamped their HR functions. One did so by making HR more centralized, whereas the other did so by making HR more decentralized. Both efforts were successful because they were designed and implemented within the context of the organization's strategy.

Strategic Reorganization of the HR Function at General Motors

We might logically assume that larger and older organizations would be less prone to dramatic changes in their operating practices; however, one of the most venerable corporations in the United States has been among the most innovative in its HR practices. General Motors (GM), like other domestic automakers, watched its market share shrink as Japanese, German, and Korean competitors captured the American consumer's dollar. When Rick Wagoner became CEO in the late 1990s, one of his primary objectives was to shake up the status quo at the organization through its HR practices. Wagoner had the head of HR join the senior management team and pushed HR into a more strategic role. At the time, the HR function at GM was totally "siloed," with a highly decentralized structure in which every GM facility administered HR in its own way. Each plant had its own HR staff, which operated with near total autonomy. Wagoner brought in Kathleen Barclay to head HR, which she revamped through a strategy she called the 3Ts: technology, talent, and transformation.

Technology was used to overhaul HR by creating an effective and accessible corporate intranet and transforming that site into a full-service HR portal. This system is described more fully in Chapter 2. The focus on talent resulted in the development of GM University, one of the largest corporate education and training programs in the world. The university has 15 separate colleges that develop training and curricula tailored to the professional needs of and challenges faced by the organization's employees. The transformation component has standardized operations, resulting in greater efficiency, improved communications and interaction, and tighter coordination of operations. The "siloed" nature of GM has been replaced by an organization that now operates as a true global entity.[23]

Strategic Reorganization of the HR Function at Wells Fargo Bank

San Francisco, California–based Wells Fargo Bank has 185 branches, more than 3,000 employees, five separate division presidents, and does more than $20 billion in business annually. In such a large organization, HR had performed many of its traditional administrative roles. To become more competitive, Wells Fargo saw the need to move toward a more strategic approach in HR management. Line managers needed specific HR solutions to help them improve their operations and impact the bottom line, but HR was unable to deliver this under its existing administrative structure. That structure was highly centralized, with all HR consultants and staffing managers assigned to separate divisions but working out of headquarters. That was changed to create a new structure in which HR staff worked at the branch level to become more integrated with operations and to support local management.

To facilitate this process, an outside trainer was brought in to work with the HR staff to refocus their responsibilities and skills. HR professionals were trained in facilitation and consultation, technical issues, and strategizing and partnering by using a four-phase consultative methodology that ranged from the creation of work agreements, problem identification, data analysis and implementation, and follow-up. The transformation occurred over a year and has reduced turnover by 19 percent and pay problems by 99 percent. By centralizing some generic administrative duties, the organization was able to save close to $1 million annually. New hire time was reduced from 14 days to 7. The end result is that the reorganization has allowed managers to reach their strategic and business goals by moving HR closer to these managers and creating value-added processes.[24]

Top management in most organizations does not realize the contribution that HR can make to overall organizational performance because they still perceive HR in more traditional ways. A contributing factor to this is that senior HR managers themselves may not understand how they can contribute to their organizations strategically. Without a holistic understanding of the organization, HR managers have limited ability to contribute to high-level strategic thinking. Until HR managers take the initiative to gain technical knowledge about their organizations, products and services, competition, and markets and learn how to work politically with other senior managers, their organizations will not be able to fully integrate HR strategy with corporate strategy and will continue to operate at less-than-optimal levels of performance and efficiency.

The key to achieving success is for HR managers to realize that strategic HR can provide three critical outcomes: increased performance, enhanced customer and employee satisfaction, and enhanced shareholder value, as outlined in Exhibit 4.10. These outcomes can be accomplished through effective management of the staffing, retention, and turnover processes; selection of employees who fit with both the organizational strategy and culture; cost-effective utilization of employees through investment in *identified* human capital with the potential for high return; integrated HR programs and policies that clearly follow from corporate strategy; facilitation of change and adaptation through a flexible, more dynamic organization; and tighter focus on customer needs, key and emerging markets, and quality.

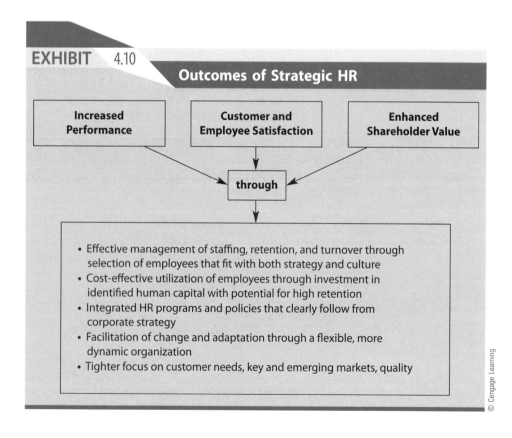

EXHIBIT   4.10

Outcomes of Strategic HR

| Increased Performance | Customer and Employee Satisfaction | Enhanced Shareholder Value |

through

- Effective management of staffing, retention, and turnover through selection of employees that fit with both strategy and culture
- Cost-effective utilization of employees through investment in identified human capital with potential for high retention
- Integrated HR programs and policies that clearly follow from corporate strategy
- Facilitation of change and adaptation through a flexible, more dynamic organization
- Tighter focus on customer needs, key and emerging markets, quality

© Cengage Learning

A model that illustrates how this can be accomplished is presented in Exhibit 4.11. This model provides the framework for the remainder of this book. At this point, we have discussed how corporate and business unit strategies are formed as well as organizational and external environment factors that need to be considered when developing strategy. Chapters 5 and 6 focus on the HR strategy component of the model, examining HR planning and the design of jobs and work systems. The remaining chapters focus on how each of the functional areas of HR can be derived from this strategy. Finally, Chapter 14 will conclude by examining strategic HR management from an international perspective.

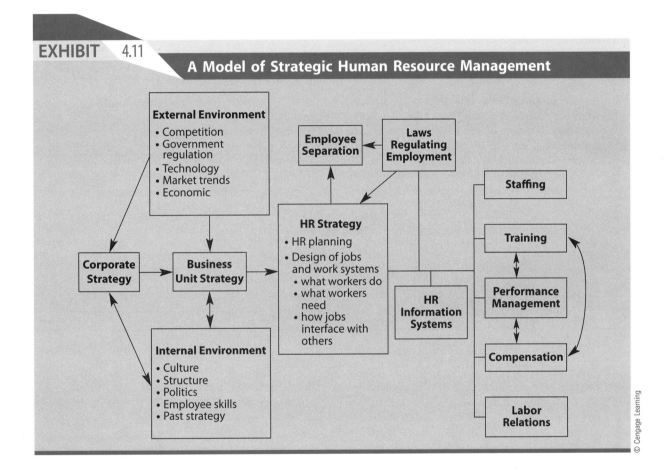

EXHIBIT 4.11

A Model of Strategic Human Resource Management

© Cengage Learning

Critical Thinking

1. Compare and contrast traditional and strategic HR. In what types of organizations might traditional HR still be appropriate?

2. What are the main barriers that prevent an organization from taking a more strategic approach to HR? Why do they exist, and how can they be overcome?

3. What is the role of HR in your current organization? What could it be? What should it be? Why does HR assume the role that it does?

4. Analyze the four HR roles presented by the Lengnick-Halls. How might the criticality of each of these roles be impacted by different strategies?

5. To be a true strategic partner, does HR need to take on a more generalized or specialized approach to its work? Why?

6. Would you want to work for a company like Netflix? Why or why not?

Reading 4.1

7. Examine each of the pairs of organizations the authors discuss. Determine whether their strategies are based on industrial organization (I/O) or resource-based view (RBV) assumptions. What does this imply about strategic planning in general?

Reading 4.2

8. What kinds of employment practices encourage employee engagement? What are the benefits of enhanced engagement?

Exercises

1. Assume the position of a consultant hired to assess the approach toward HR management taken by a client organization. What factors might you evaluate in determining whether an organization uses a traditional or strategic approach to managing its HR? Develop specific questions that need to be answered and determine which key decision makers in an organization should be asked these questions.

2. Select a local organization and investigate these factors by interviewing selected key decision makers.

3. Visit the Web site for the Society for Human Resource Management (http://www.shrm.org). SHRM is the largest professional association for HR practitioners in the world. Determine whether this organization encourages HR professionals to approach HR from a traditional or strategic standpoint. Print examples of pages that support your conclusion, and be prepared to present them to the class.

Chapter References

1. Grossman, R. J. "Tough Love at Netflix," *HR Magazine*, 55, (4), April 2010, pp. 37–41.

2. Bates, S. "Written HR Strategy Pays Off," *HR Magazine*, 48, (4), April 2003, p. 12.

3. Ibid.

4. Stockman, J. "Building a Quality HR Organization at GE," *Human Resource Management*, 38, (2), Summer 1999, pp. 143–146.

5. Ulrich, D. Human Resource Champions: *The Next Agenda for Adding Value and Delivering Results*, Boston, MA: Harvard Business School Press, 1997.

6. Forbringer, L. R. and Oeth, C. "Human Resources at Mercantile Bank Corporation, Inc.: A Critical Analysis," *Human Resource Management*, 1998, 37, (2), pp. 177–189.

7. Lengnick-Hall, M. and Lengnick-Hall, C. *Human Resource Management in the Knowledge Economy*, San Francisco, CA: Berrett Koehler, 2003.

8. Meisinger, S. "Adding Competencies, Adding Value," *HR Magazine*, 47, (8), July 2003, p. 8.

9. Zielinski, D. "Building a Better HR Team" *HR Magazine*, 55, (8), August, 2010, pp. 65–68.

10. Lepak, D. P. and Snell, S. A. "Examining the Human Resource Architecture: The Relationships among Human Capital, Employment and Human Resource Configurations," *Journal of Management*, 28, (4), pp. 517–541.

11. Hallowell, R. "Southwest Airlines: A Case Study Linking Employee Needs Satisfaction and Organizational Capabilities to Competitive Advantage," *Human Resource Management*, 35, (4), pp. 513–534.

12. Pfeffer, J. *Competitive Advantage Through People: Problems and Prospects for Change*, Boston, MA: Harvard Business School Press, 1994.

13. Ulrich, D. and Brockbank, W. *The HR Value Proposition*, Boston, MA: Harvard Business School Press, 2005.

14. Collins, C., Collins, C. J., and Smith, K. G. "Knowledge Exchange and Combination: The Role of Human Resource Practices in the Performance of High Technology Firms," *Academy of Management Journal*, 2006, 49, pp. 544–560.

15. Grossman, R. "Steering a Business Turnaround," *HR Magazine*, 53, (4), April 2008, pp. 73–80.

16. Hastings, R. R. "Broken Trust Is Bad for Business," Society for Human Resource Management, March 7, 2011. Available at http://www.shrm.org/hrdisciplines/ employeerelations/articles/pages/brokentrust.aspx

17. Rosenfeld, R. *Making the Invisible Visible: The Human Principles for Sustaining Innovation*, Xlibris Corp., 2006.

18. Schneider, B. and Paul, K. B. "In the Company We Trust," *HR Magazine*, 56, (1), January, 2011, pp. 40–43.

19. SHRM Online Staff. "Work/Life Balance, Learning Opportunities Impact Job Satisfaction," Society for Human Resource Management, February 9, 2012. Available at http://www.shrm.org/hrdisciplines/benefits/ articles/pages/jobsatisfactionimpact.aspx

20. Kerr, S. "On the Folly of Rewarding A, While Hoping for B," *Academy of Management Journal*, (18), 1975, pp. 769–783.

21. Grossman, R. J. "Remodeling HR at Home Depot," *HR Magazine*, 53, (11), November 2008, pp. 67–72.

22. Ramos, R. T. "Home Depot Laying off 1,000 Nationwide" Atlanta Journal-Constitution, January 26, 2010. Available at http://www.ajc.com/business/home-depot-laying-off-283844.html

23. Leonard, B. "GM Drives HR to the Next Level," *HR Magazine*, 47, (3), March 2002, pp. 47–50.

24. Fox, A. "HR Makes Leap to Strategic Partner," *HR Magazine*, 48, (7), July 2003, p. 34.

READING 4.1

Distinctive Human Resources Are Firms' Core Competencies

Peter Cappelli and Anne Crocker-Hefter

Find a firm with a reputation for excellence in some function, copy its practices, and your company, too, will excel. Advice such as this, under the rubric of "best practices" or "benchmarking," has flooded the popular business literature. Each article implicitly extends the argument that superior management practices are readily identifiable and can be transferred across organizations.

The best practices advocates, however, must contend with a discomforting reality: *Many firms—some very successful—stubbornly refuse to adopt those practices.* Are we to assume, perhaps, that competition drives out firms that do not adopt the most efficient techniques—and that the intractable companies will ultimately fail? Hardly the case.

To understand what is happening, we need to look at a counterpoint to the best practices approach. When it comes to explaining how and why certain firms have carved out competitive advantages, attention increasingly focuses on unique, *differentiating* resources—the notion of "core competencies" being perhaps the best known of these resource arguments.

We believe that the notion of a single set of "best" practices may, indeed, be overstated. As we illustrate below, there are examples in virtually every industry of highly successful firms that have very distinct management practices. We argue that these distinctive human resource practices help to create unique competencies that differentiate products and services and, in turn, drive competitiveness. Indeed, product differentiation is one of the essential functions of strategic management, and distinctive human resource practices shape the core competencies that determine how firms compete.

The argument that there should be a "fit" between human resource practices and business strategies can be traced back to manpower planning and is certainly not new in management circles. What is new here is the argument that people management practices are the *drivers*—the genesis of efforts to create distinctive competencies and, in turn, business strategies.

We illustrate this point by examining pairs of successful organizations competing in the same industry. We chose the paired companies by asking analysts, consultants, and other industry experts to help us identify successful organizations in their industry that appeared to have very different employee management practices. We began our investigation with financial reports and other publicly available information on the organizations, including stories in the business press over the past five years. We also contacted each organization for information and in most cases visited them. The most revealing sources of information, however, tended to be competitors and former employees. The competitors in particular, typically the other member of an industry "pair," had a keen sense for what was truly distinctive in each organization. Former employees also have a clear sense about what actually happens inside organizations, as opposed to what the written practices say.

With the help of industry experts and competitors, we then identified the distinctive competencies and competitive advantages of each organization. There was remarkably little variance across respondents in what they believed these competencies to be. In most cases, competencies were clearly associated with particular employee groups—customer service, for example, or marketing.

The next step was to describe the employment practices associated with the relevant employee group. In cases where practices have recently changed, we describe the longstanding practices that were in place when the distinctive competencies were developed. In our final step, we compared the distinctive competencies for each organization with the employment practices for the relevant employee group to suggest how these competencies were created.

When Employees Are the "Product"

The link between people management practices and the way organizations compete is most direct in industries where employees, by themselves, create what the organization sells—where the "product" is a service provided directly by employees interacting with customers. Consider the following cases.

Professional Sports

Professional sports are obviously big-businesses in their own right, and it's easy to see how "employee performance" matters in this arena. The rules governing each sport standardize the equipment, playing fields, and time limits for all competitors. Within those parameters, each club must deliver its services—an event that attracts an audience.

Sports are idiosyncratic in other ways as well. The fact that there is no "open" labor market and that teams tend to control hiring through drafts may make it easier to align organizations and employees than in other industries. Financial success and the success of the team in its sport are not always related, which may reduce somewhat the financial incentives to seek out the most effective strategies and employee matches on the field.

The San Francisco 49ers and Oakland Raiders have been among the most successful teams in American sports, yet they represent very distinct models of player management. The 49ers have succeeded by using a strategy of long-term player development—recruiting through college drafts rather than through trades, developing talent within the team, and then holding on to the best players by keeping them happy. Their salaries are among the most generous in the league, and more than in other clubs, the 49ers players have some influence on team decisions and feel that they are a part of the organization.

On the field, the club relies on experienced athletes who have worked with their coaches for years and who act as team leaders. (The coaches and management staff also have long tenure with the team.) They have a reputation for playing as a precise, well-disciplined unit. Long-tenure players also help create long-term relationships with fans, helping cement their loyalty to the club. If production language could be applied to sports, this is a "high commitment" organization that operates as a "quasi-autonomous team" on the field. The approach has apparently paid off—the 49ers have won at least ten games a year every year since 1983.

The Raiders, in contrast, do not as a rule develop their own players, but instead use trades to scoop up talented players who fail or do not fit in elsewhere. The club has a very high player turnover and a reputation as a collection of individuals who often do not fit together well. As an organization, the Raiders are not known for treating players especially well, or for letting them have much influence on team decisions. The team, which has been called "an organizational anomaly," has an autocratic owner who is personally involved in coaching and personnel decisions. No employee participation here.

On the field, the Raiders are known for their individual performances and wide-open playing style, a style that makes good use of their pool of individual talent. The players are not known for their personal discipline either, having "swashbuck-led through Bourbon Street" during Super Bowl week, for example, and recovered by game day.

The practices of these two clubs create reputations that contribute to some self-selection of players, reinforcing their systems; those comfortable working in disciplined systems go to the 49ers while players who bridle at the constraints such systems impose go to the Raiders. It makes sense for the 49ers to staff their team with inexperienced players from the college draft in order to better "stamp" them with their own system; players from other pro teams are more likely to come in with expectations and playing habits that might be incompatible with the 49ers' system. Similarly, the fact that the Raiders hire experienced players who bring disparate attitudes and reputations that are not easily blended helps create their more individualistic playing style.

How Do Management Practices Help Build Distinct Competencies?

Employee selection, i.e., the selection of employees with distinctive capabilities, provides the most obvious example of how management practices create distinct competencies. Moreover, a company's reputation for certain employment practices may attract employees and thus push the process along, aligning individual and organizational attributes. In practice, this is an imperfect mechanism. It requires that both employers and prospective employees have accurate information about each other and it assumes stable characteristics and mobility between organizations. But there is considerable evidence that this matching process between organizations and employee characteristics does occur.

In addition, each organization has its own training programs, rewards systems, and work organization, and these systems develop skills and behaviors that help an organization create distinctive competencies for attacking markets.

To some extent, football teams compete for fans the same way that firms compete for customers, and having distinct styles of play may help build a national audience. A distinctive and unusual style may be useful on the field as well, in that it demands unusual responses from the other side that may be difficult to master.

Retailing: Sales as the Service

Sears and Nordstrom are both legends in the retailing industry.

Sears was the world's largest retailer for generations and has outlasted all of its historical competitors. During the 1980s, Nordstrom set service and growth standards for the industry. Although Sears stumbled in this period—as did most department stores—it has recently reorganized with improved performance.

Sears and Nordstrom are very different companies, with different employment practices, especially with reference to sales positions—the key job in retailing. Yet each company's practices make sense for its operations.

Sears has been and remains one of the pioneering firms in the science of employee selection. It relies on some of the most sophisticated selection tests in American industry. The company has refined these tests over time to achieve extremely high predictive power. Once hired, employees receive extensive training in company practices. Management also keeps track of employee attitudes and morale through frequent and rigorous employee surveys.

Two practices are especially noteworthy in the management of sales representatives. The first is intensive training in Sears products, operating systems, and sales techniques. The second is the pay program: a great many sales employees work on straight salary—not commissions—and the commissions that are paid at Sears are modest. (They have recently been cut to one percent of sales.)

Nordstrom operates with virtually none of the formal personnel practices advanced by Sears. Indeed, its practices appear downright primitive in comparison. Nordstrom's hiring is decentralized and uses no formal selection tests. Managers look for applicants with experience in customer contact—not necessarily prior retailing experience (which is often seen as a drawback). The important qualities are a pleasant personality and motivation. The company has only one rule in its personnel handbook: "Use Your Best Judgment at All Times." Individual sales clerks run their areas almost as if they were private stores.

Nordstrom maintains a continuous stream of programs to motivate employees toward the goal of providing intensive service, but it offers very little of what could be thought of as training. The pay system is leaded toward commissions, which makes it possible for clerks to earn sizable incomes. Nordstrom sales personnel are also ranked within each department according to their monthly sales: the most successful are promoted (virtually all managers are promoted from within) and the least successful let go.

In Nordstrom's fashion-oriented retail business, the service that customers demand is not detailed knowledge of the products, but personal contact. The clerk's emotional energy is important—and hustle, running across the store to match an item, remembering an individual customer's tastes, etc. Impulse purchases are more important in fashion than in other segments of retailing, and the clerk's effort can be especially important in such sales.

The Nordstrom employment system fuels an intense level of personal motivation and customer contact. The commissions, internal competition, and motivation programs provide the drive, while autonomy and the absence of rules allow it to be exercised. Many new hires do not survive—Nordstrom's turnover ranks among the highest in the industry. But because the investment in each employee is relatively small, such turnover is not a real problem.

Sears is also in the retail business, of course, and service is part of what it sells. But it is service of a different kind, in part because housewares, rather than fashion, dominate its product line. Customers buying home appliances or hardware want information about the products and how they are used. Sears also sells financing and warranties, reasonably complicated services that require some background knowledge. As evidenced by its marketing ("The Name You Can Trust"), Sears trades, in part, on a reputation for steering the customer in the right direction.

With this strategy, training is important, and turnover is costly—hence the emphasis on selection. Salary pay systems, as opposed to commissions, create no incentives to push products irrespective of customer needs or to cut back on "non-selling time" associated with providing information. Personal relationships with customers also help build a reputation for honest and reliable service. Sears customer satisfaction data finds that the stores with the lowest employee turnover and the least temporary help have the highest satisfaction ratings. (Interestingly, Sears' problem with fraud in its automotive business a few years ago provides an exception that proves the rule—automotive managers operated on commissions and quotas that provided the incentives to encourage repairs that in many cases were apparently not needed.)

The restructuring of Sears during the past two years smashed its no-layoff policy, but left other principles of employment intact. In fact, the amount of training for sales representatives has increased and the limited commission-based pay reduced further.

Professional Service Firms: Information and Advice as the Product

Boston Consulting Group (BCG) and McKinsey & Company are among the world's leading strategic consulting firms. Both have world-wide operations, and their reputations for thoughtful leadership and quality service to management are comparable. Both firms hire from the best undergraduate and MBA programs and compete for the top students. Both have rigorous selection procedures and exceptional compensation. Yet the characteristics of the people the two firms hire, and the way each firm manages people, differ in important ways. Again, the practices relate to the companies' approaches to their markets.

BCG tends to attract candidates with very broad perspectives on business. Some have started their own businesses, and others leave BCG to found new companies. BCG also maintains something of a "revolving door" with academia, hiring business school professors as consultants and sometimes losing consultants to faculty positions in business schools. Once hired, consultants jump right into work, albeit closely supervised, and the formal training they receive is likely to be from outside courses.

BCG has an entrepreneurial environment—an expectation that each project team will come up with its own innovative approach. Each office is seen as having a slightly different culture. BCG pays less than many of its competitors, but offers more individualized incentive pay, reinforcing the entrepreneurial culture.

While BCG has some standard "products" such as time-based competition and capabilities-based strategies, these are not the source of its competency. Indeed, some products, such as the "Growth-Share" matrix, are well-publicized and basically given away. The value added comes from the customized application to the client's situation. Many of BCG's projects do not even start with these products but rather with a "clean sheet of paper" approach. What clients buy, therefore, are original solutions and approaches to their problems. And these approaches begin with consultants whose varied backgrounds and entrepreneurial spirit help produce a unique product.

McKinsey, on the other hand, has historically taken virtually all of its new hires from on-campus recruiting and rarely hires from other employers. It tends to prefer candidates with technical backgrounds, such as engineering and computer science, who have depth in some functional business area. The new entrants vary less in terms of their management experience and come in as "blank slates" in terms of their consulting ideas. If McKinsey consultants leave, they are more likely to take senior line management positions in corporations than entrepreneurial positions.

McKinsey provides new consultants with extensive training in the company's method of project execution and management, even though this is highly tailored to each client's situation. McKinsey's size—3,000 consultants compared to 800 at BCG—may create scale economies in training new entrants that make it easier for the firm to provide such programs itself. The firm expects the career path to the highest position, senior partner, to take approximately 12 years (versus six to eight at BCG), which gives the consultants a long period to learn how to fit in.

The company is known for the "McKinsey way." McKinsey believes that it is important to provide its clients with consistent services; the client knows what to expect from the project teams whose products and techniques are regarded as proprietary and are not publicized. The firm's core competency, therefore, is in the consistent products and techniques that constitute the "McKinsey way." This standardization is especially notable given the far-flung nature of McKinsey's empire. Half of its senior partners are abroad, and 27 of the 33 offices it has opened since 1980 are outside the U.S.

Business Schools

A similar pattern of employment practices applies across business schools. And because these schools serve as supply channels for business, the pattern also influences the relationships with firms that recruit at those schools.

As an employer, the Harvard Business School represents the end of the spectrum associated with internal development of skills. Harvard is well-known for identifying bright young academics who, in many cases, come from fields largely unrelated to business. Harvard hires them as assistant professors and turns them into business experts. Harvard is also known for a faculty with unique skills and abilities: a deep and practical knowledge of business problems typically acquired through clinical methods, and the ability to teach "cases" using the Socratic method. Compared with other schools, Harvard is organized more by problem areas and teaching responsibilities than by traditional academic fields.

Several personnel practices support the development of these skills. Until recently, a system of post-doctoral fellowships specifically for Ph.D.s in non-business fields helped them learn about business. The best of these fellows were then hired as assistant professors. A second practice is a longer tenure clock than at many schools—nine years—which makes it easier for candidates to make the significant investment in Harvard-specific methods and for the institution to observe who is really fitting in. The tenure evaluation is more likely to stress factors specific to Harvard, such as course development, and to rely on evaluations from internal faculty. Finally, Harvard has been much more inclined than most schools to hire its own students as faculty, providing a more direct way of ensuring that the faculty "fit" into the organization.

The Wharton School exemplifies the other end of the continuum. It seeks faculty whose work is recognized as excellent, in academic fields such as finance, accounting, and management. Like most business schools, Wharton hires its faculty from the network of Ph.D. programs and competitor schools with similar departments that make up the academic labor market. It is extremely rare that Wharton will hire one of its own Ph.D. students. Indeed, a majority of the tenured professors have been hired away from a faculty position elsewhere. The tenure decision is based largely on evaluations from faculty at other schools as a way of ensuring that successful candidates truly have skills recognized elsewhere. And a shorter tenure clock makes it easier to move faculty in and out, making use of the outside market.

What Wharton gets from its faculty, then, are skills oriented toward academic functional areas. Within the school, departments are organized according to academic fields. And the fact that it is the largest of the major business schools ensures that each department has considerable depth.

Given these different orientations, it is not surprising that the two schools produce different "products"—MBA students with different strengths. Harvard graduates are known for their general management orientation and superior discussion skills, while Wharton graduates have superior analytic skills associated with functional areas. It makes sense, therefore, that companies interested in general talent like McKinsey prefer Harvard's MBAs while those interested in specific skills, like the investment banks, prefer Wharton graduates. In 1992, for example, 26 percent of the Harvard MBA class went into consulting compared with 20 percent at Wharton, while 27 percent of the Wharton class went into commercial and investment banking compared with only 18 percent at Harvard.

Financial Services

The property and casualty section of the insurance industry is based, perhaps more directly than other businesses, on knowledge and skills. The ability to identify and assess risk in unique situations, for example, is the central issue in the business, so it may not be a surprise that employees and the practices used to manage them are at the heart of competencies in this industry.

Yet we find a very wide range of people management practices and policies in the property and casualty business, a range that once again appears to result from different competitive strategies that are driven by different competencies. The two property and casualty firms exemplifying the most marked difference with respect to people management are Chubb and American International Group (A.I.G.). Yet both are among the most profitable firms in the entire insurance business.

Chubb, often described by competitors as the "Cadillac" of its industry, is successful by being the best at what it does. Chubb does not create new markets or drive the ones that it is in through low prices. Instead, in the property business, it tries to find the very best risks that will provide a high return on its premiums. Chubb often goes after customers of other firms who it believes are good risks, identifies "gaps" or problems in their coverage, and offers them superior insurance protection. For both businesses and individuals, Chubb also looks for customers who are willing to pay a premium for superior service that is manifested by intensive customer contact. It has a reputation for being the "insurer of choice" for the very wealthy who are willing to pay a premium for superior service and customer contact.

In short, Chubb earns above-market profits by targeting those customers who will pay some premium for superior products and service and by identifying particularly good risks not spotted by competitors. These competencies—superior underwriting and service—are generated by Chubb's employee management practices.

Chubb makes a substantial investment in its employees, beginning with recruitment. Historically, it has recruited graduates, regardless of major, from the most prestigious undergraduate schools. These candidates, often from the liberal arts, come with the interpersonal and communication skills upon which insurance-specific skills can be built. The recruiters seek out applicants who "look like" Chubb's customers—i.e., who have personal contacts in the monied class and are comfortable with potential customers in that social stratum. New hires participate in several months of intensive training and testing before going to the branch into which they were hired. For the next 6 to 12 months, they work alongside established underwriters in an apprentice-like system.

With this substantial investment in skills, the company goes to great lengths to ensure that the new workers (and their skills) stay around long enough for the investment to be recouped. First, Chubb keeps its underwriters from the boredom of desk jobs, which often produces turnover elsewhere, by making them agents. The fact that underwriters go to the field to do the selling is a key factor in creating Chubb's competency. It eliminates communication problems that might otherwise exist between the sales and underwriting functions. The underwriter gets better information for assessing risks, and also provides customers with better service, including better information about their risks. The superior abilities of the underwriter/agents make it possible to combine these two roles.

Second, Chubb fills vacancies internally, moving people frequently and retraining them for new jobs. The pace of work eventually pushes some people out of the organization, but they rarely go to other insurance companies and more typically become independent agents, helping to expand the network for Chubb's business. And this turnover expands what would otherwise be very limited opportunities for career development in a reasonable stable organization.

American International Group (A.I.G.) achieves its high level of profitability in a different way, but one that also relies on its human resources. A.I.G. is a market maker. It identifies new areas of business, creates new products, and benefits from "first mover" advantages. It was the first insurer allowed into communist China and has recently entered the Russian market. A.I.G. thrives by finding markets where it has little competition, often high-risk operations that competitors avoid. Once companies that compete on price enter its markets, A.I.G. might well move on to another product.

The company's competencies, therefore, are in marketing—identifying new business areas—and in the ability to change quickly. It pursues change with a set of policies that are virtually the mirror opposite of Chubb's. Operating in a highly decentralized manner by creating literally hundreds of subsidiary companies, each targeted to a specific market, it creates new companies to attack new markets and staffs them by hiring experts with industry skills from other firms. It has been known to hire away entire operations from competitors, typically for much higher pay. For example, it hired the head and seven other members of Drexel Burnham Lambert's interest rate swap department in 1987 as part of its move into capital markets.

A.I.G. has little interest in developing commonalities across its companies. The executives in each company are managed through a series of financial targets—with generous rewards for meeting the targets—and are otherwise given considerable autonomy in running the businesses. When a market dries up or tough competition enters the picture, A.I.G. may close shop in that arena. For example, the company's top executives forced out most of the original management team at A.I.G. Global Investors after determining that the profit potential in that market was no longer there. The fact that the company changes markets so quickly would make it difficult to recoup an investment in developing employees with market-specific skills itself, so it relies on the outside labor market instead.

The advantages of speed in attacking markets effectively make other ways of competing difficult. For example, hiring experienced employees away from competitors without offering any real job security means that A.I.G. is paying top dollar to get them, an expense that would make it difficult to compete as a low-cost provider. The reverse argument could be made about Chubb, that the investment in people required to develop the competencies needed to exploit existing markets would be too slow and expensive for attacking new markets as they emerge.

Beyond Direct Services

The link between employees and product market strategy is sometimes less direct when one moves away from services. But there are still relationships between the way employees are managed, the competencies employees help produce, and the way companies compete. Let's consider two examples, one from a service industry that relies heavily on technology, the other from food and beverage manufacturing.

The Shipping Business

It is difficult to find two companies with people management systems that are more different than those at Federal Express and United Parcel Service. FedEx has no union, and its work force is managed using most of the "hot" concepts in contemporary human resource management. The company has pay-for-suggestions systems, quality-of-worklife programs, and a variety of other arrangements to "empower" employees and increase their involvement. The most important of these may be its "Survey-Feedback-Action" program that begins with climate surveys and reviews by subordinates and ends with each work group developing a detailed action plan to address the problems identified by the surveys and reviews.

Employees at FedEx play an important role in helping to design the work organization and the way technology is used, and employee hustle and motivation have helped make FedEx the dominant force in the overnight mail business. As evidence that initiatives paid off, FedEx claimed the honor of being the first service company to win the Malcolm Baldrige National Quality Award.

One of the goals at FedEx is that every employee should be empowered to do whatever is necessary to get a job done. Decentralized authority and the absence of detailed rules would lead to a chaotic pattern of disorganized decisions in the absence of a strong set of common norms and values. FedEx achieves those with an intensive orientation program and communication efforts that include daily information updates broadcast to each of its more than 200 locations. Empowering individual employees also requires that they have the information and skills to make good decisions. FedEx requires that employees pass interactive skills tests every six months. The tests are customized to each location and employee, and the results are tied to a pay-for-skill program.

UPS, on the other hand, has none of these people management practices. Employees have no direct say over work organization matters. Their jobs are designed in excruciating detail, using time-and-motion studies, by a staff of more than 3,000 industrial engineers. Drivers are told, for example, how to carry packages (under their left arm) and even how to fold money (face up). The company measures individual performance against company standards for each task, and assesses employee performance daily. There are no efforts at employee involvement other than collective bargaining over contract terms through the Teamsters' Union. The union at UPS does not appear to be the force maintaining this system of work organization. The initiative on work organization issues has been with management, which has shown little interest in moving toward work systems such as FedEx champions. Indeed, the view from the top of the company has been that virtually all of the company's problems could be addressed by improving the accountability of employees—setting standards for performance and communicating them to workers.

The material rewards for working at UPS are substantial and may, in the minds of employees, more than offset tight supervision and the low level of job enrichment. The company pays the highest wages and benefits in the industry, and it also offers employees gainsharing and stock ownership plans. UPS remains a privately held company owned by its employees. In contrast to FedEx, virtually all promotions (98 percent) are filled from within, offering entry-level drivers excellent long-term prospects for advancement. As a result of these material rewards, UPS employees are also highly motivated and loyal to the company. The productivity of UPS's drivers, the most important work group in the delivery business, is about three times higher (measured by deliveries and packages) than that at FedEx.

Why might it make sense for UPS to rely on highly engineered systems that are generally thought to contribute to poor morale and motivation, and then offset the negative effects with strong material rewards, especially when FedEx offers an alternative model with high levels of morale and motivation and lower material rewards? Differences in technology do not explain it. FedEx is known for its pioneering investments in information systems, but UPS has recently responded with its own wave of computerized operations. Yet the basic organization of work at UPS has not changed.

The employment systems in these two companies are driven by their business strategies. FedEx is much the smaller of the two companies, operating until recently with only one hub in Memphis, and focusing on the overnight package delivery service as its platform product. UPS, in contrast, has a much wider range of products. While its overnight delivery volume is only 60 percent of FedEx's, its total business is nine times as large (11.5 million deliveries per day versus 1.2 million at FedEx).

The scale and scope of UPS's business demand an extremely high level of coordination across its network of delivery hubs, coordination that may be achievable only through highly regimented and standardized job design. The procedures must be very similar, if not identical, across operations if the different delivery products are to move smoothly across a common network that links dozens of hubs.

The highly integrated system at UPS parallels the experience with assembly line production, where workers are closely coupled to each other by the line. The elimination of "buffers" or inventory stocks between work stations associated with just-in-time systems increases the coupling and dictates that the pace at which work flows be the same across all groups, substantially eliminating the scope for autonomy within groups and increasing the need for coordination across groups. The delivery business is like an extreme version of a just-in-time system in that there can be no buffers. A package arrives late from another hub, and it misses its scheduled delivery—clearly a worse outcome even than a temporary break in the flow of an assembly line. And the more points of interchange, the more the need for coordination. Changes in practices and procedures essentially have to be system-wide to be effective. Such coordination is incompatible with significant levels of autonomy of the kind associated with shop floor employee decision making. It is compatible with the system-wide process of collective bargaining, however.

In short, the scale and scope of UPS's business demand a level of coordination that is incompatible with individual employee involvement and a "high commitment" approach. UPS substitutes a system of unusually strong material rewards and performance measurement to provide alternative sources of motivation and commitment. Having historically one hub at FedEx meant that there were fewer coordination problems, allowing considerable scope for autonomy and participation in shaping work decisions at the work group level and more of a "high commitment" approach.

Food and Beverages

Few products appear to be more similar than soft drinks, yet "The Cola Wars" that marked the product market competition between Coke and Pepsi show how even organizations with highly similar products can be differentiated by their business strategies.

Coke is the most recognized trademark in the world. First marketed some 70 years before Pepsi, Coke has been a part of American history and culture. In World War I, for example, Coca-Cola set up bottling plants in Europe to supply the U.S. forces. With such enormous market recognition, Coke's business strategy centers on maintaining its position and building on its carefully groomed image. Compared with other companies its size, Coca-Cola owns and operates few ventures besides Coke (especially now that its brief fling with Columbia Pictures is over) and has relatively few bottling franchises with which to deal. Indeed, the largest franchisee, which controls 45 percent of the U.S. market, is owned by Coca-Cola itself.

Given its dominance, the Coke trademark is akin to a proprietary technology, and Coca-Cola's business strategy turns on subtle marketing decisions that build on the trademark's reputation. This is not to suggest that running Coke's business strategy is easy. Rather, the decisions are highly constrained within a framework of past practices and reputation. (One of the reasons that "New Coke" was such a debacle, it can be argued, was that it broke away from the framework represented by Coke's tradition.)

History as Influence

What determines the investments in particular employment practices in the first place is a fascinating question. Often, the differences in practices seem to be associated with the period when the organization was formed. UPS, for example, was founded in 1907 when the scientific management model for effective work organization was in full bloom. Federal Express, in contrast, was founded in 1971 when job enrichment and work reform programs were the innovations taught in every major business school. Similarly, companies like Sears (founded in 1886) grew up in the period where top-down, command-and-control systems of work organization dominated American industry. While Nordstrom began as a shoe store in 1901, it did not sell apparel until 1966 and became a major organization some time later, when more decentralized management structures became popular.

In the pairs discussed here, the older companies are the ones with employment practices that invest in their employees. Whether the different practices of the newer member of the pair resulted simply from growing up in a different period (i.e., Federal Express) or from a need to differentiate itself from the more established competitor (i.e., Pepsi), or both is an open question.

Managing Coca-Cola therefore requires a deep firm-specific understanding and a "feel" for the trademark that cannot be acquired outside the company—or even quickly inside it. What Coke does, then, is build an employment system that both creates those skills and hangs onto them. Coke typically hires college graduates—often liberal arts majors and rarely MBAs—with little or no corporate experience and provides them with intensive training. Jobs at Coke are very secure. Adequate performers can almost count on lifetime employment, and a system of promotion-from-within and seniority-based salary increases provides the carrot that keeps employees from leaving. The internal company culture is often described as family-like. Decision making is very centralized and there is little autonomy and a low tolerance for individual self aggrandizement: No one wants an unsupervised, low-level decision backfiring on the trademark. To reinforce the centralized model, performance is evaluated at the company or division level.

Coca-Cola slowly steeps its new employees in the company culture—in this case, an understanding of the trademark's image. The people management system then ensures that only career Coke managers who have been thoroughly socialized into worrying about the company as a whole get to make decisions affecting the company.

Perhaps the main point in understanding Pepsi is simply that it is not Coke. Pepsi has prospered by seeking out the market niches where Coke is not dominant and then differentiating itself from Coke. From its early position as a price leader ("Twice as Much for a Nickel") to contemporary efforts at finding a "New Generation" of consumers, Pepsi cleans up around the wake left by the Coke trademark.

Pepsi has found new markets by becoming highly diversified. Its fast food operations—Taco Bell, Pizza Hut, Kentucky Fried Chicken—provide proprietary outlets for Pepsi soft drinks. Pepsi markets more aggressively to institutional buyers like hotels and restaurants than does Coke, which is focused on individual consumers. Pepsi also has many more bottling franchises that operate with some autonomy.

Given this strategy of operating in many different markets, Pepsi faces a much more diversified and complicated set of management challenges. It relies on innovative ideas to identify market niches, and it needs the ability to move fast. Its people management system makes this possible. Pepsi hires employees with experience and advanced degrees—high-performing people who bring ideas with them. In particular, Pepsi brings in more advanced technical skills. Once in the company, Pepsi fosters individual competition and a fast-track approach for those who are successful in that competition. The company operates in a much more decentralized fashion with each division given considerable autonomy, and performance is evaluated at the operating and individual levels. The recent restructuring has moved toward further decentralization and introduced the "Sharepower" stock option program designed to push entrepreneurial action down to individual employees.

Pepsi employees have relatively little job security, which is accentuated by the absence of a strong promotion-from-within policy. One Pepsi insider commented: "Whenever anybody is either over 40 or has been in the same Pepsi job for more than four or five years, they tend to be thought of as a little stodgy." In part because of higher turnover, Pepsi employees have significantly less loyalty to the company than do their counterparts at Coke. Indeed, the main issue that unites them, some say, is their desire to "beat Coke."

What Pepsi gets from this system is a continuous flow of new ideas (e.g., from experienced new hires), the ability to change quickly (e.g., hiring and firing), and the means for attacking many different markets in different ways (e.g., decentralized decision making with individual autonomy).

Conclusions

Our paired comparisons uncover clear patterns in the relationships between business strategies and employment practices. Organizations that move quickly to seize new opportunities compete through flexibility and do not develop employee competencies from within. It does not pay to do so. Instead, these organizations rely on the outside market to take in new competencies, individualism to sustain performance, and the outside market to get rid of old competencies. Organizations that compete through their dominance in an established market or niche, on the other hand, rely on organization-specific capabilities developed internally and group-wide coordination.

Exhibit 1 illustrates the relationship between the way in which human resource competencies are generated and the business strategies that flow from them. The "flexibility" dimension is associated with "prospectors"—companies that seek first-mover advantages in attacking new markets or

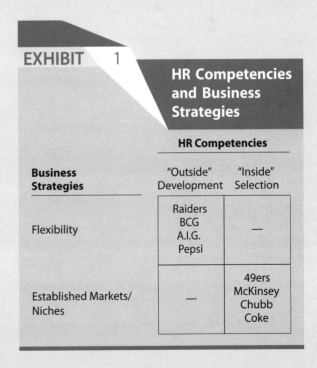

EXHIBIT 1

HR Competencies and Business Strategies

Business Strategies	HR Competencies	
	"Outside" Development	"Inside" Selection
Flexibility	Raiders BCG A.I.G. Pepsi	—
Established Markets/ Niches	—	49ers McKinsey Chubb Coke

quick responses to changing customer preferences. The "established markets" category is linked to classifications like "defenders," firms that maintain stable market niches. The most interesting part of the chart is the absence of cases in the off-diagonal quadrants. It is difficult to think of companies with a tradition of internal development that are known for their flexibility in response to markets or ones with reputations for outside hiring that have the kind of proprietary competencies associated with established products and market.

There may well be a natural equilibrium in the marketplace between the flexible and established market firms. Companies like Pepsi and A.I.G. exist in part because they have competitors like Coke and Chubb that do not (perhaps cannot) adapt quickly to new opportunities; similarly, companies like McKinsey succeed because their competitors cannot easily match the depth of competencies and long-term investments that they have established.

One factor that helps sustain this equilibrium is the difficulty in changing strategies. Historical investments in a particular approach create considerable inertia and reputations that, in turn, affect employee selection long after those investments have been exhausted. Going from an "inside" employment strategy to a market or "outside" approach, and in turn from the "established market" to the "flexibility" quadrant in business strategy, can probably be done more easily than the reverse (i.e., discarding the firm-specific assets and going to the market for new ones).

General Electric under Jack Welch may represent one of the more successful attempts to make such a change in HR competencies and in business strategy, and even there it has taken about a decade. It is very difficult, however, to find examples of mature firms that have gone from a market approach to an inside employment strategy. Start-up firms and those that are growing rapidly have no choice but to rely on a market approach to get staff, and some of these firms eventually switch to an inside strategy. But that is not the same as the transition from outside to inside for mature firms.

The fact that employment practices are so difficult to change and transfer helps explain the basic notion that core competencies should drive business strategy and not vice versa: It may be easier to find a new business strategy to go with one's existing practices and competencies than to develop new practices and competencies to go with a new strategy.

Companies that secure skills and competencies in the outside market, on the other hand, are pursuing a strategy that is not difficult to reproduce. And if these competencies are in fact available to everyone on the open market, how can they generate a unique competency and competitive advantage for any one firm? One answer is that a firm may be better at spotting talent on the open market or at managing that talent than are those competitors that are also trying to secure skills and competencies directly from the market. The Raiders' player management, for example, has been particularly good at incorporating and accommodating talented players who have trouble playing effectively under other systems. The fact that BCG is able to hire new consultants at salaries somewhat below those of its leading competitors suggests a competency in recruiting—an ability to identify underpriced talent and/or job characteristics that substitute for salary.

The Need for Change

The increase in the need for flexibility and change, pressures that virtually all firms feel, may be exacting a toll on employers that develop their own competencies. Competitive pressures may be pushing more of them toward the "outside"/ "flexibility" quadrant. UPS, for example, did not mount an overnight delivery business until 1982, despite 10 years of lessons from FedEx that customers would pay almost twice as much for it. It also delayed automating its operations until 1986. It was also slow to develop modern computer and information systems because it did not have the skills inhouse to build them and no experience in getting such skills on the outside.

A portion of IBM's recent troubles has been attributed to its inability to respond to changing markets, due in part to a lack of new talent and ideas from the outside. Sears' high-quality but high-cost sales force became a disadvantage when it confronted competition from low-cost discounters that sold reliable brand-name products. Its delay in restructuring its operations despite a decade of decline has been attributed in part to inbred management. Companies like Coca-Cola and McKinsey have begun to take in more talent from the outside, and schools like Wharton that traditionally supplied functional skills have changed curricula to ensure that their graduates are broader and more flexible. The increased need for flexibility may erode the market niches mined by firms with high competencies and specific skills like Chubb. Perhaps these firms will find lower cost ways of creating the necessary competencies in the future, possibly assembling them from the outside market.

Whether firms with highly skilled, broadly trained employees can be more flexible in their product markets than firms that hire-and-fire to change their competencies is an important empirical question. The former may well be better at creating flexibility within their current product market (e.g., "quick response" or customized production) although the latter may achieve more flexibility in moving across product markets.

Public policy discussions about changing employment practices in the nation as a whole—increased levels of employer investment in skills or introducing "high performance" systems of work organization—must be thought through very carefully in light of the above arguments. Mandated changes in employment practices could well alter the competencies of organizations and their business strategies. Some might argue that changing business strategies is a desirable outcome. The constraints on dismissing employees in European countries, for example, encourage investments in existing employees and, it is argued, shift production toward the higher quality (and higher cost) markets that make use of higher skills. But they may also drive out of business firms that rely on first-mover advantages based on very high levels of internal flexibility. The fact that distinctive ways of competing appear to be driven by competencies and capabilities that are created by unique sets of employee management practices helps explain the long-standing puzzle noted earlier: Why is there so much variance in management practices? Even practices that appear to have been demonstrated to be "best" in some firms never seem to sweep over the business community as a whole.

None of this suggests, of course, that all practices are equally good. For practices that are not central to an organization's core competency, there may indeed be best practices that clearly cut across firms; for companies with similar business strategies, hence similar core competencies, it may also be possible to identify management practices that dominate others—"lean production" among auto assemblers, for example. But it should come as no surprise that variety in employment practices, as in other aspects of life, can be a source of distinctiveness and competitive advantage.

Source: Peter Cappelli and Anne Crockett-Hefter, "Distinctive Human Resources Are Firms' Core Competencies," Organizational Dynamics, Winter 1996, pp. 7–22. Elsevier Science.

SELECTED BIBLIOGRAPHY

Resource-based arguments in the strategy field suggest that the source of competitive advantage lies within the firm, not in how it positions itself with respect to the market. See Robert M. Grant, "The Resource-Based Theory of Competitive Advantage: Implications for Strategy Formation," *California Management Review,* Vol. 33, 1993. Among the most influential of the resource-based arguments has been C. K. Prahalad and G. Hamel, "The Core Competence of the Corporation," *Harvard Business Review,* May–June 1990, which suggests that the key resource of a firm lies on the procedural side. Several articles document differences in human resource practices among otherwise similar firms. One of the most interesting of these sees the differences as relating to business strategies: Jeffrey B. Arthur, "The Link Between Business Strategy and Industrial Relations Systems in American Steel Minimills," *Industrial and Labor Relations Review,* Vol. 45, 1992.

Among more behaviorally oriented research, many studies find that the process of selection may create distinctive organizational characteristics. See Ben Schneider, "The People Make the Place," *Personnel Psychology,* Vol. 40, 1987.

Evidence about the organizations described in this article often included published material. Interesting evidence explaining the link between employment strategies and business needs at Sears is reported in Dave Ulrich, Richard Halbrook, Dave Meder, Mark Stuchlik, and Steve Thorpe, "Employee and Customer Attachment: Synergies for Competitive Advantage," *Human Resource Planning,* Vol. 41, 1992. Complete references for the company material presented in this paper are available from the authors.

READING 4.2

Employee Engagement and Commitment

A Guide to Understanding, Measuring and Increasing Engagement in Your Organization

Robert J. Vance

Employee Engagement First

[No] company, small or large, can win over the long run without energized employees who believe in the [firm's] mission and understand how to achieve it. That's why you need to take the measure of employee engagement at least once a year through anonymous surveys in which people feel completely safe to speak their minds.

Jack and Suzy Welch

Employees who are engaged in their work and committed to their organizations give companies crucial competitive advantages—including higher productivity and lower employee turnover. Thus, it is not surprising that organizations of all sizes and types have invested substantially in policies and practices that foster engagement and commitment in their workforces. Indeed, in identifying the three best measures of a company's health, business consultant and former General Electric CEO Jack Welch recently cited employee engagement first, with customer satisfaction and free cash flow coming in second and third, respectively.[1] "Reaping Business Results at Caterpillar" and "Engagement Pays Off at Molson Coors Brewing Company" show two examples of companies that benefited from enhancing engagement and commitment.

Reaping Business Results at Caterpillar

Construction-equipment maker Caterpillar has garnered impressive results from its employee engagement and commitment initiatives, including:

- $8.8 million annual savings from decreased attrition, absenteeism and overtime (European plant)
- a 70% increase in output in less than four months (Asia Pacific plant)
- a decrease in the break-even point by almost 50% in units/day, and a decrease in grievances by 80% (unionized plant)
- a $2 million increase in profit and a 34% increase in highly satisfied customers (start-up plant)

Engagement Pays Off at Molson Coors Brewing Company

At beverage giant Molson Coors, engaged employees were five times less likely than nonengaged employees to have a safety incident and seven times less likely to have a lost-time safety incident. Moreover, the average cost of a safety incident for engaged employees was $63, compared with an average of $392 for nonengaged employees. By strengthening employee engagement, the company saved $1,721,760 in safety costs during 2002. Engagement also improved sales performance at Molson Coors: Low-engagement teams fell far behind engaged teams in 2005 sales volumes. In addition, the difference in performance-related costs of low- vs. high-engagement teams totaled $2,104,823.

But what are employee engagement and commitment, exactly? This report examines the ways in which employers and corporate consultants define these terms today, and offers ideas for strengthening employee engagement. Though different organizations define *engagement* differently, some common themes emerge. These themes include employees' satisfaction with their work and pride in their employer, the extent to which people enjoy and believe in what they do for work and the perception that their employer values what they bring to the table. The greater an employee's engagement, the more likely he or she is to "go the extra mile" and deliver excellent on-the-job performance. In addition, engaged employees may be more likely to commit to staying with their current organization. Software giant Intuit,[2] for example, found that highly engaged employees are 1.3 times more likely to be high performers than less engaged employees. They are also five times less likely to voluntarily leave the company.

Clearly, engagement and commitment can potentially translate into valuable business results for an organization. To help you reap the benefits of an engaged, committed workforce at your organization, this report provides guidelines for understanding and measuring employee engagement, and for designing and implementing effective engagement initiatives. As you will see, everyday human resource practices such as recruitment, training, performance management and workforce surveys can provide powerful levers for enhancing engagement.

Employee Engagement: Key Ingredients

"Employee Engagement Defined" shows examples of engagement definitions used by various corporations and consultancies. Clearly, definitions of employee engagement vary greatly across organizations. Many managers wonder how such an elusive concept can be quantified. The term does encompass several ingredients for which researchers have developed measurement techniques. These ingredients include the degree to which employees fully occupy themselves in their work, as well as the strength of their commitment to the employer and role. Fortunately, there is much research on these elements of engagement—work that has deep roots in individual and group psychology. The sections following highlight some of these studies.

Employee Engagement Defined

CORPORATIONS

Caterpillar
Engagement is the extent of employees' commitment, work effort, and desire to stay in an organization.

Dell Inc.
Engagement: To compete today, companies need to win over the MINDS (rational commitment) and the HEARTS (emotional commitment) of employees in ways that lead to extraordinary effort.

Intuit, Inc.[3]
Engagement describes how an employee thinks and feels about, and acts toward his or her job, the work experience and the company.

CONSULTANTS and RESEARCHERS

Corporate Leadership Council
Engagement: The extent to which employees commit to something or someone in their organization, how hard they work and how long they stay as a result of that commitment.

Development Dimensions International
Engagement is the extent to which people enjoy and believe in what they do, and feel valued for doing it.

The Gallup Organization
Employee engagement is the involvement with and enthusiasm for work.

Hewitt Associates
Engagement is the state of emotional and intellectual commitment to an organization or group producing behavior that will help fulfill an organization's promises to customers – and, in so doing, improve business results.

Engaged employees:

- Stay – They have an intense desire to be a part of the organization and they stay with that organization;
- Say – They advocate for the organization by referring potential employees and customers, are positive with co-workers and are constructive in their criticism;
- Strive – They exert extra effort and engage in behaviors that contribute to business success.

Institute for Employment Studies[4]
Engagement: A positive attitude held by the employee toward the organization and its values. An engaged employee is aware of business context, and works with colleagues to improve performance within the job for the benefit of the organization. The organization must work to develop and nurture engagement, which requires a two-way relationship between employer and employee.

Kenexa
Engagement is the extent to which employees are motivated to contribute to organizational success, and are willing to apply discretionary effort (extra time, brainpower and effort) to accomplishing tasks that are important to the achievement of organizational goals.

Towers Perrin
Engagement is the extent to which employees put discretionary effort into their work, beyond the required minimum to get the job done, in the form of extra time, brainpower or energy.

Copyright Towers Watson, reprinted with permission.

Occupying the Job

Psychologist William Kahn[5] drew on studies of work roles[6] and organizational socialization[7] to investigate the degrees to which people "occupy" job roles. He used the terms "personal engagement" and "personal disengagement" to represent two ends of a continuum. At the "personal engagement" end, individuals fully occupy themselves—physically, intellectually and emotionally—in their work role. At the "personal disengagement" end, they uncouple themselves and withdraw from the role.

How do people become personally engaged in their work activities? Why do they become more engaged in some activities than others? Scholars have proposed answers to these questions based on their studies of the psychology of commitment.

Committing to the Work and the Company

Some experts define *commitment* as both a willingness to persist in a course of action and reluctance to change plans, often owing to a sense of obligation to stay the course. People are simultaneously committed to multiple entities, such as economic, educational, familial, political and religious institutions.[8,9] They also commit themselves to specific individuals, including their spouses, children, parents and siblings, as well as to their employers, co-workers, supervisors and customers.

Commitment manifests itself in distinct behavior. For example, people devote time and energy to fulfill their on-the-job responsibilities as well as their family, personal, community and spiritual obligations. Commitment also has an emotional component: People usually experience and express positive feelings toward an entity or individual to whom they have made a commitment.[10] Finally, commitment has a rational element: Most people consciously decide to make commitments, then they thoughtfully plan and carry out the actions required to fulfill them.[11]

Because commitments require an investment of time as well as mental and emotional energy, most people make them with the expectation of reciprocation. That is, people assume that in exchange for their commitment, they will get something of value in return—such as favors, affection, gifts, attention, goods, money and property. In the world of work, employees and employers have traditionally made a tacit agreement: In exchange for workers' commitment, organizations would provide forms of value for employees, such as secure jobs and fair compensation. Reciprocity affects the intensity of a commitment. When an entity or individual to whom someone has made a commitment fails to come through with the expected exchange, the commitment erodes.

Dramatic changes in the global economy over the past 25 years have had significant implications for commitment and reciprocity between employers and employees—and thus for employee engagement. For example, increasing global competition, scarce and costly resources, high labor costs, consumer demands for ever-higher quality and investor pressures for greater returns on equity have prompted organizations to restructure themselves. At some companies, restructuring has meant reductions in staff and in layers of management.

Employee Engagement Survey Items: Samples

DELL

- Even if I were offered a comparable position with similar pay and benefits at another company, I would stay at Dell.
- Considering everything, Dell is the right place for me.

DEVELOPMENT DIMENSIONS INTERNATIONAL

- My job provides me with chances to grow and develop.
- I find personal meaning and fulfillment in my work.
- I get sufficient feedback about how well I am doing.

INSTITUTE FOR EMPLOYMENT STUDIES[12]

- A positive attitude toward, and pride in, the organization.
- A willingness to behave altruistically and be a good team player.
- An understanding of the bigger picture and a willingness to go beyond the requirements of the job.

INTUIT[13]

- I am proud to work for Intuit.
- I would recommend Intuit as a great place to work.
- I am motivated to go "above and beyond" what is expected of me in my job.

TOWERS PERRIN

- I am willing to put in a great deal of effort beyond what is normally expected to help my organization succeed.
- I understand how my role in my organization is related to my organization's overall goals, objectives and direction.
- My organization inspires me to do my best work.

Copyright Towers Watson, reprinted with permission.

Although restructuring helps organizations compete, these changes have broken the traditional psychological employment "contract" and its expectations of reciprocity. Employees have realized that they can no longer count on working for a single employer long enough to retire. And with reduced expectations of reciprocity, workers have felt less commitment to their employers. Many companies, having broken both formal and psychological employment agreements, are struggling to craft effective strategies for reviving employees' commitment and thereby revitalizing their engagement.

10 Common Themes: How Companies Measure Engagement

Employers typically assess their employees' engagement levels with company-wide attitude or opinion surveys. (See "Employee-Engagement Survey Items: Samples" on page 5.) A sampling of the criteria featured in such instruments reveals 10 common themes related to engagement:

- Pride in employer
- Satisfaction with employer
- Job satisfaction
- Opportunity to perform well at challenging work
- Recognition and positive feedback for one's contributions
- Personal support from one's supervisor
- Effort above and beyond the minimum
- Understanding the link between one's job and the organization's mission
- Prospects for future growth with one's employer
- Intention to stay with one's employer

This broad array of concepts has come to be labeled *employee engagement* by virtue of *linkage research,* which relates survey results to bottom-line financial outcomes. (See "About Linkage Research.") Workforce surveys will be covered in greater detail later in this report.

About Linkage Research

Psychologist Benjamin Schneider and colleagues in 1980 developed linkage research to show that employee perceptions of service to customers correlate highly with customers' evaluations of service quality.

Linkage analysts:

- Aggregate employee-opinion survey responses at the business-unit level (summarizing by averaging across survey respondents)
- Statistically correlate aggregated employee-opinion survey responses with measures of business outcomes, such as sales volume, profitability, customer loyalty, employee safety, attendance and retention.

Employee-engagement survey items are those having the strongest correlations with business results.

The Link Between Employer Practices and Employee Engagement

How does an engaged workforce generate valuable business results for an organization? The process starts with employer practices such as job and task design, recruitment, selection, training, compensation, performance management and career development. Such practices affect employees' level of engagement as well as job performance. Performance and engagement then interact to produce business results. Figure 1 depicts these relationships.

Think about what engagement and commitment mean in your own organization. To help you get started, review the questions in "Food for Thought" below.

Food for Thought

Employee Commitment

- How do you and other managers in your organization define commitment?
- Are some employees in your company engaged in their work but not committed to the organization? Committed to staying with your firm but not exactly engaged in their work? Both engaged and committed?
- To whom are your organization's employees committed? The company? Their supervisor? Co-workers? Team members? Customers?
- What business results has commitment from employees created for your organization? For example, has commitment reduced turnover and, therefore, decreased recruitment, hiring and training costs?
- What does your company do to reciprocate employees' commitment? Is the organization living up to its side of the bargain?

Employee Engagement

- How do you and other managers in your organization define employee engagement?
- How do you know that certain employees in your company are engaged? Do they relish their jobs? Enjoy specific responsibilities or tasks? Willingly "go the extra mile"?
- In teams, departments or business units in your company that have a large number of engaged employees, what business results are you seeing? Higher productivity? Lower costs? Greater revenues? More efficiency? Lower turnover? Higher product or service quality?
- Conversely, how do disengaged employees behave, and what are the consequent costs for their teams, units and your entire company?

To engage workers as well as to benefit from that engagement, your organization must invest in its human resource practices. But just like other investments, you need to consider potential return—that is, to devote resources to the HR practices you believe will generate "the biggest bang" for your investment "buck." You must weigh how much

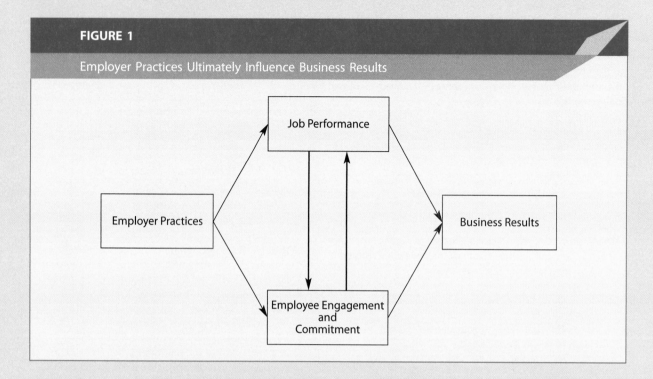

FIGURE 1

Employer Practices Ultimately Influence Business Results

engagement and commitment your company wants—and at what cost. Below, we review employer practices that affect employee engagement and commitment and examine ways to manipulate these "levers" to influence engagement or commitment or both.

To shed light on the ways in which employer practices affect job performance and engagement, Figure 2 presents a simple job performance model.[14]

As Figure 2 suggests, a person possesses attributes such as knowledge, skills, abilities, temperament, attitudes and

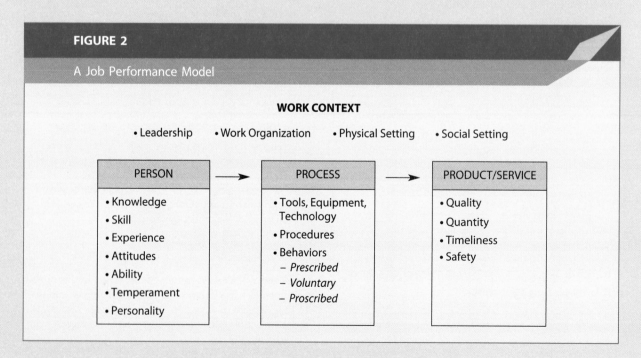

FIGURE 2

A Job Performance Model

personality. He or she uses these attributes to accomplish work behaviors according to organization-defined procedures, by applying tools, equipment and/or technology. Work behaviors, in turn, create the products and services that make an organization successful. We classify work behaviors into three categories: those required to accomplish duties and tasks specified in a job description (*prescribed* behaviors), "extra" behaviors that an employee contributes for the good of the organization (*voluntary* behaviors), and behaviors prohibited by an employer (*proscribed* behaviors, including unexcused absenteeism, stealing and other counterproductive or illegal actions).[15] Of course, job performance occurs in an organizational context, which includes elements such as leadership, physical setting and social setting.

Employers naturally want to encourage workers to perform prescribed and voluntary activities while avoiding proscribed ones. To achieve these goals, organizations use a number of HR practices that directly affect the person, process and context components of job performance. Employees' reactions to these practices determine their levels of engagement and commitment. Next we examine several such practices in greater detail.

Job and Task Design

Over the past 250 years, the nature of work and employment has evolved through a series of stages. Initially, craftspeople and laborers worked on farms and in workshops. Then cottage industries arose, in which suppliers assembled goods and products for companies that marketed them. Later, people worked for companies in increasingly formalized employment relationships. And today, the world of work is characterized by flat and agile organizations that outsource production of goods and services on a global scale.[16]

Likewise, the nature of job and task design also has evolved.[17] For example, with the advent of mass production in the early part of the 20th century, many American companies adopted the "scientific management" approach to work design. Through scientific management, companies simplified tasks to be performed by highly specialized, narrowly trained workers.[18] Though this system enhanced efficiency, it also exacted costs: Workers—unhappy with routine, machine-paced jobs that afforded little personal control or autonomy—felt dissatisfied with their work, were often absent, and left employers in search of more meaningful employment.[19] In short, fitting jobs to efficient production systems disengaged employees and eroded their commitment.

Workers' negative responses to job design in early 20th century America spurred organizational scientists to examine the human component of work more closely. By the 1950s, several theories of job satisfaction and work motivation had emerged that related to job design, particularly the beneficial effects of *job enlargement* (broadening the scope of job tasks) and *job enrichment* (providing more complex and challenging tasks).[20]

With publication of *the job characteristics* model in the early 1970s, interest in the impact of job design on worker motivation and productivity intensified.[21] This model proposed five "core" or motivational job characteristics: skill variety, task identity, task significance (which collectively contribute to a sense of work meaningfulness), autonomy and performance feedback.[22] Jobs that have these characteristics promote internal motivation, personal responsibility for performance and job satisfaction—in short, engagement. The job characteristics model became so widely accepted by management scientists that comparatively few studies of work design and motivation have been published in recent years.[23]

As employers broadened the scope of job responsibilities in flatter organizations with less management oversight, researchers also began looking at the social characteristics of work, including interdependence of job roles, feedback from others and opportunities to get advice and support from coworkers.[24] Analysis of work-design research revealed that social characteristics strongly influence both employee engagement and commitment.

In addition, researchers have recently begun investigating job enrichment's relationship to proactive work behaviors—those self-initiated "extra" contributions noted in many engagement definitions.[25,26] Findings show that managers who provide enriched work (jobs that are high in meaningfulness, variety, autonomy and co-worker trust) stimulate engagement and enthusiasm in their employees. In turn, engagement and enthusiasm encourage employees to define their work roles broadly. Broad definition of job roles then enhances workers' willingness to take ownership of challenges that lie beyond their immediate assigned tasks. These challenges inspire people to innovate and to solve problems pro-actively. Thus, job enrichment promotes engagement in both prescribed *and* voluntary work activities. Although somewhat preliminary, these studies shed valuable light on how your organization might design work to inspire employee engagement and commitment. "The Power of Job Enrichment" captures key lessons from this research.

Recruiting

The messages your organization conveys while seeking to attract job applicants also can influence future employees' engagement and commitment. If your firm has designed jobs specifically to engage employees, then you'll want to ensure that recruiting ads extol these positions' attractive features—such as challenging work assignments, a highly skilled team environment or minimal supervision. Applicants who notice and respond to these ads will more likely be motivated by these features.

Also consider how you might best seek candidates from inside your organization. When you recruit existing employees for desirable jobs, you enhance their engagement (by maximizing the person-job fit) *and* commitment (by providing growth and advancement opportunities to employees in return for

The Power of Job Enrichment

TO INCREASE ENGAGEMENT	TO ENHANCE COMMITMENT
Imbue jobs with:	Demonstrate reciprocity by providing employees with opportunities for personal development.

- meaningfulness

- variety

- autonomy

- co-worker support

With job enrichment, employee performance on prescribed tasks improves. Workers define their role more broadband willingly take on tasks outside their formal job description.

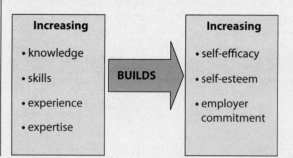

Increasing	BUILDS	Increasing
• knowledge		• self-efficacy
• skills		• self-esteem
• experience		• employer commitment
• expertise		

their loyalty). If you recruit from outside when qualified internal candidates are available, you may unwittingly suggest to current employees that your company is not willing to reciprocate their commitment. Existing staff may then begin questioning their own commitment to your firm.

By contrast, you recruit external candidates to both the job and your organization. For these candidates, ensure that recruiting messages highlight attractive job features, organizational values and commitment reciprocity. That is, in return for performance and dedication, your company offers competitive pay and benefits, flexible work hours and learning and career advancement opportunities.

Also remember that prospective employees have multiple commitments: You will inevitably have to compete with those commitments as you try to attract candidates to your firm. Most people find it easier to make a new commitment when it is compatible with their other obligations. For example, you boost your chances of recruiting a highly qualified candidate who is a single parent if you offer flexible work hours, family health benefits and on-site day care. "Recruiting for Engagement and Commitment" captures some of the principles discussed above.

Employee Selection

Once your recruiting efforts produce a pool of promising job candidates, you select among them to fill available positions. When you select the right individuals for the right jobs, your new hires carry out their work more smoothly and experience fewer performance problems.[27] The result? Greater enjoyment of—and engagement in—the job. (For more information on

Recruiting for Engagement and Commitment

TO INCREASE ENGAGEMENT

Target qualified applicants likely to find the work interesting and challenging.
Send recruiting messages that:

- Extol attractive job features to enhance person-job fit.
- Encourage those who are not suited to the work to self-select out.

TO INCREASE COMMITMENT

For internal candidates
Send recruiting messages that:

- Emphasize possibilities of movement/promotion to more desirable jobs, to signal commitment reciprocity.

For external candidates
Send recruiting messages that:

- Highlight the employer side of the exchange relationship-pay and benefits, advancement opportunities, flexible work hours.
- Recognize and address commitment congruence (e.g., work-family balance.)
- Encourage those who are not suited to the organization to self-select out.

implementing formal assessments, see the SHRM Foundation's "Selection Assessment Methods"[28] by Elaine Pulakos.)

To enhance engagement through your selection of employees, identify those candidates who are best-suited to the job *and* your organization's culture. Also use candidate-assessment methods that have obvious relevance to the job in question—for example, by asking interviewees what they know about the role and having them provide work samples. Most candidates will view these techniques more positively than tests with less apparent relevance, such as personality and integrity assessments.[29] Successful candidates feel good about having "passed the test," and see your company as careful and capable for having selected them. A positive initial impression of an employer encourages growth of long-term commitment. "Effective Employee Selection" summarizes lessons from this section.

Effective Employee Selection

TO INCREASE ENGAGEMENT

Select the right individuals for the right jobs.
Choose candidates most likely to:

- Perform prescribed job duties well.
- Contribute voluntary behaviors.
- Avoid proscribed activities

TO INCREASE COMMITMENT

- Present selection hurdles that are relevant to the job in question. Successful candidates will feel good about surmounting such hurdles to land the job.
- Create a positive first impression of your company's competence. You will set the stage for growth of long-term commitment.

Training and Development

Training and development can serve as additional levers for enhancing engagement and commitment. For new hires, training usually begins with orientation. Orientation presents several important opportunities—including explaining pay, work schedules and company policies. Most important, it gives you a chance to encourage employee engagement by explaining how the new hire's job contributes to the organization's mission. Through orientation, you describe how your company is organized, introduce the new employee to his or her co-workers, give the person a tour of the area where he or she will be working and explain safety regulations and other procedural matters. In short, you foster person-organization fit—vital for developing productive and dedicated employees.

Through training, you help new and current employees acquire the knowledge and skills they need to perform their jobs. And employees who enhance their skills through training are more likely to engage fully in their work, because they derive satisfaction from mastering new tasks. Training also enhances employees' value to your company as well as their own employability in the job market. In addition, most companies offer higher wages for skilled workers, to compensate them for their greater value and to discourage turnover.

If your company is reluctant to invest in training, consider demonstrating to executives the links between training investments, employee engagement and measurable business results.

To get the most from your training investments, also explore how you might leverage digital technology and the Internet. Whereas companies once had to deliver training to employees in the same place at the same time, you can now use technology to offer self-paced and individualized instruction for employees in far-flung locations. Such training not only reduces your company's travel expenses; it also helps employees to manage their other commitments, such as family obligations. Consequently, their commitment to your organization increases.

"Training and Development" summarizes key lessons from this section.

Compensation

Like the HR practices discussed above, compensation can powerfully influence employee engagement and commitment. Some compensation components encourage commitment to employers, while others motivate engagement in the job. It is possible to stimulate one and not the other, though it's generally better to foster both. For example, a company that offers a strong performance incentive system but no retirement plan will probably realize exceptional engagement from its workers; however, they may eventually commit themselves to another company that does offer a good retirement plan. Meanwhile, an organization that offers generous retirement benefits but a traditional seniority-based pay grade system may have committed employees; however, these workers might deliver pedestrian performance as they bide their time until retirement. In designing compensation plans, you therefore need to consider employee engagement and commitment strategically.

Compensation consists of financial elements (pay and benefits) but may also include nonfinancial elements or perks, such as on-site day care, employee assistance programs, subsidized cafeterias, travel discounts, company picnics and so on. The most effective compensation plans support your organization's strategic objectives. For example, if your company's strategy hinges on innovation, then your compensation system should encourage and reward risk-taking. A well-designed compensation plan gives your organization a competitive advantage. How? It helps you attract the best job candidates, motivate them to perform to their maximum potential and retain them for the long term.

Training and Development

TO INCREASE ENGAGEMENT	**TO ENHANCE COMMITMENT**

TO INCREASE ENGAGEMENT

Provide employee orientation to establish:

- The employer-employee exchange relationship.
- Understanding of how the job contributes to the organization's mission.

Offer skill development to enhance:

- Performance.
- Satisfaction.
- Self-efficacy.

Provide training to encourage prescribed and voluntary performance.

TO ENHANCE COMMITMENT

Signal commitment reciprocity by:

- Your investments in training.
- Modes of training delivery that accommodate employees' other commitments.

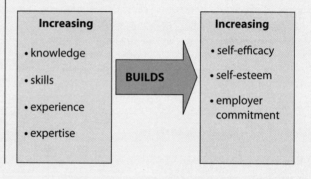

Increasing

- knowledge
- skills
- experience
- expertise

BUILDS

Increasing

- self-efficacy
- self-esteem
- employer commitment

Incentive pay, also known as pay-for-performance, can directly influence employees' productivity (and thus their engagement) as well as their commitment to your organization (as workers learn to trust that they will be rewarded for good performance). Piecework, annual bonuses, merit raises and sales commissions are familiar examples of incentive pay that rewards individual performance. You can also tie incentive pay to team or work group performance, and to organization-wide results through profit sharing, gain-sharing, and employee stock ownership plans. Most employees are motivated by financial incentives and will exert greater effort to produce more if the incentives your company offers make it worthwhile to do so.

The caveat with incentive plans, of course, is that you must first define and measure performance and then decide which aspects of performance you will tie to pay. Because incentive-plan programs can present a heavy administrative burden, many companies opt to reward performance that is easiest to quantify. But this approach can have unintended—and undesirable—consequences. For example, if you pay people based on how many units of a product they assemble per hour, you may encourage quantity at the expense of quality: Employees assemble the units as fast as they can in order to get the incentive pay, regardless of whether they're making mistakes along the way. The challenge in using incentive plans is to reward the results most important to your organization—even if those results are relatively difficult to quantify. You also need to encourage employees' willingness to "go the extra mile" rather than just doing the minimum to reap a reward. To that end, you may want to combine financial incentives and

recognition-based awards to foster the full range of performance your organization needs to stay competitive.

You might also consider competency-based (or skill-based) pay, which has grown more popular in recent years. Through competency-based pay, you reward employees not only for mastering job-relevant knowledge and skills but also for using those abilities to produce results that your organization values. This type of pay can increase engagement by fostering employees' pride in their new mastery. And it can enhance commitment because workers learn that the company is willing to help them burnish their employability.

Many companies also offer retirement plans as part of their compensation package. Although these plans are usually available to all full-time employees, the specific plans offered may depend on job, year hired, number of years employed, highest salary achieved and so on. As we've seen, well-designed and secure retirement plans can encourage long-term commitment to your organization.

In designing financial forms of compensation, consider employees' sensitivity to equity. Will they perceive compensation as commensurate with their contributions? As fair compared to pay earned by co-workers performing the same or similar jobs? Fair compared to what other jobs in the organization pay? Reasonable given what other employers are paying for the same work? Perceived inequity can cause employees to disengage and reexamine their commitment to your firm. They may ask for a raise, seek employment elsewhere or stop striving so hard to deliver top-notch results. And none of these outcomes benefits your organization.

"Strategic Compensation" distills some of the key points from this section.

Strategic Compensation

TO INCREASE ENGAGEMENT:

- **Equitable exchange:** Motivates willingness to contribute prescribed and voluntary performance, and to avoid proscribed behaviors.
- **Pay-for-performance:** Focuses employees' attention on incentivized behaviors—but be careful how you define performance.
- **Competency-based pay:** Fosters acquisition of knowledge and skill and enhance employees' performance, satisfaction and self-efficacy.

TO ENHANCE COMMITMENT:

- **Competitive pay:** Attracts qualified job candidates.
- **Equitable exchange:** Signals commitment reciprocity.
- **Flexible benefits and perks:** Facilitates commitment congruence (e.g., work-family balance matched to stage of life).
- **Retirement and seniority-graded pay plans:** Fosters long-term commitment and identification with your company.

Performance Management

The right performance management practices also can enhance employee engagement and commitment. (See the SHRM Foundation's report on "Performance Management"[30] by Elaine Pulakos for information on creating an effective system.) To design your performance management system, begin by linking job objectives to organizational objectives. What are your organization's priorities, and how will each employee help to achieve them? What results does your organization expect employees to produce? How might you help managers throughout your organization to communicate performance expectations and goals to their direct reports?

Encourage managers to include employees in the goal-setting process. This technique helps to ensure that workers understand the goals. It also promotes acceptance of challenging objectives, because people generally feel more committed to goals they have helped define.

In addition, consider how you and other managers will recognize and encourage contributions that exceed expectations. For example, when a piece of equipment malfunctions, Joe finds other ways to maintain production rather than merely shutting down the machine and waiting for the maintenance staff to fix it. Or when a less experienced co-worker encounters a new task, Sally offers friendly coaching, instead of standing by and waiting for the inevitable mistakes to crop up.

Performance management processes operate on a continuous basis. Therefore, they provide perhaps the best ongoing opportunities for employers to foster employee engagement and commitment. For example, managers can use routine discussions about performance and feedback sessions to learn which aspects of the job hold the most interest for each employee and which tasks are most challenging. During such discussions, managers also can define what "going above and beyond the call of duty" looks like and generate ideas for rewarding such contributions.

An employee's aspirations and career goals can receive careful attention during performance appraisal meetings. Without inquiring into an employee's personal life, a supervisor can nevertheless explore ways to enhance the compatibility between the worker's commitment to your organization and the employee's other life commitments. Through such means, the organization personalizes its relationship to each employee and provides support, while also expressing appreciation for their contributions—key drivers of engagement and commitment.

To further engage employees and win their commitment through your performance management programs, consider how to treat your organization's most experienced employees. In many cases, these employees understand the intricacies of a job better than their supervisors or managers do. By virtue of long identification with your organization, they may be deeply committed to high-level goals. They use their expertise to contribute in ways that newer employees simply cannot match. But many of them also may be planning to retire soon, especially if they are from the "Baby Boomer" generation. How will you transfer their knowledge to younger workers? Design a performance management system that recognizes and rewards proactive sharing of knowledge and expertise among co-workers. For example, create knowledge repositories or learning histories that can be stored in databases that employees can access, and then create incentives for people who contribute to and use these repositories.

Of course, effective performance management systems also identify employees who are not meeting expectations. Failing to address problem performance can erode other employees' engagement and commitment, as their workloads increase and they conclude that the company is willing to tolerate poor performance. If feedback, coaching and remedial training are of little avail, the manager may need to move the person to a different position within the company where he or she can make a more valuable contribution, or let the individual go if there is no good match elsewhere in the organization.

"Effective Performance Management" lists key points from this section.

Effective Performance Management

TO INCREASE ENGAGEMENT:

Provide:

- Challenging goals that align with your company's strategic objectives.
- Positive feedback and recognition for accomplishments.
- Recognition and appreciation for extra voluntary contributions.

TO ENHANCE COMMITMENT:

Manage performance to:

- Enable employees to experience success over the long term.
- Facilitate congruence between employee commitment to your organization and other life commitments.
- Value the expertise of experienced employees.

A Closer Look at Workforce Surveys

Many organizations use workforce surveys to gauge the intensity of employee engagement and assess the relationships between engagement and important business results. Findings from such surveys can shed light on which investments in engagement initiatives are paying off, which are not and how you might change your engagement-related HR practices and investment decisions.

Today's employee surveys are often shorter, more narrowly focused and more frequently administered than traditional instruments. In many cases, respondents also fill out the surveys online rather than using paper and pencil. Survey questions or statements now explicitly link employee attitudes to business objectives; for example, "I can see a clear link between my work and Dell's objectives."

Engagement surveys conducted by research firms across many organizations typically give rise to empirically grounded engagement models. Consider this example from the Corporate Leadership Council (CLC).[31] Based on extensive surveys of more than 50,000 employees of 59 global organizations representing 10 industries and 27 countries, the CLC model identifies 300-plus potential "levers of engagement" (specific employer practices that drive employee engagement). These levers collectively influence employees' rational and emotional commitment to their jobs, teams, managers and company, which in turn influences employees' discretionary efforts and intentions to remain with their employers. "Going the extra mile" and planning to stay with a company then lead to improved performance and retention, respectively.

To date, much employee engagement research has been conducted by consulting firms. Owing to their proprietary status, these studies validating engagement models have yet to appear in refereed scientific journals. Most of this research is unavailable to detailed outsider scrutiny. Nevertheless, numerous linkage research studies have been published. Based on these studies, there is evidence that aggregated employee opinions relate fairly strongly to important business outcomes.[32] But does engagement cause business outcomes to improve? Are business units profitable because their employees are engaged, or are employees engaged because they work for profitable units?[33] Do they say they hope to remain indefinitely because they wish to stick with a winner? Recent evidence suggests that the causal direction is not so straightforward.[34] It is important to understand the cause-and-effect relationships involved given the considerable cost and effort associated with organizations' attempts to improve employee engagement. One way to determine the causal direction is to conduct research specifically designed to answer these important questions in your own organization.

A summary model (Figure 3) by Jack Wiley, cofounder of Gantz Wiley Research (now part of Kenexa), shows how employer leadership practices, employee results of those practices, customer results of leadership and work practices and business performance are interrelated.[35] The model is cyclical, showing that, over time, business performance also influences leadership practices. In addition, this model suggests particular variables within each factor that may affect employee engagement.

Aside from learning how engagement is affecting business results in your organization, surveying employee opinions and attitudes—in itself—can enhance engagement and commitment. For example, by asking employees for their opinions and then taking constructive action based on survey results, you signal that the organization values them and takes their feedback seriously. This enhances engagement. Surveying employees also reinforces a two-way employer-employee relationship, strengthening commitment to your firm.

Designing Engagement Initiatives: Guidelines to Consider

The HR practices discussed above—job design, recruitment, employee selection, training and development, compensation and performance management—are just some of the practices you can leverage to improve engagement and commitment in your organization. As you consider adopting or changing these practices, keep the following guidelines in mind.

Make Sound Investments

Think strategically about how your organization currently uses its human resource practices. Which of these merit greater investment to improve engagement or commitment? What's more important to your organization—employees who are engaged in their work, or those who feel a strong sense of commitment to the organization? Or are both

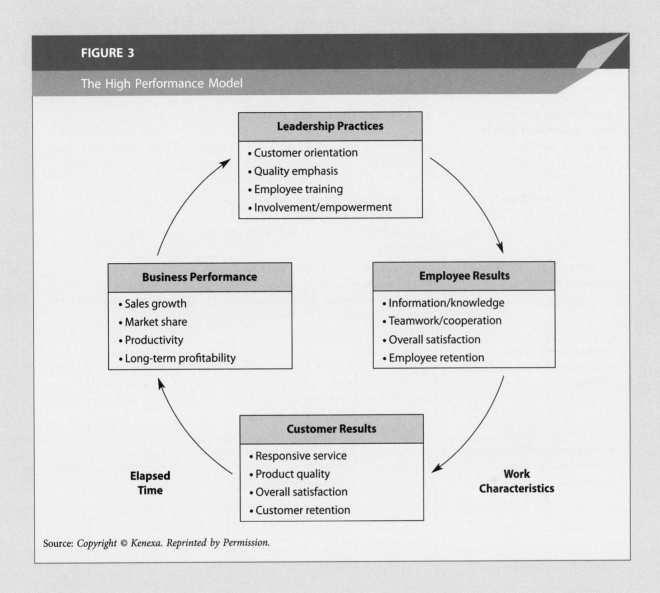

FIGURE 3

The High Performance Model

Leadership Practices

- Customer orientation
- Quality emphasis
- Employee training
- Involvement/empowerment

Business Performance

- Sales growth
- Market share
- Productivity
- Long-term profitability

Employee Results

- Information/knowledge
- Teamwork/cooperation
- Overall satisfaction
- Employee retention

Customer Results

- Responsive service
- Product quality
- Overall satisfaction
- Customer retention

Elapsed Time

Work Characteristics

Source: *Copyright © Kenexa. Reprinted by Permission.*

equally important? How much is your organization willing to invest in specific HR practices designed to foster engagement, commitment or a combination of these?

Given your organization's objectives, in some cases you may want to use specific HR practices to foster engagement in work but not commitment to your organization. In others, your goal may be employee engagement and short-term commitment. In still others, it may be maximum engagement and long-term commitment. For example, if your HR strategy relies on increasing the use of contingent workers in order to cut costs and create more flexible staffing, you'll want to take steps to enhance not only contingent workers' engagement but also their short-term commitment. "Matching Engagement and Commitment Strategies to Business Conditions" shows additional examples.

Craft compelling Business Cases for Improving Engagement and Commitment

To gain the funding needed to invest in engagement and commitment initiatives, you may need to apply your powers of persuasion. Creating a compelling business case for these initiatives can increase your chances of success. How might you make the business case for such investments to your supervisor or members of the executive team? Show how these investments have paid off for your organization or for other organizations by generating measurable business results. "Employee Engagement Drives Results at Intuit" and "Employee Engagement Drives Customer Satisfaction at a State Transportation Department" provide examples of effective business cases.

Matching Engagement and Commitment Strategies to Business Conditions

If You Are Facing This Business Condition...	Change Your HR Practices In These Ways...	To Enhance...
Restructuring to flatter organization with broader job responsibilities	• Align job/work design to new roles/responsibilities. • Recruit, select, train, compensate and manage accordingly. • Outsource or automate simple or routine work.	• Engagement • Short-term commitment • Long-term commitment
Changing technology	• If technology increases job complexity, train and compensate accordingly. • If technology simplifies work, enlarge jobs or outsource.	• Engagement
Increasing customer focus, emphasis on quality	• Recognize and reward voluntary contributions and proactive work behaviors. • Redefine performance expectations. • Provide supervisor/performance management support.	• Engagement • Short-term commitment • Long-term commitment
Increasing reliance on contingent and contract workers	Core employees: • Increase job complexity and job security. Contingent employees: • Emphasize pay-for-performance. • Provide results-based incentives. • Increase task identity.	• Engagement • Long-term commitment • Engagement • Short-term commitment
Broken employment contracts resulting from merger, acquisition or bankruptcy	• Confront the question, Commitment to whom? • Earn credibility with realistic promises, avoiding promises that can't or won't be kept.	• Engagement • Short-term commitment

Employee Engagement Drives Results at Intuit[36]

PROBLEM

Between 2003 and 2004, engagement levels among employees of Intuit's Contact Centers dropped significantly. These employees, who make up 40% of the company's workforce, provide service and assistance to customers. Intuit's engagement survey findings pointed to several areas for possible action.

SOLUTIONS

With understandable urgency, the company conducted a Six Sigma process analysis to identify the root causes of the engagement problem. Remedies initiated in 2004 targeted front-line leadership training, to provide supervisors with better coaching skills, and Intuit's performance measurement and incentive system, which the company revised to give employees greater flexibility in determining how to provide the best customer service.

RESULTS

Within two years of implementing these initiatives, Contact Center engagement scores (percent favorable) increased by 16%. There was a corresponding steady increase in the number of new-business referrals by satisfied customers. Revenue growth for 2006 rebounded and grew to 15%-the best growth rate in four years. Intuit stock rose almost 300% over this period, outperforming the Dow Jones Industrial Average, the S&P 500 and the NASDAQ Composite.

Consider Unintended Consequences

In weighing options for redesigning HR practices to foster engagement and commitment, be sure to think about the possible unintended consequences that revised policies can bring. For example, suppose you want to add flextime to your organization's overall work policies. If employee demographics differ across business units (by age, gender and so forth), the new flextime policy may generate more engagement and commitment in units populated primary by, say, single parents with young children than in units with different demographics.

Keep in mind that employees are individuals. Each one may value something different about the organization's work experience and benefits. When you plan a change to your policies or benefits, take time to consider the impact of that change on employees with different life situations—married, single, older, children at home, childless and so forth. Then be sure the change is a net positive for the majority of your workforce. If you expect that some groups of employees will not like the change, be prepared to address this honestly and directly. If possible, consider making several changes at once that benefit different groups. That way no one will feel left out.

Ground Investment Decisions in Sound Data

It is important to ground decisions about engagement and commitment initiatives in sound data. Linkage research conducted within an organization yields customized advice that highlights specific HR practices likely to produce the best results. Outcomes of this research may include short lists of the highest-impact engagement levers and actionable survey items that differentiate top-performing units in your company from less successful units. "Linking Customer Satisfaction to Employee Opinions" shows an example.

To develop sound investment decisions, be sure to measure employee engagement at least once a year. Choose a survey consulting firm to adapt a standard engagement survey to your organization by linking survey items to the organization's performance measures, which support its business strategy. Performance measures may include profitability, productivity, efficiency, quality, safety, employee attendance, employee retention, customer satisfaction and customer loyalty—and may differ for each business unit depending on that unit's role in supporting the high-level organizational strategy.

For example, if your company's strategy calls for increasing customer loyalty, you might set a goal to raise employee retention in all customer-facing departments. Since longstanding employees are more likely to establish more enduring relationships with customers, it follows that they will provide higher-quality service. You also can create your own engagement survey. If you decide to go this route, include actionable survey items (topics over which management has some control) that explicitly link employee opinions to your organization's business objectives.

Using your engagement survey results, identify top levers of engagement and drivers of measurable results for each business unit. Determine which aspects of engagement are most important for business success. Then work with unit managers to create an Employee Engagement Action Plan for each unit. Determine ownership and accountability for each action item in these plans. "Owners" may include organizational policy and executive decision makers, unit managers and team supervisors. Also identify the resources—personnel, time, funding, space, equipment—that you will need to put each plan into action.

Create an Engagement Culture

Establish a receptive foundation for your engagement initiatives by creating an "engagement culture." Communicate the value of employee engagement through your company

---

Employee Engagement Drives Customer Satisfaction at a State Transportation Department

PROBLEM

A county highway maintenance unit of a state department of transportation was plagued with low morale and a disengaged workforce. At just 36% favorable (indicating very low engagement), scores on the annual employee engagement survey were among the lowest in the state. The department had recently begun a customer-focus initiative, and customer satisfaction scores for ride quality and road maintenance were falling in this county.

SOLUTIONS

The "old school" county manager retired. His successor, a former assistant manager in another county, was selected because he demonstrated skills in employee- and customer-focused management. He proved much more open than the previous manager in his communication with employees-inviting their participation in decision-making and encouraging teamwork. Employee survey scores for each of these dimensions steadily improved by more than 50 percentage points favorable over the next three years. The new manager also encouraged innovation. Scores on process improvements and use of new equipment and technology increased from 19% to 85% favorable.

RESULTS

County employees responded well to the new management approach. Engagement scores showed steady improvement-from 36% favorable just before the change of manager to 84% favorable three years later. An important payoff was a corresponding increase in customer satisfaction, from 51% favorable to 66% percent favorable.

Linking Customer Satisfaction to Employee Opinions

Employee Opinion Items Customer Service	Average 3 Best Units*		Store 2-1	
	Agree (% Positive)	Disagree (% Negative)	Agree (% Positive)	Disagree (% Negative)
In my work unit, a frequent topic of discussion is how well we satisfy our customers' needs.	62.7%	16.9%	27.6%	29.3%
My work unit responds to customer complaints by providing prompt resolution.	67.1%	26.1%	42.7%	21.0%
My work unit obtains reliable information about customer satisfaction.	64.8%	14.4%	22.7%	28.6%

*Average 3 Best Units: The 3 stores having the best Customer Satisfaction scores from Customer Pulse Survey.
Copyright © Vance & Renz, LLC 2006,

At one retailer, employees at the three stores with the best customer satisfaction scores expressed different opinions in a survey than employees from other, lower-performing stores (e.g., Store 2-1). The differences in employee opinions across stores suggest differences in engagement levels and may stimulate ideas for changing workplace practices in stores with lower customer satisfaction scores.

mission statement and other executive communications. For example, look through the "Sample Mission Statements" from three different organizations, and think about how they emphasize the importance of engaged employees for organizational success. Follow up and ensure that all units execute their engagement action plans. Monitor progress on engagement-improvement efforts, and adjust your strategies and plans as needed. Equally important, be sure to recognize and celebrate progress and results.

Conclusion

Engaged employees can help your organization achieve its mission, execute its strategy and generate important business results. This report has highlighted ways in which different HR practices, including job design, recruitment, selection, training, compensation and performance management can enhance employee engagement. But these examples also show that employee engagement is more complex than it may appear on the surface. Organizations define and measure engagement in a variety of different ways, suggesting there is no one "right" or "best" way to define or stimulate engagement in your workforce. The decision to invest in strengthening engagement or commitment (or both) depends on an organization's strategy and the makeup of its workforce.

For these reasons, it is vital to consider your own organization's view of engagement, as well as its strategy and

Sample Mission Statements

STARBUCKS COFFEE COMPANY

Establish Starbucks as the premier purveyor of the finest coffee in the world while maintaining our uncompromising principles while we grow.

The following six guiding principles will help us measure the appropriateness of our decisions:

- Provide a great work environment and treat each other with respect and dignity.
- Embrace diversity as an essential component in the way we do business.
- Apply the highest standards of excellence to the purchasing, roasting and fresh delivery of our coffee.
- Develop enthusiastically satisfied customers all of the time.
- Contribute positively to our communities and our environment.
- Recognize that profitability is essential to our future success.

Source: *http://www.starbucks.com/aboutus/environment.cisp, October 12, 2006.*

BRIGHT HORIZONS FAMILY SOLUTIONS

The Bright Horizons Family Solutions mission is to provide innovative programs that help children, families and employers work together to be their very best.

We are committed to providing the highest-quality child care, early education and work/life solutions in the world. We strive to:

- Nurture each child's unique qualities and potential.
- Support families through strong partnerships.
- Collaborate with employers to build family-friendly workplaces.
- Create a work environment that encourages professionalism, growth and diversity.
- Grow a financially strong organization.

We aspire to do this so successfully that we make a difference in the lives of children and families and in the communities where we live and work.

Source: *http://www.brighthorizons.com/Site/pages/mission.aspx, October 12, 2006.*

WD-40 COMPANY

We are a global consumer products company dedicated to building brand equities that are the first or second choice in their respective categories.

Our mission is to leverage and build the brand fortress of WD-40 Company by developing and acquiring brands that deliver a unique high value to end users and that can be distributed across multiple trade channels in one or more areas of the world.

We strive to cultivate a learning culture based on our corporate values. We have a healthy discomfort with the status quo. We reward those who take personal responsibility in getting results to increase the profitability and growth of our business.

Source: *http://www.wd40.com/AboutUs/our_philosophy.html, October 12, 2006.*

workforce composition when deciding which HR practices will receive scarce investment dollars. The research, guidelines and examples provided in this report—as well as the annotated bibliography—can help you begin to weigh the options and to craft an investment plan that will best suit your organization's unique circumstances.

Source: "Employee Engagement and Commitment," by Robert Vance, PhD. © 2006 the Society for Human Resource Management. Reprinted by permission.

REFERENCES

1. Welch, J., & Welch, S. (2006, May 8). Ideas the Welch way: How healthy is your company? *Business Week*, 126.

2. Ramsay, C. S., & Finney, M. I. (2006). *Employee engagement at Intuit*. Mountain View, CA: Intuit Inc. Ramsay, C. S. (2006, May). Engagement at Intuit: It's the people. In J. D. Kaufman (Chair), *Defining and measuring employee engagement: Old wine in new bottles?* Symposium conducted at the Society for Industrial and Organizational Psychology 21st Annual Conference, Dallas, Texas.

3. See note 2 above.

4. Robinson, D., Perryman, S., & Hayday, S. (2004). *The drivers of employee engagement*. IES Report No. 408. Brighton, UK: Institute for Employment Studies.

5. Kahn, W. A. (1990). Psychological conditions of personal engagement and disengagement at work. *Academy of Management Journal*, 33, 692–724.

6. Katz, D., & Kahn, R. L. (1978). *The social psychology of organizations* (2nd ed). New York: John Wiley & Sons.

7. Van Maanen, J. (1976). Breaking in: Socialization to work. In R. Dubin (Ed.), *Handbook, of work, organization, and society* (pp. 67–130). Chicago: Rand McNally & Co.

8. Abrahamson, M., & Anderson, W. P. (1984). People's commitments to institutions. *Social Psychology Quarterly*, 47, 371–381.

9. Cohen, A. (2003). *Multiple commitments in the workplace: An integrative approach*. Mahwah, NJ: Lawrence Erlbaum Associates.

10. Meyer, J. P., & Allen, N. J. (1991). A three-component conceptualization of organizational commitment. *Human Resource Management Review*, 1, 61–89.

11. Meyer, J. P., Becker, T. E., & Vandenberghe, C. (2004). Employee commitment and motivation: A conceptual analysis and integrative model. *Journal of Applied Psychology*, 89, 991–1007.

12. Robinson, D., Perryman, S., & Hayday, S. (2004). *The drivers of employee engagement*. IES Report No. 408. Brighton, UK: Institute for Employment Studies.

13. See note 2.

14. Vance, R. J. (2006). Organizing for customer service. In L. Fogli (Ed.), *Customer service delivery: Research and best practices* (pp. 22–51). San Francisco, Calif.: Jossey-Bass.

15. Vance, R. J. (2006). Organizing for customer service. In L. Fogli (Ed.), *Customer service delivery: Research and best practices* (pp. 22–51). San Francisco, Calif.: Jossey-Bass.

    Organ, D. W., & Ryan, K. (1995). A meta-analytic review of attitudinal and dispositional predictors or organizational citizenship behavior. *Personnel Psychology*, 48, 775–802.

    Borman, W. C., & Motowidlo, S. J. (1997). Task performance and contextual performance: The meaning for personnel selection research. *Human Performance*, 10, 99–110.

16. Barley, S. (1996). *The new world of work*. London: British-North American Research Committee.

17. Humphrey, S. E., Nahrgang, J. D., & Morgeson, F. P. (2006). *Integrating social and motivational models of work design: A meta-analytic summary and theoretical extension of the work design literature*. Paper presented at the annual conference of the Society for Industrial and Organizational Psychology, Dallas, Texas.

18. Taylor, F. W. (1911). *The principles of scientific management*. New York: W. W. Norton.

19. Hackman, J. R., & Lawler, E. E. (1971). Employee reactions to job characteristics. *Journal of Applied Psychology Monograph*, 55, 259–286.

20. Georgopoulos, B. A., Mahoney, G. M., & Jones, M. W. (1957). A path-goal approach to productivity. *Journal of Applied Psychology*, 41, 345–353.

    Herzberg, F., Mausner, B., & Snyderman, B. B. (1959). *The motivation to work*. New York: Wiley.

    Ford, R. N. (1969). *Motivation through the work itself*. New York: American Management Association.

21. See note 19 above.

22. Hackman, J. R., & Oldham, G. R. (1980). *Work redesign*. Reading, Mass. Addison-Wesley.

23. Humphrey, S. E., Nahrgang, J. D., & Morgeson, F. P. (2006). *Integrating social and motivational models of work design: A meta-analytic summary and theoretical extension of the work design literature*. Paper presented at the annual conference of the Society for Industrial and Organizational Psychology, Dallas, Texas. Fried, Y, & Ferris, G. R. (1987). The validity of the job characteristics model: A review and meta-analysis. *Personnel Psychology*, 40, 287–322.

24. Morgeson, F. P., & Humphrey, S. E. (2006). The Work Design Questionnaire (WDQ): Developing and validating a comprehensive measure for assessing job design and the nature of work. *Journal of Applied Psychology*.

25. Parker, S. K., Williams, H. M., & Turner, N. (2006). Modeling the antecedents of proactive behavior at work. *Journal of Applied Psychology*, 91, 636–652.

26. Parker, S. K. (2006). *A broaden-and-build model of work design: How job enrichment broadens thought-action repertoires via positive affect*. Paper presented at the annual conference of the Society for Industrial and Organizational Psychology, Dallas, Texas.

27. Vance, R. J., & Colella, A. (1990). The utility of utility analysis. *Human Performance*, 3, 123–139.

28. Pulakos, E. D. (2005). *Selection assessment methods: A guide to implementing formal assessments to build a high-quality workforce*. Alexandria, Va.: SHRM Foundation.

29. Hausknecht, J. P., Day, D. V., & Thomas, S. C. (2004). Applicant reactions to selection procedures: An updated model and metaanalysis. *Personnel Psychology*, 57, 639–683.

30. Pulakos, E. D. (2004). *Performance management: A roadmap for developing, implementing and evaluating performance management systems*. Alexandria, Va.: SHRM Foundation.

31. Corporate Leadership Council (2004). *Driving performance and retention through employee engagement*. Washington, DC: Corporate Executive Board.

32. Schneider, B., Parkington, J. J., & Buxton, V. M. (1980). Employee and customer perceptions of service in banks. *Administrative Science Quarterly*, 25, 252–267.

    Schneider, B., Hanges, P. J., Smith, B., & Salvaggio, A. N. (2003). Which comes first: Employee attitudes or organizational financial and market performance? *Journal of Applied Psychology*, 88, 836–851.

Schneider, B., White, S. S., & Paul, M. C. (1998). Linking service climate and customer perceptions of service quality: Test of a causal model. *Journal of Applied Psychology*, 83, 150–163.

Ryan, A. M., Schmit, M. J., & Johnson, R. (1996). Attitudes and effectiveness: Examining relations at an organizational level. *Personnel Psychology*, 49, 853–882.

Dietz, J., Pugh, S. D., & Wiley, J. W. (2004). Service climate effects on customer attitudes: An examination of boundary conditions. *Academy of Management Journal*, 47, 81–92.

Harter, J. K., Schmidt, F. L., & Hayes, T. L. (2002). Business-unit-level relationship between employee satisfaction, employee engagement, and business outcomes: A meta-analysis. *Journal of Applied Psychology*, 87, 268–279.

33. Schneider, B., Hanges, P. J., Smith, B., & Salvaggio, A. N. (2003). Which comes first: Employee attitudes or organizational financial and market performance? *Journal of Applied Psychology*, 88, 836–851.

34. See note 33.

35. Brooks, S. M., Wiley, J. W., & Hause, E. L. (2006). Using employee and customer perspectives to improve organizational performance. In L. Fogli (Ed.), *Customer service delivery: Research and best practices* (pp. 52–82). San Francisco, Calif.: Jossey-Bass. Wiley, J. W. (1996). Linking survey results to customer satisfaction and business performance. In A. I. Kraut (Ed.), *Organizational surveys: Tools for assessment and change* (pp. 330–359). San Francisco, Calif.: Jossey-Bass Publishers.

36. Ramsay, C. S., & Finney, M. I. (2006). *Employee engagement at Intuit*. Mountain View, CA: Intuit Inc. Ramsay, C. S. (2006, May). Engagement at Intuit: It's the people. In J. D. Kaufman (Chair), *Defining and measuring employee engagement: Old wine in new bottles?* Symposium conducted at the Society for Industrial and Organizational Psychology 21st Annual Conference, Dallas, Texas.

CHAPTER 5

Strategic Workforce Planning

LEARNING OBJECTIVES

- Understand the objectives and benefits of strategic workforce planning
- Explain the link between an organization's strategy and its workforce plan
- Gain an appreciation for the need for and value of succession planning
- Appreciate the role that mentoring can play in succession planning

Developing Talent at Procter & Gamble

Consumer goods conglomerate Procter & Gamble (P&G) has had a long, successful history based on hiring at the entry level and developing and promoting its managers and executives from within. The key to this success is the organization's Build From Within program, which tracks the performance of every manager within the organization relative to his or her potential and next area for development. Each of the organization's top 50 jobs consistently has three internal replacement candidates lined up and ready to assume responsibility. Loyalty of employees is paramount to ensuring the success of such a program, and P&G's history of grooming and training its employees promotes such loyalty. Fewer than 5 percent of the organization's non-entry-level hires come from outside the organization, and its rigorous and competitive screening process, in which fewer than 5 percent of applicants are hired, ensures that P&G hires those best suited for the organization and its culture. P&G's 138,000 employees are tracked via monthly and annual performance reviews in which managers discuss business goals, personal goals, and how they've trained others to assume responsibility. The latter is a key factor in the upward mobility of any manager. P&G prides itself in being able to fill any opening internally "in an hour." All executives are required to teach in the organization's training programs, and the CEO assumes direct responsibility for the development of the organization's top 150 employees.[1]

Once the corporate and business unit strategies have been established, then the human resource (HR) strategy can be developed. The HR strategy involves taking the organization's strategic goals and objectives and translating them into a consistent, integrated, complementary set of programs and policies for managing employees.

This does not imply, however, that strategic HR is reactive in nature. Although it is derived from corporate and/or business unit strategies, HR strategy is developed in a proactive manner, with HR staff attempting to design and develop appropriate HR systems to meet the anticipated conditions under which the organization will operate. The senior HR professional, as a vital member of the top management team, should also be heavily involved in corporate or business unit strategic planning so that the top management team can include HR management concerns in its overall planning. HR needs to inform the top management team of the skills and capabilities of the organization's workforce and how they might impact strategic plans.

The first component of HR management strategy is strategic workforce planning. The second component, the design of work systems, is covered in Chapter 6. All other functional HR activities, such as staffing, training, performance management, compensation, labor relations, and employee separation, are derived and should flow from the strategic workforce planning process. When undertaking strategic workforce planning, the organization considers the implications of its future plans on the nature and types of individuals it will need to employ and the necessary skills and training they will require. The organization will also need to assess its current stock of employees as well as those available for employment externally. The key facet of strategic workforce planning is that it is a *proactive* process. It attempts to plan and anticipate what might happen in the various domains of the organization's internal and external environments and to develop plans to address these events prior to their actually happening. Rather than react to changes in the industry, marketplace, economy, society, and technological world, strategic workforce planning ensures that the organization can adapt in tandem with these changes and maintain the fit between the organization and its environment. HR planning is particularly important during periods of organizational turbulence, such as during a merger or acquisition, when labor market conditions are tight, or when unemployment is high.

Because strategic workforce planning involves making assumptions about the future, particularly the status of the economy, competition, technology, regulation, and internal operations and resources, it is critical that all strategic workforce planning initiatives be flexible. If events and circumstances materialize differently from how they are anticipated, then the organization should not be bound by prior and existing plans. Changes to any planning initiatives should not be viewed as a weakness in the planning process. Rather, they should be a positive sign that the organization is carefully monitoring its external environment and responding appropriately to any changes taking place.

To facilitate this flexibility, it is critical that key decision makers in the organization *clarify* and *write down* all assumptions they make about the external environment and the organization when developing the HR plan. If the organization has difficulty achieving its strategic objectives despite following a carefully wrought HR plan, there is a very good chance that inaccurate assumptions were made about what might happen in the future or when expectations failed to materialize.

Clarifying and writing down these assumptions make subsequent intervention and corrective action much easier. Many interventions become complicated and time-consuming because when decision makers revisit the process, the strategy seems to flow logically from the process outlined in Chapter 3. However, as previously noted, much of the assessment of the external environment involves assumptions that various conditions of the economy, technology, marketplace, competition, and regulatory environment will remain the same or change. These assumptions are often held by key decision makers but not verbalized. As a result, corrective action may be stymied because of an inability to identify the key problem.

Strategic workforce planning goes far beyond simple hiring and firing. It involves planning for the deployment of the organization's human capital in the most effective and efficient ways, in line with the organization and/or business unit strategy. In addition to hiring and/or separation, human capital management may involve reassignment, training and development, outsourcing, and/or using temporary help or outside contractors. Modern organizations need as much flexibility as possible in how they utilize human talent in the pursuit of their strategic goals.

Strategic Workforce Planning at Drexel Heritage Furnishings

Drexel Heritage Furnishings is a North Carolina-based, century-old manufacturer of premium quality furniture. To plan its workforce needs in such a competitive, volatile, and seasonally cyclical industry, the organization carefully monitors a variety of internal and external indicators. The vice president of HR carefully tracks incoming orders to monitor and project volume over the coming quarter. In addition, the Purchasing Managers Index, a monthly measure of nationwide business activity, is tracked. This index is a gauge of consumer sentiment about the economy and is based on new orders, prices, inventories, and backlogs. Additional indicators such as real estate activity—including construction activity, mortgage rates, relocations, and market prices—are also monitored by HR, as these factors can be tied to demand for home furnishings. Finally, trends in employee compensation, including bonuses and stock options, are considered, as such "add-on" compensation may be used as discretionary income for the purchase of home furnishings.[2]

The need to carefully monitor strategic workforce planning activities will become even more acute in the coming years. The U.S. Bureau of Labor Statistics estimates that during the current decade, the civilian labor force will increase by only 1 percent and that after that, the retirement of baby boomers will slow the growth to only two-tenths of a percent until the year 2025.[3] Probably nowhere is this creating more challenges than with the federal workforce. Recent reports published by the U.S. Merit Systems Protection Board (MSPB) have determined that the federal government's recruiting processes greatly hamper its ability to hire needed employees. With an average age of approximately 50 years, between one-half million and one million federal employees are expected to retire by 2020. Because little concerted effort is being made to replace such workers or to provide training for those who will remain after these retirements, the future looks grim. In addition, the process for hiring new employees has been found to be so cumbersome that many qualified workers are discouraged from applying for federal jobs.[4] However, one federal employer, the U.S. Postal Service, has developed a model for human capital management that is exemplary for government agencies.

Human Capital Management at the United States Postal Service

With more than 800,000 employees, the U.S. Postal Service (USPS) has the second-largest workforce in the country. The 230-year-old post service has an operating budget of $65 billion and has been under increased competitive pressure from organizations such as Federal Express, United Parcel Service, and Internet service providers, all of whom have eroded market share and offered alternatives to the traditional monopoly enjoyed by the USPS. Current projections are that 85 percent of its executives, 74 percent of its managers and supervisors, and 50 percent of its career workforce will be eligible to retire in the next few years.

The postal service has developed a strategy to ensure that it attracts the right people and then deploys them effectively to where they are most needed. To ensure that the best employees are retained, performance management and leadership development programs have been created to motivate and reward them. At the center of its human capital management plan are four key strategies: (1) aggressive recruitment of future leaders; (2) building of an effective, motivated workforce in which individuals and teams are recognized through a performance-based pay system; (3) establishment and maintenance of a good work environment, based on cooperative working relationships between unionized employees and management; and (4) creation of a flexible workforce that can be readily adjusted as conditions change and new needs arise.

To facilitate these goals, back-office functions have been reorganized and consolidated into 85 separate "performance clusters." Each cluster has its own HR staff that applied re-engineering principles and technology tools to repetitive transactional service work to create more self-service transactions for employees and managers. Performance management is being integrated into virtually every organizational initiative to ensure that rewards are commensurate with productivity. Succession planning and corresponding training and development initiatives have been established to ensure that vital skills are identified and transferred to up-and-coming employees. The Advanced Leadership Program has been developed as a premier program for high-potential future executives, which trains them to understand the strategic challenges being faced by the organization and to develop the skills that allow participants to creatively address those challenges.[5]

Objectives of Strategic Workforce Planning

There are five major objectives of strategic workforce planning, as outlined in Exhibit 5.1. The first is to prevent overstaffing and understaffing. When an organization has too many employees, it experiences a loss of efficiency in operations because of excessive payroll costs and/or surplus production that cannot be marketed and must be inventoried. Having too few employees results in lost sales revenue because the organization is unable to satisfy the existing demand of customers. Moreover, the inability to meet current demand for products or services due to understaffing can also result in the loss of future customers who turn to competitors. Strategic workforce planning helps to ensure that operations are not only efficient but also timely in response to customer demand.

The second objective is to ensure that the organization has the right employees with the right skills in the right places at the right times. Organizations need to anticipate the kinds of employees they need in terms of skills, work habits, and personal characteristics and time their recruiting efforts so that the best employees have been hired, fully trained, and prepared to deliver peak performance exactly when the organization needs them. Specific techniques for accomplishing this will be discussed in Chapter 8. Nonetheless, the planning process needs to consider myriad factors, including skill levels, individual employee "fit" with the organization, training, work systems, and projected demand, and then integrate these factors as a critical component of its HR strategy.

The third objective is to ensure that the organization is responsive to changes in its environment. The strategic workforce planning process requires decision makers to consider a variety of scenarios relative to the numerous domains in the environment. For example, the economy might grow, remain stagnant, or shrink; the industry might remain the same or become either more or less competitive; government regulation may remain the same, be relaxed, or become more stringent; technology may or may not be further developed. Strategic workforce planning

EXHIBIT 5.1
Key Objectives of Strategic Workforce Planning

- Prevent overstaffing and understaffing
- Ensure the organization has the right employees with the right skills in the right places at the right times
- Ensure the organization is responsive to changes in its environment
- Provide direction and coherence to all HR activities and systems
- Unite the perspectives of line and staff managers

© Cengage Learning

forces the organization to speculate and assess the state of its eternal environment. Anticipating and planning for any possible changes rather than passively reacting to such conditions can allow the organization to stay one step ahead of its competitors.

The fourth objective is to provide direction and coherence to all HR activities and systems. Strategic workforce planning sets the direction for all other HR functions, such as staffing, training, and development, performance measurement, and compensation. It also ensures that the organization takes a more systemic view of its HR management activities by understanding the interrelatedness of the HR programs and systems and how changes in one area may impact another area. A coherent HR plan will ensure, for example, that the areas in which employees are trained are being incorporated into their performance measurements and that these factors are additionally considered in compensation decisions.

The fifth objective is to unite the perspectives of line and staff managers. Although strategic workforce planning is usually initiated and managed by the corporate HR staff, it requires the input and cooperation of all managers within an organization. No one knows the needs of a particular unit or department better than the individual manager responsible for that area. Communication between HR staff and line managers is essential for the success of any HR planning initiatives. Corporate HR staff needs to assist line managers in the planning process but simultaneously acknowledge the expertise of and responsibility assigned to individual line managers in considering their input to the planning process.

Developing Employees at Costco and Xerox Europe

What do a large Seattle-based membership warehouse retailer and a European division of a U.S-based technology company have in common? Both have committed to promoting from within and developing their entry-level employees into managers. Costco promotes from within by filling 98 percent of its searches for jobs above entry level. Costco has found that training and advancement opportunities boost morale and productivity and lead to improved customer service. Because lower-level employees are the public "face" of the company, motivated workers enhance the shopping experience of members. Costco also benefits from having managers who have worked directly on the floor and know the merchandise, business, and customer base.

Xerox Europe operates a call center in Dublin, Ireland, which has employment statistics that run counter to those of the industry. Call centers are typically beset with high turnover rates due to low wages and the stresses that are inherent in dealing with unhappy customers. Xerox Europe has developed career tracks for call center employees, which attempt to counter the fundamental nature of working in a call center. Call center employees work closely with their supervisors on professional development and Xerox-provided training to enhance skills. Employees who have completed training receive preferential treatment when new positions open up in the organization. These new positions can involve either or both a promotion and a reassignment to a position that requires higher level of skills and is compensated accordingly. Call center veterans are sought after due to the fact that they have proven themselves in one of the more challenging jobs in the organization.[6]

Types of Planning

Planning is generally done on two different levels. *Aggregate planning* anticipates the needs for groups of employees in specific, usually lower-level, jobs (the number of customer service representatives needed, for example) and the general skills employees need to ensure sustained high performance. *Succession planning* focuses on key individual management positions that the organization needs to make sure remain filled and the types of individuals who might provide the best fit in these critical positions.

Aggregate Planning

The first step in aggregate planning is forecasting the demand for employees. In doing so, the organization needs to consider its strategic plan and any kinds and rates of growth or retrenchment that may be planned. The single greatest indicator of the demand for employees is demand for the organization's product or service. It is imperative, when forecasting the demand for employees, to clarify and write down any assumptions that might affect utilization of employees (new technology that might be developed or acquired, competition for retention of existing employers, changes in the production of a product or provision of a service, new quality or customer service initiatives, or redesigning of work systems).

Although there are several mathematical methods, such as multiple regression and linear programming, to assist in forecasting the demand for employees, most organizations rely more on the judgments of experienced and knowledgeable managers in determining employee requirements. This may be done through unit forecasting (sometimes called *bottom-up planning*), top-down planning, or a combination of both.

In unit forecasting, each individual unit, department, or branch of the organization estimates its future needs for employees. For example, each branch of a bank might prepare its own forecast based on the goals and objectives each branch manager has for the particular office. These estimates are then presented to subsequent layers of management, who combine and sum the totals and present them to senior management for approval.

This technique has the potential for being the most responsive to the needs of the marketplace because it places responsibility for estimating employee needs at the "point of contact" in service provision or product production. However, unless there is some mechanism for control and accountability for allocating resources, such a technique can easily lead managers to overestimate their own unit needs. Without accountability and control measures for costs and productivity, this technique can become quite inefficient as lower-level managers attempt to hoard employees without regard as to whether these human assets might better be deployed in another division of the organization. Consequently, any system of unit forecasting needs to have an accompanying program of accountability for performance based, at least in part, on headcount. This underscores the need for having integrated HR systems and programs.

Top-down forecasting involves senior managers allocating a budgeted amount for employee payroll expenditures and then dividing the pool at subsequent levels down the hierarchy. Each manager receives a budget from her/his supervisor and then decides how to allocate these funds down to the next group of managers. This technique is similar to sales and profit plans in many organizations, whereby each unit is assigned a budgeted amount and is then required to make decisions on deploying those resources in the manner most consistent with business objectives. Although this technique may be efficient, as senior management allocates HR costs within a strict organization-wide budget, there is no guarantee that it will be responsive to the needs of the marketplace. Allocations are based solely on what the organization can afford, without regard to input concerning demand and marketplace dynamics.

Unit forecasting promotes responsiveness to customers and the marketplace; top-down forecasting promotes organizational efficiency in resource allocation. Consequently, an organization can choose a planning technique that is consistent with its overall strategy. An organization whose key strategic objectives involve cost minimization can opt for top-down forecasting. An organization more concerned with change and adaptability can opt for unit or bottom-up forecasting. However, if an organization has objectives of both responsiveness and efficiency, it is possible to use both forms of forecasting and have middle levels of management responsible for negotiating the differences between the two techniques.

In addition to the demand for actual headcount of employees, the organization also needs to consider the demand for specific skills that it will require of its employees as part of the HR planning process. Changes in workplace demographics are having a significant impact on the skills that job applicants bring to an organization. Technology is also having an impact on the skills required of employees. Assessment of the demand for employees needs to consider not only numbers but also the kinds of workers who will best fit with the organization relative to personal characteristics, work habits, and specific skills.

Once demand for employees has been forecasted, the organization then has to plan for an adequate supply of employees to meet this demand. This process involves estimating the actual number of employees and determining the skills that these employees must have and whether their backgrounds, training, and career plans will provide a sufficient fit for the organization's future plans. This chapter focuses on the internal supply of labor. Chapter 8 expands the discussion to consider external labor markets.

One way to assess the abilities, skills, and experiences of existing employees is by using a skills inventory. In the past, these inventories were usually compiled and processed manually, but skills inventories are now usually computerized databases that are part of the organization's overall HR information system. Each employee provides information on his or her experience, education, abilities, job preferences, career aspirations, and other relevant personal information. This allows an organization to gain a collective sense of who their employees are and what capabilities they have. Skills inventories must be constantly updated to be of any value to an organization. Changing employee backgrounds and preferences mandate that the skills inventory be updated at least annually.

Estimate of the existing supply of HR relative to quantity is not a static measure; rather, it is dynamic. In the majority of medium and large organizations, employees change positions and job levels constantly or leave the organization. Consequently, any attempt to assess the supply of employees needs to assess mobility within the organization as well as turnover rates. This can be done through a mathematical technique known as *Markov analysis*, which describes the probability of employees staying with the job in any job category, moving to another job, or leaving the organization over a given time period, usually one year. It uses a transition probability matrix that is established based on historical trends of mobility. Markov analysis can also be utilized to allow managers identify problem departments within an organization or positions that appear to be less desirable as reflected in high rates of turnover or low rates of retention. A sample Markov analysis is illustrated in Exhibit 5.2.

The top portion of this exhibit presents a sample transition probability matrix. For the sake of simplicity, we will assume that there are three job classifications in the restaurant: servers, hosts, and bus persons. Horizontal readings show the movement anticipated during the coming year for each job classification based on historic trends. For example, 80 percent of the current

EXHIBIT 5.2 Transition Probability Matrix for a Restaurant

		One Year From Now			
		Servers	**Hosts**	**Bus persons**	**Exit**
	Servers	.80	.10	0	.10
Current Year	Hosts	.10	.70	0	.20
	Bus persons	.15	.05	.40	.40

Analysis of Matrix

Retention Levels

	Servers	80%
	Hosts	70%
	Bus persons	40%

Forecasted Levels

Incumbents		**Servers**	**Hosts**	**Bus persons**	**Exit**
60	Servers	48	6		6
10	Hosts	1	7		2
20	Bus persons	3	1	8	8
	Total	52	14	8	16

staff of servers would be expected to remain employed in that capacity one year from now; 10 percent will become hosts; none will become bus persons; and 10 percent will leave the organization.

The bottom half of the exhibit first shows retention levels, followed by a forecast of the supply of employees expected in each position. To calculate these values, we take the number of incumbents and multiply them by the percentages from the transition probability matrix. Summing each of the columns that pertain to job classifications allows us to determine, given normal movement, expected supply levels of employees one year from now.

After reliable estimates have been made for both supply and demand of employees, programs can be implemented to address any anticipated surplus or shortage of employees in a particular job category. In planning for anticipated shortages, the organization first needs to consider whether the shortage is expected to be temporary or indefinite. This has implications for whether the organization should hire temporary or permanent employees or even consider subcontracting work to an outside vendor. If permanent employees are to be hired, the plan needs to be comprehensive and consider the types of employees that should be recruited, whether they should be recruited internally or externally, how long they will need training to perform at acceptable levels, and how long the recruiting process has historically taken. Issues and strategies for addressing these concerns are discussed in Chapter 8.

Another important consideration is whether the individuals will need the latest skills or whether the organization requires more hands-on practical experience. The former strategy would suggest recruiting younger employees directly out of formal schooling or training programs; the latter strategy would suggest recruiting from competitors or possibly having older workers postpone retirement or work on a contract or part-time consulting basis.

If a surplus of employees is anticipated, a critical strategic issue that must be addressed is whether this surplus is expected to be temporary or permanent. The most extreme action to reduce a surplus is to lay off employees. Layoffs should usually be conducted only as a last resort, given the effects they can have on the morale of remaining employees as well as the significant economic costs that often result from large-scale layoffs. Surpluses can also be addressed through early retirement programs, transfer, and retraining of existing employees, and/or an across-the-board reduction in salaries or working hours. Exhibit 5.3 summarizes some strategies for managing employee shortages

EXHIBIT 5.3 Strategies for Managing Employee Shortages and Surpluses

Strategies for Managing Shortages	Strategies for Managing Surpluses
• Recruit new permanent employees	• Hiring freezes
• Offer incentives to postpone retirement	• Do not replace those who leave
• Rehire retirees part-time	• Offer early retirement incentives
• Attempt to reduce turnover	• Reduce work hours
• Work current staff overtime	• Voluntary severance, leaves of absence
• Subcontract work out	• Across-the-board pay cuts
• Hire temporary employees	• Layoffs
• Redesign job processes so that fewer employees are needed	• Reduce outsourced work
	• Employee training
	• Switch to variable pay plan
	• Expand operations

Source: *Adapted from Fisher, Schoenfeldt, and Shaw. Human Resource Management, 4d, 1999.*

Avoiding Layoffs at the University of Maryland, Baltimore

The Baltimore campus of the University of Maryland (UMB) was founded in 1807, employs approximately 6,500 faculty, and enrolls more than 6,300 students in graduate and professional degree programs offered by its Schools of Medicine, Law, Dentistry, Pharmacy, Nursing, Law, Social Work, Public Health, and Graduate Studies. Like many public institutions nationwide, UMB began to experience decreased financial support from the state government, causing budgetary shortfalls, leaving it in a quandary as it attempted to maintain employment of its faculty and staff. Even with the suspension of any pay increases, UMB faced a $2.6 million shortfall in funding to meet its payroll obligations. While layoffs would have provided an immediate solution, UMB officials felt that layoffs would have a devastating impact on morale and opted against them.

In lieu of layoffs, the university chose unpaid furloughs. Furloughs were implemented on a tiered basis by salary to minimize the financial impact on lower-salaried employees. Employees earning less than $30,000 per year were excluded from the furloughs while higher-salaried employees were required to take two to five days of unpaid furlough leave. During the subsequent year, furloughs were replaced by across-the-board temporary salary reduction, which was again tiered to have the least impact on lower-salaried employees. Employees who participated in the salary reduction plan received an additional amount of paid administrative leave to compensate for the salary reduction. The furlough plan was developed to avoid layoffs and the salary reduction plan helped to counter the disruption that had been the result of the furlough plan. During this time, turnover at the university has not increased and university officials have pledged to restore salaries and merit and cost-of-living increases as soon as the state budget situation permits.[7]

---

and surpluses. Shortages are discussed in more depth and detail in Chapter 8, while surpluses are discussed in Chapter 13.

Succession Planning

Succession planning involves identifying key management positions that the organization cannot afford to have vacant. These are usually senior management positions and/or positions that the organization has traditionally had a very difficult time filling. Succession planning serves two purposes. First, it facilitates transition when an employee leaves. It is not unusual to have a departing employee work alongside his or her successor for a given period prior to departure to facilitate the transition. Succession planning aids in this process. Second, succession planning identifies the development needs of high-potential employees and assists with their career planning. By identifying specific individuals who might be asked to assume high-level responsibilities, the organization can attempt to develop key skills in these individuals that might be needed in subsequent assignments.

Although succession planning programs are relatively easy to understand in concept, actual practice shows that even though organizations realize how critical the processes are, they may fail to implement succession planning effectively. One criticism of existing succession planning models is that their timing often does not remain in synch with ongoing and evolving business needs, resulting in constant shortages or surpluses of talent. For that reason, it is critical that succession planning programs be subject to regular review and revision, as necessary, as business conditions and the organization itself change.

Traditional succession planning utilizes a relatively simple planning tool called a *replacement chart*. Replacement charts identify key positions, possible successors for each of these positions, whether each potential successor currently has the background to assume the job responsibilities, or the expected amount of time it will take for the potential successor to be ready. Replacement

Succession Planning at K. Hovanian Enterprises

Red Bank, New Jersey–based K. Hovanian Enterprises, is one of the nation's largest home-builders. The $2.6 billion company was recently cited by Fortune as the nation's 15th fastest-growing company. As it has acquired seven other homebuilding companies within a three-year period, senior management saw the need to develop a succession planning committee to select and approve candidates who had high potential to move the organization ahead. In assessing candidates, data are collected in confidence on each candidate that consist of detailed feedback provided by 12–14 direct reports, colleagues, and senior managers. This data report is used to assess leadership ability and potential. After a candidate is accepted by the committee, that person is notified, and he or she creates a plan for personal development that reflects his or her experience and background. Employees are expected to devote 10–20 percent of their time to their personal development plan. The company has reported successful results to date. One hundred percent of the employees who have completed the program have been promoted, whereas those hired from the outside have a promotion success rate of only 50 percent.[8]

charts are easily derived from the organizational chart and are often part of the HR information system: They can narrow in on one key position and the subordinates reporting to the individual holding that position. A sample replacement chart is presented in Exhibit 5.4.

In this example, Smith is the vice president of marketing and has three direct reports: Jones, Williams, and Anderson. Beneath the three reports' job titles is the expected period of additional time each will need to be ready to assume the vice president's responsibilities. The assessments of time are generally not objective. They are usually based on the opinions and recommendations of higher-ranking managers. In this example, Smith may have provided the time estimates for the three subordinates based on subjective personal assessments.

Some organizations, however, are much more systematic about their succession planning. Their replacement charts may contain specific skills, competencies, and experiences rather than subjective estimates of time-readiness. This may help to overcome problems associated with

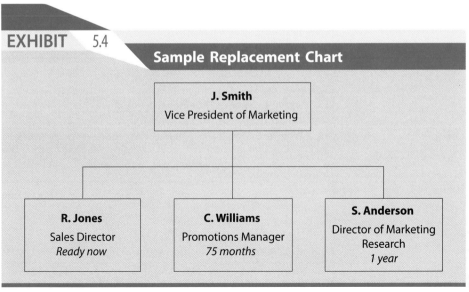

EXHIBIT 5.4

Sample Replacement Chart

J. Smith
Vice President of Marketing

R. Jones
Sales Director
Ready now

C. Williams
Promotions Manager
75 months

S. Anderson
Director of Marketing Research
1 year

© Cengage Learning

personal bias and ensure that the most qualified individuals are promoted. Moreover, it allows an organization to provide its high-potential employees with more specific feedback regarding developmental needs. Such an approach might ensure that women and minorities have equal access to high-level management positions.

Clearly, the more volatile competitive organizations of the twenty-first century may need to develop much larger pools of talent with very broad sets of skills. Consequently, many organizations are beginning to embrace the development of succession planning strategies that are based more on organization-needed competencies and flexibility than focusing on subjective assessment of "readiness."

Succession planning has traditionally been very limited in scope, focused on senior executives within the organization. One estimate is that a typical organization's succession planning process involves no more than 2 percent of the organization's workforce.[9] Much of the process of succession planning has involved CEOs and other executives secretly identifying their chosen successors from among the ranks of existing employees.[10] Wall Street analysts also consider and weigh in on likely successors and their identities in assessing an organization's ongoing potential and value. In more recent years, however, succession planning has been taking place throughout the managerial and technical ranks of organizations and become seen increasingly as a critical component of an organization's talent management and development process. While individual high-potential employees are still identified and targeted for development, many organizations now take a broader approach and focus on pools of talent to ensure depth of employee skill development throughout the organization and the development of successors for a wide range of positions than just those at the senior executive ranks.

Some guidelines for effective succession planning are presented in Exhibit 5.5. First, succession planning efforts should be tied into an organization's strategy relative to projected needs and competencies over the coming five years. It is critical that the organization modify the plan accordingly as the organization responds to unanticipated events and revamps its strategy. Second, organizations should monitor the progress of succession planning initiatives and measure outcomes as frequently as financial performance is measured (preferably quarterly). This helps to ensure that targeted efforts are producing results. Third, succession planning efforts need to ensure that all HR functions that impact the succession plan (hiring, training and development, compensation, and retention) are integrated and working in tandem. Typically, succession planning and these other areas are siloed without any coordination.[11] Planning efforts are a critical part of the organization's HR strategy and ideally function as a blueprint for all the various HR activities. Fourth, the organization needs to ensure that there is some centralized coordination of succession planning effort to ensure that top performers are not being coveted by different executives as a possible successor, potentially setting managers against each other in cannibalizing talent. Finally, succession planning efforts need to engage and involve managers throughout the organization. While HR can coordinate the

EXHIBIT 5.5 — Guidelines for Effective Succession Planning

- Tie into organization's strategy (and modified accordingly)
- Monitor the progress and measure outcomes of succession planning initiatives
- Ensure that all HR functions that impact the succession plan are iterated and working in tandem
- Ensure centralized coordination of succession planning
- Engage and involve managers throughout the organization

© Cengage Learning

process, effective succession planning requires "multiple owners" of the process. In-depth interviews with managers of business units are as critical as—if not more important than—any computer-generated information. Managers need to see the benefits of succession planning and be willing to partner with HR in developing plans for their workforce.

Succession Planning at Eli Lilly

Eli Lilly and Co. is a global manufacturer and seller of pharmaceuticals. Based in Indianapolis, the organization employs more than 38,000 worldwide. Lilly first started using succession planning in 1957 but in 2002 moved its succession planning efforts online in an attempt to allow every employee with the company to apply for any job for which he or she feels qualified. The system is assessed by several metrics, including the skill level of talent in the pipeline and the number of positions for which there is a "ready" candidate. Three potential successors are named for each senior position within the organization. Roughly 3,800 positions have been identified as "key" positions—those that will cause disruption to operations if left unstaffed and not filled in a timely manner. Managers within the organizations can query the system to identify existing positions worldwide, those candidates being groomed for any such position, and skill gaps that might adversely impact the ability to fill the position. Whenever no candidates are available for succession, the system identifies new potential trainees and proposes individual development plans. Similarly, the system detects hidden "vulnerabilities," where individuals are part of more than three separate succession tracks. Individual employees who have been targeted for succession are not informed of the organization's sense of their potential for advancement in an attempt to alleviate stress and prevent breakdowns in communication and cooperation because of perceived competition.[12]

Succession planning not only helps to ensure that key management positions remain filled, but it also helps to identify the critical training and development needs of both individual managers and the organization as a whole. Succession planning clearly involves taking an investment-oriented approach toward employees. Although the benefits of a well-developed succession planning program can be significant, such programs can also come at a significant cost to an organization. An employer should ensure that there is at least one individual able to assume every critical position if something prevents the incumbent from continuing in it; however, the more prepared an individual is for a promotion that he or she does not receive, the greater the possibility that he or she might seek such a position elsewhere. This is particularly true for succession planning programs built around defined management competencies. The end result of this process is that the organization invests in an individual and a competitor receives the return on that investment. Succession planning initiatives aimed at key managers need to be coupled with a specific retention strategy designed for potential successors who are passed over for promotions.

One key issue that organizations must address in their succession planning is the extent to which these efforts will be public and whether those targeted for grooming for higher-level assignments are informed of their "high-potential" status. These questions have been the subject of ongoing debate, as outlined in Exhibit 5.6. Telling employees that they have been identified as key potential players in the organization's future plans might reinforce these employees' decision to stay with the organization for a longer period of time in light of alternative career opportunities. At the same time, it may create expectations for these employees that advancement is guaranteed and/or imminent. In addition, it could create a kind of implied contract to workers that they are guaranteed continued employment, eroding the employment-at-will doctrine, which is discussed in Chapter 7. Not telling employees has the benefit of the employer "not committing" to employees and allows some flexibility in changing the mix of employees as business needs and the skill sets and experiences required to run the business change. On the other hand, if individuals are not aware that they have been targeted as "high potential," they may be more receptive to opportunities with other

EXHIBIT 5.6 Pros and Cons of Disclosing Succession Planning

	Disadvantages	Advantages
Do Not Tell	High performers may leave the organization, unsure of their future	Allows flexibility as business needs change
Tell	Unrealistic expectations and implied contracts	Retention strategy

© Cengage Learning

employers or consider going out on their own. One recent survey found that 37.5 percent of employers tell employees that they have been targeted; another found that 64 percent did so.[13] There is clearly no consensus as to whether such information should be kept confidential among the senior management team, and each organization should weigh the pros and cons presented in Exhibit 5.6 when deciding its strategy.

Succession Planning at Dole Food

California-based Dole Food Company, Inc., which produces and markets fruits, vegetables, and flowers, has more than 61,000 employees in more than 90 countries, with annual revenues of more than $4.6 billion. As the company grew from its humble origins, a decentralized structure was kept in place that allowed each unit to remain flexible relative to local market conditions. However, as Dole has become a worldwide conglomerate, this structure has inhibited the effective management of human capital at the executive level. To facilitate the global deployment of human capital, Dole instituted a succession planning model that revolves around four strategic competencies: accountability, business acumen, multifunctionality (cross-training), and vision/originality. Conducted entirely online, the program allows top managers access via a password. Employees provide a résumé and fill out personal data, including career interests and mobility restrictions, and assess themselves on the four competencies. The information is then made available to managers who can assess the data for promotability as well as identify those employees for whom a special retention strategy should be developed. The data are then used to create a career development plan for each employee and to keep executives informed about those internal candidates who might be best suited for an opening. The system also allows Dole to identify those areas where it has a "talent gap" so development opportunities might be provided, candidates sourced externally, or both, until those competencies are fully contained in-house.[14]

CEO Succession

A recent survey conducted by executive search firm Heidrick & Struggles in conjunction with Stanford University found that more than 50 percent of U.S. and Canadian organizations did not have any CEO succession plan in place.[15] This lack of planning persists despite the fact that the majority of respondents to the survey feel the need to have a CEO successor ready at any given time. In fact, 39 percent of respondents reported that they did not have a single viable internal CEO candidate. The study also found a lack of support for new CEOs with only 50 percent of employers providing any kind of onboarding or transition support for a new CEO.

This lack of succession planning at the top can leave an organization vulnerable in the wake of a sudden and unexpected departure of a CEO. For that reasons, CEO succession planning should be two-pronged, dealing with both the short and long terms. The short-term plan would involve a CEO who could step into the position immediately, generally within a 24- to 48-hour time frame. This individual could be a board member, retired executive, or other individual who could be trusted to keep the company on track until a permanent (long-term) successor was named. Ideally these would be two different individuals to prevent any sense of insider advantage as well as allow the organization to truly think strategically about who would provide the best fit as the next long-term CEO.

Succession planning efforts for the top executive spots have taken on more importance in recent years. With increasing pressure from boards and shareholders for continual profitability, the job of CEO has become far less attractive, particularly as the economy slows. Approximately 20 percent of the CEOs of America's 200 largest corporations were replaced in a recent year, and the average CEO tenure is currently less than three years.[16] Even more startling is the number of high-profile CEOs who have departed after 18 months or less on the job, by either resignation or ouster, including the CEOs of Procter & Gamble, Mattel, Gillette, and Maytag.[17] Although turnover at the CEO level can be beneficial for an organization, it can also be highly disruptive. Consequently, organizations need to pay special attention to planning at the CEO level.

CEO Succession Planning at General Electric

When legendary General Electric (GE) CEO Jack Welch announced his pending retirement, there was not as much concern among GE stakeholders as might be expected. In keeping with GE's reputation as one of the best organizations at grooming senior management, Welch had planned his succession for more than six years prior to his public announcement. Within one month of Jeffrey Immelt being named president and chairman-elect of GE as Welch's successor, two other top GE executives were named CEOs of Minnesota Mining and Manufacturing (3M) and Home Depot, Inc., affirming that GE is known for its superb training of senior executives for the chief executive's role.

GE's plan is relatively simple. Managers and executives are rotated from job to job every two to three years, with each new assignment being carefully designed to build experience and skills, creating a knowledgeable and experienced team of managers who have been exposed to a range of the giant corporation's divisions. Each new assignment involves a specific set of goals and expectations that must be met to ensure further advancement. The model is relatively simple and easy to duplicate; yet it takes a tremendous amount of time, energy, and commitment to make it succeed. At GE, the model is firmly ingrained in the corporate culture and creates a highly competitive system of performance management in which only the best and brightest executive will ultimately succeed.[18]

Mentoring

One key tool often used in succession planning is mentoring, whereby an individual executive or manager assumes responsibility for the development of an individual employee. Mentoring programs ideally mesh the needs of individual employees and those of the organization under the stewardship of a responsible individual senior to the individual being mentored. Exhibit 5.7 presents a model of an effective mentoring program.

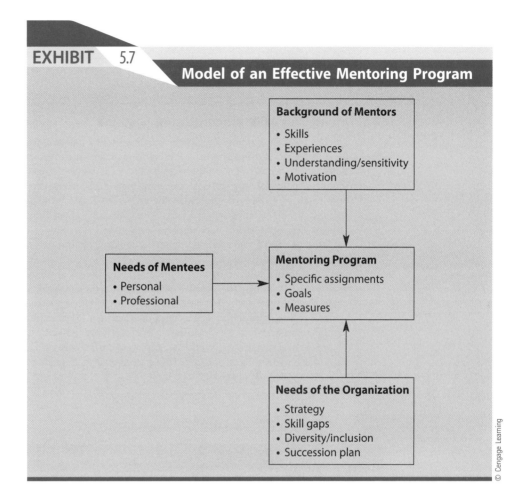

EXHIBIT   5.7

Model of an Effective Mentoring Program

Background of Mentors
- Skills
- Experiences
- Understanding/sensitivity
- Motivation

Needs of Mentees
- Personal
- Professional

Mentoring Program
- Specific assignments
- Goals
- Measures

Needs of the Organization
- Strategy
- Skill gaps
- Diversity/inclusion
- Succession plan

© Cengage Learning

In selecting individuals to be mentored, an organization will usually select an individual who has proven high levels of performance and/or is high potential in the case of a new hire. Mentoring should be holistic in nature and consider the needs of the individual being mentored, or mentee, from both personal and professional perspectives. Mentors should be selected who have the appropriate skill and experience to guide the mentee but, equally important, have a genuine interest in mentoring and some sensitivity toward the needs of the mentee. The mentoring program should be designed around specific organizational needs, considering the organization's strategy, identified skill gaps that need to be addressed and developed, and diversity and inclusion initiatives. To be effective, a mentoring program should have specific goals and measures of success identified prior to its inception. On a micro-level, these might involve performance levels and skills development of individual employees. On a macro-level, these might involve retention, knowledge transfer, and development and promotion of targeted minority groups.

Mentoring programs may be formal or informal. Informal mentoring programs have been criticized as being less effective because individual employees are prone to seeking out mentors who are like themselves, relative to demographic factors such as race, gender, ethnicity, and/or religion.[19] Organizations that have little diversity in the executive and managerial ranks may find that informal mentoring does little to alleviate this shortage. One criticism of succession planning programs is that many have perpetuated the development and succession of white males (or majority employees) at the expense of others, particularly in organizations where the demographic makeup of the executive team does not reflect the overall diversity of employees or percentage of employees from different groups in the organization's overall workforce. Reading 5.1 "Diverse Succession Planning: Lessons from the Industry Leaders," addresses this issue and presents suggestions as to how succession planning and diversity programs can work in tandem with each other.

Mentoring at Raytheon Vision Systems

Raytheon Vision Systems is a Goleta, California-based national defense contractor that produces detection and imaging devices. Several years ago, the organization came to the realization than 35 percent of its employees would be eligible to retire within five years. In many instances, potential retirees were the only individuals within the organization who knew how to do something, as they were the ones who had invented a product or process. In response to this potential talent drain, the organization created a mentoring program called Leave-A-Legacy in which older employees who had vital, proprietary knowledge were paired with high-potential subordinate employees to facilitate transfer of knowledge. Knowledge sharing involves activities such as bringing mentees to meetings, introducing them to customers, and involving them in the proposal or design stages of product development, and this is facilitated by third-party coaches who work with the employee pairs to set individualized plans. Pending retirees report that the program gives them a strong sense of purpose and value to the organization as well as ensuring that their legacies are carried on. Mentees have higher commitment to the organization and a stronger interest in remaining at Raytheon. The program is a potential model for any organization concerned about the loss of experience, skills, and contacts from a resulting large-scale retirement of employees who are part of the Baby Boom generation.[20]

Conclusion

Effective strategic workforce planning is the first key component for developing a HR strategy. Strategic workforce planning involves translating corporate-wide strategic initiatives into a workable plan for identifying the people needed to achieve these objectives; simultaneously, planning serves as a blueprint for all specific HR programs and policies. It is critical for the success of smaller, rapidly growing companies to ensure that their growth is properly managed and focused. Strategic workforce planning allows the HR function to contribute to an organization's effectiveness by laying a foundation for proactive management that is strategically focused. Reading 5.2, "The Annual HR Strategic Planning Process: Design and Facilitation Lessons From Corning Incorporated Human Resources," provides a case study example that illustrates the relationship between HR planning and overall strategic planning for the organization.

More specifically, strategic workforce planning facilitates a number of key processes within an organization. First, it facilitates leadership continuity through succession planning. It ensures that there will be no—or, at most, minimal—disruption of day-to-day operations because of unplanned departures.

Second, it facilitates strategic planning by examining the future availability of employees and their skill sets. Although strategic workforce planning follows from the strategic plan, the information collected in the strategic workforce planning process contributes to the assessment of the internal organization environment done in subsequent strategic planning.

Third, it facilitates an understanding of shifts and trends in the labor market through an examination of job requirements and employee capabilities. By assessing demographics, skills, and knowledge of employees and applicants vis-à-vis job requirements, the organization can remain ahead of its competitors in understanding the changing labor force.

Fourth, it facilitates employee development by determining the skills that are needed to achieve strategic objectives as well as to ensure future career success in the organization. Ideally, this can serve as a catalyst for investing in employees through targeted training and development programs.

Fifth, it facilitates budget planning and resource allocation by determining needs for employees in response to the organization's strategic plan. This is particularly important in labor-intensive service industries where a significant portion of the budget is assumed by direct and indirect payroll expenditures.

Sixth, it facilitates efficiency by estimating future employee surpluses and shortages. Costs of overstaffing and understaffing can be significant and are minimized by the strategic workforce planning process, allowing organizations to maintain a more competitive cost structure.

Finally, it facilitates the organization's adaptation to its environment. By assessing the external factors that can affect the organization against existing employee skills and background, the organization is better able to maintain an appropriate fit with its environment by ensuring that it has the in-house talent to manage its relationship with its environment.

Critical Thinking

1. What are the major objectives of strategic workforce planning? Why is each of these objectives critical for an organization's success? What benefits are provided by each that can result in a competitive advantage?

2. Why are aggregate and succession planning of critical importance? How might failures in these areas impact an organization's ability to compete?

3. What role might strategic workforce planning play in each of the following organizations?

   - A small, rapidly growing technology company
   - A medium-sized nonprofit social services agency
   - A state government agency
   - A professional sports franchise
   - A company planning on acquiring or merging with a key competitor

4. Discuss the implications and pros and cons for managing surpluses and shortages by using the various strategies presented in Exhibit 5.3.

5. Discuss the pros and cons of informing employees that they have been targeted as part of the organization's succession planning process. What particular business conditions and/or strategy might make telling or not telling the more advantageous option?

6. Identify the steps you might take in consulting with the federal government about strategic workforce planning. What factors would you suggest senior managers examine, and what obstacles to implementing change might exist?

7. Select three organizations in which a new CEO has assumed responsibility during the past year. Identify via news sources factors that may have led to the change at the top of the organization. What appears to be the reason for the succession, and what was the general reaction to the succession?

8. What problems are demographic shifts and layoff practices causing for succession planning? What role do competencies play in the succession planning initiatives of leading organizations?

9. Identify the positions within your school for which you feel succession planning is critical, such as deans, program directors, or department chairs. What critical skills or competencies are needed to perform these jobs? Design a succession planning program that is consistent with the strategic objectives of your school, utilizing the four phases of the succession model presented in the reading.

10. What are the advantages and disadvantages of establishing cross-cultural mentoring relationships?

Reading 5.1

11. Should special succession planning programs directed toward minorities be established? Discuss the pros and cons of identifying "best" and "best minority" candidates in succession planning, as is done at Procter & Gamble and Motorola.

Reading 5.2

12. Explain the process used for human resource planning at Corning. What obstacles might exist to implementing such a process in another organization?

Exercises

1. Explain how the dean of your school would employ techniques of strategic workforce planning to decide how many faculty and staff to employ in the coming academic year and which specific employees to retain, reassign, or release. What critical pieces of information would the dean need in order to arrive at these decisions?

2. Visit the Web site for the Human Resource Planning Society, a professional organization of those who are involved with strategic workforce planning, at http://www.hrps.org. Identify the programs that they offer that might be of value to various organizations.

Chapter References

1. Kimes, M. "P&G's Leadership Machine," *Fortune,* April 13, 2009, 159, (7), p. 22.

2. Wells, S. J. "Keeping Watch: Tracking the Evidence," *HR Magazine,* April, 2002, 47, (4), pp. 34–35.

3. Wells, S. J. "Catch a Wave," *HR Magazine,* April 2002, 47, (4) pp. 31–37.

4. Leonard, B. "Study Shows U.S. Government Needs to Restructure Recruiting, Training Tactics," *HR Magazine,* June 2003, 48, (6), p. 36.

5. Staisey, N., Treworgy, D., and Shiney, M. "Managing for the Future: Human Capital Strategies at the United States Postal Service," *The Business of Government,* Spring 2002, pp. 47–50.

6. Overman, S. "On the Right Track," *HR Magazine,* April 2011, 56, (4), pp. 73–75.

7. Barovick, L. P. "Sharing the Pain," *HR Magazine,* November 2010, 55, (11), pp. 51–54.

8. Staisey et al., op. cit.

9. Webster, L. "Leaving Nothing to Chance," *T + D,* 2009, 62, (2), pp. 56–61.

10. Kirchhoff, J. "Objective Measurement in Succession Planning." Society for Human Resource Management,

article 016356. Available at www.shrm.org/hrnews_/published/articles/CMS_016356.asp, May 2006.

11. Cooper, J. "Succession Planning: It's Not Just for Executive Anymore," *Workspan,* 2006, 49, (2), pp. 44–47.

12. Olson, S. "Lilly Relying on Technology to Spot Management Talent," *Indianapolis Business Journal,* March 2, 2009, 29, (53), p. 16.

13. Wells, S. J. "Who's Next?" *HR Magazine,* November 2003, 48, (11), pp. 45–50.

14. Roberts, B. "Matching Talent with Tasks," *HR Magazine,* November 2002, 47, (11) pp. 91–96.

15. Heidrick & Struggles and Rock Center for Corporate Governance, Stanford University, 2010 Survey on CEO Succession Planning (2010), Stanford University.

16. Leonard, B. "Turnover at the Top," *HR Magazine,* May 2001, 46, (5), pp. 46–52.

17. Ibid.

18. Ibid.

19. Tyler, K. "Cross-Cultural Connections," *HR Magazine,* October 2007, 52, (10), pp. 77–83.

20. Tyler, K. "Training Revs Up," *HR Magazine,* April 2005, 50, (4), pp. 58–63.

READING 5.1

Diverse Succession Planning: Lessons From the Industry Leaders

Charles R. Greer and Meghna Virick

Although practitioners and academics alike have argued for succession planning practices that facilitate better talent identification and creation of stronger "bench strength," there has been little attention to the incorporation of gender and racial diversity with succession planning. We discuss practices and competencies for incorporating diversity with succession planning and identify methods for developing women and minorities as successors for key positions. Improvements in strategy, leadership, planning, development, and program management processes are suggested. Recommendations for process improvement are developed from the diversity and succession planning literatures and interviews of 27 human resource professionals from a broad range of industries. © 2008 Wiley Periodicals, Inc.

Those being positioned as future leaders tend to look and act an awful lot like people in those top positions … It simply reflects an adherence to traditional methods of succession planning. (Tom McKinnon, Novations Group)

An emerging body of empirical evidence (e.g., Richard, 2000; Wright, Ferris, Hiller, & Kroll, 1995) indicates positive performance effects for diversity, and there are increasing indicators of the strategic importance of diversity to the success of companies. PepsiCo's previous CEO, Steve Reinemund, has said, "I believe that companies that figure out the diversity challenge first will clearly have a competitive advantage" (Terhune, 2005). A leading insurer, Allstate, also has embraced diversity and sees it as a source of competitive advantage, particularly in terms of expanding the number of minority policyholders (Crockett, 1999). Cosmetics maker L'Oreal attributes its global success in developing and marketing cosmetics to marketing initiatives that have drawn on international diversity (Salz, 2005).

Aside from the impact of competitive forces, some of the recent interest in succession planning may be attributed to the more active role of boards of directors in response to the Sarbanes-Oxley Act of 2002 and other regulatory developments. We see striking examples of succession planning successes and failures in organizations. For instance, GE's former CEO Jack Welch placed great emphasis on succession planning. One of his legacies was a process that allows the company, which is a veritable CEO greenhouse, to develop and promote talent from within the organization (Gale, 2001). Companies such as Bank of America, Dell, Dow Chemical, and Ely Lilly also have developed bench strength for their top positions by closely linking leadership development with succession planning (Conger & Fulmer, 2003; Karaevli & Hall, 2003). McDonald's provides an unusual example of preparedness in that the company was able to quickly designate a permanent replacement within six hours of CEO Jim Cantalupo's death, compared to the typical timetable of several months (Gibson & Gray, 2004; Hymowitz & Lublin, 2004). A few months later, when Cantalupo's successor, Charlie Bell, resigned because of terminal illness, McDonald's was able to immediately appoint Jim skinner as CEO (Gray, 2004; McGuirk, 2005).

While there have been note-worthy successes with succession planning, companies have had disappointments. At Coca-Cola, for example, Douglas Ivester replaced the late Robert Goizueta but lasted only two-and-a-half difficult years (Conger & Fulmer, 2003). While such failures may be attributed to flawed external searches, internal succession is often not an attractive option in the absence of succession planning and development. Some well-managed firms, such as Hewlett-Packard, Lincoln Electric, Southwest Airlines, and Whole Foods Markets, place heavy emphasis on promotion from within (Pfeffer, 1998) and treat succession planning as a critical process. Improved practices and competencies are needed for succession planning to meet the challenges posed by environmental turbulence, shortage of talent, and globalization (Karaevli & Hall, 2003).

Although these examples concern high-profile CEO succession, our broader approach involves succession to key managerial and professional positions and incorporates diversity initiatives. While failures in diversity are reflected in enduring underrepresentation of women and minorities in key positions, the combined effects of diverse succession planning have received little attention. Nonetheless, companies such as Allstate are using succession planning to increase diversity in key positions and women now occupy 40% of Allstate's executive and managerial positions, with 21% being held by minorities (Kim, 2003). Succession planning has also been critical to Harley-Davidson's accomplishments in diversity, as 17% of its vice presidents are women (PR Newswire, 2004).

Although we are unaware of any empirical evidence on the combined effects of diverse succession planning, the importance placed on both diversity and succession planning by several leading companies makes the topic relevant for consideration. Recent survey data also have called attention to the importance of diversity practices for increased organizational competitiveness (Esen, 2005). The significance of linking diversity management with succession planning is that more robust succession plans are produced and thus provide a strategic focus for the development of a diverse workforce. With such linkage, the planned succession of diverse talent provides more options for strategy formulation, such as the pursuit of growth in diverse and global markets or innovation-based strategies, while strategy implementation and operations benefit from the flexibility provided by a deeper talent pool.

Practitioners and academics alike have argued for succession planning practices that facilitate better talent identification and create stronger bench strength, yet there has been little attention paid to the incorporation of gender and racial diversity with succession planning. As companies attempt to revitalize their succession planning, it is a good time to address a major challenge for these efforts—specifically, integrating diversity with succession. This article addresses these concerns by identifying practices and competencies that can facilitate such integration. We draw on results of interviews with human resource professionals along with findings from the literature to identify suggestions for integrating the two processes.

Performance Effects of Diverse Succession Planning

While little research has focused on the performance effects of succession planning, some aspects of succession systems are related to financial performance (Friedman, 1986). Success factors include CEO involvement, rewards for developing subordinates, "earnestness" of performance reviews, forecasting the need for talent, and individual values consistent with organizational values (Friedman, 1986). Succession planning also has indirect impacts on measures of firm performance such as productivity and gross returns on assets (Huselid, Jackson, & Schuler, 1996). Indirect evidence of effective succession planning also is provided by the lower failure rates of insider CEOs (Charan, 2005) and the infrequency in which some very successful companies search beyond the firm to fill vacant CEO Positions. A landmark study of visionary companies found that poor succession planning caused gaps in internal supplies of leadership talent, as described in the following statement:

We found evidence that only two visionary companies (11.1 percent) ever hired a chief executive directly from outside the company, compared to thirteen (72.2 percent) of the comparison companies. Of 113 chief executives for which we have data in the visionary companies, only 3.5 percent came directly from outside the company, versus 22.1 percent of the 140 CEOs at the comparison companies. (Collins & Porras, 1994, p. 172)

Promotion-from-within policies, which require some level of sophistication in succession planning, also are positively associated with measures of organizational performance (Delaney & Huselid, 1996). In fact, researchers have concluded that external successors are likely to be effective in more limited circumstances, such as when they are brought in to help with poorly performing firms (Wei & Cannella, 2002).

The future of many organizations is likely to depend on their mastery of diverse succession planning given that building bench strength among women and minorities will be critical in the competitive war for talent. For example, the U.S. Department of Labor predicts that women and minorities will account for 70% of the new participants in the labor force in 2008 (McCuiston, Wooldridge, & Pierce, 2004). Furthermore, women account for an increasing proportion of the well-educated workforce and are forecasted to receive 60% of all bachelor's degrees, 60% of all master's degrees, and 48% of all doctoral degrees by 2014 (U.S. Department of Education, 2005). Moreover, organizations lacking effective diversity management programs often experience excessive turnover and high replacement costs, loss of investments in training, brand image problems, poor employer image, and litigation (Hubbard, 2004). Absence of diversity programs also may result in strategic opportunity costs such as unrealized market access or lack of awareness (D. A. Thomas & Ely, 1996). Indeed, if the performance impact of diversity problems is approached in terms of litigation and related costs alone, the costs for some leading companies such as Coca-Cola ($102.5 million) and State Farm ($250 million) have been breathtaking (Hubbard, 2004).

The integration of diversity with succession planning requires an appropriate approach. Typically, organizations have adopted one of three approaches to managing diversity: an assimilation view that downplays differences; an access view that focuses on building diversity in order to gain access to ethnic consumer groups; and an integrated view that emphasizes uniform performance standards, personal development, openness, acceptance of constructive conflict, empowerment, egalitarianism, and a nonbureaucratic structure that encourages challenges to the status quo (D. A. Thomas & Ely, 1996). We argue that an integrated approach and a culture of inclusiveness are critical for diverse succession planning. Next we describe the methods used to examine the interface between diversity and succession planning.

Data Sources and Analysis

Our investigation was based on a review of the succession planning and diversity literature and on 27 interviews of HR professionals from 25 different organizations in the United States and one in Canada. Interviews were conducted using a semistructured format based on a set of seven questions that were revised as other issues became evident. Questions such as the following were used for the initial inquiries: "What are some of the things that (your organization) does in terms of the succession planning of women and minorities?"; "Are there any practices that link the management of diversity to succession planning?"; and "Are there methods for increasing nominations of diverse professionals for admission to the pool of potential successors?"

Notes taken during the interviews were reviewed to identify practices or themes and then transferred to electronic files for analysis with computer search routines. Because we were concerned with identifying a broad range of practices we used qualitative "editing" and "template" analytical approaches (King, 1994; Miller & Crabtree, 1992). These approaches provide a search for meaningful content segments (Miller & Crabtree, 1992), and a codebook is compiled from the categories or themes that are created from an initial examination of the data or on an a priori basis. The codebook is then revised as themes emerge from continued searches of the data (King, 1994).

We identified several themes such as communication related to program strategy, values driving the process, and leadership involvement. Computer search routines were then used to refine the organization of content according to the themes and to reconcile the content with the narrative of our findings. We will discuss the practices that facilitate the integration of diversity with succession planning, beginning with the organization's business strategy. Information on interviewee demographics, job titles, and industries of their organizations is provided in Table 1. As indicated in Table 1, there was substantial diversity in our group of interviewees.

Practices and Competencies

Our discussion of practices and competencies follows a sequence of five processes that reflect the order of succession planning. We begin with a discussion of integration of strategy and planning. Figure 1 illustrates this integration with a feedback loop of diverse talent influencing strategy formulation. Next, we discuss leadership practices and then move on to critical planning practices. We then focus on systematic approaches to development and mentorship competencies, with special attention to paradoxes and challenges. Finally, we address program management practices and issues.

Business Strategy

The integration of diversity with business and human resource strategies, reflected in Figure 1, lays the foundation for identifying the range of competencies and for designing the developmental experiences required for succession. This integration process should be continuous and flexible, because the competencies for key personnel are likely to change in the future (McCall, 1998). The example of GE (Hymowitz & Lublin, 2004; Karaevli & Hall, 2003) demonstrates the critical role of alignment with business strategy. In GE's continuous process of succession planning, the CEO first sets objectives for the various business units. The process of setting objectives includes succession planning as a key part of the decision framework and involves attention to such issues as staffing, backups for key slots, global issues, technical workforce development, and diversity (Liebman, Bruer, & Maki, 1996). Motorola, PepsiCo, and IBM provide examples of other companies that integrate human resource development processes with business strategy (Childs, 2005; McCall, 1998). One of our interviewees stressed the importance of communication about strategy and goals of diversity initiatives. Without such communication, individuals targeted for development have no basis for comparing developmental requirements with their aspirations or for making informed decisions about program participation (Cespedes & Galford, 2004).

Leadership

Commitment and direct involvement by the CEO and the senior leadership team are clear threshold requirements for diverse succession planning. A recent comparison by Hewitt Associates of 20 top companies, including such companies as 3M, GE, IBM, Medtronic, Pitney Bowes, and Procter & Gamble, found that 100% of the CEOs in the top group (defined as companies that have built a sustainable pipeline of future leaders) were involved with leadership development relative to only 65% of other companies (Salob & Greenslade, 2005). Colgate-Palmolive, ranked among the best companies in diversity, devotes four sessions each year to developing plans for high-potential minorities (Sherwood & Mendelsson, 2005). The relevance of senior leadership involvement is revealed as follows:

> ... bringing attention to diversity into succession planning processes [requires that] ... that possible successors for key jobs are diversity-competent. Unfortunately, only a small percentage of companies take this seriously ... CEOs and others who are committed to changing the culture of their organizations to be better at welcoming and using diversity must make sure that the people most likely to replace them are strong on managing diversity. (Cox, 2001, p. 123)

Leadership support for diverse succession planning is also reflected in reporting relationships. A recent survey of 1,700 HR executives found that a relatively small percentage of the companies for which the respondents worked (30%) had direct reporting relationships between their diversity officers and their CEOs (Alleyne, 2005). On the other hand,

Table 1

Architecture for Intangibles

Gender	Interviewees
Men	18
Women	9

Race	Interviewees
Caucasian	18
African American	6
Hispanic	2
Asian	1

Job Titles	Interviewees	Job Titles	Interviewees
President	2	Director of Diversity Council	1
Executive Vice President	1	Senior Human Resource Manager	1
Senior Vice President	3	Training Manager	1
National Managing Partner	1	Workforce Diversity Manager	1
Vice President	2	Human Resource Manager	1
Partner	1	Inspector—Career Development	1
Assistant Vice President	1	Human Resource Business Partner	1
Plant Manager	1	Human Resource Generalist	1
Senior Executive and Director	1	Senior Sourcing Specialist	1
Senior Director	1	Account Manager for College Relations and Recruitment	1
Director	3		

Industries	Industries
Computer Manufacturing	Gift Manufacturing
Commercial Real Estate	Pharmaceuticals
Convenience Retailing	Public Administration
Consulting Services	Railway Transportation
Distilling	Semiconductor Manufacturing
Electronics Manufacturing	Specialty Retailing
Financial Services	Specialty Services
Food Manufacturing	Telecommunications
General Manufacturing	Wholesaling

Note: Interviewees' organizations included nine Fortune 500 publicly traded companies, with the remainder being foreign-held companies, smaller publicly traded companies, privately held companies, small and large consulting firms, and one public-sector organization. One of the interviewees had retired from his executive position to become a consultant and educator.

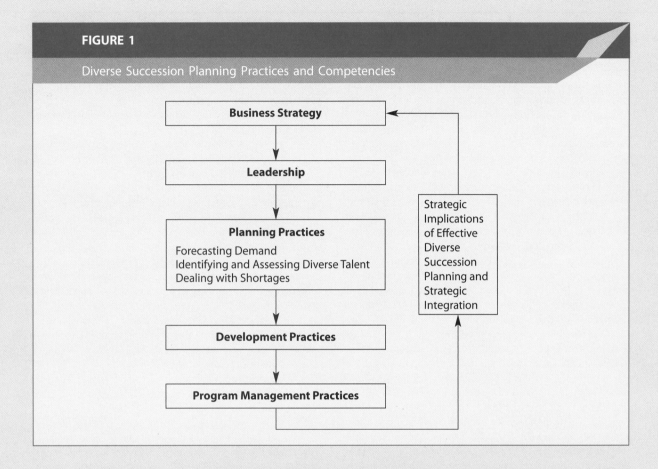

FIGURE 1

Diverse Succession Planning Practices and Competencies

positions for chief diversity officers (CDOs) or vice presidents for diversity have been created at such companies as Abbott Labs, Boeing, Colgate-Palmolive, Johnson Controls, Lockheed Martin, PricewaterhouseCoopers, and Starbucks. Approximately 20% of our interviewees noted the importance of top leadership involvement in various capacities. One interviewee emphasized the importance of a direct reporting relationship to the CEO and noted that she had power to influence inclusion of women and minorities in succession planning solely by virtue of access to the CEO. Aside from the leadership provided by CEOs and diversity officers, management of diversity should be embraced by the entire leadership team and not perceived as the exclusive domain of the HR function (Childs, 2005).

In organizations that emphasize the use of succession planning for development, managerial accountability becomes important (McCall, 1998). This may take the form of mentoring. One interviewee, who led her company's diversity efforts, noted top-level involvement through the requirement for senior executives to personally mentor a woman or minority. She also stressed the frequency of succession planning, noting that they had a biannual succession planning exercise involving the CEO and the company's top

15 executives. In contrast, an interviewee from another company with a fairly comprehensive succession planning program indicated that until recently, the company had only addressed gender diversity in a reactive manner by asking, during the process of compiling lists of high potentials, whether any women candidates ought to be considered. Slow progress on diversity issues points to the importance of having more responsive leadership.

Planning

Forecasting Demand Although the demand for talent is driven by business strategy and the approach to diversity the talents and behavioral competencies identified as requirements for future executive positions are likely to change (Charan, 2005; McCall, 1998). One of the paradoxes of planning is that with more turbulent conditions, planning is more difficult but it also becomes more valuable (Greer, 2001; Niehaus, 1988). Given the long developmental time horizons and the associated uncertainty, flexibility is best obtained with talent pool approaches to succession planning as opposed to more position-specific targeted approaches, typically referred to as replacement planning (Carnazza, 1982).

Talent Identification and Assessment Early identification of talent is important for the development of broad range of experiences needed to fill executive positions (McCall, 1998), and our interviewees stressed the need to reach deeper into the organization. Fortunately, our understanding of early talent identification is improving, especially the role of learning and learning agility, which are critical indicators of success in senior leadership positions (Lombardo & Eichinger, 2000). McCall and his colleagues have identified several learning-oriented dimensions that are helpful for early identification such as "seeks opportunities to learn," "is committed to making a differences," "has the courage to take risks," "seeks and uses feedback," and "learns from mistakes" (McCall, 1998, pp. 128–129). Measures of learning ability, defined as the ability and willingness to learn from experience, or the ability to learn as conditions change, also are available (Eichinger & Lombardo, 2004; Lombardo & Eichinger, 2000). The common problem of negative bias in performance evaluations for minorities makes measures of learning agility particularly relevant to the issue of diverse succession planning. One of our interviewees noted her company's reliance on a measure of learning agility in the use of data and on a measure of results orientation toward both deadlines and goals.

One of the most heavily utilized approaches for identifying talent for succession planning involves performance evaluations. This approach has problems, given evidence of negative bias in performance evaluations of minority managers (Kilian, Hukai, & McCarty, 2005). Companies leading the way in developing minority executives take a different approach by emphasizing results, relying on objective indicators of competency, and focusing on measurable track records to identify talent (Thomas & Gabarro, 1999). One interviewee mentioned the use of an anecdotal profile of potential successors as an important component of assessment. Another interviewee stressed the importance of objective standards of potential and readiness for promotion to offset unconscious biases against women. Assessment-center procedures are also used for succession planning and have potential for diversity initiatives (Conger & Fulmer, 2003; Klimoski, 1997; Yeung, 1997).

Additional recommendations deal with formalization, involving more decision makers, and the degree to which decisions on participation should be centralized. More specifically, it has been recommended that organizations should keep the list of high potentials subject to revision while another recommendation is to allow for self-nominations (Conger & Fulmer, 2003). An interviewee noted the value of his company's human resource inventory system in identifying employees who are ready for opportunities. Leaders in succession planning such as Eli Lilly, Hewlett-Packard, Citigroup, and the U.S. Army have adopted group approaches that have the advantage of utilizing more than one individual's perceptions of potential (Karaevli & Hall, 2003). Along this line, Deloitte & Touche has changed its succession process from one in which the departing manager selected a successor to a more centralized approach. When vacancies arise in the top ranks, senior managers across the country review short lists of candidates keeping diversity objectives in mind (Armour, 2003).

A variant of this approach, noted by one interviewee, was to have decentralized identification of high potentials, along with some centralized oversight with interwoven diversity objectives. This approach was considered to be the key to her company's success in succession planning, and is consistent with organizations such as Lockheed-Martin. When oversight reveals that women and minorities are not represented in developmental programs, managers are asked to provide explanations. The manager of organizational effectiveness has the authority to promote developmental opportunities, even if it means changing succession plans (Bogan, 2002). Replacement lists are also monitored at companies such as IBM and Dow Corning (Salomon & Schork, 2003), and several interviewees told us that their companies will not fill some jobs without conversations aimed at having a diverse slate of candidates.

Another concern for talent identification is related to the residual effects of differences in past assignments. Current successors to top-level positions often have benefited from prior advantageous developmental assignments and have sometimes been selected simply due to their similarity to past incumbents in terms of work experiences and demographic characteristics of gender, race, and age (Frase-Blunt, 2003). Such similarity biases are more likely to occur in the absence of formal succession planning (Rothwell, 2001). This heightens the need for defining competencies for senior-level positions in terms of specific behaviors with the purpose of making the process more transparent and acceptable (McKinnon, 2003).

Certain technical planning practices are also relevant to diverse succession. At Procter & Gamble, top-level managers designate three successors: an "emergency" replacement, who is typically a peer who could fill the position very quickly; a "planned" successor, who will be prepared to fill the position after some period of time if provided with the correct developmental experiences; and a potential "diversity" successor (Himelstein & Forest, 1997). In a similar vein, Motorola attempts to identify three successors: an immediate replacement, someone who could fill the position with three to five years of development, and the best qualified woman candidate beyond any already identified for the first two categories. Four years after the program's implementation, the company increased the number of minority women vice presidents from one to eleven (Caudron, 1999; Himelstein & Forest, 1997).

Dealing with Shortages One approach for dealing with shortages of diverse talent when there is no time for longer-term development is referred to as "priming the pump." This approach encourages early promotions or brings in diverse talent from the outside. The following account of a presentation to Boeing employees by James Bell, Boeing's CFO and president, provides perspective on the need for rapid progress:

> When high-potential young people from diverse backgrounds look at Boeing's organization chart—or [those of] any of a thousand large publicly traded companies—more often than not, they're seeing a picture that doesn't appropriately reflect their experience." He argued that that reality simply must change in order for Boeing to maintain its market leadership.... (Orenstein, 2005, p. 234)

Some interviewees noted the importance of developing a culture of inclusiveness as employees look upward in the hierarchy to see if there are people who look like them. Minority employees are likely to ask, "Is the environment accepting of me?" Quick-fix approaches that bypass developmental time, or methods based on expediency, can produce ill-prepared successors and cause problems in morale and turnover (Rothwell, 2001). As such, they should be viewed with caution. As Charan (2005, p. 81) noted, "A quick infusion of talent may be a company's only course, but it is no way to run a railroad." Nonetheless, we found that some organizations obtain quick infusions of talent by bringing in senior-level women and minorities from the outside or by relying on early promotions. One of our interviewees noted the symbolic importance of success stories and reported successful use of judicious pump priming with the early promotion of a high-potential woman who improved the environment for women engineers in his company.

Development

Systematic Approaches Evidence indicates that companies with good reputations for developing people, such as Colgate-Palmolive, Emerson Electric, General Electric, Johnson & Johnson, Procter & Gamble, and Sherwin-Williams (Charan, 2005), have been both systematic and persistent over a long period of time before having obtained results (Carnazza, 1982; Charan, 2005; Conger & Fulmer, 2003). Succession planning at the American Red Cross includes talented women and minorities in special developmental programs and emphasizes communication and individual career development plans (Frase-Blunt, 2003). The key to development lies in providing challenging assignments to high potentials with accountability for profit and loss and close evaluation of performance in these roles (Cappelli & Hamori, 2005; Cespedes & Galford, 2004; Charan, 2005). Women's inexperience with profit-and-loss responsibility is one of the reasons for their slow progress in obtaining senior-level jobs

(Catalyst, 2003). Many leading companies have recognized and are addressing this issue. Lateral moves are especially important in large complex companies dominated by engineering or other technical work (Flynn, 1998), since many key professional positions are not on the vertical career track.

Contact and visibility with senior leaders is also important. The Hewitt study cited earlier found that 95% of the companies in the top group create such opportunities for high potentials (Salob & Greenslade, 2005). One of our interviewees emphasized the critical importance of positioning succession planning programs so that they focus on developing high potentials rather than on diversity per se. His approach was to ensure diversity in the succession pool, with the overall emphasis being the creation of a "leadership pipeline full of good people." Special programs for women and minorities may be hindered by the stigma of special treatment (Murrell & James, 2001), and may not conform to the special consideration test proposed by Roosevelt Thomas because they are not open to everyone (R. Thomas, 1990). As Thomas has stated, "Does this program or policy give special consideration to one group? If so, it won't solve your problem—and may have caused it" (R. Thomas, 1990). Other observers (Liff, 1997) and some of our interviewees also cautioned against special succession planning programs for women and minorities. One interviewee, in reference to women and minorities in leadership ranks, stated that "the way they got there is more important than the fact that they got there." Interviewees also noted that programs championed by only a few senior leaders are unlikely to be successful in the long term because of the lack of organizational support and the absence of a systematic approach. After the champions are gone, the programs often fail.

Nonetheless, it has been argued that in the absence of special programs that are targeted specifically toward women and minorities, very little is likely to change. Special programs have had an impact in some organizations, such as GE and shell (Reinhold, 2005), Deloitte & Touche (Anderson, 2005), and IBM (D. Thomas, 2004). However, such programs reflect the reality of constrained resources that prevent unlimited access for all employees. Special programs also address the problem of small numbers. As one interviewee pointed out, if women and minorities are simply given the same assignments as everyone else, some will get interesting assignments while others will not. Because of smaller numbers, when women and minorities leave as a result of uninteresting or unchallenging assignments, there are serious problems for diversity objectives. We sometimes encountered contradictions in that interviewees initially noted the inadvisability of special programs but later mentioned that their companies provided such programs for women and minorities.

Special challenges often occur in professional settings when there are small proportions of women or minorities. In these circumstances, they are visible because of their uniqueness and isolated because they have few diverse peers

(Estlund, 2003). Interestingly, when women comprise a small proportion in a professional setting, those in early-career stages may not perceive senior women as role models because they view such women as lacking in power or behaving more like men than women (Ely, 1994; Murrell & James, 2001).

Women employed in industries that rely heavily on operations face such challenges. One interviewee told us that women sometimes faced so much difficulty in gaining acceptance in operations that they simply concluded it was not worth their effort to pursue a career in the area. Another interviewee told us that the old guard would conclude that a woman might not be suited for a position because it was a "tough job" involving 24/7 operations or unions. Other interviewees reported difficulties in obtaining representation of women in technology areas, such as chip design and manufacturing. These experience gaps are critical, because operations voids in the skill portfolios of women reduce their opportunities to move into senior executive ranks.

Mentorship   Scholars have found differences in mentoring experiences when different races and genders are involved (Noe, Greenberger, & Wang, 2002; Wanberg, Welsh, & Hezlett, 2003). For example, when women are mentored by women, they are likely to learn more about overcoming barriers to promotion and methods for achieving career and family balance (Noe et al., 2002; Ragins & McFarlin, 1990). With same-race mentorship relationships, there also tends to be more psychological or social support (Noe et al., 2002; D. Thomas, 1990). However, because of the scarcity of women and minorities in senior positions, cross-gender and cross-race mentoring relationships are prevalent (Noe et al., 2002; Ragins & Cotton, 1991; Wanberg et al., 2003). Nonetheless, cross-gender mentoring relationships can add value because they enable men and women to gain insights and perspectives about how the other gender handles workplace issues (Clawson & Kram, 1984; Noe et al., 2002).

PepsiCo, which has been cited as a leader in diversity (Sherwood & Mendelsson, 2005; Terhune, 2005), views cross-race mentorship as more than a substitute for same-race or same-gender mentoring. Its former CEO, Steve Reinemund encouraged mentoring across race and gender lines. More specifically, Reinemund required his direct reports to serve as sponsors for diversity across race and gender lines. An African American serves as the sponsor for white men, a white man sponsors African Americans, and a white woman sponsors Latinos (Terhune, 2005). PepsiCo's current CEO, Indra Nooyi, has said that the company wants its managers to be "'comfortable being uncomfortable' so they're willing to broach difficult issues in the workplace" (Terhune, 2005, p. B1).

Nonetheless, cross-race relationships require that mentors have diversity skills. With cross-gender mentoring relationships, there also can be problems unless mentors and protégés maintain appropriate levels of admiration, informality, respect, and trust, and act in a manner that does not create public image problems (Clawson & Kram, 1984). Not all mentors perform well in such roles, but some are truly exceptional. One interviewee told us that his company made this discovery when it asked approximately 100 of its minority and women employees about their experiences with mentors. When asked "Who was there for you in your darkest hour?" the group identified a very small number of mentors, and the same person was identified by as many as 20 to 25 individuals. Thus, efforts to identify exceptional mentors and leverage their skills should be a priority. Another interviewee emphasized the importance of training mentors and the value for basic guidelines such as advising mentors to avoid discussions of sensitive issues like race until the parties have established a strong relationship. Good matchups are always important, but are critical when high-level executives are involved. One interviewee told us that she personally makes the high-level match-ups and lags the notification to mentors by several days so that mentees have an opportunity to anonymously decline a mentor.

The retention of women and minorities, which is critical for program success, is being addressed with a number of different practices. A number of companies have been using affinity groups to provide informal guidance and networking assistance. For example, Nike now has such groups for African Americans, lesbians, gays, and other minorities (Jung, 2005). One interviewee told us that a great deal of coaching is needed in order to retain minorities and that the senior executive in charge of diversity needs to be heavily involved in these efforts, while another observed that succession planning is closely related to retention, but only when the company follows through with development. Another interviewee noted dramatically that organizations need to "throw their arms around women and minorities" in order to retain them and that coaching and mentoring are key for their retention. He also reported that his organization is reaching down to minority professionals, even at entry level, to help them discover the hidden messages that are critical to development in the organization's culture.

Program Management

Reward Systems   Some companies are using reward systems to motivate diverse succession. Senior executives at Denny's have a strong incentive to be responsive to diversity because the representation of minorities and women in their divisions accounts for 25% of executives' bonuses (Brathwaite, 2002). At Hyatt, where 52% of the company's managers are women, diversity goals account for 15% of bonuses (Prince, 2005). When retention levels for high potentials drop below 90% at Colgate-Palmolive, top-level managers lose money. Some companies have also implemented rewards for mentors. One interviewee told us that his company initially used only recognition as a reward for mentors who performed well, but that over time the company began to include such contributions in the performance-appraisal process and linked financial rewards to these efforts. On the other hand, intrinsic rewards may be very powerful, particularly for minority mentors who mentor other minorities (Noe et al., 2002; Ragins, 1997a, 1997b).

Confidentiality and Transparency Trade-offs As with some other issues in diverse succession planning, there are differing views on transparency. The Hewitt study noted earlier found that 68% of the top companies in leadership development informed employees of their status as high potentials while only approximately 53% in the comparison group of companies provided such information (Salob & Greenslade, 2005). With transparency, the career objectives of the candidate may be considered in developmental planning. On the other hand, complete transparency may interfere with teamwork and demotivate those not included on the list (Conger & Fulmer, 2003; Yeung, 1997). Informing employees of their readiness for promotion is a related issue. We saw varying levels of transparency. Whereas some of our interviewees stressed the importance of transparency and informing employees of their readiness in succession, other interviewees advocated the use of partial transparency, where individuals are told that they are making a contribution but are not explicitly told that they are high potentials to avoid raising expectations.

Measurement and Evaluation Ideally, evaluations should draw on both qualitative and quantitative measures. Qualitative measures may include factors such as satisfaction with the process at multiple levels of the managerial hierarchy and across gender and racial groups, as well as perceptions of fairness and usefulness. Such measures could include perceived smoothness of succession and the perceived quality of the talent pool. Quantitative metrics may include measures such as the percentage of diverse successors obtained internally, waiting time or ratios of "ready now" potentials to incumbents, and reservoirs of cross-functional or international experience, as well as attrition rates for diverse high potentials (Conger & Fulmer, 2003). One of our interviewees emphasized the importance of setting diversity targets in anticipation of the future racial composition of the United States. His pragmatic justification of his organization's adoption of special programs was that "you are not going to be successful by osmosis." Another interviewee, who stressed the importance of measuring the impact of such programs with more than one indicator, noted that her company uses 14 different measures of program effectiveness, including retention, advancement, hiring, and development. A different interviewee's company conducts periodic "pulse surveys" of employees to determine satisfaction with their career succession. Whatever the metric or diversity scorecard used, it is important to allow sufficient time, perhaps four to five years, for the effects to be evident before a program is evaluated and potentially disbanded (Carnazza, 1982).

Implications for Practitioners Industry leaders such as PepsiCo and Allstate provide examples of companies that have made diversity a part of their competitive strategies while others, such as GE, Eli Lilly, and Dell Computer provide examples of companies that are very skilled at developing talent through succession planning. We have identified a number of competencies and practices being used by industry leaders to increase diversity through the succession planning process. Those who wish to excel in this area will benefit from the knowledge of industry leaders that we have attempted to convey in this article. As we have noted, some leading companies recognize the performance effects to be gained from excellence in managing diversity and the value that may be created through such initiatives. The persuasion of others to support the development of organizational competencies in diverse succession planning requires a clear understanding of the business strategy and communication of how the process will provide a source of competitive advantage. Nonetheless, despite the rapid successes of a few leading organizations, senior leaders who seek to persuade their colleagues on the importance of diverse succession planning should understand and communicate to others that success in this area involves a longterm commitment.

Several practices appear to be important for success in this area, and a summary of these practices and competencies is provided in Table 2.

In summary, we need to understand how organizations can implement the guidance we received from one of our interviewees, that organizations should "throw their arms around women and minorities." We were deeply impressed by the passion and commitment of our interviewees, many of whom shared deep feelings with us. We point to the passion and persuasiveness of champions of diversity and talented mentors as a means of selling the importance of the process to others in the organization. Nonetheless, we acknowledge that diverse succession planning is a sensitive area in many organizations since future opportunities and limited numbers of developmental assignments are at stake, particularly where greater progress in diversity is needed. Although it is sometimes difficult to obtain candid answers about diverse succession planning practices, there is much to learn in most organizations about this issue and much to be gained in terms of competitive advantage. Further investigation of questions, such as one posed by one of our interviewees, would seem to add value. The surprising answer to his question, "Who did you turn to in your darkest hour?" indicates that there is much to learn in most organizations.

Those organizations that excel at managing diversity will need to be creative in developing programs that reduce the negative side effects of special programs for women and minorities. Such programs pose a paradox, because while the conventional wisdom is that they should not be adopted, they appear to be necessary for progress.

Table 2

Suggestions for Diverse Succession Planning

Strategic Integration
- Obtain alignment between business strategy and diverse succession planning.
- Frame programs with emphasis on developing "high potentials."
- Communicate the strategy and goals of the program.

Leadership
- Establish a values basis for diverse succession.
- Obtain commitment of top executives to personally mentor diverse successors.
- Include diversity goals in performance evaluations of executives and managers.
- Establish close contact between the CEO and the chief diversity officer.
- Establish authority and accountability for diverse succession goals.
- Involve the chief diversity officer in all succession decisions.

Planning Processes
- Identify behavioral competencies for the future while recognizing that these may change.
- Disseminate descriptions of specific behavioral competencies required for top positions.
- Conduct deep internal searches for diverse high potentials.
- Rely on assessments from credible mentors.
- Evaluate recruiting programs for their impact on diversity.
- Use valid objective testing where feasible to offset unconscious bias in assessment.
- Use valid objective indicators of performance, competence, and potential where possible.
- Use valid learning-oriented early identifiers of executive ability.
- Use valid measures of results orientation to identify high potentials.

Development Practices
- Develop behavioral competencies for training, development planning, and evaluations.
- Focus on the advantages of same-race/gender or cross-race/gender mentorship.
- Provide anonymous procedures for mentees to decline pairing with potential mentors.
- Provide opportunities for diverse high potentials to gain exposure with senior executives.
- Create critical masses of diverse talent to prevent tokenism and related effects.
- Use "pump priming" where appropriate to signal commitment and opportunity.

Program Management Practices
- Monitor flows of diverse successors into core areas as opposed to periphery functions.
- Identify effective mentors and leverage their skills.
- Include diverse succession in executive performance evaluation and reward systems.
- Inform high potentials of their inclusion in succession plans and obtain their inputs.
- Monitor succession and high-potential programs for representation of diversity.
- Evaluate diverse succession planning with multiple metrics such as retention, development, advancement, and size of the "ready now" talent pool.

Acknowledgments

The authors would like to acknowledge questions posed by Shannon Ryan, executive vice president, Stagen Leadership, Inc., which provided focus for our inquiry. In addition, they would also like to express their appreciation for insights provided by John Baum, Jim Combs, John Delaney, Mark Huselid, Shirley Rasberry, Lynn Wooten, and two anonymous reviewers.

Source: Charles R. Greer and Meghna Virick, "Diverse Discussion Planning: Lessons from the Industry Leaders," Human Resource Management, Summer 2008, Vol. 47, No.2, pp. 351–367.

REFERENCES

Alleyne, S. (2005). But can you walk the walk. Black Enterprise, 35(2), 100–106.

Anderson, R. (2005). Welcome to the diversity and inclusion initiative. Deloitte & Touche USA LLP. Retrieved February 29, 2008, from http://www.deloitte.com/dtt/article/

Armour, S. (2003, November 24). Playing the succession game. USA Today, p. 3B.

Bogan, C. (2002). Best practices in career path definition and succession planning. Chapel Hill, NC: Best Practices, L.L.C. (revised 2005).

Brathwaite, S. T. (2002). Denny's: A diversity success story. Franchising World, 34(5), 28–29.

Cappelli, P., & Hamori, M. (2005). The new road to the top. Harvard Business Review, 83(1), 25–23.

Carnazza, J. (1982). Succession/replacement planning programs and practices. New York: Center for Research in Career Development, Columbia Business School, Columbia University.

Catalyst. (2003). Women in U.S. corporate leadership: 2003. New York: Author.

Caudron, S. (1999). The looming leadership crisis. Workforce, 78(9), 72–79.

Cespedes, F. V., & Galford, R. M. (2004). Succession and failure. Harvard Business Review, 82(6), 31–42.

Charan, R. (2005). Ending the CEO succession crisis. Harvard Business Review, 83(2), 72–81.

Childs, J. T., Jr. (2005). Managing workforce diversity at IBM: A global HR topic that has arrived. Human Resource Management, 44, 73–77.

Clawson, J. G., & Kram, K. E. (1984). Managing cross-gender mentoring. Business Horizons, 27(3), 22–32.

Collins, J. C., & Porras, J. I. (1994). Built to last: Successful habits of visionary companies. New York: HarperCollins.

Conger, J. A., & Fulmer, R. M. (2003). Developing your leadership pipeline. Harvard Business Review, 81(12), 76–84.

Cox, T., Jr. (2001). Creating the multicultural organization: A strategy for capturing the power of diversity. San Francisco, CA: Jossey-Bass.

Crockett, J. (1999, May). Winning competitive advantage through a diverse workforce. HR Focus, 9–10.

Delaney, J. T., & Huselid, M. A. (1996). The impact of human resource management practices on perceptions of organizational performance. Academy of Management Journal, 39, 949–969.

Eichinger, R. W., & Lombardo, M. M. (2004). Learning agility as a prime indicator of potential. Human Resource Planning, 27, 12–15.

Ely, R. J. (1994). The effects of organizational demographics and social identity on relationships among professional women. Administrative Science Quarterly, 39, 203–238.

Esen, E. (2005). 2005 workplace diversity practices: Survey report. Alexandria, VA: Society for Human Resource Management.

Estlund, C. (2003). Working together: How workplace bonds strengthen a diverse democracy. New York: Oxford University Press.

Flynn, G. (1998). Texas Instruments engineers a holistic HR. Workforce, 77(2), 26–30.

Frase-Blunt, M. (2003). Moving past 'mini-me': Building a diverse succession plan means looking beyond issues of race and gender. HR Magazine, 48(11), 95–98.

Friedman, S. D. (1986). Succession systems in large corporations: Characteristics and correlates of performance. Human Resource Management, 25, 191–213.

Gale, S. F. (2001). Bringing good leaders to light. Training, 38, 38–42.

Gibson, R., & Gray, S. (2004, April 20). Death of chief leaves McDonald's facing challenges. Wall Street Journal, pp. A1, A16.

Gray, S. (2004, November 24). Naming Skinner CEO, McDonald's shows its executive depth. Wall Street Journal, p. B2.

Greer, C. R. (2001). Strategic human resource management: A general managerial approach (2nd ed.). Upper Saddle River, NJ: Prentice Hall.

Himelstein, L., & Forest, S. A. (1997, February 17). Breaking through. Business Week, p. 64.

Hubbard, H. E. (2004). The diversity scorecard: Evaluating the impact of diversity on organizational performance. Oxford, UK: Elsevier Butterworth–Heinemann.

Huselid, M. A., Jackson, S. E., & Schuler, R. S. (1996). Technical and strategic human resource management effectiveness as determinants of firm performance. *Academy of Management Journal,* 40, 171–188.

Hymowitz, C., & Lublin, J. S. (2004, April 20). McDonald's CEO tragedy holds lessons. *Wall Street Journal,* pp. B1, B8.

Jung, H. (2005, April 21). Few women, minorities in top positions at Nike. *The Oregonian,* p. B01.

Karaevli, A., & Hall, D. T. (2003). Growing leaders for turbulent times: Is succession planning up to the challenge? *Organizational Dynamics,* 32, 62–79.

Kilian, C. M., Hukai, D., & McCarty, C. E. (2005). Building diversity in the pipeline to corporate leadership. *Journal of Management Development,* 24, 155–168.

Kim, S. (2003). Linking employee assessments to succession planning. *Public Personnel Management,* 32, 533–547.

King, N. (1994). The qualitative research interview. In C. Cassell & G. Symon (Eds.), *Qualitative methods in organizational research: A practical guide* (pp. 14–36). London: Sage.

Klimoski, R. (1997). Assessment centers. In L. H. Peters, C. R. Greer, & S. A. Youngblood (Eds.), *Blackwell encyclopedic dictionary of human resource management* (pp. 10–12). Oxford, UK: Blackwell.

Liebman, M., Bruer, R. A., & Maki, B. R. (1996). Succession management: The next generation of succession planning. *Human Resource Planning,* 19, 16–29.

Liff, S. (1997). Two routes to managing diversity: Individual differences or social group characteristics. Employee Relations, 19, 11–26.

Lombardo, M. M., & Eichinger, R. W. (2000). High potentials as high learners. *Human Resource Management,* 39, 321–329.

McCall, M. W. (1998). High flyers: Developing the next generation of leaders. Boston: Harvard Business School Press.

McCuiston, V. E., Wooldridge, B. R., & Pierce, C. K. (2004). Leading the diverse workforce: Profit, prospects and progress. *Leadership and Organizational Development Journal,* 25, 73–91.

McGuirk, R. (2005, January 17). Cancer claims ex-McDonald's CEO Bell at 44. *Associated Press Newswires.*

McKinnon, T. (2003). Building a diversity succession plan you can really use. Presentation at the American Society for Training and Development, ASTD 2003 International Conference and Exposition. San Diego, CA.

Miller, W. L., & Crabtree, B. F. (1992). Primary care research: A multimethod typology and qualitative road map. In B. F. Crabtree & W. L. Miller (Eds.), *Doing qualitative research* (pp. 3–28). Newbury Park, CA: Sage.

Murrell, A. J., & James, E. H. (2001). Gender and diversity in organizations: Past, present, and future directions. Sex Roles, 45, 243–257.

Niehaus, R. (1988). Models for human resource decisions. *Human Resource Planning,* 11, 95–107.

Noe, R. A., Greenberger, D. B., & Wang, S. (2002). Monitoring: What we know and where we might go. In G. R. Ferris & J. J. Martocchio (Eds.), *Research in personnel and human resources management* (Vol. 21, pp. 129–173). Greenwich, CT: JAI Press.

Orenstein, E. G. (2005). The business case for diversity. *Financial Executive,* 21(4), 22–25.

Pfeffer, J. (1998). The human equation: Building profits by putting people first. Boston: Harvard Business School Press.

PR Newswire. (2004, January 15). General Electric, Harley-Davidson, and Shell Oil Company earn prestigious Catalyst Award for efforts to advance women employees.

Prince, C. J. (2005). Doing diversity. *Chief Executive,* 207, 46–49.

Ragins, B. R. (1997a). Antecedents of diversified mentoring relationships. *Journal of Vocational Behavior,* 51, 90–109.

Ragins, B. R. (1997b). Diversified mentoring relationships in organizations: A power perspective. *Academy of Management Review,* 22, 482–521,

Ragins, B. R., & Cotton, J. L. (1991), Easier said than done: Gender differences in perceived barriers to gaining a mentor. *Academy of Management Journal,* 34, 939–951.

Ragins, B., & McFarlin, D. (1990). Perceptions of mentor roles in narcissistic self-esteem management in cross gender mentoring relationships. *Journal of Vocational Behavior,* 37, 321–339.

Reinhold, B. (2005). Smashing glass ceilings: Why women still find it tough to advance to the executive suite. *Journal of Organizational Excellence,* 24, 43–55.

Richard, O. C. (2000). Racial diversity, business strategy, and firm performance: A resource-based view. *Academy of Management Journal,* 43, 164–177.

Rothwell, J. J. (2001). Effective succession planning: Ensuring leadership continuity and building talent from within (2nd ed.). New York: American Management Association.

Salob, M., & Greenslade, S. (2005), How the top 20 companies grow great leaders, 2005 Research Highlights: Hewitt Associates LLC. Retrieved February 29, 2008, from http://was4.hewitt.com/hewitt/resource/

Salomon, M. F., & Schork, J. M. (2003). Turn diversity to your advantage, *Research Technology Management*, 46, 37–44.

Salz, P. A. (2005, May 2). A vital building block in attaining that competitive edge calls for the creation of a unique corporate anatomy. *Wall Street Journal*, p. A8.

Sherwood, S., & Mendelsson, M. (2005, October). Marriott goes far beyond the numbers. *Diversity Inc.*, pp. 29–34.

Terhune, C. (2005, April 19). Pepsi, vowing diversity isn't just image polish, seeks inclusive culture. *Wall Street Journal*, p. B1,

Thomas, D. (1990). The impact of race on managers' experiences of developmental relationships (mentoring and sponsorship): An intra-organizational study. *Journal of Organizational Behavior*, 11, 479–492.

Thomas, D. (2004). Diversity as a strategy. *Harvard Business Review*, 82(9), 98–108.

Thomas, D. A., & Ely, R. J. (1996). Making differences matter: A new paradigm for managing diversity. *Harvard Business Review*, 74(5), 79–90.

Thomas, D. A., & Gabarro, J. J. (1999). Breaking through: The making of minority executives in America. Boston: Harvard Business School Press.

Thomas, R. (1990). From affirmative action to affirming diversity. *Harvard Business Review*, 68(2), 107–117.

U.S. Department of Education. (2005). Projections of education statistics to 2014. Retrieved from http://nces.ed.gov/programs/projections/projections2014/index.asp

Wanberg, C. R., Welsh, E. T., & Hezlett, S. A. (2003). Mentoring research: A review and dynamic process model. In J. J. Martocchio & G. R. Ferris (Eds.), *Research in personnel and human resources management* (Vol. 22, pp. 39–124). Greenwich, CT: JAI Press.

Wei, S., & Cannella, A., Jr. (2002). Power dynamics within top management and their impacts on CEO dismissal followed by inside succession. *Academy of Management Journal*, 45, 1195–1206.

Wright, P., Ferris, S. P., Hiller, J. S., & Kroll, M. (1995). Competitiveness through management of diversity: Effects on stock price valuation. *Academy of Management Journal*, 38, 272–287.

Yeung, A. K. (1997). Succession planning. In L. H. Peters, C. R. Greer, & S. A. Youngblood (Eds.), *Blackwell encyclopedic dictionary of human resource management* (pp. 340–341). Oxford, UK: Blackwell.

READING 5.2

The Annual HR Strategic Planning Process: Design and Facilitation Lessons from Corning Incorporated Human Resources

Debbie Bennett and Matthew Brush

Abstract

This article presents an internal perspective on the Annual HR Strategic Planning Process Corning's HR team uses to prioritize HR investments and deliver services aligned with business requirements. Over three years, this process has integrated inputs from a Human Capital Planning process, the HR function's transformation goals, and other corporate initiatives into a one-page Annual Operating Plan with supporting objectives. The authors share process, meeting design and facilitation lessons learned from their work with their clients.

Corning Corporate History

From a shatter-proof lens for railroad lanterns and a glass envelope for Edison's new light bulb filament, to premium quality LCD glass substrates and highly engineered optical fiber, Corning has established a 150-plus year legacy of technological innovation.

Through the early 1990s, Corning maintained a diverse portfolio of businesses that typically generated $4 billion to $5 billion in annual revenues; the sale of its well known consumer business (Corelle dishes, Visions cookware, etc.) funded a massive investment in the telecommunications sector and explosive growth, followed by a major retrenchment. All of which, of course, had significant impact on the HR function as well as the company overall.

Corning Human Resources History

The HR function can be described as having a sterling legacy of constructive union labor relations, innovative corporate Centers of Excellence (COEs), and responsive generalists in the business – all three of which were managed separately for a number of years until they were consolidated under a single senior vice president in April 2002. This fragmented approach caused a disconnect between the COEs and the businesses. This created dynamic tension between centralization and decentralization of strategy as the COE specialists and the business unit generalists struggled in regard to their

roles relative to strategy development and deployment. When businesses were ascendant, the pendulum swung toward decentralization and the businesses set the agenda for what HR needed to focus on; when the businesses were not performing as well, as during the telecom downturn in 2001, the pendulum swung toward centralization as a way of controlling costs and focusing the HR function on the most important work. Developing a robust Annual Operating Plan (AOP) process and applying the human capital planning process to the HR function has helped Corning HR to step out of the pendulum dynamic and better balance multiple sources of input regarding the work that HR should be doing.

Corning's HR AOP Process

This paper will examine the creation and evolution of Corning's Annual HR Strategic Planning Process – the Process that Corning's HR team uses to prioritize HR investments and deliver services aligned with business requirements. We will examine how this process has blended the inputs from an innovative Human Capital Planning process, the HR function's transformation goals, and other corporate initiatives into a one-page Annual Operating Plan with supporting objectives. These objectives are woven into our compensation programs and are used to track our progress toward our goals. Where practical, we will examine the process, meeting design, and facilitation lessons we have learned from our work with our clients – the senior leaders in Corning Human Resources.

It is important to note that the current Human Capital Planning process was built from foundational conversations with John Boudreau and Peter Ramstad (Boudreau, et al, 2003) that were then operationalized for Corning in partnership with Sibson Consulting.

Corning Human Resources – Business Context

As Corning's telecommunications businesses grew rapidly in the late 1990s, the human resources function had to change. HR was supporting explosive growth in an environment of

FIGURE 1

Corning Human Resources Transformation Goals

Strong Business Linkage + Global HR Processes + Scaleable Solutions + Continuous Cost Improvement = SUCCESS

plentiful resources. The HR leadership team developed four transformation goals (Figure 1) to guide that growth. We had to build a better connection between HR function strategy and business strategy, support growth globally, deliver scalable solutions and still manage to reach our broad cost targets.

Then, the telecommunications businesses started to contract dramatically. Although the transformation goals still made sense, the emphasis changed completely. Suddenly, it was primarily a "cost game" – with a target of spending no more than 1% of revenue on the global HR function – and scalability became focused on becoming *smaller* instead of *bigger*. The Senior Vice President of HR, Kurt Fischer, challenged his team to still deliver the global mindset and processes, as well as a strategy process that linked with the client businesses, but faster, and on a much tighter budget.

Decentralization v. Centralization

The tension between centralization and decentralization is new to no one in the organizational development field. How it played out in Corning HR was fairly classic. The field generalists were part of the business unit and the business unit provided direction, funding, appraisal and rewards. The COE folks were part of 'corporate' and their direction came primarily from large corporate initiatives emanating from the Senior Management Team or HR Function Strategy. COEs had some input from the business units but it was fragmented and often driven by whichever business happened to be the current "king of the hill". This created a situation in which the unspoken job of the generalist was often to protect the business from the COEs. The field generalists were accused of "going native" and the COE specialists were accused of not knowing what was really going on, what was really needed by the people who generated revenue.

That is not to say that no collaboration or cooperation occurred, but rather, that it was situation dependent. Then the telecommunications bust forced us to look at how ineffective and inefficient this approach had become. Accepting the fact that both centralization and decentralization have

advantages and disadvantages, the question before us was how we could better balance the two. Part of the answer came in the form of our AOP Planning Process.

Human Capital Planning as Transformation Accelerator

Realizing that the first transformation goal, linking HR strategy effectively with business strategy, represented a powerful tool for driving change in the global HR function, Fischer commissioned a next-generation Human Capital Planning process using a combination of internal and external consultants. The result was a four step process (Figure 2) that gave business unit generalists shared tools and language for deconstructing client business strategy into actionable steps for talent development, and gave the HR function as a whole a way of identifying and prioritizing needs across businesses and COEs.

Steps 1 through 3 of the process enable the identification of the talent that will *most impact the* success of business strategy, and the talent that will be *most impacted by* the success of the business strategy, enabling a multi-year look at the number, type and timing of critical talent requirements supported by rigorous gap analysis that drives staffing actions. Step 4 delivers powerful organizational effectiveness diagnostic tools and a prioritization process that balances competing inputs from the business unit HR team members.

As part of successive years of continuous improvement efforts, Corning has managed to build in opportunities for robust input from corporate COEs (compensation and benefits, workforce development and learning, talent management, and employee relations) and the regional HR leads outside the U.S. These inputs ensure that the division HR leads have an understanding of issues that will impact their global businesses, including HR technical and regulatory changes as well as regional dynamics that will impact one or more businesses that operate in greater China, Japan and Europe.

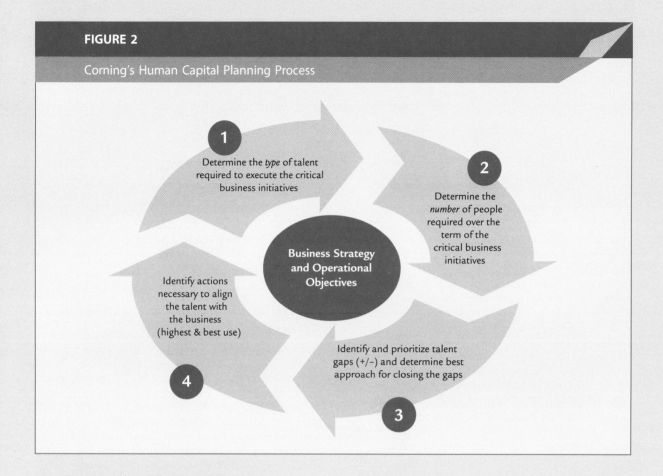

FIGURE 2

Corning's Human Capital Planning Process

1 — Determine the *type* of talent required to execute the critical business initiatives

2 — Determine the *number* of people required over the term of the critical business initiatives

3 — Identify and prioritize talent gaps (+/−) and determine best approach for closing the gaps

4 — Identify actions necessary to align the talent with the business (highest & best use)

Business Strategy and Operational Objectives

The COEs and the corporate HR leadership team have found it valuable to receive spreadsheets that consolidate the outputs from each business, allowing them to see all of the major initiatives to be undertaken by HR resources within the businesses on one sheet, and all the work being requested of the COEs by the businesses on another. This facilitates the identification of common requests across businesses that might otherwise go unidentified or might not make the final prioritized list, and forms one of the inputs for the AOP discussion.

Our annual strategic planning process (Figure 3) for HR brings together several key components including: (a) corporate strategy and the implications of that strategy for HR, (b) HR function strategy including the strategic direction for each of the COEs, and (c) the outputs of the Human Capital Planning process for each of the business units, which is essentially the HR implications of each of their business strategies. As all of these involve "strategy," they all encompass a three to five year planning process. These three discrete inputs are brought together at an annual offsite meeting of the direct reports to the senior vice president of HR, plus several facilitators, usually in October, where we further develop and build alignment around the Human Capital Planning process for HR and develop the Annual Operating Plan.

AOP Offsite – Preparation and Meeting Design

Prior to the annual offsite to develop the HR Annual Operating Plan (AOP), each of these components are analyzed for "must have's", common themes, clear conflicts in the data, and key outliers (e.g. those things that may not show up as a theme but are highly probable and will have a high impact). The senior HR leadership team owners of each component dialogue with their teams so that when they come to the HR AOP offsite they are ready to present the real core of the work. Several years ago much of this work was done during the offsite itself. We have since found that doing much of this in preparation for the offsite allows for broader participation, more ownership as the constituents are helping to provide prioritization, and a more efficient, more focused AOP session. In 2006 we actually "took our own medicine" by following the HCP Process for the HR Function as the funnel to synthesis the key inputs prior to the offsite (Figure 3).

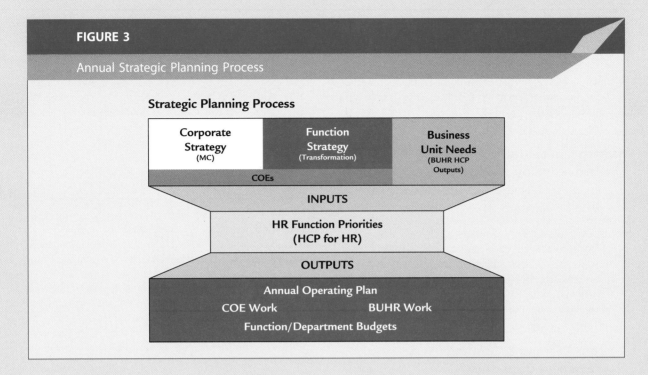

FIGURE 3

Annual Strategic Planning Process

The HR AOP offsite meeting is attended by the HR function staff, the chief of staff for business unit HR, and two internal facilitators. We have the group arrive at the off-site location the night before and have a group dinner and some team activity to help them let go of the day-to-day, often role-specific work they were focused on and get them refocused, as a team, on their function leadership role.

The first day begins with a review of the agenda, groundrules for the session and the boundary conditions. The boundary conditions are essential as no work is done in a vacuum. For our purposes the boundary conditions include our HR governance statements which include our corporate values and core deliverables; our budget for the upcoming year, the HR transformation goals (the strategic goals for the HR function) and HR HCP outputs. Throughout the process we check our work against these boundary conditions to ensure that we remain on target. That is not to say that we never go outside the boundaries, but if we do, it is in a very explicit way. For example, if we have a large initiative that will go beyond regular budget boundaries, it must be demonstrated how we can show the plan for funding that work, what is the likelihood of funding, what are the trade-offs with other projects that are then less likely to be resourced, etc.

Next, each staff member presents the pre-work they completed with their staff. During these presentations each staff member explains the objectives that they are proposing be included in the upcoming year's plan and why. The focus at this point is on understanding what conclusions were reached by the staff members, and how they were reached. This is done through facilitated dialogue and, as these are the main ingredients to success, we ensure that the tough questions and important challenges are brought out. Throughout these discussions the facilitators are capturing and testing changes so that by the time this section is complete we have a reasonable draft of the AOP. Hence this is a highly interactive and iterative session, as changes in one section often cause us to go back and revisit a previous section. Day one does not end until the group has agreed on the main elements of the AOP.

On the second day, following an evening of relaxation, we break the leadership team into sub-teams. The objectives agreed to on the previous day are divided up and the sub-teams' task is to articulate how we will measure each objective in the context of the Corning incentive compensation payout scheme by setting 50%, 100%, and 150% performance targets for each. This exercise serves several purposes including (a) providing another cross-check of the objectives themselves, often helping us to calibrate scope, complexity, timing etc., (b) tightening up our language. Having to determine how to measure something lends a lot of clarity to the goals, and (c) forces even more clarity regarding what work will be required to deliver on these objectives.

The last day of the AOP offsite has two components. Considerable time is devoted to planning the communication of the finished AOP to business unit leaders and all HR employees. The balance of the day focuses on the creation of a global HR function calendar for the following year, capturing key function activities like deployment meetings, staff meetings, communication meetings, HCP process deadlines, etc.

The outputs of the AOP offsite include: a final one-page Annual Operating Plan summary, the detailed goals behind the AOP, an understanding of the required work from both the COEs and business unit HR. While budgets are used as a boundary condition at the offsite, a follow-up staff meeting includes the reconciliation of the AOP with the relevant department budgets.

Strategy Elements in the Larger Context – Pulling It All Together

To put the various elements in context, Figure 4 illustrates the annual cycle of human capital planning, the human resources annual operating plan process, and the corporate strategy process (as discussed previously in this paper) on a single timeline. The business unit human capital planning process runs in parallel with the business unit portion of the corporate strategy process, and the two inform each other. HR completes its human capital planning process on itself using the output of the business units' work.

Lessons Learned & Continuous Improvement Opportunities

As with many HR processes, the AOP process is based on an annual cycle and the year-on-year improvements are best understood by considering each year in turn.

We have implemented the annual AOP process for each of three years. Each year, we have learned new lessons that enable us to continually improve the process. In the first year, the COE presentations were made at the April kick-off meeting. The process did not include an opportunity for the region HR leaders to provide a global perspective. Additionally, the business unit HR output was not formally prioritized before the offsite, resulting in a mix of "wish list" and duplicate requests.

Relative to the AOP offsite itself, in the first year there was no pre-agreement on what the AOP would look like or what the framework would be. As a result, this work took up considerable time in the meeting. The summary page was ultimately organized by a framework that included the following three main headings: Improve Cost Performance, Deliver Quality and Continuous Improvement, and Drive for Talent Management Excellence. While the specific objectives under these headings have changed from year to year, the headings have remained viable.

In the second year, we kept the COE presentations at the April kick-off meeting, and added time for the regional HR leads to provide input. The business unit HR team prioritized their requests in a single meeting prior to the AOP offsite, which resulted in a more coherent set of requests. The process was also modified to provide formal opportunity for COE leaders to work with their staffs on the business unit HR requests for support before coming to the offsite.

In developing the AOP itself, we re-used the framework developed in year one, saving considerable meeting time. We felt that consistency was more important than change for change's sake. This meeting went considerably smoother from facilitation standpoint, as the participants were on more familiar ground.

In pursuit of efficiency in the HCP process, we made an overcorrection in the third year by having the COE presentations done virtually, via a page on the intranet rather than during a live meeting. This was a mistake, as it sent a message to the COEs that their input was undervalued and it allowed some business unit HR people to under value the COE input. The prioritization of BUHR input was dramatically improved by facilitating a senior HR staff debrief dinner directly following the business unit HR HCP presentations in July and facilitating a business unit HR cross-business prioritization process and identifying common threads.

With regard to the annual offsite, we broke the three days into two sessions; one day for HCP for HR, and two

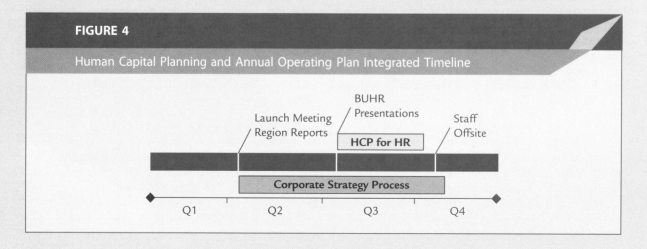

FIGURE 4

Human Capital Planning and Annual Operating Plan Integrated Timeline

days for the AOP. This made the work more manageable and resulted in more focused sessions with the senior staff. The strength of the AOP framework that we developed in year one, and retained in year two, was validated in year three when we kept the main headings consistent but were able to make accommodation for a major new initiative.

Meeting Facilitation – Basics Reconfirmed

The following points, while focused on Corning's experience with this particular set of meetings, and perhaps basic to the seasoned facilitator, have added value in our process:

- The meeting structure and overall process design must permit individuals with different work styles to process the information effectively, and to engage with their staffs as appropriate before group meetings.
- The meeting facilitators have to seek a balance between efficiency and effectiveness as the meeting unfolds – there is no substitute for frank dialog regarding thorny issues. Likewise the facilitators must provide pre-work material while resisting the urge to over-process that material for the participants. This means cleaning up the inputs without trying to do the work for the team.
- As with any leadership team working through a difficult process, facilitation was key. We found value in using someone outside the intact staff – which allows all the staffers to participate and improves facilitator independence. In addition, we found that a two person facilitation team added significant value in managing both the group dynamics and the meeting content. Using the same team year on year allowed the facilitators to develop a feel for when to push for closure and when to back off.
- Our facilitation was further improved by our ability to process the content live in the room on a computer and projector, rather than on flipcharts. Having immediate visual turnaround of the feedback greatly improved meeting effectiveness and efficiency.
- By including in the meeting design opportunities for max-mix sub teams to do break-out work and present it to the rest of the participants, we found that more issues got raised in the room and resolved productively.

Continuous Improvement Opportunities

There are still many opportunities for us to improve our strategic planning process in total. While most of the HR generalists have now embraced the human capital planning process, there are still some that struggle with the concepts and corrective action is now appropriate. As the generalists who do understand the process drive it further into their client business' strategic planning process, we expect to draw more general managers into the mid-year report-out sessions. As the HR leadership team gets more comfortable with and

confident in the process, we have an opportunity to make greater distinctions between the requests from the different businesses, driving more prioritization of projects and work requests based on their impact to the requesting business. This will drive better portfolio management decisions and help HR to achieve its goal of containing cost while delivering value to the organization.

As we transition to a new facilitation team for the annual offsite, we have articulated clear concerns about how much work the facilitator can do in preparation for the meeting without undermining the leadership team. In some departments, facilitators can save time and add value by creating "straw person" proposals that interpret the source data. However, our recommendation has been to resist that temptation and to allow the team to work directly with the raw data. This experience with the raw inputs gives them greater familiarity with the details and helps them to arrive at a shared point of view. Over-processing the inputs might save time in the meeting, but at the risk of losing the alignment of the participants.

General Conclusions

Working together, the human capital planning and annual operating plan processes reviewed in this paper have helped to build a more coherent global HR function for Corning by creating a shared understanding across the COEs and the business unit HR groups of the many client business' situations and needs, and of the technical and strategic advances in each of the COEs. While the details of such processes must differ from company to company, the creation of such integrated, structured, and repeatable processes appear to add considerable value for HR professionals and their clients. Anecdotal evidence for the value of this work has come from the number of requests from other companies to benchmark Corning on this subject.

Critical elements of a successful AOP process include a number of mechanisms for gathering input; corporate strategy input from senior management, function-specific direction from the senior leadership of the function, and business-specific input from each of the businesses supported by the HR function. The more diverse the lines of business that the company is pursuing, the more important a robust planning process similar to Corning's HCP process becomes.

The process for developing the AOP is important as well. While a certain amount of pre-work is desirable, there is no substitute for a well-facilitated meeting of the senior team where options can be identified, ideas can be discussed and alignment can be gained on the agreed-upon actions.

Finally, alignment of the HR strategy process with the corporate and discrete business unit strategy processes increases HR's ability to align the services it offers, and the way it delivers them, with the needs of businesses.

Acknowledgements

As with many Corning HR programs, the Annual Operating Plan (AOP) process originated in one of the businesses – in this case, in a best practice developed in the then Optical Fiber business. The calendar and AOP templates were introduced within Corning by Christy Pambianchi, who currently serves as Division Vice President of Business Unit HR. The current process incorporates the feedback of numerous Corning HR colleagues received by the authors in the last three years, but most importantly from the members of Kurt Fischer's staff, for whom this work was commissioned. The Human Capital Planning process that Corning has been using in its current form since 2004 has roots in the HC BRidgetm work of Dr. John Boudreau and Peter Ramstad. This work has also benefited greatly from the practical consulting approach of Don Ruse of Sibson Consulting.

Authors' Reflection

As Director of Human Capital Planning for Corning Inc., my mission was to develop, deploy and manage a process for identifying the talent implications of the business strategy each business was pursuing. Working directly for the SVP of HR, I was asked to co-develop and co-facilitate an Annual Operating Plan process with Debbie Bennett, a senior member of the in-house OD team.

As with any senior leadership team, a major challenge was to develop a process that would focus on a specific outcome – a clear, measurable plan – that would effectively balance the differing personalities and perspectives of the senior HR leadership team. Being an internal consultant was beneficial, because my co-facilitator and I were familiar with each team member's style, strengths, and weaknesses. Our ongoing relationships with the team allowed us to push the team in ways that an external consultant would not have been able to easily accomplish.

Beyond the reflections contained in our paper, we would encourage any internal consultant to carefully consider the balance between completing some of the framework of the plan prior to any working offsite meeting to maximize the effectiveness of the session for all participants, and leaving sufficient work to be done by the group in person to ensure meaningful dialog between the participants and full ownership of the final project.

Source: Debbie Bennett and Matthew Brush, The Annual HR Strategic Planning Process: Design and Facilitation Lessons from Corning Incorporated Human Resources, Organization Development Journal, Fall 2007, 25, 3; pp. P87–P93.

REFERENCES

Boudreau, J. W., Ramstad, P. M. & Dowling, P. J. (2003). "Global Talentship; Toward a Decision Science Connecting Talent to Global Strategic Success." In W. Mobley and P. Dorfman (Eds.), *Advances in Global Leadership* (Volume 3). JAI Press/Elsevier Science, 63–99.

Brush, M. C., Ruse, D. H. (2005). "Driving Strategic Success Through Human Capital Planning; How Corning Links Business and HR Strategy to Improve the Value and Impact of Its HR Function." *Human Resource Planning* (Volume 28.1). 49–60.

CHAPTER 6

Design and Redesign of Work Systems

- Understand the individual and organizational factors that affect job design
- Gain an appreciation of the need for "fit" between individuals and jobs and how such fit can be achieved
- Understand the reasons why organizations outsource and/or offshore and the pros and cons of utilizing alternative work location strategies
- Gain an appreciation of the role of HR in mergers and acquisitions
- Understand the impact that technology has on the design of jobs and work

Work Design at Johnsonville Sausage

Johnsonville Sausage is a family-owned business headquartered in Kohler, Wisconsin. Founded in 1944, the company has designed its workplace to facilitate employee involvement in all aspects of the business. Johnsonville hires "members," as opposed to employees, and supervisors are referred to as coaches or team leaders, with work units organized as teams rather than departments. From the time of hire, all members are required to learn about the entire business. During the first six months of employment, all members are required to attend a series of four 4-hour workshops that introduce them to company history and culture, teamwork, diversity, and financial management, including how the work of teams affects cash flow and profits. Production teams hold daily meetings prior to the beginning of their shifts to discuss issues of concern. The organization's "culture of empowerment" gives members the authority to shut down the production line at any time if they observe something that does not appear to be correct. Member involvement in all aspects of Johnsonville's business is reinforced with monthly bonuses that are tied to the month's production goals and profitability. Employee involvement in the business has resulted in an annual turnover rate of 8 percent at Johnsonville, which is significantly greater than the 20 percent average in the meat-packing industry.[1]

The second component in the development of human resource (HR) management strategy, in addition to strategic workforce planning, is the design of work systems. The organization must consider the implications of its future plans on how tasks and responsibilities should be assigned to individuals and groups within the organization and decide how to redesign existing work systems. A model for the design of work systems is presented in Exhibit 6.1.

Design of Work Systems

In Exhibit 6.1, three primary considerations are presented that decision makers need to consider in designing jobs: what workers do, what workers need, and how jobs interface with other jobs within the organization.

What Workers Do

One of the more challenging tasks in organizations is allocating specific tasks and job responsibilities to employees. Those who assign responsibilities need to ensure that employees are not overwhelmed by their jobs yet at the same time ensure that employees have sufficient work to keep them both productive and motivated. In addition, job titles and content serve as an important basis of comparison for employees within the organization relative to status, power, and appropriateness of compensation.

There are various strategies for the design of individual jobs. Those responsible for designing jobs and work systems need to fully assess the skills, knowledge, and abilities required by the organization both currently and in the future and consider both existing and possible future technologies. As noted in Chapter 5, a critical component of strategic workforce planning is anticipating changes in the organization's environment. Work systems need to be constantly assessed and evaluated to ensure that the organization has assigned workers tasks and responsibilities that assist in achieving organizational objectives.

Early approaches to work system design focused on individual employees' jobs. In the late nineteenth and early twentieth centuries, industrial engineering prescribed work systems with jobs that had very narrow task assignments, thus giving rise to the term "*job specialization.*"

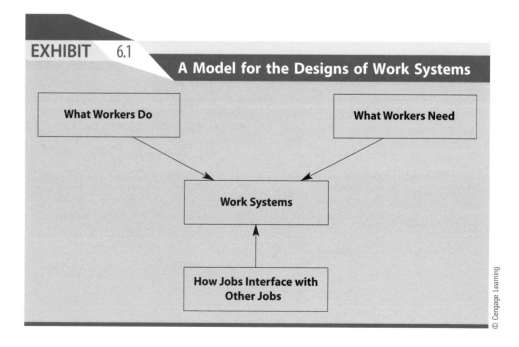

EXHIBIT 6.1

A Model for the Designs of Work Systems

What Workers Do → Work Systems ← What Workers Need

How Jobs Interface with Other Jobs → Work Systems

© Cengage Learning

These systems attempted to promote efficiency in industrial operations by allowing workers to specialize in particular tasks and gain high levels of competence in their work. Jobs had a limited number of tasks assigned that required little thought but precise execution. Not surprisingly, although these efforts toward simplified, specialized jobs provided efficiency, they also resulted in creating jobs that were boring and monotonous for employees. Because employees were not encouraged to go beyond a basic robotic function in most of their work, they were consequently unable to contribute to the organization in any meaningful way. This does not mean, however, that job specialization is inappropriate or never works. In fact, United Parcel Service, as discussed in Chapter 1, uses techniques of job specialization extensively. Job specialization can be a viable strategy for the design of work systems in organizations that require high levels of efficiency and cost minimization in order to compete effectively. It can also be appropriate for organizations that employ workers who do not seek to grow and be challenged in their careers.

Initial efforts to relieve this boredom and design more stimulating work for employees focused on providing them with tasks outside the scope of their previously narrowly defined jobs. *Job enlargement* provides some variety by increasing the number of tasks, activities, or jobs to help alleviate the boredom of highly specialized work. A variation of job enlargement is *job rotation,* where workers rotate across different specialized positions within the organization. Both techniques of designing jobs rest with providing employees with more variety in the tasks they perform. However, although these approaches add variety to tasks, they do not necessarily involve giving employees more responsibility. This does not mean that efforts to allow or require workers to perform additional tasks are necessarily useless. Employees who assume responsibility for additional tasks can have their understanding of organizational production processes enhanced and have a greater appreciation of how their specialized job contributes to the overall organization. Several studies have documented the success of both job enlargement and job rotation. Shortly after World War II, IBM instituted a job enlargement program and found a significant increase in product quality and a reduction in down or idle time.[2] Pharmaceutical company Eli Lilly utilized a popular job rotation program that allowed employees to qualify for salary increases and promotions while enhancing career development opportunities.[3]

Job rotation has become increasingly popular in recent years as a key tool by which employees are developed through exposure to different roles and functions within an organization. Job rotation has been a long-standing practice for senior executives who benefit from gaining a sense of not only how different functions operate but how they contribute to the entire organization. More recently, job rotation has been offered increasingly to employees at the middle and lower levels of the organization as a means of facilitating communication and fostering collaboration across different divisions of the organizations or across regions. Job rotation is also a means of facilitating individual professional development. A recent survey by the Society for Human Resource Management found that 43 percent of employers offer some form of job rotation to facilitate the development of proficiencies not required as part of an individual employee's current job responsibilities.[4] Younger employees in particular seek out these kinds of opportunities with prospective employers, so job rotation can aid in both attracting and retaining younger workers.

Job rotation is increasingly being seen as a key means for HR professionals to further their careers. In order for HR to be a true strategic partner, HR executives must understand fully not only the functional aspects of HR management but also the nature of the organization's business. One of the best ways to obtain this understanding is to work within the organization in an operating division outside the HR function. Ironically, for many years, HR has developed programs that rotate employees across functions such as marketing, finance, operations, and accounting, providing those in rotation with a better grasp of the entire organization and an appreciation for how individual functions contribute to overall strategy. HR executives, however, are usually not part of such programs because of the traditional "administrative" role that HR played. To participate in an organization's success at the highest levels, HR executives need to avail themselves of opportunities to "learn the business" by actually participating in and learning about the entire organization and its various units. Until they do so, they cannot contribute to the organization as a true strategic partner.

Job Rotation at General Electric

General Electric (GE) has always been a leader in employee development among large organizations. For many years, entry-level HR managers have been placed in a two-year job rotation program on joining the organization. New hires spend three 8-month rotations within the HR function. Although they might end up in different business units or divisions, these rotations were still within the HR domain and confined to areas such as labor relations, compensation, staffing, and benefits. The goal of this program was to develop strong HR generalists who could eventually become senior HR executives within GE. In the mid-1990s, GE added cross-functional rotations to the mix, whereby individuals would leave HR for at least one rotation, working in areas such as audit, marketing, finance, or operations. This rotation program can continue throughout the employee's career as new skills, competencies, experiences, and knowledge bases are sought. HR executives in GE now have far greater credibility among their non-HR peers given this experience and are also better able to understand the business and develop HR solutions to key business challenges faced by divisions.[5]

Job enrichment initiatives involve going beyond merely adding tasks to employees' jobs. Job enrichment involves increasing the amount of responsibility employees have. Work is designed so that employees have significant responsibility for their own work. In many cases, the employee becomes more accountable for his or her own performance because responsibilities for quality and productivity that were previously assigned to the employee's supervisor are redirected to the employee. This process of reassigning what were formerly supervisory responsibilities to employees is commonly referred to as *vertical loading*.

To assist organizations in designing enriched jobs, a model was developed that illustrated the relationships between redesigned jobs and ultimate performance and behavioral outcomes.[6] The Job Characteristics Model is presented in Exhibit 6.2. This model suggests that five core job characteristics can impact certain employee psychological states that will impact certain work-related outcomes. These five core job characteristics are: (1) skill variety, the extent to which the work allows an employee to use a variety of acquired skills; (2) task identity, the extent to which the work allows an employee to complete a "whole" or "identifiable" piece of work; (3) task significance, the extent to which the employee perceives that his or her work is important and meaningful to those in the organization or those outside of the organization; (4) autonomy, the extent to which the employee is able to work and determine work procedures at her or his own discretion, free of supervision; and (5) feedback, the extent to which the work allows the employee to gain a sense of how well job responsibilities are being met. The model argues that work systems can be designed to enhance motivation, performance, and satisfaction and reduce absenteeism and turnover.

Frequently, the job characteristics model can be utilized to allow workers to assemble an entire product or provide a wider range of services to customers. For example, at Motorola's Communications Division, individual employees assemble, test, and package paging devices, whereas previously these tasks were performed on an assembly line with 100 workers performing 100 different steps.[7] Similarly, the job responsibilities of a group of employees may be enriched by allowing the work group the autonomy to complete an entire range of tasks in a manner determined by the group.

Organizations are increasingly developing job requirements around specific competencies that employees are expected to have and/or develop to maintain their value to the organization in the future. Competencies are fluid, meaning that they change and evolve as the organization, its strategy, and the environment in which it operates both change and evolve. A focus on competencies helps the organization and individual employees better connect individual employee efforts with organizational results.

Competency models can be extremely difficult and time consuming to develop. Typically they involve, at a minimum, interviews of key executives, behavioral interviews of best and worst performers on various jobs, and reviews of performance data, which allow correlations to be developed between competencies and performance. A variety of competency models can be developed within any organization around four different levels of assessment:

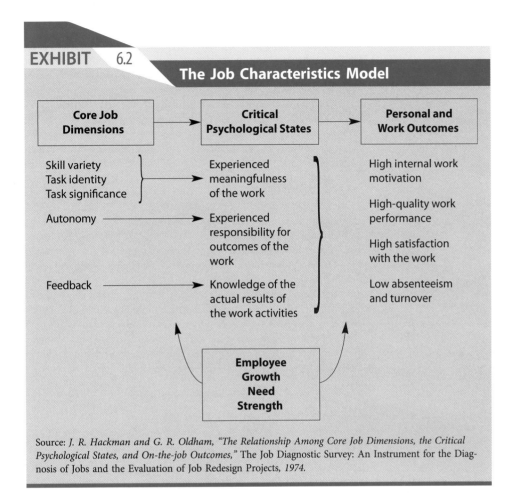

EXHIBIT   6.2

The Job Characteristics Model

Core Job Dimensions	Critical Psychological States	Personal and Work Outcomes

Skill variety
Task identity
Task significance → Experienced meaningfulness of the work

Autonomy → Experienced responsibility for outcomes of the work

Feedback → Knowledge of the actual results of the work activities

High internal work motivation

High-quality work performance

High satisfaction with the work

Low absenteeism and turnover

Employee Growth Need Strength

Source: *J. R. Hackman and G. R. Oldham, "The Relationship Among Core Job Dimensions, the Critical Psychological States, and On-the-job Outcomes,"* The Job Diagnostic Survey: An Instrument for the Diagnosis of Jobs and the Evaluation of Job Redesign Projects, *1974.*

- Organization-wide competencies are those that are important for all employees, regardless of position or level in the organization.
- Division-based competencies relate to a specific business function (such as information technology), area of operation (such as geographic region), business unit (individual product or service line), or customer group (such as business-to-business).
- Role-based competencies are those specific to a level of management (such as divisional vice president) or specific role (such as profit and loss responsibility) in the organization.
- Job-based competencies are those specific to an individual job, which have been proven to correlate to higher success in that job (such as customer service representative or accounts receivable manager).

Individual competencies often have performance of behavioral dimensions, which provide a basis for assessment and rating. As an example, Lominger International, a division of Korn/Ferry, has developed a competency called "strategic skills," which has the subcomponents of dealing with ambiguity, creativity, innovation management, perspective, and strategic ability.[8] Competency models are complex and expensive to develop, and many of these that have been developed are unnecessarily complex. Employees and managers should be directly be involved in their development because, as the end users, if these individuals have difficulty using the competency model, ambiguities about specific performance expectations can result. Competency models should be able to channel employee efforts toward organizational strategic objectives and simultaneously provide employees with a means of receiving specific feedback related to their professional development.

What Workers Need

The design of work systems also needs to consider what workers need and want in order to carry out their job responsibilities. Certainly, all employees do not work for the same reasons nor do they expect the same things from their employers. However, employers must consider a number of important universal considerations in designing work systems to ensure that workers are motivated, productive, and happy.

The first of these considerations is the changing demographics and lifestyles of the labor market. As noted in Chapter 2, there are some significant differences in the composition of the twenty-first century workforce. No longer are the majority of employees married white males who are considered the breadwinners of their families. In fact, white males now make up less than 50 *percent* of the U.S. workforce. Organizations need to realize that employees no longer have generic needs. Employees expect their employers to understand their needs and respect them as individuals. Worker needs will vary among and between those of different age groups, genders, races, religions, physical abilities, sexual orientations, and marital and family status. To perform at peak levels, employees need to remain free from bias or prejudice in hiring, treatment, performance management, compensation, and advancement decisions and programs. This diversity of worker needs creates a significant challenge for allocating work in organizations.

Organizations also need to be more aware of employee needs for work–life balance. All employees, but particularly younger employees, are far less loyal to their employers than they were a generation ago. Employers who design work systems that do not allow employees to have the balance they desire in their life activities will find workers who not only are less committed to the organization but who may also suffer from burnout and perform at less than optimal levels. One recent survey found that 42 percent of working adults were willing to assume a salary reduction in order to gain more flexibility in their work schedules and 83 percent reported that flexibility in work schedule is one of the most important factors considered when searching for a job or employer.[9]

Flexible Work at State Street

State Street is a Boston-based multinational financial service provider with more than 29,000 employees in 26 countries. In 2009, an executive committee was convened to address the need to provide for better work–life balance of its employees than the existing informal, ad hoc, practices in place. The global nature of State Street's operations also mandated flexibility in work across time zones to facilitate collaboration and decisive, timely decision making. The result was the development and implementation of a formal Flex Work Program, which has become known simply as Flex.

The program began as an employee-initiated activity to one that is manager-initiated in considering goals, strategies, and operating issues of the work unit and responsibilities of specific positions. Managers utilize Flex as a strategic business tool to enhance team efficiency, optimize workflow, and make more optimal use of physical space. 67 percent of State Street employees engage in Flex with an equal number of men and women participating. The essence of Flex is that employees and managers are given an array of options regarding how, when, and where they work, including flexible start and finish times to the work day, compressed work schedules, reduced hours, flexible work sites, and job-sharing options.

State Street reports heightened employee satisfaction, productivity and loyalty, decreased turnover, and better operating efficiencies company wide. Increased employee engagement and creativity have been reported by managers and the organization has calculated that Flex results in employees driving 140,000 fewer miles per week, resulting in time and energy consumption savings, not to mention environmental benefits.[10]

An increasing number of employers are establishing stress management programs as well as physical health and wellness programs and are contracting with outside employee-assistance programs to ensure that employees retain an essential balance among their life activities. In response to the particularly stressful work environments in which many high-technology executives find themselves, the Growth and Leadership Center of Mountain View, California, was established to work with executives from nearby Silicon Valley. Leading employers such as Sun Microsystems, Intel, and Netscape sent employees at risk for burnout to the center for weekly coaching sessions.[11] A typical 10-week program costs $12,000 per employee. Such excessive costs can be avoided through the development of work systems that are strategically designed to allow the organization's employees to retain the right balance in their life activities and can be a key catalyst to high performance.

A third consideration in determining what employees want is ensuring that employees have some form of representation, or "voice." More highly skilled and trained workers do not expect to be micromanaged. They expect to use their training and experience to make a contribution to the organization, and they expect the organization to listen to their concerns. Systems for employee input are not only motivational to employees, but they also allow the organization to fully utilize its existing human capabilities by encouraging employees to get involved in work-related issues that impact them. Work systems need to be designed so employees have sufficient voice to allow them to contribute their perspectives and expertise.

In unionized organizations, employee voice is formalized and centralized. However, less than 20 *percent* of the U.S. workforce is unionized. Unions also restrict the individual employee's right to have an independent voice, apart from the majority. In the absence of and even with a formal union, employers need to design their work systems to ensure that employees are able to communicate their needs and concerns in a constructive manner within an atmosphere of mutual respect. Both employees and the organizations win when this is accomplished.

One final consideration that needs to be incorporated in work system design under worker needs is workplace safely. The United States has established numerous guidelines for employers, administered by the Occupational Safety and Health Administration (OSHA), which oversees the Occupational Safety and Health Act. The Act largely addresses employer liability for on-the-job injuries and occupationally acquired diseases. In addition to the traditional concerns of hazardous products or waste and unsafe physical conditions, increasing attention is being paid to safety issues regarding technology. Ergonomics is a relatively new science that explores the relationship between injuries and physical office working conditions. The National Institute for Occupational Safety and Health recently reported that musculoskeletal disorders related to the neck, shoulders, elbow, hand, wrist, and back generated more than $13 billion in worker compensation claims.[12] Consequently, OSHA has been developing national standards related to ergonomics.

The near-constant use of computers with video display monitors has ignited debate concerning radiation hazard and the potential long-term effects of sustained gazing at video display monitors on an individual's vision. Because many employees also spend significant amounts of time at their desks or workstations, concern is also being addressed toward the ergonomics of worksites. Work systems and jobs need to be designed to be consistent with employees' physical capabilities and allow them to perform their jobs without any undue risks.

How Jobs Interface with Other Jobs

The final component of designing jobs is an understanding of how individual jobs may have interdependencies with other jobs as well as how individual jobs can or should interface with others. There are three traditional types of task interdependence: pooled, sequential, and reciprocal.

Pooled interdependence is where individual employees can work independently of each other in performing their tasks but utilize some coordination of their activities. Bank loan officers utilize this kind of work system. Each loan officer works independently of peers, yet the work of each officer is coordinated within the rules and procedures outlined by the bank for lending. In addition, experienced loan officers may often assist newer officers with specific tasks or questions they might have.

Sequential interdependence refers to work that flows from one individual to another, where one individual depends on the timely completion of quality work from another coworker. Mass-production assembly line workers utilize this kind of work system. Here, the output of one employee becomes the input for the next employee. Timely completion of work to be "passed on" is essential to avoid any slack or downtime, which creates inefficiencies and may strain relations between coworkers.

Reciprocal interdependence occurs when the workflow is not linear (as in sequential interdependence) but random. Employees can process work so that its flow is not necessarily predictable and often spontaneous to suit an immediate situation. Teammates on a basketball or hockey team utilize reciprocal interdependence, as would the different departments within a hospital. Employees in a reciprocal interdependence need to be flexible and are often configured as a team, with joint and shared responsibility.

When the work of one employee interfaces with another, concern must be paid to designing the work system to allow as efficient a flow as possible. Higher levels of interdependence require higher levels of coordination and attention. In designing work systems, organizations need to consider the implications that the levels of interdependence have for management practices that facilitate control of processes and communication among the interdependent tasks. For example, higher levels of interdependence might require more frequent meetings between employees, regular status reports, and more careful monitoring of performance and processes by management.

The design of organizational work systems is not an easy task. Allocation of tasks and responsibilities must be balanced with worker needs. Consideration must also be paid to the need for interdependencies among workers. Because changes in technology and changes in workforce composition continue to present ongoing challenges, the design of work systems is not a static activity.

Teams at Dow Chemical

Michigan-based Dow Chemical has been a leader in the use of employee teams since it began the practice in Europe in 1994. The large, bureaucratic organization felt that it was not using the skills and talent of its employees as well as it might, which led to a restructuring of plant operations. Work processes, from budgeting to actual production, were examined, and a three-tiered system was developed for rating the degree of autonomy each team displayed. With the goal of removing day-to-day control and responsibility from a supervisor and giving it to a team—allowing individuals to contribute more fully to the organization—Dow developed audit systems that assessed teams and their independence. Rewards were developed commensurate with team performance and autonomy. The teams have saved Dow more than $1 billion in their first 10 years of operation. The process also has allowed Dow staff engineers to spend more time on improving plant processes rather than its operations.[13]

The key strategic challenge in designing and staffing jobs is ensuring an optimal "fit" between the needs of employees and the needs of the organization. Ironically, employers are often very unaware of the needs and concerns of their own employees. A *2008 Job Satisfaction Survey Report*, prepared by the Society for Human Resource Management, surveyed the top needs of employees as well as the perceptions of HR professionals as to employees' top needs. Of the top four employee needs—which, in order, were job security, benefits, compensation, and safety—only benefits appeared on the list of responses of HR professionals. The consequences of poor "fit" between employees and employers can be significant in terms of productivity, motivation, and willingness to remain in the organization.

Work at Best Buy

In the mid-2000s, Minneapolis, Minnesota–based consumer electronics retailer Best Buy adopted a new program that allowed most of its 4,000 corporate staff employees to work off-site without restriction. The Results-Only Work Environment (ROWE) has since been rolled out to the 100,000 employees who work in Best Buy's retail stores. The program attempts to provide employees with better work–life balance and allows employees to complete their work whenever and wherever they choose. The program has required significant time and training for managers in an attempt to move the company culture from the management of people to the management of results. The program has resulted in productivity increases averaging 35 percent and voluntary turnover decreases as much as 90 percent in the divisions in which ROWE has been implemented. In one procurement division alone, turnover dropped from 36.6 percent to less than 6 percent in one year. Initially developed as a "guerrilla" operation, unknown to and unsanctioned by management and focused strictly on flextime, the early pilot run illustrated that flextime was an oxymoron and actually required much additional work to track employee's time, but, more importantly, flextime enhanced employee communication and teamwork by transcending the traditional eight-hour workday. ROWE's success is based on the three key commandments ingrained into the system: (1) There are no work schedules; (2) every meeting is optional; and (3) employees should render no judgment as to how coworkers spend their time. Best Buy has found that ROWE enhances their ability to recruit new employees and retain existing employees and has allowed the organization to refocus its performance management system on goal-setting and outcomes-based measures. The team-based nature of Best Buy's work environment ensures that employees who fail to abide by the system are pressured by their team members and eventually select out of Best Buy. The program has also resulted in significant cost savings relative to real estate and employee retention, as desktop computers and offices have been replaced with laptops, cell phones, and PDAs.[14]

Strategic Redesign of Work Systems

The redesign of work systems represents one of the most radical, yet common, changes taking place in organizations from an HR perspective. Traditional work systems that stressed individualized jobs that were specialized and hierarchical have inhibited organizations and hindered performance. Current and future work systems are becoming much more broadly defined and stress designing jobs not solely around technical measures for efficiency but around strategic choices made by management. The greater the volatility in an organization's environment, the greater the need for more flexible and adaptive work systems. In fact, a new model for organizational effectiveness requires organizations to be agile or infinitely adaptable.[15] Although redesign efforts may initially be a very time-consuming process, well-designed flexible work systems can provide an organization with the ongoing ability to respond quickly to a changing environment.

Although key decision makers can and do approach work redesign from a more macro, holistic perspective, individual employees' main concerns usually involve their individual jobs. This is not to say that employees are not concerned about larger, systemic types of organizational change; understandably, individuals have the greatest concern about changes that directly impact their careers and livelihoods. Many of the most significant change initiatives being undertaken in contemporary organizations involve job design—notably, what workers do, what workers are given and need in terms of resources, how jobs interface with each other, and skills requirements. Changes in these areas may be referred to in a number of ways, particularly re-engineering, but the bottom line is that employees' jobs are changing faster than they ever have before, particularly in light of how information-processing technology is impacting the nature of work.

The trend toward re-engineering has resulted in numerous changes in the fundamental ways in which work is carried out. Unnecessary activities that add no value are eliminated; tasks are outsourced; work is consolidated; and divisions are restructured in the interest of increased efficiency and enhanced performance. These efforts often result in the establishment of cross-functional teams that have a very high potential for conflict as areas of responsibility are redefined and positions are eliminated. At the same time, these changes can have a negative impact on employee motivation and morale, as workers may feel some threat to their job security. Therefore, management needs to consider and plan for those possible effects prior to implementation, when redesign initiatives are initially being considered.

The increased use of teams and project groups in organizations has also created a number of challenges. Because U.S. culture is so highly individualistic, there is some discomfort as to the role that teams and group decision-making should play vis-à-vis individual initiative. Employees who have been brought up in such an individualistic culture need training to be effective team members. In some instances, teams function more effectively than individuals, but in others, they do not. Although teams are becoming more prevalent, organizations still struggle with how to effectively manage them.

One increasingly common trend in the reorganization of work is the creation of a matrix organizational structure, in which a number of managers will simultaneously report to two different supervisors. This "dual hierarchy" is designed to provide greater visibility, stronger governance, and more control in large, complex organizations.[16] Typically an employee will report simultaneously to a functional supervisor as well as one who oversees a business or operating unit. An example of this might be the director of information technology in a collegiate school of business who might report to the chief information officer as well as to the dean of the School of Business. Another example might be the HR director for an individual location of a retail store who reports to both the corporate vice president for HR and store manager of the individual location.

Matrix organizations work best when the organization is facing dual pressure for both responsiveness to changes in the environment and increased efficiency for controlling costs. The functional head (VP for HR) in the above example ensures efficiency and consistency in the operation of the HR function, while the store manager ensures responsiveness to the needs of that particular store location, which might differ from those of other locations. Matrix organizations represent a very nontraditional means of organization and can be challenging to implement and oversee. Communication needs are heightened, and stress and ambiguity for employees can increase. However, when implanted effectively, matrix structures can provide great benefit to organizations and are frequently used in organizations that engage in a significant amount of merger and acquisition activity.

In designing motivating and challenging work for employees, it is critical to remember that as employees become more proficient at their jobs, they will seek new challenges and opportunities for growth and development. A model that addresses the stages of a typical employee "life cycle" is presented in Exhibit 6.3. While typical time frames associated with each life cycle stage of this model are presented, individual employees may move through these stages at varying rates. Hence, it is important to be alert to any signs of potential boredom or disengagement on the part of employees, communicate with employees, and consider alternatives in light of the employee's needs and the needs and strategy of the organization and work unit.

Outsourcing and Offshoring

Developing an organization's strategy involves, in part, an assessment of the organization's strengths and weaknesses, as discussed in Chapter 3. This process increasingly forces senior management to consider how best to leverage these strengths and minimize weaknesses.

Frequently, the result is the decision to outsource some of the work being done by in-house employees. While outsourcing originated with larger organizations, it has now become a popular practice in organizations of all sizes. Reading 6.1, "Using Outsourcing for Strategic Competitiveness in Small- and Medium-Sized Firms," illustrates how outsourcing can provide strategic advantages for smaller organizations, which may allow them to compete more effectively with their larger rivals.

Outsourcing involves contracting some of the organization's noncore work activities to outside specialists who can do the job more effectively, often for less than it costs the organization to do such work in-house. Once an organization identifies its core competencies—the things that it does better than its competitors—anything remaining may be expendable. A simple cost–benefit analysis can allow managers to determine the efficacy of outsourcing a particular function. Within HR, payroll and benefits are two areas that are frequently outsourced. Technological support is often outsourced because of the high costs involved with keeping an organization's technology support systems from becoming obsolete. Training and capital investment in this area often provide limited return because of the rate of change in the application of information technology in organizations. Such work is often better handled by outsourced specialists, usually at a lower cost to the organization.

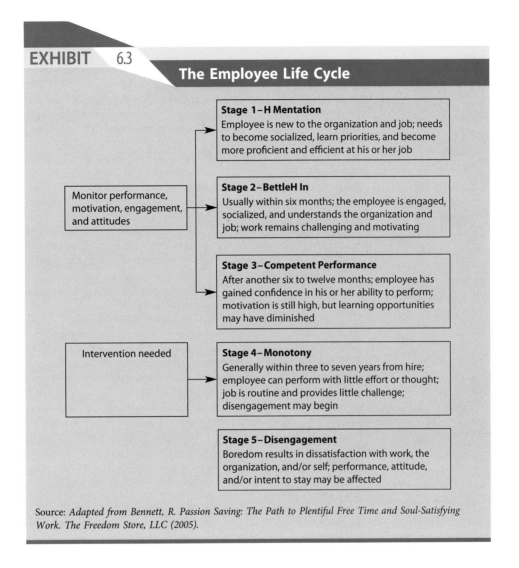

EXHIBIT 6.3 The Employee Life Cycle

Stage 1–H Mentation
Employee is new to the organization and job; needs to become socialized, learn priorities, and become more proficient and efficient at his or her job

Monitor performance, motivation, engagement, and attitudes

Stage 2–BettleH In
Usually within six months; the employee is engaged, socialized, and understands the organization and job; work remains challenging and motivating

Stage 3–Competent Performance
After another six to twelve months; employee has gained confidence in his or her ability to perform; motivation is still high, but learning opportunities may have diminished

Intervention needed

Stage 4–Monotony
Generally within three to seven years from hire; employee can perform with little effort or thought; job is routine and provides little challenge; disengagement may begin

Stage 5–Disengagement
Boredom results in dissatisfaction with work, the organization, and/or self; performance, attitude, and/or intent to stay may be affected

Source: *Adapted from Bennett, R. Passion Saving: The Path to Plentiful Free Time and Soul-Satisfying Work. The Freedom Store, LLC (2005).*

Outsourcing by Federal and State Governments

The popularity of outsourcing is not limited to for-profit organizations. In late 2002, President Bush announced plans to put out for bid up to 850,000 federal jobs, close to half of the nonpostal civilian positions within the federal government. One successful outsourcing bid involved the merging of 22 separate payroll systems into only two systems, at a projected savings of more than $1 billion over the coming decade. Florida has been a leader in outsourcing, taking its entire HR function for 189,000 state employees and elected officials and outsourcing it under a seven-year, $280 million contract. This action is anticipated to save the state an average of $24 million annually, in addition to the $65 million to $90 million it avoided having to spend to update its antiquated software system. The contractor operates "employee care service centers" in Jacksonville and Tallahassee to handle administrative work, and remaining HR employees with the state now focus on strategic issues such as collective bargaining and specialized training and staffing.[17]

One recent study showed that more than 75 *percent* of organizations outsource at least one HR function.[18] A particular benefit for HR in outsourcing is that the assignment of transactional and administrative work, such as payroll and benefits administration, can free up HR staff to focus on more strategic issues. In considering whether to outsource any function, either within or outside of HR, decision makers need to consider not only costs but also whether the contractor can deliver a higher level of performance; where control and responsibility will lie, particularly in areas where compliance with laws is necessary; and how outsourcing might affect employees whose jobs might be lost as well as the morale of remaining employees.

The importance of the compliance aspect of outsourcing cannot be overemphasized. In October 2003, Wal-Mart made headlines not for increasing its sales, profits, and market share but for the raids by federal agents at 60 of its stores that rounded up 250 illegal workers. The employees were cleaners, employed by a contractor to whom Wal-Mart outsourced this area of its retail operations. Two weeks later, a number of these workers turned around and sued both Wal-Mart and the cleaning contractor, alleging that they did not receive overtime pay to which they were entitled and that taxes and workers' compensation premiums were not being withheld from their wages. Employers who outsource may be considered "joint employers" if they exert a certain level of control over these employees. An organization can give contractors complete latitude in their hiring and compensation practices, but the organization may still face legal liability if a court finds that the organization exerts control over the work performed by the subcontractor's staff.

Decisions to outsource some or all of the work being done in an organization are usually driven by projected cost savings. Employers in our information- and service-based economy frequently have labor as their chief expense. While many domestic outsourcing contractors can provide cost savings relative to labor, they are often limited by laws that mandate minimum wages and/or by the forces of supply and demand relative to the market value of certain skills and competencies. As a result, many organizations are taking outsourcing one step further by using a practice known as "offshoring." Offshoring involves the exporting of tasks and jobs to countries where labor costs are significantly less than comparative costs in the United States. Offshoring was once considered a threat only to manufacturing and assembly jobs that required relatively low levels of skill and education. Many domestic workers in these jobs were unionized, with correspondingly high wages, particularly relative to those that could be earned in less-developed countries. Because these jobs required basic manual skills that were easily taught, organizations began to enjoy significant cost savings when they exported such jobs to Mexico and underdeveloped areas in Central America and Asia. More recently, many white-collar, professional jobs have been the target of offshoring, and decisions by organizations to engage in such practice have been controversial.

Chief among the jobs that are offshored are those in the information technology sector, computer programming, back-office accounting, and customer service call centers.[19] India remains the largest market for offshoring, accounting for as much as 90 *percent* of the industry.[20] The workforce there is largely fluent in English and highly educated, with approximately 2 million university graduates annually, many with science and engineering backgrounds.[21] Most important to organizations, however, is the fact that wages for these workers—at approximately 10 *percent* of those that would be paid for the same work done in the United States—are considered good by local standards.[22] Oracle Corporation recently offshored more than 2,000 software development jobs to India. China, Russia, and Ireland are also popular locations for the offshoring of white-collar jobs.

Offshoring has presented an unprecedented challenge to organizations via the means of managing virtual global teams. The projected cost savings that can be realized by offshoring some work can be lost if employees from different regions of the world fail to work together effectively. A nonstop, 24-hour work environment creates a dispersed global team with sequential and reciprocal interdependence. Managers responsible for such dispersed teams need to exercise tight organizational and operational control to ensure coordination and communication.

Virtual teams can provide significant advantages to organizations. Employees who function best as part of a virtual team are those who are self-motivated, self-disciplined, don't mind ambiguity and unstructured situations, and have exceptionally strong written communication skills.

One study found that virtual work teams result in increases in productivity, which range from 10 to 43 percent, and that virtual work when combined with flexible work schedules have a strong positive effect on employee retention.[23]

Offshoring is certainly a controversial practice, as was seen, when an IBM company memo was leaked to the *Wall Street Journal*. Meant for internal consideration, the memo reported that IBM could save $168 million annually by offshoring programming jobs to China, where the going wage rate was 20 *percent* of that in the United States.[24] Offshoring has been criticized for a number of reasons, but its proponents argue not only its merit but its necessity if domestic organizations are to continue to be successful and build the U.S. economy. These pros and cons are illustrated in Exhibit 6.4.

The chief advantage of—and often the motivating factor behind—the decision to offshore is the savings that can be realized through reduced labor costs. It has been argued that this can make the U.S. economy more efficient and competitive and is necessary to allow domestic organizations to compete with their foreign counterparts who already enjoy such reduced labor costs. In addition, offshoring can extend the workday around the clock. This can be particularly beneficial for functions such as software development, allowing production time to be reduced considerably as the work is transferred across time zones. Call center operations can also claim enhanced 24-hour customer service through offshoring. The biggest criticism of offshoring involves the fact that offshored jobs usually result in job loss for domestic workers, hampering our domestic economy. In addition, offshoring often involves the transfer of technical knowledge overseas, developing the workforces of other countries rather than benefitting domestic employees. Job losses through offshoring can also be detrimental to the morale and loyalty of employees who remain, fearing that their jobs might next be exported. Finally, because offshoring can be viewed as unpatriotic, organizations who offshore have to be concerned about their public image and take steps to maintain the loyalty of their customers, the public, and government agencies and officials who have decried the practice of offshoring.

However, at the same time, many jobs are being offshored, negative outcomes associated with offshoring are causing many employers to consider alternatives to sending jobs abroad. Complaints from customers concerning language and communication barriers as well as the inability of call center employees to be responsive to their needs and the corresponding loss of business associated with this dissatisfaction have resulted in many organizations "reshoring" their customer services operations. In many instances, customer service operations are being handled by contract employees who work from their homes. This reshoring trend reverses the movement of jobs overseas and is expected to involve more than 300,000 jobs as organizations such as Office Depot, J. Crew, Wyndham Hotels, Sears, and Victoria's Secret, among others, return customer service operations domestically.[25] In these and other organizations, domestic call center staff usually work as independent contractors, receiving few or no benefits, and provide their own technology, which can reduce employer costs by as much as 80 percent over those associated with offshoring.

EXHIBIT 6.4	Advantages and Disadvantages of Offshoring
Advantages	**Disadvantages**
• Cost savings	• Loss of domestic jobs
• Extend workday to 24 hours (continuous)	• Transfer of technical knowledge
	• Demoralizing
	• Public image/loyalty concerns

© Cengage Learning

Because these individuals work from their own homes, this practice is sometimes referred to as "homeshoring" and expands an employer's potential labor pool by allowing individuals to work, who otherwise might not have the opportunity to do so. These workers also tend to be better educated, as 70–80 percent of home-based call center employees have college degrees, compared with 30–40 *percent* who work in conventional call centers.

Homeshoring at JetBlue Airlines

JetBlue Airlines has utilized home-base call center employees since the organization's inception in 2000. These individuals are full-time employees of JetBlue, receiving all company benefits, and live in the greater Salt Lake City area, where JetBlue bases its reservations operations. JetBlue employs more than 1,500 agents who work from their homes—70 percent of whom are stay-at-home mothers, while 30 percent of these agents work part-time, and JetBlue strives to maintain the ratio of 70 percent : 30 percent part-time/full-time staff because part-timers have a higher retention rate. The system provides JetBlue with a competitive advantage in its service operations, as employees can still be "on the job" during periods of severe weather, when customer service needs increase greatly.[26]

Mergers and Acquisitions

Throughout the 1990s and into the twentieth century, merger and acquisition activity in the United States has grown at a frenetic pace. An increasing number of domestic organizations are merging and/or being acquired by both domestic and international partners. While most merger activity is fairly well planned relative to financial, product line, and operational decisions, the human element of mergers and acquisitions is often ignored. In a study of merger activity in the banking industry, the International Labour Organization (ILO) found that neglecting HR activities in merger and acquisitions results in a much higher risk of failure.[27] It found that mergers are pursued for a variety of reasons, including economies of scale in operations, consolidation in saturated markets, and improving competitive position through a larger asset base. Employees, however, often first gain knowledge of pending merger and acquisition activity through the news media rather than from their employers. This lack of communication erodes trust and loyalty, resulting in increased job insecurity and workplace stress. The ILO report states that a full two-thirds of mergers fail to achieve their objectives, largely because of the inability to merge cultural and other human factors into the combined enterprise or a blatant failure to even consider such issues.

Consistent with international findings in the banking industry and despite the proliferation of high-profile domestic merger and acquisition activity in recent years, three out of four merger and acquisitions undertaken in the United States fail to achieve the targeted strategic and financial goals sought through with the combination.[28] Merger and acquisition activity creates uncertainty among customers, suppliers, creditors, the financial community, and, most of all, employees because of the uncertainty surrounding the future of their employment. It has been argued that the management of people's expectations, fears, and concerns is the most important job a CEO can perform during merger and acquisition activity.[29] Ideally, the new organization created by the merger or acquisition should involve a mission and vision that encompasses the best parts of the separate organizations and the creation of a new organization that builds on strengths and synergies that allows it to be stronger than either of the separate organizations. To accomplish this, however, focus needs to be placed on the similarities of the cultures of the separate organizations rather than their differences. The key challenge for success is retaining and continuing to motivate good employees and creating a HR strategy that addresses employee needs as well as the mission and vision of the new organization.

The Human Side of Creating AOL Time Warner

The $162 billion merger of America Online (AOL) with Time Warner was the largest in corporate history. Whereas much has been written about the strategic and financial aspects of the merger, little insight has been shared as to the role that HR played in the merger to ensure its success. HR focused on five critical areas in attempting to merge the organizations as seamlessly as possible. First, HR restructured itself. Some operating units didn't need a full-time HR presence, so HR managers divided their time among units as necessary. Routine administrative work was outsourced to allow HR to focus on strategic and HR planning. Second, the foreign HR staff was flown to corporate headquarters to collaboratively work on global strategy. Foreign operations were centralized in London, Paris, and Hong Kong to speed up both production and communication. Third, talent profiles were developed for 300 key executives to assist with the most efficacious deployment of talent worldwide. Fourth, recruiting practices were redesigned to facilitate an expedited review process as well as the sharing of applicant information across the different business units. Finally, an Internet tutorial, AOL Time Warner 101, was developed that explained the reasons for the merger as well as the benefits that it could provide to employees. As one of the most closely watched business transactions ever undertaken, the AOL Time Warner merger has been facilitated by the involvement of HR as a true strategic partner from the initial stages of merger planning onward.[30]

Successful merger and acquisition activity has been described as progressing through four distinct stages.[31] The first is the pre-deal, or selection of the target organization. The second is due diligence, during which time the parties meet and disclose all information relevant to the merger or, in the case of a hostile takeover, the acquiring company gathers its information on its own. The third is integration planning, or premerger activity just prior to the formal launch. The fourth is the actual implementation. HR plays a critical role in each of these stages, as identified in Exhibit 6.5.

EXHIBIT   6.5

HR's Role in Mergers/Acquisitions

	Stage of Merger/Acquisition			
	Pre-deal	**Due Diligence**	**Integration Planning**	**Implementation**
HR roles	• Identifying people-related issues • Assessing individual's fit with new needs • Assessing "cultural fit" between organizations • Educating top management on HR aspects of transaction	• Estimating employee-related costs • Estimating employee-related savings • Assessing cultural issues as potential challenges	• Developing communication strategies • Designing talent retention programs • Planning for overcoming resistance	• Managing employee communication • Aligning rewards with organizational needs • Monitoring the new culture and employee dynamics

© Cengage Learning

Impact of Technology

One of the most significant trends affecting HR and people in organizations is technology. Simply defined, an organization's technology is the process by which inputs from an organization's environment are transformed into outputs.[32] Technology includes tools, machinery, equipment, work procedures, and employee knowledge and skills. All organizations, be they manufacturing or service, public or private, large or small, employ some form of technology to produce something for the open marketplace or for a specific group of constituents.

With constant advances in technology and work processes, organizations are under increased competitive pressure to implement, if not develop on their own, more efficient means of operations. However, the financial considerations of whether to adopt a new technology must be balanced with a number of strategic issues and, more specifically, a number of specific strategic HR issues, as shown in Exhibit 6.6. The specifics of these issues are discussed in greater detail in Chapter 4 but are presented here to give the reader a sense of how technological initiatives need to be considered from a holistic perspective that transcends the sole consideration of economic costs. At this juncture, we will address three ways in which work is changing, as illustrated in Exhibit 6.7.

As newer technologies are developed and implemented, the skills and work habits required of employees also change. There is a much greater need to continue to upgrade existing employee skills today than there has ever been at any time in the past. Gone are the days when employees utilized the same skills and equipment to perform their jobs for decades at a time.

At the same time that technological change is creating demand for workers with more sophisticated training and skills, a significant number of new workforce entrants have limited technical skills and, in some cases, little or no training beyond basic literacy. For at least the first decade of the twenty-first century, immigrants will represent the largest increase in the workforce in the United States.[33] This is compounded by the fact that the growth in our economy and the greatest number of jobs being created are in the service sector, particularly services related to information processing. Service organizations are relatively easy to establish and expand, and they provide significant entrepreneurial opportunities. However, service sector employees need different skills than those utilized in manufacturing.[34] Rather than manual dexterity, service sector employees need strong interpersonal and communication skills as well as the ability to be flexible in handling a variety of problems related to serving clients. Customers of service organizations need much more "customized" or individualized output. For example, the clients of a real estate brokerage do not all wish to purchase the same kind of housing. However, many organizations are finding it quite challenging to bridge the gap between the skills new workforce entrants possess and those required in the marketplace in an expeditious, efficacious manner.

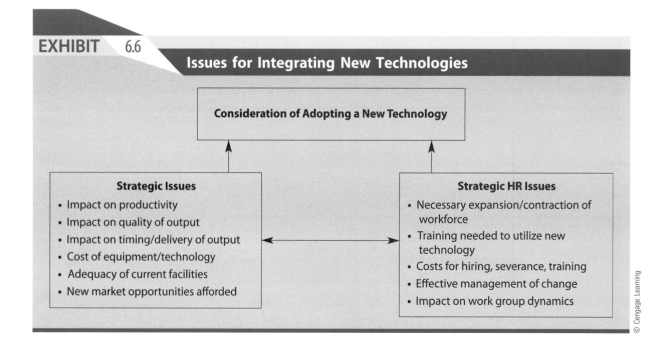

EXHIBIT   6.6

Issues for Integrating New Technologies

Consideration of Adopting a New Technology

Strategic Issues
- Impact on productivity
- Impact on quality of output
- Impact on timing/delivery of output
- Cost of equipment/technology
- Adequacy of current facilities
- New market opportunities afforded

Strategic HR Issues
- Necessary expansion/contraction of workforce
- Training needed to utilize new technology
- Costs for hiring, severance, training
- Effective management of change
- Impact on work group dynamics

© Cengage Learning

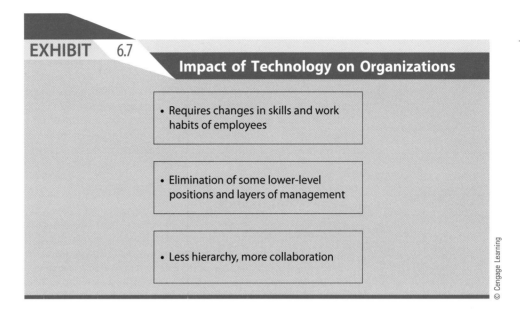

<figure>
EXHIBIT 6.7

Impact of Technology on Organizations

- Requires changes in skills and work habits of employees

- Elimination of some lower-level positions and layers of management

- Less hierarchy, more collaboration

© Cengage Learning
</figure>

The implementation of advanced technologies has also resulted in many organizations eliminating lower-level positions held by employees who performed tasks that can now be accomplished through automation. This has resulted in reduced employee headcounts, with those remaining employees having higher levels of training and skills. Automated technologies require more technically trained employees who act as trouble-shooters to repair, adjust, or improve existing processes.[35] Consequently, organizations have been able to reduce and, in some cases, eliminate layers of management and move toward "flatter" organizational structures with fewer levels in the hierarchy. At the same time, because these technical workers have advanced training, the power bases in many organizations have been rearranged from management to technical workers. It is not uncommon today for managers to have limited understanding of the technical dimensions of their subordinates' work. This is a dramatic departure from traditional supervision and creates unprecedented challenges for managers.

Technological change has resulted in hierarchical distinctions being blurred and more collaborative teamwork where managers, technicians, and analysts work together on projects. This, in part, is reflected in the growing trend for organizations to offer total quality management (TQM) initiatives for employees that focus on collaborative attempts to improve organizational processes to ensure continual improvement in the quality of the organization's product or service. Similarly, technology has created more flexible, dynamic organizational structures that facilitate change and adaptation to changes in the organization's environment. These alternative structures take the form of unbundled corporations, autonomous groupings or subsidiaries, or smaller, streamlined units designed to be more responsive to changing customer needs and competitive pressures.[36]

HR Issues and Challenges Related to Technology

In addition to impacting how work is organized and organization structure, technology has created three new areas of concern for HR and organizations: telework, workplace monitoring and surveillance, and e-HR.

Telework

Telework, the process by which employees work from home, is increasing dramatically in popularity in both small and large organizations. The key factors that have facilitated this trend are the advances taking place in information processing and telecommunications technologies. Telework involves more than merely an agreement between employees and supervisors that the subordinate can work at home. It involves a management system that allows employees a tremendous amount of discretion as to how they fulfill their job responsibilities.

The number of Americans who work remotely for at least part of the workweek has been estimated to be as high as 44.4 million employees.[37] Two-thirds of *Fortune 100* companies currently have telework programs, half of which were implemented over the past three years. Of the remaining *Fortune 100* organizations, 60 percent are planning to implement a telework program. Of the employers listed on *Fortune*'s "100 Best Companies to Work for" 82 offer their employees telework options. Ten of those organizations have 40 percent or more of their employees engaging in telework during at least 20 percent of their workweek.[38]

Telework at Deloitte

Global accounting and professional services company Deloitte started its telework program in 1996 and now allows most of its 45,000 United States—based employees the option to engage in telework as many as five days each week. Expired leases on office spaces were not renewed, permitting savings of 30 percent on rent and energy costs. Given that 86 percent of Deloitte employees engage in telework at least one day each week, Deloitte was able to redesign its facilities to accommodate mobile employees who did not need permanent desk, resulting in a savings of $30 million.[39]

Telework programs can provide a number of benefits. Stringent environmental regulations, such as the Clean Air Act, have put pressure on many urban areas to reduce employee commuting on roadways. It is estimated that if 5 percent of Los Angeles commuters worked from home once a week, 9.5 million gallons of gasoline would be saved annually, and 94 million fewer tons of pollutants would be dumped into the atmosphere. Telework can be used as a retention aid, as a more flexible work environment can allow an employee to balance multiple roles. Telework can help employers to retain their investment in employees in situations where the employee needs to relocate for personal reasons as well as when the organization needs to relocate and the employee is unable to do so. Telework also creates flexibility in recruiting and allows employers to hire from a broader prospective applicant pool. Organizations can gain significant savings relative to real estate costs, which are often high in larger urban areas. Additional studies also show that telework can significantly increase productivity. One such survey reports that teleworkers enjoyed significantly lower stress levels, were more loyal to their employers, and were able to achieve a great work–life balance.[40]

Despite these benefits, there is often strong resistance to telework from direct supervisors of workers who would engage in telework, primarily over the issue of measuring performance and monitoring the progress of employees who are working remotely. Although the criteria for performance and accountability standards need not be different for those who engage in telework vis-à-vis those employees who do not, the fact that there is no face-to-face contact is disconcerting to many supervisors.

A clear performance measurement system is the key component of a successful telework program. The telework employee should have a clearly defined set of measurable objectives, which can be integrated into a telework agreement. Organizations such as Hewlett-Packard and Cisco Systems have successfully implemented objectives-based performance management programs that have facilitated telework arrangements.

A second issue is deciding how many and which employees are offered participation in the telework program. Care has to be exercised to avoid creating resentment or morale problems among nonparticipants. A key factor to be considered is the extent to which an individual's job responsibilities can be performed effectively away from the office. Attention also must be paid to individual employee characteristics. Telework generally requires employees to have strong organizational and time management skills as well as be self-motivated.

Another consideration is the expense of purchasing equipment for the employee's home office. Similarly, liability for injuries incurred while working at home must be factored in. Because the home workspace is considered an extension of the company, the liability for job-related injuries continues to rest with the employer.

A final issue is that many managers are just not comfortable having their direct reports away from the office. Unfortunately, this is because of the fact that many managers have had no prior telework experience themselves. Training programs aimed at both—those engaged in telework and those who supervise such employees—that cover issues such as goal setting, time management, and project reporting could help mitigate some of these concerns.

Attention also needs to be paid to the investment that a networking system will require and the capacity of that system to support the volume of remote access for teleworkers. A technological feasibility assessment is as important as ensuring that the appropriate employees are allowed to participate in the program.

One study has shown that a well-designed and implemented telework program can reduce turnover by an average of 20 percent, boost productivity by up to 22 percent, and reduce absenteeism by nearly 60 percent.[41] More recently, telework has been used to aid succession planning, particularly in cases of high potential, high performing employees whose services the employer does not want to lose but who are unable or unwilling to relocate for career advancement. In such cases, employees may periodically commute to company headquarters or some other site while primarily working offsite.[42]

Telework at the U.S. Patent and Trademark Office

Most federal government agencies are slow to adapt to changes, particularly changes in how work is performed. However, the U.S. Patent and Trademark Office (USPTO) has been a leader among federal agencies in the use of telework as a central component of its business strategy. Its program, involving the participation of more than 40 percent of the agency's 3,600 employees, was designed to promote higher productivity, efficiency, and performance, reduce traffic congestion and air pollution around the nation's capital, and reduce real estate costs. The agency started its telework program as a pilot and saw that productivity and retention were immediately impacted in a positive way. Because the nature of trademark examination work lends itself to ease of reporting and documentation, performance for employees who engage in telework is easily measurable. The agency has determined that its program saves more than 613,000 gallons of gasoline consumption and $1.8 million in fuel costs annually.[43]

Telework at Merrill Lynch

Financial services giant Merrill Lynch did not rush into the decision to offer its employees the option to engage in telework. The program was the product of four years of study, research, and planning that resulted in a well-designed, strategized approach to telework that fits the organization's strategic objectives and culture. A 21-page managers' guide was developed that explained the nature and benefits of alternative work arrangements. Workshops are required in which employees and managers confront issues that could be affected by telework, including productivity measurement, time management, coworker communication, and career planning. Prior to allowing an employee to start telework, a two-week "simulation lab" experience is required, during which prospective teleworkers work in isolation from their managers and coworkers. During that time, communication is allowed by phone or e-mail only, as it would be if the employee were working at home. Employees also receive training in troubleshooting problems with computer hardware and software that will be used at home. During the first year of the program, productivity among teleworkers increased 15–20 percent, turnover declined by 6 percent, and fewer sick days were used by teleworkers. The program has also been used effectively as a recruiting tool and allowed the organization to retain many workers it would have lost when it moved its headquarters[44]

Employee Surveillance and Monitoring

Most employers and employees agree that technology, particularly access to the Internet, has enhanced employees' abilities to do their jobs: The dizzying array of information available on demand on the Internet allows more comprehensive and faster data collection when addressing issues and problems at work. Online technology also makes it far easier for employees to work at home via either telework or on the employee's own time. As employees perform more of their job responsibilities on "nonwork" time, they may feel much more free to take care of their personal needs during work hours, as long as their job responsibilities are being fulfilled. One study found that 90 *percent* of employees admitted to visiting nonwork-related Web sites while at work, spending an average of more than two hours per week taking care of personal work and needs.[45] Much of this activity centers around banking, bill paying, and shopping, but there is also significant employee visits to adult Web sites, chat rooms, daring sites, and gaming sites during the working day.

In response, an increasing number of employers have implemented electronic monitoring of their employees, using software to track employee Internet use. More than 80 *percent* of large employers are now utilizing such technology, which can monitor not only Internet usage but also e-mails, computer files, and voice mail and telephone usage. Such monitoring raises serious concerns about employee rights to privacy and can also have a detrimental effect on employee morale and loyalty. As heightened job demands require employees to spend more and more time at the office and do work-related business at home, the line between work and personal life blurs. Hence, employers have to balance the need for employee productivity with employees' rights to privacy and their need to maintain a balance between work and personal life. These issues are outlined and explained in Reading 6.2, "Monitoring Employee E-mails: Is There Any Room for Privacy?"

In addition to the monitoring of employees' Internet usage, employers are also monitoring specific employee work activity with greater scrutiny than in the past. Advances in digitization of information have made it possible to store large amounts of data on portable storage devices as small as two inches in length. Given the fact that an organization's most important documents are usually prepared and stored electronically, such information can be vulnerable to access by those who might use it for purposes contrary to the organization's best interests. An increasing number of employers are availing themselves of digital forensics, which allows tracking of employee activity, including access and storage of information.[46] Video surveillance of workplaces is also on the increase with a recent survey finding that 48 percent of employers utilize some form of video monitoring in the workplace.[47]

Employees actually have very limited privacy rights in the area of workplace monitoring. The Electronic Communications Privacy Act (ECPA), passed in 1986, is the only federal law that addresses employer monitoring of electronic communications in the workplace. While the ECPA prohibits the intentional interception of employees' oral, wire, and electronic communications, it contains two important workplace exceptions. The first is the "business purpose exception," which allows the monitoring and interception of employee communications as long as the employer can show a legitimate business reason for doing so. The second is the "consent exception," which allows for monitoring of employee communications when employees have provided the employer with their permission to do so, thereby relinquishing employee claims for invasion of privacy.

The ECPA also provides that employers may monitor oral telephone communications if they normally do so within the course of their business. This is important for telemarketing and customer service operations where employers have particular concerns related to professionalism, productivity, and quality control. However, the ECPA requires that employers refrain from listening to employee telephone conversations the moment they determine that such calls are personal in nature.

Because many employers have taken punitive action against employees for their use of technology for personal purposes during working hours, there is the potential for increased tension between employees and employers surrounding the use of telecommunications technology. Employers who chose to monitor employee use of telecommunications equipment should implement a clear and succinct policy and communicate this policy to all employees. Monitoring should be kept to a minimum and be consistent with "business necessity" or with performance problems or deficiencies dealt with as part of the employer's performance management system. As employee loyalty continues to decline, employers need to ensure that their policies do not create additional distrust on the part of their employees.

In addition to surveillance and monitoring of employee computer usage, maintaining the security of information obtained by employers is a critical concern that organizations must address. As an increasing amount of employee personal information is collected and stored in automated databases, organizations have a heightened responsibility to ensure that reasonable measures of security have been put in place to prevent access to and leakage of employee information, particularly to those outside the organization. With incidents of identity theft on the rise, inappropriate access to employee personal information contained in employment records could cause tremendous harm to both employees and the employer. Leakage of such information can result in a loss of employee and consumer confidence, harm the organization's reputation, and expose the organization to legal liability.[48] While the body of case law in this domain is still under development, an increasing number of state legislatures are passing laws that hold employers responsible for safeguarding all employee information and records.[49]

e-HR

Technological advances have also provided HR with an incredible opportunity to deliver many of its transactional types of services online, freeing HR staff to work on more strategic issues. Payroll, employee benefits, scheduling, recruiting, training, and career development are just some of the areas that are being delivered in a self-service format to employees. While there are many examples of how various employers are using e-HR to benefit both employees and the organization, the examples provided here illustrate the range of HR activities that are being delivered electronically as well as the scope of how "deep" such delivery can go.

Time Warner Cable, Inc., in Houston, Texas, has more than 1,660 employees, spread out over 27 locations. The majority of these employees work a great distance from any HR office or staff. In response to the mandate for better delivery of HR services, Time Warner installed kiosks at its remote locations to provide better service to installers and service center personnel in these locations. Initially designed to facilitate the delivery of HR programs and services, many other departments in the organization soon wanted to become a part of the communications vehicle. Employees can now do everything from participating in open enrollment for benefits to learning about the activities of the public affairs department via the kiosks.[50]

In 2003, the city of Dallas stopped issuing paychecks to its employees. This was not because of the inability of the city to pay its employees but rather was a result of the full elimination of paper paychecks. Many employees had been receiving their pay through direct deposit, but for those without bank accounts, the city began issuing debit cards. The distribution of paper paychecks was expensive and time consuming for the city; the move to "electronic pay" resulted in a $150,00 annual savings, in addition to the freed-up time of HR staff. Payroll debit cards can be used to obtain cash at automated teller machines as well as purchase goods from most retailers. In addition to the Dallas city government, employers such as Little Caesars pizza, Sears, Office Depot, and Chicago's public school system have eliminated the use of paper paychecks in lieu of plastic.[51]

American Airlines, Inc., was one of the early pioneers in using the Internet for customer service. It has since expanded its use of online technology for managing its more than 100,000 employees worldwide. American has a highly mobile workforce, with more than 25 *percent* in the air at any time and more than 50 *percent* with no office. Consequently, it needed an effective means to communicate with employees at a time and place that was convenient for each employee. A program was launched to assist employees with the purchase of low-cost personal computers to facilitate the implementation of American's "jetnet" program. Under this program, employees and retirees can complete benefits enrollment and book travel. Pilots and flight attendants, who bid for monthly flight schedules through a preference system, saw the time required for this activity reduced from four to five hours monthly to less than thirty minutes Jetnet has allowed American to not only greatly reduce costs but to also provide its mobile workforce with a tremendous added time-saving convenience.[52]

One of the most comprehensive examples of electronic delivery of HR services can be seen at General Motors (GM). GM sees itself not as the world's largest manufacturer of automobiles but rather as an e-commerce organization that just happens to manufacture cars. A special unit of GM, e-GM, has been created to produce consumer Web sites and business-to-business portals and to deliver e-HR services. The delivery of e-HR, through GM's "Employee Service Center," is designed to allow HR to move away from transactional issues and focus more on strategic issues. The ESC allows different information to be displayed to different employee groups, in line with each group's needs. Access to the center is not limited to the workplace; employees can access it anywhere via the Internet. The site receives more than 15 million hits per month and allows employees to enroll in classes online, develop a career development plan that can be reviewed with their supervisor, view job postings, manage their benefits, and review their employment history. GM has rolled out its ESC to its international divisions and sees the project as continuous, with an updated re-release of the site planned every six months.[53]

Social Networking

As Internet-based social networking sites have proliferated and their membership mushroomed, employers have begun to see the benefits that online social networking can have for the workplace. Some smaller employers have embraced existing sites, such as Facebook, and encouraged their employees to join and use their membership as a means of getting to know coworkers, particularly those who work at different locations, and to promote the organization and its business.[54] However, while many employers favor bringing dispersed workers closer together virtually, the idea of having the organization co-opt with a large general public provider may be unappealing. Many employers have developed their own in-house corporate network that would permit social networking among employees but maintain oversight of the site under the command-and-control features of the organization's firewall. Dow Chemical has developed its own social networking site as a critical means of maintaining contact with former employees and retirees. Given the episodic, temporary, project-based nature of work at Dow, the site is used to recruit back retirees for temporary projects as well as stay in touch with and recruit back former employees for permanent employment. Use of the site for recruiting has significantly reduced recruiting and hiring costs.[55]

Social Networking at Capital One

Capital One, a 26,500 employee banking and financial services organization based in McLean, Virginia, has long maintained its own employee intranet, called Oneplace. Oneplace was largely a depository of materials related to basic HR services, such as benefits information and forms, training schedules, and the employee handbook. Realizing that the workplace was not as collaborative as senior management wished, the organization decided to add a social networking site to Oneplace in 2008. Employees are allowed to post personal profiles, photographs, and information about their jobs and areas of expertise and interest. Bulletin boards allow communication about any area of interest, regardless of whether it is work-related or personal. Contained within Oneplace is a feature called "communities of practice," where employees can post tips or seek advice on various aspects of their jobs. While the site is new and no measures of its success are yet available, 96 percent of Capital One employees visit the site at least once a month, and the typical employee visits 14 different days during the month, accessing 85 pages of content.[56]

Social networking is being seen increasingly as a means of facilitating collaboration among employees, particularly given the fact that coworkers and collaborators are frequently not in the same physical space. With increased used of geographically dispersed teams to support global operations and more employers working remotely, social networking is being used to share information, facilitate discussion and even meetings, and to share information and knowledge in a timely manner. Occasionally project teams may involve customers and/or vendors, and the participation of such "outsiders" is greatly facilitated by the use of social networks.[57] Social networking is viewed by many employers as more efficient than e-mail particularly when teams need to collaborate on projects and also as a means to allow more close communication and collaboration with senior executives.[58] One recent study by Towers Watson & Co. found that organizations with the most effective communication strategies, which include social media tools, had higher shareholder returns than organizations with less comprehensive strategies.[59] Clearly, there is a payoff related to effective internal social networking.

Social Networking at 7-Eleven

Dallas, Texas–based convenience store chain rolled out its own social networking platform, Yammer, in May 2011. It is used primarily to assist field consultants, who work with local franchise owners, in sharing best practices across locations. Displays or other forms of visual merchandising and product placement can be photographed and shared instantly. The application serves as a kind of "virtual water cooler," where information can be shared and formal documentation stored related to effective strategies and best practices.[60]

Understanding Change

The pressure to change can be a constant force in many organizations. Small organizations try to grow to gain the economic and market advantages that come with larger size. At the same time, larger organizations try to become smaller—either by streamlining operations or dividing into smaller subsidiaries—to increase efficiency and responsiveness to marketplace changes. Multinational organizations try to change to adapt to different economic, political, social, and market conditions faced in various locations around the world.

Despite the need for and pressure to change, any change initiatives in organizations are often met with resistance. There are several reasons for such resistance. One is the real or perceived costs of change. Change involves disrupting the status quo and entering areas of uncertainty. It also generally involves commitment of resources (financial, time, capital, human) that could be deployed otherwise. Particularly when there is a mentality of "If it ain't broke, don't fix it," the opportunity cost of the resources being committed to an uncertain change initiative may be questioned. If employees fail to see any real need to change the design of work systems, they are less likely to support changes in their job or work environment, particularly if they enjoy things as they are.

Resistance to change can also be found when those involved with and impacted by the change efforts fail to perceive any benefits for themselves. Rank-and-file employees, in particular, may have no incentive to do things differently, be retrained, or have their jobs restructured if they see no personal benefit. Employees may adopt the attitude that the organization is trying to get them to do more without compensating them for their efforts. This can be particularly problematic in union settings where union representatives often reject any initiatives that may alter the collective bargaining agreement in spite of the benefits they may provide.

A third barrier to change involves risk and the uncertainly inherent in doing something differently. There is no assurance that the change initiatives will result in higher performance, greater efficiency, better working conditions, or improved morale. Older workers with greater tenure in an organization are more likely to be creatures of habit and find the risk to greatly outweigh any return they or the organization might receive. Employees who question the utilization of and need for new technology or distrust team-based responsibility may be particularly resistant to work redesign.

Finally, poor coordination and communication often undermine change initiatives. Managers are well aware that change initiatives are often met with some resistance, and therefore, they may refrain from informing workers about new projects and programs that are being considered or developed. Unfortunately, the organization's grapevine invariably gets a sense that something may be happening and often produces exaggerated and/or more threatening rumors than what is actually being planned. Although senior managers may wish to develop change initiatives in a vacuum, that vacuum always has leaks. Misinformation unrefuted by managers can result in the departure of employees who may sense a threat to their jobs.

Managing Change

The management challenge then becomes how to overcome resistance to change. First, organizations need to plan to promote and implement change so it provides benefits to the users—those who will be most affected by the change. This might be in the form of incentives to learn, an understanding of how it will make a job easier or more enjoyable, enhanced marketability of skills, an upgrading of a position, or some form of "gain sharing" of the results for employees. Work redesign strategies need to consider the employee perspective as to how the changes will improve work and organizational life for them.

Second, those responsible for change initiatives need to promote and invite participation. Employees will generally be much more committed to any course of action they have been consulted on and agreed to than one that is forced upon them. In addition, the organization stands to benefit from the most fundamental rule of managing people in organizations: No one knows a job better than the person doing it. An employee who "lives" with a job day in and day out can provide far keener insights as to how to improve the job, working conditions, or efficiency than virtually anyone else. Consider how many senior managers in organizations know what it is like to work in a mailroom day after day, week after week, year after year; how many have ever worked swing shifts, cleaning the offices after everyone has left; how many have ever worked at a fast-paced reception desk or switchboard all day long. An individual does not need an advanced degree in management to be able to make significant recommendations and contributions relative to work design based on their own *real* experiences in living with a job.

Finally, change is facilitated by open, two-way communication. In addition to seeking input from those affected by change, managers also need to keep all employees informed of what is being considered and planned. This is particularly true when nothing has yet been decided. A lack of any information at all can cause employees to suspect that something significant may be in the works. Again, the informal rumor mill will often manufacture scenarios that are far more threatening than anything that might be under consideration. Employees who are apprehensive and have dubious perceptions of what management might be planning will be more stressed and less productive. Seeking employee input is not only motivating and beneficial for the organization in soliciting relevant expertise, but communicating with employees also fosters an atmosphere of trust and allows the organization to determine where resistance might lie prior to implementation of change rather than after.

The HR function is increasingly being called upon to facilitate change within organizations. A strategic approach to HR involves the HR function identifying trends and business conditions that might imply the need for change, consulting with senior management on the design of any change initiatives, leading and implementing the change, and monitoring its result to ensure that it is producing the desired results for the organization. Indeed the 2012 Human Resource Competency Study prepared by the University of Michigan and the consulting firm RBL Group identified the critical role of "change champion" for HR professionals.[61] Hence we can expect increasing expectations for the HR function to be centrally involved with change initiatives.

Conclusion

The changing nature of work requires organizations to strategically manage change processes as part of work design and redesign. Redesigning work to create more flexible, responsive organizations is probably the biggest unmet need in modern organizations and a key, ongoing strategic issue for organizations of all sizes, in all industries, and in all locations.

Restructuring an organization is a risky undertaking and provides no guarantee of success. One 18-year study of Standard and Poor's 500 companies found no correlation between an organization's decision to downsize and its profitability.[62] To optimize performance, organizations need to determine the factors that distinguish successful reorganizations and restructurings from those that are less successful. Cascio has identified the practices that correlate with successful restructuring as:

- Skills training and continuous learning
- Increased employee participation in the design and implementation of work processes
- Flattened organizational structures
- Labor-management partnerships
- Compensation linked to organizational performance[63]

Clearly, HR plays a critical role in the success of any restructuring efforts. In partnering with senior executives on strategic objectives and how the organization's human capital might best be deployed toward those objectives, HR can facilitate the effective implementation of change that accompanies restructuring decisions and increase the probability that such efforts will be successful.

A strategic approach to HR management involves HR acting as a change agent to drive, facilitate, and strategize change in organizations. Although some areas and functions, notably marketing, may respond to and/or drive change external to the organization, no other area drives change within the organization as the HR function does.

Critical Thinking

1. Obtain the job description for your current or most recent job (prepare one yourself if one does not exist). Redo this description by using the job characteristics framework presented in Exhibit 6.2. Design a job that would be more interesting, challenging, and enjoyable for you.

2. What are the critical factors to consider in the design of work systems? What particular role does technology play in the design of work systems?

3. Compare and contrast job enlargement, rotation, and enrichment. How are they similar to and different from each other?

4. What barriers to change exist in most organizations, and how can they be overcome?

5. Describe a successful and unsuccessful attempt at job redesign that you have experienced or observed. What factors contributed to the success or failure of the change initiative? How could the unsuccessful attempt have been managed better?

6. Debate how offshoring might impact the U.S. economy. Do you feel that it will cause domestic organizations to become more competitive in the global marketplace through increased efficiency and reduced costs or will it simply result in higher unemployment and an erosion of the consumer segment of our economy?

Reading 6.1

7. How might the HR function be affected by outsourcing decisions in small- and medium-sized organizations? What roles can and should HR play in such decisions?

Reading 6.2

8. As an employee, how would you feel about having your employer monitor your e-mail? As an employer, why would you choose to monitor employee e-mail? How can employee morale be maintained when an employer monitors employee e-mail?

Exercises

1. Apply the job characteristics model in Exhibit 6.2 to the following positions:

   - An order-taker at McDonald's
   - An usher in a movie theater
   - A receptionist
   - A manager of an auto rental company
   - A computer programmer
   - An insurance salesperson

2. Visit the Web site for Kaiser Permanente Health Maintenance Organization (HMO) at http://www.kaiserpermanente.org. If you are a member, go to Kaiser Permanente Online. This site allows the organization to extend member services to the Web by allowing community members to interact with one another and with physicians in moderated sessions. Members can also research their own healthcare needs as well as arrange appointments. The goal of this site is to improve outcomes and lower operating costs by fostering preventive care. This form of "redesigning" the work of healthcare enables Kaiser to get feedback that can be used to improve the delivery of services.

Chapter References

1. Pomeroy, A. "Great Places, Inspired Employees," *HR Magazine*, July 2004, 49, (7), pp. 46–54.

2. Walker, C. R. "The Problem of the Repetitive Job," *Harvard Business Review*, 1950, 28, pp. 54–58.

3. Campion, M. A., Cheraskin, L. and Stevens, M. J. "Career-Related Antecedents and Outcomes of Job Rotation," *Academy of Management Journal*, 1994, 37, pp. 1518–1542.

4. Weber, L. and Kwoh, L. "Co-Workers Change Places," *Wall Street Journal*, February 21, 2012, B8.

5. Grossman, R. J. "Putting HR in Rotation," *HR Magazine*, March 2003, pp. 51–57.

6. Hackman, J. R. and Oldham, G. R. "The Job Diagnostic Survey: An Instrument for the Diagnosis of Jobs and the Evaluation of Job Redesign Projects," *Technical Report No. 4*, New Haven, CT: Department of Administrative Sciences, Yale University, 1974.

7. Gomez-Meija, L. R., Balkin, D. B. and Cardy, R. L. *Managing Human Resources*, 3rd ed., Upper Saddle River, NJ: Prentice Hall, 2001.

8. Krell, E. "Competency Modeling Meets Talent Management," September 8, 2011. Available at http://www.shrm.org/hrdisciplines/orgempdev/articles/pages/competencymodelingmeetstalentmanagement.aspx

9. SHRM Online Staff. "U.S. Workers Willing to Earn Less for Workplace Flex." Available at mhttp://www.shrm.org/hrdisciplines/benefits/articles/pages/earn-less.aspx.

10. Quirk, A. "The Business Case for Flex," *HR Magazine*, April 2012, 57, (4), pp. 44–46.

11. "Tough Love for Techie Souls," *Business Week*, November 29, 1999, p. 164.

12. Gomez-Meija, et al., op. cit.

13. Bates, S. "Accounting for People," *HR Magazine*, October 2002, 47, (10), pp. 3137.

14. Jossi, F. "Clocking out," *HR Magazine*, June 2007, 52, (6), pp. 47–50.

15. Shafer, R. A. "Only the Agile Will Survive," *HR Magazine*, July 2000, 45, (7), pp. 50–51.

16. Krell, E. "Managing the Matrix," *HR Magazine*, April 2011, 56, (4), pp. 69–71.

17. Overman, S. "Federal, State Governments Fishing for Business Process Outsourcing Bounties," *HR Magazine*, September 2003, 48, (9), p. 32.

18. Pomeroy, A. "Telecom Leaders Share HR Outsourcing Tips." Available at www.shrm.org/hrnews_published/articles/CMS_003846.asp.

19. "Job You Like May Be Going Overseas Soon," *Baltimore Sun*, December 30, 2002, p. 14D.

20. Babcock, P. "America's Newest Export: White-Collar Jobs," *HR Magazine*, April 2004, 49, (4), pp. 50–57.

21. Schramm, J. "Offshoring," *Workplaces Visions*, Society for Human Resource Management, 2004, No. 2.

22. "Job You Like May Be Going Overseas Soon," *Baltimore Sun*, December 30, 2002, p. 14D.

23. Leonard, B. "Managing Virtual Teams," *HR Magazine*, June 2011, 56, (6), pp. 39–42.

24. Babcock, P. "America's Newest Export: White-Collar Jobs," *HR Magazine*, April 2004, 49, (4), pp. 50–57.

25. Frase-Blunt, M. "Call Centers Come Home," *HR Magazine*, January, 2007, 52, (1), pp. 85–89.

26. Ibid.

27. "Financial Sector Workforce Hit by Mergers and Acquisitions," " 'Human Factor' is Key Element in Success Rates for Merged Companies," International Labour Organization. Available at www.ilo.org/public/english/burea/inf/pr/2001/06.htm.

28. Marks, M. and Mirvis, P. "Making Mergers and Acquisitions Work: Strategic and Psychological Preparation," *Academy of Management Executive*, 2001, 15, (2), pp. 80–92.

29. Carey, D. and Ogden, D. *The Human Side of M&A*, New York: Oxford University Press, 2004.

30. Adams, M. "Making a Merger," *HR Magazine*, March 2002, 47, (3), pp. 52–57.

31. Schmidt, J. A. "The Correct Spelling of M&A Begins with HR," *HR Magazine*, June 2001, 46, (6), pp. 102–108.

32. Perrow, C. "A Framework for the Comparative Analysis of Organizations," *American Sociological Review*, 1967, 32 pp. 194–208; Rousseau, D. M. "Assessment of Technology in Organizations: Closed Versus Open Systems Approaches," *Academy of Management Review*, 1979, 4, pp. 531–542.

33. Harvey, B. H. "Technology, Diversity and Work Culture—Key Trends in the Next Millennium," *HR Magazine*, July 2000, 45, (7), p. 59.

34. Bowen, D. E. and Lawler, E. III. "The Empowerment of Service Workers: What, Why, How and When," *Sloan Management Review*, Spring 1992, pp. 31–39.

35. Daft, R. L. *Organization Theory and Design*, 6th ed., Cincinnati, OH: South-Western College Publishing, 1998, pp. 126–130.

36. Ibid.

37. Listed, K. How Many People Actually Engage in Telework? Available at: http://www.workshifting.com/2010/02/how-many-people-actually-engageintelework.html

38. http://money.cnn.com/magazines/fortune/best-companies/2012/benefits/telework.html.

39. Meinert, D. "Make Telework Pay Off," *HR Magazine*, June 2011, 56, (6), pp. 33–37.

40. SHRM Online Staff. Survey: Engage in teleworkers Are Happier and Healthier. Available at http://www.shrm.org/hrdisciplines/benefits/articles/pages/engage in teleworkrshappier.aspx.

41. Wells, S. J. "Two Sides to the Story," *HR Magazine*, October 2001, 46, (10), p. 41.

42. Yost, C. *Work + Life: Finding the Fit That's Right for You*, New York: Riverhead Books, 2005.

43. Overman, S. "Most Federal Agencies Don't Measure Telework Program Results," Society for Human Resource Management, article 023659, published at www.shrm.org/hrnews_/published/articles/CMS_023659.asp, November 2007.

44. Wells, S. J. "Making Telecommuting Work," *HR Magazine*, October 2001, 46, (10), pp. 34–45.

45. Society for Human Resource Management, *Workplace Visions*, No. 5, 2001, p. 5.

46. Lytle, T. "Cybersleuthing," *HR Magazine*, January 2012, 57, (1) Available at http://www.shrm.org/Publications/hrmagazine/EditorialContent/2012/0112/Pages/0112tech.aspx.

47. Nelson, Jr., C. H. and Tyson, L. "HR Undercover," October 2010, *HR Magazine*, 55, (10), pp. 107–110.

48. Caterinicchia, D. "Safeguarding HR Information" *HR Magazine*, November 2005, 50, (11), pp. 55–59.

49. Cadrian, D. "Liability for Employee Identity Theft Is Growing" *HR Magazine*, June 2005, 50, (6), pp. 35–40.

50. Robb, D. "Kiosks Bring HR Services to All Employees," *HR Magazine*, October 2002, 47, (10), pp. 109–114.

51. Demby, E. R. "Plastic Paychecks," *HR Magazine*, April 2003, 48, (3), pp. 89–94.

52. Roberts, B. "Portal Takes Off," *HR Magazine*, February 2003, 48, (2), pp. 95–99.

53. Jossi, F. "Taking the E-HR Plunge," *HR Magazine*, September 2001, 46, (9), pp. 96–103.

54. Roberts, B. "Social Networking at the Office" *HR Magazine*, May 2008, 53, (5), pp. 81–83.

55. Ibid.

56. Zeidner, R. "Employee Networking," *HR Magazine*, November 2008, 53, (11), pp. 58–60.

57. Roberts, B. "Developing a Social Business Network," *HR Magazine*, October 2010, 55, (10), pp. 54–60.

58. Raice, S. "Social Networking Heads to the Office," *Wall Street Journal*, April 2, 2012, R6.

59. Roberts, B. "Developing a Social Business Network," *HR Magazine*, October 2010, 55, (10), pp. 54–60.

60. Ibid.

61. Meinert, D. "HR Competency Model Updated," January 4, 2012. Available at http://www.shrm.org/hrdisciplines/orgempdev/articles/Pages/HRCompetencyModelUpdated.aspx.

62. Cascio, W. *Responsible Restructuring*, San Francisco, CA: Berrett-Koehler, 2002.

63. Ibid.

READING 6.1

Using Outsourcing for Strategic Competitiveness in Small and Medium-sized Firms

B. Elango

Introduction

Outsourcing of activities which started largely in the manufacturing sector to secure lower cost supplies is also growing widely throughout the service sector. Its growing importance has made it a major concern for industry, government and the public at large. The consequences of outsourcing in today's business landscape cannot be ignored. The global outsourcing market is estimated at $386 billion and is estimated to be growing at a rate of 25 percent (Tagliabue, 2007). It is estimated that almost 80 percent of *Fortune* 500 firms are involved in some form of outsourcing already and continue to be involved in more outsourcing work. This pattern in outsourcing is also reflected in Europe where the offshore practices of European firms are predicted to grow about 30–40 percent during the years 2003–2008 (Kshetri, 2007). The growth of newer communication and computing technologies which facilitate outsourcing in the service sector, coupled with globalization, seem to be driving this growth in outsourcing services.

While many firms have used outsourcing effectively to achieve important cost saving, additional potential to exploit outsourcing still exists. While cost reduction is important, one time cost reduction does not offer sustained competitive advantage for firms only till rivals catch up. For instance, about 97 percent of companies report cost reduction to be a big motivation in a survey of companies involved in outsourcing conducted by Lewin and Peeters (2006). A much lower percentage of companies cited strategy to be the factor driving their outsourcing decision. This paper seeks to contribute to managerial practice by showing that outsourcing of certain activities within the core of the company can potentially lead to strategic innovation.

In particular, one untapped arena is where outsourcing can be effectively exploited by small and medium-sized firms to enhance their competitive advantage through strategic innovation. Based on an outsourcing matrix, this paper explains how outsourcing can facilitate strategic innovation, apart from the traditional roles played by outsourcing, namely enhancing operational efficiency and flexibility. In particular, this approach gives small and medium-sized firms an option to become more creative in strategy innovation (i.e. creation of newer services and products), potentially leveling the playing field with larger rivals. Using the financial services industry as a context for illustration, this paper presents various options of outsourcing based on the outsourcing matrix and suggests steps a company should take to achieve strategic innovation. This paper is structured into six sections inclusive of this introductory section. The second section presents the methodological approach used in this paper, and the third contain outlines the conceptual overview of the matrix. In the following section, the outsourcing matrix is presented and elucidated using a case study. This section also presents suggestions as to how the matrix may be implemented for strategic innovation. The final two sections present the managerial implications of this paper and conclude with suggestions for future research.

Methodological Approach

The methodological approach followed in this study is of an explanatory case study (Yin, 1993, 2003). This approach tries to understand the casual structure of the specific phenomenon to provide a basis of new theory generation or new understanding of the event studied. This approach is in contrast to explorative and descriptive case studies common in the literature, where the motivation is to develop a grounded theory. According to Yin, in an exploratory case study the goal is "analytic generalization." This approach fits well with the goals for this paper, as it allows for us to build upon and understand the typology presented. Therefore, we present the conceptual underpinnings of the typology, follow it with the background of the industry and integrate the case study in illustrating the model's logic. For this case study, we use secondary as well as primary data from several interviews with the founders of the firm and industry experts to present the underlying logic of the matrix. The combination of the two sources of data ensured a certain level of convergence and completeness in our explanations. However, considering the strategic importance of this topic to the firm as well as the political sensitivity of this topic, it should be noted the interviews were offered under strict conditions of anonymity and confidentially. In fact, one of the interviewees let it be known that any breach in the agreement would lead to prompt legal action by his firm. Hence, all names or any identifying information is deliberately obscured.

Conceptual Overview

In management literature, outsourcing has been defined as moving activities that had previously been performed within the organization externally (Parkhe, 2007). In this paper, we use the term outsourcing in instances of the outsourcing activity done locally (within a country's borders) and in other countries. We make this point to clarify to the reader that even though in the popular press there is a tendency to use offshoring and outsourcing interchangeably, it should be noted that offshoring can also be done within the company; i.e. captive outsourcing (UNCTAD, 2004). Traditionally, in strategy literature, the outsourcing decision was viewed within the transaction cost framework (Grant, 2008). Under this framework, the focus was on optimizing the costs/risks given the tradeoffs between conducting the activity internally or externally. This perspective usually applies to firms who outsource activities which were deemed non-core (i.e. non-critical), such as payroll maintenance. While not challenging the importance and usefulness of this transaction cost view, it brings in firm resources to show how a firm can expand the concept of outsourcing by further differentiating its core activities into supplementary and complementary activities. By doing so, firms are able to transform themselves by redefining their business strategies. In the literature, others have referred to such changes as third generation outsourcing (Brown and Wilson, 2005) or transformational outsourcing (Linder, 2004). While the suggestions presented in this paper are applicable to small and large-sized firms, it is more critical for smaller firms, as they do not have the choice of captive offshoring. In this type of offshoring, large corporations can internalize some of the benefits of outsourcing through the establishment of foreign affiliates. For instance, firms like IBM have restructured themselves as a globally integrated enterprise. In such cases, firms locate operations and functions anywhere in the world—based on the right cost, the right skills and the right business environment, integrating those operations horizontally (Palmisano, 2006). Considering the fact that larger firms have capitalized on the information revolution, wherein the flow of information has expanded the scope of tradable services (Blinder, 2006), small and medium-sized firms need to "rethink" more effective ways to compete (Ali, 2006).

Outsourcing Matrix

The goal of this matrix is to allow firms to link outsourcing decisions with strategic planning rather than using them just as a means of cost reduction. Understanding this link is

critical, as one of the major reasons for failure of outsourcing projects is the failure to clarify the strategic objectives of the onset of the project (Robinson and Kalakota, 2005). While the process of outsourcing involves moving internal activities externally, the outcomes achieved by a firm through outsourcing vary, based on the particular activity outsourced. To explain the varied outcomes and the implications for competitive advantage, this paper presents an outsourcing matrix (Figure 1). The following paragraphs discuss each of the three outcomes (Cell A: efficiency, Cell B: synergy and legitimacy, and Cell C: core-enhancing) of outsourcing. The fourth cell (shaded in grey) will not be discussed, as this option represents strategic suicide for a firm.

The vertical axis of the matrix represents the generic role played by outsourcing based on similar articulation on information strategy literature (Elango, 2000). When outsourcing leads to replacement of one or more of the value activities currently done by the firm internally, we call this role supplementary. Examples of such activities include tasks such as building maintenance, payroll processing and payments, web site maintenance, etc. to external parties. In a situation where outsourcing leads to supporting a value activity within a firm, causing it to be done more effectively, we call this role complementary. Examples of such roles could include accounting or marketing activities. For instance, the usage of professional accounting firms or advertising firms is the norm in many firms. In these cases, while the services of these external firms are used, it does not mean that these activities are eliminated within the firm. Typically, what we see happening is that some activities where the firm does not have expertise (i.e. expert knowledge) are done outside and some activities are carried inside where the firm is more effective in accomplishing the task.

The horizontal axis of the matrix represents degree of strategic importance of a particular value activity. Here, we split activities into two groups: core and non-core activities. Core activities refer to value activities which fall within the core-competence of a firm and non-core activities refer to activities outside it. Core competence is the collective learning in an organization and refers to the ability to integrate diverse streams of knowledge (Barney and Hesterly, 2008). Further differentiation of core vs non-core activities are presented in subsequent sections. Within the two axes presented, the outsourcing matrix consists of four cells, three of which offer viable outsourcing options. Each of these three cells offers specific options for firms to pursue, and these roles will be expanded with examples from the case study from the financial services sector following a presentation of the context of the industry studied.

Contextual Background

The examples used in this paper are based on a medium-sized investment firm called Boutique Asset Management (BAM) in the financial services industry. This firm operates

FIGURE 1

Outsourcing Matrix

		Strategic Importance	
		Non-Core	Core
Outsourcing Role	Supplementary	Cell 1 Efficiency (*e.g., Record-Keeping, Web-Site Maintenance*)	
	Complementary	Cell 2 Synergy & Legitimacy (*e.g., Joint Marketing, Financial Reporting*)	Cell 3 Core-Enhancing (*e.g., Research*)

in the Portfolio Management (NAICS code: 52392) segment of this industry. In this industry, the prime source of revenue for firms is fees or commissions received for managing the assets of others. The activities of firms in this industry include management of mutual funds, pension funds, portfolio funds, and investment trusts. It is estimated that this industry employs around 200,000 individuals, has a combined revenue of $84 billion and industry gross product of $ 44.5 billion, and grew about 7.7 percent in 2005 (IBISWorld, 2006). It is estimated there are 7,977 mutual funds holding around $8905 billion worth of assets (US Census Bureau, 2007). In this industry, about 62 percent of firms have outsourcing arrangements and about 31 percent say they will be increasing their outsourcing in the next two years (Maxey, 2007). Estimates of the services outsourcing by the financial services industry is about $40 billion.

BAM was started in 1997 by two friends Sammie Bjior-shein (henceforth referred to as Sam) and Raja Tamil (henceforth referred to Raj). They initially met in a required financial modeling class as they were working on their PhDs in Economics and Business, respectively, at the City University of New York. Raj, who had extensive background and contacts in financial markets, felt there existed a market for mutual fund firms whose stock picking strategy was based on econometric models infused with neural networks. He was also very impressed by Sam's capabilities in advanced

mathematical models incorporating complexity theory by virtue of skills he had developed earlier while getting his PhD in Mathematics. The usage of complexity theory with neural networks allowed Sam's models to infuse technical and fundamental modeling concepts seamlessly. So, he broached the idea to Sam that starting a firm could make them rich. To his surprise, Sam jumped at the offer. Both of them dropped out of the PhD program to start BAM. Within eight months, they completed the regulatory requirements along with the certification exams required to operate in this industry and secured seed capital. BAM was born in the basement of a multistory building near Wall Street, with two state-of-the-art computers and Raj's wife as part-time secretary without pay. The initial startup capital of $130,000 was raised with contributions from family members, while investments (i.e. assets) were secured from wealthy friends and contacts in the industry.

After going through initial start-up pains, BAM prospered due to its ability to produce consistently high returns for its initial investors. BAM quickly become a favorite among investors who sought this type of stock-picking methodology. BAM' reputation for consistency improved significantly in a short time, as its returns were not even affected by the 2000 and 2003 market meltdowns. The consistency and market-leading performance of BAM led to a short article in one of the country's largest newspapers, wherein BAM was noted for being the "best" in its niche. Soon thereafter, investors were pouring money into BAM. However, this also invited new competition in its product segment.

By late 2006, there were about 20 direct competitors and an equal number of indirect competitors (ETFs) compared to only one or two during its initial days in 1997. Moreover, some of the newer competitors were broad financial conglomerates with interests in banking and insurance. Raj and Sam felt the pressure to reduce management fees (the prime source of revenue) as well as a demand for additional services (e.g. web-based access). On the cost side, they found their expenses continuing to increase. Over the last nine years, they had added about 46 members to their firm. Additionally, the salaries for good business graduates in New York City had gone up by 80 percent during the same time period. While BAM was doing well by most industry metrics, the risks of competing with larger conglomerates worried both partners. BAM was already one of the pioneers in using outsourcing, having begun as early as 1996, which allowed it to keep its costs low. Both partners felt there was a need for them to plan for the reinvigoration of the firm. Raj came across an article titled "Global sourcing" by Forbath and Brooks (2007). This article claimed the next wave of outsourcing would lead to "non-financial" benefits like faster time-to-market, ancillary revenue streams, and process improvement. This convinced Sam and Raj that maybe there were other options in outsourcing which would allow them to chart a better future for their firm. Given this situation, they hired a former PhD colleague (who was also a professor) to conduct strategic analysis and offer suggestions for BAM on outsourcing options.

Outsourcing Matrix Applied

In this sub-section, we apply the outsourcing matrix to BAM to show potential options of outsourcing and its varied outcomes.

Cell 1. This cell represents noncore-activities wherein the external service provider supplements (i.e. replaces) a value activity that is done internally. The activities in the cell do not represent the core of the firm and, coupled with ability of a firm to achieve cost savings along with reduced administrative burden, makes their outsourcing a logical choice for most firms. Examples of this type of outsourced activity include record-keeping, data warehousing, development of web pages, etc. The prime driver of this type of outsourcing is efficiency. BAM, as mentioned earlier, had outsourced these activities, because Raj and Sam felt these activities consumed too much time and attention. They felt it was more cost-effective to secure services from outside firms rather than keep them internally.

Cell 2. This cell represents non-core-activities wherein the external service provider complements a value activity within a firm. In these activities, firms do not have the scale, legitimacy, or synergy to get the task done internally.

Therefore, firms use outside providers to complement their services. Examples of this type of outsourced activity include marketing, computer infrastructure maintenance and auditing services. The driver of this type of outsourcing is synergy and legitimacy. For instance, to promote its products, a firm needs a distribution network. BAM, being a smaller firm, did not have the scale to run its own distribution network. Therefore, it had secured the services of a large financial service firm to market its products along with several firms on a fee/commission basis.

As is the case with many firms, BAM had already exploited the options (efficiency and synergy and legitimacy) provided by Cells 1 and 2. These two cells represent traditional outsourcing space and have been well exploited by firms for several decades. The exploitation of these two cells is also referred to as the first and second wave of outsourcing (Brown and Wilson, 2005). However, a key limitation of these two cells is that once similar cost reductions are achieved by rivals, they do not offer any strategic advantage. Therefore, the key focus of this paper is Cell 3, wherein firms seek to enhance their strategic core by outsourcing to generate strategic innovations.

Cell 3. This cell represents core-activities of the firm which can be complemented by outsourcing. Conventional logic on outsourcing dictates that value activities within this cell should be conducted within the company, as these activities are of strategic importance. While this paper concurs with the notion that the core competence of an organization should be protected, we believe some fine tuning of this notion will allow greater benefits to small and medium-sized organizations.

To illustrate this point, in the case of BAM, its core competence *(raison d'etre)* is the ability to pick the "right" stocks based on specific requirements of its portfolio models and customer mix. Therefore, BAM should not outsource this activity (i.e. strategic suicide). However, what BAM can do is look for activities outside its core which will enable it to pick stocks. For instance, to sustain this core competence, BAM needs a continuous stream of stock market research to be conducted on firms both within and outside its portfolio. Such research costs are estimated to comprise about 30–40 percent of operating costs in this industry. If BAM can outsource its research activities more efficiently and effectively than its current operations, it will enhance its core, allowing for strategy innovation. Obviously, BAM, through outsourcing, gains cost parity with larger rivals who may be conducting such activities internally. Therefore, outsourcing may allow BAM to tap specialized knowledge and processing capabilities at a reasonable cost which might not have been possible before.

As mentioned earlier, such options are critical for small and medium-sized firms. This is because when large firms face twin pressures to reduce costs and conduct these activities internally, they typically internationalize operations through captive off-shoring, as they have the resources to buy out local firms or set up greenfield operations on their own. For instance, according to the *Wall Street Journal* (Kelly, 2007), Merrill Lynch & Co. has taken minority stake in the research firm Copal Partners to create "deal books" for corporate mergers and acquisitions. For firms such as BAM, choosing to offshore operations internally is usually not viable in terms of scale and costs. Moreover, smaller firms do not have the resources or capabilities to set up ventures in foreign countries, unlike large firms. Therefore, this matrix offers small and medium-sized firms new options with outsourcing of Cell 3 activities to enhance their strategic innovation.

Exploiting Strategic Innovation

In this sub-section, we explain how Cell 3 activities can be used for enhancing strategic innovations. Let us assume that BAM uses outsourcing firms for stock and market research activities. Through these firms, BAM can contract CAs in India (equivalent of CPAs in the USA) with about five to ten years' experience to conduct financial analysis. Currently, the cost for such services in Indian outsourcing markets is between $20,000 and $30,000 (inclusive of benefits and other costs). For comparison, this is about $20,000 to 30,000 lower than the starter compensation package an average business undergraduate would receive in the USA. Hiring CPAs in the USA with comparable experience could cost three times as much as outsourcing. While there have been increases in hiring costs for such professionals in India and elsewhere, it should be noted they are typically in offshoring hubs such as Bangalore or Moscow (Farrell, 2006). It is estimated that more than 90 percent of such people are located in less well-known cities like Coimbatore in India or Zlin in the Czech Republic. Therefore, this option not only allows for operational cost reductions (even relative to lesser qualified talent secured locally), but also provides for a significant upgrade in BAM's capabilities. For instance, BAM can use the Indian CAs to conduct scenario-forecasting on tax policies based on accounting principles. While these services are available in the USA, for BAM the fees and costs are unviable, forcing senior management to make judgment calls based on heuristics. By outsourcing Cell 3, BAM has access to new research at about 50 percent of the current costs (Kentouris, 2005) endowed with greater skills, allowing for BAM to innovate strategically by finding new competitive positions against rivals.

Porter (1996) suggests new competitive positions (need, access, and variety based) can help firms draw new customers into the market or draw customers from rivals. The various strategic options BAM could consider include:

- offering additional personalized services which were previously unviable for its "medium network" clients (i.e. need-based position);
- reducing its entry point for its clients from, say, $1 million to a much lower figure (i.e. access-based position); and
- increasing its scope of operations, for instance, BAM may have kept itself out of BRIC countries due to the high cost of information collection in these emerging markets.

However, lower operational costs and newer capabilities will allow it to add a market segment which was not possible before (i.e. variety-based position). Without outsourcing these activities, BAM's strategic options were limited to broad segments which were not too specialized, in which larger firms operate. The key notion being advanced here is that outsourcing Cell 3 activities allows BAM' to avail itself of cutting-edge services at a low cost, thereby creating an arsenal of new options for strategic innovation.

Therefore, Cell 3 allows BAM to exploit capabilities outside the organization to leverage its own ability to offer newer services and products, improve quality, speed and responsiveness and achieve operational scale previously impossible. In this approach BAM, rather than being boxed in a corner by newer rivals, can compete by offering newer services and products which are hard for rivals to replicate. At the least, it creates a level playing field. While the earlier example focused on research activities to explicate the benefits of Cell 3 outsourcing, other activities for BAM to consider for outsourcing include fund accounting and management reports, statutory accounting and compliance audits, investor reporting and investor relations.

Managerial Implications

This section of the paper offers suggestions for managers implementing core-enhancing outsourcing. First, while Cell 3 represents an opportunity for strategic innovation, differentiating value activities of the core suitable for outsourcing is critical. Any wrong choice in identifying the elements to outsource will result in a diminished strategic position for the firm. In order to differentiate core activities that can be outsourced, firms may want to question if the knowledge required to complete the outsourced task is explicit or implicit (Polanyi, 1967; Szulanski, 2003). Explicit knowledge is knowledge about a particular concept or phenomenon which is explainable, whereas implicit knowledge is tacit and cannot be explained, usually characterized by understanding of insights and acquired through experience. Explicit knowledge is conducive to transfer from one person to another through formal languages, manuals, blueprints, etc. and therefore can be outsourced. Moreover, since the underlying principles are usually well-understood, the firm is unlikely to face any additional strategic threat through outsourcing. Implicit knowledge, on the other hand, is embedded knowledge within the firm and involves factors which cannot and should not be articulated, as this can result in strategic risk for the firm.

Again, using BAM as an example, let us apply this concept of explicit and implicit knowledge. Assume that BAM has several proprietary stock selection models for stock screening and selection. BAM would be faced with minimal competitive risk if it outsourced and asked CAs from India to review financial reports of firms around the world and to generate input information for its stock selection model or generate reports. There are several reasons for this. First, this is a case of explicit knowledge wherein most individuals with financial analysis training would be aware of such models. Training a few more individuals does not pose an additional strategic threat. Moreover, information generated through outsourcing by itself is not proprietary, as it is based on information which can be acquired by others. However, in the case of implicit knowledge the reverse will hold true. Therefore, BAM should not outsource the running or refinement of its proprietary stock selection models, nor share any insight into the specifics of its outsourcing model, such as weighting criteria of input parameters. In fact BAM should make efforts to "wall-off" (Hamel *et al.*, 1989) such knowledge, by building institutional barriers between personnel, records and processes within BAM and outsourcing firms.

Second, while there are many risks to outsourcing, activities in Cell 3 have relatively higher risks compared to those in Cells 1 and 2. Therefore, firms may need to be careful to avoid these pitfalls. First, if a firm outsources part of its core activities, specific guarantees need to be sought that information collected will not shared with (i.e. resold to) others. Therefore, apart from careful screening of vendors, specific safeguards should be negotiated and protected through legal means. For instance, BAM should demand that outsourcing work be carried out in a facility that is not shared and that information generated by employees in the facility is secured. Second, monitoring the quality of the outsourcing supplier is much more difficult in activities related to Cell 3. For instance, non-systemic errors in research reports cannot be identified easily and the consequences of such errors are significantly high. Therefore, firms need to be careful to identify supplier firms who have good reputations. Additionally, firms should also use an in-house employee to institute random quality control checks. Despite these risks, small and medium-sized firms may find it worthwhile to exploit this opportunity of outsourcing, not as a means for cost reduction alone, but also as a means for enhancing their core competencies, thereby serving as a tool of strategic innovation.

Third, managers of core-enhancing outsourcing need to careful not to create a "hollow corporation." Firms should not completely lose in-house capabilities of core related activities. For instance, BAM should always retain some capability in research however effective the outsourced partner is in providing research services. This will allow BAM an exit strategy (Lorber, 2007) to rebuild such operations in-house if needed.

Fourth, managers should not forget that core-enhancing outsourcing is more costly in terms of managerial time and commitment relative and requires different approaches compared to the options presented in Cells 1 and 2. For instance, each of the five costs of outsourcing (Kelly and Jude, 2005): cost of knowledge transfer; cost of contracting; cost of communications; cost of quality; and cost of change will be higher for Cell 3.

Finally, managers need to recognize that a collaborative approach is needed with core enhancing outsourcing to get its full benefits. Firms need to find partners who have higher operation and ethical standards, reputation, trust, and competence, as an agnostic attitude does not work for Cell 3 initiatives. Failure of managers to adapt to this requirement increase the possibility of firms failing in Cell 3 outsourcing despite successful experience in Cells 1 and 2 outsourcing previously. Therefore, firms need to make realistic commitment of resources and refinement of strategies to ensure the plans of such outsourcing are achieved.

Conclusion

In this section, we conclude by offering suggestions for future research. This paper's primary goal was to develop an outsourcing matrix to illustrate how outsourcing can be used by small and medium-sized firms to gain competitive advantage. To this extent, a typology was presented and supported through the explanatory case study. We believe this paper offers practicing managers of medium and small businesses a tool for using outsourcing as a means to compete effectively with large firms. Additionally, compared to the outsourcing literature's traditional focus on large firms, this paper is one of the few which posits the perspective of the small or medium sized firm.

While we hope this paper serves as a foundation for future work and theory building on this topic, we believe this paper suffers from the inherent limitations due to the case study methodology employed. Therefore, we also offer two fruitful avenues for researchers working on this topic. The choice for the case study was made considering the newness in the execution of the particular option of outsourcing suggested in this paper. Therefore, replication of the matrix at a later date using broader samples may offer needed refinements to the model presented. Second, in order to implement core-enhancing outsourcing strategies, we believe much work is needed on the topic of services outsourcing risk management. Our review of the literature found that, while academic work on this nascent topic of outsourcing is emerging, work on implementing risk management programs (Whitmore, 2006) during outsourcing in service firms seems to be rather scarce. This topic needs attention, as the typical contractual risk mitigating mechanisms commonly used in outsourcing (McIvor, 2005) may not work in a knowledge-based transaction. In this regard, we hope this paper serves as a foundation for future scholars working on implementing outsourcing strategies.

Source: B. Elango, "Using Outsourcing for Strategic Competitiveness in Small and Medium-Sized Firms" in Competitiveness Review *pp. 322–331, Vol. 18, No. 4, 2008, © Emerald Group Publishing Limited.*

REFERENCES

Ali, A. (2006), "Rethinking competition," *Competitiveness Review*, Vol. 16, pp. 171–2.

Barney, J. B. and Hesterly, W. S. (2008), *Strategic Management and Competitive Advantage*, Pearson Prentice-Hall, Upper Saddle River, NJ.

Blinder, A. (2006), "Offshoring: The next industrial revolution?," *Foreign Affairs*, Vol. 85, pp. 113–28.

Brown, D. and Wilson, S. (2005), *The Black Book of Outsourcing: How to Manage the Changes, Challenges, and Opportunities*, Wiley, New York, NY.

Elango, B. (2000), "Do you have an internet strategy?," *Information Strategy*, Vol. 17, pp. 32–8.

Farrell, D. (2006), "Smarter offshoring," *Harvard Business Review*, June, pp. 85–92.

Forbath, T. and Brooks, P. (2007), "Global service providers: outsourcing's next wave," *Financial Executive*, April, pp. 21–4.

Grant, R. M. (2008), *Contemporary Strategy Analysis*, Blackwell, Malden, MA.

Hamel, G., Doz, Y. and Prahalad, C. K. (1989), "Collaborate with your competitors—and win," *Harvard Business Review*, January/February, pp. 133–9.

IBISWorld (2006), *Industry Report: Portfolio Management in the US: 52392*, IBISWorld, New York, NY.

Kelly, K. (2007), "Mergers' India connection: Merrill joins rivals in outsourcing grunt work," *Wall Street Journal*, June 16, p. C3.

Kelly, M. and Jude, M. (2005), "Making the outsourcing decision," *Business Communication Review*, December, pp. 28–31.

Kentouris, C. (2005), "New outsourcing target: private equity funds," *Securities Industry News*, January 9, p. 11.

Kshetri, N. (2007), "Institutional factors affecting offshore business process and information technology outsourcing," *Journal of International Management*, Vol. 13, pp. 38–56.

Lewin, A. Y. and Peeters, C. (2006), "Growth strategies: the top-line allure of offshoring," *Harvard Business Review*, March, pp. 22–4.

Linder, J. C. (2004), "Transformational outsourcing," *Supply Chain Management Review*, Vol. 8, pp. 54–61.

Lorber, L. (2007), "An expert's dos and don'ts for outsourcing technology," *Wall Street Journal*, May 7, p. B8.

Mclvor, R. (2005), *The Outsourcing Process: Strategies for Evaluation and Management*, Cambridge University Press, Cambridge.

Maxey, D. (2007), "Fund's outsourcing may be boon to investors," *Wall Street Journal*, May 29, p. C2.

Palmisano, S. (2006), "The globally integrated enterprise," *Foreign Affairs*, Vol. 85, pp. 127–36.

Parkhe, A. (2007), "International outsourcing of services: introduction to the special issue," *Journal of International Management*, Vol. 13, pp. 3–6.

Polanyi, M. (1967), *The Tacit Dimension*, Anchor Books, Garden City, NY.

Porter, M. (1996), "What is strategy?," *Harvard Business Review*, November/December, pp. 61–78.

Robinson, M. and Kalakota, R. (2005), *Offshore Outsourcing: Business Models, ROI and Best Practices*, Mivar Press, Inc., Alpharetta, GA.

Szulanski, G. (2003), *Sticky Knowledge: Barriers to Knowing in the Firm*, Sage, London.

Tagliabue, J. (2007), "Eastern Europe becomes a center for outsourcing," *The New York Times*, April 19, p. B2.

UNCTAD (2004), *World Investment Report*, United Nations, New York, NY.

US Census Bureau (2007), *Statistical Abstract of the United States: 2000*, Department of Commerce, Washington, DC.

Whitmore, H. B. (2006), "You've outsourced the operation, have you outsourced the risk?," *Financial Executive*, November, pp. 41–3.

Yin, R. K. (1993), *Application of Case Study Research*, Sage, Newbury Park, CA.

Yin, R. K. (2003), *Case Study Research: Design and Methods*, Sage, London.

READING 6.2

Monitoring Employee E-mails: Is There Any Room for Privacy?

William P. Smith and Filiz Tabak

Executive Overview

This paper reviews the current knowledge about e-mail monitoring and draws conclusions for practice. The discussion entails justifications for employers' e-mail monitoring along with an analysis of supporting statutory and case law, Web-based private e-mails, and international implications of e-mail monitoring. The paper also provides evidence of work outcomes of e-mail monitoring regarding employee attitudes and behaviors such as organizational commitment, job satisfaction, and performance. The paper explores these considerations within the framework of existing research evidence and presents practical implications not only for e-mail monitoring, but also potentially for the broader issue of privacy in the workplace.

Communication is a rich process underlying all information exchange, decision making, and cooperative effort. New technologies such as e-mail, the Internet, global positioning systems, and wireless communication have expanded the types and scope of communication media used in organizations. These new media present two interesting implications for managers. First, they enable a wider range of monitoring practices that can capture and retrieve messages exchanged in the workplace. Second, new communication devices increase the speed and accessibility of information exchanges between organizational members and consequently are at least partially responsible for the blurring of work-life boundaries. As a result of these trends employees find themselves at a vortex of

cross-currents. Employers can now require fuller, more continual forms of engagement while simultaneously expanding the range of employee communications to be monitored. More engagement means a wider range of communication contexts to be encountered and for which to be accountable.

The pervasiveness of e-mail in particular highlights the ubiquitous role of digital communication in the workplace. The American Management Association's 2007 annual review of workplace monitoring and surveillance reported that 84% of employers have e-mail-use policies in place, 43% engage in some active form of e-mail monitoring, and 28% have terminated employees for inappropriate e-mail use (American Management Association, 2007). The 2007 survey suggested that e-mail monitoring by employers is connected with growing legal exposure associated with e-mail use; 24% of organizations had e-mail records subpoenaed in the year prior to the report (American Management Association, 2007). Employer monitoring of instant messages (IMs) and blogs so far is lagging behind; 43% have policies aimed at IM use, and 12% address employees' work-related blogs. Recent estimates place the growth rate for e-mail monitoring software at about 30% per year (Tam, White, & Wingfield, 2005).

The U.S. legal system does not currently address rights and responsibilities associated with e-mail in the workplace. In spite of this legal vacuum, courts have consistently supported the rights of employers to monitor employee e-mails (Muhl, 2003; Rustad & Koenig, 2003). This paper first reviews the justifications for e-mail monitoring in the workplace and provides an analysis of supporting statutory and case law. However, the story does not end there. While there may be little in the way of legal impediments to monitoring, legitimate questions about employee privacy claims remain. The legality of monitoring becomes less certain as e-mail evolves to include more Web-based hosting services and transcends national boundaries. Finally, under certain circumstances monitoring may trigger a sequence of counterproductive attitudinal and behavioral responses from employees. Our paper addresses the attitudinal, behavioral, privacy, ethical, and international implications of e-mail monitoring and raises questions about its perceived benefits and costs for organizations.

The authors wish to gratefully acknowledge the assistance of the associate editor and comments of two anonymous reviewers, Dr. Deborah Kidder (University of Hartford), and Mr. Steven Schwartzman, Esq. (Hodes, Pessin, & Katz) in the preparation of this manuscript. Any remaining errors are the responsibility of the authors.

William P. Smith (wsmith@towson.edu) *is Associate Professor of Management at Towson University.*
Filiz Tabak (ftabak@towson.edu) *is Professor of Leadership and Management at Towson University.*

Why Employers Monitor E-mail

Given the volume of e-mail traffic, why do employers go to the expense and effort to monitor all those messages? The basic answer lies in the twin goals of performance management and creation of a positive work environment. More specifically, monitoring advocates provide three basic justifications: (a) protecting the firm from liability risks, (b) protecting company assets, and (c) ensuring job performance.

Monitoring Reduces Legal Liabilities

While e-mail is known for being an easy, quick, and inexpensive method to send a message anywhere in the world, these virtues have a dark side. Whether through negligence, foolishness, or deliberate hostility, employees may transmit messages that are damaging to the employer or other parties. When objectionable or sensitive material is involved, employers may be held legally liable for any resulting damages. Implementing a message monitoring system represents a good-faith attempt to minimize this liability exposure (Echols, 2003; Hoffman, Hartman, & Rowe, 2003; Rustad & Paulsson, 2005). Sarbanes-Oxley also requires firms to store all e-mails related to financial transactions (Holton, 2009).

Employer responsibility for employee conduct while on the job is rooted in the legal doctrine of "respondeat superior."[1] Someone who has sustained damage through the misconduct of an employee may hold the employer accountable if the employer knew about the misconduct but failed to prevent it, or even if the employer was unaware of the misconduct but should have known (Fazekas, 2004). Sexual harassment provides a good example of this doctrine (Areneo, 1996). For example, Chevron Oil agreed to a $2.2 million settlement with a group of employees who were offended that an inappropriate e-mail ("25 Reasons Why Beer Is Better Than Women") was allowed to circulate on the company's e-mail system. The plaintiffs were able to establish that Chevron failed to provide the proper controls to prevent offensive messages from being circulated (Sherman, 2007).

Monitoring Protects Company Assets

Not only do firms face liability consequences if employee e-mails cause harm to stakeholders, but there is also the risk that e-mails might directly damage the firm. Two types of risks can be identified. First is the possibility that an e-mail might compromise the firm's intellectual property or other intangible assets (Areneo, 1996; Echols, 2003; Greenlaw & Prundeanu, 1999). For example, it is quite easy to attach a document to an e-mail that could contain the company's most recent pricing decisions, its customers' records, technical details for a patented product, trade secrets, or similar sensitive information. Preventing the dissemination of such information or determining the source of damaging disclosures is clearly consistent with any firm's self-interest.

In addition to protecting intellectual property, most firms find it necessary to monitor and control the efficient use of network resources (Hornung, 2003). As total e-mail volume (both business and personal) increases, firms may find their existing network systems less able to handle the traffic. Monitoring e-mail usage is a way of ensuring that a firm's systems are not being excessively stressed by unauthorized use. Further, the more frequently e-mail is used for nonwork purposes, the more likely employees are to encounter virulent software in attachments and embedded links that might compromise network security. Since the employer has paid for the equipment and related support, it is appropriately within its purview to ensure that those resources are not compromised by careless e-mail practices.

Monitoring Helps Ensure Productivity

Curtailing lost productivity due to excess e-mail use by employees is another often-cited motive for employer monitoring (Echols, 2003; Greenlaw & Prundeanu, 1999; Hoffman, Hartman, & Rowe, 2003; Hornung, 2003; Rustad & Paulsson, 2005; Sherman, 2007). Again, the ease and accessibility of e-mail seems almost to invite overuse. In an extensive literature review Taylor, Fieldman, and Altman (2008) cited several ways in which e-mail can dampen productivity, including the time spent during message engagement (as compared with face-to-face messages) and characteristics of e-mail that can make it a particularly stressful form of communication. E-mail has become so prolific that some firms have begun to limit employee access to preapproved addresses (Reiter, 2006).

Legal Foundations Associated with E-mail Monitoring

E-mail monitoring is a widely practiced method of ensuring that employer interests are protected. But are employer interests consistent with prevailing legal standards, particularly in the United States? Are there privacy issues at stake that might mitigate against an employer's right to monitor e-mails? Three levels of legal analysis help provide insight into these questions: (a) constitutional, (b) tort-related, and (c) statutory.

Constitutional Sources of Employee Privacy

The U.S. Constitution, including the Bill of Rights and all subsequent amendments, is silent on the issue of privacy. Despite the lack of explicit recognition, two sections of the Constitution have general implications with respect to privacy (Hor-nung, 2005; Rustad & Paulsson, 2005). The Fourth Amendment guarantees that "the right of the people to be

---

[1]A common-law doctrine that makes an employer liable for the actions of an employee when the actions take place within the scope of employment.

secure in their persons, houses, papers, and effects, against unreasonable searches and seizures, shall not be violated." In certain circumstances the Fourth Amendment can extend to public-sector employees' claims to privacy rights while at work. The 14th Amendment, Section 1 (also known as the "equal protection clause"), ensures that "no State shall make or enforce any law which shall abridge the privileges or immunities of citizens of the United States; nor shall any State deprive any person of life, liberty, or property, without due process of law; nor deny to any person within its jurisdiction the equal protection of the laws." The concept of liberty, similar to though not the same as privacy, is at issue here. The 14th Amendment has been at the heart of controversial topics such as abortion rights and same-sex marriages.

Most important, the Constitution outlines the rights of citizens and corresponding claims that can be made against the federal government (Hodson, Englander, & Englander, 1999; Oyama, 2006). These claims do not apply to nongovernmental entities. In fact, private-sector employees in the United States have no constitutional protections for privacy while they are at work (Rustad & Paulsson, 2005). At the state level, only ten states currently provide constitutional guarantees to their citizens.[2] State courts have found that varying degrees of privacy do exist in the workplace, but that the plaintiff must prove a reasonable expectation of privacy (Hodson et al., 1999). As of this writing, however, state constitutional guarantees have failed to establish a right to privacy in e-mail cases (Rustad & Paulsson, 2005).

Torts and Privacy

Privacy claims do not always arise from legislation. There is also the possibility that the body of common law, or tort law, can provide protection if one party's actions result in damages to another, even when a formal contract or relationship is absent. Tort law can be used as the basis for privacy claims in four ways (Prosser, 1960). One basis, intrusion upon seclusion, is probably most relevant to the workplace and e-mail monitoring.[3] An actionable claim based on intrusion upon seclusion must meet two conditions: (a) the employee must have a reasonable expectation of privacy, and (b) the intrusion must be considered highly offensive to a reasonable person.[4] Case law is an important guide to understanding how these two conditions have been applied in actual monitoring situations.

A reasonable expectation of privacy is most likely to occur when the actions of the employer suggest that such

privacy is a condition of work. This was apparently the situation in *Smyth v. Pillsbury* (1996), one of the most commonly cited e-mail monitoring cases. When the company introduced an intranet-based e-mail system, it also issued a policy that messages on this system would remain confidential. Michael Smyth then sent several provocative e-mails to his supervisor. One message allegedly referred to the firm's sales management team with a comment to "kill the backstabbing bastards." Another e-mail labeled a company social occasion as "the Jim Jones Kool-Aid affair." Despite the confidentiality policy the company reviewed these communications, determined the messages to be unprofessional, and dismissed Michael Smyth. Pillsbury's monitoring and Smyth's resulting dismissal were upheld because Smyth could not establish that he had a reasonable expectation of privacy. The judge's ruling emphasized that e-mail communications are entirely voluntary (unlike other monitoring efforts such as drug testing) and that employers' interests in preventing unprofessional comments in the workplace take precedence over employee privacy expectations (Echols, 2003; Rustad & Paulsson, 2005).

The *Smyth* case is one of the early cases of e-mail monitoring and helped established precedent for future cases. At the John Hancock Company two female employees were fired for forwarding sexually explicit e-mails. Following a complaint by another employee, the employer searched the contents of the plaintiffs' e-mail folders. Both employees were terminated for violating company policy regarding offensive e-mails. The plaintiffs argued that e-mail policy was deficient in several respects and that they had reason to believe that the contents of their messages would be kept private. The court reaffirmed the essential precedents from the Pillsbury case: the primacy of the employer's interests in preventing harassment and ensuring a professional work environment (Echols, 2003; Rustad & Paulsson, 2005).

Another important case illustrates how difficult it can be for employees to establish a reasonable expectation of privacy for workplace communications. During an investigation into inventory shortages and sexual harassment, managers at Microsoft found a directory labeled "personal folders" on an employee's computer. The employee, Michael McLaren, had sought to limit access to his computer and its contents through the use of passwords. Objectionable material was found on McLaren's computer, and he was dismissed. McLaren maintained that marking folders as "personal" and protecting them with passwords established a reasonable expectation of privacy. The court disagreed, ruling that the employer's ownership of the computers and the network preempted any reasonable expectation of privacy. Further, once e-mail messages had been transmitted to other persons on the network there could no longer be an expectation of privacy (Rustad & Paulsson, 2005).

Perhaps the sole example of a legal decision acknowledging the potential for privacy claims in employees'

---

[2] Alaska, Arizona, California, Florida, Hawaii, Illinois, Louisiana, Montana, South Carolina, and Washington.

[3] The other three tort-based privacy violations are public disclosure of embarrassing private facts, publicity that places someone in a false light, and appropriation of a person's name or likeness.

[4] As Hornung (2005) observed, it is difficult to imagine a situation in which one of these standards applies and the other does not (e.g., there is no expectation of privacy but the monitoring is considered highly offensive).

e-mails is a case in the 1990s involving Burke Technologies. At the time, Burke Technologies had an internal e-mail system, but no policy and no notification about possible monitoring. After a supervisor informed the company president that an employee, Neil LoRe, was a frequent user of the system, the president used a special password to access LoRe's e-mail. He found several e-mails between LoRe and another employee, Laurie Restuccia, with nicknames for the president and with reference to an extramarital affair between the president and another employee. LoRe and Restuccia were both fired for excessive use of e-mail (the content of messages was never cited as a basis for the dismissals), and the two sued, claiming they had a reasonable expectation of privacy that the employer violated.

The final disposition of the case is a bit confusing. The employees claimed that their messages were unlawfully intercepted. The court disagreed. But when Burke Technologies sought to have the employees' complaints of a privacy violation dismissed, the court declined to do so, citing "general issues of material fact as to whether the plaintiffs had a reasonable expectation of privacy in their e-mail messages" (Sargent, 1997). From here the trail goes cold: There are no further references about the continuation of this case, suggesting that there was an out-of-court resolution. The denial of the employer's motion to dismiss LoRe and Restuc-cia's claims of privacy invasion makes this a unique case (Rustad & Paulsson, 2005).

All of these cases clearly demonstrate that court decisions on workplace e-mail monitoring have been decidedly pro-employer. Both of the requirements necessary to establish privacy-violation torts—that a reasonable expectation of privacy exists and that the intrusion is highly offensive—have been elusive for employees. Courts are not sympathetic to "reasonable expectations of privacy" claims given the inherently nonprivate nature of most work environments and the employer's ownership of the computer and network resources (Gabel & Mansfield, 2003). "Highly offensive to a reasonable person" is also a difficult standard to meet, as monitoring employee work behavior is typically an employer prerogative (Fazekas, 2004).

Statutory Guidelines and Privacy
In the United States the critical piece of federal legislation defining the extent and limits of employer monitoring is the Electronic Communications Privacy Act (ECPA) of 1986. Title I of the ECPA amends the Omnibus Crime Control and Safe Streets Act of 1968 (known more commonly as the Wiretap Act). The original law's focus was the interception of wire and aural messages. The ECPA extends these prohibitions to wire communications and makes it a crime to "intentionally intercept, endeavor to intercept, or procure any other person to intercept or endeavor to intercept, any wire, oral or electronic communication." Title II of the ECPA is known as the Stored Communications Act (SCA). This act makes it illegal "to access without authorization a facility through which an electronic communication service is provided" (Oyama, 2006, p. 506).

Even though e-mail was in its earliest stages of development when the ECPA was passed, federal court decisions have ruled that the provisions of the ECPA apply to e-mail. The law allows persons to initiate civil actions against any party they believe have violated rights outlined in the ECPA (Areneo, 1996). The privacy of e-mail communications is protected by both sections of the ECPA, depending on whether the communication is in transit or in electronic storage (Hornung, 2005). Title I covers transmission of e-mail messages. Title II limits the access of those messages from storage (Rustad & Paulsson, 2005). E-mail monitoring by employers is usually not considered illegal because of exceptions in both Title I and II.

The ECPA has four exemptions that give employers wide latitude in monitoring their employees' e-mails (Hornung, 2005). First, interception is allowable if it occurs through a device or component that is associated with the ordinary course of business (King, 2003). Since network software that tracks and stores e-mail is a necessary part of network administration, the ordinary course of business exception can be easily applied. Second, service providers are allowed to monitor messages through proprietary communication systems. Hence, when an e-mail system is owned and maintained by the employer, as would be the case through operation of branded systems such as Microsoft Outlook and Novell GroupWise, there is no violation of the ECPA. Third, exceptions are made when users provide prior consent. Company policies and login messages usually inform employees of monitoring and make system use dependent on agreeing to these conditions. Such notification effectively establishes employees' consent to potential review of their e-mails. Finally, interception must meet the "contemporaneity requirement," i.e., e-mail interception is illegal only during message transmission. For instance, in the case *U.S. v. Steve Jackson Games* (Oyama, 2006), the Secret Service seized a computer owned by the defendant company and read and deleted electronic bulletin board system e-mails stored on the computer's hard drive. The court found that the e-mail messages were in electronic storage and not subject to interception provisions of the ECPA.[5] The Jackson case reaffirmed the concept of contemporaneity, that is, that interception of communication must occur during transit (Hornung, 2005).

Obviously, the contemporaneity requirement of Title I of the ECPA tends to exclude most e-mail monitoring. E-mail messages do not create a dedicated link between a sender and a receiver as would be the case in phone conversations. Most e-mail messages follow a "store and forward" basis of distribution. The extent to which messages can be located at any point in time depends on server capacities at

---

[5]Legal analysis (Oyama, 2006) says that Title II doesn't apply here.

several points during delivery. Further, once e-mails are sent, received, and even deleted on a personal computer, service providers or employers (in the case of workplace e-mails) retain copies of those messages. Monitoring software can then be applied to gauge traffic patterns for each account, or message content can be reviewed with keyword searches.

Hence, employer review and monitoring of employee e-mails involves retrieval of communication, not interception. Rustad and Paulsson (2005, p. 853) concluded that Title I is basically "useless" to employees seeking to limit employer surveillance of workplace e-mails. Case interpretations of the ECPA have been consistent: Monitoring may occur with or without employee consent and with or without notice (Gabel & Mansfield, 2003).

The Stored Communications Act, Title II of the ECPA, has greater applicability to employer monitoring of e-mails, given the essential characteristics of e-mail and the nature of most monitoring software. Like Title I of the ECPA, the SCA provides exemptions for service providers and participant consent. These exemptions support e-mail monitoring practices, since most employers establish and maintain these systems for the benefit of their employees and with the intent of supporting work-related purposes (Oyama, 2006; Rustad & Paulsson, 2005). In addition, the law provides specific exceptions when participants in the system have consented to have their communications monitored and stored (Echols, 2003). Hence, the SCA has also provided a limited basis for employee claims to privacy in their e-mail communications.

In summary, there are few legal impediments to employer monitoring of employee e-mails. There is no constitutional recognition of privacy rights that applies to employment contracts. It is possible in principle for employees to seek tort-based remedies for privacy violations, provided that they can establish a "reasonable expectation for privacy" and that monitoring conducted by the employer is "highly offensive to the average person." Practical experience has proved these legal standards to be unattainable in the vast majority of circumstances. Existing statutory provisions, specifically Titles I and II of the Electronic Communications Privacy Act, have limited applicability to the privacy of employee e-mail messages during both transmission and storage stages. Not surprisingly, legal scholars Rustad and Koenig asserted that "in a decade of Internet-related workplace privacy cases, private employers have prevailed in every case" (2003, p. 95).

Challenges for Employer Monitoring

Given the compelling incentives to engage in monitoring and the strong legal justifications for doing so, the popular press often advises people to assume that the boss is reading everything. We cannot discredit either the basis for this advice or the logic that allows monitoring to continue. However, we offer four considerations that may limit the propriety of unfettered surveillance in the workplace: (a) remaining questions about privacy in the workplace, (b) e-mails using Web-based personal accounts, (c) international implications and varying legal and cultural standards around the world, and (d) attitudinal and behavioral implications of e-mail monitoring.

Remaining Questions About Privacy in the Workplace

Philosophers typically consider some level of privacy to be a right for individuals because it is necessary in the exercise of self-determination (Rogerson, 1998) or as a basis for self-protection (Velasquez, 2006). These interests are somewhat mitigated because most workplaces can be considered public (Fazekas, 2004), and employers generally provide advance notification of monitoring. Both conditions tend to argue forcefully against any legitimate expectation of privacy in e-mail communications made at work. However, there are other issues that support employees' privacy claims in workplace communications (including e-mail messages).

It is worthwhile to consider the implications that personal communication and reasonable expectations of privacy are not relevant considerations in the workplace. This line of thought may have been consistent with prevailing management practices during the time of Frederick Taylor, but seems ill-suited to the workplace of the 21st century. It is difficult to conceive of any working person today, whether at a desk, on an assembly line, or in an executive suite, who doesn't conduct some personal business during the course of the workday. The practice is widespread, and with good reason. Occasional personal communications (e-mail, phone, text messages) allow employees to take more control over their lives and their work. With the proliferation of modern communication tools (cell phones, PDAs, laptops) come overlapping boundaries between work and personal life. If work messages can intrude into evenings, weekends, and vacations, one can reasonably argue that an e-mail message to a spouse or family member can take place between 9:00 a.m. and 5:00 p.m.

We should also acknowledge that some measure of privacy already exists in the workplace. For example, employers initiate and implement systems that protect employee privacy in areas such as access to personnel records, genetic testing, drug testing, searches of employee property and personal effects, and other forms of communication (e.g., personal conversations, written correspondence). If employees expect privacy regarding such employer practices, is it reasonable to expect privacy in e-mail communications as well?

Finally, even if privacy claims can be easily dismissed it is worth asking the question: Can there be too much monitoring? Digital communication has the advantages of being relatively inexpensive, easy to use, widely accessible, and instantaneous in delivery. However, these advantages are realized only to the extent that people use, and trust, such communication. Monitoring is counterproductive to the extent that it leads to a lack of trust, discourages open and free exchange of ideas, and reduces creativity. Certain forms of monitoring might go too far. An example is keystroke monitoring. If, in the heat of the moment, an employee types a comment such as "the boss is an idiot," but changes his or her mind, backspaces and deletes "an idiot," and types "mistaken" (or something more diplomatic), even if there is no e-mail sent or received, keystroke monitoring will record the original "idiot" entry. Has the employee engaged in any communication? Or is this a thought crime? These are questions employers need to consider before implementing e-mail monitoring systems in their organizations.

E-mails Using Web-Based Personal Accounts

As currently written and interpreted, U.S. law is extremely clear. Private-sector employees have very limited privacy rights associated with e-mails sent or received through employer-hosted e-mail accounts. However, Internet access allows employees the opportunity to establish Web-based e-mail accounts such as through Yahoo, Gmail, or Hotmail. While employees may be accessing these accounts using equipment and Internet access provided by the employer, Web-based e-mail presents a set of characteristics worthy of consideration. For instance, employers cannot claim that the e-mail system is exclusively their property. Lack of complete ownership may be a particularly relevant factor, since employees frequently access these accounts from a variety of locations, and not just while they are at work. If an employee accesses a Hotmail account on one occasion while at work, is all prior and subsequent e-mail traffic in and out of that Hotmail account subject to employer review? Employees may have more compelling claims of "reasonable expectation of privacy" given that these accounts are established and maintained outside of the immediate work environment. As long as the use of these Web-based accounts is not too frequent (leaving aside for the moment the specific standards that would establish such limits), employees' privacy expectations may be more legitimate. In addition, the monitoring software for Web-based e-mails is fundamentally different than that for internal e-mail. Copies of Web-based e-mails are not automatically stored on the company's server (Echols, 2003). Commercially available software can record keystrokes, enable views of computer screens, or make and return copies of outgoing messages on chat programs or Web-based mail servers. Installing these special programs that create copies of such messages tends to crowd the definition of interception (Hornung, 2005).

There are two cases involving employer monitoring of employees' Web mail accounts: *Fischer v. Mt. Olive Lutheran Church* (2002) and *Booker v. GTE.net* (2003). In the first case, the plaintiff served as a youth counselor for a church. Church employees overheard Fischer involved in sexually provocative

conversations over the church phone. Church officials then hired a computer expert, conducted a search of Fischer's Hotmail account, and found evidence of sexually oriented e-mails. Fischer was terminated and subsequently sued his former employer for defamation, invasion of privacy, and ECPA violations. The court granted Mt. Olive's petitions for summary judgments on defamation but denied summary petitions for ECPA and privacy violations. Hornung (2005, p. 149) analyzed the court's decision and suggested that the Fischer case "does not say much about the ECPA when it is applied in the context of employer monitoring of Web-based mail." Given the trend of pro-employer decisions, however, an ambiguous decision may signal a foothold for privacy advocates.

The second case, *Booker v. GTE.net* (2003), is also complex and does not provide clear guidelines for monitoring employee Web-based accounts. Jarmilla Booker, an employee in the office of the Kentucky attorney general, was questioned about an e-mail sent to a Verizon customer via a Web-based account and bearing Booker's signature. A summary of the problematic e-mail, allegedly from Booker, follows:

> *I would just like to take a moment and tell you how disgusted I am that someone would waste so much time over INTERNET ACCESS! You sir are pathetic and I would greatly appreciate it if you would take me OFF of your ridiculous e-mail list! If you are having this much trouble getting INTERNET ACCESS, then go through another company. This is not a difficult thing to understand. The whole reason we de-regulate such things is to give you, the customer, the opportunity for more selection.*
>
> *I sympathize with you over your troubles, but come on [Verizon customer], why don't you put on your pampers and ask for your bobba OR cancel the service altogether! Your repeated e-mails lambasting people for doing the job for which they were trained to do is baseless and petty. You sir are a grumpy, horrible man who needs to grow up and realize that you are on earth, not some crazy place where everything works out for [Verizon customer] and company!*
>
> *Frankly, I hope you NEVER get this internet service and sit on perpetual hold, waiting for a "live" human to answer the phone.*
>
> *[Verizon Customer], if you want to waste precious time spreading libel around about Verizon, which by the way is illegal, then that is your business. Please stop sending me these despicable e-mails at once!!*
>
> *Sincerely,*
> *Mrs. Booker (Booker v. GTE.net, 214 F. Supp. 2d 746)*

Further investigation determined that two ill-meaning Verizon employees, not Booker, were responsible for the message, which was intended either as a prank or as true sabotage. Booker sued Verizon based on principles of vicarious liability and respondeat superior. It can be argued that the messages were sent within the employees' scope of employment and thereby establish Verizon's respondeat superior responsibility because the messages were created at work, on Verizon equipment, and communicating via e-mail was part of the employees' job responsibilities. However, the court was swayed by Verizon's defense that the employees acted outside of their job responsibilities, since sending intentionally offensive e-mails is not expected from employees.

The Booker decision stopped significantly short of resolving questions about monitoring Web-based e-mail accounts. Echols (2003) and Hornung (2005) reaffirmed the potential for employer liability arising from Web-based accounts, whereas Sherman (2007) argued that the Booker case acknowledges limits to employer liabilities and consequently impedes employer interests related to such monitoring. Lasprogata, King, and Pillay (2004) argued that the ECPA does not clearly provide any protections for Web-based email. However, their analysis suggests that monitoring of off-site e-mail accounts not provided by the employer may run the risk of violating the ECPA.

International Implications: Legal and Cultural Considerations

Business is an increasingly global endeavor. Because e-mail can quickly and cheaply link people anywhere in the world, it has become an important medium of business communication. Moreover, since e-mail messages can easily traverse geographical boundaries they face differing legal and cultural conditions with respect to monitoring. Employers can face more stringent conditions on monitoring employee e-mail and different cultural expectations about privacy, particularly in the European Union.

Variation in Laws and Regulations Privacy in the United States is operationalized in a different manner than in countries such as Canada or members of the European Union. In the United States, privacy can be viewed as a commodity, meaning that it can be bartered away when individuals feel it is in their interests to do so. In Europe, however, privacy is viewed as more fundamental, something that persons cannot be induced to forfeit. At the center of European public policy is Article 8, a policy directive[6] originating from the 1995 European Convention for the Protection of Human Rights and Fundamental Freedoms. Article 8 was established to protect personal privacy during an era of accelerating computer and information technologies (Laspro-gata, King, & Pillay, 2004; Rustad & Paulsson, 2003). It recognizes that individuals have a right to secrecy of correspondence that extends to

communications made while at work (Lasprogata, King, & Pillay, 2004). The directive acknowledges that "everyone has a right to respect for his private and family life, his home and his correspondence" (Rustad & Paulsson, 2003, p. 872). Article 8 has been extended to include business relations and electronic correspondence. Yet employer monitoring of employee e-mail can be justified if it meets standards such as "necessity" and "legitimacy."

The implications of public policy instruments relevant to e-mail monitoring can be far-reaching. A case illustration (*Onof v. Nikon*) from France is helpful in illustrating the notion that not all countries take the same approach as we do in the U.S. In 2001, Nikon retrieved and read an employee's stored e-mails marked "personal." The employee, Onof, was dismissed for engaging in personal pursuits in violation of company policy. The French supreme court ruled that the employer is not permitted to read employee e-mail and that doing so is a "violation of the fundamental right of secrecy in one's private correspondence even if that correspondence is conducted on the employer's e-mail system and in violation of company policy" (Lasprogata, King, & Pillay, 2004, p. 54). Even though this case has similarities to *McLaren v. Microsoft*, the legal principles used to resolve the dispute were very different. Establishing a reasonable expectation of privacy is easier for employees in France than in the United States. In another recent case (2007), *Copland vs. United Kingdom*, Lynette Copland, an employee of Carmarthenshire College in Wales, won a judgment against her employer for monitoring her phone calls and e-mails.

Cultural Differences About Privacy

Legal systems can be viewed as a country's formalized set of expectations for its citizens. Other values, not always so formalized, are also important when considering the appropriateness of particular practices. As argued here, employer monitoring of employees goes to the heart of critical assumptions about what types of information employers may collect about their employees. We would expect that cultural perceptions of privacy will shape stakeholder perceptions about this issue.

Milberg, Smith, and Burke (2000) tested a conceptual model on the interrelationships between cultural values, corporate privacy policies, and government regulation by surveying information systems analysts from 25 countries. Their research focused on perceptions of privacy for consumer information, which may offer some early insight into cross-cultural dimensions of employee privacy. Milberg and her colleagues reported that the United States and Japan tend to have "low involvement" or "hands off" (p. 36) tendencies for government's role in workplace privacy; European nations tend toward more government regulation. Consequently, the United States and Japan adhere to market-based approaches to privacy, whereas in Europe government regulations are more likely. These control strategies are rooted in cultural values such as those proposed by Hofstede

---

[6]Such directives, per se, do not have the force of law. EU directives do represent areas of public policy agreement among member nations. Each nation is expected to harmonize its national practices to be consistent with the directives.

(2000). Milberg and her colleagues reported that the cultural dimensions of power distance (power inequalities are acceptable), individualism (individual rights and interests tend to supersede those of a collective), and masculinity (traditional masculine values such as achievement and competition are emphasized over more feminine virtues such as caring) are positively associated with privacy concerns, whereas uncertainty avoidance (preference for unambiguous and structured situations) has an inverse association. These same dimensions also explain, in similar directions, a country's tendency to use public policy instruments to ensure privacy interests. The findings from this research are in need of replication (particularly as related to workplace privacy) and its implications are rather complex; still, the fundamental conclusion is relevant: "[S]ocieties' values and assumptions about privacy vary greatly" (2000, p. 53). The inclusion of survey respondents from many nations argues in favor of the study's generalizability, though its reliance on a single professional category may be a compromising factor.

Strong implications also exist for a growing trend: global virtual teams (GVTs). GVTs offer several advantages to employers, including fast response to rapidly changing business conditions, increased ability to pool cross-functional expertise across geographically dispersed locations, and reduced travel costs (Bergeil, Bergeil, & Balsmeier, 2008). Given the dual trends of globalization and technological advancements, it is not surprising that there is a growing interest in understanding how and under what circumstances GVTs can be effective. Much of this research tends to be descriptive and rather basic in nature, but more substantial inquiries are beginning to emerge. For instance, GVTs tend to be inherently multicultural and lacking in opportunities to establish familiarity and intimacy, characteristics that are more conducive to misunderstandings among team members. In contrast, dysfunctional forms of politics and influence tactics are less prominent in GVTs than in face-to-face groups (Elron & Vigoda-Gadot, 2006). In another exploratory study, Kankanhalli, Tan, and Wei (2007) reported that GVTs that rely extensively on e-mail as the primary communication medium tend to encounter high levels of task conflict due to information overload and lack of feedback immediacy. Malhotra, Majchrzak, and Rosen's (2007) field research suggested that confidentiality is a common norm for virtual teams and instrumental in establishing trust between members.

We have yet to see any investigations on how e-mail monitoring may influence processes or outcomes of GVTs. Will monitoring e-mails be beneficial or detrimental to these teams? The complexity of coordination and the need for accountability argue for a system where messages can be readily retrieved for verification. However, early research emphasizes the importance of establishing trust and overcoming cultural differences among members. It is likely that the nature of monitoring rather than its existence will be especially critical with GVTs. There may be benefits to allowing these teams access to media that are not subject to unfettered review by managers.

Attitudinal and Behavioral Issues Associated with E-mail Monitoring

Obviously, there are several perceived advantages for companies engaged in e-mail monitoring that may be measured in terms of increased productivity through decreased time spent on personal emails. However, there are also many disadvantages that may be somewhat indirectly associated with the bottom-line measures of increased cost and reduced productivity. For example, employees' feelings of being degraded, stressed, and frustrated (Ariss, 2002; Zimmerman, 2002) may increase voluntary turnover rates and may lead to performance declines.

Critics argue that negative job attitudes and reduced morale are likely to result from employers' electronic monitoring (Kemper, 2000; Tabak & Smith, 2005). Employees who are aware that they are monitored may have a difficult time getting involved and committing themselves to work, as they know that they are constantly being watched. Organizational commitment may suffer in an environment where distrust exists, leading to higher levels of stress and frustration (Tabak & Smith, 2005). Electronic monitoring, in general, may increase levels of stress at work and lower job satisfaction, and is likely to be viewed as unwelcome and intrusive (Aiello, 1993; Aiello & Kolb, 1995; Hodson, Englander, & Englander, 1999; Kallman, 1993). Many employees are also concerned that their basic rights such as privacy and due process are being violated as a result of e-mail monitoring in the workplace (Ambrose, Alder, & Noel, 1998), which may result in less engagement in organizational citizenship behaviors due to the negative impact on employees' perceptions of privacy and fairness as well as employee resistance (Alge, 2001; Stanton, 2000; Taylor & Bain, 1999).

Initiation and implementation of e-mail monitoring systems at work may be an antecedent condition to the beginning of a decline of trust between the employees and the employer. The employer by the very act of starting to monitor essentially signals that the employees are no longer viewed as trustworthy (Tabak, 2006). Further, there is evidence that organizational monitoring reduces trust in virtual teams in that members become more watchful and nontrusting of teammates who are perceived as unreliable, engaging in more monitoring themselves (Piccoli & Ives, 2003). Hence, monitoring may erode the current levels of trust among employees as well as between management and employees, and actually create an atmosphere of mistrust (Manning, 1997).

Why is this important? Researchers through several years of empirical and conceptual research have recognized the significance of relational trust in leadership (McAllister, 1995; Tabak, 2006). There is meta-analytic evidence that trust in leadership is directly related to work attitudes of increased job satisfaction, increased organizational commitment and goal commitment, and increased satisfaction with the leader (Dirks & Ferrin, 2002). On the behavioral side, trust is significantly and positively related to organizational citizenship behaviors and performance, and negatively to intent to quit (Dirks & Ferrin, 2002).

In an electronic monitoring study, Alder, Noel, and Ambrose (2005) found that giving employees advance notice about electronic monitoring and perceived organizational support significantly and positively affected postimplementation trust. According to Alder et al.'s study, trust, measured as "organizational trust" using McAllister's (1999) scale, also significantly affected employees' job satisfaction, organizational commitment, and turnover intentions. Increased levels of control can then be associated with managers' and employees' lack of trust and may lead to employee outcomes such as increased voluntary turnover and lower organizational commitment (Tabak & Smith, 2005). There is also evidence that individual task performance declines when performance is monitored unless individuals have control over monitoring (Douthitt & Aiello, 2001). In summary, this line of research strongly supports the conclusion that it is prudent for organizational decision makers to consider these employee outcomes before implementing e-mail monitoring. Even though e-mail monitoring may lead to short-term productivity gains, decision makers need to take into account longer term effects of turnover and performance declines resulting from increased negative work attitudes as well as individual forms of resistance, such as falsely giving impressions of doing work under intense monitoring when actually no work is being done (Taylor & Bain, 1999). Last but not least, since e-mail monitoring is already so pervasive in organizations, those organizations that have such monitoring systems in place might need to reconsider the costs and benefits of continuing the practice.

Electronic monitoring can be associated with organization structure as well as management's desire for control. For example, bureaucratic cultures and mechanistic structures may respond more favorably to electronic performance monitoring than supportive cultures and organic structures (Adler, Noel, & Ambrose, 2001). In an early work on trust and power, Luhmann (1979) explained monitoring and trust as alternative control mechanisms for organizations, which still seems to be applicable today. However, e-mail monitoring may also originate from a desire to cut costs and focus on tight controls to monitor levels of productivity. This is especially true for organizations following a cost leadership strategy in their markets (Porter, 1980). For these organizations, tight cost control requiring frequent and detailed control reports and intense supervision of labor, as well as a structured system of responsibilities, are common characteristics that could easily accommodate and justify e-mail monitoring. In fact, there is evidence that low trust in terms of expected employee performance leads to increased monitoring by employers (Alge, Ballinger, & Green, 2004).

Bottom Line: Is Monitoring Employees' E-mails Acceptable?

The answer to this question isn't easily available. E-mail monitoring is a complex issue. We have identified several important reasons such monitoring can be justified. But these reasons have their limits, because employer interests are only part of the picture. We have sought to provide a balanced review of the monitoring question and have advocated that initiatives aimed at monitoring employee e-mails, in particular the common "capture and retrieve" methods, should balance advantages against potential concerns.

We have summarized the important arguments on both sides of the monitoring question and presented them in Table 1. We hope practitioners and academics will find the items listed in the table useful in developing an understanding of the implications of e-mail monitoring. Again, we begin with the recognition that it is every organization's right to protect its resources and investments and manage its workforce to achieve high performance. Employers are also obliged to follow the law in those instances where monitoring may be necessary (e.g., Sarbanes-Oxley) and when liability risks must be reduced. Correspondingly, we also share a view similar to that advocated by Freeman and Gilbert (1988): Individuals are entitled to some measure of autonomy and self-determination while at work. Organizations need not be viewed as coercive entities with interests detached from their members, but rather can be communities of persons committed to mutually supportive interactions. Idealism acknowledged, we advocate that legal acceptability is an insufficient basis to establish the unfettered legitimacy of employer monitoring of e-mail.

Table 1 reminds us that when properly introduced, personal expression and privacy represent opportunities for employers. Many organizations are experimenting with new forms of performance management that allow employees greater personal control over how, where, and when they do their jobs (Conlin, 2006). Emerging and innovative forms of social networking, more often than not driven by new technologies, encourage rethinking assumptions about individual-group-organizational linkages. The "heavy hand" of monitoring, with its focus on conformity and suppressed individuality, may be at odds with the social and economic benefits of these new technologies. It is well beyond the scope of this paper to identify all the situational factors that explain when e-mail monitoring is appropriate and when it is not. With more time and experience we look forward to the creation of a framework where such explanations are possible.

A specific illustration of this point may be seen in the *Smyth v. Pillsbury* case. Smyth's e-mail message was perceived to be extreme, and from a strictly legal perspective, Smyth failed to meet the necessary standards for a reasonable expectation of privacy. Yet from an ethical and behavioral perspective, we believe there is still room to consider the advantages and disadvantages of Pillsbury's actions, particularly in light of

Table 1

Countervailing Factors Influencing the Appropriateness of Monitoring Employee E-mails*

Factors That Support the Monitoring of E-mails	Factors That Make Monitoring Potentially Problematic
• The firm's liability exposure is limited, because reckless employee conduct and communications (e.g., sexual harassment) can create problems. • Firms are legally responsible for employee conduct ("respondeat superior").	• Externally hosted e-mail accounts may limit organizations' claims based on property rights and the extent of employer liability.
• Monitoring assets and resources is appropriately within the organization's domain. • Monitoring may be necessary to protect intellectual property and network security.	• Employee privacy interests always exist in the workplace; some personal/nonwork communication is inevitable, and in certain circumstances it may be in the organization's interests to protect it.
• Employees' efforts are appropriately directed. Excessive time spent on e-mail (or Internet sites) may constitute time theft.	• Excessive or poorly implemented monitoring programs can become counterproductive. Reduced trust and openness and increased stress may be unintended consequences of monitoring. • Cultural values about privacy vary around the world.
• In the United States monitoring is strongly supported by court rulings and interpretations of the Electronic Communications Privacy Act. • Monitoring may be legally mandated in specific instances, such as Sarbanes-Oxley compliance and financial reporting.	• Legal standards about e-mail and workplace privacy vary around the world. • Legal justifications do not always ensure desired results.

*These factors have been presented in parallel formats for the convenience of organization, not as assertions that these are well-defined continua.

earlier assurances of confidentiality. How exactly should other Pillsbury employees interpret this situation? Pillsbury may have justifiably terminated an employee for inappropriate and unprofessional comments, but the company very likely paid a price for doing so, and subsequent assurances, whether about e-mail confidentiality, job security, or any other matter of policy, may no longer be trusted.

Where Do We Go From Here?

Collectively, research on e-mail monitoring has shown that monitoring has significant negative effects on employee attitudes such as job satisfaction, stress, and trust. Future research should look into the mediating mechanisms that explain the link between e-mail monitoring practices at organizations and employee attitudes; such mechanisms could be individual and group cognition, and attribution processes. What does

implementation of monitoring indicate to the employees? What message is being delivered? How are such practices perceived? How do characteristics of monitoring programs influence these relationships? This line of research could help managers introduce and implement such practices in ways that would alleviate employee concerns and not foster distrust.

Another beneficial area for investigation is the fit between organizational culture and monitoring practices. For example, the competing values framework (Cameron, Quinn, Degraff, & Thakor, 2006) proposes a culture typology based on the dimensions of organizational focus (internal/external) and organizational preference for flexibility/discretion or stability/control. It would be interesting to investigate whether employees in some organizational cultures are more accepting of e-mail monitoring practices than those in others. It would be prudent for managers in certain organizational cultures to show more care and attention to the type and extent of e-mail monitoring systems they choose to implement. The fit may determine the success of the initiation and implementation of monitoring systems. It will also be worthwhile to investigate how various techniques to foster ethical behavior in organizations (e.g., anonymous hotlines, employee ethics training and development) can be used to control and prevent undesirable employee behavior so that electronic monitoring becomes unnecessary.

It is also worth noting that the current class of college graduates, the next generation of managers, have spent their entire lives online. A major portion of their communication has occurred through instant messaging, texting, and social networking sites. What significance do concepts such as "privacy," "monitoring," and "control" hold for this new cadre of workers with hundreds of friends on Facebook? We expect that age will be an important demographic variable to consider for research in this area.

What does all this mean for practitioners? E-mail monitoring, like many other workplace programs, involves careful consideration of multiple trade-offs that can enhance yet also damage employee well-being. In parallel, organizational decision makers need to design e-mail monitoring systems based on the fit among organizational environment, technology, structure, and culture. For example, decision makers in an organic structure with a clan culture may find it more cost-effective to rely on informal methods of control such as social pressure, group dynamics, and trust than on electronic monitoring methods. Further, it might be more cost-effective for many organizations to pursue avenues designed to foster ethical behavior among employees or to combine techniques such as hotlines and training with less intrusive forms of electronic monitoring.

Finally, it is important to bear in mind how the pace of technological change continues to shape our thinking about workplace monitoring. E-mail grew in popularity in the 1990s but today is only one of many types of electronic communication. (Consider that students are likely to send e-mails when communicating with their professors, but among themselves use primarily text messaging.) The misuse of company computers is a much broader issue than simple e-mail monitoring, including nonwork-related surfing, shopping, and gambling on the Internet. The cases and scenarios described in this paper are mostly based on relatively straightforward examples of employees sending e-mails during work hours, while at designated work locations, and using company-owned computers, e-mail software and servers. In such circumstances employer property rights and the primacy of work responsibilities establish a strong legitimacy for monitoring. However, the current trend with communication technologies is toward cheaper, portable, multifunctional devices that make use of multiple access points (e.g., Wi-Fi). We will certainly see a wider variety of corporate-issued devices enabling communication (work- and nonwork-related) to take place anywhere and anytime. These innovations will bring with them new questions for which old

answers are insufficient. It remains likely that employees (particularly those in the United States) will find weak legal protections when it comes to privacy of electronic messages. Still, we emphasize that trust remains a core virtue of high-performing work environments and that privacy is a necessary component in trusting relationships. Managers, as they always have been, will be challenged to ensure the viability of their enterprises, including understanding the trade-offs between properly protecting the firm from legal liabilities and dysfunctional practices on one hand and respecting, even nurturing, the creative and occasionally chaotic contributions of a talented workforce on the other.

Source: Academy of Management.

REFERENCES

Aiello, J. R. (1993). Computer-based work monitoring: Electronic surveillance and its effects. *Journal of Applied Social Psychology*, 23(7), 499–507.

Aiello, J. R., & Kolb, K. J. (1995). Electronic performance monitoring and social context: Impact on productivity and stress. *Journal of Applied Psychology*, 80(3), 339–353.

Alder, G. S., Noel, T. W., & Ambrose, M. L. (2006). Clarifying the effects of Internet monitoring on job attitudes: The mediating role of employee trust. *Information & Management*, 43(7), 894–903.

Alge, B. J. (2001). Effects of computer surveillance on perceptions of privacy and procedural justice. *Journal of Applied Psychology*, 86(4), 797–804.

Alge, B. J., Ballinger, G.A., & Green, S. G. (2004). Remote control. *Personnel Psychology*, 57, 377–410.

Ambrose, M. L., Alder, G. S., & Noel, T. W. (1998). Electronic performance monitoring: A consideration of rights. In M. Schminke (Ed.), *Managerial ethics: Moral management of people and processes*. Mahwah, NJ: Lawrence Erlbaum & Associates.

American Management Association. (2007). AMA/ePolicy 2007 survey of electronic monitoring & surveillance survey. Retrieved July 21, 2008, from http://press.amanet.org/press-releases/177/2007-electronic-monitoring-surveillance-survey/

Areneo, J. (1996). Pandora's (e-mail) box: E-mail monitoring in the workplace. *Hofstra Law Review*, 14, 339–365.

Ariss S. (2002). Computer monitoring: Benefits and pitfalls facing management. *Information & Management*, 39(7), 553–558.

Bergeil, B. J., Bergeil, E. B., & Balsmeier, P. W. (2008). Nature of virtual teams: A summary of their advantages and disadvantages. *Management Research News*, 31, 99–110.

Booker v. GTE.net., 6th Cir., 350 F.3d 515, Dec. 5, 2003.

Brown, W. S. (1996). Technology, workplace privacy, and personhood. *Journal of Business Ethics*, 15, 1237–1248.

Cameron, K. S., Quinn, R. E., Degraff, J., & Thakor, A. V. (2006). Competing values leadership. Northampton, MA: Edward Elgar.

Conlin, M. (2006, December 11). Smashing the clock. *Business Week*, 60–68.

Day, D. V., Schleicher, A. L., & Hiller, N. J. (2002). Self-monitoring personality at work: A meta-analytic investigation of construct validity. *Journal of Applied Psychology*, 87(2), 390–401.

Dirks, K. T., & Ferrin, D. L. (2002). Trust in leadership: Meta-analytic findings and implications for organizational research. *Journal of Applied Psychology*, 87(4), 611–62.

Douthitt, E. A., & Aiello, J. R. (2001). The role of participation and control in the effects of computer monitoring on fairness perceptions, task satisfaction, and performance. *Journal of Applied Psychology*, 86(5), 867–874.

Echols, M. (2003). Striking a balance between employer business interests and employee privacy: Using respon-deat superior to justify the monitoring of web-based, personal electronic mail accounts of employees in the workplace. *Computer Law Review and Technology Journal*, 7, 273–300.

Elron, E., & Vigoda-Gadot, E. (2006). Influence and political processes in cyberspace: The case of global virtual teams. *International Journal of Cross Cultural Management*, 6, 295–318.

Fairweather, N. B. (1999). Surveillance in employment: The case of teleworking. *Journal of Business Ethics*, 22(1), 39–49.

Fazekas, C. P. (2004). 1984 is still fiction: Electronic monitoring in the workplace and U.S. privacy law. *Duke Law and Technology Review*, 15.

Freeman, R. E., & Gilbert, D. R. (1988). *Corporate strategy and the search for ethics*. Englewood Cliffs, NJ: Prentice Hall.

Fried, C. (1968). Privacy (a moral analysis). *Yale Law Journal*, 77(1), 475–493.

Gabel, J. T. A., & Mansfield, N. R. (2003). The information revolution and its impact on the employment relationship: An analysis of the cyberspace workplace. *American Business Law Journal*, 40(2), 301–353.

Grant, A. M., Christianson, M. K. & Price, R. H. (2007). Happiness, health, or relationships? Managerial practices and employee well-being tradeoffs. *Academy of Management Perspectives*, 21(3), 51–63.

Hodson, T. J., Englander, F., & Englander, V. (1999). Ethical, legal, and economic aspects of employer monitoring of employee electronic mail. *Journal of Business Ethics*, 19(1), 99–108.

Holton, C. (2009). Identifying disgruntled employee systems fraud risk through text mining: A simple solution for a multibillion dollar problem. *Decision Support Systems*, 46(4), 853–864.

Hornung, M. S. (2005). Think before you type: A look at e-mail privacy in the workplace. *Fordham Journal of Corporate & Financial Law*, 11, 115–160.

Johnson, D. G. (2001). *Computer ethics* (3rd ed.). Upper Saddle River, NJ: Pearson Education Inc.

Kallman, E. (1993). Electronic monitoring of employees: Issues and guidelines. *Journal of Systems Management*, 44(6), 17–21.

Kankanhalli, A., Tan, B. C. Y., & Wei, K. (2007). Conflict and performance in global virtual teams. *Journal of Management Information Systems*, 23, 237–274.

Kemper, C. L. (2000). Big brother. *Communication World*, 18(1), 8–12.

King, N. J. (2003). Electronic monitoring to promote national security impacts workplace privacy. *Employee Responsibilities and Rights Journal*, 15(3), 127–147.

Lasprogata, G., King, N. J., & Pillay, S. (2004). Regulation of electronic employee monitoring: Identifying fundamental principles of employee privacy through a comparative study of data privacy legislation in the European Union, United States and Canada. *Stanford Technology Law Review*, 4.

Luhmann, N. (1979). *Trust and power*. Palo Alto, CA: Stanford University Press.

Malhotra, A., Majchrzak, A., & Rosen, B. (2007). Leading virtual teams. *Academy of Management Perspectives*, 21(1), 60–70.

Manning, R. C. (1997). Liberal and communitarian defenses of workplace privacy. *Journal of Business Ethics*, 16(8), 817–823.

McAllister, D. J. (1995). Affect and cognition based trust as foundations for interpersonal cooperation in organizations. *Academy of Management Journal*, 38(1), 24–59.

McAllister, D. J. (1999). *Cynicism at work: The social dynamics of extreme distrust in organizations*. Paper presented at the 1999 Annual National Academy of Management Meetings, Chicago, IL.

Milberg, S. J., Smith, H. J., & Burke, S. J. (2000). Information privacy: Corporate management and national regulation. *Organization Science*, 11(1), 35–57.

Moore, A. D. (1998). Intangible property: Privacy, power, and information control. *American Philosophical Quarterly*, 35, 365–378.

Muhl, C. J. (2003). Workplace e-mail and internet use: Employees and employers beware. *Monthly Labor Review*, 126(2), 36–45.

Nehf, J. P. (2005). Incomparability and the passive virtues of ad hoc privacy policy. *University of Colorado Law Review*, 76, 1–56.

Oyama, K. A. (2006). Cyberlaw note: E-mail privacy after *United States v. Councilman:* Legislative options for amending ECPA. *Berkeley Technology Law Journal*, 21, 499–529.

Piccoli, G., & Ives, B. (2003). Trust and the unintended effects of behavior control in virtual teams. *MIS Quarterly*, 27(3), 365–395.

Porter M. E. (1980). *Competitive strategy*. New York: Free Press.

Prosser, W. L. (1960). Privacy. *California Law Review*, 48, 383–423.

Rachels, J. (1975). Why privacy is important. *Philosophy and Public Affairs*, 4, 323–333.

Reiter, C. (2006, May 8). Managing technology; Missed messages: As complaints about e-mail mount, some companies look for new ways to communicate. *Wall Street Journal*, p. R8.

Rogerson, S. (1998). Computer and information ethics. *Encyclopedia of Applied Ethics, vol. 1*. Dubuque, IA: Kent-Hall.

Rosen, J. (2000). Why privacy matters. *Wilson Quarterly*, 24(4), 32–38.

Rustad, M. L., & Koenig, T. H. (2003). Cybertorts and legal lag: An empirical analysis. *Southern California Interdisciplinary Law Journal*, 13, 77–140.

Rustad, M. L., & Paulsson, S. R. (2005). Monitoring employee e-mail & internet usage: Avoiding the omniscient electronic sweatshop: Insights from Europe. *University of Pennsylvania Journal of Labor & Employment Law*, 7, 829–904.

Sargent, C. F. (1997). Electronic media and the workplace: Confidentiality, privacy and other issues. *Boston Bar Journal*, 41(May/June).

Sherman, M. A. (2007). Webmail at work: The case for protection against employer monitoring. *Touro Law Review*. Retrieved August 1, 2007, from http://ssrn.com/abstract=978075.

Stanton, J. M. (2000). Reactions to employee performance monitoring: Framework, review, and research directions. *Human Performance*, 13, 85–113.

Tabak, F. (2007). The role of trustworthy behaviors and cognitive categorization in organizational settings: Links to leader-member exchange behaviors and employee work outcomes. *Proceedings of the 2007 Annual Meeting of the Southern Management Association*, Clearwater Beach, FL.

Tabak, F., & Smith, W. P. (2005). Privacy and electronic monitoring in the workplace: A model of managerial cognition and relational trust development. *Employee Responsibilities and Rights Journal*, 17(3), 173–189.

Tam, P. W., White, E., Wingfield, N., & Maher, K. (2005, March 9). Snooping e-mail by software is now a workplace norm. *Wall Street Journal*, p. B1.

Taylor, H., Fieldman, G., & Altman, Y. (2008). E-mail at work: A cause for concern? The implications of the new communication technologies for health, wellbeing and productivity at work. *Journal of Organisational Transformation and Social Change*, 5(2), 159–173.

Taylor, P., & Gain, P. (1999). An assembly line in the head: Work and employee relations in the call center. *Industrial Relations*, 30(2), 101–117.

Traub, S. H. (1996). Battling employee crime: A review of corporate strategies and programs. *Crime and Delinquency*, 42(2), 244–252.

Velasquez, M. G. (2006). *Business ethics: Concepts and cases* (6th ed.). Upper Saddle River, NJ: Pearson Prentice Hall.

Employment Law

- Describe the doctrine of employment-at-will and its impact on the employment relationship
- Understand the provisions and enforcement of federal laws that impact the employment relationship
- Understand the positions and arguments in favor of and against affirmative action
- Gain an appreciation of the issues surrounding the management of sexual harassment in organizations
- Gain an awareness of trends in employment litigation and the challenges they present to employers

Racial Harassment at Lockheed Martin

In January 2007, the Equal Employment Opportunity Commission (EEOC) announced a settlement with Lockheed Martin, the Bethesda, Maryland–based *Fortune 100* corporation and world's largest military contractor. As part of the settlement, Lockheed paid $2.5 million to an employee who had complained about racial discrimination and harassment and terminated four coworkers and the supervisor who were alleged to have participated in the harassment. The employee who brought the charges had been a field service worker who was called the "N-word" and physically threatened while working on military aircraft on team assignments in Florida, Washington, and Hawaii. The only black worker on the team, the complainant was subjected to weekly mock "newsletters" in the employee break room for Ku Klux Klan meetings, racist graffiti in restrooms, threatened with lynching, told how easy it would be to make him disappear on the isolated worksites, and subjected to coworkers repeatedly circling the block by his home late at night. After complaining to Lockheed's human resources (HR) office, the harassment escalated and the complaining employee was kept on the same team as the harassing coworkers. When the complaining employee filed his allegations with the EEOC, corporate HR became angry and told him, "We're Lockheed Martin. We never lose." upon firing him. In addition to the monetary award and firings, Lockheed was required to provide annual antidiscrimination training to all employees and report annually to the EEOC as to whether any new claims of discrimination had been levied and what actions had been taken in response.[1]

The increasing scope, complexity, and ambiguity of federal laws that regulate the employment relationship have contributed to making employment law more of a critical strategic issue for employers than it has been in the past. Organizations that knowingly or unknowingly violate these laws can be saddled with significant litigation costs, negative press and public relations, and lowered employee morale, even if the organization is eventually cleared of the allegations. When employers are found to have violated laws, the consequences can be even more severe.

Employment law can have a significant impact on an organization's cost structure. The establishment and maintenance of internal mechanisms, such as training and reporting systems, to ensure compliance with laws can be time consuming and costly. Violations of the law can result in significant monetary penalties and can damage an organization's name and reputation.

Several federal laws protect individuals from unfair treatment in the workplace. Congressional intent in passing these laws is to ensure that all Americans receive equal access to and treatment in employment. In other words, all Americans should enjoy equal opportunity in employment. From an organizational perspective, there are two reasons why it makes sense to be an equal opportunity employer. First, federal laws provide for a variety of penalties for organizations that violate such laws. Second it is in an organization's best interest to hire the most qualified applicant for any job or to promote the most qualified individual, regardless of factors that do not impact the individual's ability to perform the job in question.

A critical component of the strategic management of human resources (HR) involves attracting, developing, and retaining the highest quality workforce. Decisions regarding staffing, compensation, and other HR programs and policies are mitigated by laws regulating employment, as noted in Chapter 4. Employment law has a significant impact on an organization's ability to implement strategic HR management for two reasons. First, any strategic HR initiatives must be tempered and structured within the context of applicable laws that regulate the employment relationship. Second, there is a significant cost to organizations for noncompliance with these laws. Pretrial costs to defend an allegation of illegal employment discrimination can exceed $1 million. These costs are incurred regardless of whether the complaints are judged to be valid. Additional costs include the impact of litigation and publicity on the organization's reputation with customers and prospective employees as well as on the morale and productivity of current employees.

Employment-at-Will

Contrary to popular belief, most employees in the United States receive very limited protection against unfair treatment at work. The reason for this is the fact that the doctrine of "employment-at-will" is applied to the employment relationship. Originally developed as part of British common law, employment-at-will argues that the employment relationship should allow either an employer or an employee the right to terminate their relationship at any time, without giving the other party prior notice. Even in the twenty-first century, employment-at-will remains the fundamental rule on which employment and job security are based. Cursory "two-week notices" that employees often give to employers are not required by law nor does the employer need to give an employee any advance notice about the termination of employment under employment-at-will.

The only exceptions to employment-at-will are (1) conditions specified in a collective-bargaining agreement (union contract), which is discussed in Chapter 12, (2) express written contracts between an employee and employer that are not part of a collective-bargaining agreement, (3) terms of implied contracts between an employer and employees, (4) judicially determined "public policy exceptions" to employment-at-will, and (5) federal and state statutes that expressly prohibit the discrimination against individuals who are members of certain "protected classes."

Express employment contracts are often used for middle- and executive-level management positions to ensure these individuals some degree of security with their employment and income. Middle- and executive-level managers often give up positions of significant responsibility and income with other employers to assume a position with a new organization and consequently usually receive some form of written guarantee that their employment and/or income will be guaranteed for a given time period. Implied contract exceptions are the most widely recognized exceptions to pure employment-at-will. Implied contracts involve some reassurance to an employee or group of employees that their employment cannot be terminated at-will. Implied contracts are usually based on terms found in an organization's employee handbook or policy manual or through some oral promise or representation by a supervisor that employment is something other than at-will. Public policy exceptions to employment-at-will are generally judicially manufactured and usually based on state law. The doctrine of public policy exceptions to employment-at-will is based on the belief that an employer should not be allowed to terminate an employee for engaging in some activity that, while detrimental to the employer, is beneficial to public welfare. The most frequently acknowledged activity covered under this doctrine is "whistleblowing," where the employee reports the employer's actions to a law enforcement or regulatory agency, but also included in the protections of public policy are refusal to commit an illegal or unethical act, exercising legal rights (such as filing a worker's compensation or sexual harassment claim), good-faith assistance of a coworker who has filed a claim against the employer, and the performance of a legal, civic duty (such as military service or jury duty). Specific laws that regulate the employment relationship are discussed below.

Scope of Laws

Laws passed by Congress at the federal level are binding on each of the 50 United States as well as the U.S. territories. Individual states can pass their own additional, supplemental laws as long as these laws do not violate or contradict federal laws. These state laws are then binding on all cities, towns, and municipalities in that state. Individual municipalities can also pass their own laws that extend state laws, as long as the municipal laws do not contradict or violate state and, consequently, federal laws. For example, no federal law currently prohibits discrimination in employment on the basis of sexual orientation. Although such a bill has been proposed in Congress, it has not received sufficient support to be passed into law at this writing. However, 10 individual states have decided to offer this protection at the state level. California is one such state. One municipality within California, San Francisco, has decided to extend this protection under the law even further and prohibit discrimination based on gender orientation or that directed at transgendered individuals. In this example, each lower level of government has exercised the freedom to extend or supplement the laws that have been passed by higher legislative bodies.

An organization that operates in multiple states or even within multiple municipalities within a single state may find that it needs to comply with different legal requirements in different locations. This would require the employer to have separate HR programs and policies at different locations or one blanket policy that covers all locations and considers state and local laws in all locations in which it operates.

The process of selecting applicants for positions requires employers to discriminate in their selection decisions. The process of discrimination, in and of itself, is not an illegal action. To discriminate simply means "to make or note a distinction." Employers do this all the time; they discriminate, for example, regarding the number of years' prior experience and levels of education applicants have. Discrimination becomes illegal, however, when it is directed at groups that Congress has decided to protect under federal law. Groups that enjoy protection against illegal job discrimination are referred to as "protected classes."

Federal Antidiscrimination Laws

The first law passed by Congress that impacted the employment relationship was the Civil Rights Act of 1866. This law literally gave all citizens the right to enter into contracts as "white citizens." Although this terminology may sound racist, it is important to interpret this language within its historical context. The year 1865 marked the end of the Civil War and the abolition of slavery. Congress's intent in passing this law was to ensure that the former slaves enjoyed freedom in their lives and were able to obtain gainful employment on an equal basis with Caucasians. Congress, however, was a bit naive in assuming that just because it passed a law, employers would comply. No remedies for unjust treatment were provided in this law when it was passed. Not surprisingly, racial discrimination did not end upon passage of the law; however, those discriminated against had no recourse. Consequently, Congress passed the Civil Rights Act of 1871, which gave individuals the right to sue if they felt that they had been deprived of their rights under the Civil Rights Act of 1866.

Equal Pay Act

Nearly a century passed before Congress ratified another law aimed at protecting workers from discrimination in employment. In 1963, Congress passed the Equal Pay Act, which prohibits wage discrimination based on sex or gender for jobs that require equal skill, effort, and responsibility and are performed under similar working conditions. In short, it states that women cannot be paid less than men for doing the same jobs. However, more than 50 years have passed since the passage of this act, and women still make, on average, somewhere around 80–85 cents on the dollar of what men make.

One reason for this discrepancy is that Congress provided four exceptions, or exclusions, to the law. If satisfied, these conditions allow an employer to legally pay women less than men. The first exception is a bona fide seniority system. When compensation is based on seniority and men have held jobs longer than women, pay differentials are legitimate. Throughout American labor history, Congress and the courts have readily embraced the idea of seniority as a legitimate criterion in making employment-related decisions because it is an objective standard. The term "bona fide" in describing a seniority system refers to the fact that the seniority system must not be self-serving as a means of facilitating wage discrimination. It must be an existing, legitimate, and enforced system of managing various aspects of employee relations.

The second exclusion to the Equal Pay Act is differences in quality of performance. If the employer can show that men perform at higher levels than women, then the pay differential is justified. This, however, can be problematic, as most assessments of performance are highly subjective in nature. Organizations need to ensure that any merit-based pay system does not intentionally or inadvertently discriminate against women. This is discussed in greater detail in the chapter on performance management systems.

The third exception to the law is pay plans that are based on quantity of output. Traditionally called "piece-rate" systems in manufacturing organizations, compensation is based on how much an individual produces. This is somewhat analogous to commission-based sales in today's organizations or wages based on the number of transactions completed or customers serviced.

The final exception is for "factors other than sex." Although this term is often treated with cynicism, Congress realized when passing the law that it could not anticipate every possible contingency that might arise in establishing a basis of equity in pay. Therefore, it allowed this exclusion to give employers some latitude if they had some other means of compensation that resulted in gender-based pay differentials that did not take gender into account. This is one of many laws that Congress has passed that has included a provision allowing somewhat of an open option for employers to articulate a legitimate, nondiscriminatory means for treating employees as it does.

Civil Rights Act of 1964

The following year, Congress passed the Civil Rights Act of 1964, which is often regarded as being the single-most important piece of social legislation of the twentieth century. The act is broken into a number of different sections, called *titles;* Title VII pertains to employment. As a result, when referring to this particular Act, most employers, policymakers, and members of the legal and judiciary communities simply refer to it as "Title VII."

Title VII prohibits discrimination in employment based on race, color, religion, sex, and national origin. Conditions of employment included under Title VII include hiring, firing, promotion, transfer, compensation, and admission to training programs. Title VII applies to all private employers with 15 or more employees as well as state and local governments, colleges and universities, and employment agencies and labor unions.

The law also established the Equal Employment Opportunity Commission (EEOC), which was charged with overseeing Title VII. Prior to the passage of this law, employees who felt that they had been discriminated against had no means by which to pursue their complaints outside of hiring a private attorney. Because many employees could not afford the kind of costly legal counsel that their employers could, the playing field was hardly level. Consequently, Congress saw a need to establish a federal agency to enforce federal labor laws and receive employee complaints. In addition to Title VII, the EEOC is also charged with oversight of the Equal Pay Act of 1963 and all other federal labor laws subsequently discussed in this chapter.

Racial Discrimination at Coca-Cola

In late 2000, Coca-Cola made the largest settlement in history related to a race discrimination case. The organization agreed to pay $192.5 million to a group of African-American employees and former employees and also agreed to institute significant changes in its employment practices relative to the ways it manages and promotes minority employees. The lawsuit began when four employees came forward with their allegations; the case escalated into a highly publicized event as 45 current and former employees traveled from Coke's Atlanta headquarters to Washington, D.C, on a "bus ride for justice." Reverend Jesse Jackson joined the fray by calling for a consumer boycott of the company and its products.

In addition to paying the monetary settlement, Coke created a panel of outside monitors to perform independent audits of the organization's performance on diversity issues as well as to mandate changes in HR practices. The panel's recommendations are binding on the organization, unless Coke can prove in court that they are financially impossible to implement. In addition to the panel, Coke's board of directors also agreed to establish a Public Issues and Diversity Review Committee to oversee corporate equal employment opportunity programs and devise a strategy for tying executive compensation to successful EEO efforts.[2]

Sex Discrimination at Novartis ... and its aftermath

In 2010, multinational pharmaceutical manufacturer Novartis was found guilty of engaging in a pattern of discriminating against women. These behaviors included discrimination in both compensation and promotion decisions and against employees who were pregnant for which a jury awarded a group of more than 6,200 past and present female Novartis employees $250 million in damages. Ironically this decision was based on charges that took place at the same time that Novartis had been declared one of the 100 best companies for which to work by *Working Mother* magazine.[3] At the time of the verdict, Novartis expressed the intent to appeal the verdict but both parties opted to settle the case for $175 million to avoid the appeal. Amazingly each of the female plaintiffs in the case only received $16,173 while the plaintiffs' 68 attorneys each received an average of $625,000.[4]

Age Discrimination in Employment Act of 1967

The Age Discrimination in Employment Act (ADEA) of 1967 prohibits employment discrimination against employees who are aged 40 or older and prohibits the setting of mandatory retirement ages (although mandatory retirement ages are allowed in some occupations that deal with public safety). This Act was amended in 1990 by the Older Workers Protection Act, which prohibits employers from discriminating based on age when providing benefits to employees or from asking older workers to sign waivers of any future age discrimination claims when being laid off. The

EEOC—as well as the federal government—has oversight of this law, which applies to all employers covered under Title VII in addition to the federal government.

The ADEA has been frequently cited in actions against employers who conduct any kind of large scale layoffs or reductions-in-force. If a disproportionate percentage of employees being terminated are over the age of 40, an ADEA challenge is likely. Typically, large-scale layoffs attempt to reduce layers of management, often eliminating one of several layers of mid-management employees who are likely to be predominantly over the age of 40.

Age Discrimination at 3M

In 2011, Minnesota-based global technology company 3M agreed to pay $3 million to a group of former employees who had been laid off as part of a series of reductions-in-force. The EEOC found that the laid-off workers were all older and had been denied leadership training opportunities. The CEO himself had admitted in an e-mail that 3M's "vision for leadership development" was that "we should be developing 30-year-olds with general manager potential" and that 3M should "tap into youth as participants in leadership development." As a result of the EEOC investigation, 3M agreed to pay $3 million in monetary relief to 290 former employees, develop and implement a review process for terminations, and provide company-wide training on how to prevent age bias.[5]

Rehabilitation Act of 1973

The Rehabilitation Act of 1973 prohibits discrimination by organizations with federal contracts against applicants or employees who are handicapped. It should be noted that by requiring compliance only by federal contractors, the majority of private employers are not covered under this Act. The Act has a three-pronged definition of what constitutes an individual with a handicap: (1) an individual with a physical or mental impairment that substantially limits one or more major life activities; (2) an individual with a history or record of such impairment; (3) an individual regarded as having such an impairment. The act requires individuals with these conditions to be "otherwise qualified" to perform job responsibilities (in spite of their handicap) in order to receive protection against discrimination and also requires employers to provide "reasonable accommodation" to such qualified individuals with handicaps. The Supreme Court has ruled that "reasonableness" of an accommodation would be determined on a case-by-case basis relative to the specific facts of the case, including the cost of the accommodation, the resources of the employer, the nature of the job, workplace safety issues, and any relevant collective-bargaining provisions.

Pregnancy Discrimination Act of 1978

The Pregnancy Discrimination Act of 1978 prohibits employers from discriminating against pregnant employees by requiring employers to allow pregnant employees to take leave for pregnancy and childbearing, as it would for any other medical condition. In short, the law requires the employer's existing policy on disability leave to be extended to include pregnancy. This act does not require the employer to reinstate the employee in the same job upon return from leave and does not allow the employer to determine the dates of leave. It further prohibits employers from refusing to hire or promote because of pregnancy or from providing health insurance plans that do not cover pregnancy.

Americans with Disabilities Act of 1990

The Americans with Disabilities Act (ADA) of 1990 greatly extends the protection first offered under the Rehabilitation Act. The act covers all public and private employers with 15 or more employees and utilizes much of the same language as the Rehabilitation Act. The ADA's definition of disability is adapted from the Rehabilitation Act, and the ADA retains the Rehabilitation Act provisions for being "otherwise qualified" and providing "reasonable accommodation."

The extension of the coverage of the Rehabilitation Act under the ADA to so many additional Americans with disabilities has resulted in a flood of litigation. The courts have found many of the provisions of the ADA to be quite ambiguous and open to interpretation. For example, there is some concern as to whether certain medical conditions really are impairments and whether they limit any major life activity. This is particularly problematic when a condition can be controlled by medication or some prosthetic device. Courts have issued ambiguous rulings in this regard related to a number of medical conditions, including diabetes, epilepsy, asthma, HIV, hypertension, and lymphoma. They have also disagreed as to whether any major life activities other than earning a living are relevant to consider in employment discrimination cases.

The courts have ruled that "otherwise qualified" and "reasonable accommodation" need to be determined on a case-by-case basis. Some courts have been sympathetic to those with disabilities by granting great latitude to employees or applicants stating a claim; others have been very strict in their interpretations of the provisions of the ADA in ruling for employers. Similarly, some courts have granted wide latitude as to what constitutes a disability. In certain instances, aspects of physical appearance, including weight and poor dental health, have been considered disabilities under the third prong of the definition in the statute. Although the ADA has provided more than 43 million Americans with disabilities wide protection against discrimination in employment and in other areas of their lives, the statute as it stands is very vague, flexible, and open to the interpretation and whim of the courts. One recent study concluded that despite more than 20 years of ADA protection strong perceptions still exist in both workplaces and society concerning both mental and physical disabilities, which prohibit the goals of the ADA from being realized.[6]

Employees with Disabilities at IBM

Since 1995, Armonk, New York–based IBM has sponsored an employee disabilities taskforce. One of eight diversity task forces within IBM, this group was asked first to address four issues. The first is what IBM could do to make employees with disabilities feel welcome and valued. The second was what IBM could do to maximize disabled employees' productivity. The third was what IBM could do to maximize business opportunities with consumers with disabilities. The fourth was an inquiry as to what community organizations employees would like to see IBM participate in. The task force was designed with a dual purpose: to assist in the recruiting and retention of employees with disabilities and to capitalize on new market opportunities. As part of its initiatives, IBM has created a partnership with the American Association for the Advancement of Science, which recruits and screens undergraduate students with disabilities to receive training in math- and science-related disciplines for positions at IBM. It has also allowed IBM to develop a number of products that make workplace and home technology more accessible to individuals with disabilities.[7]

In response to some controversial Supreme Court rulings under the ADA, Congress amended the ADA through passage of the ADA Amendments Act of 2008 (ADAAA). The terms of the ADAAA went into effect January 1, 2009, and greatly expand the protection offered for individuals with disabilities as well as expand coverage to individuals whose protection was not provided or ambiguous under the original ADA. The ADAAA has five major provisions that expand on the ADA. First, the ADAAA specifies that an impairment must be evaluated without the consideration of mitigating measures, such as medication, hearing aids, or other devices. This provision was in direct response to a Supreme Court decision that found that mitigating measures should be considered in assessing whether an impairment limited a major life activity. Second, the ADAAA specifies that impairments that are episodic or in remission are to be considered disabilities. Hence, individuals who have had cancer, mental illness, diabetes, epilepsy, or any other condition that is not currently "active" are covered. Third, the ADAAA expressly identifies major life activities to include "eating, sleeping, walking, standing, lifting, bending, reading, concentrating, thinking and communicating" as well as all bodily functions. Fourth, the ADAAA lowers the standard in determining whether an individual is "regarded" as having a disability by not requiring that the perceived condition limit any major life activity. Finally, the ADAAA directs the EEOC to reinterpret its equation of the ADA terms "substantially limits" to "significantly restricts." Congress found this language too limiting and asked the EEOC for a broader interpretation of "substantially limits."

Remaining intact under the ADAAA is the requirement that an employee be able to perform the essential duties of her/his job, which are to be determined by the employer. The ADAAA also left unchanged the requirement that an individual not pose a safety threat to themselves or others in order to receive protection under the statute. The employee is also required to cooperate with employers as part of an interactive process that attempts to determine any reasonable accommodation that can be provided by the employer. The net effect of the ADAAA is the shifting of the main issue in ADA litigation from whether an employee is covered under the ADA to whether the employer engaged in an interactive process with the employee who attempted to find a reasonable accommodation. The express expanded coverage of what constitutes a "disability" under the ADA will leave little subjectivity as to whether an individual employee is protected under the ADA.

Since the passage of the ADAAA, there has been a marked increase in telework as a reasonable accommodation for employees with disabilities.[8] This is largely attributable to the fact that the ADAAA expressly provides protection to individuals to a much broader segment of the workforce, particularly those who have short-term or episodic impairments who might be unable, for example, to drive to work yet still remain able to perform their job responsibilities. As an increasing number of employers see the benefits of telework, as discussed in Chapter 6, telework will probably continue to be utilized increasingly as an accommodation for employees with disabilities.

Civil Rights Act of 1991

Congress extended the rights of individuals protected under Title VII when it passed the Civil Rights Act (CRA) of 1991. This law has four specific provisions that amend the coverage of Title VII: (1) it extends the protection of Title VII to federal government employees; (2) it allows litigants to sue for compensatory and punitive damages, in addition to back pay, benefits, and attorney's costs; (3) it requires a heavier "burden of proof" on the part of employers in rebutting claims of unlawful discrimination; and (4) it provides for "extraterritorial enforcement" of federal labor laws, protecting U.S. employees on overseas assignments unless compliance would violate laws of the foreign country where the employee is on assignment. The additional protection and benefits offered to employees under the CRA of 1991 have resulted in a dramatic increase in Title VII filing with the EEOC.

Family and Medical Leave Act of 1992

The Family and Medical Leave Act (FMLA) of 1992 requires employers to provide up to 12 weeks unpaid leave for the birth, adoption, or serious illness of a child, family member, or the employee during any 12-month period. It only covers organizations with 50 or more employees. In order to receive protection, an employee has to have been employed a minimum of 25 hours per week for one year, or 1,250 hours in total. Employees whose salaries are among the highest 10 percent of the employer's workforce do not receive FMLA protection.

The employer is required to continue the employee's group health insurance during the leave, and the employee must be allowed to return to the same job or an equivalent position upon returning to work. The employer may require that the employee utilize any accrued vacation or sick time as part of the leave. It is important to remember that this law sets a minimum federal standard for compliance. Any organization is obviously free to provide more generous options, such as longer leave, paid leave, or other accommodations, such as working at home when the leave time period has been completed.

Interestingly enough, when President Clinton signed the Family and Medical Leave Act into law, its passage was hailed as a major victory for families and parents. It had taken a number of years and several congressional revisions of the Act before it was finally passed. Although an earlier version had been passed by Congress, it had been vetoed by President George H. W. Bush. However, despite its family-friendly provisions, the FMLA provides far less extensive coverage than comparable laws of other industrialized countries. European countries, for example, tend to be far more generous in both the length of the leave that they provide as well as the compensation and benefits offered to employees. Sweden offers up to one full year parental leave for either parent, with the first 38 weeks at 90 percent salary, with guaranteed job security. Italy provides mothers with up to 40 weeks, with 100 percent salary for the first 22 weeks, with guaranteed job security. Finland provides either parent 35 weeks of leave at 100 percent salary, with guaranteed job security. It is worth noting, however, that citizens of these countries are taxed at a significantly higher rate than those in the United States. However, these European countries share a philosophy that children are a "national resource" to be properly nurtured and developed and that the future of the nation depends on proper childrearing. The United States, on the other hand, considers children to be the "personal property" of parents, with responsibility for childrearing resting with the parents rather than the state, unless the state can find abusive treatment of the child.

However, a recent report, The Future of Children, which was prepared by Princeton University and the Brookings Institution, found that workplace policies such as paid parental leave and paid leave to care for sick children exist in many countries that remain economically competitive in the global marketplace. Of the 17 countries studied, the United States was the only one which did not provide some form of paid leave for new mothers and all but the United States and Switzerland provide paid leave for new fathers. Australia, for example, guarantees 18 weeks of paid leave at the federal minimum wage rate for primary caregivers who earn less than $150,000 per year. All of the countries in the study provide a minimum of 14 paid weeks of leave for new mothers with much of the cost for the leave coming from a social insurance system.

The study found that guaranteed paid parental leave for new parents as well as for those with a sick child would be nothing to jeopardize the United States economic position. With more than half of working Americans not covered under the FMLA, the United States lags woefully behind all other developed countries in considering support for working families.[9]

While the terms of the FMLA are relatively straightforward, implementation of the provisions of the statute are quite challenging because of the fact that most individual states have their own leave laws, many of which provide more generous coverage than the FMLA. The FMLA expressly states that its terms do not supersede any terms of comparable state or local laws that pertain to employee leave. Consequently, if a state provides more generous leave than the FMLA, the state statute requirements must be met as long as they are not in violation of any terms of the FMLA.

The most common areas of disparity between state leave laws and the FMLA are those involving coverage; namely, which employers are covered, which employees are protected, and what specific types of leave are covered. Usually, state law provides more generous coverage than the FMLA in one or more of these areas. For example, some states, such as Hawaii, Massachusetts, and Oregon, provide leave for employees after 6 months rather than 12 months, while others, such as Connecticut, New Jersey, Wisconsin, and the District of Columbia, provide leave after only 1,000 hours rather than 1,250 hours. Eight states and the District of Columbia provide leave for the care of a parent-in-law or domestic partner, which is not included in the FMLA. Many state statutes also cover smaller employers, with Kansas, Minnesota, Montana, and the District of

Columbia covering employers with as few as one employee, Iowa covering those with at least four employees, Maine and Vermont covering those with 15 or more employees, and Louisiana and Oregon covering those with 25 or more employees. Connecticut and the District of Columbia each provides up to 16 weeks leave over a 24-month period.

Complicating this mosaic even further, it is not uncommon for an employer to have to provide separate consecutive leaves to an employee, first providing FMLA leave and then upon the end of the FMLA leave, giving additional leave under state law for a condition that is not covered under the FMLA. Leave may run concurrently when the applicable terms and conditions of the FMLA and relevant state statute are identical; however, this is frequently not the case. As an example, the New Jersey Family Leave Act (NJFLA) does not provide leave for an employee's own medical condition. Hence, an employee in New Jersey in a given year could take 12 weeks leave for her/his own medical condition under the FMLA and another 12 weeks under the NJFLA for any other reason provided in the NJFLA, including one that might also be covered under the FMLA. Even without considering state law, it is possible for an employee to be granted 24 consecutive weeks of leave under the FMLA, depending on how the employer determines the 12-month period. Such a process is calling "stacking." As an example, if an employer uses a simple calendar year approach in the determination of the 12-month period, it is possible for an employee to take leave for the last 12 weeks of one calendar year and the first 12 weeks of the subsequent calendar year. The FMLA allows employers to determine how the 12-month period is calculated, including (1) calendar year; (2) any other "fixed" year (such as an employee's date of hire); (3) a "forward" year (in which leave is calculated from the first day an employee takes leave); or (4) a "backward" year (in which leave is calculated backward from each date the employee uses leave). While the first two methods are easiest, they also allow for the potential of employees to "stack" leave and have a single leave extend past 12 weeks. Some states have weighed in on this issue and require that the leave period be calculated in a specified manner. Rhode Island requires the use of a calendar year, while California requires a forward-year calculation. Needless to say, FMLA compliance is greatly complicated given the variance, scope, and inconsistencies between individual state laws related to leave.

Genetic Information Nondiscrimination Act of 2008

The Genetic Information Nondiscrimination Act (GINA) of 2008 prohibits the use of genetic information in decisions related to health insurance and employment. Genetic discrimination takes place when an individual is treated unfairly because of the makeup of his or her DNA might increase the likelihood of contracting a certain disease. A health insurer might refuse to give coverage or charge a higher premium to a woman whose DNA might indicate a heightened risk for breast cancer. Employers are prohibited from considering any genetic information they may have about a job applicant or employee in decisions related to hiring, termination, discipline, promotion, compensation, or other terms and conditions of employment.

The challenge for employers in attempting to comply with GINA is that an employer might inadvertently discover information about an employee or applicant that could be the basis for a discrimination claim. While few, if any, employers collect genetic information or data as part of the screening and employment process, there is a more covert side of GINA, which would apply to almost any employer. Inquiring about the health status of a blood relative of an employee could trigger a GINA charge, regardless of motive. If an employee's father, for example, was diagnosed with prostate cancer, inquiring about the father's health or treatment and/or whether the employee himself had been tested could trigger a GINA claim, even if the inquiry was a means of showing concern or support for the employee and his or her family. Genetic information, as defined by GINA, includes information about an employee or family member's medical tests and any family medical history, and it is illegal to use this information for employment purposes. Hence, managers and supervisors need to proceed with caution in inquiring about employee or immediate family member illnesses and medical conditions.

Enforcement of Federal Laws Under the EEOC

As previously mentioned, Title VII created the EEOC to oversee and enforce federal labor laws. Any individual who feel that their rights under Title VII have been violated may file a complaint with the EEOC in an attempt to remedy the situation. During its 2011 fiscal year, the EEOC received an all-time record number of complaints, 99,947.[10] The procedures that are followed in an EEOC investigation are outlined in Exhibit 7.1.

The first requirement is that the charge be filed within 180 days of the alleged discriminatory act. The charge can be filed with the federal EEOC office or a state or local agency responsible for overseeing claims of employment discrimination. If charges are initially filed with a state or local agency and the complainant is dissatisfied with the outcome, the individual may refile the charge with the EEOC within 30 days of the initial decision.

The EEOC will then investigate the complaint to determine if there is reasonable cause to believe that discrimination has occurred. If no cause is found, the complaint will be dismissed, although the complainant still retains the right to hire a private attorney. If cause is found, the EEOC will notify the employer of the charge and attempt to mediate the dispute with the employer on behalf of the complainant. The EEOC will first meet with the complainant to determine what would constitute a satisfactory settlement and then attempt to have the employer sign a conciliation agreement. If the employer refuses, the EEOC may file suit on behalf of the complainant or issue the complainant a "right to sue" letter.

In proving illegal discrimination, the burden of proof first falls with the employee or applicant to establish a prima facie case. *Prima facie* means "on the surface" or "at first look," and prima facie status is established by showing either disparate treatment or disparate impact. It should be noted that disparate treatment/impact is sometimes referred to as *adverse treatment/impact.*

Disparate or adverse treatment happens when an employee is treated differently from others based on some dimension of protected-class status, such as age, race, sex, religion, national origin, or disability. Disparate or adverse impact is a bit more subtle. Here, the same standards and treatment are applied to all workers, but the outcomes or consequences of this treatment are different for different groups. For example, a requirement that all employees be a certain height might result in adverse impact for an applicant who uses a wheelchair. Similarly, an employment test in which individuals from one ethnic or religious background consistently score higher than individuals from other backgrounds would establish adverse impact. Disparate impact is usually illustrated statistically by using the four-fifths rule. Under this, if the selection rate for a protected group is less than 80 percent of the selection rate for a majority group, then adverse impact is established. For example, if an employment test resulted in 20 out of 100 males being qualified, then at least 16 out of 100 (16 being four-fifths of 20) females should be assessed similarly to refute the fact that the test results in disparate impact.

Once the complainant has established disparate treatment or impact, the burden of proof then shifts to the employer to provide a legally justifiable, nondiscriminatory reason for the action. There are essentially four ways in which an employer can rebut a prima facie case.

The first is through showing job-relatedness. To do this, the employer illustrates that the criteria utilized to select applicants is essential for performance of the job. Proving job-relatedness is not easy; employers usually have to perform validation studies of tests or other criteria used to screen applicants or provide performance data of past employees to support their contentions.

The second means is by claiming a bona fide occupational qualification (BFOQ) defense. This defense requires the employer to explain why it is essential for the employee to be a member of a certain group. This defense has been utilized most frequently in gender and religious discrimination cases. It would be legitimate, for example, to deny a woman a job as a men's locker room attendant. Customer preferences for a certain "type" of individual do not support the BFOQ defense. When an airline refused to hire male flight attendants, claiming that being female was a BFOQ because of "customer preferences," they were found in violation of Title VII.

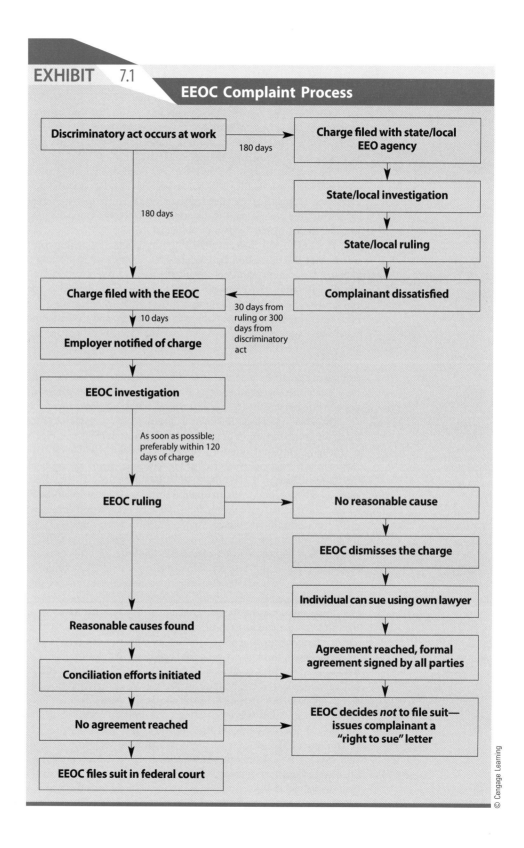

EXHIBIT 7.1

EEOC Complaint Process

The third defense is a bona fide seniority system. As previously discussed, courts support the use of seniority in employment decisions because of the objectivity of seniority. As long as the system is bona fide, meaning it was not set up to discriminate or perpetuate discrimination, seniority systems are a justifiable defense. When the city of Memphis used seniority as the criterion to lay off firefighters, African-American firefighters who had been hired under an affirmative action program were disproportionately affected. Because the department had traditionally used seniority in making other personnel decisions, the criterion was upheld, even though it had significant adverse impact on a protected class.

The final defense is "business necessity." This defense requires the employer to show that the criteria used are essential to the safe and efficient operation of the enterprise. However, the courts have rejected business necessity claims that were based on profitability or other economic concerns of the business owners. Instead, this condition applies more to factors related to the safety of employees and customers. For example, a postal worker who was of short stature sued the U.S. Postal Service when it refused to provide him with a reasonable accommodation in the form of a stepstool so he could reach mail slots that were beyond the reach of his arms. The postal service successfully argued that having an employee constantly climbing up and down a stepstool would be unsafe for the employee and coworkers around him.

Although the EEOC has broad oversight of federal antidiscrimination laws, it does not serve as a judiciary authority and has limited power over employers. It is empowered by Congress to perform only a conciliatory role between employers and those who file discrimination charges and relies on the federal court system to enforce charges it brings against employers. Currently, the EEOC has a backlog of tens of thousands of cases because it is being called upon to play a different role than that envisioned by Congress when it passed Title VII. This backlog is severely undermining Congress's intentions to have discrimination-free workplaces. Under a new chair, the EEOC has recently taken a very aggressive stance in attempting to reduce the backlog of cases on its docket. Over 95,000 private sector charges were filed in 2008 and the average time to process these complaints declined to 171 days, despite the increased caseload.[11] To assist with the resolution of claims, the EEOC Web site now has a special page that assists employers with investigations. Much of the EEOC's success can be attributed to its strategic plan, which provided much-needed direction to agency activities and initiatives. This plan is presented in Exhibit 7.2.

Perhaps the EEOC initiative that has had the most impact on resolving discrimination charges against employers has been its voluntary mediation program. While the program has been in existence since the early 1990s, it really had not had a tremendous impact until the new chair decided to emphasize its use. Mediation involves the employee and employer attempting to resolve their differences outside of a courtroom through the assistance of an EEOC mediator. The process is designed to be fair, impartial, and unbiased and has met with resounding success.

EXHIBIT 7.2

Strategic Plan of the Equal Employment Opportunity Commission

- Prevent discrimination through education and partnerships with other like-minded organizations.
- Efficiently track and resolve charges of discrimination, evaluate data, and report trends to employers.
- Develop efficient working relationships between attorneys and investigators for more strategic enforcement and litigation.
- Expand the mediation program and increase use of external mediators.
- Become a model workplace and an example for the private sector to follow.

© Cengage Learning

Ninety-six percent of employers and 91 percent of employees who engaged in EEOC-assisted mediation reported that they would do so again. However, when offered mediation services by the EEOC, only 30 percent of employers agreed to mediation, as opposed to 83 percent of employees.[12] Despite the fact that the EEOC uses what it calls "facilitative mediation," many employers initially view EEOC-assisted mediation with some skepticism because the EEOC was established to ensure compliance with federal laws as well as to assist employees with their claims. Employers may also reject mediation when they are certain that the claims against them will eventually be judged unfounded after an investigation. Also, by refusing mediation, employers may force the employee to go to court, becoming involved in an often lengthy, expensive resolution process that the employee may not be able to afford either financially or emotionally. To an extent, when an employer refuses mediation, it "dares" the employee to continue the process. This dare, however, is not without risk: Litigation is time consuming and expensive for the employer as well as the employee. It also can be disruptive to the employer's workplace during the investigatory process and may result in hard feelings toward the employer among other employees, who may sympathize with the charging employee. Essentially, the decision by an employer to accept or reject EEOC-assisted mediation may come down to a simple cost–benefit analysis. However, even though many of those costs and benefits can be estimated, their certainty of incurrence is unknown.

Executive Orders

In addition to federal laws that regulate the employment relationship, certain employers are required to comply with executive orders. Executive orders are issued by the president and apply to all federal agencies and organizations with federal contracts. Executive Orders 11246 and 11375, taken together, prohibit those organizations from discriminating against the same protected classes that Title VII does. Compliance with executive orders is overseen by the Office of Federal Contracts Compliance Programs (OFCCP), an agency of the U.S. Department of Labor, which performs similar investigatory functions as the EEOC. However, unlike the EEOC, the OFCCP actively monitors compliance with laws and executive orders instead of waiting for employees or job applicants to file complaints. The OFCCP also has enforcement power, unlike the EEOC, allowing it to levy fines and punishments, including revocation of the federal government contracts.

Affirmative Action

Executive orders also require organizations with 100 or more employees *and* $50,000 or more in federal contracts to develop, implement, and maintain a program of affirmative action. The concept of affirmative action addresses the fact that there has been significant past discrimination in employment and other aspects of life in the United States and attempts to remedy these injustices. Affirmative action requires organizations to make special efforts to ensure that their workforce is representative of the society where the business operates. Affirmative action rests on the assumption that we still have not progressed to the point, as a society, where we can treat all individuals equally and that the only way to rectify past injustices is to provide individuals from protected classes special consideration and treatment in employment opportunities.

Although the doctrine of equal employment opportunity (EEO) requires that organizations provide a discrimination-free workplace, it does not imply that organizations should attempt to go back and correct past injustices. EEO rests on the assumption that any initiative to show preference to any member of a protected class would be, in and of themselves, illegal and just turn the tables by unfairly discriminating against the majority. Therefore, the only way to ensure a discrimination-free society and workplace is to wipe the slate clean. History cannot be rewritten, and past injustices cannot be corrected by discriminatory treatment in the present. In short, EEO argues that "two wrongs do not make things right."

Affirmative action plans, however, are usually meant to be temporary measures that require organizations to take corrective action to address "underutilization" of certain protected classes. Preferential treatment, in this regard, is a means of allowing the organization to ensure that its workplace is well represented by various protected classes. Nonetheless, critics of affirmative action have called for dismantling affirmative action programs because of the problems of reverse discrimination that they create. Proponents of affirmative action argue that such programs are necessary because our society is not yet blind to personal characteristics that have nothing to do with the ability to perform a given job. Reading 7.1, "In Defense of Preference," illustrates that affirmative action is problematic in both concept and practice but argues that society without affirmative action is worse off than with it.

Affirmative action plans are filed with the Department of Labor and monitored by the OFCCP. They consist of four separate sections. The first section is a utilization analysis in which the employer identifies its employees by gender, race, ethnicity, religion, physical ability, and any other protected class. This is merely a counting and summation and is often performed for various levels of employment in the organizational hierarchy rather than being aggregated to ensure that representation of protected classes is not limited to low-level positions. The second portion is an availability analysis that examines the availability for employment of all protected classes in the immediate recruiting vicinity. The third portion is an identification of problem areas in which the employer notes over- and underutilization of certain groups in the employee mix. The final section is a narrative statement of a corrective action in which the organization details plans with timetables to rectify the discrepancies between utilization and availability.

Those who support and those who oppose affirmative action do agree on one thing: Our society has unfairly and unlawfully discriminated against a variety of protected classes for a long period of time. Where they disagree is the means of correcting such injustices. Those who argue that EEO laws are sufficient without affirmative action feel that affirmative action does nothing more than perpetuate the discrimination that federal law tries to prohibit by merely shifting the target of unfair treatment from the minorities to the majorities. This group argues that our society *can* treat all individuals equally. Proponents of affirmative action argue that discrimination is still rampant in our society, and the only way to remedy this is to force organizations to employ and promote individuals from all protected classes through government regulation because the organizations themselves are not capable of doing this on their own. Even proponents of affirmative action realize that it can be problematic: Individuals in protected classes often argue that they are never really sure whether they receive jobs or promotions because of their protected-class status or their own individual abilities, qualifications, and accomplishments.

Affirmative action does not require organizations to hire individuals who are not qualified to hold positions for which they apply. If the organization has a clear job description and qualifications that it can prove are specifically job related—and can show that it has made a sincere effort to recruit individuals from underutilized populations—it may continue to show discrepancies between utilization and availability.

Sexual Harassment

In 1986, the Supreme Court ruled in *Meritor Savings Bank v. Vinson* that sexual harassment constituted a form of sex discrimination under Title VII. To date, the majority of sexual harassment cases have involved situations where a man sexually harasses a woman who holds a lower or equal position. In 1998, the high court further ruled in *Oncale v. Sundowner Offshore Services, Inc.,* that same-sex harassment was also actionable under Title VII. Every year, organizations pay workers millions of dollars in claims involving allegations of sexual harassment. In addition to the direct monetary costs of sexual harassment, there can also be significant costs in terms of negative public relations and damaged employee morale. Managing sexual harassment becomes even more complicated in light of the fact that sexual attraction and even interoffice romances between consenting adults do happen in the workplace. As a result, sexual harassment compliance remains one of the more challenging aspects of legal compliance for employers.

What Sexual Harassment Is

Courts have identified several key concepts that influence whether behavior constitutes sexual harassment. The first is that the advances are of an "unwelcome" nature. It is imperative in sexual harassment cases that the individual who is the target of the harassment make clear that the behavior is considered offensive and inappropriate. Two individuals may be privy to the same behavior; although one may find the behavior offensive, the other may find it perfectly acceptable. Sexual harassment, being subjective in nature, places the initial burden on the complainant to communicate the "unwelcome-ness" to the alleged harasser.

The second key concept is the nature of the harassment. The courts have identified two kinds of harassment: quid pro quo and hostile environment. Quid pro quo, which translated from the Latin means "this for that," happens when certain benefits are promised to an individual in return for sexual favors or threats of punishment are made if sexual favors are withheld. Hostile environment constitutes the majority of sexual harassment claims and is much more subtle than quid pro quo. Hostile environment happens when an employee is subjected to an offensive working environment. However, the subjective nature of what constitutes an offensive or hostile working environment can make it difficult for employers to identify whether sexual harassment is taking place.

One potential complicating factor in addressing hostile environment claims is whether at any time a consensual sexual relationship existed between the parties to the harassment charge. While many employers have attempted to defend sexual harassment charges by providing evidence that the complainant had consensually agreed to the relationship, hence removing the "unwelcome" factor, any time a supervisor or manager becomes involved in a relationship with a subordinate the relationship needs to be framed within the power dynamics that exist between supervisor and subordinate. The complaining employee could argue that (s)he felt coerced into the relationship given the status of the other individual in the organization. Indeed a rejected paramour could easily file a sexual harassment charge as a means of vindication. In addition, it is important to realize that sexual harassment is not just limited to male/female relationships and that intimacy need not be the goal of the harasser.[13]

In an attempt to alleviate the uncertainty of defining a working environment as "offensive," the courts have utilized the standard of "reasonable woman." Realizing that in some cases that employee claims of harassment may be unwarranted, the courts have attempted to apply a neutral standard to determine whether the working environment is indeed offensive. This involves an assessment of how a reasonable woman (or reasonable person, if the complainant were male) would be expected to react to such working conditions.

Another key consideration in sexual harassment claims concerns whether a pattern of behavior was displayed. Isolated incidents of alleged harassment usually carry less weight with the courts than continued harassment of an individual or ongoing harassment of a number of individuals perpetrated by a single individual. The courts will also attempt to determine whether the organization took any action if and when it was made aware of earlier allegations of harassment in determining ultimate liability for the conduct and the full extent of such liability.

A final concern is that many incidents of harassment involve the words of one employee against those of another and can be difficult to prove. Allegations need to be provable and verifiable. Such evidence is often provided through witnesses and/or written or printed documentation that supports the allegations of harassment.

Cleaning Up Sexual Harassment at Dial

Sexual harassment can be very costly to an organization. In 2003, Dial Corporation agreed to pay $10 million in settlement of a federal lawsuit brought when women at its Aurora, Illinois, plant argued that the employer had ignored their sexual harassment complaints. The suit charged that 90 current and former female employees had been groped, shown pornography, and called names on the job. This settlement was eclipsed by one involving Mitsubishi Motors in 1998. Facing allegations that women working on an assembly line were groped and insulted and their complaints then met with indifference, Mitsubishi settled this case, which involved 486 plaintiffs, for $34 million?[14]

Problems in Managing Sexual Harassment

In managing sexual harassment, organizations have to deal with four specific problems. The first is that many workers and managers are not aware of what sexual harassment is and what constitutes harassment. Several key management challenges need to be addressed in remedying this: Employees have different perceptions and standards of what is offensive; sexual harassment can be difficult to identify; and the intention of the harassing party is irrelevant relative to how the receiving party interpreted the behavior or action.

These challenges can be dealt with effectively through training that centers on discussion rather than merely knowledge or skills. Awareness of and attitudes toward sexual behavior at work need to be addressed among both men and women. Perceptions need to be shared and clarified, and employees, particularly managers, need to be aware of different ways of understanding or framing action and behaviors that may be sexual in nature.

The second problem is that although an organization may have a policy that prohibits sexual harassment, many employees may be unaware of the policy or know that there is a policy but not know what it says. A challenge that management faces in addressing this problem is that although every allegation of sexual harassment is unique, any established policy needs consistency in application but flexibility in enforcement to suit the specific circumstances and their severity. This issue can be dealt with through training that focuses on procedures, policies, and processes. Employees need to understand exactly the organization's position on sexual harassment and how it will be enforced. This type of training is probably most effective when conducted in conjunction with training that deals with attitudes and awareness.

The third problem in managing sexual harassment is that employees often fear reporting any incidents of sexual harassment. For the average employee, reporting sexual harassment means challenging the power base of the organization and often confronting a direct supervisor. Employees need to know that their claims will be taken seriously. Although Title VII expressly prohibits retaliation against any employee who files a claim under the law, it is not difficult for a supervisor or an organization to "dance around the law" and make an employee's life miserable without running afoul of the law. Employees often feel that challenging the organization is a losing proposition in which the individual employee is pitted against a large, powerful, resource-abundant organization. This also has significant implications for those who investigate any such charges within the organization. This individual or these individuals need to be objective. If employees distrust the process or investigator, they are more likely to allow acts of harassment to continue. To encourage reporting of sexually offensive behavior, it is important to create a climate of trust within the organization. Employees need to be assured of some confidentiality and provided with some support in continuing in their jobs during the course of the investigation into the allegations. Investigations also need to be conducted by an impartial, preferably neutral, outside source to prevent bias.

The fourth problem is determining how best to investigate allegations of sexual harassment. The challenges to doing this effectively involve the fact that there are two sides to every story, and there are neither witnesses nor evidence to support the claims levied by one or both parties. To facilitate the investigation, those looking into claims of sexual harassment should seek out all others who may have knowledge about the effects of the harassment, particularly on the complainant, or of other incidents that might support or disclaim the allegations of harassment. Complaints should also be investigated immediately. This might help in curtailing any ongoing harassment or offensive behavior, and it is also generally looked upon favorably by the courts. In investigating claims of sexual harassment, if the charges cannot be proven, it can be useful to notify the accused party in writing that if the conduct did occur, it would constitute sexual harassment and be in violation of company policy. A notification using neutral language serves notice to the employee without accusing the employee of wrongdoing and setting up a potential defamation claim. Exhibit 7.3 summarizes how to overcome some of the problems inherent in addressing sexual harassment in organizations.

EXHIBIT 7.3

Problems and Challenges in Managing Sexual Harassment

Problems	Challenges	Strategies

• Workers/managers still not sure what it is	• Perceptions
	• Difficult to identify
	• Intention irrelevant, interpretation important
		• Training
		  • Centering on discussion between men and women
		  • Not skills; awareness and attitudes

• Workers unaware of policy or know there's a policy but not what it says	• Need consistency in application (to ensure fair and legal treatment of employees) but flexibility in enforcement (to suit special circumstances)	• Training • Centering on policy, processes, etc.
• Fear of reporting	• Retaliation • Biases of investigators	• Create climate of trust • Investigation by impartial, outside source • Confidentiality • Support those filing allegations
• How to investigate	• Two sides to every story • Often no outside witnesses	• Seek out others for any knowledge about effects, other incidents • Investigate immediately while issue is still "fresh"; also looks good with courts • If no resolution, notify accused in writing that if conduct did occur, it would constitute sexual harassment

© Cengage Learning

Sexual Harassment at W.R. Grace & Co.

On June 1, 2000, the U.S. EEOC announced that a subsidiary of W.R. Grace & Co. and a company that subsequently operated one of its facilities had agreed to pay $1 million to the victims of widespread sexual harassment at one of its food-processing plants in Laurel, Maryland. The class-action lawsuit had been filed by the EEOC on behalf of 22 Hispanic females, all recent immigrants from Central America who spoke limited English, who had been routinely subjected to unwanted groping and explicit requests for sexual favors from male managers and coworkers over a period of several years.

The harassment directed at the workers took many forms. One woman was locked in a freezer by her supervisor upon turning down his request for a sexual favor. Two other women, who were pregnant at the time, were asked to perform sexual favors and subsequently demoted and fired following their refusal to comply with the requests. Many of the other women had their job duties reassigned to especially menial or difficult tasks when refusing requests for sexual favors from plant management.

EEOC Chairwoman Ida L Castro noted that the EEOC would "remain vigilant to ensure that no worker endures this type of discrimination in order to earn a paycheck and support their family."[15]

Strategy for Managing Sexual Harassment

Exhibit 7.4 presents some general guidelines organizations can use to strategically manage sexual harassment in the workplace and minimize both legal liability and other adverse consequences of sexual harassment. First, the organization should investigate *all* allegations of harassment. Lack of knowledge or ignorance concerning the harassment would not be an acceptable defense in court. Second, a thorough and prompt investigation of all charges should be conducted. Determining potential liability is critical, as is dealing with the charges and curtailing any harassment in a timely manner. Third, the investigator that is appointed needs to be unbiased and objective. This is critical in avoiding company politics and preventing conflicts of interest. An improperly or poorly conducted investigation will not only be a waste of time and resources but may further damage employee trust and morale. Fourth, steps should be taken to ensure that no retaliation takes place against the complainant. As stated, such action is prohibited under Title VII, regardless of whether the allegations of harassment are ultimately proven. Even if no harassment has taken place, a Title VII violation may be found in how the complainant was subsequently treated. Unfounded claims do not remove the retaliation protection offered by Title VII. Fifth, the accused employee must be treated fairly. There are two sides to every story, and the story of the accused should be heard in a nonjudgmental manner. Many unfairly accused employees have turned around and successfully sued their employers for wrongful discharge. Sixth, both parties should sign written statements that outline facts and completely disclose all pertinent information and clarify where they stand. This assists the investigator and prevents the parties from subsequently changing their stories. Seventh, in cases where harassment is found, employers need to take prompt action to rectify the situation and equate the consequences with the behavior. Any and all appropriate measures should be taken to ensure that the behavior never happens again. Finally, the organization needs to develop a clear, well-defined investigative process. This process should be applied consistently across cases and involve extensive written documentation of every step of the investigation. Information collected should be held in confidence due to its sensitive nature.

EXHIBIT 7.4   Guidelines for Managing Sexual Harassment in the Workplace

- Investigate *all* allegations (lack of knowledge, ignorance not a defense)
- Conduct a thorough and prompt investigation (determining actual liability often easier at this point)
- Ensure that investigator is unbiased, objective (avoid company politics, conflicts of interest)
- Ensure that no retaliation takes place (could result in additional Title VII liability)
- Treat accused employee fairly (hear his or her side, avoid wrongful discharge)
- Have both parties sign written statements (prevents "facts" in stories from changing)
- Take prompt action and equate consequences with behavior (goal is to ensure that behavior never happens again)
- Have clear, defined process for investigation (apply consistently, document everything)

© Cengage Learning

Sexual Harassment at Tyson Foods

Tyson Foods is the world's second-largest producer of processed meat products. In 2010, it was found in violation of Title VII of the Civil Rights Act due to the harassing behavior to which an employee was subjected. At the time of hire, Amanda West, a new female employee in one of Tyson's processing plants in Kentucky, was informed that company policy required any employee who suffered harassment to his or her direct supervisor and any employee aware of harassment was required to report such harassment to management. The policy further stated that all claims would be investigated within two weeks.

During her third week of work, West informed her supervisor and her trainer about harassing behavior to which she was being subjected. The supervisor told her that she should not take offense and that she was "hot." The supervisor requested that West not contact the HR department and offered to move her to a different production line. Two weeks later the harassment had not subsided and after West was followed to her car one night, she resigned. During her exit interview, she informed HR about what she had experienced, including the disclosure to her supervisor. The HR manager promised to investigate but did not. West filed a complaint with the EEOC and filed suit against Tyson. The court awarded West a $1.2 million judgment, despite her having been employed for only 5 weeks by Tyson, which was upheld on appeal by Tyson. In reaching its verdict, the court found that West had followed company policy and that her supervisor justified and perpetuated the harassment.[16]

The lesson to be learned from the Tyson case is that it is not enough to simply have a sexual harassment policy. Employees need to be trained regarding what constitutes harassment and any claims related to harassment charges need to be investigated thoroughly and in an expeditious manner.

Complications Abroad

The increasing rate at which U.S. organizations set up operations abroad has some significant implications for how sexual harassment is handled. Although the Civil Rights Act of 1991 provides for extraterritorial enforcement of U.S. labor laws, many cultures do not acknowledge sexual harassment as a workplace or societal problem. Ethical dilemmas arise concerning how such behavior should be tolerated when it is not considered inappropriate in another culture.

In managing sexual harassment in the workplace, employers *always* have a chance to rectify wrongdoings if they have a policy in place. Although courts place a responsibility on complainants to inform harassers that advances or behaviors are "unwelcome," this does not relieve the employer of the burden of establishing, communicating, and implementing a clear policy on sexual harassment. Sexual harassment can and will happen in virtually any workplace. Clear measures can be taken to strategically manage this form of unlawful discrimination, ensuring that all employees have a workplace more conducive to high performance.

Trends in Employment Litigation

As can be seen from the previous discussion, the legal dimensions of the employment relationship are complex and require careful management. Within this arena, there are a number of trends taking place in employment-related litigation that are evolving and impacting the employment relationship. First among these is the trend away from blatant to subtle discrimination. As our society and workplaces have become more tolerant and accepting of individual differences, at least on the surface, and employers have been subjected to significant penalties for violating anti-discrimination statutes, the nature of discrimination has changed. The EEOC has noted that during the twentieth century discrimination tended to be very blatant and pervasive. Today, however, it often takes more subtle forms, which can be just as unnerving to employees yet much more difficult to prove. Rather than taking the form or hate speech or physical violence, for example, discrimination today might involve shunning, non-inclusion, or marginalization of employees, sometimes referred to as micro-inequities. Such behaviors might involve negative and/or extreme facial expressions or tones of voice, leaving individuals off of distribution of team or group e-mails or other correspondence, not including an individual in meetings, mistaking an executive of color for a support or cleaning staff member, repeatedly mistaking individuals from a common ethnic or racial background for each other, repeatedly mispronouncing a coworker's name after having been corrected several times, mocking or copying accents or interrupting continuously when a minority group member is speaking, or continuously asking questions of such an individual in an attempt to discredit her or him.[17]

A second trend in employment litigation is the use of electronically produced and stored evidence. Most employees find e-mail the most simple, direct, and expeditious means of communicating with coworkers, customers, and supervisors, particularly in cases where individuals are located at different sites. E-mail is also advantageous for employees in that it can be conveniently archived and referenced as need be. However, there is also a potential problem with e-mail, as its informal nature often invites employees to make spontaneous, emotional comments to each other that once "sent" can usually not be rescinded. Such communications can later be used against the organization as evidence in legal proceedings. This same caveat is true for instant messaging that may be utilized at work. Employers need to establish formal policies regarding the content of electronic conversations and communication and train managers, in particular, to keep such communication fact based, with more sensitive information communicated in person or by telephone. Employers have a legal obligation under amendments to the Federal Rules of Civil Procedure to preserve all electronically stored information relevant to current or reasonably foreseeable future litigation. Hence, employers need to set policy relative to how long electronic information not subject to litigation holds should be backed up and stored, balancing the potential benefits of retaining data for legal and operational benefits versus the potential costs of storage and loss associated with not retaining it.

A third trend is the increasing number of complaints by employees and former employees regarding employer retaliation for employee assertion of their employment rights. Title VII of the Civil Rights Act prohibits retaliation against employees or coworkers who have aided in the filing of Title VII or other claims. Despite this, the number of retaliation claims filed with the EEOC increased by 35 percent over the past decade and in 2011 retaliation charges became the most common complaint filed with the EEOC, surpassing racial discrimination complaints and accounting for more than 36 percent of the complaints filed.[18] A recent Supreme Court ruling, *Burlington Northern & Santa Fe Railway Co. v. White,* made it easier for workers to file retaliation claims by allowing suits even when an employment action does not diminish pay or benefits or cause any kind of economic or monetary loss for the employee as well as ruling that antiretaliation behavior extends to nonwork-related employer conduct. In early 2011, the Supreme Court took retaliation one step further when it ruled unanimously in *Thompson v. N. Am. Stainless LP* that close family members of employees who had filed charges against their employer could file their own allegations of retaliation.

One particularly challenging feature of the Title VII antiretaliation provision is the fact that HR managers are exempt from its protection. This has created some complex ethical dilemmas for HR professionals, as the antiretaliatory provision creates dual, conflicting loyalties for HR managers relative to whether or not he or she is representing the employee or employer. If the HR manager is not perceived to be as an advocate of the employee, the employee may be prompted to seek redress outside the organization. This is clearly not in the employer's best interest. However, the higher an individual's rank in an organization the greater the expectation on the part of the employer for loyalty. Hence, an HR manager who is not protected from retaliation will feel the pressure to comply with the employer's wishes, even when the HR manager has determined that the employer might be liable for unlawful discrimination. Even the Code of Ethics of the Society of Human Resource Managers (SHRM) has somewhat conflicting statements relative to the role of the HR professional in providing employee support and organizational loyalty.[19]

This can be further complicated when an HR manager her or himself is subject to discrimination and/or retaliation. Given that HR managers typically have access to highly confidential employment records as well as generally assist in investigating and resolving charges brought by employees, their job responsibilities provide them with access which could be tremendously damaging to an employer should the HR manager take legal action against the employer. The full "duty of confidentiality" of HR managers in this regard has not been fully tested in the courts at this point in time.

A fourth trend in employment litigation is the movement toward employer settlement of charges in an expeditious manner. Litigation has many economic and noneconomic costs for both employers and employees, and while the EEOC has advocated the use of its mediation program, such a process can still be time consuming. From the perspective of the employers, unless the organization is successful in having charges dismissed by a judge via summary judgment, settlement is often the best option for a speedy resolution. The questions surrounding settlement, however, are when and at what cost. One study found that in cases of gender, age, disability, or religious discrimination, employers generally initially denied claims but settled out-of-court within one year. In cases involving race, most employers sought quick settlement and promised to adopt policies to prevent future claims of race discrimination by employees. Sexual harassment claims usually involved denied charges, retaliation, and a refusal to settle.[20] Quicker settlements generally incur lower costs. One study found that cases that settled in two years cost employers double that of those that settled in one year, and cases that settled in three years cost two-and-a-half times those that settled in one year—in both attorney fees and settlement amounts.[21] Employers, however, often resist early settlements because of (1) a sense that the organization did nothing wrong and that justice should prevent a dishonest employee from benefitting, (2) a need for vindication of the individuals involved, and (3) a fear of "opening the floodgates" for all kinds of frivolous employee litigation if the employer gains a reputation of settling quickly and easily and not defending charges. Hence, employers need to consider these balancing act factors in deciding if and when to settle an employment discrimination claim.

A fifth trend is the use of employment practices liability insurance (EPLI) by employers to prevent having to pay large settlements in discrimination cases. EPLI is becoming increasingly popular, as large settlements are offered and judgments are rendered against employers. EPLI assumes some of the risk incurred by an employer's illegal or questionable employment practices. With employment law becoming an increasingly complicated dimension of the employment relationship, it is more likely that managers and supervisors unversed in the changing aspects of the law may commit violations. Premiums for EPLI are dependent on the size of the employer and the frequency of past serious claims. Much like various kinds of consumer insurance, EPLI assesses an employer based on risk. Insurers who offer EPLI look favorably on employers who provide ongoing training for managers and supervisors and have strong policies against sexual harassment—and all kinds of discrimination—as well as procedures that call for a quick, thorough, and impartial investigation of complaints.

A final trend in employment litigation is the use of various kinds of language rules in the workplace. Because national origin discrimination is expressly prohibited in Title VII of the Civil Rights Act of 1964, employers who adopt "speak-English-only" rules in their workplaces may be putting themselves at risk of Title VII violations. This is also true of English language proficiency for job applicants and employers. This challenge is heightened by the fact that by the year 2050, 19 percent of Americans will be immigrants. By that time, Hispanics are expected to grow to 29 percent of the U.S. population from the current 14 percent proportion. More so, certain populous border states, such as California, Texas, and Florida, have much higher percentages of immigrants and non-English-speaking residents. In 2009, Hispanics constituted 62 percent of the population in Miami-Dade County. In 2007, the EEOC received 9,396 complaints of national origin discrimination, many of which involved language restrictions and policies. The EEOC has adopted a blanket rule that English-language only rules will automatically constitute national origin discrimination unless the employer can argue for its policy. This rule has been rejected by some courts but embraced by others. A key factor in determining whether such policies are justified is business necessity. English-at-all-times rules have been found burdensome to employees but acceptable, for example, when communicating with customers, coworkers, or supervisors who only speak English, in emergency situations to promote safety, and for cooperative and teamwork assignments. Clearly, this is an area of employment law and litigation that will evolve as different courts interpret the EEOC's position and our workplaces and society become more diverse.

Conclusion

Although employment law is a key strategic area for HR, it remains the single area in which managers throughout organizations are most uninformed and ill-prepared to manage. The laws regulating employment relationships are numerous, complex, and ambiguous. Although no manager can be expected to be a legal expert, the move toward decentralized operations and the establishment of autonomous subsidiaries and work groups requires line managers to increasingly have full responsibility for HR issues. However, of all the traditional HR functions, employment law is probably the most difficult to manage effectively. Not only are there myriad laws and technical details as to how the laws have been interpreted by the courts, but there is also ambiguity in most of the newer laws (and also many of the older laws) that requires informed strategic decision making by managers at all levels in an organization.

Laws that regulate the employment relationship attempt, in part, to neutralize the power disparity between employers and employees, particularly in light of the prevalence of the employment-at-will doctrine in employee handbooks and court decisions. Employment laws set minimum standards for compliance relative to the fair and just treatment of employees. Organizational justice has been found to be a key factor that impacts employee motivation, performance, and commitment. However, justice goes far beyond simple legal compliance and extends to a variety of organizational activities and policies. Reading 7.2, "The Management of Organizational Justice," introduces the types and components of organizational justice and explains how concepts of fair and just treatment extend beyond employment laws to the design, implementation, and maintenance of a variety of HR systems, which are discussed in Part II of this book.

Critical Thinking

1. What is a protected class, and what laws exist that safeguard the rights of each protected class?

2. Explain the process under which an EEOC complaint is processed. To what extent is it more advantageous for an employee to file an EEOC complaint at the local or federal level?

3. How can an employer lawfully respond to an allegation of employment discrimination?

4. Why does illegal discrimination persist nearly 40 years after the passage of Title VII?

5. What constitutes sexual harassment? What rights and responsibilities does an alleged recipient of sexual harassment have?

6. To what extent do cultural norms influence how other societies and cultures deal with the issue of sexual harassment in the workplace?

7. What are the pros and cons of mediation for an employer? What factors might influence whether an employer agrees to the mediation of an employee charge? What can be done to make mediation more attractive to employers?

Reading 7.1

8. Why is affirmative action such a controversial issue? Is society better served with or without affirmative action? In small groups, take a position either in favor of or against affirmative action and then debate the issue within your group.

Reading 7.2

9. Explain the different components of organizational justice and the outcomes of perceived organizational justice and injustice.

Exercises

1. In small groups, investigate any laws that prohibit employment discrimination in the European Union, Australia, Japan, or China. Note similarities and differences from American laws. What values or assumptions do the laws of these countries make about the employment relationship?

2. You are an HR manager for a medium-sized financial services institution. You overhear an employee, Pat, tell a coworker, Chris, that a third employee, Jamie, told Pat about being the recipient of harassing behavior from Chris. How would you handle this situation? Role-play this with several classmates, and have the remainder of the class critique the approach used.

3. Evaluate California law A.B. 2222. Does it go too far in protecting the rights of employees with disabilities? Break into two groups, with one arguing the need for the provision of the law and the other arguing against the law.

4. Visit the EEOC Web site at http://www.eeoc.gov. Identify current trends in complaints being filed with the EEOC and the processes by which claims are being resolved. Review the EEOC press releases posted on the site. What appear to be the agency's current priorities, and how appropriate do you feel these priorities are for the U.S. society?

Chapter References

1. Gurchiek, K. "Lockheed Martin Settlement Sends 'Powerful Message,'" *Society for Human Resource Management,* article 024101, published at www.shrm.org/hrnews_/published/articles/ CMS_024101.asp, January 4, 2008.

2. Schafer, S. "Coke to Pay $193 Million in Bias Suit," *Washington Post,* November 17, 2000, p. A1.

3. Reuters. Novartis Fined $250 Million in Sex Discrimination Suit, May 19, 2010, *NY Times.* Available at http://www.nytimes.com/2010/05/20/business/20drug.html

4. Edwards, J. "In Novartis Sex Discrimination Case, Lawyers Get $40M But Women Get Just $16K," November 22, 2010, *CBS News.* Available at http://www.cbsnews.com/8301-505123_162-42846523/in-novartis-sex-discrimination-case-lawyers-get-40m-but-women-get-just-16k/

5. Equal Employment Opportunity Commission Press Release, August 22, 2011. Available at http://www.eeoc.gov/eeoc/newsroom/release/8-22-11a.cfm

6. Hastings, R. R. "Has the Americans With Disabilities Act Made a Difference?" July 9, 2010. Available at http://www.shrm.org/hrdisciplines/Diversity/Articles/Pages/HastheADAMadeaDifference.aspx

7. Wells, S. "Is the ADA Working?" *HR Magazine,* April 2001, 46, (4), pp. 38–46.

8. Marks, J. "Telework as ADA Accommodation on the Rise," November 17, 2011. Available at http://www.shrm.org/hrdisciplines/technology/Articles/Pages/TeleworkADA.aspx

9. Maurer, R. "Report: Paid Leave Policies Support Workplace Flex in Competitive Economies," October 28, 2011. Available at http://www.shrm.org/hrdisciplines/global/Articles/Pages/PaidLeaveWorldwide.aspx

10. Equal Employment Opportunity Commission Press Release, November 15, 2011. Available at http://www.eeoc.gov/eeoc/newsroom/release/11-15-11a.cfm

11. Equal Employment Opportunity Commission. Fiscal Year 2008 Performance and Accountability Report. (2009).

12. Barrier, M. "The Mediation Disconnect," *HR Magazine,* May 2003, 48, (5), pp. 54–58.

13. Deschenaux, J. "Nontraditional Workplace Harassment Lawsuits Increasing," May 28, 2011. Available at http://www.shrm.org/LegalIssues/FederalResources/Pages/NontraditionalHarassment.aspx

14. "Dial to Pay $10 Million to Settle Sexual Harassment Case," *Baltimore Sun,* April 30, 2003, p. 9C.

15. EEOC Press Release, "EEOC Obtains $1 Million for Low-Wage Workers Who Were Sexually Harassed at Food Processing Plant," June 1, 2000. Available at http://www.eeoc.gov

16. Schaecher, S. M. "Five-Week Employee Wins $1.2 Million in Harassment Claim," *HR Magazine*, July, 2010, 55, (7), p. 66.

17. Hastings, R. "Little Slights Can Erode Employee Engagement," *Society for Human Resource Management*, article 023952, published at www.shrm.org/hrnews_/published/articles/CMS_023952.asp, December, 2007.

18. Smith, A. "Retaliation Becomes Most Common Charge," *HR Magazine*, March 2011, 56, (3), p. 16.

19. Mello, J. A. "The Dual Loyalty Dilemma for HR Managers Under Title VII Compliance," *Society for the Advancement of Management Advanced Management Journal*, 2000, 65, (1), pp. 10–15, 51.

20. James, E. and Wooten, L. "Diversity Crises: How Firms Management Discrimination Lawsuits," *Academy of Management Journal*, December 2006, 49, (3), pp. 1103–1118.

21. Parauda, J. and Janove, J. "Settle for Less," *HR Magazine*, November 2004, 49, (11), pp. 135–139.

READING 7.1

In Defense of Preference

Nathan Glazer

Affirmative action is bad. Banning it is worse.

The battle over affirmative action today is a contest between a clear principle on the one hand and a clear reality on the other. The principle is that ability, qualifications, and merit, independent of race, national origin, or sex should prevail when one applies for a job or promotion, or for entry into selective institutions of higher education, or when one bids for contracts. The reality is that strict adherence to this principle would result in few African Americans getting jobs, admissions, and contracts. What makes the debate so confused is that the facts that make a compelling case for affirmative action are often obscured by the defenders of affirmative action themselves. They have resisted acknowledging how serious that gaps are between African Americans and others, how deep the preferences reach, how systematic they have become. Considerably more than a mild bent in the direction of diversity now exists, but it exists because painful facts make it necessary if blacks are to participate in more than token numbers in some key institutions of our society. The opponents of affirmative action can also be faulted: they have not fully confronted the consequences that must follow from the implementation of the principle that measured ability, qualification, merit, applied without regard to color, should be our only guide.

I argued for that principle in a 1975 book titled, provocatively, *Affirmative Discrimination*. It seemed obvious that that was what all of us, black and white, were aiming to achieve through the revolutionary civil rights legislation of the 1960s. That book dealt with affirmative action in employment, and with two other kinds of governmentally or judicially imposed "affirmative action," the equalization of the racial proportions in public schools and the integration of residential neighborhoods. I continued to argue and write regularly against governmentally required affirmative action, that is, racial preference, for the next two decades or more; it was against the spirit of the Constitution, the clear language of the civil rights acts, and the interests of all of us in the United States in achieving an integrated and just society.

It is not the unpopularity of this position in the world in which I live, liberal academia, that has led me to change my mind but, rather, developments that were unforeseen and unexpected in the wake of the successful civil rights movement.

What was unforeseen and unexpected was that the gap between the educational performance of blacks and whites would persist and, in some respects, deepen despite the civil rights revolution and hugely expanded social and educational programs, that inner-city schools would continue to decline, and that the black family would unravel to a remarkable degree, contributing to social conditions for large numbers of black children far worse than those in the 1960s. In the presence of those conditions, an insistence on color-blindness means the effective exclusion today of African Americans from positions of influence, wealth, and power. It is not a prospect that any of us can contemplate with equanimity. We have to rethink affirmative action.

In a sense, it is a surprise that a fierce national debate over affirmative action has not only persisted but intensified during the Clinton years. After twelve years under two Republican presidents, Ronald Reagan and George Bush, who said they opposed affirmative action but did nothing to scale it back, the programs seemed secure. After all, affirmative action rests primarily on a presidential executive order dating back to the presidencies of Lyndon Johnson and Richard Nixon which requires "affirmative action" in employment practices from federal contractors—who include almost every large employer, university, and hospital. The legal basis for most of affirmative action could thus have been swept away, as so many noted at the time, with a "stroke of the pen" by the president. Yet two presidents who claimed to oppose affirmative action never wielded the pen.

Despite the popular majority that grumbles against affirmative action, there was (and is) no major elite constituency strongly opposed to it: neither business nor organized labor, religious leaders nor university presidents, local officials nor serious presidential candidates are to be found in opposition. Big business used to fear that affirmative action would undermine the principle of employment and promotion on the basis of qualifications. It has since become a supporter. Along with mayors and other local officials (and of course the civil rights movement), it played a key role in stopping the Reagan administration from moving against affirmative action. Most city administrations have also made their peace with affirmative action.

Two developments outside the arena of presidential politics galvanized both opponents and defenders of affirmative action. The Supreme Court changed glacially after successive

Republican appointments—each of which, however, had been vetted by a Democratic Senate—and a number of circuit courts began to chip away at the edifice of affirmative action. But playing the largest role was the politically unsophisticated effort of two California professors to place on the California ballot a proposition that would insert in the California Constitution the simple and clear words, taken from the Civil Rights Act of 1964, which ban discrimination on the basis of race, national origin, or sex. The decision to launch a state constitutional proposition. Proposition 209, suddenly gave opponents the political instrument they needed to tap the majority sentiment that has always existed against preferences.

While supporters of affirmative action do not have public opinion on their side, they do have the still-powerful civil rights movement, the major elites in education, religion, philanthropy, government, and the mass media. And their position is bolstered by a key fact: how far behind African Americans are when judged by the tests and measures that have become the common coin of American meritocracy.

The reality of this enormous gap is clearest where the tests in use are the most objective, the most reliable, and the best validated, as in the case of the various tests used for admission to selective institutions of higher education, for entry into elite occupations such as law and medicine, or for civil service jobs. These tests have been developed over many years specifically for the purpose of eliminating biases in admissions and appointments. As defenders of affirmative action often point out, paper-and-pencil tests of information, reading comprehension, vocabulary, reasoning, and the like are not perfect indicators of individual ability. But they are the best measures we have for success in college and professional schools, which, after all, require just the skills the tests measure. And the test can clearly differentiate the literate teacher from the illiterate one or the policeman who can make out a coherent arrest report from one who cannot.

To concentrate on the most hotly contested area of affirmative action—admission to selective institutions of higher education—and on the group in the center of the storm—African Americans: If the Scholastic Assessment Test were used for selection in a color-blind fashion, African Americans, who today make up about six percent of the student bodies in selective colleges and universities, would drop to less than two percent, according to a 1994 study by the editor of the *Journal of Blacks in Higher Education.*

Why is this so? According to studies summarized in Stephan and Abigail Thernstrom's book, *America in Black and White,* the average combined SAT score for entering freshmen in the nation's top 25 institutions is about 1300. White applicants generally need to score a minimum of 600 on the verbal portion of the test—a score obtained by eight percent of the test-takers in 1995—and at least 650 on the mathematics section—a score obtained by seven percent of the test-takers in 1995. In contrast, only 1.7 percent of

black students scored over 600 on the verbal section in 1995, and only two percent scored over 650 on the math. This represents considerable progress over the last 15 years, but black students still lag distressingly far behind their white counterparts.

There is no way of getting around this reality. Perhaps the tests are irrelevant to success in college? That cannot be sustained. They have been improved and revised over decades and predict achievement in college better than any alternative. Some of the revisions have been carried out in a near-desperate effort to exclude items which would discriminate against blacks. Some institutions have decided they will not use the tests, not because they are invalid per se, but because they pose a barrier to the increased admission of black students. Nor would emphasizing other admissions criteria, such as high school grades, make a radical difference. In any case, there is considerable value to a uniform national standard, given the enormous difference among high schools.

Do qualifications at the time of admission matter? Isn't the important thing what the institutions manage to do with those they admit? If they graduate, are they not qualified? Yes, but many do not graduate. Two or three times as many African American students as white students drop out before graduation. And the tests for admission to graduate schools show the same radical disparities between blacks and others. Are there not also preferences for athletes, children of alumni, students gifted in some particular respect? Yes, but except for athletes, the disparities in academic aptitude that result from such preferences are not nearly as substantial as those which must be elided in order to reach target figures for black students. Can we not substitute for the tests other factors—such as the poverty and other hardships students have overcome to reach the point of applying to college? This might keep up the number of African Americans, but not by much, if the studies are to be believed. A good number of white and Asian applicants would also benefit from such "class-based" affirmative action.

(I have focused on the effect of affirmative action—and its possible abolition—on African Americans. But, of course, there are other beneficiaries. Through bureaucratic mindlessness, Asian Americans and Hispanics were also given affirmative action. But Asian Americans scarcely need it. Major groups—not all—of Hispanic Americans trial behind whites but mostly for reasons we understand: problems with the English language and the effect on immigrant children of the poor educational and economic status of their parents. We expect these to improve in time as they always have with immigrants to the United States. And, when it comes to women, there is simply no issue today when it comes to qualifying in equal numbers for selective institutions of higher and professional education.)

How, then, should we respond to this undeniable reality? The opponents of affirmative action say, "Let standards prevail whatever the result." So what if black students are reduced to two percent of our selective and elite student bodies? Those who gain entry will know that they are properly qualified for entry, that they have been selected without discrimination, and their classmates will know it too. The result will actually be improved race relations and a continuance of the improvements we have seen in black performance in recent decades. Fifteen years from now, perhaps three or four percent of students in the top schools will be black. Until then, blacks can go to less competitive institutions of higher education, perhaps gaining greater advantage from their education in so doing. And, meanwhile, let us improve elementary and high school education—as we have been trying to do for the last 15 years.

Yet we cannot be quite so cavalier about the impact on public opinion—black and white—of a radical reduction in the number of black students at the Harvards, the Berkeleys, and the Amhersts. These institutions have become, for better or worse, the gateways to prominence, privilege, wealth, and power in American society. To admit blacks under affirmative action no doubt undermines the American meritocracy, but to exclude blacks from them by abolishing affirmative action would undermine the legitimacy of American democracy.

My argument is rooted in history. African Americans— and the struggle for their full and fair inclusion in U.S. society—have been a part of American history from the beginning. Our Constitution took special—but grossly unfair—account of their status, our greatest war was fought over their status, and our most important constitutional amendments were adopted because of the need to right past wrongs done to them. And, amid the civil rights revolution of the 1960s, affirmative action was instituted to compensate for the damage done to black achievement and life chances by almost 400 years of slavery, followed by state-sanctioned discrimination and massive prejudice.

Yet, today, a vast gulf of difference persists between the educational and occupational status of blacks and whites, a gulf that encompasses statistical measures of wealth, residential segregation, and social relationships with other Americans. Thirty years ago, with the passage of the great civil rights laws, one could have reasonably expected—as I did—that all would be set right by now. But today, even after taking account of substantial progress and change, it is borne upon us how continuous, rooted, and substantial the differences between African Americans and other Americans remain.

The judgment of the elites who support affirmative action—the college presidents and trustees, the religious leaders, the corporate executives—and the judgment even of many of those who oppose it but hesitate to act against it— the Republican leaders in Congress, for example—is that the banning of preference would be bad for the country. I agree. Not that everyone's motives are entirely admirable; many conservative congressmen, for example, are simply afraid of being portrayed as racists even if their opposition to affirmative action is based on a sincere desire to support meritocratic

principle. The college presidents who support affirmative action, under the fashionable mantra of diversity, also undoubtedly fear the student demonstrations that would occur if they were to speak out against preferences.

But there are also good-faith motives in this stand, and there is something behind the argument for diversity. What kind of institutions of higher education would we have if blacks suddenly dropped from six or seven percent of enrollment to one or two percent? The presence of blacks, in classes in social studies and the humanities, immediately introduces another tone, another range of questions (often to the discomfort of black students who do not want this representation burden placed upon them). The tone may be one of embarrassment and hesitation and self-censorship among whites (students and faculty). But must we not all learn how to face these questions together with our fellow citizens? *We* should not be able to escape from this embarrassment by the reduction of black students to minuscule numbers.

The weakness in the "diversity" defense is that college presidents are not much worried about the diversity that white working-class kids, or students of Italian or Slavic background, have to offer. Still there is a reputable reason for that apparent discrepancy. It is that the varied ethnic and racial groups in the United States do not, to the same extent as African Americans, pose a test of the fairness of American institutions. These other groups have not been subjected to the same degree of persecution or exclusion. Their status is not, as the social status of African Americans is, the most enduring reproach to the egalitarian ideals of American society. And these other groups have made progress historically, and make progress today, at a rate that incorporates them into American society quickly compared to blacks.

This is the principal flaw in the critique of affirmative action. The critics are defending a vitally important principle, indeed, the one that should be the governing principle of institutions of higher education: academic competence as the sole test for distinguishing among applicants and students. This principle, which was fought for so energetically during the 1940s and 1950s through laws banning discrimination in admission on the basis of race, national origin, or religion, should not be put aside lightly. But, at present, it would mean the near exclusion from our best educational institutions of a group that makes up twelve percent of the population. In time, I am convinced, this preference will not be needed. Our laws and customs and our primary and secondary educational systems will fully incorporate black Americans into American society, as other disadvantaged groups have been incorporated. The positive trends of recent decades will continue. But we are still, though less than in the past, "two nations," and one of the nations cannot be excluded so throughly from institutions that confer access to the positions of greatest prestige and power.

On what basis can *we* justify violating the principle that measured criteria of merit should govern admission to selective institutions of higher education today? It is of some significance to begin with that we in the United States have always been looser in this respect than more examination-bound systems of higher education in, say, Western Europe: we have always left room for a large degree of freedom for institutions of higher education, public as well as private, to admit students based on nonacademic criteria. But I believe the main reasons we have to continue racial preferences for blacks are, first, because this country has a special obligation to blacks that has not been fully discharged, and second, because strict application of the principle of qualification would send a message of despair to many blacks, a message that the nation is indifferent to their difficulties and problems.

Many, including leading black advocates of eliminating preferences, say no: the message would be, "Work harder and you can do it." Well, now that affirmative action is becoming a thing of the past in the public colleges and universities of California and Texas, we will have a chance to find out. Yet I wonder whether the message of affirmative action to black students today really ever has been, "Don't work hard; it doesn't matter for you because you're black; you will make it into college anyway." Colleges are indeed looking for black students, but they are also looking for some minimal degree of academic effort and accomplishment, and it is a rare ambitious African American student seeking college entry who relaxes because he believes his grades won't matter *at all.*

One of the chief arguments against racial preference in college and professional school admissions is that more blacks will drop out, the quality of blacks who complete the courses of instruction will be inferior, and they will make poorer lawyers, doctors, or businessmen. Dropping out is common in American higher education and does not necessarily mean that one's attendance was a total loss. Still, the average lower degree of academic performance has, and will continue to have, effects even for the successful: fewer graduating black doctors will go into research; more will go into practice and administration. More blacks in business corporations will be in personnel. Fewer graduating black lawyers will go into corporate law firms; more will work for government.

And more will become judges, because of another and less disputed form of affirmative action, politics. Few protest at the high number of black magistrates in cities with large black populations—we do not appoint judges by examination. Nor do we find it odd or objectionable that Democratic presidents will appoint more black lawyers as judges, or that even a Republican president will be sure to appoint one black Supreme Court justice. What is at work here is the principle of participation. It is a more legitimate principle in politics and government than it is for admission to selective institutions of higher education. But these are also gateways to power, and the principle of participation cannot be flatly ruled out for them.

Whatever the case one may make in general for affirmative action, many difficult issues remain: What kind, to what extent, how long, imposed by whom, by what decision-making

process? It is important to bear in mind that affirmative action in higher education admissions is, for the most part, a policy that has been chosen (albeit sometimes under political pressure) by the institutions themselves. There are racial goals and targets for employment and promotion for all government contractors, including colleges and universities, set by government fiat, but targets on student admissions are not imposed by government, except for a few traditionally black or white institutions in the South.

Let us preserve this institutional autonomy. Just as I would resist governmentally imposed requirements that these institutions meet quotas of black admissions, so would I also oppose a judicial or legislative *ban* on the use of race in making decisions on admission. Ballot measures like Proposition 209 are more understandable given the abuses so common in systems of racial preference. But it is revealing that so many other states appear to have had second thoughts and that the California vote is therefore not likely to be repeated. (A recent report in *The Chronicle of Higher Education* was headlined "LEGISLATURES SHOW LITTLE ENTHUSIASM FOR MEASURES TO END RACIAL PREFERENCES"; in this respect, the states are not unlike Congress.)

We should retain the freedom of institutions of higher and professional education to make these determinations for themselves. As we know, they would almost all make room for a larger percentage of black students than would otherwise qualify. This is what these institutions do today. They defend what they do with the argument that diversity is a good thing. I think what they really mean is that a large segment of the American population, significant not only demographically but historically and politically and morally, cannot be so thoroughly excluded. I agree with them.

I have discussed affirmative action only in the context of academic admissions policy. Other areas raise other questions, other problems. And, even in this one area of college and university admissions, affirmative action is not a simple and clear and uncomplicated solution. It can be implemented wisely or foolishly, and it is often done foolishly, as when college presidents make promises to protesting students that they cannot fulfill, or when institutions reach too far below their minimal standards with deleterious results for the academic success of the students they admit, for their grading practices, and for the legitimacy of the degrees they offer. No matter how affirmative action in admissions is dealt with, other issues remain or will emerge. More black students, for example, mean demands for more black faculty and administrators and for more black-oriented courses. Preference is no final answer (just as the elimination of preference is no final answer). It is rather what is necessary to respond to the reality that, for some years to come, yes, we are still two nations, and both nations must participate in the society to some reasonable degree.

Fortunately, those two nations, by and large, want to become more united. The United States is not Canada or

Bosnia, Lebanon or Malaysia. But, for the foreseeable future, the strict use of certain generally reasonable tests as a benchmark criterion for admissions would mean the de facto exclusion of one of the two nations from a key institutional system of the society, higher education. Higher education's governing principle is qualification—merit. Should it make room for another and quite different principle, equal participation? The latter should never become dominant. Racial proportional representation would be a disaster. But basically the answer is yes—the principle of equal participation can and should be given some role. This decision has costs. But the alternative is too grim to contemplate.

Testing Texas

The University of Texas Law School is ground zero of the post–affirmative action world. In a 1996 case, *Hopwood v. Texas,* the Fifth Circuit Court of Appeals struck down the law school's affirmative action policy. To ensure that each entering class of 500 or so included about 75 black and Hispanic students, the law school had been operating, in effect, a "dual" admissions system under which minority and nonminority students were being admitted by separate criteria—a method that the Supreme Court had struck down in the 1978 Bakke case. This fall, at the beginning of the first semester since *Hopwood,* 26 Mexican-American students, and four blacks, enrolled in Texas's first-year class—only a few more than the law school had had during the late '60s. Back then, the lack of minority representation hadn't been a big issue at the law school. Now, it is seen as a political and marketing disaster. Qualified minority students, whom schools fight over like star quarterbacks, are proving reluctant to apply to Texas. And so are the kind of progressively minded, out-of-state white students who help make the law school a national, rather than local, institution. "There have been times at recruitment events when majority and minority students approach the table together and say 'What does the entering class look like?'" Shelli Soto, the law school's assistant dean of admissions, told me.

Since *Hopwood the* law school has labored mightily to thread the eye of a legal needle—to admit large numbers of minority students without applying explicitly racial or ethnic criteria. The law school's application now includes an optional "Statement on Economic, Social or Personal Disadvantage"—an effort to tease more minority applicants out of the pool. "'Qualified' really means a combination of your accomplishments and your experiences," Soto explains. But this effort to side-step such statistical criteria as LSAT results doesn't really work. Black students do not have more extracurricular activities than whites and do not have better grade-point averages relative to their LSAT scores. And, because so few black students from truly disadvantaged backgrounds do well enough academically to qualify even under affirmative action criteria, "class-based" affirmative action doesn't help either. It seems the only way to admit large numbers of blacks is to admit them *because* they are black.

When I posed this problem to William Cunningham, the chancellor of the U.T. system, he said that the University of Texas Medical School had already adjusted its admissions criteria. "They want to look at people's motivation," the chancellor said, "the human traits that have to do with their wanting to be doctors." Was this being done in the hope that it would have a "race-positive effect"? I asked. Cunningham paused for a long, careful moment. "I don't want to say 'race-positive,'" he said. It wasn't clear what he *could* say without violating *Hopwood.* "We want to have a diverse student body," he said, "and we want to look at broader criteria than we have in the past to insure that we have a diverse student body." I told Cunningham that some law school faculty members were concerned about diluting admissions standards. The chancellor said very carefully, "I do think this is a time for us to be thoughtful and flexible." Was it possible to be "flexible" without either violating the terms of *Hopwood* or lowering standards? "It is," Cunningham signed, "a difficult problem."

U.T.'s administrators are also looking over their shoulders at the Texas state legislature. A quarter of a century ago, it was virtually all white; now it has significant, and growing, black and Hispanic representation. As Russell Weintraub, a professor of contracts at the law school who was uneasy about affirmative action, says: "If the majority of people in this state are going to be Mexican-American and African American, and they are going to assume many of the leadership roles in the state, then it's going to be big trouble if the law school doesn't admit many minority students—it's going to be a bomb ready to explode."

Indeed, a few small bombs have detonated already. Soon after the *Hopwood* decision the state legislature passed a law that would require the University of Texas undergraduate college to accept the top ten percent of graduates from every high school in the state. This law, which would increase minority enrollment by automatically admitting the best students from heavily minority high schools, effectively reinstated a rule the college had abandoned three years ago in order to strengthen its standards.

The legislature then passed another law that requires public universities to apply the minimum grade-point average demanded of entering students to everyone—including athletes admitted on scholarship. The law, whose interpretation is now a matter of debate, would destroy the Texas Longhorn football team. Its sponsor, Ron Wilson, is a black State Assemblyman from Houston who attended both U.T. and U.T. Law. Wilson freely admits that the bill was designed to punish the university, which he saw as complicit in the Hopwood ruling. "If you're just a regular African American student with a two-point-five grade-point average, you can't get into the University of Texas," he told me. "But, if you can play the court jester out there on the football field and earn the university a million dollars, you can get it. As far as I'm concerned, that's hypocrisy. My bill says you can't have it both ways."

Wilson's real goal, of course, is not to exclude the athletes but to force the university to take everyone else. One solution, Wilson said, was "open admission." I asked if that wouldn't lead to a lowering of standards. Wilson said: "I don't look at academic standards as the Bible for academic excellence. There hasn't been enough input into those standards from African Americans and Hispanics to make them relevant to their community." And he added one more threat: if the university couldn't counteract the effect of *Hopwood*, he said, "We're going to move the money to follow the students to historically black colleges, if necessary."

The revenge of the legislature implies that the costs of doing away with affirmative action may turn out to be higher than the costs of keeping it. One of the most intriguing documents of the post-affirmative action era is an amicus brief which three professors at U.T. Law submitted to the Supreme Court in an affirmative action case last year. The three made the usual case in favor of affirmative action—but added a more novel, purely pragmatic argument: "A large public institution that serves the whole state cannot maintain its legitimacy if it is perceived to exclude minority students." The authors described the two bills that had passed the Texas legislature and noted that the University of California system is considering waiving its SAT requirement. If *Hopwood* becomes law for the country as a whole, the authors declared apocalyptically, "there will eventually be no great public universities—not for the nation and not for the white plaintiffs either."

In other words, affirmative action represents not a threat to academic standards but the surest means of preserving them. This argument sounds so perverse that it's hard to take seriously, but it's not without foundation. Douglas Laycock, one of the authors of the brief, said: "We're in the middle of a full-blown attack on every means we have to measure merit and on the very idea of merit, and it's mostly driven by the issue of race." What Laycock was suggesting is that, in a straightforward battle between the old meritocratic principle on which conservatives make their stand on the new ideals of diversity and inclusion, meritocracy is likely to lose. And, several weeks later, *The New York Times* inadvertently confirmed his point in a front-page story headlined, "COLLEGES LOOK FOR ANSWERS TO RACIAL GAPS IN TESTING." Donald M. Stewart, president of the College Board, lamented the "social cost" of relying on standardized tests on which minority students fare poorly. "America can't stand that," Stewart said.

Should we regret the political and marketplace dynamics that essentially *force* institutions like the University of Texas Law School to practice affirmative action? The original rationale for affirmative action was that it helped disadvantaged students overcome the effects of discrimination, both current and historical. No one questions that U.T. Law is guilty of past discrimination. The school was off-limits to black students as a matter of state law until a celebrated 1950 Supreme court decisions, *Sweatt v. Painter*. But most of the black students who attend the law school now come from other states, and they are scarcely more likely than the white students to come from a disadvantaged background.

What about "diversity"? The diversity argument has rapidly eclipsed the past-discrimination argument, because it is so much rosier and more consensual. It's hard to dispute the notion that institutions benefit from "diverse" points of view. But is that a large enough good to justify disadvantaging whites? And there's something arbitrary about the math. Randall Kennedy, a professor at Harvard Law School and another uneasy supporter of affirmative action, says: "I have my problems with the idea that we've got to have diversity because in the year 2000 the census says this and this about a jurisdiction. Does that mean that, if you're in Maine, you don't have to have more than one black student?"

The simple and painful truth is that affirmative action rests on a bedrock of failure. The reason why the University of Texas Law School needed affirmative action in the first place is that, according to a university deposition in *Hopwood*, only 88 black students in the entire country had a combination of grades and law boards in 1992 that reached the mean of admitted white students; only one of those black students came from Texas. One lesson of *post-Hopwood* Texas is that eliminating affirmative action would virtually wipe out the black presence in top schools. For conservatives, that's just the way the meritocratic cookie crumbles, but for most Americans, justly proud of the extent to which our leading institutions have been integrated over the last quarter century, that's likely to be an unacceptable outcome.

Affirmative action is, at bottom, a dodge. It allows us to put off the far harder work: ending the isolation of young black people and closing the academic gap that separates black students—even middle-class black students—from whites. When we commit ourselves to that, we can do without affirmative action, but not before.

James Traub

READING 7.2

The Management of Organizational Justice

Russell Cropanzano, David E. Bowen and Stephen W. Gilliland

Executive Overview

Organizational justice has the potential to create powerful benefits for organizations and employees alike. These include greater trust and commitment, improved job performance, more helpful citizenship behaviors, improved customer satisfaction, and diminished conflict. We demonstrate the management of organizational justice with some suggestions for building fairness into widely used managerial activities. These include hiring, performance appraisal, reward systems, conflict management, and downsizing.

> *Justice, Sir, is the greatest interest of man on earth*
> —Daniel Webster

Business organizations are generally understood to be economic institutions. Sometimes implicitly, other times explicitly, this "rational" perspective has shaped the relationship that many employers have with their workforce (Ashforth & Humphrey, 1995). Many organizations, for example, emphasize the quid pro quo exchange of monetary payment for the performance of concrete tasks (Barley & Kunda, 1992). These tasks are often rationally described via job analysis and formally appraised by a supervisor. Hierarchical authority of this type is legitimized based upon the manager's special knowledge or expertise (Miller & O'Leary, 1989). Employee motivation is viewed as a quest for personal economic gain, so individual merit pay is presumed to be effective. Using the rational model, one can make a case for downsizing workers who are not contributing adequately to the "bottom line." And the rational model is found at the heart of the short-term uptick in the stock price of firms that carry out aggressive cost-cutting measures (Pfeffer, 1998).

Businesses certainly are economic institutions, but they are not *only* economic institutions. Indeed, adherence to this paradigm without consideration of other possibilities can have problematic side effects. Merit pay is sometimes ineffective (Pfeffer & Sutton, 2006), downsizing often has pernicious long-term effects (Pfeffer, 1998), and bureaucratic management can straitjacket workers and reduce innovation. We should attend to economic matters, but also to the sense of duty that goes beyond narrowly defined quid pro quo exchanges. It includes the ethical obligations that one party has to the other. Members may want a lot of benefits, but they also want something more. Organizational justice—members' sense of the moral propriety of how they are treated—is the "glue" that allows people to work together effectively. Justice defines the very essence of individuals' relationship to employers. In contrast, *in*justice is like a corrosive solvent that can dissolve bonds within the community. Injustice is hurtful to individuals and harmful to organizations.

In this paper we will discuss organizational justice, with an emphasis on how it can be brought to the workplace. We first define justice, paying careful attention to its three core dimensions: distributive, procedural, and interactional. We then examine why justice is important; we will consider various criterion variables that justice favorably influences. Once we understand the nature of justice we will be in a better position to describe how it can be brought about. The lesson here is that organizational justice actually has to be managed. This paper will provide specific techniques and recommendations for doing so.

What Is Organizational Justice?

Prescription vs. Description

Philosophers and social commentators were writing about justice long before management scientists were. Among the ancient Greeks, for example, Herodotus' *History* and Plutarch's *Lives* described the achievements of the lawgiver Solon, who reformed Athenian government. These are the *prescriptive* approaches, since they seek to logically determine what sorts of actions *truly are just*. As such, they reside comfortably within the domain of business ethics.

While organizational justice borrows from these older traditions, it has its own distinctions. Unlike the work of philosophers and attorneys, managerial scientists are less concerned with what *is* just and more concerned with what people *believe* to be just. In other words, these researchers are pursuing a *descriptive* agenda. They seek to understand why people view certain events as just, as well as the consequences that follow from these evaluations. In this regard, justice is a subjective and descriptive concept in that it captures what individuals believe to be right, rather than an objective reality or a prescriptive moral code. As defined here, organizational justice is a personal evaluation about the ethical and moral standing of managerial conduct. It follows from this approach that producing justice requires management to take the perspective of an employee. That is, they need to understand what sorts of events engender this subjective feeling of organizational justice. On this important competency, many fall short.

Why Employees Care About Justice

Managers too often assume that justice, in the minds of employees, means only that they receive desirable outcomes. These managers are confusing outcome *favorability* with outcome *justice*. The former is a judgment of personal worth or value; the latter is a judgment of moral propriety. Evidence shows that outcome justice and outcome favorability are distinct (Skitka, Winquist, & Hutchinson, 2003) and correlated between .19 and .49, depending on where and how the variables are measured (Cohen-Charash & Spector, 2001). In so many words, it's important to get what you want, but other things matter as well. For this reason it is useful to consider three reasons justice matters to people (for details, see Cropanzano, Rupp, Mohler, & Schminke, 2001).

Long-Range Benefits People often "sign on" for the long haul. Consequently, they need to estimate *now* how they are likely to be treated *over time*. A just organization makes this prediction easy. According to the "control model," employees prefer justice because it allows them to predict and control the outcomes they are likely to receive from organizations. According to the control model of justice, appropriate personnel policies signal that things are likely to work out eventually. Most of us understand that every personnel decision cannot go our way, but justice provides us with more certainty regarding our future benefits.

For this reason the control model proposes that people are often motivated by economic and quasi-economic interests (cf. Tyler & Smith, 1998). People want fairness because fairness provides things they like. There is more than a little truth to this idea. For instance, when individuals are rewarded for successfully completing a task they report being happy (Weiss, Suckow, & Cropanzano, 1999) and having pride in their performance (Krehbiel & Cropanzano, 2000). This is so even when their success resulted from cheating. At the same time, these individuals also report feeling guilty for their unfair behavior, suggesting that individuals can recognize and react to injustice, even when it is personally beneficial.

There is sometimes a certain tension between getting what we want and playing by the rules. The two tend to go together, but less so than many believe. For example, pay satisfaction is only modestly correlated with perceptions

of pay justice (Williams, McDaniel, & Nguyen, 2006). If "justice" were based exclusively on obtaining benefits, then one would expect a higher association. Later we shall discuss evidence suggesting that individuals can accept an unfortunate outcome as long as the process is fair and they are treated with interpersonal dignity (e.g., Goldman, 2003; Skarlicki & Folger, 1997).

Social Considerations People are social animals. We wish to be accepted and valued by important others while not being exploited or harmed by powerful decision-makers. In the "group-value model," just treatment tells us that we are respected and esteemed by the larger group. We are also at less risk for mistreatment. This sense of belonging is important to us even apart from the economic benefits it can bring (Tyler & Blader, 2000; Tyler & Smith, 1998). As you might expect, this can pose a potential problem for organizations. To the extent that justice signals our value to an employer, the more we care about the organization the more distressed we become when we are treated unfairly. Brockner, Tyler, and Cooper-Schneider (1992) assessed the commitment of a group of employees before a layoff occurred. After the downsizing those people who were initially the *most* committed responded the *most* negatively to the downsizing. When we treat workers unfairly, we may end up doing the most harm to those who are most loyal.

Ethical Considerations People also care about justice because they believe it is the morally appropriate way others should be treated (Folger, 2001). When individuals witness an event they believe is ethically inappropriate, they are likely to take considerable risks in the hopes of extracting retribution (Bies & Tripp, 2001, 2002). Such unfortunate (from the organization's point of view) reactions may occur even when an employee simply witnesses the harm and is not personally wronged (Ellard & Skarlicki, 2002; Spencer & Rupp, 2006). Consider, for example, a day-to-day problem faced by many service workers. When these employees see a customer treating one of their coworkers unfairly, the observing worker is apt to experience stress symptoms. Through this mechanism, injustice may spread ill will throughout a workgroup.

Three Components of Justice

Research has shown that employees appraise three families of workplace events. They examine the justice of outcomes (distributive justice), the justice of the formal allocation processes (procedural justice), and the justice of interpersonal transactions they encounter with others (interactional justice). These are shown in Table 1.

Distributive, procedural, and interactional justice tend to be correlated. They can be meaningfully treated as three components of overall fairness (Ambrose & Arnaud, 2005;

Table 1

Components of Organizational Justice

1. Distributive Justice: Appropriateness of outcomes.
   - Equity: Rewarding employees based on their contributions.
   - Equality: Providing each employee roughly the same compensation.
   - Need: Providing a benefit based on one's personal requirements.

2. Procedural Justice: Appropriateness of the allocation process.
   - Consistency: All employees are treated the same.
   - Lack of Bias: No person or group is singled out for discrimination or ill-treatment.
   - Accuracy: Decisions are based on accurate information.
   - Representation of All Concerned: Appropriate stakeholders have input into a decision.
   - Correction: There is an appeals process or other mechanism for fixing mistakes.
   - Ethics: Norms of professional conduct are not violated.

3. Interactional Justice: Appropriateness of the treatment one receives from authority figures.
   - Interpersonal Justice: Treating an employee with dignity, courtesy, and respect.
   - Informational Justice: Sharing relevant information with employees.

Ambrose & Schminke, 2007), and the three components can work together. However, if one's goal is to promote workplace justice, it is useful to consider them separately and in detail. This is because each component is engendered in distinct ways, arising from different managerial actions.

Distributive Justice

Researchers call the first component of justice *distributive justice* because it has to do with the allocations or outcomes that some get and others do not. Distributive justice is concerned with the reality that not all workers are treated alike; the allocation of outcomes is differentiated in the workplace. Individuals are concerned with whether or not they received their "just share." Sometimes things are distributively just, as when the most qualified person gets promoted. Other times they are not, as when advancement goes to corporate "insiders" with a political relationship to upper management.

Equity Theory   Perhaps the earliest theory of distributive justice can be attributed to Aristotle. In his *Nicomachean Ethics,* the philosopher maintained that just distribution involved "something proportionate," which he defined as "equality of ratios." Specification, and a bit of rearrangement, led Adams (1965) to represent his influential equity theory of distributive justice with the following equation:

$$\frac{O_1}{I_1} = \frac{O_2}{I_2}$$

According to equity theory, we are interested in how much we get (outcomes or O_1) relative to how much we contribute (inputs or I_1). Such a ratio is meaningless, however, unless anchored against some standard. To accomplish this, we examine the outcomes (O_2) and inputs (I_2) of some referent. Usually, though not necessarily, this is another person who is similar to us. Things are "equitable" when the ratios, not the individual terms, are in agreement. When the ratios are out of alignment, employees may feel uneasy. They are motivated to "balance" the equation by modifying the terms. For example, one who is underpaid might reduce inputs by a corresponding amount.

This simple equation leads to a number of predictions, some of which are not obvious. For example, an individual who earns less than another may still be satisfied, as long as he or she also contributes less. Likewise, a person who is paid equally to another may feel unjustly treated if he or she also contributes substantially more to the organization. These consequences often do not occur to managers, but they make good sense in light of equity theory. But by far the most famous prediction from equity theory is the "over-reward effect"—that is, what happens when the equation is unbalanced in one's own favor.

According to equity theory, when one is *overpaid* the two sides of the ratios are misaligned. Consequently, one must work harder (i.e., increase inputs) in order to be equitable. These effects seem to occur. Greenberg (1988) studied managers who were temporarily moved to higher- or lower-status offices than their position actually warranted. Those moved to higher-status offices boosted performance, whereas those moved to lower-status offices showed decrements. These gains and losses later disappeared when individuals were returned to status-appropriate office spaces. Apart from its impact on performance, inequity can also cause workplace sabotage (Ambrose, Seabright, & Schminke, 2002) and employee theft (Greenberg, 1993). It is personally painful for employees, as distributive injustice is associated with stress symptoms (Cropanzano, Goldman, & Benson, 2005).

Recent Advances in Distributive Justice As Table 1 makes clear, there is more to distributive justice than simple equity. These different standards can be in conflict with one another. Generally speaking, we can distinguish three allocation rules that can lead to distributive justice if they are applied appropriately: equality (to each the same), equity (to each in accordance with contributions), and need (to each in accordance with the most urgency). These rules map onto Aristotle's famous dictum that all men wish to be treated like all other people (equality), like some other people (equality), and like no other person (need). While it is no mean task to find the correct alchemistic combination among these three allocation rules, there are three basic suggestions that can be helpful.

First, it is useful to consider one's strategic goals (Colquitt, Greenberg, & Zapata-Phelan, 2005). Equity tends to provide individual rewards for high performance, whereas equality tends to build esprit de corps among teammates. If one desires to stimulate individual motivation, err toward equity. If one desires to build group cohesion, err toward equality. We shall return to this issue later when we discuss reward systems.

Second, organizations can balance these considerations by mixing equality and equity together. It need not be either-or. Experiments with work groups suggest that it is often best to provide team members with a basic minimum of benefit. This is analogous to equality. Above that minimum, however, it can be useful to reward based on performance. This is analogous to equity. This sort of hybrid approach has been adopted by many organizations. Their compensation systems contain a "fixed" base; everyone in a particular job class and with a particular tenure receives this base. Employees are also encouraged to go beyond this minimum, earning additional pay through the allocation of merit bonuses (Milkovich & Newman, 2005, see especially Chapters 9 and 10).

Third, different rewards should be provided in accordance with different rules. Equity works well for some things, such as money, but less well for others, such as status symbols. Among American managers, it is often seen as fair to allocate economic benefits in accordance with equity (i.e., those who perform better might earn more). On the other hand, social-emotional benefits, such as reserved parking places, are best allocated equally (Martin & Harder, 1994). Employees often see themselves and their peers as belonging to a group or, in the most beneficial case, a community. Allocating social-emotional rewards equally signals that everyone in the organization matters and is worthy of respect.

Procedural Justice

Procedural justice refers to the means by which outcomes are allocated, but not specifically to the outcomes themselves. Procedural justice establishes certain principles specifying

and governing the roles of participants within the decision-making processes. In three papers, Leventhal and his colleagues (Leventhal, 1976, 1980; Leventhal, Karuza, & Fry, 1980) established some core attributes that make procedures just; these are displayed in Table 1. A just process is one that is applied consistently to all, free of bias, accurate, representative of relevant stakeholders, correctable, and consistent with ethical norms. Though surprising to some, research has shown that just procedures can mitigate the ill effects of unfavorable outcomes. Researchers have named this the "fair process effect."

To illustrate let us consider the case of strategic planning. Kim and Mauborgne (1991, 1993) reported that when managers believed that their headquarters used a fair planning process, they were more supportive of the plan, trusted their leaders more, and were more committed to their employers. In their well-known book, *Blue Ocean Strategy*, Kim and Mauborgne (2005) explain why. Fair processes lead to intellectual and emotional recognition. This, in turn, creates the trust and commitment that build voluntary cooperation in strategy execution. Procedural injustice, on the other hand, produces "intellectual and emotional indignation," resulting in "distrust and resentment" (p. 183). Ultimately, this reduces cooperation in strategy execution.

We can go further. Procedural justice seems to be essential to maintaining institutional legitimacy. When personnel decisions are made, individuals are likely to receive certain outcomes. For instance, one may or may not be promoted. According to Tyler and Blader (2000), outcome favorability tends to affect satisfaction with the particular decision. This is not surprising. What is more interesting is that procedural justice affects what workers believe about the organization as a whole. If the process is perceived as just, employees show greater loyalty and more willingness to behave in an organization's best interests. They are also less likely to betray the institution and its leaders.

Interactional Justice

In a sense, *interactional justice* may be the simplest of the three components. It refers to how one person treats another. A person is interactionally just if he or she appropriately shares information and avoids rude or cruel remarks. In other words, there are two aspects of interactional justice (Colquitt, Conlon, Wesson, Porter, & Ng, 2001). The first part, sometimes called *informational justice* refers to whether one is truthful and provides adequate justifications when things go badly. The second part, sometimes called *interpersonal justice,* refers to the respect and dignity with which one treats another. As shown in Table 1, both are important.

Because interactional justice emphasizes one-on-one transactions, employees often seek it from their supervisors. This presents an opportunity for organizations. In a quasi-experimental study, Skarlicki and Latham (1996) trained union leaders to behave more justly. Among other things, these leaders were taught to provide explanations and apologies (informational justice) and to treat their reports with courtesy and respect (interpersonal justice). When work groups were examined three months later, individuals who reported to trained leaders exhibited more helpful citizenship behaviors than individuals who reported to untrained leaders.

Working Together: The Three Components of Justice Interact

Maintaining the three components of justice simultaneously is a worthwhile task, but it may also seem daunting. Fortunately, there is good news. Evidence suggests that the three components of justice interact (Cropanzano, Slaughter, & Bachiochi, 2005; Skarlicki & Folger, 1997). Though this interaction can be described in different ways, the key point is this: The ill effects of injustice can be at least partially mitigated if at least one component of justice is maintained. For example, a distributive and a procedural injustice will have fewer negative effects if interactional justice is high.

To understand this phenomenon one can look at a study by Goldman (2003). Goldman studied the relationship between justice and filing legal claims for alleged workplace discrimination. He found that claimants were most likely to purse litigation when distributive, procedural, and interactional justice were all low. If just one component of justice was judged to be high, the likelihood of a legal claim dropped. This is good news, because it suggests that organizations have three bites at the apple. If they can get at least one component of justice right, some important benefits should result. We will consider the beneficial consequences of justice in our next section.

The Impact of Organizational Justice

Over the past few decades a considerable body of research has investigated the consequences of just and unjust treatment by work organizations. This literature has been summarized in three different meta-analytic reviews (Cohen-Charash & Spector, 2001; Colquitt et al., 2001; Viswesvaran & Ones, 2002). While these quantitative reviews differ in some specifics, they all underscore the propitious effects of workplace justice. We will look at each of the findings individually.

Justice Builds Trust and Commitment

Trust is a willingness to become vulnerable with respect to another party. As one might expect given our comments so far, Colquitt and his colleagues (2001) found that all three components of justice (distributive, procedural, and interactional) predict trust. These relationships can be quite strong. For example, the association between perceptions of just procedures and trust can be as high as .60. In a like fashion, justly treated employees are also more committed to their employers. Findings again vary somewhat with how justice is measured, but the correlation of

perceived justice and affective commitment can range between .37 and .43 (Cohen-Charash & Spector, 2001).

Justice Improves Job Performance

As is true for other scholars, we use the term "job performance" to refer to formal job duties, assigned by organizational authorities and evaluated during performance appraisals (for a similar discussion, see Organ, 1988). Workplace justice predicts the effectiveness with which workers discharge their job duties (Colquitt et al., 2001), though more so in field settings and less so in the undergraduate laboratory (Cohen-Charash & Spector, 2001). As Lerner (2003) observed, justice effects are often strongest in real life. In part, this is because, over time, fairness leads to strong interpersonal relationships. In two studies, Cropanzano, Prehar, and Chen (2002) and Rupp and Cropanzano (2002) examined whether supervisors treated their reports with interactional justice. When they did, the leader and the subordinate had a higher-quality relationship. This strong relationship, in turn, motivated employees to higher job performance. Supervisors worried that just pay and process are expensive and time-consuming might take heart. These costs may be partially defrayed by higher productivity.

Justice Fosters Employee Organizational Citizenship Behaviors

Organizational citizenship behaviors (OCBs) are employee behaviors that go beyond the call of duty (Organ, 1988). Several studies have found that justly treated employees are more likely to comply with workplace policies, show extra conscientiousness, and behave altruistically toward others (Cohen-Charash & Spector, 2001). Indeed, workers tend to tailor their citizenship behaviors carefully, doling them out to those groups or individuals who have treated them justly and withholding them from those who have not.

To illustrate this point, consider the case of temporary employees. A contingent worker is likely to be associated with two different organizations—the temporary agency and the organization that contracts with it. In an interesting study, Liden, Wayne, Kraimer, and Sparrowe (2003) surveyed contingent workers who were assigned to a Fortune 500 manufacturing firm. Liden and his colleagues discovered that citizenship behaviors toward this manufacturing organization were influenced by the procedural fairness with which the manufacturing company treated the workers. Contingent employees who received just processes from the contracting organization (the manufacturing firm) performed more OCBs. However, the procedural justice these workers received from the employment agency did nothing to boost citizenship behaviors toward the manufacturing firm. In other words, individuals repaid procedural justice with hard work, but they reciprocated only to the organization that treated them justly in the first place. The manufacturing firm did not benefit from the temporary agency's efforts at procedural justice. If you want justice to work to your benefit, you have to do it yourself.

Justice Builds Customer Satisfaction and Loyalty

Justice-inspired employee OCBs, such as behaving altruistically toward others, sound much like employee customer service–oriented behaviors, such as helping others and listening carefully to their needs. Building on this, Bowen, Gilliland and Folger (1999) suggested that just treatment of employees would lead to OCBs that "spill over" to customers. This "just play" results in customers feeling appropriately treated, thereby yielding customer satisfaction and loyalty. These types of internal-external relationships have been empirically validated by such scholars as Masterson (2001) and Maxham and Netemyer (2003). For example, Masterson (2001) asked a large group of university instructors how they were being treated. When teachers felt that they received distributive and procedural justice they tended to report higher organizational commitment. This commitment, in turn, improved student responses toward the instructor. Since small gains in customer loyalty can translate into much larger gains in profitability (e.g., Heskett, Sasser, & Schlesinger, 1997; Smith, Bolton, & Wagner, 1999), these are very potent effects.

Thoughts Before Moving On

More broadly, we suggest that justice can be a core value that defines an organization's identity with its stakeholders, both internally and externally. When justice is espoused as a core value of an organization's management philosophy and enacted through a set of internally consistent management practices, it can build a "culture of justice," a system-wide commitment that is valuable and unique in the eyes of employees and customers, and tough to copy in the minds of competitors. And that can translate into the makings of sustainable competitive advantage. In our next section, we will look at management practices that can help develop a culture of justice.

How to Create Perceptions of Justice

We will now turn to common and important workplace situations, discussing a variety of managerial and personnel functions. These are displayed in Table 2. In each case, we will provide a lesson for promoting justice, including some normative recommendations regarding how individuals should be treated. And in each case we will return to one or more of our conceptual observations, such as the fair process effect and the two-factor model, illustrating how these phenomena affect real-life organizations.

Selection Procedures: Positive Job Candidates

For most job candidates, the recruiting and selection process is their first introduction to an organization. How they are

Table 2
Building Justice Into Management Systems
1. Positive Job Candidates: The Justice Paradox in Selection Procedures.
2. Justly Balancing Multiple Goals: The Two-Factor Model in Just Reward Systems
3. You Don't Have to Win: How the Process by Outcome Interaction Helps Us Resolve Conflicts
4. Softening Hardship: The Fair Process Effect in Layoffs
5. Keeping Score Fairly: A Due Process Approach to Performance Appraisal.

treated at this time can have ramifications later. Applicants who feel justly treated are more likely to form positive impressions of the organization (Bauer et al., 2001) and recommend it to their friends (Smither, Reilly, Millsap, Pearlman, & Stoffey, 1993). And the flip side is also true. When applicants feel unjustly treated they are more likely to consider litigation as a potential remedy (Bauer et al., 2001). This research suggests that it pays for organizations to put their best foot forward. By treating applicants justly in the hiring process, organizations are setting the foundation for a relationship of justice and trust when those applicants become employees.

The research on job candidates' reactions to recruiting and hiring processes suggests that it is about much more than whether or not someone gets the job. Further, because applicants don't often know why they didn't get the job or the qualifications of the person who did, distributive justice is less of a concern in selection. However, managers do need to be mindful of procedural and interactional justice. It is also important to realize that the selection process begins with recruiting and initial communication, and encompasses all contact with job candidates up to and including extending an offer and rejecting an individual for a job (Gilliland & Hale, 2005). In terms of procedural justice, research has identified two broad sets of concerns:

- *Appropriate questions* and *criteria* are *critical for procedural justice. Job candidates expect interview questions and screening tests to be related to the job, or at least to appear to be related to the job (Gilliland, 1994; Ryan & Chan, 1999). Overly personal interview questions and some screening tests, such as honesty tests, are often seen as inappropriate and an invasion of candidates' privacy (Bies & Moag, 1986; Kravitz, Stinson, & Chavez, 1996).*

• *Adequate opportunity to perform* during the selection process means giving job candidates the chances to make a case for themselves and allowing sufficient time in interviews (Truxillo, Bauer, & Sanchez, 2001). If standardized tests are used to screen applicants, justice can be enhanced by allowing candidates to retest if they feel they did not perform their best (Truxillo et al., 2001).

On the face, these two criteria seem reasonable and pretty straightforward. However, when compared with recommended hiring practices, managers are often faced with a "justice paradox" (Folger & Cropanzano, 1998). That is, many of the selection procedures with the highest predictive validity—those that are the best screening tools—are unfortunately those that fail to satisfy these justice concerns. Consider cognitive ability and personality tests. These screening methods have high demonstrated validity (Schmidt & Hunter, 1998), but both are seen by job applicants as not particularly fair (Steiner & Gilliland, 1996). Questions on these tests are often not related to the job, and applicants don't feel they have an opportunity to present their true abilities. The converse is also observed with the justice paradox. Traditional unstructured interviews have long demonstrated weak predictive validity, not much better than chance (Huffcutt & Arthur, 1994). However, job applicants perceive these interviews as having high procedural justice because they are able to demonstrate their qualifications (Latham & Finnegan, 1993). Adding structured situations and questions to the interview increases predictive validity, but decreases perceptions of procedural justice.

So how can this justice paradox be managed effectively? We have three suggestions. First, there are some screening tools that have both predictive validity and procedural justice. Work sample tests and performance-based simulations demonstrate reasonable predictive validity (Roth, Bobko, & McFarland, 2005) and are also seen as procedurally just (Steiner & Gilliland, 1996). A second solution is to modify existing screening tools to increase job applicants' perceived procedural justice. Smither and colleagues (1993) found that cognitive ability tests with concrete, rather than abstract, items tended to be viewed more positively by job applicants. Based on the observation that applicants perceive greater justice in unstructured interviews, Gilliland and Steiner (1999) suggest a combined interview that has both structured behavioral questions to maximize predictive validity and unstructured questions to allow applicants the "opportunity to perform."

The third suggestion is based on our earlier discussion of interactional justice. Recall that interactional justice can attenuate the negative effects of procedural injustice. Research has demonstrated that interactional justice is very important for job candidates (Bies & Moag, 1986; Gilliland,

1995). With attention to considerate interpersonal treatment, honest information, and timely feedback, organizations can create hiring processes that embody interactional justice. Research has demonstrated that the informational components are particularly important if there are unanticipated delays or unusual screening procedures involved in the process (Rynes, Bretz, & Gerhart, 1991).

Reward Systems: Justly Balancing Multiple Goals

At the most basic level, rewards systems need to accomplish two goals: They need to motivate individual performance, and they need to maintain group cohesion. While both goals are worthwhile, distributive justice research tells us that it is difficult to accomplish them simultaneously. Equity allocations, which reward for performance, can spur individual effort. But the resulting inequality that is likely to occur can be disruptive. In a study of academic faculty, Pfeffer and Langton (1993) examined wage dispersion in their home departments. When wage dispersion was high, faculty reported less satisfaction and less collaboration with colleagues. Overall research productivity dropped as well. This is not what merit pay is supposed to do.

Paying everyone the same thing, though, is not the answer either. Indeed, equality distributions can boost group harmony, but they bring troubles of their own. A key problem is one of external equity. High-performing employees, or those with rare skills, may be worth more in the external marketplace. If their salaries are "capped" to maintain internal equality, these workers may seek employment elsewhere. This is just another way of saying that no matter how people are paid, not everyone will be satisfied.

How then to position rewards? The research discussed earlier underscores an opportunity. To be sure, individuals who do not receive the compensation they desire will want more. However, they often remain loyal to their employer if the pay administration procedures are viewed as fair. Consequently, if an organization needs to maintain external equity, it can do so and risk internal inequality, but only as long as the allocation process is just. To illustrate, McFarlin and Sweeney (1992) surveyed more than 600 banking employees. As expected, when distributive justice was low, workers reported less pay satisfaction and less job satisfaction. This is bad news, but it is partially compensated for by the procedural justice results. When procedural justice was high, workers experienced higher organizational commitment and a positive reaction to their supervisors. This is the two-factor model in action. Individuals who were not necessarily satisfied with their pay were still unlikely to derogate the organization when the procedures were just.

In addition to procedural justice, interactional justice can be helpful in administering pay fairly. To illustrate this point, let us consider a situation that everyone dislikes: pay cuts. Greenberg (1993) found that differences in how pay cuts were managed at two manufacturing plants produced dramatically different outcomes. The key is interpersonal treatment. In one, an executive politely, but quickly in about 15 minutes, announced a 15% pay cut. In the other, an executive spent about an hour and a half speaking, taking questions, and expressing regrets about making an identical pay cut. During a subsequent 10-week period, employee theft was about 80% lower in the second case, and employees in that plant were 15 times less likely to resign. No one wanted to have his or her pay cut. But workers understood why it happened, appreciated the supportive interpersonal treatment, and did not vent their ire on the organization.

Conflict Management: You Don't Have to Win

Thomas and Schmidt (1976) tell us that managers may spend about 20% of their time settling disputes among employees, and they are not always successful (Schoorman & Champagne, 1994). Conflict resolution is likely to be most difficult when one or both parties is intransigent. At this point the manager may listen to both disputants, but will need to impose a settlement on them. This is called arbitration, and it is ultimately autocratic. As a result, arbitration may sound risky because it hazards a distributive injustice; the settlement is imposed and not approved in advance by other parties.

There is good news, however. If *any* component of justice is present during arbitration (distributive or procedural or interactional), the overall appraisal of the situation will be improved (Goldman, 2003). Because arbitration preserves procedural justice, an unfortunate outcome is less destructive than one might imagine. Or, we might say, managers can make hard choices, but they have to make them justly (for details see Folger & Cropanzano, 1998). This illustrates a simple yet powerful lesson from research on conflict resolution: If you can't give people the outcome they want, at least give them a fair process.

Layoffs: Softening Hardship

So far we have reviewed evidence pertaining to justice in the context of hiring, reward systems, and conflict resolution. These are everyday events in a large organization, and each will function more effectively if justice is taken into account. Even a reader willing to indulge our arguments so far might be wondering whether justice helps when something really bad happens.

Among common management situations that affect employees, downsizing is among the worst (Richman, 1993). Layoffs have pernicious effects, harming the victims while undermining the morale of survivors who remain employed. Though downsizing is a widely used cost-cutting strategy, it is highly risky. The costs of workforce reductions often outweigh the benefits (Kammeyer-Mueller, Liao, & Arvey, 2001). In these circumstances people not only lose, they lose big. The event can be so negative that a sense of

distributive injustice is virtually a given. Can the guidelines suggested in this paper do any good at all?

As a matter of fact, they can. When a layoff is handled with procedural and interactional justice, victims are less likely to derogate their former employers (Brockner et al., 1994, Study 1). Indeed, justice can have direct bottom-line effects. Lind, Greenberg, Scott, and Welchans (2000) interviewed a large number of layoff victims. Many of these individuals considered legal action following their downsizing, and almost a quarter of the victims went so far as to speak to an attorney. The single best predictor of willingness to take legal action was the justice of the treatment they received at the time of their discharge. Among those who felt unjustly treated, Lind and his colleagues found that a full 66% contemplated litigation. Among those who felt justly treated, this dropped to just 16%. These are impressive findings. Although managers are often coached by attorneys or HR representatives to avoid apologizing—an apology can be seen as an admission of guilt—these results suggest that an apology may help promote the feelings of interactional justice that actually reduce the risk of litigation. Justice, it would seem, provides a useful way to survive a crisis with one's business reputation intact.

While we have so far discussed the victims of layoffs, workforce reductions also affect survivors. Those left behind, though retaining their jobs, tend to suffer from "survivor guilt" (Brockner & Greenberg, 1990). However, if organizations provide a good explanation as to why the downsizing is necessary—an aspect of interactional justice—the remaining employees respond much less negatively (Brockner, DeWitt, Grover, & Reed, 1990). Providing unemployment benefits is also advantageous, as one might expect. However, if these benefits are lacking, an advance warning that a layoff is about to occur will blunt the negative reactions that might otherwise transpire (Brockner et al., 1994, Studies 2 and 3).

Performance Appraisals: Keeping Score Fairly

In order to assign rewards, identify candidates for promotion, and develop human capital, most large organizations conduct performance evaluations. While these appraisals are useful, concerns remain, and their implementation is often troubled. For example, scholars have observed a phenomenon called the "vanishing performance appraisal" (for a review, see Folger & Cropanzano, 1998). When surveyed, most managers reported having provided performance reviews, while many of their subordinates reported never receiving one. Other research suggests that evaluations are affected by political considerations (Longenecker, Gioia, & Sims, 1987), cognitive processing limitations of the rater (DeNisi & Williams, 1988), and the social context in which they are conducted (Levy & Williams, 2004). These concerns tell us that the performance appraisal process often contains a good deal of ambiguity as well as room for reasonable people to disagree.

For this reason, it is helpful to approach performance evaluations with an eye to their subjectivity. Historically, much of the advice academics provided to practitioners encouraged them to think of the performance review as a sort of test, whereby the central task is to assign a valid rating to a more-or-less objective quantity. For example, raters have been advised to "become expert at applying principles of test development" (Banks & Roberson, 1985, p. 129) and that "psychometric issues surrounding performance measurement [are] more relevant than ever" (DeVries, Morrison, Shullman, & Gerlach, 1981). This venerable, measurement-oriented understanding of performance appraisal has been termed the "test metaphor" (Folger, Konovsky, & Cropanzano, 1992).

More recent performance appraisal work has taken a broader perspective, emphasizing the social setting (Levy & Williams, 2004) and input from multiple sources (Smither, London, & Reilly, 2005). In this vein, Cawley, Keeping, and Levy (1998) meta-analyzed 27 field studies, each of which examined employee participation in performance appraisal. They found that when employees had a voice they were more satisfied, saw the process as more fair, and were more motivated to do better. This is interesting, but probably not terribly surprising. The really impressive finding was that these effects occurred even when participation could not affect the rating. Simply being able to speak one's mind (what Cawley and coauthors termed "value-expressive" participation) caused employees to be more favorable toward the performance appraisal system. Notice how these findings are consistent with the fair process effect mentioned earlier.

Research on organizational justice is providing a new paradigm for understanding performance review. Consistent with Folger, Konovsky, and Cropanzano (1992), we call this the due process approach to performance appraisal. Adopting a due process metaphor sensitizes one to the distinct interpretations, potential conflicts of interest, and legitimate disagreement about facts. The due process approach to performance review has three core elements: adequate notice, just hearing, and judgment based on evidence.

- *Adequate notice,* as one might expect, involves letting people know in advance when they will be appraised and on what criteria they will be appraised. However, from a justice point of view, it goes beyond this. It is also useful to have workers involved in devising performance standards and making these widely available. Of course, it follows that feedback should be provided regularly.
- *Just hearing* means limiting the feedback review to "admissible" evidence, such as worker performance rather than personal attacks. It also means providing workers with a chance to provide their own interpretation of events, including disagreeing with the supervisor where this is appropriate.
- *Judgment based on evidence* means that the standards should be accurate, data should be gathered, and decisions should be based on this formal process. Steps should be taken to provide rater training, so as to improve accuracy and to keep the process free of political influence.

Taylor, Tracy, Renard, Harrison, and Carroll (1995) redesigned the performance appraisal system of a large state agency so that it included these principles of due process. They discovered that workers preferred the new system, finding it fairer and more effective. Managers liked it as well, believing that it allowed them to be honest and feeling that it was more effective for solving work problems. This occurred even though workers in the due process system received *lower* ratings than did workers under the older approach.

This is all to the good, but there are risks involved. Adequate notice, just hearing, and judgment based on evidence are complicated to administer. A key problem is that they may raise expectations while simultaneously providing employees with a set of tools for making their discontent felt. Consider the case of two companies studied over six years by Mesch and Dalton (1992). Each firm was in the same region, and workers in each were represented by the same union. In fact, grievances at both organizations were assigned to the same union local. After 36 months, one of the firms decided to improve its grievance process by adding a fact-finding intervention. Before the grievance process began, both the union and management provided a "fact finder" to determine the merits of the case, prevent concealment of information, and encourage negotiated settlements. This provided an additional stage of process protection. The result? The number of grievances filed skyrocketed at the firm with the new procedural safeguard, but stayed roughly constant at the other organization. After about two years, the fact-finding intervention was abandoned, and the grievance rate returned to normal. The new intervention seems to have raised expectations and thereby encouraged workers to complain about real and imagined ill-treatment. In the long run this was counterproductive. The implications of Mesch and Dalton's (1992) study need to be appreciated. If procedures are not designed appropriately, they could create more problems than they solve.

Concluding Thoughts

There are two sides to the justice coin. On the negative side, the absence of justice is likely to provide problems for organizations. There is strong evidence that injustice can provoke retaliation, lower performance, and harm morale (Cohen-Charash & Spector, 2001; Colquitt et al., 2001; Viswesvaran & Ones, 2002). On the positive side, justice can do more than forestall these unfortunate outcomes. Justice acts as a sort of buffer, allowing employees to maintain respect and trust for an organization even when things do not go as they would have liked (Brockner & Wiesenfeld, 1996). It is inevitable in life that things will not always go our way. However, the negative effects of an unfortunate event are less severe if an organization is able to maintain procedural and interactional justice (Goldman, 2003; Skarlicki & Folger, 1997).

Justice provides an excellent business opportunity, from reaping specific returns such as stronger employee commitment to gaining an overall tough-to-copy competitive edge that resides in a "culture of justice." In this paper we have examined justice from the perspective of five managerial tasks: hiring, reward systems, conflict management, layoffs, and performance appraisals. These tasks are diverse, but they all involve a degree of risk. Each has the potential to designate some as "winners" and others as "losers." After all, there will always be people who fail to get the job, receive a lower than expected performance appraisal, or are downsized in the face of business exigencies. As a result, organizations hazard the ill will of employees simply because they are making the sorts of decisions necessary to run their businesses. Organizational justice allows managers to make these tough decisions more smoothly. Just play certainly does not guarantee all parties what they want. However, it does hold out the possibility that power will be used in accordance with normative principles that respect the dignity of all involved. This is sound business advice. *It is also the right thing to do.*

Source: "The Management of Organizational Justice," by Russell Cropanzano, David E. Bowen, and Stephen W. Gilliland, pp .34–45. Academy of Management Perspectives. ©2007 the Academy of Management. Reprinted by permission.

REFERENCES

Adams, J. S. (1965). Inequity in social exchange. In L. Berkowitz (Ed.), *Advances in experimental social psychology* (Vol. 2, pp. 267–299). New York: Academic Press.

Ambrose, M. L., & Arnaud, A. (2005). Are procedural justice and distributive justice conceptually distinct? In J. A. Colquitt & J. Greenberg (Eds.), *Handbook of organizational justice* (pp. 85–112). Mahwah, NJ: Lawrence Erlbaum Associates.

Ambrose, M. L., & Schminke, M. (2007). Examining justice climate: Issues of fit, simplicity, and content. In F. Dansereau & F. J. Yammarino (Eds.), *Research in multilevel issues* (Vol. 6, pp. 397–413). Oxford, England: Elsevier.

Ambrose, M. L., Seabright, M. A., & Schminke, M. (2002). Sabotage in the workplace: The role of organizational injustice. *Organizational Behavior and Human Decision Processes*, 89, 947–965.

Ashforth, B. E., & Humphrey, R. H. (1995). Emotion in the workplace: A reappraisal. *Human Relations*, 48, 97–125.

Banks, C. G., & Roberson, L. (1985). Performance appraisers as test developers. *Academy of Management Review*, 10, 128–142.

Barley, S. R., & Kunda, G. (1992). Design and devotion: Surges of rational and normative ideologies of control in managerial discourse. *Administrative Science Quarterly*, 37, 363–399.

Bauer, T. N., Truxillo, D. M., Sanchez, R. J., Craig, J., Ferrara, P., & Campion, M. A. (2001). Applicant reactions to selection: Development of the selection procedural justice scale (SPJS). *Personnel Psychology*, 54, 387–419.

Bies, R. J., & Moag, J. S. (1986). Interactional justice: Communication criteria for justice. In B. Sheppard (Ed.), *Research on negotiation in organizations* (Vol. 1, pp. 43–55). Greenwich, CT: JAI Press.

Bies, R. J., & Tripp, T. M. (2001). A passion for justice: The rationality and morality of revenge. In R. Cropanzano (Ed.), *Justice in the workplace* (pp. 197–208). Mahwah, NJ: Lawrence Erlbaum Associates.

Bies, R. J., & Tripp, T. M. (2002). "Hot flashes, open wounds": Injustice and the tyranny of its emotions. In S. W. Gilliland, D. D. Steiner, & D. P. Skarlicki (Eds.), *Emerging perspectives on managing organizational justice* (pp. 203–221). Greenwich, CT: Information Age Publishing.

Bowen, D. E., Gilliland, S. W., & Folger, R. (1999). HRM and service justice: How being just with employees spills over to customers. *Organizational Dynamics*, 27, 7–23.

Brockner, J., DeWitt, R. L., Grover, S., & Reed, T. (1990) When it is especially important to explain why: Factors affecting the relationship between managers' explanations of a layoff and survivors' reactions to the layoff. *Journal of Experimental Social Psychology*, 26, 389–407.

Brockner, J., & Greenberg, J. (1990) The impact of layoffs on survivors: An organizational justice perspective. In J. S. Carroll (Ed.), *Applied social psychology and organizational settings* (pp. 45–75). Hillsdale, NJ: Erlbaum.

Brockner, J., Konovsky, M., Cooper-Schneider, R., Folger, R., Martin, C., & Bies, R. J. (1994). Interactive effects of procedural justice and outcome negativity on victims and survivors of job loss. *Academy of Management Journal*, 37, 397–409.

Brockner, J., Tyler, T. R., & Cooper-Schneider, R. (1992). The influence of prior commitment to an institution on reactions to perceived unfairness: The higher they are, the harder they fall. *Administrative Science Quarterly*, 37, 241–261.

Brockner, J., & Wiesenfeld, B. M., (1996). An integrative framework for explaining attractiveness of decisions: The interactive effects of outcomes and processes. *Psychological Bulletin*, 120, 189–208.

Cawley, B. D., Keeping, L. M., & Levy, P. E. (1998). Participation in the performance appraisal process and employee reactions: A meta-analytic review of field investigations. *Journal of Applied Psychology*, 83, 615–633.

Cohen-Charash, Y., & Spector, P. E. (2001). The role of justice in organizations: A meta-analysis. *Organizational Behavior and Human Decision Processes*, 86, 278–321.

Colquitt, J. A., Conlon, D. E., Wesson, M. J., Porter, C. O. L. H., & Ng, K. Y. (2001). Justice at the millennium: A meta-analytic review of 25 years of organizational justice research. *Journal of Applied Psychology*, 86, 425–445.

Colquitt, J. A., Greenberg, J., & Zapata-Phelan, C. P. (2005). What is organizational justice? A historical overview. In J. Greenberg & J. A. Colquitt (Eds.), *Handbook of organizational justice* (pp. 3–56). Mahwah, NJ: Lawrence Erlbaum Associates.

Cropanzano, R., Goldman, B., & Benson, L., III. (2005). Organizational justice. In J. Barling, K. Kelloway, & M. Frone (Eds.), *Handbook of work stress* (pp. 63–87). Beverly Hills, CA: Sage.

Cropanzano, R., Prehar, C. A., & Chen, P. Y. (2002). Using social exchange theory to distinguish procedural from interactional justice. *Group and Organizational Management*, 27, 324–351.

Cropanzano, R., Rupp, D. E., Mohler, C. J., & Schminke, M. (2001). Three roads to organizational justice. In J. Ferris (Ed.), *Research in personnel and human resources management* (Vol. 20, pp. 1–113). Greenwich, CT: JAI Press.

Cropanzano, R., Slaughter, J. E., & Bachiochi, P. D. (2005). Organizational justice and black applicants' reactions to affirmative action. *Journal of Applied Psychology*, 90, 1168–1184.

DeNisi, A. S., & Williams, K. J. (1988). Cognitive research in performance appraisal. In K. Rowland & G. S. Ferris (Eds.), *Research in personnel and human resources management* (Vol. 6, pp. 109–156). Greenwich, CT: JAI Press.

DeVries, D. L., Morrison, A. M., Shullman, S. L., & Gerlach, M. L. (1981). *Performance appraisal on the line*. New York: Wiley.

Ellard, J. H., & Skarlicki, D. P. (2002). A third-party observer's reactions to employee mistreatment: Motivational and cognitive processes in deservingness assessments. In S. W. Gilliland, D. D. Steiner, & D. P. Skarlicki (Eds.), *Emerging perspectives on managing organizational justice* (pp. 133–158). Greenwich, CT: Information Age Publishing.

Folger, R. (2001). Justice as deonance. In S. W. Gilliland, D. D. Steiner, & D. P. Skarlicki (Eds.), *Research in social issues in management* (Vol. 1, pp. 3–33). New York: Information Age Publishing.

Folger, R., & Cropanzano, R. (1998). *Organizational justice and human resource management*. Beverly Hills, CA: Sage.

Folger, R., Konovsky, M. A., & Cropanzano, R. (1992). A due process metaphor for performance appraisal. In B. M. Staw &

L. L. Cummings (Eds.), *Research in organizational behavior* (Vol. 14, pp. 129–177). Greenwich, CT: JAI Press.

Gilliland, S. W. (1994). Effects of procedural and distributive justice on reactions to a selection system. *Journal of Applied Psychology*, 79, 691–701.

Gilliland, S. W. (1995). Justice from the applicant's perspective: Reactions to employee selection procedures. *International Journal of Selection and Assessment*, 3, 11–19.

Gilliland, S. W., & Hale, J. (2005). How do theories of organizational justice inform just employee selection practices? In J. Greenberg & J. A. Colquitt (Eds.), *Handbook of organizational justice: Fundamental questions about justice in the workplace* (pp. 411–438). Mahwah, NJ: Erlbaum.

Gilliland, S. W., & Steiner, D. D. (1999). Applicant reactions to interviews: Procedural and interactional justice of recent interview technology. In R. W. Eder & M. M. Harris (Eds.), *The employment interview: Theory, research, and practice* (pp. 69–82). Thousand Oaks, CA: Sage.

Goldman, B. M. (2003). The application of reference cognitions theory to legal-claiming by terminated workers: The role of organizational justice and anger. *Journal of Management*, 29, 705–728.

Greenberg, J. (1988). Equity and workplace status: A field experiment. *Journal of Applied Psychology*, 73, 606–613.

Greenberg, J. (1993). Stealing in the name of justice: Informational and interpersonal moderators of theft reactions to underpayment inequity. *Organizational Behavior and Human Decision Processes*, 54, 81–103.

Heskett, J. L., Sasser, W. E., Jr., & Schlesinger, L. A. (1997). *The service profit chain: How leading companies link profit and growth to loyalty, satisfaction, and value*. New York: The Free Press.

Huffcutt, A. I., & Arthur, W. Jr. (1994). Hunter and Hunter (1984) revisited: Interview validity for entry-level jobs. *Journal of Applied Psychology*, 79, 184–190.

Kammeyer-Mueller, J., Liao, H., & Arvey, R. D. (2001). Downsizing and organizational performance: A review of the literature from a stakeholder perspective. In G. R. Ferris (Ed.), *Research in personnel and human resource management* (Vol. 20, pp. 269–230). Amsterdam: JAI Press.

Kim, W. C., & Mauborgne, R. A. (1991). Implementing global strategies: The role of procedural justice. *Strategic Management Journal*, 12, 125–143.

Kim, W. C., & Mauborgne, R. A. (1993). Procedural justice, attitudes, and subsidiary top management compliance with multinationals' corporate strategic decisions. *Academy of Management Journal*, 36, 502–526.

Kim, W. C., & Mauborgne, R. A. (2005). *Blue ocean strategy: How to create uncontested market space and make competition irrelevant*. Cambridge, MA: Harvard Business School Press.

Kravitz, D. A., Stinson, V., & Chavez, T. L. (1996). Evaluations of tests used for making selection and promotion decisions. *International Journal of Selection and Assessment*, 4, 24–34.

Krehbiel, P. J., & Cropanzano, R. (2000). Procedural justice, outcome favorability, and emotion. *Social Justice Research*, 13, 337–358.

Latham, G. P., & Finnegan, B. J. (1993). Perceived practicality of unstructured, patterned, and situational interviews. In H. Schuler, J. L. Farr, & M. Smith (Eds.), *Personnel selection and assessment: Individual and organizational perspectives* (pp. 41–55). Hillsdale, NJ: Erlbaum.

Lerner, M. J. (2003). The justice motive: Where social psychologists found it, how they lost it, and why they may not find it again. *Personality and Social Psychology Review*, 7, 388–389.

Leventhal, G. S. (1976). Justice in social relationships. In J. W. Thibaut, J. T. Spence, & R. C. Carson (Eds.), *Contemporary topics in social psychology* (pp. 211–240). Morristown, NJ: General Learning Press.

Leventhal, G. S. (1980). What should be done with equity theory? New approaches to the study of justice in social relationships. In K. Gergen, M. Greenberg, and R. Willis (Eds.), *Social exchange: Advances in experimental and social psychology* (Vol. 9, pp. 91–131). New York: Plenum.

Leventhal, G. S., Karuza, J., & Fry, W. R. (1980). Beyond justice: A theory of allocation preferences. In G. Mikula (Ed.), *Justice and social interaction* (pp. 167–218). New York: Springer-Verlag.

Levy, P. E., & Williams, J. R. (2004). The social context of performance appraisal. *Journal of Management*, 30, 881–905.

Liden, R. C., Wayne, S. J., Kraimer, M. L., & Sparrowe, R. T. (2003). The dual commitments of contingent workers: An examination of contingents' commitment to the agency and the organization. *Journal of Organizational Behavior*, 24, 609–625.

Lind, E. A., Greenberg, J., Scott, K. S., & Welchans, T. D. (2000). The winding road from employee to complainant: Situational and psychological determinants of wrongful termination claims. *Administrative Science Quarterly*, 45, 557–590.

Longenecker, C. O., Gioia, D. A., & Sims, H. P. (1987). Behind the mask: The politics of employee appraisal. *Academy of Management Executive*, 1, 183–193.

Martin, J., & Harder, J. W. (1994). Bread and roses: Justice and the distribution of financial and socioemotional rewards in organizations. *Social Justice Research*, 7, 241–264.

Masterson, S. (2001). A trickle-down model of organizational justice: Relating employees' and customers' perceptions of and reactions to justice. *Journal of Applied Psychology*, 86, 594–604.

Maxham, J. G., & Netemyer, R. G. (2003). Firms reap what they sow: The effects of shared values and perceived organizational justice on customers' evaluations of complaint handling. *Journal of Marketing*, 67, 46–62.

McFarlin, D. B., & Sweeney, P. D. (1992). Distributive and procedural justice as predictors of satisfaction with personal and organizational outcomes. *Academy of Management Journal*, 35, 626–637.

Mesch, D. J., & Dalton, D. R. (1992). Unexpected consequences of improving workplace justice: A six-year time series assessment. *Academy of Management Journal*, 5, 1099–1114.

Milkovich, G. T., & Newman, J. M. (2005). *Compensation* (8th Ed.). Boston: McGraw-Hill.

Miller, P., & O'Leary, T. (1989). Hierarchies and American ideals: 1900–1940. *Administrative Science Quarterly*, 14, 250–265.

Organ, D. W. (1988). *Organizational citizenship behavior: The good soldier syndrome*. Lexington, MA: Lexington Books.

Pfeffer, P. (1998). *The human equation: Building profits by putting people first*. Cambridge, MA: Harvard Business School Press.

Pfeffer, J., & Langton, N. (1993). The effect of wage dispersion on satisfaction, productivity, and working collaboratively: Evidence from college and university faculty. *Administrative Science Quarterly*, 38, 382–407.

Pfeffer, J., & Sutton, R. I. (2006). *Hard facts, dangerous half-truths, and total nonsense: Profiting from evidence-based management*. Cambridge, MA: Harvard Business School Press.

Richman, L. S. (1993, September 20). When will the layoffs end? *Fortune*, pp. 54–56.

Roth, P. L., Bobko, P., & McFarland, L. A. (2005). A meta-analysis of work sample test validity: Updating and integrating some classic literature. *Personnel Psychology*, 58, 1009–1037.

Rupp, D. E., & Cropanzano, R. (2002). The mediating effects of social exchange relationships in predicting workplace outcomes from multifoci organizational justice. *Organizational Behavior and Human Decision Processes*, 89, 925–946.

Ryan, A. M., & Chan, D. (1999). Perceptions of the EPPP: How do licensure candidates view the process? *Professional Psychology*, 30, 519–530.

Rynes, S. L., Bretz, R. D., & Gerhart, B. (1991). The importance of recruitment on job choice: A different way of looking. *Personnel Psychology*, 33, 529–542.

Schmidt, F. L., & Hunter, J. E. (1998). The validity and utility of selection methods in personnel psychology: Practical and theoretical implications of 85 years of research findings. *Psychological Bulletin*, 124, 262–274.

Schoorman, F. D., & Champagne, M. V. (1994). Managers as informal third parties: The impact of supervisor-subordinate relationships on interventions. *Employee Responsibilities and Rights Journal*, 7, 73–84.

Skarlicki, D. P., & Folger, R. (1997). Retaliation in the workplace: The roles of distributive, procedural, and interactional justice. *Journal of Applied Psychology*, 82, 434–443.

Skarlicki, D. P., & Latham, G. P. (1996). Increasing citizenship behavior within a labor union: A test of organizational justice theory. *Journal of Applied Psychology*, 81, 161–169.

Skitka, L. J., Winquist, J., & Hutchinson, S. (2003). Are outcome justice and outcome favorability distinguishable psychological constructs? A meta-analytic review. *Social Justice Research*, 16, 309–341.

Smith, A. K., Bolton, R. N., & Wagner, J. (1999). A model of customer satisfaction with service encounters involving failure and recovery. *Journal of Marketing Research*, 36, 356–372.

Smither, J. W., London, M., & Reilly, R. R. (2005). Does performance improve following multisource feedback? A theoretical model, metaanalysis, and review of empirical findings. *Personnel Psychology*, 58, 33–66.

Smither, J. W., Reilly, R. R., Millsap, R. E., Pearlman, K., & Stoffey, R. W. (1993). Applicant reactions to selection procedures. *Personnel Psychology*, 46, 49–77.

Spencer, S., & Rupp, D. E. (2006, May). *Angry, guilty, and conflicted: Injustice toward coworkers heightens emotional labor.* Paper presented at the Annual Meeting of the Society for Industrial and Organizational Psychology, Dallas, TX.

Steiner, D., & Gilliland, S. W. (1996). Justice reactions to personnel selection techniques in France and the United States. *Journal of Applied Psychology*, 81, 134–141.

Taylor, M. S., Tracy, K. B., Renard, M. K., Harrison, J. K., & Carroll, S. J. (1995). Due process in performance appraisal: A quasi-experiment in procedural justice. *Administrative Science Quarterly*, 40, 495–523.

Thomas, K. W., & Schmidt, W. H. (1976). A survey of managerial interests with respect to conflict. *Academy of Management Journal*, 19, 315–318.

Truxillo, D. M., Bauer, T. N., & Sanchez, R. J. (2001). Multiple dimensions of procedural justice: Longitudinal effects on selection system justice and test-taking self-efficacy. *International Journal of Selection and Assessment*, 9, 330–349.

Tyler, T. R., & Blader, S. L. (2000). *Cooperation in groups: Procedural justice, social identity, and behavioral engagement.* Philadelphia: Psychology Press.

Tyler, T. R., & Smith, H. J. (1998). Social justice and social movements. In D. Gilbert, S. T. Fiske, & G. Lindzey (Eds.), *Handbook of social psychology* (Vol. 4, pp. 595–629). Boston: McGraw-Hill.

Viswesvaran, C., & Ones, D. S. (2002). Examining the construct of organizational justice: A meta-analytic evaluation of relations with work attitudes and behaviors. *Journal of Business Ethics*, 38, 193–203.

Weiss, H. M., Suckow, K., & Cropanzano, R. (1999). Effects of justice conditions on discrete emotions. *Journal of Applied Psychology*, 84, 786–794.

Williams, M. L., McDaniel, M. A., & Nguyen, N. T. (2006). A meta-analysis of the antecedents and consequences of pay level satisfaction. *Journal of Applied Psychology*, 91, 392–413.

Implementation of Strategic Human Resource Management

PART 2

CHAPTER **8**

Staffing

Strategic Staffing at Kroger Supermarkets

Kroger Co. is currently the nation's largest supermarket chain with over 1,400 supermarkets, 200,000 employees, 500 convenience stores, 40 manufacturing plants, and $27 billion in annual sales. Faced with a constant need to hire new employees and with problems concerning the quality of new hires, Kroger set out to improve its selection processes. Kroger's goal was to enhance the effectiveness of its ability to hire and retain outstanding customer service employees. Its traditional structured interview approach was very time consuming. Numerous interviewers needed to be trained and certified, and each interview took an average of 45 minutes of management time. At the same time, Kroger faced pressures to develop a system that was efficient and cost-effective. The answer was a computer-based, self-administered employee selection system.

Kroger began by conducting a survey of its customers to gather information regarding customer perceptions of customer service. This information was then converted to scales that measured the knowledge, skills, and competencies that impact outstanding customer service. The end result—an employability index—was able to evaluate an applicant's thought process, management of job-related stress, self-control, and general job-related attitudes. The index was determined entirely by an online, interactive interview with applicants; a recommendation was then offered as to whether the individual should be offered a job. This innovative approach is designed to improve both effectiveness and efficiency by matching selection criteria with carefully chosen strategic objectives. Although the program has not been formally evaluated, Kroger has already determined the three criteria by which it will assess the program: customer service measures, turnover rate, and employee safety.[1]

S taffing, the process of recruiting applicants and selecting prospective employees, remains a key strategic area for human resource (HR) management. Given that an organization's performance is a direct result of the individuals it employs, the specific strategies used and decisions made in the staffing process will directly impact an organization's success or lack thereof.

Decisions made as part of the staffing process can have a significant impact on an organization's bottom line. One study found that 45 percent of companies calculated the cost of turnover at more than $10,000 per person, while 10 percent calculated it at more than $40,000 per person.[2] Turnover costs tend to rise as the level of the job and its complexity increase. In technology companies, the costs of turnover can be staggering. Agilent Technologies of Palo Alto, California, estimates an average turnover cost of $200,000 per departing employee and $250,000 per software engineer.[3]

The activities performed as part of recruiting and selection offer an organization numerous choices for finding and screening new employees. These options can have a significant impact on an organization's efficiency because some are much more extensive, costly, and time consuming than others. Organizations have great latitude to select from a variety of staffing techniques, each of which offers various degrees of sophistication and selectivity; however, such benefits come at a price.

In addition to the time and financial costs involved with staffing, many changes are taking place concerning how work is performed. Trends such as broader job scope and responsibilities, the move toward leaner staffing and operating with fewer full-time permanent employees, smaller autonomous units, pay for company-wide performance, and flatter organization structures affect the types of individuals and skills that organizations seek and influence how organizations find and screen applicants. The staffing process must be more strategically focused: Newer challenges and considerations must be directly incorporated into an organization's staffing strategy.

Staffing takes on even greater importance in the service sector, which continues to create the largest number of jobs in our economy. However, a service-based economy requires different skills and has higher turnover costs than those associated with manufacturing. In addition, payroll typically assumes a higher percentage of overall costs in service organizations. Companies in this traditionally high-turnover sector need strategic staffing initiatives that allow them to attract and retain productive employees, thereby minimizing operating expenses.

Probably most important is ensuring that employees fit with the culture of the organization. Technical skills alone do not guarantee high performance, particularly as organizations move toward process- and project-oriented work teams.

Recruiting

Temporary Versus Permanent Employees

When an organization needs to increase its headcount, the first strategic choice is whether to hire temporary or permanent employees. To do this, the organization must accurately forecast how long it expects the employee shortage to last. Temporary employees obtained from an agency usually cost more per hour to employ than permanent workers; however, unlike permanent employees, temporary employees are not paid when there is no work for them to do, particularly if they are hired on a project basis. Temporary employees are not provided benefits and cannot file claims for unemployment compensation when their employment ends. Temporary employees also provide flexibility for employers because payroll can be quickly and easily contracted during downturns without having to result in layoffs.

Staffing agencies, rather than the employer, are generally liable for the workplace injuries of temporary employees. As a result, despite the fact that temporary employees may be paid at a higher hourly rate than permanent employees, they can provide the employer with significant cost savings in light of the above facts.

The use of temporary employees has been increasing dramatically in recent years. During 2011, nearly 15 percent of the jobs added in the U.S. economy were staffed by temporary employees. Twenty-four percent of U.S. businesses with 100 or more employees, including the majority of

Fortune 500 employers, use temporary employees, and the rate of growth of use of such workers is expected to be twice the rate of overall job growth between 2008 and 2018.[4]

Care must be used, however, in determining whether temporary employees are actually "employees" of the organization that is contracting for their services rather than employees of the staffing agency. In 1997, Microsoft Corp. was accused of misclassifying thousands of present and past employees as temporary independent contractors rather than as Microsoft employees. A lower court ruled against Microsoft who appealed the decision but then settled the case for $97 million prior to the final ruling.[5]

In addition to hiring temporary employees from an agency, an organization can subcontract work to an outside vendor; this is usually done on a project basis. Larger organizations can also move permanent employees from department to department as needs dictate. This promotes efficiency through lower costs and flexible utilization of employees. These in-house "temporary" employees have more permanent status, including benefits; are generally more committed to the organization; and know the inside workings of the organization. They can be extremely useful when regular employees take extended vacation or sick leaves. In-house temporary employees provide the organization with more flexibility and efficiency than it would garner from outside temporary employees; also, in-house employees have more variety in their work assignments.

The use of temporary employees has greatly increased in recent years and to the point where an entire industry has been created for the employment of temporary workers. The "contingent workforce" industry involves 5.7 million workers, or 4 percent of the U.S. workforce.[6] Employees in almost every job category are now being considered and employed on a temporary-for-permanent basis without any promise or legal obligation for continued employment. Short-term temporary employment has also found its way into the executive ranks, including the CEO office.[7] Interim CEOs are typically retired or laid-off senior executives who wish to return to work for a limited time commitment to help a particular organization or contribute and build their résumés and professional networks while they seek more permanent employment. Similar to other levels of temporary employment, contingent executives can also allow a trial period of employment for consideration of permanent employment. Reading 8.1, "Temporary Help Agencies and the Making of a New Employment Practice," traces the rise of the temporary employment movement and explains its current uses and potential.

Internal Versus External Recruiting

If an organization decides to hire permanent employees, the first critical question it needs to address is whether to recruit internally or externally. Recruiting from the current employee pool can benefit the organization in a number of ways. First, the organization already has performance data on employees. Ample opportunity has been afforded to observe the applicant's work habits, skills and capabilities, ability to get along with others, and fit with the organization.

Second, promotion from within motivates employees. Employees feel that the organization is trying to provide them with promotional and developmental opportunities in reward for their performance and loyalty. Third, training and socialization time are reduced. Current employees know the organization, its procedures, politics, and customers and have already established relationships with coworkers. Consequently, they need far less formal or informal socialization time than those hired from the outside. Finally, internal recruiting is often much faster and far less expensive than going outside of the organization for applicants.

Internal Recruiting at Cisco Systems

Cisco Systems, Inc. is a San Jose, CA–based multinational designer and manufacturer of networking equipment. With more than 65,000 employees worldwide, Cisco has constant and evolving staffing needs as a leading global technology company. To assist with internal recruiting, Cisco has developed a program called Talent Connection, which seeks to identify qualified employees who might not necessarily be looking for another position in the company. Employees are encouraged to create profiles on an internal website that company recruiters can peruse to recruit internal candidates, much in the same way they recruit external candidates. To date, half of Cisco's employees have registered with Career Connection, and these internal "passive candidates" have saved the organization millions of dollars in search-firm fees and other recruiting costs while simultaneously raising employee satisfaction with career development opportunities by nearly 20 percentage points.[8]

Internal recruiting can provide significant productivity gains for employers as well. A recent study conducted at the University of Pennsylvania found that salaries received by external recruits are, on average, 18 percent higher than those paid to internal recruits. Perhaps more important, external recruits received lower performance reviews than internal recruits during their first two years on the job.[9] Another study that analyzed the 2,500 largest publically traded companies around the world found that chief executives recruited from the outside are twice as likely to fail and be forced out than those promoted from within.[10] This result is attributable to the fact that insiders typically have a strong ability to understand how to bring about change in an organization. As a result, insiders typically deliver better returns for shareholders.[11]

Although internal recruiting has advantages, this approach also has some disadvantages. First, internal recruiting can become very political and competitive, particularly when coworkers apply for the same position. Dysfunctional conflict may result, and collegiality and interpersonal relationships can be strained. Second, those employees not selected for the position can suffer from diminished morale and performance, particularly when they feel equally or better qualified than the candidate selected.

Third, the organization can become inbred through excessive internal recruitment. Continuing to promote from within can encourage maintaining the status quo. An organization that needs to improve organizational processes should usually recruit from the outside. Finally, excessive internal recruitment can cause inefficiency by creating multiple vacancies. For instance, if a senior-level manager leaves the organization and is replaced by a direct subordinate, that subordinate's job will then need to be filled. As this promotion chain continues down the hierarchy, an initial vacancy could spur promotions for a large number of people. Nearly all employees require a certain period of time to learn a new job. Even when an employee has worked in the organization for several years, a new position requires adjusting to new responsibilities and redefining interpersonal relationships with coworkers. Internal recruiting can exacerbate this effect by creating a large number of employees having new positions. Until these employees gain the level of competence that their predecessors had and sufficiently redefine their working relationships, inefficiency will result.

Internal recruiting has its advantages and disadvantages. It is probably best utilized when the organization pursues a strategy related to stability, faces few major threats from its external environment, and is concerned with maintaining the status quo relative to its operating systems. When time and/or money are limited, internal recruiting can also be beneficial.

External recruiting also has advantages and disadvantages. Not surprisingly, the advantages of external recruiting are consistent with the disadvantages of internal recruiting. External recruiting facilitates change and tends to be more useful for organizations with volatile external environments. External recruiting can allow an organization to expand its knowledge base beyond that of its existing employees and bring in new ideas and viewpoints; external recruits are not bound by existing ways of thinking or doing things. They can bring a fresh approach to problems that have plagued the organization. At the senior level, candidates are often recruited for their history of bringing about high-level change in other organizations.

External recruiting, however, can be expensive and time consuming. Employees from outside the organization will often need a longer socialization period to know the organization, its products or services, coworkers, and customers. External recruits are also unknown entities in that the organization has no experience working with them. Although an applicant may have outstanding skills, training, or experience and may have had past success in another organization, those factors do not guarantee similar success with a new organization or an ability to fit with a new organization's culture. Finally, external recruiting can have detrimental effects on the morale of those employees who have applied for the job internally but have not been selected. Exhibit 8.1 summarizes the strategic issues surrounding internal versus external recruiting.

EXHIBIT 8.1 — Advantages and Disadvantages of Internal and External Recruiting

	Advantages	Disadvantages	When Useful
Internal	Have performance data available	Possible politics	Stability strategy
	Motivation	"Loser" effects	Stable external environment
	Less training/socialization time	Inbreeding	Limited time and money
	Faster	Promotion chains	
	Less expensive		
	Advantages	**Disadvantages**	**When Useful**
External	Fresh ideas and viewpoints	Unknown entities	Need for change
	Expand knowledge base	Detrimental to internal applicants	Volatile external environment
		Training and socialization time	
		Time consuming	
		Can be expensive	

© Cengage Learning

When recruiting employees from outside the organization, employers have a variety of applicant sources from which to choose. Proper sourcing can save not only time and money but can also reduce the time it takes to have new employees actually on the job. A recent survey of recruiters found that the top five recruitment goals were (1) generating high-quality employment applications; (2) generating the best possible return on investment; (3) stimulating a desire to work for the organization; (4) filling specific positions; and (5) generating diversity.[12]

When recruiting externally, employers can utilize an active or a passive approach. Passive recruiting involves simply posting and/or advertising openings in selected communications media and "waiting" to see who applies as well as the overall composition of the applicant pool. Selected communications media are often chosen based on their target audience to assist the organization in communicating openings to and hopefully attracting a diverse applicant pool, often in support of mandated Equal Employment Opportunity Commission (EEOC) goals and guidelines. These efforts, however, have had mixed results in attracting both the best candidates and most diverse applicant pool. Active recruiting involves the targeting recruiting of specific individuals within professional networks to ensure the best and most broad pool of applicants. This is accomplished by reaching out to prospective applicants at professional conferences, industry trade shows, networking events, and other face-to-face venues as well as through social media. This personalized approach can also attract candidates who may not be actively looking for a new job as well as allow the employer to satisfy any EEOC requirements.

When and How Extensively to Recruit

Regardless of whether recruiting is done internally or externally, effective planning and strategizing are essential to the success of the process. An organization needs to know that it has the right employees with the right skills in the right places at the right time. This involves determining (1) how large an applicant pool is needed and (2) when recruiting efforts should begin. Both these questions can be answered by reviewing data from past recruiting efforts. A recruiting pyramid can be constructed by using yield ratios that show, traditionally, how many employees pass from one stage of the recruiting process to the next. This can help the organization determine how large an applicant pool to seek. An example of a recruiting pyramid is presented in Exhibit 8.2. In this

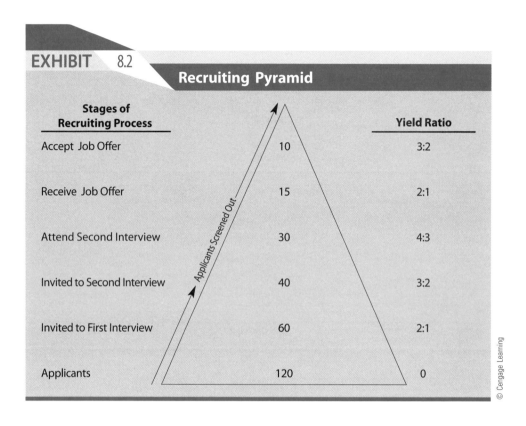

EXHIBIT 8.2 — Recruiting Pyramid

Stages of Recruiting Process		Yield Ratio
Accept Job Offer	10	3:2
Receive Job Offer	15	2:1
Attend Second Interview	30	4:3
Invited to Second Interview	40	3:2
Invited to First Interview	60	2:1
Applicants	120	0

Applicants Screened Out

© Cengage Learning

case, the organization could use historic yield ratios to determine how extensively to recruit. For example, if the organization is seeking 20 new employees, it should obtain 240 résumés.

An organization must determine when to begin its recruiting efforts to ensure that trained employees will be ready when the organization needs them. Timelines of past recruiting efforts can help the organization determine when to time its recruiting efforts. Here, an organization works backward from the time employees will be needed to determine when to begin recruiting. An example of a recruiting timeline is presented in Exhibit 8.3. In this case, the organization should begin recruiting 14 weeks before the intended start date.

One caveat must be issued concerning the use of recruiting pyramids and timelines. Because they are based on past recruiting data, they may need to be adjusted if labor market conditions have changed dramatically. Higher or lower unemployment, changes in the competitiveness of the industry, and/or the attractiveness of the employer vis-à-vis competitors might make the staffing process easier or more difficult than it had been in the past. Managers should assess how any changed conditions might impact the size of the applicant pool, the ratios, and the timeline.

Methods of Recruiting

Small organizations often do their recruiting very informally. Job openings or new positions may be communicated by word of mouth or by allowing the direct supervisor to find someone of his or her own choosing. Most larger organizations do their internal recruiting through some means of formal job posting. This process involves posting the available position where all employees have access, such as a physical or online bulletin board. Employees then decide whether they want to apply for any position.

When such a system is used and several people apply for the job, the detrimental effects of nonselection on employee morale can be minimized by providing nonselected employees with specific, objective feedback concerning the screening process. These employees should also be counseled

EXHIBIT   8.3

Recruiting Timeline

Stages of the Recruiting Process	Normal Time Taken to Complete
Candidate begins work	2 weeks
Acceptance of offer by candidate	1 week
Making an offer to candidate	1 week
Second interview cycle	1 week
Arranging second interviews	2 weeks
First interview cycle	1 week
Arranging first interviews	2 weeks
Screening résumés	2 weeks
Recruiting for position	3 weeks

© Cengage Learning

regarding how they might enhance their skills and experience if they plan to apply for future job openings. However, no guarantee or promise of appointment or promotion should be made.

If the organization maintains employee information in a computerized database, the skills inventory component of the HR information system can be used to assist in internal recruiting. The employee database can be searched for employees having skills, experiences, and personal qualities that are required for a job. This can save the organization a great deal of time in identifying strong internal candidates for a job. These candidates can then be contacted to determine their interest in a position.

External recruiting may also be done informally through contact with friends and acquaintances of existing employees; this process is usually limited to small organizations. However, informal recruiting tends to be the norm at the executive level. A recent survey found that 64 percent of executives found their jobs through peer networking.[13] Many job openings that are advertised are actually nonexistent because a desired candidate, either internal or external, has already been identified and applications are sought simply to create an applicant pool. This is particularly true at the middle-management level where approximately 50 percent of positions are filled by informal means.[14] In recent years, the number of CEOs who have been directly recruited from outside their organization has doubled.[15]

A primary source of recruiting for larger organizations is targeted advertising in selected media. In writing and designing a help-wanted ad, it is important to be accurate and specific and provide sufficient information about the position and organization to encourage applicants to apply. Interestingly, studies have shown that fewer than 20 percent of those who read help-wanted ads are actively looking for employment. Competitors, current employees, investors, stockbrokers and analysts, recruiters, and regulators also read such ads to gain information about organizations. Consequently, employers who use recruitment advertising need to take these audiences into account without losing sight of the need to attract strong applicants.

Recruiting on the Internet is one of the fastest-growing recruitment methods. More than 70 percent of HR professionals are using the Internet for recruiting.[16] Most found using the Internet more cost-effective than newspaper advertising.[17] Internet recruiting can be extremely effective in generating applicants because of its low cost, speed, and ability to target applicants with technical skills. A recent survey of undergraduate and graduate students found that 75 percent used the Internet for job searches.[18] Information on the organization is readily available, which allows applicants to assess their interests and needs with the employer's offerings. However, poorly designed or user-unfriendly Web sites can damage an organization's reputation and its ability to attract applicants. The same survey found that 25 percent of job candidates rejected a potential employer on account of its Web site.[19]

Because Internet recruiting is worldwide, it gives an employer global exposure to potential applicants, which can be critical if particular language skills or cultural backgrounds are needed. Technology-based employers have found the Internet to be a fertile recruiting ground for applicants who are technologically savvy. For example, Cisco Systems receives more than 80 percent of its résumés electronically.[20]

The main reason employers use the Internet for recruiting is to attract "passive job candidates," those who might not be actively seeking a new job. Eighty-four percent of employers stated that the recruiting of passive job candidates was the main reason they used the Internet, and particularly social networking sites, for recruiting. Cost-effectiveness and opportunities for employment branding, to be discussed later in this chapter, were given as secondary reasons for recruiting online.[21]

Interestingly, the strategies used by recruiters often do not fit the job search strategies being used by applicants. Networking, or the use of personal and professional contacts to obtain employment, is the strategy of choice for the majority of job seekers: Seventy-eight percent use this approach.[22] Sixty-seven percent of recruiters, however, find that the Internet is their top source for attracting new employees.[23] This is not to say that job seekers do not use the Internet, as they have been shown to utilize more search tactics than recruiters,[24] but, rather, implies that HR professionals need to think carefully about their recruiting sources and think strategically about how best to achieve the recruitment goals they have set.

Internet recruiting has become increasingly popular with employers and can cut the search process time by as much as 75 percent.[25] Sophisticated technology allows employers to quickly process large numbers of applications through the use of spiders, which are programs that search résumés for specific characteristics or words. One recent survey found that the percentage of large employers who utilize software programs to screen résumés was in the high 90 percent range.[26] Employers such as Starbucks, which received 7.6 million applications for employment in the past year, and Procter & Gamble, which received nearly 1 million applications for 2,000 vacancies during the same time period, need to place a heavy reliance on electronic screening of résumés. Such screening systems can be programmed to scan for keywords related to skills, experience, former employers, schools attended, or any other means by which an employer seeks to identify applicants with particular backgrounds and result in significant cost savings for the employer. A typical large employer spends approximately 7 percent of its recruiting budget on applicant screening and tracking systems.[27]

Many employers attempt to attract applicants by developing Web sites that provide information about the organization that can allow applicants to determine if there might be an optimal "fit" between their career goals and the goals of the organization, guide candidates through the application process, and even allow prospective applicants to take a virtual tour of the organization. While Internet recruiting can speed up the employment process, it is also fraught with some potential challenges that must be weighed by an organization considering Internet recruiting.[28]

The first of these challenges is ensuring security. Online recruiting means that the employer will be receiving electronic inquiries from unknown sources. Many of these communications will include attached files, making viruses a security concern; another consideration is ensuring that those visiting the Web site do not obtain access to unauthorized areas of the site. A second challenge is that overreliance on Internet recruiting can result in a disparate impact against certain protected classes of applicants. Studies have shown that members of certain ethnic minority groups, women, and older individuals either may not have access to or be less likely to use the Internet.[29] A survey conducted by the Society for Human Resource Management found that 95 percent of employers utilized LinkedIn to recruit job applicants.[30] Another recent study found that 85 percent of LinkedIn users are white and 63 percent are male.[31] Similarly, Facebook is used by 58 percent of employers to recruit candidates[32] and 78 percent of Facebook users are white.[33] Employers tend to use LinkedIn more for professional and managerial positions and Facebook more for hourly positions.[34] Individuals with disabilities may also have conditions that limit or prevent their ability to easily access the Internet as well.

Consequently, employers may unintentionally screen out large groups of potential applicants who are members of protected classes in the interest of the efficiency afforded by Internet recruiting. Finally,

Internet recruiting can complicate reporting of data related to compliance with federal and state laws. A difficult question arises as to whether an individual who sends an unsolicited résumé via the Internet needs to be "counted" and considered an "applicant" for the purpose of federal reporting. The EEOC and Office of Federal Contracts Compliance Programs (OFCCP) have continuously wrestled with the definition of "job applicant" for reporting purposes; combining this with the greatly increased number of job applicants that result from Internet recruiting creates a challenging situation for employers.

E-cruiting at Air Products and Chemicals, Inc.

One organization that has developed a satisfactory strategy for reporting its Internet recruiting activities to federal agencies is Air Products and Chemicals, Inc. (APC). Based in Allentown, Pennsylvania, APC supplies gases and chemicals to various industries as well as to the federal government. With 16,000 employees worldwide, including 9,000 in the United States, APC falls under the purview of the OFCCP as a government contractor. As APC began to use the Internet for recruiting with greater frequency, a conflict arose relative to its reporting with the OFCCP. The OFCCP considered résumés submitted electronically as an expression of interest in employment, and APC's reading of that résumé constituted acceptance of it, making the submitting party an "applicant" for reporting purposes. Because the organization could not control who submitted unsolicited résumés, it found itself at a disadvantage relative to its affirmative action goals. APC eventually solved the dilemma. Each unsolicited résumé received an automatic e-mail reply, instructing the individual to apply for a specific open position listed on the company Web site. Only when a position was chosen would the individual be considered an "applicant." In addition, applicants were required to submit information identifying their race and gender. This system met with the OFCCP's enthusiastic approval and has allowed APC to reap the benefits of Internet recruiting while satisfying the OFCCP's reporting requirements for federal contractors.[35]

An organization's existing employees can often be a very valuable source for recruiting new employees. Consumer products manufacturer Johnson & Johnson relies extensively on its employee referral program to recruit new hires. Johnson & Johnson offers up to $1,500 for each employee recruit, paid in full two weeks after the new employee's start date.[36] Hartford-based Lincoln Financial's referral program results in 55 percent of all external hires and saves the organization more than 97 percent of the costs it would incur by using an executive search firm.[37] One innovative approach to staffing has existing employees recruit themselves, as illustrated in the following vignette.

Staffing at St. Peter's Health Care

St. Peter's Health Care is an Albany, New York–based hospital that, like many healthcare institutions, suffered from a severe shortage of qualified nurses. Nurses hired from outside agencies to assume unstaffed shifts not only commanded a premium price but were also unfamiliar with operations and procedures at St. Peter's. To alleviate this problem, St. Peter's launched an online bidding system by which any nurse could bid for an open shift. Nurses must be existing employees or approved to work for the hospital and bid on shifts for a certain pay rate per hour. Nurse managers have the authority to accept or reject any bid, and applicants whose bids have been rejected are free to rebid at a lower pay rate. Because the hospital cannot mandate overtime for workers, this system allows maximum flexibility for both St. Peter's and nurse-employees. St. Peter's recently filled 43,400 available hours under the bidding system at an average pay rate of $37 per hour. Two-thirds of those hours were filled by existing employees. Outside agency nurses would have cost the hospital $54 per hour. In addition to the cost savings, turnover among nurses has decreased from 11 percent to below 5 percent annually, and both patient and employee satisfaction have increased.[38]

Organizations can also address their staffing needs by turning to other organizations and outsourcing all or part of their staffing. Employment agencies, more commonly called staffing agencies or staffing services, can locate and prescreen applicants for an employer. Because locating and prescreening applicants are often the most time consuming, expensive, and laborious processes for managers, many organizations are quite willing to use staffing agencies to perform these functions. In addition, the risk of running afoul of the law and having initial screening influenced by the biases of current employees is minimized because the staffing service is often able to bring a more objective perspective to the process.

In addition to traditional staffing agencies, there are several other kinds of organizations that may help an employer with external recruiting. The first of these are state job service agencies. State job service agencies are public funded by the federal government but are operated by individual states. All citizens who file unemployment compensation claims are required to register with the state job service agency and remain actively looking for work as a condition of receiving ongoing unemployment compensation. Employers can call and list positions with their state job service agency for no fee and, at the same time, assist those who have lost their jobs.

Another source of prospective employees is the Private Industry Council (PIC), a local agency that administers federal funds to assist individuals who are hard to employ in finding jobs. These individuals are generally those who depend on public welfare assistance but have either limited or no marketable job skills or lack the means to obtain appropriate training. Employers who are willing to train individuals for entry-level jobs can obtain assistance in locating such applicants from the local PIC. If the organization provides training and then subsequently hires the individual referred from the PIC for a permanent position, then the employer can seek partial reimbursement for the wages paid during the training period from the PIC. The PIC receives federal money for such reimbursement under the Job Training Partnership Act.

Executive search firms are a specialized type of staffing agency that assist organizations in filling skilled technical and senior- and executive-level management positions. Executive search firms usually charge significant fees for their services; these fees are paid by the employer. Searches are usually conducted for a contracted period of time and for a set fee, which is paid regardless of whether the search is successful. Estimates are that fewer than 50 percent of searches are successful during the contracted time period.[39]

Despite their relatively low rates of success, the services of executive search firms continue to be in demand because search firms provide employers with several benefits. First, search firms are usually better and faster than the organization's in-house recruiters in locating talent. The majority of search firms focus on specific industries, and they have extensive networks and numerous contacts. Consequently, they can locate and attract candidates who are not actively looking for new jobs. Although most employers would not directly call someone who works for a competitor to recruit that individual, an executive search firm can and does. The executive search firm can also keep the organization's identity confidential during the recruiting and prescreening process. Some organizations have hired executive search firms to contact their own employees in efforts to determine whether the employees might have any interest in leaving the organization. Although this kind of behavior may be unethical, it shows that executive search firms can offer an organization a means of secretly recruiting candidates. Finally, executive search firms will often, upon request, provide their client organizations with a written and signed "anti-raiding" agreement, whereby the search firm promises not to contact or recruit any of the organization's employees for a given time period in searches being conducted for other client organizations.

One recent study of executive search firms criticized their common practice of identifying potential recruits based on their job titles and the match of these titles with those for the positions being recruited rather than focusing on the skills of candidates and the responsibilities of jobs. As a result, many search firms promote only lateral moves, rather than placing recruits into new job functions or positions of increased responsibility. Similarly, search firms were found to limit applicant pools by focusing their recruiting on large, well-known, high-performing organizations.[40]

Outsourced Recruiting at Kellogg

Michigan-based cereal manufacturer Kellogg recently revamped its recruiting function for all its nonhourly employees. With more than 14,000 employees worldwide, coordination of the recruiting function had become cumbersome, prompting Kellogg to outsource its entire exempt recruiting operation. Because the industry is highly cyclical, Kellogg did not want to have to continuously hire and lay off recruiting staff and sought a system that was more flexible and better aligned with its business needs and strategy. When Kellogg needed to hire 200 new salespeople in a short time, the vendor was able to fill the positions much more quickly and efficiently than Kellogg would have been using its own staff and an outside search firm. The vendor's performance is overseen by a project manager at Kellogg and evaluated according to a variety of metrics, including cost, timeliness, quality of applicants, service to managers, and diversity. During the first year of implementation, the outsourced recruiting program saved Kellogg more than $1.3 million and reduced the average cost per hire by more than 35 percent.[41]

In contrast to Kellogg, an increasing number of larger organizations are bringing their executive recruiting functions in-house. Time Warner found that bringing their previously outsourced executive recruitment function in-house saved time, improved retention, and allowed its recruiters to better determine candidate "fit" with the company culture. It also has saved the organization more than $100 million in search firm fees in less than 10 years.[42] Sears Holdings, Hilton Worldwide, and PepsiCo, along with more than 25 percent of other *Fortune 500* companies, have all recently moved their executive search functions in-house, largely facilitated by the use of social media sites such as LinkedIn. Campbell Soup Co. saved more than $3.5 million by moving its executive recruiting in-house and cites the added benefit of ensuring that candidates who have been passed over remain on good terms with the organization.[43]

Many organizations use college and university on-campus recruiting as a means of attracting a relatively large number of qualified applicants. Campus recruiting can generate a large applicant pool in a short time period at a minimal cost and, therefore, create efficiency in the recruiting process. However, this can also create inefficiencies because of having to screen an excessively large number of applicants. Campus recruiting can often result in motivated, highly skilled, energetic applicants, but these applicants are usually available only at certain times of the year; they may also have very limited prior work experience. Success in the classroom does not necessarily translate to success in the workplace. Campus recruiting involves higher risk, given the practical inexperience of most applicants; however, there is a potential for higher return, given the intelligence, level of training, energy, and ambition that many applicants possess.

To alleviate some of the difficulties associated with campus recruiting, an increasing number of employers are offering co-op and/or internship programs. Such programs allow both the employer and student a trial period with no obligation. Employers have an advantage in recruiting interns for permanent positions; students gain marketable experience for their résumés. This experience can provide interns with an advantage when they apply for full-time employment upon graduation. Seventy percent of HR professionals prefer to hire a candidate who has an internship in the candidate's career field over an applicant who has more general experience.[44]

College Recruiting via Internships at Microsoft

Redmond, Washington–based Microsoft is one of the most sought-after employers in the world. The software giant receives upwards of 50,000 résumés a month and is clearly an "employer of choice" for many applicants. One way to heighten one's chances of obtaining employment with Microsoft is through interning at the organization. While the internship program itself is highly competitive, it provides Microsoft and interns with an opportunity to try each other out for a limited time period. Microsoft provides paid internships to approximately 800 college students each summer. After a rigorous screening process, fewer than 10 percent of applicants eventually end up with Microsoft for the summer. Those who are selected receive "competitive salaries," company-subsidized housing, training, and full benefits. Microsoft, with employee turnover at less than 6 percent, hires as much as 45 percent of its interns for permanent positions. Microsoft expects that after the 12-week internship concludes, each intern will be ready for permanent full-time employment.[45]

While internships are becoming increasingly popular among both employers and students, organizations need to be mindful of potential legal issues involving internships. The United States Department of Labor has taken the position that interns should be paid at least the federal or relevant state or local minimum wage by private section for-profit employers. Public section and nonprofit organizations are generally afforded greater latitude regarding compensation for interns, particularly if these workers are classified as "volunteers" or "trainees."[46] Such classification of workers is typically not found in the private, for-profit sector unless there is a partnership with an educational institution whereby the student receives academic credit and the skills being acquired can be used in a variety of employment settings rather than being specific to the organization providing the internship.

Employers also need to be wary of intentionally or unintentionally discriminating on the basis of age for internship applicants who may be older, particularly those who have lost their jobs and are seeking a career change or who have retired. Finally, employers of interns need to ensure that workers have the legal right to work in the United States and that their policies comply with federal and state immigration laws. This is particularly important as an increasing number of foreign students come to study domestically.

Selection

Once a sufficient pool of applicants has been recruited, critical decisions need to be made regarding applicant screening. Selection decisions can and do have significant economic and strategic consequences for organizations, and these decisions need to be made with great care. Before the application of any selection tools or criteria, the organization needs to determine if the methods being employed are both reliable and valid.

Reliability refers to the consistency of the measurement being taken. Ideally, the application of any screening criteria should elicit the same results in repeat trials. For example, if an applicant is asked to take a pre-employment test, the test should have consistent results each time it is administered to an applicant. Similarly, when different interviewers evaluate an applicant's ability to make spontaneous decisions, they should assess the applicant's skill level similarly. Consequently, in planning a screening process, the organization needs to ensure that there is reliability on two levels: across time and across evaluators.

Because many factors can impact assessment, 100 percent reliability is rarely, if ever, achieved. An individual might score poorly on a test on a given day because of a preoccupation with personal matters. Interrater reliability, which is the correlation among different judges who interview an applicant, is often low because these evaluators may bring different perceptions and biases to the process. However, low interrater reliability is not always bad. A supervisor might evaluate an applicant by using different criteria from those a subordinate might use. Such differences in perception are important in getting a holistic assessment of a potential employee.

Low reliability is often the result of one of the two types of errors in assessment. The first of these is deficiency error. Much as the name implies, deficiency error occurs when one important criterion for assessment is not included in the measure. For example, if the test for an applicant for an editor's position did not attempt to measure the applicant's writing ability, deficiency error would be present.

The second type of error is contamination error. Contamination error is caused by unwanted influences that affect the assessment. If an interviewer is under intense time pressure to complete other tasks and rushes the interview process so that it is impossible to gather sufficient information on a candidate, contamination error would result. Similarly, if a test measures knowledge, skills, or abilities that are not essential for the job and the evaluation of these noncritical factors impacts the ratings for the more important dimension, contamination error would result.

Reliability is a prerequisite for validity. A test cannot be valid without first being reliable. Validity refers to whether what is being assessed relates or corresponds to actual performance on the job. It examines whether the skills, abilities, and knowledge being measured make a difference in performance. Validity is critical not only to ensure proper selection, but it also becomes the chief measure by which employers defend discrimination allegations in court. Although no laws specifically require employers to assess the validity of their screening devices, illustrating that specific criteria are valid selection measures and are, therefore, job related is the major way for employers to respond to such claims.

There are two types of validity that support selection criteria. The first is content validity. Content validity illustrates that the measure or criterion is representative of the actual job content and/or the desired knowledge that the employee should have to perform the job. Content validity is determined through the process of job analysis, which is discussed in Chapter 6. For example, to receive a real estate license and work as a licensed salesperson or broker, an individual must pass an examination that tests knowledge of job-related concepts, activities, and processes. Content validity, in and of itself, does not guarantee successful performance on the job, much as completing a prerequisite course in a degree program does not guarantee successful completion of a later course.

The second validity measure is empirical, or criterion-related, validity. This measure demonstrates the relationship between certain screening criteria and job performance. If individuals who obtain higher scores or evaluations on these screening criteria also turn out to be high performers on the job, then this type of validity is established.

It is important to realize that reliability alone is not sufficient for determining the appropriate screening criteria. These criteria must also be valid. Validity not only ensures the best possible strategic fit between applicant and job, but it also ensures that the organization will have a readily accepted means of defending discrimination charges at hand. Criteria cannot be valid that are not already reliable. Conversely, criteria can be reliable without being valid. It is critical for decision makers to understand this difference and develop their screening criteria accordingly.

Interviewing

The first set of critical decisions in the selection process involves the interviewing process. Employers first need to determine who should be involved in interviewing applicants. A number of different constituents can provide input.

Prospective immediate supervisors, peers, and/or subordinates might be asked to participate in interviewing candidates. Coworker input can be critical in organizations that emphasize teams and project groups. The input of customers might also be sought, particularly for employers in service industries. Those involved in selecting appropriate interviewers must consider the different perspectives that different individuals or groups offer and the relevance of these perspectives for selecting the best applicant. Interviewers should be chosen from diverse racial, ethnic, age, and gender backgrounds. Another decision must be made as to whether interviews will be conducted in an individual or group format. Group interviews can save time for both the organization and applicant, but they often involve creating a less personal atmosphere for applicants. Group interviews may make it more difficult for interviewers to get a sense of the applicant's interpersonal style.

Interviewing applicants involves making subjective assessments of each applicant's qualifications for a job. However, interviewers commonly make interpretation errors that should be avoided in an effective interviewing process. Among these are similarity error, in which the interviewer has a positive disposition toward an applicant considered to be similar to the interviewer in some way; contrast error, in which the candidates are compared to each other during the interview process instead of the absolute standards and requirements of the job; first impression error, in which the interviewer immediately makes a positive or negative assessment of the candidate and uses the remaining interview time to seek information to support that contention; halo error, in which a single characteristic, positive or negative, outweighs all other dimensions; and biases that are based on the interviewee's race, gender, religion, age, ethnicity, sexual orientation, or physical condition rather than factors that relate to job performance.

One recent study examined the effects of interviewee behavior on the assessments made by those conducting interviews.[47] Two different interviewee behaviors, ingratiation and self-promotion, were examined related to interview outcomes. Ingratiation involves displaying behavior that is perceived to conform to the desires of the interviewer, while self-promotion involves the assertion of the interviewee's own strengths and competencies. The study found that ingratiation played a bigger role in interview outcomes than any other factor, including objective credentials. This added potential bias on the part of interviewers needs to be controlled to ensure the efficacy of the interview process.

Group interviewing allows different interviewers to compare and contrast their interpretations of the same interview information. Consequently, this often helps overcome many of the errors that individual interviewers might make.

One interviewing technique that has become increasingly popular in recent years is behavioral interviewing, which involves determining whether an applicant's anticipated behavior in a variety of situations and scenarios posed in interview questions would be appropriate for the employer. Behavioral interviewing can be used with experienced applicants as well as with those who have little or no professional work experience because it asks about situations the candidate might likely find him or herself facing on the job. Behavioral interviewing with candidates who have professional experience can also involve candidates presenting real-life situations in which they were involved and how they handled them.

To use behavioral interviewing, the first step is to determine the most important behavioral characteristics required for a given job or to work in a certain unit. These can be identified by examining the key traits displayed by high-performing incumbents. Behavioral interviewing assumes that candidates have already been screened for technical skills and focuses more on the human interaction traits and people skills an applicant would bring to a job. Questions might be what an applicant did in a certain past situation or might do in a given situation as well as things he or she most enjoyed, least enjoyed, and would opt to change about a given situation. Behavioral interviewing is used extensively by Dell Computer, AT&T, and Clean Harbors Environmental Services.[48] Dell collects data from 300 of its executives to determine the qualities most needed for success within the organization. AT&T has developed a series of behavioral questions that address the core competencies of organization, interpersonal communication style, decision making, and problem analysis. Clean Harbors, which specializes in cleanups of hazardous materials in the environment, looks for problem-solving ability, openness to new ideas, and enthusiasm.[49]

Behavioral interviewing generally reduces potential employer liability because of its focus on specific behaviors that are considered critical for effective performance. Typically, in asking interviewees to provide examples of behavior, job candidates might be asked to describe situations, explain actions taken and the reasons for such actions, and explain outcomes. Proper behavioral interviewing will involve all three dimensions of questioning: situations, actions, and outcomes. Exhibit 8.4 provides some examples of behaviorally based questions.

Regardless of who conducts the interviews and whether they are administered in a group or individual format, a decision needs to be made as to whether the actual format or process of the interviews should be structured or unstructured. Structured interviews follow a set protocol: All interviewees are asked the same questions and are given the same opportunity to respond. There is standardization in that it becomes easier to compare applicant responses to identical questions, and legal liability can be minimized because all applicants are treated the same. However, structured interviewing provides limited opportunity to adapt the interview process to any unique circumstances surrounding any applicant.

An unstructured interview is totally spontaneous and one in which questions are not planned in advance. The topics of discussion can vary dramatically from one candidate to another. Such a process allows interviewers to gain a greater sense of the applicant as an individual, but it often makes comparison among different candidates difficult. A semistructured interview would fall somewhere between these two extremes. With a semistructured interview, the interviewer asks

EXHIBIT   8.4

Sample Behavioral Interview Questions

Describe a situation in which you experienced conflict with a coworker (or supervisor).

Provide an example of your seeing a project from conceptualization to implementation and the challenges encountered.

Provide an example of a problem that you failed to anticipate.

Provide an example of a decision you made that you would make differently if given the opportunity again.

Describe a situation in which you had to manage a problem employee or confront a performance problem.

each candidate a set of standard questions. However, the interviewer can determine exactly which questions each candidate is asked and can be flexible and probe for specifics when answers are provided. Although structured interviews provide the greatest consistency, unstructured interviews provide the greatest flexibility. The organization must determine which is more important strategically. For example, in interviewing for jobs that require a great degree of creativity, the interviewer may wish to use a less-structured approach to determine how the applicant handles an unstructured situation. If it is critical to compare candidates closely across several criteria, a more structured approach might be more advantageous.

Regardless of interview structure, the selection process is aided when the interviewer asks specific, pointed questions. Asking candidates to describe behaviors they have engaged in or actions they have taken in specific situations is far more meaningful for assessment purposes than closed-ended "yes or no" questions. This strategy of behavioral interviewing has become increasingly popular in organizations. Candidates can and should be presented with scenarios they might expect to encounter on the job for which they are being interviewed and be asked how they would handle the situation. This can assist the organization in determining the fit between the applicant and organizational culture and processes. Interviewing by itself generally has relatively low reliability and validity. Consequently, it is critical to employ other criteria in the screening process to increase the likelihood of selection of the best applicants.

A number of employers are now utilized using virtual interviews as part of the screening process. Engaging in videochat sessions via Skype can allow organizations to interview candidates from a distance without incurring travel expenses or inconveniences associated with travel. More sophisticated platforms allow for recorded interviews, which can be reviewed or viewed by others in an organization. One survey found that the number of employers utilizing some kind of Web-based video interviewing jumped from 10 to 42 percent in a single year.[50] Juice and food producer Ocean Spray sends job candidates an e-mail link that invites candidates to respond to preset interview questions while being recorded on a webcam. This process allows consistency across candidates, illustrates more of the candidate's personality than a phone interview could provide and also allows the candidate to "interview" at a convenient time. It also saves the organizations a tremendous amount of time and money while also allowing more efficient processing and screening of applicants.[51] Wal-Mart uses a similar video interview process for its pharmacist candidates, allowing the employer to better assess a candidate's potential ability to interact with customers.[52]

Testing

Another critical decision in the selection process involves applicant testing and the kinds of tests to use. The needs of the organization and job structure (specific responsibilities, interpersonal relationships with others, and so forth) will determine whether any or all of the following should be assessed: technical skills, interpersonal skills, personality traits, problem-solving abilities, or any other job-related performance indicators. The key variable that should influence testing is job requirements. Any testing that is not specifically job related could be legally challenged, particularly if adverse impact can be shown.

The timing of testing can vary from organization to organization. Traditionally, testing has been conducted after the interviewing and screening process because of the expense of testing and time required to score and evaluate test results. However, some organizations are now testing earlier in the selection process because costs involved with interviewing often exceed the costs of testing. Clearly, it makes sense for an employer to use more cost-effective screening techniques earlier in the selection process.

Perhaps the most useful types of tests are work sample and trainability tests. Work sample tests simply involve giving the applicant a representative sample of work that would be part of the job and asking the individual to complete it. These tests are useful when the employer needs employees who will be able to perform job responsibilities from the first day of employment. Trainability tests measure an applicant's aptitude and ability to understand critical components of the job that the company may be willing to teach once the employee is hired. They are useful when the employer needs some familiarity with the nature of the work but seeks to train the new employee in the organization's way of doing things.

Both work sample and trainability tests can provide candidates with realistic job previews. Traditionally, organizations emphasized only the positive aspects of jobs during the recruiting process. This approach kept the applicant pool large and allowed the organization to reject the applicant, instead of vice versa. However, by hiding negative aspects of jobs, employers often hired individuals who became disillusioned once employed and left the organization shortly after hire. This results in a waste of both time and money and loss of efficiency. The idea behind realistic job previews is to make applicants aware of both the positive and negative aspects of the job. If the applicant is hired, the new employee has realistic expectations and is less likely to become dissatisfied with the job and quit. Realistic job previews also increase the likelihood of a candidate's self-selecting out of a position; however, this is in both the applicant's and employee's best interests. The predictive power of work sample and trainability tests for an appropriate fit between an applicant and job/organization has been found to be quite high.

Applicants might also be asked to provide samples of their previous work. A means of assessing the validity of collected information (such as samples of work and past work projects) also needs to be determined. Such work may be falsified. Its integrity can be verified by asking candidates detailed questions about its content or the process by which it was completed.

Other types of testing need to be administered very carefully. Personality testing often centers around what have been called the "Big Five" personality dimensions.[53] These traits are considered most relevant to performance in any kind of work environment. As illustrated in Exhibit 8.5, they

EXHIBIT 8.5

The Big Five Personality Dimensions

Personality Dimension	Characteristics of a Person Scoring Positively on the Dimension
(1) Sociability	Gregarious, energetic, talkative, assertive
(2) Agreeableness	Trusting, considerate, cooperative, tactful
(3) Conscientiousness	Dependable, responsible, achievement oriented, persistent
(4) Emotional stability	Stable, secure, unworried, confident
(5) Intellectual openness	Intellectual, imaginative, curious, original

are sociability, agreeableness, conscientiousness, emotional stability, and intellectual openness. Personality testing can be useful to anticipate how employees might behave, particularly on an interpersonal level, but personality tests can be problematic on two levels. First, personality testing has been successfully challenged in many courts because of the impact of certain questions on members of protected classes. Second, few, if any, jobs require one specific type of personality to ensure success. No employer has ever been able to argue successfully in court that a specific personality type or dimension was necessary for effective job performance. As a result, 82 percent of employers do not utilize personality testing in the hiring or promotion of employees. The few organizations that do utilize this testing tend to limit its use to mid-level managers and executives.[54]

Personality testing is easier to defend, however, when certain personality traits can be directly attributed to superior job performance and an absence of such traits attributed to poorer performance. Yankee Candle, based in South Deerfield, Massachusetts, asks each of its managers to complete a standard personality assessment and then compares the results with individual store performance. This has allowed the organization to develop a behavioral profile of high-performing managers, which considers traits such as sense of urgency, independence, motivation, communication style, and attention to detail, and becomes the basis for assessing applicants for future employment.[55]

Under the Americans with Disabilities Act, physical testing can be done only after a job offer has been made unless an employer can show that there are specific, critical physical requirements for job performance. The use of honesty testing has been declining since Congress passed the Employee Polygraph Protection Act in 1988. This Act, which prohibits such tests, is problematic and generally unreliable. Research has shown that employee theft is usually influenced more by factors external to the individual (pay inequity, working conditions, or abusive treatment from superiors) than internal factors, such as inherent dishonesty. Drug testing has been challenged in the courts under the legal doctrine of invasion of privacy; however, no federal right-to-privacy statutes prohibit testing of either on- or off-the job drug use by employees. Drug testing is, however, coming under increased scrutiny by the courts, and rulings favoring employers versus employees/applicants have been inconsistent. If any drug testing is conducted, those who sanction and administer the tests need to ensure that they do not unduly target members of protected classes.

Call Center Staffing at Capital One

Capital One is one of the largest suppliers of consumer MasterCard and Visa credit cards in the world, with more than 44 million cardholders and more than 20,000 employees. More than 75 percent of its employees are call-center customer service associates, and 3,000 new call-center employees are hired annually. The tremendous growth of the organization required that it develop a strategy for staffing its call centers that would recruit and retain the best individuals, reduce turnover and associated costs, and increase sales volume. After a three-year planning period, Capital One rolled out its company information-based strategy (IBS). A major component of IBS is the proprietary database software that allows Capital One to achieve its staffing goals. Applicants for call-center associate jobs can either call a toll-free telephone number and proceed through a battery of screening questions or answer the same questions online. These questions relate to the job characteristics deemed to be most critical to success as a call-center associate at Capital One. Those who receive acceptable scores are invited to a regional assessment center, where they undergo an average of five hours of additional computer-based tests and assessments spread over a two-day period. The IBS uses multiple technologies, including real-time automated decision making, simulations, and online videos. The IBS has decreased time-to-hire by 52 percent, increasing the rate at which Capital One can hire by 71 percent. Moreover, the system has resulted in a 12 percent increase in the number of calls handled per hour, a 36 percent increase in the rate of closing sales, an 18 percent decrease in unproductive downtime, and a 75 percent decrease in involuntary attrition during the first six months on the job.[56]

The most important criterion for determining whether testing will be effective and withstand any potential legal challenges is whether the testing is specifically related to the job for which an applicant has applied. Job relatedness is most commonly shown through validation of a specific test. There are three types of validation: content validity, criterion-related validity, and construct validity. Content validity involves the use of specific job requirements as a means of testing, where the applicant is tested on skills that will be used on the job. For example, an applicant for a bookkeeping or accounting position might be asked to post ledger entries or prepare a financial statement accurately. Criterion-related validity involves the testing of attributes that have been shown to correspond to successful performance on the job. For example, an applicant could be asked to complete a simulation based on actual experiences incumbents in the position have encountered. Construct validity is similar to criterion-related validity but focuses on traits, such as honesty and integrity, rather than on specific skills.

Simulation Testing at Toyota

In 2005, Toyota Motors needed to fill 2,000 jobs from tens of thousands of applicants for its new $800 million assembly plant in San Antonio, Texas. Applicants for these positions began their application process not via an application form or interview but, rather, at a computer screen, performing a job simulation. Skills such as the reading of dials and gauges, identification of safety issues, and assemblage of components and processes were measured as well as candidates' abilities to assess and solve problems and learn. Applicants were also provided with video links where they could actually see and hear about the jobs for which they were applying from current employees. Those who successfully completed the simulation were invited to return for a hands-on opportunity to demonstrate their skills. Online simulations such as these allow employers to make better hiring decisions, allow prospective employees a better sense of the reality of their jobs, and reduce both recruiting costs and employee turnover. Toyota estimates that the use of this screening process saved the organization $2.6 million associated with the opening of the San Antonio plant. The assembler testing process has been cited as a "best practice" at Toyota and is being used to assist with the opening of new plants in Canada and Europe. The simulation process is also being expanded for administrative jobs.[57]

References and Background Checks

Reference checking is usually part of the selection process; however, most prospective employers do little more than waste valuable time during this process. Generally, employers contact individuals whose names have been provided by the applicant, despite the fact that common sense dictates that an applicant would not submit a reference who would provide a negative recommendation. However, few employers bother to investigate the applicant's background any further. Employers can and should call individuals other than those named by the applicant. When contacting references the applicant has provided, requests can be made for additional contacts within or outside of the organization. Once an individual has worked within a given industry in a given geographical location for a few years, he or she becomes well networked within the local industry. These contacts can and should be used for checking references. There are often far fewer degrees of separation between an applicant and an employer than the employer might imagine.

Much like testing, reference checking was often done after the interviewing process and usually as the final step in the selection decision. More recently, however, many organizations have begun checking references prior to interviewing to allow them to eliminate candidates and gather information to be used later in the interviewing process.

One potential limitation with reference checking is that many past employers will not provide any information at all; they may do nothing more than verify the dates of employment, position held, and/or salary level. Increasing liability for libel, slander, and defamation of past employees has caused more organizations to adopt a policy of not commenting on past employees' employment history. This can be overcome at times through a well-established professional network, whereby individuals will confidentially tell those in other organizations whom they know and trust about a problem former employee.

Reference checking has become more critical for organizations because courts have been holding employers responsible for an employee's acts if the employer did not conduct a reasonable investigation into the employee's background. The doctrine of negligent hiring requires employers to balance an applicant's right to privacy, with the responsibility for providing a safe workplace for employees and customers. Fifty-five percent of employers cite the risk of legal liability for negligent hiring as a reason for checking references.[58] At the very least, the employer should verify all dates of employment and education and investigate any time gaps on an applicant's résumé.

In attempting to balance the need to avoid defamation suits brought by former employees with the need to avoid possible negligent referral charges for failure to warn another employer about a past employee's suspected potential to cause harm, employers are faced with a catch-22: Giving either too much or too little information can expose them to a lawsuit. As a public policy issue, many states have adopted laws that provide qualified immunity to an employer who provides reference information in good faith. Employers who knowingly provide false or misleading information are not immune from liability. To date, 35 states have enacted such legislation, which has been supported by the Society for Human Resource Management.[59]

Many employers also now check candidate backgrounds through social media sites. One survey found that more than 45 percent of recruiters admit to checking candidate profiles on social media sites and 70 percent of this group reports to having rejected a job applicant based on information the recruiter found online.[60] However, another survey found that the percentage of organizations that use any kind of online search engines to screen job candidates decreased from 34 to 26 percent from 2008 to 2011.[61] Using social media to check a candidate's background can be risky for several reasons. First, it might uncover information related to the protected class status of an applicant, which might not be known otherwise to the organization. Second, a social media search might uncover information that is irrelevant to the position for which the candidate has applied (and should not be considered) yet causes the applicant to be viewed in an otherwise more positive or negative manner. For example, the applicant may show an interest in certain outside hobbies or pursuits that are similar to those of the recruiter or engage in certain political activities that are at odds with the beliefs and preferences of the recruiter.

International Assignments

One final challenge that organizations face in staffing is selecting among current employees for overseas assignments. Traditionally, such assignments have been made based on past proven successes within the organization and the employee's work-related technical skills. Although technical ability is certainly a valid selection criterion, the main reason employees fail on international assignments has less to do with technical skills than with interpersonal and acculturation abilities. Lack of adaptation of not just the employee but the employee's family has caused problems for numerous organizations in their international operations as well as with relations with foreign officials, customers, and business partners.

Organizations are now realizing that assessing the technical backgrounds of such employees is merely an initial screening criterion. To ensure the success of overseas assignments, employers are increasingly testing employees' adaptability, open-mindedness, ability to tolerate uncertainty and ambiguity, and independence. Similarly, many are also interviewing and screening family members who would be accompanying the employee on the assignment. In certain cases, the employee is able to adapt, but problems with family members adapting either require the employee to return home before the end of the assignment or have a negative impact on the employee's performance. Screening employees as part of staffing international operations has consequently become much more elaborate and strategic to ensure the success of the assignment.

As the economy and workforces have become more diverse and global, organizations have developed a much heightened interest in assessing how well an individual might function in an increasingly global and multicultural work environment. Consequently, a large number of assessment tools have been developed that attempt to measure an individual's adaptability, cultural sensitivity, and values. These instruments are useful not only for employees who are being considered for international assignments but also for domestic employees in organizations that have global customer and/or employee bases and/or value an understanding of and appreciation for cross-cultural sensitivity. Reading 8.2, "Assessment Instruments for the Global Workforce," identifies and explains 18 different tools for measuring these traits and qualities in individuals.

One significant challenge with international staffing involves the sourcing and acquisition of talent in emerging economies. The tremendous potential for growth in the economies of countries such as Brazil, Russia, India, and China has set off a near-frenzy of organizational entry into these markets. However, in many cases, the demand for workers with certain skills exceeds the supply available locally. Economic activity in the emerging "BRIC" (Brazil, Russia, India, and China) economies is experiencing 40 percent annual compounded rates of growth, compared to 2–5 percent in the west and Japan. The competition for talent in these markets is intense, and employees there are experiencing employment choices and have high career expectations for the first time in their lives. Employers who simply try to export their domestic talent to these locations often experience abysmal results.

Those organizations that are to be the most successful in attracting and retaining talent in such markets need to focus on four means of distinguishing themselves as employers to attract talent. These means are purpose, brand, culture, and opportunity.[62] Purpose involves a strong guiding mission and values, evidence of global citizenship, and a perceived commitment to the region and its people. Brand involves a reputation for global reputation for excellence and inspirational leadership. Culture involves transparency of operations and processes and a merit- and talent-based recognition system. Opportunity involves challenging work, accelerated career tracks, continuous opportunities for training and development, and competitive compensation practices.

Documentation of Employment Eligibility

One of the chief challenges employers face in the hiring of low-skilled employees is ensuring that applicants have the legal right to work in the United States. Because there is no widespread, reliable system for verification of the legitimacy of documentation an applicant might provide, employers have to utilize extra caution in hiring. If documentation is suspect but later found to be valid, an employer can face unlawful discrimination charges. On the other hand, in spite of stiffer penalties and increased enforcement of worker eligibility, some employers feel that they have no choice but to hire illegal immigrants because of the unduly slow process associated with obtaining work visas vis-à-vis the employer's need for employees. This is particularly true in industries such as agriculture and hospitality and seasonal businesses that rely on large numbers of foreign employees.

Employers who wish to hire foreign workers who have not obtained citizenship first need to prove that there are no domestic workers with the skills and availability to perform the responsibilities of a given job and that the employment of foreign workers will have no adverse impact on wages and working conditions. Even once an employer decides to hire a foreign employee whose documentation appears to be valid, verification of the authenticity of the documentation by the Social Security Administration can take months.

It is estimated that there are more than 11 million foreign individuals working illegally in the United States and that these individuals account for nearly 5 percent of the U.S. labor force.[63] In many instances, these individuals work in low-skilled jobs that are being shunned by an increasingly educated U.S. citizenry. In 1960, 50 percent of employees in the United States had not completed high school; currently, that figure is less than 10 percent.[64] Simply deporting such workers, even if were logistically possible, would decimate certain sectors of our economy. The economic arguments both in favor of and against the employment of illegal workers are compelling. These individuals tend to pay less in taxes than the financial burdens they impose on services such as medical care and education. However, they also contribute billions of dollars annually into the

Social Security system, for whose benefits they are ineligible. They also pay state and local sales and properly taxes in the communities in which they reside.

While the political and economic debates concerning foreign workers will continue, this area of employment provides both tremendous opportunities for employers to fill their ranks with low-skilled workers for whom there is a demand, but at the same time, ensuring the legality of such individuals' employment status is fraught with delays, possible penalties, and ambiguity. Employers need to carefully and strategically monitor employment of foreign workers as well as maintain their currency in the relevant and evolving laws and regulations in this area.

New Trends in Staffing

Three notable trends are taking place in organizations related to their staffing programs. The first of these is employment branding. Employment branding involves the creation of an image of the organization as an employer, much like an organization may attempt to create a brand around its products and services. An employer's employment brand involves the dissemination of information that allows current and prospective employees as well as the business community to perceive the organization in a certain way. Numerous "best" lists are published each year, which employers strive to be a part of, including best employers for women, older workers, workers with disabilities, gay and lesbian employees, working mothers, and so on. Organizations may brand themselves through their advancement opportunities, higher-than-market compensation, flexible work arrangements, prestige of the employer's reputation, or the organization's social consciousness. Branding initiatives generally involve an attempt to make an employer the "employer of choice" for at least a certain segment of the workforce.

Employers create an employment brand by first making a candid assessment of their strengths as an employer. Employee satisfaction and attitude surveys can provide data as to what aspects of their employment current employees most value. Applicant cover letters can also contain information regarding why applicants seek employment with a given organization. Once these factors have been identified, employers need to consider if they are currently attracting the applicant pool they seek to employ. If not, surveys can be conducted to determine why desired applicants are not seeking employment with the organization.

Once this information has been collected, an employer can then develop its message for prospective employees regarding what the organization is and what it aspires to be. Follow-through requires careful oversight and management of the organization's culture, mission, and employment policies and practices. A critical part of an organization's employment branding is its culture, particularly relative to relationships, authority, and accountability.[65] Meetings and interviews with prospective employees should communicate the organization's culture as part of the employment brand. Ideally, strong employment branding combined with effective recruitment and selection processes should result in higher retention rates, lower overall recruitment costs, and improved company image.

Employment Branding at W. L. Gore

In 2010 Newark, DE–Delaware–based W. L. Gore and Associates launched a global branding campaign designed to attract the most qualified professionals in medical research, engineering, and other technical fields to the organization. Using the theme "join Gore and change your life," Gore developed a platform on the Careers section of its website for its existing employees to tell individual stories concerning how the products they have personally helped to design and market have changed lives. Included with these stories is information about the hierarchy-free environment of the workplace and the organization's culture and key values, which combine to create a workplace with no job titles. The bottom line message is that working at Gore allows individual to make a difference in the lives of others as well as make the world a better place.[66]

The second trend in staffing is candidate relationship management (CRM). CRM involves building a relationship with job applicants that transcends the current hiring cycle and process. Similar to employment branding, CRM is designed to engage candidates in an ongoing manner and heighten the image of the organization as a desirable place to work. It may be the case that a position is not available for a strong candidate at the time of candidate inquiry, there may be more desirable candidates than there are current openings, or a candidate may have personal circumstances that prevent acceptance of an offer of employment at a particular point in time. CRM involves the creation of an ongoing relationship with potential employees that can be capitalized on when a position becomes available within the organization and/or the candidate becomes available. The end result of this activity is the creation of a pipeline of talent that remains interested in and available for employment with an organization over time.

CRM activities usually center on the creation and maintenance of a database of possible candidates for employment as well as regular communication with these individuals to keep them engaged and their interest level elevated. Many CRM activities parallel those that organizations have developed with key customers to maintain and nurture the client relationship. Prospective employees can be sent e-mails, newsletters, links to blogs, birthday cards, and other correspondence to keep the organization in the forefront of their minds. Such activities tend to be extremely cost-effective relative to later savings realized in terms of both time and direct out-of-pocket recruiting expenses.[67]

CRM at Whirlpool

Whirlpool Corporation is a global manufacturer of major home appliances under brand names that include Maytag, Amana, KitchenAid, and Jenn-Air. Candidate recruiting at Whirlpool is treated as an opportunity to market both the organization and its product lines. Every job candidate is an existing or potential customer, so Whirlpool's Exceptional Candidate Experience (ECE) program was designed to develop both the employer brand and customer loyalty.

The ECE involves a three-stage process—initial candidate touch points, candidate engagement, and candidate closings—with the goal of providing an exceptional experience to ensure that the candidate leaves with a positive impression of the organization, regardless of whether an offer of employment is made. The first stage-initial candidate touch points focuses on consistent, positively branded messages about the organization and its products, which are designed to create an inviting image. Candidate engagement ensures that every candidate is treated warmly and engaged during the interview process. This includes gifts of Whirlpool products in appreciation for the time candidates spend during the interview process. The final stage—candidate closings—attempts to ensure that all job candidates remain customers for life, regardless of the outcome of the interview.

Whirlpool realizes that prospective and existing employees have many choices for employment and that top performers have near-limitless choices. The ECE is designed to ensure that Whirlpool is not only successful in recruiting the best available talent but that the process also creates ambassadors of the company and its products.[68]

CRM activities go beyond simply engaging current and prospective applicants in seeking to attract applicants from unconventional places. Two commonly overlooked sources of employees are customers and former employees. Recruiting employees from an organization's customer base can be convenient, cost-effective, and result in highly qualified, enthusiastic employees who already believe in the organization and its products or services. Targeting customers who may not currently be on the job market can increase both the quantity and quality of the employer's applicant pool. Existing customers have experience with the organization's products and services and can provide additional insights into the development and marketing of the organization's offerings. A perennial favorite on *Fortune* magazine's "TOO Best Companies to for Work For" list is The Container Store, which recruits employees almost exclusively from its customer base.[69]

A number of organizations are increasingly utilizing former employees as a target applicant pool. This activity has been prompted by a fundamental shift in the employment relationship from the traditional, long-term "loyalty" paradigm to one that is more short-term and transactional in nature.[70] Former employees can be a valuable resource to an employer, given that they know the organization's products/services, culture, market, and customers. Many employers are also creating alumni networks for former employees, keeping these individuals in touch via social events and written and electronic communications. Former employees can be similar to internal hires in that they result in lower recruiting costs and a shortened time-to-hire cycle, given that they are known entities within the organization. Former employees can also bring a heightened sense of the marketplace, depending on their interim employment. Former employees also tend to be more productive because of the loyalty and goodwill created by the employer as part of the re-employment decision.[71] Returning employees have higher retention rates than other employees, and re-employment also allows employers to recoup some of the training and development costs of these former employees as well as benefit from any additional training and skill development that the employee has obtained since leaving the organization.[72]

CRM has another important dimension: public and customer relations. Job candidates who have a negative experience as part of the application process can affect an organization's sales and reputation. One recent survey found that 8 percent of job applicants who had a negative experience with an organization had sufficient anger and resentment to cause them to end their relationship with the organization as customers and share this resentment with others.[73] Job applicants may resent the fact that the organization considers them "good enough" to be a customer but not so as an employee. CRM, particularly in those organizations who market directly to consumers, need to ensure that all job applicants, particularly those who were not hired, are treated with respect throughout the application (and rejection) process.

The third trend in staffing is a heightened awareness of fit between an applicant and the organization's culture. An increasing number of employers are using various types of assessments in screening employees to determine whether there is an optimal "fit" between an applicant's interpersonal style and preferences for certain types of work environments and the organization's culture. One recent study found that more than half of hiring managers ranked fit as more important to their hiring decisions than either analytical thinking of communication skills, citing its positive impact on retention.[74] Assessments can take various forms including complex surveys, in-depth questioning, and spending extended periods of time with prospective coworkers. They can also involve simple questions such as "if you could be any superhero, who would it be?" (AT&T), "what color best represents your personality?" (Johnson & Johnson), "what animal are you?" (Bank of America), and "describe your perfect last meal" (Whole Foods).[75]

Assessments for fit can allow job candidates to self-select out of the application process and help to avoid some of the above-mentioned issues, which can be associated with candidates who are not selected by the employer. While these assessments can become an important part of an organization's staffing strategy, they run the risk of having employers select candidates who might not be the most skilled or talented applicants. On the other hand, fit is a stronger predictor of retention than skills and can result in significant savings for an employer relative to recruiting and orientation or onboarding costs. Online retailer Zappos doesn't assess job candidates for fit but realizes its importance in creating a high-performance work environment. As a result, the organization will offer new employees who might be struggling $40004,000 to resign after a week of employment rather than continue to invest in training an employee who simply doesn't get along with coworkers.[76]

The potential downside to "hiring for fit" is the risk that hiring managers and employees may be biased in favor of candidates who are similar to themselves. Diversity initiatives may be thwarted by assessing and measuring how well an individual fits in. Innovation, creativity, and suggesting new and better ways of doing things can also be derailed if the process of hiring for fit is blind toward the developmental needs of the organization and some of the specific employee skills that may be needed to accomplish strategic objectives. Numerous studies have documented the benefits and competitive advantages that diverse workforces provide to employers. Diverse workforces have also been shown to produce an average of 15 times more sales revenue than those that are less diverse.[77] Hiring for fit and promoting diversity need not be at odds with each other if the organization's culture stresses the value of a diverse work place and incorporates these considerations when determining "fit." In asking nonjob-related questions regarding personal out-of-work activities, favorite vacation spots, and so on, employers can show preference toward non-typical responses in light of the contribution this diversity might provide to the organization's culture and its performance.

Conclusion

An organization can only be successful and reach its strategic objectives by employing individuals who have the capacity and desire to contribute to its mission. The staffing function, therefore, plays an important role in facilitating an organization's success. When unemployment is low, organizations face even greater challenges in staffing because the forces of supply and demand drive wages up and provide greater career opportunities with other organizations.

An effective staffing strategy requires in-depth planning for the recruiting process to ensure efficiency and generation of a qualified applicant pool. How selection will proceed relative to the process and the kinds of applicant information needed must also be determined. The strategic decisions organizations need to make relative to staffing are summarized in Exhibit 8.6. Staffing is the key or core component that forms the backbone of an integrated, strategic system of HR

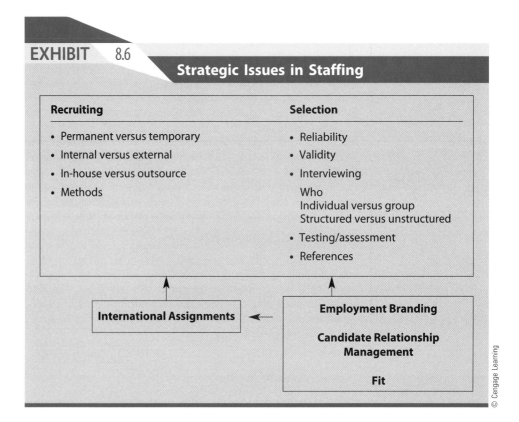

EXHIBIT   8.6

Strategic Issues in Staffing

Recruiting	**Selection**
• Permanent versus temporary	• Reliability
• Internal versus external	• Validity
• In-house versus outsource	• Interviewing
• Methods	Who
	Individual versus group
	Structured versus unstructured
	• Testing/assessment
	• References

International Assignments ← **Employment Branding**

Candidate Relationship Management

Fit

© Cengage Learning

management by ensuring that there is an optimal fit between employees and the strategic needs of the organization. If an organization's staffing is deficient, the effectiveness of its HR programs and policies will be impaired. As one HR professional commented, "Good training will not fix bad selection."

Critical Thinking

1. How does an organization's investment in staffing benefit the organization after an applicant becomes an employee?

2. What problems can result from cutting corners to save time or money in the staffing process?

3. What are the major strategic choices an organization faces concerning staffing? What are the advantages and disadvantages of each alternative?

4. What are the pros and cons (from the employer perspective) of conducting executive searches in-house versus outsourcing the function? What are the pros and cons of internal versus external executive search from the applicant's perspective?

5. Devise a staffing strategy for the following organizations:

   • A church-based soup kitchen staffed with volunteers
   • A professional baseball team
   • A small Internet startup
   • A publisher of a large daily newspaper in a major city
   • A police department
   • A 400-room luxury hotel

6. Develop a set of behaviorally based interview questions for the following jobs:

   • High school principal
   • Nursing supervisor
   • Factory foreman
   • Chief medical resident
   • Police chief

7. Discuss the challenges organizations face associated with the employment of foreign workers.

8. How might an employer create an employment branding strategy?

9. What are the pros and cons of establishing a CRM program?

10. What are the pros and cons of hiring for "fit?" How can an employer best ensure that new employees will fit with the company culture while simultaneously managing diversity and ensuring that the most qualified candidate will be hired?

Reading 8.1

11. Evaluate the future potential and possibilities for the contingent employment market and industry.

Reading 8.2

12. What types of positions in what types of industries might each of the eighteen inventories be used to assess?

Exercises

1. Visit a major employer's Web site (such as those provided here or any others). Apply for a specific job with the same company both via online means and through submitting a résumé by postal mail. Compare and contrast the processes. As an applicant, which did you find preferable and why?

Cisco Systems	http://www.cisco.com
GE Energy	http://www.gepower-careers.com
Advanced Micro Devices	http://www.amd.com
Booz Allen Hamilton	http://www.bah.com
Bank of America	http://www.bankofamerica.com
Hewlett-Packard Computer	http://www.hp.com
Eastman Kodak	http://www.kodak.com
Specialized Bicycles	http://www.specialized.com

2. In small groups, discuss your experiences with and determine the pros and cons of online recruiting from the employer's perspective.

3. Develop a behavioral interviewing protocol for your current or most recent job.

Chapter References

1. Murphy, T. E. and Zandvakili, S. "Data- and Metrics-Driven Approach to Human Resource Practices: Using Customers, Employees and Financial Metrics," *Human Resource Management*, 2000, 39, (1), pp. 93–105.

2. Joinson, C. "Capturing Turnover Costs," *HR Magazine*, July 2000, 45, (7), pp. 107–119.

3. Ibid. p. 118.

4. Grossman, R. J. "Strategic Temptations," *HR Magazine*, 57, (3), March 2012. Available at http://www.shrm.org/Publications/hrmagazine/EditorialContent/2012/0312/Pages/0312grossman.aspx

5. *Vizcaino v. Microsoft Corp.*, 120 F.3d 1006 (9 Cir. 1997).

6. Tyler, K. "Treat Contingent Workers with Care," *HR Magazine*, 53, (3), March 2008, pp. 75–79.

7. Frase-Blunt, M. "Short-term Executives," *HR Magazine*, 49, (6), June 2004, pp. 110–114.

8. Silverman, R. E. and Weber, L. "An Inside Job: More First Opt to Recruit From Within," *Wall Street Journal*, May 30, 2012, B1.

9. Ibid.

10. Kwoh, L. "Chief Executives Hired Internally Outlast, Outperform Their Rivals," *Wall Street Journal*, May 30, 2012, B8.

11. Ibid.

12. McConnell, B. "Recruiting How-tos as Important as Who-tos, SHRM Survey Reveals," *HR News*, December 2002, pp. 2, 5.

13. Miraz, P. "Networking: An Executive Recruiter's Best Friend," *HR Magazine*, September 2000, 45, (9), p. 22.

14. Weber, L. and Kwoh, L. "Beware the Phantom Job Listing," *Wall Street Journal*, January 9, 2013, B1.

15. Miraz, P. "Where Are All the Home-Grown CEOs?," *HR Magazine*, September 2000, 45, (9), p. 22.

16. Leonard, B. "Online and Overwhelmed," *HR Magazine*, August 2000, pp. 37–39.

17. Ibid.

18. Leonard, B. "Job Candidates Judge Employers by Their Web Sites," *HR Magazine*, July 2000, 45, (7), pp. 30–31.

19. Ibid.

20. Martinez, M. N. "Get Job Seekers to Come to You," *HR Magazine*, August 2000, 45, (8), pp. 45–52.

21. Schramm, J. "The Rapid Rise of Social Media as a Recruiting Tool," *Society for Human Resource Management*, Workplace Visitions, 2, 2012. Available at http://www.shrm.org/research/futureworkplacetrends/documents/12-0331%20workplace%20visions%20issue%202%202012_fnl.pdf

22. "Networking Rules, Say Job Seekers and Employers," *HR News*, 20, (5), May 2001, p. 2.

23. Leonard, B. "Job-Hunting Professionals Rank Networking over Internet," *HR Magazine*, May 2002, 47, (5), pp. 25–26.

24. "Networking Rules, Say Job Seekers and Employers," *HR News*, 20, (5), May 2001, p. 2.

25. McConnell, 2002, op. cit.

26. Weber, L. "Your Resume vs. Oblivion," *Wall Street Journal*, January 24, 2012, B1.

27. Ibid.

28. Grensing-Pophal, L. "The Perils of Internet Recruiting," Available at www.shrm.org.hrresources.whitepapers_published/CMS_000408.asp

29. Ibid.

30. SHRM Research Spotlight: "Social Networking Websites and Staffing," *Society for Human Resource Management*, June, 2011 Available at http://www.shrm.org/research/surveyfindings/articles/pages/socialnetworkingwebsitesforidentifyingandstaffingpotentialjobcandidates.aspx

31. Huntley, D. "Proceed with Caution When Recruiting Online," *Society for Human Resource Management*, July 14, 2011. Available at http://www.shrm.org/hrdisciplines/technology/articles/pages/socialrecruiting.aspx

32. SHRM Research Spotlight, op. cit.

33. Huntley, 2011, op. cit.

34. Wright, A. D. "Social Recruiting Goes Viral," *Society for Human Resource Management*, March 12, 2012. Available at http://www.shrm.org/hrdisciplines/technology/articles/pages/socialrecruitingviral.aspx

35. Roberts, B. "System Addresses 'Applicant' Dilemma," *HR Magazine,* September 2002, 47, (9), pp. 111–119.

36. Martinez, M. N. "The Headhunter Within," *HR Magazine,* August 2001, 46, (8), pp. 48–55.

37. Ibid.

38. Robinson, K. "Online Bidding Fills Nursing Jobs," *HR Magazine,* December 2003, 48, (12), p. 44.

39. Fisher, C. D., Schoenfeldt, L. F. and Shaw, J. B. *Human Resource Management,* 4th ed. Boston, MA: Houghton Mifflin Co, 1999, p. 274.

40. Hamori, M. "Who Gets Headhunted—And Who Gets Ahead?" *Academy of Management Perspectives,* November 2010, pp. 46–59.

41. Martinez, M. N. "Recruiting Here and There," *HR Magazine,* September 2002, pp. 95–100.

42. Lublin, J. S. "More Executive Recruiting Shifts In-House," *Wall Street Journal,* October 10, 2012, B8.

43. Ibid.

44. Taylor, S. "The Lowdown on Internship Programs," *HR Magazine,* November 2010, 55, (11), pp. 46–48.

45. Hirsh, S. "Software King Builds Young Careers, Too," *Baltimore Sun,* March 9, 2003, p. 1 D.

46. Thornton, G. R. "Employing Interns," *Society for Human Resource Management,* July 14, 2011. Available at http://www.shrm.org/templatestools/toolkits/pages/employinginterns.aspx

47. Higgins, C. and Judge, T. "The Effect of Applicant Influence Tactics on Recruiter Perceptions of Fit and Hiring Recommendations: A Field Study," *Journal of Applied Psychology,* 89, (4), pp. 622–632.

48. Poe, A. C. "Graduate Work," *HR Magazine,* October 2003, 48, (10), pp. 95–100.

49. Ibid.

50. Zielinski, Dave. "The Virtual Interview," *HR Magazine,* July 2012, 57, (7), pp. 55–57.

51. Ibid.

52. Ibid.

53. Goldberg, L. R. "An Alternative 'Description of Personality': The Big-Five Structure," *Journal of Personality and Social Psychology,* 59, (6), December 1990, pp. 1216–1229.

54. SHRM Poll: Personality Tests for the Hiring and Promotion of Employees. *Society for Human Resource Management,* December 16, 2011. Available at http://www.shrm.org/research/surveyfindings/articles/pages/shrmpollpersonalitytestsforthehiringandpromotionofemployees.aspx

55. Krell, E. "Personality Counts," *HR Magazine,* 50, (11), November, 2005, pp. 47–52.

56. Romeo, J. "Answering the Call," *HR Magazine,* October 2003, 48, (10), pp. 81–84.

57. Winkler, C. "Job Tryouts Go Virtual," *HR Magazine,* 51, (9), September 2006, pp. 131–134.

58. Meinert, D. "Seeing Behind the Mark," *HR Magazine* February 2011, 56, (2), pp. 31–37.

59. "SHRM Board Oks Investment Advice, Safety, Reference Positions," *HR News,* May 2002, p. 11.

60. Meinert, 2011, op. cit.

61. "The Use of Social Networking Websites and Online Search Engines in Screening Job Candidates," *Society for Human Resource Management,* August 25, 2011. Available at http://www.shrm.org/research/surveyfindings/articles/pages/theuseofsocialnetworkingwebsitesandonlinesearchenginesinscreeningjobcandidates.aspx

62. Ready, D. A., Hill, L. A. and Conger, J. A. "Winning the Race for Talent in Emerging Markets," *Harvard Business Review,* November 2008, pp. 63–70.

63. Ladika, S. "Trouble on the Hiring Front," *HR Magazine,* 51, (10), October 2006, pp. 56–61.

64. Ibid.

65. Brandon, C. "Truth in Recruitment Branding," *HR Magazine,* 50, (11), November 2005, pp. 89–96.

66. Fleck, C. "Not Just a Job," *Staffing Management,* 6, (1), April 1, 2010. Available at http://www.shrm.org/Publications/StaffingManagementMagazine/EditorialContent/Pages/0410fleck.aspx

67. Frase, M. "Stocking Your Talent Pool," *HR Magazine,* 52, (4), April 2007, pp. 67–74.

68. Weirick, K. "The Perfect Interview," *HR Magazine,* 53, (4), April 2008, pp. 85–88.

69. Arnold, J. "Customers as Employees," *HR Magazine,* 52, (4), April 2007, pp. 77–82.

70. Pulley, J. "When the Grass Wasn't Greener," *Staffing Management,* 2, (3), September 2006. http://www.shrm.org/Publications/StaffingManagementMagazine/EditorialContent/Pages/0607_pulley.aspx

71. Weaver, P. "Tap Ex-Employees' Recruitment Potential," *HR Magazine,* 51, (7), July 2006, pp. 89–91.

72. Pulley, 2006, op. cit.

73. Weber, L. "Angry Job Applicants Can Hurt Bottom Line," *Wall Street Journal*, March 14, 2012, B8.

74. Rivera, L. A. "Hiring as Cultural Matching: The Case of Elite Professional Service Firms," *American Sociological Review*, 77, (6), pp. 999–1022.

75. Poundstone, W. "How to Ace A Google Interview," *Wall Street Journal*, December, 2011 C1-2, pp. 24–25.

76. Hill, L. "Only BFFs Need Apply," *Bloomberg Business Week*, January 7–13, 2013, pp. 63–65.

77. Herring, C. "Does Diversity Pay? Race, Gender, and the Business Case for Diversity," *American Sociological Review*, 74, April 2009 pp. 208–224.

READING 8.1

Temporary Help Agencies and the Making of a New Employment Practice

Vicki Smith and Esther B. Neuwirth

Executive Overview

Over the past 50 years in America, we have gone from a system of work characterized by lifetime employment at a single employer to a patchwork system characterized by low security and high volatility. A major player in our new world of work is the temporary help agency, which serves as the intermediary between workers and companies. Traditionally, temporary help agencies have been regarded, at best, as a necessary evil, and, at worst, as machines that eat up and spit out workers. In fact, the reality is far more nuanced. When job seekers' options are unemployment or degraded employment, working with the staff of an agency that has an investment in promoting its profit-making commodity—good temporary workers—gives them a distinct advantage. Agency staff help applicants and valued workers improve résumés and refine their job expectations in productive ways, and often advocate for better wages, higher-level positions, and more humane, safer working conditions for their temps. Temporary employment today is thus a double-edged sword. While, on average, agency temps receive lower wages, rarely can purchase health insurance, and have virtually no employment security, they can also be buffered from the worst aspects of new employment relations by labor market intermediaries such as temporary placement agencies.

Fifty years ago, temporary employment was such a, marginal labor practice that the Bureau of Labor Statistics did not track the size or composition of the temporary workforce, nor did it collect systematic data about employers' use of such workers (Watson, personal communication, 2007). This occupational ghetto appears to have been staffed almost exclusively by married women who lacked viable employment alternatives (Goldin, 1990) and often had weak labor market attachments (Moore, 1965). Employers and managers used temps, mostly in office positions, on a short-term, stopgap basis, bringing them in to cover for permanent employees. In post-World War II offices, the jobs were permanent; it was the workers who were temps.

This model of temporary employment has experienced a sea change since the mid-20th century. Far from being a marginal labor practice, temporary employment today is widespread and normalized. Employers hire temporary workers—almost three million each day (Berchem, 2008, Fig. 3)—as a routine staffing strategy rather than simply to fill in for permanent workers on a stopgap basis. Many companies today have limited budgets for hiring permanent workers but ample resources—and top management approval—for hiring temps.[1] Companies that are reluctant to add to their permanent workforces instead create short- and long-term temporary positions, the latter evidenced by the steady growth of "permatemps."[2] In 2005, for example, 35% of temporary agency workers held a single temp job for more than a year, compared to 24% in 1995 (Mishel, Bernstein, & Allegretto, 2007, p. 241, Table 4.8). In contrast to the post-World War II era, now, both the jobs and the workers are temporary.

Temps today are about as likely to be adult men as adult women, with women comprising 52.8% and men comprising 47.2% of temporary agency workers (Mishel, Bernstein, & Allegretto, 2007, p. 242, Table 9). They can be found in low (those we refer to as temporary agency workers) and high (contract workers) ranks of the occupational and professional structure, in blue- and white-collar jobs, in services and manufacturing.

The temporary help service (THS) industry has grown exponentially. The number of THS offices surged from about 800 in the early 1960s to 5,000 by 1981 to nearly 40,000 today. Temporary help service revenue has likewise exploded over the years; annual earnings expanded from about $250 million in the early 1960s to $73.5 billion in 2007. Growth in industry earnings was paralleled by growth in the size of the temporary workforce, which was a little over 11 million in 2007 (Berchem, 2008; Mangum, Mayall, & Nelson, 1985; Moore, 1965). The growth of temporary employment has mixed effects for workers, which has been confirmed in numerous studies by labor economists, sociologists, and organizational scholars. On the one hand, the majority of those who work in temp jobs prefer permanent work (they are involuntary temps), they experience high levels of job insecurity, and they lack health benefits and mobility opportunities. On the other hand, temporary jobs provide opportunities to earn income when job seekers can't get hired into a permanent or regular job; they have become a valuable source of employment, often on a long-term, albeit destabilized, basis.

How did temporary employment evolve from a small, peripheral practice to one that is large and central to contemporary hiring practices? Much is known about the historic rise of the temporary help services industry, which actively worked to enlarge and legitimate this previously marginal employment relationship. In the 1970s and '80s representatives of the industry directly marketed their product—temporary laborers—to hiring managers, overcoming their resistance to using nonpermanent workers (Ofstead, 1999). Convincing hiring managers to transition from the stopgap to the staffing model of using temps required work and persuasion. Temporary staffing agencies had to appease hiring managers' anxieties about the logistical complexities of bringing in temps, and overcome their reluctance to change long-standing employment practices of hiring permanent workers. Industry representatives worked to convince hiring managers that using temps would not compromise trade secrets, that the costs associated with training and retraining workers would not be prohibitive, and that temps could be loyal to the companies that employed them (Vosko, 2000, p. 149).

The THS industry also fought its case in the courts and reshaped labor law, striving to generate new demand for its product and improve the competitive conditions under which it operated (Gonos, 1997). The industry lobbied and worked through state and federal courts to become legal employers of temporary workers. This accomplishment had two profound implications: First, it meant that the temporary agency, rather than the hiring company, became the employer of record and that firms rid themselves of legal obligations to a subset of their workers. Second, given that managers in hiring firms did not actually have to fire and hire temps themselves—given that they could simply inform agencies if they didn't want a particular temp to return or if they needed a fresh supply of temps—the corporate world gained great latitude in its use of labor.

On top of these institutional and legal changes, THS industry leaders cultivated a new, positive image of temporary workers in the popular media, paving the way for greater acceptance of temps and greater skepticism about permanent workers' productivity and work ethic (Smith & Neuwirth, 2008). Writing articles in personnel and business magazines, many THS leaders highlighted the value of their new product, emphasizing the hidden costs of permanent labor; discussing groups of people (besides married women) who had the capacity to be good temporary workers; and identifying new occupations, industries, and task niches where temporary workers could be used. Through these combined measures, the industry engaged extensively in market-making activities.

But what few understand is the active work undertaken by temporary help placement agencies to create a high-quality, marketable product: good temporary workers and workforces. Since the late 1990s we have interviewed and observed temporary workers, interviewed production and hiring managers, and worked in the office of a temporary help service agency in Silicon Valley (an agency we call Select Labor).[3] Our focus during this time has been on the labor market segment that includes office, assembly, warehouse, and other types of entry-level temporary agency workers and the agencies that employ them. Although there are other types of temporary workers, such as high-level contractors (Barley & Kunda, 2006), day laborers (Bartley & Roberts, 2006), and contract company employees, temporary agency workers constitute the largest proportion of the temporary workforce (Dey, Houseman, & Polivka, 2007). We found that both temporary help service agencies and the industry at large have a significant interest in constructing a labor force of good temporary employees, creating temporary jobs, and reshaping managerial practices to optimize outcomes for both temps and hiring firms.

Our findings help correct an outdated image of temporary employment and temporary workers. Contrary to the perception of temporary help agencies as machines that eat and spit out workers, treating them as if they were disposable, even interchangeable commodities, temporary help agencies have created a set of practices that buffer their workers from the most insecure and exploitative aspects of temporary employment. Indeed, some of their screening, selection, and retention practices closely resemble those used when companies hire workers on a standard basis. Temporary workers, frequently assumed to be disposable, are in contrast often valued workers whom companies and agencies seek to use on a steady, long-term basis.

The paper unfolds as follows: First, we look at the economics of temporary help agencies as a way of understanding their unique position of serving two "masters": their temporary workers (their products) and the companies who employ their workers (their clients). In the second and third sections of the paper, we look at Select Labor, a temporary help agency that we studied over several years, and use the case to show how temporary agencies work to get the best possible employees and also how they must negotiate and work with client companies to ensure a good "fit" for the temporary workers they place there.

The Economics of Temporary Help Agencies

To understand the rise of temporary agencies, it is first important to look at the economics of THS agencies. These agencies compete with one another and earn their profits in a variety of ways. Most fundamentally, they sell services: expertise and ability to assist with recruitment, screening, hiring, placing, monitoring, and firing temporary workers and managing payroll (temps are on the agencies' payroll, not the payroll of the hiring companies) (Pfeffer & Baron, 1988). They also help companies develop and manage temp-to-perm programs, set up on-site offices ("vendor on premises"), and sometimes transport temps to their work sites (Vosko, 2000).

Agencies can compete for new clients (the hiring companies that need temps) by offering smaller markups than their competitors do. An agency profits from every hour its temps are employed because of the markup, a standard practice whereby a client firm pays an hourly wage for each temp plus a negotiated additional amount that goes directly to the agency and constitutes the agency's profits (Gonos, 2000/01). Hourly wages for temporary workers are often benchmarked to prevailing regional wages for entry-level jobs, although agency representatives often play a role in negotiating higher wages for their temps (Smith & Neuwirth, 2008).

Beyond being economically competitive, agencies can also compete with one another by selling quality temporary workers. Temporary workers are the grist for the THS mill, and agencies work in a field that is dense with other agencies striving to place their product first.[4] The increased emphasis on providing quality temps parallels the larger preoccupation with "quality service" that has swept through American business over the past few decades. As companies compete to survive, they strive to distinguish themselves by the high quality of the goods and services they provide to consumers (Martin, 1994). Client firms play their own role in pressuring agencies to produce a pool of good temps: They threaten to use the temps of other agencies if they are not satisfied with one agency's workers (Peck & Theodore, 1998). Companies may demand "good" quality temps because they are concerned with productivity, skills, effort, and motivation (Nollen & Axel, 1998, p. 138).

Promoting an image of temporary workers as good workers and actually creating temporary workers who can live up to that image leads THS agencies to adopt a unique set of practices. A good temp, we argue, is a specific type of worker but also an image, a sales pitch, and a source of competitiveness for the THS industry. Sometimes temporary workers measure up to this ideal; sometimes they don't. Sometimes people want to be good temps; sometimes they don't. What is important is that promising then constructing good temporary workers is at the heart of the mainstream temporary placement industry.

Characteristics of a Good Temporary Employee

There are multiple dimensions that can come into play in selecting and making an employee not simply a good worker but a good temporary worker, and ensuring that an agency is not simply a purveyor of generic labor but of a reliable, on-call workforce of temps. In theory, a good temp has specific characteristics. The first concerns attitude. Agencies look for job applicants with attitudes and dispositions appropriate for temporary work (Cappelli, 1995). Successful temporary workers must understand and accept the unique terms of temporary employment. When people are new to temporary employment it is imperative that they are or become familiar with the concept of "at will" employment and the fact that there is no employment guarantee; that a job might last just a few days but that it might last several months or more with no guarantee of a permanent position; that the agency will receive a portion of every hour's wages paid by the client firm as a result of the markup; that their hourly wage almost certainly will be lower than the hourly wage of their permanent counterparts, even though they may work side by side doing exactly the same tasks[5]; and that the agency, not the client firm, is their boss.

These conditions can signal to applicants that they are second-class citizens, posing a challenge to the companies that hire them. For example, these terms may be troubling to an individual who is determined to land a permanent, secure job—and as American Staffing Association data show, the majority of people who take a temporary job do so with the hope that it will lead them to permanent employment (Berchem, 2006, Figure 6). An individual with predictable resentment, anxiety, and possible confusion about having to accept temporary employment would likely be a difficult person to place and keep on the job.

Even a person who prefers a temp job because it allows him to attend school or raise a family can find it impossible to succeed in these pursuits given the inherent unpredictability of a "no guarantee" job. This person may not want a permanent job but still may desire something relatively stable. For these reasons, a desirable attitude might consist of a demonstrable level of mental flexibility and a willingness to work on an open-ended basis. We expect such characteristics of good employees, but the idea that good attitude would be expected of temporary workers runs counter to traditional notions of temps as disposable labor. It is incumbent on agencies to select or create workers with reasonable attitudes, as illustrated by our data.

The second characteristic of a good temp has to do with a minimum level of competence, responsibility, and adaptability. Even jobs that appear to be unskilled nearly always require some ability and judgment. An ideal temp would be able to walk into a variety of situations and get to work. A materials handler position, for example—where someone delivers materials and supplies to various production units in a workplace—might be thought of as a position requiring primarily physical strength and endurance, but it can entail greater complexity (such as social-relational competencies). Language competencies might be essential in such jobs, as might the capacity for teamwork. Individuals with previous experience in an environment characterized by authoritarian management might be ill equipped to survive in a production setting that stresses participation and initiative. Someone who has worked in a professional position in a law office may feel qualified for a white-collar work environment and be frustrated and resentful if sent to a comparatively de-skilled white-collar job, repetitively entering data. For these reasons, we might say that a good temp will be adaptable and able to learn, and that agencies must engage in selection methods more extensively than might be anticipated (Wilk & Cappelli, 2003).

Additional Challenges Affecting Temporary Help Agencies

A good temporary *workforce* is something above and beyond a good temporary worker. Temp placement agencies need to be able to guarantee that if a hiring company places an order for a batch of temps, the agency will be able to quickly produce decent temporary workers in volume, a strong motivation for having a just-in-time pool of good temporary workers.

Inherent in the promise of producing a batch of temps on demand is the promise of a steady stream of temps who can be sent and will stay for the duration of a project, whether it is fulfilling a one-time order that requires assembling 1,000 servers or, testing circuit boards in a company that has a freeze on hiring permanent workers but has authorization to hire temporary workers—all in positions that are defined as temporary, may last months, and will ultimately disappear. For this reason, agencies can be committed to retention and minimizing turnover of good temps (Autor, 2001). In the era of widespread and long-term use of temporary workers, agencies lose if turnover is too high. As when companies hire permanent workers, invest in their training, and pay a cost if they quit prematurely, temporary placement agencies invest in their temps and pay a cost if temps walk off the job without completing the job assignment or refuse to return to an assignment. Having to continually create new temps becomes a burden to the agency.

This cost has been underestimated in previous studies, which insinuate that, from the perspective of the agency, entry-level temporary workers are interchangeable, almost disposable. On the contrary, THS agencies incur fixed costs that they strive to minimize. Every new job applicant must be administratively processed: tested, screened, and interviewed for a job. Agency staff must nurture their social relationships with temps, particularly good temps who are valued members of a temporary pool and will work diligently for long periods of time in one temporary position. Since the agency profits from every hour a temp is employed, it is ideal that any given temp work as long as possible in one position, without disruption or the need to find a replacement. These relations build momentum and endure, and losing them means the agency has to begin all over again with new "raw material."

Hiring companies (the clients of the temp agencies), too, must train and retrain new temps, leading shop-floor managers to try to avoid turnover of long-term temps (Smith, 2001). Having to deal with a hiring company where bad management practices lead temps to quit their assignments poses a distinct challenge for a placement firm that wishes to maintain a steady and reliable supply of temporary workers. In the following pages we use case study data to detail how an agency manages these contradictory issues. These strategies, we argue, are at the center of the growth, the normalization, and the continuation of temporary employment in the United States.

How an Agency Constructs Good Temporary Workers and Workforces

For Select Labor, a pseudonym for the agency we studied, attracting, developing, keeping, and controlling good temps was by no means automatic or straightforward. Just as the THS industry has had to work over decades to achieve legitimacy for a new type of employment relationship, so too did Select Labor have to repeatedly build and control its temp workforce. We cannot take this process for granted. Agencies have to construct good, qualified temps to cultivate and maintain marketable workforces. What sells in the world of temporary employment is not simply warm bodies; it is good workers who are willing to work on a temporary basis.

According to Select Labor's marketing brochures, the agency promised temps who were "productive," "committed to quality performance," and "reliable," and who "would make significant contributions to [hiring company] products." Agency staff had many reasons to guard against hiring people they suspected wouldn't succeed as temps, whether because they would not be productive, wouldn't cooperate with supervisors and managers, or in other ways didn't show potential for positive work performance. Having a reliable stream of quality temporary workers supported the agency's reputation, attracted additional client firms, and added to the bottom line. Sending temporary workers who wouldn't last on a job was directly counterproductive to these goals. We found that these interwoven imperatives led Select Labor to adopt a variety of strategies to improve the quality of its temporary labor and the quality of its services (for a fuller analysis see Smith & Neuwirth, 2008).

Selective Recruitment

Like virtually every business in America, Select Labor (SL) advertised its services in customary places and ways. Anybody wishing to find employment—whether as a temporary worker or as a temporary who could convert to a permanent worker—could find out about SL on its Web site, in the yellow pages of the local telephone directory, in a regional *Employment Guide and Career Source* magazine, and at community colleges and training centers. In addition to these impersonal methods of advertising, SL staff widely and selectively recruited people who could help secure the firm's claim to sell a high-quality temporary workforce.

For one thing, SL staff attended local job fairs when possible. Job fairs are fascinating terrain for anyone studying contemporary employment practices. Visitors can find dozens if not hundreds of employers hawking their products, services, and reputations to potential employees. Fairs, particularly large urban fairs, attract thousands of the job-seeking unemployed as well as employed people just curious about what the labor market has to offer. Job fairs encompass a surprising number of employers and industries (including government agencies, goods and service providers, Internet companies and high-tech firms, and temp/staffing agencies). When Select Labor staff sponsored tables at a fair, they could keep their eyes open for job seekers who were looking for permanent work but were receptive to learning about the advantages and disadvantages of temporary jobs. At the same time, the staff used this opportunity to discourage those job seekers for whom temporary employment would be an unacceptable alternative to permanent jobs: In other words, agency staff engaged in nurturing some potential applicants and weeding out others before they even came to the agency office.

Reeling in job fair attendees by offering promotional items such as chocolates, pens, calendars, and notepads, agency reps collected résumés from attendees (as do virtually all those who staff the tables at job fairs). They conducted impromptu interviews, speaking with and taking notes on potential job candidates about their preferred hours of work and wages. Conversations at these fairs gave SL reps an opening to educate job seekers about temporary work and collect information for their database of potential recruits to the industry.

Staffing specialists tried to recruit competitive, good temporary workers through networks with job development specialists in the region. These job development specialists worked for state agencies (both training and placement); they worked with community colleges, and they worked for for-profit training schools and colleges. One staff member in the SL office, for example, sent off job announcements each week to a group of job specialists in the region with whom he had developed close relations throughout his career in the staffing industry, trusting that they would direct these announcements to appropriate individuals. Alex, an energetic recruiter at Select Labor, said of his systematic approach:

Many of these people don't make money by placing people—they either work for the county, the city, or the state, and it's their job to help people find work. So if I have a job opening, I'll go down my list and start calling these folks and say, "Hey, I need this type of candidate with these skills" and so on. I'll ask if they have anyone they can send my way. And every Monday morning I try and type out a spreadsheet with all my job openings. Then I fax this list to over 33 agencies, schools, and places like

that. I'll follow that up with a phone call or even a visit if I have time. Sometimes I'll go ahead and visit the place and post a flyer with my open job orders, and I'll attach an envelope to the flyer with my business cards.

Other staff routinely telephoned their contacts at agencies and schools to find out about new graduates who might be good "material" for temporary positions.

Trust is an important ingredient in hiring new workers, and as sociologists and labor economists well know, relying on established networks is a common way for employers to recruit good workers they can trust (Granovetter, 1995; Smith, 2005). Select Labor recruited reliable temps by tapping the networks of the temps already on its payroll. SL had a formal program that offered modest bonuses to temporary workers who recommended friends or family members for jobs with SL. (The parent company estimated that approximately 50% of SL's recruits were friends and family members of current employees.) To maximize the quality of those who were referred, SL gave temps the bonus only if the recommended person was able to work in good standing for several weeks of full-time temporary employment. On occasion, SL staff declined to hire someone recommended by one of their regular temps, a person who was good enough to be sent out to some jobs but just questionable enough to make Select Labor staff wary of his recommendations. In other words, agency staff did not leave the quality of their temporary labor pool to chance, or passively wait for the right kind of temps: They sought job applicants who might be reasonably compatible with temporary positions.

Screening for Good and Weeding Out Undesirable Applicants

Selective recruitment doesn't guarantee that a temp will succeed on the job. Once the agency succeeded in persuading people to visit the office, follow-up measures were critical. SL staff used a rigorous intake process as a filter to separate questionable from promising temps. What is surprising is the high level of quality control agency representatives used to select the members of their temporary employment pool. While we would expect that a company hiring a permanent worker for a complex or demanding job might use rigorous selection measures (Wilk & Cappelli, 2003), we would not have the same expectation for those who hire workers who are commonly thought of as "disposable."

The primary objective of the intake process was the inextricably entwined work of weeding out unacceptable candidates and identifying acceptable ones. First, minimal skills tests were administered in the office: SL had one room in the facility dedicated to testing the computer skills (word processing, graphics, and database management) of candidates for office positions, and the soldering skills of applicants for positions with integrated circuit producers who needed expert solderers. Beyond their technical skills, job applicants were assessed on their understanding of the parameters of temporary employment. SL placement specialists were trained to carefully follow a scripted interview protocol when new temps came in seeking work. SL staff gave job seekers a pamphlet outlining the features of temporary employment, including minimum standards of job participation (arriving on time for an assignment, observing all client rules, volunteering for more tasks once on the job), the importance of maintaining confidentiality about the client's business, and covering how payroll was handled.

Staff were instructed to use the interview to find out how much the candidate knew about temping. Training literature exhorted them to consider: "What does the candidate hope we can do for him/her? How flexible is he/she regarding assignments and pay? How realistic is the candidate? Do they understand the meaning of 'at will' employment?" The brochure went on to implore recruitment specialists to "set forth Select Labor's expectations, policies regarding communication and commitment, business dress and attendance. Gauge what you emphasize by the strengths/weaknesses/problems you suspect."[6] If a recruitment specialist suspected that an applicant's expectations were way out of line, or that an applicant misrepresented his skills or wasn't really serious about taking a temporary position, the specialist would attempt to discourage him and, more notably, "encourage poor candidates to register at other services."

Agency staff were primed to detect behaviors believed to predict an applicant's potential for good and bad work performance. Promising applicants were said to have some combination of these good traits: positive attitude, responsibility, reliability, loyalty, energy, intelligence, honesty, and trustworthiness; these traits, in turn, were associated with close to 100 examples of "good" behavior. Questionable applicants were said to have a set of traits that were the polar opposites of those typical of the promising applicants and were similarly associated with close to 100 behavioral propensities, all "bad."

Placement specialists were asked to check off other traits during the interview, using categories for grooming, verbal facility, awareness, and behavior. Each category contained a list of characteristics ranging from very desirable to unacceptable. Under "grooming," for example, job seekers were ranked as to whether they appeared to be management and professional or "casual" material, fit for light industrial or clerical work, unkempt or unhygienic, "counselable," or unacceptable. Under "awareness," a job seeker could be interpreted as excellent, with strong understanding of expectations, all the way down to unsatisfactory, "shows total lack of understanding of expectations." And under "behavior" someone seeking temporary employment could be interpreted as extremely good with a positive attitude, all the way down to "unacceptable, exhibits poor attitude."

SL staff engaged in quality control of temps after they were placed in jobs by collecting and studying data on worker performance, monitoring temps at job sites, and rewarding good temps while sanctioning problematic temps. For example, agency staff sent a survey to the managers at client companies asking managers to evaluate individual temps. The short survey created a track record about general aptitudes and behaviors rather than specific skill sets: "production" and "skill level" (both undefined), attendance, judgment, cooperation, dress/grooming, and accuracy—with a telling question, "Would you accept his/her return?" concluding the survey.

Quality control was exercised in other ways as well. Agency staff were required to conduct a "quality check" by calling hiring managers within 30 minutes of the arrival of a new temp or batch of temps to make sure their transition into the workplace had been successful. Had the temp or temps arrived on time? Had they been able to understand and follow directions? SL staff always hoped that the new temps would blend into the client company in a relatively seamless way. As further follow-up, agency staff would conduct unannounced "spot checks," visiting different work sites to check in with managers, touch base with the temps they had hired, and observe the work site to make sure that everything was in place. At companies where they had on-site offices—vendor-on-premise arrangements—staff were easily able to monitor temps on the job for evidence of satisfactory behavior and attitude. All these methods allowed agency staff to identify the good performers and gather ammunition for weeding out the bad.

SL staff used incentives to reward and reinforce good temp behaviors. By using an employee reward system that set a bar for quality work performance, they communicated what they expected of all their temporary workers, simultaneously acting to retain good temps. The employee recognition program awarded bonuses to temps who were deemed of the highest quality, with good temps receiving cash, paid days off, and gift cards. SL staff encouraged client firms to have employee-of-the-month award programs for temporary workers as well.

On the other hand, agency staff could refuse to rehire or replace temps who, for various reasons, didn't succeed on the job. Agencies are not legally bound to place or replace applicants once they have hired them. And on the other side of the employment relationship, hiring firms can easily request that a temp not be sent back to them. Select Labor staff could cast off substandard or "suboptimal" (Peck & Theodore, 1998, p. 670) temps, noting who was unsatisfactory, who was making managers at client firms unhappy, and who was unlikely to make it as a temp in the long run. Agency staff occasionally sent a temporary worker off to interview for a position at a company, only to hear later that the individual never arrived. When and if the job candidate called the agency begging for a second chance, Select Labor's staff had the option of deactivating his job application. SL staff generally gave temps with problems a second chance but usually stopped before giving them a third. Occasionally, the placement staff at SL would tell job seekers after an infraction (such as not showing up for an interview or a job, or failing to meet the minimum standards for job performance) that they weren't able to find another position for them, a passive antiretention strategy. The agency's guarantee that Select Labor would not charge a client firm for the final eight hours of a "failed" temp's work subtly reminded staff about the financial cost of keeping a bad temp.

Maximizing Fit, Modifying Workers' Aspirations

Successful sales in the staffing industry come from knowing how to place the right worker in the right job. Select Labor management continually stressed that the work of agency representatives was not primarily to help workers who wanted excellent employment opportunities. Rather, their primary goal was to give employers what they wanted. And part and parcel of that goal was to know how to avoid setting up temps for failure, which would of course redound on SL's reputation. Time and again, SL staff would refrain from sending a job applicant out to a job the individual was particularly interested in but was not qualified for. Staff also worked to modify job applicants' aspirations, encouraging them to postpone immediate goals that were unrealistic and adjust their expectations to the realities of existing opportunities. In both cases, Select Labor's goal was to eliminate or at least narrow the mismatch between temporary worker and temporary job, and increase the success of the former on the latter. A successful placement, with a maximum of fit between job seeker and job, was one where a temp could fulfill the terms of the contract, and doing so was an integral element of good temporary performance.

For example, Rowena, a Filipina-American in her late 30s, came to SL to find a job as an assembler, explaining that she had previously worked for a photocopy company that was subcontracted through a legal firm. She worked for the photocopy firm for several years and had experienced some upward mobility, but had tired of the job and desired change. Her goal was to work as a circuit board assembler, and eventually rise to the ranks of management. However, Lisa, SL's branch manager, cognizant of the lack of bridge jobs between assembly and management positions (not to mention between most temporary positions and the ranks of management), advised Rowena to rethink her strategy for achieving upward mobility. Lisa, who had several years of experience placing people in circuit board assembly and manufacturing jobs, explained to Rowena during an interview:

> From what I've seen in all the years I've been placing people in circuit board assembly line jobs, it is not easy to rise to a managerial position. At these places, they typically use people up and spit them out. These jobs are draining, and they work people very hard and replace them often. Surely people become managers and rise in the ranks, but I've rarely seen that in the whole time I've been placing people.

Lisa advised Rowena to give her résumé to the SL clerical and administrative recruiters, who might be able to place her in a position that was more appropriate to her skills and experience. Rowena had strong word processing skills, she was an excellent communicator, and she was fluent in Tagalog. Lisa could easily have placed Rowena in an assembler position; SL had many such job orders, and Rowena would easily have qualified for these jobs. Lisa, however, believed that Rowena would quickly become frustrated with that type of work and quit (an indicator of an unsuccessful placement), so she tried to help place Rowena in a job that she thought better suited her skills and background and that provided a more realistic path to management, possibly to the supervision of other white-collar, entry-level workers. Eventually Select Labor was able to place Rowena in a position that seemed to have the potential to become a permanent position: as a customer service representative in a company that was looking for a bilingual English-Tagalog speaker, a job that paid more than assembly line work and had opportunities for upward mobility.

Some workers came to the agency with recently acquired skills but little or no job experience in their new skill area. Silicon Valley was and continues to be a land of dream making and dream breaking, and many people hoped to capitalize on the prosperity of the high-tech industry. Some SL job applicants had paid significant amounts of money for training in various areas of the hightech industry only to learn that getting a job in their field was extremely difficult without experience and connections.

Job applicants often invested in training programs with little real understanding of how they would deploy their newfound skills or whether their training programs would link them to actual jobs. SL reps recognized the potential of these applicants but were aware that they were not going to be able to place them until they had gotten a foot in the door of a desirable company, possibly in an entry-level temporary job that had little to do with their newly acquired area of expertise. Entering a company or a field this way could help the job applicant connect to helpful networks for landing jobs. SL advisers worked with these applicants to modify their goals, to gradually adjust and maneuver their way into new fields, and to maximize their fit to particular job assignments.

Mark, for example, was working on getting an MCSE (Microsoft Certified Systems Engineer) certificate and wanted to know what SL might have for him. Mark was employed as a tester (a fairly low-level position in high tech) inspecting hard drives, printers, and hardware, but he wanted to get into the software industry. He had decided to take the MCSE course because he was persuaded by Microsoft's claim that people possessing this certificate would be very marketable. He wanted a high-paying, better job but was not sure how to find one, so he had decided to learn UNIX because he believed that companies were looking for people proficient with that operating system. SL staff convinced him that starting with a temporary job as a PC technician at one of the local computer manufacturing firms would be a good bridge job for him, increasing the chances that he would eventually obtain the position he hoped for.

Often, when one of the agency's good temporary workers was seeking a temp job but didn't possess the requisite skills for an advertised position, SL placement staff would go out of their way to talk to the manager at the client firm to discern whether there might be other opportunities for the individual. Good temps were something to retain, and SL went to lengths to do so. In one instance, SL sent Navit, a long-term temp, to interview at a company for a technician position. In the course of the interview, the manager determined that Navit was not qualified for the position and communicated this to the Select Labor placement specialist. The latter, however, was impressed by Navit's previous record and felt that he would be a good fit with this particular company, a firm that assembled computer components. She spent a fair amount of time telephoning other contacts she had in the company to see if anyone had a need for a trustworthy, hardworking temporary worker. Navit's case and others like it highlight how temporary workers can receive better career advice and be the recipients of advocacy efforts in ways superior to what regular employees might experience.

Agency staff used other seemingly small but important measures to retain valued temps. A branch manager at SL, for example, personally gave a cash advance from her own pocket to a regular temp whose paycheck had not come through. When one valued temp, a woman who had contracted for several jobs through Select Labor and had been working in a clerical position for more than nine months, asked for an additional day off over a long weekend so that she could spend it with her young child, the agency staff found a temp to fill her place for that short time—a temp filling in for a temp. On the whole, the agency attempted to pursue and optimize its chances for building and retaining the best temporary workforce possible. This workforce was the agency's cutting edge, its competitive commodity, and staff devoted an enormous amount of time to its manufacture.

Reshaping Managerial Practices and Creating Good Enough Temporary Jobs

Shaping labor supply—doing what they could to improve the quality of their temporary workers, increase the likelihood that their temps would succeed on the job, and hold turnover rates to a minimum—constituted one part of agency staff's work. They also worked to shape the demand side of temporary employment. Specifically, agency staff brokered relations between the temporary workforce and the supervisors and managers in hiring companies. They had to be attentive to the practices of the hiring companies and the ways in which those practices potentially could compromise the quality and output of temporary workers. Agency staff had to interpret hiring companies' distinct cultures and markets and learn how to work with and around them. They had to teach managers in client firms how to effectively use temps and gain their compliance. If agency staff placed temps at companies with bad work conditions—work sites that were unsafe or were managed by supervisors who resented the addition of temps to their units or acted "rough and tough," as one agency staff member put it—they had to deal with an increasing volume of complaints and labor turnover.

Recalibrating Abusive Managers

Caricatures of hiring company supervisors and managers and the way they deal with temporary employees abound. Researchers have blamed onsite managers for degrading temporary employees' work, for subjecting temps to toxic and hazardous work conditions (McAllister, 1998; Parker, 1994), and for sexual harassment (Rogers & Henson, 1997) and homophobia (Henson, 1996). This portrayal of managers, although partial (Smith, 2001), contains a kernel of truth: One of the major factors shaping the work experiences of Select Labor's temps was the attitude, interpersonal style, and management philosophy of the person for whom the temp worked. Whether the temp was integrated into a workforce of regular employees or worked in an enclave of other temporary workers, on-site supervisors and managers gave directions, kept an eye on the pace at which temps worked, commented on the products temps turned out, and reprimanded or praised temps for the quality of their work. Moreover, some supervisors and managers held implicit and explicit biases toward temps qua temps.

Select Labor staff had to moderate and rationalize—recalibrate—the behavior of on-site managers who were abusive, despotic, or confused when carrying out their normal oversight functions. In some cases, managers and supervisors on the shop floor were engaged in statistical discrimination, assuming temporary workers on the whole were untrustworthy and ignoring the laudable qualities or attributes of any individual temp. Occasionally managers baldly revealed their contempt for temps and attacked their vulnerable status. The comments of a disgruntled temp who had been sent for an interview revealed the humiliation that at least some managers were willing to heap upon "the temp." The temp, upon returning from the interview, reported the interaction in this way:

> I told Steve [the hiring manager] that I hoped to earn $10 an hour. Steve laughed at me and said, "With your lack of skills and knowledge of computers, you should just be happy with the salary I'm offering and just be happy to have the job."

In other cases, managers were disrespectful and injurious to all subordinates, permanent and temporary workers alike. Morale at firms could be severely affected when there was a sense of unfair or capricious treatment or when workers perceived that management did not care about their complaints. Demoralization registered strongly in the agency when temps' complaints about a particular boss added up. As study after study of work has shown, despotic or coercive managers can create significant organizational costs (to productivity, efficiency, and quality) and can lead to high turnover, resistance, and even sabotage (Hodson, 2001; Jacoby, 1985). Supervisors of temporary workers are no exception to this rule: They can incur obvious and concealed costs when they act out their contempt for temps.

One day the senior human resources manager at Computers R Us (CRU) invited Lisa, SL's branch manager, to sit in on a special staff meeting convened to review Rina's performance. Rina, a production supervisor, oversaw both temporary and permanent workers. Lisa was already well aware that Rina was causing problems for workers. Temporary workers assigned to CRU had complained to SL placement specialists about the routine humiliation Rina handed out: She was rude to them on the shop floor, snapped at them on a regular basis, and had even yelled at them. Some refused to return to CRU for their assignments.

Lisa expressed concern for her two equally pressing constituencies: "her workers"—Select Labor's temps—and the client firm. The human resource manager at CRU told Lisa that she needed her help, that she wanted her to give Rina direct feedback from temporary workers. After a meeting between Lisa and Rina, Rina's behavior appeared to improve. In the weeks that followed SL had far fewer complaints from the workers Rina supervised. Rina's actions had had a destabilizing effect on CRU's ability to hold on to its much-needed temporary workers, and SL willingly stepped in to help ameliorate the problem. In so doing, SL took on aspects of the traditional HR function, participating in performance appraisal, representing employees' grievances, and helping to manage tensions between the temporary and permanent workforce.

SL was asked on another occasion to help manage another problematic supervisor at CRU, to again assist HR in communicating employee grievances to him. Alex, a Select Labor placement specialist, was brought in to deal with Steve, the facilities management supervisor at CRU. Steve, like Rina,

evoked many complaints from temporary workers. The HR person in charge of temporary workers at CRU had not wanted to approach Steve about his attitude but finally felt there was no alternative but to confront him: Steve's actions were negatively affecting morale and retention of temporary workers. Alex explained:

> Steve's a rough and tough guy. I haven't met him but I've placed a few janitors with him, and he takes a lot of workers. But he gets people and spits them out. Like, he waits to sign timecards and then sends them in after they are due. He also talks rough with his workers—so people don't want to stay working for him for 10 bucks an hour and get that kind of treatment. Laura [a human resources manager at Computers R Us] wants me to talk with Steve about these issues—she wants me to handle these things and keep her out of having these kinds of talks with managers. She's relying on me to have these talks. I'm not sure what to do, but I'll have a talk with him. Maybe I'll take him out to lunch.

Alex's solution was to address Steve outside the workplace and to "socialize" him about some of the distinct issues facing temporary workers, and to educate Steve about the fact that the SL temps were usually very willing to work hard and comply with orders if they were treated respectfully. A significant goal of these one-on-one interventions was to eliminate capriciousness in the handling of temps.

In yet another company, Lisa had a series of conversations with a line manager at a client firm, criticizing his harsh attitude and actions toward Select Labor temps. Lisa had heard from a number of temporary workers, as well as from SL office staff, that this particular manager was intimidating temps when he interviewed them. And once they started the job, the manager often required the temps to work very long shifts on short notice. Lisa perceived this manager as being unresponsive to her concerns and decided to go over his head to the manager of the company's HR department. After his conversation with Lisa, this senior-level HR manager reprimanded the abusive line managers, leading Lisa to feel that she had succeeded in communicating to both of them that rude and thuggish behavior toward temporary workers would not be tolerated.

Agency staff did not always succeed in improving bad workplaces. The financial power of a client could limit the agency's ability to battle that client's damaging management practices. With a client that was a significant source of revenue, the agency could only try to contain the disgruntlement and turmoil. For example, SL staff had placed a number of workers in a firm, packaging computers. Although SL staff had visited the job site and determined that the quality of the worksite and the health and safety standards were acceptable, over time it emerged that some African American male and female temps felt that the line manager was discriminating against them. SL staff had wondered why many of their workers came back to Select Labor requesting new placements and tried to determine the source of the problem. A handful had walked off the job and returned to SL with complaints that were so vague that SL staff had trouble pinning down the precise problem. It took several weeks of inquiry for SL staff to get a handle on this particular manager's racism. The line manager, SL staff discovered, had publicly stated that he favored male Vietnamese workers and was perceived as treating all the female workers and men of a different racial or ethnic background unfairly. Workers of the "wrong" gender or ethnicity told Rosa (a specialist at SL) that the foreman yelled at them, pressured them to work harder, and gave them tasks they claimed were "dirty" or "demeaning." Select Labor staff met with upper management at the firm and complained about the line manager's actions. However, the line manager remained in the position and SL continued to place workers at this job site: The hiring firm was taking on so many of its temps that SL feared the loss of the considerable revenue. SL's goal to create decent work conditions could not be perfectly achieved all the time, but the issue was of ongoing concern nevertheless.

Socializing Managers

Agency staff did not limit themselves to trying to recalibrate "bad" managers. Their larger goal was to socialize managers across the board, to familiarize everyone with the administrative logistics of temporary employment. Staffing agency placement specialists would teach hiring managers how to use temporary workers and how to use staffing services in general. Partly this entailed building an infrastructure in which agency staff could support line managers on the shop floor. Many managers lacked experience working on a regular basis with this different set of employment arrangements. While acquainting managers about the unique aspects and virtues of working with temps, SL staff were trying to rationalize and standardize the way the latter were deployed.

The experience of one Select Labor staff member, Jill, who managed a vendor-on-premises (VOP) unit at Technology Pathways (TP or Tech Path), highlights this process. Jill's desk was situated among the desks of other administrative staff. To anyone who was not in the know, Jill was indistinguishable from other permanent company employees. When not attending to daily paperwork and administrative tasks at her desk, Jill walked around the TP "campus" visiting with managers, informally instructing them on how to use SL's services. Jill mused that:

When people come off the street to Technology Pathways to apply for temporary jobs, they go on our payroll if they are to start as a temp, but Tech Path doesn't yet understand that they can send the person directly to me and I'll handle that paperwork. Now they are putting the person into their system and making a lot of work for themselves.

I'll have to teach them and explain the options and possibilities for me to help them out. We can handle all that and save them time: I'm not sure why they are doing all that themselves.

In her first few weeks, Jill spent a great deal of time with managers, getting to know them and learning about their hiring needs, advising them on how SL could save them time by searching for and interviewing potential employees. Working on-site, Jill also attended regular HR meetings to gain insight into and shape personnel practices at the company. SL had a vested economic interest in successfully teaching managers how to use temps, at TP and at all client work sites. The following example explains this interest.

When SL first started its VOP program at Technology Pathways, there were approximately six temporary workers at the company. Three months later there were a total of 76 temps working at TP (35 of whom were recruited by Select Labor). Jill explained:

Even though some of these temps were not recruited by us, we make money on all of them because we have a primary vendor contract with Technology Pathways, so we have a subcontracting relationship with the other agencies—they are subcontracting with us to have temps at Technology Pathways.

These multiple layers of subcontracting were common with VOP arrangements, and Jill's presence on-site at TP facilitated both the growth of Technology Pathway's contingent workforce and Select Labor's share of this growth. Simply put, the larger the workforce of temps at Technology Pathways, the larger the flow of revenue to Select Labor.

At various sites, Jill advised managers on how to enlist SL's help in getting the kinds of workers they needed quickly and efficiently. She wrote and designed job descriptions after discussions with managers about their labor force needs. Jill conducted the orientation for temporary employees, helping them with necessary paperwork, giving them a tour of the facility, and training them in matters related to safety and the grievance process. She oversaw performance appraisals for temporary workers, conducted ergonomic evaluations of workstations, and made recommendations to managers for improvements. She had regular access to managers through meetings and informal encounters, and often these interactions afforded Jill a significant impact on the direction of HR management at the firm. She even negotiated on behalf of temporary Workers for higher wages when hiring managers offered pay rates that she thought were too low given prevailing market wages for temps. As Jill explained about another company where SL had a VOP account:

I'm shocked at how low the pay rates are [at Company X]. They don't realize the current pay rates in the Valley now and how competitive things are and how much more people are making these days…. I'll try and negotiate with them, and I know I'll have to advocate for some candidates.

Negotiating higher pay for temps was not uncommon for SL staff. Elsewhere, Select Labor staff had been cultivating an account with Building Blocks (BB), working as consultants with BB management when the company relocated from the west side to the east side of the San Francisco Bay. Managers at BB initially insisted to SL staff that they intended to pay temporary workers the minimum wage. The SL salesperson told them there would be trouble if they paid minimum wage: She stated bluntly that no one competent or reliable would come work for them. After lengthy negotiations the BB managers agreed to start temps at two dollars above minimum wage, a low wage to be sure, but high enough to increase the chance of filling positions and minimizing turnover.

As Jill's experiences at Technology Pathways highlight, agency staff could be called upon to assess unanticipated work orders, predict employers' needs, and then prepare job descriptions for hiring companies. One manager from Computer Driven called SL to place a job order. She needed some temporary workers who could work as testers but had not prepared a description for the position. She requested that Alex (the SL recruiter mentioned earlier) write up a job description and let her review it, after which she planned to authorize SL to recruit people for the position. In addition to specifying the production schedule and the length of the job, the tasks it entailed, and the minimal skills required, the Computer Driven manager wanted Alex to benchmark this position by comparing it to prevailing wages for testers that CD would consider and possibly use. Alex used job descriptions that were on file in the agency as a template for CD's positions. In this way, Computer Driven relied on the signaling from Select Labor about what constituted a reasonable job, reasonable job expectations, and prevailing wages. In turn, Alex was able to transmit to CD a normative model for a temporary placement.

For all intents and purposes, agency staff were production engineers and organizational consultants, trained to size up jobs, workforce head counts, labor processes, and production procedures and figure out what was necessary to achieve outcomes in optimally efficient ways. If managers did not request the right types or numbers of temps, the ensuing mismatch between worker and position could undermine the likelihood for a successful temporary placement, and SL staff had a strong commitment to avoiding failure on this score.

Assessing Workplace Safety
Occasionally temps found themselves working at sites where they faced genuine risks to their bodily well-being. Being denied appropriate tools or laboring in workplaces where physical arrangements were dangerously configured had the potential to inflict meaningful damage on workers. Temps complained of dangerous work settings, and some refused to return to these jobs. These combined factors led agency staff to go to lengths to ensure that risk was minimized and safety maximized.

Agency staff were advised to "hire safe workers," "give all temps safety training," and "make sure clients have safe workplaces and good supervision." On top of this, agency staff were instructed to ask themselves: Were they providing appropriate safety training? What office procedures did they have in place for responding to accidents? Did they know for sure that the work sites where they were sending temps were safe? Were they "sending temps with proper experience, skill, strength, and attitude"? On several occasions agency staff refused to open accounts with companies that were reputedly negligent about work conditions and let go of accounts with companies that didn't comply with Select Labor's requests for improvement. Temps repeatedly told agency staff that one client firm, McTech, was a "bad" place to work, claiming that supervisors were abrasive and forced the temps to do the most dirty, heavy-lifting tasks. SL began the process of managing out the account, slowly shrinking the number of placements there. Similarly, agency staff were in the process of phasing out another company that routinely ignored requests to improve the safety conditions where temps worked. Select Labor staff also simply dropped a client firm that refused to correct a situation where heavy boxes kept falling on top of the temporary workers.

Select Labor staff believed that the best way they could keep tabs on what their temps were walking into was to conduct a thorough evaluation of different work sites. When possible, recruitment specialists would inspect the work sites when they set up new accounts with hiring companies. They might make recommendations for improving a work site. They made routine spot checks, visiting a client's site unannounced to monitor work conditions, and when they worked in VOP setups they scoped out potential risks to their temps. At a corporate training session an SL vice president warned participants from the agency office:

You have to make sure that you are eyeballing the job sites where you are sending people. Think to yourself, would I want to work here? Don't just send people to a site you know nothing about. It helps to do on-site visits when possible and see as many places as you can. Yes, we are the legal employer of temps, but we have dual—joint—employment so companies can't totally clean their hands of bad practices. As placement specialists, you should be getting detailed job descriptions when possible and remind the client about their joint employment responsibilities. Do as much quality control as possible. Visit clients when possible and develop a rapport with them.

Conclusion

This study of the active work that goes into sustaining good temps and good temp workforces helps us understand how a trivial labor practice became a significant one and how temporary employment has become so entrenched in today's economy. Regularizing a system of temporary employment, building it from the ground up, as agency staff do, contributes enormously to the normalization of temporary work. For temporary workers themselves there are unexpectedly positive consequences. Applicants seeking temporary positions and individuals who work as temps on an ongoing basis receive advice and mentoring not otherwise available to them as job seekers on the open labor market. Agency staff help applicants and valued workers improve résumés and refine their job expectations in productive ways; they help workers anticipate what can be expected of them in various production settings (which can help the worker succeed on the job); agency staff often advocate for better wages, higher-level positions, and more humane, safer working conditions for their temps.

In general, agency staff, in striving to construct good temps and maintain a pool of decent and available temporary workers, engage in practices that benefit a segment of the labor force that might otherwise be stranded high and dry by the shifting currents of labor market practices in today's economy. When job seekers' options are unemployment or degraded employment, working with the staff of an agency that has an investment in promoting its profit-making commodity—good temporary workers—gives them a distinct advantage.

Temporary employment today is thus a double-edged sword. While, on average, agency temps receive lower wages, rarely can purchase health insurance, and have virtually no employment security, they can also be buffered from the worst aspects of new employment relations by virtue of the practices of labor market intermediaries such as temporary placement agencies. Researchers have identified additional benefits that can accrue to some workers because of access to temporary employment: Working at temporary jobs allows individuals who otherwise can't find permanent work to stay in the labor market (Farber, 1999); some workers segue from temporary jobs to permanent jobs (Autor, 2003); people who would be considered high-risk hires can gain work experience through temporary positions (Houseman & Erickcek, 2002); and disadvantaged job seekers can improve the extent and quality of their social networks that can be so vital to finding a good job (Benner, Leete, & Pastor, 2007). In general, temporary employment represents a path of mobility for diverse groups of workers.

Ironically, in an era when more workers are shouldering the risks of employment and when fewer workers are protected by unions, temporary help placement agencies in the United States can play a vital role insulating job seekers from the more precarious aspects of the labor market. Moreover, given the kinds of services that agencies such as Select Labor extend to their temporary workers, workers may feel greater loyalty and commitment to agencies—where they work on a regularly destabilized basis—than they do to "regular" employers, a sad comment on the state of employment relations today.

However, our analysis should not be construed as an endorsement of profit-making temporary help service agencies or the industry as a whole. The fact that the practices we've discussed take the edge off of temporary employment, in our view, is a by-product of the explicit profit-seeking strategies of private-sector business, profits that are earned from the labor of temporary workers. Nevertheless, as temporary employment has become widespread, normalized, and arguably permanent, the infrastructure of the temporary help industry may provide unusual forms of assistance and protections for workers who lack options for better jobs.

Source: Academy of Management Perspectives, 23, (1), 56–72 (2009). Reprinted by permission of the CCC.

ENDNOTES

1. This issue is explored in Smith (2001), Hiring temporary instead or permanent workers allows companies to avoid paying federal insurance contributions, unemployment, taxes, Social security taxes, health care, sick leave, and vacation and holiday pay. When budgets for fixed labor decrease while funds for variable labor increase, managers can be forced to hire temps even when they may prefer permanent workers.

2. The term permatemps seems to have first been used to characterize a class of high-technology contractors who worked at Microsoft in the 1990s for extremely long periods of time. These contractors sued Microsoft on the grounds that they worked side by side with permanent Microsoft workers and performed the same type of work, yet they were denied access to Microsoft's benefits and the company's lucrative stock option plan because they lacked employee status. The Ninth Circuit Court of Appeals ruled that these permatemps were "common law" employees of Microsoft and therefore eligible for the same benefits and rights as permanently employed workers (DuRivage, 2001, p. 386).

3. The insider's view of these processes was acquired on the job. Neuwirth was employed full time for four months as a placement specialist at Select Labor, a pseudonym for a staffing firm in Silicon Valley. As a participant observer at Select Labor (SL). Neuwirth was trained directly by SL's branch manager. In her job, she interviewed and placed applicants in temporary jobs, conducted skills training tests, worked with managers and human resources specialists in hiring companies, went through SL corporate training

seminars, attended industry-relevant workshops and job fairs, and, in general, engaged in all aspects of agency life. She visited the sites of client firms, interacting with line and human resource managers and observing temps on the job. In all, Neuwirth logged approximately 1,400 hours of participant observation and collected massive amounts of industry data for the study of temporary help staffing firms. Neuwirth worked at Select Labor in 2000, a time when the high-tech economy of the Valley was hot: robust and with a considerable amount of churning in the labor market for temporary workers. For understanding the dynamics of temporary employment, the timing was perfect, as it meant that the full range of agency practices and agency/firm relationships was in play and observable. However, because the labor market in Silicon Valley was tight, hiring companies' dependence on the agency may have been greater than normal, giving the latter greater leverage over the former (Houseman, Kalleberg, & Erickcek, 2003). Further, a tight labor market may have forced agency representatives to craft more beneficial policies for temps in order to attract them. However, based on Neuwirth's extensive fieldwork in the Valley and our reading of the now-voluminous literature on temporary employment (including Benner, Leete, and Pastor's excellent comparative study of agencies in Silicon Valley and Milwaukee [2007]), we have a fair degree of confidence that the practices of Select Labor were extremely similar to those of other moderately sized agencies.

4. Approximately 37,000 of the 64,000 firms in the employment services industry are temporary help placement, firms, making this a densely populated business field (Bureau of Labor Statistics 2005).

5. Virtually all studies find that temporary agency workers earn lower wages than do their permanent co-workers, even when they do the same work.

6. Quotes come from Select Labor training literature on how to interview and select workers.

REFERENCES

Autor, D. (2001). Why do temporary help firms provide free general skills training? *Quarterly Journal of Economics*, 116(4), 1409–1448.

Autor, D. (2003). Outsourcing at will: The contribution of unjust dismissal doctrine and the growth of employment outsourcing. *Journal of Labor Economics*, 21(1), 1042.

Barley, S., & Kunda, G. (2006). Contracting: A new form of professional practice. *Academy of Management Perspectives*, 20(1), 45–66.

Bartley, T., & Roberts, W. (2006). Regional exploitation: The informal organization of day labor agencies. *Working USA: The Journal of Labor and Society*, 9(4), 41–58.

Benner, C., Leete, L., & Pastor, M. (2007). *Staircases or treadmills: Labor market intermediaries and economic opportunity in a changing economy.* New York: Russell Sage Foundation.

Berchem, S. (2006). *A profile of temporary and contract employees.* American Staffing Association. Available at http://www.americanstaffing.net/statistics/pdf/Staffing_Employee_Survey_Executive_Summary.pdf.

Berchem, S. (2008). *Uncharted territory: Annual economic analysis puzzles through the data and explains the trends.* American Staffing Association. Available at http: www.americanstaffing.net/statistics/pdf/American_Staffing_2008.pdf.

Bureau of Labor Statistics. (2005). Employment services outlook: Employment services. Accessed January 13, 2009, from www.bls.gov/oco/cg/cgs039.htm.

Cappelli, P. (1995). Is the skills gap really about attitudes? *California Management Review*, 37(4), 108–124.

Dey, M., Houseman, S., &. Polivka, A. (2007). Outsourcing to staffing services: How manufacturers' use of staffing agencies affects employment and productivity measurement. *Employment Research*, 14(1), 4–6.

DuRivage, V. (2001). CWA's organizing strategies: Transforming contract work into union jobs. In F. Carre, M. Ferber, L. Golden, &. S. Herzenberg (Eds.), *Nonstandard work: The nature and challenges of changing employment relations* (pp. 377–392). Champaign, IL: Industrial Relations and Research Associates and University of Illinois Press.

Farber, H. (1999). Alternative and part-time employment relationships as a response to job loss. *Journal of Labor Economic*, 17(4, pt. 2), S142–169.

Goldin, C. (1990). *Understanding the gender gap.* New York: Oxford University Press.

Gonos, G. (1997). The contest over "employer" status in the postwar United States: The case of temporary help firms. *Law & Society Review*, 31(1), 81–110.

Gonos, G. (2000/2001). Never a fee! The miracle of the postmodern temporary help and staffing agency. *Working USA*, 4(3), 9–36.

Granovetter, M. (1995). *Getting a job: A study of contacts and careers.* Chicago: University of Chicago Press.

Henson, K. (1996). *Just a temp.* Philadelphia: Temple University Press.

Hodson, R. (2001). *Dignity at work.* Cambridge, England: Cambridge University Press.

Houseman, S., & Erickcek, G. (2002). Temporary services and contracting out: Effects on low-skilled workers. *Employment Research*, 9(3), 1–3.

Houseman, S., Kalleberg, A., & Erickcek, G. (2003). The role of temporary agency employment in tight labor markets. *Industrial and Labor Relations Review*, 57(1), 105–127.

Jacoby, S. (1985). *Employing bureaucracy: Managers, unions, and the transformation of work in American industry, 1900–1945.* New York: Columbia University Press.

Mangum, G., Mayall, D., & Nelson, K. (1985). The temporary help industry. *Industrial and Labor Relations Review*, 38(4), 599–611.

Martin, J. (1994). *Command performance: The art of delivering quality service.* Boston, MA: Harvard Business School Press.

McAllister, J. (1998). Sisyphus at work in the warehouse: Temporary employment in Greenville, South Carolina. In K. Barker & K. Christensen (Eds.), *Contingent work: American employment relations in transition* (pp. 221–242). Ithaca: Cornell/ILR Press.

Mishel, L., Bernstein, J., &. Allegretto, S. (2007). *The state of working America: 2006/2007.* Economic Policy Institute and Ithaca, NY: Cornell University/ILR Press.

Moore, M. (1965). The temporary help service industry: Historical development, operation, and scope. *Industrial and Labor Relations Review*, 18(4), 554–569.

Nollen, S., & Axel, H. (1998). Benefits and costs to employers. In K. Barker & K. Christensen (Eds.), *Contingent work: American employment relations in transition* (pp. 126–143). Ithaca, NY: Cornell/ILR Press.

Ofstead, C. (1999). Temporary help firms as entrepreneurial actors. *Sociological Forum*, 14(2), 273–294.

Parker, R. (1994). *Flesh peddlers and warm bodies: The temporary help industry and its workers.* New Brunswick, NJ: Rutgers University Press.

Peck, J., & Theodore, N. (1998). The business of contingent work: Growth and restructuring in Chicago's temporary employment industry. *Work, Employment, and Society*, 12(4), 655–674.

Pfeffer, J., & Baron, J. (1988). Taking the workers back out: Recent trends in the structuring of employment. *Research in Organizational Behavior*, 10, 257–303.

Rogers, J. K., & Henson, K. (1997). Hey, why don't you wear a shorter skirt? Structural vulnerability and the organization of sexual harassment in temporary clerical employment. *Gender and Society*, 11(2), 215–237.

Smith, S. (2005). "Don't put my name on it": (Dis) trust and job-finding assistance among the black urban poor. *American Journal of Sociology*, 111(1), 1–57.

Smith, V. (2001). Teamwork vs. tempwork: Managers and the dualisms of workplace restructuring. In D. Cornfield, K. Campbell, & H. McCammon (Eds.), *Working in restructured workplaces: Challenges and new directions for the sociology of work* (pp. 7–28). Thousand Oaks, CA: Sage Publications.

Smith, V., &. Neuwirth, E. B. (2008). *The good temp.* Ithaca, NY: Cornell University/ILR Press.

Vosko, L. (2000). *Temporary work: The gendered rise of a precarious employment relationship.* Toronto: University of Toronto Press.

Wilk, S., & Cappelli, P. (2003). Understanding the determinants of employer use of selection methods. *Personnel Psychology*, 56(1), 103–124.

READING 8.2

Assessment Instruments for the Global Workforce

Douglas Stuart

Spurred by the demands of globalization, international relocation and the increasingly multicultural workplace, intercultural assessment instruments have proliferated in the last decade. The growing supply of instruments reflects the increasing importance of selecting appropriate people for international assignments or positions in multicultural work environments and preparing them for these unfamiliar circumstances. Because such positions often require competencies beyond the standard set of professional knowledge and skills needed for familiar first-culture work environments, international human resource professionals responsible for selection and development seek tools to assess and enhance aptitude, awareness and skills.

There are dozens of commercially available and increasingly sophisticated instruments purporting or measure various aspects of intercultural adaptability or suitability; intercultural sensitivity, development or competence; or work style and/or cultural values orientation. It has become increasingly difficult to keep up with what tools are available in the market, what they measure and whether they are appropriate for particular needs.

This paper summarizes various aspects of competence required for successful performance in the global environment, organizes commercially available instruments that attempt to measure some aspects of that competence according to their appropriate application—selection or development—and describes several appropriate instruments in each category with respect to purpose and design, supporting research, presentation languages, source and other pertinent or unique attributes. Part 1 focuses on instruments particularly applicable to the selection process. Part 2 focuses on instruments primarily designed for the development process.

In total 18 tools are included, originating in the United States (10), United Kingdom (3), Netherlands (3), Canada (1) and the United Arab Emirates (1). For quick reference, all instruments discussed are summarized in a table at the end of this paper.

Global Intercultural Competence: A Cluster of Traits, Attitudes, Knowledge and Skills

Although a lot of research has examined the traits and skills associated with success in international assignments and, more recently, success in the multicultural workplace domestically or abroad, the selection and development process is still more of an art than a science. With respect to international assignments, there are so many variables affecting the outcome that it is difficult to predict success or failure. One must look at the personal situation of the candidate—single or married, with or without children, of what ages, separation issues with respect to extended family or support group, point in career path, etc. Variables in the assignment itself include location (developed or undeveloped economy, urban versus rural setting, remoteness, degree of cultural difference and language challenge, climate, number of other expatriates at the workplace and in the community, experience of the local workforce with foreigners, etc.) and the nature of the work (a technical versus a management focus, the relative importance of external relationship-building with client, customer, local government and community versus internal management, and more).

There are many variables affecting the nature and the degree of challenge of an assignment. The fundamental question is: what factors, beyond technical competence, predict success in the global business environment? *In general, the global workplace requires the ability to operate comfortably and effectively within a broad spectrum of difference—human, cultural and environmental,* all of which overlap naturally. While research has identified numerous attitudes, traits and skills that make up this broad ability or competence, here is a short and reasonably comprehensive list:

1. Action orientation (conscientiousness).
2. Flexibility.
3. Emotional stability.
4. Openness (open-mindedness).
5. Sociability (extraversion, agreeableness).
6. Cultural empathy (cultural sensitivity, cultural intelligence).

Taken as universal across cultures, the first "big five" attributes listed above are transparent and make common sense with respect to fostering comfort and competence in unfamiliar and diverse situations. Such traits are generally not learned but rather part of one's personality, their presence or absence appearing early in life. Although traits are generally considered stable rather than trainable competencies, the latter, more social dimensions, have been shown to increase as a result of training or living abroad. For convenience, let us associate the "big five" cluster with *adaptability*.

Cultural empathy, however, differs from the others. As noted by Milton Bennett, empathy requires a shift in frame of reference, an experiencing of a situation from another person's perspective.[1] Research in social neuroscience, as reviewed recently by Daniel Goleman, confirms ever more strongly that empathy, the major component of cultural sensitivity, is learned and that cultural sensitivity plays a primary role in intercultural competence.[2] We will associate this factor with *competence*.

The successful global manager, whether expatriating, simply working in a multicultural environment or supporting a multicultural workforce, exhibits a complex *global competence* that comprises the following:

1. Knowledge of one's own and other pertinent cultures.
2. Recognition of specific differences between cultures.
3. Understanding of how culture influences behavior in the workplace.
4. Ability to empathize with, adapt to and/or manage differences, as expressed in business structures, systems and priorities, within multicultural work environments.

Together with the factors discussed above, this emotional, cognitive and behavioral set provides the foundation for successful participation in global business.

Tools for Building the Global Workforce

Whether the task is selecting employees to fill sensitive positions or development planning for managers, there are sophisticated and well-researched tools for measuring and developing various aspects of intercultural competence. It is crucial to understand the attitudes, knowledge and skills needed for management of the global workplace and to be able to measure and develop these. The instruments discussed below present a strong and consistent basis for these processes.

The somewhat artificial separation of *adaptability* and *competence* above allows us to group the nine instruments of Part 1 into two sections.

Part 1

Tools for the Selection Process: Adaptability

When selecting candidates for international or multicultural assignments from a pool of personnel of roughly equal technical qualifications, it is useful to assess both intercultural adaptability and intercultural competence. Ideally, candidates are offered the confidential opportunity to complete instruments relating to both categories in order to self-select into or

out of consideration for a specific assignment. There are numerous instruments designed to assess adaptability or intercultural competence or some combination of both. We will first look at adaptability instruments.

Adaptability instruments were the first assessment tools developed in response to the globalization of business and the increase of international assignments. Some have been available for more than 30 years, and new ones continue to be developed. Most of these instruments are based primarily on a self-assessment of a set of personality traits (listed above under Global Competencies for Global Work) associated with adaptability to new situations.

Note that HR personnel often elect to review the individual profiles resulting from these instruments. This can compromise the results because, in many cases, the questions are quite transparent in terms of what the desirable answers might be. Thus, if a candidate suspects that his or her profile, as revealed by the instrument, might be a factor in an employment decision, he or she may not answer the questions candidly.

Questions focusing on adaptability traits generally employ five- or six-point Likert scales expressing degrees of agreement or disagreement. Typical questions, taken from several of the instruments described below, include:

- I can think of very few people who dislike me.
- I try to understand people's thoughts and feelings when I talk to them.
- My closest friends are similar to me in terms of their religious affiliations.
- I like to get the opinions of others when making decisions at work.
- I could live anywhere and enjoy life.
- I generally eat my meals at the same time each day.
- When I meet people who are different from me, I tend to feel judgmental about their differences.
- I can laugh at myself and not take myself too seriously.
- Most of what I do is governed by the demands of others.

Recognizing the transparency of such questions, it is advisable to use these tools for self-selection prior to offering international assignments.

Note also that use of such instruments in employment decisions can entail legal liability, since the tools are generally not job-specific. That is, if the candidate's profile from an instrument influences the hiring decision and the candidate is unhappy with the decision, he or she may have legal recourse in protesting that the instrument was irrelevant to the job and thus used inappropriately. This can work both ways, in rejecting an employee for a desired position or in selecting an employee for an assignment that results in failure. Instruments designed to assist the management decision process are so noted.

Here are six quite different instruments that assess variations of these traits or these plus other competencies. Four of these tools below were developed in the United States, one in Canada and one in the Netherlands. Tools developed outside of the United States are marked. Throughout the paper, instruments are ordered alphabetically by acronym to avoid any implication of ranking:

- Cross-Cultural Adaptability Inventory (CCAI).
- International Assignment Profile (IAP).
- International Personnel Assessment tool (iPASS) *Canada*.
- Overseas Assignment Inventory (OAI).
- Multicultural Personality Questionnaire (MPQ) *Netherlands*.
- Self-Assessment for Global Endeavors (SAGE).

Cross-Cultural Adaptability Inventory (CCAI) The CCAI, developed by Colleen Kelley, Ph.D. and Judith Meyers, PsyD, was copyrighted in 1987. It is designed to provide information to an individual about his or her potential for cross-cultural effectiveness. Both versions consist of 50 questions that assess four components of cross-cultural adaptability. Initial statistical studies indicated that the CCAI had sufficient reliability and validity for a training instrument. While some recent research has questioned the validity of the four-factor structure, other research has correlated it with emotional intelligence. The CCAI remains a convenient tool for the self-selection process because of its simplicity and low cost. The instrument can be purchased in any quantity and does not require certified administrators. It can be used as a standalone instrument for self-selection for international assignments, as part of a larger selection battery, for pre- and post-testing or as part of a cross-cultural training. There is a follow-up training tool, called the CCAI Action-Planning Guide, that suggests actions to address factors assessed as weak, and there is also a Facilitator's Guide and Cultural Passport to Anywhere for use in group debriefs. The Multi-Rater Kit provides 360-degree feedback with three observers. The CCAI is available in two versions, a self-scoring paper-and-pencil instrument that provides immediate turnaround and an online version that provides the scoring and a printed feedback report, from Pearson Performance Solutions at 1-800-922-7343 or www.pearsonps.com under Solutions/Performance Management/Organization Surveys/CCAI.

International Assignment Profile (IAP) It is common knowledge that family adjustment is the most significant threat to the success of an international assignment. The IAP, from International Assignment Profile Systems, is a unique and technologically sophisticated tool designed primarily as a preparation instrument to assist those selected for international assignment to prepare well for their destination. Its goal is to make a good match between the employee, the family and the particular destination. However, the tool has selection implications; if the IAP report indicates that the required support is too onerous or extensive, then manager and employee may want to reconsider the timing or

destination. The IAP is a multi-faceted process that gathers and organizes extensive information about a family anticipating international assignment and integrates it with information about the destination to which they are being sent. It also provides the means of archiving this information for learning and future research. The IAP recognizes the client company and can be customized to convey specific information; it can be modified, customized or "branded" to fit a client's or vendor's specific requirements.

The IAP report summarizes family information in a comprehensive, easily understood format identifying core issues that need to be addressed prior to departure:

- Critical planning issues and adjustments that must occur to ensure assignment success.
- A list of "sleeper" issues that could emerge post-arrival to compromise the assignment.
- Information on "back home" issues that may affect the assignment.
- "Pleasant surprises"—essential or important things to the family that will meet or exceed expectations in the destination.
- Destination information on spousal employment and spousal impact.
- Traits and behaviors that may hinder or enhance cultural adjustment.

The two-part questionnaire can be completed in approximately 35 minutes per section for employee and spouse. The survey is secure and does not have to be completed in one sitting. The report is typically generated within 24 hours but can be received more quickly if necessary. While information on how to use and interpret the IAP is available from IAP Systems, the IAP requires no special training. (No information on research support was offered.) More information is available from *www.iapsystems.com*.

International Personnel Assessment tool (iPASS) With Part 2 still under development, iPASS is already a comprehensive, behaviorally based tool to assess intercultural effectiveness and readiness for undertaking an international assignment. Designed for HR and recruiting specialists in the international field, iPASS is being developed by the Centre for Intercultural Learning, Foreign Affairs department, Canada. *In contrast to most intercultural assessment instruments, iPASS is intended to provide a strong, reliable basis for HR and management in employment decisions.* Part 1, available now in French and English, is the Behavioral-Based Interview Kit, providing a reliable intercultural competency interview. Based on 35+ years of research, the interview kit employs seven competencies for intercultural effectiveness: cultural adaptation, knowledge of the host country, sensitivity and respect, network and relationship building, intercultural communication, intercultural leadership, and personal and professional commitment. Each competency has four levels of mastery. A client chooses three competencies necessary for success in the intended assignment as well as the level of each competency required for adequate functioning. Based on this, a customized interview kit is then prepared for the iPASS-certified HR/recruiter specialist with a set of comprehensive questions appropriate to the selected competencies and levels, including questions on motivation, interest and attitude toward cultural difference as well. These questions are then addressed during a two-hour interview.

Part 2, a 40-question Situational Judgment test based on actual intercultural conflict situations, will provide an additional screening tool when completed. Qualification for use of the Behavioral-Based Interview Kit is obtained through a three-day training delivered for 8–12 people wherever required. For further information, go to http://www.dfait-maeci.gc.ca/cfsi-icse/cil-cai/iPAss-en.asp?IVI=6 or contact the project leader, Nicole Paulun, at nicole.paulun@international.gc.ca (access from www.intercultures.gc.ca).

Multicultural Personality Questionnaire (MPQ) Karen I. Van der Zee, Ph.D., and Jan Pieter Van Oudenhoven, Ph.D., University of Groningen, the Netherlands developed the Multicultural Personality Questionnaire of 91 items as a multidimensional instrument to measure intercultural effectiveness. Developed in 1998 and revised in 2000, the MPQ measures five traits: cultural empathy, open-mindedness, social initiative, emotional stability and flexibility. Designed primarily for self-assessment, it can be used as well for risk assessment as part of the selection process. More information on the MPQ can be found at www.interculturalcontact.org or www.intercultureelcontact.nl/en/. The Questionnaire is available through Van der Maesen Personnel Management in Dutch, English, German, Italian (all research-supported) and French online at www.psychecommerce.nl; a report is generated and available immediately for download.

Overseas Assignment Inventory (OAI) Developed by Michael Tucker, Tucker International, the OAI was the first major instrument assessing suitability for an international assignment. Available since the early 1970s and first designed for the U.S. Navy, the self-awareness questionnaire examines six factors of acceptance, knowledge, affect, lifestyle, interaction and communication found crucial for successful adaptation to another culture. The factors include 14 specific motivations, expectations, attributes and attitudes, including motivations for accepting or wanting an international assignment. Studies of validity and reliability have been conducted at intervals on various populations since its implementation, and the OAI has undergone significant redevelopment. It continues to be well-known and respected in the relocation industry.

The questionnaire is available in booklet form or online, although the reports, in two versions—one to the candidate and another to HR or management—are furnished in hard copy only and may take several weeks for delivery.[3] Reports are self-explanatory and do not require certified administrators. However, for the corporate selection process, the OAI can be combined with a behavioral interview; in this case, HR must be certified in the interview technique incorporating the OAI report. The OAI report can be integrated into intercultural training as well. Use of the OAI can be arranged through Tucker International www.tuckerintl.com in English, French and German. Tucker International also offers several other assessment instruments. The OAI is appropriate for self-selection and may be helpful for HR in its decision process. The OAI provides a limited basis for professional development in preparation for an international assignment, and its debrief can become a major component of cultural training.

Self-Assessment for Global Endeavors (The SAGE)

The SAGE was developed by Paula Caligiuri, Ph.D., Director of the Center for Human Resource Strategy at Rutgers University, at the time of writing. Available since 1997, the instrument was designed to assist individuals and families as a confidential tool in their decision process of whether to accept an international assignment. The tool's three sections address issues of personality (six factors), motivation and family situation. Validity and reliability is supported by considerable research. The SAGE is available in two versions—one for the employee and a second for the accompanying partner—online in English with the report immediately available for reading online or printing. Paper-based versions are also available in French, Japanese, Mandarin and Taiwanese. These versions are not merely translation/back translations but recreations of the instrument using cultural resources to assure the appropriateness of the questions. The first two sections, on traits and motivation, are scored with ranges marked in green, yellow or red as indications of one's suitability and readiness for assignment. The third section, on family, is not scored but is designed to facilitate the family conversation necessary for an informed decision about seeking and accepting an assignment. While designed to support the self-selection process, the SAGE report can also be within a pre-departure or post-arrival cultural training program. Information on The SAGE is available at www.cali-giuri.com; the tool can be purchased from RW[3] LLC, 212-691-8900 or www.rw-3llc.com.

Tools for the Selection Process: Competence

While the dividing line between adaptability and competency instruments is blurry because many—such as the OAI and iPASS above—incorporate aspects of both, there are a number of tools designed more for the assessment of competencies than for adaptability. The next three disparate instruments focus more on the complex skills essential for effective functioning in international assignments. Proprietary considerations prevent the presentation of sample questions, and in any case, because of the complexity of these tools, the presentation of a few sample questions would not be illustrative and might be misleading.

- Global Candidate Assessment (GCA 360°)
- Intercultural Development Inventory (IDI)
- Survey on Intercultural (Relocation) Adaptability (SIA, SIRA)

Global Candidate Assessment[SM] **(GCA 360°)** The Global Candidate Assessment is an elaborate 3-step online assessment process, developed by Aperian Global, that involves self-assessment and assessment by up to 10 colleagues, supervisors and subordinates on the same items (not identified in the available description), including written commentary on selected questions about the candidate's attitudes and abilities. While the assessment examines workplace behaviors and adaptability, the instrument does not focus specifically on intercultural competencies as defined above. Once the surveys are completed, the tool generates an instant compilation, the Candidate Summary Report, which is viewable by the client assessment administrator. This includes overall scores, a combined visual display, a gap analysis indicating difference between the candidate's and others' scores, and a compilation of written comments. Administrative functions can be performed by Aperian or by a client HR person. Step Two is a three-hour interview with the candidate conducted by an Aperian consultant. This may include the spouse or partner as well and covers motivation, challenges, relocation issues, career impact, personal strengths/weaknesses and self-rating of adaptability, all resulting in a verbal summary report to client HR. Step Three is a candidate meeting with client HR to debrief the process and indicate current level of commitment to an international assignment. As an optional Step 4 after the candidate has been accepted, the candidate and key colleagues in the new position can take the GlobeSmart Assessment Profile (GAP), which compares a profile of the candidate with that of the selected colleagues and generates a report to each suggesting various behavior modifications to enhance collaboration. *Clearly the GCA 360° is designed to support employment decisions.* (No information on research support was offered.) More information on the Global Candidate Assessment is available from www.aperianglobal.com, which also offers a number of other Web-based tools.

Intercultural Development Inventory[TM] **(IDI)** The IDI is a theory-based instrument, developed by Mitchell Hammer, Ph.D., and Milton Bennett, Ph.D., that measures intercultural sensitivity as conceptualized in Bennett's Development Model of Intercultural Sensitivity (DMIS—1986, 1993). First introduced in 1997 and revised in 2002, the 50-item instrument measures people's reaction to cultural

difference along a developmental six-stage scale of cognitive structures or "worldviews" reflecting increasing intercultural sensitivity or competence. These worldviews range from denial and defense through minimization to acceptance, adaptation and integration, with the first three labeled as ethnocentric and the last three—ethnorelative. Intercultural competence minimally requires development into the acceptance/adaptation stage of intercultural sensitivity. The IDI is supported by impressive reliability and validity studies, available from www.intercultural.org, and *can be used with confidence in both the selection process and developmental planning,* where it predicts the kind of intervention most effective for development according to the revealed stage of intercultural sensitivity. It is equally applicable for measuring the intercultural competence of work or leadership teams (as an average) and for planning further competence development.

The IDI is available as a paper-and-pencil instrument or online in 12 languages: Bahasa Indonesia/Malay, Chinese, English, French, German, Italian, Japanese, Korean, Norwegian, Portuguese, Russian and Spanish. While inexpensive to purchase, it must be purchased and debriefed by a certified interpreter. Further information is available at www.intercultural.org.

Survey on Intercultural (Relocation) Adaptability (SIA & SIRA) From Grovewell LLC, SIA and SIRA are online 360° assessment instruments for global leadership or relocation candidates. For global leadership candidates, the SIA assesses seven skills/qualities that facilitate successful adaptation to global realities: flexibility, non-judgmentalness, interest in different views and values, awareness of others' feelings, attention to relationships, responding well in unclear situations and self-confidence. The 360° process (up to 12 raters) also assesses 20 behaviors that undermine relationships with diverse counterparts. For global relocation candidates, the SIRA adds a self-assessment (not 360°) for candidate and separately for the spouse or partner of motivations, concerns and expectations around long-term living and working in an unfamiliar environment. The Feedback Report of these instruments is provided directly and solely to the user, who is advised to share results with HR or management. While no certification is required for the administration of these instruments, a separate manual plus phone consultation is provided to HR and EAP professionals in contracting firms. Usage prices are available on the Web site at www.grovewell.com/expat-360-assessment.html.

Conclusion: Part 1

Part 1 described nine varied instruments in support of the selection process for international assignments or entry into the multicultural workplace, with respect to both adaptability and intercultural competence. These were selected from a larger pool for various reasons, including design, research support, commercial availability and application to varied needs. As a final comment, users of selection instruments are often concerned about their reliability and validity, often because of a desire to use the tool to predict performance success and thus tie it to employment decisions. It is important to understand that although many of these instruments are well supported by significant research, the linking of their results to the probability of assignment success is problematic since such instruments (with the exception of iPASS and GCA 360°) are not job-specific in their design. That is, the need for adaptability and intercultural competence varies greatly with the job and the work and living environments. Therefore, results of these instruments (again, with the exception of iPASS, GCA 360° and, to some extent, the IDI) should not be used as the sole or even the primary basis of employment decisions.

Part 2 below describes another set of instruments primarily suited for the development of intercultural competence.

Part 2

Tools for the Development Process: Intercultural Awareness

Intercultural research by authors ranging from Florence Kluckhohn and Fred Strodbeck in the 1950s through Edward Hall in the 1960s and 1970s and Geert Hofstede and Fons Trompenaars (with Charles Hampden-Turner) in the 1980s and 1990s, plus the large value surveys such as the World Values Survey, Shalom Schwartz's work in Europe and most recently the seminal publication of *Culture, Leadership, and Organizations: The GLOBE Study of 62 Societies*,[4] The contrast of cultures through the lens of value dimensions has provided a research-supported, practical means of comparison in which values can be predictably linked to patterns of behavior in a variety of situations. Such information forms the basis of the knowledge component of intercultural competence and can be invaluable in the preparation for an international assignment, working in a multicultural environment or leading a global team. It is no surprise, then, that a number of assessment instruments have been developed to enable people to understand their own cultural value preferences and compare these with core values of other cultures in order to understand the challenges these differences might present in the work environment.

Since each of the following instruments focuses on value preferences, a list of sample questions will provide an idea of how these tools are designed (because of their proprietary nature, the tools from which the questions are drawn are not identified):

- You take more pride in…
  - Your contributions to your company.
  - The accomplishments of your company.

- Outperforming co-workers is a motivator for you.
  - Yes.
  - No.
- It is more important that business decisions be made in accordance with…
  - General principles and theories.
  - The particular circumstances.
- Most organizations would be better off if conflict could be eliminated forever. (Five-point Likert scale of disagreement/agreement)
- In order to have efficient work relationships, it is often necessary to bypass the hierarchical lines. (Five-point Likert scale)
- Gaining consensus is more important than decisive action. (Five-point Likert scale)

Below are descriptions of six instruments (three from the United States and one each from the United Kingdom, the United Arab Emirates and the Netherlands) with a focus on cultural values and their impact on how we work. These tools are not evaluative and are not designed to support employment decisions by candidates or management.

- Argonaut Assessment (AA) U.K.
- Cultural Mapping and Navigation© Assessment Tool (CMNAT) U.A.E.
- Cultural Orientation Indicator (COI)
- Culture in the Workplace Questionnaire (CWQ)
- Intercultural Awareness Profiler (IAP) Netherlands
- Peterson Cultural Style Indicator (PCSI)

Argonaut™   Developed by Coghill & Beery International in the United Kingdom, ArgonautOnline™ is a suite of cross-cultural e-learning tools that includes an assessment instrument. The Argonaut Assessment (AA) instrument, available in English only, employs a 20-minute questionnaire involving 12 dimensions (communication, conflict, problem solving, space, use of time, time spans, fate, rules, power, responsibility, group membership, tasks) to produce a graphical map allowing comparison of the learner's self-perception, home culture and target cultures from a list of 50+ countries. This contrastive mapping provides a basis for the formation of "personal strategies for international success." Results from the AA instrument can be combined with other online learning tools, including personalized feedback and interactive tutorials. Access to the AA is gained through accreditation as a trainer or coach to use the ArgonautOnline tool suite. For more information, visit www.argonautonline.com.

Cultural Mapping and Navigation© Assessment Tool (CMNAT) Created by Knowledgeworkx in the United Arab Emirates, this tool employs a 72-question online inventory to produce a personal profile that details preferences on 12 bipolar cultural dimensions affecting workplace behaviors: growth (people vs. material), relationship (universal vs. situational), outlook (tradition vs. Innovation), destiny (directed vs. directive), context (informal vs. formal), connecting (exclusive vs. inclusive), expression (reveal vs. conceal), decision making (relationship vs. rules), planning (people vs. time), communication (direct vs. indirect), accountability (community vs. individual) and status (ascribed vs. achieved). The CMNAT profile is incorporated in the second level of a four-level program (three days of training for Levels 1–3 and ongoing coaching toward intercultural excellence in Level 4). The goal is the growth and application of intercultural intelligence to achieve intercultural excellence within multicultural teams. The Assessment Tool is also integrated with other (noncultural) assessment instruments (the Diamond Profiling Process) as part of intercultural leadership consultation. There is a five-day intensive program for certification in the delivery of Levels 1–3 of the Cultural Mapping & Navigation Program® suite of products. More information is available at www. KnowledgeWorkx.com.

Cultural Orientations Indicator® (COI) Developed by Training Management Corporation (TCM), the COI is a Web-based self-reporting instrument that assesses individual preference within 10 cultural dimensions (environment, time, action, communication, space, power, individualism, competitiveness, structure, thinking) drawn from the social science research mentioned at the beginning of Part 2, plus other contributors, such as Edward Stuart, Milton Bennett and Stephen Rhinesmith. The 108-question inventory yields a profile of preferences along a series of continua–17 in all, as several of the 10 dimensions have sub-continua. The profile of preferences (restricted to work-related behaviors and situations) enables comparison to other team members and national norms, allowing "gap analysis" and the coaching of strategies for bridging differences. Group or team aggregate reports are also available. The COI is also integrated into the Cultural Navigator™, an online learning portal, and other programs offered by TMC. Test construction has been psychometrically validated (but not all the 10 dimensions have been validated globally). The COI is available in Chinese, English, French, German, Italian, Japanese and Spanish. The COI is supported by the *Cultural Orientations Guide* (4th edition), which supplies a context for understanding the instrument and its applications. Further information is available at www. tmcorp.com.

Culture in the Workplace Questionnaire™ (CWQ) Based on the research and developed with the support of Geert Hofstede,[5] the CWQ, recently revised and Web-enabled, provides individual cultural profiles incorporating five cultural dimensions validated by extensive research: individualism, power distance, certainty (uncertainty avoidance), achievement (masculinity) and time orientation (long-term orientation). The instrument is available through ITAP International,

which licenses the Culture in the Workplace Questionnaire™ from Professor Hofstede. Profiles can be compared to average national values (established through the research of Hofstede and others) of 60 countries.

The 60-question inventory is completed online, resulting in a seven-page personal report, which can be downloaded and printed by the user or saved for later distribution by a facilitator. The individual profile illustrates the user's score on each dimension in comparison with national averages of up to 15 selected countries. The report explains each dimension, lists the impact on work style of values at either end of the dimension, such as individual vs. group orientation, and illustrates in a scenario the misunderstanding and conflict typical of interaction between individuals holding different orientations. It also provides specific analyses on the user's score on each dimension and the implications of the differences between the user scores and the comparison country averages and adaptive recommendations.

The CWQ can be used with individuals or groups and also provides team reports for printing or download. Group averages can be compared in PowerPoint slides to numerous countries' average values, and the scores of individual members of the group can be confidentially compared with respect to each dimension, which is very useful for global teams. The CW Questionnaire is currently available in a simple world business English; by the end of 2007 it will be available in multiple languages. Clients can also add special demographic fields so that, for example, data can be analyzed by location of multiple users.

CWQ profiles must be requested and debriefed by trainers or consultants certified in CW profile interpretation. More information on the CWQ is available from www.itapintl. com

Intercultural Awareness Profiler (IAP) Created by Fons Trompenaars, the IAP employs Trompenaars' seven cultural dimensions or polarities, a list drawn from sociological theories of the 1950s and 1960s: universalism vs. particularism, individualism vs. communitarianism, specific vs. diffuse cultures, affective vs. neutral, achievement vs. ascription, sequential vs. synchronic, internal vs. external control. A diagnostic questionnaire, available online, is used to produce a personal cross-cultural orientation against a reference model. Further questions provide sub-group identifications of organizational culture, functional areas and other variables. The analysis is cross-referenced against the Trompenaars' cross-cultural database, including the data of 55,000 + managers in many countries gathered over a 10-year period. The personal report offers advice for doing business and managing in and with other cultures. For information on using the IAP, contact Trompenaars Hampden-Turner (THT) Consulting at www.thtconsulting.com.

Peterson Cultural Style Indicator™ The PCSI, designed by Brooks Peterson of Across Cultures, Inc., consists of a 20-question online inventory that generates a five-dimensional profile. The five bipolar dimensions are hierarchy/equality, direct/indirect, individuality/group, task/relationship and risk/caution. One's profile is comparable to 70 country "norms" (chosen scores based on comparing various studies and updated in 2004), with strategic recommendations for increasing business success. Research supporting the instrument is discussed on the Web site, which includes a list of corporate clients. The PCSI, designed as a stand-alone instrument, can be accessed immediately online for $50 per use, including the comparison of your profile with other countries and suggestions for bridging gaps based on your score. For more information, go to www .acrosscultures.com.

Tools for the Development Process: Intercultural Coaching

One of the tools introduced in Part 1 of this paper, Tools for the Selection Process: Competence, the *Intercultural Development Inventory,* is equally suitable for the development process, particularly in a coaching environment. The explanatory material provided in an IDI profile contains descriptions for each of its scales, including behaviors or attitudes associated with particular scores, the strengths associated with these and the developmental tasks. With the help of an intercultural coach, a user can create and implement a developmental plan.

Here are three more instruments, two developed in the United Kingdom and one in the Netherlands, all intended to be used developmentally. The first of these instruments focuses on competencies, the second incorporates cultural values and an overlay of workplace behaviors, while the third focuses on adaptability and workplace behaviors. Again, proprietary considerations prevent the presentation of sample questions, and because of the complexity of these tools, a few sample questions would not be illustrative and might be misleading.

- Intercultural Readiness Check (IRC) Netherlands
- The Spony Profiling Model (SPM) U.K.
- The International Profiler (TIP) U.K.

Intercultural Readiness Check (IRC) The intercultural readiness check was developed in 2002 by Ursula Brinkman, Ph.D., of Intercultural Business Improvement in the Netherlands. Focused entirely on learnable complex skills crucial to effective intercultural interaction, the IRC examines the following four competencies: intercultural sensitivity, intercultural communication, building commitment and preference for certainty (defined as "ability to manage the greater uncertainty of intercultural situations"). The tool can be used before entering a multicultural environment or during and international assignment. In the debrief of the personal profile, a participant is advised of potential pitfalls and provided practical suggestions for development. In collaboration with an intercultural trainer or coach, the participant can then create a plan for applying strengths and developing weak points, which can be carried out with or without continued coaching. Reliability and validity research was conducted on an international business population of Europeans, U.S. Americans and others. Studies show high reliability (reconfirmed based on a population of more than 2,600 individuals) and sufficient validity to make the IRC a useful instrument for specific developmental training on any of the four competencies. Research continues on the instrument, and scores can be compared to a large data bank of more than 7,000 respondents. The questionnaire can be accessed online, but results must be presented by a licensed intercultural consultant. Information concerning use of the IRC and certification is available from www.ibi-net.nl and www.irc-center.com.

The Spony Profiling Model (SPM) Offered by Future-ToBe in the United Kingdom, the SPM is a unique integrated online instrument that combines aspects of cultural values and work style instruments with 360° reporting on communication style (three work colleagues). It can be used to produce individual, team and organizational culture profiles using the same concepts and frameworks, thereby providing consistency, rigor and integration between the development of individuals, the building of teams and the strategic alignment of organizations. Developed over eight years of research and testing in Britain and France by Dr. Gilles Spony at the Cranfield School of Management, the SPM incorporates the work of cross-cultural psychologist Shalom Schwartz as well as the research of Geert Hofstede to produce profiles of work style preferences. These are graphically displayed on a values framework of two perpendicular Universal axes, the vertical RELATIONSHIP axis of Self-Enhancement vs. Consideration for Others and the horizontal TASK ORIENTATION axis of Group Dynamics vs. Individual Dynamics. This results in a profile of 12 attitudinal orientations that yield 12 operational styles with a total of 36 subdivisions. The individual profile is then overlaid on a cultural values map in order to understand how work style may fit into or clash with various national cultures. The 230 questions of the work style questionnaire require about 45 minutes, while the communication style questionnaire for colleagues takes about 15 minutes. Because of the SPM's sophistication and complexity, accreditation in its use requires a three-day training plus one day of assessment in order to use the instrument to a professional standard with respect to individuals, teams and organizations. Candidates for accreditation are preferred to be holders of a Certificate of Competence in Occupational Testing (Level A) from the British Psychological Society and/or to have experience with other management models. More information on the SPM is available at www.futuretobe.net/.

The International Profiler (TIP) TIP, developed by World-Work Ltd. in the United Kingdom, is a Web-based questionnaire and feedback process, available in English, German, French and Italian, to assess the development needs of managers and other professions for international work. It is based on a set of 10 competencies with 22 associated skills, attitudes and areas of knowledge derived from intercultural research and the practical experience of international professionals. The competencies are openness, flexibility, personal autonomy, emotional strength, perceptiveness, listening orientation, transparency, cultural knowledge, influencing and synergy. TIP is an online psychometric inventory of 80 questions requiring about 45 minutes and generating a scored report within a hefty Feedback Book for the certified consultant and client that provides structured feedback in terms of the energy, emphasis and attention the user typically brings to a competency set. The feedback session, face-to-face or by telephone, consists of a structured discussion of the report with respect to the user's present or future international challenges. The intent is to identify three or four qualities requiring greater energy in the future. This results in a completion of a Personal Development Plan by the user entailing developmental areas, expected benefits from the development and an action plan. The licensing process, required in order to employ TIP, provides a Coaching Manual.

WorldWork Ltd. also offers **Global View 360°**, a panoramic version of the TIP providing feedback from 6–10 international colleagues, clients, friends, etc. who have observed the user in international contexts. It employs a reduced questionnaire (55 questions) focusing solely on the 10 key competencies and provides a gap analysis in the feedback report of the difference between the level of importance given to selected behaviors as compared with the perceived level of performance. Two free fields allow for open-ended commentary. The Global View 360° can be administered in its entirety by its subject. For more information on both instruments, email **info@worldwork.biz** or go to **www.worldwork.biz**.

Conclusion: PART 2

The six value orientation tools described in section titled "Tools for the Development Process: Intercultural Awareness" incorporate the concept of differing behaviors (generally in a business context) rather predictably according to deeply held cultural preferences on values spectra that have undergone extensive global research over the last 50+ years. The instruments differ with respect to the value dimensions they employ, but they all produce personal profiles for comparison with other individuals and group or national averages. Such instruments can be powerful teaching tools for the knowledge component of intercultural competence, both before and during an assignment or while in a multicultural

team; they provide a structured comparative bases for intercultural training and can also be used for coaching.

Two of the instruments described in the section "Tools for the Development Process: Intercultural Coaching" look at workplace behaviors—one from an adaptability and the other from a cultural values perspective. The third tool examines complex skills in the work environment. All these tools are more appropriate to a coaching than a training process.

The increasing demands of globalization raise the stakes of cultural due diligence, both in the selection of appropriate personnel for sensitive positions in the multicultural workforce at home and abroad and in the preparation of employees for the intercultural demands of these assignments.

In making employment decisions with intercultural implications, no assessment instrument by itself can replace a thorough and systematic selection process that includes job-specific performance evaluation and interviews with candidates, colleagues, superiors, direct reports and family (in the case of international assignments). On the other hand, with the availability of the instruments described above, it is equally inexcusable to make such decisions without the support of an appropriate intercultural assessment tool.

Whether you intend to help an employee or family decide whether to accept an international assignment; gather significant information for HR and management to assist in a culturally sensitive employment decision; choose the most culturally competent manager from a pool of candidates to lead a virtual multicultural team; determine the intercultural competence of a work group or leadership team; prepare a manager for an international assignment or a multicultural leadership position; prepare an individual or team for work with a specific cultural group; coach an international transferee or the leader of a multicultural team; provide developmental input to a multicultural team; or affect any other situation involving a need to select for or further develop intercultural competence, there are competitive choices among the sophisticated and powerful assessment tools described in this paper to assist you in that task.

Assessment Instruments for the Global Workforce I: Tools for the Selection Process: Intercultural Adaptability and Intercultural Competence.

Source: Stuart, D. Assessment Instruments for the Global Workforce. Society for Human Resource Management White Paper 022010, June, 2007.

ENDNOTES

1. Bennett, M. J. (1993). Towards ethnorelativism: A developmental model of intercultural sensitivity. In R. Michael Paige (Ed.), *Education for the intercultural experience*. Intercultural Press, pp. 53–54.

2. Goleman, D. (2006). *Social intelligence: The new science of human relationships*. United States: Random House.

3. Information concerning commercially available instruments is based on what was readily available publicly at the time of writing. Because all these instruments are proprietary, full information on availability and cost may be provided solely to potential purchasers.

4. House, Hanges, Javidan, Dorfman, & Gupta (Eds.). (2004). *Culture, leadership, and organizations: The GLOBE Study of 62 Societies.* Sage Publications.

5. Dr. Hofstede is Professor Emeritus, the University of Limburg at Maastricht, Director (Emeritus) of the Institute for Research on Intercultural Cooperation (IRIC), the Netherlands, and author of *Culture and Organizations: Software of the Mind* (McGraw Hill, 1991) and *Culture's Consequences: Comparing Values, Behaviors, Institutions, and Organizations across Nations,* which presents the research basis for the CWQ.

CHAPTER 9

Training and Development

- Understand how training and development activities can contribute to an organization's strategic objectives
- Describe how to conduct a needs assessment as part of a training program
- Explain the different modes of delivery of training and how to maximize transfer of training
- Gain an appreciation for the various levels of evaluation of training and the benefits and limitations of each
- Describe the role of organizational development in promoting change with an organization
- Understand the critical link between training, performance management, and compensation in ensuring the success of training

Using Training to Rebrand Sofitel Hotels

With an increasingly competitive marketplace in the high-end hotel industry, worldwide luxury hotel chain Sofitel embarked on a rebranding program in 2008 to position itself as an exclusive chain that offered its guests a unique experience. To facilitate this, an extensive employee training program was put in place across all 40 countries in which Sofitel operates to make every one of the organization's 25,000 employees "ambassadors" for the brand. Every employee, from new hires to the most long-term employees, from hourly employee to executives, went through a two-year long onsite training program at the individual hotel site in which the employee works. Training was provided by a corporate training team that traveled from location to location. Training centered on how to create a sense of luxury for customers, empowering employees at all levels with the freedom to make unique and personalized experiences for any guests on the spot. Employees are issued "passports" for their training, which are stamped upon completion of individual training units with stamps rewarded through gift certificates, celebrations, accreditation, and heightened responsibilities. Ongoing monthly training is provided to employees who have successfully completed the initial two-year training. The program has resulted in significant improved guest satisfaction and greatly aided in employee retention.[1]

f an organization considers its employees to be human assets, training and development represents an ongoing investment in these assets and one of the most significant investments an organization can make. Training involves employees acquiring knowledge and learning skills that they will be able to use immediately; employee development involves learning that will aid the organization and employee later in the employee's career. Many organizations use the term *learning* rather than *training* to emphasize the point that the activities engaged in as part of this developmental process are broad based and involve much more than straightforward acquisition of manual or technical skills.

Learning implies ongoing development and continuously adding to employees' skills and knowledge to meet the challenges the organization faces from its external environment. A focus on learning, as opposed to training, emphasizes results rather than process, making such an approach more palatable to senior executives. Any kind of employee learning that is not reinforced by the organization's reward system has little chance of impacting employee behavior and performance.

Employee training and development is increasingly becoming a major strategic issue for organizations for several reasons. First, rapid changes in technology continue to cause increasing rates of skill obsolescence. To remain competitive, organizations need to continue training their employees to use the best and latest technologies available. Managing in such a turbulent environment has created the need for continuous learning among managers.[2] Second, the redesign of work into jobs having broader responsibilities (that are often part of self-managed teams) requires employees to assume more responsibility, take initiative, and further develop interpersonal skills to ensure their performance and success. Employees need to acquire a broader skill base and be provided with development opportunities to assist with teamwork, collaboration, and conflict management. Third, mergers and acquisitions have greatly increased. These activities require integrating employees of one organization into another having a vastly different culture. When financial and performance results of merger and acquisition activity fall short of plans, the reason usually rests with people management systems rather than operational or financial management systems. Fourth, employees are moving from one employer to another with far more frequency than they did in the past. With less loyalty to a particular employer and more to the employees' own careers, more time must be spent on integrating new hires into the workplace. Finally, the globalization of business operations requires managers to acquire knowledge and skills related to language and cultural differences.

These strategic challenges for training exist alongside standard types of training that are done for new organizational hires (orientation and socialization) and for those employees assuming new job responsibilities. In organizations that emphasize both promotion from within and the career development of existing employees, continual training and development opportunities are critical. Employees must be updated in industry best practices and changing technology. For an employer who hires a significant number of skilled workers from outside the organization, new employees need to understand rules, policies, and procedures and be socialized into company operations and employee networks.

New employee orientation can be a daunting challenge for employers. New hires are often inundated with forms, procedures, and people but lack a strong sense of the business and operations in which they have begun to work. Coworkers can be critical catalysts in helping new employees obtain information they need to be productive.[3] While new-hire orientation programs can attempt to assist new employees in their transition into the workplace, if the programs were not developed in tandem with any strategic objectives or in concert with other human resources (HR) programs and/or critical operational areas of the organization, they often do not have a significant impact on the new hire's ability to fully understand the entire organization and their place in it. Ideally, new employee orientation programs will teach employees not only about their jobs and the organization's culture and strategy but also how their individual jobs are critical to the organization's success. Orientation training, sometimes called "onboarding," should allow employees the opportunity to ask questions and interact with those providing information as well as facilitate the development of a network of work relationships for employees. Exemplary new employee orientation and training programs have been developed at Black and Decker and MicroStrategy.

New Employee Training at Black and Decker

Towson, Maryland–based tool manufacturer Black and Decker (B&D) has developed a new employee training program that literally puts employees to work. College grads who gain entry-level professional employment in sales with B&D traditionally received their training via a three-ring binder that provided information about B&D products. New employees would study and learn the material to assist them with their selling. Establishing credibility was not part of the training equation, and many trainees never even touched the products they were selling, let alone used them. Black and Decker has recently revamped its sales training for new hires to combine classroom training, online courses, and, most important, a training floor where new hires engage in hands-on learning about construction and tool use. This program, a component of Black and Decker University, enrolls 100–200 new sales and marketing employees annually. B&D University has a staff of 15 employees and an annual budget of $3 million. As part of their training, sales and marketing trainees take an online course that explains the four basic applications of tools: cutting, removing, fastening, and making holes. They then go to work in a product training area, where they must use the tools to build things, such as roofs, moldings, and stairs. Such experience allows them to go to retailers and fully explain product features and benefits. As a result of its program, Black & Decker has drastically reduced turnover, sent out more credible sales staff, enhanced the Black & Decker name, and reported higher employee satisfaction and loyalty.[4]

Boot Camp at MicroStrategy

MicroStrategy is a Vienna, Virginia–based organization that provides data mining services and has long held a spot on Fortune's best employers' list. With a strong corporate culture, based on the convictions and beliefs of its founder, Michael Saylor, MicroStrategy has developed a new-hire orientation program that attempts to infuse elements of its culture into employees from the first day of work The program, known as "boot camp," goes beyond mere orientation and is a written requirement in every employment contract for MicroStrategy employees, who work in 18 states and 35 countries. It is an intensive immersion into MicroStrategy culture to which Saylor wants each employee exposed and committed. There are three different variations of boot camp, each targeted to a different group of employees. The first is a three-day general boot camp that concludes with a 20- to 25-question examination that covers information such as MicroStrategy's products and company structure. The second is a two-week sales boot camp that culminates in a mock marketing presentation. The third is a five-week technical boot camp that features continuous testing. Despite its intensity, employee feedback on boot camp has been very positive and the only complaint heard is that it is too short.[5]

Another approach to new-employee training is rotation. Discussed in Chapter 6, rotational programs can have an added benefit for new employees, particularly those who have limited full-time professional work experience. Rotations allow new hires to sample different kinds of work within the organization and determine an optimal fit between their needs and interests and those of the organization. Rotation programs can be expensive in the short run, but they represent a longer-term investment in employees who can provide significant benefits to an organization. Employers benefit in that rotation programs allow more flexibility in work assignments. Employees who have been cross-trained not only better understand how their individual jobs contribute to the whole but can also be reassigned as business and organization conditions change. Rotational programs also have the benefit of minimizing the chance that specialized knowledge will be vested in only one individual in the organization, causing disruptions when such an individual resigns, retires, or otherwise leaves the organization. In addition to helping develop a knowledgeable and flexible workforce, rotation programs can enhance retention because the versatility they offer allows employees to pursue more opportunities within the organization.[6]

Organizations that wish to remain competitive must consider the types of employees they should hire and the skills and knowledge these employees will need to ensure optimal performance over time. Ironically, however, training budgets and programs are usually some of the first expenses organizations cut in response to economic downturns. Many key decision makers consider these to be luxury expenditures for prosperous times instead of the necessary investments in the organization's future that they are.

Training and development activities are equally important to both employees and employers. One recent survey found that 96 percent of job applicants reported that the opportunity to learn new skills was very important when evaluating a prospective employer.[7] Employers also see a bottom-line benefit from strategically designed training activities. One study found that employers who were in the top quartile of their peers relative to the average training expenditure per employee experienced 24 percent higher-gross profit margins, 218 percent higher income generation per employee, and a 26 percent higher price-to-book value of company stock price relative to those employers in the bottom quartile.[8] Investment in training and development, however, remains a catch-22 for employers. While additional training can improve bottom-line operating results, that same training can make employees much more attractive targets of competitors' recruiting efforts. This is particularly true for technical employees, a majority of whom view training primarily as an opportunity to obtain another job.[9]

Benefits of Training and Development

Training involves some kind of change for employees: changes in how they do their jobs, how they relate to others, the conditions under which they perform, or changes in their job responsibilities. Although some employees may find any kind of change threatening, change that results from employee training and development has nothing short of win-win outcomes for both employees and employers. Strategically targeted training in critical skills and knowledge bases adds to employee marketability and employability security that is critical in the current environment of rapidly developing technology and changing jobs and work processes. Organizations continue to seek out and employ knowledge workers rather than workers with narrowly defined technical skills.

Organizations can benefit from training, beyond bottom-line and general efficiency and profitability measures, when they create more flexible workers who can assume varied responsibilities and have a more holistic understanding of what the organization does and the role they play in the organization's success. Providing employees with broader knowledge and skills and emphasizing and supporting ongoing employee development also help organizations reduce layers of management and make employees more accountable for results. Everyone (employees, employers, and customers) benefits from effective training and development programs. The key strategic issue then becomes how to make training effective.

In order for organizations to provide effective employee training and development, key decision makers must consider employees from the investment perspective described in Chapter 1. Training and development quite frequently involve short-term costs (for design and delivery of the learning activities) and long-term benefits. Particularly with issues of employee development, there may be no return on investment for the immediate time period. Organizations that are bound by short-term financial performance indicators are less likely to value training and less likely to create and support a culture that fosters employee development.

One critical decision that can impact the benefits and outcomes achieved by training is whether training activities will be centralized or decentralized within the organization. Centralized training provides economies of scale and can allow the organization tighter control over all training initiatives. This can ensure that all training programs are consistent with the organization's strategy and each other as well as ensure that there is little to no duplication of effort. Decentralized training moves training into each individual business unit and can facilitate stronger alignment between division needs and training. This is particularly true when considering that different divisions within an organization may have drastically different responsibilities and make significantly different contributions to the organization's strategy.

Organizations that take a strategic approach to HR can find that employee training can be much more efficacious as part of an integrated approach to HR. For example, training and development are greatly assisted by having appropriate and well-thought-out staffing strategies. Judicious recruitment and selection of new employees will not only allow more targeted training that addresses specific needs but also minimize the need to conduct any extensive or remedial training among new employees.

Planning and Strategizing Training

There are two keys to developing successful training programs in organizations. The first is planning and strategizing the training. This involves four distinct steps: needs assessment, the establishment of objectives and measures, delivery of the training, and evaluation. A model for planning and strategizing training is presented and explained in Exhibit 9.1.

Needs Assessment

The first step—needs assessment—involves determining why specific training activities are required and placing the training within an appropriate organizational context. Needs assessment involves three levels of analysis: organizational, task, and individual. At the organizational level, the training is considered within the context of the organization's culture, politics, structure, and strategy. This analysis considers how the training will assist the organization or unit in meeting its objectives and how the training may affect day-to-day workplace dynamics between and among different units. It also considers the cost of training relative to the benefits that may be expected and considers the opportunity costs of foregoing the training.

Task-level assessment involves looking at specific duties and responsibilities assigned to different jobs and the types of skills and knowledge needed to perform each task. This level also considers whether the learning can or should take place on or away from the job, the implications of mistakes, and how the job can be designed to provide the employee with direct feedback on his or her performance. This level also involves determining whether the training needs of certain jobs are similar to or different from the training needs of other jobs in the organization.

The individual level of assessment considers the people to be trained. It requires an analysis of their existing levels of knowledge and skills as well as factors relating to their preferred learning styles, personality, interpersonal styles in interacting with others, and any special needs individual employees might have, such as any physical or mental condition that might need to be addressed in the design and delivery of the training. The three levels of needs analysis are summarized in Exhibit 9.2.

EXHIBIT 9.1 Strategizing Training

Assessment	Objectives and Measures	Design and Delivery	Evaluation
• Organization		• Interference • On the job	
• Task		• Transfer • Off the job	
• Individual		• Online	

© Cengage Learning

EXHIBIT 9.2

Levels of Needs Assessment

Organizational Level

- How does the training relate to organizational objectives?
- How does the training impact day-to-day workplace dynamics?
- What are the costs and expected benefits of the training?

Task Level

- What responsibilities are assigned to the job?
- What skills or knowledge are needed for successful performance?
- Should the learning setting be the actual job setting?
- What are the implications of mistakes?
- How can the job provide the employee with direct feedback?
- How similar to or different from the training needs of other jobs are the needs of this job?

Individual Level

- What knowledge, skills, and abilities do trainees already have?
- What are the trainees' learning styles?
- What special needs do the trainees have?

© Cengage Learning

Objectives

After training needs have been assessed, objectives for the training activities must be developed. These objectives should follow directly from the assessed needs and be described in specific, measurable terms. Measures should be stated in terms of both desired employee behaviors as well as the results that are expected to follow such behavior. A common problem at this stage is that an organization's objectives may be so vague that success in achieving them cannot be accurately measured or evaluated. On the other hand, an organization may have no plan for measuring these objectives. Training programs that cannot be evaluated are of little value to the organization in the long run. One important source of information in setting objectives can be the data contained in the organization's performance management system, which is discussed in detail in Chapter 10. Specific training objectives can be derived from the performance deficiencies noted in the performance feedback process. Both individual and group training can be developed around these measures.

Design and Delivery

After objectives and measures have been set, the next step is the design and delivery of the training itself. Two critical issues must be considered in the design of the training prior to its delivery. The first is interference. Interference occurs when prior training, learning, or established habits act as a block or obstacle in the learning process. Anyone who learned to drive an automobile having an automatic transmission and later attempted to drive a manual or standard transmission probably experienced interference in their learning. The more experience someone has in behaving in a certain way, the more difficult it may be to modify the response he or she displays. When individuals are stressed, they tend to revert to conditioned behavior.

The second critical issue that must be addressed in design is transfer. Transfer refers to whether the trainee or learner can actually perform the new skills or use the new knowledge on the job. In other words, transfer is the extent to which the trainee or learner is able to "transfer" the learning to the actual job setting. Many training programs that are conducted away from the worksite have been criticized for their lack of transfer because the conditions under which employees have been trained are vastly different from those in which they actually work. Obviously, it is inefficient to conduct training and receive no benefit from it in terms of employee job performance; those responsible for training need to ensure that it provides maximum transfer.

The delivery of the training should anticipate any interference that might be present, and a strategy should be planned to overcome it and ensure transfer. Interference is not caused only by conditioned or learned behavior. The attitudes of supervisors or peers may also produce interference. Coworkers who publicly express negative concerns about the training may cause learners to be predisposed against the training. When trainers examine the potential sources of interference, they need to look beyond the backgrounds, skills, and habits of the trainees themselves to the broader organizational context, which includes culture, politics, and organization structure. Training and development will not be effective unless it is conducted within a larger supportive organizational environment. Having the CEO or other senior executives attend training sessions communicates strong organizational support for training.

Transfer can be facilitated by delivering the training in an environment that simulates the actual job conditions as much as possible. In some cases, it may be feasible to provide direct on-the-job training where the employee is trained under the exact working conditions in which he or she will be expected to perform. However, in other cases, on-the-job training may not be feasible, and the delivery of the training should then replicate exact working conditions as much as possible. Airline pilots do not learn to fly by going up in an airplane and being told what to do. Their training involves extensive exposure to simulated flight conditions on the ground, which tests their learning and ability to react to a variety of situations, including crisis situations.

On-the-job training may help to maximize transfer, but it is obviously not feasible for all jobs. In addition, off-the-job training allows learners to focus on their learning by minimizing interruptions or distractions that might take place in the actual work environment. An increasing amount of training is being conducted away from the workplace. This sort of training utilizes techniques that attempt to simulate what happens on the job. Instructional techniques that facilitate such simulation involve the use of case studies, role plays, and interactive and experiential methods of learning. Individuals being trained are asked to assume a role and the responsibilities that they might have on the job and then perform accordingly.

An increasing amount of organizational training is being conducted online. Many organizations have entire training libraries that consist of skills-related training and information- or knowledge-based learning that have been packaged into computer-based instruction modules or programs. Colleges and universities are offering an increasing number of courses and even entire degree programs online. However, despite its increasing popularity, online learning has been subject to some criticisms. Reading 9.1, "Confronting the Bias Against On-line Learning in Management Education," addresses and refutes some of these criticisms while presenting some guidelines to promote more acceptance of online learning.

Computer-Based Training at QUALCOMM

San Diego, California–based QUALCOMM is unquestionably one of the leaders in computer-based training for its employees. The 6,000-plus employee organization, which invented the multiple access technology used in digital wireless communication worldwide, offers more than 250 custom-designed courses online. These courses include offerings in both technical and professional/management development areas and were initially designed for delivery to fit different learning schedules and different learning styles. Online courses are offered 24 hours a day, 7 days a week, but certain courses are still available in a traditional classroom delivery setting for those who prefer this type of learning environment.

Probably most critical is the fact that the training is strategically focused. All instruction is developed in concert with QUALCOMM's culture and business needs. Learning specialists are assigned to track the needs of various business units by attending staff meetings, meeting regularly with senior management, and conducting group needs assessments. They are then charged with identifying training needs and working with vendors and management to define the course and create appropriate and unique content geared to the needs of the business unit and QUALCOMM.

Training at QUALCOMM is tightly integrated with the organization's competency management initiative, MySource. MySource is an intranet-based employee development tool that allows employees to access their employment records and view their skills and accomplishments. Individuals can map out career options and then enroll in the appropriate learning modules to facilitate promotion and skill development.

In moving to computer-based training, QUALCOMM has saved millions of dollars from the cost of ineffective centralized training. More important, its system successfully unleashes the full potential of its employees through training and skill development, career planning, and competency management.[10]

Online computer-based instruction provides a number of benefits. It is self-paced, allowing different individuals to learn and absorb material at their own level of comfort and understanding. It is adaptive to different needs and can be customized for different employees. It is also easy to deliver: All an employee has to do is turn on a computer at a workstation or at home. There is no need to leave one's desk or coordinate schedules with trainers or trainees or have trainers and trainees in the same physical space. Computer-based training is also usually less expensive to administer when different units in the organization are geographically dispersed. Finally, training can be conducted whenever it is convenient for the employee. An employee who has finished assigned work early no longer needs to look busy or find a way to kill time. The training can be undertaken without any advance scheduling.

The popularity of online training cannot be underestimated. A recent survey of 100 companies with an average of 15,000 employees found that 42 percent currently used online learning applications. More importantly, however, 92 percent of the respondents planned to introduce or accelerate the volume of online training within 12 months.[11] More recently, mobile learning, where employee training is conducted via smartphones and tablet computers, has been gaining in popularity. Heavily based on short instructional video presentations, the number of large organizations using mobile learning for formal training increased from 21 to 42 percent from 2011 to 2012.[12]

Despite its popularity, there are some drawbacks to computer-based instruction. First, learners must be self-motivated and take both initiative and responsibility for their learning. Second, the cost of producing online, interactive materials can be quite high. The content of the learning can become outdated quickly and require revision and possible redesign of the entire online learning environment. Finally, the lack of both interaction with others and two-way communication may work against the needs and preferred learning styles of many employees, particularly adult learners. Consequently, computer-based training can either be advantageous for an employer or a waste of time, resources, and money. Clearly, it needs to be considered within the larger context of the training objectives and the assessed organizational task and individual considerations discussed previously.

E-Learning at EMC Corporation

EMC is a Hopkinton, Massachusetts–based supplier of software, networks, and services for data and information storage. Dramatic improvements in technology related to data storage and retrieval have made product life cycles at EMC increasingly short. This has prompted a need for continuous new product development and, consequently, training. The use of traditional classrooms to meet these accelerated training needs would have involved great expense, as it required the building or leasing of physical space as well as the cost of moving employees out of the field to the training site. As EMC expanded globally, there was also a need to deliver more standardized training to prevent inconsistencies that were taking place in different locations relative to content and approach. In response to these challenges, EMC installed a single learning management system that moved training from a traditional instructor-led process to an integrated e-learning process. This move has allowed new employees to complete product training in five months rather than the nine months previously required, and the sales staff is now able to meet quotas in four months rather than nine to twelve months. Perhaps the biggest benefit has been realized with new product launches. Updated courses are available to coincide with a new product's release, resulting in increased customers' willingness to become early adapters. Customers also are now more prone to buy multiple products, knowing that online support is readily available for them. While EMC initially developed its e-learning program with an eye on costs, the longer-term investments in this area are also yielding significant productivity and revenue gains.[13]

Evaluation

After the training has been delivered, it needs to be evaluated. This evaluation should be an integral part of the overall training program. The organization needs to receive feedback on the training and decide whether the training should be continued in its current form, modified, or eliminated altogether. The ultimate evaluation criteria should also be assessed prior to training delivery to provide a comparison basis for post-training assessment. Evaluation techniques that are not developed when objectives are set will usually have little value to the organization. The decision of how to evaluate training should be made at the same time the training objectives are set.

A highly regarded model has been developed for training evaluation that suggests that evaluation can take place on four levels and that these levels form a hierarchy, meaning that lower levels are prerequisites for higher levels.[11] In other words, if one of the lower-level measures is not affected, then those measures that follow it will automatically not be affected. These levels are reaction, learning, behavior, and results and are illustrated in Exhibit 9.3.

Reaction measures whether the employees liked the training, the trainer, and the facilities; it is usually measured by a questionnaire. If employees have less-than-favorable reactions to the program, it is unlikely that other employees will have an interest in the training or that employees attending the training received anything of value from it. A favorable reaction, in and of itself, does not ensure that the training was effective.

Learning measures whether the employees know more than they did prior to undertaking the training. Knowledge-based training can be measured by tests; skills-based training can be measured through demonstrations or simulations. If employees did not learn anything, then obviously we can expect no change in their behavior on the job. For any change to occur as a result of training, the trainees must have learned something.

Behavior measures what employees do on the job after the training. This measure allows organizations to assess not only whether transfer has taken place but also whether the employees are able to do anything differently (skills-based training) or think or solve problems in different ways (knowledge-based training). Behavioral impact is usually measured through performance appraisal, which is done by those who are able to witness and observe the employee. If there is no change in behavior, we cannot expect employees' performance to have been enhanced.

Evaluation of results looks at the overall outcomes of the training and the impact that the training has had on productivity, efficiency, quality, customer service, or any other means the organization uses to measure contributions and performance of employees. This can be assessed by budget and cost reports, sales figures, production, customer surveys, or any other means that correspond to the organization's performance measures. However, results of training programs are often not immediate. Training programs may be ongoing or involve employees' developing a level of proficiency, which takes time to achieve and master. Although results-based measures of training are

EXHIBIT 9.3

Four Levels of Training Evaluation

Level	Questions Being Asked	Measures
Results	Is the organization or unit better because of the training?	Accidents Quality Productivity Turnover Morale Costs Profits
Behavior	Are trainees behaving differently on the job after training? Are they using the skills and knowledge they learned in training?	Performance appraisal by superior, peer, client, subordinate
Learning	To what extent do trainees have greater knowledge or skill after the training program than they did before?	Written tests Performance tests Graded simulations
Reaction	Did the trainees like the program, the trainers, the facilities? Do they think the course was useful? What improvements can they suggest?	Questionnaires

© Cengage Learning

usually the most meaningful and economically significant for an organization, undue reliance on them may cause key decision makers to abandon training programs that do not produce immediate short-term results. In addition, there are those who question whether results-based approaches are always the most appropriate measures for training evaluation. One study found that training related to leadership and professional development might best be assessed by measuring learning rather than results.[14] Given the limitations of each of the four levels of training evaluation, it is advisable to consider all four levels of training evaluation, either in part or in total, contingent on the organization's strategy when making a determination of how training will be evaluated.

Organizational Development

The majority of training programs and initiatives are designed to address the training needs of individual employees or small groups of employees. Largely focused on skill acquisition and development, these programs attempt to provide employees with the knowledge and skills that will result in improved productivity as well as a workforce that is more able to achieve the organization's strategic objectives. However, to continue to survive and prosper in a rapidly changing global environment, organizations need to respond to changes in their external environments by undertaking large-scale organization-wide changes. These activities constitute organizational development (OD), which focuses on the entire organization rather than individual employees or employee groups. OD initiatives attempt to improve an organization's overall effectiveness through planned interventions that are undertaken in response to the organization's strategy. While training and development focuses on the micro-aspects of organizational needs and responsiveness, OD focuses on the macro- or organization-wide perspective of performance and responsiveness.

OD initiatives generally involve organizational processes as well as organization's culture. Typical OD interventions might include culture change, facilitating mergers and acquisitions, organizational learning, knowledge management, process improvement, and organization design and structure.[15] In addition to considering issues related to performance, efficiency, and profitability, OD interventions also consider the organization's people. Initiatives are driven by humanistic values, such as respect, inclusion, authenticity, and collaboration, with desired outcomes of values, norms, attitudes, and management practices that result in a positive organizational climate that engages employees and acknowledges and rewards their efforts.[16]

Such changes require a clear understanding of organization-wide issues and consideration of the organization as an open system of interrelated functions and processes. The open systems model of organizations acknowledges the importance of examining the organization within the broader context of external influences on the organization. It also considers the fact that organizations consists of a variety of different functions and processes that influence each other, resulting in the need for a holistic analysis of any planned intervention of change initiative. Those involved must consider not only the organization's relationship with external constituents but also how changes undertaken in one part of the organizations might impact other parts of the organization.

Organizations can undertake a variety of interventions as part of organizations development. A variety of tools are available to assist the organization with such initiatives. These include individual self-assessment tools, such as personality inventories, coaching and mentoring, performance feedback, and career planning and progress charting. At the organizational level, team-building initiatives, brainstorming, knowledge transfer and retention programs, conflict–resolution sessions, and process feedback consultation aid in organizational development.

Knowledge Transfer and Retention at Hewlett-Packard

Palo Alto, California–based Hewlett-Packard (HP) is the world's largest seller of personal computers and the world's largest technology organization. HP has recognized the need for knowledge retention as its workforce has become more transient and key individuals have approached retirement. To assist with knowledge retention, the organization has developed a program called "Knowledge Briefs" (KB), which facilitates knowledge transfer and retention through a documentation process and incentive scheme. The program is based on the premise that employee turnover can be unpredictable and that resultant knowledge transfer needs to happen on a regular, continuous basis and is best accomplished within the context of an employee's everyday work and without time pressures.

The KB program asks key technical employees to document in writing their main technical responsibilities as well as "best practices" they have observed in their work Given that so much of the work at HP involves knowledge and process generation, such documentation allows employees to communicate their individual experiences, perspectives, and successes to others. These technical reports, or knowledge briefs, can be no more than 10 pages long and can be prepared by any employee at HP. They must address a technical topic of the employee's choice in a precise and succinct manner and be prepared by using specific written guidelines and a template format. Once written, KBs are subject to a strict internal review process to ensure quality and uniformity and provide authors with feedback from those unfamiliar with the content of the brief. Incentives and awards, which include monetary bonuses and publication in an in-house technical journal, are provided to employees who produce accepted KBs. The program now has more than 4,000 KBs available to HP employees, with approximately 600 new KBs published annually. HP has attempted to measure the value of the KB program relative to cost savings associated with the transfer of knowledge. To date, the program has incurred just under $13 million in costs and has produced $75 million in value relative to knowledge retention.[17]

In taking a more macroperspective on the organization and its need to change and evolve, key attention must be paid to the development of appropriate interpersonal relationships. This is particularly true relative to the development of leaders and the management of groups and group processes. Leadership development has been positively correlated to an organization's financial performance. Organizations with strong leadership development programs frequently display strong financial performance, particularly relative to organizations that do not focus on developing leaders.[18] Early career leaders, in particular, face distinct challenges to which organizations must respond, as illustrated in Reading 9.2, "Becoming a Leader: Early Career Challenges Faced by MBA Graduates." Ongoing development of leaders is discussed in part in Chapter 5 in the discussion of succession planning. However, the specific means and strategies for leadership development need to be addressed. Exhibit 9.4 presents a model that was developed by NASA for the development of global leaders, which focuses on six different core competencies.[19]

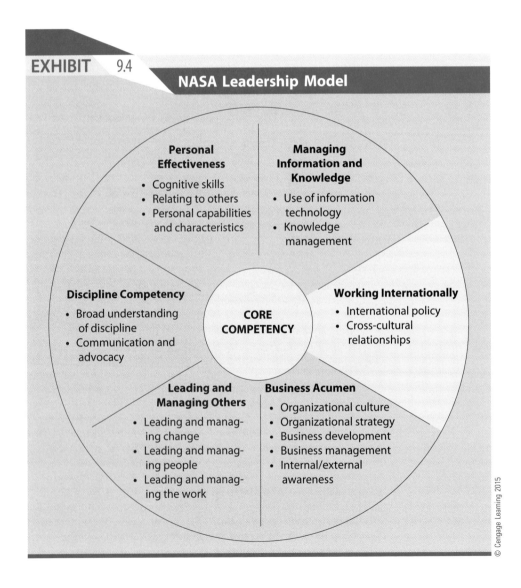

EXHIBIT 9.4

NASA Leadership Model

Personal Effectiveness
- Cognitive skills
- Relating to others
- Personal capabilities and characteristics

Managing Information and Knowledge
- Use of information technology
- Knowledge management

Discipline Competency
- Broad understanding of discipline
- Communication and advocacy

CORE COMPETENCY

Working Internationally
- International policy
- Cross-cultural relationships

Leading and Managing Others
- Leading and managing change
- Leading and managing people
- Leading and managing the work

Business Acumen
- Organizational culture
- Organizational strategy
- Business development
- Business management
- Internal/external awareness

Leadership Development at Virgin Atlantic Airlines

With 37 aircraft, more than 9,000 employees and more than 4.5 million annual passengers, Virgin Atlantic is Britain's second-largest airline. Established in 1985, the organization has been successful in building a brand and image that resonates with consumers. However, the rapid demand for its services created a challenge for staffing the organization's executive ranks. Given Virgin's strong corporate culture and desire to maintain this culture by promoting from within, Virgin realized that it quickly needed to develop its young and inexperienced but enthusiastic management team. To accomplish this, Virgin developed its own leadership development program. Centered on strategic business objectives, Virgin's executive team started by identifying those traits it felt had contributed most to Virgin's success. It then followed this with a comprehensive assessment of the strengths and weaknesses of Virgin's management team. All the organization's 120 managers were sent to external personal development workshops, which consisted of personality testing and reviews of performance feedback from within the organization. The results were individual assessments, coaching sessions, and personal development plans. Ongoing efforts consist of activities that instill Virgin's culture and values into leadership development cohorts of six managers who met regularly to monitor and discuss their own progress and share ideas. The program has increased both motivation and retention and increased the ratio of management positions filled internally by 20 percent.[20]

The increasing use of work groups and teams is addressed in Chapter 6. Teams and groups can be temporary or permanent, live or virtual, within functions or cross-functional, and domestic or global. However, all teams and groups present different learning and training challenges than do individuals. Successful organizational development initiatives need to consider how groups evolve and learn and incorporate these theories and concepts into the design and delivery of any intervention initiatives.

One significant OD-related practice that many organizations are undertaking is the establishment of corporate universities (CUs). The activities of CUs usually involve both training and organizational development activities. A CU is an in-house operation that attempts to develop both individuals and the organization toward the organization's strategic objectives and facilitate and manage any planned change initiatives. It is estimated that there are currently more than 2,000 existing CUs, which exist either physically or virtually.[21] CUs tend to evolve through several stages prior to becoming full-fledged CUs as illustrated in Exhibit 9.5.

Activities of CUs may be developed in-house or in full or partial consultation with consultants and/or traditional universities. In some cases, programs and activities of a CU may be custom designed or consist of standard assessments, programs, and activities. Successful CUs need to have the support of top management, including financial support, a well-defined mission and business plan, high-quality instruction and corresponding student satisfaction, strong internal marketing, a high level of online instruction, and the ability to document the impact of CU activities on the organization's outcomes, particularly financial outcomes.[22] Effective CUs can contribute to an organization's leadership development, employee engagement, talent management, organizational change initiatives, and innovation, each of which can be significant sources of competitive advantage.[23]

Organizational development interventions can be used as a key catalyst to facilitate global initiatives an organization may be undertaking. Such activities might include cross-cultural communication, understanding and team building, training and placement for employees abroad, and integration of domestic and foreign operations. However, because OD interventions are built on a foundation of humanistic approaches to work and organization, care must be exercised when attempting to implement OD initiatives abroad. The United States's social values of democracy, participation, and human dignity are not globally accepted, so OD initiatives undertaken abroad must be developed with an appreciation for and empathy toward cultural differences. These issues are discussed in greater depth in Chapter 14.

EXHIBIT 9.5 — Stages of Corporate University (CU) Development[26]

Stage	Operational	Tactical	Strategic
Focus	Consolidation of existing training activities	Development of targeted programs to address specific needs	Knowledge management, development, and retention
Goal	Efficiency	Alignment with organization needs	Competitive advantage
Strategic perspective	Random and reactive	Targeted and reactive	Targeted and proactive
Man activity	Centralizing training functions and activities	Matching activities to organizational strategy	Strategic partnership

Liverpool Virtual University

With 63 stores and more than 33,000 employees, Mexico City–based Liverpool is the largest department store chain in Mexico. Several years ago, the organization began creating what would evolve into Liverpool Virtual University. With an initial $2 million investment, Liverpool created a corporate television network, which provided employees access to two different learning management systems. Today, Liverpool Virtual University (LVU) offers 22 separate programs. Ten of these are academic programs, ranging from a high school degree to master degree programs in leadership and finance, while 12 are corporate programs focused on various aspects of management and leadership. Liverpool directly attributes increased employee retention and improved productivity to the activities and programs offered by LVU.

The organization has already recouped its $2 million investment through the elimination of costs associated with external trainer fees, rental and maintenance of training facilities, and employee transportation costs associated with attending in-person training. Liverpool is preparing to turn LVU into a profit center by enrolling employees of other organizations on a contract basis. In addition, LVU is supporting Liverpool's commitment to social responsibility by signing a partnership agreement with the National Institute for Adult Education (NIAE) of Mexico, under which LVU will provide NIAE employees and their children opportunities to finish their secondary school studies.[24]

Integrating Training with Performance Management Systems and Compensation

The second key factor in strategizing training programs is to ensure that the desired results of training are reinforced when employees achieve or accomplish them. In larger organizations, it is not uncommon to see an entire department devoted solely to employee training and development. This unit may be separate and autonomous from other HR functions, such as performance measurement (appraisal) and compensation and benefits administration. When employees expend the effort to learn new skills and knowledge and are expected to implement such learning in their jobs, there should be some incentive to do so and some acknowledgment and reinforcement of that performance once it is achieved. However, when training, performance measurement, and compensation are administered separately and not integrated within a larger, integrative HR strategy, there is less chance of that appropriate and necessary reinforcement.

When employees are asked to learn critical new skills and/or absorb important new knowledge and apply this in their jobs, the means by which their performance is assessed must reflect these changes. The more critical the skills and knowledge are to the organization's strategy, the greater the emphasis that should be placed on assessing them in the organization's performance management system. Similarly, compensation should reflect the results of training. If employees have learned new skills and knowledge and successfully implemented this learning to enhance the performance of the organization, they should be compensated accordingly in a way that is significant to them. A training program that is not linked to the organization's performance management and compensation systems, as indicated in Exhibit 9.6, has far less chance of success than one that does. Training should be conceptualized, designed, and delivered within a larger strategic context and receive an organization-wide commitment to ensure its success.

Strategizing Training and Performance Management at Anheuser-Busch

The past decade has seen a tremendous boom in the use of online training programs. One of the most comprehensive was developed by St. Louis, Missouri–based beer brewer Anheuser-Busch. Anheuser-Busch has developed its Wholesaler Integrated Learning (WIL) program for its 13 company-owned branch operations, 12 breweries, and 700 independent distributors. The WIL took more than a year to develop, starting with data collection related to employee skills, knowledge, and attributes that was used to create a competency database, which in turn was used to create unique job descriptions based on almost 400 different competencies. The WIL allows employees to access the company Web site from virtually anywhere to take advantage of e-learning opportunities and measure proficiencies deemed critical for a given job description. Immediate feedback is offered and a gap analysis prepared that shows employee skill levels relative to those needed for a position, along with specific suggestions that might include classroom training, online training, reference materials, apprenticeships, coaching, and on-the-job training for bridging any gap. The WIL is far from being a simple testing and assessment program though; the program also ties a comprehensive performance management system into its training components. The WIL analyzes employee performance relative to individual jobs and increases manager accountability by tracking when managers evaluate their employees, whether the manager has produced a development plan for each employee, and how the employee acts on that plan throughout the year.[25]

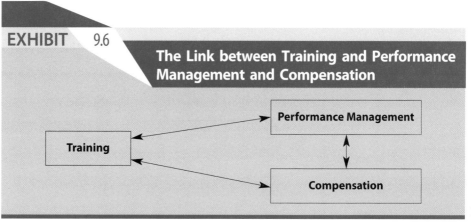

EXHIBIT 9.6

The Link between Training and Performance Management and Compensation

© Cengage Learning

Conclusion

Training and development of employees is a key strategic issue for organizations: It is the means by which organizations determine the extent to which their human assets are viable investments. Because much of the return on investment in training and development may be difficult to quantify, particularly in the short run, organizations should take a holistic view of training and development, particularly with regard to the kinds of employees and the skills and knowledge bases necessary to achieve strategic objectives. Changes in how work is performed and the organizational contexts in which work is conducted mandate that organizations conduct specific, targeted, strategic training and development initiatives as a prerequisite for continued success.

Critical Thinking

1. Why is training such a critical strategic issue for organizations?

2. What is transfer, and how can it best be facilitated?

3. What are the advantages and disadvantages of on-the-job, off-the-job, and online training? For what types of training is each approach most appropriate?

4. How is training likely to change in the future?

5. Using Exhibit 9.1, develop a training module to teach your classmates about your company and job responsibilities.

6. Explain the relationship between training and organizational development. How might each contributes to strategic HR management?

Reading 9.1

7. What criticisms have been levied against online learning? What strategies can be employed to increase the acceptance of online learning?

Reading 9.2

8. What specific and distinct challenges do new leaders face in organizations? How can employers best address these challenges?

Exercises

1. In small groups, develop a tool to evaluate the learning/training taking place in the course in which you are enrolled. Be sure to consider the needs of the organization, task, and individuals; specific objectives; and design and delivery issues.

2. Trace the growth and evolution of the corporate university of your choice. Share your findings with classmates and determine specifically how each CU contributes to its organization's strategy.

3. Visit the Web site for Bright Hub (ww.brighthub.com) and click on the "Business" link. How useful might this Web site be for organizational training and development issues?

Chapter References

1. Overman, S. "Hotel Chain's Rebranding Focuses on Living, Training (in Luxury)," October 26, 2012. Available at http://www.shrm.org/hrdisciplines/orgempdev/articles/Pages/Hotel-Training-in-Luxury.aspx

2. Alutto, J. A. "Just-in-time Management Education for the 21st Century," *HR Magazine*, July 2000, 45, (7), p. 57.

3. Rollag, K., Parise, S., and Cross, R. "Getting New Hires up to Speed Quickly," *MIT Sloan Management Review*, 46, (2), Winter 2005, pp. 35–41.

4. Henry, K. "Local Grad School Teaches Power Tools," *Baltimore Sun*, October 13, 2002, pp. 1C, 8C.

5. Garvey, C. "The Whirlwind of a New Job," *HR Magazine*, June 2001, 46, (6), pp. 111–118.

6. Frase-Blunt, M. "Ready, Set, Rotate," *HR Magazine*, October 2001, 46, (10), pp. 46–53.

7. Leonard, B. "Training Can Be a Valuable Job Perk," *HR Magazine*, February 2001, 46, (2), p. 37.

8. Wells, S. "Stepping Carefully," *HR Magazine*, 46, (1), January 2001, pp. 44–49.

9. Leonard, 2001, op. cit..

10. Greengard, S. "Keyboarding Courses at Work or Home," *Workforce*, March 2000, pp. 88–92.

11. Anonymous. "Growing Number of Employers Jump on E-Learning Bandwagon," *HR Magazine*, September 2000, 45, (9), p. 34.

12. Roberts, B. "From E-learning to Mobile Learning," *HR Magazine*, August 2012, 57, (8), pp. 61–65.

13. Silberman, R. "E-Learning Is Strategic Corporate Move, Not Just Cost-Saver," *HR News*, May 2002, p. 15.

14. Seijts, G. H. and Latham, G. P. "Learning Versus Performance Goals: When Should Each Be Used?" *Academy of Management Executive*, 19, (91), 2005, pp. 124–131.

15. Yaeger, T. and Sorenson, P. "Strategic Organization Development: Past to Present," *Organization Development Journal*, 24, (4), Winter 2006, pp. 10–17.

16. McLean, G. and McLean, D. "If We Can't Define HRD in One Country, How Can We Define It in an International Context?," *Human Resource International*, 4, (3), 2001, pp. 313–326.

17. Gotthart, B. and Haghi, G. "How Hewlett-Packard Minimises Knowledge Loss," *International Journal of Human Resources Development and Management*, 9, (2/3), 2009, pp. 305–311.

18. Pollitt, D. "Leadership Success Planning Affects Commercial Success," *Human Resource Management International Digest*, 13, (91), 2005, pp. 36–39.

19. Brower, D., Newell, T. and Ronayne, P. "The Imperative of Developing Global Leaders." In Lawrence, P. (ed.), *The Business of Government*, IBM Business Consulting Services, pp. 18–24 (2002).

20. Martindale, N. "Virgin Atlantic's HR in Practice: High-Flying Management," *Personnel Today*, August 20, 2007, article 41937.

21. Knight, R. "Move to a Collaborative Effort," *Financial Times*, 19 March, 2007, p. 2.

22. Adapted from Jansink, F. "The Knowledge-Productive Corporate University," *Journal of European Industrial Learning*, 29, (1), 2005, pp. 40–57.

23. Graebner, R. and Lockwood, N. "Corporate Universities," *Society for Human Resource Management Research Brief*, October 2007.

24. Tyler, K. "Take E-Learning to the Next Step," *HR Magazine*, February 2002, 47, (2), pp. 56–61.

25. Ibid.

26. Moss, D. "A Lesson in Learning," *HR Magazine*, 52, (11), November 2007, pp. 51–52.

READING 9.1

Confronting the Bias Against On-Line Learning in Management Education

Lindsay Redpath

Despite abundant research evidence that on-line learning is just as effective as classroom learning, a bias toward face-to-face delivery continues to influence business educators and evaluators. Drawing on the comparative research, I dispute the assumption that on-line delivery lacks the kind of interaction, collaborafion, and learning outcomes that are necessary to support a quality business education. Recommendations are made to confront the bias by leveraging the research and removing some barriers that prevent wider acceptance and adoption of on-line teaching and learning.

On-line learning has grown dramatically during the past 2 decades, as advancements in information technology have revolutionized the way that individuals and organizations communicate and engage in productive activities. In the United States, where statistics about on-line learning are readily available, enrollments in on-line courses have far outpaced those in classroom courses. Between 2002 and 2009, the annual compound rate of growth for on-line courses was 19%, compared to 2% for campus-based courses (Allen & Seaman, 2010). By 2009, almost one third of higher education students in the United States were enrolled in at least one on-line course, and enrollments continued to rise during the economic downturn (Allen & Seaman, 2010). The Open University, the largest distance provider in the United Kingdom, recently reported an "unprecedented" increase of 34% in younger students (18–24 years) doing distance-learning degree programs (BBC Mobile News, 2010). The phenomenal growth of distance and cross-border education worldwide has opened up greater possibilities to meet the education needs of a wider range of people, particularly in developing countries (Altbach, Reisberg, & Rumbley, 2009).

In the United States, the proportion of higher education institutions with fully on-line programs in business was estimated to be about 33% in 2008 (Allen & Seaman, 2008). On the surface, it appears as though the management education community has embraced e-learning. Blended and fully online programs have proliferated, millions have been sunk into technology enhancements for teaching and learning, and on-line tools have been incorporated successfully with conventional teaching methods. With the growing acceptance and popularity of on-line communication and social networking in current generations of students, it would seem inevitable that on-line education be accepted as a normative form of management education today. The door is not fully open; in fact, it is firmly closed in the minds of some.

Perceptions of On-Line Teaching and Learning

Among many higher education leaders and faculty members in mainstream academia, attitudes tend to marginalize on-line learning (Allen & Seaman, 2009; Kim & Bonk, 2006; McCarthy & Samors, 2009; Puzziferro & Shelton, 2009). In the United States, one third of higher education institutions and two thirds of those without experience in on-line offerings rate on-line courses and programs inferior to face-to-face offerings (Allen & Seaman, 2009). Over 80% of public university faculty with no on-line teaching experience believe that on-line learning outcomes are inferior to face-to-face, while a majority of those with on-line teaching experience say that on-line learning outcomes are as good as or better than face-to-face learning outcomes (Seaman, 2009). Higher education leaders are reluctant to integrate on-line learning into the academic and operational structures of their institutions (McCarthy & Samors, 2009). Significant attitudinal and systemic barriers stand in their way (Bates, 2011).

> *With the growing acceptance and popularity of on-line communication and social networking in current generations of students, it would seem inevitable that on-line education be accepted as a normative form of management education today. The door is not fully open; in fact, it is firmly closed in the minds of some.*

Attitudes in business education have been slow to change. On-line and distance schools face significant barriers

Thank you to colleagues and students at Athabasca University, Feedback from AMLE reviewers, and from Marilyn Wangler and Dr. Stephen Murgatroyd, was greatly appreciated.

in meeting criteria for business school accreditation or participating in media rankings that are based on conventional approaches to teaching and learning. Standards for accreditation, membership in business school organizations, and media rankings continue to emphasize the amount of face-to-face instructional time and other criteria that favor traditional classroom delivery. For example, executive MBA programs (EMBA) that do not have 50% or more of their curriculum delivered face-to-face are excluded from participating in the *Financial Times Executive EMBA Rankings* (*Financial Times*, 2010).

Instead, they are relegated to a separate list of on-line MBAs that is not ranked and receives far less attention (*Financial Times*, 2011). The distinction, based on an arbitrary rule related to method of delivery, has nothing to do with the quality of teaching or learning in MBA programs. How is the *Financial Times* qualified to determine that one mode of delivery merits ranking over another or that delivering one half of a program on-line is acceptable but more than that justifies exclusion? How is blended learning assessed according to the 50% rule? The distinction between ranked EM-BAs and those delivered on-line has the effect, intended or not, of implying that on-line MBAs are not up to par with those delivered face-to-face. This impression extends to employers as well, who may be reluctant to accept on-line degrees as equivalent to traditional ones (Carnevale, 2005, 2007).

Certainly, there have been efforts by the business school accreditation bodies to acknowledge distance education and on-line learning, particularly as they focus more on learning outcomes (AACSB [Association to Advance Collegiate Schools of Business] International, 2007). As more accredited schools adopt on-line learning courses and programs, it will be difficult to draw the line. A survey of AACSB-accredited schools in 2005 reported that 53% offered distance or on-line courses, up from 39% in 1999 (Popovich & Neel, 2005). According to data collected from the AACSB Business School Questionnaire, the percentage of members offering at least one on-line program, that is "programs that may be completed in full by students enrolled only in courses taught on-line" increased from 9% in 2001–2002 to 24% in 2008–2009 (AACSB International, 2010).

Despite the trend toward on-line programs among AACSB member schools, on-line delivery continues to be relegated to second-class status in the business education community. "On-line" has become synonymous with "lower quality" regardless of research evidence to the contrary. By exploring the bias and examining the research evidence, I aim to inform, confront, and perhaps even convert business educators who have little or no exposure to on-line teaching and learning.

Exploring the Bias

As management educators and lifelong learners, our biases play a role in how we perceive teaching and learning. Mine stem from years of experience developing, teaching, and directing an on-line executive MBA program in a university with a longstanding mandate for distance delivery. Skepticism toward a new model of delivery was expected when our on-line program entered the market in the early 1990s. That skepticism has persisted throughout the years. Although technology has been incorporated into the classroom, the traditional lecture mode remains the dominant form of delivery in business schools. Teaching students about the impact of technology on business and other professions does not seem to have provoked widespread consideration of how technology might affect our teaching methods.

What makes attitudes toward teaching so impermeable to change in the academic community? The image of the professor lecturing to a group of attentive students in a classroom or lecture theater is deeply ingrained in our assumptions about what it means to teach or learn at the postsecondary level. Psychologists might suggest that early role models and experiences with education continue to influence how we perceive education and teaching. Although many people are involved in on-line communication and social networking, they may not have a sense of how learning occurs in a formal on-line education environment. Until one has experienced learning or teaching in an active and collaborative on-line environment, it is difficult to understand how it works. Perhaps participation in on-line teaching and learning has not yet reached a sufficient critical mass to generate momentum for change.

Academics who are critical of on-line delivery often view it as a means for administrators to reduce costs and to increase managerial control over the education process (Noble, 1997; Stahl, 2004; CAUT [Canadian Association of University Teachers], 2004). These "advantages" have negative, rather than positive, connotations for faculty members used to fighting cutbacks and higher teaching loads. Faculty resistance is exacerbated by declining proportions of public funding and the globalization of postsecondary education that have increased competition for resources and market share. Since many high-profile on-line providers are private or distance education institutions, there has been a tendency for established business schools to question the quality and legitimacy of on-line delivery in general. While concerns about the quality of some providers may be valid, the method of delivery should not be confounded with the quality of an institution, its programs, or its teaching and learning effectiveness. In an era of scarce resources and increased competition, however, established business schools and their stakeholders may have vested interests in marginalizing on-line providers to protect their market share and status. Institutional theory might offer some insights into the mimetic, coercive, and normative forces at play in reinforcing traditional forms of teaching and learning (Morphew, 2009; Oliver, 1991).

While concerns about the quality of some providers may be valid, the method of delivery should not be confounded with the quality of an institution, its programs, or its teaching and learning effectiveness.

Lack of awareness about on-line research and practice is also a factor in reinforcing the bias against on-line teaching and learning. The first comprehensive review of the research in on-line learning in business disciplines emerged fairly recently (Arbaugh, Godfrey, Johnson, Pollack, Nien-dorf, & Wresch, 2009). Many business educators, including those involved in on-line teaching, are not aware of the theory and evidence emanating from the comparative research in the business education or the on-line education literature. Wider dissemination of research and cross-fertilization between academic disciplines would help to inform both the believers and the nonbelievers (Arbaugh et al., 2009). Still, a sufficient amount of information is available to make one wonder why negative attitudes toward on-line learning prevail.

A recent article in the *Harvard Business Review* serves to illustrate the way that on-line education continues to be viewed as an inferior mode of delivery (Barker, 2010). Arguing against the professionalization of business education, Barker offers his opinions about what a good management education should entail, emphasizing the value of creating learning environments through sharing and collaboration. His views about on-line learning, while a minor point in the article, defy logic. He begins with the statement that "First and foremost, business education should be collaborative" (59). A brief discussion about the pedagogical advantages of sharing and collaborative learning follows. Hence, he asserts, "business education cannot be delivered exclusively on-line, because online delivery is a teaching mechanism not a learning environment" (60). This statement precedes a quotation by a former United States business school dean indicating that "going on-line" will not help to "maximize the quality of what we deliver" (60).

While Barker's article is not about on-line learning per se, the argument that he presents clearly implies that on-line delivery equates to a lower quality of learning. It also implies that on-line learning does not involve sharing and collaboration. Neither assertion is substantiated. Certainly, on-line delivery is a "teaching mechanism" or a mode of delivery. However, a mode of delivery is not a determinant of the teaching methods employed or the learning environment experienced by students. Following Barker's logic, it would be just as valid to state that *business education cannot be delivered exclusively in the classroom because classroom delivery is a teaching mechanism and not a learning environment.* As educator Richard Clark contends, the instructional method, not the medium, is the critical factor in determining the quality of instruction and learning outcomes (see Clark, 1983, 1994). Research evidence confirms that good-quality business education can be achieved using classroom, blended, or on-line delivery. On-line delivery does not necessarily equate to lower quality learning for students, according to the comparative research to date. Furthermore, collaboration has always been fundamental to on-line pedagogy and practice, as early research demonstrates (Alavi, 1994; Hiltz, 1988; Leidner & Fuller, 1997; Leidner & Jarvenpaa, 1995).

Certainly, researchers and others have raised concerns about on-line education, including faculty rights, skills, and resources; pressures to expand enrollments and reduce costs; and the lack oi technical, administrative, and financial support required to deliver quality on-line learning (Cleary, 2001; Dyrud, 2000; Parthasarathy & Smith, 2009; Sarker & Nicholson, 2005; Tanner, Noser, & Totaro, 2009). Some warn that the rapid expansion of online learning may lead to a growing disparity between those who can afford and access classroom delivery and those who cannot (Carr-Chellman, 2005). A few express direct opposition to on-line delivery, viewing it as the harbinger of commoditization and commercialization of higher education (Cox, 2005; Noble, 1997; Stahl, 2004). However, Barker's comments tend to reflect the attitudes of many business educators who simply assume that on-line learning cannot possibly be as good as face-to-face learning.

The following discussion refutes Barker's key points, providing evidence that on-line "teaching mechanisms" support quality learning that is comparable to classroom learning outcomes and that on-line learning environments are often highly collaborative. To suggest otherwise is inaccurate, misleading, and disingenuous.

Comparing On-Line and Face-To-Face Learning Outcomes

Academic debate about technology-mediated delivery and classroom delivery has been going on for decades. Many critics, however, have failed to keep up with the evolution of research and practice in on-line teaching and learning (Gaytan, 2007). The early-to-mid-1990s marked the turning point when new information technologies and collaborative learning platforms significantly changed the way that computer-mediated learning was delivered; hence, comparative studies published in the past 20 years are more likely to reflect contemporary on-line learning methods (Zhao, Lei, Yan, Lai, & Tan, 2005). Over the same time, the quality of comparative research has also improved, with the adoption of meta-analytical techniques, quasi-experimental designs, pre- and posttesting, and better controls for student characteristics and instructional methods.

Although some maintain that the evidence is inconclusive (Shachar, 2008), a substantial body of research evidence indicates that there is no significant difference in learning outcomes for students who learn on-line compared to those who learn in the classroom. Meta-analytical studies comparing classroom with distance and on-line learning reveal considerable variations at the disaggregate level but no significant differences overall between modes of delivery (Allen, Bourhis, Burrell, & Mabry, 2002; Bernard et al., 2004; Jahng, Krug, & Zhang, 2007; Machtmes & Asher, 2000; Shachar & Neumann, 2003; Sitzmann, Kraiger, Stewart, & Wisher, 2006; U.S. Department of Education, 2009; Williams, 2006; Zhao et al., 2005). Just over half of the 26 studies considered in a qualitative comparative analysis reported that Internet-supported learning outcomes were better than the classroom; no significant differences were reported in the rest (Bekele & Menchaca, 2008). As confirmed by a recent review of the literature, a majority of researchers examining a variety of learning outcomes across different subject areas agree that on-line instruction is at least as effective as traditional classroom teaching (Tallent-Runnels, Thomas, Lan, Cooper, Ahern, Shaw, & Liu 2006).

What may be surprising to many management educators is the high quantity and quality of research comparing on-line and classroom delivery in the business disciplines. Most comparative studies involving business courses support the argument that students learn just as effectively online as they do in the classroom—and in some cases, more effectively (Alavi, Yoo, & Vogel, 1997; Arbaugh, 2000b; Brower, 2003; Bryant, Campbell, & Kerr, 2003; Connolly, MacArthur, Stanfield, & McLellan, 2007; Friday, Friday-Stroud, Green, & Hill, 2006; Glenn, Jones, & Hoyt, 2003; Hansen, 2008; Hiltz, Coppola, Rotter, Turoff, & Benbunan-Fich, 2000; Iverson, Colky, & Cyboran, 2005; Lady-shewsky, 2004; Lapsley, Kulik, Moody, & Arbaugh, 2008; Larson & Sung, 2009; Lim, 2002; Lim, Morris, & Kupritz, 2007; Piccoli, Ahmad, & Ives, 2001; Sitzmann et al., 2006; Weber & Lennon, 2007). Contributions across subject areas are uneven, with the bulk of studies occurring in information systems, management, and marketing, and very few in economics and finance. There is some conjecture that learning on-line may be more effective in applied and qualitative subjects than in pure and quantitative subjects (Anistine & Skidmore, 2005; Arbaugh, Bangert, & Cleveland-Innes, 2010; Arbaugh & Rau, 2007; Smith, Heindel, & Torres-Ayala, 2008; Vamosi, Pierce, & Slotkin, 2004). Nevertheless, a comprehensive review of research in on-line and blended learning in the business literature concluded that performance outcomes in courses delivered face-to-face and those delivered on-line are not significantly different; moreover, differences in learning outcomes appear to be decreasing as more students and instructors gain on-line experience.

Arbaugh and colleagues' (2009) compilation and analysis of the research from the various disciplines has made an enormous contribution to the current state of knowledge about online learning in business education. Recent reviews of on-line education, as the authors point out, have included little evidence from the business schools, partly due to the tendency of business faculty to publish in discipline-specific journals rather than journals related to technology-mediated and on-line learning. The substantive amount of research by business faculty identifies the range of methodological approaches and conceptual frameworks that require further testing. The review highlights the multiple factors that influence on-line learning, including both student and instructor characteristics, perceptions, and behaviors. Most interesting are the findings around disciplinary effects. When learning outcomes are considered, instructor behaviors may be more important that the effects

of the discipline taught; whereas disciplinary effects explain the majority of the variance in student satisfaction with on-line learning (83). To date, research indicates less success with on-line learning in upper level economics and statistics courses; however, it is not clear whether lack of success is due to ineffective on-line teaching strategies or the nature of the subject. The question, as the authors conclude, is not which mode of delivery is the best but what is the optimal mode or blend for a given learning situation?

The question, as the authors conclude, is not which mode of delivery is the best but what is the optimal mode or blend for a given learning situation?

While the overall findings from the research support the argument of "no significant difference," there are differences in various dimensions of learning outcomes and the ways in which students perceive learning on-line compared to the classroom. For example, students sometimes report better perceived learning or satisfaction with face-to-face learning even where learning outcomes are comparable, and these perceptions may change over time (Glenn et al., 2003; Kock, Verville, & Garza, 2007; Nemanich, Banks, & Vera, 2009; Pri-luck, 2004; Rivera & Rice, 2002; Spiceland & Hawkins, 2002; Sweeny & Ingram, 2001; Weber & Lennon, 2007). Measurement of learning outcomes is a challenge for comparative researchers, particularly as the validity of student self-assessment is questioned (Sitzmann, Ely, Brown, & Bauer, 2010). Many comparative studies have used grades or other objective performance indicators, while other studies rely on subjective indicators of learning outcomes. Perceptions of learning provide crucial insights into on-line learning processes. Tanner and colleagues (2009) found that faculty and students may differ in their perceptions and evaluations of on-line learning. Both perceptions of learning and learning outcomes may change throughout the duration of a course or a program, as students and faculty learn to adapt to on-line environments (Kock et al., 2007; Yoo, Kanawattanachai, & Citurs, 2002). While it has been suggested that the relationship between learner self-assessments and direct measures of cognitive learning may be weaker in on-line compared to classroom instruction, both types of measures are useful in evaluating learning (Benbunan-Fich, 2010; Richardson, Maeda, & Swan, 2010; Sitzmann et al., 2010).

Learner characteristics and behaviors are also considered in studies comparing learning outcomes across different modes of delivery. For example, women may perform better than men in some aspects of on-line learning and communication (Arbaugh, 2000a, 2000b, 2005a; Friday et al., 2006). Ethnicity may also have a bearing on how students respond to on-line environments (Sankaran, Sankaran, & Bui, 2000; Sweeny & Ingram, 2001). Researchers have explored differences across levels of learning, finding, for example, that undergraduates may require more direct teaching intervention than do graduate students (Arbaugh, 2010a; Arbaugh & Rau, 2007; Tallent-Runnels et al., 2006; Zhao et al., 2005). Learning styles, preferences, and student attitudes and behaviors may also influence learning outcomes (Aragon, Johnson, & Shaik, 2002; Kulchitsky, 2008; Peters & Hewitt, 2010). A study involving undergraduate students in a Principles of Management course found that student enjoyment had a more positive effect on learning for classroom students, while student learning ability had more impact on learning for on-line students (Nemanich et al., 2009). Research incorporating learner characteristics, attitudes, and behaviors, then, deepens our understanding of how learners respond to different modes of delivery.

What figures prominently in the results is that instructional pedagogy and methods explain a good deal of the variation in learning satisfaction and learning outcomes, just as Clark (1983, 1994) predicted and others have since concluded (Arbaugh & Benbunan-Fich, 2006; Arbaugh & Rau, 2007; Bernard et al., 2004; Hiltz et al., 2000; Rivera & Rice, 2002). Research in on-line learning has contributed significantly to understanding the dynamics of student–instructor, student–student, and student–content interactions, their relative importance, and how they affect learning outcomes (Arbaugh, 2000b, 2005b; Arbaugh & Rau, 2007; Bernard et al., 2009; Kellogg & Smith, 2009; Liu, Bonk, Magjuka, Lee, & Su, 2005; Peltier, Schibrowsky, & Drago, 2007; Peltier, Drago, & Schibrowsky, 2003; Rovai, 2002). The complex interactions between pedagogy, instructional design, instructor methods, learner characteristics, and other variables that affect learning outcomes and experiences raise many questions for further research (Arbaugh et al., 2009; Arbaugh & Benbunan-Fich, 2006; Bekele & Menchaca, 2008; Bernard et al., 2004; Bernard et al., 2009; Peltier et al., 2007; Tallent-Runnels et al., 2006). Most researchers agree, however, that there are likely to be minimal gains from additional studies to prove which mode of learning is better. A more productive approach is to focus on testing and developing the theories and models emerging from the literature with a view to improving teaching and learning in all modes of delivery (Arbaugh et al., 2009; Bernard et al., 2009; Kim & Bonk, 2006).

Far from supporting Barker's contention that online delivery is inferior to face-to-face delivery, then, the empirical evidence demonstrates that while students may experience learning differently, learning outcomes in both modes of delivery are comparable. Furthermore, research comparing on-line to face-to-face learning challenges our traditional assumptions about learning and teaching effectiveness, demonstrating how technology can be used to engage learners beyond the confines of the classroom.

The Importance of Collaboration in On-Line Learning

Contrary to Barker's (2010) inference, collaboration has always been a prominent factor in on-line learning practice and research (Alavi, 1994; Harasim, 2000; Hiltz, 1988; Leidner &

Fuller, 1997). Research comparing on-line to face-to-face delivery reflects the growing use of asynchronous on-line delivery and active on-line communities (Bekele & Menchaca, 2008). The challenge of engaging students at a distance using technologies to support interaction and collaboration has led to the current generation of on-line teaching, which is less "didactic" or "expository" than conventional classroom teaching (U.S. Department of Education, 2009). A constructivist pedagogy, emphasizing self-directed discovery and construction of meaning rather than one-way transfer of knowledge from instructor to student, has become the dominant trend in on-line learning (Bekele & Menchaca, 2008; Kim & Bonk, 2006; Rovai, 2002). Only recently has the constructivist approach been questioned by researchers, suggesting that objectivist pedagogy may be just as effective, or more effective, in online learning, so long as collaborative instructional methods are employed (Arbaugh & Benbunan-Fich, 2006; Kellogg & Smith, 2009).

In short, on-line learning is optimal when it involves a high degree of interaction and collaboration (Arbaugh, 2005a, 2010b; Arbaugh & Benbunan-Fich, 2006; Peltier et al., 2007; Tallent-Runnels et al., 2006). Many of the barriers to working on-line and at a distance can be overcome through course design and instructional strategies that ensure that learning objectives as well as the task-oriented, cognitive, and social-emotional needs of students are met (Brower, 2003; Lim et al., 2007; Liu et al., 2005; Rovai, 2002).

Engaging Students On-Line

The roles and relationships between students and instructors in on-line courses are somewhat different from those in the traditional classroom. Students have more control over their learning activities and a greater responsibility for initiating participation. Collaboration is a shared task between students and teachers, and the instructor's role is more facilitative than directive; yet an active teaching presence, a well-developed construct in on-line education, is essential to effective online learning (Arbaugh, 2010b, 2008; Arbaugh & Benbunan-Fich, 2006; Arbaugh & Hwang, 2006; Drago, Peltier, & Sorensen, 2002; Garrison, Anderson, & Archer, 2000; Ke, 2010; Kim & Bonk, 2006). Teaching presence (course design, facilitation, and direct instruction), cognitive presence (the ability to construct knowledge and meaning through communication), and social presence (development of interpersonal relationships, group cohesion, and identity with the community), are essential elements of the community of inquiry (CoI) framework that has shown promise in predicting effective on-line teaching and learning outcomes (Arbaugh, 2008, 2010b; Arbaugh & Benbunan-Fich, 2006; Garrison et al., 2000; Garrison, Anderson, & Archer, 2010; Heckman & Annabi, 2005; Ke, 2010; Shea et al., 2010). A critical component of teaching presence is facilitating discourse, which includes identifying areas of agreement and disagreement, encouraging and reinforcing contributions to learning; promoting exploration of ideas and productive dialogue; probing and reflection, and summarizing discussions, all of which can be achieved through on-line delivery (Arbaugh, 2008; Arbaugh & Benbunan-Fich, 2006; Ivancevich, Gilbert, & Konopaske, 2009; Shea et al., 2010).

Research demonstrates that the physical presence of an instructor is not required to establish teaching presence, to foster critical thinking and deep level learning, or to create dynamic learning communities. The lack of face-to-face interaction can be overcome by "creating a context where students can learn collectively and collaboratively" (Arbaugh, 2000b: 229). Communication immediacy and richness, typically an advantage of classroom learning, can be overcome by effective on-line instructional techniques and students' ability to adapt to on-line environments (Kim & Bonk, 2010; Kock et al., 2007; Liu et al., 2005; Nemanich et al., 2009). The use of humor, personal anecdotes, and the shorthand and emoticons that are part of the lexicon for on-line communication are simple ways to counteract the absence of body language in on-line environments (Arbaugh, 2008; Lim et al., 2007). Instructors can create safe environments for meaningful and honest communications by establishing a sense of trust and fairness, disclosing more about themselves and their interests, and employing a variety of pedagogical and social roles that facilitate on-line collaboration and learning (Ke, 2010; Liu et al., 2005; Shea et al., 2010).

In some ways, on-line environments can be more conducive than the typical classroom setting to promoting participation, collaboration, and knowledge transfer. An advantage of on-line interaction is that time is not limited to specific classroom hours, so that participation tends to be more evenly distributed. Written communication provides the opportunity to think, check facts, and to reflect before responding, which can facilitate a higher level of discourse (Arbaugh, 2000b; Brower, 2003; Connolly et al., 2007; Hansen, 2008; Heckman & Annabi, 2005; Sautter, 2007; Sweeny & Ingram, 2001). The ability to bring together more diverse populations of students and instructors can be a significant advantage for on-line learners in that it provides a wider range of perspectives and information sharing. A virtual classroom consisting of students living across the nation and in other countries, as well as working in different organizations and industries, provides opportunities for interactions that do not exist in programs where students are typically drawn from a particular region where certain industries and cultures are dominant.

Hence, certain learning outcomes, such as application and transfer of learning and effective group decision making, may be more evident in virtual learning environments (Hansen, 2008; Heckman & Annabi, 2005; Iverson et al., 2005; Jonassen & Kwan, 2001; Yoo et al., 2002). For example, on-line students demonstrated greater ability to apply their knowledge in the development and presentation of marketing plans than did students in classroom sections of an undergraduate marketing course (Hansen, 2008). Researchers concluded that a stronger sense of community and independence

led to greater cooperation among team members. Greater participation was evident in the on-line groups, who could converse whenever they wanted and who were less inhibited from "speaking" openly. Participants in the classroom discussions were more reluctant to speak out, and conversations tended to be dominated by a small group of students (Hansen, 2008). Similarly, students in an on-line section of a capstone course were more involved in creating the social environment and in "teaching" each other compared to students in the classroom who relied more on the instructor to facilitate discussion and exploration. The on-line students demonstrated higher levels of abstract cognitive/analytic processes and a focus on the concrete details compared to classroom students. Finally, a case study comparing on-line with face-to-face student discussions in an MBA course found that higher scores for social presence and integrative complexity (ability to combine different facts and perspectives into a coherent logical argument) were evident in the on-line group (Yoo et al., 2002). Diversity of perspectives (resulting from removal of geographic barriers) and opportunities to reflect and think more about issues were cited as advantages for the on-line students. Researchers concluded that once students grow accustomed to on-line environments, collaborative learning processes and outcomes may be just as effective, and in some ways more effective, than what occurs in the classroom (Yoo et al., 2002).

Challenges for On-Line Collaboration

On the other hand, collaborative learning on-line can be challenging for both students and instructors. On-line discussions, researchers point out, are less linear in sequence compared to the classroom discussions because students and instructors are participating at different times over longer durations of time (Heckman & Annabi, 2005). Several discussions may be occurring simultaneously, making it more challenging to follow the flow of arguments, provide timely feedback, and to conclude discussion topics. Student–student interaction is more prevalent in on-line environments, and while there are benefits to sharing and learning from each other, heavy emphasis on group discussion may be more time-consuming and frustrating for participants (Kellogg & Smith, 2009). Another drawback is that students in on-line courses may have less confidence in the instructor's expertise than do students who sit face-to-face with instructors in classrooms, possibly due to the lack of visual clues and less immediacy of responses to questions (Nemanich et al., 2009).

Facilitating on-line learning and collaboration, then, requires a delicate sense of timing and balance in performing various instructional roles (Arbaugh, 2010b; Liu et al., 2005; Shea et al., 2010). Too much or too little instructor involvement may have a negative effect on the quality and quantity of student participation (Arbaugh, 2010b; Ke, 2010; Kellogg & Smith, 2009; Mazzolini & Maddison, 2007). Students expect the instructor to have a strong social as well as a teaching presence, creating a sense of "being there" through acknowledgment and response (Ke, 2010). Contrary to what some expect, overparticipation, rather than underparticipation, is likely to be a problem for on-line participants. On-line instructors and students often report feeling overwhelmed by the volume and length of postings and the vigilance required to keep conversations on topic (Brower, 2003; Peters & Hewitt, 2010). Coping behaviors, including skimming over comments, avoiding complex topics or issues, pitching for instructor favor, or forming online cliques, may have negative effects on learning outcomes (Ke, 2010; Peters & Hewitt, 2010). Students often express dissatisfaction with superficial postings that add no value to the learning conversation (Ke, 2010). Many of these problems can be mitigated by effective course design and instructional techniques.

The Role of Instructional Design

Meaningful, engaging interaction and collaboration do not happen simply by opening up a discussion board (Puzziferro & Shelton, 2009). Discussion and collaboration must be consciously incorporated into the design of the course and properly facilitated by instructors (Arbaugh, 2005b, 2010b; Peltier et al., 2007). Course content, some argue, may be the most important factor in how students and faculty perceive the quality of on-line teaching and learning (Drago et al., 2002; Peltier et al., 2007). Orientation to on-line learning platforms and guidance on how to promote effective learning dialogue are essential for both students and instructors. As in the classroom, dysfunctional group dynamics, social loafing and time constraints must be managed for on-line learning to be effective (Brower, 2003; Kellogg & Smith, 2009; Mullen & Tallent-Runnels, 2006). A strong rationale for incorporating group activities, a good balance between individual and group work, and clear directions and support for managing group dynamics (e.g., guidelines for teamwork, peer evaluation, avoiding "group think," conflict management, and dealing with "slackers") are important aspects of instructional design. If collaborative activities and group projects are not assessed, low participation is likely (Brower, 2003; Lim, 2002). Group size and composition are important and may vary across different activities (Arbaugh, 2005b; Arbaugh & Rau, 2007; Hewitt & Brett, 2007; Ladyshewsky, 2004; Larson, 2002). Providing structure and setting the rules of engagement are more crucial to on-line collaboration than they are to classroom collaboration (Sautter, 2007). Without clear guidelines emphasizing the quality of participation, students may engage in strategies that are counterproductive to intended learning outcomes (Peters & Hewitt, 2010). Instructional design, then, acts as a surrogate for the physical structure and instructional presence that occur in a classroom (Arbaugh, 2010b; Arbaugh & Rau, 2007). Again, instructional methods and design are more important than mode of delivery in ensuring successful collaborative learning.

In sum, collaboration is vital to effective on-line teaching and learning that is increasingly informed by theoretical constructs applicable to business education (Arbaugh & Benbunan-Fich, 2006; Garrison et al., 2000, 2010; Nemanich et al., 2009; Peltier et al., 2007). Contrary to what many believe, choice of instructional method is not necessarily a choice between "high tech" and "high touch" (Kulchitsky, 2008). To reiterate. Barker's assumptions that on-line delivery is not capable of supporting collaboration or quality teaching and learning are unsupported by the research evidence.

Changing Mind-Sets

Given the amount of research available about online learning, the business education community seems surprisingly ignorant about the quality of communication, collaboration, and learning outcomes that can be achieved through on-line delivery. Uninformed opinions about on-line learning must be challenged, as I contend here, by faculty and administrators who are aware of the research and practice in on-line teaching. Management educators like Barker may never change their point of view but, at the very least, they should base their comments on valid evidence. They should also consider current and future generations of Internet-savvy students who might expect business schools to embrace technology, including on-line teaching and learning, as a tool for engaging students. Sadly, greater effort seems to be devoted to preserving the status quo. What might help to overcome biased perceptions about on-line education? I offer three recommendations for consideration: leverage the research, incent and enable faculty, and remove systemic barriers.

Leverage the Research

Within postsecondary institutions, senior administrators often know little about the use of technology for learning and its strategic and resource implications for their institutions (Alavi & Gallupe, 2003; McCarthy & Samors, 2009). Administrators should be better informed about the research, challenges, and benefits related to on-line teaching and learning. Lack of awareness may be somewhat due to the way the research is disseminated. Research related to on-line education has not been easily accessible to business educators and the broader business community, partly because it is published in journals related to distance education and education technology (Arbaugh et al., 2009). As well, many of the comparative studies involving business students have appeared in discipline-specific journals, particularly in the areas of information systems management and marketing. Hence, those at the forefront of on-line teaching have found it difficult to pull the evidence together in a form that is accessible for students, program evaluators, and the media. Articles in the *Chronicle for Higher Education* or *Biz Ed* magazine (whether positive or negative) tend to be based on opinions and experience rather than evidence (Benton, 2009; Clift, 2009; de l'Etraz, 2010).

Now that a comprehensive review of the research about online teaching in the business disciplines has brought the evidence to the forefront, key findings need to be communicated succinctly through media that will reach administrators, faculty, students, and employers (Arbaugh et al., 2009). For those of us involved in on-line teaching and research, educating our colleagues who have little or no exposure to alternate forms of delivery is perhaps the best place to begin.

We know much more about what leads to effective on-line teaching and learning than we did 20 years ago. Development and testing of theoretical frameworks must continue, along with cross-disciplinary collaboration (Arbaugh, 2008; Arbaugh, Bangert et al., 2010; Arbaugh, Cleveland Innes, Diaz, Garrison, Ice, Richardson, & Swain, 2008). Greater attention should be paid to closing the gap between research and practice, a gap that is certainly evident even at my former university where distance education is a research priority. Furthermore, on-line teaching methods considered to be innovative 10 or 15 years ago have now become somewhat "traditional" themselves. A long-standing theme in the literature on technology-mediated learning is that choices about technology should be pedagogically driven, an argument that has been reinforced by Adams and Morgan (2007). They argue for greater alignment between pedagogy and technology in what they refer to as the "second generation" of e-learning (Morgan & Adams, 2009). Research and teaching practices should be more aggressive in exploring the application of new technologies (including social networking, knowledge building, and mobile computing) and innovations in teaching methods that will engage the next generations of learners (Farmer, Yue, & Brooks, 2008; Johnson, Levine, Smith, & Stone, 2010; Kulchitsky, 2008; Li, 2007; McKerlich & Anderson, 2007; Twining, 2009). Business schools might question how well they will be able to accommodate students who may be self-directed and widely connected, and who may prefer more personalized learning environments (Puzziferro & Shelton, 2009).

There will be a continuing need for business faculty to produce research related to on-line and blended pedagogy in various subject areas. Many contributors to the research are drawn to it as a result of their experiences teaching on-line, yet few are continuing to pursue research agendas focused on pedagogy (Arbaugh et al., 2009). Business schools, working in partnership with experts in education and learning technology, should do more to encourage pedagogical research across business and other academic disciplines. The future advantage may lie with those schools that promote innovation in teaching regardless of mode of delivery.

Incent and Enable Faculty

Negative perceptions about on-line delivery are most evident among faculty members who have no on-line experience, whereas the majority of those who have taught on-line are positive about their experiences (Seaman, 2009). The latter group has a lot to say about how to improve support for on-line and blended learning (Alexander, Perreault, Zhao, & Waldman, 2009; Baglione & Nastanski, 2007; Seaman, 2009). Business school leaders should tap into this resource to promote greater awareness of the challenges and benefits of on-line teaching and learning.

The additional time required to develop courses and teach on-line is likely the most significant barrier to faculty participation in on-line delivery. A study conducted by the Association of Public and Land-Grant Universities found that nearly 64% of faculty said it takes more effort to teach on-line compared to face-to-face (cited in Seaman, 2009). Faculty respondents rated their universities as "below average" in providing support and incentives for on-line course development and delivery (2009). The extra time required for on-line course development and teaching, they reported, was not rewarded by additional compensation nor was it acknowledged for tenure review or promotional purposes. Lack of incentives and rewards was more of a concern for junior faculty compared to senior faculty, likely due the pressures of achieving tenure and promotion. Technological competence, on the other hand, was less of a concern even for senior faculty members.

A misconception about on-line delivery is that is a less costly and more scalable alternative to face-to-face delivery. Yet significant investments in technology, electronic library resources and learning materials, instructional design expertise, and course administration are necessary to support online delivery on a wider scale. Furthermore, instructor-student ratios for on-line courses are often lower than what is sustainable through classroom delivery. Research indicates that there is a negative relationship between larger class sizes and the quality of interaction and student satisfaction with on-line learning (Arbaugh & Rau, 2007; Hewitt & Brett, 2007). Hence, administrators must be prepared to reassess course-load requirements, at least in the initial stages of moving to on-line delivery (Sarker & Nicholson, 2005). Criteria for tenure-and-promotion review, evaluation of teaching, and measures of instructional time or student contact hours must be developed to reflect the differences between on-line and face-to-face instruction.

Particular attention must be paid to minimizing instructor time devoted to technical and course administration support (Liu et al., 2005). Provision of IT support, including help-desk services outside of normal hours, and instructional design and editorial support will help to ease the burden on instructors and course developers. Faculty resources are best focused on substantive teaching activities such as fostering meaningful dialogue, inquiry, and critical thinking. Hence, decisions around on-line learning platforms must be driven by pedagogy and not the other way around.

In addition to time, faculty members are also concerned about training for on-line teaching. They often lack knowledge of the pedagogy, instructional techniques, and technical skills employed in on-line learning environments (Bates, 2010; Liu et al., 2005; Yang & Cornelius, 2005). Training for faculty and students can also help to mitigate the time and effort required to facilitate online learning. Students at my former university receive a 1-week orientation course prior to beginning the first course in the MBA program. First time instructors must attend a 1-day orientation to the on-line pedagogy, instructional techniques, and the learning platform. They are paired with an experienced instructor before they begin teaching independently. Students and faculty have access to comprehensive handbooks and other on-line resources that include instructions about expectations for instructor–student and student–student interaction. Behaviors that contribute to effective "learning conversations" are clearly outlined.

Training, alone, will not be sufficient to support effective on-line teaching. Creation of an active on-line learning community where faculty can share experiences on a continuous basis is more likely to sustain faculty commitment and skills development (Liu, Kim, Bonk, & Magjuka, 2007; Yang & Cornelius, 2005). For example, my former university holds an annual conference for on-line instructors, located in various parts of the world, to network, share teaching strategies and techniques, and to keep up-to-date with changes in technology, pedagogy, and course administration. Databases are created for each course, where instructors can confer about teaching methods, course content and design, and student learning issues. These examples illustrate how transfer of knowledge and continuous improvement can be supported within and across course offerings. Online delivery, then, requires significant investments in faculty time, training, and development.

Why would administrators and faculty members choose to invest more time in on-line delivery if the learning outcomes are comparable to those for classroom delivery? In addition increasing recruitment opportunities, student needs for greater access and flexibility should be the primary motivator for adopting on-line and blended delivery (Seaman, 2009). Indeed, the desire for faculty to contribute to positioning the business school as being more progressive and responsive to market trends is perhaps the greatest incentive for faculty to participate in on-line teaching (Parthasarathy & Smith, 2009).

Beyond altruistic and strategic motivations, online delivery has the potential to benefit faculty more directly. Many of these benefits are yet to be fully explored. The option to choose when and where they teach can be a significant advantage to faculty members with family or elder care responsibilities, mobility and other health issues, or for those who must commute long distances (Alexander et al., 2009; Liu et al., 2007; Parthasarathy & Smith, 2009). On-line delivery allows a business school to access specialized instructors who reside elsewhere or who travel extensively for work. Pressures for classroom space are reduced, and flexibility in deploying faculty resources is increased. Options for faculty members to continue to teach a course if they are away at a conference or conducting research can increase opportunities for travel during the academic term (Liu et al., 2007). Faculty may opt to teach additional courses on-line to supplement regular salaries. Finally, there are many reasons why faculty enjoy on-line teaching, including the ability to attract a greater diversity of students, which can enhance learning experiences (Liu et al., 2007; Seaman, 2009; Yoo et al., 2002). In many ways, the increased accessibility and flexibility afforded to faculty members may serve as an effective recruitment-and-retention strategy as business schools struggle to attract and maintain academically qualified faculty.

Faculty resistance to on-line delivery is not solely due to lack of knowledge or acceptance. There are practical impediments that need to be addressed through policy changes and incentives to encourage experimentation with alternative teaching modes and methods. While changes to some policies and practices can be made at the faculty level, others require adaptations at the institutional level or beyond.

Remove Systemic Barriers

Whether it is for accreditation, rankings, approval of government bodies, program reviews, membership in affiliated associations, or policies for transfer credit, criteria for assessment should be applicable to different forms of delivery (Bates, 2011; Gaytan, 2007). For example, there is no basis for an institution to refuse transfer credit simply because a course is delivered on-line. Regional degree-granting and approval bodies should re-examine their policies around transfer credit to ensure that they do not unjustifiably penalize students who take courses or complete programs on-line. Institutional-level policies, such as those related to intellectual property rights, require review and adjustment as alternate forms of delivery are adopted (Dyrud, 2000; Seaman, 2009; Wallace, 2007). While many distance-education institutions retain the rights to on-line course content, this is not the norm in most post-secondary institutions where faculty rights over teaching materials prevail. Copyright policies, then, must consider the balance between the rights of the creators of teaching materials and recognition of the investments that institutions have made in the development and distribution of on-line teaching and learning materials and systems.

Accreditation bodies, too, must adapt more quickly to on-line delivery. For example, AACSB International developed special guidelines for distance education a number of years ago, yet the application of accreditation standards continues to reflect the classroom model of delivery (AACSB International, 2007). Despite increasing emphasis on learning outcomes, face-to-face instructional hours are used as a proxy measure for the quantity and quality of instruction. This does not work well for evaluating on-line learning, where the instructional process is less direct and significant instructional elements are incorporated into the course materials and activities. Instructional hours, particularly with asynchronous delivery, are not usually prescribed by a specific time frame and often extend over a longer duration than is normally required for classroom participation. Students may spend no face-to-face time with an instructor, but they often spend more hours per week interacting with other students and their instructors than do students and instructors who meet for a specified class time each week.

Responsibility also resides with researchers and institutions involved with on-line delivery to develop and recommend appropriate metrics for evaluating on-line teaching and learning. For example, Rovai, Wighting, Baker, and Grooms (2009) have proposed an instrument for measuring perceived learning that is relevant to on-line, blended, and classroom delivery no matter what instructional methods or philosophies are used. Moreover, as emphasis shifts to the development of objective measures of learning outcomes, there is an opportunity to address how these outcomes may be achieved through different modes of delivery.

Both AACSB and institutions that have experienced the accreditation process indicate that business schools that deliver programs almost entirely on-line have a difficult road to navigate in achieving accreditation. The problem may have less to do with the accreditation standards and more to do with how teaching is perceived by volunteer committee members who may have little or no experience with, or understanding of, on-line teaching methods. This is likely to change as more distance- and on-line learning institutions gain accreditation, and measures of effectiveness focus more on learning outcomes.

Many business schools will, for good reasons, choose to focus on classroom teaching, and some faculty members will never make the transition to on-line teaching (Clift, 2009). However, resistance to on-line learning is beginning to thaw as more of the elite schools incorporate on-line and blended learning. Still, negative perceptions and misinformation prevail. Faculty resistance persists, and policies and practices remain rooted in the traditional model of classroom delivery. The proposed recommendations may generate constructive debate around the barriers that prevent more widespread consideration and adoption of on-line delivery as an effective alternative or complement to face-to-face delivery.

Concluding Remarks

The results and observations drawn from the comparative research, along with the knowledge that has accrued about effective on-line pedagogy and instruction, illustrate why management educators must be better informed and more open-minded toward on-line learning. Measures of teaching and learning must accommodate different modes of delivery and instructional approaches. Attitudinal biases that assume face-to-face interaction and the physical presence of the instructor necessarily constitute a superior method of delivery are simply no longer valid.

An abundance of comparative research supports what many on-line educators and researchers have been saying all along: Success is rooted in pedagogy, more than in technology or mode of delivery (Arbaugh & Benbunan-Fich, 2006; Hiltz et al., 2000). While there are differences in the way that communication, interaction, and instruction occur in on-line and classroom delivery, learning outcomes are not necessarily more or less effective in one mode or another. This is not a new revelation, but it is one that should be more fully recognized in the business education community.

On-line researchers and practitioners must do more to leverage the research evidence about online learning, not only to counter prevailing beliefs, but also to inform research and teaching practice across business and other academic disciplines. Indeed, research agendas have been directed more toward improving and evaluating online and blended modes of teaching and learning, and less toward using traditional teaching models as a basis for assessing effectiveness. Common principles inform models of classroom and on-line delivery even though methods of teaching may differ (Bangert, 2004; Liu et al., 2005). Now that research about pedagogy and instructional methods has been recognized as an area of intellectual contribution for business faculty, continuing research regarding technology and learning for all modes of delivery is more likely to flourish (AACSB, 2003).

On-line learning will continue to grow as people demand greater access to business education no matter where they are located and as emerging technologies continue to impact the way that education is delivered (Johnson et al., 2010). Given the research evidence, there is no excuse for business educators to view on-line learning as a second-class instructional method. As Barker's (2010) comments suggest, traditional beliefs about education are strongly entrenched in the ways in which online distance programs are perceived and assessed. Until this message is more widely disseminated and accepted, the bias toward face-to-face instruction is likely to persist, particularly among educational gatekeepers.

Source: Academy of Management

REFERENCES

AACSB International. 2007. Quality issues in distance learning. Tampa: AACSB International. Retrieved from: http://www.aacsb.edu/Resource_Centers/DeansResources/quality-issues-final.pdf. Accessed 09/23/2009.

AACSB International. 2010. AACSB member schools are increasing on-line program offerings. In eNewsline: Management education news from AACSB. Tampa: AACSB International. Retrieved from: http://www.aacsb.edu/publications/enewsline/archives/2010/vol9-issue3-datadirect.pdf. Accessed 07/ 06/2011.

AACSB. 2003. [Association to advance collegiate schools of business] international. *Sustaining Scholarship in Business Schools.* Report of the Doctoral Faculty Commission to

AACSB International's Board of Directors.Tampa: AACSB International.

Adams, J., & Morgan, G. 2007. "Second generation" e-learning: Characteristics and design principles for supporting management soft-skills development. *International Journal on E-Learning*, 6: 157–185.

Alavi, M. 1994. Computer mediated collaborative learning: An empirical evaluation. *MIS Quarterly*, 18: 159–174.

Alavi, M., & Gallupe, R. B. 2003. Using information technology in learning: Case studies in business and management education programs. *Academy of Management Learning and Education*, 2: 139–153.

Alavi, M., Yoo, Y., & Vogel, D. R. 1997. Using information technology to add value to management education. *Academy of Management Journal*, 40: 1310–1333.

Alexander, M., Perreault, H., Zhao, J., & Waldman, L. 2009. Comparing AACSB faculty and student on-line learning experiences: Changes between 2000–2006. *Journal of Educators On-line*, 6: 1–20.

Allen, I. E., & Seaman, J. 2008. *Staying the course: On-line education in the United States*. Needham, MA: Sloan Consortium.

Allen, I. E., & Seaman, J. 2009. *Learning on demand: On-line education in the United States*. Needham, MA: Sloan Consortium.

Allen, I. E., & Seaman, J. 2010. *Class differences: On-line education in the United States.* Needham, MA: Sloan Consortium. Retrieved from: http://sloanconsortium.org/publications/survey/pdf/class_differences.pdf. Accessed 04/03/2011.

Allen, M., Bourhis, J., Burrell, N., & Mabry, E. 2002. Comparing student satisfaction with distance education to traditional classrooms in higher education: A meta-analysis. *American Journal of Distance Education*, 16: 83–97.

Altbach, P. G., Reisberg, L., & Rumbley, L. E. 2009. Trends in global higher education: Tracking an academic revolution. A report prepared for the UNESCO 2009 World Conference on Higher Education. In *Executive summary*. Paris, France: United Nations Educational, Scientific and Culture Organization. Retrieved from: http://unesdoc.unesco.org/images/0018/001831/183168e.pdf. Accessed 10/29/2010.

Anistine, J., & Skidmore, M. 2005. A small sample study of traditional and on-line courses with sample selection adjustment. *Journal of Economic Education*, 36: 107–127.

Aragon, S. R., Johnson, S. D., & Shaik, N. 2002. The influence of learning style preferences on student success in on-line versus face-to-face environments. *American Journal of Distance Education*, 16: 227–244.

Arbaugh, J. B. 2000a. An exploratory study of the effects of gender on student learning and class participation in an internet-based course. *Management Learning*, 31: 533–549.

Arbaugh, J. B. 2000b. Virtual classroom versus physical classroom: An exploratory study of class discussion patterns and student learning in an asynchronous internet-based MBA course. *Journal of Management Education*, 24: 213–233.

Arbaugh, J. B. 2005a. How much does "subject matter" matter? A study of disciplinary effects in on-line MBA courses. *Academy of Management Learning and Education*, 4: 57–73.

Arbaugh, J. B. 2005b. Is there an optimal design for on-line MBA courses? *Academy of Management Learning and Education*, 4: 135–149.

Arbaugh, J. B. 2008. Does the Community of Inquiry framework predict outcomes in on-line MBA courses? *International Review of Research in Open and Distance Learning*, 9: 1–21.

Arbaugh, J. B. 2010a. Do undergraduates and MBAs differ online? Initial conclusions from the literature. *Journal of Leadership and Organizational Studies*, 17: 129–142.

Arbaugh, J. B. 2010b. Sage, guide, both, or even more? An examination of instructor activity in on-line MBA courses. *Computers and Education*, 55: 1234–1244.

Arbaugh, J. B., Bangert, A., & Cleveland-Innes, M. 2010. Subject matter effects and the Community of Inquiry (CoI) framework: An exploratory study. *Internet and Higher Education*, 13: 37–44.

Arbaugh, J. B., & Benbunan-Fich, R. 2006. An investigation of epistemological and social dimensions of teaching in online learning environments. *Academy of Management Learning and Education*, 5: 435–447.

Arbaugh, J. B., Cleveland-Innes, M., Diaz, S. R., Garrison, D. R., Ice, P., Richardson, J. C., & Swain, K. 2008. Developing a community of inquiry instrument: Testing a measure of the Community of Inquiry framework using a multi-institutional sample. *Internet and Higher Education*, 11: 133–136.

Arbaugh, J. B., Godfrey, M., Johnson, M., Pollack, B., Niendorf, B., & Wresch, W. 2009. Research in on-line and blended learning in the business disciplines: Key findings and possible future direction. *Internet and Higher Education*, 12: 71–87.

Arbaugh, J. B., & Hwang, A. 2006. Does "teaching presence" exist in on-line MBA courses? *Internet and Higher Education*, 9: 9–21.

Arbaugh, J. B., & Rau, B. L. 2007. A study of disciplinary, structural, and behavioral effects on course outcomes in on-line MBA courses. *Decision Sciences Journal of Innovative Education*, 5: 65–95.

Baglione, S. L., & Nastanski, M. 2007. The superiority of on-line discussion: Faculty perceptions. *Quarterly Review of Distance Education*, 8: 139–150.

Bangert, A. W. 2004. The seven principles of good practice: A framework for evaluating on-line teaching. *Internet and Higher Education*, 7: 217–232.

Barker, R. 2010. No, management is not a profession. *Harvard Business Review*, 88: 52–60.

Bates, T. 2011. 2011 Outlook for on-line learning and distance education. Sudbury, ON: Contact North. Retrieved from http://elearnnetwork.ca/?q=node/540. Accessed 03/18/2011.

BBC. Mobile News. 2010, August 7. Young open university student numbers increase. Retrieved from: http://www.bbc.co.uk/news/education-10903088. Accessed 10/30/2010.

Bekele, T. A., & Menchaca, M. P. 2008. Research on internet-supported learning: A review. *Quarterly Review of Distance Education*, 9: 373–405.

Benbunan-Fich, R. 2010. Is self-reported learning a proxy metric for learning? Perspectives from the information systems literature. *Academy of Management Learning and Education*, 9: 321–328.

Benton, T. 2009, September 18. On-line learning: Reaching out to the skeptics. Chronicle of Higher Education. Retrieved from http://chronicle.com/article/On-line-Learning-Reaching-Out/48375/. Accessed 03/19/2011.

Bernard, R. M., Abrami, P. C., Borokhovski, E., Wade, C. A., Tamin, R. N., Surkes, M. A., & Bethel, E. C. 2009. A meta-analysis of three types of interaction treatments in distance education. *Review of Educational Research*, 79: 1243–1289.

Bernard, R. M., Abrami, P. C., Lou, Y., Borokhovski, E., Wade, C. A., Wozney, L., Wallet, P. A., Fiset, M., & Huang, B. 2004. How does distance education compare with classroom instruction? A meta-analysis of the empirical literature. *Review of Educational Research*, 74: 379–439.

Brower, H. H. 2003. On emulating classroom discussion in a distance-delivered OBHR course: Creating an on-line learning community. *Academy of Management Learning and Education*, 2: 22–36.

Bryant, K., Campbell, J., & Kerr, D. 2003. Impact of web-based flexible learning on academic performance in information systems. *Journal of Information Systems Education*, 14: 41–50.

Canadian Association of University Teachers (CAUT). 2004. *Policy Statement on Distance Education* (revised February 2009). Retrieved from: http://www.caut.ca/pages.asp?page=263&lang=l. Accessed 03/24/2011.

Carnevale, D. 2005. Employers still prefer traditional degrees over on-line learning, study finds. *Chronicle of Higher Education*, 52: A43.

Carnevale, D. 2007. Employers often distrust on-line degrees. *Chronicle of Higher Education*, 53: A-28.

Carr-Chellman, A. (Ed.). 2005. *Global perspectives on e-learning: Rhetoric and reality.* Thousand Oaks, CA: Sage.

Clark, R. E. 1983. Reconsidering research on learning from media. *Review of Educational Research*, 53: 445–459.

Clark, R. E. 1994. Media and method. *Educational Technology Research and Development*, 42: 7–10.

Cleary, S. P. 2001, March 12. The downside: Why some critics give web-based education less than stellar grades. *Wall Street Journal:* R32.

Clift, E. 2009, May 21. I'll never do it again. *Chronicle of Higher Education.* Retrieved from http://chronicle.com/article/Ill-Never-Do-It-Again/44250/?sid=at. Accessed 03/18/2011.

Connolly, T. M., MacArthur, E., Stanfield, M., & McLellan, E. 2007. A quasi-experimental study of three on-line learning courses in computing. *Computers and Education*, 49: 345–359.

Cox, R. 2005. On-line education as institutional myth: Rituals and realities at community colleges. *Teachers College Record*, 7: 1754–1787.

de l'Etraz, P. 2010, November/December. *What can an on-line program do for you?* BizEd: 34–39.

Drago, W., Peltier, J., & Sorensen, D. 2002. Course content or the instructor: Which is more important in on-line teaching? *Management Research News*, 25: 69–83.

Dyrud, M. A. 2000. The third wave: A position paper. *Business Communications Quarterly*, 63: 81–93.

Farmer, B., Yue, A., & Brooks, B. 2008. Using blogging for higher order learning in large cohort university teaching: A case study. *Australasian Journal of Educational Technology*, 24: 123–136.

Financial Times. 2010. EMBA rankings 2010. Retrieved from: http://rankings.ft.com/businessschoolrankings/emba-rankings-2010. Accessed 07/26/2011.

Financial Times. 2011. On-line MBA 2011 listing. Retrieved from: http://rankings.ft.com/businessschoolrankings/on-line-mba-2011. Accessed 07/26/2011.

Friday, E., Friday-Stroud, S. S., Green, A. L., & Hill, A. Y. 2006. A multi-semester comparison of student performance between multiple traditional and on-line sections of two management courses. Journal of Behavioral and Applied Management, 18. Retrieved from: http://www.ibam.com/ pubs/jbam/articles/vol8/no1/JBAM_8_l_4.pdf. Accessed 09/ 23/2009.

Garrison, D. R., Anderson, T., & Archer, W. 2000. Critical inquiry in a text-based environment: Computer conferencing and higher education. *Internet and Higher Education*, 2: 87–105.

Garrison, D. R., Anderson, T., & Archer, W. 2010. The first decade of the community of inquiry framework: A retrospective. *Internet and Higher Education*, 13: 5–9.

Gaytan, J. 2007. Visions shaping the future of on-line education: Understanding its historical evaluation, implications and assumptions. *On-line Journal of Distance Learning Administration*, 10. Retrieved from: http://www.westga.edu/ ~distance/ojdla/summer102/gaytan102.htm. Accessed 03/27/ 2011.

Glenn, L. M., Jones, C. G., & Hoyt, J. E. 2003. The effect of interaction levels on student performance: A comparative analysis of web-mediated versus traditional delivery. *Journal of Interactive Learning Research*, 14: 265–299.

Hansen, D. E. 2008. Knowledge transfer in on-line learning environments. *Journal of Marketing Education*, 30: 93–105.

Harasim, L. 2000. On-line education as a new paradigm in learning. *Internet and Higher Education*, 3: 41–61.

Heckman, R., & Annabi, H. 2005. A content analytic comparison of learning processes in on-line and face-to-face case study discussions. *Journal of Computer Mediated Communication*, 10: 141–150. Retrieved from: http://jcmc.indiana.edu/ vol10/issue2/heckman.html. Accessed 04/30/2011.

Hewitt, J., & Brett, C. 2007. The relationship between class size and on-line activity patterns in asynchronous computer conferencing environments. *Computers and Education*, 49: 1258–1271.

Hiltz, S. R. 1988. Collaborative learning in a virtual classroom: Highlights of findings. In *Proceedings of the 1988 ACM Conference on Computer-Supported Cooperative Work*. New York: Association for Computing Machinery. Retrieved http://delivery.acm.org/10.1145/70000/62289/p282-hiltz.pdf? key1=62289&key2=4582668921&coll=DL&dl=ACM&ip= 131.232.21.119&CFID=11568730&CFTOKEN=78152180. Accessed 03/15/ 2011.

Hiltz, S. R., Coppola, N., Rotter, N., Turoff, M., & Benbunan-Fich, R. 2000. Measuring the importance of collaborative learning for the effectiveness of ALN: A multi-measure, multi-method approach. *Journal of Asynchronous Learning Networks*, 4. Retrieved from: http://www.aln.org/publications/ jaln/v4n2/pdf/v4n2_hiltz.pdf. Accessed 09/23/2009.

Ivancevich, J. M., Gilbert, J. A., & Konopaske, R. 2009. Studying and facilitating dialogue in select on-line management courses. *Journal of Management Education*, 33: 196–218.

Iverson, K. M., Colky, D. L., & Cyboran, V. 2005. E-learning takes the lead: An empirical investigation of learner differences in on-line and classroom delivery. *Performance Improvement Quarterly*, 18: 5–29.

Jahng, N., Krug, D., & Zhang, Z. 2007. Student achievement in on-line distance education compared to face-to-face education. In *European Journal of Open, Distance and E-Learning*, 1. Retrieved from: http://www.eurodl.org/? p=archives&year=2007&halfyear=l&article=253. Accessed 09/24/2009.

Johnson, L., Levine, A., Smith, R., & Stone, S. 2010. *The 2010 Horizon report*. Austin, TX: New Media Consortium. Retrieved from: http://net.educause.edu/ir/library/pdf/ CSD5810.pdf. Accessed 10/29/2010.

Jonassen, D. H., & Kwan, H. I. 2001. Communication patterns in computer mediated versus face-to-face group problem solving. *Educational Technology Research and Development*, 49: 35–52.

Ke, F. 2010. Examining on-line teaching, cognitive, and social presence for adult students. *Computers and Education*, 55: 808–820.

Kellogg, D. L., & Smith, M. A. 2009. Student-to-student interaction revisited: A case study of working adult business students in on-line courses. *Decision Sciences Journal of Innovative Education*, 7: 433–455.

Kim, J., & Bonk, C. J. 2010. Towards best practices in on-line teaching: Instructional immediacy in on-line faculty experiences. *International Journal of Instructional Technology and Distance Learning*, 7. Retrieved from: http://www.itdl.org/ Journal/Aug_10/article02.htm. Accessed 10/28/2010.

Kim, K., & Bonk, C. J. 2006. The future of on-line teaching and learning in higher education: The survey says … *Educause Quarterly*, 29(4): 22–30.

Kock, N., Verville, J., & Garza, V. 2007. Media naturalness and on-line learning: Findings supporting both the significant and no significant difference perspectives. *Decision Sciences Journal of Innovative Education*, 5: 333–355.

Kulchitsky, J. D. 2008. High-tech versus high-touch education: Perceptions of risk in distance learning. *International Journal of Educational Management*, 22: 151–167.

Ladyshewsky, R. K. 2004. E-learning compared with face to face: Differences in the academic achievement of postgraduate business students. *Australian Journal of Educational Technology*, 20: 316–336.

Lapsley, R., Kulik, B., Moody, R., & Arbaugh, J. B. 2008. Is identical really identical? An investigation of equivalency theory and on-line learning. *Journal of Educators Online, 5.* Retrieved from: http://www.thejeo.com/Archives/Volume5-Number1/LapsleyetalPaper.pdf. Accessed 10/25/2010.

Larson, D. K., & Sung, C. H. 2009. Comparing student performance: On-line versus blended versus face-to-face. *Journal of Asynchronous Learning Networks*, 13: 31–42.

Larson, P. D. 2002. Interactivity in an electronically delivered marketing course. *Journal of Education for Business*, 77: 256–245.

Leidner, D. E., & Fuller, M. 1997. Improving student learning of conceptual information: GSS supported collaborative learning vs. individual constructive learning. *Decision Support Systems*, 20: 149–163.

Leidner, D. E., & Jarvenpaa, S. L. 1995. The use of information technology to enhance management school education: A theoretical view. *MIS Quarterly*, 19: 265–291.

Li, X. 2007. Intelligent agent-supported on-line education. *Decision Sciences Journal of Innovative Education, 5:* 311–331.

Lim, D. H. 2002. Perceived differences between classroom and distance education: Seeking instructional strategies for learning applications. *International Journal of Educational Technology, 2.* Retrieved from: http://www.ed.uiuc.edu/ijet/v3n1/d-lim/index.htmlAGES. Accessed 09/23/2009.

Lim, D. H., Morris, M. L., & Kupritz, V. W. 2007. On-line vs. blended learning: Differences in instructional outcomes and learner satisfaction. *Journal of Asynchronous Learning Networks*, 10: 27–42. Accessed 07/27/2011.

Liu, S., Kim, K., Bonk, C. J., & Magjuka, R. 2007. What do on-line professors have to say about on-line teaching? On-line *Journal of Distance Learning Administration*, 10. Retrieved from: http://www.westga.edu/~distance/ojdla/summer102/liu102.htm.

Liu, X., Bonk, C. J., Magjuka, R. J., Lee, S. H., & Su, B. 2005. Exploring four dimensions of on-line instructor roles: A program level case study. *Journal of Asynchronous Learning Networks*, 9: 29–48.

Machtmes, K., & Asher, J. W. 2000. A meta-analysis of the effectiveness of telecourses in distance education. *Journal of Education for Business*, 69: 273–277.

Mazzolini, M., & Maddison, S. 2007. When to jump in: The role of the instructor in on-line discussion forums. *Computers & Education,* 49(2): 193–213.

McCarthy, S. A., & Samors, R. J. 2009. On-line learning as a strategic asset, vol. 1, A resource for campus leaders. In

A report on the On-line Education Benchmarking Study Conducted by APLU-Sloan National Commission on On-line Learning. Washington, DC: Association of Public and Land-grant Universities, Office of Public Affairs.

McKerlich, R., & Anderson, T. 2007. Community of inquiry and learning in immersive environments. *Journal of Asynchronous Learning Networks,* 11: 35–52.

Morgan, G., & Adams, J. 2009. Pedagogy first: Making web-technologies work for soft skills development in leadership and management education. *Journal of Interactive Learning Research*, 20: 129–155.

Morphew, C. 2009. Conceptualizing change in the institutional diversity of U.S. colleges and universities. *Journal of Higher Education*, 80: 243–269.

Mullen, G. E., & Tallent-Runnels, M. K. 2006. Student outcomes and perceptions of instructors' demands and support in on-line and traditional classrooms. *The Internet and Higher Education,* 9(4): 257–266.

Nemanich, L., Banks, M., & Vera, D. 2009. Enhancing knowledge transfer in classroom versus on-line settings: The interplay among instructor, student, content, and context. *Decision Sciences Journal of Innovative Education*, 7: 123–148.

Noble, D. 1997. Digital diploma mills: part 1. In *The automation of higher education.* Retrieved from: http://communication.ucsd.edu/dl/ddm1.html. Accessed 04/03/2011.

Oliver, C. 1991. Strategic responses to institutional processes. *Academy of Management Review*, 16: 145–179.

Parthasarathy, M., & Smith, M. A. 2009. Valuing the institution:An expanded list of factors influencing the adoption of on-line education. On-line *Journal of Distance Learning Administration*, 12. Retrieved from: http://www.westga.edu/~distance/ojdla/summer122/parthasarathy122.html. Accessed 04/03/2011.

Peltier, J. W., Drago, W., & Schibrowsky, J. A. 2003. Virtual communities and the assessment of on-line marketing education. *Journal of Marketing Education,* 25: 260–276.

Peltier, J. W., Schibrowsky, J. A., & Drago, W. 2007. The interdependence of the factors influencing the perceived quality of the on-line learning experience: A causal model. *Journal of Marketing Education,* 29: 140–153.

Peters, V. L., & Hewitt, J. 2010. An investigation of student practices in asynchronous computer conferencing courses. *Computers and Education*, 54: 951–961.

Piccoli, G., Ahmad, R., & Ives, B. 2001. Web-based virtual learning environments: A research framework and a preliminary assessment of effectiveness in basic IT skills training. *MIS Quarterly*, 25: 401–426.

Popovich, C. J., & Neel, R. E. 2005. Characteristics of distance education programs at accredited business schools. *American Journal of Distance Education*, 19: 229–240.

Priluck, R. 2004. Web-assisted courses for business education: An examination of two sections of principles of marketing. *Journal of Marketing Education*, 26: 161–173.

Puzziferro, M., & Shelton, K. 2009. Challenging our assumptions about on-line learning: A vision for the next generation of on-line higher education. *Distance Learning*, 6: 9–20.

Richardson, J. C., Maeda, Y., & Swan, K. 2010. Adding a web-based perspective to the self-assessment of knowledge: Compelling reasons to utilize affective measures of learning. *Academy of Management Learning and Education*, 9: 329–334.

Rivera, J. C., & Rice, M. J. 2002. A comparison of student outcomes and satisfaction between traditional and web based course offerings. On-line *Journal of Distance Learning Administration*, 5. Retrieved from: http://www.westga.edu/~distance/ojdla/fall53/rivera53.html. Accessed 10/29/2010.

Rovai, A. P. 2002. A preliminary look at the structural differences of higher education classroom communities in traditional and ALN courses. *Journal of Asynchronous Learning Networks*, 6. Retrieved from: http://www.whateverproductions.net/Rovai-1.pdf. Accessed 10/29/2010.

Rovai, A. P., Wighting, M. J., Baker, J. D., & Grooms, L. D. 2009. Development of an instrument to measure perceived cognitive, affective, and psychomotor learning in traditional and virtual classroom higher education settings. *Internet and Higher Education*, 12: 7–13.

Sankaran, S., Sankaran, D., & Bui, T. 2000. Effect of student attitude to course format on learning performance: An empirical study in web vs. lecture instruction. *Journal of Instructional Psychology*, 27: 66–73.

Sarker, S., & Nicholson, J. 2005. Exploring myths about on-line education in information systems. *Informing Science*, 8: 55–73.

Sautter, P. 2007. Designing discussion activities to achieve desired learning outcomes: Choices using mode of delivery and structure. *Journal of Marketing Education*, 29: 121–131.

Seaman, J. 2009. On-line learning as a strategic asset, vol. 2, The paradox of faculty voices: Views and experiences with online learning. *Results of aNational Faculty Survey (Ed.), Part of the On-line Education Benchmarking Study Conducted by the APLU-Sloan National Commission on On-line Learning.* Washington, DC: Association of Public and Land-grant Universities, Office of Public Affairs.

Shachar, M. 2008. Meta-analysis: The preferred method of choice for the assessment of distance learning quality factors. *International Review of Research in Open and Distance Learning*, 9. Retrieved from: http://www.irrodl.org/index.php/irrodl/article/view/493/0. Accessed 10/29/2010.

Shachar, M., & Neumann, Y. 2003. Differences between traditional and distance education academic performance: A meta-analytic approach. *International [Review] of Research in Open and Distance Education*, 4(2): 1–20. Retrieved from http://www.irrodl.org/index.php/irrodl/article/view/ 153/704. Accessed 10/29/2010.

Shea, P., Hayes, S., Vickers, J., Gozza-Cohen, M., Uzuner, S., Mehta, R., Valchova, A., & Rangan, P. 2010. A re-examination of the community of inquiry framework: Social network and content analysis. *Internet and Higher Education*, 13: 10–21.

Sitzmann, T., Ely, K., Brown, K., & Bauer, K. 2010. Self-assessment of knowledge: A cognitive learning or affective measure? *Academy of Management Learning and Education*, 9: 169–191.

Sitzmann, T., Kraiger, K., Stewart, D., & Wisher, R. 2006. The comparative effectiveness of web-based and classroom instruction: A meta-analysis. *Personnel Psychology*, 59: 623–664.

Smith, G., Heindel, A., & Torres-Ayala, A. 2008. E-learning commodity or community: Disciplinary differences between online courses. *Internet and Higher Education*, 11: 152–159.

Spiceland, J. D., & Hawkins, C. P. 2002. The impact on learning of an asynchronous active learning course format. *Journal of Asynchronous Learning Networks*, 6: 68–75.

Stahl, B. C. 2004. E-teaching: The economic threat to the ethical legitimacy of education? *Journal of Information Systems Education*, 15: 155–161.

Sweeny, J. C., & Ingram, D. 2001. A comparison of traditional and web-based tutorials in marketing education: An exploratory study. *Journal of Marketing Education*, 23: 55–62.

Tallent-Runnels, M. K., Thomas, J. A., Lan, W. Y., Cooper, S., Ahern, T. C., Shaw, S. M., Liu, X. 2006. Teaching courses on-line: A review of the research. *Review of Educational Research*, 76: 93–135.

Tanner, J. R., Noser, T. C., & Totaro, M. W. 2009. Business faculty and undergraduate students' perceptions of on-line learning: A comparative study. *Journal of Information Systems Education*, 20: 29–40.

Twining, P. 2009. Exploring the educational potential of virtual worlds: Some reflections from the SPP. *British Journal of Educational Technology*, 40: 496–514.

U.S. Department of Education. 2009. *Evaluation of evidence-based practices in on-line learning: A meta-analysis and review of on-line learning studies.* Washington, DC: Office of Planning, Evaluation, and Policy Development.

Vamosi, A. R., Pierce, B. G., & Slotkin, M. H. 2004. Distance learning in an accounting principles course: Student satisfaction and perceptions of efficacy. *Journal of Education for Business*, 79: 360–366.

Wallace, L. 2007. On-line teaching and university policy: Investigating the disconnect. *Distance Education*, 22: 87–100. Retrieved from: http://www.jofde.ca/index.php/jde/article/view/58. Accessed 07/27/2011.

Weber, J. M., & Lennon, R. 2007. Multi-course comparison of traditional versus web-based course delivery systems. *Journal of Educators On-line*, 4. Retrieved from: http://www.thejeo.com/Archives/Volume4Number2/Weber%20Final.pdf. Accessed 04/05/2011.

Williams, S. L. 2006. The effectiveness of distance education in allied health science programs: A meta-analysis of outcomes. *American Journal of Distance Education*, 20: 127–141.

Yang, Y., & Cornelius, L. 2005. Preparing instructors for quality on-line instruction. On-line *Journal of Distance Learning Administration,* 8(4). Retrieved from: http://www.westga.edu/~distance/ojdla/spring81/yang81.htm. Accessed 07/27/ 2011.

Yoo, Y., Kanawattanachai, P., & Citurs, A. 2002. Forging into the wired wilderness: A case study of a technology-mediated distributed discussion-based class. *Journal of Management Education*, 26: 139–163.

Zhao, Y., Lei, J., Yan, B., Lai, C., & Tan, H. S. 2005. What makes the difference? A practical analysis of research on the effectiveness of distance education. *Teachers College Record*, 107(8): 1836–1884.

Dr. Lindsay Redpath, vice president of Academic and Student Services at University Canada West in Vancouver, has a PhD from the University of Alberta. Formerly with Athabasca University, Redpath led the development of a pioneering on-line MBA program. Her research interests include underemployment, cross-cultural issues, and management education.

READING 9.2

Becoming a Leader: Early Career Challenges Faced by MBA Graduates

Beth Benjamin
Charles O'Reilly

Leadership development is often cited as an important orga-nizational priority. Despite the criticisms of MBA education, MBA graduates represent one important source of future lea-ders. Although we have amassed significant knowledge about the roles and functions of senior leaders, we know far less about the challenges faced by younger ones. Indeed, Linda Hill's seminal work on new managers is predicated on the study of only 19 recently promoted sales managers from two companies (Hill, 1992). Our work here investigates the early career challenges of 55 young leaders who had graduated from an MBA program in the past decade. Based on in-depth inter-views, we identified three types of transition that these young leaders described as particularly important to their develop-ment, and the four most common challenges they struggled with throughout these transitions. The process of working through these challenges led many of these young leaders to fundamentally change the way they thought about and prac-ticed leadership, thereby facilitating their evolution from indi-vidual contributor to experienced leader. Drawing on these observations, we provide suggestions for how MBA programs can be modified to help students prepare for the experiences they will likely have to navigate early in their careers.

> *"In content and pedagogy, the education many business schools provide does little to prepare managers for their day-to-day realities (Porter & McKibbin, 1988: 258)."*
>
> *"Business schools appear to be producing MBA grad-uates ill-equipped for the challenges of the real world (Chia & Holt, 2008: 471)."*

In their well-known evaluation of the state of business schools, Porter and McKibbin (1988) lamented the fact that business schools, in their quest for rigor, had lost their relevance. In the two decades since, little seems to have changed. Critics still charge business schools with being largely irrelevant to leader-ship and the practice of management (e.g., Bennis & O'Toole,

2005; Ghoshal, 2005; Pfeffer & Fong, 2004). Mintzberg (2004) has put it most pun-gently, claiming that we are teaching the wrong material with the wrong methods to the wrong stu-dents. If these claims are true, why have business schools failed so abysmally? Critics have identified a number of potential reasons, one of which is that recent MBA graduates lack the skills necessary to effectively manage people. Conger (2004) argues that academic models of leadership typically adopt a one-size-fits-all approach rather than acknowledging that lead-ership requirements may vary across levels and circumstances. Compounding this, MBA programs typically concentrate on the skills needed by general managers but largely ignore or are ignorant of those needed by their graduates to succeed in their early careers. Indeed, in a symposium on leadership development, Steve Kerr, a scholar-practitioner, observed that "[t]he developmental needs of 'early' employees are usually not well known" (Kerr, 2004: 120).

The primary mission of business schools is to prepare people to practice their skills in the business world. Unfortu-nately, many academics do a poor job of developing and organizing new knowledge in a way that can be useful to practicing managers. Instead of teaching what the students need, we often teach what we know—our disciplinary exper-tise (Tushman & O'Reilly, 2007). An unanswered question is do we know what our students need to know? In their cri-tique of MBA education, Pfeffer and Fong (2002) suggest that business school faculty need to do three things to improve the relevance of MBA education: be more problem or phe-nomenon focused, listen more to our subjects, and be con-cerned with applicability as well as theory.

> *Managers clearly would benefit most if these developmen-tally challenging experiences occurred earlier in their careers rather than later.*

To address this problem, several prominent researchers in leadership development have suggested straightforward solutions. Hill (1992), for example, suggests that "[M]anage-ment training should focus on what it means to be and what it feels like to be a manager" (249). McCall (2010) argues that development efforts should "focus not on attributes of the leaders we might call effective leaders, but on the experiences that teach lessons that might, over time, produce effective leaders" (681). These suggestions all argue for a greater understanding of the real challenges faced by younger leaders as opposed to the current preoccupation with theoretical and analytic skills. Hackman and Wageman (2007) note that we need a better understanding of both *what* should be taught as well as *how* leaders can be helped to learn.

Leadership Development

There can be little doubt that leadership development is an important topic. A Google search on leadership reveals 141 million hits. Friga, Bettis, and Sullivan (2003) report that corporations spend more than $2.2 trillion on education and training. Hannah and Avolio (2010) estimate that $10 billion is spent on leadership development alone. Mintzberg (2004) notes that the United States produces more than 130,000 MBA graduates annually and that in 1998, 42% of the *Fortune*-100 CEOs had MBA degrees. Pfeffer and Fong (2002) even point out that management and management skills have been identified as a core competence for economic prosperity.

Yet, evidence for the failures in leadership abound. Several books have documented the failure of large firms and attributed these to failures in leadership (e.g., Carroll & Mui, 2008; Finkelstein, 2003). McCall (2010) observes that "[c]onsidering the damage done by lousy leadership, and the possibilities for good in extraordinary leadership, it seems obvious that it is important, indeed crucial, to invest in developing leadership talent" (705). In a study of managerial derailment within one company, Lombardo, Ruderman, and McCauley (1988) estimated the cost of a single failed manager at $500,000. Even the American public seems to regard leadership as lacking in the United States. A 2005 Yankelovich study using interviews with more than 1,300 people reported that 73% believed that leaders were out of touch with the average person and only 27% were the "best and the brightest."

Leadership is an individual capability. It is about what you do, how you think, and who you are. The acquisition of these skills may be partly dispositional, but much comes through learning and experience. From this perspective, improvements in leadership development could be well served by better understanding what aspects of "doing" leaders struggle with and why. Understanding the early "doing" challenges will likely produce significant insight into the other aspects of leadership as well.

MBA Programs—Problem or Solution?

Although academics love to debate whether leaders are born or made, the evidence is quite clear: "It is not a matter of whether leaders are born or made. They are born and made" (Conger, 2004: 136). Avolio, Rotundo, and Walumbwa (2009) estimate that 30% of leadership is heritable, while 70% is developed. These estimates are consistent with the finding that successful performance in most domains can be attributed to experience, practice, and coaching rather than innate talent (Gladwell, 2008). Other evidence suggests that there can be significant positive returns to the investment in leadership development (Avolio, Avey, & Quisen-berry, 2010).

However, to be effective, leadership development should start early in a person's career and, as McCall (2004) notes, "pay special attention to crucial transition points" (128). One such transition occurs as students move from MBA programs into jobs that require them to manage others.

If we want our graduates to flourish, it is imperative that we help them acquire the skills, abilities, attitudes, and knowledge required to do so. But do we know what it is that our students need to know? Wren, Halbesleben, and Buckley (2007), in a study of 525 members of the Academy of Management, argue that academics in business schools don't always see their jobs as developing and organizing new knowledge in a way that it can be useful to practicing managers. Chia and Holt (2008: 471) illustrate how a preference for abstract causal explanation over practical knowledge has led to detached contemplation rather than involved action when it comes to business school teaching. Indeed, in a survey of the curricula of top-rated business schools, Navarro (2008) found a lack of emphasis on the integration and experiential components needed to develop leaders.

Many authors agree that beginning to develop leader-managers early in their careers is important. McCall (2004) observes that most organizations begin executive development processes at very senior levels, but to be truly effective he suggests that leadership development should begin much earlier. Hill (1992) also notes that "[t]here can be significant benefits to intensive education for younger managers" (2). Although many scholars have observed that experience, rather than formal training, may be the best way to develop leaders, educational training that replicates developmentally challenging experiences can enhance leadership skills by motivating people to think critically about the situation, teaching them to analyze underlying causes and consequences of problems, and enabling them to develop new ways of dealing with others (DeRue & Wellman, 2009). Managers clearly would benefit most if these developmentally challenging experiences occurred earlier in their careers rather than later.

We expect that educational experiences could be especially impactful if the form and content of what is being taught reflects the specific requirements of the leadership audience's near-term needs. Thus, in teaching leadership to MBAs, that we design experiences to reflect the actual challenges our students will face early on is critical, in addition to more abstract theories. When designing development efforts, the ideal is to present the right challenges at the right time to people who are motivated to learn such that they are prepared to extract all that their subsequent experiences have to offer. This requires that we have a good understanding of the specific situations and challenges that young managers typically face.

The First-Time Manager

In her book *Becoming a Manager* (1992) Linda Hill followed 19 first-time managers for a year and documented the challenges they encountered. She characterized the challenge of becoming a manager as one of a transformation in identity, which also challenged new managers to develop new skills—skills which their previous experiences had not prepared them for. Because the nature and significance of this transformation required not only learning new skills but also changes in attitude and self-awareness, Hill surmises much of the emphasis on imparting managerial knowledge through classroom learning may be misplaced—the education many business schools provide may do little to prepare managers for their day-to-day realities. To address this misalignment, Hill advocates training that emphasizes the specific challenges faced by new managers with a focus on what it means to be and feel like a new manager. But what are the specific challenges faced by recent MBA graduates? Hill's study focused on 19 first-line sales managers from two firms—10 branch managers in a securities firm (average age 36) and 9 sales managers in a computer company (average age 30). Whether any were MBAs or how their experiences might generalize to the roles and responsibilities of recent business school graduates in other firms or industries is unclear. Would the specific challenges be the same? We set out to extend Hill's work by focusing directly on the experiences of new managers who have graduated from an MBA program.

Methods

Study Design

To identify specific leadership challenges faced by MBA graduates early in their careers, we gathered data from managers across a variety of organizations. Our goal was to understand the experience of recently minted MBAs—from their perspectives—with a focus on the types of situations they found most difficult to navigate. Specifically, we wanted to know: (1) Were there particular experiences that MBA graduates frequently fumbled or struggled with? (2) if so, what was it about these situations that they found particularly difficult or surprising? and (3) what insights or lessons, if any, could be learned from these experiences? Because we wanted to understand the world from the eyes of those who lived it, we relied on key informant interviews as described by Gilchrest (1992). *Key informant interviewing* is an ethnographic approach used across a variety of disciplines including anthropology, medical sociology, and education. It is sometimes described as "research listening" (Miller & Crabtree, 1992) because the goal is not to test a set of specific hypotheses, but to discover a sense of reality that is shared by a given group or constituency. The difference in orientation is important to note because researchers using key informant interviews seek to learn *from* people and understand their informants' interpretation of events rather than studying people and forming interpretations of their own (Spradley, 1979). This approach allows for the discovery of phenomena that might not have been considered otherwise, in addition to new ways of conceptualizing and analyzing problems of interest.

Sample Selection

Key informants are individuals who possess special knowledge or status; who are willing to share their knowledge; and who have access to perspectives, experiences, or observations that are not directly available to the researcher (Goetz & LeCompte, 1984). In addition, Gilchrest (1992) points out that key informants differ from other informants in the nature of their relationship to the researcher. In many cases, the relationship may be one of longer duration, it may span different settings, and it may be more intimate or familiar. Notably, key informants are not selected randomly. Random sampling is based on the assumption that the phenomenon under study is represented equally across the population—in this case, graduates of MBA programs. We make no assumption that the knowledge or perspective we are seeking—perceived challenges experienced by early-career managers—and the ability to share these challenges, is equally distributed among the population of MBA graduates. Our intention was to learn as much as possible about the situations described most frequently as difficult or hazardous to a novice manager's career.

With these considerations in mind, we wanted to interview a set of informants who would have unique insight into the types of leadership challenges that MBA graduates pursuing a managerial career are likely to struggle with early on. To generate our sample, we obtained a listing of all students who had graduated from the MBA program of a top-ranked U.S. business school between the years of 1997 and 2006. The listing included each subject's date of graduation, current organizational affiliation, their title, the city within which they worked, and relevant contact information. The data set was sorted by graduation date and organization, allowing us to compare graduates on the basis of their career progression within and across comparable companies.

Consistent with ethnographic methods, our sampling aimed to yield a reasonable number of informants who could provide a representative picture of the types of leadership challenges experienced by the population of MBA graduates pursuing a management career. The sampling was purposeful and strategic, guided by our theoretically formed judgments (Johnson, 1990). Because we were explicitly interested in the challenges associated with managing others, we excluded from the sampling pool graduates working for organizations with a partnership governance structure (i.e., management consulting, private equity, venture capital, and investment banking). Although interesting in their own right, we were concerned that the career paths, election processes, and equity requirements in these firms could introduce unique variation that might not generalize to firms with more traditional corporate governance structures. We also dropped from our sample those who were clearly not in management roles (e.g., technical specialists, such as analysts, buyers, staff engineers, etc.).

For each graduating class we identified graduates whose current job title suggested that they held a role with significant managerial responsibility. We reasoned that individuals who had advanced to more senior positions during a given period, or who had founded and led their own organizations, were likely to have had a broader range of experiences. In addition, Fetterman (1989) and others have recommended that key informants, ideally, should be individuals who are articulate, thoroughly enculturated, and currently active within the domain-of-interest, in this case management. Our previous discussions with more experienced leaders suggested that individuals occupying more senior roles were no less likely to encounter significant leadership challenges on their way up. Rather, they were simply more likely to have learned from the challenges they experienced (McCall, 2010). Ultimately our interviews appeared to support this claim: We discovered that despite their apparent success, many of our informants had experienced significant setbacks at some point during the first 5–10 years of their careers. Last, we aimed to select informants representatively across industry and cohort (i.e., number of years since graduation).

To the extent young managers were able to figure out which assumptions and behaviors to leave behind and which new ones to incorporate into their evolving repertoire, they accomplished the learning necessary for making important transitions in their leadership.

We sent e-mail invitations to 62 graduates, inviting these former students to take part in a 60–90 minute interview as part of our "Young Leaders" study. Fifty-five of the 62 graduates agreed to participate. One declined our request and six failed to respond to the invitation, possibly due to outdated contact information. Figure 1 reports the distribution of respondents by class year, gender, and company size. The sample reflects a representative distribution of graduates by gender, with a slight oversampling of those who had graduated 4–6 years prior to the study to ensure that we identified challenges associated with newer managers.

Interviews

Once a graduate-informant agreed to be interviewed, we sent a list of discussion topics to review prior to the conversation. We conducted interviews in person at the informant's workplace, at a convenient location nearby, or by telephone when the participant's schedule or location made meeting in person prohibitive. Phone interviews typically lasted 60–75 minutes and in-person interviews typically lasted 90 minutes, although a few ran as long as 2 hours. A single interviewer—one of the coauthors—conducted all interviews to maintain consistency.

Because our goal was to uncover patterns and generate new insight, we began each discussion with some broad, open-ended questions that allowed the informant to set the stage for the rest of the discussion (Gilchrest, 1992; Spradley, 1979). After describing the career path since graduating and the scope of current responsibilities, each informant was asked to recount the most challenging leadership issues faced in their career to date. These questions focused the discussion on the specific situations, management dilemmas, and personal issues that these early-career leaders found as

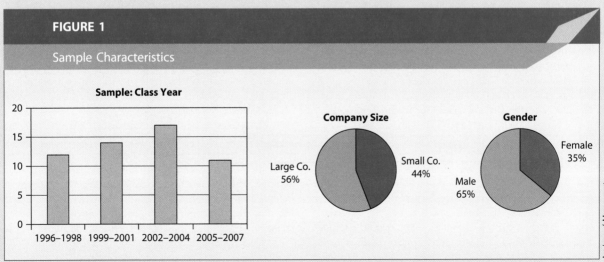

FIGURE 1

Sample Characteristics

most challenging, surprising, or difficult. We asked our informants to describe each situation in-depth and to articulate what made the issue particularly difficult. We also asked how their business education had either prepared or failed to prepare them to handle the challenges.

Last, we asked what, if anything, our informants had taken away from their experiences—what had they learned or changed? We did not assume that the informants had learned anything from the experiences they described or that any of their take-aways were necessarily the "right" lessons. They were merely an accurate rendering of the managers' perceptions as they had experienced a given challenge. Once we exhausted our discussion of the first issue, we asked informants to recount others, repeating the process until the individuals could recall no additional examples or until we ran out of time.

After each interview, the interviewer transcribed the discussion, creating a detailed set of interview notes. These notes included descriptions of the informants' career histories, their characterization of the most challenging experiences they had faced since business school, the context in which these experiences occurred, what actions they took, and any reported learning. In many cases, participants described their learning in terms of how their leadership views had changed and what they would do differently if the situation occurred today. When relevant, direct quotes were included in the interview notes, capturing the participants' experiences in their own words.

After all the interviews were completed, we independently reviewed the transcribed notes to identify and group the challenges and discover themes that emerged from the data. We iterated back and forth to compare interpretations, discuss thematic categories, and resolve any differences in coding or conclusions (Glaser & Strauss, 1967). This coding process yielded approximately 125 separate descriptions of incidents or problems.

As the final part of our study, we contacted 15 of the graduate-managers whose transitions, challenges, and learning appeared to be most representative or informative of the full sample. We conducted two additional interviews with each participant, exploring and documenting in greater depth the leadership issues they described. The second interview was videotaped and used to produce a series of leadership video vignettes that we created for teaching purposes.

Three Types of Transition

The first goal of our study was to identify the situations that MBA graduates struggled with early in their careers. The logic driving our investigation was simple: If leadership learning is cumulative, as some research suggests (Charan, Drotter, & Noel, 2001; McCall et al., 1988), then it is important to understand what leaders must learn early in their development if they are to progress and perform well in more senior

roles. To the extent that developing managers struggle early on or fail to learn the right lessons from their experiences, they are less likely to establish the foundation needed to navigate and learn from even more demanding experiences later (McCall, 2010). Moreover, should they handle the learning process poorly, the initial impressions they make on others may have strong and lasting effects, which could easily limit or slow their access to subsequent opportunities (Willis & Todorov, 2006). As we tried to characterize the situations and challenges described by our key informants, it became evident that most involved change and transition. In almost all cases, the informants described struggling with something they had not encountered before, usually a new set of circumstances that required them to tackle multiple challenges all at once. Often these challenges included rethinking (and letting go of) old assumptions, developing new skills and attitudes, negotiating new relationships, renegotiating existing ones, and most difficult of all, changing their behavior and self-concept. As McCall (2010) has pointed out, "When situations change dramatically, as is the case when a person is given an assignment that is quite different from what he or she has done before, either development or derailment may result" (701).

Previous research on careers and leadership development has demonstrated that transitions are critical periods for learning and development and can be a defining element in managerial success or failure (e.g., Ibarra, 2003; Nicholson & West, 1988). When things go well, individuals move from one level of mastery to the next. For example, Hill's seminal study of first-time managers showed that the transition from individual contributor to manager was a time when individuals began developing "not only managerial knowledge and skills, but also managerial interests and a managerial temperament" (Hill, 1992:159). That said, there is no guarantee that the right learning—or any learning, for that matter— will occur simply because managers encounter a transitional moment. The situational and psychological demands of transition can be quite taxing and, if experienced as too stressful, may preclude some individuals from expending the cognitive energy needed to adapt their existing routines. Indeed, research by DeRue and Wellman (2009) suggests that leadership skill development begins to diminish when experiences move beyond an optimal level of difficulty, when there is little access to feedback, or when an individual lacks the necessary learning orientation.

The extent to which a young leader successfully navigated the leadership transitions described in our study depended on their ability to learn from the challenges brought about by a change in their immediate context—for example, a job change or changes in important relationships. As we listened to our informants' accounts, we came to realize that the experiences they described weren't just about *managing* transitions, they, in fact, created transitions.

There is an important distinction here that is worth clarifying, namely, the difference between change and transition.

Bridges (2004) observes that change is situational, whereas *transition* is psychological. The circumstances that create a new situation—for example, a promotion, changing business conditions, or differences with a boss—represent change. Transition, by contrast, is the process by which individuals work through, learn, and come to terms with the new challenges and conditions that change creates. The emerging leaders in our study had to contend with changes that presented specific challenges, which in turn, forced them to reexamine some of their most fundamental assumptions, working models, and practices. In short, they were forced to reevaluate and often adjust the very things that had made them successful to date. To the extent young managers were able to figure out which assumptions and behaviors to leave behind and which new ones to incorporate into their evolving repertoire, they accomplished the learning necessary for making important transitions in their leadership. If they did not, they would continue to struggle with the same challenges until they ultimately mastered the appropriate learning or derailed.

As we analyzed our data, we were able to group the transitions described by our informants into three broad categories. Each category was (1) triggered by a particular change in context, (2) had the potential to instill a specific type of learning, and (3) could be characterized by a single dominant question (Table 1).

The first category was *role transitions*. As the name suggests, these were transitions that occurred after a manager took on a new role. The specific role transitions described by our informants involved the move from individual contributor to first-time manager; from managing a few individuals to being accountable for a team; from managing teams to managing other managers; and, from leading one functional domain to leading a different function or much broader business unit. Through these transitions, emerging leaders learned how to lead new and different types of people and how to shift priorities as they assumed responsibility for larger, more complex units. Surprisingly, new role requirements were rarely spelled out for early-career managers. Although they often discussed the business objectives of a new role with their superiors, and they generally understood that the parameters of a new position would be different (e.g., more people, different people, and different objectives), they were not usually prepared for how their leadership would have to change to address these differences. They had to learn through trial and error about new demands, expectations, and ways of working. And, through this trial and error, they sometimes discovered that their previous leadership practices were not only insufficient to the demands of their new role, but also capable of producing unintended consequences that made the new job even more difficult. Ultimately, the

Table 1

Early Career Transitions

	Role Transitions	Business Transitions	Personal Transitions
Type of instigating change **Incidents identified by informants**	Change in Role • From individual contributor to first-time manager • Taking responsibility for team performance • Managing other managers • Managing transitions in function or scope	Change in business/stage in organizational life cycle • Launching a new initiative or business • Managing growth • Turning around a group or business • Taking a team/business to the next level	Situation creating values conflict • Managing strategic differences with a boss • Navigating and correcting ethically questionable practices • Blending work, life, and family • Dealing with professional setbacks
Learning	Role Requirements *"What does it mean to be a leader in this new role?"*	New Strategies and Tactics *"How can I get things done in a diiierent business context?"*	Judgment and Integrity *"How do I stay true to myself?"*

fundamental question that characterized the transition around role change was "What does it mean to be a leader in this new role?"

Business transitions—more specifically, being responsible for leading a significant change in the business—were the second type of transition that our informants struggled with. As with role change, leading a significant business change challenged implicit assumptions and rendered previous leadership tactics insufficient for dealing with new demands. The difficulties that managers experience when leading during times of organizational change has been described by Greiner (1998) and others who have studied the organizational life cycle. This research suggests that transitions between an organization's developmental phases rarely go smoothly due to an inevitable paradox: The very leadership styles and practices that help organizations thrive during one evolutionary stage become entirely unsuitable for sustaining them into the next. Consistent with our informants' accounts, Greiner observed that this paradox often "haunts and confuses the managerial psyche," as leaders struggle to understand how the practices they used successfully at one point "eventually sow the seeds of their own decay" (Greiner, 1998: 5, 8).

Business transitions appeared to be less about role and more about context. Consistent with the task-related characteristics of developmental jobs described by McCauley, Ruderman, Ohlott, and Morrow (1994), these transitions were triggered by challenges that emerged because of changing business conditions. In some cases, our informant-managers remained in the same role, but the business around them changed significantly. These situations often involved managing growth. In other cases, managers kept their role but were asked to head up new organizational initiatives designed to fend off stagnation and enhance a company's competitiveness. Last, some managers were placed in new roles specifically to lead a business transition, for example, a turnaround effort. These leadership transitions could be especially difficult because they challenged relatively inexperienced managers to master new role requirements while simultaneously requiring them to figure out how to lead strategic changes or organizational transformation efforts. The fundamental question characterizing this type of transition was "How can I get things done in a very different business context?"

We labeled our third category *personal transitions*. These involved personal conflicts that often put a developing leader's values to the test. The fundamental question characterizing personal transitions was "How do I stay true to myself in the face of competing values?" Personal transitions were often triggered by situations that required young managers to work their way through delicate issues such as managing strategic differences with a boss, dealing with ethically questionable practices, or balancing the demands of work- and family-life. These transitions also

sometimes occurred in the wake of major mistakes or setbacks that forced young leaders to acknowledge limitations and carefully evaluate what was most important to them.

Personal transitions were often very emotionally charged. In fact, several young leaders in our study chose to leave their jobs rather than deal with the emotional tensions surrounding a given situation. Unlike those who worked through the challenges more effectively, managers who decided to leave their jobs typically believed there was nothing they could do to resolve the situation—they saw themselves as essentially powerless. Unfortunately, leaving the situation tended to slow their learning. It allowed them to avoid self-examination and sidestep issues they found particularly upsetting. In contrast, when young managers chose to work through these values dilemmas or other emotionally charged situations, the learning appeared to be quite significant. Emerging leaders began to realize that managing values conflicts was not a one-time occurrence, but rather an inevitable and fundamental part of being a leader.

Four Challenges

To better equip graduates for these key transitions, we wanted to identify and understand the specific challenges they struggled with. A review and parsing of the more than 125 incidents generated by the 55 interviews suggested a host of challenges that confronted these managers early in their careers. Based on our coding and review, we identified four main themes or types of problems reported across a majority of respondents (see Table 2). These four types could be further organized into two broad categories: (1) Challenges associated with managing others, and (2) Challenges associated with managing oneself. Challenges managing others could be further segmented into *difficulties managing and motivating subordinates,* and *difficulties managing relationships with peers and bosses.* Similarly, challenges managing oneself could be divided into *developing a leadership mind-set* and *coping with personal setbacks and disappointments.* Many of the individual challenges did not map neatly onto specific transitions; rather, any one transition might involve challenges from any number of these categories. Our data are too limited to definitively assess whether specific challenges were more prevalent during some transitions than others. Nonetheless, a preliminary review suggests that developing a leadership mind-set and difficulties managing and motivating subordinates were common challenges mentioned when describing role transitions. Similarly, difficulties managing relationships with peers and bosses appeared to be more prevalent when navigating business transitions. Coping with setbacks and disappointments were central to successfully navigating personal transitions.

Table 2

Four Common Leadership Challenges

Managing Others

1. Managing and motivating subordinates
   - Understanding others with different values and motives
   - Appreciating the importance of B and C players—not just A players
   - Listening to others rather than problem solving
   - Establishing credibility—especially when others have more experience
   - Being clear about what your value added is as a manager
   - Dealing with poor performers and problem employees
   - Setting clear expectations

2. Managing relationships with peers and bosses
   - Recognizing the importance of relationships—process and content
   - An inability to resolve differences with a boss
   - The importance of understanding others' priorities—not just your own
   - Balancing competition and cooperation among peers
   - Being right versus being effective—appreciating that peer conflicts taint all involved, regardless of who is "right"

Managing the Self

3. Developing a leadership mind-set
   - Understanding that individual skill and effort are no longer what makes you successful
   - Looking to solve problems—not simply identifying them
   - Developing others
   - Being intentional
   - Deriving satisfaction from others' success

4. Coping with setbacks and disappointments
   - Maintaining poise and composure under pressure
   - Understanding how you react to a setback may be more important than the setback itself
   - Being overwhelmed
   - Balancing work and family pressures

Managing Others

When asked to describe their most difficult leadership challenges to date, informants typically began by describing issues or problems they experienced in their efforts to manage subordinates. This is understandable because these issues frequently coincided with their very first managerial assignments. In addition, however, many informants also described problems managing difficult relationships with other individuals, namely, their peers or bosses. As such, these challenges required emerging leaders to learn important lessons about managing laterally and upward, as well as downward.

Managing and Motivating Subordinates The most common theme mentioned in one form or another by almost all informants centered on the challenge of managing and motivating people with different skills and values from themselves. A common tendency of young managers, especially high achievers, is to assume that others share their values and motivations. In her study of new managers, Hill (1992) came to a similar conclusion, noting that young managers often assumed they could use themselves as role models in understanding how to manage their subordinates and, over time, came to realize "how limiting it was to use themselves as models for predicting how others would interpret situations or respond to their actions" (170).

The critical recognition for these new leaders was appreciating that their performance was no longer a function of their own skill and effort but contingent on their ability to unleash the talent of those who worked for them.

Confronted with the reality that not all people shared their levels of motivation and skill, several respondents talked about the challenge of managing "real" people—and the importance of getting the engagement of all employees. As one former Navy SEAL said, "You can't project your level of motivation onto others." An entrepreneur with his own start-up talked about the need to create a "crusade" to motivate his employees, since he could not afford to motivate them with money. Another young leader in the entertainment business described how important it was to not only find the "A players … but also about developing the B, C & D players." Acknowledging these differences, many of the informants came to realize:

No one model works to motivate all people … You have to understand each person and their interests … My job is to get people not to hit the snooze button on the alarm each morning.

[Business School] doesn't prepare you to manage a wide swatch of people … the most difficult part of my job is the people aspect.

One informant who was failing in his role as a manager lamented:

Managing people is a headache … you have to deal with different personalities, performance reviews, and (all their) problems … You feel responsible for their career development and guilty if there aren't opportunities for them.

To succeed, young managers came to appreciate the importance of listening without judgment and demonstrating empathy to build trust. A young divisional manager expressed surprise at the number of personal problems he had to deal with. "The technical aspect is not all that hard … my people typically come to me with problems about people." Reflecting this challenge, another young manager in a large financial institution described how he kept an ongoing document with notes about each employee so that he could be more helpful in providing feedback. Often, this feedback was not about problem solving but simply about demonstrating interest and concern: "As a new manager you have to recognize that your direct reports do not always want you to 'fix' or 'solve' their problems. Often, they just want to be heard and understood." The risk, as another observed, was that if a manager was always providing answers for subordinates, they would fail to create a team that felt responsible for results. Instead, the team would always look to the leader for solutions.

But this advice, to listen and be empathetic, also had a downside when it came to dealing with poor performers. Here, too, new managers often struggled. Confronted with a problem employee, young managers often either ignored the issue or became overly involved in trying to help the poor performer. Others unfortunately, often misinterpreted their attention as legitimating the problematic behavior. As the CEO of a start-up noted, "One negative person affects everyone." In her study of new managers, Linda Hill recognized this problem. "When asked to identify what was most stressful about their jobs, most new managers replied without hesitation that it was the problem subordinate" (1992: 133).

With experience, young managers came to realize the importance of dealing with poor performers quickly. Many started to realize that "[i]n almost every case, peers were relieved to see the poor performer go."

I delayed for 6 months in letting the person go, which was regrettable and tainted the organization. It slowed our growth rate and led to internal politics. Then the person quit with only 7 days notice—which created a hardship for the team.

Saying "no" and discussing poor performance is a challenge for a lot of [MBA] students because most haven't had setbacks. But, in the real world, 7 out of 10 things go wrong. You must be able to discuss performance issues and expectations without being an [expletive].

The common underlying theme when dealing with people issues again had to do with beliefs and assumptions our informants had drawn from their own past experiences and success. Often, their tendency was to assume that their subordinates held the same motivations and aspirations that they did when, in fact, the subordinates often did not. A variant of this was to assume that subordinates understood and agreed about what they were supposed to accomplish. But young managers frequently discovered that they had failed to adequately clarify expectations at the outset. For instance, one respondent described how he initially treated his subordinates as "partners" (rather than underlings), only to realize that doing so confused people about expectations and, therefore, made it more difficult to call people on poor performance. Another informant echoed this lesson and talked about how she learned that being clear about performance expectations helped her feel "less guilty" when she had to fire people who weren't living up to those expectations. She went on to note that letting go of poor performers was critical because invariably poor performers affected their teams. "It is," she said, "disrespectful to the team *not* to let the poor performer go." Another young manager observed that unless he set clear standards, it was hard for people to hear critical feedback.

In the absence of clear expectations, early-career managers tended to avoid performance issues or tried to solve subordinates' problems themselves. With their analytic skills and strong problem solving capabilities, many MBAs simply forgot about the people aspect: "The people part of my job, it's never top of mind for me … I need to consciously think about it." As they developed their managerial capabilities, some informants began to realize that setting clear expectations was only part of the solution; it was also important to articulate a vision that motivated subordinates to pursue expectations by engaging them emotionally. "Employees see past the money," said one. "You need to make people feel like they are invaluable, irreplaceable ... even though no one really is." A young vice-president in a large financial institution confessed that she was initially uncomfortable with the concept of a vision statement, considering such efforts as too "airy-fairy." But as she experimented with new approaches, she was surprised by how much her employees responded to having a well-articulated vision. "They'd been in the desert and needed some water." In talking about the importance of setting a vision, another informant argued that it was essential for subordinates to see the big picture to get them motivated and excited about their work. In short, a key lesson for many young managers was learning how to express emotion in ways that allowed them to convey passion and create authentic connections with their subordinates.

Relationships With Peers and Bosses Many of the managers we interviewed described difficult relationships with peers and bosses as another significant challenge. As with the previous theme, working through these challenges often produced significant learning, which, in turn, facilitated the leadership transitions described earlier. Once again, these difficulties often arose because of the propensity to prioritize task-related concerns over relationship-building concerns. Young managers initially had a tendency to apply their own skills and effort to resolving problems rather than undertaking the messier task of involving others. As with the first theme, these were sometimes exacerbated by the assumption that others shared the same goals and motivations as the rookie manager. Over time, however, young managers came to understand that performance in organizations was seldom a matter of individual achievement or even a single group. They began to appreciate that being successful often required coordination and cooperation across unit boundaries.

I was 2–3 years out of business school and I was used to being in situations where you could get by on intellect and hard, diligent work. I now realize how important social relationships are—if there are relationship building opportunities (i.e., social), you should be there.

How well you work with peers is important because you need to be able to get things done and accomplish your goals. You don't get anything done by yourself. You have to be able to work with others across functions and divisions to be successful.

Even if you think you know the answer, you have to bring others along. This is especially critical when you have

to reach decisions that cross functional areas. You have to win people over one by one.

One young manager described how in his first role in a business development function he vied aggressively to get visibility with his superiors. As a result, he demonstrated he could do deals and was subsequently promoted to head his unit. But his competitiveness alienated his peers, and three of the five people in his group quit shortly after he was promoted. As one might imagine, this didn't send a particularly good signal. Luckily, because of this experience, he quickly learned "[y]ou can't be successful in a new role if those below you with critical knowledge and experience leave or don't cooperate." Afterward, his advice to younger managers was always to "treat your peers as though they might someday be your boss or direct reports."

Several informants reflected on how poor relationships with peers made both sides look bad— regardless of who was actually responsible for a conflict. For example, one manager described a conflict with a peer who was heading another unit but failing to provide the support she believed was appropriate.

He wasn't as smart as I was ... I thought he was a whiner. He wasn't managing his team well. I thought he was an idiot. I didn't see it as my job to solve his problem ... he needed to [expletive] lead his team.

For the MBA graduates in our study, transitional periods were a time of great potential and great risk.

As she continued to struggle with her peer, she came to realize, "my problem with my peer was a problem *for* my boss, and you don't want to be a problem for your boss." With more experience, she learned to soften her interactions: "It doesn't matter who is right or who is wrong, if your boss has to resolve the conflict both parties are tainted." Like other managers, she concluded that it was more important to be effective than to be right.

Perhaps the most troubling of these relationship issues occurred when problems arose with the person's boss. Several respondents acknowledged that problems with a boss had led to missed promotions or, in several cases, the manager's decision to leave the organization. For example, several graduates described taking jobs where subsequent disagreements with their bosses necessitated their leaving, either because of what they felt were ethical issues or because the relationship led to unfavorable performance reviews. In two of these cases, rather than emphasizing their achievements, the managers' performance evaluations highlighted their lack of teamwork and sensitivity to others. In a third case, the person delivered what he believed to be a success only to learn that he had failed to clarify important priorities with his boss, and therefore, missed the mark.

In several other cases, however, differences with a boss were resolved successfully. In one instance, the subordinate was able to build a coalition of others who helped to overturn what she believed was an ethical breach by the superior. In another, the young manager was able to calmly articulate his differences with his boss, which led his boss to change his views. Because of these experiences, many informants emphasized the importance of clarifying priorities and expectations with the superior as early as possible. This could be done in a variety of ways, such as putting priorities in writing or getting to know the boss at a personal level to facilitate open exchanges and keep the boss in the loop with frequent updates. Studies of management careers have shown that the inability to craft a successful relationship with a superior can be a significant derailer (McCall, 1998; Van Velsor & Leslie, 1995).

As with the previous theme, the challenges of managing difficult relationships with peers and superiors again reflect the respondents' earlier strengths of problem solving and individual achievement. If unchecked, the tendency of many of these young managers was to assume that others shared their focus on getting the right answer and to ignore or underplay the importance of relationships. When faced with conflict, many resorted to logic and analysis. "I'm used to presenting a powerful case—the logic and course of action necessary—and it's easy for me to fall into this pattern and enter into a debate. I'm trying not to do this," said a manager in the entertainment business. For many, it was only after a setback that they realized the importance of clarifying expectations and nurturing relationships.

Managing Oneself

Although the proximal problems described by young managers often began with the challenges of managing others, many of our informants ultimately recognized that their own thinking needed to change if they were to be effective leaders longer term. Not only did they have to think differently about their role, they also had to think differently about their goals and priorities, their orientation toward others, and the basis of their accomplishments. In short, to be effective they had to shift their mind-set about who they were and what they needed to accomplish. This also entailed figuring out how to weather the inevitable mistakes and setbacks that would be a critical part of their learning and personal growth.

Developing a Leadership Mind-Set Having worked in roles where hard work, intelligence, and strong analytic skills were expected and rewarded, most informants had become successful by demonstrating their ability to solve problems on their own. However, as managers, the very things that had made them successful in their individual contributor roles were no longer as important—and in some cases were problematic. Many young managers discovered that trying to gain visibility for themselves, demonstrating their analytic

prowess, and simply working longer and harder would not serve them well when leading others. They had to change—not only their behavior, but the very assumptions that guided their behavior. What was required was a new set of assumptions—a new leadership mind-set.

Looking back on some of their most trying experiences, many of these emerging leaders commented on the difficulty of letting go of old assumptions and work habits:

It was a big shift for me to let go of my expertise (i.e., doing things myself). My job became setting goals, motivating, holding people accountable, providing resources, and assigning projects. I didn't get much training in this. If you continue to use the "just put your head down and work approach," you'll shoot yourself in the foot ... you'll crash and burn. You have to get your work done through others, even when there are only 2–3 people.

For instance, one graduate described his attitude as a young manager: "I was a real pain in the ass for my boss. I would fire off missives identifying all sorts of problems." Later he realized that his role as a manager was not just to identify problems but to take responsibility for solving them, often without being asked and even when they were beyond his formal scope of responsibility. This usually entailed working with and through others. The leader of a private school described moving from a mind-set of thinking about how he could get the most out himself to one where "I can develop others and help them get better." Making such recognitions required these emerging leaders to fundamentally shift their assumptions about their roles from independence to interdependence.

The critical recognition for these new leaders was appreciating that their performance was no longer a function of their own skill and effort but contingent on their ability to unleash the talent of those who worked for them. "[Y]our performance is completely a function of other peoples' performance. Your primary responsibility is building a team, not just fixing immediate problems," said one respondent. Several informants noted how threatening this recognition was. If they could no longer rely on those strengths that made them successful in the past, what was their added value as new managers—especially when, as young managers, they were managing people who were more experienced and knew far more than they did? They began to realize that their earlier mind-set about the importance of demonstrating their own capabilities was less useful than a new set of assumptions about the importance of helping others to develop. This new perspective often required more listening and less problem solving.

It's about listening, hearing and digesting, rather than reacting and debating ... Younger leaders often mistakenly think it's more important to articulate their logic and demonstrate that they're right. In many cases, there's no upside to this.

As they began to better understand the value they added as leaders, they also became more aware of the significance of their words and actions. As leaders they were constantly being scrutinized and therefore had to be especially intentional about what they said and did: "Now I'm in the spotlight where I can't really afford to blow it" said one. Another described how she needed to be careful about making flip comments. When she jokingly commented in a public setting that "the business was in the toilet" it was translated as "she's saying we're all t**ds." One successful start-up CEO came to realize that what he said was often taken as gospel—sometimes with negative consequences. Another noted how over time, he began to prepare more carefully for meetings, became less spontaneous, and learned to stay on message.

Leadership is all about "intention." You must think carefully about how you want to "show up" and what you want to accomplish in each interaction … If I only have one interaction a month with someone, I have to be intentional about what I want to accomplish.

A final element in the adoption of a managerial mindset was the recognition that success no longer came from actually doing the work but from deriving satisfaction from the accomplishments of others. One respondent working for a pharmaceutical company noted that, unlike an individual contributor, managers often don't get a lot of positive reinforcement from the people above them. "This means you have to derive satisfaction from your impact on the organization and the people below you—you get 90 percent of your enjoyment from the people below you." For some, this is a difficult transition and doesn't provide the fulfillment of being an individual contributor.

I'm the caretaker for something larger than myself… It's not about me, it's about finding the right answer … It's about something larger than yourself … it's something that you're stewarding. It's not personal.

There are a lot of things I hate about being a manager. I no longer get to do things that allow a lot of self-expression and creativity. Now I simply set goals and oversee. I have to get satisfaction from corporate performance. I now get more excited by the accomplishment of team goals. It's different—a shift in pride.

Overall, this required a shift in mind-set from one that emphasized individual skills and visibility to one that focused on growing others and deriving satisfaction from their accomplishments. It meant changing their assumptions about what their roles were and what success looked like. It also meant that they had to be more conscious and intentional in how they dealt with others.

Coping With Setbacks and Disappointments A final theme that was frequently mentioned, especially when discussing personal transitions, was the importance of learning from mistakes and personal setbacks. Prior to business school, most participants had enjoyed a lifetime of professional success. They had yet to experience major setbacks or professional challenges that couldn't be fixed by simply working harder and doing more of what they had always done well. Therefore, when they experienced setbacks, failures, and values dilemmas that seemed beyond their control it came as a shock to many. In some cases, these setbacks came in the form of a surprisingly negative performance review:

I got a 360 that showed that I didn't involve peers in decision making, I didn't make people comfortable with dissenting views, I wasn't seen as collaborative, I hoarded knowledge, and didn't coach others … I was totally blind to this. From my perspective I was the heroic, decisive leader.

Things were growing, I'm getting awards, and my ego went up. Then [my boss] called me into his office. I was expecting the best … that we would talk about growth plans. What I got instead was some really tough, slap-in-the-face feedback that [our division] wasn't going as well as we thought. The experience was really humbling. It was the worst day of my life.

In some cases, setbacks came in the form of disappointing business results or personal relationships that caused young managers to feel unappreciated or even betrayed. People responded to these setbacks in a variety of ways. At one extreme, some young managers hit a wall and essentially fell apart. For example, one junior manager found himself failing in a new position and didn't know how to turn things around:

"I was way in over my head … I was literally pushing paper from one side of my desk to the other, not knowing how I could impact the business."

Without an understanding of the transitional challenges he was stepping into, the manager lost credibility with his team and experienced a "total loss of confidence … Life got out of control to the point where I ceased operating." Luckily, such dramatic reactions usually only lasted a short time. However, because the jolts were rarely anticipated, they were particularly poignant and could have dramatic effects ranging from job loss to significant learning and self-discovery.

Some managers responded to setbacks by denying responsibility and blaming their perceived misfortunes on others. When one manager was passed over for a promotion, he responded by challenging the person who was promoted ahead of him, constantly finding fault with his new manager's decisions. Looking back several years later, he acknowledged that such behavior had simply made him look cocky, uncooperative, and professionally immature. He had missed an opportunity to better understand his own shortcomings and had, in effect, reinforced the very impressions that caused him to be passed over.

Resigning or leaving one's job was another common, but unfortunate response to a setback or values conflict (Gentile, 2008). Young managers who lacked appropriate coping skills appeared to be slower to learn from their setbacks and mistakes. Rather than reflecting on their behavior, accepting feedback, and believing they could change, they tended to feel victimized. For example, one young manager simply wouldn't accept the feedback he was given and subsequently decided to leave his job rather than acknowledge his mistakes:

> I walked into my review and what really irked me about the whole thing was he said, "Listen, you alienated your peers and you really need to be careful about that. You really kind of missed the boat on culture." I stepped back and said "You're kidding me, right? Let me ask you this: If I had developed (the product) three months late, but was nice along the way, as opposed to bruising some toes ... do you think I'd be having a better review right now?" He said "yes" and I said "I frankly don't agree with that."
>
> [Before] I fundamentally believed in meritocracy— that if you did good work and achieved your objectives, the rest would follow. I don't believe that anymore.

Young managers who had difficulty working through setbacks often extracted lessons that had less to do with changing their own behavior than protecting themselves from the behavior of others they saw as unreasonable or out for political gain. Nonetheless, they still tended to feel powerless or ill-equipped to deal with the unpleasant issues they faced and often decided to avoid the situation altogether by leaving. Ironically, escaping the situation also denied them the opportunity to experiment with actions that would have helped to build the very influence skills they lacked.

Fortunately, several of the managers in our study seemed to have developed critical coping skills early in their careers. It wasn't that these young leaders were somehow smarter or made fewer mistakes, they were simply hardier and did things that allowed them to learn and recover from their mistakes more quickly. We noted several similarities in the how these resilient young managers responded to the mistakes and setbacks they experienced. First, they all appeared to engage in some form of emotional regulation (Goleman, Boyatzis, & McKee, 2002; Reivich & Shatte, 2002). Although the setbacks they experienced uniformly generated strong emotional reactions, resilient young leaders refrained from making rash decisions or acting impetuously. They took time to decompress and get away from their emotionally charged surroundings. As one disappointed manager remarked after being demoted to a less attractive position: "I didn't go off the deep *end*. I was gracious about the choices given me ... I didn't show all of my hurt... I cried at home, not at work."

Second, those who handled setbacks best sought out feedback and social support. Rather than withdrawing or quitting, successful coping involved getting a realistic understanding of the situation, no matter how painful. This meant talking with others, getting their assessment, and asking for input. In almost all cases, reaching out helped people to see the situation more objectively and reduced the tendency to interpret it as more catastrophic than it actually was. Perhaps even more important, young managers discovered that setbacks and mistakes could be an opportunity to strengthen relationships rather than run from them (Maddi & Khoshaba, 2005). As one young manager noted, "I clearly failed; but others were very understanding because they knew I would learn. They took it as a huge sign that I was capable of change and development."

Finally, those who weathered setbacks well came to realize that *how* they responded to the setback was more important than the setback itself. They took a longer term perspective, saw their situation as an inevitable part of the learning process, and recognized that the initial unpleasantness would ultimately lead to a better outcome for the organization or themselves (Maddi & Khoshaba, 2005). They also engaged in a great deal of personal reflection and often came to terms with specific shortcomings or errors. Through this process of self-examination, emerging leaders opened themselves up to important learning, became more skillful at managing their emotions, and ultimately gained greater self-confidence. They also developed a clearer sense of personal resolve and began to build the strength, judgment, and professional maturity required to handle similar challenges in the future. In other words, they learned and worked their way through yet another important leadership transition.

Discussion

We designed this study to explore the challenges confronting MBA graduates as they moved into leadership roles. Consistent with previous research (Charan et al., 2001; Dotlich, Noel, & Walker, 2004; Hill, 1992), the 55 in-depth interviews confirmed that to be successful, young managers must deal with both a significant set of transitions and a set of common challenges. These results reinforce several important findings from previous research and highlight some new insights that have implications for how we might improve leadership education for MBA students and other managers in the early stages of their careers.

First, adopting a leadership mind-set is not a trivial matter. It involves developing a fundamentally different way of thinking about one's role and what it means to be effective and successful. For the most part, the MBA graduates in this study did not appear to fully grasp the implications of these differences until they began managing people after business school. It is important to point out that relatively few of the graduates in our study had much direct management experience prior to business school and few moved right into managerial roles immediately after. Instead, most took jobs as functional specialists, joined training programs, or launched their own endeavors. These early job experiences served to further reinforce the notion that success meant distinguishing oneself from peers and others competing for opportunities. However, as these recent grads moved into managerial roles, they began to realize that self-promoting attitudes were counterproductive to managerial success. Difficulties motivating subordinates or gaining cooperation from fellow managers often stemmed from perceptions that the rookie managers cared more about their own interests than those of their subordinates or peers. As young managers began to shift their orientation in an effort to understand and support the needs and motivations of the people they worked with, they discovered that their teams (and colleagues) often reciprocated by taking more responsibility for their collective success.

The enormity of this shift in mind-set was not always immediately apparent to the new managers. As individual contributors, their goal had been to stand out from others. As managers, their goal was to help their subordinates stand out. Where before they had labored intensely to perform at the highest levels for their bosses, now they had to take responsibility for the mistakes and indifference of subordinates who didn't always share the same values or ambitions. Where before they had relied on their managers to coordinate their activities and smooth the way, now they were expected to resolve issues with their peers on their own. For high achievers who had long based their self-esteem on being competent and doing things right, this responsibility-without-control was particularly unsettling. Having not yet internalized what it meant to be a leader, they felt powerless—almost victimized—when subordinates showed little enthusiasm for work, ignored or challenged their direction or, in some cases, quit jobs or transferred to other units. Over time, they gradually came to realize that their power, and their success, rested in their ability to help others—both subordinates and peers—become more effective and more satisfied in performing their own work.

This shift in mind-set had three significant benefits. First, it changed the way emerging leaders interacted with their teams, as well as their peers. When they saw their role as growing and enabling others, they reported becoming less competitive and more collaborative. Second, it gave them back some of the control they thought they had lost. With a leadership mind-set, they no longer felt like helpless victims when their subordinates made mistakes or lacked motivation. Instead, they felt responsible for developing people who had the capacity to learn and improve. By valuing and accepting people—rather than judging and dismissing them—they discovered that they had far more leverage to make their situation better. Last, when emerging leaders saw their role in terms of others (rather than themselves), they seemed to be more adept at controlling their emotions and taking difficult relationships less personally. Rather than viewing difficult relationships (or people) as a statement about themselves,

they began to realize that "it wasn't *all* about them." With this insight, emerging leaders were able to remain less emotionally embroiled and were better equipped to explore conflicts dispassionately.

Another theme that was pervasive in our study was the tendency for inexperienced managers to over-rely on previous strengths when entering unfamiliar territory. This is especially troubling for junior managers for two reasons. First, it has been well documented that under conditions of stress, people fall back on overlearned skills that have worked well for them in the past (Fiedler, 1996). This can be quite effective when someone has a broad range of experiences to draw on but is far less effective when experiences are limited. A number of empirical studies suggest that when situational stress is high, high leader intelligence can impair performance (Fiedler, 1996; Fiedler & Garcia, 1987). In other words, leader intelligence and experience may actually interfere with each other when leaders perceive situations as highly stressful due to interpersonal conflicts or otherwise. Clearly this does not bode particularly well for intelligent business school graduates who are moving into challenging (potentially stressful) leadership roles, especially when they have a fairly narrow range of nonmanagerial experience to fall back on.

As we saw in this study, it was not unusual for MBAs to be placed in roles or situations that challenged them in significant ways. However, as we've discussed, it is precisely when situations are perceived as stressful (as these early management transitions often were), that leaders tend to draw less on their intellect and more on their experience. Because rookie managers have relatively little experience, it is especially important that we provide metacognitive strategies (Clark, 1992) that can help them to anticipate and prepare for stressful periods and that will allow them to leverage their cognitive strengths and analytic capabilities more effectively. Arming them with an understanding of the key transitional periods they are likely to experience, knowledge of what those transitional experiences may feel like, and strategies for handling them more productively may vastly improve the efficiency and effectiveness of a young leader's early-career development (e.g., Bridges, 2004; Maddi & Khoshaba, 2005; Reivich & Shatte, 2002; Watkins, 2009).

Without question, transitions represented particularly critical moments in a young leader's developmental journey. As McCall (2010) notes, while one can debate the number of transitions that are needed on the path to effective leadership, there is little question that these are times when much is on the line. For the MBA graduates in our study, transitional periods were a time of great potential and great risk. For some, working through difficult transitions, making mistakes, and learning from their successes and failures produced significant growth and development. For others, the transitions were more disorienting. It was clear that some of these young managers struggled with the adaptive challenges of specific transitions for months, and even years, as they tried to make sense of their personal experiences.

One of the most striking findings in our investigation was the sheer number and diversity of transitions that our emerging leaders weathered. This is important because recently it has been argued that understanding and improving key transitions precipitated by early job experiences could go a long way toward improving development over an entire career (McCall, 2010). The results of this study take us a step in that direction. When many people think of leadership transitions, their first thoughts go mainly to role transitions, much like the first category we describe in Table 1 (e.g., Charan et al., 2001; Hill, 2004). The early-career leaders in this study pointed to a variety of situations— beyond role changes—that produced significant transitions in the way they thought about and practiced leadership. These included leading significant business changes, much like those described by Watkins (2003), and dealing with situations that required clarifying and standing up for personal values and interests (Gentile, 2008).

One of the reasons we think that emerging managers sometimes struggled with their transitions, or failed to complete them, was because they typically didn't recognize that they were actually going through one. Transitions tend to take place over a period that often begins before people are fully aware of what is happening (Ibarra, 2003). Moreover, these can be particularly confusing and lonely times, even when the changes that sparked the transition are seemingly positive ones. For example, although an exciting new job with a bigger title can feel good initially, later it can seem like a mistake as a (previously successful) manager struggles to understand a new role, tries to navigate a new culture, and misses the old colleagues and well-worn networks of the previous job. This is because people interpret events partly by their past experience and expectations (Fiske & Taylor, 1991), which means that managers at different points in their development are likely to have different transitional experiences in response to the same change. One young manager may reflect on the circumstances, reevaluate old assumptions, and use the experience to learn and move on. Another may not yet have the knowledge base, learning orientation, or skills needed to draw out the appropriate learning and will likely repeat the process in a different context or with different people (Bridges, 2004; DeRue & Wellman, 2009). Unfinished transitions are destined to repeat themselves because when the necessary learning does not happen, inexperienced managers tend to exit—mentally or physically—without realizing that it is not the situation that needs to change, but themselves. Perhaps one of the most critical transitions for early-career leaders was the personal adaptation required to cope successfully with a professional setback. Those in our study who had done particularly well in terms of career advancement almost invariably mentioned the valuable lessons they had learned in dealing with a significant mistake or failure. In fact, most credited these transitions for subsequent promotion opportunities or job offers. To the extent that young managers developed resilience and professional maturity in working through these transitions, they built not only confidence, but credibility. However, if they let their emotions rule and failed to take the actions necessary for learning, they sometimes lost confidence and credibility and, at least for a time, lost their way. As such, the personal transitions that occurred in response to life's inevitable setbacks had perhaps the greatest impact on an emerging leader's career, either opening up new and greater opportunities or substantially derailing their development.

Implications for MBA Education

The raison dêtre for MBA programs is to prepare students to be managers and leaders of organizations. Unfortunately, as Pfeffer (2009) observes, many faculty in business schools choose to focus on topics that have only minor implications for the problems that managers face. Of equal concern is the lack of attention to the significant challenges and hurdles that managers do have to overcome, especially those that occur early in a career. It isn't that our research is irrelevant but rather that, unlike our colleagues in medical schools, faculty too often are unfamiliar with the actual problems that managers encounter in their day-to-day business (McGrath, 2007). In Jean Bartunek's terms (2007), our research and teaching often lack "intended rationales for action."

If we are to help our MBA students acquire the skills, abilities, attitudes, and knowledge needed to be effective leaders, our challenge is to ensure that our curricula not only provide abstract concepts and frameworks but are also grounded in the real problems that our students will have to navigate. McCall (2010) asserts that this requires "[s]marting from what managers do rather than what they are like" (681). Hill (2004) echoes this sentiment, noting that "[s]pecial emphasis should be given to matters on which new managers are prone to make mistakes" (256). The data from this study can help in this respect by informing us about some of the most difficult challenges that young managers struggle with and the important transitions that must occur if they are to develop as leaders. By understanding these challenges, we can design highly relevant content that can be directly applied in their new roles, and therefore, have a greater impact on their performance (Conger, 2004).

Assuming that we have identified the right challenges and transitional experiences, the next task is figuring out how to design our pedagogical material to adequately support the development of something as complex as leadership. To understand how, we need only turn to the work on human performance technologies. Based on more than 40 years of research, cognitive scientists striving to improve human performance in the workplace generally agree that there are two very different types of knowledge that people can acquire: (1) *procedural knowledge,* which tells us how things are done, and (2) *declarative knowledge,* which tells us *why* things work the way they do (Clark, 1992). People use procedural knowledge to master job tasks that can be accomplished in discrete steps or stages; whereas they use declarative knowledge to understand (or explain) why things work in certain ways or to predict how things will turn out if we engage in certain actions. Procedural knowledge has the advantage of becoming automatic with practice and can be accomplished without attention. Declarative knowledge has the advantage of being more flexible and allowing for creativity, but people can only think about a limited number of declarative things at once because declarative knowledge requires conscious attention (Clark, 1999). This is likely why people revert to overlearned behavior when dealing with stressful situations—it requires less cognitive expenditure.

Leadership is best characterized as a combination of both procedural and declarative knowledge. The declarative aspects of leadership allow managers to apply principles, concepts, and facts to creatively address problems in each new situation. They also help managers form procedures and decide when to use them. Over time, as procedures are applied consistently and produce positive outcomes, they become automatic. So, for example, young managers may learn about the importance of establishing clear expectations and providing feedback (declarative knowledge) and receive instruction on the discrete steps involved in conducting feedback conversations (procedural knowledge). If they practice consistently and receive feedback on their performance, over time, the steps involved may become more or less automatic.

There are problems, however, with how these seemingly straightforward aspects of leadership are taught in many business schools. First, there is a common misconception that skill development and knowledge development are best learned—and should be taught—in different ways. As such, many business schools relegate skill development to special classes, labs, cocurricular modules, and so on, that are largely experiential, and knowledge development to more traditional classes, which are largely case-based. The experiential classes emphasize practice and feedback with a light concept introduction, while the case-based classes typically focus on frameworks and strategy, leaving skill development to others. The problem is that when it comes to learning, our minds make no distinction between knowledge and skills—they only pay attention to the procedural or declarative aspects of what we're trying to learn. Most important, both skills- and knowledge-based tasks (e.g., active listening and empowering others) require procedural and declarative knowledge to support successful application (Clark, 1999). As such, classes focusing on one or the other type of task or knowledge may be insufficient for learning the complex bundle of knowledge that translates into well-performed leadership acts. Moreover, simply assuming that students will be able to combine and integrate knowledge across classes on their own is not only unrealistic, it is unfair. As many faculty will acknowledge, the coordination of pedagogical material across classes is typically loose at best, even if the school's marketing efforts claim otherwise. And, even if our coordination were better, expecting novices to accurately integrate complex knowledge introduced from varying perspectives devoid of any real context or cross-curricular support seems unreasonable.

Second, just because novice leaders remember and understand a concept does not guarantee they will be able to apply it effectively. And, just because someone can apply a concept does not mean that they are necessarily fully aware of how they did it. Memory and application of both procedural and declarative knowledge operate independently (Clark, 1992). Again, this has two implications for current pedagogical practices. First, teaching leadership principles without sufficient application opportunities runs the risk of making complex leadership concepts appear simple and obvious. Certainly, it is easy to cognitively grasp the importance of being empathetic or making other people successful, but it is difficult to appreciate the challenges or subtleties involved without actually trying to do it when other things are at stake. This may lead some students to underestimate the value or significance of our leadership offerings. Second, many business schools attempt to bridge the application gap by having practitioners teach leadership electives or speak in classes about their leadership experience. While this can have many benefits, such as exposing students to real-life situations and different leadership styles, practitioners with extensive experience have often reached the point of automaticity. That is, they may not be able to accurately articulate exactly how they do complex leadership tasks such as delegation or trust building, even when they think they can.

Last, the transfer of knowledge from the educational context to the work setting is a complicated process. It involves both *near transfer*—routine uses of knowledge— and *far transfer*—creative uses of knowledge (Clark, 1999). We know from behavioral psychology that near transfer is greatly facilitated when the specific problems presented in the training context closely mirror the application setting and corrective feedback is provided. We also know that far transfer is enhanced when educators help students to link seemingly unrelated, yet actually similar events to new problems, thereby clarifying a broader concept or honing a practical insight (Conger & Xin, 2000). But there are ways that far transfer can actually be inhibited if the pedagogical approach overemphasizes near transfer and vice-versa. The increasingly behavioral orientation of many schools' skill-building efforts—much like the overuse of competencies in the organizational context—runs the risk of throwing the proverbial baby out with the bathwater. While leadership skills, such as giving feedback, setting goals, active listening, communication and influence techniques are certainly important, repeatedly practicing a specific skill on similar types of problems (e.g., role-plays with peers) can inhibit creativity and give young leaders the false impression that by following recommended steps to the letter, they are in fact practicing good leadership. Without the relevant declarative knowledge and interpretive frames (i.e., mind-sets), young leaders may lack the capacity to reflexively adapt their responses in ways that are consistent with the concepts they are trying to apply.

One solution to these pedagogical misalignments is to create courses and other offerings designed to enhance creative problem solving while at the same time promoting the development of practical skill. Approaches that combine procedural and declarative knowledge building increase the chances that students will be able to apply what they learn in the classroom to the ever-evolving leadership challenges they face on the job. To this end, we created a series of short (10 min) leadership video vignettes designed purposely to develop both forms of knowledge relevant to leadership. Our goal was to truly integrate problem solving and skill development.

These video vignettes portray early-career leaders trying to manage their way through real situations fraught with the challenges described by the young managers in our study. They also capture some of the emotion that these problems contain, which enhances engagement and learning (Bar-tunek, 2007; Weick, 1999). The videos are interactive, allowing students to analyze the situation in class, discuss what they might do, and then see how it might play out. Faculty moderate the discussion, often incorporating role-plays so that students gain practice applying their suggestions, using specific procedures, or experimenting with concepts. Faculty can selectively combine vignettes in a way that allows them to build on previous learning or, more importantly, vary specific parameters of a given leadership challenge. By changing aspects of the problems, faculty can help students learn how to adapt their responses to different circumstances and contexts which, in turn, makes future managers more adept at applying the leadership concepts to real situations.[1]

The video vignettes can also be used to underscore the importance of a leadership mind-set. In our experience, the topic of leadership mind-set gets relatively little attention in many business schools. We know from a long tradition of research in social cognition and other fields that individuals actively construct their own reality based on the organized beliefs or social schema they hold. Schemas about roles and self shape our perceptions and the inferences we make (Fiske & Taylor, 1991). Recently, Dweck (2006) has argued convincingly that the mind-sets leaders hold about ability can dramatically shape many of the practices they put in place in their organizations, as well as the quality of their interactions with peers and subordinates. When students see firsthand through the video vignettes how mind-sets play out in very real situations and how they can undermine their leadership efforts in tangible ways, the learning can be quite powerful. When they begin to actively experiment with leadership mind-sets, they become more self-aware and better able to regulate their behavior in ways that are consistent with the leadership concepts we emphasize in class.

Conclusions

In recent years the debate about the relevance and legitimacy of business schools and what we teach has increased (e.g., Khurana, 2007; Pfeffer, 2009). Tushman and O'Reilly (2007) argue that business school faculty face a more difficult challenge than faculty in disciplinary departments. We are required not only to develop new knowledge (rigor), but also to ensure that this knowledge can be applied (relevance). This applies to our teaching as well. Unlike students in conventional academic departments where the goal is the acquisition of knowledge per se, we need to provide our students with knowledge and skills that can be applied (Tyson, 2005).

To succeed at this, we need to understand at some level of granularity the specific problems our students struggle with as young managers. This study has identified three significant transitions and four common challenges faced by young managers. These challenges, and the associated transitions they require, are both conceptual (e.g., adopting a managerial mind-set, dealing with setbacks and failure) and practical (e.g., motivating others, resolving difficult relationships). As such, they challenge us as educators to both make our students aware of these issues and to help them develop the skills needed to confront the issues successfully. Part of this can be done through a curriculum design that highlights these challenges. We can also benefit from a better understanding of the cognitive processes that enable the development, transfer, and application of complex knowledge. Pfeffer and Fong (2004) argue that "[b]usiness schools could be more relevant to the management profession they ostensibly serve, possibly even more relevant and useful than they are today ..." (1515). We agree. By identifying specific challenges that young manager's face and creating teaching materials that help students confront these challenges, extract the appropriate learning, and make the necessary psychological transitions, we can improve the relevance and the rigor of leadership development in the business school context.

Source: Academy of Management

ENDNOTE

1. The course syllabus and teaching notes are available from the authors. The video vignettes are available for free from the Stanford Center for Leadership Development and Research. See www.leadershipinfocus.net for a further description and access to these materials.

REFERENCES

Avolio, B. J., Avey, J. B., & Quisenberry, D. 2010. Estimating the return on leadership development investment. *Leadership Quarterly,* 21: 633–644.

Avolio, B. J., Rotundo, M., & Walumbwa, F. O. 2009. Early life experiences and environmental factors as determinants of leadership emergence: The role of parental influence and rule breaking behavior. *Leadership Quarterly,* 20: 329–342.

Bartunek, J. M. 2007. Toward a relational scholarship of integration. *Academy of Management Journal,* 50: 1323–1333.

Bennis, W. G., & O'Toole, J. 2005. How business schools lost their way. *Harvard Business Review,* May: 96–104.

Bridges, W. 2004. *Transitions: Making sense of life's changes.* Cambridge, MA: DaCapo Press.

Carroll, P. B., & Mui, C. 2008. *Billion dollar lessons: What you can learn from the most inexcusable business failures of the last 25 years.* New York: Portfolio.

Charan, R., Drotter, S., & Noel, J. 2001. *The leadership pipeline.* San Francisco: Jossey-Bass.

Chia, R., & Holt, R. 2008. The nature of knowledge in business schools. *Academy of Management Learning and Education,* 7: 471–486.

Clark, R. E. 1992. How the cognitive sciences are shaping the profession In H. D. Stolovich, & E. J. Keeps (Eds.), *Handbook of human performance technology: Improving individual and organizational performance worldwide* (1st ed.). San Francisco: Jossey-Bass.

Clark, R. E. 1999. The cognitive sciences and human performance technology In H. D. Stolovich, & E. J. Keeps (Eds.), *Handbook of human performance technology: Improving individual and organizational performance worldwide* (2nd ed.). San Francisco: Jossey-Bass.

Conger, J. A. 2004. Developing leadership capability: What's inside the black box?. *Academy of Management Executives,* 18: 136–139.

Conger, J. A., & Xin, K. R. 2000. Executive education in the 21st century. *Management in Education,* 24: 73–101.

DeRue, D. S., & Wellman, N. 2009. Developing leaders via experience: The role of developmental challenge, learning orientation, and feedback availability. *Journal of Applied Psychology,* 94: 859–875.

Dotlich, D. L., Noel, J. L., & Walker, N. 2004. *Leadership passages: The personal and professional transitions that make or break a leader.* San Francisco: Jossey-Bass.

Dweck, C. S. 2006. *Mindset: The new psychology of success.* New York: Ballantine Books.

Fetterman, D. M. 1989. *Ethnography: Step-by-step.* Newbury Park, CA: Sage.

Fiedler, F. E. 1996. Research on leadership selection and training: One view of the future. *Administrative Science Quarterly,* 41: 241–250.

Fiedler, F. E., & Garcia, J. E. 1987. *New approaches to effective leadership: Cognitive resources and organizational performance.* New York: Wiley.

Finkelstein, S. 2003. *Why smart executives fail and what you can learn from their mistakes.* New York: Portfolio.

Fiske, S. T., & Taylor, S. E. 1991. *Social cognition* (2nd ed.). New York: McGraw-Hill.

Friga, P. N., Bettis, R. A., & Sullivan, R. S. 2003. Changes in graduate management education and new business school strategies for the 21st century. *Academy of Management Learning and Education,* 2: 233–249.

Gentile, M. 2008. Giving voice to values: Ways of thinking about our values in the workplace. www.AspenCBE.org.

Ghoshal, S. 2005. Bad management theories are destroying good management practices. *Academy of Management Learning and Education,* 4: 75–91.

Gilchrest, V. J. 1992. Key informant interviews In B. F. Crabtree, & W. L. Miller (Eds.), *Doing qualitative research.* London: Sage.

Gladwell, M. 2008. *Outliers: The story of success.* New York: Little, Brown.

Glaser, B., & Strauss, A. 1967. *The discovery of grounded theory: Strategies for qualitative research.* New York: Aldine de Gruyter.

Goetz, J. P., & LeCompte, M. D. 1984. *Ethnography and qualitative design in educational research.* Orlando, FL: Academic Press.

Goleman, D., Boyatzis, R., & McKee, A. 2002. *Primal leadership: Realizing the power of emotional intelligence.* Boston: Harvard Business School Press.

Greiner, L. E. 1998. Evolution and revolution as organizations grow. *Harvard Business Review,* May–June.

Hackman, J. R., & Wageman, R. 2007. Asking the correct questions about leadership. *The American Psychologist,* 62: 43–47.

Hannah, S. T., & Avolio, B. J. 2010. Ready or not: How do we accelerate the developmental readiness of leaders? *Journal of Organizational Behavior,* 31: 1181–1187.

Hill, L. A. 1992. *Becoming a manager.* Boston: HBS Press.

Hill, L. A. 2004. New manager development for the 21st century. *Academy of Management Executive,* 18: 121–126.

Ibarra, H. 2003. *Working identify: Unconventional strategies for reinventing your career.* Boston: HBS Press.

Johnson, J. C. 1990. *Selecting ethnographic informants.* Newbury Park, CA: Sage.

Kerr, S. 2004. Introduction: Preparing people to lead. *Academy of Management Executive,* 3: 118–120.

Khurana, R. 2007. From *higher aims to hired hands: The social transformation of American business schools and the unfulfilled promise of management as a profession.* Princeton, NJ: Princeton University Press.

Lombardo, M. M., Ruderman, M. N., & McCauley, C. D. 1988. Explanations of success and derailment in upper-level management positions. *Journal of Business and Psychology,* 2: 199–216.

Maddi, S., & Khoshaba, D. 2005. *Resilience at work: How to succeed no matter what life throws at you.* New York: AMA-COM.

McCall, M. W. 1998. *High flyers: Developing the next generation of leaders.* Boston: Harvard Business School Press.

McCall, M. W. 2004. Leadership development through experience. *Academy of Management Executive,* 18: 127–130.

McCall, M. W. 2010. The experience conundrum. In N. Nohria, & R. Khurana (Eds.), *Handbook of leadership theory and practice: A Harvard Business School Centennial Colloquium.* Boston: Harvard Business Press.

McCall, M. W., Lombardo, M. M., & Morrison, A. M. 1988. The lessons of experience: How successful executives develop *on* the job. *Lexington Books.*

McCauley, C. D., Ruderman, M. N., Ohlott, P. J., & Morrow, J. E. 1994. Assessing the developmental components of managerial jobs. *Journal of Applied Psychology,* 79: 544–560.

McGrath, R. G. 2007. No longer a step-child: How the management field can come into its own. *Academy of Management Journal,* 50: 1365–1378.

Miller, W. L., & Crabtree, B. F. 1992. *Doing qualitative research.* Newbury Park: Sage.

Mintzberg, H. 2004. *Managers not MBAs: A hard look at the soft practice of managing and management development.* San Francisco: Berrett-Kohler.

Navarro, P. 2008. The MBA core curricula of top-ranked U.S. business schools: A study in failure? *Academy of Management Learning and Education,* 7: 108–123.

Nicholson, N., & West, M. 1988. Transitions, work histories, and careers In M. Arthur, D. Hall, & B. Lawrence (Eds.), *Handbook of career theory:* 188–199. New York: Cambridge University Press.

Pfeffer, J. 2009. Renaissance and renewal in management studies: Relevance regained. *European Management Review,* 6: 141–148.

Pfeffer, J., & Fong, C. T. 2002. The end of business schools? Less success than meets the eye. *Academy of Management Learning and Education,* 1: 78–95.

Pfeffer, J., & Fong, C. T. 2004. The business school "business": Some lessons from the U.S. experience. *Journal of Management Studies,* 41: 1501–1520.

Porter, L. W., & McKibbin, L. E. 1988. *Management education and development.* New York: McGraw-Hill.

Reivich, K., & Shatte, A. 2002. *The resilience factor.* New York: Random House.

Spradley, J. P. 1979. *The ethnographic interview.* New York: Holt, Rinehart & Winston.

Tushman, M. L., & O'Reilly, C. A. 2007. Research and relevance: Implications of Pasteur's quadrant for doctoral programs and faculty development. *Academy of Management Journal,* 50: 769–774.

Tyson, L. D. 2005. On managers, not MBAs. *Academy of Management Learning and Education,* 4: 235–236.

Van Velsor, E., & Leslie, J. B. 1995. Why executives derail: Perspectives across time and cultures. *Academy of Management Learning & Education,* 9: 62–72.

Watkins, M. 2003. *The first 90 days: Critical success strategies for new leaders at all levels.* Boston: Harvard Business School Press.

Watkins, M. 2009. *Your next move: The leader's guide to navigating major career transitions.* Boston: Harvard Business School Press.

Weick, K. E. 1999. That's moving: Theories that matter. *Journal of Management Inquiry,* 8: 134–142.

Willis, J., & Todorov, A. 2006. First impressions: Making up your mind after a 10-MS exposure to a face. *Psychological Science,* 17: 592–598.

Wren, D. A., Halbesleben, J. R., & Buckley, M. R. 2007. The theory-application balance in management pedagogy: A longitudinal update. *Academy of Management Learning & Education,* 6: 484–492.

Performance Management and Feedback

Performance Management at Microsoft Corporation

Redmond, Washington–based global software giant Microsoft recently redesigned its performance management system to allow its integration with the company's compensation program and provide a transparent process to facilitate differentiated rewards for various performance levels. During its early years, Microsoft, like most technology start-ups, relied heavily on stock options as a means of compensation, which was welcome by employees as the company's stock price surged. After the 2000 dot-com bust, compensation was altered to provide a greater percentage of compensation in the form of cash. As the stock price stabilized, Microsoft shifted its remaining equity compensation away from stock options in favor of restricted stock units, which reward performance over time and retention of employees.

In 2011, Microsoft simplified its performance management process by having one assessment of performance conducted by an employee's direct supervisor, who simply rated performance on a scale of 1(highest) to 5 (lowest). This single performance rating was a composite of three factors: (1) employee performance during the year relative to individual goals and performance of peers; (2) the behavior displayed in achieving results; and (3) employees' overall capabilities and perceived future value in tandem with performance history.

Targeted distribution levels set guidelines for supervisor relative to the number or percentage of employees who could receive each rating. The performance rating was considered alongside the employee's job family and discipline to allow Microsoft to reward highest performers who held positions that were most critical to the company's success and strategy. Employees were given access to an intranet portal to allow them to see how their compensation would shift given differential performance ratings. Employee satisfaction increased as a result of the new system and Microsoft executives reported an enhanced ability to "attract and retain key talent by delivering the highest compensation to the highest performing employees."[1]

An organization's long-term success in meeting its strategic objectives rests with its ability to manage employee performance and ensure that performance measures are consistent with the organization's needs. Consequently, performance management—also called *performance evaluation, performance appraisal,* or *performance measurement*—is becoming more of a strategic issue for organizations than in the past. The term *performance feedback* will be used frequently in this chapter to stress that the performance management system needs to be understood and accepted by the organization's employees and must provide them with meaningful information if it is to be effective. Effective performance management systems require employees and supervisors to work together to set performance expectations, review results, assess organizational and individual needs, and plan for the future. On the other hand, the terms *performance appraisal* and *performance evaluation* imply a one-sided judgmental approach to performance management, where employees have little involvement in the process.

Traditional performance appraisal simply involves evaluative supervisory comments on past performance. Such a process does not involve any kind of management, per se, as the only performance that can be managed is present and future performance. Performance appraisal involves hierarchical, downward communication from supervisor to subordinate concerning the value the supervisor places on the subordinate's performance. Feedback involves a mutual exchange of information that both parties share, discuss, and jointly assess in planning future work activities. Appraisals often put employees in a defensive position, whereas feedback is usually perceived as more neutral and a process over which employees have some control and influence. Exhibit 10.1 summarizes the key differences between performance feedback and performance appraisal.

Performance management systems need not be formal to be effective, although a recent survey conducted by the Society for Human Resource Management found that 98 percent of employers have a formal performance management process.[2] The most important concern in designing a performance management system is its fit with the organization's strategic objectives, and the most important concern in providing performance-related feedback is its fit with the organization's culture. SAS, an international, 8,000-employee software company headquartered in Cary, North Carolina, decided to do away with formal performance feedback entirely. Instead, SAS opted for a system that provides continuous dialogue on performance-related matters. Executives report that the system works well because it is built on the values of open communication, trust, and

EXHIBIT 10.1 Performance Feedback Versus Performance Appraisal

	Performance Feedback	Performance Appraisal
Time period	Past, present, and future	Past
Focus	Link employee work activities to specific business objectives and strategy	Create records; document performance problems
Nature of communication	Two-way	One-sided, downward, directive; "rebuttal" sometimes allowed
Employee role	Active participant	Passive
Formality	Informal, verbal	High formality, written forms with signatures
Timing	Spontaneous, ad hoc needed	As prescribed (usually annual)
Basis of relationship	Collegiality	Power
Role of supervisor	Coach, motivator, partner	Authority figure
Outcomes	Participation; enhanced, targeted performance; improved relationships	Compensation decision; task directives

self-motivation of employees to do their best. Moreover, any performance-related issues are dealt with in a timely manner because the lack of formality in the process allows feedback to be provided on an ongoing basis.[3]

The trends toward more streamlined organizations and hierarchies with fewer employees having broader job assignments have resulted in performance feedback taking on a more critical role than it has assumed in the past. Organizations today cannot afford to have weak links or unproductive employees. More than ever, organizations need broader measures of employee performance to ensure that (1) performance deficiencies are addressed in a timely manner through employee development programs that meet the changing needs of the organization and its markets; (2) employee behaviors are being channeled in the appropriate direction toward performance of specific objectives that are consistent with the work unit and the organization's strategy; and (3) employees are provided with appropriate and specific feedback to assist with their career development. The importance of performance management for organizations has led to the establishment of an American National Standard, developed by the Society for Human Resource Management and approved by the American National Standards Institute. This standard provides employers with guidance and suggestions relative to the development and analysis of performance standards, goal setting, and performance improvement.[4]

An effective performance management process can be conceptualized as one that connects three time periods, as illustrated in Exhibit 10.2. It utilizes data about past performance to set goals, plans, and objectives for the present that should result in high levels of performance in the future. However, a number of critical strategic issues must be addressed to establish an effective performance management system, as will be discussed in the following sections.

Use of the System

An organization faces five strategic decisions in establishing its performance management system, as illustrated in Exhibit 10.3. The first is a determination of the purpose of the system and how it will be used. A performance management system can serve multiple purposes, and it is important for the organization to strategize why the system is being used before further design decisions can be made. If the system is developed to serve several purposes, the organization also needs to ensure that these purposes are at odds with each other and that any purpose does not undermine data collection for the other(s).

One purpose of performance management systems is to facilitate employee development. By assessing deficiencies in performance levels and skills, an organization can determine specific training and development needs. In fact, the performance feedback process can be designed to provide information to fuel the organization's training and development programs. Assessing individual and team strengths and weaknesses can allow employee and team development plans to be established. A reciprocal relationship exists between the two, as the desired outcomes of training and development initiatives must be incorporated into the performance management system, as

EXHIBIT 10.2	Performance Management Timeline	
Past	**Present**	**Future**
Data related to past performance, →	allows work plans, goals, and development opportunities to be set, →	resulting in the achievement of strategic objectives.

© Cengage Learning

EXHIBIT 10.3

Strategic Choices in Performance Management Systems

How System Will Be Used
- Employee development
- Determine rewards and compensation
- Enhance motivation
- Facilitate legal compliance
- Facilitate human resource planning

Link with Training

Who Evaluates
- Supervisor
- Peers
- Subordinates
- Customers
- Self

Link with Compensation

What to Evaluate
- Traits
- Behaviors
- Results

How to Evaluate
- Absolute
- Relative

Flexible/ Standardized

Means of Evaluation
- Graphic rating scale
- Weighted checklist
- BARS
- BOS
- Critical incident
- Objectives-based

Individual/ Team

Time Periods

discussed in Chapter 9. At the same time, the performance management system provides data that impact the needs assessment of training and development, as displayed in Exhibit 10.4.

A second purpose of performance management systems is to determine appropriate rewards and compensation. Salary, promotion, retention, and bonus decisions are frequently based on data collected as part of performance measurement. Therefore, employees must understand and accept the performance feedback system as a prerequisite for accepting decisions made relative to rewards and compensation. Any perceived unfairness of the performance feedback system on the part of employees will result in a perceived unfairness of the compensation system.

A third purpose of managing performance is to enhance employee motivation. A formal process that allows for employee acknowledgment and praise can reinforce the behaviors and outcomes that are beneficial to the unit or organization. Employees can be told specifically what the

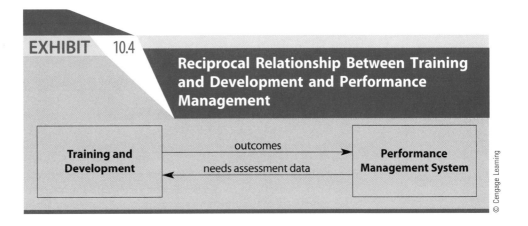

EXHIBIT   10.4

Reciprocal Relationship Between Training and Development and Performance Management

Training and Development → outcomes → Performance Management System

Performance Management System → needs assessment data → Training and Development

© Cengage Learning

organization's expectations for them are, and employees can inform their employers of the types of job assignments and responsibilities they desire.

A fourth purpose of performance management systems is to facilitate legal compliance. Claims of unfair dismissal and/or Title VII violations are best supported when the organization has documentation of performance deficiencies. Such information is often admitted into court to prove nondiscriminatory means of taking remedial action against employees and for termination of employment. Data showing unacceptable performance, particularly over a period of time, is a strong defense against such charges of unlawful bias.[5]

Finally, performance management systems facilitate the human resource (HR) planning process. Performance data can alert the organization to deficiencies in the overall level and focus of employee skills and can be used in critically planning for future staffing needs relative to the skills and abilities of current employees. Because performance feedback can perform multiple functions in any organization, the organization must determine how it will be used prior to developing the system. This will keep the system focused—rather than random—and allow the organization to determine the specifications of its design.

Who Evaluates

The second strategic decision that must be made relative to the development of the performance management system concerns who provides performance data. Traditionally, performance evaluation was performed by the employee's immediate supervisor, who communicated to the employee the supervisory assessment of performance. This system offered very little opportunity for input or feedback from the employee. This approach, by itself, can be problematic for a number of reasons. Immediate supervisors often do not have the appropriate information to provide informed feedback and do not observe the employee's day-to-day work enough to assess performance accurately. It is also common in today's organizations for supervisors not to be current on the technical dimensions of a subordinate's work, which may be best evaluated by peers, customers, or other external constituencies. Technical line managers often have no training in or appreciation for the process and can see it as nothing more than an administrative burden. Finally, performance assessment is an inherently subjective process that is prone to a variety of perceptual errors by supervisors.

These errors include the halo effect, in which the rater allows one positive or negative trait, outcome, or consideration to influence other measures (e.g., if an employee is often late for work, that fact may impact ratings having nothing to do with tardiness); stereotyping or personal bias, in which the rater makes performance judgments based on characteristics of the employee rather than on employee performance (e.g., a bias that older workers are more resistant to change, less mentally agile, and less capable than younger workers of working longer hours); contrast error, in which the employee's assessment is based on those being given to other employees; regency error, in which the evaluation is biased toward events and behaviors that happened immediately prior to the time the evaluation is completed, with little or no consideration given to events occurring earlier in the evaluation period; central tendency error, in which the evaluator avoids the higher and lower ends of performance assessment ratings in favor of placing all employees at or near the middle of the scales; and leniency or strictness error, in which employees are generally all rated well above the standards (making the supervisor look effective and/or attempting to appease employees) or well below the standards (making the supervisor look demanding). Personal biases and organizational politics may have a significant impact on the ratings employees receive from their supervisors.

There may also be a number of reasons why supervisors might intentionally inflate or deflate employee ratings. For example, an empathetic supervisor might inflate the rating given to an employee having difficulties with personal matters. Conversely, a supervisor who sees a subordinate as a threat to the supervisor's job might intentionally deflate performance ratings. The performance management process can be inherently political in many organizations. In most instances, when supervisors conduct performance evaluations, they personally have job and career issues at stake in the ratings they give to their employees.

In addition to these errors, supervisors and subordinates may agree on levels of performance but disagree on the causes for such performance. Research has shown that supervisors are much more likely to place the responsibility for poor performance with the employee, whereas the employee is likely to cite organizational factors outside his or her control for performance deficiencies.[6] Employees are much more likely to attribute their own job success to their own behaviors rather than to external factors, such as easy job assignments or assistance from others.

For these reasons, organizations have been moving away from traditional means of performance feedback where only one assessment of an employee's performance is conducted and completed by the immediate supervisor. In addition to supervisory input, performance feedback can also be sought from peers, subordinates, customers, and/or the employee. Feedback from peers can be useful for developmental purposes, but peer feedback systems must be administered with care. They can be very political and self-serving in organizations where employees compete with each other either formally or informally. When a peer has personal gain or loss at stake in the assessment of a colleague, he or she can hardly be expected to exercise objectivity. Competitive organizational cultures could cause a peer evaluation system to raise havoc throughout the organization by escalating conflict. This could have detrimental effects on morale and teamwork. Peer feedback systems can only be effective when political considerations and consequences are minimized (meaning that peers have nothing at stake in their assessments of colleagues) and employees have a sense of trust in the organization and its performance measurement system.

Peer Assessment at Coffee & Power

Coffee & Power is a small San Francisco, California—based start-up where individuals can "buy and sell" small jobs. As part of its performance management and rewards process, each of its 15 full- and part-time employees is annually given 1,200 stock options to distribute to their coworkers in whatever way they see fit. Options may be given entirely to one individual or distributed to as many other coworkers as an employee decides. The only restrictions are that employees cannot give shares to themselves or to the company founders.

The system is designed to reward employee contribution, which might not always be recognized by management and also holds workers accountable for managing relationships with coworkers, a critical success factor in small start-ups where employees work closely together over long hours. Because the company is still privately held, the options only hold paper value at the present time. However, individual employee cash bonuses are tied in to this allocation system. Employees learn of the options and bonuses they receive but not who rewarded them. The owners prepare a distribution curve of all bonus grants without attaching individual names to allow employees see the highest and lowest bonuses as well as where they fit individually within the company distribution.[7]

Performance feedback from subordinates can provide insights into the interpersonal and managerial styles of employees and can assist the organization in addressing employee developmental needs, particularly for high-potential employees. Subordinate evaluations are also excellent measures of an individual's leadership capabilities. However, subordinate evaluations can suffer from the same political problems as peer evaluations. They can also be used by either the supervisor or subordinates to retaliate against each other. However, in assessing an employee's ability to manage others, valuable performance data pertaining to behavior and skills can be uniquely provided from subordinates.

Because our economy is becoming increasingly service oriented and because many organizations emphasize customer service as a key competitive and strategic issue, customers are increasingly being sought for feedback on employee performance. In most instances, customers can provide the feedback that is most free from bias: They usually have little or nothing at stake in their assessment of employees. Feedback from customers can be critical for facilitating employee development and determining appropriate rewards because it is most clearly related to the organization's bottom line.

Self-evaluations allow employees to provide their own assessments and measures of their own performance. Although it should be obvious that self-evaluation can be self-serving, allowing employees to evaluate their own performance has at least two important benefits for organizations. First, it can be motivating because it allows the employee to participate in a critical decision that impacts his or her employment and career. Second, the employee can provide insights, examples, and a more holistic assessment of performance than that provided by supervisors or peers, who generally spend a limited time observing and interacting with each employee. Individual employees are far more likely to remember significant examples of effective performance than their supervisors, and they can often provide specific examples of behaviors and outcomes rather than the generalities often cited by supervisors. Individual employees may also be able to provide performance information of which others may be unaware.

Performance management systems that solicit the input and advice of others besides the immediate supervisor are referred to as multirater systems or 360-degree feedback systems. These systems can be beneficial because the organization and employee gain multiple perspectives and insights into the employee's performance. Each of these sources of performance feedback can balance each other relative to any inherent organizational politics that may be at play in the process. However, there is a cost to such systems: They can be very time consuming and laborious to administer. Data from numerous sources need to be analyzed, synthesized, and, occasionally, reconciled. There is inherently a cost–benefit aspect to any type of multirater performance feedback system. The more performance data collected, the greater the overall facilitation of the assessment and development of the employee. At the same time, larger volumes of data are costly to collect and process. At some point, the collection of additional data will undoubtedly provide diminishing returns.

Performance Management at Otis Elevator

Farmington, Connecticut–based Otis Elevator is the world's largest manufacturer, installer, and servicer of elevators, escalators, moving walkways, and other vertical and horizontal passenger transportation systems. Otis's products are offered in more than 200 countries worldwide, and the company employs more than 63,000 people. Among its many installations are the human transport systems of the Eiffel Tower, Sydney Opera House, Vatican, ON Tower (Toronto), and Hong Kong Convention Center.

For years, the company had an ineffective performance management system that was excessively time consuming and inspired little confidence among employees or managers. In revamping its performance management, Otis moved toward a system that provided performance feedback based on critical strategic competencies related to the company's new focus on project teams. For this realignment into project teams to be successful, managers were required to demonstrate specific competencies in both team leadership and project management as well as remain accountable for the financial and operating results of projects.

Realizing that critical feedback in these areas could not come exclusively from immediate supervisors, Otis had a custom-designed 360-degree feedback system developed that provided managers with feedback from those most directly affected by their performance: their subordinates, peers, and customers. The system provides ratings on several critical core competencies and is administered entirely online via the company intranet. The online system is easy to use, employs encryption technology to secure all data, and allows a performance review to be completed in 20 minutes. The system allows Otis to provide performance feedback in tandem with the organization's strategic objectives; is far more efficient than the previous paper-driven system; and, perhaps most importantly, has restored employee faith in the company's performance feedback system.[8]

The popularity and use of 360-degree feedback programs have increased dramatically in recent years: More than 65 percent of organizations now use some form of multirater feedback, despite the fact that 360-degree feedback programs have been associated with a 10.6 percent decline in shareholder value.[9] The reason appears to be that many organizations have jumped on the 360-degree bandwagon without careful planning and strategizing about why and how the program is being used within the organization. Unless each rater has a consistent view of effective performance relative to the organization's strategy, disagreements can cause unexpected conflicts and problems and result in communication breakdowns that require time to resolve. Despite their popularity, 360-degree feedback programs can create severe problems if not designed, implemented, and managed carefully. The organization's strategy and culture must support such a system. Otherwise, the organization runs the risk of performance problems that will inevitably impact bottom-line profitability and value.

Despite the advantages of multirater systems, collecting additional performance data results in a greater economic cost (relative to opportunity cost of the time of those involved in the process) and a more complex process in attempting to process and analyze the data to provide meaningful feedback to employees. If not designed and implemented carefully, 360-degree feedback systems can result in the collection and processing of excessive amounts of information that provide no benefit to either the organization or the employee. Such data overload can cause the most relevant, critical performance data to be lost or obscured in the process.

What to Evaluate

The next strategic question that needs to be addressed involves determining what is to be evaluated. Essentially, employee evaluations can be based on their traits, their behaviors, or the results or outcomes they achieve. Traits-based measures focus on the general abilities and characteristics of the employee. They might include dimensions such as loyalty to the organization, industriousness, and gregariousness. Although assessment of traits can often allow the organization to determine how the employee fits with the organization's culture, such measures ignore what the employee actually *does*. Traits-based measures, therefore, are of limited use or value; the subjective nature of such nonperformance-related criteria would probably not hold up well in court in a discrimination complaint.

Behavior-based measures focus on what an employee does by examining specific behaviors of the employee. Factors assessed here might include the employee's ability to get along with others, punctuality, willingness to take initiative, and ability to meet deadlines. Behavioral measures are very useful for feedback purposes because they specify exactly what the employee is doing correctly and what the employee should do differently. This is critical as work-related behaviors are generally within the control of most employees. Of particular attention to most employers is the behavior of leaders, as discussed in Reading, 10.1, "Effective Leadership Behavior: What We Know and What Questions Need More Attention." However, it is possible for employees to engage in appropriate behaviors but not achieve results for the organization. Although employees may do the right things, their performance may not make a difference for the organization in terms of performance that relates to strategic objectives.

The third basis for performance feedback is to assess outcomes or results. Results-based measures focus on specific accomplishments or direct outcomes of an employee's work. These might include measures of number of units sold, divisional profitability, cost reduction, efficiency, or quality. Unlike traits and behaviors, results-based measures are often criteria that can be measured objectively. More important, results are generally more meaningful to the organization due to their more direct correlation with performance relating to the divisional or organizational strategy.

Although results may be a more significant measure of performance than traits or behaviors, there are some imitations to the utilization of results-based feedback measures. First, it may be difficult to obtain results for certain job responsibilities. Any tasks that involve dealing with the future (i.e., forecasting and planning relative to competition or assessing other dimensions of the external environment) will not show immediate results nor will the quality or accuracy of the work be assessable until sometime in the future. Second, results are sometimes beyond an individual employee's control. Budget cuts and resource availability may be at the discretion of others, but they may impact the employee's ability to generate specific performance objectives. Third, results—taken by themselves—focus on the ends or outcomes while ignoring the means or processes by which the results were obtained. An employee might achieve targeted goals but do so in an unproductive way by incurring excessive costs, alienating coworkers, or damaging customer relations. Finally, results are limiting in that they fail to tap into some critical areas—such as teamwork, initiative, and openness to change—of performance for modern organizations. The need for organizations to remain flexible and responsive to change in their environments requires them to have internal processes to facilitate internal change. Results-based measures would ignore these processes.

As can be seen, all three types of performance measures have some limitations. However, the strengths of one approach can offset the limitations of the others. Nothing prevents an organization from utilizing any combination of traits, behaviors, and results-based measures in attempting to develop a performance feedback system that is in sync with the organization's strategic objectives. In short, the decision of what to evaluate is contingent upon what the organization seeks to achieve.

In addition to traits, behaviors, and outcomes, one area that employers are beginning to measure is the job performance competencies the employee displays. Competencies can often be closely tied to an organization's strategic objectives and therefore provide a more critical measure of performance—as well as more valuable feedback for employees in their careers. A competency-based performance management program can take a tremendous amount of time to establish, must be communicated clearly to employees, and should also tie in with the organization's reward structure. A recent survey conducted by the Society for Human Resource Management found that 69 percent of employers utilize organization-wide competency models and 61 percent have developed organization-wide competency models, which allow variation in competencies by job level.[10] Core competencies should be limited in number to those most central to the organization's success, and corresponding opportunities should be established by which employees can obtain and build on these competencies. Exhibit 10.5 presents a sample competency model for managers that cuts across organization size and industry.

Competency-Based Performance and Development at Capital One

Capital One, one of the world's fastest growing consumer credit companies, utilizes a competency-based performance management system, known as the Success Profile, which is designed to support the organization's strategy and long-term growth objectives. The Success Profile is designed to provide specific measurable performance feedback as well as to allow employees to plan their own professional development activities. The Success Profile contains 23 competencies that are seen as critical to the mission and objectives of Capital One. These competencies are grouped together into five access factors, as illustrated in Exhibit 10.6. Each competency is measured on a behavioral-based rating scale containing up to four stages. Employees receive detailed performance feedback and work with their managers to develop a personal development plan for the future.

EXHIBIT 10.5 — Multilevel Corporate Competency Model

Core Managerial Competencies

- Flexible and adaptive to change
- Able to cope with stress
- Customer service minded
- Open minded
- Team player
- Appreciate diversity
- Understand the "big picture"

Senior Manager Competencies

- Able to lead change
- Persuasive communicator
- Strategic initiator
- Delegate appropriately
- Able to develop others

Middle Manager Competencies

- Change implementer
- Creative thinker
- Strategic implementer
- Team builder
- Participation oriented
- Facilitator

Source: *Adapted from Elmer Burack, Wayne Hockwarter, and Nicholas Mathys, "The New Management Development Paradigm,"* 3rd *ed.,* Human Resource Planning, *Vol. 80(1), 1997, pp. 14–21.*

EXHIBIT 10.6 — Capital One Competencies

Success Factors	Competencies
Builds relationships	1 Communicates clearly and openly
	2 Treats others with respect
	3 Collaborates with others
Applies integrative thinking	4 Analyzes information
	5 Generates and pursues ideas
	6 Develops and shapes strategies
	7 Identifies and solves problems
	8 Applies integrated decision making
Drives toward results	9 Focuses on strategic priorities
	10 Organizes and manages multiple tasks
	11 Directs and coordinates work
	12 Gets the job done
Leads in a learning environment	13 Recruits talent
	14 Motivates and develops
	15 Builds and leads teams
	16 Influences others
	17 Promotes the culture

Success Factors	Competencies
Takes personal ownership	18 Takes responsibility
	19 Learns continuously
	20 Embraces change
	21 Initiates opportunities for improvement
	22 Shows integrity
	23 Maintains perspective

© Cengage Learning

How to Evaluate

The next strategic decision that must be addressed in designing the performance management system is how to assess employees. Performance feedback can be performed on an absolute or relative basis. Absolute measures evaluate employees strictly according to the performance requirements or standards of the job; relative measures evaluate employees in comparison to coworkers. Relative measures may further involve slotting employees into categories, such as the top 10 percent of the employees in the work unit receiving an overall outstanding evaluation, similar to what is known in education as grading on a curve.

Relative assessment of employees can be useful in allowing the organization to identify overall top performers, much as high schools provide class rank to their students to facilitate college and university assessments for admission. However, if performance is not normally distributed, skewed results can provide misleading data: If all employees are outstanding performers, some will still be ranked poorly. Conversely, if all employees are deficient in performance, some will still be ranked as outstanding. For example, in a classroom setting, assume that there are 30 students in a class and that on a midterm examination, all 30 students score 90 or above. If performance was ranked on a relative basis, a student who scored 90 would be ranked 30th out of 30, despite the fact that the student did "A" work in absolute means. Similarly, if on the final exam, the highest grade was a 55, that student would be ranked 1st out of 30, despite the fact that, on an absolute basis, the student failed the exam. Relative measures can easily facilitate distorted perceptions of performance when all employees are superior or deficient. Although they are useful in identifying the best employees, they should not be used without some supplementary absolute assessment and ratings that are specifically related to strategic objectives.

One popular—although controversial—means of relative assessment is forced ranking. Forced ranking, or forced distribution, involves placing employees into clusters or groupings based on a distribution schema. Forced ranking is premised on a social science theory that finds that human phenomena tend to distribute normally along a bell-shaped curve when measured by using sufficiently large samples.[11] Forced rankings ideally can help build a high-performance organization by ensuring that managers clearly distinguish among employee performance levels.

Forced ranking systems were pioneered by General Electric (GE) under former CEO Jack Welch. At GE, employees are sorted into three groups: the top 20 percent on whom rewards, promotions, and stock options are showered; the "high-performing" middle 70 percent with promising futures; and the bottom 10 percent, whose employment is terminated, either voluntarily or involuntarily.[12] Other large employers who use forced ranking systems include Cisco Systems, Hewlett-Packard, Microsoft, Sun Microsystems, and Pepsico.[13]

Those who favor forced ranking argue that it is the best way to identify both the highest-performing employees, who should receive generous incentives, and bottom performers, who should be helped up or out. It also provides data-driven bases for compensation decisions and forces managers to make and justify sometimes tough decisions and will not allow them to avoid giving employees needed feedback. Critics, however, argue that forced ranking can be arbitrary, unfair, and expose an organization to law suits.[14] Ford Motor Company abandoned its practice of forced rankings when it settled two class-action lawsuits for $10.5 million.[15] To avoid some of the inherent subjectivity that might come with the final rankings, some employers outsource the final distributions to outside consultants who are able to analyze trends and correct biases in final ratings.[16]

Forced rankings can also help to overcome some problems associated with inflated reviews as well as remedy the dilemma presented when a supervisor rates everyone on a "satisfactory" basis. Most performance management systems leave top performers feeling unrecognized and other employees upset that poor performers are not handled appropriately.[17] Forced ranking prevents these problems, particularly if the system involves measures to terminate consistently low-ranked employees.

While forced rankings may be controversial, they tend to be more effective in organizations with a high-pressure, results-driven culture.[18] Forced rankings are certainly not appropriate for every organization, but in concept, forced rankings are consistent with a strategic approach toward HR management because they emphasize differentiating employees by performance level and investing more resources in those human assets that have displayed the highest returns.

Measures of Evaluation

Another strategic decision that needs to be made in the design of the performance management system is the means of evaluation. There are a variety of tools or formats to use in measuring performance. These include graphic rating scales, weighted checklists, behaviorally anchored rating scales (BARS), behavioral observation scales (BOS), critical incident measures, and objectives-based measures.

Graphic rating scales are one of the most widely used assessment and feedback devices. Relatively easy to design, use, and update as job requirements change, they involve a scale that gives the evaluator the performance measures for traits, behaviors, or results. Some examples of graphic rating scales are illustrated in Exhibit 10.7.

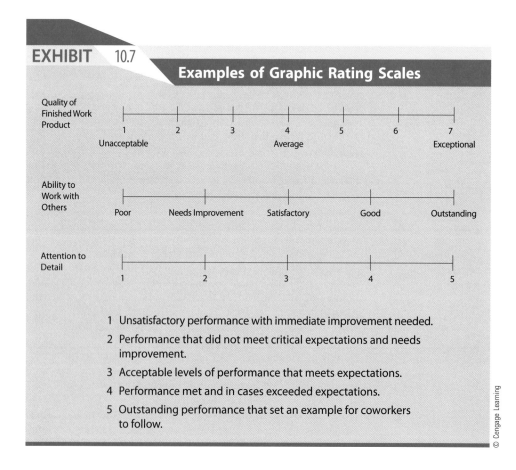

EXHIBIT 10.7 — Examples of Graphic Rating Scales

Quality of Finished Work Product

1 2 3 4 5 6 7
Unacceptable   Average   Exceptional

Ability to Work with Others

Poor   Needs Improvement   Satisfactory   Good   Outstanding

Attention to Detail

1   2   3   4   5

1 Unsatisfactory performance with immediate improvement needed.
2 Performance that did not meet critical expectations and needs improvement.
3 Acceptable levels of performance that meets expectations.
4 Performance met and in cases exceeded expectations.
5 Outstanding performance that set an example for coworkers to follow.

© Cengage Learning

EXHIBIT 10.8

Example of a Weighted Checklist

Instructions: Check all those qualities that are accurate assessments of the employee's performance.

	Weight
_____ Is able to address routine day-to-day problems effectively.	4.2
_____ Maintains cordial and productive relationships with coworkers.	3.7
_____ Displays the ability to delegate effectively and develop subordinates.	4.1
_____ Works well without direct supervision.	5.1
_____ Is able to meet deadlines and follow through on commitments.	4.8
_____ Engages in appropriate activity to further individual career development.	2.9
_____ Adheres to rules, procedures, and standard operating protocols.	3.4

Note: *The weights are not included on the actual rating form that the evaluator completes. Higher values indicate more critical requirements for the job.*

© Cengage Learning

Weighted checklists provide the evaluator with specific criteria on which performance is to be assessed and ask the evaluator to check those criteria that apply to the employee. The different dimensions are weighted based on their importance to the organization; weights are unknown to the evaluator as the checklist is being completed. A sample weighted checklist is presented in Exhibit 10.8.

A BARS is a more specific type of graphic rating scale. The evaluator is given specific descriptions of behaviors along a numerically rated scale and is asked to select the behavior that most corresponds to the employee's performance for the time period being evaluated. A BARS can be difficult and time consuming to develop, but it can help to overcome some of the subjectivity and biases that may result when evaluators are given no set descriptions for performance measures. A sample BARS is presented in Exhibit 10.9.

A potential problem with a BARS may be that an employee's behavior is inconsistent. Sometimes, the employee might merit a 6 on a scale of 1–7; at other times, performance would be closer to 2. A BOS addresses the problem of inconsistent employee performance by measuring frequencies along the scale. Instead of providing examples of different behaviors as would be presented in a BARS, a BOS determines which behavior of a BARS is optimal and asks for an assessment of the frequency with which the employee displays it. A sample BOS is presented in Exhibit 10.10.

Critical incident measures do not generally utilize a scale. The evaluator provides specific examples of the employee's critical behaviors or results—either outstanding or problematic—during the performance period. The evaluator must maintain a log or diary for each employee and make periodic notation of noteworthy behaviors or results that were particularly effective or ineffective. This process can be very time consuming, but it allows the feedback to cite specific examples of performance measures instead of general impressions. Feedback that is specific and directed is not only more meaningful to the employee, but it can also be targeted to specific objectives of the work unit or organization. The critical incident technique can be utilized by itself or incorporated into a rating scale where space is provided for open-ended comments by the evaluator.

A final way to assess performance is to base feedback on predetermined, negotiated work objectives. Traditionally called *management by objectives* (MBO), this process involves having the employee meet with his or her immediate supervisor prior to the time period for which

EXHIBIT   10.9

Example of a Behaviorally Anchored Rating Scale

Position: _____

Job Dimension: _____

Plans work and organizes time carefully in order to maximize resources and meet commitments.	9	
	8	Even though this associate has a report due on another project, he or she would be well prepared for the assigned discussion on your project.
	7	This associate would keep a calendar or schedule on which deadlines and activities are carefully noted and which would be consulted before making new commitments.
	6	As program chief, this associate would manage arrangements for enlisting resources for a special project reasonably well but would probably omit one or two details that would have to be handled by improvization.
Plans and organizes time and effort primarily for large segments of a task. Usually meets commitments but may overlook what are considered secondary details.	5	This associate would meet a deadline in handing in a report, but the report might be below the usual standard if other deadlines occur on the same day the report is due.
	4	This associate's evaluations are likely not to reflect abilities because of over-commitments in other activities.
	3	This associate would plan more by enthusiasm than by timetable and frequently have to work late through the night before an assignment is due, although it would be completed on time.
	2	This associate would often be late for meetings, although others in similar circumstances do not seem to find it difficult to be on time.
Appears to do little planning. May perform effectively, despite what seems to be a disorganized approach, although deadlines may be missed.	1	This associate never makes a deadline, even with sufficient notice.

Source: *Anthony, W. P. et al. Human Resource Management, 3rd ed., Dryden, 1999, p. 389.*

performance is to be assessed. The two parties jointly agree on the employee's work objectives for the forthcoming time period. The process of negotiation is important here. Ideally, this process involves setting objectives that are simultaneously consistent with the organization's strategy and satisfy job requirements and also provide challenging work assignments that are consistent with the employee's developmental needs and career aspirations.

Objectives-based performance management systems are based on a goal-setting theory, which was pioneered by Edwin Locke.[19] Goal-setting theory assumes that motivation is enhanced when individuals work toward a specific, targeted goal or goals and also receive feedback as to their progress toward reaching their goals.[20] Even though objectives are determined for a set time

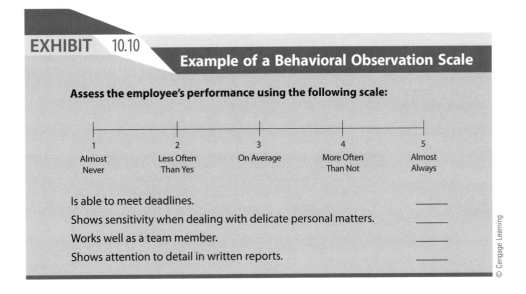

EXHIBIT 10.10

Example of a Behavioral Observation Scale

Assess the employee's performance using the following scale:

1	2	3	4	5
Almost Never	Less Often Than Yes	On Average	More Often Than Not	Almost Always

Is able to meet deadlines. _____

Shows sensitivity when dealing with delicate personal matters. _____

Works well as a team member. _____

Shows attention to detail in written reports. _____

© Cengage Learning

period, commonly six months or one year, this does not mean that performance feedback should be withheld until the end of the time period. Informal, regular feedback is more effective; particularly when it is provided immediately following some outcome or behavior, it has a far stronger and more constant impact on motivation than feedback that is only provided annually in a more formal manner.

Objectives-based performance measurement systems often result in enhanced employee motivation because employees are allowed to provide input in determining their job responsibilities and in discussing critical organizational goals to which they can contribute.[21] Employee commitment is also usually enhanced; employees can be expected to be far more committed to reaching performance objectives that they have agreed to and negotiated for themselves rather than having objectives determined for them by the organization.[22] When an employee participates in this process, the employee's trust and dependability are placed on the line. Nonperformance cannot be as readily dismissed through claims that the supervisor does not understand the job or the pressures inherently involved with it or that the objectives set were therefore unrealistic.

Three common oversights can inhibit the effectiveness of any objectives-based feedback system. These oversights are (1) setting objectives that are too vague, (2) setting objectives that are unrealistically difficult, and (3) not clarifying how performance will be measured, particularly when the objective itself is not quantifiable and requires some subjectivity in evaluation. Any objectives set as part of such a process must be specific, measurable, and within the employee's control if the feedback system is to be beneficial to the organization and to the employee. Objectives also need to be challenging yet obtainable. Unrealistic goals may hamper motivation; supervisors need to have faith in their employees' abilities yet realize where to draw the line. When the objectives are set, the parties must also reach agreement as to how the performance criteria will be measured and assessed. This is particularly important when there are no objective measures available for assessing performance.

The objectives selected must also be valid. Much as selection measures need to be valid, objective performance measures must also be valid. Occasionally, inappropriate objective measures may be selected. These measures may be easily quantifiable and accurately measurable but not directly related to performance. For example, a teacher could be evaluated on the test scores of students. Although this is an objective measure, it might encourage the teacher to teach students to maximize test scores rather than learn. A salesperson could similarly be evaluated on sales volume, which is easily measurable, but not get evaluated on expenses incurred, customer service, returns, or professional demeanor. Most employees will focus on the behavior or outcome that is evaluated and rewarded at the expense of other elements of the job.[23]

These various means of measuring performance are not mutually exclusive. Nothing prevents an organization from using some combination of methods. However, it should be remembered that much like the decision of who should provide performance feedback, more is not necessarily better. Organizations need to ensure that the methods employed in measuring performance are not cumbersome, contradictory, or excessively laborious. The methods of providing performance data must be consistent with the uses of the system and the organization's strategic objectives.

Other Considerations

In addition to the five strategic design decisions previously outlined, several other critical factors must be considered when developing an effective performance management system. First, the organization needs to ensure the link between the performance management system and the training and development and compensation systems. This link was explained in Chapter 9, but it bears reiteration here. Training and development goals and objectives must be reflected in performance feedback systems. Subsequently, the criteria by which performance is evaluated must be incorporated into the compensation or reward system. If either of these two links is not established and maintained, the performance management system will be of limited value. The performance management system lies within the much larger framework of HR management systems and must be conceptualized and designed with this strategic perspective in mind.

Traditional performance evaluation systems stress the most recent, immediate time period and evaluate individual employee performance. However, many organizations have strategic initiatives that involve long-range planning and growth, requiring the use of criteria that cannot be measured based on performance during the immediate past time period. In addition, many organizations are moving toward more flexible job assignments and responsibilities. Organizations having self-managed work teams place more responsibility for performance on the group rather than at the individual level. Traditional means of performance evaluation may need to be significantly recast in the light of changes taking place in contemporary organizations. There are few, if any, models of evaluation systems that can assess work responsibilities associated with longer range objectives or team-based evaluation. Reading 10.2, "Managing the Life Cycle of Virtual Teams," provides some insights as to how teams—specifically increasingly popular virtual teams—function and the implications that team life cycle stages have for the management of team performance.

A final consideration is the degree of standardization or flexibility of the performance management system. Standardization is important to prevent job bias or allegations of discriminatory treatment. Flexibility in the system is important because jobs have different levels of responsibility and accountability and require different types and mixes of skills (technical, interpersonal, or administrative). Organizations need to strike a balance between having some consistency (standardization) and some variance (flexibility) in their performance feedback systems. The single most important criterion in addressing this issue is the nature of the job responsibilities assigned to the employee. Specific job-related criteria are not only most meaningful for feedback and developmental purposes but are also most defendable under the law. This does not imply that each individual job should have a unique means and method for measuring performance. That is clearly impractical and unrealistic. It does mean, however, that there is no one appropriate way to develop a performance management system in any organization; the system must be tailored to the objectives of the organization.

Why Performance Management Systems Often Fail

Despite the importance of performance management systems, many managers and executives are not committed to providing performance feedback. The process is often seen as time consuming and cumbersome and can make managers uncomfortable. This dissatisfaction is also seen in the

HR suite. One survey of HR directors and executives found that 90 percent felt that their performance management system needed reform.[24] Another survey of employees found that 87 percent of employees and 94 percent of chief executives felt that their organization's performance review process was ineffective.[25] Exhibit 10.11 outlines some of the reasons managers may resist—or totally ignore—performance management processes.

First, many managers are disheartened by the complexity of the process. Performance data may be subject to multiple levels of review and/or require the collection of large amounts of data that must be analyzed and condensed. A system that requires the collection of data from multiple individuals may further require that contradictory and/or inconsistent feedback be reconciled. Second, unless the performance management process involves some planning by which managers and subordinates use the performance data to set clear goals for future performance, there may be little, if any, impact on subsequent job performance. An ideal performance management system connects data about recent past performance to future plans that incorporate the employee's career goals and the strategic goals of the organization and/or unit. Third, when salary, promotion, and retention decisions are made based on performance management data, claims of unlawful discrimination may be made by employees who did not feel appropriately rewarded. The inherently subjective nature of performance management data fuels this possibility and, as a result, may cause organizations to limit the performance feedback given and/or how such feedback is used. Fourth, many managers feel that they have little control over the process by which they manage their subordinates' performance. When standards related to expectations of the end results are set by senior management, managers may feel that the process is less than legitimate. Fifth, employees and managers alike lament the fact that many performance management systems are totally divorced from the organization's reward system. If there are no consequences, results, or outcomes from the performance management process, it most likely will be short changed and not taken seriously by those at all levels in the organization. Finally, the forms and paperwork that often accompany the performance management system can be lengthy and complex. A process that takes managers away from their day-to-day responsibilities for an unduly long time may result in them looking for shortcuts that compromise the efficacy and integrity of the overall process.

Addressing the Shortcomings of Performance Management Systems

The challenge then becomes how to get buy-in from managers to improve the performance management system. Exhibit 10.12 highlights some strategies for addressing some of the managerial reluctance or resistance to fully commit to performance management. First, managers should be involved in the design of the system. Because they are its true users, their input as "consumers" should be sought to facilitate the design of a system that works both for them and the

---

EXHIBIT   10.11

Reasons Managers Resist or Ignore Performance Management

- Process is too complicated
- No impact on job performance
- Possible legal challenges
- Lack of control over process
- No connection with rewards
- Complexity and length of forms

Source: *Adapted from Grensing-Pophal, L "Motivate Managers to Review Performance"* HR Magazine, *March 2001, pp. 45–48.*

EXHIBIT 10.12 — Strategies for Improving the Performance Management System

- Involve managers in the design of the system
- Hold managers accountable for the performance and development of their subordinates
- Set clear expectations for performance
- Set specific objectives for the system
- Tie performance measures to rewards
- Gain commitment from senior management

© Cengage Learning

organization. Second, managers should be held accountable for the performance of their subordinates as well as for the development of their direct reports. By tying managers' performance in meeting organization and divisional goals to their effective use of the performance management system, managers are more likely to take the system seriously. Third, clear expectations should be set for individual performance at all levels of performance review to facilitate a timely review of recent performance data and allow more specific feedback to be provided to employees. Fourth, the organization should identify the specific purpose and goals of its performance management system. Clarification of the relationship of the system to the organization's strategy makes the system more salient and relevant to organizational participants and further legitimizes the entire process. Fifth, performance measures should be clearly linked to rewards, solidifying the legitimacy of the system. Finally, absolute commitment to the performance management system needs to be gained from top management. One recent survey found that at the executive level, 42 percent of executives do not even review the performance management system at all.[26] When senior managers publicly support and personally use the performance management system, a strong message is sent regarding its importance to all employees. Commitment of top management to the process of performance management as well as to the specific process used by the organization sends a strong message to employees and influences a performance-based culture.

Conclusion

Performance management systems can significantly impact organizational performance and processes. However, there is no single optimal way to develop and design an effective performance management system. Organizations face a number of strategic choices as to how they measure performance and provide employees feedback on the process.

Although effective performance management systems need to be developed within the context of specific organizational contingencies, five critical guidelines should be followed in any performance management system: (1) Any feedback provided to employees should be specific rather than general; (2) feedback should only be provided from credible, trustworthy sources that have ample opportunity and background to make an assessment of performance; (3) feedback should be provided as soon as possible after events, behaviors, or outcomes take place to be of maximum benefit; (4) performance measures should be based on clear, measurable goals; and (5) the process should involve a dialogue between the employee and the manager that addresses the most recent period and also plans for the future.

Critical Thinking

1. Identify the major strategic issues an employer faces in designing a performance management system.

2. What are the major purposes of a performance management system? To what extent can all the purposes be realized simultaneously?

3. What are the advantages and disadvantages of 360-degree feedback systems? How should an organization decide whose feedback to seek?

4. Describe the strengths and weaknesses of traits, behaviors, and outcomes-based measurements. For what kinds of positions is each appropriate?

5. Do performance management systems usually measure the right things? How can performance management systems encourage performance that is more consistent with long-range rather than short-term issues?

6. Devise an appropriate performance management system for your current position.

7. Debate the pros and cons of forced rankings. What kinds of organizations would most benefit from forced ranking systems?

8. How does performance appraisal differ from performance feedback?

Reading 10.1

9. What are the most critical behaviors related to leadership? Are these behaviors equally important in all organizations or do certain industries or types of organizations need certain types of leaders?

Reading 10.2

10. What are the stages of a virtual team's life cycle, and what performance issues arise during the life cycle stages?

Exercises

1. Individually or in small groups, select one occupation from the following list and then design a performance management system for this position.
   - University professor
   - Convenience store clerk
   - Attorney
   - Marriage counselor
   - Software engineer
   - Clergy member

2. Develop a competency-based performance management system for a student in the degree program in which you are enrolled. How would you go about determining and measuring important competencies? What benefits might such a system provide?

3. In an organization of your choosing, briefly interview three managers who work in different divisions/departments/units and are at different levels of managerial responsibility. How does each feel about performance management in the organization?

4. This chapter contained a description of a 360-degree performance management system at Otis Elevator that is administered electronically. What are the pros and cons of an intranet-based performance management system compared to a paper-based system? Investigate the costs of moving a traditional, paper-based performance management system to an online system in economic, technical, and human terms.

Chapter References

1. Miller, S. "Integrating Performance Management and Rewards at Microsoft," *Society for Human Resource Management*. Available at http://www.shrm.org/hrdisciplines/compensation/articles/pages/rewardsatmicrosoft.aspx, May 25, 2012.

2. SHRM Poll: "Performance Management and Other Workplace Practices," *Society for Human Resource Management*, December 15, 2011.

3. Johnson, C. "Making Sure Employees Measure Up," *HR Magazine*, March 2001, 46, (3), pp. 36–41.

4. http://www.shrm.org/HRStandards/Documents/Performance%20Management%20ANS%20(2012).pdf

5. Janove, J. "Reviews—Good for Anything?" *HR Magazine*, June 2011, 56, (6), pp. 121–126.

6. Carson, K. P., Cardy, R. L. and Dobbins, G. H. "Performance Appraisal as Effective Management or Deadly Management Disease: Two Empirical Investigations," *Group and Organization Studies*, 16, 1991, pp. 143–159.

7. Silverman, R. E. "My Colleagues, My Paymaster," *Wall Street Journal*, April 3, 2012. Available at http://online.wsj.com/article/SB100014240527023047504045773220311128520506.html

8. Grote, D. *Forced Ranking*, Boston, MA: Harvard Business School Press, 2005.

9. Pfau, B. and Kay, I. "Does 360-Degree Feedback Negatively Affect Company Performance" *HR Magazine*, June 2002, 47, (6), pp. 55–59.

10. SHRM Poll: "Performance Management and Other Workplace Practices," *Society for Human Resource Management*, December 15, 2011.

11. Guralnik, O. and Wardi, L. "Forced Distribution: A Controversy," www.shrm.org/research/articles/articles/pages/CMS_005247.aspx. Society for Human Resource Management White Paper, August 2003.

12. Grote, D. "Are Most Layoffs Carried Out Fairly? Yes," available at www.mbadepot.com/content/2756.

13. Ibid.

14. Guralnik, O. and Wardi, L. "Forced Distribution: A Controversy," available at www.shrm.org/research/articles/articles/pages/CMS_005247.aspx. August 2003

15. Bates, S. "Forced Ranking," *HR Magazine*, July 2003, 48, (7), pp. 63–68.

16. Guralnik, O. and Wardi, L. "Forced Distribution: A Controversy," available at www.shrm.org/research/articles/articles/pages/CMS_005247.aspx. August 2003

17. Grote, D. *Forced Ranking*, Boston, MA: Harvard Business School Press, 2005.

18. Bates, S. "Forced Ranking," *HR Magazine*, July 2003, 48, (7), pp. 63–68.

19. Locke, E. "Toward a Theory of Task Moves and Incentives," *Organizational Behavior and Human Performance*, 3, 1968, pp. 157–189.

20. Pinder, C. *Work Motivation*, Glenview, Illinois: Scott Foresman, 1984.

21. Ibid.

22. Ibid.

23. Kerr. S. "On the Folly of Rewarding A, While Hoping for B," *Academy of Management Journal*, 18, 1975, pp. 766–783.

24. Grensing-Pophal, L. "Motivate Managers to Review Performance," *HR Magazine*, May 2001, 46, (5), pp. 45–48.

25. Janove, J., 2011, op. cit.

26. "Performance Management Gaps Need Filled, Survey Says," *HR News*, November 2000, pp. 14, 21.

READING 10.1

Effective Leadership Behavior: What We Know and What Questions Need More Attention

Gary Yukl

Executive Overview

Extensive research on leadership behavior during the past half century has yielded many different behavior taxonomies and a lack of clear results about effective behaviors. One purpose of this article is to describe what has been learned about effective leadership behavior in organizations. A hierarchical taxonomy with four meta-categories and 15 specific component behaviors was used to interpret results in the diverse and extensive literature and to identify conditions that influence the effectiveness of these behaviors. Limitations and potential extensions of the hierarchical taxonomy are discussed, and suggestions for improving research on effective leadership behavior are provided.

The essence of leadership in organizations is influencing and facilitating individual and collective efforts to accomplish shared objectives. Leaders can improve the performance of a team or organization by influencing the processes that determine performance. An important objective in much of the leadership research has been to identify aspects of behavior that explain leader influence on the performance of a team, work unit, or organization. To be highly useful for designing research and formulating theories, leader behavior categories should be observable, distinct, measurable, and relevant for many types of leaders, and taxonomies of leader behaviors should be comprehensive but parsimonious.

Thousands of studies on leader behavior and its effects have been conducted over the past half century, but the bewildering variety of behavior constructs used for this research makes it difficult to compare and integrate the findings (Bass, 2008; Yukl, in press). The behavior taxonomies guiding past research have substantial differences in the number and type of behaviors they include. Some taxonomies have only a few broadly defined behavior meta-categories, whereas other taxonomies have a larger number of narrowly defined behavior categories. Some taxonomies are intended to cover the full range of leader behaviors, whereas others include only the behaviors identified in a particular leadership theory. Some taxonomies describe leader behaviors used to motivate individual subordinates, whereas other taxonomies describe behaviors used to lead groups or organizations. Some taxonomies include other types of constructs along with behaviors, such as leader roles, skills, and values. Additional confusion is created by lack of consistency in the use of category labels. Sometimes different terms are used to refer to the same type of behavior, and sometimes the same term is used for different forms of behavior.

The primary purpose of this article is to review what has been learned about effective leadership behavior from research conducted over more than half a century. To integrate results from a large number of studies with many different ways of classifying and measuring leadership behavior, it was first necessary to develop a comprehensive behavior taxonomy. The article begins by describing how decades of behavior research provides the basis for a hierarchical taxonomy with four broad meta-categories and 15 specific component behaviors. Next is a brief overview of research on the effects of widely used behavior categories, followed by a more detailed description of what has been learned about the relevance of each specific behavior in the hierarchical taxonomy. Several conditions that influence the effects of the behaviors are described, and the need for more research on them is explained. The article ends with a summary and suggestions for improving future research.

Research on Behavior Taxonomies

The method used most often to identify categories of leadership behavior is factor analysis of behavior description questionnaires. This method is most useful when clear, relevant items are selected for the initial questionnaire and respondents are able to remember the leader's past behavior and provide accurate ratings. Unfortunately, the selection of behavior items for a questionnaire is usually influenced by preconceptions about effective leadership or the desire to develop a measure of key behaviors in a leadership theory. The sample of respondents is seldom systematic, and the accuracy of most behavior questionnaires is seriously reduced by respondent biases and attributions. Finally, the basic assumptions of factor analysis (high correlation among examples from the same category) do not apply very well when a behavior category includes several alternative ways to achieve the same objective and a leader needs to use only one or two of them. The limitations of this method may help to explain the substantial differences among leader behavior taxonomies.

Another common method for identifying distinct behavior categories is to have subject matter experts sort behavior descriptions into categories based on similarity of purpose and content, but this method also has limitations. The selection of categories may be biased by prior assumptions and implicit leadership theories, and disagreements among subject matter experts are not easily resolved. A behavior taxonomy is more likely to be useful if it is based on multiple methods and is supported by research on the antecedents and outcomes of the behaviors.

From 1950 to 1980 most of the research on leadership behavior was focused on explaining how leaders influence the attitudes and performance of individual subordinates. In the early survey research, factor analysis of leadership behavior questionnaires found support for two broadly defined behavior categories involving task-oriented and relations-oriented behaviors. Different labels were used for these meta-categories, including initiating structure and consideration (Fleishman, 1953; Halpin & Winer, 1957), production-centered and employee-centered leadership (Likert, 1961), instrumental and supportive leadership (House, 1971), and performance and maintenance behavior (Misumi & Peterson, 1985). The specific behaviors defining the two meta-categories varied somewhat from one taxonomy to another, and some relevant behaviors were not adequately represented in any of these taxonomies. Finding the two meta-categories was a good start, but researchers failed to conduct systematic follow-up research to build on the initial discoveries.

Leadership behaviors directly concerned with encouraging and facilitating change did not get much attention in the early leadership research. Change behaviors are more relevant for executives than for the low-level leaders studied in much of the early research, and they are more important for the dynamic, uncertain environments that have become so common for organizations in recent decades. In the 1980s one or two specific change-oriented behaviors were included in questionnaires used to measure charismatic and transformational leadership, but leading change was still not explicitly recognized as a distinct meta-category. Researchers in Sweden and the United States (Ekvall & Arvonen, 1991; Yukl, 1999; Yukl, Gordon, & Taber, 2002) eventually found evidence for the construct validity of a leading-change meta-category. The classification of change-oriented behavior as a distinct and meaningful meta-category provided important new insights about effective leadership.

In most of the early research on leadership behavior the focus was on describing how leaders influence subordinates and internal activities in the work unit. Leader behavior descriptions were usually obtained from subordinates who had little opportunity to observe their leaders interacting with people outside the work unit. Thus, it is not surprising that few leadership studies examined external ("boundary-spanning") behavior, and only a few leader behavior taxonomies included any external behaviors (e.g., Stogdill, Goode, & Day, 1962). However, in the late 1970s and early 1980s, descriptive research on managers found that it is important to influence bosses, peers, and outsiders as well as subordinates (Kaplan, 1984; Kotter, 1982; Mintzberg, 1973), and later research on teams found that boundary-spanning behavior is important for effective team performance (e.g., Ancona & Caldwell, 1992; Joshi, Pandey, & Han, 2009; Marrone, 2010). The importance and uniqueness of external leadership behavior provides justification for classifying it as a separate meta-category.

Hierarchical Behavior Taxonomy

The hierarchical taxonomy proposed in this article describes leadership behaviors used to influence the performance of a team, work unit, or organization. The four meta-categories and their component behaviors are shown in Table 1. Each meta-category has a different primary objective, but the objectives all involve determinants of performance. For task-oriented behavior the primary objective is to accomplish work in an efficient and reliable way. For relations-oriented behavior the primary objective is to increase the quality of human resources and relations, which is sometimes called "human capital." For change-oriented behavior the primary objectives are to increase innovation, collective learning, and adaptation to the external environment. For external leadership behavior the primary objectives are to acquire necessary information and resources, and to promote and defend the interests of the team or organization. In addition to these differences in primary objectives, each meta-category includes unique specific behaviors for achieving the objectives. The relevance of each component behavior depends on aspects of the situation, and the effect is not always positive for the primary objective or for other outcomes.

The proposed taxonomy builds on the extensive factor analysis research by Yukl and colleagues (2002), and it also reflects findings in other taxonomic research linking specific behaviors to the performance of a team or organization. The three meta-categories in the Yukl and colleagues (2002) taxonomy were retained, but another component on

Table 1

Hierarchical Taxonomy of Leadership Behaviors

Task-oriented	Clarifying
	Planning
	Monitoring operations
	Problem solving
Relations-oriented	Supporting
	Developing
	Recognizing
	Empowering
Change-oriented	Advocating change
	Envisioning change
	Encouraging innovation
	Facilitating collective learning
External	Networking
	External monitoring
	Representing

research conducted from 1960 to 1980. Reviews and meta-analyses of results from hundreds of studies concluded that both meta-categories are related to independent measures of leadership effectiveness (DeRue, Nahrgang, Wellman, & Humphrey, 2011; Judge, Piccolo, & Ilies, 2004).

Since the 1980s, much of the research on the effects of leadership behavior has been based on theories of transformational and charismatic leadership (Avolio, Bass, & Jung, 1999; Bass, 1985; Conger & Kanungo, 1987; House, 1977; Shamir, House, & Arthur, 1993). As in the earlier research, most of these studies reported results only for composite scores on behavior meta-categories included in the theory. Reviews and meta-analyses of this research found that transformational leadership was related to indicators of leadership effectiveness in a majority of studies, but results were inconsistent for transactional leadership and charismatic leadership (De Groot, Kiker, & Cross, 2000; Judge & Piccolo, 2004; Lowe, Kroeck, & Sivasubramaniam, 1996; Wang, Oh, Courtright, & Colbert, 2011; Yukl, 2013).

The research on effects of broadly defined behaviors has limitations that make the results difficult to interpret. The limitations include differences in the way behavior is defined and measured from study to study, use of composite scores based on diverse component behaviors that do not have the same effects, the exclusion of other relevant behaviors likely to be confounded with the measured behaviors, and over-reliance on weak research methods such as same-source survey studies. The results found for independent measures of leadership effectiveness were much weaker than results found for same-source measures, especially when objective performance measures were used (Burke et al., 2006; Kaiser, Hogan, & Craig, 2008).

The popularity of survey research on meta-categories may have inhibited research on effects of specific behaviors, because the number of studies on them is much smaller. The research on effects of specific leadership behaviors included several types of studies. Some studies used a behavior description questionnaire, but other studies used behavior descriptions from observation, diaries, or critical incidents. Several multiple-case studies used interviews, records, and other data collection methods to investigate how leader decisions and actions influenced performance for a team or organization, and the behavior of effective and ineffective leaders was usually compared. A few studies used laboratory or field experiments in which leader behavior was manipulated to assess the effects on subordinate performance. The findings in this research provide evidence that each of the 15 specific behaviors in the proposed taxonomy is relevant for effective leadership.

task-oriented behavior (problem solving) was added, consulting and delegating were combined into a broader relations-oriented component (empowering), and taking risks to promote change was included in a broader change-oriented component (advocating change). The new taxonomy also includes a fourth meta-category (external behavior). Two of the component behaviors (networking and representing) were not included in the questionnaire used for the Yukl and colleagues (2002) research, and the third component (external monitoring) was in their questionnaire but it was included in the change-oriented meta-category.

Overview of Research on Effects of Leader Behavior

Much of the research on effects of leader behavior has been guided by popular leadership theories that emphasized one or two broadly defined behaviors. Early leadership theories such as path-goal theory (House, 1971), leadership substitutes theory (Kerr & Jermier, 1978), situational leadership theory (Hersey & Blanchard, 1977), and the managerial grid (Blake & Mouton, 1964) emphasized task-oriented and relations-oriented behavior, and these meta-categories were used in much of the

Effectiveness of Specific Leader Behaviors

In this section, the relevance of each specific component behavior is briefly explained, and the research linking it to effective leadership is cited. The research includes studies on dyadic, group, and organizational leadership. Most studies examined effects of behavior by individual leaders and included an independent source of information about leadership effectiveness, such as ratings by superiors or objective performance measures.

Task-Oriented Behaviors

As noted earlier, the primary purpose of task-oriented behaviors is to ensure that people, equipment, and other resources are used in an efficient way to accomplish the mission of a group or organization. Specific component behaviors include planning and organizing work-unit activities, clarifying roles and objectives, monitoring work-unit operations, and resolving work-related problems.

Planning This broadly defined behavior includes making decisions about objectives and priorities, organizing work, assigning responsibilities, scheduling activities, and allocating resources among different activities. More specifically, activity planning involves scheduling activities and assigning tasks in a way that will accomplish task objectives and avoid delays, duplication of effort, and wasted resources. Project planning includes identifying essential action steps; determining an appropriate sequence and schedule for them; deciding who should do each action step; and determining what supplies, equipment, and other resources are necessary. The planning often requires information provided by other people such as subordinates, peers, bosses, and outsiders. Negative forms of this behavior include making plans that are superficial or unrealistic. Several types of research provide evidence that planning can enhance a leader's effectiveness, including survey studies (e.g., Kim & Yukl, 1995; Shipper, 1991; Shipper & Dillard, 2000; Shipper & Wilson, 1992; Yukl, Wall, & Lepsinger, 1990), incident and diary studies (e.g., Ancona & Caldwell, 1992; Morse & Wagner, 1978; Yukl & Van Fleet, 1982), and multiple-case studies (e.g., Kotter, 1982; Van Fleet & Yukl, 1986).

Clarifying Leaders use clarifying to ensure that people understand what to do, how to do it, and the expected results. Clarifying includes explaining work responsibilities; assigning tasks; communicating objectives, priorities, and deadlines; setting performance standards; and explaining any relevant rules, policies, and standard procedures. Setting clear, specific, and challenging but realistic goals usually improves performance by a group (Locke & Latham, 1990). Negative forms of clarifying include failing to provide clear assignments, setting vague or easy goals, providing inconsistent instructions that create role ambiguity, and giving excessively detailed directions (micromanaging). Evidence that clarifying can enhance leadership effectiveness is provided by survey studies (e.g., Kim & Yukl, 1995; Shipper, 1991; Shipper & Dillard, 2000; Shipper & Wilson, 1992; Yukl & Kanuk,

1979; Yukl et al., 1990), incident and diary studies (e.g., Amabile, Schatzel, Moneta, & Kramer, 2004; Yukl & Van Fleet, 1982), comparative case studies (e.g., Van Fleet & Yukl, 1986), an executive team simulation study (Zalatan, 2005), a laboratory experiment (Kirkpatrick & Locke, 1996), and field experiments (Latham & Baldes, 1975; Latham & Yukl, 1976).

Monitoring Leaders use monitoring to assess whether people are carrying out their assigned tasks, the work is progressing as planned, and tasks are being performed adequately. Information gathered from monitoring is used to identify problems and opportunities and to determine if changes are needed in plans and procedures. Information from monitoring can also be used to guide the use of relations-oriented behaviors such as praise or coaching. There are many different ways to monitor operations, including directly observing activities, examining recorded activities or communications, using information systems, examining required reports, and holding performance review sessions. Negative examples include types of monitoring that are intrusive, excessive, superficial, or irrelevant. Evidence that monitoring can improve leadership effectiveness is provided by survey studies (e.g., Kim & Yukl, 1995; Wang, Tsui, & Xin, 2011; Yukl et al., 1990), studies using direct observation or diaries (e.g., Amabile et al., 2004; Brewer, Wilson, & Beck, 1994; Komaki, 1986), comparative case studies (e.g., Peters & Austin, 1975; Van Fleet & Yukl, 1986), and a laboratory experiment (Larson & Callahan, 1990).

Problem Solving Leaders use problem solving to deal with disruptions of normal operations and member behavior that is illegal, destructive, or unsafe. Serious disruptions of the work usually require leadership intervention, and other terms for problem solving include "crisis management" and "disturbance handling." Effective leaders try to quickly identify the cause of the problem, and they provide firm, confident direction to their team or work unit as they cope with the problem. It is important to recognize the difference between operational problems that can be resolved quickly and complex problems likely to require change-oriented behaviors and involvement by other leaders. Problem solving also includes disciplinary actions in response to destructive, dangerous, or illegal behavior by members of the work unit (e.g., theft, sabotage, violation of safety regulations, falsification of records). Problem solving can be proactive as well as reactive, and effective leaders take the initiative to identify likely problems and determine how to avoid them or minimize their adverse effects. Many things can be done to prepare the work unit or organization to respond effectively to predictable types of disruptions such as accidents, equipment failures, natural disasters, health emergencies, supply shortages, computer hacking, and terrorist attacks. Negative forms of problem solving include ignoring signs of a serious problem, making a hasty response before identifying the cause of the problem, discouraging useful input from subordinates, and reacting in ways that create more serious problems. Evidence that problem solving is related to leadership effectiveness is provided by survey studies (e.g., Kim & Yukl, 1995; Morgeson, 2005; Yukl & Van Fleet, 1982; Yukl et al., 1990), studies using critical incidents or diaries (e.g., Amabile et al., 2004; Boyatzis, 1982; Yukl & Van Fleet, 1982), and comparative case studies (e.g., Van Fleet & Yukl, 1986).

Relations-Oriented Behaviors

Leaders use relations-oriented behaviors to enhance member skills, the leader–member relationship, identification with the work unit or organization, and commitment to the mission. Specific component behaviors include supporting, developing, recognizing, and empowering.

Supporting Leaders use supporting to show positive regard, build cooperative relationships, and help people cope with stressful situations. Examples include showing concern for the needs and feelings of individual team members, listening carefully when a member is worried or upset, providing support and encouragement when there is a difficult or stressful task, and expressing confidence that someone can perform a difficult task. Supporting also includes encouraging cooperation and mutual trust and mediating conflicts among subordinates. A significant relationship between supporting and leadership effectiveness was found in survey studies (e.g., Dorfman, Howell, Cotton, & Tate, 1992; Kim & Yukl, 1995; McDonough & Barczak, 1991; Yukl & Van Fleet, 1982; Yukl et al., 1990), in studies using incidents or diaries (e.g., Amabile et al., 2004; Druskat & Wheeler, 2003; Yukl & Van Fleet, 1982), and in a laboratory experiment (Gilmore, Beehr, & Richter, 1979). Negative forms of supporting include hostile, abusive behavior. Research on abusive supervision finds that it reduces trust, elicits resentment, and invites retaliation (Mitchell & Ambrose, 2007; Tepper, 2000).

Developing Leaders use developing to increase the skills and confidence of work-unit members and to facilitate their career advancement. Examples of developing include providing helpful career advice, informing people about relevant training opportunities, making assignments that allow learning from experience, providing developmental coaching when it is needed, asking a group member to provide instruction to a new member, arranging practice sessions or simulations to help members improve their skills, and providing opportunities to apply new skills on the job. Developing is mostly done with a subordinate or team, but some aspects may be used with a colleague or an inexperienced new boss. A positive relationship between developing subordinate skills and indicators of leadership effectiveness was found in survey studies (e.g., Kim & Yukl, 1995; Yukl et al.,

1990), in research using critical incidents and interviews (e.g., Morse & Wagner, 1978), in comparative case studies (e.g., Bradford & Cohen, 1984; Edmondson, 2003b; Peters & Austin, 1985), and in an experiment (Tannenbaum, Smith-Jentsch, Salas, & Brannick, 1998).

Recognizing Leaders use praise and other forms of recognition to show appreciation to others for effective performance, significant achievements, and important contributions to the team or organization. Recognizing may involve an award presented in a ceremony, or the leader's recommendation for a tangible reward such as a pay increase or bonus. Effective leaders are proactive in looking for things that deserve recognition, and they provide recognition that is sincere, specific, and timely. Negative examples include providing excessive recognition for trivial achievements, failing to recognize an important contribution, and taking credit for another person's ideas or achievements. Evidence for the positive effects of praise and recognition on subordinate performance is provided by survey research (e.g., Kim & Yukl, 1995; Shipper, 1991; Shipper & Wilson, 1992; Yukl & Kanuk, 1979), research with incidents or diaries (e.g., Amabile et al., 2004; Atwater, Dionne, Avolio, Camobreco, & Lau, 1996), and descriptive case studies (e.g., Kouzes & Posner, 1987; Peters & Waterman, 1982). A field experiment found that increased use of praise by supervisors improved performance by employees (Wikoff, Anderson, & Crowell, 1983).

Empowering Leaders can empower subordinates by giving them more autonomy and influence over decisions about the work. One empowering decision procedure called consultation includes asking other people for ideas and suggestions and taking them into consideration when making a decision. An even stronger empowering decision procedure called delegation involves giving an individual or group the authority to make decisions formerly made by the leader. When used in appropriate ways, empowerment can increase decision quality, decision acceptance, job satisfaction, and skill development (Vroom & Yetton, 1973; Yukl, in press). Ineffective forms of the behavior include using the supposedly empowering decision procedures in a way that allows no real influence, and giving too much autonomy or influence to people who are unable or unwilling to make good decisions.

The term "participative leadership" is sometimes used to describe extensive use of empowering decision procedures, and many studies have assessed the effects on subordinate attitudes and performance. Meta-analyses of this research found a weak positive relationship with leadership effectiveness (e.g., Miller & Monge, 1986; Spector, 1986; Wagner & Gooding, 1987). Stronger evidence that specific empowering decision procedures are related to leadership effectiveness has been provided by survey studies that measured a leader's use of consultation and delegation (e.g., Kim & Yukl, 1995; Shipper & Wilson, 1992; Yukl et al., 1990), by research with critical incidents and diaries (e.g., Amabile and colleagues, 2004; Druskat & Wheeler, 2003), by comparative case studies (e.g., Bradford & Cohen, 1984; Edmondson, 2003b; Kanter, 1983; Leana, 1986), and by field experiments (Bragg & Andrews, 1973; Coch & French, 1948; Korsgaard, Schweiger, & Sapienza, 1995).

Change-Oriented Behaviors

Leaders use change-oriented behaviors to increase innovation, collective learning, and adaptation to external changes. Specific component behaviors include advocating change, articulating an inspiring vision, encouraging innovation, and encouraging collective learning. The first two component behaviors emphasize leader initiation and encouragement of change, whereas the second two component behaviors emphasize leader facilitation of emergent change processes.

Advocating Change Explaining why change is urgently needed is a key leadership behavior in theories of change management (e.g., Kotter, 1996; Nadler et al., 1995). When changes in the environment are gradual and no obvious crisis has occurred, people may fail to recognize emerging threats or opportunities. Leaders can provide information showing how similar work units or competitors have better performance. Leaders can explain the undesirable outcomes that are likely to occur if emerging problems are ignored or new opportunities are exploited by competitors. Influencing people to accept the need for change involves increasing their awareness of problems without creating an excessive level of distress that causes either denial of the problem or acceptance of easy but ineffective solutions (Heifetz, 1994). Resistance to change is common in organizations, and courage is required to persistently push for it when the leader's career is at risk. It is easier to gain support for making innovative changes when a leader can frame unfavorable events as an opportunity rather than a threat. The leader can propose a strategy for responding to a threat or opportunity, but involving people with relevant expertise usually results in a better strategy and more commitment to implement it. Negative forms of the behavior include advocating a costly major change when only incremental adjustments are necessary (McClelland, Liang, & Barker, 2009), or advocating acceptance of a costly new initiative without considering the serious risks and obstacles (Finkelstein, 2003). Evidence that advocating relevant change is related to effective leadership is provided by comparative case studies (e.g., Beer, 1988; Edmondson, 2003b; Heifetz, 1994; Kotter & Cohen, 2002; Tichy & Devanna, 1986) and by an experiment using a simulated team task (Marks, Zaccaro, & Mathieu, 2000).

Envisioning Change An effective way for leaders to build commitment to new strategies and initiatives is to articulate a clear, appealing vision of what can be attained by the work unit

or organization. A vision will be more inspiring and motivating if it is relevant to the values, ideals, and needs of followers and is communicated with colorful, emotional language (e.g., vivid imagery, metaphors, stories, symbols, and slogans). An ambitious, innovative vision is usually risky, and members of the team or organization are more likely to accept it if the leader can build confidence that they will be successful (Nadler, 1988). However, an appealing vision based on false assumptions and wishful thinking can divert attention from innovative solutions that are more likely to be successful (Mumford, Scott, Gaddis, & Strange, 2002). Consistently pursuing a risky and unrealistic vision is a major reason for serious performance declines in organizations with a charismatic leader (Finkelstein, 2003). Evidence that articulating an appealing and inspiring vision is relevant for effective leadership is provided by survey studies (e.g., Baum, Locke, & Kirkpatrick, 1998; Elenkov, Judge, & Wright, 2005; Keller, 2006; Kim & Yukl, 1995; Wang, Tsui, & Xin, 2011; Yukl et al., 1990), comparative case studies (e.g., Bennis & Nanus, 1985; Emrich, Brower, Feldman, & Garland, 2001; Kotter & Cohen, 2002; Roberts, 1985; Tichy & Devanna, 1986), and laboratory experiments (e.g., Awamleh & Gardner, 1999; Kirkpatrick & Locke, 1996).

Encouraging Innovation There are many ways leaders can encourage, nurture, and facilitate creative ideas and innovation in a team or organization. Other terms that describe aspects of this behavior include "intellectual stimulation" and "encouraging innovative thinking." Leaders can encourage people to look at problems from different perspectives, to think outside the box when solving problems, to experiment with new ideas, and to find ideas in other fields that can be applied to their current problem or task. By creating a climate of psychological safety and mutual trust, a leader can encourage members of the team or organization to suggest novel ideas. Leaders can also help to create an organizational culture that values creativity and entrepreneurial activities, they can provide opportunities and resources to develop new products or services, and they can serve as champions or sponsors for acceptance of innovative proposals. Evidence linking this type of change behavior to indicators of effective leadership is provided by survey studies (e.g., Bass & Yammarino, 1991; Elenkov, Judge, & Wright, 2005; Howell & Avolio, 1993; Keller, 2006; Waldman, Javidan, & Varella, 2004; Zhu, Chew & Spangler, 2005), comparative case studies (e.g., Edmondson, 2003b; Eisenhardt, 1989; Kanter, 1983; Peters & Austin, 1985), a laboratory experiment (Redmond, Mumford, & Teach, 1993), and a field experiment (Barling, Weber, & Kelloway, 1996).

Facilitating Collective Learning There are many ways leaders can encourage and facilitate collective learning of new knowledge relevant for improving the performance of a group or organization (Berson, Nemanich, Waldman, Galvin, & Keller, 2006; Popper & Lipshitz, 1998). Collective learning may involve improvement of current strategies and work methods (exploitation) or discovery of new ones (exploration). Leaders can support internal activities used to discover new knowledge (e.g., research projects, small-scale experiments) or activities to acquire new knowledge from external sources. Leaders can use practices that facilitate learning by an operations team (e.g., after-activity reviews, benchmarking) or a project development team (e.g., providing resources and opportunity to test new ideas). By helping to create a climate of psychological safety, leaders can increase learning from mistakes and failures. To enhance collective learning from both successes and failures, leaders must avoid common tendencies to misinterpret causes and over-generalize implications (Baumard & Starbuck, 2005). Leaders can help their teams to better recognize failures, analyze their causes, and identify remedies to avoid a future recurrence (Cannon & Edmondson, 2005). Leaders can also influence how new knowledge or a new technology is diffused and applied by explaining why it is important, guiding the process of learning how to use it, and encouraging the use of knowledge-sharing programs. Leaders can help people develop a better understanding about the determinants of organizational performance. More accurate, shared mental models will improve strategic decisions and organizational performance. Evidence that facilitating collective learning is related to effective leadership is provided by comparative case studies (e.g., Baumard & Starbuck, 2005; Beer, 1988; Edmondson, 1999; Edmondson 2002, 2003a) and by experiments with teams (e.g., Ellis, Mendel, & Nir, 2006; Tannenbaum, Smith-Jentsch, & Behson, 1998).

External Leadership Behaviors

In addition to influencing internal events in the work unit, most leaders can facilitate performance with behaviors that provide relevant information about outside events, get necessary resources and assistance, and promote the reputation and interests of the work unit. Three distinct external behaviors include networking, external monitoring, and representing.

Networking It is important for most leaders to build and maintain favorable relationships with peers, superiors, and outsiders who can provide information, resources, and political support (Ibarra & Hunter, 2007; Kaplan, 1984; Kotter, 1982; Michael & Yukl, 1973). Networking includes attending meetings, professional conferences, and ceremonies; joining relevant associations, clubs, and social networks; socializing informally or communicating with network members; and using relationship-building tactics (e.g., finding common interests, doing favors, using ingratiation). In addition to developing their own networks, leaders can encourage relevant networking by subordinates. Networking is a source of information that facilitates other leadership behaviors, but there are potential costs if it is overdone (e.g., time demands, role

conflicts). Evidence that networking can facilitate leadership effectiveness is provided by survey studies (e.g., Kim & Yukl, 1995; Yukl et al., 1990); studies with incident diaries, interviews, or observation (e.g., Amabile et al., 2004; Ancona & Caldwell, 1992; Druskat & Wheeler, 2003; Luthans, Rosenkrantz, & Hennessey, 1985); and comparative case studies (e.g., Katz & Tushman, 1983; Tushman & Katz, 1980).

External Monitoring This external behavior includes analyzing information about relevant events and changes in the external environment and identifying threats and opportunities for the leader's group or organization. Information may be acquired from the leader's network of contacts with outsiders, by studying relevant publications and industry reports, by conducting market research, and by studying the decisions and actions of competitors and opponents. Other terms for external monitoring are "environmental scanning" or "scouting." The extent to which top executives accurately perceive the external environment of their organization is related to financial performance (Bourgeois, 1985), and it is more important when the environment is dynamic and competitive. For a team or work unit in an organization, the importance of external monitoring depends on how much their performance is likely to be affected by external events. Likewise, the need to closely monitor events in other subunits is determined by dependence on them. Evidence that external monitoring is related to indicators of effective leadership is provided by survey research (Dollinger, 1984), research with critical incidents and diaries (e.g., Druskat & Wheeler, 2003; Katz & Tushman, 1981; Luthans et al., 1985), research with comparative cases (e.g., Geletkanycz & Hambrick, 1997; Grinyer, Mayes, & McKiernan, 1990; Van Fleet & Yukl, 1986), and a study using an executive team simulation (Zalatan, 2005).

Representing Leaders usually represent their team or organization in transactions with superiors, peers, and outsiders (e.g., clients, suppliers, investors, and joint venture partners). Representing includes lobbying for resources and assistance, promoting and defending the reputation of the team or organization, negotiating agreements, and coordinating related activities. Other terms used to describe this type of leadership responsibility include "promoter," "ambassador," and "external coordinator." Leaders of project teams have more successful projects when they have sufficient influence to obtain essential resources and support from top management (Katz & Allen, 1985). For work units that have high interdependence with other subunits of the organization or with outsiders such as suppliers, clients, and distributors, it is important for the leaders to coordinate activities, resolve disagreements, and buffer work-unit members from interference (Ancona & Caldwell, 1992). Top executives need to influence external stakeholders whose confidence and support are important to the success and survival of the organization

(Fanelli & Misangyi, 2006). Representing also includes some political tactics that can be used to influence decisions relevant for a leader's work unit or organization, but research on the use of political tactics by leaders in organizations is still very limited. Evidence that representing is related to effective leadership is provided by research using survey questionnaires (e.g., Ancona & Caldwell, 1992; Dorfman, Howell, Cotton, & Tate, 1992; Yukl, Wall, & Lepsinger, 1990), research with incident diaries and interviews (e.g., Amabile et al., 2004; Ancona & Caldwell, 1992; Campbell, Dunnette, Arvey, & Hellervik, 1973; Druskat & Wheeler, 2003), and comparative case studies (e.g., Ancona & Caldwell, 1992; Edmondson, 2003b; Kanter, 1983; Van Fleet & Yukl, 1986).

Future Research

Much of the research on effects of leader behavior has examined how often the behavior is used, but the effects also depend on other conditions that are seldom considered. To improve leadership theory and practice we need to know more about how much the behaviors are used, when they are used, how well they are used, why they are used, who uses them, the context for their use, and joint effects on different outcomes. This part of the article explains the need for more research on the quality and timing of behavior, patterns of behavior, leader skills, leader values, trade-offs for multiple outcomes, situational variables, the joint effects of multiple leaders, and the joint effects of behavior and formal programs.

Quality and Timing of Behavior

Most leader behavior studies emphasize how much the behavior is used rather than how well it is used. Few studies have examined the quality and timing of the behavior or checked the possibility of a non-linear relationship between behavior and the performance criterion. There is growing evidence that most types of leadership behavior can be overused as well as underused, and the optimal amount of behavior is often a moderate amount rather than the maximum amount (e.g., Fleishman & Harris, 1962; Gebert, Boerner, & Lanwehr, 2003; Pierce & Aguinis, in press). For example, too much clarifying can limit innovation, empowerment of subordinates, and development of their problem-solving skills, but too much autonomy can result in coordination problems, lower efficiency, and inconsistent treatment of clients. Even when doing more of a behavior does not reduce the benefits or have negative side effects, spending more time than necessary on a behavior means that the leader is losing the opportunity to use more beneficial types of behavior.

Timing is often a critical determinant of effectiveness for a behavior, and acting too early or too late can reduce the effectiveness of many behaviors. For example, taking action to avoid a problem or resolve it quickly is usually more effective than waiting until the problem becomes very serious and difficult to resolve. Praise for an achievement or contribution is usually more effective when it is given promptly rather than waiting months to mention it in a formal performance review. Research is needed to identify optimal levels of the behaviors and when the behaviors are most likely to be effective.

Patterns of Behavior

In most research on the effects of leader behavior the focus is on the independent effects of each meta-category or individual behavior, but in many cases the effects depend in part on what other behaviors the leader uses. To understand why a leader is effective requires that we examine how different behaviors interact in a mutually consistent way. The effective pattern of behavior may involve multiple components of the same meta-category or component behaviors from different meta-categories. For example, monitoring operations is useful for discovering problems, but unless something is done to solve the problems, monitoring will not contribute to leader effectiveness. Monitoring is more effective when used together with other behaviors such as problem solving, coaching, and recognizing.

The descriptive research on effective leaders suggests that they use complementary behaviors woven together into a complex tapestry, and the whole is greater than the sum of the parts (Kaplan, 1988). Similar results were found in research using incident diaries from team members (Amabile et al., 2004). The pattern of specific component behaviors is usually more important than how much each behavior is used, and more than one pattern of behavior may be used to accomplish the same outcome. Sometimes it is necessary for a leader to find an appropriate balance for behaviors that appear inconsistent, such as directing versus empowering (Kaiser & Overfield, 2010). More research is needed to determine how interacting behaviors are used effectively by leaders in different situations.

Multiple Outcomes and Trade-Offs

Each specific type of leadership behavior can influence more than one type of outcome or performance determinant. For example, developing is classified as a relations-oriented behavior because the primary objective is usually to help people improve their capabilities and advance their careers. But some types of developing are used to improve performance in the current job (a task objective) or facilitate the successful use of an innovative new technology (a change objective). Consulting with team members about the action plan for a new project may increase member commitment (human relations), improve the use of available personnel and resources (efficiency), and identify more innovative ways to satisfy clients (adaptation).

Specific behaviors with positive outcomes for more than one objective are desirable and can increase a leader's effectiveness. However, some leader behaviors have unintended side effects that are negative rather than positive. A behavior can have positive effects for some outcomes and negative effects for other outcomes. For example, delegating responsibility for determining how to do a task to someone with little experience may increase learning for the person, but it can reduce short-term efficiency (e.g., more errors, slower task completion, lower quality). Some decisions intended to benefit employees (e.g., increasing pay and benefits) may increase costs and reduce short-term financial performance. Some decisions intended to reduce costs can reduce human relations and resources (i.e., downsizing can result in less commitment for remaining employees and loss of unique knowledge). Some decisions made to reduce costs (e.g., reducing research activities, outsourcing operations that involve unique knowledge) can also reduce future adaptation. The trade-offs for different outcomes are described by leadership theories such as competing values theory (Quinn & Rohrbaugh, 1983) and flexible leadership theory (Yukl, 2008). More research is needed to discover how effective leaders use specific behaviors that enhance multiple outcomes, minimize negative side effects, and balance difficult trade-offs.

Situational Variables

The effects of a leader's behavior also depend on the situation. Each meta-category includes behaviors that are often relevant for influencing performance outcomes, but aspects of the situation determine which component behaviors are relevant. Effective leaders analyze the situation and identify the specific behaviors that are relevant. The ability to use a wide range of specific behaviors and adapt them to the situation is sometimes called "behavioral flexibility," and it is related to effective leadership (Hart & Quinn, 1993; Hooijberg, 1996; Yukl & Mahsud, 2010). Unfortunately, most studies on situational moderator variables have used behavior meta-categories, and the results are weaker and more difficult to interpret for a broad category than for specific behaviors. For example, the research testing contingency theories about the effects of task-oriented and relations-oriented behaviors failed to find strong, consistent results (Podsakoff, MacKenzie, Ahearne, & Bommer, 1995). There has been less research on situational moderators for the other meta-categories, and there is little systematic research to identify situations where specific leadership behaviors are most likely to impact performance outcomes. More research is needed to learn how leaders adapt their behavior to changing situations and to assess the importance of behavioral flexibility for different types of leaders. The common practice of examining one situational variable at a time is less useful than examining how the situational variables that define common situations for leaders jointly determine which behaviors are most relevant.

Leader Skills

Skills involve the ability to perform some type of activity or task, and some studies on effective leadership use skills rather than observable behaviors as the independent variables. Different taxonomies have been proposed for classifying skills, and some scholars define them more broadly than others. The early research identified three broadly defined skills (Katz, 1955; Mann, 1965): Technical skills are primarily concerned with things, interpersonal skills are primarily concerned with people, and conceptual skills are primarily concerned with ideas and concepts. Other types of skills that have been used in leadership research include political skills (Ferris, Treadway, Perrewé, Brouer, Douglas, & Lux, 2007), administrative skills, and competencies involving the ability to use specific types of behavior such as planning and coaching (e.g., Mumford, Campion, & Morgeson, 2007). Skills are not equivalent to actual behavior, but they can help us understand why some leaders are able to select relevant behaviors and use them more effectively. A combination of skills and traits can help to explain why some leaders are able to recognize what pattern of behavior is relevant, how much of each behavior is optimal, and when to use the behaviors. The research on how skills can enhance the effects of leader behavior is still very limited, and more studies are needed to discover how a leader's skills and personality traits influence the choice of behaviors and leader flexibility in adapting behavior to different situations.

Leader Values and Integrity

The effects of the specific component behaviors also depend on how much the leader is trusted by people he or she wants to influence. Most types of leadership behavior can be used in ethical or unethical ways, and a leader who is not trusted will have less influence. Leader values and integrity did not get much attention in the early research on effective leadership, but interest in them has increased in recent years (Brown & Trevino, 2006). Values such as honesty, altruism, compassion, fairness, courage, and humility are emphasized in servant leadership theory (Greenleaf, 1970), spiritual leadership theory (Fry, 2003), and authentic leadership theory (Avolio, Gardner, Walumbwa, Luthans, & Mayo, 2004; George, 2003). Proponents of these theories contend that leaders whose behavior reflects these values will be more effective. However, research on these subjects is still very limited, and more studies are needed to understand how leader values influence the use of the specific behaviors and the effects of the behaviors.

Multiple Leaders and Shared Leadership

Most of the research on the outcomes of leadership behavior examines relationships only for individual leaders. However, organizations have many leaders who can influence important decisions and determine how successfully they are implemented (Mintzberg, Raisinghani, & Theoret, 1976; Schweiger, Anderson, & Locke, 1985). Sometimes two or more leaders have shared responsibility for an activity or project, and sometimes leaders have different but interdependent responsibilities. The performance of an organization depends in part on the level of cooperation and coordination among interdependent leaders (Yukl, 2008; Yukl & Lepsinger, 2004). It is more difficult to achieve a high level of cooperation when the leaders do not share the same objectives or have the same priorities. In some cases, one leader's actions to improve subunit performance can be detrimental to the performance of other subunits and the overall organization. For example, a subunit leader may gain control of resources that other subunits need and could use more effectively. Several scholars have discussed how shared or distributed leadership is related to team or organizational effectiveness (e.g., Brown & Gioia, 2002; Carson, Tesluk, & Marrone, 2007; Denis, Lamothe, & Langley, 2001; Friedrich, Vessey, Schuelke, Ruark, & Mumford, 2009; Pearce & Conger, 2003). However, more research is needed to discover how the use of the specific behaviors by different leaders can influence their effectiveness.

Behaviors and Formal Programs

Management programs and systems can enhance the effects of direct leadership behaviors. For example, encouraging innovative thinking is more likely to increase innovation when an organization has a climate of psychological safety for risk taking and appropriate rewards for creative ideas about improving products and processes. Programs and structures can also limit the use of leadership behaviors or nullify their effects. For example, it is difficult to empower subordinates when they must follow elaborate rules and standard procedures for doing the work. Management programs and systems can also serve as substitutes for some types of direct behaviors. For example, company-wide training programs for widely relevant skills can reduce the amount of training that managers need to give their immediate subordinates. Top executives have responsibility for implementing and revising programs, and the effectiveness of programs depends on support by lower-level managers. The effects of leader behavior and management programs have been examined separately, but more systematic research is needed to examine their joint and interacting effects on organizational performance.

Summary and Recommendations

The proposed hierarchical taxonomy facilitates the integration of important findings in research on leader behavior constructs and research about the effects of specific behaviors on team or organizational performance. More than half a century of research provides support for the conclusion that leaders can enhance the performance of a team, work unit, or organization by using a combination of specific task, relations, change, and external behaviors that are relevant for their situation. Why the behaviors are important for effective leadership is explained better by theories about the determinants of group and organizational performance than by leadership theories focused on motivating

individual followers. A limitation of the conclusions about effective leadership is that enhancing performance is not the only basis for evaluating effectiveness, and the importance accorded different criteria affects the selection of relevant behaviors for a taxonomy.

The hierarchical taxonomy can be used to explain results found in the extensive research on behavior meta-categories not used in the taxonomy, such as transformational and transactional leadership. The results found in survey research on transformational leadership can be explained as effects of specific behaviors used to compute the composite score for each leader (e.g., Yukl, 1999; Yukl, O'Donnell, & Taber, 2009). Individualized consideration includes supporting and developing, inspirational motivation includes envisioning change, and intellectual stimulation includes aspects of encouraging innovation. Idealized influence is primarily a measure of perceived leader integrity involving consistency between leader actions and espoused values. Transactional leadership includes one task-oriented behavior (monitoring), one relations-oriented behavior (recognizing), and communication of reward contingencies, which are usually specified by the formal compensation program.

The taxonomy described in this article should not be viewed as the final solution for classifying leadership behavior. Behavior constructs are conceptual tools, and there is no objective reality for them. They are most useful when they can be measured accurately, they can predict and explain leader influence on important outcomes, and they can improve leadership development programs. Future research may discover additional component behaviors that should be included (e.g., implementing change). Some component behaviors may need to be expanded to include forms of the behavior not explicitly included in the current descriptions. Some of the broader component behaviors in the current taxonomy may need to be subdivided in the future if it is found that narrower components would provide a better explanation of leadership effectiveness. However, at this time it does not appear worthwhile to make the taxonomy any more complex. The current version is easy to remember and easy to use for developing an observation checklist or a coding guide (the behavior definitions are provided in the appendix).

Future research may also provide justification for adding more meta-categories, and a possible candidate is ethical and socially responsible leadership. One component of this meta-category could be leadership behavior that encourages ethical practices. Some examples are communicating ethical standards, encouraging ethical conduct, modeling ethical behavior, and opposing unethical conduct. Another component could be leadership behavior that encourages corporate social responsibility. Examples include making decisions that consider the needs of different stakeholders, encouraging support of worthy community service activities, encouraging improvements in product safety, and recommending practices that reduce harmful effects for the environment.

Leadership decisions and actions intended to benefit employees, customers, or the environment are controversial if they do not also benefit the organization (Cameron, 2011; Waldman, 2011; Waldman & Siegel, 2008). Research on the effects of ethical and responsible leadership is still very limited, and more research is needed to identify relevant behaviors and assess their short-term and long-term effects. The focus of this article is on leadership behaviors intended to improve performance, and more research is needed to determine if ethical and responsible leadership should be included as a separate meta-category in a taxonomy for describing performance-enhancing behaviors.

The hierarchical taxonomy provides a broad perspective for understanding the types of behavior that determine how effective a leader will be, but the specific component behaviors are much more useful than the meta-categories for developing better contingency theories and practical guidelines for leaders. Moderator variables for some of the specific behaviors have been suggested (Yukl, 2013), but more research is needed on the joint effects of situational variables. Other relevant conditions that need more attention in future research include nonlinear relationships between behavior and outcomes, reciprocal causality, lagged effects, effects for different outcomes, effects of negative forms of the behaviors, effects of different combinations of specific behaviors, mediating processes that explain why the behaviors influence performance, the joint effects of multiple leaders, multi-level effects of behaviors, and joint effects for behaviors and programs.

When designing future studies on leadership it is important to select research methods that are appropriate for the type of knowledge sought rather than merely using a method that is familiar or convenient. Each research method has limitations, and it is desirable to use multiple methods whenever feasible. Strong research methods should be used more often, including longitudinal field studies and experiments with manipulation of leader behaviors in simulated teams or organizations to assess immediate and delayed effects. More studies should include incident diaries or video recording of leaders. When behavior questionnaires are used, more effort should be made to improve measurement accuracy and minimize respondent biases (e.g., train respondents to understand and recognize the behaviors). If a survey is conducted for a sample of homogeneous leaders (e.g., project team managers, coaches of athletic teams, public administrators), it should include some behavior items that are directly relevant for the sample rather than relying only on a behavior questionnaire with generic examples. Leadership effectiveness should be assessed from the perspective of multiple stakeholders and with multiple criteria that include objective measures of work unit or organizational performance.

Finally, it is important to recognize that observable leadership behaviors are not the same as skills, values, personality traits, or roles. These other constructs can be useful for understanding effective leadership, but they differ in important ways from observable behaviors. When feasible, future studies should investigate how the different types of constructs jointly explain leader influence on work unit performance and other outcomes.

REFERENCES

Amabile, T. M., Schatzel, E. A., Moneta, G. B., & Kramer, S. J. (2004). Leader behaviors and the work environment for creativity: Perceived leader support. *Leadership Quarterly*, 15(1), 5–32.

Ancona, D. G., & Caldwell, D. F. (1992). Bridging the boundary: External activity and performance in organizational teams. *Administrative Science Quarterly*, 37, 634–665.

Atwater, L. E., Dionne, S. D., Avolio, B. J., Camobreco, J. F., & Lau, A. W. (1996). *Leader attributes and behaviors predicting emergence of leader effectiveness* (Technical Report 1044). Alexandria, VA. U.S. Army Research Institute for the Behavioral and Social Sciences.

Avolio, B. J., Bass, B. M., & Jung, D. I. (1999). Re-examining the components of transformational and transactional leadership using the multifactor leadership questionnaire. *Journal of Occupational and Organizational Psychology*, 72, 441–462.

Avolio, B. J., Gardner, W. L., Walumbwa, F. O., Luthans, F., & Mayo, D. R. (2004). Unlocking the mask: A look at the process by which authentic leaders impact follower attitudes and behaviors. *Leadership Quarterly*, 15, 801–823.

Awamleh, R., & Gardner, W. L. (1999). Perceptions of leader charisma and effectiveness: The effects of vision content, delivery, and organizational performance. *Leadership Quarterly*, 10(3), 345–373.

Barling, J., Weber, T., & Kelloway, E. K. (1996). Effects of transformational leadership training on attitudinal and financial outcomes: A field experiment. *Journal of Applied Psychology*, 81, 827–832.

Bass, B. M. (1985). *Leadership and performance beyond expectations*. New York: Free Press.

Bass, B. M. (2008). *Handbook of leadership: Theory, research, and managerial applications* (4th ed.). New York: Free Press.

Bass, B. M., & Yammarino, F. J. (1991). Congruence of self and others' leadership ratings of naval officers for understanding successful performance. *Applied Psychology: An International Review*, 40(4), 437–454.

Baum, R. J., Locke, E. A., & Kirkpatrick, S. (1998). A longitudinal study of the relation of vision and vision communication to venture growth in entrepreneurial firms. *Journal of Applied Psychology*, 83, 43–54.

Baumard, P., & Starbuck, W. H. (2005). Learning from failures: Why it may not happen. *Long Range Planning*, 38, 281–298.

Beer, M. (1988). The critical path for change: Keys to success and failure in six companies. In R. H. Kilmann & T. J. Covin (Eds.), *Corporate transformation: Revitalizing organizations for a competitive world* (pp. 17–45). San Francisco: Jossey-Bass.

Berson, Y., Nemanich, L. A., Waldman, D. A., Galvin, B. M., & Keller, R. T. (2006). Leadership and organizational learning: A multiple levels perspective. *Leadership Quarterly*, 17, 577–594.

Blake, R. R., & Mouton, J. S. (1964). *The managerial grid*. Houston: Gulf Publishing.

Bourgeois, L. J. (1985). Strategic goals, perceived uncertainty, and economic performance in volatile environments. *Academy of Management Journal*, 3, 548–573.

Boyatzis, R. E. (1982). *The competent manager*. New York: John Wiley.

Bradford, D. L., & Cohen, A. R. (1984). *Managing for excellence: The guide to developing high performance organizations*. New York: John Wiley.

Bragg, J., & Andrews, I. R. (1973). Participative decision making: An experimental study in a hospital. *Journal of Applied Behavioral Science*, 9, 727–735.

Brewer, N., Wilson, C., & Beck, K. (1994). Supervisory behavior and team performance amongst police patrol sergeants. *Journal of Occupational and Organizational Psychology*, 67, 69–78.

Brown, M. E., & Trevino, L. K. (2006). Ethical leadership: A review and future directions. *Leadership Quarterly*, 17(6), 595–616.

Brown, M. W., & Gioia, D. A. (2002). Making things click: Distributive leadership in an online division of an offline organization. *Leadership Quarterly*, 13, 397–419.

Burke, C. S., Stagl, K. C., Klein, C., Goodwin, G. F., Salas, E., & Halpin, S. M. (2006). What types of leadership behaviors are functional in teams? *Leadership Quarterly*, 17, 288–307.

Cameron, K. (2011). Responsible leadership as virtuous leadership. *Journal of Business Ethics*, 98, 25–35.

Campbell, J. P., Dunnette, M. D., Arvey, R. D., & Hellervik, L. W. (1973). The development and evaluation of behaviorally based rating scales. *Journal of Applied Psychology*, 57, 15–22.

Cannon, M. D., & Edmondson, A. C. (2005). Failing to learn and learning to fail (intelligently): How great organizations put failure to work to improve and innovate. *Long Range Planning Journal*, 38(3), 299–320.

Carson, J., Tesluk, P., & Marrone, J. (2007). Shared leadership in teams: An investigation of antecedent conditions and performance. *Academy of Management Journal*, 50, 1217–1234.

Coch, L., & French, J. R. P. Jr. (1948). Overcoming resistance to change. *Human Relations*, 1, 512–532.

Conger, J. A., & Kanungo, R. (1987). Toward a behavioral theory of charismatic leadership in organizational settings. *Academy of Management Review*, 12, 637–647.

De Groot, T., Kiker, D. S., & Cross, T. C. (2000). A meta-analysis to review organizational outcomes related to charismatic leadership. *Canadian Journal of Administrative Sciences*, 17(4), 356–371.

Denis, J. L., Lamothe, L., & Langley, A. (2001). The dynamics of collective leadership and strategic change in pluralistic organizations. *Academy of Management Journal*, 44(4), 809–837.

DeRue, D. S., Nahrgang, J., Wellman, N., & Humphrey, S. E. (2011). Trait and behavioral theories of leadership: An integration and meta-analytic test of their relative validity. *Personnel Psychology*, 64(1), 7–52.

Dollinger, M. J. (1984). Environmental boundary spanning and information processing effects on organizational performance. *Academy of Management Journal*, 27(2), 351–368.

Dorfman, P. W., Howell, J. P., Cotton, B. C. G., & Tate, U. (1992). Leadership within the "discontinuous hierarchy" structure of the military. In K. E. Clark, M. B. Clark, & D. P. Campbell (Eds.), *Impact of leadership* (pp. 399–416). Greensboro, NC: Center for Creative Leadership.

Druskat, V. U., & Wheeler, J. V. (2003). Managing from the boundary: The effective leadership of self-managed work teams. *Academy of Management Journal*, 46(4), 435–457.

Edmondson, A. (1999). Psychological safety and learning behavior in work teams. *Administrative Science Quarterly*, 44, 350–383.

Edmondson, A. (2003a). Framing for learning: Lessons in successful technology implementation. *California Management Review*, 45(2), 34–54.

Edmondson, A. (2003b). Speaking up in the operating room. *Journal of Management Studies*, 40, 1419–1452.

Edmondson, A. C. (2002). The local and variegated nature of learning in organizations: A group-level perspective. *Organization Science*, 13, 128–146.

Eisenhardt, K. M. (1989). Making fast strategic decisions in high-velocity environments. *Academy of Management Journal*, 32(3), 543–576.

Ekvall, G., & Arvonen, J. (1991). Change-centered leadership: An extension of the two-dimensional model. *Scandinavian Journal of Management*, 7, 17–26.

Elenkov, D. S., Judge, W., & Wright, P. (2005). Strategic leadership and executive innovation influence: An international multi-cluster comparative study. *Strategic Management Journal*, 26, 665–682.

Ellis, S., Mendel, R., & Nir, M. (2006). Learning from successful and failed experience: The moderating role of kind of after-event review. *Journal of Applied Psychology*, 91(3), 669–680.

Emrich, C. G., Brower, H. H., Feldman, J. M., & Garland, H. (2001). Images in words: Presidential rhetoric, charisma, and greatness. *Administrative Science Quarterly*, 46, 527–557.

Fanelli, A., & Misangyi, V. F. (2006). Bringing out charisma: CEO charisma and external stakeholders. *Academy of Management Review*, 31(4), 1049–1061.

Ferris, G. R., Treadway, D. C., Perrewé, P. L., Brouer, R. L., Douglas, C., & Lux, S. (2007). Political skill in organizations. *Journal of Management*, 33, 290–320.

Finkelstein, S. (2003). *Why smart executives fail*. New York: Portfolio.

Fleishman, E. A. (1953). The description of supervisory behavior. *Personnel Psychology*, 37, 1–6.

Fleishman, E. A., & Harris, E. F. (1962). Patterns of leadership behavior related to employee grievances and turnover. *Journal of Applied Psychology*, 15, 43–56.

Friedrich, T. L., Vessey, W. B., Schuelke, M. J., Ruark, G. A., & Mumford, M. D. (2009). A framework for understanding collective leadership: The selective utilization of leader and team expertise within networks. *Leadership Quarterly*, 20(6), 933–958.

Fry, L. W. (2003). Toward a theory of spiritual leadership. *Leadership Quarterly*, 14(6), 693–727.

Gebert, D., Boerner, S., & Lanwehr, R. (2003). The risks of autonomy: Empirical evidence for the necessity of balance in promoting organizational innovativeness. *Creativity and Innovation Management*, 12(1), 41–49.

Geletkanycz, M. A., & Hambrick, D. C. (1997). The external ties of top executives: Implications for strategic choice and performance. *Administrative Science Quarterly*, 42, 654–681.

George, B. (2003). Authentic leadership: Rediscovering the secrets to creating lasting value. San Francisco: Jossey-Bass.

Gilmore, D. C., Beehr, T. A., & Richter, D. J. (1979). Effects of leader behaviors on subordinate performance and satisfaction: A laboratory experiment with student employees. *Journal of Applied Psychology*, 64, 166–172.

Grinyer, P. H., Mayes, D., & McKiernan, P. (1990). The sharpbenders: Achieving a sustained improvement in performance. *Long Range Planning*, 23, 116–125.

Halpin, A. W. & Winer, B. J. (1957). A factorial study of the leader behavior descriptions. In R. M. Stogdill & A. E. Coons (Eds.), *Leader behavior: Its description and measurement*. Columbus, OH: Bureau of Business Research, Ohio State University.

Hart, L. S., & Quinn, E. R. (1993). Roles executives play: CEOs, behavioral complexity, and firm performance. *Human Relations*, 46(5), 543–575.

Heifetz, R. (1994). *Leadership without easy answers*. Cambridge, MA: Belknap Books of Harvard University Press.

Hersey, P., & Blanchard, K. H. (1977). *The management of organizational behavior* (3rd ed.). Englewood Cliffs, NJ: Prentice Hall.

Hooijberg, R. (1996). A multidimensional approach toward leadership: An extension of the concept of behavioral complexity. *Human Relations*, 49(7), 917–947.

House, R. J. (1971). A path-goal theory of leader effectiveness. *Administrative Science Quarterly*, 16, 321–339.

House, R. J. (1977). A 1976 theory of charismatic leadership. In J. G. Hunt & L. L. Larson (Eds.), *Leadership: The cutting edge* (pp. 189–207). Carbondale, IL: Southern Illinois University Press.

Howell, J. M., & Avolio, B. J. (1993). Transformational leadership, transactional leadership, locus of control, and support for innovation: Key predictors of consolidated business unit performance. *Journal of Applied Psychology*, 78, 891–902.

Ibarra, H., & Hunter, M. (2007). How leaders create and use networks. *Harvard Business Review*, 85(1), 40–47.

Joshi, A., Pandey, N., & Han, G. H. (2009). Bracketing team boundary spanning: An examination of task-based, team-level, and contextual antecedents. *Journal of Organizational Behavior*, 30, 731–759.

Judge, T. A., & Piccolo, R. F. (2004). Transformational and transactional leadership: A meta-analytic test of their relative validity. *Journal of Applied Psychology*, 89(5), 755–768.

Judge, T. A., Piccolo, R. F., & Ilies, R. (2004). The forgotten ones? The validity of consideration and initiating structure in leadership research. *Journal of Applied Psychology*, 89(1), 36–51.

Kaiser, R. B., Hogan, R., & Craig, S. B. (2008). Leadership and the fate of organizations. *American Psychologist*, 63(2), 96–110.

Kaiser, R. B., & Overfield, D. V. (2010). Assessing flexible leadership as a mastery of opposites. *Consulting Psychology Journal: Practice and Research*, 62, 105–118.

Kanter, R. M. (1983). *The change masters.* New York: Simon & Schuster.

Kaplan, R. E. (1984). Trade routes: The manager's network of relationships. *Organizational Dynamics, Spring,* 37–52.

Kaplan, R. E. (1988). The warp and woof of the general manager's job. In F. D. Schoorman & B. Schneider (Eds.), *Facilitating work effectiveness* (pp. 183–211). Lexington, MA: Lexington Books.

Katz, R. (1955). Skills of an effective administrator. *Harvard Business Review,* 33–42.

Katz, R., & Allen, T. J. (1985). Project performance and the locus of influence in the R&D matrix. *Academy of Management Journal,* 28, 67–87.

Katz, R., & Tushman, M. L. (1981). An investigation into the managerial roles and career paths of gatekeepers and project supervisors in a major R&D facility. *R&D Management,* 11, 103–110.

Katz, R., & Tushman, M. L. (1983). A longitudinal study of the effects of boundary spanning supervision on turnover and promotion in research and development. *Academy of Management Journal,* 26, 437–456.

Keller, R. T. (2006). Transformational leadership, initiating structure, and substitutes for leadership: A longitudinal study of research and development project team performance. *Journal of Applied Psychology,* 91, 202–210.

Kerr, S., & Jermier, J. M. (1978). Substitutes for leadership: Their meaning and measurement. *Organizational Behavior and Human Performance,* 22, 375–403.

Kim, H., & Yukl, G. (1995). Relationships of self-reported and subordinate-reported leadership behaviors to managerial effectiveness and advancement. *Leadership Quarterly,* 6, 361–377.

Kirkpatrick, S. A., & Locke, E. A. (1996). Direct and indirect effects of three core charismatic leadership components on performance and attitudes. *Journal of Applied Psychology,* 81, 36–51.

Komaki, J. L. (1986). Toward effective supervision: An operant analysis and comparison of managers at work. *Journal of Applied Psychology,* 71(2), 270–279.

Korsgaard, M. A., Schweiger, D. M., & Sapienza, H. J. (1995). Building commitment, attachment, and trust in strategic decision-making teams: The role of procedural justice. *Academy of Management Journal,* 38(1), 60–84.

Kotter, J. P. (1982). *The general managers.* New York: Free Press.

Kotter, J. P. (1996). *Leading change.* Boston: Harvard Business School Press.

Kotter, J. P., & Cohen, D. S. (2002). *The heart of change: Real-life stories of how people change their organizations.* Boston: Harvard Business School Press.

Kouzes, J. M., & Posner, B. Z. (1987). *The leadership challenge: How to get extraordinary things done in organizations.* San Francisco: Jossey-Bass.

Larson, J. R., & Callahan, C. (1990). Performance monitoring: How it affects work productivity. *Journal of Applied Psychology,* 75, 530–538.

Latham, G. P., & Baldes, J. J. (1975). The "practical significance" of Locke's theory of goal setting. *Journal of Applied Psychology,* 60, 122–124.

Latham, G. P., & Yukl, G. A. (1976). Effects of assigned and participative goal setting on performance and satisfaction. *Journal of Applied Psychology,* 61(2), 166–171.

Leana, C. R. (1986). Predictors and consequences of delegation. *Academy of Management Journal,* 29, 754–774.

Likert, R. (1961). *New patterns of management.* New York: McGraw-Hill.

Lowe, K. B., Kroeck, K. G., & Sivasubramaniam, N. (1996). Effectiveness of correlates of transformational and transactional leadership: A meta-analytic review of the MLQ literature. *Leadership Quarterly,* 7, 385–425.

Luthans, F., Rosenkrantz, S. A., & Hennessey, H. W. (1985). What do successful managers really do? An observational study of managerial activities. *Journal of Applied Behavioral Science,* 21, 255–270.

Mann, F. C. (1965). Toward an understanding of the leadership role in formal organization. In R. Dubin, G. C. Homans, F. C. Mann, & D. C. Miller (Eds.), *Leadership and productivity.* San Francisco: Chandler.

Marks, M. A., Zaccaro, S. J., & Mathieu, J. E. (2000). Performance implications of leader briefings and team-interaction training for team adaptation to novel environments. *Journal of Applied Psychology,* 85, 971–986.

Marrone, J. A. (2010). Team boundary spanning: A multilevel review of past research and proposals for the future. *Journal of Management,* 36, 911–940.

McClelland, P. L., Liang, X., & Barker, V. L. (2009). CEO commitment to the status quo: Replication and extension using content analysis. *Journal of Management,* 36, 1251–1277.

McDonough, E. F., & Barczak, G. (1991). Speeding up new product development: The effects of leadership style and source of technology. *Journal of Product Innovation Management,* 8, 203–211.

Michael, J., & Yukl, G. (1993). Managerial level and subunit function as determinants of networking behavior in organizations. *Group and Organization Management*, 18, 328–351.

Miller, K. I., & Monge, P. R. (1986). Participation, satisfaction, and productivity: A meta-analytic review. *Academy of Management Journal*, 29, 727–753.

Mintzberg, H. (1973). *The nature of managerial work*. New York: Harper & Row.

Mintzberg, H., Raisinghani, D., & Theoret, A. (1976). The structure of unstructured decision processes. *Administrative Science Quarterly*, 21, 246–275.

Misumi, J., & Peterson, M. (1985). The performance-maintenance (PM) theory of leadership: Review of a Japanese research program. *Administrative Science Quarterly*, 30, 198–223.

Mitchell, M. S., & Ambrose, M. L. (2007). Abusive supervision and workplace deviance and the moderating effects of negative reciprocity beliefs. *Journal of Applied Psychology*, 92(4), 1159–1168.

Morgeson, F. P. (2005). The external leadership of self-managed teams: Intervening in the context of novel and disruptive events. *Journal of Applied Psychology*, 90, 497–508.

Morse, J. J., & Wagner, F. R. (1978). Measuring the process of managerial effectiveness. *Academy of Management Journal*, 21, 23–35.

Mumford, M. D., Scott, G. M., Gaddis, B., & Strange, J. M. (2002). Leading creative people: Orchestrating expertise and relationships. *Leadership Quarterly*, 13, 705–750.

Mumford, T. V., Campion, M. A., & Morgeson, F. P. (2007). The leadership skills strataplex: Leadership skill requirements across organizational levels. *Leadership Quarterly*, 18, 154–166.

Nadler, D. A. (1988). Organizational frame bending: Types of change in the complex organization. In R. H. Kilmann & T. J. Covin (Eds.), *Corporate transformation: Revitalizing organizations for a competitive world* (pp. 66–83). San Francisco: Jossey-Bass.

Nadler, D. A., Shaw, R. B., Walton, A. E., et al. (1995). *Discontinuous change: Leading organizational transformation*. San Francisco: Jossey-Bass.

Pearce, C. L., & Conger, J. A. (2003). *Shared leadership: Reframing the hows and whys of leadership*. Thousand Oaks, CA: Sage.

Peters, T. J., & Austin, N. (1985). *A passion for excellence: The leadership difference*. New York: Random House.

Peters, T. J., & Waterman, R. H., Jr. (1982). *In search of excellence: Lessons from America's best-run companies*. New York: Harper & Row.

Pierce, J. R., & Aguinis, H. (in press). The too-much-of-a-good-thing effect in management. *Journal of Management*.

Podsakoff, P. M., MacKenzie, S. B., Ahearne, M., & Bommer, W. H. (1995). Searching for a needle in a haystack: Trying to identify the illusive moderators of leadership behaviors. *Journal of Management*, 21, 423–470.

Popper, M., & Lipshitz, R. (1998). Organizational learning mechanisms: A structural and cultural approach to organizational learning. *Journal of Applied Behavioral Science*, 34(2), 161–179.

Quinn, R. E., & Rohrbaugh, J. (1983). A spatial model of effectiveness criteria: Toward a competing values approach to organizational analysis. *Management Science*, 29, 363–377.

Redmond, M. R., Mumford, M. D., & Teach, R. J. (1993). Putting creativity to work: Leader influences on subordinate creativity. *Organizational Behavior and Human Decision Processes*, 55, 120–151.

Schweiger, D. M., Anderson, C. R., & Locke, E. A. (1985). Complex decision making: A longitudinal study of process and performance. *Organizational Behavior and Human Decision Processes*, 36, 245–272.

Shamir, B., House, R J., & Arthur, M. B. (1993). The motivational effects of charismatic leadership: A self-concept based theory. *Organization Science*, 4, 1–17.

Shipper, F. (1991). Mastery and frequency of managerial behaviors relative to subunit effectiveness. *Human Relations*, 44, 371–388.

Shipper, F., & Dillard, J. E., Jr. (2000). A study of impending derailment and recovery of middle managers across career stages. *Human Resource Management*, 39(4), 331–345.

Shipper, F., & Wilson, C. L. (1992). The impact of managerial behaviors on group performance, stress, and commitment. In K. Clark, M. B. Clark, & D. P. Campbell (Eds.), *Impact of leadership* (pp. 119–129). Greensboro, NC: Center for Creative Leadership.

Spector, P. E. (1986). Perceived control by employees: A meta-analysis of studies concerning autonomy and participation at work. *Human Relations*, 39, 1005–1016.

Stogdill, R. M., Goode, O. S., & Day, D. R. (1962). New leader behavior description subscales. *Journal of Psychology*, 54, 259–269.

Tannenbaum, S. I., Smith-Jentsch, K., & Behson, S. J. (1998). Training team leaders to facilitate team learning and performance. In J. A. Cannon-Bowers & E. Salas (Eds.), *Making decisions under stress: Implications for individual and team training* (pp. 247–270). Washington, DC: American Psychological Association.

Tepper, B. J. (2000). Consequences of abusive supervision. *Academy of Management Journal*, 43(2), 178–190.

Tichy, N. M., & Devanna, M. A. (1986). *The transformational leader*. New York: John Wiley.

Tushman, M. L., & Katz, R. (1980). External communication and project performance: An investigation into the role of gatekeepers. *Management Science*, 26, 1071–1085.

Van Fleet, D. D., & Yukl, G. (1986). *Military leadership: An organizational perspective*. Greenwich, CT: JAI Press.

Vroom, V. H., & Yetton, P. W. (1973). *Leadership and decision making*. Pittsburgh, PA: University of Pittsburgh Press.

Wagner, J. A., & Gooding, R. Z. (1987). Shared influence and organizational behavior: A meta-analysis of situational variables expected to moderate participation-outcome relationships. *Academy of Management Journal*, 30, 524–541.

Waldman, D. A. (2011). Moving forward with the concept of responsible leadership: Three caveats to guide theory and research. *Journal of Business Ethics*, 98, 75–83.

Waldman, D. A., Javidan, M., & Varella, P. (2004). Charismatic leadership at the strategic level: A new application of upper echelons theory. *Leadership Quarterly*, 15, 355–380.

Waldman, D. A., & Siegel, D. (2008). Defining the socially responsible leader. *Leadership Quarterly*, 19, 117–131.

Wang, G., Oh, I.-S., Courtright, S. H., & Colbert, A. E. (2011). Transformational leadership and performance across criteria and levels: A meta-analytic review of 25 years of research. *Group and Organization Management*, 36, 223–270.

Wang, H., Tsui, A. H., & Xin, K. R. (2011). CEO leadership behaviors, organizational performance, and employee attitudes. *Leadership Quarterly*, 22, 92–105.

Wikoff, M., Anderson, D. C., & Crowell, C. R. (1983). Behavior management in a factory setting: Increasing work efficiency. *Journal of Organizational Behavior Management*, 4, 97–128.

Yukl, G. (1999). An evaluative essay on current conceptions of effective leadership. *European Journal of Work and Organizational Psychology*, 8, 33–48.

Yukl, G. (2008). How leaders influence organizational effectiveness. *Leadership Quarterly*, 19, 708–722.

Yukl, G. (2013). *Leadership in organizations* (8th ed.). Englewood Cliffs, NJ: Prentice Hall.

Yukl, G., Gordon, A., & Taber, T. (2002). A hierarchical taxonomy of leadership behavior: Integrating a half century of behavior research. *Journal of Leadership and Organizational Studies*, 9, 15–32.

Yukl, G., & Kanuk, L. (1979). Leadership behavior and effectiveness of beauty salon managers. *Personnel Psychology*, 32, 663–675.

Yukl, G., & Lepsinger, R. (2004). *Flexible leadership: Creating value by balancing multiple challenges and choices*. San Francisco: Jossey-Bass.

Yukl, G., & Mahsud, R. (2010). Why flexible, adaptive leadership is important. *Consulting Psychology Journal*, 62(2), 81–93.

Yukl, G., O'Donnell, M., & Taber, T. (2009). Leader behaviors and leader member exchange. *Journal of Managerial Psychology*, 24(4), 289–299.

Yukl, G., & Van Fleet, D. (1982). Cross-situational, multimethod research on military leader effectiveness. *Organizational Behavior and Human Performance*, 30, 87–108.

Yukl, G., Wall, S., & Lepsinger, R. (1990). Preliminary report on validation of the managerial practices survey. In K. E. Clark & M. B. Clark (Eds.), *Measures of leadership* (pp. 223–238). West Orange, NJ: Leadership Library of America.

Zalatan, K. A. (2005). Inside the black box: Leadership influence on team effectiveness (Unpublished Doctoral Dissertation). University of Albany School of Business.

Zhu, W., Chew, I. K. H., & Spangler, W. D. (2005). CEO transformational leadership and organizational outcomes: The mediating role of human-capital-enhancing human resource management. *Leadership Quarterly*, 16(1), 39–52.

Appendix: Definitions of 15 Specific Leadership Behaviors

Planning: develops short-term plans for the work; determines how to schedule and coordinate activities to use people and resources efficiently; determines the action steps and resources needed to accomplish a project or activity.

Clarifying: clearly explains task assignments and member responsibilities; sets specific goals and deadlines for important aspects of the work; explains priorities for different objectives; explains rules, policies, and standard procedures.

Monitoring: checks on the progress and quality of the work; examines relevant sources of information to determine how well important tasks are being performed; evaluates the performance of members in a systematic way.

Problem Solving: identifies work-related problems that can disrupt operations, makes a systematic but rapid diagnosis, and takes action to resolve the problems in a decisive and confident way.

Supporting: shows concern for the needs and feelings of individual members; provides support and encouragement when there is a difficult or stressful task, and expresses confidence members can successfully complete it.

Recognizing: praises effective performance by members; provides recognition for member achievements and contributions to the organization; recommends appropriate rewards for members with high performance.

Developing: provides helpful feedback and coaching for members who need it; provides helpful career advice; encourages members to take advantage of opportunities for skill development.

Empowering: involves members in making important work-related decisions and considers their suggestions and concerns; delegates responsibility and authority to members for important tasks and allows them to resolve work-related problems without prior approval.

Advocating Change: explains an emerging threat or opportunity; explains why a policy or procedure is no longer appropriate and should be changed; proposes desirable changes; takes personal risks to push for approval of essential but difficult changes.

Envisioning Change: communicates a clear, appealing vision of what could be accomplished; links the vision to member values and ideals; describes a proposed change or new initiative with enthusiasm and optimism.

Encouraging Innovation: talks about the importance of innovation and flexibility; encourages innovative thinking and new approaches for solving problems; encourages and supports efforts to develop innovative new products, services, or processes.

Facilitating Collective Learning: uses systematic procedures for learning how to improve work unit performance; helps members understand causes of work unit performance; encourages members to share new knowledge with each other.

Networking: attends meetings or events; joins professional associations or social clubs; uses social networks to build and maintain favorable relationships with peers, superiors, and outsiders who can provide useful information or assistance.

External Monitoring: analyzes information about events, trends, and changes in the external environment to identify threats, opportunities, and other implications for the work unit.

Representing: lobbies for essential funding or resources; promotes and defends the reputation of the work unit or organization; negotiates agreements and coordinates related activities with other parts of the organization or with outsiders.

READING 10.2

Managing the Life Cycle of Virtual Teams

Stacie A. Furst, Martha Reeves, Benson Rosen, and Richard S. Blackburn

Executive Overview

In the fast-paced, technology-driven 21st century, virtual project teams represent a growing response to the need for high-quality, low-cost, rapid solutions to complex organizational problems. Virtual project teams enable organizations to pool the talents and expertise of employees (and non-employees) by eliminating time and space barriers. Yet, there is growing evidence that virtual teams fail more often than they succeed. To understand the factors that contribute to virtual team effectiveness, we tracked six virtual project teams from a large food distribution company from inception to project delivery. We identified factors at each stage of the virtual-team life cycle that affected team performance. These results provide specific examples of what managers can do, at various points in time, to increase a virtual team's chances to fully develop and contribute to firm performance.

FOODCO* has grown dramatically over the last several years as the result of numerous acquisitions. One of the nation's largest food distributors, FOODCO has more than 20 operating companies located throughout the United States. To maximize long-term performance, FOODCO executives wanted to tap into the knowledge and expertise of employees located throughout the newly expanded company. In particular, executives wanted to encourage the sharing of best practices across operating companies, streamline work processes, prepare managers for promotion, and develop a unified culture. To address these issues intelligently, quickly, and effectively, FOODCO created virtual project teams.

Virtual project teams represent a recent response to the demand for high-quality, rapid solutions to complex issues such as those faced by FOODCO. Virtual project teams include individuals who are geographically dispersed and interact primarily through telecommunications and information technologies to accomplish specific objectives within specified timeframes.[1] Assignments for these teams might include designing new products, developing strategies, and revising operating procedures. Virtual project teams allow organizations to pool the talents and expertise of employees regardless of employee location, overcoming time and

distance barriers to accomplish critical tasks quickly and effectively.

But simply establishing virtual project teams does not guarantee success. In fact, virtual teams are often less effective than face-to-face teams on many outcome measures.[2] Virtual project teams can experience difficulties at every stage of their development. Improved understanding of how virtual project teams develop and mature will provide managers with important insights that might increase a team's contributions to firm performance.

The authors were able to follow six virtual project teams at FOODCO from inception through project delivery to assess how teams developed and to determine what factors contributed to performance at each stage of the project-team life cycle. We surveyed and interviewed team members throughout an eight-month project period and gathered information on how top executives at FOODCO and outside experts evaluated each team's deliverables. Our data provide useful insights about virtual project team development, the challenges encountered at various points in team life cycles, and suggestions for overcoming these challenges. We discuss the implications of our findings for organizations planning to adopt or currently using virtual project teams. We also offer specific recommendations for coaching virtual teams at each stage of their life cycle.

The Emergence of Virtual Teams

Globalization and technological advancements have led to an increase in virtual team use over the last decade. Estimates suggest that in the US alone, as many as 8.4 million employees are members of one or more virtual teams or groups.[3] Numerous studies of virtual teams document how they operate and how they compare to traditional, face-to-face teams. For example, *The Executive* has published several articles discussing the birth of virtual teams as an alternative work form, the advantages and disadvantages of virtual work, and the specific challenges confronting virtual teams.[4]

Virtual teams afford many advantages to organizations, including increased knowledge sharing and employee job satisfaction and commitment, as well as improved organizational performance.[5] However, virtual teams can also face a

---

* FOODCO is a pseudonym being used to protect the anonymity of the company.

number of unique challenges that often prevent them from obtaining successful outcomes. Broadly, these challenges include (1) logistical problems, such as communicating and coordinating work across time and space, (2) interpersonal concerns, such as establishing effective working relationships with team members in the absence of frequent face-to-face communication, and (3) technology issues, such as identifying, learning, and using technologies most appropriate for certain tasks.[6]

There is an abundance of advice to managers on how to motivate virtual teams to high levels of performance. Some authors encourage managers to help virtual teams draft mission statements, set goals, and coordinate their work. Others emphasize the importance of teambuilding exercises to create a team identity and strengthen interpersonal relationships. Much of this advice is based on single observations or laboratory studies with student virtual teams. Our goal is to understand how virtual teams of real employees develop through every phase of a team life cycle from team formation through product delivery. Our focus is on helping managers understand the special challenges that virtual project teams confront at each stage of development and how to time intervention strategies so that teams can make smooth transitions.

The Life Cycle of Virtual Project Teams

Teams are more effective when members can combine their individual talents, skills, and experiences via appropriate working relationships and processes.[7] Two models that describe how teams evolve through this process have been proposed by Tuckman (1965) and Gersick (1988).[8]

Tuckman's Stage Model of Development
Based on an extensive analysis of groups located in one place, Tuckman identified four distinct stages of team development: forming, storming, norming, and performing. During the forming stage, team members share information about themselves and their task explicitly through discussions or implicitly through non-verbal cues, such as status symbols or physical traits. Ideally, team members also establish trust, clarify group goals, and develop shared expectation's in this stage. Efforts to resolve these issues often surface differences of opinions, and in the storming stage, conflicts emerge as team members work to identify appropriate roles and responsibilities. Groups able to resolve conflicts move to the norming stage. In this stage, teams recognize and agree on ways of working together, strengthen relationships, and solidify understanding of member obligations, all of which increase levels of trust, mission clarity, and coordination. Finally, teams reach the performing stage during which team members work toward project completion, actively helping and encouraging each other.

Gersick's Punctuated Equilibrium Model
Gersick examined the impact of deadline pressures on the development processes of work teams. She described a "punctuated equilibrium" model of development in which a team's evolution is marked by two periods of stability—Phase I and Phase II—punctuated by abrupt changes at the project midpoint that occurs halfway to the deadline.[9] Phase I begins with the first team meeting and continues until the team is halfway to a project's deadline. During Phase I, teams try to establish a working agenda and to develop norms that guide early project efforts. These activities parallel Tuckman's forming, storming, and norming stages. At the project midpoint, a transition occurs as teams assess the norms and assumptions set during Phase I. Teams dissatisfied with their progress may seek advice from an outside leader or facilitator in order to develop more effective norms. Teams satisfied with their performance maintain the status quo. With a successful transition, team members focus on their performance for the duration of the project (Phase II). This transition is usually followed by a burst of activity to insure that the team meets the deadline with an acceptable outcome.

Some evidence shows that virtual teams evolve through processes similar to those described by Tuckman and Gersick, although differences in the speed and pattern of development appear to exist.[10] These findings provide some clues that the evolution of virtual project teams may be more complex and challenging than for co-located teams. For instance, reliance on electronic communication may slow the establishment of trust, limit conflict resolution, promote free riding, and inhibit team synergy and performance. Similarly, it may be more difficult for virtual project teams to (re) assess their progress, reflect on collective work ethics, and recommit to task completion within designated time frames, as described by the punctuated equilibrium model. These issues, which we detail in the next section, are summarized in Table 1.

The Challenges Associated with Virtual Team Development

Forming
In co-located teams, face-to-face interactions during the early stages of a project provide opportunities for building relationships based on common interests and permit individuals to analyze their colleagues' trustworthiness based on observation and conversation. Developing high-quality relationships is more difficult and takes longer when team members are geographically dispersed because reliance on electronic communications often diminishes communication frequency.[11] Proximity enables team members to engage in informal work and non-work related conversations that can occur over coffee, at the water cooler, or during lunch.[12] More frequent interaction increases opportunities to break the ice,

Table 1

Stages of Virtual Project Team Development

Tuckman: Gersick:	**Forming**	**Storming Phase I**	**Norming Midpoint Transition**	**Performing Phase II**
		Model		
Description of Team Behavior During Each Stage	Team members get to know each other, exchange information about themselves and the task at hand, establish trust among group members, and clarify group goals and expectations	Similarities and differences are revealed and conflicts surface as the group attempts to identify appropriate roles and responsibilities among the members	Team members recognize and agree on ways of sharing information and working together; relationships are strengthened, and team members agree on member obligations and team strategy	Team members work toward project completion, actively helping and encouraging each other
Challenges to Virtual Teams	Fewer opportunities for informal work- and non-work-related conversations; risk of making erroneous stereotypes in the absence of complete information; trust slower and more difficult to develop	Reliance on less rich communication channels may exacerbate conflicts by provoking misunderstandings; ease of withdrawing behaviors; diversity of work contexts; reliance on an emergent or assigned team leader	Difficulty in developing norms around modes of communication, speed, and frequency of responding, and commitment to use special software	Vulnerability to competing pressures from local assignments, frustrations over free-riding or non-committed teammates, and communication discontinuities due to asynchronous communication

establish lines of communication, and identify points of similarity, all of which are critical for successful team formation.

Reliance on electronic communications also increases the potential for faulty first impressions and erroneous stereotypes.[13] In the absence of visual or audio cues provided by some technologies, team members may develop incorrect stereotypes based on geographic and cultural differences, or differences in functional expertise. These mistaken stereotypes or presumed differences between team members can undermine relationship-building efforts.[14] In particular, teams may struggle to form a collective identity that promotes a shared commitment to a common goal.[15]

Successful navigation through the forming stage requires that team members establish a sense of trust.[16] In face-to-face teams, trust develops based on social and emotional attachments. In virtual teams, trust develops based on more identifiable actions as timely information sharing, appropriate responses to electronic communications, and keeping commitments to virtual teammates.[17] These actions signal that team members are competent and want to help the team, but they take time to occur in the virtual environment.

Storming

As Table 1 notes, past research on co-located teams suggests that disagreement and conflict characterize the storming stage of team development. In the virtual environment, the use of communication technologies may prolong these conflicts. Without the benefit of the subtle social cues associated with face-to-face communications (body language, tone of voice, and facial expressions), misunderstandings can occur more readily.[18] Electronic communication can exacerbate conflict when team members simply refuse to respond to electronic messages. This explains why virtual teams, particularly those working on complex, non-technical issues, take longer to reach consensus on team process issues than do co-located teams.[19]

The presumed diversity of work settings can also inhibit conflict resolution for virtual teams. For example, in some work settings, technology and support staff are available to support virtual teams. In less advanced settings, even minor technical problems can be disruptive for teams and team members. Similarly, in some settings, managers or team members may view virtual team participation as a high priority, while others may view it as a distraction from more immediate concerns. Team members in different work settings can form different expectations regarding how to coordinate work and accomplish team objectives.[20]

In the storming stage, virtual project team sponsors can appoint team leaders to help minimize conflicts that can occur over role assignments. When leadership selection is based on the skills critical for virtual team success, including conflict management, virtual teams are more likely to survive the storming stage.[21] However, self-managed virtual project teams are created without a formal leader, and other teams are formed with a misplaced emphasis on a leader's technical as opposed to interpersonal skills. In such cases, the emergence of an informal or social leader may be an agonizingly slow process. And, if virtual teams are low in trust, the absence of an emergent or formal leader can have serious consequences for later team performance.[22]

Norming

Table 1 shows that in the norming stage of development, virtual teams work to strengthen relationships, solidify norms around team processes, and reach consensus regarding obligations, timetables, and deadlines. These efforts mirror the activities that teams may engage in at Gersick's "midpoint transition." At this point, teams assess whether their work processes have been effective or if they need to be revised. Special challenges confronting virtual teams in the norming stage include coordinating work, developing a shared understanding around modes of communication, and the speed and frequency of responding.

Virtual teams must establish norms governing both work processes and communication content. Agreements on timetables and individual areas of responsibility are essential for virtual team effectiveness.[23] Structured schedules and timelines enable virtual team members to coordinate work across time zones and to manage variations in team members' "local" work schedules and demands. Working virtually also requires keeping all members informed. Unfortunately,

some members may initially lack the discipline to follow virtual team agreements with respect to information sharing. For example, phone calls and emails between a subset of team members may feel comfortable and appear efficient but could prove to be self-defeating when other members are deprived of critical information or made to feel like second-class team members.[24] Creating new habits around the use of shareware and other technology platforms which allow members to archive documents and use message boards are among the challenges facing virtual teams during the norming stage.

Norms must also address the quality and candidness of communication. In any team, members may be reluctant to share creative but potentially divisive ideas with their teammates. In the virtual context, it is not easy to test the waters, gauge potential reactions, and/or modify ideas based on the subtle feedback often available in co-located teams. Virtual team members may also withhold message postings critical of teammate suggestions to spare others from embarrassment. Thus, norms that require complete information sharing have the paradoxical effect of making virtual team members more cautious when it comes to publicly sharing untested ideas or offering criticisms of others.[25] Clearly, establishing trust in earlier stages of team development is a necessary condition for solidifying these kinds of norms at this stage.

Performing

The performing stage of development requires that teams effectively collect and share information, integrate members' inputs, look for creative solutions to problems, and prepare deliverables for outside sponsors. At this stage, virtual team members are able to collaborate and sustain a task focus across multiple assignments.[26] This is "crunch time" as teams become aware of impending deadlines and increase their activity to ensure that the deadline is met.

Maintaining team performance and synergy during this stage is particularly challenging for virtual project teams. Virtual team members can face competing pressures from local assignments, frustrations over free-riding teammates, and communication problems associated with asynchronous communication. Without a formal leader of maintain team morale and motivation, virtual team members may lose focus. Failure to meet deadlines, poorly written reports, and ill-conceived recommendations may have serious career consequences for all concerned. Hence, the performing stage of team development can be a period of great satisfaction and/or stress.

The experiences of virtual project teams throughout their life cycles are more complex and challenging when compared to face-to-face project teams. For managers charged with supporting virtual project teams, additional insights may be gained from studying multiple "real life" virtual teams as they move through their life cycles. Of specific interest are the factors associated with performance effectiveness at each stage of team development.

FOODCO: A Longitudinal Study of Virtual Project Teams

To learn more about how virtual project teams develop, we followed six virtual project teams from FOODCO, one of the nation's leading food service distributors. The six project teams were formed as part of an Executive Leadership Institute (ELI) commissioned by FOODCO's top executives at a major southeastern university in the US. FOODCO executives requested that a key component of the ELI be projects requiring participants to work in cross-disciplinary virtual project teams addressing business issues that executives deemed "critical" to company performance. ELI administrators assigned four to five participants to each project team, ensuring that each team had cross-functional representation and included at least one participant with expertise relevant to the issue under investigation. Team assignments, listed in Table 2, required the collection of archival data, interviews with key employees in the company, analysis and synthesis of this information, and the development of recommendations and presentations for these projects. A complete description of the ELI goals and objectives, the virtual team assignments, and the methodology used to assess the evolution of virtual teams is provided in the Appendix.

The project design allowed team members to work briefly face-to-face during each of three residency periods prior to the project presentations. However, the majority of their work was necessarily completed while team members worked in their home offices. Technology available to the teams included phone, email, fax, conference calling, and other resources necessary to work collaboratively. FOODCO assigned a senior sponsor to each virtual team to assist in the project. Sponsors were company executives who had a vested interest in seeing the team succeed and were willing to help obtain needed resources, overcome organizational barriers, and provide guidance on how to approach and complete the team's work.[27] Teams were instructed to initiate contact with their senior sponsors, as needed, throughout the eight-month project period. Sponsors would not do a team's work nor be responsible for the quality of the team's deliverables.

Next, we summarize our survey and interview findings for each time period.

The Virtual Team Life Cycle

Time 1: Forming—Unbridled Optimism

During the first residency period, team members' perceptions of the likelihood of team success reflected a sense of unbridled optimism, which is also characteristic of most non-virtual work teams. Team members were able to meet briefly with their project teammates, and survey results following these early meetings suggested that teams started on an equal footing. There were no differences in team members' initial assessments of their time available to work on the project, their comfort with technology, and their confidence in working virtually. Perceptions regarding the meaningfulness of their assignment, the support for the project in their local offices, and the availability of resources to carry out the project also did not differ.

Team members felt confident that they could meet the desired performance goals despite the nature of the virtual task. Responses to open-ended questions illustrated invariably high levels of optimism regarding how easily team members expected to complete their projects and how well they

Table 2

Project Team Assignments

Team	Name	Project Objective
1	ACQUIRE	To develop an integration strategy for acquisitions
2	ITECH	To determine how to efficiently transfer information technology from one subsidiary company to other parts of the firm
3	TRANSFER	To determine how to transfer best practices from one division of the company to another
4	AP	To streamline the accounts payable process
5	COMM	To conduct a corporate communications audit
6	CAREER	To develop career paths of specific jobs

would work together. Some representative comments included:

"I believe we have a great team and will work well together. We all understand the importance of the project and intend to take it seriously." (ACQUIRE team member)

"I feel the team will work well together, and I expect us to be very effective." (COMM team member)

"I think the team will work very well together. We all agree on the substance and the goal." (CAREER team member)

Time 2: Storming—Reality Shock

A second survey was administered early in the second residency, approximately two months later. At this time, several teams reported having spent little, if any time working on their virtual team projects since their initial meeting. Other teams reported spending several hours a week on their projects. Asked to describe which stage of development best characterized their team at Time 2, one team reported that they had already reached the performing stage ("Team members are clear about their responsibilities, and we are making excellent progress"). Other teams felt they were still in the forming stage ("We're just getting started").

At Time 2, we noted several differences between team members' perceptions of mission clarity, team trust and support, involvement of senior sponsors, and productivity. Most teams had not yet identified a leader by this point in the program. Some teams neglected boundary management issues—failing to keep sponsors informed of problems or developing strategies for using sponsors to assist with resource acquisition, for instance. One team member, indicating that his team had been delayed by the absence of senior sponsor input, remarked, "Due to other business problems, our senior sponsor has been unavailable. This has made it difficult for us to get a clear focus on the project."

More than half of the program participants indicated that their teams had encountered some difficulties working on their project in the virtual environment between Times 1 and 2. Lack of commitment from some team members became evident at this point as several teams reported occurrences of "free riding." While it is not uncommon for members of co-located teams to express concern over some team members not doing "their fair share," the frustrations that our virtual team members expressed with non-performers appeared amplified because team members could not directly observe or influence one another's behavior. Specific comments reflected four primary issues with which some groups had struggled: establishing leadership roles, setting direction, coordinating work, and building commitment to the task. Comments in these areas included,

"No one has taken a leadership role. We have not made the project the priority that it deserves." (ITECH team member)

"Team members' day-to-day tasks are being used as an excuse to avoid doing the project." (ITECH team member)

"It has been difficult to get all members to attend each conference call. Out of 5 calls there has not been perfect attendance yet." (AP team member)

These comments reflect a variety of issues impeding trust-building and commitment. To their credit, many teams began to address these issues during the second ELI residence period. The opportunity for face-to-face interaction allowed some teams to "clear the air" and deal with passive and destructive individual and team behaviors. Resolution of team issues provided a basis for the establishment of team norms, reflecting an example of "punctuation" where some teams discussed and changed their work processes.

Time 3: Norming—Refocus and Recommit

By Time 3 (during the third residency period, approximately mid-way through the project life cycle), most teams recognized the need for reaching agreement on how they would operate going forward. Teams had revisited (and reinforced) existing norms or had established new norms regarding information collection, document sharing, task responsibilities, acceptable attendance at conference calls, and team commitment. Teams discussed ways in which members could be held more accountable for timely delivery of project assignments and openly confronted problems that might interfere with the completion of their projects. Teams also expressed some regret about their initial passivity, lack of initiative, and delays in collecting information.

Our survey and interview data at this point suggested that teams now differed with respect to perceived levels of team trust, sponsor support, and team performance (the percentage of work completed to date). For example, several teams reported high levels of trust in their teammates, while others reported minimal intra-team trust. At Time 3, the ACQUIRE and AP teams reported making the most progress, indicating that they had completed more than half of their projects. ITECH members reported making the least amount of progress on their assignment, having completed only a quarter of their planned work.

We used team-member perceptions of progress toward project completion as a proxy for team performance and examined what factors measured at Time 2 predicted team performance at Time 3. Results indicated that progress at Time 3 was associated with greater levels of communication, knowledge sharing, and confidence in performing the task at Time 2. Participant comments indicated that several teams struggled with issues of commitment and accountability during the norming stage that likely inhibited their progress. Developing norms required each team member to fulfill his/her assigned role, share important information, and meet deadlines. A majority of comments reflected the desire for greater commitment to the project, more discipline in working on the project, and better time management, communication, and coordination. Below are several illustrative comments:

"Virtual teaming is something that requires discipline." (ACQUIRE team member)

"We need to develop a sense of urgency." (ITECH team member)

"It is difficult to get people to do what they say." (TRANSFER team member)

"You must make firm commitments to specific time schedules." (CAREER team member)

These observations prompted some team members to increase their commitment levels and their communications with one another. When asked "What additional changes, if any, do you need to make to deliver an outstanding project?" many participants reported the need to develop a greater sense of urgency about the project, to speed up their work, and to communicate responsibilities more explicitly. Representative comments included:

"We may need to buckle down to get to work. Devoting the necessary time to the project has it challenges." (CAREER team member)

"We really need to communicate each team member's responsibilities" (ACQUIRE team member)

"We need to refocus our energy on moving forward." (COMM team member)

Time 4: Performing—A (Sometimes Mad) Dash to the Finish

At Time 4, differences among teams emerged with respect to levels of team commitment, sponsor involvement, coordination, intra-team trust, and member "loafing." During the final week of the ELI, the teams presented their project findings and recommendations to the other ELI participants, seven senior FOODCO executives, including the CEO, CFO, and president, and five faculty members. These twelve nonparticipants evaluated each project for content, quality, and anticipated effectiveness. Aggregated team scores from these observations provided the performance data used to assess how a variety of factors affected team effectiveness.

Project team effectiveness as measured above was found to be a function of team members' perceptions of the availability of resources at Time 1. Teams that perceived greater amounts of resource availability at the onset of their projects performed better at the end of the project. At Time 2, teams with greater mission clarity, more time to examine work process effectiveness, and higher perceived levels of sponsor support were more effective at Time 4. At Time 3, none of the variables we examined predicted team performance at Time 4.

At Time 4, we also asked participants to reflect on their experiences and to consider what they had learned from their virtual projects. Responses suggest that the teams clearly underestimated the challenges associated with working virtually. During the "honeymoon period" (Time 1), they had anticipated minimal conflict, strong individual contributions from team members, and few obstacles to project completion. By the end of the project, participants uniformly remarked that virtual interactions were far more difficult than they had expected. Participants' responses to the question "If you could turn back the clock and start over, what would you do differently?" included,

"Better define what the project was. We had a lot of problems at the beginning not knowing about what we were to work on." (AP team member)

"We could have included our mentor (sponsor) more in the planning phase of the project; this would have helped eliminate any wrong paths." (CAREER team member)

"More discipline in hitting timeline." (TRANSFER team member)

Additionally, when asked "What advice would you give future virtual teams?" nearly three quarters of the participants replied "Start earlier!" stressing the importance of establishing a clear mission and structured work processes from the outset. Representative comments included:

"Start early, meet often, and hold each other accountable to timelines and workloads." (TRANSFER team member)

"Communicate a lot in the early stages. Find out what each person's strengths are, and get everyone involved. Hold members accountable." (AP team member)

"Start early and talk at least every other week. Set firm deadlines." (CAREER team member)

Comparing the Most and Least Effective Teams

A profile of the "best" team shows that at each step of the life cycle this team was proactive, focused, resourceful, and unafraid to seek support and guidance as needed. Specifically, evaluations of team effectiveness demonstrated that among the six virtual teams, CAREER was the most effective while AP was the least effective. A comparison of these teams at each data collection period reveals the significant issues that successful virtual teams resolve at various stages of their development. At Time 2, CAREER had developed much stronger consensus regarding team mission compared to the AP team. CAREER also reported greater levels of sponsor support and more frequent assessments of team processes than the AP team. These differences likely reflect the amount of time that the CAREER team committed to their project at the beginning of the assignment compared to their colleagues on the AP team.

Results at Time 3 revealed other differences between the CAREER and AP teams. For instance, the CAREER team recognized that they had developed effective working procedures but were not fully clear about responsibilities. Team members realized that their work processes might need to be revised to meet their deadline and perform well. The AP team, in contrast, struggled with how they could best accomplish their work. CAREER was also more confident than AP that they could deliver an outstanding product and that their recommendations would be acted upon by the firm.

At Time 4, differences between the two teams were even more apparent. In particular, CAREER reported maintaining higher levels of mission clarity, communication, commitment, and trust among team members. These differences suggest that between Times 3 and 4 the CAREER team recognized what changes needed to be made and successfully adapted their work processes to deliver an outstanding final product.

Guiding Virtual Teams Through the Life Cycle: Guidelines for Managers

This study represents one of the few research efforts that follow virtual project teams from project inception to completion. We were fortunate to have access to six virtual teams situated in an organization, dealing with real issues that required a tangible outcome for top management. Our findings thus provide a rare glimpse into the dynamics of "real life" virtual teams. Our data enabled us to explore which factors at each stage of development contribute to team performance and to identify the special challenges confronting virtual project teams as they develop. Importantly, however, our results should be interpreted with some caution as the experiences of our 29 participants and the six teams they formed as part of the ELI may not have been captured fully in our data nor may their experiences be applicable to all virtual project teams. For example, we do not know the extent to which the teams were evenly distributed in talent and capabilities or the extent to which team sponsors or local managers encouraged team members to take the endeavor seriously. These limitations notwithstanding, we offer our insights into how managers can guide virtual project teams through the project life cycle.

Not surprisingly, we found that working virtually delayed team progress through the forming stage by diminishing opportunities to communicate. Indeed, many of the virtual project teams communicated infrequently (if at all) during the early, forming stages of their projects. The lack of communication among team members reduced mission clarity and productivity at the project's onset, stifling early momentum and sending these teams into a spiral of failure. Contrary to our expectations and past research on virtual student teams, trust was not particularly difficult to establish at the beginning of the teams' projects. In fact, for almost all of the teams, perceptions of trust peaked at Time 2 and declined thereafter. Perhaps team members recognized that participation in the ELI was highly selective and inferred that teammates should be competent, hard working, and trustworthy. As the projects progressed and some team

members failed to demonstrate competence and commitment to the team during the storming and norming stages, disillusionment set in, and perceptions of trust eroded.

Our findings underscore the critical role that senior sponsors can play in assisting virtual project teams through the early stages of development. The most successful teams we observed actively sought and initiated senior sponsor involvement at the early and middle stages of team life cycles. Sponsors helped these teams define their mission, set guidelines and accountabilities, and build confidence, facilitating team formation and reducing the length of the storming stage. In contrast, teams without early sponsor involvement lacked direction and momentum during this formative period. The lack of support prevented these teams from successfully navigating through the storming stage, often undermining team members' confidence and motivation to learn through the remainder of the projects. Indeed, our observations of the ELI teams are consistent with prior research in the project management literature which suggests the importance of early, pre-project planning and leadership support. This literature concludes that successful project teams invest time upfront with project managers to deal with the "fuzzy front end" of their projects which are often characterized by an ill-defined purpose, ambiguity regarding roles and responsibilities, and the uncertainty of acquiring resources and support. Hackman has recently offered the same insights in his discussion of the role of leaders in managing successful teams.[28]

As the ELI teams entered the norming stage of development and attempted to more clearly define work processes, many struggled with coordination and commitment issues. Team members expressed doubts about one another's commitment to the projects and raised concerns of possible "free riding" by some members, reflected in missed meetings, scheduling conflicts, and unreturned emails and phone calls. These behaviors may have been due to more pressing local work demands or technological breakdowns. However, without the benefit of direct observation and a full understanding of team members' local work contexts, both of which are typically afforded to co-located teams, virtual team members attributed the lack of participation and communication to a lack of commitment. Managers should encourage communication between team members to clarify whether lapses in participation are due to a lack of commitment or competing demands.

Consistent with prior research on virtual teams, we found that periodic face-to-face meetings marked periods of "punctuation" and provided teams with an opportunity to (re)assess their progress. For some teams, a pattern emerged in which energy devoted to working on the projects peaked shortly before each residency and quickly dissipated when team members dispersed. However, our best performing teams took advantage of the time between residencies to maintain momentum and developed a learning orientation by continuously sharing information and knowledge with one another. This disciplined approach to managing their

Table 3

Managerial Interventions During the Virtual Project Team Life Cycle

Formation	Storming	Norming	Performing
• Realistic virtual project team previews	• Face-to-face team building sessions	• Create customized templates or team charters specifying task requirements	• Ensure departmental and company culture supports virtual team work
• Coaching from experienced team members	• Training on conflict resolution	• Set individual accountabilities, completion dates, and schedules	• Provide sponsor support and resources for team to perform
• Develop a shared understanding and sense of team identity	• Encourage conflicting employees to work together to find common ground	• Establish procedures for information sharing	
• Develop a clear mission	• Shuttle diplomacy and mediation to create compromise solutions	• Distinguish task, social, and contextual information; design procedures appropriate for each	
• Acquire senior manager support		• Assign a team coach with skills for managing virtually	

"virtual" activities enabled teams to be more confident of their ability to deliver an outstanding project and more confident that their recommendations would be implemented.

Our observations and analyses suggest important implications for organizations considering the use of virtual project teams. Based on prior research regarding on-site team development and supported by findings derived from our longitudinal observations of the six ELI virtual teams, we offer suggestions for possible interventions appropriate to each stage in the virtual team life cycle. These interventions, described below, are summarized in Table 3.

Interventions at the Forming Stage

Our findings highlight a degree of unbounded but perhaps unrealistic optimism about potential virtual team success during the forming stage. This was often followed by the shock of slow progress, concern about teammates' commitment levels, problems with sponsor support, and anxiety over pending deadlines during later stages of team development. All six of our teams reported that their first experience working virtually was surprisingly difficult, and many commented that the opportunity provided valuable lessons that would help them in any future virtual team assignments. Frustrations stemming from unrealistically high expectations are not uncommon to project teams.[29] However, we believe that managerial prescriptions for helping virtual teams establish reasonable expectations must be sensitive to the unique challenges of virtual work.

Providing virtual project team members with insights from those who have served in similar situations is one way we suggest to improve team formation, as it should alert new teams to potential problems and pitfalls.[30] For example, Sabre uses realistic previews to focus virtual team members' attention on the importance of getting off to a fast start, contacting sponsors early, and scheduling opportunities for synchronous communication well in advance. Previews might also include other specific insights gained from previous virtual project team experience or might profile the characteristics of successful virtual teams as a benchmark against which new teams can chart their progress.

At the forming stage, care should be taken to help the virtual project team establish a shared team identity to prevent team members from abandoning the virtual project when they return to their home offices. Initial communications, whether face-to-face, teleconference, videoconference, or on-line, should encourage the exchange of personal information about backgrounds, skills, and experiences designed to help team members get to know one another and identify common ground. To help the team create a unique identity, teams might develop their own language or jargon to engage members or develop logos/symbols to serve as a constant visual reminder of the team and its mission.[31]

Our findings complement prior research on work teams by highlighting the importance of involving a senior sponsor early in the team's life cycle and gaining "unequivocal support from the top of the organization."[32] Indeed, the least effective sponsors we observed proceeded with their roles in a laissez-faire manner, did not proactively contact the teams, and did not attend their final presentations. Moreover, these sponsors failed to clarify their teams' missions until the teams had completed a considerable amount of work. This created enormous frustration when midway through the projects the sponsors expressed concern that the teams were not meeting expectations.

Effective senior sponsors can help virtual project teams clarify their mission and ensure that team members have the resources needed to accomplish their tasks, such as funding travel costs for intermittent face-to-face meetings.[33] Senior sponsors can also be used to provide pertinent information and an "expert opinion" on the teams' task. For example, in the virtual teams that Lipnack and Stamps observed from Eastman Chemical Co. and Sun Microsystems, senior sponsors advised teams on their task, were invited to key meetings, and were included in email correspondence between team members.[34] Finally, sponsors can help teams create "small wins" upfront that provide a springboard for future performance. For example, one of the more successful virtual teams we followed used their sponsor to help develop and administer a survey shortly after the initial meeting. The launch of the survey energized team members and provided a confidence boost for their efforts going forward. This practice has been used successfully at IBM where virtual team sponsors assist teams in creating an important 30-day goal upfront that requires full team participation. Similar to the team we observed, teams at IBM use these 30-day projects as vehicles to come together and build early momentum.[35] An important intervention at the forming stage requires managers to foster a collaborative partnership between sponsors and their virtual teams.

Interventions at the Storming Stage
Much has been written about the self-fueling spiral of success or failure experienced by many types of teams.[36] In particular, teams that experience early success gain confidence and motivation, which fuels future efforts and continued success. Conversely, teams that struggle initially lose confidence and momentum, stifling motivation and sending these teams into a spiral of failure. The importance of teams getting off to a fast start and building on early successes to generate momentum cannot be overemphasized. The virtual project team members we followed consistently pointed to the need for teams to build consensus around the team mission, work out role assignments, commit to goals, and confront conflicts. The most effective virtual teams reported the eventual development of greater mission clarity and higher levels of coordination and agreement around monthly goals, all of which reflected the time that these teams invested up front on their projects and the active, early involvement of the senior sponsor. Less successful teams reported early ambiguity around the project's purpose, unresolved coordination problems, and conflict over some members' lack of commitment, all symptoms of the self-fueling spiral of failure.

Though sometimes costly and inconvenient, a face-to-face team-building session for virtual teams is highly recommended early in the team development process to reduce the impact of an unsuccessful storming stage on team development. The senior sponsor could assign an experienced team facilitator or "coach" to help virtual team members focus on building consensus around a team's mission, differentiating roles, clarifying assignments, and resolving conflicts. Meeting face-to-face provides the richest possible communication context, often proving critical for overcoming problems encountered early in a virtual team's development.[37]

In situations where early face-to-face meetings are not possible, alternatives such as video or teleconferencing meetings can still provide a relatively rich opportunity for exchanges and can offer many, but not all, of the advantages of face-to-face meetings. If conflict cannot be resolved at such meetings, teams may employ more overt techniques aimed at addressing specific points of conflict.[38] For instance, a team leader or facilitator may ask conflicting team members to work together to resolve a problem and to foster greater understanding and appreciation of each other's perspective. In rare cases where a consensus regarding protocol or other coordination issues cannot be reached, teams may consider using "shuttle diplomacy" or mediation.[39] Specifically, a facilitator will communicate with team members individually to hear issues, concerns, or ideas, and then consolidate these viewpoints to come up with a compromise solution.

Interventions at the Norming Stage
Our teams reported that problems with information gathering, commitment from some team members, and free riding by others became more apparent at the norming stage of development. Teams acknowledged that their current work pace would make it nearly impossible to meet deadlines. The seriousness of these shortcomings led many teams to markedly increase their work efforts. For the best teams, a renewed

commitment proved critical for project completion. For those teams hopelessly behind, norms governing commitment and productivity developed too late, the teams became stressed, and the final results were relatively disappointing.

We believe that early managerial intervention will increase the likelihood that teams develop norms governing commitment, accountability, and productivity, as our successful teams did. Managers who observe teams struggling with scheduling and coordination conflicts, miscommunications between distal team members, and gaining team members' commitment to the task can provide virtual teams with templates that identify strategies for improved team coordination.[40] Teams can then customize a template to include specific task requirements, individual accountabilities, expected completion dates, and mechanisms for collecting, collating, and sharing information. Managers can also help virtual teams identify norms regarding communication content, including how to share contextual information. For example, managers at Intel encourage virtual team members to send a "face" depicting their mood on any given day so that team members can better understand how to interpret and respond to team member communications.[41]

Some virtual teams may benefit from using electronic decision support systems to stimulate brain-storming and group decision-making.[42] Managers should provide training to ensure that team members know how to use these technologies and use them appropriately, as needed. Virtual team leaders at Novartis recommend that training team members in the use of more complex collaborative technologies should be incremental, allowing team members to become comfortable with various features of a given technology over time.[43]

In addition to the impact of a supportive senior sponsor, another possible intervention is to assign project teams "coaches" skilled in virtual management to nurture virtual project teams through the early development stages. Senior sponsors may not have had experience managing virtual teams and/or may not be sufficiently accessible to team members to provide the type of personal suggestions a "coach" could provide. In addition to providing team members with a realistic preview of the virtual team experience, coaches could counsel team members on- or off-line, model the appropriate use of communication and collaboration technologies, and reinforce the value of managing boundary relationships.[44] Indeed, our most successful teams were particularly proactive, seeking out informal sources of coaching and support. Once team members experience success working virtually, they should become well situated to coaching new virtual project members and teams.

Interventions at the Performing Stage

As these results suggest, many factors contribute to virtual project team effectiveness. We have emphasized how team processes can contribute to or detract from team performance. However, it is equally important to recognize that virtual team members do not function in isolation. Corporate and sub-unit cultures may also influence virtual team effectiveness.

Virtual project team sponsors may need to intervene to shape a more supportive corporate and sub-unit context within which virtual teams can flourish. In most instances, serving on a virtual project team is a part-time assignment. Team members must balance competing local demands for their time with commitments made to their virtual project teams. Virtual team sponsors must be sensitive to these dual demands and, as needed, be willing to negotiate with local executives the relative importance and time commitment required for successful virtual project team participation.

One of our least successful teams reported minimal support for their project activities among executives in the divisions represented on this team. Team members also believed that their performance evaluation and compensation for their "real (non-virtual) job" were at risk if they made more than a token commitment to the virtual project team. In contrast, our most successful virtual team reported complete support for their virtual project efforts by senior managers in all of the divisions represented by the team. By providing team members with the necessary time and resources to work on both their local and virtual projects, senior management signaled that outcomes of the virtual project team were valued. The lesson seems obvious: To thrive, virtual project teams must be embedded in supportive corporate cultures.

In addition to providing sufficient resources, managers can use other strategies to create a supportive culture. For example, virtual team leaders at ARCO reported that to support their virtual team's efforts, team leaders "buffer" interference from on-site work demands.[45] When virtual team members are relieved from some of their typical local demands, they may focus more energy on the virtual team assignment without fear of reprisal from their local managers.

The creation of virtual teams will likely require that managers realign recognition and reward systems to better assess and reward virtual team performance.[46] For example, Sabre uses a balanced scorecard approach for tracking virtual team performance that provides quantitative and qualitative information including growth, profitability, process improvement, and customer satisfaction.[47] Teams may wish to complement this objective performance data with 360 degree evaluation procedures to capture unique individual contributions. By realigning recognition and reward systems, managers help their virtual teams discover how various stakeholders, including customers, other team members, and outsiders perceive the quality of their work.[48]

Conclusion: Timing the Interventions

To mobilize virtual project teams, managers need insights into the challenges associated with each stage of the virtual team life cycle. Based on our comparison of flourishing and floundering virtual teams, it appears that managers who can recognize the signs of steady progress as well as the signs of distress associated with virtual team development will be in stronger positions to keep their teams on track. Similar to the concept of a "teachable moment" for introducing skills training at the point where these skills are most salient, managers must learn to time the introduction of interventions to virtual team life cycle challenges.[49] To conclude, we suggest a number of stage-appropriate interventions.

In the formation stage, realistic previews, exercises surrounding the creation of mission statements, and assistance in building team identity are all potentially useful strategies for helping virtual project teams get off to a fast start. The active involvement of a senior sponsor to clarify the team's mission and to ensure that the team has the resources it needs to perform can also boost early success. Because teams typically experience frustration and conflict in the storming stage, most teams should benefit from managerial interventions to help select appropriate procedures for working through conflicts, pushing teams more quickly to the norming stage of team development. Encouraging teams to establish a strong work ethic and to create mechanisms for holding members accountable for meeting deadlines are interventions particularly important at the norming stage.

At the performing stage, managerial interventions to facilitate brainstorming, decision making, and monitoring of progress against objectives and timelines will enhance team performance. Finally, and perhaps most important, are ongoing managerial efforts to embed virtual teams in supportive work contexts. Similar to other virtual team experiences chronicled in the literature, our six teams struggled to balance their virtual team demands with home office priorities.[50] To combat these competing demands, managerial interventions could take the form of negotiating work priorities with on-site supervisors and aligning reward systems to recognize virtual team contributions.

Certainly, sponsors, coaches, managers, and virtual team leaders and members have many intervention options to assist struggling virtual teams. But, as with so many organizational activities, timing is everything. Introducing interventions at the appropriate stage of development represents an important tool for leveraging virtual team performance. Having the tools in the toolkit is only the beginning. Knowing which tool to use when is the sign of the true master craftsman.

Appendix: Descriptive Information Regarding the Six Virtual Project Team Participants

The members of the six virtual project teams that we followed were employed by FOODCO. This company distributes food products to schools, hospitals, fast-food chains, and individually owned and operated restaurants, and manufactures a limited number of its own products. Executives at FOODCO commissioned a large university located in the southeastern US to create an Executive Leadership Institute (ELI) that would (1) align organizational learning with strategic business needs, (2) establish cross-organizational networks to encourage the sharing of best practices, (3) prepare managers for expanded organizational roles, (4) integrate new managers from FOODCO's recent acquisitions, and (5) develop a unified company culture across its multiple operating companies.

The 29 participants in the ELI program held positions of substantial responsibility in human resources, finance, marketing, sales, and operations areas. Superiors nominated participants for the program based on their potential to contribute to the company beyond their current levels of responsibility. Fourteen participants were from the executive ranks, while the remaining participants held middle-management positions.

Summary of Methodology Used to Study Virtual Project Teams at FOODCO

To assess the factors that contributed to virtual project team performance at various stages of the teams' life cycles, we collected survey and interview data throughout the eight-month project period. Specifically, during each of the four residence sessions, ELI participants completed surveys and participated in interviews designed to assess their attitudes and behaviors during the virtual project team assignment.

Participant surveys included both quantitative and qualitative questions. The quantitative data we collected at each time period varied slightly to reflect anticipated differences in development issues. During the first residency, participants were asked about the meaning of their project, its usefulness to the firm, the impact that the project would have on the company, how competent they felt to complete the project, and the anticipated climate for teamwork. During subsequent residence periods, survey questions focused on team process variables, such as perceptions of mission clarity, trust levels among team members, learning capacity, extent of sponsor support, and specific performance outcomes, including percentage of project completed, perceptions of team productivity, and perceived efficacy of completing an outstanding project.

Surveys also included several open-ended questions allowing participants to describe their views of the project, the challenges associated with virtual work, and their teams' responses to these challenges. For instance, during the first residency, we asked participants to "Describe your expectations for how you think your team will work together." Questions at the third residency focused on what individuals had learned about working virtually and what they would do differently had they been able to start over. During the final residency, we asked participants to reflect on their experience, to discuss what they learned about team processes that they could carry over to their current jobs, and to consider what advice they might give future virtual teams.

At the end of the fourth residency, teams presented their analysis and recommendations to a group of FOODCO's top executives and ELI administrators. This group rated the quality and content of each team's analysis of the critical business issue they researched and the quality of the recommendations they provided. They also rated the quality of the presentation delivered by each team. Each observer calculated an overall score for each team based on these three dimensions. We aggregated and averaged ratings for each team and used the result as the measure of team performance in further analyses.

Source: Academy of Management Executive, 18, (2), 6–20 (2004). Reprinted by permission of the CCC.

ENDNOTES

1. Townsend, A. M., DeMarie, S. M., & Hendrickson, A. R. 1998. Virtual teams: Technology and the workplace of the future. *The Academy of Management Executive*, 12(3): 17–29.

2. Potter, R. E., & Balthazard, P. A. 2002. Understanding human interaction and performance in the virtual team. *Journal of Information Technology Theory and Application*, 4: 1–23; Baker, G. 2002. The effects of synchronous collaborative technologies on decision making: A study of virtual teams. *Information Resources Management Journal*, 15(4): 79–93.

3. Ahuja, M. K., & Galvin, J. E. 2001. Socialization in virtual groups. *Journal of Management*, 29: 1–25.

4. Townsend, et al., 1998, op. cit.; Cascio, W. F. 2000. Managing a virtual workplace. *The Academy of Management Executive*, 14(3): 81–90; Kirkman, B. L., et al. 2002. Five challenges to virtual team success: Lessons from Sabre, Inc. *The Academy of Management Executive*, 16(3): 67–79.

5. See, for example, Banker, Lee, Potter, & Srinivasan, 1996; Wellins, Byham, & Dixon, 1994; Cohen & Ledford, 1994; and Cordery, Mueller, & Smith, 1991.

6. For studies that investigate coordination, communication interpersonal dynamics, and technology issues in virtual or computer-mediated teams, see Straus, S. G. 1996. Getting a clue: The effects of communication media and information distribution on participation and performance in computer-mediated and face-to-face groups. *Small Group Research*, 27: 115–42; Lipnack. J., & Stamps, J. 2000. *Virtual teams: People working across boundaries with technology*. 2nd ed. New York: Wiley; Daft, R. T., & Lengel, R. H. 1986. Organizational information requirements, media richness, and structural design. *Management Science*, 32: 554–571; and Straus, S. G., & McGrath, L. E. 1994.

Does medium matter? The interaction of task type and technology on group performance and member reactions. *Journal of Applied Psychology*, 79(1): 87–97.

7. Hackman, J. R. 1990. *Groups that work (and those that don't): Creating conditions for effective teamwork*. San Francisco: Jossey-Bass.

8. Tuckman, B. W. 1965. Development sequence in small groups. *Psychological Bulletin*, 63: 384–399; Gersick, C. J. G. 1988. Time and transition in work teams: Toward a new model of group development. *Academy of Management Journal*, 31: 9–41.

9. Gersick, C. J. G. 1994. Pacing strategic change: The case of a new venture. *Academy of Management Journal*, 37: 9–45.

10. See, for example, in Bordia, P., DiFonzo, N., & Chang, A. 1999. Rumor as group problem solving: Development patterns in informal computer-mediated teams. *Small Group Research*, 30: 8–28. For further evidence of pacing differences, see Gluesing, J. C., et al. 2002. The development of global virtual teams. In C. B. Gibson & S. G. Cohen (Eds.), *Virtual teams that work: Creating conditions for virtual team effectiveness*: 353–380. San Francisco: Jossey-Bass. For evidence of the punctuated equilibrium model in virtual teams, see Maznevski & Chudoba, 2000, op. cit.

11. Caproni, P. J. 2001. *The practical coach: Management skills for everyday life*. Upper Saddle River, NJ: Prentice-Hall (see specifically Chapter 8, entitled, "Diverse teams and virtual teams: Managing differences and distances," 247–287).

12. Cramton, C. D. 2001. The mutual knowledge problem and its consequences for dispersed collaboration. *Organization Science*, 12: 346–371.

13. Tsui, A. S., Egan, T. D., & O'Reilly III, C. A. 1992. Being different: Relational demography and organizational attachment. *Administrative Science Quarterly*, 37: 549–579.

14. Cramton, C. D. 2002. Finding common ground in dispersed collaboration. *Organizational Dynamics*, 30: 356–367.

15. Shapiro, D. L., et al. 2002. Transnational teams in the electronic age: Are team identity and high performance at risk? *Journal of Organizational Behavior*, 23: 455–467.

16. Handy, C. 1995. Trust and the virtual organization. *Harvard Business Review*, 73(9): 40–48.

17. Jarvenpaa, S. L., Knoll, K., & Leidner, D. E. 1998. Is anybody out there? Antecedents of trust in global

virtual teams. *Journal of Management Information Systems*. 14; 29–64.

18. Cramton, 2002, op. cit.

19. Hollingshead, A. B., & McGrath, J. E. 1995. Computer assisted groups: A critical review of the empirical research. In Guzzo, R., & Salas, E. (Eds.), *Team effectiveness and decision making in organizations*, San Francisco: Jossey-Bass: 46–78.

20. Hinds, P. J., & Weisband, S. P. 2002. Knowledge sharing and shared understanding in virtual teams. In C. B. Gibson & S. G. Cohen (Eds.), *Virtual teams that work: Creating conditions for virtual team effectiveness*: 221–36. San Francisco: Jossey-Bass.

21. Blackburn, R. S., Furst, S. A., & Rosen, B. 2002. Building a winning team: KSAs, selection, training, and evaluation. In C. B. Gibson & S. G. Cohen (Eds.), *Virtual teams that work: Creating conditions for virtual team effectiveness*: 95–120. San Francisco: Jossey-Bass.

22. Tyran, K. L., Tyran, C. K., & Shepard, M. 2002. Exploring emerging leadership in virtual teams. In C. B. Gibson & S. G. Cohen (Eds.), *Virtual teams that work: Creating conditions for virtual team effectiveness*: 183–195. San Francisco: Jossey-Bass.

23. Furst, S. A., Blackburn, R. S., & Rosen, B. 1999. Virtual team effectiveness: A proposed research agenda. *Information Systems Journal*, 9: 249–269.

24. Kirkman, et al., 2002, op. cit.

25. Jarvenpaa, et al., 1998, op. cit.; Cascio, 2000, op. cit.

26. Gluesing, et al., 2002, op. cit.

27. Kossler, M., & Prestridge, S. 2004. *Leading dispersed teams: Ideas into action guidebook*. Greensboro, NC: Center for Creative Leadership.

28. Hackman, J. R. 2002. *Leading teams: Setting the stage for great performances*: 199–232. Boston: Harvard Business School; Jiang, J. J., Klein, G., & Discenza, R. 2002. Pre-project partnering impact on an information system project, project team and project manager. *European Journal of Information Systems*, 11: 86–97; Zhang, Q., & Doll, W. J. 2001. The fuzzy front end and success of new product development: A causal model. *European Journal of Innovation Management*, 4(2): 95–112.

29. Wetlaufer, S., et al. 1994. The team that wasn't. *Harvard Business Review*, 72(6): 22–38.

30. Kirkman, et al., 2002, op. cit.

31. Malhotra, A., et al. 2001. Radical innovation without collocation: A case study at Boeing-Rocketdyne. *MIS Quarterly*, 25: 229–249.

32. Kossler & Prestridge, 2004, op. cit.

33. Ibid.

34. Lipnack, J., & Stamps, J. 2000, op. cit.

35. Rosen, B., et al. 2001. Is virtual the same as being there?: Not really! Paper presented at the National Academy of Management Meetings, Toronto.

36. Hackman, J. R. 1990. *Groups that work (and those that don't)*. San Francisco: Jossey-Bass.

37. Joinson, C. 2002. Managing virtual teams. *HR Magazine*, 47(6): 69–73.

38. Gluesing, et al., 2002, op. cit.

39. Ibid.

40. Montoya-Weiss, M. M., Massey. A. P., & Song, M. 2001. Getting it together: Temporal coordination and conflict management in global virtual teams. *Academy of Management Journal*, 44: 1251–1262.

41. Rosen, et al., 2001, op. cit.

42. Lam, S. S. K., & Shaubroeck, J. 2000. Improving group decisions by better pooling information: A comparative advantage of group decision support systems. *Journal of Applied Psychology*, 85(4): 565–573.

43. Rosen, et al., 2001, op. cit.

44. Jarvenpaa, S., & Leidner, D. 1998. Communication and trust in global virtual teams. *Organization Science*, 10(6): 791–815.

45. Ibid.

46. Lawler, E. E. 2002. Pay systems for virtual teams. In C. B. Gibson & S. G. Cohen (Eds.), *Virtual teams that work: Creating conditions for virtual team effectiveness*: 121–144. San Francisco: Jossey-Bass.

47. Kirkman, et al., 2002, op. cit.

48. Blackburn, et al., 2002, op. cit.

49. Ibid.

50. Reeves, M. & Furst, S. 2004. Virtual teams in an executive education training program. In S. H. Godar, & S. P. Ferris (Eds.), *Virtual and collaborative teams: Process, technologies, and practice*: 232–252. Hershey, PA: Idea Publishing Group; Gluesing, et al., 2002, op. cit.: Hackman, et al., 2002, op. cit.

Compensation

Strategic Compensation at Jamba Juice

Founded in 1990, San Francisco, California–based Jamba Juice has expanded to 300 stores that employ more than 4,000 workers in 15 states. Jamba is a leading retailer of blended-to-order fruit smoothies, fresh-squeezed juices, and healthful soups and breads. Since its inception, one of Jamba's chief challenges has been finding and retaining qualified managers. In a high-growth company that has intense competition within the industry, Jamba is additionally challenged by its location in the San Francisco Bay area, which provides many other career opportunities to the younger employees—Jamba recruits. A large number of these employers are technology based and offer more generous financial incentives than the typical food retailer.

To expand, Jamba must attract and retain these younger workers. To assist them in this objective, Jamba has developed an innovative compensation policy that allows it to compete not only within the growing juice industry but also with the technology-based employers who attract the same young employees. Jamba's "J.U.I.C.E. Plan" allows general managers to receive a percentage of the store's cash flow, predicated on the financial performance of their business. To keep good managers on board, Jamba provides opportunities for general managers to share in store profits over a three-year period. When general managers increase year-to-year sales in their operation, money accrues in a retention account, which is payable only in three-year cycles. Much like stock options that vest over three or five years in technology companies, Jamba's retention account not only provides short-term performance incentives but it also provides incentives to stay with Jamba. On top of this, Jamba also provides all employees at the managerial level with traditional stock options. When assistant managers are promoted, their general managers also receive a cash bonus of $1,000 for their development efforts.

In a fiercely competitive industry characterized by high turnover, Jamba was able to reduce turnover among managers during the first year of operating its J.U.I.C.E. Plan. Jamba has also received inquiries from Australia and Europe from prospective employees, managers, and franchisees. Ironically, the company's strategically designed compensation program has also provided the unintended benefit of fueling its growth.[1]

ompensation—a key strategic area for organizations—impacts an employer's ability to attract applicants, retain employees, and ensure optimal levels of performance from employees in meeting the organization's strategic objectives. Compensation is also a key economic issue: Compensation programs continue to assume an increasingly larger share of an organization's operating expenses. This is particularly true in service industries, which are highly labor intensive. A critical balancing act must occur to ensure that compensation attracts, motivates, and retains employees; at the same time, compensation should allow the organization to maintain a cost structure that enables it to compete effectively and efficiently in its markets.

Compensation, as part of an organization's total reward system, has been evolving relative to the changing needs of organizations and employees in recent years in a number of ways.[2] First, greater emphasis is being placed on employee performance and contribution, rather than seniority, in compensation decisions. Second, employers are taking a more holistic approach to compensation in offering enhanced and flexible benefits to meet individual employee needs and preferences. Third, greater emphasis is being placed on more immediate and intermittent rewards, rather than waiting for the annual performance review to announce compensation decisions. Fourth, organizational rewards are becoming more directly linked to the organization's mission, strategy, and goals. Fifth, compensation decisions and rewards are becoming more individualized, rather than applied equally, "across the board," to all employees.

An organization's compensation system usually consists of three separate components, as illustrated in Exhibit 11.1. The first and largest component is the base compensation or salary system. The second is the incentive system, where employees receive additional compensation based on individual, divisional, and/or organization-wide performance. Third is the indirect compensation system, where employees are provided with certain benefits, some of which are legally required and others are provided at the discretion of the employer. This chapter focuses on the strategic and policy issues associated with compensation, as opposed to presenting details concerning many of the components of indirect compensation.

Equity

In designing the overall compensation system, an organization needs to be concerned with the perceived equity or fairness of the system for employees. All employees should feel that they are being compensated fairly relative to their coworkers and to individuals who hold comparable jobs in other organizations. The equity theory of motivation holds that workers assess their perceived inputs to their work and their outcomes to those of others, as depicted in Exhibit 11.2.[3]

When individuals perceive that they are being treated inequitably relative to their peers, they usually try to establish equity by increasing their outcomes or decreasing their inputs. Increasing outcomes might involve asking for additional compensation or pilfering from the organization. In the latter case, the individual might use the inequity to justify the theft. Decreasing inputs might involve not working as hard, taking longer breaks, coming in late, leaving early, or resigning.

The design of an equitable compensation system must incorporate three types of equity: internal, external, and individual. These perceptions of equity directly impact motivation, commitment, and performance on the job, as illustrated in Exhibit 11.3. It is important to remember that employee assessments of equity are, in fact, perceptions. They may be based, in part, on incomplete or inaccurate information. Few employees really know the extent of their coworkers' inputs unless they are together throughout the workday.

One critical policy decision employers must make is the extent to which compensation levels will be made public or kept private. Public employers usually have no choice in this matter, as relevant state laws may require full disclosure and reporting of and public access to such information. However, privately held and publically traded organizations have the option of disclosing the compensation of individuals and/or the compensation ranges associated with specific positions. Even if that information is not disclosed, employers frequently have policies that forbid employees from disclosing their compensation to others. Reading 11.1 "Exposing Pay Secrecy," explores the reasons for such policies as well as the advantages and disadvantages of such a practice.

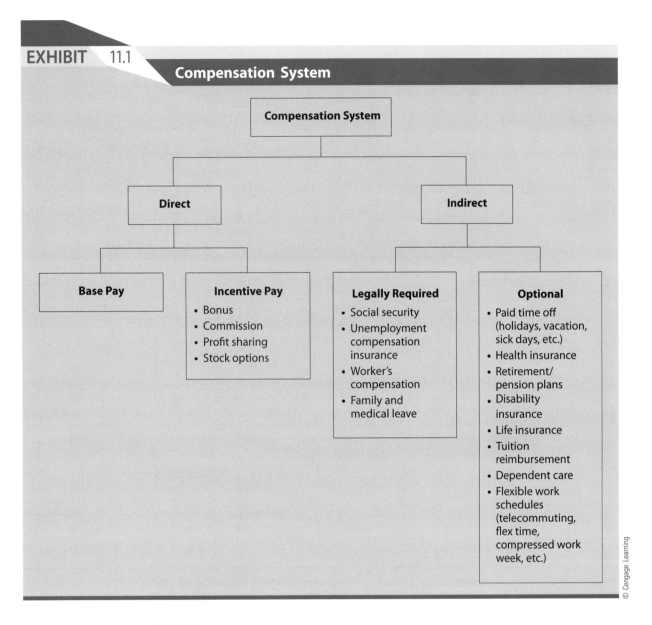

EXHIBIT 11.1

Compensation System

Compensation System

Direct

Indirect

Base Pay

Incentive Pay
- Bonus
- Commission
- Profit sharing
- Stock options

Legally Required
- Social security
- Unemployment compensation insurance
- Worker's compensation
- Family and medical leave

Optional
- Paid time off (holidays, vacation, sick days, etc.)
- Health insurance
- Retirement/ pension plans
- Disability insurance
- Life insurance
- Tuition reimbursement
- Dependent care
- Flexible work schedules (telecommuting, flex time, compressed work week, etc.)

© Cengage Learning

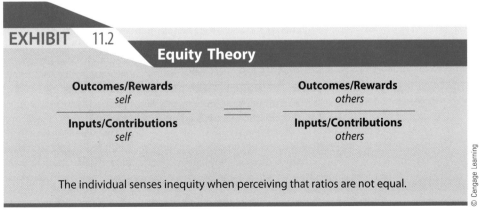

EXHIBIT 11.2

Equity Theory

$$\frac{\text{Outcomes/Rewards}_{\textit{self}}}{\text{Inputs/Contributions}_{\textit{self}}} = \frac{\text{Outcomes/Rewards}_{\textit{others}}}{\text{Inputs/Contributions}_{\textit{others}}}$$

The individual senses inequity when perceiving that ratios are not equal.

© Cengage Learning

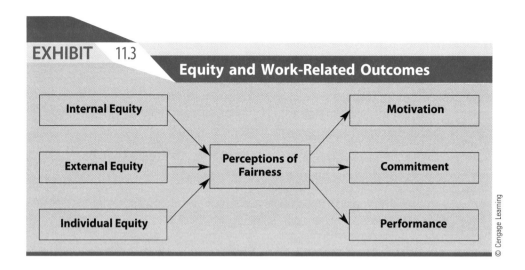

The confidentiality of many compensation programs can also make it difficult for employees to obtain accurate information on coworker compensation. Nonetheless, these perceptions impact motivation, commitment, and performance and must be effectively managed. Although compensation is not the only work-related outcome employees receive, it is often the basis by which employees conclude that they are being treated appropriately.

The Internet can provide a wealth of information to employees about comparable salary data. A recent Google search turned up more than 28,000 hits for the search "salary comparison" sites. The most popular of these sites, www.salary.com, averages more than 26 million hits annually and hosts 1.7 million different visitors monthly. The *Wall Street Journal* even offers its own site, www. careerjournal.com.[4] Much of the salary information found by employees may be inaccurate, dated, or based on samples that are irrelevant to the individual employee's job. Employers, however, add to the confusion by failing to communicate compensation policy with employees. Although 60 percent of workers in one recent survey reported that their pay compares unfavorably to pay levels elsewhere, only 43 percent of that same group reported that their employers do a good job of explaining how pay is determined.[5] Hence, with the abundance of salary information available to employees, it is more important than ever that employers develop an equitable compensation system and explain it to employees.

Internal Equity

Internal equity involves the perceived fairness of pay differentials among different jobs within an organization. Employees should feel that the pay differentials between jobs are fair, given the corresponding differences in job responsibilities. In attempting to establish internal equity, employers can evaluate jobs by using four techniques: job ranking, job classification, point systems, and factor comparison.

Job ranking is a relatively simple, nonquantitative means of determining equity in compensation in smaller, less complex organizations. Senior management makes judgments as to which jobs are most challenging and ensures that the more challenging jobs receive higher compensation. This method, which is somewhat random and nonscientific, is more concerned with the hierarchical position of jobs rather than with the differential amounts of compensation. Because it is random, job ranking is used infrequently and usually only in small, informal organizations.

Job classification systems group jobs requiring similar effort, ability, training, and responsibility into predetermined grades or classes and compensates each job within a grade similarly. This method is more scientific than job ranking, but it has been criticized for lack of flexibility. Organizations must force each job into a specific category, and subjectivity is involved in classifying jobs, given the nonquantitative nature of the process.[6] However, job classification systems are easy to understand and explain and can be widely administered in large organizations. The federal government, for example, has an elaborate system of 18 job classes, each of which is distinguished by 10 levels of job difficulty or challenge; this impacts the compensation of more than 3 million federal employees. Exhibit 11.4 provides a sample of several of these job grades.

Point systems involve making a quantitative assessment of job content and are more scientific than job ranking or classification. Point systems are easy to understand and explain and—although difficult to design—are easy to implement once they are operational. The organization first creates a list of compensable factors—things that the organization is willing to pay its employees for, such as education, experience, specific skills, working conditions, and responsibility. Each of these compensable factors is then assigned a factor scale, which describes progressive levels of mastery or accomplishment of each factor. Points are assigned to each level of each scale, and compensation is determined by the overall number of points that correspond to the job. A sample point system is presented in Exhibit 11.5. Note that some compensable factors receive higher points than others. For example, level one in technical skills receives 30 points; level one in working conditions receives only 5 points. Employers can determine the relative worth of each compensable factor by

EXHIBIT 11.4

Grade Description and Representative Job Titles from the Classification System used by the Federal Government

Grade Level	Grade Description	Jobs Included in Grade
GS 1	Includes those classes of position the duties of which are to perform, under immediate supervision, with little or no latitude for the exercise of independent judgment: • The simplest routine work in office, business, of fiscal operations; or • Elementary work of a subordinate technical character in a professional, scientific, or technical field.	Typist, Messenger
GS 2	Includes those classes of position the duties which are: • to perform, under immediate supervision, with limited latitude for the exercise of independent judgment, routine work in office, business, or fiscal operations, of comparable subordinate technical work of limited scope in a professional, scientific, of technical field, requiring some training or experience; or • to perform other work of equal importance, difficulty, and responsibility, and requiring comparable qualifications.	Engineering aide
GS 5	Includes those classes of positions the duties which are: • to perform, under general supervision, difficult and responsible work in office, business, or fiscal administration, or comparable subordinate technical work in a professional, scientific, or technical field, requiring in either case; • considerable training and supervisory or other experience; • broad working knowledge of a special subject matter or of office, laboratory, engineering, scientific, or other procedure and practice; and • the exercise of independent judgment in a limited field; • to perform other work of equal importance, difficulty, and responsibility, and requiring comparable qualifications.	Chemist, Accountant, Engineer (civil), Statistical clerk

Source: *From* The Management of Compensation *by Alan, N. Nash and Stephen J. Carroll. Copyright © 1976 by Wadsworth, Inc.*

EXHIBIT   11.5

Sample Point System

Factors	Level				
	1	2	3	4	5
Education	15	30	45	60	75
Experience	20	40	60	80	100
Technical skills	30	60	90	120	150
Working conditions	5	10	15	20	25
Responsibility	25	50	75	100	125

The compensable factor "technical skills" might have its five levels defined as follows:

Knowledge

This factor measures the knowledge or equivalent training required to perform the job duties.

1st Degree

Use of reading and writing, adding and subtracting of whole numbers; following of instructions; use of fixed gauges, direct reading of instrument, and similar devices; where interpretation is not required.

2nd Degree

Use of addition, subtraction, multiplication, and division of numbers, including decimals and fractions; simple use of formulas, charts, tables, drawings, specifications, schedules, wiring diagrams; use of adjustable measuring instrument; checking of reports, forms, records, and comparable data; where interpretation is required.

3rd Degree

Use of mathematics with the use of complicated drawings, specifications, charts, tables; various types of precision measuring instruments. Equivalent to one to three years' applied traders training in a particular or specialized occupation.

4th Degree

Use of advanced trades mathematics, together with the use of complicated drawings, specifications, charts, tables, handbook formulas; all varieties of precision measuring instruments. Equivalent to complete accredited apprenticeship in a recognized trade, craft or occupation; or equivalent to a two-year technical college education.

5th Degree

Use of higher mathematics involved in the applications of engineering principles and the performance of related practical operations, together with a comprehensive knowledge of the theories and practices of mechanical, electrical, chemical, civil, or like engineering field. Equivalent to complete four years of technical college or university education.

Source: *Adapted from* Compensation, *3/c by George T. Milkovich and Jerry M. Newman. Copyright © 1990 by Richard D. Irwin.*

assessing its criticality for the organization's strategic objectives. The more a compensable factor relates to goals and objectives, the higher the values that should be present in the factor scales.

A special type of point system is often used for administrative and managerial positions. Developed by the consulting group Hay Associates, this system is known as the "Hay Plan" and is used by most of the *Fortune 500* companies as well as over 5,000 organizations in more than

30 countries. The Hay Plan utilizes three factors, called "universal factors," which are common to all managerial and administrative jobs: know-how, problem solving, and accountability. Know-how pertains to the technical knowledge required to do the job. Problem solving assesses the amount of independent thinking and decision making required in the job. Accountability considers the direct responsibility for people, resources, and results. A brief summary of the Hay Plan is presented in Exhibit 11.6.

Factor comparison is somewhat similar in concept to the point system. However, instead of assessing jobs independently of each other relative to compensable factors, factor comparison utilizes five standard factors in evaluating all jobs: responsibility, skills required, mental effort, physical effort, and working conditions. Jobs are evaluated relative to each other on each of these five dimensions to determine appropriate compensation. For example, an employer would try to determine whether the job of a paralegal required more or less responsibility, skill, mental effort, physical effort, or unusual working conditions relative to the job of an accounting clerk to determine appropriate compensation for each job. Factor comparison can be difficult to administer in organizations where job content and responsibilities change frequently. It has also been criticized for its assumption that the five factors are universal to and equally important in all jobs. Factor comparison is best utilized in organizations where there is limited change and job responsibilities and content remain somewhat stable.

EXHIBIT 11.6

Hay Compensable Factors

Know-How

Know-how is the sum total of every kind of skill, however acquired, necessary for acceptable job performance. This sum total, which comprises the necessary overall "fund of knowledge" an employee needs, has three dimensions:
- Knowledge of practical procedures, specialized techniques, and learned disciplines.
- The ability to integrate and harmonize the diversified functions involved in managerial situations (operating, supporting, and administrative). This know-how may be exercised consultatively as well as executively and involves in some combination the areas of organizing, planning, executing, controlling, and evaluating.
- Active, practicing skills in the area of human relationships.

Problem-Solving

Problem-solving is the original "self-starting" thinking required by the job for analyzing, evaluating, creating, reasoning, and arriving at conclusions. To the extent that thinking is circumscribed by standards, covered by precedents, or referred to others, problem-solving is diminished and the emphasis correspondingly is on know-how.

Problem-solving has two dimensions:
- The environment in which the thinking takes place.
- The challenge presented by the thinking to be done.

Accountability

Accountability is the answerability for an action and for the consequences thereof. It is the measured effect of the job on end results. It has three dimensions:
- Freedom to act—the degree of personal or procedural control and guidance.
- Job impact on end results.
- Magnitude—indicated by the general dollar size of the areas(s) most clearly or primarily affected by the job (on an annual basis).

Source: *Courtesy of the Hay Group, Boston, MA.*

The consequences of having a compensation system that employees perceive to be inequitable can be severe. Employers have a choice of four systems for developing an internally equitable compensation system based on whether they wish to consider complete or specified job factors as well as whether they wish to compare jobs to each other or to some standard. Exhibit 11.7 compares the four techniques, noting the relative strengths and weaknesses of each technique. Regardless of the method chosen, employees must understand and accept the system to ensure optimal motivation, commitment, and performance.

A more recent issue that has arisen relative to the management of internal equity is salary compression. Salary compression happens when new hires earn higher salaries than employees who have more experience and/or tenure within the organization. It is the result of rising starting salaries in fields for which demand for employees exceeds supply. Salary compression has become a common and particularly problematic issue for faculty in colleges and universities.

Salary compression can be exacerbated in organizations in which individual salaries are made public. It can lead to severe morale problems due to the sense of inequity felt by long-term employees who may have shown tremendous loyalty to their employers. It can be difficult to remedy, as its effects are often far reaching throughout the organization. Simply adjusting salaries to address salary compression can create additional problems relative to the basis for such adjustments as well as the availability of resources to support such adjustments. Frequently, the only solution for those employees who are on the short end of salary compression is to leave their organization and seek employment elsewhere on the open market at the going salary rates. When an organization realizes that its compensation system suffers from salary compression, there is no simple answer as to how to best remedy the situation, but action is necessary to retain top-performing employees. Chapter 13 provides some recommendations as to how to retain such individuals.

EXHIBIT 11.7

Comparison of Job Evaluation Methods

Basis of Comparison	Unit of Analysis	
	Whole Job	**Selectors Factors of Job**
	Job Ranking	**Factor Comparisons**
Job vs. Job	• Identify jobs based on "worth" to organization relative to other jobs	• Define compensable factors and evaluate jobs on these factors relative to other jobs
	▲ Simple, inexpensive, easy to understand	▲ Ease of employee comprehension
	▼ Random, subjective, not useful in large organizations	▼ Cumbersome and requires constant updating; universal importance of factors in all jobs questionable
	Job Classification	**Point Method**
Job vs. Standard	• Prepare job grades/classification and assign job to appropriate class	• Define compensable factors and levels of accomplishment and determine levels for each job
	▲ Apply to large number of varied jobs; easy to understand; flexible	▲ Simple to understand and administer; easy for employees to aspire to high levels
	▼ Detailed and time-consuming to develop; lack of flexibility	▼ Extremely time consuming to develop; lack of universal applicability of compensable factors

External Equity

External equity involves employee perception of the fairness of their compensation relative to those outside the organization. Obviously, employees would not be thrilled to discover that those who do similar work in other organizations receive greater compensation. Employers need to be aware of salary structures of competitors and understand that this can impact motivation, commitment, and productivity.

Assessing external equity is relatively a straightforward process. Organizations should first collect wage and salary information to determine market wage rates. This information, which can be collected in-house or through sources external to the organization, is usually readily available relative to the industry and geographic area through professional associations, human resource (HR) consulting firms, or through the organization's own primary research. When making assessments of external equity, it is important to consider not only salaries but also other forms of compensation, such as bonus and incentive plans and benefits packages. Information pertaining to these additional forms of compensation may be more difficult to obtain, but it must be incorporated into the analysis, especially for higher level managerial and executive positions that may have a significant portion of the overall compensation based on incentive pay.

After an investigation of the market has been completed, the organization then determines its own pay strategy relative to the market. The three strategies an employer can choose are a lead, lag, or market policy. A lead policy involves paying higher wages than competitors to ensure that the organization becomes the employer of choice. In other words, this strategy assumes that pay is a critical factor in an applicant's decision in choosing an employer and attempts to attract and help retain employees of the highest quality. In short, the employer desires to be the first-choice employer; that is, the organization wants first selection from available talent. However, any organization that offers higher compensation than its competitors needs to ensure that it has a means of remaining competitive relative to its cost structure and market prices. This requires the organization to have operational efficiencies that its competitors lack, a higher rate of employee productivity than its competitors, and/or a product or service for which consumers are willing to pay a premium price.

With a lag policy, the organization compensates employees below the rates of competitors. An organization employing this strategy attempts to compensate employees through some other means, such as opportunity for advancement, incentive plans, good location, good working conditions, or employment security. The organization believes that work-related outcomes are multifaceted and, more important, that employees consider more than just salary in weighing their employment options. An organization employing a lag policy needs strong insights into the personal and lifestyle choices of the employees it recruits to allow it to tailor compensation options for these individuals that will allow them to accept a lower base salary than that offered by the competition.

With a market policy, the organization sets its salary levels equal to those of competitors. An employer following this strategy attempts to neutralize pay as a factor in applicant decisions, assuming that it can compete in the labor market in attracting employees by other means such as those listed in the discussion of lag policy. It should come as no surprise that the majority of employers set their salary levels at or very near market levels. Such a strategy assumes that employees are less likely to leave if their salaries would remain the same with a new employer.

Individual Equity

Individual equity considers employee perceptions of pay differentials among individuals who hold identical jobs in the same organization. Determining individual salary levels and pay differentials among employees in identical jobs can be done in a number of ways. The most basic is basing pay on seniority. Seniority-based systems determine compensation according to the length of time on the job or length of time with the employer. Although this rewards a stable and experienced workforce, it has no direct relationship to performance on the job. Seniority systems are very common in union settings. They are also usually looked upon favorably by the court system because they are objective in nature. However, they provide little incentive to be more productive, and they encourage workers who may be mediocre or substandard performers to remain with the organization.

Merit pay systems compensate individuals for their proven performance on the job. Ideally, they provide an incentive for employees to work harder and accomplish more. Merit pay is generally permanently added to an employee's base pay. However, in practice, merit pay can be quite problematic. Because merit-based pay systems are anchored by the organization's performance feedback system, they can extend the subjectivity that is inherent in the feedback system. If an employee believes that the performance feedback process is biased or unfair, a compensation system that is based on this process can further add to the employee's perceptions of unfairness. Any merit-based pay plan must ensure that the performance feedback upon which it is built is understood and accepted by employees.

An increasing number of organizations are using incentive pay to compensate their employees. Incentive plans allow the employee to receive a portion of his or her compensation in direct relation to the financial performance of the individual, unit, or entire organization. Incentive pay is provided for a given time period and is not added to the base salary. Consequently, it must be re-earned in subsequent time periods and can have a greater motivational impact than merit pay.

The philosophy behind this compensation system is to reward higher levels of performance by returning financial rewards to the employees who have been responsible for creating them. Incentive pay programs also allow organizations to adjust their compensation expenses based on organizational performance. These plans can take a variety of forms, such as commission sales plans, profit-sharing plans, gain-sharing plans (in which cost savings are partially distributed to those responsible for them), and stock ownership, distribution, or option plans. Incentive plans also differ from merit pay plans in that the former are based on objective, measurable financial performance; the latter are based on subjective, generally nonfinancial performance-related criteria. A well-designed incentive pay plan can be the deciding factor in an applicant's decision to accept or reject a job offer when base compensation is set at market level and nondistinguishable from that of competitors.[7]

Performance-based pay that is variably tied into an employee's, work unit's, or organization's results is popular with both employers and employees. Performance-based pay—which was until recently offered to senior executives only—is now extended to many other employees, as organizations realize how variable compensation programs can impact individual employees' behavior and performance. Approximately two-thirds of U.S. companies offer some form of variable performance-based pay, and about 10 percent of all compensation paid in the United States is variable.[8] More important, one survey found that employers who provide variable performance-based pay to their top employees are 68 percent more likely to report outstanding bottom-line financial performance than those who do not.[9]

Performance-based pay plans are not limited to the private sector. Pay-for-performance plans have also been implemented successfully in the public sector, as illustrated in Reading 11.2, "The Development of a Pay-for-Performance Appraisal System for Municipal Agencies: A Case Study," which further illustrates the critical link between performance management and compensation programs.

One important consideration in the shift from straight salary to incentive compensation is the fact that incentive compensation will usually lower the base salary an individual receives in exchange for incentives that could significantly raise overall compensation. Not all employees, however, will find such a trade-off attractive, as illustrated below.

Joe Torre and the New York Yankees

In October 2007, the sporting world was stunned when Joe Torre parted ways with the New York Yankees baseball franchise. Torre had managed the Yankees for 12 seasons, and in each of those seasons had led the Yankees to the postseason, including four World Series championships. However, the 2007 season ended for the Yankees with elimination during the first round of the playoffs for the third consecutive year. At the time, Torre was the highest paid manager in baseball, having earned $7.5 million for the 2007 season.

Team owner George Steinbrenner, hungry for another World Series championship, decided to offer Torre an incentive compensation package. Torre's base salary for 2008 would be reduced to $5 million but with incentives of an additional $3 million possible, with $1 million being awarded for each successive level of Yankee postseason success. The incentive-laden, short-term contract with a 33 percent decreased in base salary caused Torre to leave the Yankees and sign a $13 million, 3-year contract with the Los Angeles Dodgers two weeks later.

Incentive pay is popular with employers, in part because it is self-funded. Because it is tied to specific financial performance of a division or the entire organization and is not paid unless specific measurable financial metrics are achieved, it can and should appeal to even the most fiscally conservative organizations. The flexibility of variable compensation programs allows them to be tailored to organization-wide, divisional, team, or individual performance—or some combination thereof—depending on the interdependence present in jobs as well as organizational strategy. Perhaps their greatest value is that variable compensation programs, if well communicated and implemented, allow employees to fully understand the organization's goals and objectives as well as how their individual jobs impact organizational performance.

Pay-for-performance plans have been identified as a means of aligning the interests of employers and owners. One study compared pay-for-performance plans with a fixed salary compensation program and found that the former resulted in significantly higher productivity and overall financial performance.[10] This is because pay for performance generally attracts higher quality applicants, which has a net effect of lowering unit cost of production or service delivery. Not surprisingly, higher performing employees show a marked preference for pay-for-performance compensation programs over salaried compensation without incentives. However, employers need to monitor such programs to ensure that employees do not focus excessively on incentive-producing tasks and behaviors that result in individual financial rewards at the expense of other important tasks or goals.

Team-Based Incentive Pay at Children's Hospital Boston

The accounts receivable department at Children's Hospital Boston was suffering from low morale and inefficiencies after an unsuccessful change to a new billing system. With an average of more than 100 days from billing to payment, the organization was facing serious cash flow concerns in its fiscal operations. To alleviate this, the management developed a team-based incentive plan that would allow employees to see the relationship between quarterly cash flow and the number of days a bill spent uncollected in accounts receivable. Employee centered, the program allowed team members to set three possible goal levels—threshold, target, and optimal—with corresponding rewards of $500, $1,000, and $1,500 for the attainment of each. Meetings were set up with employees to explain the program and obtain employee input and support. Employees suddenly began to feel important, empowered, and energized: Weekly progress reports allow employees to self-monitor their progress. During the first year, the average number of days a bill spent in accounts receivable was reduced from more than 100 days to 76, and during the second year, the average was reduced to the mid-60s—and the satisfaction with the program has reduced employee turnover in the department.[11]

While performance-based rewards can be tremendous motivators and allow employees to see a stronger connection between their performance and organizational performance, they are clearly not for every organization. Cultural barriers, both institutional and national, can act as impediments to the successful implementation of a performance-based pay plan. Japanese conglomerate

Fujitsu was the first Japanese organization to implement such a compensation plan. Hailed as a breakthrough and revolutionary when first introduced, the program ignited a trend in Japanese organizations to abandon archaic pay systems based almost entirely on seniority in favor of performance-based plans. After eight years, however, Fujitsu abandoned the program, calling it "flawed" and a poor fit with Japanese culture that respects and rewards loyalty and seniority. In addition, to maintain a positive self-image, employees fought to keep the performance standards under the plan as low as possible for fear of falling short and being embarrassed. Innovation was stifled, as employees resisted change, fearing that results might not accompany the change.[12]

Skill-based pay systems have been increasing in popularity in recent years because of the ease of measurement of many specific skills and because skills relating to the organization's strategy can be readily identified. Skill-based pay involves basing the employee's compensation on the acquisition and mastery of skills used on the job. Skill-based pay programs not only give employees incentives to learn new skills or upgrade existing ones, but they also promote flexibility for the organization. They can easily be linked with training programs and the strategic needs of the organization. During the strategic planning process, the organization must determine which kinds of employee skills are most critical to its objectives and future success. Then, the organization must hire employees either with these skills or with the capacity to learn these skills.

Despite their popularity, skill-based pay systems are not without problems. Employers should remember that the acquisition of skills and improved performance are two different things. Skill-based pay systems are often based on the acquisition of skills, without regard to whether the employee has successfully transferred the training to the work setting or achieved any results from the skill-based training. In a rapidly changing work environment, skill obsolescence may result in a pay system that compensates employees for previously learned skills that have become outdated and are no longer of value to the employer. Most employees would find it unfair for the organization to reduce compensation because it no longer values certain employee skills, particularly if the organization has not provided opportunities for employees to upgrade their skills. Employers need to implement skill-based pay plans very carefully and with a clear sense of what the future might hold for how work is performed.

Team-based pay plans are also becoming more prevalent in many organizations. With more work and responsibility being centered on self-managed teams, such compensation plans provide incentives to cooperate and be more flexible in working with others in achieving group and organizational objectives. Administering team-based pay systems can be less time consuming than administering individual reward systems. However, team-based pay plans may impact group dynamics and can adversely impact and intensify conflict within a unit, particularly if team members feel that certain teammates are not doing their share of the work and living up to their responsibility to the team. Such free riders can also greatly damage morale and enthusiasm for the plan.[13] Team-based pay plans present a key strategic issue for organizations in determining the percentage of overall employee compensation that should be based on team rather than individual performance. Consequently, team-based pay plans may require the oversight and attention of supervisors, particularly in their early stages of implementation.[14]

Team-based pay systems need a decentralized decision-making system that gives the team some autonomy and responsibility to be successful; they also need to be tied into specific measures of accountability and results. To the extent that they foster unhealthy competition and conflict among different teams within an organization, they can have adverse effects on overall performance. Although team-based pay plans may make sense given the changing nature of work and the emphasis on project teams and groups, their potential impact on both individual teams and intra-team relations and performance needs to be assessed before the plan is implemented. Despite the changing nature of job design, technology, and work relationships, certain organizations may find that their culture does not support the team-based pay concept. Team-based pay plans must be implemented within the context of an organizational culture that values sharing and collaboration, cooperation, and open communication.

While many employers realize the critical role that effective teams play in the success of their organization, few have been able to implement compensation systems that encourage and reward team effort. The few that have done so find that three criteria influence the success of such a plan.

First, there has to be a high level of communication with employees regarding the details of the plan. Second, employees should have a voice and provide input into the design and implementation of the plan. Third, team members need to feel that the system is fair and equitable.[15]

Team-Based Pay at Phelps Dodge

Phoenix, Arizona–based Phelps Dodge has a copper-mining operation that employs more than 4,200 individuals at six North American locations. When the employees decided to decertify their existing labor union, the management saw a golden opportunity to create a more incentive-based compensation system. The new plan involves a base salary, with bonuses awarded for meeting team-based goals set for a specific location or mine. Goals are set by team members, and the compensation is constantly being evaluated through the feedback provided by employees.[16]

Legal Issues in Compensation

Those designing compensation systems must also bear in mind that compensation is a condition of employment covered under Title VII of the Civil Rights Act of 1964. The design of any compensation system that intentionally or unintentionally discriminates against any protected class can subject the organization to legal action. The Equal Pay Act of 1963 also partially regulates compensation and must be considered when designing and administering compensation programs. These laws were discussed in Chapter 7.

Critics of the Equal Pay Act have noted that it has been of limited value because men and women are often not employed in the same jobs, and the Act only requires equal pay for equal work. To combat this limitation, the concept of comparable worth has been advanced. Comparable worth argues that the standards of equal pay for equal work should be replaced with the doctrine of equal pay for equal value. Because many occupations, although becoming more gender integrated, are still somewhat gender segregated, women and men generally do not hold the same jobs or do the same work in our economy, so the Equal Pay Act does nothing to relieve the lower wages that women receive relative to men. For example, in a warehouse, men might be working on the loading dock, and women might be working in the office. Men will invariably be paid more, but the Equal Pay Act cannot address this because the jobs being performed by men and women are not the same. Comparable worth would argue that the work being done in the office (bookkeeping, clerical, and switchboard) has as much value as and is as important to the organization as that being done on the loading dock and should be compensated similarly.

Comparable worth of two different jobs, however, remains very difficult to prove because of the lack of objective, measurable data that would support an assessment of job value. Gender stereotyping of certain jobs creates an additional obstacle in this regard. For example, the majority of schoolteachers (particularly in elementary schools), secretaries, nurses, and flight attendants are female. Although the courts have been sympathetic to arguments for comparable worth, they have been extremely reluctant to take action because the doctrine falls outside existing federal law. In addition, the value of a particular job is very difficult to objectively determine and prove in a legal arena. Comparable worth may be our society's best hope for narrowing the gender gap in wages, in which women consistently have been found to earn 70–75 cents on the dollar of what men earn.[17] This is particularly true given that the Equal Pay Act does have exclusions that allow gender-based pay differentials to exist. Comparable worth, however, will most likely remain an unenforceable ideal until laws are passed that specifically address it. Equal pay for equal work is still the standard; the courts have refused to manufacture standards and policies that have not been legislated.

One additional law that impacts compensation is the Fair Labor Standards Act (FLSA) of 1938, which regulates the federal minimum wage, overtime policies, and the use of child labor.

It exempts from minimum wage and overtime requirements certain groups of employees (managers, administrators, outside salespeople, and professionals) who exercise independent judgment in carrying out their job duties. However, there has been significant controversy concerning whether certain types of sales positions, temporary employees, and independent contractors are legally considered employees and/or covered under the FLSA. As nontraditional employment relationships continue to develop, this Act will require the courts to increase scrutiny of the legal status of such nontraditional employees. In the interim, companies that employ these workers will have to exercise caution when designing compensation programs to ensure that they follow the law.

The FLSA has caused numerous problems for employers in recent years. Because it was written and passed long before our economy became based on services, knowledge, and information technology, Congress was unable to anticipate many of the changes that would take place relative to the nature of jobs, work, and organizational life. Problems have arisen because of the ambiguity of the law regarding specifically who is covered under the Act and is therefore eligible for overtime pay. In response, there have been a number of high-profile class-action lawsuits that have resulted in major payouts by employers. RadioShack recently settled a class-action lawsuit for $30 million that was filed by managers who claimed that they were classified improperly under the Act in an attempt to avoid paying them overtime.[18] Similar settlements were offered by Starbucks ($18 million), Rite Aid ($25 million), and Pacific Bell (two separate cases settled for $35 million and $27 million).[19] Such responsibilities and consequences are not limited to large organizations. A small chain of three Asian restaurants in the New York City suburbs was recently fined more than $1 million by the U.S. Department of Labor to settle violations of minimum wage and overtime provisions for 255 employees. In addition to these payments for back wages and interest, the employer was also required to pay nearly $100,000 in civil penalties.[20] While the U.S. Department of Labor offers employers a comprehensive FLSA compliance assistance program, much confusion still exists and lawsuits continue to be filed.

In 2006, Congress amended the FLSA to provide some additional clarification as to which employees are exempt from its provisions. Under the revised FLSA standards, an employee is exempt from FLSA coverage if he or she is paid a minimum salary of $455 per week, has primary duties that involve "management," customarily oversees at least two employees, and has the authority to hire and fire or provide recommendations for hiring and firing. This standard of hiring/firing decision making or participation has become critical in determining FLSA exempt status.

Executive Compensation

One important and controversial area of compensation concerns the pay received by executives. There is no real average or standard for executive compensation, largely because of differences between industries as well as between organizations within a given industry. The demand for talented CEOs and other chief officers who can generate results for shareholders often results in significant compensation packages. Typically, a senior executive receives no more than 20 percent of annual compensation in the form of salary, with the remainder usually divided between annual (30 percent) and long-term (50 percent) incentives.[21]

Executive compensation has been criticized for its excessiveness as well as for the fact that it is often unrelated to actual performance. In 1980, the average CEO made 42 times the average hourly worker's pay; by the year 2000, average CEO pay had grown to 531 times the average hourly workers pay.[22] *Forbes* magazine reported that in 2013 utility company CEOs were earning 475 times the average employee salary in that sector.[23] More so, a *CNNMoney* report noted that Apple CEO Tim Cook's 2011 $378 million salary was 6,258 times the annual pay of the average Apple employee.[24] These compensation differentials are even more noteworthy in comparison to Great Britain, Canada, and Japan, where average CEO pay is 22, 20, and 11 times that of the average employee wage, respectively.[25]

Recent corporate accounting scandals in which executives reaped millions of dollars in compensation while their organizations were going bankrupt has drawn even more attention to executive compensation. The lesson learned from the Enron scandal is that heavy reliance on stock options as part of executive compensation can create a culture obsessed with improving stock performance at the expense of all other concerns. Nonetheless, stock options remain a key component of executive compensation packages.

In response to the growing number of corporate scandals of the early 2000s, Congress passed the Dodd-Frank Wall Street Reform and Consumer Protection Act of 2010. Dodd-Frank requires all publically traded companies to enact executive compensation policies under which employers could recover any and all incentive-based compensation paid out to executives during the previous three years when company financial reports or performance were restated or revised. These "clawback" provisions apply to all company executives and greatly expanded the scope of the Sarbanes-Oxley Act of 2002, which allowed such action only against the CEO and chief financial offer and then only when the subjected individual had consciously engaged in fraudulent reporting. Dodd-Frank allows retrieval of financial benefits paid to executives regardless of whether or not any error was deliberate or the affected executives were aware of the error.

Stock options provide employees with the opportunity to purchase shares at some future date, at a price that is determined at the time the options are awarded. They are designed to focus employee attention on creating shareholder value, and in doing so, employees are also able to reap the benefits of the organization's financial performance. However, stock options can prompt executives to engage in creative accounting practices in which revenues and profitability are artificially inflated, driving up the value of the stock and the options. In addition, stock options are deductible on corporate income taxes despite the fact that they do not have to be reported as expenses in the organization's financial reports.[26]

Several large organizations, including Coca-Cola and Bank One Corp., however, have voluntarily decided to expense stock options offered to employees. Designed to ease concerns in the investment community in light of the recent accounting scandals, this move will make earnings appear lower. Ideally, this may reduce the use of stock options, particularly among rank-and-file employees, as stock options and cash will cost the organization an identical amount. With stock options requiring more time and recordkeeping for the organization and oversight by employees, both employers and employees might find simple equivalent cash compensation more efficient than stock options. Regardless of the decisions that individual organizations make regarding the future of stock options, those organizations that continue to offer stock options to executives as well as other employees will now find their compensation practices more carefully scrutinized by those outside the organization.

A number of employers have been moving away from stock options and instead compensating employees, particularly executives, with stock grants.[27] Stock grants require that the organization meet specific financial goals, such as a given return on capital or return on assets, as a condition of their issuance. At the same time that organizations have been moving away from stock options, there has been a marked trend in privately held organizations offering equity stakes as part of executive compensation packages. Designed largely to allow these privately held organizations to compete with publically held organizations for executive talent, such plans are now offered by 43 percent of private employers. A recent study from Pricewaterhouse Coopers found that the typical compensation package for executives at the fastest growing privately held organizations generally consists of 74 percent base salary, 16 percent annual performance incentives, and 5 percent each of long-term cash and equity-based incentives. The survey further found a trend toward privately held employers basing an increasing percentage of executive compensation on performance and longer-term measures.[28]

The "pay for performance" trend among executives has also made its way into the boardroom. Coca-Cola recently announced a radically new plan for director compensation. Typical director compensation includes cash and/or stock options. In Coke's case, this amounted to $50,000 cash and $75,000 in options annually. However, under the new plan, all director compensation was to be performance based. Directors would receive annual $175,000 option packages only if the organization posted annual compound growth in earnings per share of 8 percent. Coke saw this as a necessary step in light of the fact that the organization had been struggling financially for a number of years, as sales of its flagship products slipped and its expansion into noncarbonated drinks produced mixed results.[29]

Executive compensation decisions are among some of the most important policy decisions made today. Because the demand for seasoned, talented executives greatly exceeds the supply of such and with increasing rates of turnover in CEO positions, organizations need to carefully strategize their executive compensation packages.

Conclusion

Organizations face a number of key strategic issues in setting their compensation policies and programs. These include compensation relative to the market, the balance between fixed and variable compensation, utilization of individual versus team-based pay, the appropriate mix of financial and nonfinancial compensation, and developing an overall cost-effective program that results in high performance.

In addition to these strategic issues, the fast pace of change in our society and the corresponding need for organizations to respond to remain competitive create challenges for all HR programs but particularly for compensation. Probably more now than at any time in the past, organizations need to re-evaluate their compensation programs within the context of their corporate strategy and specific HR strategy to ensure that they are consistent with the necessary performance measures required by the organization. Overly rigid compensation systems inhibit the flexibility needed by most contemporary organization's competitive strategies, so it is no surprise to see such flexibility being incorporated into compensation systems.

At the same time, organizations wishing to be more innovative may need to alter their compensation systems to promote more intrapreneurial behavior that encourages employees to act as risk-taking entrepreneurs. Similarly, smaller entrepreneurial organizations will usually need different compensation systems than their larger counterparts. Organizations taking a strategic approach to compensation realize the need for creativity to meet strategic objectives. Also, within a given organization, different compensation programs may be needed for different divisions, departments, or groups of employees. Compensation systems must grow and evolve in the same manner as the organization to ensure that what is actually being rewarded is consistent with the organization's strategic objectives. This link between strategy and compensation is essential for ensuring optimal performance.

Critical Thinking

1. Does money motivate employees? Why or why not?

2. Why should compensation systems be equitable? How can an organization design an equitable compensation system?

3. Compare and contrast the four job evaluation methods. Give an example of an organization in which each of the four methods might provide an optimal strategic fit.

4. Discuss the pros and cons of employee pay being fixed versus variable and dependent on performance. How might such decisions impact recruiting, motivation, and retention?

5. Analyze your current job responsibilities. Determine whether the method by which you are compensated is appropriate.

6. Is performance-based pay effective? Why or why not? How can performance-based pay systems be better designed to ensure optimal results?

Reading 11.1

7. What are the advantages and disadvantages of organizational policies that mandate pay secrecy? Consider this question from the perspective of managers, employees, and owners. Is pay secrecy a good practice?

Reading 11.2

8. What obstacles exist to developing pay-for-performance plans in the public sector? How can these obstacles best be overcome? Do public sector pay-for-performance plans differ from those found in the private sector?

Exercises

1. Briefly interview an employee in his or her 20s, 30s, 40s, 50s, 60s, and 70s. Determine what motivates workers from different generations and design compensation plans for each generation that would result in high performance.

2. Is salary compression an issue at your college or university? If so, what are its effects, and how is it being handled? Interview administrators and individual faculty to gain a sense of the extent of the problem, how serious it is perceived as being, and how it is being managed.

3. Visit the Web site http://www.salary.com. Click on "salary trends" and then prepare a brief report on the latest developments in compensation practice.

4. At the same Web site, click on "salary wizard." Select a job category and then determine the median compensation figures for this position in eight different locations within the United States. Should an organization that operates in these different locations pay different salaries for identical work? Is cost of living a sufficient explanation for an employee who senses inequity?

Chapter References

1. Sunoo, B. P. "Blending a Successful Workforce," *Workforce*, March 2000, pp. 44–48.

2. Chen, H.-M. and Hsieh, Y.-H. "Key Trends of the Totals Reward System in the 21st Century," *Compensation and Benefits Review*, 38, (6), Nov–Dec 2006, pp. 64–70.

3. Adams, J. S. "Toward an Understanding of Inequity," *Journal of Abnormal and Social Psychology*, October 1963, pp. 422–436.

4. Wellner, A. S. "Salaries in Site," *HR Magazine*, May 2001, 46, (5), pp. 89–96.

5. Shea, T. F. "Send Employees a Message—About Their Pay," *HR Magazine*, December 2002, 47, (12), p. 29.

6. Fisher, C. D., Schoenfeldt, L. F. and Shaw, J. B. *Human Resource Management,* 4th ed, Boston: Houghton Mifflin Co., 1999, p. 560.

7. Williams, V. L. and Grimaldi, S. E. "A Quick Breakdown of Strategic Pay," *Workforce*, 78, (12), December 1999, pp. 72–75.

8. Bates, S. "Pay for Performance," *HR Magazine*, January 2003, 48, (1), pp. 31–38.

9. Ibid.

10. Cadsby, C, Song, F. and Tapon, F. "Sorting and Incentive Effects of Pay for Performance: An Experimental Investigation," *Academy of Management Journal*, 50, (2), 2007, pp. 387–405.

11. Cadrain, D. "Put Success in Sight," *HR Magazine*, May 2003, pp. 85–92.

12. Tanikawa, M. "Fujitsu Decides to Backtrack on Performance-Based Pay," *New York Times*, March 21, 2001, p. W1.

13. Heneman, F. and Von Hippel, C. Interview in the *Wall Street Journal*, November 28, 1995, p. A1.

14. Albanese, R. and VanFleet, D. D. "Rational Behavior in Groups: The Free-Riding Tendency," *Academy of Management Review*, 10, 1985, pp. 244–255.

15. McClurg, L. N. "Team Rewards: How Far Have We Come?" *Human Resource Management*, 40, (1), pp. 73–86.

16. Garvey, C. "Steer Teams with the Right Pay," *HR Magazine*, May 2002, 47, (5), pp. 71–78.

17. U.S. Bureau of the Census. *Current Population Reports,* No. P60-197, Washington, DC: U.S. Government Printing Office, 1997.

18. "RadioShack Agrees to Pay $30 Million to Settle Suit," *Baltimore Sun*, July 17, 2002.

19. Clark, M. M. "FLSA: Will Ya Still Need Me When I'm 64?" *HR News*, October 2002, p. 3.

20. FLSA Violations Cost Restaurant Chain More than $1M. Society for Human Resource Management, January 22, 2013. Available at http://www.shrm.org/legalissues/stateandlocalresources/pages/ny-FLSA-Violations-Restaurant.aspx

21. Overman, S. "Executive Compensation to Undergo Intense Scrutiny," *HR News*, May 2002, p. 1.

22. Patel, D. "The Evolution of Compensation," *Work Visions*, No. 3, 2002.

23. Silverstein, K. "Are Utility CEO Pay Packages Fair Compared to Average Workers?" *Forbes*, April 7, 2013. Available at http://www.forbes.com/sites/kensil verstein/2013/04/07/are-ceo-pay-packages-fair-compared-to-average-workers/

24. *Fortune 50* CEO Pay vs. Our Salaries. Available at http://money.cnn.com/magazines/fortune/fortune500/2012/ceo-pay-ratios/

25. Cossack, N. "Designing Executive Compensation Plans," Society for Human Resource Management, December 29, 2011. Available at http://www.shrm.org/templatestools/toolkits/pages/executivecompensationplans.aspx

26. Bates, S. "More Firms Take High Road by Expensing Stock Options," *HR Magazine*, August 2002, 47, (8), p. 10.

27. Gerena-Morales, R. "Balancing Pay and Performance," *South Florida Sun-Sentinel,* May 23, 2003, p. 1 E.

28. "Public, Private Exec Comp Programs Increasingly Similar," *HR Magazine, 53,* (1), January 2008, p. 12.

29. Terhune, C. and Lubin, J. "In Unusual Move, Coke Ties All Pay for Directors to Earnings Targets," *Wall Street Journal*, April 6, 2006, pp. A1, A11.

READING 11.1

Exposing Pay Secrecy

Adrienne Colella, Ramona L. Paetzold, Asghar Zardkoohi and Michael J. Wesson

Pay secrecy is a contentious issue in many organizations and a controversial one in our society. However, there has been little scholarly research on this topic. We hope to address this void by exposing the complexity of pay secrecy as a construct. What are its costs and benefits? What factors affect the link between pay secrecy and the extent to which it is a cost or benefit? This article reveals the complexity of pay secrecy and, we hope, generates ideas for much new research in the broad management field.

Pay secrecy in organizations is a contentious issue and has been for a long time. Take, for example, the following memoranda that were exchanged in October of 1919:

POLICY MEMORANDUM (October 14, 1919) Forbidding Discussion among Employees of Salary Received

It has been the policy of the organization to base salaries on the value of services rendered. We have, therefore, a long established rule that the salary question is a confidential matter between the organization and the individual.

It is obviously important that employees live up to this rule in order to avoid invidious comparison and dissatisfaction. Recently several cases have come to the notice of management where employees have discussed the salary question among themselves.

This memorandum should serve as a warning that anyone who breaks this rule in the future will be instantly discharged.

POLICY MEMORANDUM (October 15, 1919) Concerning the Forbidding of Discussion among Employees

We emphatically resent both the policy and working of your policy memorandum of October 14. We resent being told what we may and what we may not discuss, and we protest against the spirit of petty regulation which has made possible the sending out of such an edict (Robert Benchley, cited in Steele, 1975: 102–103).

The authors of the second memorandum then walked around the office with signs stating their salaries hanging from their necks, leading the organization to give up its pay secrecy policy. This anecdote describes the managerial viewpoint toward pay at a magazine where humorist Robert Benchley worked in 1919. Although Benchley and his coworkers chose a witty manner in which to voice their discontent with the magazine's pay secrecy policy, one perhaps different from how you or we would have chosen to respond, pay secrecy itself remains a serious, contentious issue in organizations today.

For example, Mary Craig, an assistant cook for an Ohio nursing home, was fired in 1997 after discussing her pay with her coworkers. Although the nursing home had told her never to discuss pay so as to avoid "hard feelings" among employees, she violated the mandate after listening to other workers' complaints of being shortchanged on overtime or not receiving a promised raise. A federal appellate court affirmed the National Labor Relations Board's (NLRB) determination that the nursing home had to reinstate her with back wages (*NLRB v. Main Street Terrace Center*, 2000).

Intuition tells us that there must be detriments flowing from pay secrecy. What is the big deal about how pay is distributed if we are not supposed to know about it? Why is our organization treating us as though we cannot handle knowledge of others' pay? What if our pay reflects illegal discrimination? And, if we cannot determine what pay levels are possible, wouldn't pay secrecy actually demotivate us so that our performance levels would be expected to drop?

In fact, the limited empirical research has shown that pay secrecy leads to employee dissatisfaction and low motivation (e.g., Burroughs, 1982; Futrell & Jenkins, 1978). In the scanty compensation literature addressing pay secrecy, researchers argue, in general, that pay secrecy is bad for organizations, also demonstrating lowered motivation (Bartol & Martin, 1988; Lawler, 1965a,b, 1967; Leventhal, Karuza, & Fry, 1980; Milkovich & Anderson, 1972). Thus, the state of empirical knowledge continues to suggest that pay secrecy is negative for both individuals and organizations. Further, evidence of the negative effects of pay secrecy include its being viewed as a way for organizations to hide pay discrimination. In fact, England recently passed legislation permitting employees who suspect pay discrimination to request detailed pay information from their supervisors (BBC News, 2004), suggesting a growing awareness that pay secrecy may be costly to society by covering discriminatory practices.

However, current attitudes and practices suggest that there may be beneficial aspects to pay secrecy. First, surveys asking how people feel about pay secrecy indicate that the majority of U.S. workers are in favor of it (*Hrnext.com Survey*, 2001; Walsh, 2000). Furthermore, many organizations seem to employ some form of pay secrecy. Employer surveys (Balkin & Gomez-Mejia, 1985; *Hrnext.com Survey*, 2001) and anecdotal data (e.g., Pappu, 2001; Walsh, 2000) indicate that some form of pay secrecy is prevalent in many organizations, despite its potential illegality (e.g., Fredricksburg Glass and Mirror, 1997; *NLRB v. Main Terrace Center* 2000). This evidence seems to suggest that individual employees and many organizations find pay secrecy useful and desirable.

Thus, although the academic research of the 1960s and 1970s (e.g., Futrell & Jenkins, 1978; Lawler, 1965a,b, 1967; Milkovich & Anderson, 1972) seems to leave us with one view of pay secrecy—that it presents costs to organizations because, among other things, individual employees should not want it—there has been no scholarly investigation that we are aware of since then to determine whether there may also be benefits to organizations. No organizational scholars have investigated how individual demands and organizational practices can continue to be at such odds with this dated academic knowledge.

In this article we discuss the apparently contradictory positions about pay secrecy and argue that there is no simple answer to the question of whether pay secrecy is beneficial or detrimental to individuals and organizations. Instead, we posit that the effects of pay secrecy depend on a variety of factors that render it sometimes valuable or of benefit to employers and employees and other times costly. Throughout the course of our discussion, we examine arguments based on management, economics, psychology, and cultural perspectives to look at the role of pay secrecy in our lives and to suggest avenues for further study. Our ultimate goal is to reopen the discussion of pay secrecy in organizations so that new empirical work in this area can be generated. We first turn to a definition of pay secrecy.

What Is Pay Secrecy?

Although there is no one definition of pay secrecy, it can simply be viewed as a restriction of the amount of information employees are provided about what others are paid. In practice, however, pay secrecy can become quite complex. First, there is the issue of availability of information. An employer may keep pay information secret by never providing for its publication or release. Second, the employer may restrict the type of pay information made available. For example, it may choose to provide certain aggregate

information about pay, such as pay ranges and/or average pay raises, but fail to give precise individual-level information about employees. Third, the employer may restrict the manner in which pay information is disseminated. For example, the employer may encourage strong norms against discussing pay, even if pay information is technically publicly available. In this case the employer may actually threaten to impose heavy sanctions against employees who disclose pay or engage in discussions about it.

The traditional venue for discussions of pay—the compensation literature—identifies several dimensions of pay: pay level, pay structure, the basis for pay, and the form of pay (see Gerhart & Rynes, 2003). Although pay secrecy can range across these various dimensions, the traditional focus has been on pay level itself (i.e., the average pay across jobs; Gerhart & Rynes, 2003). Because we are interested in advancing the discussion about pay secrecy as a general construct, and because we also do not want to limit ourselves to a micro human resource (HR) focus but intend, rather, to write for a much broader audience, we focus on pay-level discussions and avoid the complexities of compensation systems. In other words, when we speak of pay secrecy, we are talking about the lack of information that employees have about the level of other employees' pay in the organization.

Although much prior research has conceptualized pay secrecy as all-or-nothing, we argue that it is best understood along a continuum. Thus, for us, pay secrecy is conceptualized as representing the amount of information about pay available to employees. Burroughs (1982) was the first to hint at such a continuum when he referred to examples of how different organizations could have varying levels of pay secrecy, with the most secret anchor being represented by organizations in which no information is provided to employees other than their own pay and salary increase. The least secret (or most open) anchor reflects organizations where information about specific pay levels and increases for individuals is made available to all employees. We base our view on Burroughs'. In addition, we assume that any costs and benefits of pay secrecy become more extreme as pay becomes more secret.

Finally, we assume throughout that organizations are making good faith efforts to provide equitable compensation and that compensation accurately reflects an individual's contribution to the organization, however that is determined. Because equity is ultimately in the eye of the beholder, we recognize that employees' views on whether they receive pay that is fair may deviate from those of the organization. Thus, our discussion of pay secrecy will rely heavily on the perceptions it creates in the minds of employees.

Why Is Pay Secrecy Interesting?

Based on earlier discussion, we find pay secrecy interesting because it obviously has the potential to apply to many people across jobs, organizations, and industries (Balkin & Gomez-Mejia, 1985; *Hrnext.com Survey*, 2001). Since pay secrecy reflects a lack of information, one way of conceptualizing pay secrecy is in terms of pay uncertainty. Humans are generally motivated to reduce uncertainty or the discomfort that arises from it (Lind & van den Bos, 2002) and, thus, can be expected to engage in a variety of behaviors as a means of eliminating, reducing, or otherwise coping with pay uncertainty. In particular, a host of cognitive biases in information processing are known to result when judgments must be made under uncertainty (Kahneman & Tversky, 1973). Thus, the possible breadth of application of pay secrecy policies immediately raises controversial issues about the extent to which U.S. employees are making less than optimal decisions about jobs and career choices and what the impact might be on American society. Although the answer to such a question is beyond the scope of this article, the very nature of this consideration enhances our interest in thinking about pay secrecy.

Additionally, part of the fascinating character of this topic stems from the fact that it is not a new concern but, rather, one of continuing debate without many insights over the years. For example, pay secrecy was a major difficulty around the time of the passage of the National Labor Relations Act ([NLRA], 1935), because it was determined to interfere with the attempts of employees to unionize. Because information about pay is so critical to employee behaviors and decision making, the NLRA continues to make enforced pay secrecy illegal in order to promote maximal employee information about their job circumstances and workplace fairness (Bierman & Gely, 2004; Gely & Bierman, 2003). Given this historical background, we would have expected two things. First, its sheer illegality should have deterred employers from using pay secrecy over the period since the initial enforcement of the NLRA. Quite to the contrary, many employers willingly announce and promote their pay secrecy policies. For example, a survey of U.S. employers found that 36 percent of respondents indicated their companies prohibited discussion of pay (*Hrnext.com Survey*, 2001). Second, the controversial nature of this topic should have promoted extensive research in this area to build a nomological network of understanding about the costs and benefits of pay secrecy for individuals, organizations, and even society. No such comprehensive course of study exists.

Pay secrecy also seems to reflect current social or cultural values that are expressed or facilitated through its practice. One key value is that of privacy. Today, privacy concerns are reawakening, as evidenced by relatively new legislation or new awareness of older legislation (such as the Family Educational Rights and Privacy Act [FERPA], 1974, and the Health Insurance Portability and Accountability Act [HIPAA], 1996), as well as public outrage about technologically possible behaviors, such as identity theft. Pay secrecy promotes the notion that our own pay should be kept private—that *we, not the employer*, should have the right to

determine whether to disclose our pay and to whom. Thus, its social and personal salience appears to be grounded in the general resurgence of privacy concerns that are part of our evolving world.

One final, but not less important, aspect of pay secrecy that renders it interesting to us is the fact that it might well be a culturally bound construct. Investigations of collectivist and individualist societies (Triandis, 1989) have indicated that Western cultures and economies reflect autonomous, individualistic goals and values, whereas Eastern cultures and economies tend to reflect collectivistic, group-based goals and values. Thus, pay secrecy may not be as controversial an issue in an Eastern culture. There, the tendency would be toward values that favor the collective (Triandis, 1989, 1994). Moreover, members of the collective typically are not truly recognized as "others" completely distinct from the self, causing the very notion of "others' pay" and "referent others for comparison" to be ill-defined. In addition, the collectivist's sense of trust in the group or organization might be expected to accompany lack of concern for what people other than oneself are making in the workplace. The interdependence that accompanies collectivism further suggests that a view of "what is good for one of us is good for all of us" would also tend to dominate and render pay secrecy less controversial (Markus & Kitayama, 1991). Finally, individuals in collectivist cultures typically do not want to stand out from the group or compete with others in the group; pay secrecy would allow this to flourish. Thus, pay secrecy may always be positive in an Eastern culture.

In contrast, in Western cultures, individuals engage in self-construal that tends not to include general "other in self" enhancements (at least outside of close partners and friends; Mashek, Aron, & Boncimino, 2003). Thus, each individual in the workplace is seen as fairly autonomous and a competitor for resources. Independence instead of interdependence is associated with individualistic societies, implying that each person's welfare depends on his or her own efforts and rewards. Pay secrecy reflects values emanating from this type of culture, and it is both supported and promoted by more capitalistic societies that promote individual competitiveness (Markus & Kitayama, 1991). It may only be within Western culture that pay secrecy can produce the costs that are associated with it.

What Are the Costs and Benefits of Pay Secrecy?

Before turning to the focus of our article—that the costs and benefits of pay secrecy depend on a variety of previously undiscussed factors—it is essential to first lay out the costs and benefits themselves. In this section we first review the apparent costs of pay secrecy before turning to a discussion of the benefits. Perhaps surprisingly, some aspects of pay secrecy can turn out to be both costs and benefits, as we will show. Further, factors adding an even greater level of complexity will be addressed in the next section of the paper. For now, we try to elucidate the major costs and benefits as seen by researchers and practitioners.

Costs

There are at least three major costs to pay secrecy, according to research scholars (who continue to challenge the use of pay secrecy by organizations). First, employee judgments about fairness and their perceptions of trust may be sacrificed. Second, employee performance motivation can be expected to decrease. Third, from an economics perspective, the labor market may be less efficient because employees will not move to their highest valued use. This would mean that organizations are not obtaining the best employees for the jobs. Why, and from where, would these costs occur?

Pay secrecy is about lack of information, thus producing uncertainty for employees and an asymmetrical information status between employees and the organization. Based on this lack of information, employees may *infer* that pay outcomes and procedures for distributions are unfair, even when the organization is making a good faith effort to provide equitable compensation based on individual contributions. (Recall that this was an underlying assumption we made earlier.)

One reason this might occur is because the uncertainty of not knowing where employees stand with respect to others and the extent to which their contributions are valid may lead to general anxiety about workplace worth. According to recent work in the organizational justice literature on uncertainty management theory (Lind & van den Bos, 2002), increased uncertainty enhances the degree to which people care about fairness, because apparent fairness is one way of coping with the anxiety generated by uncertainty. When the environment is uncertain, people are able to gain some degree of predictability of their future treatment by looking at how fairly they recently have been or now are being treated. When treated fairly, people can develop trust and reduce their fears of being exploited in the future. When treated unfairly, however, they may take a defensive stance in an attempt to avoid exploitation. Thus, ceteris paribus, employees who are faced with pay secrecy should be more concerned about whether their pay is fair than employees who are in positions where pay information is open. As a result, they may be more vigilant about the extent to which pay and pay determination processes are fair, and this becomes a cost when fairness judgments are negative.

Unfortunately, under high levels of pay secrecy, judgments can be expected to be negative for all three general types of fairness judgments: informational, procedural, and distributive (Bies & Moag, 1986; Colquitt, Conlon, Wesson, Porter, & Ng, 2001; Leventhal, 1976; Thibaut & Walker, 1975). Obviously, judgments about informational fairness can be expected to be negative because information is being withheld. Judgments about procedural fairness can be expected to be negative because, for example, the lack of information restricts employee voice, permits inferences of bias, and suggests that decision making about pay may be done without accurate information. These deficits violate the known requirements for procedural justice to be perceived (Leventhal et al., 1980; Thibaut & Walker, 1975).

Distributive fairness judgments can be expected to be negative for two major reasons. First, inaccurate estimates about what referent others (Dornstein, 1989) are being paid can be expected owing to the lack of information about pay. Lawler's seminal research (1965a,b) indicated that, in the absence of individual pay information, managers overestimated the salaries of other managers at their own and lower levels and underestimated the salaries of managers at higher organizational levels. (In other words, they tended to compress the pay range.) The fact that those at lower levels of the organization were perceived as having higher pay than was actually the case would lead to judgments of distributive unfairness, because they would arguably be making lesser contributions to the organization than was commensurate with their perceived pay.

Second, fairness heuristic theory (Lind, 2001) states that people are likely to base specific fairness judgments on their general impression of organizational fairness in the absence of other information. Thus, in the absence of information about pay, distributive fairness concerning pay level cannot be known, and judgments about it will be inferred based on judgments about other aspects of fairness. If procedural and informational fairness judgments are negative, as indicated above, then distributive fairness judgments should be negative as well (van den Bos, Lind, Vermunt, & Wilke, 1997). This reliance on other fairness judgments generally may be viewed as akin to use of the availability heuristic in prospect theory (Kahneman & Tversky, 1973). In the absence of specific pay information, employees would be expected to rely on recent or vivid information that was readily available or accessible in memory. This information might well be other judgments about fairness regarding aspects of the organization—that is, even fairness judgments beyond those regarding pay could become relevant under pay secrecy.

Related to unfairness judgments resulting from pay secrecy is the notion of distrust in the organization. We follow Mayer, Davis, and Schoorman's definition of trust as "the willingness of a party to be vulnerable to the actions of another party based on the expectation that the other will perform a particular action important to the trustor, irrespective of the ability to monitor or control that other party" (1995: 712). Pay secrecy should generally be expected to lower employees' organizational trust. Research on organizational trust all points to the importance of managers' openness with both themselves and others (Butler, 1991), since this behavior suggests that management has both integrity and benevolence. Such openness has been shown to be a primary driver of trust (Mayer et al., 1995; Mishra, 1996).

Two other key factors strongly suggest that organizational trust should be affected by pay secrecy and its ensuing judgments of unfairness. First, media attention to young, self-made millionaires during the technology boom of the 1990s, astronomical executive pay levels, and corporate scandals have highlighted the wide discrepancy in pay in American society, tending to enhance perceptions that pay may be unfair. Pay secrecy in this environment enhances views of this unfairness and corruption, suggesting that organizations cannot be trusted. Second, pay secrecy signals that the organization does not trust its employees.

Pay secrecy should also reduce work motivation. Because a pay-performance linkage underlies many theories of motivation, one can argue that pay secrecy will reduce motivation by breaking that linkage. The only study we are aware of that examines this connection was conducted by Futrell and Jenkins (1978), who found that moving from pay secrecy to pay openness resulted in increased performance on the part of their sample of salespeople, suggesting that motivation was hampered by pay secrecy. This result appeared to stem from an equity theory explanation: since managers acting under pay secrecy compressed the managerial pay scale in their estimates, as mentioned earlier, the link between pay and performance was weakened, and there was less motivation to perform.

Other theories of work motivation also depend on linking pay to performance; without perceptions of this link, employees lack an essential driver of motivation. For example, expectancy theorists (Naylor, Pritchard, & Ilgen, 1980; Vroom, 1964) argue that the motivation to perform is a direct function of the subjective probability that engaging in a certain level of performance will result in given outcomes (i.e., instrumentality). Goal theorists suggest that performance goals employees are committed to drive motivation (Locke & Latham, 1990), and goal commitment is partially determined by the valence of outcomes associated with achieving a goal (Klein, Wesson, Hollenbeck, & Alge, 1999). Thus, if employees do not know the relative worth of their outcomes, they may be less likely to be committed to goals that assure the achievement of the desired outcomes. They may make poor estimates of their subjective probabilities or the valence of their outcomes.

Pay secrecy can also have an important and deleterious effect on the labor market, thereby imposing a cost on some businesses and society. Economic theory is based on the assumption of perfect information in order to have perfect markets so that resources can migrate to their most valued use (i.e., market efficiency). Labor markets would be one type of market to which this argument should apply (Brickley, Smith, & Zimmerman, 2000). Pay secrecy, by hindering information to employees, generates information *asymmetry* between workers and organizations, thus preventing workers from moving to better-fitting jobs. In other words, if a top-quality engineer is not aware of a higher-paying job that he or she could perform in his or her current company or in another company with a pay secrecy policy, then that engineer may stay in the "wrong" job and be underemployed. Employers cannot "lure" or "pull" good employees away from other employers if they maintain pay secrecy, because they cannot advertise current wage or salary levels. Thus, pay secrecy is one factor that prevents labor markets from clearing in an efficient manner. This represents a cost to employees who could hold better jobs, as well as to organizations that would prefer to hire these employees. Economists would argue that there are social costs imposed because of the inefficient use of human capital in society (Williamson, 1985).

Benefits

Although pay secrecy may have the foregoing costs, it is clear that it must also have benefits attached to it since it continues to be relatively pervasive in organizational practice. Here we identify three major benefits—organizational control, protection of privacy, and decreased labor mobility—which we now discuss in detail.

One benefit of pay secrecy would be that it appears to enhance efforts at organizational control. One major way in which organizations prefer to control employees is by maintaining a civil, peaceful workplace, free from conflicts. In fact, avoiding conflicts is one of the main reasons managers give for enforcing pay secrecy (Gomez-Mejia & Balkin, 1992; Steele, 1975). There are many reasons to believe that pay secrecy is a major source of avoiding or reducing conflict in the workplace.

First, for example, differentials in pay are hidden under pay secrecy, thus preventing problems in corps de sprit and levels of satisfaction among workers. As Sally J. Scott, a partner in a Chicago law firm stated, "[Pay secrecy] would create morale problems if one person were allowed to boast about their huge merit bonus" (Walsh, 2000). Second, social psychologists (e.g., Leventhal et al., 1980; Leventhal, Michaels, & Sanford, 1972) have argued that people who allocate resources have a motivation not only to maintain equity but also to avoid conflict. If pay were open, managers might feel that they would have to keep the pay distribution artificially narrow in order to avoid conflict (Leventhal et al., 1980; Major & Adams, 1983). Pay secrecy, however, allows them to provide maximal separation in reward for performance (Bartol & Martin, 1988), while at the same time avoiding negative reactions by those who end up at the lower end of the distribution (Gomez-Mejia & Balkin, 1992; Leventhal et al., 1972). Finally, economists (Brickley et al., 2000) have argued that employers engage in pay secrecy because the cost of the political behavior (such as influence activities) and conflict resulting from pay openness policies makes pay openness inefficient.

In addition, pay secrecy allows organizations to correct pay inequities that arise (even despite good faith efforts to avoid them) without having to face employees' negative reactions to those inequities (Gomez-Mejia & Balkin, 1992). (Ironically, although pay secrecy may generate inferences of pay discrimination, as alluded to earlier, it may also prevent employee awareness of an unintentional pay inequity, thus precluding moderate reactance to or even charges of pay discrimination.) Pay secrecy can therefore be beneficial, because it can actually avoid perceptions of unfairness when pay inequities do exist and can minimize claims of discrimination or other organizational wrongdoing.

Furthermore, if we think of cooperation as the opposite of conflict, it seems clear that organizations, although major players in our capitalistic economic system, prefer some level of cooperation among employees and like to maintain competition in the workplace at a "healthy" or otherwise nondeleterious level. We can think of employers in North America as operating within an individualistic culture but seeking to transcend it by encouraging more of a tempered collectivistic culture within the workplace. For example, organizations may prefer that employees form identities that include the organization (Ashforth & Mael, 1989). The recent emphasis on teamwork in organizations means that organizations want to encourage employees, under many circumstances, to be good team players instead of striving for "superstardom" at the expense of the team. Pay secrecy should give employers operating in individualistic societies the opportunity to introduce a more interdependent approach to culture and values in the workplace.

Another way in which pay secrecy can serve as a form of organizational control is by being a form of organizational paternalism—a way of treating employees as children and limiting their autonomy, supposedly for their own benefit (cf. Colella & Garcia, 2004). Organizational sociologists and economists (e.g., Jackman, 1994; Padavic & Earnest, 1994) have often discussed how organizations use paternalism to control their employees. Pay secrecy can be viewed as a paternalistic policy when managers argue that pay should be kept secret for the benefit of their employees, because (1) employees really want pay kept secret, (2) it will upset them to know what others are making, or (3) they may make "irrational" decisions (such as leaving) if they know what others are being paid. In each case, managers are assuming that they know what is in employees' best interests while limiting their autonomy by failing to provide them with full pay information.

From the organization's point of view, using pay secrecy as a form of paternalistic control would be a benefit of pay secrecy. It would allow the organization to control its employees, but at the same time would let the employers feel good about it, since they were supposedly acting in the best interest of their employees (Abercrombie & Hill, 1976). It is unclear whether this would be a benefit from the employees' perspective. Some argue that paternalism always causes harm to its targets (Jackman, 1994), but targets often welcome paternalistic behavior (Jost & Banaji, 1994). An employee may reason, for example, that an organization really cares about her

because, by enforcing pay secrecy, it protects her privacy rights. Regardless of the impact on targets, paternalism is generally seen as an organizational benefit.

A second benefit of pay secrecy would be expected to be the enhanced privacy that comes from having one's own pay kept secret from others. Stone and Stone (1990), in a review of the organizational privacy literature, found that employees' perceptions of privacy led to many positive organizational outcomes, such as performance (Klopfer & Rubenstein, 1977; Sundstrom, Burt, & Kamp, 1980), satisfaction and commitment (Klopfer & Rubenstein, 1977; Sundstrom et al., 1980), and retention (Sundstrom, 1978).

In today's society, in general, as previously mentioned, privacy has become a major concern. Living in an age of technology, we have all become more sensitized to the troublesome ease with which information about us is available and how it can be used to our disadvantage. Much information about us is requested by, and potentially available from, our employers (e.g., in order to work, we must present an official form of ID and a social security number; employers perform credit and sometimes criminal background checks). Given this, it is perhaps not at all surprising that surveys of employees often find that the majority of employees are in favor of pay secrecy policies (Markels & Berton, 1996). In addition, in North American culture there continues to be a strong norm against discussing one's pay (Steele, 1975). Many people prefer not to have their pay discussed by coworkers (Pappu, 2001; Sim, 2001). Most people would be more comfortable answering questions about personal family matters such as religion—or even perhaps sex—than about their salary (BBC News, 2004; Bierman & Gely, 2004). In addition, the discomfort of discussing pay may result from another's revealing too much information about himself or herself (Paetzold, Boswell, & Belsito, 2004).

Of course, some of us might be curious about the pay of others and, thus, be willing to trade off some secrecy about our own pay in order to learn something about how much referent others are making. To date, there is no empirical research that tests this notion. Based on employee surveys, we conclude that the desire for privacy about oneself and one's own pay dominates and overrides the desire to know pay information about others.

Finally, pay secrecy can actually benefit organizations with respect to labor market immobility. Although the labor market inefficiency resulting from pay secrecy may be a cost to society as a whole and some employers in particular, as mentioned above, other employers can profit from this inefficiency by reducing the mobility of their productive workers. For example, Danzinger and Katz (1997) argue that a policy of pay secrecy prevents employees from comparing their wages with others inside the firm, as well as wages of the firm with those in the job market. Such comparisons are needed for employees to switch jobs when it is to their advantage to do so. Thus, pay secrecy reduces this source of information and prevents employees from recognizing other good employment opportunities. A net benefit can accrue to the organization requiring pay secrecy, not only because the pay secrecy facilitates the organization's ability to keep productive employees but also because the organization can avoid costs associated with labor transitions—for example, recruiting and training. Thus, it is clear that pay secrecy can be advantageous for some employers, presumably those who continue to use it.

A related construct in the organizations literature is that of continuance commitment, which reflects an employee's commitment to an organization because of a need to remain with the organization (Meyer, Allen, & Gellatly, 1990). It is not necessary that the employee have positive feelings about the organization; instead, continuance commitment is a function of the opportunities that an employee perceives he or she has. As indicated above, pay secrecy operates by reducing the perceived number of alternative job possibilities, because pay information about other jobs is lacking and appropriate pay comparisons cannot be made. Hence, continuance commitment is increased. At the same time, pay secrecy also prevents "poaching" from other companies, because it keeps competitors from knowing what they must offer to lure good employees away (Sim, 2001). (Notice that we mentioned this earlier as a social cost and a cost to some organizations. Here, it is an organizational benefit.)

Trading off Costs and Benefits

As indicated so far in our discussion, there are both costs and benefits to pay secrecy, but it should also be clear that not all organizations will experience the costs and benefits to the same degree. This would appear to depend, in part, on the quality of employees, their individual needs and perceptions, and the history of those employees with the employer. Employers can therefore be "profiled" based on their employees in order to predict which of them should choose pay secrecy policies. For example, an organization that has many high-quality employees whom it would like to retain and also has high recruiting and training costs, all else being constant, should be more likely to use pay secrecy than an organization that does not.

Once we remove the constraint that all else is being held constant, pay secrecy can look even better for this organization. Consider that work motivation may not be as much of a concern if the "good" employees are intrinsically motivated (so that pay secrecy will not work to reduce their level of work motivation) and tend to have a lot of accumulated trust in the organization stemming from other aspects of the work relationship. Such an employer (who uses pay secrecy) may enjoy, therefore, the benefit of lack of labor mobility (continuance commitment), in addition to not suffering the costs associated with reduced work motivation and lack of trust in the organization.

Other employers with different cost/benefit trade-offs should be expected not to employ pay secrecy. An organization with employees having a low need for privacy, but with a history of organizational unfairness and distrust, should *not* use a pay secrecy policy. For this organization, pay openness could help with perceptions of fairness and trust, as well as potentially improve work motivation and performance. In addition, this organization may prefer to enhance the mobility of its dissatisfied employees and, thus, should prefer pay openness as a way of making outside opportunities more appealing. For example, as discussed above, the pay distribution under pay openness would tend to be narrower than under pay secrecy so that opportunities for pay raises would appear to be small. Although we mentioned that this has the benefit of reducing conflict, we must also note that it will tend to encourage employees to move to other positions, where they can be put to their "most valued use."

Thus, separate consideration of costs and benefits does not reveal the whole picture of pay secrecy; their joint consideration is relevant. In joint consideration, these costs and benefits can help us to identify why some employers may prefer pay secrecy while others do not; characteristics of individual employees, for example, suggest that some employers should prefer pay secrecy while others should not.

But individual characteristics cannot tell us the whole picture either. In fact, the *context* or *contextual factors* employers face may be the most important determinant of why some employers engage in pay secrecy policies while others do not. The relationships between pay secrecy and its costs or benefits are not fixed but depend on these contextual factors. Organizations and their environments are complex, and there are a number of contextual factors that are likely to accentuate or minimize the costs and benefits mentioned above. For example, which employees should respond more positively to pay secrecy—those who hold knowledge and skills specific to the organizations or those who do not? The answer to this and similar questions suggests that context, or a variety of contextual factors, helps to determine whether pay secrecy is costly or beneficial for organizations. This consideration has never been addressed in the academic literature, and our presentation of it follows.

When Do Costs and Benefits of Pay Secrecy Occur?

In addition to identifying that there are legitimate benefits to pay secrecy, despite its costs, we also view the thrust of our work as identifying a set of contextual factors that make pay secrecy more likely to be either a benefit or a cost—that is, they make it more likely for organizations to incur the costs or reap the benefits of pay secrecy. Because many organizations seem to prefer pay secrecy today, and because we have presented our discussion from the perspective of highlighting reasons why such a policy may be beneficial, we now assume that pay secrecy is operating throughout the discussion that follows. We identify contextual factors that exist at different levels of the organization and write from the perspective of how they mitigate the costs and help to make the benefits realizable for those organizations employing pay secrecy. We discuss, in order, the nature of human capital, the criteria used for pay allocation, and the gauging of employees' relative pay status.

We do not claim that these are the only contextual factors that can affect how organizations experience pay secrecy, but we view them as three major contexts that share commonality of importance for many organizations.

Contextual Factor 1: Nature of Human Capital

Consider the following scenario. Heather has worked at AAB (Anti-Ad-Bot) for just a few years, but she has reached a high rung on the internal employment ladder—operations manager. To accomplish this, she has held a variety of positions, beginning as a programmer and working her way up, one job after the other. She has received training and experience along the way that has enabled her to perform all jobs below her current position, and that training has also been essential to her knowledge of the unique culture at AAB. Eric started working at AAB at the same time as Heather, but he remains a programmer. He has never undergone specialized training, remaining in a "dead-end" position within AAB. Between Eric and Heather, who should react to AAB's pay secrecy policy more positively?

We would posit that Eric should. Because Eric has only lower-level skills and no firm-specific training about particular jobs within AAB, Eric also has no special, firm-specific value to AAB beyond what he would have to similar firms. Thus, Eric should be able to go outside the organization in the labor market that is pertinent to programmer jobs for pay information (Milgrom & Roberts, 1992). Heather, however, has such firm-specific skills that she probably cannot find another firm where her talents could be as valuable as they are to AAB. The market for her skills—the one inside AAB—does not allow her to find pay information because it maintains a policy of pay secrecy.

Firm-specific human capital refers to the skills, abilities, knowledge, and/or interpersonal relationships that positively affect employees' performance in their current employment but that are relatively useless if the employee moves to another organization (Williamson, 1985). Therefore, when employees hold primarily firm-specific human capital, external labor market information is less useful to them. In contrast, general human capital refers to human capital with value that remains the same across various organizations. For example, mathematics teachers are likely to provide the same value across various schools. Similarly, carpenters may move across sites to build homes without much change in their duties across those various sites. In both cases, employees can be replaced, requiring little, if any, additional training, and pay is relatively difficult to hide from employees having general human capital.

This means that although there is a relationship between pay secrecy and labor immobility (continuance commitment), the nature of the relationship is highly dependent on the type of human capital workers possess. Looking inside the firm for pay information, employees with firm-specific human capital will find their efforts to learn about pay levels thwarted. Employees with general human capital, however, can look to the external labor market and find little hindrance to obtaining pay information.

Similarly, because of the availability of external information, privacy should be less of a concern to employees with general human capital. These employees cannot keep their pay completely secret if an industry compensation norm exists. They may also be less likely to make incorrect fairness judgments, because they can use external comparison others. If the firm is paying market rates, then employees with general human capital should perceive that their pay is fair. (Those with firm-specific human capital lack external comparison others and may be more likely to make incorrect comparisons.) Also, pay secrecy should have less of an effect on motivation when employees have general human capital, because the employees should want to maintain high enough performance levels to make them attractive to other firms.

Thus, having general human capital should mitigate the costs of pay secrecy and enhance any benefits, at least marginally (assuming that an asymptotic level of benefits has not been reached). In our scenario, Heather cannot easily benefit from any outside pay information, but Eric perhaps can. The benefits of having no firm-specific skills accrue to him when pay secrecy is operating. The organization does not suffer costs from pay secrecy with regard to its general human capital employees—and is free to enjoy all the benefits—even though it may incur costs associated with its firm-specific human capital employees.

Contextual Factor 2: Criteria for Pay Allocation

The criteria for pay allocation are those elements or aspects of effort or performance used to determine pay levels. Pay criteria may be measured either *objectively* or *subjectively*, and we suggest that the nature of measurement helps to determine whether costs or benefits will be experienced during pay secrecy. Using objective criteria for pay allocation should mitigate the costs of pay secrecy.

Consider, for example, Ryan and Natasha, supervisors of two different sales teams at a retail outlet. Ryan's manager stresses "management by objectives" and has specific sales goals that Ryan's sales team must reach in order for Ryan to be evaluated highly. Natasha's manager uses more subjective criteria for evaluating her performance, including her communication skills, leadership abilities, and commitment to diversity. Assume that the retailer maintains pay secrecy policies for its employees. For which supervisor will the retailer be more likely to incur the benefits of pay secrecy?

We posit that it should be for Ryan. Recall that one major cost of pay secrecy is that any pay differentials that may exist—here, between Ryan and Natasha—will lose their power to motivate because they are unknown. In order to counter this difficulty, organizations can provide a clear linkage between pay and performance in order to create work incentives for employees (Thompson & Pronsky, 1975). One factor that would enable the pay-for-performance linkage to be clear would be the use of objective performance criteria. Here, Ryan's raises could be justified to him clearly, whereas Natasha's could not. Thus, if Natasha believes she is underpaid, her manager cannot point to objective performance criteria to justify her pay and attempt to convince her that her pay is commensurate with the goals that he or she has specified for Natasha. It would be difficult to discuss "how much" leadership or "how many" skills were necessary for Natasha to satisfy her supervisor's requirement. Ryan's manager would be in just such a position to get that specific, however. And when employees perceive a specific pay-performance linkage, they are more likely to be satisfied with their pay (Huber, Seybolt, & Venemon, 1992).

Second, the performance appraisal literature (DeNisi, 1996; Murphy & Cleveland, 1995) states that when there is objective information on which to base appraisals, managers are less likely to engage in biases when evaluating employees, and employees are more likely to perceive the appraisal as fair. Such perceptions of fairness will attenuate the general unfairness in justice perceptions that accompany pay secrecy, making the costs of pay secrecy less likely to be incurred and providing for greater organizational trust. This would be true regardless of the strength of the pay-for-performance link, but the two together provide a strong basis for arguing that the costs of pay secrecy will not be incurred.

Third, privacy, a benefit of pay secrecy, is not automatically threatened by having objective performance criteria. Just because performance may be measured more objectively, and hence may be more visible to others, this does not guarantee that pay will be. Privacy issues, however, may be of less concern to employees in this situation, because when objective performance criteria are clearly linked to pay, there is a somewhat natural transparency concerning what people are paid.

Thus, although pay secrecy is operating, an organization that uses objective performance criteria is more likely to experience benefits than one using subjective performance criteria. In addition, however, beyond the question of whether pay criteria are measured objectively or subjectively, is the question of whether pay criteria are *known and not secret*. We suggest also that when the criteria for pay—what we call the basis for one's pay—are known, then the costs of pay secrecy are less likely to be incurred, and the benefits are more likely to be reaped.

When the basis of pay is secret, individuals do not know why they receive the pay they get. The negative effects of pay secrecy (which, recall, has been *pay-level* secrecy by assumption)

should be amplified, and the positive effects with respect to cooperation will be mitigated. Why? Go back to Ryan and Natasha, who, under pay basis secrecy, do not know whether their pay is based on leadership, diversity initiatives, communication skills, sales performance, or some other criteria. The level of uncertainty is even higher than under ordinary pay secrecy such that uncertainty management theory (Lind & van den Bos, 2002) suggests even more negative assessments than before, but for all of the same reasons.

Employees cannot predict their pay into the future. For all they know, chance factors, mistakes, and bias play a role in determining their pay. Fairness assessments will be highly negative and lead to a lack of trust. As employees seek out information about pay (which they are more predisposed to do under uncertainty management theory), they will be able to learn even less than before, thereby creating the possibility of greater conflict. The organization may have passed the point at which individuals are willing to keep their own pay information secret, because a need for uncertainty reduction may lead to an enhanced desire to know *others'* pay as a way of judging one's own.

Clearly, therefore, organizations that provide for pay secrecy should also provide *known* bases for pay if they want to highlight the benefits of the pay secrecy policy and incur fewer costs. In other words, it is not only the issue of measurement of pay criteria that determines whether costs or benefits will be experienced but also knowledge of those very criteria themselves.

Contextual Factor 3: Gauging of Relative Pay Status

Our last factor is at the most micro of the levels we consider, but it is nonetheless important. Employees may always attempt to "guess" where they stand or rank against the pay distribution, even though the distribution itself is unknown. In other words, even under pay secrecy, employees will believe that they are better or worse employees and, thus, closer to the top or bottom of the pay scale. We argue that this affects the organization's consequences of using pay secrecy.

For example, assume that LaToya has always been successful in her work as a loan officer and therefore believes that she probably falls near the top of the pay distribution for bank loan officers at Fifth National Bank. Jonathan, however, doesn't have as much confidence in his work, notices that a lot of the loan officers seem to be more successful than he is, and decides that he is probably closer to the bottom of the pay distribution for loan officers at the same bank. Which of the two loan officers will respond more favorably to pay secrecy?

We argue that employees who perceive their relative pay to be closer to the top of the relevant pay distribution should have a more positive reaction to pay secrecy, so we expect LaToya to respond more favorably than Jonathan. It has been demonstrated that high performers desire pay secrecy more than low performers (Schuster & Colletti, 1973). First, since these employees believe they are being paid more than others, they may also believe that pay secrecy will prevent them from becoming targets for conflict. Second, because these employees already believe they are being paid more than others, they will be less likely to make judgments that pay levels are distributively unfair. Third, because people who are successful and paid more are more likely to attribute pay to internal causes (Miller & Ross, 1975), they will likely attribute their pay to their own superior performance and, thus, be more motivated, regardless of pay secrecy. Finally, because managers may narrow pay distributions when pay is open, as previously discussed, those who believe they are highly paid may fear that they would be paid less relative to those at the bottom of the distribution were pay to become open.

In summary, therefore, employees who perceive that they have high relative pay will tend not to suffer from judgments of unfairness or decreases in motivation under pay secrecy. Thus, because pay secrecy was described as a potential cost in the previous section, the implication is that this expectation holds for employees who view themselves as being at the bottom of the pay distribution (i.e., probably the lower performers). We predict that what previously appeared to be costs of pay secrecy—lack of fairness perceptions and lowered work motivation—would tend to occur most strongly for those employees who believe they are paid low relative to relevant others.

But does this make sense? What is it about these employees that could render pay secrecy even more negative for them? For example, we might argue that the employees who perceive themselves as making low relative pay may also perceive themselves as having low value in the organization.

In that case, they should see pay secrecy as a benefit. As one worker stated:

I worked in a place where a lot of people knew others' salaries.... I was humiliated when I found out that others at my title and experience level were making vastly higher amounts of money.... If management had kept that information to themselves, and discouraged discussion, they would have prevented a lot of problems (Cohen, 2003).

The "humiliation" spoken of by this worker suggests a privacy violation: he or she experienced negative affect when allowed to compare his or her own pay with that of others. The humiliation was undoubtedly not only due to the realization that others at the same title and level of experience were making more but also that coworkers could realize that this worker was making *much less.* This type of privacy issue is the one we identified as a benefit to pay secrecy.

However, employees who perceive themselves as being paid less than others are more likely to experience an array of negative outcomes from pay secrecy for a variety of interrelated reasons that do not concern privacy. First, they will intuitively be more likely to experience conflict with decision makers about pay and perhaps other coworkers whom they

perceive to be paid at higher levels—a negative factor. Second, employees who experience negative pay outcomes are more likely to perceive them as distributively unfair. It is under conditions of judgments of distributive unfairness that employees will also be most concerned about procedural fairness of pay allocation decisions (Brockner & Weisenfeld, 1996), which we have already described as tending to be negative under pay secrecy. Finally, employees who experience negative outcomes will be more likely to attribute the cause of those outcomes to external sources, such as bias on the part of the decision maker. This might increase the likelihood of conflict and reduce motivation (Miller & Ross, 1975). Thus, pay secrecy should clearly be linked to costs of judgments of unfairness and lowered work motivation in this situation.

In addition, perceptions of being paid less than relevant others could increase perceptions of mobility by making relatively low offers or lesser opportunities from the outside look more appealing than they otherwise would, particularly if the employees are attributing low pay level to unfairness or bias (Hulin, Roznowski, & Haichya, 1985). Thus, those who believe themselves to be at the lower end of the pay scale should experience pay secrecy in a more negative manner than those who believe they are at the higher end.

What Remains to be Known About Pay Secrecy?

In short, much. In this article we have entered into a discussion of pay secrecy with multiple goals in mind. The notion of pay secrecy jumped into our research minds when one of us, Asghar Zardkoohi, discussed with the rest of us a news article he had just read on the topic. As conversation evolved, we realized that we knew and had heard very little about this topic. Our own investigation of early research efforts indicated that scant scholarly work existed on this topic, and most of it had been done many years ago. It seemed that most of what we thought we knew about pay secrecy was anecdotal.

Numerous discussions later, we emerged with this framework for discussing pay secrecy. Our hope is to regenerate an interest in the topic, one that this time will engage more scholars and produce more scholarship. We hope that our framework provides many research questions that academics will find interesting. No longer need we make the intuitive jump, as many organizational researchers have, that pay secrecy is obviously bad for organizations. No longer need we embrace economists' intuitive belief that pay secrecy must be good for organizations or organizations would not use it.

In addition, we have attempted to suggest that pay secrecy is not just a human resources issue. It has individual and societal consequences that cannot be ignored, even beyond their impact on the organization. For example, the very concept of privacy is an important social value during the early twenty-first century. Pay secrecy may not only reflect this value but may be critical for promoting this value more strongly in American society. Future research could focus more generally on the role that pay secrecy in organizations plays in helping society maintain or even attain a level of individual privacy that allows American citizens or residents to live in comfort, experience important freedoms, or even achieve other goals that we, as a society, see as valuable.

What is the overall impact of pay secrecy on society? Does it maximize the differential between higher- and lower-paid employees? What is its net effect on wages? If it is true, as we have conjectured, that pay secrecy will enable supervisors and managers to create larger pay differentials among employees, then we expect that high-performing employees could make even more in wages or salary than they would tend to under pay openness. Also, the pay differential should be wider under pay secrecy, because there is less of a concern about conflict when employees do not know what others are making, as we have discussed. Thus, society could experience an even bigger gap between those who are highly paid and those who receive little pay. This topic should be of particular interest to a broad range of management scholars. For example, is it even possible for all organizations to hold pay secrecy policies at the same time in a capitalist society? What benefits would be expected to accrue to the "first mover"—the first organization to offer pay openness? What would characterize the first-mover organization?

Pay secrecy also can be important in the study of international management or cross-cultural management, as we have alluded to in this article. First, further study regarding the notion that organizations operating in a capitalistic society may nonetheless try to instill the values associated with collectivist societies is interesting to explore in and of itself. What happens when American businesses locate in countries having cultural values different from our own? Is it true that pay secrecy has a different impact in more collectivist cultures? (Here, it might be interesting to consider whether pay openness leads those at the top of the pay distribution in Eastern cultures to be the most embarrassed for "sticking out," whereas in Western cultures those at the top may be the most proud, even if they want to avoid being the targets of conflict.) What happens when workers from different cultural backgrounds and expectations must work alongside each other in the same organization? The strategic considerations accompanying pay secrecy simply should not be ignored, but research is needed to inform us of the importance of culture to strategic decision making in this regard.

One aspect of organizational control not considered in this article is the manner in which pay secrecy is "enforced." We believe this variable falls along a continuum, from implicit to explicit enforcement. At the more lenient end is a situation where there are no explicit norms or organizational policies regarding the discussion of pay—where pay secrecy might exist only because individual employees choose

not to discuss their pay with each other. At the most restrictive level—the more explicit of the two poles—there is an enforced and formal organizational policy that prohibits discussion of pay. Along the continuum are levels that include varying degrees of pay secrecy. For example, somewhat beyond the more lenient of the poles is a level where pay secrecy is enforced by group or departmental norms alone, despite no formal organizational policy existing about the discussion of pay. Closer to the more restrictive pole is a level where there are strong organizational norms or informal policies against sharing pay information—for example, a statement emphasizing that pay discussion should not take place, but without sanctions in place.

The manner in which pay secrecy is enforced is likely to affect how employees will respond to it. On the one hand, when pay secrecy stems from either individual choices or informal group norms not to discuss pay, employees are signaling that they value the privacy avoidance of conflict that they obtain from pay secrecy to a greater degree than they value information about what others are being paid. It is unlikely that this situation would arise if there were suspicions of bias in the pay distribution or if there were substantial negative fairness inferences regarding the organization. On the other hand, when the enforcement of pay secrecy is tied to the organization and is not volitional on the part of employees, employees may view this as over-reaching, providing a basis for suspicion that the organization has something to hide and may be biased and unfair. Research on this issue could help to elucidate the trade-offs employees make regarding privacy choices about their own pay, as well as shed light on broader issues of organizational control.

Certainly, strategic HR academics can pursue many research questions stemming from pay secrecy. For example, the question of internal alignment (i.e., the degree to which different HR practices fit together and work with the overall strategy of the organization) is related to compensation strategies and, thus, potentially, to pay secrecy. Corporate strategy may influence the effectiveness of a pay secrecy policy in conjunction with whether the firm is pursuing a defender strategy or a prospector strategy (see Miles & Snow, 1978, for a review of these strategies).

Gomez-Mejia and Balkin (1992) have proposed two different compensation strategies that would be appropriate for these different business strategies: algorithmic and experiential strategies. An algorithmic strategy is one characterized by pay based on individual performance, internal equity, above-market salary and benefits, and *pay secrecy*. An experiential strategy, in contrast, is characterized by pay based on level of skills, external equity, below-market salary and benefits (but salary plus incentives above market), and *pay openness*. Gomez-Mejia and Balkin hypothesized, and have found support for the idea, that defenders would use algorithmic compensation strategies, whereas prospectors would employ experiential compensation strategies (Balkin & Gomez-Mejia, 1987, 1990).

However, our analysis makes it unclear as to the extent to which these aspects of a compensation system *should occur* together if a firm wishes to achieve the benefits of pay secrecy. For example, a firm following an algorithmic strategy would appear to be attracting top employees, paying them along internal hierarchical distinctions in individual performance (which could be relatively wide), and would probably invest in firm-specific training for them. Both the relatively wide pay distribution and the firm-specific investments for the employees suggest that the employer would suffer the costs of a pay secrecy policy instead of realizing the benefits. *Pay openness* would appear to be more appropriate for firms in this situation.

If a firm followed an experiential strategy, however, it would appear to be maintaining general human capital for its employees and encouraging weaker employees to leave the organization by paying below market. The incentive pay system should lead to wider pay distributions, providing perceptions that pay is unfair and potentially leading to conflicts. Pay openness would seem inappropriate in this situation. Instead, the benefits of having pay secrecy could be achieved (privacy and lack of conflict; maintaining high-quality employees) while its costs would be mitigated (perceptions of unfairness and lack of trust; subjecting good employees to poaching). Thus, *pay secrecy and not pay openness* would be desirable in this situation. Further investigation of Gomez-Mejia and Balkin's contingency approach to compensation strategies should be conducted as a result of our research.

Additional HR strategy issues may also be generated from our work by considering pay-level secrecy in conjunction with other pay system characteristics more generally. Clearly, based on the above, HR strategy can influence the effectiveness of pay secrecy policies. We have examined pay-level secrecy in isolation from other pay system characteristics and corporate strategy (implying a "best practices" approach), but future work is needed to expand our approach.

Pay secrecy continues to be a contentious and interesting issue in our society today. Nonetheless, there has been little scholarly research over the past several decades. We hope that our efforts here will reignite research on this timely and provocative topic and serve as a guide for future research.

Source: A. Colella, et al., Exposing Pay Secrecy. Academy of Management Review, 32, (1), 55–71 (2007). Reprinted by permission.

REFERENCES

Abercrombie, N., & Hill, S. 1976. Paternalism and patronage. *British Journal of Sociology*, 27: 413–429.

Ashforth, B. E., & Mael, F. 1989. Social identity theory and the organization. *Academy of Management Review*, 14: 20–40.

Balkin, D. B., & Gomez-Mejia, L. R. 1985. Compensation practices in high tech industries. *Personnel Administrator*, 30: 111–123.

Balkin, D. B., & Gomez-Mejia, L. R. 1987. Toward a contingency theory of compensation strategy. *Strategic Management Journal*, 8: 169–183.

Balkin, D. B., & Gomez-Mejia, L. R. 1990. Matching compensation and organizational strategies. *Strategic Management Journal*, 11: 153–169.

Bartol, K. M., & Martin, D. C. 1988. Effects of dependence, dependency threats, and pay secrecy on managerial pay allocations. *Journal of Applied Psychology*, 74: 105–113.

BBC News. 2004. *Salary secrecy "penalises women."* http://news.bbc. co.uk/1/hi/business/3392937.stm, January 14.

Bierman, L., & Gely, R. 2004. Love, sex, and politics? Sure. Salary? "No way": Workplace social norms and the law. *Berkley Journal of Law and Employment*, 25: 167–191.

Bies, R. J., & Moag, J. F. 1986. Interactional justice: Communication criteria of fairness. *Research on Negotiations in Organizations*, I: 43–55.

Brickley, J. A., Smith, C. W., Jr., & Zimmerman, J. L. 2000. *Managerial economics and organizational architecture* (2nd ed.). New York: McGraw-Hill.

Brockner, J., & Weisenfeld, B. M. 1996. An integrative framework for explaining reactions to decisions: Interactive effects of outcomes and procedures. *Psychological Bulletin*, 120: 189–208.

Burroughs, J. D. 1982. Pay secrecy and performance: The psychological research. *Compensation Review*, 14: 44–54.

Butler, J. K. 1991. Toward understanding and measuring conditions of trust: Evolution of a condition of trust inventory. *Journal of Management*, 17: 643–663.

Cohen, S. 2003. Keeping pay details away from friends. *WSJ.com College* Journal. http://www.collegejournal.com/salaryinfo/negotiation-stips/20030106-jobspectrum.html.

Colella, A., & Garcia, M. F. 2004. *Paternalism: Hidden discrimination?* Paper presented at the annual meeting of the Academy of Management, New Orleans.

Colquitt, J. A., Conlon, D. E., Wesson, M. J., Porter, C. O. L. H., & Ng, K. Y. 2001. Justice at the millennium: A meta-analytic review of 25 years of organizational justice research. *Journal of Applied Psychology*, 86: 425–445.

Danziger, L., & Katz, E. 1997. Wage secrecy as a social convention. *Economic Inquiry*, 35: 59–69.

DeNisi, A. S. 1996. *Cognitive approach to performance appraisal: A program of research.* London: Routledge.

Dornstein, M. 1989. The fairness judgments of received pay and their determinants. *Journal of Occupational Psychology*, 62: 287–299.

Fredricksburg Glass and Mirror. 1997. 323 NLRB 165.

Futrell, C. M., & Jenkins, O. C. 1978. Pay secrecy versus pay disclosure for salesmen: A longitudinal study. *Journal of Marketing Research*, 15: 214–219.

Gely, R., & Bierman, L. 2003. Pay secrecy/confidentiality rules and the National Labor Relations Act. *University of Pennsylvania Journal of Labor and Employment Law*, 6: 121–156.

Gerhart, B., & Rynes, S. L. 2003. *Compensation: Theory, evidence, and strategic implications.* Thousand Oaks, CA: Sage.

Gomez-Mejia, L. R., & Balkin, D. B. 1992. *Compensation, organizational strategy, and firm performance.* Cincinnati: South-Western Publishing.

Hrnext.com Survey. 2001. www.hrnext.com/content.

Huber, V. L., Seybolt, P. M., & Venemon, K. 1992. The relationship between individual inputs, perceptions, and multidimensional pay satisfaction. *Journal of Applied Social Psychology*, 22: 1356–1373.

Hulin, C. L., Roznowski, M., & Haichya, D. 1985. Alternative opportunities and withdrawal decisions: Empirical and theoretical discrepancies and an integration. *Psychological Bulletin*, 97: 233–250.

Jackman, M. 1994. *The velvet glove: Paternalism and conflict in gender, class, and race relations.* Berkeley: University of California Press.

Jost, J. T., & Banaji, M. R. 1994. The role of stereotyping in system-justification and the production of false consciousness. *British Journal of Social Psychology*, 33: 1–27.

Kahneman, D., & Tversky, A. 1973. On the psychology of prediction. *Psychological Review*, 80: 237–251.

Klein, H. J., Wesson, M. J., Hollenbeck, J. R., & Alge, B. J. 1999. Goal commitment and goal setting process: Conceptual clarification and empirical synthesis. *Journal of Applied Psychology*, 84: 885–896.

Klopfer, P. H., & Rubenstein, D. I. 1977. The concept of privacy and its biological basis. *Journal of Social Issues*, 33: 52–65.

Lawler, E. E. 1965a. Managers' perceptions of their subordinates' pay and of their supervisors' pay. *Personnel Psychology*, 18: 413–422.

Lawler, E. E. 1965b. Should managers' compensation be kept under wraps? *Personnel*, 42: 17–20.

Lawler, E. E. 1967. Secrecy about management compensation: Are there hidden costs? *Organizational Behavior and Human Performance*, 2: 182–189.

Leventhal, G. S. 1976. The distribution of rewards and resources in groups and organizations. *Advances in Experimental Social Psychology*, 9: 92–131.

Leventhal, G. S., Karuza, J., Jr., & Fry, W. R. 1980. Beyond fairness: A theory of allocation preferences. In G. Mikuyla (Ed.), *Justice and social interaction:* 167–218. New York: Springer.

Leventhal, G. S., Michaels, J. W., & Sanford, C. 1972. Inequity and interpersonal conflict: Reward allocation and secrecy about reward as methods of preventing conflict. *Journal of Personality and Social Psychology*, 23: 88–102.

Lind, E. A. 2001. Fairness heuristic theory: Justice judgments as pivotal cognitions in organizational relations. In J. Greenberg & R. Cropanzano (Eds.), *Advances in organizational behavior:* 56–88. Stanford, CA: Stanford University Press.

Lind, E. A., & van den Bos, K. 2002. When fairness works: Toward a general theory of uncertainty management. *Research in Organizational Behavior*, 24: 181–223.

Locke, E. A., & Latham, G. P. 1990. *A theory of goal setting and task performance.* Englewood Cliffs, NJ: Prentice-Hall.

Major, B., & Adams, J. B. 1983. Role of gender, interpersonal orientation, and self-presentation in distributive justice behavior. *Journal of Personality and Social Psychology*, 45: 598–608.

Markels, A., & Berton, L. 1996. Executive pay: A special report. *Wall Street Journal*, April 11: R10.

Markus, H. R., & Kitayama, S. 1991. Culture and the self: Implications for cognition, emotion, and motivation. *Psychological Review*, 98: 224–253.

Mashek, D. J., Aron, A., & Boncimino, M. 2003. Confusion of self with close others. *Personality and Social Psychology Bulletin.* 29: 382–392.

Mayer, R., Davis, J. H., & Schoorman, F. D. 1995. An integrative model of organizational trust. *Academy of Management Review*, 20: 709–734.

Meyer, J. P., Allen, N. J., & Gellatly, L. R. 1990. Affective and continuance commitment to the organization: Evaluation of measures and analysis of concurrent and time-lagged relations. *Journal of Applied Psychology*, 75: 710–721.

Miles, R. E., & Snow, C. C. 1978. *Organizational strategy, structure, and process.* New York: McGraw-Hill.

Milgrom, P., & Roberts, J. 1992. *Economics, organizations, and management.* Upper Saddle River, NJ: Prentice-Hall.

Milkovich, G. T., & Anderson, P. H. 1972. Management compensation and secrecy policies. *Personnel Psychology*, 25: 293–302.

Miller, D. T., & Ross, M. 1975. Self-serving biases in attribution of causality: Fact of fiction? *Psychological Bulletin*, 82: 213–225.

Mishra, A. K. 1996. Organizational responses to crisis: The centrality of trust. In R. M. Kramer & T. R. Tyler (Eds.), *Trust in organizations: Frontiers of theory and research*: 261–287. Thousand Oaks, CA: Sage.

Murphy, K. R., & Cleveland, J. N. 1995. *Understanding Performance appraisal: Social, organizational, and goal-based perspectives*. Thousand Oaks, CA: Sage.

Naylor, J. C., Pritchard, R. D., & Ilgen, D. R. 1980. *A theory of behavior in organizations*. New York: Academic Press.

NLRB v. Main Street Terrace Center. 2000. 218 F.3d 531 (6th Cir.).

Padavic, I., & Earnest, W. R. 1994. Paternalism as a component of managerial strategy. *Social Science Journal*, 31: 389–405.

Paetzold, R. L., Boswell, W. R., & Belsito, C. A. 2004. *Theorizing with the need for privacy construct*. Paper presented at the annual meeting of the Academy of Management, New Orleans.

Pappu, S. 2001. Whispered numbers. *Money*, August: 23.

Schuster, J. R., & Colletti, J. A. 1973. Pay secrecy: Who is for and against it? *Academy of Management Journal*, 16: 35–40.

Sim, V. 2001. Commentary on "When salaries aren't secret." *Harvard Business Review*, 79(5).

Steele, F. 1975. *The open organizations: The impact of secrecy and disclosure on people and organizations*. Reading, MA: Addison-Wesley.

Stone, E. F., & Stone, D. L. 1990. Privacy in organizations: Theoretical issues, research findings, and protection mechanisms. *Research in Personnel and Human Resource Management*, 8: 349–411.

Sundstrom, E. 1978. Crowding as a sequential process: Review of research on the effects of population density on humans. In A. Baum & Y. M. Epstein (Eds.), *Human responses to crowding*: 31–116. Hillsdale, NJ: Lawrence Erlbaum Associates.

Sundstrom, E., Burt, R. E., & Kamp, D. 1980. Privacy at work: Architectural correlates of job satisfaction and job performance. *Academy of Management Journal*, 23: 101–117.

Thibaut, J. W., & Walker, L. 1975. *Procedural justice: A psychological analysis*. Hillsdale, NJ: Lawrence Erlbaum Associates.

Thompson, P., & Pronsky, J. 1975. Secrecy or disclosure in management compensation? *Business Horizons*, 18(3): 67–74.

Triandis, H. C. 1989. The self and social behavior in differing cultural contexts. *Psychological Review*, 96: 506–520.

Triandis, H. C. 1994. *Culture and social behavior*. New York: McGraw-Hill.

van den Bos, K., Lind, E. A., Vermunt, R., & Wilke, H. A. M. 1997. How do I judge my outcome when I do not know the outcome of others? The psychology of the fair process effect. *Journal of Personality and Social Psychology*, 72: 1034–1046.

Vroom, V. 1964. *Work and motivation*. New York: Wiley.

Walsh, M. W. 2000. Workers challenge employers' policies on pay confidentiality. *New York Times*, July 28, accessed at http://www.nytimes.com/library/financial/072800discuss-pay.html.

Williamson, O. E. 1985. *The economic institutions of capitalism*. New York: Free Press.

READING 11.2

The Development of a Pay-for-Performance Appraisal System for Municipal Agencies: A Case Study

Michael A. Mulvaney, PhD, William R. McKinney, PhD, and Richard Grodsky

Well-designed employee performance appraisal instruments assume great importance by providing agencies with information that can guide administrative and developmental decision-making about their most important asset—their human resources. Administratively, performance appraisals serve as the formal evaluation tool used by managers when making decisions about the distribution of pay increases and the promotion and demotion of an employee. Developmentally, performance appraisals assist agencies in identifying issues such as employee training needs and cross training opportunities.[1] Despite its importance, both employees and management often view the performance appraisal process as frustrating and unfair. These frustrations are largely attributed to a reliance on performance appraisal instruments that: are not job related; have confusing or unclear rating levels, and; are viewed as subjective and biased by staff.[2] This study was undertaken to identify steps for creating a more effective pay-for-performance system for public agencies. Specifically, this case study: (1) identified a systematic procedure for creating performance appraisal instruments; (2) described the appropriate training for those conducting an appraisal interview; (3) implemented performance reviews using the developed instruments and appraisal interview/review training, and; (4) evaluated employee attitudes toward the newly developed system. Survey results identified significant mean differences between employee attitude toward the original pay-for-performance instrument and appraisal interview process and the newly developed system. Results of the case study are analyzed and discussed.

Introduction

Performance appraisal has become a general heading for a variety of activities through which organizations seek to provide feedback to their employees, develop their competencies, enhance performance, and distribute rewards.[3] An agency's performance appraisal system impacts individual and organizational operations by prompting decisions regarding compensation and merit salary increases, training and development opportunities, performance improvement, promotion, termination, organizational climate, and financial management. Despite expected benefits, poor design often leads both administration and staff to resist the process as a painful annual exercise.

Recognizing that one of the major difficulties with performance appraisal stems from various competing objectives (i.e., development, promotion, termination, staff training, etc.), but that salary decisions account for nearly 80% of its use,[4] this study provides a case study of the collaborative steps involved in creating a performance appraisal system used for merit salary increase decisions. It then assesses the staff's attitude toward the new vs. the old appraisal system.

Review of Related Research

In describing the cognitive and affective value of employee participation in the development of appraisal systems, research has identified five benefits: (1) employee participation is an

Dr. Michael Mulvaney is an assistant professor in the Department of Recreation Administration at Eastern Illinois University. He received his PhD from the University of Illinois. Before enrolling at the University of Illinois, he was employed with the Decatur Park District, Decatur, Illinois in a variety of capacities, including assistant manager of the Decatur Indoor Sports Center, fitness coordinator, and special recreation supervisor. His teaching and research interests include employee training and development, learning technologies in human resource development, and performance appraisal practices in parks and recreation.

Dr. William R. McKinney serves as an associate professor in the Department of Recreation, Sport & Tourism at the University of Illinois. McKinney has authored numerous articles dealing with comprehensive planning, personnel psychology and personnel management. His public service engagements include demonstration projects, educational programs, and direct consultation to park and recreation agencies and organizations.

Richard Grodsky is retired with 37 years of experience, focusing on agency reorganizations. He is a member of the American Academy for Park and Recreation Administration, currently serving as executive director.

effective tool for enhancing job-related autonomy, a necessary precondition for employee growth; (2) appraisal participation provides employees with a voice into the appraisal process. If employees are confident in the fairness of the appraisal process, they are more likely to accept performance ratings, even adverse ones; (3) employees possess valid, unique, and relevant performance information that is unavailable or unobservable by the rater, therefore the quality, quantity, accuracy and validity of performance appraisal information increases; (4) employee ownership in the process provides a personal stake in the success of the system, enhancing employee acceptance; (5) employee participation generates an atmosphere of cooperation and employee support.[5]

This study is situated within a Strategic Human Resource Management (SHRM) framework that places great importance on the employees and managers in the success of agency operations.[6] SHRM is cognizant of the value of an agency's material resources (i.e, financial and physical), but asserts that it is equally, if not more, important to give attention to an agency's human resources. This approach is particularly appropriate within the service fields of municipal government where human resources convert material resources into services and programs, and where labor typically accounts for more than 60% of municipal agencies operational budgets.[7]

A SHRM framework suggests that managers tailor their pay systems to support their agency's strategic objectives. This approach is based on contingency notions, suggesting that differences in an agency's strategy should be supported by corresponding differences in the agency's human resource strategies, including compensation.[8] The underlying premise of SHRM, as it relates to compensation, is that the greater the alignment, or fit, between the agency's objectives and the compensation system, the more effective the agency.[9]

Pay-for-performance systems have been described as one of the most effective methods of motivating and increasing employee performance.[10] These plans theoretically forge a link between pay expenditures and individual productivity.[11] A well-developed pay-for-performance appraisal instrument also addresses the norm of distributive justice, or the commonly held belief that individuals should be rewarded in proportion to their contributions. An adequately developed appraisal instrument potentially diffuses employee concerns about equity and fairness while motivating employees to increase performance.[12]

An agency's appraisal instrument serves as the tool to accurately discriminate outstanding performers from those who are below average. Likewise, it satisfies the increasing demand for wise fiscal management practices in the public sector.[13] Pay-for-performance plans signal a movement away from an entitlement orientation where all employees receive the same raise annually for simply showing up to work. However, creating a valid and legally defensible pay-for-performance plan requires three things: (1) a definition of job specific performance that leads to the creation of an appraisal instrument that clearly

outlines low to high performance measures; (2) a well-conducted performance appraisal interview process, and; (3) equitable decisions regarding the amount of merit increases that will be given for different levels of performance.[14] This research is the first of a two-part study and focuses on the process of creating the performance appraisal instruments and conducting the performance appraisal reviews. The second part of the investigation will address the distribution of merit salary increase monies (see the winter 2012 issue).

Even the most well-developed pay-for-performance system is predisposed to problems, if it is viewed negatively by staff.[15] Researchers assert that perceptions of unfairness and dissatisfaction in the process of evaluations can doom any appraisal system to failure.[16] Thus, it is clear that assessment of reaction to the performance appraisal instrument and interview process is important.[17]

Research on performance appraisal reactions has identified two general areas of interest: First, there is satisfaction with the appraisal instruments and fairness of the appraisal.[18] This is the most widely studied reaction and it has been primarily conceptualized into two subcategories: satisfaction with the appraisal interview and satisfaction with the overall appraisal system.[19] Satisfaction with the appraisal interview refers to the employee's attitudes toward the structure and implementation of the performance review. Satisfaction with the overall appraisal system represents a more global measure of the entire appraisal system, including the interview and subsequent actions following the interview.[20]

Fairness of the appraisal is the second area of interest and it has also been conceptualized into two subcategories: procedural justice and distributive justice.[21] In this case, procedural justice is defined as the perceived fairness of the processes and procedures used in the agency's performance appraisal system. Distributive justice is defined as perceived fairness in the distribution of outcomes (i.e., merit salary increase amounts).

Focus of the Study

A Strategic Human Resource Management framework was applied to the development of a performance appraisal system for the Elmhurst Park District (Elmhurst, Illinois), the municipal agency serving as the representative case study. The Elmhurst Park District sought to accomplish three goals with the development of a new performance appraisal system. First, Elmhurst Park District was interested in improving employee motivation and job performance while controlling costs. By doing this, the Elmhurst Park District hoped to further establish a high performance culture. Second, Elmhurst Park District sought to increase "employee buy-in" toward their performance appraisal system. Specifically, managers wanted to improve employees' perceptions of fairness and accuracy, and to increase overall satisfaction with the agency's appraisal process. Third, managers expressed a need to motivate staff to "keep up" with the highly demanding nature of today's park and recreation users. A recognized method for inspiring the quick adoption of new technologies and approaches to constituent service is through the establishment of a valid pay-for-performance plan that rewards high performing employees while not rewarding employees whose performance has been less than standard.

Once the pay-for-performance system was implemented, the study assessed the employees' attitudes toward the newly developed system compared to the agency's previous system. Specifically, it sought to address the following questions:

1. What are the specific steps involved in developing a pay-for-performance system for a public park and recreation agency?
2. What are the effective procedures for conducting the performance appraisal review?
3. Did employee attitude toward the newly developed system change when compared to the previous system?
4. Did employee perception of procedural justice toward the newly developed system change when compared to the previous system?

Although a case study with a limited number of respondents can't be widely generalized, the results should be of interest to management researchers and directors of municipal agencies who think critically about ways to increase employee performance and seek methods to improve the management of pay-for-performance dollars available within an agency's operating budget. The need to develop a pay-for-performance appraisal system that motivates staff, is cost effective, and assists the agency in meeting its goals is arguably a problem, or opportunity, that has applications across the field of municipal management.

Methods

Case Study Site
The Elmhurst Park District was established in 1920 in portions of Cook and Du-Page counties in the state of Illinois; it oversees approximately 460 park acres, 25 buildings, and 27 park sites and serves approximately 44,500 residents. The district employs approximately 70 full-time, 550 part-time and seasonal employees, is governed by seven members of a publicly elected board of commissioners, and has an equalized assessed valuation of approximately 1.8 billion dollars.

Prior to the study, the Elmhurst Park District utilized a generic (agency-wide) performance appraisal instrument for all employees of the agency. The instrument was divided into two sections. The first section asked supervisors to evaluate employee skills/capabilities that affected job performance. Each employee's job performance was evaluated in the following areas: job knowledge, productivity, attendance, planning, communication, attitude, dependability, leadership/subordinate development, creativity, quality of work, and public contact. These skills/capabilities were applied across the agency to every full-time employee. This universal application was problematic

as managers were forced to evaluate employees on several non-job specific traits (i.e., overnight facility maintenance staff evaluated on public contact, lower-level employees evaluated on creativity, senior level employees on productivity). These skills/capabilities were evaluated on a six-point scale (1 = needs improvement … 6 = exceptional). The second section asked the supervisor to identify the level (on a five-point scale) that best represented the employee's overall performance for the year. This single assessment provided the basis for the annual pay-for-performance decision.

Data Collection Procedures
Quantitative data was collected to compare employee attitude between the original performance appraisal system and the newly developed system. Prior to starting the workshops to develop a new pay-for-performance appraisal instrument, every full-time employee completed an existing performance appraisal reaction instrument. Testing was then done to assess attitude toward the existing system.[22] At the completion of the workshops, a "trial run" was conducted using the new system. The "trial run" was conducted instead of an actual live implementation due to the developmental timeline of the new appraisal system.

Following the completion of the "trial run", the employees repeated the Keeping and Levy[23] survey instrument to measure their attitudes toward the newly developed system. Every full-time employee completed the entire Keeping and Levy[24] instrument with two of the four sections (satisfaction with the performance appraisal review session and procedural justice of the performance appraisal system) being evaluated for this portion of the study (the remaining two sections are examined in Part II of this study). Specifically, the two sections of the instrument used were: (1) employee satisfaction with the appraisal interview/session, and; (2) perceptions of procedural justice of the appraisal system. Previous studies in both private and public agencies have supported the construct validity of the items with factor loadings ranging from .76 to .97, with an average loading of .89.[25] In addition, reliability measures for each area have been high, ranging from .91 to .96.[26] The two sections of Keeping and Levy's[27] survey instrument are provided in Figure 1.

Data Analysis
Based upon previous research utilizing Keeping and Levy's performance appraisal reaction instrument, the survey data was analyzed in two ways.[28] The data were first examined descriptively according to the scoring protocol for each item: mean scores and standard deviations were obtained. Next, to assess mean differences, the data was subjected to dependent samples t-tests.

Outcomes

Defining Job Performance and the Creation of an Appraisal Instrument
An employee's job description is often used to identify job performance standards.[29] In particular, the job description

FIGURE 1

Keeping & Levy's (2000) Employee Reactions Performance Appraisal Instrument

Satisfaction with the performance review session

1.) I felt quite satisfied with my last review discussion.

1	2	3	4	5	6
Strongly Disagree	Moderately Disagree	Slightly Disagree	Slightly Agree	Moderately Agree	Strongly Agree

2.) I feel good about the way the last review discussion was conducted.

1	2	3	4	5	6
Strongly Disagree	Moderately Disagree	Slightly Disagree	Slightly Agree	Moderately Agree	Strongly Agree

3.) My manager conducts a very effective review discussion with me.

1	2	3	4	5	6
Strongly Disagree	Moderately Disagree	Slightly Disagree	Slightly Agree	Moderately Agree	Strongly Agree

4.) The performance review system does a good job indicating how an employee has performed in the period covered by the review.

1	2	3	4	5	6
Strongly Disagree	Moderately Disagree	Slightly Disagree	Slightly Agree	Moderately Agree	Strongly Agree

Procedural Justice

5.) The procedures used to evaluate my performance were fair.

1	2	3	4	5	6
Strongly Disagree	Moderately Disagree	Slightly Disagree	Slightly Agree	Moderately Agree	Strongly Agree

6.) The process used to evaluate my performance was fair.

1	2	3	4	5	6
Strongly Disagree	Moderately Disagree	Slightly Disagree	Slightly Agree	Moderately Agree	Strongly Agree

7.) The procedures used to evaluate my performance were appropriate.

1	2	3	4	5	6
Strongly Disagree	Moderately Disagree	Slightly Disagree	Slightly Agree	Moderately Agree	Strongly Agree

8.) The process used to evaluate my performance was appropriate.

1	2	3	4	5	6
Strongly Disagree	Moderately Disagree	Slightly Disagree	Slightly Agree	Moderately Agree	Strongly Agree

must clearly identify the major job domains and tasks of a job. Performance standards can flow directly from a job description.[30]

Researchers have suggested conducting a thorough job analysis to define the appropriate content domains and tasks for job descriptions.[31] Thus, conducting job analyses for every full-time position in the Elmhurst Park District appeared to have merit as a starting point in the creation of job specific pay-for-performance appraisal instruments. In describing this initial step (and the subsequent steps), this study provides an overview of the research that guided the step(s), and a description of what occurred during the implementation of each of six steps.

Step #1: Job analysis   Job analyses are a systematic way to gather and analyze information about the content of jobs.[32] The job analysis process should identify the job under review, the participants involved, existing documentation (including the existing job description), the identification of the major job content domains contained within the job, and a developed list of tasks to be fulfilled under each domain.[33]

In completing job analyses, research has indicated that involvement of employees at all levels facilitates acceptance of the system and increases cooperation.[34] Employee involvement in the performance appraisal and development process is critical. Because it can lower the system's credibility, researchers caution against attempts to save time by bypassing employee and manager input.[35] If managers, acting alone, produce a system that does not meet staff needs, it damages the perceived connection between pay and performance and loses the performance-enhancing effect on employees.

Building upon this argument for employee participation, researchers have suggested that agencies that genuinely respect their employees find ways to involve them—from top to bottom—in decision-making activities that will later affect them. Staff involvement is often an expression of the importance the agency places on its individual members and can be effective in motivating agencies to a higher commitment to and valuation of its employees. Many companies that involve their employees in problem identification and decision making discover that employees become happier, costs decrease, and quality, productivity, and profits increase.[36]

The involvement of staff also provides an opportunity for the employee to know their job better. In particular, the employee is placed into an environment where he/she must examine the job domains and tasks of their job title in great detail and discuss these roles with their supervisor. Job domains are the major areas of responsibility a job may entail. Tasks are the specific actions an employee completes under each domain. When taken together, the sum of all tasks equal the job domain and the sum of all job domains equal the job title.[37]

Subscribing to this approach, job analyses were completed for every full-time job title at the Elmhurst Park District.[38] To complete each job analysis, a meeting between the employee and their supervisor was conducted for every full-time position. In conducting the job analyses, the employee and supervisor collectively reviewed the current job description. Job descriptions of similar positions from other agencies were also reviewed to guide the employees in brainstorming a list of job domains and tasks performed. During this meeting, the employee and supervisor collectively identified between six and 10 job domains that represented the job title. Once the general content domains were identified, the employee and supervisor discussed and identified a list of specific tasks within each job domain. On average, 10-15 tasks were identified for each job domain. Consistent with previous research, the tasks: (1) began with an action verb; (2) included only one specific task, and; (3) described what the employee did.[39]

Step #2: Rating of tasks   Once an agreed-upon list of job domains and tasks were developed, "weights" were created for each task to further describe its significance. This procedure followed that advocated by a number of authors as a means of ensuring the validity of job descriptions.[40] The employee and supervisor independently reviewed the list of tasks and rated each on two, seven-point scales. The first scale, "importance" (1 = low, 7 = high) rated their perception of the importance of each task to overall job performance. The second scale, "time/frequency" (1 = low, 7 = high) assessed the time/frequency that each task required in comparison to all other tasks. The values from each scale were multiplied and a total "weight" for each task was created. The employee and supervisor each independently completed the task rating form. An example of a portion of a task rating form completed by an employee is provided in Figure 2. This example provides the rating for only one of the seven domains in this job description. Next, a meeting was scheduled between the employee and supervisor to review the weights. The intent of this discussion was to agree upon the overall importance and the time that should be spent on each task. If the supervisor and employee(s) had any disagreements about the overall weight of a task, the ultimate decision was that of the supervisor. However, the dialog between the supervisor and employee prompted an in-depth discussion about the significance of each task. This discussion was guided by research suggesting that if employees have a clear perception of their tasks, and the importance their managers place on those tasks, it's likely the employee's successful accomplishment of the tasks will occur.[41] After discussing any discrepancies in the weight assignments, a final list was completed. Figure 3 provides an example.

Step #3: Creation of appraisal instrument   The information collected during the job analysis provides the content for the appraisal instrument.[42] Performance appraisal instruments are often divided into two general formats: ranking and rating. Ranking formats require the rater to compare employees against each other. Rating formats have two elements: (1) they require raters to evaluate employees on some absolute standard rather than relative to other employees, and; (2) each performance standard is measured on a scale where appraisers can check the point that best represents the employee's performance level.[43]

In deciding which appraisal format is most appropriate for an agency scholars suggest that an understanding of the type of tasks being performed is needed.[44] As the task statements that were developed during the job analyses phase

FIGURE 2

Task Statement Rating Form

TASK STATEMENT RATING FORM	IMPORTANCE	TIME/FREQUENCY	TOTAL
Name: _____ Agency: _____ Title: Division Manager - Recreation Date: _____ Length of time in title: _____	Please rate each task statement on a 0-7 scale that reflects, in your opinion, how important that task statement is to overall job performance. Use the scale below as a guide to help you rate. 0 1 of no importance 2 3 moderately important 4 5 very important 6 7 of greatest importance	Please rate each task statement on the 0-7 scale shown below. Looking at the whole job over approximately a one-year period, how would you allocate the task statements in terms of the time/frequency with which each is done? 0 1 of no importance 2 3 moderately important 4 5 very important 6 7 of greatest importance	
TASK STATEMENTS			
Programming Domain			
Develops programs that provide for the physical needs of participants	5	4	20
Develops programs that provide for the societal needs of participants	4	5	20
Develops programs that provide for the educational needs of participants	4	5	20
Provides programs according to participants' demographic characteristics	4	5	20
Provides programs according to participants' leisure needs	6	5	30
Provides structured programs	4	4	16
Provides unstructured programs	4	4	16
Plans seasonal programs	6	6	36
Evaluates recreational programs	7	7	49
Utilizes participant groups in program planning and development	3	3	9
Adapts programs to meet ADA needs as requested	5	5	25
Oversees outdoor aquatic operations	6	6	36
Responsible for building rentals	4	6	24

FIGURE 3

Task Statement Rating Form

TASK STATEMENT RATING FORM

Name: _____

Agency: _____

Title: Division Manager - Recreation

Date: _____

Length of time in title: _____

TASK STATEMENTS

Programming Domain	Supervisor's Rating	Incumbent's Rating	Agreed Rating
Develops programs that provide for the physical needs of participants	25	20	25
Develops programs that provide for the societal needs of participants	25	20	25
Develops programs that provide for the educational needs of participants	25	20	25
Provides programs according to participants' demographic characteristics	12	20	12
Provides programs according to participants' leisure needs	49	30	49
Provides structured programs	42	16	42
Provides unstructured programs	42	16	42
Plans seasonal programs	49	36	36
Evaluates recreational programs	20	49	36
Utilizes participant groups in program planning and development	16	9	16
Adapts programs to meet ADA needs as requested	20	25	25
Oversees outdoor aquatic operations	35	36	36
Responsible for building rentals	24	24	24

included written statements of what the employee does, the Elmhurst Park District chose to incorporate an "anchored" rating format. An anchored rating format describes performance variation along a continuum from good to bad.[45] It is the type and number of descriptors used in anchoring the continuum that provide the major differences in rating scales. Organizational research has indicated the reliability of a performance appraisal instrument is strongest when using between three and seven descriptive anchors.[46] The Elmhurst Park District selected a three-anchor approach. As a result, each task was evaluated against three anchors on a performance continuum: (1) below standards, (2) meets standards,

and (3) exceeds standards. A "not applicable" rating was also included. Figure 4 is the performance appraisal instrument for the Division Manager of Recreation.

Step #4: Identifying raters Once a performance appraisal instrument has been developed, the agency must identify who will rate the performance (i.e., supervisor, subordinate, coworkers).[47] In particular, the agency must be concerned with improving the accuracy of performance ratings by focusing their attention on who is most likely to be precise. Management research documents a variety of rater methods that have been implemented in organizations, including

FIGURE 4

Division Manager of Recreation Performance Appraisal Instrument

Response Scale:

    0 = Not Applicable The task is not performed/not observed

    1 = Below Standard The performance is below standards

    2 = Meets Standard The performance meets standards

    3 = Exceeds Standard The performance exceeds standards

Programming	Not Applicable	Below Standard	Meets Standard	Exceeds Standard
Develops programs that provide for the physical needs of participants				
Develops programs that provide for the societal needs of participants				
Develops programs that provide for the educational needs of participants				
Provides programs according to participants' demographic characteristics				
Provides programs according to participants' leisure needs				
Provides structured programs				
Provides unstructured programs				
Plans seasonal programs				
Evaluates recreational programs				
Utilizes participant groups in program planning and development				
Adapts programs to meet ADA needs as requested				
Oversees outdoor aquatic operations				
Responsible for building rentals				

Financial Management	Not Applicable	Below Standard	Meets Standard	Exceeds Standard
Prepare and monitor division budget				
Coordinate purchase of division supplies, materials, and equipment				
Develop and implement program pricing policies				
Manage internal and external assistance payments and delinquent accounts				
Manage bid specs for major purchases				

Organizational Planning	Not Applicable	Below Standard	Meets Standard	Exceeds Standard
Serve as member of the Parks and Recreation Services Management Team and other appointed committee assignments				
Attend staff meetings				
Prepare annual T-shirt bid				
Develop and implement customer service standards				

FIGURE 4

Division Manager of Recreation Performance Appraisal Instrument *(continued)*

Communications/Customer Service	Not Applicable	Below Standard	Meets Standard	Exceeds Standard
Develop and maintain cooperative relationships and effective oral and written communications with internal and external customers				
Promote District programs to patrons, guests, and staff				
Prepare written and verbal bullet points, updates, and reports as required				
Act as a liaison to affiliates, community groups, and governmental units				
Design and distribute information for public distribution				
Coordinate seasonal brochure productions				

Safety	Not Applicable	Below Standard	Meets Standard	Exceeds Standard
Encourage and demonstrate safe work habits through use of established safety program guidelines				
Serve as member of the District's Crisis Management Team				
Maintain CPR and AED certification, and ensure that all staff within supervision do the same				

Personnel Management	Not Applicable	Below Standard	Meets Standard	Exceeds Standard
Recruit, hire, and train staff				
Manage and evaluate staff				
Provide ongoing direction, foresight, and motivation to staff				
Prepare for and conduct staff meetings and trainings as needed				

Registration	Not Applicable	Below Standard	Meets Standard	Exceeds Standard
Manage program registration process				
Manage program cancellation/expansion/addition process				
Manage permit and rental registrations				

360-degree feedback, a system that uses supervisors as raters, peers as raters, self as raters, customers as raters, and subordinates as raters.[48] In deciding which approach to take, research suggests that organizations identify those individuals who possess the most complete information on the performance of the ratee.[49] Research has also found the immediate supervisor to be the most frequently used.[50] In addition, a comparison of the reliability of raters suggests supervisor ratings tend to be more reliable than those from other sources.[51]

Step #5: Rater training The next step in the construction of a performance appraisal system is to understand how and where raters make mistakes. In describing how raters process information about the performance of employees they rate, scholars identify five stages. First, the rater observes the behavior of the ratee. Second, the rater encodes this behavior as part of a total picture of the ratee. Third, the rater stores this information in memory. Fourth, during the evaluation phase, the rater reviews the performance dimensions and retrieves the stored information (i.e., observations, impressions, etc.) to determine their relevance to the performance dimensions. Finally, the information is reconsidered and integrated with other available information as the rater decides on the final ratings.[52] Quite unintentionally, this process can produce information errors and they can occur at any stage.

One approach to limiting errors is through appraiser rater training.[53] Surprisingly, managers frequently report that they receive little training beyond a description of the rating form.[54] An effective formal performance appraisal system can't exist without the ongoing education of all key appraisers in the appraisal process.[55] Developing the skills necessary to conduct effective performance appraisals, including an understanding of psychometric errors, can be completed through appraiser training.[56]

Training sessions subscribing to the previously mentioned principles were conducted with the employees of the Elmhurst Park District. Integrating the previously mentioned principles, employees were provided with a three-hour training session that focused on three error categories: (1) rater-error training; (2) performance dimension training, and; (3) performance standard training. During the rater-error training session, employees were introduced to several psychometric errors (i.e., leniency, halo effect, recency) and offered suggestions for addressing these problematic areas. The performance dimension training session involved a collective discussion on the performance dimensions between the raters and ratees. Finally, the performance standard training focused on providing the raters with a standard of comparison or frame of reference for making appraisal decisions.

Step #6: Performance appraisal interview There is a large body of research indicating that the level of employee participation in the interview is associated with a variation in various desirable appraisal-related outcomes, including appraisal system fairness, appraisal satisfaction, supervisory support, satisfaction with supervisors, appraisal system acceptance, and greater acceptance of feedback.[57] In particular, self-evaluation provides employees with the opportunity to systematically assess their performance. A common method to facilitate self-evaluation is to require employees to complete their own appraisal and present the draft for discussion with the supervisor. The supervisor can review the draft with the employee and compare the employee's self-appraisal ratings to the supervisor's appraisal ratings of the employee.

Adopting this participative process of self-appraisal, a "trial run" was conducted for the newly developed performance appraisal instruments. The "trial run" allowed the Elmhurst Park District to test the appraisal process and instruments with no consequences assigned to the results. The "trial run" was conducted instead of an actual live implementation due to the developmental timeline of the new appraisal system.

The "trial run" was initiated with the employee and supervisor independently completing the appraisal instrument. To assist in the final calculations, the appraisal instruments were created in a Microsoft Excel format. Paper copies of the spreadsheet-formatted instrument were printed and provided to the employee and supervisor (see Figure 4).

Once the employee and supervisor had independently completed the appraisal instrument they met and discussed the ratings. During this time the employee and supervisor reached an agreed upon rating for each task statement. At this point, the appraisal was completed and signed by both the employee and supervisor. The Elmhurst Park District Human Resource Specialist applied the previously established "weights" for each task statement to determine a final percentile score for each employee (see Figure 5). Statistically, this procedure involved: (1) multiplying the score of the task (i.e., "1" – below standard, "2" – meets standard, "3" – exceeds standard) by the "weight" of each task (tasks receiving a "not applicable" rating were voided from the computations); (2) determining the total points possible (i.e., the sum of each task's "weight" multiplied by "3 – exceeds standard"), and; (3) dividing the total possible points by the total points earned by the employee to obtain a final percentile score. For example, in Figure 5, the Division Manager's final percentile score was 68.42%.

Findings with Employee Assessments

In addition to describing the steps involved in creating a pay-for-performance appraisal system for a municipal agency, this study used Keeping and Levy's appraisal reaction instrument to assess every full-time employee's reactions toward the newly developed process.[58]

Preliminary Analysis

Prior to testing the research questions, the data were examined for accuracy of data entry, missing values, and outliers. A review of the raw data entries identified two participants who had not fully completed both the pre and post surveys. Specifically, the two participants had completed the pre survey instrument, but had voluntarily left the agency before completing the workshops and post survey. As a result, these participants were removed from the study, thus yielding a response rate of 97% (n = 56).

The instruments used in the study were then examined for internal consistency. In particular, reliability measures were obtained for the satisfaction with the performance

FIGURE 5

Finalized Division Manager of Recreation Performance Appraisal Instrument

Response Scale:

0 = Not Applicable	The task is not performed/not observed
1 = Below Standard	The performance is below standards
2 = Meets Standard	The performance meets standards
3 = Exceeds Standard	The performance exceeds standards

Programming	Not Applicable	Below Standard	Meets Standard	Exceeds Standard	Score	Weight	Weighed Score	Total Possible
Develops programs that provide for the physical needs of participants			X		2	25	50	75
Develops programs that provide for the societal needs of participants		X			1	25	25	75
Develops programs that provide for the educational needs of participants			X		2	25	50	75
Provides programs according to participants' demographic characteristics		X			1	12	12	36
Provides programs according to participants' leisure needs				X	3	49	147	147
Provides structured programs		X			1	42	42	126
Provides unstructured programs			X		2	42	84	126
Plans seasonal programs			X		2	36	72	108
Evaluates recreational programs		X			1	36	36	108
Utilizes participant groups in program planning and development			X		2	16	32	48
Adapts programs to meet ADA needs as requested				X	3	25	75	75
Oversees outdoor aquatic operations				X	3	36	108	108
Responsible for building rentals			X		2	24	48	72

(continued)

FIGURE 5

Finalized Division Manager of Recreation Performance Appraisal Instrument *(continued)*

Financial Management	Not Applicable	Below Standard	Meets Standard	Exceeds Standard	Score	Weight	Weighed Score	Total Possible
Prepare and monitor division budget		X			1	36	.36	108
Coordinate purchase of division supplies, materials, and equipment				X	3	25	75	75
Develop and implement program pricing policies				X	3	6	18	18
Manage internal and external assistance payments and delinquent accounts			X		2	12	24	36
Manage bid specs for major purchases				X	3	5	15	15
Organizational Planning	**Not Applicable**	**Below Standard**	**Meets Standard**	**Exceeds Standard**	**Score**	**Weight**	**Weighed Score**	**Total Possible**
Establish and monitor division goals and objectives		X			1	36	36	108
Serve as member of the Parks and Recreation Services Management Team and other appointed committee assignments		X			1	49	49	147
Attend staff meetings			X		2	30	60	90
Prepare annual T-shirt bid		X			1	15	15	45
Develop and implement customer service standards				X	3	25	75	75
Communications/Customer Service	**Not Applicable**	**Below Standard**	**Meets Standard**	**Exceeds Standard**	**Score**	**Weight**	**Weighed Score**	**Total Possible**
Develop and maintain cooperative relationships and effective oral and written communications with internal and external customers			X		2	49	98	147
Promote District programs to patrons, guests, and staff			X		2	36	72	108
Prepare written and verbal bullet points, updates, and reports as required			X		2	16	32	48
Act as a liaison to affiliates, community groups, and governmental units				X	3	16	48	48
Design and distribute information for public distribution				X	3	9	27	27
Coordinate seasonal brochure productions				X	3	20	60	60

Safety	Not Applicable	Below Standard	Meets Standard	Exceeds Standard	Score	Weight	Weighed Score	Total Possible
Encourage and demonstrate safe work habits through use of established safety program guidelines			X		2	49	38	147
Serve as member of the District's Crisis Management Team			X		2	21	42	63
Maintain CPR and AED certification, and ensure that all staff within supervision do the same			X		2	49	98	147
Personnel Management	**Not Applicable**	**Below Standard**	**Meets Standard**	**Exceeds Standard**	**Score**	**Weight**	**Weighed Score**	**Total Possible**
Recruit, hire and train staff				X	3	36	108	108
Manage and evaluate staff				X	3	15	45	45
Provide ongoing direction, foresight, and motivation to staff				X	3	24	72	72
Prepare for and conduct staff meetings and trainings as needed				X	3	36	108	108
Registration	**Not Applicable**	**Below Standard**	**Meets Standard**	**Exceeds Standard**	**Score**	**Weight**	**Weighed Score**	**Total Possible**
Manage program registration process			X		2	36	72	108
Manage program cancellation/expansion/ addition process				X	3	25	75	75
Manage permit and rental registrations				X	3	16	48	48
						TOTALS	2227	
						TOTAL POSSIBLE	3255	3255
						PERCENT-AGE (%)	68.42	

Table 1

Satisfaction with the Performance Review Session

Variable	Original Appraisal System (n = 56)		Newly Developed Appraisal System (n = 56)		t statistic	p-value
	Mean	S.D.	Mean	S.D.		
I felt quite satisfied with my last review discussion	4.05	1.74	4.81	1.39	2.321	0.023
I feel good about the way the last review discussion was conducted	4.23	1.63	4.92	1.40	2.166	0.033
My manager conducts a very effective review discussion with me	4.21	1.59	5.30	1.024	3.992	0.000
The performance review system does a good job of indicating how an employee has performed in the period covered by the review	3.46	1.34	4.46	1.02	5.458	0.000

review session and procedural justice of the performance appraisal system instruments. The four-item satisfaction with the performance review session yielded an alpha coefficient of .93. The four-item procedural justice of the performance appraisal system instrument was found to have acceptable internal consistency (.97).

Satisfaction with the Performance Review Session

Once the employees completed the workshops and the trial run of the newly developed system, they completed the performance appraisal reaction instrument again to assess their attitudes toward the new system. Four items were used to assess the employees' satisfaction with the performance review session. Responses were indicated on a six-point Likert scale, with "1" representing strongly disagree and "6" representing strongly agree.[59] Table 1 represents the measures of central tendency and t-test results for the satisfaction with the performance review session measures. Significant mean differences were found for all of the items measuring employees' satisfaction with the performance review session ($p < .05$). In particular, significant mean differences were found in favor of the new system for "I felt quite satisfied with my last review discussion," "I feel good about the way the last review discussion was conducted," "My manager conducts a very effective review discussion with me," and "The performance review system does a good job of indicating how an employee has performed in the period covered by the review."

Procedural Justice of Performance Appraisal System

Employee perceptions of procedural justice were assessed on Keeping and Levy's performance appraisal reaction instrument.[60] Procedural justice was assessed with a four-item measure on a seven-point Likert scale ranging from strongly disagree to strongly agree. Table 2 presents the measures of central tendency and t-test results for the procedural justice measures. Significant mean differences were found for all four items measuring the employees' perceptions of procedural justice toward the performance appraisal ($p < .05$). In particular, significant mean differences between the new and previous performance appraisal instrument were found in favor of the new system for "The procedures used to evaluate my performance were fair," "The process used to evaluate my performance was fair," "The procedures used to evaluate my performance were appropriate," and "The process used to evaluate my performance was appropriate."

Discussion

Results from the measures of employee reaction to the pay-for-performance system yielded some interesting findings. Significant mean differences between employee attitude toward the original pay-for-performance interview/review sessions and the newly developed sessions were found for all four of the "satisfaction with the performance review session" items. Employee perception of fairness, operationalized as procedural justice, also indicated significant mean differences on all four measures.

Table 2

Procedural Justice of Performance Appraisal System

Variable	Original Appraisal System (n = 56)		Newly Developed Appraisal System (n = 56)		t statistic	p-value
	Mean	S.D.	Mean	S.D.		
The procedures used to evaluate my performance were fair	4.41	1.75	5.43	1.37	3.157	0.002
The process used to evaluate my performance was fair	4.29	1.72	5.51	1.07	4.236	0.000
The procedures used to evaluate my performance were appropriate	4.23	1.72	5.30	1.22	3.494	0.001
The process used to evaluate my performance was appropriate	4.32	1.73	5.05	1.29	2.337	0.022

Management Implications, Limitations & Future Research
These results provide further support to the cognitive and affective value of employee participation in the creation of an agency's pay-for-performance appraisal system. The findings are further supported by a comment obtained from one of the supervisors, stating:

"… it was somewhat difficult to tell Employee 'A' that he is a '1' (below standards performance rating), but it was worth it. I was surprised—Employee 'A' showed little disagreement with the rating (during the performance review session) and I saw immediate and continued improvement in Employee 'A's' attitude and performance."

According to the supervisor, the opportunities for employee voice in the appraisal process resulted in the employee displaying little resistance to his performance ratings. Furthermore, the supervisor's feedback identified very specific, job deficient areas for the employee to improve upon. Taken together, the employee's participation in the appraisal process and the clearly stated areas for employee improvement, led to higher perceptions of fairness and acceptance of the supervisor's ratings. In turn, these high levels of employee acceptance and understanding will likely enhance the employee's motivation and job performance.

This case study of the Elmhurst Park District sought to provide an empirically grounded overview of the steps involved in developing a pay-for-performance system for municipal agencies. Future research with different and larger samples is needed to further understand pay-for-performance appraisal practices in the public sector. Although park districts represent the norm in the state of Illinois, public park and recreation departments housed within municipal or county government represent a predominant type of leisure service organization in the United States. Thus, additional research examining the development of a pay-for-performance system within other municipal or county departments is needed.

In addition, research that examines the social context of performance appraisal development in municipal agencies could provide additional insight into the role of employee participation. As research in the management field has suggested, research efforts examining the effects of the social context of the agency, such as feedback culture, group dynamics, politics, impression management, and other environmental variables, are needed.[61] Future studies examining these issues within municipal agencies are suggested, and could help in providing a richer understanding of important management issues related to performance appraisal.

Another limitation is the "trial run." The "trial run" of the performance appraisal process was implemented similar to a "live performance appraisal" process, but without the consequences (i.e., using results to make merit salary increase decisions). Employees were aware of the lack of consequences from the "trial run."

In summary, this study adopted a two-pronged approach to understanding performance appraisal systems in municipal agencies. First, the study sought to identify the steps needed to develop a pay-for-performance appraisal system for a municipal agency. Next, the study was interested in examining employees' reactions toward a system that adopted these steps. The Elmhurst Park District served as a representative case study for this investigation. The study identified positive employee reactions to a performance appraisal system adopting these steps with strong indicators found of an increased satisfaction and perception of procedural justice in the new system.

Source: IPMA-HR

NOTES

1. Milkovich, G. T. & Newman, J. (2005). *Compensation* (8th ed.). Boston, MA: Irwin McGraw-Hill Companies, Inc.

2. Mathis, R. L. & Jackson, J. H. (2006). *Human resource management* (11th ed.). Mason, OH: Thomas Learning.

3. Grote, D. (2000). Public sector organizations. *Public Personnel Management*, 29(1), 1–20.

4. Mathis, R. L. & Jackson, J. H. (2006). *op. cit.*; Thomas, S. L. & Bretz, R. D. (1994). Research and practice in performance appraisal: Evaluating employee performance in America's largest companies. *SAM Advanced Management Journal*, 59(2), 28–34; Smith, B. N., Hornsby, J. S., & Shirmeyer, R. (1996). Current trends in performance appraisal: An examination of managerial practice. *SAM Advanced Management Journal*, 1, 20.

5. Roberts, G. E. (2003). *op. cit.*

6. Tompkins, J. (2002). Strategic human resources management in government: Unresolved issues. *Public Personnel Management*, 31(1), 95–111; Wright, P. M. & McMahan, G. C. (1992). Theoretical perspectives for strategic human resource management. *Journal of Management*, 18(2), 295–320.

7. Chelladurai, P. (1999). *Human Resource Management in Sport and Recreation*. Champaign, IL. Human Kinetics; Edginton, C. R., Hudson, S. D., & Lankford, S. V. (2001). *Managing recreation, parks, and leisure services: An introduction*. Champaign, IL: Sagamore Publishing; McKinney, W. R., & Yen, T. H. (1989). Personnel management in large U.S. park and recreation organizations. *Journal of Park and Recreation Administration*, 7(2), 1–25.

8. Milkovich, G. T. & Newman, J. (2005). *op. cit.*

9. Dyer, L. & Reeves, T. (1995). Human resource strategies and firm performance: What do we know and where do we need to go? *International Journal of Human Resource Management*, 6(3), 656–670; Milkovich, G. T. & Newman, J. (2005). *op. cit.*

10. Levy, P. E. & Williams, J. R. (2004). The social context of performance appraisal: A review and framework for the future. *Journal of Management*, 20(6), 881–905; Moss, S. E. & Martinko, M. J. (1998). The effects of performance attributions and outcome dependence on leader feedback behavior following poor subordinate performance. *Journal of Organizational Behavior*, 19, 3, 259–274.

11. Campbell, D. J., Campbell, K. M., & Chia, H. B. (1998). Merit pay, performance appraisal, and individual motivation: An analysis and alternative. *Human Resource Management*, 37(2), 131–146.

12. Levy, P. E. & Williams, J. R. (2004). *op.cit.*

13. Bartlett, K. R., & McKinney, W. R. (2004). A study of the role of professional development, job attitudes, and turnover among public park and recreation employees. *Journal of Park and Recreation Administration*, 24(4), 63–81; Edginton, C. R., Hudson, S. D., & Lankford, S. V. (2001). *Managing recreation, parks, and leisure services: An introduction*. Champaign, IL: Sagamore Publishing.

14. Milkovich, G. T. & Newman, J. (2005). *op. cit.*

15. Cardy, R. L. & Dobbins, G. H. (1994). *Performance appraisal: alternative perspectives*. Cincinnati, OH: South-Western Publishing; Keeping, L. M. & Levy, P. E. (2000). Performance appraisal reactions: Measurements, modeling, and method bias. *Journal of Applied Psychology*, 85(5), 708–724; Murphy, K. R. & Cleveland, J. N. (1995). *Understanding performance appraisal: Social, organizational, and goal-based perspectives*. Thousand Oaks, CA: Sage Publications.

16. Cardy, R. L. & Dobbins, G. H. (1994). *op. cit.*

17. Keeping, L. M. & Levy, P. E. (2000). *op. cit.*

18. Giles, W. F. & Mossholder, K. W. (1990). Employee reactions to contextual and session components of performance appraisal. *Journal of Applied Psychology*, 75, 371–377; Greller, M. M. (1978). The nature of subordinate participation in the appraisal interview. *Academy of Management Journal*, 21, 646–658; Keeping, L. M. &

Levy, P. E. (2000). *op. cit*; Smither, J. W. (1998). Lessons learned: Research implications for performance appraisal and management practice. In J. W. Smither (Ed.), *Performance appraisal: State of the art in practice.* San Francisco, CA: Jossey-Bass.

19. Keeping, L. M. & Levy, P. E. (2000). *op. cit.*

20. Ibid

21. Ibid

22. Ibid

23. Ibid

24. Ibid

25. Ibid; Levy, P. E. & Williams, J. R. (2004). *op. cit.*

26. Keeping, L. M. & Levy, P. E. (2000). *op. cit.*

27. Ibid

28. Levy, P. E. & Williams, J. R. (1998). The role of perceived system knowledge in predicting appraisal reactions, job satisfaction, and organizational commitment. *Journal of Organizational Behavior,* 19, 53–65; Levy, P. E. & Williams, J. R. (2004). *op. cit*; Keeping, L. M. & Levy, P. E. (2000). *op. cit.*

29. Mathis, R. L. & Jackson, J. H. (2006). *op. cit*; Rotundo, M. & Sackett, P. R. (2002). The relative importance of task, citizenship, and counter productive performance to global ratings of job performance: A policy-capturing approach. *Journal of Applied Psychology,* 87, 66–80; Scullen, S. E., Goff, M., & Mount, M. K. (2000). Understanding the latent structure of job performance ratings. *Journal of Applied Psychology,* 24, 419–434; Van Scotter, J. R., Motowidlo, S. J., & Cross, T. C. (2000). Effects of task performance and contextual performance on systematic rewards. *Journal of Applied Psychology,* 85, 526–535.

30. Wojcik, J. (2000). Focus on performance. *Business Insurance,* July, 20.

31. Viswesvaran, C. & Ones, D. S. (2000). Perspectives on models of job performance. *International Journal of Selection and Assessment,* 8(4), 216–226.

32. Mathis, R. L. & Jackson, J. H. (2006). *op. cit.*

33. Ibid.

34. Levy, P. E. & Williams, J. R. (2004). *op. cit*; Longenecker, C. O. & Fink, L. S. (1999). Creating effective performance appraisals. *Industrial Management,* 41(5), 18–24; Longenecker, C. O. & Fink, L. S. (2003). Benchmarks for effective performance rating instruments. *Journal of Compensation and Benefits,* 19(2), 24–31.

35. Longenecker, C. O. & Fink, L. S. (1999). *op. cit.*

36. Roberts, G. E. (2003). Employee performance appraisal system participation: A technique that works. Public Personnel Management, 32(1), 89–99.

37. Mathis, R. L. & Jackson, J. H. (2006). *op. cit.*

38. Viswesvaran, C. & Ones, D. S. (2000). *op. cit.*

39. Mathis, R. L. & Jackson, J. H. (2006). *op. cit.*

40. Ibid; Drauden, G. & Peterson, H. (1974). *A domain sampling approach to job analysis.* St. Paul, MN: Test Validation Center.

41. Mathis, R. L. & Jackson, J. H. (2006). *op. cit.*

42. Milkovich, G. T. & Newman, J. (2005). *op. cit.*

43. Ibid.

44. Keeley, M. (1978). A contingency framework for performance evaluation. *Academy of Management Review,* 3, 428–438; Tziner, A. & Kopelman, R. E. (2002). *op. cit.*

45. Milkovich, G. T. & Newman, J. (2005). *op. cit.*

46. Arvey, R. D. & Murphy, K. R. (1998). Performance evaluation in work settings. *Annual Review of Psychology,* 49,141–168.

47. Milkovich, G. T. & Newman, J. (2005). *op. cit.*

48. Harris, M. M. & Schaubroeck, J. (1988). A meta analysis of self-supervisor, self-peer and peer-supervisor ratings. *Personnel Psychology,* 4, 43–62; Ones, D. S., Schmidt, F. L., & Viswesvaran, C. (1996). Comparative analysis of the reliability of job performance ratings. *Journal of Applied Psychology,* 81(5), 557–574.

49. Milkovich, G. T. & Newman, J. (2005). *op. cit.*

50. Ones, D. S., Schmidt, F. L., & Viswesvaran, C. (1996). *op. cit.*

51. Ibid.

52. Landy, F. S. & Farr, J. L. (1980). Performance rating. *Psychological Bulletin,* 87, 72–107.

53. Wilson, J. P. & Western. S. (2001). Performance appraisal: An obstacle to training and development? *Career Development International*, 6, 2/3, 93–102.

54. Longenecker, C. O. & Fink, L. S. (1999). *op. cit.*

55. Ibid.

56. Schweiger, I. & Sumners, G. E. (1994). Optimizing the value of performance appraisals. *Managerial Auditing Journal*, 9(8), 3–7

57. Roberts, G. E. (2003). *op. cit.*

58. Keeping, L. M. & Levy, P. E. (2000). *op. cit.*

59. Ibid.

60. Ibid.

61. Levy, P. E. & Williams, J. R. (2004). *op. cit.*

CHAPTER 12

Labor Relations

- Understand the provisions of the National Labor Relations Act (NLRA), which apply to all employers, regardless of whether their workforce is unionized
- Explain the reasons why employees form and join unions
- Describe the restrictions the NLRA places on union organizers and employer behaviors during organizing campaigns
- Gain an appreciation of the reasons for decline in union membership and the challenges organized labor faces in a global information-based economy
- Understand the process of collective bargaining and the various types of bargaining items
- Appreciate the role of alternative dispute resolution when collective bargaining has been unsuccessful

Labor Unrest at the New York MTA

On the morning of December 20, 2005, New Yorkers who relied on public transit to get to their places of employment or around town to complete their holiday shopping woke up to find that the subway and public bus systems had been shut down by a strike of the 34,000 workers who were members of the Transport Workers Union Local 100 of the Metropolitan Transportation Authority (MTA). Negotiations for a new contract had broken down because of a failure to agree on retirement or pension provisions and wage increases. The strike was seen as a particular hardship for lower-income residents of the outer boroughs of New York City.

While the strike itself lasted only 60 hours, it took another day to get the transit system fully up and running. Nonetheless, the strike had a significant impact on New York. Public schools were affected and had to operate on a delayed schedule, while many private schools were forced to close completely. Public safety was impacted detrimentally because of the increased congestion on streets and sidewalks. The financial impact of the strike was significant, as the city estimated that it lost more than $300 million per day and other revenues.

The strike was illegal under the New York State Public Employees Fair Employment Act, more commonly known as the Taylor Law, which prohibits municipal workers from striking and provides alternative means for resolution of labor-related disputes. This law, which had been enacted in response to a previous transit strike, which took place in 1966, also provides for criminal penalties, including imprisonment for union officials and fines to be levied against both the union and striking employees. Local 100 did not have the support of its parent union—the International Transport Workers Union—for the strike, with the parent union ordering Local 100 workers to return to work as soon as it became aware of what had transpired. As a result of the strike, Local 100 president Roger Toussaint was sentenced to ten days in jail and the union was fined $2.5 million. $300,000 in strike-related penalties were levied against union members and deducted from the paychecks of striking workers.[1] The aftermath of the strike involved a tremendous amount of published analysis of the political behavior of the union as well as local elected officials, particularly Mayor Michael Bloomberg, illustrating the politically charged realities in which organized labor operates.

Labor relations is a key strategic issue for organizations because the nature of the relationship between the employer and employees can have a significant impact on morale, motivation, and productivity. Workers who feel that the terms and conditions of their employment are less than advantageous will not be as committed to perform and to remain with an employer. Consequently, how organizations manage the day-to-day aspects of the employment relationship can be a key variable affecting their ability to achieve strategic objectives.

Workers who have unionized create special challenges for human resource (HR) management. When workers form unions, the employment relationship becomes more formal through a union contract and is subject to special provisions of the National Labor Relations Act. This Act allows unions to be formed and exist as employee organizations that have the legal right to bargain with management over various terms and conditions of employment. Unions provide membership solely for employees; managers are prohibited by law from joining employee unions or from forming their own unions.

Organized labor in the United States has had a cyclical history, generally consisting of short periods of sharp growth in union membership and activity followed by extended periods of decline.[2] In the early part of the twentieth century, employee-centered management practices were eroding interest in unionization. The Great Depression then ignited strong interest in unions with the resultant creation by John Lewis of the Congress of Industrial Organizations (CIO). At that time, both the CIO and the American Federation of Labor (AFL) were able to unionize large segments of the workforce. These organizing efforts were largely focused on second-generation immigrants, particularly Catholics, Italians, and Jews, as unions attempted to provide these individuals with the full benefits of working in the WASP-dominated economy.

Unions continued to enjoy increased membership until World War II. Interest in unions declined post-War until the mid-1960s, when unions began to reach out to African Americans during the drive for civil rights and subsequently enjoyed a renewed popularity. Also at that time, Cesar Chavez founded the National Farm Workers Association, drawing attention to the plight of Latino and Filipino farm workers who had been forced to endure deplorable working conditions and substandard wages. Chavez's efforts led to a grape boycott that was observed by more than 17 million Americans and, more generally, resulted in widespread awareness and distrust of exploitation of workers by employers. These successes also led to a flurry of union organization among public sector employees that continued until the early 1980s.

August 3, 1981, is considered to be a significant day in the history of American labor. On that date, more than 12,000 employees of the Federal Aviation Administration (FAA) who were members of the Professional Air Traffic Controllers (PATCO) union walked off of their jobs. When President Reagan ordered them back to work within 48 hours, 11,325 of them refused and were fired immediately, as the FAA commenced hiring permanent replacements. Since the unsuccessful PATCO strike, strikes have nearly disappeared in the United States. During the 1950s, organized labor successfully orchestrated an average of 344 work stoppages annually.[3] However, post-PATCO, that number had continuously been in decline and by 2008 had dipped to just 15, with 9 of these 15 lasting for 10 days or less.[4] The PATCO strike greatly influenced public perceptions against organized labor stoppages and affirmed the right for employers to hire permanent replacements for striking workers. This shift has turned the strike into a present-day near-suicide tactic for unions.

Union membership in the United States has been steadily declining for a number of years. In 1970, approximately 30 percent of the private workforce was unionized, in addition to a majority of public sector employees. By 1999, the U.S. Department of Labor reported that only 13.9 percent of the workforce was unionized. By 2013 union membership had dropped further to 11.3 percent of the workforce. Public sector employees were more than five times more likely to be union members than private sector employees (36 percent versus 6.6 percent), and more than 50 percent of union members lived in seven states (California, New York, Illinois, Pennsylvania, Michigan, New Jersey, and Ohio).[5] These numbers represented declines in overall union membership as well as in both the public and private sector union density.[6]

The decline in union membership can be attributed to a number of factors. First, many workers have become disenfranchised from their unions. Allegations of union corruption and misuse of funds—combined with the fact that workers sometimes feel that the costs of union membership outweigh the benefits—have eroded union membership. Second, many organizations have moved their manufacturing and assembly operations outside the United States. Unions have traditionally had their strongest bases of support among these blue-collar workers, and the movement of those jobs overseas has hurt unions. Third, changes in the nature of work and technology have eliminated many of the traditional manual labor jobs in which union members were employed. Finally, many unions have refused to be flexible enough to allow organizations to grow and adapt in relation to the changes taking place in their industries, markets, and the technological, economic, and sociocultural environments. The traditional model of American labor unions, which guard employee rights by attempting to maintain the status quo, no longer benefits employers or employees. Unions of the future will have to be based on a different model and have different relationships with the organizations whose workers they represent—if they continue to exist.

Although overall union membership is declining, it is important to understand organized labor relations for at least three reasons. First, in many industries, unionization is the norm. Many public sector workplaces are unionized. In the private sector, industries such as transportation, construction, hospitality, publishing, education, and healthcare are usually highly unionized. In fact, the transportation industry has the highest level of private sector union membership, at 25.5 percent.[7] Managers and business owners in these industries have no choice but to be well versed on the laws that regulate the relationship with union employees. Second, competitors may be unionized, and settlements in those organizations may impact HR practices, programs, and policies needed to remain competitive in recruiting and retaining productive employees. Arguably, the most important reason for employers to have a sense of the labor relations landscape is that the National Labor Relations Act provides all employees—rather than just those who have unionized—with specific rights. Consequently, many employers who operate in nonunion environments may be unfamiliar with some of the terms and conditions of employment outlined in the Act. Section 7 of the Act grants all employees, including those who are not members of unions, the right to engage in activities that support their "mutual aid or protection." There are six notable provisions under this section that employers must know to avoid violations of the Act.[8]

First is the right of employees to discuss employment terms. In order for employees to consider whether they wish to organize, they must be able to discuss the terms and conditions of employment, including compensation, harassment, and discrimination. This right, however, does not extend to the disclosure of confidential information, such as salaries, to which an employee might have access as part of his or her job. Second, employees reserve the right to complain to third parties, such as customers, clients, and the media, about their treatment by the employer. Again, however, the employer retains the right to prohibit disclosure of any confidential or proprietary information. Third, employees have the right to engage in a work stoppage or collective walkout to protest working conditions without fear of retaliation. Any employee who is disciplined or discharged for engaging in such behavior has a valid claim against the employer under the National Labor Relations Act. Fourth, employees have the right to honor picket lines without fear of retaliation. This is considered protected activity regardless of whether the employee is a member of the picketing union or merely sympathetic to the cause and plight of the workers on the picket line. Fifth, employees have the conditional right to solicit and distribute union literature. Such behavior can be restricted but not fully prohibited, as will be discussed shortly. Finally, employers cannot unilaterally ban employees' access to the worksite while off duty. Restrictions may be imposed that limit access to the interior of the facility if applied consistently to all employees for all purposes, but employees still retain the right to be present on company property, such as the employee parking lot, after working hours to engage in behaviors protected under the Act.

It cannot be emphasized enough that nonunion employees enjoy significant protection against arbitrary, capricious, or harassing conduct by employers. This standard was established by the Supreme Court in the 1962 case of *NLRB v. Washington Aluminum Co.,*[9] where the Court found that employee activity that was concerted for mutual aid or protection (in this case, walking off the job in protest of poor working conditions) was lawful. As long as the employee's or group of employees' actions are beyond that of a personal complaint pursued in self-interest, such behavior is protected without the presence of a formally recognized union. These rights have consistently been reinforced in numerous court cases since the initial ruling in *Washington Aluminum.*

Just because an organization is not unionized today does not mean that it may not be in the future. Managers in such organizations need to know why workers form or join unions, how the law requires the employer to behave during any union-organizing campaign and after a union has been voted in, how the collective-bargaining process is conducted, and how impasses may be settled. Some management advisors who work with organizations on labor relations have even gone as far to encourage employers to have their supervisors talk openly with employees about possible union representation in a proactive manner before any possible organizing efforts begin.[10] Critical to such a strategy, however, is training of managers on what they are allowed to say to employees (facts, opinions, and examples) and what they are not allowed to say or do (threats, interrogation, promises, and surveillance).[11]

The word "union" means that workers have agreed to work together in dealing with and negotiating the terms and conditions of their employment with management. The Latin root *uni* means *one*, in the sense of a union; it means that a plurality of workers has united to speak with "one voice."

Organized labor presents a number of key strategic challenges for management. First, when workers unionize, the power based within the organization is redistributed. Employers can find that their ability to manage workers at their discretion to achieve the organization's strategic objectives has been severely curtailed. Second, the process of unionization involves bringing in outside players: union representatives, who then become an additional constituency whose support must be gained for any new or ongoing management initiatives. Finally, a unionized work setting can greatly impact the organization's cost structure, particularly payroll expenses and work processes that may contribute to or retard efficiency in operations.

Why Employees Unionize

Employees usually form or join unions because of the perceived benefits that unionization might provide them. These benefits can be economic, social, and/or political. Economic benefits can result from a union's ability to negotiate higher wages, better or expanded benefits, greater job or employment security, and improved working hours and conditions. Social benefits can be derived from the affiliation and sense of community that workers share when they are unionized. Their personal issues and needs relating to their jobs and lifestyles can often be integrated within the union agenda, with corresponding support gained from coworkers. Unions also often sponsor social events for their members and their families. Is it not surprising that many unions have the word "brotherhood" in their name; this attempts to signify the family or community atmosphere the union tries to create for its members.

Political benefits can be gained through the sense of power in numbers. In negotiating with management over terms and conditions of employment, individual employees are relatively powerless. They often need the organization (to earn a living) far more than the organization needs them (individual workers can be easily replaced). When workers unionize and speak with one voice, they leverage their individual power against management and equalize the balance of power within the organization. Management may be able to do without individual employees, but they cannot do without their entire workforce. Unions can allow workers far greater say and involvement in negotiating and setting critical terms and conditions of employment and in ensuring fair treatment from the organization. Unions can often provide additional political benefits in a literal sense in that the power and strength of their united membership can be used to support and influence political races and legislation passed at the local, state, and federal levels.

No benefits come without some cost, and union membership is no exception. Union members pay at least two significant costs for their benefits. First are the economic costs of the fees or dues that unions charge their members to support the initiatives the union undertakes on behalf of its employees. Second are the political costs employees assume when they relinquish their individual freedom to deal with their employer and be represented by the union. Individual employees may not agree with the terms and conditions negotiated for them or the tactics and strategies the union uses in negotiating. Although individual employees do vote on the decision to strike, an employee who does not wish or cannot afford to go out on strike is basically stuck in accepting the majority position and then assumes any risk associated with deviating from the union majority.

The National Labor Relations Act

In 1935, Congress passed the National Labor Relations Act (NLRA), also called the Wagner Act, which gave employees the right to unionize and to regulate union and management relations. This Act has been amended several times, most notably in 1947, with amendments known as the Taft-Hartley Act, and in 1959, with amendments known as the Landrum-Griffith Act.

The NLRA created the National Labor Relations Board (NLRB) to oversee the provisions of the Act. Among other duties, the NLRB is responsible for overseeing union elections, certifying a particular union as the official bargaining representative of a group of employees, and hearing allegations of violations of the Act from employers, unions, and employee groups.

As a first step in establishing a union, a group of employees petitions the NLRB, often through the assistance of a union representative, to conduct an election. As a prerequisite for an election, the NLRB requires at least 30 percent of the employees to have signed authorization cards, which indicate an expressed interest in having union representation from a specific union. Most petitions to the NLRB involve the presentation of authorization cards from a far greater number of employees than 30 percent. These authorization cards are not a vote for the union; they are merely the means for establishing the level of employee interest to conduct an election. Some employees who are not in favor of union representation often sign authorization cards under peer pressure or to facilitate the election process. Union-organizing campaigns often create very stressful working conditions, and some employees who are against unionization may sign authorization cards to ensure that the election be held as soon as possible.

Once the NLRB has received the authorization cards and determined that there is sufficient interest to conduct an election, it will attempt to determine the appropriate bargaining unit. A bargaining unit is a group of employees who have similar wages, skill levels, working conditions, and/or levels of professionalism. The NLRB will determine whether the organization should have one bargaining unit that covers all employees or separate bargaining units for different groups of employees, given the differences in their jobs.

For example, airlines have separate bargaining units for flight attendants, pilots, and ramp workers, given the differences in job responsibilities, training, hours, and working conditions. Newspapers have separate unions for writers, printers, and press people because of similar differences. A restaurant, on the other hand, might have one bargaining unit that includes wait staff, cooks, hosts, bartenders, and bus staff. When a unionized organization has more than one bargaining unit, each bargaining unit negotiates a contract with management separately; however, the individual units are often impacted by what the other units negotiate, and each unit often lends support to the others during periods of labor unrest.

When the NLRB conducts an election, the option that receives the majority of the votes (50 percent plus one) wins the election. There may, however, be more than two options (union or no union) on the ballot. Given that the NLRB requires authorization cards from only 30 percent of employees, it is mathematically possible for more than one union to be part of an election. This has been the case when there has been public knowledge of dissatisfied employees and thus more than one union attempted to organize workers simultaneously. If there were three options on the ballot (no union, Union A, Union B) and none of them received more than 50 percent of the initial vote, then the option receiving the least support would be dropped and a second ballot would be issued. Eventually, one option will have the support of more than 50 percent of the employees in the prospective bargaining unit.

Behavior During Organizing Campaigns

Union-organizing campaigns often present difficult working conditions for employees, who are often continuously subjected to opposing information from management, union representatives, and prounion coworkers in support of their respective positions. In passing the NLRA, Congress determined that it should regulate the behavior of management and union representatives in union-organizing campaigns to ensure that one does not have an unfair advantage over the other in communicating positions to employees.

The NLRA outlines specific provisions pertaining to employer conduct during union-organizing campaigns in its discussion of unfair labor practices. Section 8(c) of the Act provides that "the expression of views, arguments or opinions, or the dissemination thereof, whether in written, printed, graphic or visual form shall not constitute or be evidence of an unfair labor practice … if such expression contains no threat of reprisal or force or promise of benefit." Therefore, employers have free rein to communicate their position concerning unionization to employees during working hours, which is only appropriate because the employers are paying employees for that time. However, employers are forbidden from making any threat or promise pending the outcome of the election. The reason for this directive is that allowing employers to do so would give employers an unfair advantage in the election. The union does not have the power to make any such promises, and so to ensure a level playing field, the NLRB also prohibits employers from doing so. Employers need to treat employees more favorably *before* the NLRB has stepped in and established employee interest in conducting an election.

The Act also allows prounion employees the full right to approach their coworkers at work and express their support of the union, as long as such contact takes place during nonworking periods in nonworking areas (such as the employee cafeteria during lunch breaks, the parking lot after leaving work, or in a restroom during a scheduled break). This is consistent with the constitutional guarantee of freedom of speech. Employers can prohibit employees who support the union from communicating this support to coworkers at any other time.

A more difficult question concerns the extent to which employers can prevent employee solicitation by union representatives at the worksite. The U.S. Supreme Court has issued several rulings in this area that continue to redefine the relative positions of unions and management. Generally, an employer can restrict nonemployee access to employees if two conditions have been met: (1) The nonemployee—in this case, a union organizer—must have some reasonable means to access and communicate with employees outside the workplace, such as electronic or print media, and (2) the employer must have a general ban on all nonemployee solicitation. The latter condition is not limited to union solicitation; it might also include charitable appeals, blood drives, or employer-sponsored outings for which employees have to pay. If these two conditions are met, then the employer can restrict union organizers' access to employees.

Historically, this issue of access to employees has involved somewhat of a "chess game" between employers and union organizers. Subsequent to the Supreme Court rulings described above that restrict union organizer access to employees, unions have turned to a strategy called "salting" the workplace. Salting involves a paid union organizer applying for employment with an employer whose employees are the target of an organizing drive. The Supreme Court has held that under the NLRA, an employer cannot discriminate against a person solely on the basis of his or her status as a salt and intention to organize the workplace. Employers have since countered salting efforts through the use of restricted hiring criteria that have the effect of eliminating salts from employment consideration. The portrayal of union organizing efforts and management responses as a chess game relates to the fact that each side is attempting to develop a response to counter the other side's most recent "move" or court victory. Reading 12.1, "A Big Chill on a 'Big Hurt': Genuine Interest in Employment of Salts in Assessing Protection Under the National Labor Relations Act," illustrates the tensions that exist between unions and employers in organizing campaigns.

Employees who are dissatisfied with their union representative may elect to decertify the union. The process for decertification happens in exactly the same manner as certification—utilizing authorization cards and requiring a 50 percent plus one majority employee vote. The NLRA does, however, require employees to wait at least one year from certification until a decertification election can be held. This is to ensure that the union has had appropriate time to work on behalf of the employees and to ensure that employees do not drain the time and resources of the NLRB by continually calling for certification and decertification elections. Similarly, if a union loses an organizing campaign, the NLRA prohibits another organizing campaign and election for at least one year.

Collective Bargaining

When a union is elected to represent employees, the union representative and employer are jointly responsible for negotiating a collective-bargaining agreement that covers various terms and conditions of employment. There are no set requirements as to the term or content of any collective-bargaining agreement, but the NLRA classifies bargaining items as mandatory, permissive, or prohibited. Mandatory items must be negotiated in good faith if one party chooses to introduce them to the negotiations. They consist of many of the economic terms of employment, such as wages, hours, benefits, working conditions, job-posting procedures, or job security provisions. Mandatory items also include management rights clauses and union security clauses. The two parties are not required to come to an agreement on these items, but they are legally required to discuss them and bargain in good faith if requested by the other party. "Mandatory" simply means that one party cannot refuse to discuss one of these items if the other party requests to do so.

Permissive items can be discussed if both parties agree to do so. Neither party can legally force the other party to negotiate over a permissive item nor can either party pursue a permissive item to the point of impasse. Permissive items include things such as changes in benefits for retired employees, supervisory compensation and discipline, and union input in pricing of company products and services. Prohibited items are things neither party can negotiate because these items are illegal. They include featherbedding (requiring the employer to pay for work not done or not requested), discrimination in hiring, or any other violation of the law or illegal union security clauses. A listing of some of the items that fall under each classification is presented in Exhibit 12.1.

Unions often attempt to negotiate security clauses into the collective-bargaining agreement. These clauses are a mandatory bargaining item and an attempt to ensure that the union enjoys some security in its representation of employees and that the cost of the union's efforts on behalf of employees is covered. The two types of union security clauses are union shop agreements and agency shop agreements. Union shop agreements require all newly hired employees who are not union members to join the union within a specified time period after beginning employment. Agency shop agreements do not require employees to join the union but require all nonunion members who are part of the bargaining unit to pay the union a representation fee, usually equivalent to the amount of dues paid by union members. The rationale for collecting such fees is that although individual employees can maintain the freedom of being nonunion, as bargaining unit members, they reap the advantages of what the union negotiates. Therefore, it is only fair that they should share equally in the cost of obtaining what the union is able to achieve for the bargaining unit. Although union security clauses are a mandatory bargaining item, the NLRA allows individual states to pass right-to-work laws that prohibit union and agency shop arrangements. To date, nearly half the 50 states have passed such laws. When Michigan, the birthplace of the United Auto Workers and the U.S. labor movement, became the 24th right-to-work state in December 2012, the move was seen by many as a crushing blow to the future of organized labor in the United States.[12]

A third type of union security agreement that was originally allowed under the NLRA has since been outlawed. Closed-shop agreements required the employer to hire only applicants who

EXHIBIT 12.1

Types of Bargaining Items

Mandatory	Permissive	Illegal
Base wages	Union representation on board of directors	Closed-shop agreements
Incentive pay	Benefits for retirees	Featherbedding
Benefits	Wage concessions	Discrimination in hiring
Overtime	Employee ownership	
Paid time off	Union input into company pricing policy	
Layoff procedures		
Promotion criteria		
Union security clauses		
Management rights clauses		
Grievance procedures		
Safety and health issues		

© Cengage Learning

were already union members. Congress found such arrangements to be detrimental to labor because individuals without income were forced to pay union dues without the benefit of any employment. There was no guarantee that an applicant who belonged to a union subsequently would be hired, and so closed-shop agreements were eventually outlawed.

Failure to Reach Agreement

When the union and the employer are unable to agree on the terms of the collective-bargaining agreement, workers have the right—under the NLRA—to strike. Whether employers are obligated to rehire striking employees at the conclusion of the strike depends on the kind of strike.

An economic strike is one in which the parties have negotiated in good faith but have been unable to settle on a contract or collective-bargaining agreement. The organization has the right to continue to operate during such a strike and often does so by utilizing management employees, hiring temporary workers, and/or hiring permanent replacements. The discretion of how to proceed rests with the organization. Economic strikers cannot be terminated simply for engaging in collective strike activity. At the conclusion of the strike, they must be reinstated if two conditions are met: (1) Their individual jobs still exist and (2) permanent replacements have not been hired. Economic strikers run the risk that the employer may eliminate their jobs or hire replacements; both activities are protected under the NLRA.

An unfair labor practice strike is one in which employees strike in response to some action of management that the NLRA identifies as an unfair labor practice. These behaviors are outlined within the statute, and workers who go out on such a strike have a guaranteed legal right to reinstatement by the employer even if the employer has hired permanent replacements in the interim.

A wildcat strike is one in which workers decide not to honor the terms of the collective-bargaining agreement and walk out in violation of their obligation to the employer under the agreement. Because wildcat strikers have breached their contractual obligations to the employer, they have no right to reinstatement in their jobs. Wildcat strikes can be caused by perceived unfair treatment of an employee by management or a worksite may be perceived as hazardous or dangerous, such as those found in the mining and construction industries. In certain industries, management will attempt to resolve the issue if the claims are deemed to have merit in lieu of fighting the union in court. In addition, federal workers are prohibited by law from striking for any reason, including an economic strike. Any strike by federal employees is not protected under the NLRA, and striking employees have no legal rights to return to their jobs. Such was the case in the early 1980s when the PATCO union struck, and President Reagan immediately fired and replaced the striking workers.

The incidence of labor strikes in the United States is decreasing as both employees and employers realize that everyone loses during a strike. The company gets hurt financially and in the public domain; workers get hurt financially and emotionally; customers may be hurt operationally and financially, particularly if there are no substitute providers. Organizations can prevent strike activity in two principal ways: through the use of a formal grievance procedure or through the alternate dispute resolution (ADR) processes of mediation or arbitration.

Grievance procedures are a permissive bargaining item under the National Labor Relations Act, as indicated in Exhibit 12.1. Grievance procedures outline how conflicts or disagreements between workers and management over the terms of the collective-bargaining agreement are handled. Grievance procedures are often the catalyst to resolving problems before the conflict escalates to a strike. They are also useful in helping union leaders and management identify weaknesses or oversights in the collective-bargaining agreement that can be addressed during the negotiations over subsequent collective-bargaining agreements. Grievance procedures are also useful as a means of communicating to management firsthand work-related sources of employee dissatisfaction that can hamper morale and productivity.

An increasing number of collective-bargaining agreements are calling for mediation or arbitration of labor disputes as a means of avoiding strikes. Mediation involves an outside third party who has no binding decision-making authority assisting both sides in reaching a settlement. This individual assists the two sides in finding some middle ground on which they can agree and in facilitating dialogue and concessions. Arbitration works in a similar manner: It involves an outside, unbiased third party who listens to the arguments presented by both sides. However, the arbitrator renders a ruling or decision that binds both parties. Both sides agree to abide by the decision of the arbitrator prior to entering the arbitration hearing. Mediation is frequently used in public sector organizations where strike activity is outlawed at the federal level and often greatly restricted at the state and local levels. Arbitration is used quite frequently in professional sports in resolving salary disputes between union players and the owners of their teams.

Arbitration has been controversial in that it has been perceived as depriving employees of their rights to pursue claims in courts of law and have their cases heard by a jury and replacing this process with an employer-controlled system that is less likely to result in a favorable decision for the employee. However, history has shown that this is not the case. Employment-related cases heard in federal district courts historically have resulted in a 12 percent rate of success for employees, while general employment arbitration has favored employees in 33 percent of cases decided, and labor arbitration—heard under a collective-bargaining agreement—has favored employees in 52 percent of cases.[13]

Unions Today

One way in which unions are attempting to maintain their viability in light of declining membership is to recruit in organizations and industries with which they have no previous affiliation. With the demise of their traditional manufacturing base, many domestic unions have expanded their missions, as efforts to recruit new members have become a top priority. Such recruiting efforts are seen as so central to the ongoing livelihood of unions that the AFL-CIO now earmarks one-third of its operating budget for organizing, compared to just 5 percent 10 years ago.[14] Consider the diversity now present in some of the leading labor unions: the United Steelworkers of America, established in 1936 to represent steelworkers, now includes employees from Good Humor/Breyers, the Baltimore Zoo, and Louisville Slugger; the United Auto Workers, established in 1935 to represent auto workers, now includes employees from Miller Beer, Planter's nuts, Kohler bathroom fixtures, Yamaha musical instruments, and Folger's Coffee; the International

Brotherhood of Teamsters, established in 1903 to represent drivers in the freight-moving industry, now includes flight attendants, public defenders, and nursing home employees. There is no consensus regarding the value of such diversification by unions. Some argue that it provides more power to unions and their members by strengthening their numbers and preventing their dependence on one particular industry. On the other hand, critics argue that this prevents unions from being very influential in setting wages and policy in a particular industry, given the need to spread time and resources across multiple industries. However, given the demise of traditional manufacturing jobs from which unions originated and relied on for their support and power, unions have little choice but to reach out to new industries. The critical issue is whether this diversification is really strategic for the union or merely opportunistic.

Another new development in how unions operate is their reliance on technology. Unions have been using the Internet effectively to recruit new members, particularly those in technology-based industries, and to gain support from others in their organizing efforts. The South Bay Central Labor Council, based in California's Silicon Valley, consists of 110 affiliated unions that represent more than 100,000 employees in the area. The Council is using the Internet to communicate with and, it is hoped, organize contingent workers.[15] Similarly, the Service Employees International Union undertook a campaign to organize janitorial workers in the Silicon Valley. The union successfully used the Internet to publicize its case against Apple Computer, Oracle, and Hewlett-Packard worldwide via electronic bulletin boards that informed engineers and programmers about the wages and working conditions of those who cleaned their offices at night.[16] Finally, the Oakland-based Local 2850 of the Hotel Employees & Restaurant Employees International Union used the Internet in a campaign against software giant PeopleSoft. In attempting to organize workers from a hotel used extensively by PeopleSoft and its corporate partners and unable to gain the support of PeopleSoft, the union launched an Internet campaign that caused PeopleSoft's stock value to decline by more than $63 million, according to the company's own estimates.[17]

The NLRB has also considered the role of technology as it relates to worker rights under the NLRA. Given its charge to ensure that employees are able to communicate freely with each other about wages and all other conditions and terms of employment, the NLRB has endorsed e-mail communication between employees as a means of safeguarding those rights. Only when an employee's behavior is disruptive does NLRA protection cease. As a result, employer policies that ban all nonbusiness and/or personal use of e-mail may interfere with the right to self-organize and therefore constitute a violation of the NLRA. A key issue here is the extent to which employees normally use the employer's computer system for their regular work and communication with coworkers. Employees who normally use a computer system in carrying out their regular job responsibilities are considered differently from employees who generally do not use computers or e-mail to carry out their regular job responsibilities. In addition, the more e-mail is normally used in the workplace, the less restrictive a policy an employer can implement that regulates communication that might be considered protected concerted activity under the NLRA.[18]

In recent years, the proliferation of social media has greatly altered the means by which employees communicate with each other, both inside and outside of the workplace. The National Labor Relations Board has provided protection to some employees who have had adverse action taken against them by their employers due to their social media communications and postings. Reading 12.2, "Social Media, Employee Privacy and Concerted Activity: Brave New World or Big Brother?," discusses issues surrounding employee privacy and how social media posting by employees may fall with NLRA protection.

Broader employer policies regarding employee electronic communications have also been targeted by the National Labor Relations Board. Warehouse retailer Costco had a policy which prohibited employees from making defamatory statement deemed unlawful by the NLRB. Specifically, the policy stated, "Employees should be aware that statements posted electronically (such as to online message boards or discussion groups) that damage the company, defame any individual or damage any person's reputation or violate policies outlined in the Costco Employee Agreement, may be subject to discipline, up to and including termination of employment." The NLRB found the prohibition to be too broad and designed to squelch employee concerted communications with each other.[19] As part of the same decision, the NLRB also struck down Costco rules that prohibited employees from (1) posting, distributing, removing, or altering any material on company property; (2) discussing "private matters of members and other employees … including topics such as, but not limited to, sick calls, leaves of absence, FMLA call-outs, ADA accommodations, workers' compensation injuries, personal health information, etc."; (3) sharing, transmitting, or storing for personal or public use without prior management approval sensitive personal information such as membership, payroll, confidential credit card numbers, Social Security numbers, or employee personal health information.[20]

To guide employers, the NLRB has prepared three separate updated social media reports, which describe all social media cases reviewed by the agency. These documents provide guidance to employers in formulating social media policies that will comply with federal labor laws.[21] Their two main advisories for employers are (1) employer policies should not be so sweeping that they prohibit the kinds of activity protected by federal labor law, such as the discussion of wages or working conditions among employees; and (2) an employee's comments on social media are generally not protected if they are mere gripes not made in relation to group activity among employees.[22]

Conclusion

Unions have a long and deep history in the United States and enjoy strong support under federal law. However, union membership is declining in America; unions in this country probably will not survive if they continue to display traditional adversarial relationships with employers. Traditional approaches to negotiation usually involved the union trying to gain concessions from management and winning the negotiation. To be successful in the future, unions must develop partnerships with employers and seek win–win outcomes to collective bargaining that strengthen both the union's position and employees' rights and enhance the performance of the organization. Rigid posturing by unions in attempting to maintain the status quo works against the many initiatives and innovations organizations develop as they attempt to respond to changes in their environments and remain more competitive.

Given the changing nature of organizations and work, unions clearly need to reinvent themselves. Unions need to consider that the jobs of today and those of the future are quite different from the jobs of the past. Increasing global competition, changing technology, the heightened pace of merger and acquisition activity, the move toward smaller businesses and autonomous divisions, and the increasing diversity in the workforce represent broad changes for unions in the United States. The jobs being created in our economy are more service- than manufacturing-oriented; are much more complex, multifaceted, and broadly designed; involve teams, cooperation, and working with others; and involve more self- or peer supervision than supervision by management. Countries such as Japan and Germany have extensive unionization and produce some of the highest quality, most technologically advanced products. Their unions facilitate worker involvement, development, and participation programs; also, the unions partner with employers in creating beneficial change rather than inhibiting change and attempting to ensure workers' rights by maintaining the status quo.

As unions decline in number and stature, workers become less powerful. Without union representation, employee interests can only be advanced through increased government regulation of the employment relationship or through innovative and responsive HR programs that organizations initiate themselves. Increased legislation may ensure worker rights, but it can also inhibit organizational flexibility and change. Innovative HR programs can provide workers with benefits, but usually, the organization retains power and control over the workers, who maintain their individual status in dealing with separate issues with the employer. Legislation preserves rights and empowers workers to a limited extent, but it inhibits change. Organization-designed initiatives can promote change but still leave individual workers at a disadvantage when dealing with employers on issues of equity. Hence, policymakers need to take a critical look at the institution of collective bargaining to determine whether it has lived up to the ideals Congress established for it under the NLRA.

Very few unionized companies have developed effective worker participation programs because unions are interested in keeping workers insulated from management issues. Ironically, however, successful employee participation programs in nonunionized organizations have actually increased workers' power and voice in dealing with management. Union leaders need to create a new model of worker representation if they plan to survive in the twenty-first century. This can only be done if union leaders rethink their roles and adopt collective-bargaining strategies that allow both the employees and employers to benefit. Union leaders need not only political and negotiating skills but also management skills in understanding the whole organization: strategic issues facing the employer and the organization's environment. Instead of seeing themselves as adversaries to management, they should envision themselves as facilitators and consultants. Although employers clearly need to consider labor relations from a strategic perspective, union representatives must do so even more if they are to keep their unions viable for tomorrow's organizations.

Critical Thinking

1. With unionization on the downturn, why should an organization be concerned about labor relations?

2. What benefits are received and what costs are incurred when workers unionize?

3. Describe the process by which workers unionize.

4. What are the possible outcomes of failure to reach consensus on a collective-bargaining agreement?

5. Contrast the style of labor unions in the United States to that found in other countries.

6. Does union diversification make unions stronger or weaker? How would you feel as an auto worker to see the United Auto Workers representing employees outside the auto industry?

7. What rights and responsibilities do employers and employees have regarding the use of social media communications under the National Labor Relations Act?

Reading 12.1

8. Assess the status of employer and union recruiter behaviors in union-organizing campaigns. How much access should union organizers have to employees? What new behaviors are likely from employers and union organizers in response to the actions of the other party?

Reading 12.2

9. How can social media impact the rights of employees under the National Labor Relations Act? Can or should any restrictions be placed by employers on workplace discussions that take place through social media?

Exercises

1. Locate a local unionized organization. Interview both a manager and a union employee to determine the level of satisfaction each has with the employment relationship. What types of union activity/inactivity contribute to these positions?

2. Investigate one large union, such as the United Auto Workers, United Steelworkers, or Teamsters, in depth and then examine its member base and recent activity on behalf of its members. Does it appear that diversification has made this union more or less effective?

3. Investigate the nature of collective bargaining in Australia, Canada, and Mexico and the countries that constitute the European Union and then compare and contrast the nature and state of collective bargaining in these areas as well as determine the implications this has for global business.

4. Visit the Web sites for the AFL-CIO (http://www.aflcio.org) and Teamsters (http://www.teamsters.com). What programs does each union offer its members? What are the main issues each union appears to be pursuing? Do these programs and issues appear to be well matched to the needs of the U.S. labor force?

5. Visit the Web site for the National Labor Relations Board (http://www.nlrb.gov). Of what value is this Web site for employers? Of what value is this Web site for union leaders?

6. Design a social media policy for an employer that would optimally serve both the employers and the employee without running afoul of the National Labor Relations Act.

Chapter References

1. Wikipedia. "2005 New York City Transit Strike," available at http://en.wikipedia.org/wiki/2005_New_York_City_transit_strike.

2. Caudron, S., et al. "The Labor Movement to War," *Workforce*, January 2001, pp. 27–33.

3. McCartin, J. "PATCO, Permanent Replacement and the Loss of Labor's Strike Weapon," *Perspectives on Work*, 10, (1), Summer 2006, pp. 17–19.

4. Bureau of Labor Statistics, available at http://www.bls.gov/news.release/wkstp.nr0.html.

5. U.S. Bureau of Labor Statistics, Union Members Summary, January 23, 2013. Available at http://www.bls.gov/news.release/union2.nr0.htm.

6. U.S. Bureau of Labor Statistics, Labor Force Statistics from the Current Population Survey, Union Members, available at http://stats.bls.gov.

7. Ibid.

8. Segal, J. A. "Labor Pains for Union-Free Employers," *HR Magazine*, March 2004, 49, (3), pp. 113–118.

9. *NLRB v. Washington Aluminum Co.* 370 U.S. 9 (1962).

10. Smith, A. "Talk, Talk Talk About Unions," *Society for Human Resource Management*, November 14, 2012. Available at http://www.shrm.org/Pages/login.aspx?ReturnUrl=%2fhrdisciplines%2flaborrelations%2farticles%2fpages%2forganizing-discussions.aspx.

11. Ibid.

12. Linn, A. "Michigan's Right-to-work Laws Will Ripple Across the U.S." *NBC News*. Available at http://www.nbcnews.com/business/economywatch/michigans-right-work-laws-will-ripple-across-us-1C7559684.

13. Wheeler, H., Klaas, F. and Mahony, D. *Workplace Justice Without Unions*. W.E. Upjohn Institute for Employment Research, 2004.

14. Hirsh, S. "Unions Reach Everywhere for Members," *Baltimore Sun*, January 25, 2004, p. ID.

15. Newman, N. "Union and Community Mobilization in the Information Age," *Perspectives on Work*, 6, (2), pp. 9–11.

16. Ibid.

17. Ibid.

18. Lyncheski, J. E. and Heller, L. D. "Cyber Speech Cops," *HR Magazine*, January 2001, 46, (1), pp. 145–150.

19. *Costco Wholesale Corp. and United Food and Commercial Workers Union, Local 371*, 358 NLRB No. 106 (2012).

20. Ibid.

21. NLRB, Office of the General Counsel, (Third) Report of the Acting General Counsel Concerning Social Media Cases (Memorandum OM 12-59) (May 30, 2012).

22. Deschenaux, J. "NLRB Issues Second Social Media Report," *Society for Human Resource Management*. January 31, 2012. Available at http://www.shrm.org/legalissues/federalresources/pages/nlrbsocialmediareport.aspx.

READING 12.1

A Big Chill on a "Big Hurt:" Genuine Interest in Employment of Salts in Assessing Protection Under the National Labor Relations Act

Jeffrey A. Mello

Abstract

As union membership has continued to decline steadily in the US, union organizers have become more creative and vigilant with their organizing strategies. Chief among these strategies has been "salting," a process by which unions attempt to organize employees from the inside rather than the outside. The Supreme Court has ruled that, under the National Labor Relations Act, "salts" cannot be discriminated against solely on the basis of their status as salts. This paper examines employer responses to resist salting efforts, including a recent decision by the National Labor Relations Board, which redefines the landscape under which salting activities can be conducted and considered protected activity.

Union membership has been declining steadily in the US since the US Bureau of Labor Statistics began tracking such numbers 25 years ago. At that time, 20.1% of the US workforce was unionized. By 2008, only 12% of workforce was unionized with a continuous steady decline having been recorded over that time. In 2008, public sector unionization stood at 35.9% while private sector unionization had declined to 7.4%, with both percentages having each lost a full percentage point over the preceding 3 years (Bureau of Labor Statistics 2008). This steady 25 year decline, however, was not a new trend but rather the continuation of a trend that pre-dated the Bureau of Labor Statistics tracking (Curms *et al.* 1990).

This decline can be attributed to a number of factors. First, the movement of many traditionally union-held jobs to developing countries overseas to take advantage of lower labor costs has been increasingly dramatically in recent years. Second, changes in the nature of the employment relationship, including the increased transience of the workforce and the erosion of the assumption, or presumption, of lifetime employment and the growing trend toward part-time and contract employment have impacted workers' interest in being represented by unions. Third, the rise in undocumented or illegal workers who are unprotected or afraid to protest and/or organize has affected unions.

Fourth, many of the jobs being created in our economy are in areas in which unions have no experience organizing, such as call centers, and involve workers who work from their homes or remote locations, rather than at the employer's physical facility. Fifth, an increasing number of employers are resisting and fighting union organizing attempts more so than in the past. More than 75% of employers confronted with union organizing campaigns now hire consultants and an entire new industry of "union avoidance firms," often consisting of former union leaders, has been established over the past three decades with anti-union success rates that generally exceed 90% (Maher 2005; Logan 2006). Sixth, unions themselves have been blamed for not keeping up with the times and failing to address the concerns of the fastest growing segments of the hourly labor force, including women, minorities and immigrants. Finally, the alleged antiunion doctrine and teachings of business schools have been cited as promoting and encouraging more adversarial relations between employers and unions (Gould 2008; Anonymous 2003).

Unions have responded to declines in membership by becoming much more aggressive in their recruiting tactics. One of the main strategies now being employed by unions is "salting," a process by which union organizers attempt to organize a workplace internally. Originally implemented in the early 1970s in the construction industry (Raudabaugh 2008), salting involves a union representative applying for and subsequently obtaining employment with the organization whose workers are being targeted for unionization. Salting provides union organizers with more direct and regular access to employees who are the target of the unionization drive that would be realized by organizing from the outside. More recently salting activity has evolved into a means of political and economic warfare against employers as the basis for unfair labor practice allegation filings with the National Labor Relations Board (NLRB). This paper discusses the legal foundation upon which salting activities are based, the recent court activity and NLRB rulings in salting cases, subsequent management reactions to curtail salting activity and the judgments on the legality of such activities under the National Labor Relations Act (NLRA; 29 U.S.C. § 151 et. seq.). These decisions have significant implications not only for unions as they attempt to maintain their viability but also for employers in ensuring that their management practices and actions do not run afoul of the NLRA.

Supreme Court Provides Protection to Salts Under the National Labor Relations Act

The Supreme Court first addressed salting in *NLRB v. Town and Country Electric, Inc.* (116 S. Ct. 459, 1995) where it found that paid union representatives who attempt to gain employment with a specific employer whose workers they are trying to organize cannot be discriminated against *solely* on the basis of their status as "salts." Even though a salt may have no intention of remaining with the employer subsequent to a successful organizing drive, the Court found that union salts are considered "employees" under the NLRA and hence, are entitled to the full range of rights expressly provided to employees under the statute. As a result, any failure to consider or hire otherwise qualified salts, as well as the decision to terminate a salt once the salt's intentions are made known or union organizing activities begin, solely based on salt status, is unlawful under the NLRA. While an employer has no per se obligation to hire a salt, no job applicant can be denied employment solely based on her or his status as a salt.

Town and Country constituted what was described as a "chess match" between employers and union organizers as each attempted to assert their rights under the NLRA (Mello 1998). A previous Supreme Court ruling, *Lechmere, Inc. v. NLRB* (112 S. Ct. 841, 1992), had strengthened management rights in resisting organizing activity by disallowing the practice of union organizers approaching employees on the employer's property; in this case, the employer-owned employee parking lot. Salting served as a union response to the restrictions placed on union organizer access to employees in *Lechmere* and the *Town and Country* decision validated the use of salting as a tactic to organize workers. While *Town and Country* was a significant victory for organized labor in prohibiting employers from refusing to hire an applicant or subsequently terminate an employee who is attempting to organize its workers, the decision didn't address the question of whether a salt can intentionally lie as part of her or his employment application process about his or her status as a salt and/or the intention to organize the workplace. More so, to the extent that *Town and Country* gave unions the upper hand in the "chess match," the decision certainly gave employers incentive to respond by monitoring more closely the specific activities of union organizing efforts.

Intentional Misrepresentation in the Employment Application Process

In 2002 the Seventh Circuit addressed the extent to which a salt may lie about organizing intentions in *Hartman Bros. Heating and Air Conditioning, Inc.* v. *NLRB* (280 F.3d 1110, 2002). Hartman Bros., an Indiana-based heating and air-conditioning contractor, hired Starnes, who had stated on his employment application that he had been laid off from his previous job which paid him $11 per hour. The truth was that Starnes had taken a formal leave of absence from his position so that he might work for a union to assist with its organizing efforts. As the position at Hartman for which Starnes had applied paid only $8.50 per hour, suspicions might have been aroused if Starnes stated that he was still employed at a job which paid $11 per hour. Immediately upon being hired, Starnes informed Hartman Bros. that he was a union salt who intended to organize the company. Hartman responded by telling Starnes to leave the workplace without formally terminating him.

The job for which Starnes had applied and been hired required driving. Consequently, as part of his application Starnes was required to provide information about his driving history and stated that he had received one speeding ticket. Hartman Bros. then informed him that its liability insurer would need to check his driving record and that Starnes would be ineligible for employment if, as a result of this investigation, the insurer refused to provide liability coverage for his driving. Four hours after Starnes had been ordered off the premises for declaring his salting intentions, the insurer contacted Hartman Bros. and disclosed that Starnes had received not one, but two speeding tickets and that he would be denied coverage. Starnes was immediately discharged as a result of this misrepresentation and his disqualification for insurance coverage.

Around the time Starnes applied for a position with Hartman, Till also applied for employment. Till, however, was accompanied by a known union organizer, who declared that he was a union organizer and wore a baseball cap with the union's logo. Hartman refused to hire Till.

The court found Hartman Bros. in violation of the NLRA in its refusal to hire Till as it found that this refusal was motivated solely by hostility toward unions. Hartman was ordered to cease and desist in its discriminatory practices against salts and other union supporters and to hire Till with backpay, in line with the Supreme Court ruling in *Town and Country*.

Starnes' case was more complicated than Till's. In justifying its decision to terminate Starnes, Hartman cited an Indiana law which prohibits any person from knowingly or intentionally making a false or misleading written statement in seeking employment. The court, however, found that if the state statute was being cited as a means for an employer to deny employment to an individual based on an applicant's lies about salt status, the statute would be pre-empted by the National Labor Relations Act. Any lie about salt status would be immaterial to the hiring decision nor to an applicant's qualifications for the job for which (s)he had applied and be based on a presumably erroneous employer assumption that the individual would not be a bona fide employee at any point in time. The court further found that criminalizing any applicant deception over salting intentions could only be a strong-arm means of discouraging salting, which would be further at odds with the Supreme Court's decision in *Town and Country*. The fact that Starnes lied about his being laid off by his previous employer would not be grounds for dismissal as it was done solely to hide his salting intentions and the NLRA would preempt the Indiana statute that prohibits individuals from making false or misleading statements as part of an employment application.

The Seventh Circuit did concur with the earlier NLRB ruling that the discharge of Starnes based on his driving record was legitimate as the action was done pursuant to a company policy that had been uniformly applied to all employees without animus toward an employee's participation with or attitudes toward unions. Hartman Bros. was, however, required to pay Starnes backpay, for the 4 h that had elapsed between his arrival at work and being sent home upon receipt of the insurance report. The court further ruled that the unfair labor practice committed by Hartman Bros. was not the discharge of Starnes but rather, sending him home and depriving him of the opportunity to begin organizing prior to the arrival of the insurance report.

Implications

Hartman Bros. dealt employers another post-Town *and Country* blow in finding that paid union organizers *can* lie on their job applications about their affiliation with unions as salts but *cannot* misrepresent facts about their credentials, skills or qualifications for employment. Lying about salt status is not material to a hiring decision because, under *Town and Country,* an employer cannot reject a job applicant solely on the basis of being a salt, union employee or union supporter. Any applicable state statutes which might make it illegal for applicants to lie or make misrepresentations on their employment applications are preempted by the National Labor Relations Act when any such lies or misrepresentations pertain to any union affiliation or activity.

The *Hartman Bros.* decision represented another victory for unions that further put employers on the defensive. Under *Hartman Bros.,* unions have less difficulty placing paid organizers in the employ of companies they are attempting to organize. To prevent unfair labor practice charges from being levied, employers need to be sure that any criteria used for screening and selection of employees is objective, valid, essential for job performance and not based, in any way, on

an applicant's actual or perceived salt status. Although no cases have been heard relative to "perceived" salt status, the Seventh Circuit's ruling in *Hartman Bros.* makes it likely that those applicants perceived to be salts would enjoy the same protection as actual salts. One weapon employers might have to counter salting in light of *Hartman Bros.* would be the implementation of a policy that prohibits any employee from simultaneously holding any full or part-time employment with another employer, particularly one within the same industry. Any such policy may or may not be upheld in a given jurisdiction based on local laws and general attitudes toward labor but its chances of success are more likely if enforced in a uniform manner toward all employees.

Employers Fight Back—Use of Preferential Hiring Criteria

The Seventh Circuit provided unions with a significant victory in *Hartman Bros* which affirmed their rights to use aggressive salting tactics as a means of organizing a workplace. As unions have gained the upper hand in their "chess match" with employers, employers have not been passive in fighting aggressive union organizing efforts. A post-Hartman Seventh Circuit ruling, *Operating Engineers Local 150* v. *NLRB* (325 F.3d 818, 7th Cir, 2003), provided employers with a significant victory in their efforts to fight union salting tactics.

Local 150 involved Brandt Construction Company, an Illinois highway contractor, which provides municipal road construction, bridge building, concrete and asphalt paving, sewer and water utility work and demolition work. Brandt had utilized a long-term preferential hiring policy whereby employment applications submitted by current or former employees and those filed by individuals referred by current employees received preferential consideration over applications received from non-referred walk-in applicants. Brandt also gave preferential consideration to applicants referred by equal employment opportunity service providers under a prior conciliation agreement entered into with the US Department of Labor which required Brandt to increase the numbers of women and minorities employed on each job pursuant to federal, state and local equal employment opportunity regulations. Brandt allowed any of these applicants who receive preferential treatment to apply for employment at any time without an appointment while walk-in applications were only accepted on Mondays and only when the company was hiring.

These hiring practices and policies were formalized and posted at the time Brandt entered into its agreement with the Department of Labor. The posting noted that applications would only be "considered current for a period of two weeks.... After fourteen days the employment application expires and any individual interested in employment must complete a new application, if they are being accepted. We do not accept applications when we are not hiring."

The posting further specified that Brandt showed preference for applicants in the following descending order; (1) current employees of the company; (2) past employees with proven safety, attendance and work records; (3) applicants recommended by supervisors; (4) applicants recommended by current non-supervisory employees; (5) unknown (walk-in) applicants.

Shortly after the conciliation agreement and Brandt's award of a large job, Local 150 sent some of its members to Brandt to apply for employment. The union members had been told by Local 150 to apply wearing union hats or other insignia and further instructed to indicate on their applications that they were salts and had been sent by the union for the express purpose of organizing Brandt. At the same time, Brandt received 32 referral applications as well as 20 additional non-union walk-in applications. Brandt hired a total of eight applicants, all of whom had been referred. For the remainder of that year, Brandt hired 29 additional applicants, 28 of whom were referrals, from a pool of 67 referrals. Consistent with posted policy, all new hires were offered employment within 14 days of their application.

In response to the hiring, Local 150 filed an unfair labor practice charge against Brandt with the National Labor Relations Board. The union alleged that Brandt had "changed, limited and made more onerous its hiring practices and procedures with the purpose of making it more difficult for applicants with pro-union sentiments to apply or obtain employment," in direct violation of Section 8(a)(1) of the National Labor Relations Act. Several months later Local 150 filed an additional unfair labor charge against Brandt, alleging that the company refused to hire union members despite the fact that all of new hires at Brandt at that point had been former employees, referrals from current employees or supervisors or referrals from equal employment opportunity service providers and the company had also not accepted any walk-in applications. Local 150 later filed a third unfair labor charge which alleged that Brandt "has in effect and continues to maintain and apply a hiring practice of giving preference in hiring to referred applicants regardless of their skill level over walk-in or unknown applicants" and that "such policy is designed to discriminate, interfere and prevent union-affiliated applicants from being considered for employment ... and is designed to deter the effects of union organization in violation of the Act."

The court found that while Brandt's policy clearly made it more difficult for union applicants and salts to gain employment, it did not violate the NLRA as the manner in which all applicants had been hired, by referral, excluded *all* walk-in applicants, regardless of whether or not these individuals were affiliated with a union. In issuing this decision in favor of the employer the court relied on two earlier NLRB rulings. The first was *Zurn/N.E.P.C.O.* (329 N.L.R.B. 484, 1999), which held that a hiring policy which gives preference to current and former employees, as well as referrals by

management, did not discriminate on the basis of union activities because "the policy does not on its face preclude or limit the possibilities for consideration of applicants with union preferences or backgrounds." The second, *Custom Topsoil, Inc.* (328 N.L.R.B. 446, 1999), held that an employer did not discriminate on the basis of union membership when it differentiated between "stranger" and "familiar" applicants as this differentiation did not involve a per se distinction between union and nonunion applicants.

In issuing its ruling favoring Brandt, the court relied on the fact that Brandt applied its preferential hiring policy in a nondiscriminatory manner with applications submitted by all walk-ins rejected under a long-standing and consistently applied policy, absent of any direct anti-union animus. The court also noted and commended Brandt for improving its employment of women and minority applicants pursuant to its conciliation agreement with the Department of Labor. The court found that the critical factor that prevented Local 150 members from being hired was the fact that they freely chose to apply as walk-ins, traditionally the applicants of last choice for Brandt under its publicized policy. Brandt gave union applicants exactly the same consideration as all other walk-in or unknown applicants and union members were in no way prevented from obtaining a referral from a preferential applicant source if they so chose.

The NLRB ruling in *Local 150* has found support in subsequent cases. The Board also ruled in favor of another employer who used preferential hiring criteria in *Ken Maddox Heating and Air Conditioning, Inc.* (340 N.L.R.B. No. 7, 2003). Maddox, an Indiana HVAC contractor, gave preference in hiring to applicants it had previously employed as well as to applicants referred by current employees and business associates, similar to Brandt. This long-standing policy was challenged when only one of 37 qualified overt union applicants was hired while 55 nonunion applicants were hired to fill 56 vacancies. The NLRB noted that because Maddox's policy had been in place for some time, this fact invalidated the allegation that the policy was specifically implemented to counter a salting campaign. The Board further found that the policy "was not inherently destructive of employee rights" or "sufficient, by itself, to establish animus." Citing *Brandt* as precedent the NLRB found that the general use of referral policies is a legitimate and justifiable employment practice. In *Maddox* the referral practice did not create a closed hiring system, which effectively screened out union applicants, nor was it applied in any kind of inconsistent or disparate manner.

Employers Find Additional Support for Their Use of Restricted Hiring Criteria

The victory for employers in *Local 150* was only the beginning as other employers have succeeded in their attempts to fight union organization and salting through the use of restricted, rather than preferential, hiring criteria. *Kanawha Stone*

Company, Inc. (334 N.L.R.B. No. 28, 2001) involved an employer whose hiring policy consisted of an assessment of specific hiring needs on a particular job, based on applications filled out on the employee's first day of work. The company did not maintain any applicant pool or hiring lists unless some kind of mass hiring was being conducted. All hiring was handled by superintendents at individual job sites rather than at the main office. Kanawha's hiring criteria restricted hiring to three groups of individuals; (1) employees on temporary lay off, (2) former employees and (3) referrals from existing employees. Applicants not falling into one of these categories were not considered for employment. This long-standing policy had been in effect since the company's inception. After a group of union members applied for employment at the main office, rather than at an individual job site, and who did not fit the above criteria were not hired, the union filed charges with the National Labor Relations Board.

Refusal to hire cases are considered under a burden-shifting scheme established by the Third Circuit in *NLRB v. FES (A Division of Thermo Power;* 301 F.3d 83, 3rd Cir., 2002). This case established the following criteria by which refusal-to-hire cases are analyzed:

> To establish a discriminatory refusal to hire, the General Counsel must ... first show: (1) that the respondent was hiring, or had concrete plans to hire, at the time of the alleged unlawful conduct; (2) that the applicants had experience or training relevant to the announced or generally known requirement of the position for hire, or in the alternative, that the employer has not adhered uniformly to such requirement, or that the requirements were themselves pretextual or were applied as a pretext for discrimination; and (3) that anti-union animus contributed to the decision not to hire the applicants. Once this is established, the burden will shirt to the respondent to show that it would not have hired the applicants even in the absence of their union activity or affiliation.

When the NLRB applied this criterion to *Kanawha,* it found that while union applicants were excluded from consideration for employment and some anti-union animus appeared to be present, Kanawha met its burden of proof by showing that it lawfully failed to consider the union applicants because they simply failed to meet any of its legitimate hiring criteria.

While *Kanawha* dealt with a flat-out refusal to hire, an employer in another case found a more specific means of excluding union members from consideration for employment. This criteria, refusal to hire based on wage incompatibility, was challenged in the NLRB ruling *Kelley Construction of Indiana, Inc* (333 N.L.R.B. No. 148, 2001). Kelley utilized the hiring criterion that new employees be accustomed to earning wages in line with those paid by Kelley. This policy ideally would allow Kelley to retain employees for as long as

possible and minimize disruptions and costs incurred through excessive turnover. When Kelley refused to hire 27 union applicants based on this criterion, the union filed charges with the NLRB. The NLRB had previously established a precedent for wage disparity as a legitimate means of selecting applicants in the absence of evidence of disparate application to union members in *Wireways, Inc* (309 N.L.R.B. 245 1992). In *Kelley,* the Board applied the *FES* burden-shifting criterion in concluding that Kelley's hiring decisions were made without regard to the prospective salts' union affiliation because the salts did not satisfy the neutral and legitimate hiring criteria of wage compatibility.

Subsequent to *Kelley,* however, the NLRB was presented with another salting case involving wage incompatibility criteria in which it ruled that wage disparity was not a legitimate justification for denial of employment. In *Contractors Labor Pool* (CLP; 335 N.L.R.B. No. 25, 2001) the employer enforced a "30% rule," which involved rejection of any applicant whose most recent wages differed by more than 30% from CLP's starting wages. When challenged by a union, CLP's 30% rule had been newly established and based on a study of worker retention which calculated the "break point" at which employees would be less likely to remain in the employ of CLP.

The NLRB found that while CLP had shown a legitimate business reason for adopting the policy that appeared not to be motivated by anti-union animus, the policy was "inherently destructive" of employees' NLRA rights to organize as the net effect of the policy was to "disqualify automatically virtually all applicants who had recently earned union contract wages" which "directly penalizes those who have exercised their protected right to work in an organized workforce and imposes a formidable threshold barrier to protected organizational activity in the unorganized workforces of CLP and its contractor clients." The Board considered this outcome analogous to the theory of disparate impact applied to anti-discrimination cases heard under Title VII of the Civil Rights Act of 1964. In disparate impact cases, all individuals are treated the same but the treatment results in different outcomes or consequences for different groups.

While the NLRB acknowledged that the 30% policy impacted both union and non-union applicants, this fact did not mitigate the "obvious and profound discriminatory effect" it had on those who rights were "expressly protected under the NLRA." This was based on the finding that the policy, regardless of its intent, excluded virtually *all* applicants with union history while only excluding *some* applicants with nonunion wage history. The outcome was that the only way to gain employment with CLP was through prior employment with another nonunion employer.

Despite the fact that the NLRB accepted the employer's legitimate business interest in employee retention as the basis for its wage compatibility policy, it held that a balancing act was necessary between the legitimate rights of CLP's business interests and those of employees under the NLRA. Because the 30% rule was "not essential to the successful operation of CLP's business," the "destructive direct, broad, severe and enduring impact of this rule on employee rights" had to receive priority in the balancing act.

The Board did note that it was not making a blanket ruling in *CLP* on the legitimacy of any other wage compatibility rules "that may have a lesser exclusionary effect or that may be more narrowly drawn and essential to an employer's business operation." While *Kelley* provided affirmation for employer wage disparity policies, *CLP* refined that ruling by articulating the need for wage disparity cases to be examined on a case-by-case basis relative to balancing employer needs with employee rights. The end result is that while employers may be able to justify wage disparity employment screening policies, they clearly need to be able to show that such policies have a non-disparate impact on union members and/or prospective salts.

The Latest Chapter—Genuine Interest in Employment

As the courts and NLRB have ruled on wage disparity policies and clarified the criteria under which they should be considered, another issue has arisen regarding salting and employer responses to salting activities. This issue concerns whether prospective salts need to show a genuine interest in actually working for the employer to which they've applied in order to received protection of their salting activities under the NLRA.

In *Phelps Dodge Corp. v. NLRB* (313 U.S. 177, 1941), one of the first Supreme Court cases under the NLRA, it was held that the statute made it an unfair labor practice by an employer to discriminate against applicants for employment in addition to actual employees. As noted, the Supreme Court ruled in *Town and Country Electric* that job applicants who are also salts are considered "employees" under the NLRA and entitled to protection afforded by the statute, particularly section 8(a)(3) which prohibits an employer from "discrimination in regard to hire or tenure of employment or any term or condition of employment to encourage or discourage membership in any labor organization." In other words, job applicants are de facto "employees" under the NLRA. Such protection has served as the foundation for salting activities by union organizers but a new NLRB ruling, *Toering Electric Company* (Toering Electric Company and Foster Electric, Inc., and Local Union No. 275, International Brotherhood of Electrical Workers, 351 NLRB No. 18, 2007), answered the question of whether an applicant needed to be genuinely interested in employment to qualify for protection under the NLRA.

In 1987 the President of the International Brotherhood of Electrical Workers (IBEW) announced an aggressive campaign to begin targeted nonunion employers for unionization via salting. Indeed in a videotaped speech produced and distributed at that time he encouraged local unions to unite with him in "driving the non-union element out of business." In tandem with this, the IBEW issued a Construction Organizing Membership Education Training (COMET) manual, which provided guidance for local unions on how to conduct effective salting campaigns. The COMET manual emphasized organizing strategies that would cause employers to scale back their businesses, be forced to leave the union's jurisdiction entirely or even completely go out of business. The driving force behind such economic outcomes would be the filing of unfair labor practices charges against employers at every opportunity. Such charges would impose immediate and usually substantial costs on employers as they attempted to defend themselves as well as disrupt the employer's workforce and operations via a series of continuous and ongoing unfair labor practice allegations.

In 1994 Toering Electric became a target of Local 275 of the IBEW's salting campaign. IBEW filed charges alleging that Toering refused to hire or even consider any union-affiliated individuals who applied for employment, in violation of section 8(a)(3) of the NLRA. In 1995 Toering agreed to settle the allegations by offering employment to six members of Local 275 but all six failed to show up for work. Prior to the settlement, Local 275 boasted in its newsletter that it succeeded in inflicting "a big hurt" on Toering's business.

In 1996 Local 275 again targeted Toering via a salting campaign. The head of Local 275 submitted 18 resumes to Toering. Of these resumes, five contained no work history dates, five were "stale," meaning that they were not current, outdated by as much as 6 years, and one was from one of the six individuals who had failed to show up for work when hired the previous year under the settlement agreement. Because the resumes were mostly stale or incomplete, Toering declined to hire any of the individuals whose resumes were submitted by Local 275. This action prompted another set of unfair labor practices charges to be filed by Local 275 against Toering. Toering Electric argued that the applicant salts should not be entitled to protection under the NLRA as they had no intention of ever working for Toering, as evidence by the fact that none of the applicants to whom employment offers had been made the previous year ever showed up for work. Instead, Toering argued that the only purpose of the charges was to induce economic harm on Toering and such behavior should not be protected under the NLRA.

In considering the merit of Local 275's allegations, the NLRB considered that under *Phelps Dodge,* protection against discrimination is not limited to individuals who are actually employed by the employer and extends to job applicants as well. This interpretation was further reinforced by the Supreme Court in *Town and Country Electric* in 1995 in which the Court considered whether salts could receive any protection under the NLRA. In this latter case, the Court stated that the term "employee" did not necessarily exclude paid union organizers but stopped short of saying that paid union organizers enjoyed blanket protection under the NLRA. The NLRB was asked to determine in *Toering* whether in order for a job applicant to receive protection under the NLRA that such applicant have a genuine interest in employment with the employer to whom he had applied.

The NLRB found that *Phelps Dodge* was distinguishable from *Toering* as the applicants in *Phelps Dodge* were clearly interested in employment with the employer. The NLRB held in *Toering* that in order for a job applicant to receive protection under the NLRA the applicant had to be "genuinely interested in seeking to establish an employment relationship with the employer." The NLRB found that the salt applicants at Toering had incurred no harm as the employment they were being denied was not something they actually sought and that the filing party, the union, had to prove an individual's genuine interest in actually seeking to establish an employment relationship with the employer as a prerequisite for filing a charge. The Board found that it had an obligation to "allay reasonable concerns that the Board's processes can be too easily used for the private, partisan purpose of inflicting substantial economic injury on targeted nonunion employers rather than for the public, statutory purpose of preventing unfair labor practices that disrupt the flow of commerce." In considering the request for backpay for the rejected applicants, the Board found that Section 10(c) of the Act did not provide for any kind of punitive damages and was limited to effecting "a restoration of the situation, as nearly as possible, to that which would have obtained but for the illegal discrimination." Hence, there was no basis for any action or award to the salt applicants, even if Toering had been found to have committed an unfair labor practice in violation of the NLRA. The board found that "submitting an application with no intention of seeking work but rather to generate meritless unfair labor practice charges is not protected activity" under the NLRA.

Perhaps what is most significant about *Toering* is the fact that the Board realized that the automatic presumption of an applicant's genuine interest in employment with an employer is a flawed assumption. Because it had not been previously necessary to prove this as the basis for filing a charge, unions could easily inflict "big hurts" on employers by engaging in such tactics used by Local 275. Employers would indeed incur significant costs and disruption of operations. More so, the resources of the NLRB ended up being diverted to cases and protracted litigation where there was no actual loss of the opportunity to work as applicants never intended to work for the employer in the first place. Hence, in *Toering*, the Board shifted the burden of the employer needing to prove that the applicant was indeed interested in employment back to the union and applicant in requiring that this evidence of "genuine interest" be submitted in justifying the unfair labor practice allegation. Hence, the Board felt the need to "abandon the implicit presumption that anyone who applied for a job is protected" under the NLRA. Most important for employers is that the employer's motivation for engaging in the behavior that constitute the alleged discrimination act does not become relevant until the burden of proof has been satisfied that the applicant does indeed have a genuine interest in employment.

Implications

The Supreme Court decision in *Town and Country Electric* represented the beginning of a new era in labor relations in the US (Mello 2004). At the time of the decision, unions were suffering from declining memberships and finding little success as they attempted to employ more creative and aggressive organizing strategies. In its *Town and Country* decision, the Supreme Court validated the right of labor organizers to salt the workplace, handing organized labor a significant victory. As salting has become a more prevalent union organizing strategy, employers have attempted to counter salting by attempting to force salts to disclose their union affiliations if the salts have not blatantly done so and are attempting to organize in a more discreet manner. The Seventh Circuit handed unions and labor organizers an additional major victory in *Hartman Bros.*, which will bolster union efforts to continue to test the extent of their NLRA support in the courts.

These pro-labor rulings have enticed employers to devise new strategies to prevent their workplaces from becoming unionized. Chief among these have been the use of preferential and restricted hiring criteria. Employers do not appear to be in violation of the NLRA when they employ preferential hiring policies as evidence in *Local 150*, where the Seventh Circuit affirmed an employer's right to do so, as long as the policies were consistently applied to both union and nonunion applicants. Restricted hiring criteria cases, heard under the FES burden-shifting scheme, are a bit ambiguous. Initially affirmed by the NLRB relative to the right of an employer to exclude non-refereed applicants from hiring consideration, those cases involving wage disparity are less clear-cut as the Board has stressed the need to consider them based on their individual facts and circumstances.

Even though employers have enjoyed some success with the use of restricted hiring criteria, such policies should be implemented with caution. While both the courts and NLRB have found that referral-only policies do not directly violate the National Labor Relations Act, such policies may violate anti-discrimination in employment provisions of the Civil Rights Act of 1964. To the extent that an employer has a homogeneous workforce, referrals may logically come from the same population, which could expose an employer to a possible discrimination charge if non-hired salts were not part of this population. Under the theory of disparate impact, all employees/applicants are treated equally but the treatment results in different outcomes for different classes of individuals.

This may be particularly true when an employer has a racially homogeneous workforce. In such case, a union might simply target employers whose workforces are entirely Caucasian by using an African–American, Hispanic–American or Asian–American salt. While the consequences of using such a strategy have not yet been tested in the courts, the civil rights of individual salts might easily trump employer rights and responsibilities under the NLRA and ultimately impede an employer's ability to use restricted hiring criteria and remain salt and union-free in the long run.

In *Toering,* the NLRB addressed the fact that union organizing campaigns in which prospective salts applied for employment had turned, in many instances, from those in which there was a genuine interest in organizing the employer's workforce, which is protected activity under the NLRA, to adversarial processes which were designed intentionally to inflict substantial harm on employers. The shifting of the burden of proof from employer to applicant under *Toering* greatly alters the landscape under which salting activities can and will be conducted in the future. Union organizers, on the other hand, will now be forced to consider salting as originally intended; a means of organizing the employer's workforce from the inside, an activity that is clearly within the protection of the National Labor Relations Act, rather than one that is used to coerce employers into responses that form the basis for unfair labor practices allegations. Ironically this "pro-employer" decision could greatly benefit unions. By realizing the limitations of the protection afforded to salting efforts to "gain entry" into an employer's workforce can allow unions to fine-tune their campaign organizing strategies.

It is also probably safe to say that the issues confronted by the NLRA in *Toering* have not been put to rest. The case was decided by a slim 3–2 margin and in a lengthy and scathing dissent the minority points out several problems with the majority's decision. First is the fact that Congress has expressly chosen not to amend the NLRA relative to the issue of genuine interest or intent of job applicants through a number of anti-salting bills which have been introduced since *Town and Country.* Second, and perhaps more notable, is concern over the difficulty of assessing "genuine interest," given the multitude of factors which enter into a job applicant's decision whether to accept or not to accept employment. Of course, the importance of such factors can vary from one applicant to another so certainly the issues addressed in *Toering* have not been fully resolved and give unions the opportunity to test the ambiguities inherent in the decision. While *Toering* constitutes a victory of sorts for employers there is no question that unions, many of whom are fighting for their livelihood, will be further resolved in their organizing efforts as a result of the decision. More so, the slim majority in this case could easily be overturned in the future by political appointees to the NLRB from another political party or even by those from the same party with different ideologies.

Organized labor in the US continues to find itself at a critical juncture. As jobs traditionally performed manually by union members have become automated, filled by undocumented/illegal workers, and/or moved overseas, unions have to be aggressive and creative in maintaining and expanding their membership bases if they are to survive. This will need to happen at the same time that many employers take actions to cut costs by eliminating positions held by union members and/or reducing benefit levels of unionized employees. The stakes are high for both sides with the parties continuing to see collective bargaining as a zero-sum game. Recent court decisions have provided both employers and unions added incentive to continue their adversarial behavior. As both sides test the limits of the NLRA, the courts and the NLRB will ultimately determine who wins not only individual battles but the ongoing war as ambiguous sections of the National Labor Relations Act are challenged interpreted. Ladies and gentlemen, the chess match is far from over.

Source: Employee Responsibilities and Rights Journal, 21, (1), 37–49 (2009). Reprinted by permission.

REFERENCES

Anonymous (2003). Special Report: Deja Vu?—Trade Unions. *The Economist* 367(8327). 77–80.

Bureau of Labor Statistics (2008). Report USDL 08-092 (issued 25 January, 2008). http://www.bls.gov.cps.

Curms, M. A., Hirsch, B. T., & MacPherson, D. A. (1990). Union membership and contract coverage in the United States, 1983–1988. *Industrial and Labor Relations Review*, 44(1), 5–33.

Gould, W. B. (2008). LERA and industrial relations in the United States. *Perspectives on Work*, 11(2), 6–9.

Logan, J. (2006). The union avoidance industry in the United States. *British Journal of Industrial Relations*, 44(4), 651–676.

Maher, K. (2005). Unions' new foe: Consultants. *The Wall Street Journal*, August 15, 2005, p. Bl.

Mello, J. A. (1998). Redefining the rights of union organizers and responsibilities of employers in union organizing drives. *Society for the Advancement of Management Advanced Management Journal*, 63(2), 4–9.

Mello, J. A. (2004). Salts, lies and videotape: Union organizing efforts, management responses and their consequences. *Labor Law Journal*, 55(1), 42–52.

Raudabaugh, J. (2008). National Labor Relations Board 2007 year in review: Fueling unions' demand for Euro-centric labor lab reform. *Labor Law Journal*, 59(1), 16–25.

READING 12.2

Social Media, Employee Privacy and Concerted Activity: Brave New World or Big Brother?

Jeffrey A. Mello

Introduction

Advances in technology which allow tremendous portability and affordability of personal computers, personal digital assistants and tablet devices combined with the proliferation of social media networking sites have changed the way in which we communicate, both privately and publically. Individuals are now afforded the means to communicate with friends, co-workers and even strangers via networks that until very recently were not available. While e-mail has existed for several decades, new social media, particularly Facebook and Twitter, have not only greatly altered how both individuals and organizations communicate, but also changed the ways in which business is conducted as well as how people interact with each other in many of their personal and professional dealings.

As of December 2011, Facebook had more than 800 million active users, half of whom log on to the site on a daily basis and half of whom access Facebook through their mobile devices.[1] Roughly 200 million of these members are in the United States, representing two-third of the population.[2] Facebook is currently available in more than 70 languages around the world[3] and is estimated to reach 30 percent of global internet users.[4] Twitter has approximately 300 million users,[5] although participation in both sites continues to expand in both numbers of members and volume of communications.

The use of social networking is not limited to personal communications. 46 percent of information technology professionals believe that online social networking is an important business tool and 31 percent of that number considered it to be essential to contemporary business. More than 25 percent of organizations with 500 or more employees have developed some sort of social networking presences as a business tool.[6] A recent poll conducted of human resource professionals by the Society for Human Resource Management found that 68 percent of organizations were using social media for external communications, recruiting and marketing to engage customers, potential customers and potential employees.[7] Employers see tremendous benefit from social networking which include facilitating collaboration among employees, improved efficiencies in operations, facilitation of orientation and learning, internal brand building, employee and organizational development and faster development of new products and services.[8] However, 85 percent of IT professionals acknowledge that they are aware of employees visiting social networking sites for personal usage while at work.[9] The use of online social media has contributed to the further blurring of the separation between employees' work and personal lives.

Traditional Employer Monitoring—E-mail and Internet Usage

A significant number of employers monitor the communications and online activities of their employees in the workplace.[10] In fact, 43 percent of employers were actively monitoring their employees' internet use in 2007, the most recent year in which a reliable widespread survey was administered.[11] Most large employers have electronic communications policies that alert employees that the employer reserves the right to conduct such monitoring. E-mail activity is also widely monitored.[12] Most of this monitoring is accomplished not manually but electronically via software programs which can track time, content, size, attachments and recipients.[13] This tracking can also be used on personal e-mail accounts (such as those from AOL, yahoo and Google) which are accessed from the employer's network.[14] 96 percent of employers who monitor their employee e-mails track incoming as well as outgoing messages.[15] It is, however, more difficult for employers to monitor text and e-mail messages sent from employees' personal personally-owned communication devices than from those provided by the employer.

There are many reasons why employers engage in monitoring the electronic communications of their employees.

The first is to protect the employer from a variety of legal liabilities which could come about as the result of the content of such communications. Reporting requirements imposed under the Sarbanes-Oxley require the retention and storage of all e-mails related to financial transactions.[16] In the event of any kind of employee misconduct, the employer can be held liable if the employer knew of the conduct and did nothing about it as well as if the employer was unaware of the conduct but was presumed that the employer "should have known" about the conduct.[17] Such an obligation on the part of employers requires a heightened level of sensitivity toward the activities of individual employees which might necessitate the monitoring of communications taking place at work, on employer-owned equipment and networks and within the context of an employee's job. Additional liability can be incurred through the sending and transmission of sexually explicit or provocative e-mails, with or without graphic images, and display of materials on pornographic websites which can serve as a basis for a sexual harassment lawsuit.[18]

Second, employers also might engage in employee monitoring to determine the extent to which employees are actually doing their jobs during work hours and not engaging in distracting personal business. In addition to paying employees for work which is not being performed during regular working house, excessive personal use of employer networks and servers can result in lost productivity and efficiency for a work unit, data storage problems and/or slower network operations.[19]

A third reason for employer monitoring rests with the fact that electronic media can be a means for disgruntled employees to transmit confidential files or provide access to secure parts of the employer's website or intranet.[20] Employers need to ensure that confidential documents, files, information and/or trade secrets are not disseminated to those outside of the organization who have no legitimate business interests in accessing such information.[21] The challenge here is that electronic transmission of proprietary information is quick and relatively easy but can also be "undone" if detected in a timely manner, justifying the need for vigilant monitoring.

How widespread are these alleged transgression activities? A recent American Management Association survey found that 14 percent of employees admitted to e-mailing confidential or proprietary information about their employer its people, products and services to outside parties; 14 percent admitted to sending third parties potentially embarrassing and confidential company e-mail that is intended strictly for internal readers; 89 percent of employees admitted to using the office system to send jokes, gossip, rumors or disparaging remarks to outsiders; and 9 percent admitted using company e-mail to transmit sexual, romantic or pornographic text or images.[22]

Despite the justifications for employer monitoring, there can be a significant downside to this activity. Employees can often view electronic monitoring by employers as an invasion of their privacy which serves to erode any trust relationship which exists between employees and employers. Eroded trust can have detrimental effects on employee morale, commitment, performance, retention and self-esteem.[23] Employees, however, can and do circumvent employer monitoring though the usage of personal e-mail accounts, rather than those of the employer, and/or use a variety of personal communications devices, such as their own laptop computers, cell phone, Blackberrys, i-Phones or other portable digital assistant devices to communicate during work hours for personal communications, web browsing, shopping, checking sports scores, pleasure reading or any other kind of personal activity. A typical supervisor may not have the time to monitor each subordinate to determine whether the device being used is owned by the employer or the employee. In addition, the portability of such devices can make them difficult to conceal and their similarity to the typical hardware provided makes personal usage difficult to determine.

28 percent of employers who monitor employee e-mail admit to having terminated one or more employees due to what was discovered as a result of monitoring.[24] In two-thirds of these cases the terminations were the result of inappropriate or offensive language, content or both. In other cases the dismissal was attributable to excessive personal use of the internet during working hours.[25]

Legality and Privacy

Generally speaking, employer monitoring of employee communications is not only legal but also practical, given the nature and reach of electronic communications. E-mail monitoring has not been found to be unlawful, regardless of whether or not employees had been informed of company policy,[26] mainly because the employer usually owns the hardware that is being used for communications as well the network access on which the e-mail has been sent and received. Employer internet monitoring is generally protected because employees cannot expect any reasonable expectation of privacy relative to websites they visit while they are at work and being paid by the employer for their services.[27] In short, there is no statutory right to privacy afforded to employees regarding their employment-related electronic communications.

To date, courts have consistently held that employees do not have any reasonable expectation of privacy regarding online communication, including internet usage and work e-mail systems.[28] The early precedent-setting case regarding e-mail monitoring, *Smyth v. Pillsbury*,[29] was heard in 1996. The court found that employees have no reasonable expectation of privacy because e-mail communications are voluntary and employer's interests in maintaining professionalism and preventing harassment in the workplace take precedent over any privacy expectations of employees. This reasoning was extended in another case, *McLaren v. Microsoft*,[30] where

Michael McLaren, a Microsoft employee, had labeled some folders as "personal" on his computer and created private passwords by which he accessed them. The court found that the employer's ownership of the computer and the network preempted any presumption or expectation of privacy on the part of the employee. The court further held that any alleged privacy claims were rendered moot when an e-mail was transmitted to another person, hence becoming public.[31]

The Next Wave of Monitoring—Social Networking Sites and Search Engines

Social networking, as noted above, is the latest significant trend in personal communications. However, a significant number of businesses have embraced social networking sites as a critical means of communication, public relations, promotion and marketing and branding. Social media is also being used to communicate with employees as well as with prospective employees about job opportunities and the employment relationship in general.

The combination of employer business use of social networking combined with its popularity among individuals who use it for personal reasons creates two strong simultaneous forces driving the proliferation of social networking. Use of social networking sites by employees is easy and inexpensive. Similarly, monitoring of employees' social network activities by employers is easy and inexpensive. No special technology or customized software program is needed for such monitoring. To conduct any kind of monitoring activity, an employer would only need to create a free account, even under a disguised identity, on a social networking site to gain access to the activities of any or all of its employees. Unless users of a social networking site restrict their personal account to "friends only," the accounts they create and their content are publically available. Some employees are aware of the possibility of employer monitoring as 29 percent of employees report having become both more private and conservative in their social networking endeavors for fear of employer discovery and retribution.[32] This is an especially risky issue for employees as an employer can shield their identity by using a pseudonym allowing them to learn about employee's off-work, personal life in a manner that the employee may not know who has actually gained access to the information the employee has posted.

Monitoring through the use of search engines is as equally quick, easy and inexpensive. Google or Yahoo searches, for example, can turn up information about employees which they employee may not have personally chosen to make public and/or information which was posted by others. Much of this information can be potentially embarrassing, such as information about legal proceedings.[33] However, it is probably much easier for an employer to find

discomforting information about an employee on a social networking site as the purpose of such sites is to share information which is personal and sites such as Facebook seem to encourage individual self-expression.

Employers face an ethical question relative to whether, as part of due diligence in the hiring process, they should scour online networks and sources to discover information about prospective hires. A 2011 survey of HR executives conducted by the Society for Human Resource Management found that 26 percent of organizations were using search engines and 18 percent were using social networking sites to *screen,* rather than recruit,[34] applicants for employment. Of this group, 15 percent were using information gathered via search engines to disqualify candidates and 30 percent had used information found on social networking sites to disqualify an applicant.[35] However, a more general survey found that 95 percent of employers admitted to using social media sites to discover additional information about job applicants.[36] A third survey found that 45 percent of employers research social media sites as part of the routine screening of job applicants.[37]

While the survey results vary, it is very clear that employers are utilizing search engines and social media to discover information about job applicants and, in some cases, use this information to screen out applicants. Arguments in favor of utilizing such practices would include the desire to ensure that the applicant provides the best "fit" with the company, particularly in light of how expensive recruiting activities can be. Many employers condone, if not encourage, hiring managers and human resources personnel to conduct such due diligence, feeling that the practice is certainly not unlawful and, given potential costs and risks associated with hiring the wrong candidate, an ethical if not necessary practice. Privacy advocates would argue that visiting the Facebook profile of a job applicant as part of the employer's screening of potential employees is both unnecessary and an invasion of privacy.

Once a job applicant becomes an employee, the appropriateness of such searches becomes even more ambiguous. While the same information obtained via social networking and search engine monitoring may be available post–hire as well as pre–hire, one could question the motivation of an employer's searches into existing employees' private personal lives outside of work. Once the practice became public within the workplace, such post-hire searches might greatly affect employee morale and trust[38] as in most cases an employer might monitor an employee's social networking activities and posts as a means of collective evidence to use against an employee for disciplinary purposes rather than simply wanting to get to know the employee better.

A number of recent situations have illustrated the consequences for employees of employer monitoring of employee activity online. After thirteen members of the Virgin Atlantic Airlines cabin crew expressed their impressions of employer, its planes and passengers as part of a Facebook group Virgin terminated them.[39] The airline could not find any "justification for using [Facebook] as a sounding board for staff of any company to criticize the very passengers who ultimately pay their salaries." When Boston-based Anglo Irish Bank employee Kevin Colvin told his supervisor he had to miss work due to a family emergency in New York, his supervisor checked his Facebook page the following day and discovered that Colvin had posted Halloween party pictures from the previous night with Colvin dressed as a green fairy holding a wand and can of beer. Colvin was fired for lying after his supervisor forwarded the photo to everyone in the office.[40]

Mario County FL Sherriff's office fired deputy Brian Quinn after Quinn posted a picture of himself on his MySpace page in full uniform with comments about women's breasts, binge drinking and nude swimming for "conduct unbecoming of an officer."[41] Dan Leone, a Philadelphia Eagles parking lot attendant, was terminated after six years of service when he posted derogatory comments on his Facebook page which criticized the Eagles for their failure to resign a player.[42] In yet another case, a server at Brixx Pizza in North Carolina berated a couple who left her a small tip on her Facebook page, mentioning her employer (Brixx) by name, and was fired as a result. In defending its action, Brixx claimed a violation of company policy against disparaging customers and criticizing the restaurant.[43]

These incidents illustrate the fact that issues related to work and employment which were previously "vented" among co-workers at the water cooler, in the cafeteria or in the rest room and now being vented publically online for a much wider audience. A disgruntled employee doesn't have to wait to get back to the office to express her or his feelings. Online networks provide an immediate opportunity to deal with issues and express feelings. While such public venting allows for spontaneity of expression, posts also cannot often be retracted and may continue to exist and be accessed long after the employee has "calmed down" or even had a change or heart about any specific incident. More so social network monitoring of existing employees can allow employers to monitor activities and discover personal information which may or may not be work-related. The ethical issue for employers is that much of which may be discovered online is not related to job performance and how is such information to be used once it is discovered.

Where We Stand

As the above discussion illustrates, the American legal system has not kept up with the technological advances which have greatly altered how we communicate. The creation of new communication media which were previously unavailable and the availability of the means to monitor the usage and content by which people communicate raise the issue of the appropriateness of employer monitoring.

The only existing law which impacts communications, the Electronic Communications Privacy Act (ECPA),[44] was enacted in the 1980s in response to the kinds of electronic communications which were being utilized at that time. Title I of the EPCA[45] addresses electronic communications solely from the perspective of the interception of wire and aural messages. Despite the fact that e-mail was in its earliest stages of development at the time the EPCA was passed and social networking as we know it was non-existent, federal court decisions have applied the terms and conditions of the EPCA to e-mail. However, Title I provides for the express exemptions from the statue communications related to the normal course of business as well as those conducted on proprietary communication networks and systems. Consequently, employers have prevailed in every case in which employees have objected to monitoring as a violation of their privacy rights.[46]

Hence, employees currently enjoy no specific privacy rights in their communications and very limited protection against employer monitoring (unless such monitoring was targeted at a specific employee who alleges the monitoring was based on protected class status) and the possible consequences employers take in response to what they discover as part of any monitoring. Courts have also not overturned firings which have been based solely on derogatory postings on social networking sites. Employers have generally not been liable for adverse employment actions resulting from employee postings on social media sites unless the employer gained access to the information in violation of the website's agreed terms of usage or without consent.[47] However, because social networking is still a relatively new phenomenon in personal, mass public communication, it is understandable that no specific laws have yet been developed regarding employee and employer rights and responsibilities.

National Labor Relations Act and Concerted Activity

Prior to the advent of social networking, the first case which tested the extent to which electronic communication by employees was protected under any federal law involved an online bulletin board system. In *Konop v. Hawaiian Airlines*,[48] the Ninth Circuit Court of Appeals held that an online bulletin board, established and maintained by a company pilot, used to discuss and criticize the employer's relationship with the employee union was protected concerted activity under the Railway Labor Act (RLA). Because the *Konop* court relied upon National Labor Relations Act (NLRA) in reaching its decision, which is typical in RLA cases, the *Konop* holding was considered precedent for interpretation of the NLRA relative to this issue.[49]

Given the advent of social networking and online employer monitoring of employees, the question has been raised as to whether the NLRA might provide employees some kind of protection against employer actions taken in regard to employee postings online. At this juncture, several complaints have been filed with the National Labor Relations Board (NLRB).

The first complaint was filed with the NLRB in November 2010. Danwmarie Souza, a union member/employee of the American Medical Response of Connecticut (AMR) ambulance service, posted negative comments about her supervisor on her Facebook page from her home computer after a work request she submitted had been denied. When some of her co-workers posted supportive comments in direct response to her post, Souza posted further negative comments and was subsequently fi red for alleged violation of the AMR's internet policy which prohibits employees from posting anything about AMR without express permission. While the employer stated that Souza was fi red due to "multiple, serious complaints about her behavior," the NLRB reasoned that because Souza was communicating with her co-workers about her supervisor, even though it was in a public forum which could be accessed by others, she was engaging in concerted activity rather than being disloyalty to her employer. Concerted activity is protected under Section 7 of the NLRA, which prohibits employers from interfering with employees' efforts to work together to improve the terms and condition of their workplace and their employment. There was no court ruling in the case as the parties settled in February 2011. As part of the settlement AMR agreed to revise its company policies regarding employees' rights to communicate with each other about work-related matters.[50]

However, in April 2011, the NLRB did not fi nd unlawful another employer's decision to fi re an employee because of inappropriate post to his Twitter account. When the Arizona Daily Star newspaper discovered tweets from one of its reporters which made sarcastic and derogatory comments about copy editors the employee was told by the managing editor that he was prohibited from airing grievances or commenting publically about the Daily Star. Subsequent to this incident the reporter posted additional sarcastic tweets which criticized both the Tucson police and the reporting of a local television station. When the reporter was terminated he fi led a complaint with the NLRB who held that the reporter's behavior was neither protected nor concerted activity under the NLRA because it did not related to terms and conditions of employment nor did it seek to involve other employers on matters related to employment. While the associate general counsel of the NLRB recommended that the charge be dismissed, he did note that the employer had made statements which could be interpreted as impeding employees' Section 7 rights, specifi -cally noting that the

managing editor had told the employee that he was not allowed to tweet about anything related to work.[51]

In the AMR example, it is noteworthy that Souza was part of a unionized workplace. Employers need to remain cognizant, however, of the fact that nonunionized employees enjoy the same rights under the NLRA as those who already belong to unions, including the right to communicate with coworkers about working conditions in a concerted manner. In May 2011, the NLRB announced that it was suing Hispanics United of Buffalo, a nonprofi t agency which provides various social services to low-income clients. After an employee of Hispanics United alleged that the organization's employees did not do enough to assist its clients, fi ve co-workers responded to this statement, through Facebook postings, by criticizing their workloads and working conditions. Hispanics United terminated the Facebook-posting employees on the grounds of harassment of their co-worker who made the initial statement. The NLRB argued that the Facebook postings constitute protected concerted activity under Section 7 because they pertain to terms and condition of employment. In September 2011 an NLRB administrative law judge ruled against the employer, accepting the MLRB argument, and ordered that the fi ve employees be reinstated with back pay.[52]

Section 7 of the NLRA provides all covered employees the right to engage in "concerted activities for the purpose of collective bargaining or other mutual aid or protection." It is critical however, that in order to receive protection that the employee's actions or communications not be simply on her or his own behalf nor should the employee disparage the employer, display blatant insubordination or distribute or publicize confi dential information to which the employee is privy.[53] Section 7 protection would not be afforded in such instances.

Regardless of whether a workplace is unionized or non-union, any employer policy which attempts to impede employees' abilities and rights to communicate outside of the workplace regarding wages, hours, supervision or working conditions would be subject to a Section 7 challenge. Such protected concerted activity could include online discussion boards, as noted in the *Konop* case, or even the case of a single employee who discusses issues related to supervision. Although there has been little commentary about how social media could be used as a means of organizing workplaces, the NLRB interpretation issued in AMR could easily be seen by union organizers as a new means to communicate with workers who are being recruited by the union for representation. Both pro-union employees and organizers themselves are afforded opportunities to communicate with workers via social media and networks that were previously unavailable, more cumbersome and/or more costly. Social networking has changed the way in which we communicate and this is particularly so for employees who wish to express themselves about working terms and conditions which apply to others. Given the above discussion it seems inevitable that social media will be embraced by labor unions as a means and strategy for not only communicating with existing union members but, perhaps more important, a means to communicate with employees of companies which are being targeted for organization.

Summary

Social networking is here to stay as not only have individuals embraced it as a vital means of communication, organizations have similarly embraced it as a vital 21st century means of marketing and promotion and conducting business. The question remains as to whether employees are entitled to a reasonable amount of privacy in their personal, public communications on social networking sites. At this juncture, unless such postings can be considered concerted activity, employers are free to take action against employees based on postings which do not sit well with the employer. However, the NLRB is apparently readily to vigorously investigate any allegations of alleged suppression of or intimidation related to concerted activity but even then there is some presumption of a duty of loyalty to the employer and limitations as to how far an employee can go.

While numerous states have passed laws which restrict employer actions which are the result of an employee's legal off-duty conduct, there is no body of law which addresses the issue of employer monitoring of and resultant discovery of information posted on social networking sites. Employers can be fair-minded in developing policies which balance business needs and any reasonable perceived privacy expectations employees could have but in the interim, until such case law is developed, the only protection employees potentially have against employer actions based on discovery of social networking posts is the defense of protected concerted activity under the NLRA. However, while the NLRB has been quick to file suit in such cases, no court has yet to rule on this interpretation. In the meantime, employees need to use discretion and judgment with their posts, realizing the perpetuity issue associated with hitting the "send" or "enter" button on the keyboard.

Source: © *2012 by Jeffrey A. Mello*

ENDNOTES

1. Wikipedia, http://en.wikipedia.org/wiki/Facebook, retrieved 6 January 2012.

2. New York Times, http://topics.nytimes.com/top/news/business/companies/facebook_inc/index.html, retrieved 6 January 2012.

3. Wikipedia, *supra* note 1.

4. Jeremiah Owyang, *A Collection of Social Networks Stats for 2010*, http://www.web-strategist.com/blog/2010/01/19/a-collection-of-social-network-stats-for-2010/, retrieved 6 January 2012.

5. Wikipedia, http://en.wikipedia.org/wiki/Twitter, retrieved 6 January 2012.

6. Lauren Leader-Chivee and Ellen Cowan, *Networking the way to success: online social networks for workplace and competitive advantage*, http://findarticles.com/p/articles/mi_6768/is_4_31/ai_n31909656/, retrieved 6 January 2012.

7. Society for Human Resource Management, *SHRM Survey Findings: The Use of Social Networking Websites and Online Search Engines in Screening Job Candidates*, 25 August, 2011.

8. Leader-Chivee, *supra* note 6.

9. Sarah Perez, *A Growing Acceptance of Social Networking in the Workplace*, http://www.readwriteweb.com/enterprise/2009/07/a-growing-acceptance-of-social-networking-in-the-w.php, retrieved 6 January 2012.

10. See Am. Mgmt. Ass'n & The ePolicy Inst., *2007 Electronic Monitoring & Surveillance Survey 4* (2008), *available at* http://www.plattgroupllc.com/jun08/2007ElectronicMonitoringSurveillanceSurvey.pdf (surveying employer monitoring practices in various areas such as the Internet, e-mail, computer usage, etc.)

11. *Id.* at 1.

12. *Id.* at 5 (stating that twenty-six percent of employers monitor all employees' e-mail accounts and seventeen percent of employers only monitor the e-mail accounts of employees in selected job categories).

13. *Id.* (reporting that seventy-three percent of all employers that monitor employee e-mails do so via software monitoring programs).

14. *Online Spying: Remote Computer Spyware Software*, Online-Spying.com, http://www.online-spying.com/webmail-spy.html (last visited Oct. 7, 2010). See *also* Rachel Konrad & Sam Ames, *Web-Based E-mail Services Offer Employees Little Privacy*, cnet News (Oct. 3, 2000), http://news. cnet.com/2100-1017-246543. html (stating that, "unfortunately, security experts say many employees would be surprised to know that Web-based email services also offer little privacy. Messages sent via a Yahoo or Hotmail account ... are just as accessible [as employer-created e-mail accounts] to nosy employers.").

15. Am. Mgmt. Ass'n & The ePolicy Inst., *supra* note 10, at 1.

16. Carolyn Holton, *Identifying disgruntled employee systems fraud risk through text mining: A simple solution for a multi-billion dollar problem*, 4 Decision Support Systems, 46, 853–864 (2009).

17. Christopher Pearson Fazekas, *1984 Is Still Fiction: Electronic Monitoring In the Workplace and U.S. Privacy Law*, 15 Duke L. & Tech. Rev. 1-16 (2004).

18. See, *e.g.*, Blakey v. Cont'l Airlines Inc., 751 A.2d 538, 543–44 (N.J. 2000) (discussing the facts of a sexual harassment case filed by a female airline pilot claiming, among other things, that her coworkers posted sexually explicit comments about her on Continental Airlines' online bulletin board).

19. See, *e.g.*, Lisa Scott & Ross Tate, *Monitoring Internet Usage—Spring 2010*, Ass'n of Local Gov't Auditors (2010), http://www.governmentauditors.org/index.php?option=com_content&view=ar ticle&catid=47:accounts&id=594:monitoring-internet-usage-spring-2010&ltemid=123 (reiterating that employee Internet use for personal reasons can cause "[b]andwidth and storage shortages [sic] [particularly] from peer to-peer [sic] file sharing and audio/video streaming."); and William P. Smith and Filiz Tabak, *Monitoring Employee E-mails: Is There Any Room for Privacy?* 23 Academy of Management Perspectives, (4), 33–48 (2009).

20. See, *e.g.*, Jared A. Favole, *Ex-Bristol-Myers Employee Charged with Stealing Trade Secrets*, Barclays Latitude Club (Feb. 3, 2010), http://www.barclays.com/latitudeclub/er_gr_global_news_article.html?ID_NEWS=133949142 (discussing accusations against a Bristol Myers' technical operations associate for allegedly stealing company trade secrets in order to form a competing company in India); Elinor Mills, *Microsoft Suit Alleges Ex-Worker Stole Trade Secrets*, cnet News (Jan. 3, 2009), http://news.cnet.com/8301-10805_3-10153616-75. html (stating that an ex-employee "allegedly downloaded confidential documents onto his company-issued laptop ... and then allegedly used a file-wiping program and a 'defrag' utility designed to overwrite deleted files in order to hide the tracks.").

21. Smith and Tabak, *supra* note 19, at 34.

22. Laura P. Petrecca, *More employers use tech to track workers*, USA Today, 17 March, 2010.

23. See, *e.g.*, Mia Shopis, *Employee Monitoring: Is Big Brother a Bad Idea?*, SearchSecurity.com (Dec. 9, 2003), http://searchsecurity.techtarget.com/news/interview/0,289202,sid14_gci940369,00. html (quoting an expert in electronic monitoring who stated that "[e]mployee monitoring is a bad idea ... when it's used for Big Brother and micromanagement purposes. Organizations would be better off not doing it if they're going to scrutinize their employees' every move. If it creates a morale problem (and it will if it's not handled properly) all of its value is diminished."). More generally, employee monitoring can have the following negative effects: 1. An employee may suffer loss of self-esteem if she interprets the monitoring to indicate a lack of trust in her.; also, Smith and Tabak, *supra* note 19, at 43.

24. Am. Mgmt. Ass'n & The ePolicy Inst., *supra* note 10, at 1.

25. *Id.* at 8–9.

26. Encouragingly, seventy-one percent of employers monitoring employee e-mail notify such employees prior to any monitoring. *See id.* at 5 (stating that eleven percent of employers do not notify employees while another eighteen percent do not know whether e-mail monitoring took place).

27. See, *e.g., Doe*, 887 A.2d at 1167 (upholding an employer's Internet monitoring policy, questioning whether, "with actual or imputed knowledge that Employee was viewing child pornography on his computer, was defendant under a duty to act, either by terminating Employee or reporting his activities to law enforcement authorities, or both?" and concluding that such a duty exists).

28. Tanya E. Milligan, *Virtual Performance: Employment Issues in the Electronic Age*, 38 Colorado Lawyer (2), 29–36 (2009).

29. 914 F. Supp. 97, 100 (ED Pa. 1996).

30. 1999 WL 339015, 1999 Tex. App. LEXIS 4103 (Tex. App.-Dallas May 28, 1999).

31. Michael Rustad and Sandra R. Paulsson, *Monitoring Employee E-Mail And Internet Usage: Avoiding The Omniscient Electronic Sweatshops: Insights From Europe*, 7 University of Pennsylvania Journal of Labor & Employment Law, 829–904 (2005).

32. See, *e.g.*, Deloitte, *Social Networking and Reputational Risk in the Workplace 4* (2009), *available* at http://www.deloitte.com/assets/Dcom-UnitedStates/Local%20Assets/Documents/us_2009_ethics_workplace_survey_220509.pdf., at 12.

33. See, *e.g.*, Corey A. Ciocchetti, *The Eavesdropping Employer: A Twenty-First Century Framework for*

Employee Monitoring, 48 American Business Law Journal, (2), 285–369 (2011).

34. A different survey, also conducted by the Society for Human Resource Management in 2011, found that 56% of organizations use social media sites to *recruit* applicants, with 95% using Linkedin, 58% using Facebook and 42% using Twitter. This 56 % represented an increase from 34% just three years earlier in 2008. SHRM Research Spotlight: Social Networking Website and Staffing, http://www.shrm.org/Research/Survey Findings/Documents/Social%20Networking%20 Flyer_FINAL.pdf, retrieved 6 January 2012.

35. Society for Human Resource Management, *supra* note 7.

36. Alexis Madrigal, *What You Shouldn't Post on Your Facebook Page If You Want A Job*, http://www. theatlantic.com/technology/archive/2011/10/what-you-shouldnt-post-on-your-facebook-page-if-you-want-a-job/246093/, retrieved 6 January 2012.

37. Damian R. LaPlaca and Noah Winkeller, *Legal Implications of the Use of Social Media: Minimizing* the *Legal Risks for Employers and Employees*, 5 J. Bus. Tech L. Proxy 1 (2010), http://www.law.umaryland. edu/academics/journals/jbtl/proxy/5/5_001_LaPlaca. pdf, at 8.

38. Ciocchetti, *supra* note 33.

39. John Browning, *Employers Face Pros, Cons with Monitoring Social Networking*, Houston Bus. J. (Feb. 27, 2009), http://www.bizjournals.com/houston/stories/ 2009/03/02/smallb3.html.

40. *Id.*

41. *Id.*

42. Kabrina Krebel Chang, *Facebook Got Me Fired*, Builders and Leaders, http://www.bu.edu/builders-leaders/2011/05/18/facebook-got-me-fired/34-35, retrieved 6 January 2012.

43. *Id.*

44. Pub. L. 99-508,Oct. 21, 1986, 100 Stat. 1848, 18 U.S.C. §2510-2522.

45. Stored Communications Act, 18 U.S.C. §§ 2701-12

46. Smith and Tabak, *supra* note 19, at 38.

47. LaPlaca and Winkeller, *supra* note 36, at 7.

48. 236 F.3d 1035 (9th Cir.2001).

49. Scott Grubman, *Think Twice Before You Type: Blogging Your Way to Unemployment*, 42 Georgia Law Review 615 (2008); Carson Strege-Flora, *Wait! Don't fire that blogger! What Limits Does Labor Law Impose on Employer Regulation of Employee Blogs?*, 2 Shidler J. L. Com. & Tech. 11 (Dec. 16, 2005), *at* <http://www. lctjournal.washington.edu/Vol2/a011Strege.html>

50. Chang, *supra* note 41, at 35.; Maria Greco Danaher, *NLRB Settles Complaint Based on Facebook Posts as 'Concerted Activity'*, http://www.shrm.org/LegalIssues/ FederalResources/Pages/NLRBSettlesComplaintFace book.aspx, 9 February 2011, retrieved 6 January 2012.

51. Allen Smith, *NLRB: Discharge of Employee for Inappropriate Tweets Was Lawful*, http://www.shrm.org/ LegalIssues/FederalResources/Pages/NLRBInappro priateTweets.aspx, 13 May 2011, retrieved 6 January 2012.

52. Maria Z. Stearns, *NLRB Actively Engaged in Examining Employee Social Media Use*, http://www.rutan.com/ files/Publication/46b9dcfa-2034-4c1f-a7ce-5907c824 a6de/Presentation/PublicationAttachment/e806e8b8- 2e0d-48ae-9ed3-5f095a222d18/Society%20for%20 Human%20Resource%20Management.pdf, 16 September 2011, retrieved 6 January 2012

53. Nancy King, *Labor Law for Managers of Non-Union Employees in Traditional and Cyber Workplaces*, 40 American Business Law Journal, (4), 827–883 (2003); Robert Sprague, *Fired for Blogging: Are There Legal Protections for Employees Who Blog?*, 9 U. Pa. J. Lab. & Emp. L. 355 (2007).

CHAPTER 13

Employee Separation and Retention Management

Retention Management at Kraft Foods

Information technology (IT) is one of the most difficult areas for organizations to staff. The short supply of trained, experienced workers coupled with the increasingly strong demand has presented almost limitless career opportunities for IT professionals. Most large organizations experience annual turnover in the 20 percent range. Kraft Foods, however, has developed a retention program that has resulted in the reduction of the turnover rate of its nearly 1,000 full-time IT professionals to a staggering 5 percent.

The program involved Kraft's chief information officer (CIO) partnering with human resource (HR) to help HR understand the unique challenges being faced by IT. Kraft's retention program involves more than just the standard attractive stock options; it involves a holistic and integrated set of HR programs. Many of Kraft's IT professionals have come directly from its college internship program. Interns are given early responsibility for learning different technologies and are held accountable for rigorous performance outcomes early on. Seventy percent of IT interns who are offered permanent jobs accept.

Once hired on a permanent basis, employees are expected to engage in an objectives-based management system. Managers are specially trained to provide ongoing feedback and conduct developmental performance feedback sessions. Employees are allowed to pursue one of two career tracks within IT: technical or managerial. To assist with development, an intranet site provides learning tutorials, links to job postings, formal training courses, and both division and functional area Web sites that discuss competencies required in these areas. Consequently, employees are allowed to develop a plan for career development within Kraft. IT employees are further encouraged to devote 10 working days per year exclusively to career development pursuits. In addition to in-house development opportunities, a tuition reimbursement plan is offered for outside programs of study.

Employees also become part of the IT Leadership Program, where junior employees are paired with an executive mentor. The one-year program involves about 30 days of joint work activities and provides additional exposure to leadership and technology issues.

Probably most importantly, IT employees at Kraft note that the top reason they stay is the sense of family they find at work. Ideas are solicited and accepted from every level in the organization, and inclusion is a strong company value. Kraft also understands the needs of its younger workers who populate the IT division. It offers flexible hours, telecommuting and part-time work options, a casual dress code, and a new campus that includes a company store and an onsite health club.[1]

Organizations can expect continuing pressure to change and adapt. Societal changes affecting lifestyles, technology, and the economy create threats and opportunities for nearly all organizations. The organization of yesterday that was able to serve the same customers in the same markets, use the same production technology, and operate in a relatively stable domestic economic landscape no longer exists. Profitable markets invite entry of new competitors; technological changes in production impact efficiency; lifestyle changes alter preferences for certain types of products and services; and economic decisions must be made within a global context.

Contemporary organizations that wish to remain competitive need to be flexible and responsive to their environments. These organizations must develop ways to deal with increasing skill obsolescence among their employees and the labor market in general; they must also consider alternative forms of organization structure due to downsizing operations, selling off subsidiaries, and merger and acquisition options. From an HR perspective, this often involves employee training and development. In an increasing number of scenarios, however, the organization must strategically analyze its workforce and objectives and make decisions to sever relationships with employees. Similarly, employees today spend less time with individual employers than workers did in the past and make a greater number of career changes during their working years. Personal lifestyle decisions, opportunities with other organizations, and entrepreneurial motivations are causing many employees to leave their organizations.

The pressure to remain competitive and efficient—coupled with the fact that employees are less committed to individual employers than in the past—makes the process of employee separation a key strategic issue for organizations. An effective HR strategy involves managing the process by which employees leave the organization, regardless of whether such departure is by the employer's or employee's choice. Organizations can manage this separation process to ensure that transitions are smooth for both employers and employees, that operations are not disrupted, and that important professional relationships are not damaged. The three major ways that employees leave the organization are through reductions in force (initiated by the employer), turnover (initiated by either the employer or employee), or retirement. Organizations should have strategies for managing each form of separation.

Reductions in Force

Reductions in force or employee layoffs are attempts by employers to reconfigure their workforces. Reductions in force are becoming increasingly common in nearly all industries and are often caused by organizational restructuring following merger or acquisition activity. A reduction in force is sometimes used to make an organization more competitive by reducing costs.

Organizations reduce the size of their workforces for three main reasons: inefficiency, lack of adaptability in the marketplace, and a weakened competitive position within the industry. In all regards, efficiency is a major driving force: In many organizations, labor or payroll is one of the largest expenses. This is particularly true in service organizations, which are making up an increasingly significant portion of our economy and gross national product (GNP). Efficiency is sought by attempting to reduce labor costs and accomplishing more work with fewer individuals by redesigning work processes. Interestingly, an organization's stock price often skyrockets when layoffs are announced. Such decisions create expectations among investors of improved short-term financial performance.

One federal law regulates employer actions taken as part of reductions in force. The Worker Adjustment Retraining and Notification Act (WARN) went into effect in 1989 and requires employers with 100 or more employees to provide affected employees with a minimum of 60 days' written notice of any facility closings or large-scale layoffs of 50 or more employees. WARN does not apply to federal, state, or local government agencies. Employers found to be in violation of the law can be required to provide back pay, expenses, and benefits to all workers dismissed without appropriate notice in addition to fines.

Employers who conduct layoffs often provide affected employees with 60 days' notice and immediately relieve them of their job duties. The employees remain on the payroll for two months but are able to use the two-month period to adjust, seek new employment, and transition out of the organization. This not only assists the employee in his or her transition and job search, but it also helps to ensure that laid-off employees will be less likely to file for unemployment compensation insurance. State unemployment compensation insurance programs are funded by employers, with the percentage rate determined by the use of the funds by the employers' former employees. An employer who lays off a large number of employees who file for and collect unemployment compensation will have to reimburse the compensation insurance program proportionately.

To facilitate the transition (and ensure that their unemployment insurance payments remain lower), many organizations implement outplacement programs for laid-off employees. Outplacement services, which may be conducted in-house or contracted to an external vendor, not only help laid-off employees land on their feet but also serve as a public relations tool: These services help to retain the support and goodwill of remaining employees by making them feel that the organization will look out for them if future reductions are necessary. In addition to helping maintain the morale and motivation of remaining employees, outplacement programs reduce the risk of litigation by disgruntled former employees.

Realizing that in certain circumstances it might be unrealistic, impossible, or unfair to require employers to provide such written notification, Congress allowed several exceptions to WARN. These exceptions are for (1) a "faltering company" that is actively seeking capital to retain its scope of operations and reasonably believes that giving employees a warning will jeopardize the financing; (2) an "unforeseeable circumstance," such as a strike at a supplier's business; (3) a natural disaster, such as a fire, flood, earthquake, or hurricane; and (4) any operation set up as a "temporary facility," where employees who were hired were informed that the facility and employment were nonpermanent.

Layoffs can sometimes be avoided through proper planning. The main benefit of strategic HR planning is to ensure that supply and demand of employees are equated while avoiding the costs associated with severe overstaffing and understaffing. Effective HR planning in most instances can reduce or eliminate the need for any kind of large-scale reductions in force or layoffs. Regardless of the size of the surplus, employers must identify the real reason for the excess number to determine an appropriate response. This strategic perspective determines whether the surplus is expected to be temporary or permanent to assist in developing a plan of action with a corresponding time frame. For example, longer range surpluses can often be managed without the need for layoffs by utilizing hiring freezes, not replacing departing employees, offering early retirement incentives, and through cross-training of certain employees to allow them to develop skills that the organization anticipates needing. Short-run surpluses can be managed through loaning or subcontracting employees, offering voluntary leaves, implementing across-the-board salary reductions, or redeploying workers to other functions, sites, or units.

Two more policy-oriented solutions to remedy overstaffing might involve (1) tying a greater portion of compensation to division or organization performance and/or (2) regularly staffing the organization at less than 100 percent and making up the difference with temporary employees or offering overtime. The former strategy creates a flexible or variable pay plan to control costs because payroll expenses are directly related to the organization's profitability. Therefore, overstaffing is somewhat less of a concern. The latter strategy creates a flexible or variable workforce that can be expanded or contracted to meet business needs and conditions. These strategies are summarized in Exhibit 13.1.

As part of any layoff plan, an organization also needs to develop an appropriate strategy for managing the survivors. A key management challenge that is often overlooked is ensuring that the retained employees can adjust to the changes. It should not be assumed that these individuals will automatically be relieved (and thrilled) to have retained their jobs during the layoff and will still be motivated and productive. These individuals may feel less secure about the jobs they have retained; be asked to perform more work than previously without a corresponding increase in pay; have lost long-term friends and coworkers; and may have damaged morale and fear that they are vulnerable to future layoffs. Consequently, they may be less loyal to the employer and have strong incentives to leave the organization. Studies have shown that employees who survive layoffs have decreased morale, less commitment to their work environments, more negative

EXHIBIT 13.1

Strategies for Managing Employee Surpluses and Avoiding Layoffs

Long Run	Short Run	Policy
• Hiring freezes • Attrition • Offer early retirement incentives • Cross-training of employees	• Loaning or subcontracting labor • Voluntary leaves • Across-the-board salary reductions • Re-deploying employees	• Greater percentage of compensation tied to performance • Staff at less than 100 percent

© Cengage Learning

attitudes toward their employers and higher turnover intention.[2] The organization needs a separate strategy in addition to its layoff strategy to ensure that these retained employees remain committed, loyal high performers. That strategy needs to include a comprehensive communication plan whereby management communicates openly and honestly with survivors to counterbalance the negative effects of the downsizing on employee attitudes toward the organization. Communication of the reasons for the downsizing as well as future plans and strategies can have a strong mitigating "damage control" effect on possible employee attrition.[3] This is of critical importance to employers because retention of these employees and their levels of productivity will probably determine whether the organization will survive. Ironically, downsizing organizations often ignore this critical fact and assume that retained workers will be happy to still have their positions and work harder than ever. Reality has shown that nothing could be farther from the truth.

Layoffs at Kodak

A critical component of the successful outcome of any layoff is the manner in which the survivors are managed. Rochester, New York–based Kodak actually had its surviving employees defend the organization's decision to lay off colleagues to the media during recent job cuts. When Kodak decided it needed to lay off 3,500 employees worldwide, it immediately considered how this decision would impact not only the employees being cut but those who were staying. One key to the positive response to the layoffs was the manner in which communications were handled. To help minimize uncertainty and anxiety, complete and honest information was provided to employees as soon as it was available. Employees were informed that details had not been worked out yet but that the downsizing was not temporary and would affect only certain, specified parts of the organization. A range of services was provided to those employees being let go, including a termination allowance of two weeks' pay for each year of employment; retained medical, dental, and life insurance for four months; outplacement counseling; and a retraining allowance of up to $5,000 for schooling. By strategically planning and implementing the layoffs, Kodak was able to enjoy the continued support of its remaining employees and customers.[4]

While the decision to lay off employees should usually be done as a "last resort," it is inevitable that sometimes an employer has no other choice. However, many layoff decisions by senior management are misguided and create additional problems for the organization. While the investment community may react to a layoff announcement with initial enthusiasm, the long-term performance results are often disappointing. One study found that employers that laid off more than

3 percent of their workforces saw little or no gain in their stock price over a three-year period, whereas those that laid off 15 percent or more of their workforces performed significantly below average over the same time period.[5] Layoffs tend to have better results when done strategically as part of a merger or repositioning rather than as a means to cut costs or impact stock price in the short term. Sears, Roebuck & Company recently eliminated 2,400 jobs and closed 89 stores as part of a strategic restructuring. In the same year, Praxair, Inc., a $5 billion producer of specialty gases, eliminated 900 jobs as part of a plan to change its product mix. In both cases, the value of the company stock rose 30 percent in three months.[6] The lesson here is that layoffs alone will not turn around a company whose strategy is ineffective. However, when layoffs are conducted as part of a strategic restructuring that involves fundamental changes in the direction of an organization, they have a higher probability of success.

Unfortunately, too many layoffs are conducted as a short-term strategy to improve financial performance rather than as strategic initiatives. The majority of organizations that have undertaken downsizing initiatives have failed to report any kind of increased efficiency, productivity, or profitability.[7] A good deal of this failure has been attributed to poor management of the survivors of the downsizing,[8] many of whom subsequently display behavior and attitudes that are dysfunctional to the organization's success.[9] In addition, one study found that considerable costs result from unanticipated increases in voluntary turnover that follow layoffs. Post-downsizing turnover increases can be staggering as, on average, layoffs that reduce an employer's workforce by 1 percent generally result in a 31 percent increase in voluntary post-downsizing turnover rates.[10]

Studies have shown that layoff decisions rarely produced the sought-after financial outcomes.[11] In addition more recent attention has been paid to the less-quantifiable human consequences of layoffs, which have been shown to be potentially devastating for individuals, their families, and entire communities.[12] These effects provide additional support for the contention that while reductions in force may not be completely avoidable, they should be utilized as a last, rather than first, resort. Employers always have additional cost-reduction options available beyond layoffs and should weigh the pros and cons of such options in determining their overall strategy.[13]

A framework is presented in Exhibit 13.2, which enables organizations to minimize, defer, or avoid any large-scale reductions in force, layoffs, or downsizing through the implementation of strategic cost-reduction strategies. Various strategic options are presented, which relate to short-, medium-, and long-range cost adjustments and allow employers to consider sequential stages that may be followed in leading up to or hopefully avoiding layoffs.

Strategic Downsizing at Charles Schwab

San Francisco, California–based discount brokerage Charles Schwab was hit hard in the early 2000s by the downturn in the stock market. However, given the cyclical nature of the economy, it was likely that many workers who were no longer needed might be needed again in the undeterminable future. In March 2001, when the company laid off 3,400 employees, each received a transition package that consisted of 500–1,000 stock options, cash payments to cover COBRA costs for benefits continuation, a stipend of up to $20,000 to cover tuition for schooling, and a full range of outplacement services. More important, however, was the $7,500 bonus to be provided to any employee who was rehired within 18 months of separation. This program greatly assisted in the quick rehiring of knowledgeable, trained employees when business improved, saved the organization a tremendous amount of money, and secured the goodwill of customers and remaining employees. Perhaps more important, when across-the-board pay cuts of 5 percent for rank-and-file employees were announced, it was also announced that any manager at the vice-presidential level or higher would be receiving a 25 percent pay cut. Schwab was cited as a model responsible employer within the business community and continued to be one of the most sought-after employers in the country.[14]

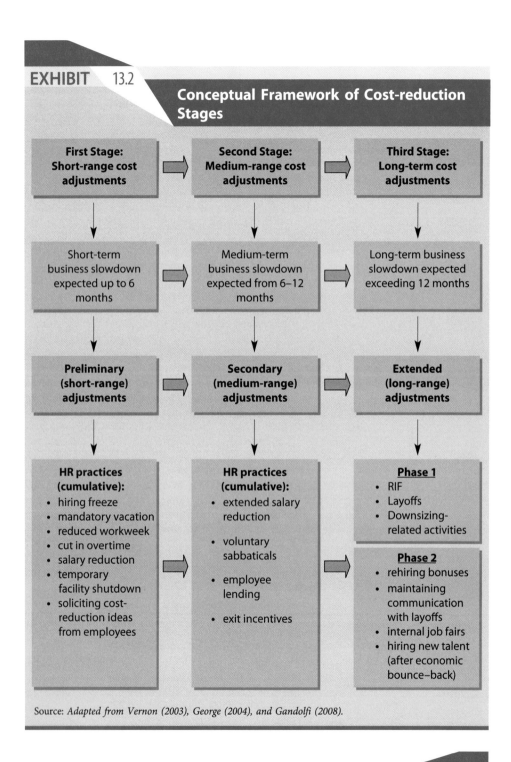

EXHIBIT   13.2

Conceptual Framework of Cost-reduction Stages

| First Stage: Short-range cost adjustments | Second Stage: Medium-range cost adjustments | Third Stage: Long-term cost adjustments |

Short-term business slowdown expected up to 6 months → Medium-term business slowdown expected from 6–12 months → Long-term business slowdown expected exceeding 12 months

Preliminary (short-range) adjustments → Secondary (medium-range) adjustments → Extended (long-range) adjustments

HR practices (cumulative):
- hiring freeze
- mandatory vacation
- reduced workweek
- cut in overtime
- salary reduction
- temporary facility shutdown
- soliciting cost-reduction ideas from employees

HR practices (cumulative):
- extended salary reduction
- voluntary sabbaticals
- employee lending
- exit incentives

Phase 1
- RIF
- Layoffs
- Downsizing-related activities

Phase 2
- rehiring bonuses
- maintaining communication with layoffs
- internal job fairs
- hiring new talent (after economic bounce–back)

Source: *Adapted from Vernon (2003), George (2004), and Gandolfi (2008).*

Turnover

Employees who leave the organization at the organization's request (involuntary turnover) as well as those who leave on their own initiative (voluntary turnover) can cause disruptions in operations, work team dynamics, and unit performance. Both types of turnover create costs for the organization. In some cases, these costs may be short term but have longer-term benefits; in other cases, the costs may be significant and longer lasting. Costs of turnover include the direct economic costs of staffing and training new hires as well as the indirect costs of the downtime needed for the new employee to gain proficiency in his or her job and to become fully socialized and integrated into the organization. In addition, those responsible for training the new employee are pulled away from their regular job responsibilities. If an organization has made significant investment in training and developing its employees, that investment is lost when employees leave. Excessive turnover can also impact the morale of employees and the organization's reputation as being a good place to work, which makes retention and recruitment more challenging and time consuming.

The economic costs of turnover can be staggering. In Chapter 8, it was noted that one technology company calculated turnover costs to average $200,000 per employee.[15] Merck and Company, the pharmaceutical giant, has estimated that its turnover costs are between 150 percent and 250 percent of the employee's annual salary.[16] Sears, Roebuck estimated that turnover among its retail sales staff amounted to $110 million annually, which constituted 17 percent of its operating income.[17] Sears also found a strong negative correlation between employee turnover and customer satisfaction. Merck and Sears are not alone; most large employers suffer from excessive turnover costs. A recent survey found that at companies with more than 1,000 employees, annual voluntary resignations averaged 21 percent.[18] For employers with more than 5,000 employees, the rate climbed to 26 percent.

Turnover can, however, be beneficial. It can allow the organization to hire new employees with more current training who are not locked into existing ways of doing things. Fresh ideas from outsiders can be critical to organizations that have become stagnant and are in need of innovation. Turnover can also lower the average tenure of employees and translate into lower payroll expenses. Turnover also affords opportunities to promote talented, high performers. Finally, when poor performers or disruptive employees leave the organization, morale can improve among coworkers.

It may be assumed that voluntary turnover generally provides more costs than benefits and that involuntary turnover is beneficial for the organization from a cost perspective. Both these assumptions are often false. First, voluntary turnover may allow the organization to find an even better performer than the employee who left, possibly at a lower salary. Second, involuntary turnover often results in much higher costs than training or counseling an employee with performance deficiencies. These and other commonly held assumptions about turnover are addressed in Reading 13.1, "Retaining Talent: Replacing Misconceptions With Evidence-Based Strategies," which uses evidence-based research practices to more clearly explain the causes and sources of turnover.

Both voluntary and involuntary turnover can be managed strategically to allow the organization to maximize the benefits of turnover and minimize the costs incurred with the process. Exhibit 13.3 presents a Performance-Replaceability Strategy Matrix that was developed by Martin and Bartol as a tool to allow organizations to manage turnover strategically.[19] The model on which this matrix is based argues that turnover in organizations, while unavoidable, can be strategically managed to allow organizations to minimize the disadvantages of turnover and maximize its advantages.

Martin and Bartol have classified turnover as being functional (beneficial) or dysfunctional (problematic) for an organization. Whether turnover is functional or dysfunctional depends on two factors: the individual employee's performance level and the difficulty the organization would have replacing the individual. In Exhibit 13.3, replaceability is depicted on the X axis and performance level on the Y axis. Each of the six cells is then classified as resulting in functional or dysfunctional turnover, and appropriate strategies for managing employees who fit into each of the cells are provided. Clearly, the more dysfunctional the turnover, the greater the attention that will be required by management to retain the employee. Retention strategies for such employees might involve additional career development opportunities, incentive compensation that rewards high performance, or innovative benefits that are tailored to the needs of the employee. Regardless of the performance level, backups should be developed by the organization for any employees who would be difficult to replace. Ideally, the strategy for managing turnover involves keeping high performers rewarded through innovative compensation and recognition and reward programs while engaging in HR planning to

EXHIBIT 13.3	**The Performance-Replaceability Strategy Matrix**

REPLACEABILITY

		Difficult	Easy
PERFORMANCE	**High**	High performers—difficult to replace Highly Dysfunctional Turnover Retain/invest in employee: develop backups	High performers—easy to replace Dysfunctional Turnover Retain/invest in employee
	Average	Average performers—difficult to replace Dysfunctional Turnover Retain/provide performance incentives: develop backup	Average performers—easy to replace Dysfunctional Turnover if Replacement Costs Are High Retain/provide performance incentives
	Low	Poor performers—difficult to replace Short-Term Dysfunctional/Long-Term Functional Turnover Improve performance or terminate: develop backup	Poor performers—easy to replace Functional Turnover Improve performance or terminate

Source: *Adapted from Martin, David C. and Bartol, Kathryn M.* "Managing Turnover Strategically' Personal Administrator," *Volume 30, #11, November 1985, p. 63.*

ensure that as few employees as possible occupy positions that will make them difficult to replace.

Exhibit 13.4 presents the eventual outcomes of a successfully managed employee turnover and retention program. All employees whose turnover would be disruptive would be reclassified as easy to replace once appropriate backups had been trained. At the same time, performance incentives and counseling should be provided to low performers to encourage and motivate them to become average performers. Similar incentives should be provided to average performers to encourage and motivate them to become high performers. If these lower performers do not improve in time, they should be terminated.

In cases of involuntary turnover or termination, employers need to have a strategy and standard policy that, if followed, would allow the employer to defend a charge of wrongful termination. In recent years, courts have been increasingly open to hearing complaints that an employer violated the public policy exception to employment at will, as discussed in Chapter 7. Although there may be no legal responsibility to continue to employ individuals, many courts have found that employers have an ethical responsibility to discharge employees only for just cause. Consequently, employers who discharge their employees should have strong evidence of just cause that has been documented and communicated to the employee over time. Otherwise, the employer could incur significant costs in defending itself against the charges or face negative publicity and dissension among the ranks of its employees. The Martin and Bartol model argues that the organization's goal should not necessarily be to reduce all turnover but to reduce dysfunctional turnover by developing appropriate HR programs and policies.

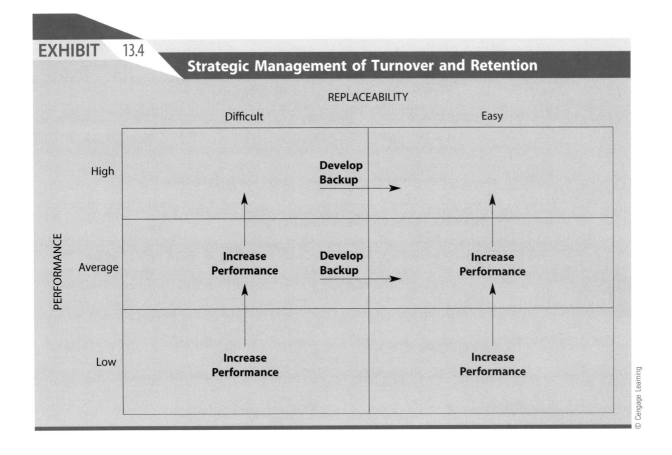

EXHIBIT 13.4 Strategic Management of Turnover and Retention

Managing Retention at Sprint PCS

In the early 2000s, Sprint PCS, a provider of consumer cellular telephone services, suffered from excessively high turnover, which exceeded 100 percent annually. Employees were leaving faster than new hires could be brought on board. Unfortunately, many of the organization's highest performing employees were among those departing. Sixty-eight percent of employees reported in exit surveys that the organization could have done something to retain them. To address this, Sprint developed a strategy to address retention that focused not on pay and programs but on developing managers to become "retention agents." Through survey data, Sprint learned that employees were leaving not because of issues related to compensation or benefits but because their managers were not seen as individuals who knew and understood them and therefore were deemed to be untrustworthy. Ten retention competencies were designed for managers: trust builder, esteem builder, communicator, climate builder, flexibility expert, talent developer and coach, high-performance builder, retention expert, retention monitor, and talent finder. Assessments were then done in five pilot customer contact centers to rate each manager on each of these competencies via 360-degree surveys. Each manager then received a plan that identified at least four competencies to be developed through e-learning modules. A survey was taken of over 7,000 PCS employees, with their response compiled into a database; that information illustrates three categories of factors that impact employee retention: organization-wide conditions, job conditions, and leader behaviors. Managers use this database to share specific "best practices" relative to retention with each other and to create a learning community around employee retention. The result is that every pilot site reported lower attrition and resultant cost savings, projected in the millions of dollars, than the control sites. The program is about to be rolled out to remaining customer service sites.[20]

Retention of top employees continues to be a vexing problem for a large number of employers. One study of HR professionals found that 75 percent of those surveyed reported that retention of high performers was the top HR problem they confronted.[21] A critical strategic issue for employers is the development of policies and programs that help retain high performers and/or those employees who are difficult to replace. It has been suggested that retention can be aided by using a customer-service approach whereby employers treat their best employees as they would treat their best customers, focusing on things like organizational culture, employee development opportunities, and enhanced supervisory relations.[22] However, employer-provided training has been found to be associated with higher employee turnover due to the enhanced marketability of employees with sought-after skills.[23] Hence, any retention strategy must be strategic and holistic in design whereby, for example, enhanced employee training is coupled with other individually determined incentives that motivate employees to remain with the employer.

Strategic Retention at United Airlines

United Airlines recently developed a "key employee retention program" that focuses on 600 workers identified as critical to the organization's efforts to emerge from bankruptcy. These individuals, who were employed in the organization's information services division, received a cash payment equal to 20 percent of their base pay. Because these individuals were deemed to have highly marketable skills, be highly expensive to replace, and be critical to United's survival objectives, United justified the payments even as other employees were being laid off. Turnover rates among these technical workers had risen to 11 percent, while the company's overall turnover rate stood at 7 percent. The plan, while popular with technical employees, was criticized by United's Association of Flight Attendants, which argued that the retention bonuses would come at the expense of other workers.[24]

When attempting to retain talented employees and top performers, employers face competition not only from other organizations but also from the very employees they are attempting to retain. Particularly in service- and information-related industries, startup costs for new businesses are often relatively low, creating opportunities for employees to start their own organizations. The access to information, such as client lists and marketing and strategic plans, which many employees have in the course of doing their jobs can provide strong support for such endeavors. In addition, these employees may have also built strong relationships with customers that transcend loyalty to the organization on the part of both parties. The number of lawsuits that involve employee startup companies has increased greatly in recent years, and many employers now require employees to sign "noncompete" agreements. However, such noncompete agreements frequently are not seen as legally valid and binding. For example, the courts in California, a state with some of the highest startup activity, do not recognize any noncompete agreements. When an employee decides to engage in an entrepreneurial endeavor, an employer essentially has two ways in which it can respond: It can treat the new business as an adversarial competitor or it can attempt to enter into a partnership with the new enterprise.[25] Many large organizations, including Xerox, General Motors, Sun Microsystems, and Microsoft, have been involved in the funding of new startup organizations created by their employees. This funding, however, comes in exchange for some involvement with and control of the new enterprise.

Retaining Talent at Intel

One of the employers that not only supports but actively embraces startup operations by employees is Intel. The Oregon-based computer chip manufacturer has an internal program called the New Business Initiative (NBI) that not only funds startups but actively solicits proposals for new businesses from Intel employees. The NBI has its own staff to examine proposals and determine whether NBI will provide funding. If approved, the employee works with the NBI to develop the project, becoming an entrepreneur while still remaining on the Intel payroll. Successful new enterprises may operate as independent organizations; others may be integrated into Intel's operations. The program is consistent with Intel's innovation strategy and entrepreneurial culture and has also served very successfully as both a retention and a training and development tool. Employees who decide to abandon their projects return to their jobs at Intel with new job skills and a stronger commitment to the organization. Employees are allowed to chase their dreams as technical entrepreneurs without the financial risk of investing in the business and having to leave their full-time employment. The program has also helped the company to retain many of the employees who have come on board as part of one of the many mergers or acquisitions completed by Intel.[26]

Retention of employees, particularly in a strong employment market and for those employees who are top performers, can be a significant challenge for organizations. While many employers appropriately attempt to retain top employees by offering opportunities for growth and development, interesting work, a congenial work environment, and strong values-driven management, the reality is that many top performers still remain focused on their salary, particularly relative to the marketplace.[27] Yet, in other cases, employees may be willing to stay with an employer at a lower salary than could be obtained elsewhere because of the nonsalary-related factors noted previously.[28] The ultimate decision for an employee to voluntarily leave an organization is a function of whether (1) the inducements to stay are sufficiently attractive and (2) the ease with which the employee could depart and is willing to sever or rearrange personal and social networks established.[29] A related factor could also be the transitions necessary for the employee's family, which might result from a decision to change employers. The significant challenge for employers in managing retention of top employees is the fact that different employees are motivated by different factors relative to their desire to stay with an employer. Hence, any retention program needs to be individualized based on the needs of the key employees who have been targeted for retention.

Smaller organizations face special challenges relative to retention of employees. Individuals who choose to work in small organizations generally do so for the unique benefits and challenges associated with small companies. Small companies offer a fast-paced work environment with less bureaucracy, near-constant change, less structure, constant interface with coworkers, including senior management, opportunities for growth and development, and the chance to shape a new organization's future. Small companies may also provide significant opportunities to share in the organization's future financial success, sometimes in tandem with a more modest starting salary. However, as smaller organizations become more successful, they change. Growth usually mandates more formality and bureaucracy, which can greatly alter the work environment employees have come to enjoy. Many smaller organizations simply cannot retain many of their early employees who opt to move on to other smaller startups. Some smaller organizations attempt to become more creative as they grow and organize, with smaller units or divisions that retain the characteristics of the initial startup. Others attempt to create a strong and unique vision or mission that keeps employees engaged as the internal environment of the organization becomes more formalized. Small organizations face some unique challenges relative to employee retention and hence need to be creative in developing the necessary means to engage and retain their top performers.

One key tool employers can use to gauge the effectiveness of their retention efforts is the exit interview. Exit interviews provide employers with the opportunity to gain candid feedback from departing employees in a manner that might not be possible if conducted within the context of an ongoing employment relationship. Departing employees are more likely to be forthcoming and honest in their assessments of their employer without fear of repercussions, and assuming that departing employees have been interviewing with other organizations, they are able to provide employers with information as to how the organization compares with other employers who recruit from the same talent pool. Exit interviews can serve three purposes: (1) provide the organization with feedback to allow it to better compete in the recruiting marketplace; (2) ensure that departing employees are able to voice their concerns and respond to such to keep the employer's reputation strong; and (3) provide, in some cases, an opportunity to retain the employee by addressing concerns in a satisfactory manner.[30] Effectively conducted exit interviews can be a catalyst for maintaining an ongoing relationship with departing employees who might be recruited back to the organization at some point in the future. The data that can be obtained in the exit interview process can provide key insights as to how well an employer is doing relative to delivery of its overall HR strategy and branding initiatives. Departing employees can also influence the perceptions of others who might be possible future employees and/or customers of the organization. Employers need to be cognizant of the value of the exit interview from multiple perspectives as well as understand the role of the exit interview from the perspectives of data collection and communication.

Retirement

Employees also leave the organization through retirement. Except for certain occupations dealing with public safely (such as airline pilots), the Age Discrimination in Employment Act of 1967 prohibits an employer from setting a mandatory retirement age. Because medical advances are allowing individuals to live longer and stay healthier longer, older workers are maintaining a strong and increased presence in the workforce. Ironically, however, many older workers tend to be set in their ways and resistant to change, particularly to technological change. Employers have a distinct challenge in finding ways to keep older workers motivated and productive and ensuring that they do not violate the legal rights of these employees.

When older workers retire, the organization can hire new employees to replace older workers who may have less physical or mental energy or skills that have become dated or obsolete. These new employees may cost less than the older workers relative to salaries and health insurance premiums. Because many older workers are higher in the organizational hierarchy, promotion opportunities may be made available when they retire.

However, significant costs are often associated with retirement. Retirees who have worked for the organization for many years usually have a wealth of knowledge about the industry and the marketplace. They also have extensive historical knowledge about the organization and experience with organizational processes, politics, and culture. Although fresh ideas from outsiders can be critical to an organization, knowledge and experience can be equally important, and decision makers need to ensure that the organization capitalizes on both to assist in meeting its objectives. The challenge again becomes how to maximize the benefits of retirement while simultaneously minimizing the costs. Reading 13.2, "Knowledge Management Among the Older Workforce," presents some insights as to the needs and interests of senior employees as well as some strategies for managing both older workers and the process of knowledge management and retention.

Older workers will become more prominent in the workplace. Employers can usually not set mandatory retirement ages, force employees to retire, or treat older workers in a discriminatory manner in any employment decision. Particularly when conducting layoffs, employers must ensure that there is no adverse treatment of older employees, which would violate the Age Discrimination in Employment Act. Indeed, many large-scale reductions in force have been accompanied by lawsuits that allege discrimination based on age. This issue may be exacerbated in the very near future as the baby boom generation moves through middle age.

Older workers are becoming a reality for employers. A recent study by the American Association of Retired Persons found that 80 percent of the baby boom generation intends to continue to work during retirement.[31] This statistic helps to counteract existing fears concerning the mass retirement of baby boomers in the coming years In fact, the number of Americans aged 65 and older in the labor force recently grew by 7 percent, to a total of 4.5 million individuals.[32] One survey of executives found that 44 percent intend to continue working past the age of 64, while 15 percent plan to continue working past the age of 70.[33]

In addition to the many seniors who wish to keep working, there are a number of them who have to keep working: Lack of adequate health insurance in post-employment years is keeping some seniors in the workforce.[34] Others feel the need to continue working because of the perceived inadequacy of their organization's retirement benefits programs, many of which have been altered in recent years because of the economic downturn.[35] Those workers who are part of the baby boom generation are also known to have a strong work ethic and, in many cases, wish to continue to contribute to their organizations. Another survey of baby boomers reported that 67 percent of this group stated that their main motivation to stay working in later years was the mental stimulation and challenge associated with work.[36] Consequently, employers may face not the anticipated worker shortage but rather an older workforce.

Many older individuals seek to cut back on their working hours in what is known as a "phased retirement" stage of their careers. Employees who opt for phased retirement show a significant lower probability of ever retiring completely compared to those who move from full-time employment to full retirement.[37] However, phased retirement can impact an employee's ability to collect retirement pensions, so it is critical that such programs be structured to benefit both the employee and the organization.[38] As part of overall HR planning, employers need to determine how to deploy human assets for maximum organizational benefit. Many employers who have offered early retirement incentives have found that a larger-than-anticipated number of employees chose to participate in the program, leaving the employer in a bind, at least for the short term. Phased retirement can allow employers to engage in much more effective HR planning. Assisting with retirement planning has become a critical strategic HR function of which phased retirement programs may be a vital component.

Employers can develop programs to give older employees incentives to retire or to take early retirement as long as employees are not coerced into doing so. When older employees retire, the organization can replace them with younger workers, but the organization can lose a great wealth of knowledge and expertise. To remedy this, many employers rehire retirees on a part-time or consulting basis. This allows the organization to retain the benefits these older workers bring to the company and gives these individuals the opportunity to gradually transition into a shorter workweek or semi-retirement. Retirees can enjoy more leisure time and work at a less hectic pace but also continue to make meaningful contributions to their employers, maintain their careers, and stay alert and challenged.

Strategic management of the retirement process results in everyone winning: Retirees gain the best of both worlds; the organization retains their knowledge and experience base; existing employees are afforded opportunities to be promoted; and new employees may be hired and learn from the experiences and knowledge bases of seasoned veterans.

Alumni Relations

An increasing number of employers are not only paying very careful attention to the processes by which employees leave the organization (to minimize potential liability) but also to maintaining communications and good will with these individuals. It has been noted that departing employees are "ambassadors" for an organization and are not only potential continued customers but also important referral sources for additional business and the recruitment of new employees.[39] Former employees who leave on positive and amicable terms, often due to reasons outside of the control of the organization, such as a family relocation, might also be able to return to the organization at some point in the future.

Employer outreach to former employees has been aided by the growing presence of online professional networks. Many employers establish Web sites, postings, or discussion groups on professional social media Web sites such as Linkedin to continue to build and enhance their employer brand. Employers are also able to continue to follow and track former employees in whom they have invested and maintain a professional business relationship. Audit and tax advisory firm KPMG has more than 100,000 alumni, 36,000 of whom are registered on KPMG Connect, a restricted membership alumni Web site that provides company updates, information on activities and events and professional development information for this specific group of former employees.[40]

Alumni Relations at Ernst & Young

Global professional services firm Ernst & Young (E & Y) employs more than 167,000 employees in more than 140 countries. The organization also has an estimated 500,000 alumni worldwide, approximately 200,000 of whom are located in North America. E & Y employs a 20-person staff dedicated to alumni relations who maintain a dedicated alumni Web site and database, publish a semi-annual print and online magazine, organize and publicize events and maintain a prolific social media presence on sites which include LinkedIn, Facebook, and Twitter as well as a video series on YouTube related to entrepreneurship and careers. The Web site has aided in the recruitment of new employees, in partnership with HR, as a critical component of the organization's candidate relations management system and has also facilitated the hiring of 19 percent of the organization's hires at the management level and above from the ranks of alumni who choose to return to E & Y.[41]

Conclusion

Organizations have only recently begun to pay attention to the HR function of employee separation. The increased pace of merger and acquisition activity as well as downsizings have made HR programs and policies that address employee separation a key strategic issue in ensuring the new organizations' success.

For many years, managing turnover has been ignored, taken for granted, or assumed to be a simple process of automatically terminating poor performers and trying to fill the gaps when employees involuntarily left the organization. It was more of a coping process than any kind of active strategic management. Organizations today, however, are realizing that the effective strategic management of turnover can be a critical factor affecting overall performance.

Retirement is no longer a process of filing paperwork as employees reach mandatory retirement age. Effective management of employee retirement can provide organizations with an important competitive advantage: the means of retaining knowledge, expertise, experience, loyalty, and positive role models while simultaneously allowing an infusion of new ideas and energy. The development of creative, mutually beneficial programs and policies related to retirement will become even more critical as our population ages and baby boomers approach traditional retirement age.[42]

The reality of employee separation is that the organization relinquishes key assets. Every employee represents an investment by the organization in terms of direct and indirect expenditures relative to staffing, training, compensation, and benefits. Strategically managing employee separation entails determining the value of human assets from an investment perspective and considering the costs of discarding these assets. How this process is managed may be one of the most important investment decisions an organization makes.

Critical Thinking

1. Why is it important to manage the process of employee separation?

2. What short-run, long-run, and policy options are available to employers in lieu of layoffs?

3. Under what conditions might layoffs be advantageous to an employer?

4. What costs are associated with turnover? What benefits can be derived from turnover?

5. Explain the Martin and Bartol matrix for managing turnover. How does this relate to taking an investment approach to HR?

6. Because workers live and stay healthy longer, the workforce is aging. How might this impact an organization's competitive position?

7. Discuss the ways an organization might attempt to retain its most valued employees.

Reading 13.1

8. What are the most common misconceptions regarding employee turnover and how can an evidence-based perspective allow organizations to develop more effective retention strategies?

Reading 13.2

9. What are some of the techniques that employers can use to address the needs of senior workers, keep these individuals motivated, and also ensure effective knowledge retention and transfer from these employees?

Exercises

1. Calculate the turnover costs for a university professor who voluntarily resigns, retires, or is dismissed. Be sure to consider both economic and noneconomic costs in your analysis. How difficult is it to gain an accurate accounting of these costs? How might you recommend to the university president that these costs be managed?

2. Select an organization of your choice and examine the extent to which it has established any processes or procedures to ensure knowledge retention of departing employees.

3. Visit the Web site. www.aarp.org. What unique characteristics and needs do older workers have? What special contributions can older workers make to an organization? How might organizations best strategically employ older workers?

Chapter References

1. Melymuka, K. "Kraft's 5% Solution," *Computerworld*, 32, (44), November 2, 1998, pp. 69–71.

2. Maertz, Jr., C. P., Wiley, J. W., LeRouge, C., and Campion, M. A. "Downsizing Effects on Survivors: Layoffs, Offshoring, and Outsourcing. Industrial Relations," *A Journal of Economy and Society*, 49, (2), 2010, pp. 275–285.

3. Ibid.

4. Juezens, J. "Motivating Survivors," *HR Magazine*, July 2001, 46, (7), pp. 92–99.

5. Jossi, F. "Take the Road Less Traveled," *HR Magazine*, July 2001, 46, (7), pp. 46–51.

6. Cascio, W. F. "Corporate Restructuring and the No-Layoff Policy," *Perspectives On Work*, 7, (1), pp. 4–6.

7. Glebbeek, A. and Bax, E. Is High Employee Turnover Really Harmful? An Empirical Test Using Company Records. *Academy of Management Journal*, 47, 2004, pp. 270–286.; Kacmar, K., et al., "Sure Everyone Can Be Replaced … But At What Cost? Turnover As A Predictor of Unit-level Performance," *Academy of Management Journal*, 49, 2006, pp. 133–144; Macky, K. "Organisational Downsizing and Redundancies: The New Zealand Worker's Experience," *New Zealand Journal of Employment Relations*, 29, (1), 2004, pp. 63–87.

8. Devine, K., Reay, T., Stainton, L. and Collins-Nakai, R. "The Stress of Downsizing: Comparing Survivors and Victims," *Human Resource Management*, 42, 2003, pp. 109–124.

9. Beylerian, M. and Kleiner, B. "The Downsized Workplace," *Management Research News*, 26, 2003, pp. 97–108.

10. Trevor, C. and Nyberg, A. "Keeping Your Headcount When All About You Are Losing Theirs: Downsizing, Voluntary Turnover Rates and the Moderating Role of HR Practices," *Academy of Management Journal*, 51, (2), 2008, pp. 259–276.

11. Cascio, W. F., Young, C. and Morris, J. "Financial Consequences of Employment-Change Decisions in Major U.S. Corporations," *Academy of Management Journal*, 40, (5), 1997, pp. 1175–1189.

12. Macky, K. "Organizational Downsizing and Redundancies: The New Zealand Workers' Experience,"

New Zealand Journal of Employment Relations, 29, (1), 2004, pp. 63–87.

13. Gandolfi, F. *Corporate Downsizing Demystified: A Scholarly Analysis of a Business Phenomenon*, Hyderabad, India: ICFAI University Press, 2006.

14. Jossi, F. "Take the Road Less Traveled," *HR Magazine*, July 2001, 46, (7), pp. 46–51.

15. Joinson, C. "Capturing Turnover Costs," *HR Magazine*, July 2000, 45, (7), pp. 107–119.

16. Bacarro, J. P. "The Hidden Cost of Employee Turnover," *Grant Thornton Benefits and HR Advisor*, Grant Thornton, 1992.

17. Schlesinger, L. A. and Heskett, J. A. "The Service-Driven Service Company," *Harvard Business Review*, 69, September–October 1991, pp. 71–81.

18. Barrette, D. L. "Survey Highlights Retention Concerns," *HR News*, 19, (10), October 2000, Alexandria, VA: Society for Human Resource Management, pp. 11–16.

19. Martin, D. C. and Bartol, K. M. "Managing Turnover Strategically," *Personnel Administrator*, November 1985.

20. Taylor, C. R. "Focus on Talent," *Training & Development*, December 2002, pp. 26–31.

21. Ibid.

22. Cardy, R. L. and Lengnick-Hall, M. L. "Will They Stay or Will They Go? Exploring a Customer-Oriented Approach to Employee Retention," *Journal of Business and Psychology*, 26, 2011, pp. 213–217.

23. Haines, III, V. Y., Jalette, P. and Larose, K. "The Influence of Human Resource Management Practices on Employee Voluntary Turnover Rates in the Canadian Non-Governmental Sector," *Industrial and Labor Relations Review*, 63, (2), 2010, pp. 228–246.

24. Cole, A. "Attendants Fight United Retention Plan," *CBS.Market-Watch.com*, July 7, 2003.

25. Leonard, B. "Inside Job," *HR Magazine*, October 2001, 46, (10), pp. 64–68.

26. Ibid.

27. MacLean, B. "Rewarding Contribution, Not Job Title: A Base Pay Strategy to Retain Peak Performers," *Society for Human Resource Management*, article 015913, published at www.shrm.org/hrnews/published/artides/CMS Q20036.asp, January, 2007; Gurchiek, K. "Lack of Career Advancement Main Reason Workers Consider Leaving," *Society for Human Resource Management*, article 024814, published at www.shrm.org/hrnews/published/articles/CMS 016356.asp, February 29, 2008.

28. Branham, L. "The 7 Hidden Reasons Employees Leave," AMACOM (2005).

29. Daniel, T. "Managing for Employee Retention," *Society for Human Resource Management*, published at www.shrm.org/research/articles, March 1, 2009.

30. Frase-Blunt, M. "Making Exit Interviews Work," *HR Magazine*, 49, (8), August 2004, pp. 109–113.

31. Carpenter, D. "Looking Forward to a Long Goodbye," *South Florida Sun-Sentinel*, September 18, 2002, p. 10D.

32. Ibid.

33. Pomeroy, A. "They Keep Going (and Going…)," *HR Magazine*, 50, (6), June 2005, p. 20.

34. Grensing-Pophal, L. "Departure Plans," *HR Magazine*, July 2003, 48, (7), pp. 83–86.

35. Pomeroy, 2005, op. cit.

36. Gurchiek, K. "Workers Taking Phase Retirement: A Special Breed," *Society for Human Resource Management*, article 015913, published at www.shrm.org/hrnews/published/articles/CMS 016356.asp, February 23, 2006.

37. Gurchiek, K. "Workers Taking Phase Retirement: A Special Breed," *Society for Human Resource Management*, article 015913, published at www.shrm.org/hrnews/published/articles/CMS 016356.asp, February 23, 2006.

38. Hirschman, C. "Exit Strategy," *HR Magazine*, December 2001, 46, (12), pp. 52–57.

39. Herring, II, W. W. Issuing Final Payments to Departing Employees. *Society for Human Resource Management*, 2013. Available at http://www.shrm.org/hrdisciplines/compensation/Articles/Pages/Final-Payments.aspx

40. Tucker, M. A. "Don't Say Goodbye," *HR Magazine*, August 2011, 56, (8), pp. 71–73.

41. Ibid.

42. Leonard, S. "The Aging Workforce; As Baby Boomers Retire, Employers Will Face New Challenges," *Workplace Visions*, No. 1. Alexandria, VA: Society for Human Resource Management, 2000.

READING 13.1

Retaining Talent: Replacing Misconceptions with Evidence-Based Strategies

David G. Allen, Phillip C. Bryant, and James M. Vardaman

Executive Overview

Despite extensive scholarly research and organizational interest in employee turnover, there remains a gap between science and practice in this area. This article bridges this gap and replaces several misconceptions about turnover with guidelines for evidence-based retention management strategies focused on shared understanding of turnover, knowledge of cause-and-effect relationships, and the ability to adapt this knowledge and apply it to disparate contexts. We provide new tools such as an illustration of the relative strength of turnover predictors, a summary of evidence-based HR strategies for managing turnover, and a new framework for implementing evidence-based retention strategies. We conclude with a research agenda to build on this evidence-based understanding.

Employee retention remains a critical issue for organizations and managers: the costs associated with recruiting, selecting, and training new employees often exceed 100% of the annual salary for the position being filled (Cascio, 2006), and the Bureau of Labor Statistics reports that the national annual voluntary quit rate in the United States typically approaches 25%. The direct costs, work disruptions, and losses of organizational memory and seasoned mentors associated with turnover are significant issues. Many organizations are also increasingly concerned about their ability to retain key employees (e.g., high performers and employees with high-demand or difficult-to-replace skill sets). These concerns may also have broader implications for organizational competitiveness in an increasingly global landscape, and for how to address social and demographic trends such as an aging and increasingly diverse workforce. Despite the

The authors gratefully acknowledge the SHRM Foundation for supporting portions of this work, and Chuck Pierce and members of the 2010 EMBA class at the University of Memphis for helpful comments and suggestions.

importance of turnover to business there remains a gap between science and practice in the understanding of the management of employee retention. Here we fill that gap by developing an evidence-based understanding of the domain.

Even when voluntary turnover rates drop because of unfavorable labor markets, it would be shortsighted to ignore retention management. For example, there is evidence that high unemployment rates have little impact on the turnover of high-performing employees or those with in-demand skill sets (Trevor, 2001). Aggressive recruitment of valuable employees still occurs, and the retention of high performers remains critical (Smith, 2009). In fact, large-scale layoffs in difficult times often lead to higher turnover among survivors (Trevor & Nyberg, 2008). Further, concerns remain about an eventual talent shortage in both the overall supply of talent and in the specialized skills and competencies most valued by organizations. Coupled with the likelihood that many current employees may remain with their organizations only because there are fewer external opportunities, the possibility exists for substantial pent-up turnover to occur when labor markets become more favorable for employees. A recent survey reported that 54% of employed adults, including 71% of those between the ages of 18 and 29, are likely to seek new jobs once the economy improves (Adecco, 2009).

Despite extensive research on employee turnover, there are few resources that effectively and comprehensively bridge scholarly evidence concerning employee retention and practitioner employee retention efforts. As a result, many managers hold important misconceptions about turnover. For example, many managers may believe that turnover is uniformly bad, that most employees quit their jobs because of pay, that job dissatisfaction is the primary reason people leave, that there is little managers can do to affect individual turnover decisions, or that generic best practices are the best way to manage retention. These misconceptions can be harmful to organizations and to managerial careers because they may lead managers to enact ineffective retention strategies that fail to reduce turnover, that are not cost-effective, or even that retain the wrong employees while chasing away the most important ones.

Our objective is to replace these common misconceptions about turnover with evidence-based retention management information, as summarized in Table 1. Evidence-based management refers to translating knowledge and principles based on the best available scientific evidence into organization practice, enabling managers to make decisions informed by social science and organizational research (Rousseau, 2006). Effective evidence-based management requires accessible systematic reviews of evidence such as those that we present here (Briner, Denyer, & Rousseau, 2009). Figure 1 illustrates our evidence-based approach.

Creating a Shared Understanding

Misconception #1: All Turnover Is the Same, and It Is All Bad

Employee turnover can certainly be problematic and in some cases devastating for organizations. However, turnover is a complex phenomenon that comes in many shapes and sizes. It is not always harmful, and in some cases may even be beneficial for organizations. Developing and implementing effective evidence-based guidelines for managing turnover requires that the parties involved (e.g., line managers, executives, and human resource managers) have a shared understanding and frame of reference for interpreting what turnover is and how it

Table 1

Five Common Misconceptions About Employee Turnover

Turnover Misconception	Evidence Based Perspective
Misconception #1 All turnover is the same, and it is all bad	• There are different types of turnover • Some turnover is functional • Turnover costs vary
Misconception #2 People quit because of pay	• Pay level and pay satisfaction are relatively weak predictors of individual turnover decisions • Turnover intentions and job search are among the strongest predictors of turnover decisions • Key attitudes such as job satisfaction and organizational commitment are relatively strong predictors • Management/supervision, work design, and relationships with others are also consistent predictors
Misconception #3 People quit because they are dissatisfied with their jobs	• Job dissatisfaction is the driving force in fewer than half of individual turnover decisions • There are multiple paths to turnover decisions • Different paths have different retention implications • It is also important to consider why people stay
Misconception #4 There is little managers con do to directly influence turnover decisions	• There are evidence-based human resource practices associated with turnover • Recruitment, selection, and socialization practices during organizational entry affect subsequent retention • Managers can influence the work environment and turnover decisions through training, rewards, and supervisory practices
Misconception #5 A simple one-size-fits-all retention strategy is most effective	• Context-specific evidence-based strategies are more effective • Turnover analysis helps diagnose the extent to which turnover is problematic • Organizational context matters for interpreting turnover data • Multiple data collection strategies enable more targeted and effective retention strategies

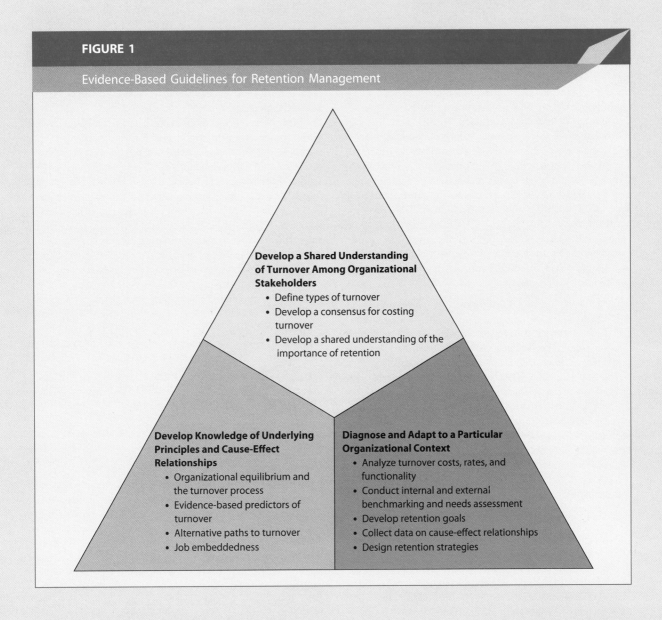

FIGURE 1

Evidence-Based Guidelines for Retention Management

Develop a Shared Understanding of Turnover Among Organizational Stakeholders
- Define types of turnover
- Develop a consensus for costing turnover
- Develop a shared understanding of the importance of retention

Develop Knowledge of Underlying Principles and Cause-Effect Relationships
- Organizational equilibrium and the turnover process
- Evidence-based predictors of turnover
- Alternative paths to turnover
- Job embeddedness

Diagnose and Adapt to a Particular Organizational Context
- Analyze turnover costs, rates, and functionality
- Conduct internal and external benchmarking and needs assessment
- Develop retention goals
- Collect data on cause-effect relationships
- Design retention strategies

affects the organization. Creating a shared understanding entails defining types of turnover, understanding the costs and benefits associated with turnover, and emphasizing the importance of turnover to organizations.

Defining Turnover Employees leave organizations for a wide variety of reasons such as taking a better paying job, leaving an abusive supervisor, going back to school, following a relocating spouse, or getting fired. Although there may be shared characteristics and outcomes associated with each incidence of turnover, there are different types of turnover, each with its own implications. Types of turnover can be described across three dimensions (Griffeth & Hom, 2001). One important

distinction is between *voluntary* and *involuntary* turnover. Voluntary turnover is initiated by the employee, while involuntary turnover is initiated by the organization, often because of poor job performance or organizational restructuring. Effectively managing involuntary turnover is important, but the loss of these employees is generally viewed as being in the best interests of the organization. Retention management typically focuses on voluntary turnover, because these employees are often individuals the organization would prefer to retain.

Even within instances of voluntary turnover, however, there is an important distinction between *dysfunctional* and *functional* turnover (Dalton, Todor, & Krackhardt, 1982). Dysfunctional turnover is harmful to the organization, such as the exit of high performers or of employees who have difficult-to-replace skill sets. Functional turnover, although disruptive, may not be harmful, such as the exit of employees who are easy to replace, and may even be beneficial, such as the exit of poor performers. Retention management strategies typically focus more on dysfunctional turnover.

Finally, even if an organization invests substantially in the retention of key employees, some of those employees would still leave. Thus, while some turnover is *avoidable*, some turnover will always be *unavoidable* (Abelson, 1987). Avoidable turnover occurs for reasons that the organization may be able to influence, such as low job satisfaction, poor supervision, or higher pay elsewhere. Unavoidable turnover occurs for reasons that the organization may have little or no control over, such as health or dual career issues. The distinction is important because it may make little strategic sense to invest a great deal in reducing turnover that is a function of largely unavoidable reasons.

Understanding Turnover Costs When employees leave, it costs the organization time and money. The total costs associated with turnover can range from 90% to 200% of annual salary (Cascio, 2006; Mitchell, Holtom, & Lee, 2001). In addition to the obvious direct costs associated with turnover, such as accrued paid time off and staffing costs associated with hiring a replacement, there are a wide range of other direct and indirect costs associated with turnover. Consider Table 2, which identifies two primary types of costs associated with voluntary turnover: separation costs and replacement costs. PriceWaterhouse Coopers (2006) estimates that turnover-related costs represent more than 12% of pretax income for the average company, and nearly 40% for companies at the 75th percentile for turnover rate. However, as we pointed out in the previous section, turnover is not always dysfunctional for the organization. Table 2 also illustrates some of the potential benefits associated with an employee's leaving. From a strategic perspective, organizations need a clear shared understanding of the costs and benefits associated with turnover to develop an effective retention management plan. There is no single appropriate formula to determine turnover costs. What is more important is that there is an internal consensus within the organization that the metrics used are appropriate, so that any analysis and subsequent conclusions and recommendations are based on a shared understanding and seen as credible.

Addressing the Growing Importance of Turnover Not only is turnover costly, but a growing body of research evidence links turnover rates to organization-level performance indicators. For example, research shows that reducing turnover rates is linked to sales growth and improved employee morale; also, research has found that high-performance human resources practices increase firm profitability and market value in part by reducing organization turnover rates (Batt, 2002; Huselid, 1995). The impact of turnover rates on organizational performance may also be a function of who is exiting the organization. For example, research shows that turnover among employees with high social capital (e.g., wide relationship networks) has a strong negative impact on firm performance (Shaw, Delery, Jenkins, & Gupta, 1998; Shaw, Gupta, & Delery, 2005).

Turnover remains important even as challenging economic times may temporarily make retention seem a less pressing issue. For example, many organizations are concerned about the future availability of skilled labor. In a white paper, staffing firm Manpower noted, "Demographic shifts (aging populations, declining birthrates, economic migration), social evolution, inadequate educational programs, globalization, and entrepreneurial practices (outsourcing, offshoring, on-demand employment) are between them causing shortages, not only in the overall availability of talent but also—and more significantly—in the specific skills and competencies required" (2006, p. 1). Furthermore, the effects of globalization and an increased reliance on technology may create demand for workers with skill sets that U.S. colleges and universities are not providing (Gordon, 2005). There is an emerging consensus that it may soon become more challenging for organizations to retain their key employees. Organizations and managers who have a shared understanding of turnover effects and trends may achieve a competitive advantage.

Knowledge of Underlying Principles and Cause-Effect Relationships

Misconception #2: People Quit Because of Pay

It is true that compensation matters for retention, and employees often leave organizations to take higher paying jobs elsewhere. However, when we consider what leads employees to seek out these other opportunities to begin with, we find that pay level and pay satisfaction are relatively weak predictors of individual turnover decisions (Griffeth, Hom, & Gaertner, 2000). To effectively develop and implement evidence-based guidelines for managing turnover requires knowledge of underlying principles and cause-effect relationships. Thus, we review the research evidence concerning how and why individuals make turnover decisions and what organizations can do about it. The model in Figure 2 summarizes the general processes from research on why and how employees decide whether to stay with or leave organizations.

Organizational Equilibrium and the Turnover Process The idea of organizational equilibrium serves as a foundation for most turnover research: individuals will continue to participate in the organization as long as the inducements offered by the organization are equal to or greater than the contributions required by the organization; these judgments are affected by both the desire to leave and the ease of leaving the organization (March & Simon, 1958). Note that while

Table 2

Voluntary Turnover Costs and Benefits

Separation Costs	*Tangible*
	HR staff time (e.g., salary, benefits, exit interview)
	Manager's time (e.g., salary, benefits, retention attempts, exit interview)
	Accrued paid time off (e.g., vacation, sick pay)
	Temporary coverage (e.g., temporary employee, overtime for current employees)
	Intangible
	Loss of workforce diversity
	Diminished quality while job is unfilled
	Loss of organizational memory
	Loss of clients
	Competition from quitter if he/she opens a new venture
	Contagion—other employees decide to leave
	Teamwork disruptions
	Loss of seasoned mentors
Replacement Costs	*General Costs*
	HR staff time (e.g., benefits enrollment, recruitment, selection, orientation)
	Hiring manager time (e.g., input on new hire decision, orientation, training)
	Recruitment
	Advertising
	Employment agency fees
	Hiring inducements (e.g., bonus, relocation, perks)
	Referral bonuses
	Selection
	Selection measure expenses (e.g., costs of RJP, work samples, selection tests)
	Application expenses
	Orientation and Training
	Orientation program time and resources
	Formal and informal training (time, materials, equipment, mentoring)
	Socialization (e.g., time of other employees, travel)
	Productivity loss (e.g., loss of production until replacement is fully proficient)
Turnover Benefits	Savings may be achieved by not replacing leaver
	There is an infusion of new skills or creativity into the organization
	Vacancy creates transfer or promotion opportunity for others
	Cost savings may be achieved by hiring a replacement with less experience or seniority
	Replacement could be a better performer and organization citizen
	Replacement could enhance workplace diversity
	Departure may offer the opportunity to reorganize the work unit

Source: Adapted from Fitz-enz (2002) and Heneman & Judge (2006).

FIGURE 2

Voluntary Turnover Model

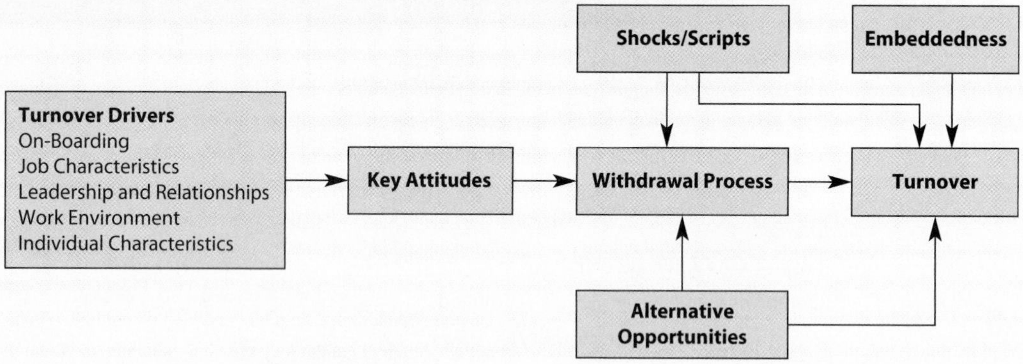

inducements can be specific, tangible rewards such as pay, there can also be other types of inducements such as working conditions, relationships, or future opportunities. Further, these inducements are evaluated in light of the attractiveness and attainability of alternative opportunities affecting the ease of movement. Thus, organizations and managers can actively manage individual turnover decisions by managing the inducements-contributions balance.

Evidence has also shown that many turnover decisions involve a process in which individuals evaluate their current job against possible alternatives, develop intentions about what to do, and engage in various types of job search behavior (Hom & Griffeth, 1991; Mobley, 1977; Steel, 2002). In general, specific organizational and individual factors that cause turnover have direct effects on key job attitudes such as job satisfaction and organizational commitment that can initiate the withdrawal process. This withdrawal process typically involves thoughts of quitting, job search, evaluation and comparison of alternative opportunities, turnover intentions, and eventually turnover behavior. Organizations and managers can monitor and manage key aspects of the work environment that influence employee desire to stay or leave, while also considering the availability and attractiveness of alternatives. When alternatives are plentiful and employees perceive many options, they tend to evaluate the work environment and their own attitudes against a higher standard than when options are sparse. Thus, plentiful opportunities become an especially difficult issue for retention: not only do employees have high ease of movement, but they may also be more difficult to keep satisfied.

Turnover Predictors   Numerous studies have been conducted to determine the specific drivers of turnover, examining issues related to the work environment, job design, the

external environment, individual demographics, job performance, and the withdrawal process. Meta-analysis is a technique used to summarize the results of numerous individual studies into a single useful estimate of the strength of a relationship. Figure 3 summarizes the results of the most recent and comprehensive meta-analyses of relationships with turnover (Bauer, Bodner, Erdogan, Truxillo, & Tucker, 2007; Griffeth et al., 2000; Phillips, 1998). These studies provide the best available research-based estimates of the relative importance of a wide variety of turnover predictors. In Figure 3, positive values indicate that as the predictor increases the likelihood of turnover increases; a negative value indicates that as the predictor increases the likelihood of turnover decreases. Although these estimates represent summaries, and some relationships may differ depending on each unique context and setting, there are implications that generally apply across settings.

The strongest turnover predictors tend to be related to the withdrawal process, such as turnover intentions and job search; it is critical for organizations to monitor and manage these variables (e.g., via employee surveys) and to understand the causes of these variables in their context. Organizational commitment and job satisfaction are two of the most important turnover drivers; organizations need to monitor and manage these key attitudes. The relationship an individual employee has with his/her immediate supervisor/manager plays a critical role in many turnover decisions; organizations that better prepare supervisors and managers for these relationships may improve retention. Role clarity and role conflict are important; organizations need to work to ensure that roles and expectations are clearly defined, communicated, and supported. Job design and the work environment matter: work satisfaction, job scope, promotion opportunities, communication, and

FIGURE 3

Meta-Analytical Relationships with Turnover

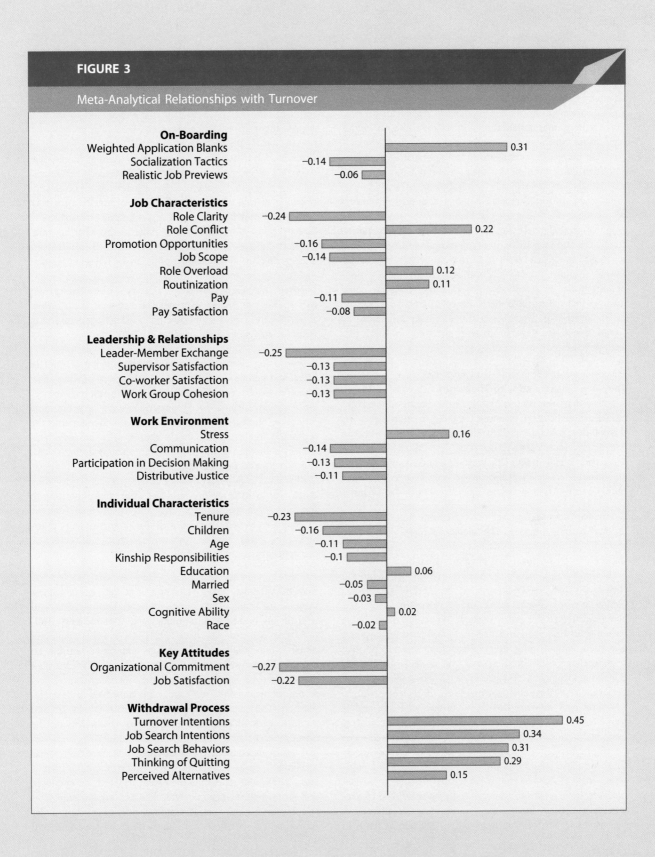

participation in decision making are moderately related to turnover; organizations that can design jobs and the environment consistent with these findings may realize improved retention. Coworker relationships matter: workgroup cohesion and coworker satisfaction are moderately related to turnover. Organizations that foster a supportive and cohesive culture may realize improved retention.

Pay may not matter as much as many managers expect. Although compensation is clearly important, pay level and pay satisfaction are typically relatively weaker predictors of individual turnover decisions; pay increases may not always be the most efficient way to address turnover issues. Demographics are relatively weak predictors: education, marital status, sex, and race are only weakly related to turnover; organizations may instead want to focus on how members of different groups might respond differently to various organizational interventions. For example, research could uncover that the turnover decisions of a particular subgroup of employees (e.g., women) are more strongly influenced by certain issues or interventions (e.g., changing work-life balance policies and resources).

Misconception #3: People Quit Because They Are Dissatisfied with Their Jobs

It is true that job dissatisfaction is one of the most consistent attitudinal predictors of turnover. However, research is showing that job dissatisfaction might be the driving force in fewer than half of individual turnover decisions (Lee, Mitchell, Holtom, McDaniel, & Hill, 1999). Understanding underlying principles and cause-effect relationships also entails knowledge of the multiple pathways to decisions about whether to stay or leave.

Alternative Paths to Turnover Not everyone follows the traditional path to quitting. The *unfolding model* of turnover identifies four primary paths to turnover, and suggests that these paths to turnover are often initiated by a shock: an event that leads someone to consider quitting his or her job (Lee & Mitchell, 1994). Shocks can be expected (e.g., completing a professional certification) or unexpected (e.g., being mistreated by a co-worker); job-related (e.g., being passed over for a promotion) or non-job-related (e.g., spouse offered an opportunity in another location); and positive (e.g., receiving a job offer), neutral (e.g., a merger or acquisition announcement), or negative (e.g., receiving a negative performance evaluation) (Mitchell et al., 2001).

One path involves leaving an unsatisfying job, and is characterized by the traditional view of the turnover process described earlier. Retention strategies in this case would focus on common retention management activities such as assessing workplace conditions and attitudes and managing common causes of dissatisfaction and turnover. Some employees, however, leave jobs with which they are quite satisfied. A second path involves leaving for a more attractive alternative. Because this path may not involve dissatisfaction, it tends to be driven by external market forces, and may be initiated by a shock such as an unsolicited job offer. Retention strategies in this case focus on ensuring the workplace is externally competitive in terms of rewards, opportunities, and the work environment, and having a strategy for responding to external opportunities for valued employees.

A third path involves individuals who have scripts or plans in mind that involve considering quitting in response to certain events, such as completing a particularly marketable training program, or after receiving a retention bonus (e.g., planning to find a new job when one completes an MBA). Although it may be difficult for organizations or managers to directly affect individual scripts, some scripts may be influenced by linking rewards to tenure (e.g., service requirements after paying for an educational program, or retention bonuses tied to length of service). Further, organizational research may uncover particularly prevalent scripts in a particular context that may be amenable to a tailored response (e.g., revised maternity and family-supportive policies for large numbers of family-related scripts) (Mitchell et al., 2001).

Finally, a fourth path involves individuals who quit despite being relatively satisfied, without having a script in place, and perhaps even without searching for an alternative. These are likely impulsive quits, typically in response to negative shocks such as being passed over for a promotion. Retention strategies in this case focus on investigating the types and frequencies of shocks that are driving employees to leave, providing training to minimize negative shocks (e.g., on how to provide negative feedback and on minimizing harassment or perceptions of unfair treatment), providing employees realistic job previews and clear communication to minimize unexpected shocks, and providing support mechanisms to help employees deal with shocks (e.g., grievance procedures, flexible work arrangements, and employee assistance programs) (Mitchell et al., 2001).

Job Embeddedness Just as important as why people leave may be why they stay. The concept of job embeddedness involves the multiple ways that employees become embedded in their jobs and their communities over time (Mitchell, Holtom, Lee, Sablynski, & Erez, 2001). Over time, employees develop connections and relationships both on and off the job that form a network. To the extent that leaving a job would require severing or rearranging these connections, employees who have many connections are more embedded in the organization. There are three types of connections: links, fit, and sacrifice. Each of these connections may be focused on the organization or on the surrounding community.

Links are connections with other people, groups, or organizations, such as coworkers, work groups, mentors, friends, and relatives. Fit represents the extent to which an employee sees himself as compatible with his job, organization, and community. For example, an employee who values community service would be more embedded in an organization and community that provided extensive opportunities to get involved in community service. Sacrifice represents what would be given up by leaving a job, and could include financial rewards based on tenure, a positive work environment, promotional opportunities, and community status. Employees with numerous links to others in their organization and community, who fit better with their organization and community, and who would have to sacrifice more by leaving are more embedded and more likely to stay.

This research leads to several practical implications (Mitchell et al., 2001). To foster links, organizations should design work in teams, provide mentors, encourage employee referrals, and support community involvement. To foster fit, organizations should provide realistic information during recruitment, incorporate organization fit into employee selection, provide clear communication about organization values and culture, recruit locally when feasible, provide relocating employees with extensive information about the community, and build organization ties to the community. To foster sacrifice, organizations should tie financial incentives to tenure, provide unique incentives that might be hard to find elsewhere, encourage home ownership through home-buying assistance, and develop career paths that do not require relocation.

Misconception #4: There Is Little Managers Can do to Directly Influence Turnover Decisions

Many managers believe that most voluntary turnover is unavoidable. They may think that most people quit in response to external job offers that the organization can do little about, or because of events unrelated to work such as moving with a relocating spouse. It is true that some instances of turnover are unavoidable; however, there is evidence regarding specific cause-effect relationships and human resource management practices that can help organizations manage turnover. Table 3 summarizes some of the most robust findings, which we discuss in terms of two phases: managing organization entry and the work environment.

There are specific evidence-based practices managers can employ in terms of the recruitment, selection, and socialization of new employees entering the organization. Recruitment practices that provide applicants the most comprehensive picture of the organization, such as realistic job previews and referrals by current employees, reduce the likelihood of subsequent turnover. Selection methods that assess applicant fit with the job and organization, as well as the use of weighted application blanks, enable the hiring of individuals more likely to remain with the organization. Socialization practices that provide connections to others, positive feedback, and clear information also reduce the likelihood of turnover in the critical first year after organizational entry.

There are also specific evidence-based practices managers can employ in managing the work environment. Training and development opportunities tend to reduce the desire to leave an organization, and linking these opportunities to tenure (e.g.,

requiring tuition reimbursement to be repaid if the employee leaves within a certain time frame) helps the organization retain the competencies acquired. In addition to making rewards market-competitive, perceived fairness of reward decisions, flexibility in tailoring rewards to individual preferences, and linking some rewards to tenure reduce the likelihood of turnover. Given the important role of supervisors in many turnover decisions, providing effective leadership training, incorporating retention metrics into manager evaluations, and effectively managing toxic or abusive supervisors can also reduce turnover. Finally, more engaged employees are less likely to quit, so designing work to foster employee engagement can also be effective. Specific approaches include providing autonomy and task variety, fostering a team environment, providing and supporting specific challenging goals, and recognizing employee contributions.

Misconception #5: A Simple One-Size-Fits-All Retention Strategy Is Most Effective

It is true that there are best practices likely to be associated with improved retention across organizations, such as those identified in Table 3. However, investing significant resources in retention initiatives without understanding the nature of turnover in a particular context is unlikely to maximize the return on these investments. Effective evidence-based management requires integrating multiple sources of data within a particular context (Briner et al., 2009). Designing a strategic, evidence-based approach to addressing turnover requires the ability to diagnose the extent to which turnover is a problem and adapt an understanding of underlying retention principles to a particular organizational context. Effective retention management requires ongoing diagnosis of the nature and causes of turnover, a strategic approach to determining in what human capital markets retention has the largest impact on organizational success, and the development of an appropriately targeted and organized bundle of retention initiatives.

There are two primary types of retention strategies: systemic strategies are based on general principles of retention management and are intended to help reduce turnover rates across the board; targeted strategies are based more specifically on organization-specific turnover drivers and are intended to address organization-specific issues and often to influence turnover among certain populations of employees (Allen, 2008, Steel, Griffeth, & Hom, 2002). These are not mutually exclusive: general retention best practices can help retain specific employees and determine which organization-specific turnover drivers to measure; at the same time, data collected on organization-specific drivers can help reduce overall turnover rates. Strategically, though, it is advantageous to focus on the types of data collection and retention efforts that are most closely tied to an organization's competitive strategy and the nature of its particular turnover problem.

Table 3

Evedence-Based HR Management Strategies for Reducing Turnover

Recruitment (Breaugh & Starke, 2000)	• Providing a realistic job preview (RJP) during recruitment improves retention. • Employees hired through employee referrals tend to have better retention than those hired through other recruitment sources.
Selections (Griffeth & Hom, 2001; Hunter & Hunter, 1984; Kristof-Brown, Zimmerman, & Johnson, 2005)	• Biodata (biographical data) and weighted application blanks (WAB) can be used during the selection process to predict who is most likely to quit. • Assessing fit with the organization and job during selection improves subsequent retention.
Socialization (Allen, 2006; Kammeyer-Mueller & Wanberg, 2003)	• Involve experienced organization insiders as role models, mentors, or trainers. • Provide new hires with positive feedback as they adapt. • Structure orientation activities so that groups of new hires experience them together. • Provide clear information about the stages of the socialization process.
Training and Development (Hom & Griffeth, 1995)	• Offering training and development opportunities generally decreases the desire to leave; this may be particularly critical in certain jobs that require constant skills updating. • Organizations concerned about losing employees by making them more marketable should consider job-specific training and linking developmental opportunities to tenure.
Compensations and Rewards (Griffeth & Hom, 2001; Heneman & Judge, 2006)	• Lead the market for some types of rewards and some positions in ways that fit with business and HR strategy. • Tailor rewards to individual needs and preferences. • Promote justice and fairness in pay and reward decisions. • Explicitly link rewards to retention.
Supervision (Aquino, Griffeth, Allan, & Hom, 1997; Griffeth, Hom, & Gaertner, 2000; Tepper, 2000)	• Train supervisors and managers how to lead, how to develop effective relationships with subordinates, and other retention management skills. • Evaluate supervisors and managers on retention. • Identify and remove abusive supervisors.
Engagement (Ramsay, 2006; Vance, 2006)	• Design jobs to increase meaningfulness, autonomy, variety, and coworker support. • Hire internally where strategically and practically feasible. • Provide orientation that communicates how jobs contribute to the organizational mission and helps new hires establish relationships. • Offer ongoing skills development. • Consider competency-based and pay-for-performance systems. • Provide challenging goals. • Provide positive feedback and recognition of all types of contributions.

Dealing with turnover, like many other issues, requires managers to make decisions with incomplete and uncertain information. One major barrier to good decision making is the tendency to use a narrow decision frame that minimizes uncertainty and ambiguity by pretending that knowledge is complete (Larrick, 2009). To improve decision making, managers should broaden their decision frames in three ways: they should consider multiple objectives and issues, not only those that are most salient at a particular point in time; evaluate alternative expected outcomes that could arise; and consider multiple alternatives, not just the first to arise (Larrick, 2009). Consider a manager who is told that turnover rates are up slightly and exit interview data indicates that 75% of quitting employees are dissatisfied with their pay. Concluding that turnover is a concern, that pay is the major issue influencing turnover, and that increasing compensation is the best strategy would suggest a narrow decision frame.

Alternatively, Figure 4 presents the major steps in developing a strategic evidence-based approach to retention management that encourages a broader decision frame and multiple sources of information (Briner et al., 2009; Larrick, 2009). The first step is to conduct a thorough turnover analysis to diagnose the extent to which turnover is a problem. Instead of focusing on only the most currently salient concerns (e.g., the data showing increased turnover and exit interviews indicating pay dissatisfaction), this analysis encourages a wider consideration of turnover costs, rates,

and functionality. The second step is to interpret this analysis through the lens of a particular organizational context. A slightly increasing turnover rate is difficult to interpret without considering past, present, and future trends (both internal and external to the organization) that provide a broader range of possible outcomes that could arise. The third step is to collect data to diagnose and adapt cause-effect relationships in a particular organizational context. Relying on one source of data (e.g., exit interviews) and one immediately accessible alternative (e.g., changing compensation) may be too narrow a decision frame—consider that most of the employees who don't quit could also be dissatisfied with their pay. Evidence-based retention strategies sit at the intersection of turnover analysis data interpreted through the lens of context and turnover diagnosis. Each step is discussed more fully below.

Developing the Ability to Diagnose and Adapt

Turnover Analysis to Diagnose the Extent to Which Turnover Is a Problem

The first step in adapting knowledge of underlying turnover principles and cause-effect relationships is to diagnose the extent to which turnover is problematic in a particular organizational context. Recall that turnover is not necessarily dysfunctional for the organization, and some turnover is likely

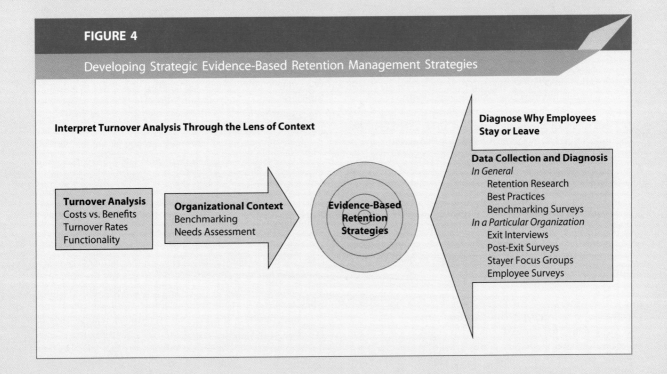

FIGURE 4

Developing Strategic Evidence-Based Retention Management Strategies

inevitable. It would be extremely expensive, and in most cases impossible, to prevent every employee from leaving. As such, most organizations expect and may even encourage some turnover. However, turnover becomes problematic when the wrong people are leaving, or when the turnover rate becomes high enough that the costs and instability outweigh the benefits and harm organizational competitiveness. Thus, determining the extent to which turnover is a problem involves conducting an ongoing turnover analysis addressing three issues: turnover rates, turnover costs, and the functionality of which employees are leaving.

The turnover rate over a given time period (e.g., monthly, yearly) can be calculated as the number of employees leaving divided by the average number of employees (Heneman & Judge, 2006). In addition to measuring the overall turnover rate, in many cases it is also useful to track these data in terms of types of turnover (e.g., avoidable or unavoidable), job category, job level, geographic location, relative impact, or any other categorization that may be of interest (e.g., performance level). These breakout data enable an evaluation of whether turnover rates in different locations or among particular types of employees are especially problematic.

Diagnosing the extent to which turnover is a problem also requires a consideration of turnover costs. Many retention initiatives require investment of time, money, or other resources; thus, a clear idea of turnover costs and benefits is needed to design interventions that will have a positive benefit at a reasonable cost. Incorporating the costs and benefits outlined earlier, it is possible to determine a cost formula that enables the calculation of total turnover costs as well as costs per incidence of turnover. Formulae need not be identical for every job, but often vary based on factors such as job type or level, employee type, and employee performance level.

In addition to analyzing turnover rates and costs, the issue of who is leaving is particularly important for assessing the extent to which turnover is functional or dysfunctional. Not every employee is of equal value to the organization. The retention of certain positions or individuals may be particularly important for organizational success; however, improving retention beyond a certain point may present diminishing marginal returns (Boudreau & Ramstad, 2007). Thus, turnover beyond a certain rate would be highly dysfunctional; however, turnover rates below the point of diminishing marginal returns, although perhaps not ideal, might not represent an optimal focus of resources. For highly pivotal positions or individuals, changes in retention continue to have a significant impact on organizational success.

View Turnover Analysis Through the Lense of Organizational context

Because turnover rates vary greatly (e.g., by industry), interpreting turnover data requires a careful consideration of context (Allen, 2008). Benchmarking and needs assessment are methods for assessing turnover data in relation to both internal and external circumstances. Benchmarking provides a useful standard of comparison for evaluating turnover rates. External benchmarking compares organization turnover rates against industry and competitor rates. If organization turnover rates are significantly higher than those of competitors, that could place the organization at a competitive disadvantage; alternatively, low turnover rates may be a source of competitive advantage. Internal benchmarking considers organization turnover rates over time, enabling the organization to track trends. If turnover is increasing, either overall or among particular groups or locations, retention may be a larger concern than if turnover rates are stable or decreasing. There are some cases where stable or even decreasing turnover could be considered problematic, such as if the organization is retaining too many poor performers, or if organizational plans call for changing the makeup of the workforce.

Needs assessment is a function of workforce planning, and enables an evaluation of turnover in *the* context of future labor demand and availability. External needs assessment considers trends in labor markets that may affect supply and demand of human capital. Trends likely to increase demand for employees valued by the organization (e.g., industry growth) or restrict supply (e.g., slowing rates of labor supply growth or retiring baby boomers) would tend to make relative turnover levels more problematic than the same levels under trends likely to decrease demand (e.g., industry contraction) or increase supply (e.g., growth in relevant educational programs). Internal needs assessment considers the future strategic direction of the organization and how that influences supply and demand for labor. Plans leading to increased demand (e.g., expansion) would tend to make relative turnover levels more problematic than those likely to decrease demand (e.g., outsourcing, offshoring, contraction). Plans designed to influence supply may require more targeted consideration. For example, plans to decrease the size of the workforce through offering early retirement or severance packages are designed to encourage turnover among some employees, while simultaneously placing an emphasis on retaining certain other key employees (Allen, 2008).

Turnover data analysis viewed through the lens of organizational context enables the organization to develop data-based retention goals. These goals could be system-wide (e.g., decrease turnover by 5%) or targeted (e.g., increase the retention rate of minority scientists by 12%), or consist of multiple systemic and targeted goals. The criteria of turnover costs, rates, and functionality can be used to identify the appropriate strategic investment required (Allen, 2008). For example, when turnover costs are tolerable, turnover rates are acceptable, and turnover is functional in terms of who is leaving, retention is not a critical issue and it is appropriate to focus on monitoring the situation. When costs are tolerable, but those quits are dysfunctional, low investment strategies targeted at leavers are appropriate. When costs are tolerable, but it is the number or rate of quits that is problematic, low investment but more system-wide strategies to reduce turnover rates are appropriate. When both the turnover rate and who is leaving are problematic, both types of strategies are warranted. When turnover costs are too high to tolerate, the same approaches apply, except it may be appropriate to consider a range of both targeted and systemic strategies that may be resource-intensive to implement but still provide a positive return on investment. When neither the rate nor who is leaving is problematic but turnover costs are too high, the most appropriate option may be to attempt to streamline exit and replacement processes and reduce the costs associated with each quit.

Collect Data to Diagnose and Adapt Cause-Effect to a Particular Context

Recall that systemic strategies such as across-the-board market-based salary increases or improving the work environment are broad-based retention strategies directed at the entire organization or at large subsystems, and are intended to address overall retention rates (Steel et al., 2002). However, an evidence-based approach to identifying the appropriate strategy requires collecting data on the systemic strategies that are most likely to be effective. The data to help organizations determine an appropriate strategy can come from several sources, including the retention research summarized earlier on the strength of relationships with turnover and on specific human resource practices, best practices drawn from the experiences of other organizations, and benchmarking surveys.

Organizations often desire to determine more specific drivers of turnover in their context, or drivers of turnover among specific subpopulations of employees (e.g., highly important or pivotal ones). The data to help organizations determine an appropriate strategy can come from several sources, including exit interviews, post-exit surveys, current-employee focus groups, linkage research, predictive survey studies, and in-depth qualitative studies. One result of the data collection and diagnosis process may be finding that some groups or types of employees leave for different reasons than others. For example, turnover analysis may show that a particular division has more dysfunctional turnover than others; linkage survey results may show that high-performing employees of that division report less positive relationships with supervisors and lower satisfaction with promotional opportunities, and that these differences are related to differences in turnover rates. As a result, the organization may decide to target an intervention (e.g., supervisor training or high potential mentoring) at that particular division or location, which may be more cost-effective than implementing it system-wide. Alternatively, turnover analysis may uncover that a particular type of employee with a high demand and hard-to-replace skill set (e.g., computer scientist) has particularly high and costly turnover; exit interviews and focus groups

with key employees suggest that departing computer scientists are particularly unhappy with their compensation. As a result, the organization may be able to address its compensation structure with a focus on the engineering labor market, which may be more cost-effective than adjusting compensation system-wide.

Putting It Into Practice

Consider an example of how a manager might follow the steps in this framework, and contrast it with the common approach of deciding that turnover is an organization-wide problem and focusing on increasing job satisfaction across all employees. A human resource manager at a large hypothetical corporation suspects that employee turnover may be a problem in her organization. Wanting to approach the problem from an evidence-based perspective, she begins with a turnover analysis to determine if turnover is really a problem. She arrives at departmental turnover rates by dividing the number of employees who leave the department during a given month by the average number of employees in the department during the same period. She also implements a reporting structure for department managers to identify who left and why and to give a brief estimate of the costs and benefits associated with each turnover incident in their respective departments. From these data, she is able to assess the turnover rates, costs, and functionality by department and by job type.

She then interprets these results through the lens of her particular context. She finds that the overall departmental turnover rates are largely in line with industry norms; however, she also identifies two particularly problematic issues. First, turnover rates among new hires are somewhat higher than those of competitors and have been rising. Second, there is a particularly pivotal position largely housed in one department that is experiencing high and dysfunctional turnover. This leads her to conclude that it is appropriate to maintain the status quo and monitor turnover in most departments and job types, develop a blanket strategy to address new hire turnover, and develop a targeted strategy to reduce turnover in the problematic pivotal job.

Next, she collects data to develop specific strategies. She turns to data collected from exit interviews, employee surveys, and focus groups of key employees (all of which she designed based on her knowledge of turnover frameworks and research). She discovers two key findings: new hires routinely report being unpleasantly surprised at certain elements of the work environment (she recognizes this as a shock), and the high-turnover pivotal employees in particular report these unpleasant surprises, along with difficulty becoming integrated into work groups (she recognizes this as an element of embeddedness). Based on her knowledge of turnover research, she develops and implements a simple realistic job preview during the recruitment process to reduce negative shocks among all new hires, and she redesigns the socialization process just for employees in the high-turnover pivotal job to emphasize embeddedness.

Future Directions

We set out to narrow the gap between science and practice with respect to employee turnover and retention by replacing several common misconceptions with evidence-based strategies, and by providing current and future organizational leaders, HR and line managers, educators, and scholars an accessible guide to understanding turnover with sound evidence-based strategies for influencing employee turnover and retention. To maximize the potential of evidence-based retention management, however, requires that organizational scholars research issues of most interest and potential impact for practitioners. Our analysis suggests several avenues of future research directions for turnover scholars.

One is to conduct more research on boundary conditions that specify under what conditions turnover theories hold for what subgroups of employees. Turnover scholars are often motivated to develop generalizable principles to advance scientific understanding; managers and practitioners, on the other hand, are often most interested in findings directly applicable to their own context. Future research that explores the effects of industry, competitive environment, and organizational and national culture, as well as effects on the retention of key subgroups of employees (e.g., high performers, hard-to-retain occupational groups, or diverse employees) would be valuable. In-depth qualitative research that provides rich data about a very specific context is uncommon in management research on turnover and may be warranted.

A second is to conduct more research involving interventions and experimental or quasi-experimental designs. Most turnover studies consist of correlational designs that limit the ability to draw firm conclusions about causality. Future research that manipulates turnover antecedents with appropriate controls for alternative explanations would be valuable for scientists and practitioners. For example, it may be possible to manipulate elements of an employee orientation program designed to increase embeddedness among new hires. As another example, creative researchers might take advantage of naturally occurring manipulations that could represent turnover shocks, such as a merger announcement. It may also be fruitful to explore the use of simulation and scenario studies that allow the controlled manipulation of parameters without directly disrupting organizational functioning.

A third is to conduct research more broadly on the effectiveness of evidence-based management in general. Reay, Berta, and Kohn (2009) argued that there is little evidence that evidence-based management is effective. Future research that compares the effectiveness of evidence-based approaches to retention management with alternative approaches could provide important evidence as to whether scholarly research on turnover adds significantly to managerial experience and judgment in retention management.

REFERENCES

Abelson, M. A. (1987). Examination of avoidable and unavoidable turnover. *Journal of Applied Psychology, 72*(3), 382–386.

Adecco. (2009). *American workplace insights survey.* PRNewswire, June 25, Melville, NY.

Allen, D. G. (2006). Do organizational socialization tactics influence newcomer embeddedness and turnover? *Journal of Management, 32,* 237–256.

Allen, D. G. (2008). Retaining talent: A guide to analyzing and managing employee turnover. SHRM *Foundation Effective Practice Guidelines Series,* 1–43.

Aquino, K., Griffeth, R. W., Allen, D. G., & Hom, P. W. (1997). An integration of justice constructs into the turnover process: Test of a referent cognitions model. *Academy of Management Journal, 40,* 1208–1227.

Batt, R. (2002). Managing customer services: Human resource practices, quit rates, and sales growth. *Academy of Management Journal, 45,* 587–597.

Bauer, T. N., Bodner, T., Erdogan, B., Truxillo, D. M., & Tucker, J. S. (2007). Newcomer adjustment during organizational socialization: A meta-analytic review of antecedents, outcomes, and methods. *Journal of Applied. Psychology, 92,* 707–721.

Boudreau, J. W., & Ramstad, P. (2007). *Beyond HR: The new science of human capital.* Boston: Harvard Business School Press.

Breaugh, J. A., & Starke, M. (2000). Research on employee recruitment: So many studies, so many remaining questions. *Journal of Management, 26,* 405–434.

Briner, R. B., Denyer, D., & Rousseau, D. M. (2009). Evidence-based management: Concept cleanup time? *Academy of Management Perspectives, 23*(4), 19–32.

Cascio, W. F. (2006). *Managing human resources: Productivity, quality of work life, profits* (7th ed.). Burr Ridge, IL: Irwin/McGraw-Hill.

Dalton, D. R., Todor, W. D., & Krackhardt, D. M. (1982). Turnover overstated: A functional taxonomy. *Academy of Management Review, 7,* 117–123.

Fitz-enz, J. (2002). *How to measure human resources management* (3rd ed.). New York: McGraw-Hill.

Gordon, E. E. (2005). *The 2010 meltdown.* Westport, CT: Praeger.

Griffeth, R. W., & Hom, P. W. (2001). *Retaining valued employees.* Thousand Oaks, CA: Sage.

Griffeth, R. W., Hom, P. W., & Gaertner, S. (2000). A meta-analysis of antecedents and correlates of employee turnover: Update, moderator tests, and research implications for the next millennium. *Journal of Management, 26,* 463–488.

Heneman, H. G., &. Judge, T. A. (2006). *Staffing organisations* (5th ed.). Burr Ridge, IL: Irwin/McGraw-Hill.

Hom, P. W., & Griffeth, R. W. (1991). Structural equations modeling test of a turnover theory. *Journal of Applied Psychology, 76,* 350–376.

Hom, P. W., & Griffeth, R. W. (1995). *Employee turnover.* Cincinnati, OH: South-Western.

Hunter, J. E., & Hunter, R. F. (1984). Validity and utility of alternative predictors of job performance. *Psychological Bulletin, 96,* 72–88.

Huselid, M. (1995). The impact of human resource management on practices, on turnover, productivity, and corporate financial performance. *Academy of Management Journal, 38,* 291–313.

Kammeyer-Mueller, J. D & Wanberg, C. R. (2003). Unwrapping the organizational entry process: Disentangling multiple antecedents and their pathways to adjustment. *Journal of Applied Psychology, 88,* 779–794.

Kristof-Brown, A. L., Zimmerman, R. D., & Johnson, E. C. (2005). Consequences of individuals' fit at work: A meta-analysis of person-job, person-organization, person-group, and person-supervisor fit. *Personnel Psychology, 58,* 281–342.

Larrick, R. P. (2009). Broaden the decision frame to make effective decisions. In E. A. Locke (Ed.), *Handbook of principles of organizational behavior* (pp. 461–480). Maiden, MA: Blackwell.

Lee, T. W., & Mitchell, T. R. (1994). An alternative approach: The unfolding model of voluntary employee turnover. *Academy of Management Review, 19,* 51–89.

Lee, T. W., Mitchell, T. R., Holtom, B. C., McDaniel, L. S., & Hill, J. W. (1999). The unfolding model of voluntary turnover: A replication and extension. *Academy of Management Journal, 42,* 450–462.

Manpower. (2006). *Confronting the coming talent crunch: What's next?* (White Paper). Available at http://files.shareholder.com/downloads/MAN/0x0xl59662/641f597e-7340-4b90-9ad62laf2843f2a9/AM08_WEF_Partner%20 Doc_Manpower%20Inc._White_Paper_Confronting_the_ Talent_Crunch.pdf.

March, J. G., & Simon, H. A. (1958). *Organizations.* New York: John Wiley.

Mitchell, T. R., Holtom, B. C., & Lee, T. W. (2001). How to keep your best employees: Developing an effective retention policy. *Academy of Management Executive, 15,* 96–108.

Mitchell, T. R., Holtom, B. C., Lee, T. W., Sablynski, C. J., & Erez, M. (2001). Why people stay: Using job embeddedness to predict voluntary turnover. *Academy of Management Journal, 44,* 1102–1121.

Mobley, W. H. (1977). Intermediate linkages in the relationship between job satisfaction and employee turnover. *Journal of Applied Psychology, 62,* 237–240.

Phillips, J. M. (1998). Effects of realistic job previews on multiple organizational outcomes: A meta-analysis. *Academy of Management Journal, 41,* 673–690.

PricewaterhouseCoopers Saratoga Institute. (2006). *Driving the bottom line* (White Paper). Available at http://www .pwc.com/en.US/us/hr-saratoga/assets/saratoga-improving-retention.pdf.

Ramsay, C. S. (2006). Engagement at Intuit: It's the people. *Society of Organizational and Industrial Psychology 21st Annual Conference,* Dallas, TX.

Reay, T., Berta, W., & Kohn, M. K. (2009). What's the evidence on evidence-based management? *Academy of Management Perspectives, 23*(4), 5–18.

Rousseau, D. M. (2006). Presidential address: Is there such a thing as "evidence-based management"? *Academy of Management Review, 31,* 256–269.

Shaw, J., Delery, J., Jenkins, G., & Gupta, N. (1998). An organization-level analysis of voluntary and involuntary turnover. Academy *of Management Journal, 41,* 511–525.

Shaw, J. D., Gupta, N., & Delery, J. E. (2005). Alternative conceptualizations of the relationship between voluntary turnover and organizational performance. *Academy of Management Journal, 48,* 50–68.

Smith, R. C. (2009, February 7). Greed is good. *Wall Street Journal,* p. Wl.

Steel, R. P. (2002). Turnover theory at the empirical interface: Problems of fit and function. *Academy of Management Review, 27,* 346–360.

Steel, R. P., Griffeth, R. W., & Hom, P. W. (2002). Practical retention policy for the practical manager. *Academy of Management Executive, 16,* 149–161.

Tepper, B. (2000). Consequences of abusive supervision. *Academy of Management Journal, 43,* 178–190.

Trevor, C. O. (2001). Interactions among actual ease of movement determinants and job satisfaction in the prediction of voluntary turnover. *Academy of Management Journal, 44*, 621–638.

Trevor, C. O., & Nyberg, A. J. (2008). Keeping your head-count when all about you are losing theirs: Downsizing, voluntary turnover rates, and the moderating role of HR practices. *Academy of Management Journal, 51*, 259–276.

Vance, R. J. (2006). *Employee engagement and commitment.* SHRM Foundation. Available at http://www.talentmap.com/knowledgecentre/pages/case%20studies/shrm_employeeengagementonlinereport.pdf.

READING 13.2

Knowledge Management Among the Older Workforce

Floor Slagter

Introduction

The world is never standing still. The world is quickly changing; internationalization increases, regulations change and costumers demand flexibility, speed and quality. This makes it difficult for an organization to keep up with its environment, or even be competitive. Literature has devoted a lot of attention to these topics and new concepts made their entry, like total quality management, business process reengineering and learning organizations. It becomes more and more obvious that the optimal generation and application of knowledge is one of the most important keys to success. An organization needs to be flexible in order to keep up with their competitors and knowledge is needed to obtain that flexibility. Knowledge management is a discipline that recognizes the importance of knowledge and assists organizations in optimally using the knowledge that is present in the organization.

Another issue that is being extensively discussed in journals now a day is the ageing workforce; between 2005 and 2015 the so-called baby boomers are going to retire *en masse*. A well-planned and effective knowledge transfer between the different generations of the workforce is of great importance. Knowledge about the organization, the processes within the company, and much more critical organizational knowledge need to be transferred to the other generation of employees. If this does not happen then this knowledge will disappear and the knowledge level of many organizations will become unbalanced. Especially in knowledge intensive industries this can have disastrous consequences. Knowledge management is an activity that can help organizations to overcome these threats.

This article will bring these two topics together; the senior employee and knowledge management. First the two topics will be discussed separately in order to create clarity about their content and meaning. Secondly, the issues will be combined and aligned. Furthermore this article will provide a number of guidelines for human resource (HR) managers, which they can use as a starting point when coping with this problem.

Knowledge Management: Definition and Processes

There exists a lot of discussion about what the proper definition of knowledge management is or should be. Scholars, practitioners, and others in field of business management are still debating about the concepts and definitions related to knowledge management (KM) and its definition is currently still evolving. To give an impression of what kind of concepts are used in the different definitions, below a few of them will be discussed. One definition of KM is one by Groff and Jones (2003):

> Knowledge management is the tools, techniques, and strategies to retain, analyze, organize, improve, and share business expertise.

This definition places the emphasis on the KM processes that take place within an organization and especially the IT facilities that support these processes. This definition is more about managing explicit knowledge, by the use of IT. The human factor is not mentioned.

Another widely accepted definition is the following of Dr. Yogesh Malhotra:

> Knowledge management caters to the critical issues of organizational adaptation, survival, and competence in face of increasingly discontinuous environmental change ... Essentially, it embodies organizational processes that seek synergistic combination of data and information processing capacity of information technologies, and the creative and innovative capacity of human beings (Dr. Yogesh Malhotra).

This definition is more encapsulating the human factor that is needed to manage knowledge. This leads us to the following definition of Rastogi (2000), who really emphasizes the importance of the human factor in his definition. This definition focuses on the ability of individuals and groups to enable knowledge creation, use and sharing. The definition is:

> Knowledge management as a systematic and integrative process of coordinating organization-wide activities of acquiring, creating, storing, sharing, diffusing, developing, and deploying knowledge by individuals and groups in

pursuit of major organizational goals. It is the process through which organizations create and use their institutional and collective knowledge.

This article will use this definition of KM, since this definition recognizes the importance of the human factor in KM by focusing on the ability of individuals and groups to enable knowledge creation, use and sharing. This article will focus on KM among senior employees and places its emphasis on how KM can be optimized among this group of employees. The human factor is therefore very important to take into account.

Although there exist not yet agreement about what the definition of knowledge management should be, researchers agree that KM is an important activity for an organization to undertake.

But why is KM so important? To stay, or even become competitive it is extremely important for organizations to be flexible and to be able to adapt quickly. Knowledge is thereby an important factor.

Knowledge management focuses on ways of sharing, storing and maintaining knowledge, as a means of improving efficiency, speed, and competency of individuals within an organization, and therefore increasing the profitability, flexibility and adaptability.

Within literature a lot of different processes that form KM can be distinguished. However it is possible to bring these activities back to four processes in which the basic operations of KM are realized. In Figure 1 these processes are depicted.

This article is mostly concerned with the processes of guaranteeing existing knowledge and the distribution of knowledge, since these are the first two processes that come to the front when employees leave the organization (in case of this article the senior employee).

The Ageing Workforce

To be able to clarify why this article is focusing on knowledge management among the senior employee and why this is becoming so increasingly important it is necessary to take a look at the recent developments within the labor force and the characteristics of the senior employee.

The percentage of employees in the age group 50 to 60 increased significantly the last ten years. The increase of senior employees within organization has certain consequences for managers, and it also means that the upcoming years many of the senior employees will retire. Most organizations are not fully aware of the serious consequences that the loss of this large source of labor can have (Ekamper et al., 2001). Research has shown that individual managers do not seem to have a sense of urgency that they need to anticipate and act on this development (Ekamper et al., 2001). However, there is a need to act and anticipate since these employees have a great pool of knowledge at their disposal.

After discussing these developments it is necessary to discuss how to define the senior employee exactly. This

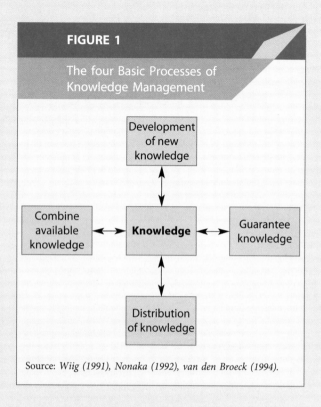

FIGURE 1

The four Basic Processes of Knowledge Management

Source: *Wiig (1991), Nonaka (1992), van den Broeck (1994).*

article will use the definition of employees within the age group 54–60 years. This because a lot of studies and research concerning the senor worker use the same definition and in this way it is easier to apply the knowledge gained in those researches to the problem discussed in this article.

The Managers' Perspective on the Senior Worker

There is of course no single "managers' perspective" on senior workers, and it is important to emphasize that, in all different literature that exist about this issue, there is evidence of both positive and negative images of senior workers, and of good practice and bad. However there are some themes that often come to the fore, when discussing senior workers with managers. To illustrate this, the findings in this area within the 1990s and some current findings will be discussed.

Two studies performed in the 1990s (Institute for Manpower Studies, 1990; Lynn and Glover, 1998) of manager attitudes to senior workers suggested that managers associated certain characteristics with age. These are shown in Table 1 and can be seen in both a positive and negative way.

A recent study performed by Remery et al. (2001) found out that a lot of managers tend to associate an increase in the average age of their workforce with higher labor costs. Managers also tended to lock upon senior staff as employees with a high level of absenteeism and a resistance to change. But managers also associate an older workforce with higher levels of experience and an increase in know-how.

Table 1

Positive and Negative Characteristics of Senior Employees According to Managers

Positive Characteristics	Negative Characteristics
Responsibility and maturity	Lack of flexibility
Commitment to work	Slow to adapt or resistance to change
Experience	Outdated skills, particularly in relation to new technology
"Staying put" in a job	Lack of mobility
	Difficult to retrain
	Prone to ill-health

These presumptions narrow the mindsets of managers; when they think mainly negatively about the senior employee, they will not initiate activities for these employees that demand flexibility, change, etc., since managers are convinced that this age group is incapable of living up to these demands. In this way the senior employee never gets a chance to "prove" him/herself.

It might be the case that managers bring all these presumptions to the fore to cover their true reason why they do not like to employ senior employees; the high costs. But when managers want to get rid of senior employees as soon as possible, because of the high costs, they tend to overlook one important thing; by firing the employee the knowledge gained by the employee over the years go with him/her.

From the information above we can conclude that the perspective that managers have on senior employees has not changed significantly over the years. But what is actually true about these presumptions? Different studies (McIntosh, 2000; Society for Human Resource Management, 1998) affirmed that, in general, senior workers:

- had low turnover rates;
- were flexible and open to change;
- possessed up-to-date skills;
- were interested in learning new tasks;
- had low absentee rates; and
- had few on-the-job accidents.

The only area where professionals expressed their concern was the area of senior employees and new technology (McIntosh, 2000).

It is interesting to see the contradictions that exist. But how do we find out what is true? This issue will be addressed under "recommendations".

Characteristics of the Senior Employee

Senior employees have other characteristics than younger employees. This part of the article will discuss the most important differences.

Motivation and Job Satisfaction

There are a lot of theories about what motivates employees. One of the earliest ones was Maslow's (1954) theory. He explains a certain hierarchy of human needs; five levels of needs that can be visualized in a pyramid (see Figure 2).

In order to motivate employees a manager needs to satisfy their needs. The satisfaction of these needs can be realized by:

- money (material needs; level 1 and 2);
- a say in things and involvement (level 3 and 4); and
- a certain degree of autonomy or independence (level 5).

As a human being grows to maturity, the need for experiencing respect increases, implying both respect for others and self-respect. The same is true for the needs for self-actualization. Both needs function as a motivator for the senior worker (Keuning, 1998).

Also, as employees grow older, interesting work becomes more of a motivator. A report by Heymann and Terlien shows that senior employees want work that has a meaning; they want to feel useful on the work floor. These researchers also emphasize that respect and recognition are highly valued by senior employees. Managers should keep these changes among adulthood in mind, to be able to employ their employees as efficient and effective as possible through all stages of life. Research performed by Diekstra (2003) also recognizes the importance of job significance among senior employees.

Job satisfaction shows consistently that work-related attitudes are more positive with increasing age in surveys of employed adults. Senior workers may have a different perspective

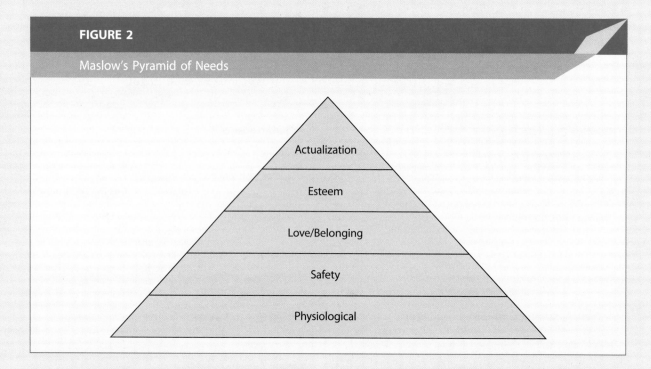

FIGURE 2

Maslow's Pyramid of Needs

on work than younger adults. For senior workers, survival needs are less likely to be urgent as they will probably have reached the maximum income for their jobs. Senior workers report that job satisfaction is more closely related to intrinsic or internal rewards of work (Sterns and Miklos, 1995). This theory supports the findings of Keuning, related to Maslow's theory.

As people grow older they find it important to reach a certain balance between their work and their private life. This is also linked up with their changing needs. Senior workers demand for flexible working hours, also keeping health issues in the back of their minds. The degree to which the employer can adjust to these needs affects the level of job satisfaction of the senior employee.

Self-development among Senior Employees

Today's society has self development high in its standard. The younger generation is used to setting goals for themselves with regard to what they want to achieve. A lot of managers are of opinion that employees are responsible themselves for their development and career. However, a lot of senior employees expect their managers to come up with initiatives concerning their development and career path (Heymann and Terlien, 2003). They are not used to taking initiative in this area. A coaching leadership style would be very appropriate for this age group. In that way the manager can show the different possibilities and the employee gets a better overview of what is possible for him/her and can subsequently make his/her decision.

Knowledge of the Senior Employee

A study of Kanfer and Ackerman (2004) explains that there exists a strong positive association between adult age and knowledge level. Tacit knowledge needs to be transferred from the senior employee to the younger one, since senior employees have built up a lot of experience and organizational know-how. Senior employees can be reticent in sharing their knowledge with younger employees, being afraid to become redundant afterwards.

Currently a lot of organizations are thinking about how to convince their senior workers to stay longer, because employers might face the loss of a significant amount of knowledge and know-how. However, several recent studies have shown (Henkens, 1998) that a vast majority of the senior workers themselves would like to withdraw from the labor force at the earliest possible opportunity. A well known question among senior employees is: "How long do you still have to work?". It is therefore important that managers start considering how they can transfer the knowledge that is present in these senior employees before they leave. This leads us to the problem definition of this article.

Problem Definition

From all the information above we can draw a couple of interesting conclusions. The first conclusion is that a lot of managers do not see the urgency of taking measures with regard to their ageing workforce and that they are not aware of the serious problems the massive retirement can cause with regard to the loss of knowledge. Another conclusion we can draw is that KM is an activity that can contribute to the preservation of knowledge and the distribution of it. When we combine these two findings we see that KM can serve as a tool to help managers to transfer the knowledge that is present in the senior employee in order to overcome the imminent loss of knowledge. The question is how this can be done adequately. To determine this, we need to take a look at the factors that determine the success of KM and how these factors can be applied to the senior employee. This brings us to the goal and problem definition of this article.

The goal of this article is to come to a number of guidelines in which the specific characteristics of the senior employee are coupled to the critical success factors (CSFs) of knowledge management. By using these guidelines as a starting point the human resource manager will be able to manage knowledge among this particular age more effectively than before.

This brings us to the following problem definition: which critical success factors of knowledge management can be aligned to the senior employee to enhance the effectiveness of this activity (among this age group)?

This problem definition is going to be discussed by using the following sub-questions:

1. What are the CSFs of KM?
2. How can these CSFs be aligned to the senior employee?
3. What are the implications for the HR manager?

Before starting to answer the problem definition, the limitations of this article need to be discussed.

Limitations

Knowledge management is a broad concept and definitions of KM are still developing. This article will focus on the human factor of knowledge management, using the definition provided by Rastogi.

A lot of studies (e.g. Abou-Zeid, 2002; Malhotra and Galletta, 2003) argue that information technology can assist KM in an important way. Although this article recognizes the importance of information systems within KM it will not address this aspect of KM. It will focus on the human and social processes of KM.

A lot of different processes are incorporated in KM; this article will focus on guaranteeing knowledge and distributing knowledge, since these are the two basic processes of KM that come to the front when employees leave the organization. These basic processes involve underlying processes, which includes knowledge sharing. Knowledge sharing is one of the most important processes when knowledge needs to be transferred, since these processes are mutually exclusive.

Furthermore it is important to stress the intention of this article. This is not to provide managers with a recipe that needs to be followed to solve the problem. Therefore

organizations are far too diverse, and unique. Other limitations due to organizational culture and business sector are therefore also relevant to mention; specific organizational cultures and business sectors may require different approaches.

In addition, national or society cultures can have their influences. For example, in Asian countries senior employees are much more respected since values of respect for the elderly are ingrained in Asian cultures. While the level and forms of respect are swiftly changing, the value of older persons is still recognized in most Asian and Pacific region societies (ESCAP, 2001). These cultural differences between nations and societies can have influence on how processes of KM take place.

This article explores the opportunities for HR managers in a broad context and its intention is to provide a number of general guidelines to HR managers how they can prevent the loss of knowledge when senior employees leave the company; a starting point where they can begin to address this issue.

This article is based on extensive literature review and conversations in the field with MA M. Diekstra, she is the project leader of the project "Exploration of labor prospects by senior employees' (see Appendix for further details). This project had the main focus to develop a route for senior employees to assist them in their self development, by looking at their past experiences, discovering where they are now and where they want to go in the future.

The information from the literature review and the conversations were used to come to the characteristics of senior employees and the critical success factors of knowledge management.

Critical Success Factors of Knowledge Management

The success of a KM initiative depends on many factors, some within human control, some less or not at all. A critical success factor is a performance area of critical importance in achieving consistently high productivity. There exist two categories of critical success factors: business processes and human processes. This article will focus on the human processes.

Theorists do not completely agree on what the critical success factors of KM are. Below several views will be discussed, thereafter the final five will be presented, which will be used in this article.

Bixel's Four-pillar Model and Davenport's and Probst's List

Different theorists describe different CSFs for KM. Bixler (2002) is one of them. He developed a four-pillar model to describe success factors for KM implementation. These four pillars consist of: leadership, organization, technology, and learning. Leadership is concerned with the fact that managers develop business and operational strategies to survive and position for success in today's environment. The pillar "organization" stresses the fact that the value of knowledge creation and collaboration should be intertwined throughout an organization. Operational processes must align with the KM framework and strategy, including all performance metrics and objectives. Technology enables and provides the whole infrastructure and the tools where KM can rely on. Furthermore Bixel stresses the fact that without learning a KM strategy will not survive; managers must recognize that knowledge resides in people, and knowledge creation occurs in the process of social interaction and learning.

Davenport and Probst developed a similar, but a more extensive list of CSFs. Their CSFs are leadership, performance measurement, organizational policy, knowledge sharing and acquisition, information systems structure, and benchmarking and training.

The Five CFSs of KM
After the literature review of above and after consulting additional articles and research (Holowetzki, 2002; Chourides et al., 2003) this article will use the following five CSFs that emphasize the human factor within knowledge management:

1. Coaching leadership style.
2. Structure, roles, and responsibilities.
3. Emphasis on learning and education.
4. Attention to motivation, trust, reward and recognition.
5. Establishing the right culture.

Below these different success factors will be discussed in more detail.

Coaching Leadership Style
Management support is essential for the success of KM initiatives. Coaching leadership shown by the managers enhances the value and strategic quality of KM initiatives and sends a signal to all employees that managers view KM as an important activity in their organization to undertake. It is important that the leader fosters open knowledge sharing by creating an environment that is built on trust.

Structure, Roles and Responsibilities
The organizational structure has to support sharing of knowledge. The collection and validation of knowledge, the availability of the appropriate IT infrastructure, and "help systems" that enable employees to share knowledge, all require appropriate structures within the organization. The organizational structure should also encourage the formation of teams, work groups, and communities of practice. Furthermore it is important that knowledge sharing is encouraged across role and functional boundaries.

Emphasis on Learning and Education
By focusing on (earning and education, new knowledge is created, which can help an organization to develop new innovative ideas. But during a learning process knowledge is also shared among individuals and they can learn from each other. In this way a bonding process between senior and the younger employee is initiated.

Attention to Motivation, Trust, Reward and Recognition
It is important that the contributors of knowledge and re-users of knowledge are assured that they have nothing to fear or be anxious about being discarded when giving knowledge "away" or by using "other people's" knowledge; a trustful environment is therefore an important goal to achieve. In business organization, trust has been identified as an essential condition for people to share knowledge and expertise (Nottingham, 1998).

The knowledge provider has to be specifically rewarded and compensated for doing something that is not explicitly stated in his or her contract. It is therefore important to reward sharing of knowledge. The reward system should be in balance with regard to intrinsic and extrinsic motivators.

Establishing the Right Culture
Creating the right culture for KM, considering the factors mentioned above, is very important, especially since other success factors are influenced by the organizational culture. Establishing a culture that enhances KM is a process and cannot be achieved overnight; it might take several years to adapt an organizational culture. However, when the right culture has been established KM can take place very effectively. Wah (1999) suggests that no KM program can succeed a shift in the culture of the organization.

Alignment of the Senior Worker to the CSFs of KM
In this part of the article possibilities to tailor the critical success factors to the senior employee are discussed, so that KM among this age group can take place as effective as possible.

A coaching Leadership Style
This leadership style is important for knowledge management since employees become conscientious about the fact that management values knowledge sharing. On the other side a coaching leadership style (as discussed earlier) has also a positive influence on the self-development of senior employees. When a manager sits down with his/her employee and reflects on things achieved in their lives and what is still possible in the future, senior employees can regain their enthusiasm and start to feel more committed to the organization (again). This increases job satisfaction and also benefits knowledge sharing. Career planning is often only done with younger employees (Zetlin, 1992), but this can be also an important tool to motivate the senior employee.

Structures, Roles and Responsibilities
Senior employees value the feeling of usefulness in their daily activities at work. This possibility could be created by letting the senior employee actively share their experience and know-how with younger employees. By giving senior employees responsibility and an active role in knowledge transfer and sharing they feel useful at work. This again increases the motivation (the senior employee experiences

the intrinsic rewards) which also benefits knowledge sharing. By creating this opportunity the knife cuts two ways.

Emphasis on Learning and Education

Senior employees are willing to learn and want to develop themselves, but they need an active approach from their managers, who help them to see where their area of interests lays. Most of the time this active style is absent and seniors are not offered the opportunity to engage in new projects or trainings. A lot of HR managers do not really offer senior employees educational trainings, since they do not see the benefits this can deliver to the company. This critical success factor of KM needs a lot of improvement with regard to the senior employee.

Attention to Motivation, Trust, Rewards and Recognition

Older employees are motivated in a different way, as described earlier in this article. They value the intrinsic rewards of work, life experiencing feelings of respect and recognition. This could be achieved by creating opportunities for senior employees in which they can feel appreciated and respected, for example, in a mentor relationship with a younger employee. I will come back to this possibility later on.

Trust is an important factor to reassure that people share their knowledge and know-how. It is important that the environment in which the senior employee works feels safe, so that they do not have the idea that when they share their knowledge they will became superfluous in the eyes of their managers.

Establishing the Right Culture

A senior employee needs an organizational culture where there exists trust and respect. A culture in which there are possibilities for flexible working hours and where their knowledge and know-how is recognized and appreciated. In a lot of organizations this is not the case and managers have negative images and ideas about the senior employee, this makes it difficult to create a culture that stimulates KM among this particular age group. A study performed by Taylor and walker (1998), also acknowledges the importance of establishing the right culture, since the culture of an organization acts as a key factor in shaping orientations towards senior employees.

Implications for the Human Resource Manager

In order for managers to effectively manage all the knowledge that is present in the senior worker, it is first important that these managers become conscientious of the value of senior employees. They should step out the mindset that holds all the negative images and presumptions about the senior employee. A positive vision that senior employees can still be of great importance to the organization and that they are a great value should replace the old, negative vision. Only after this goal is obtained the next (more practical) steps towards effective knowledge management can take place.

Managers should start talking with senior employees about what their self development needs are and where they want to go with respect to their careers. They should show their senior employees that they value them and encourage them to undertake new activities.

Managers should establish teams or work groups that contain both senior and junior employees. In this way the cooperation between the younger and the more experienced employee is stimulated and they can inspire each other and learn from each other, by sharing their knowledge. Developing mentor relationships is also a possibility, in these relationships specific organizational know-how can be transferred and shared.

Managers should also reward knowledge transfer between generations. This means creating confidence that experienced employees who pass on their knowledge to younger colleagues not need to be afraid of being replaced by them. This also has to do with building up a certain level of trust within the organization.

Managers must be aware of the fact that senior employees have other needs and therefore maintain a life-phase oriented HR development strategy. This strategy should make clear that senior employees have needs for flexible working hours and a balance between work and private life.

A culture which fosters the senior employee and in which KM can prosper needs to be created. Figure 3 visualizes this culture.

This culture entails factors that are important for stimulating knowledge sharing among senior employees, but also entails factors that are critical to the success of KM in general. By establishing a culture as depicted above KM can start to take place in a more effective way among senior employees.

An organizational culture is, of course, not only created by HR managers, the whole organization needs to contribute to its establishment. However, a lot of activities that are undertaken by the HR manager can add to the right culture for KM.

Conclusion

This article has quite extensively discussed the issues of KM and the developments within the workforce that took place over the last couple of years. The main reason for doing this is the lack of understanding that turns out to exist among managers about the impact the great loss of organizational knowledge and know-how, that is threatening many organizations, can have within the upcoming years. By discussing the issues in more detail the author hopes HR managers start to become conscientious about the possible problems.

In today's literature, the two topics (KM and the senior employee) discussed in this literature review, have received only little attention from researchers; this literature review is one of the first scientific articles that does explicitly link the senior employee to the process of KM.

However, some organizations are starting to understand the need for knowledge transfer among their own senior

FIGURE 3

The Ideal Culture for Effective KM among Senior Employees

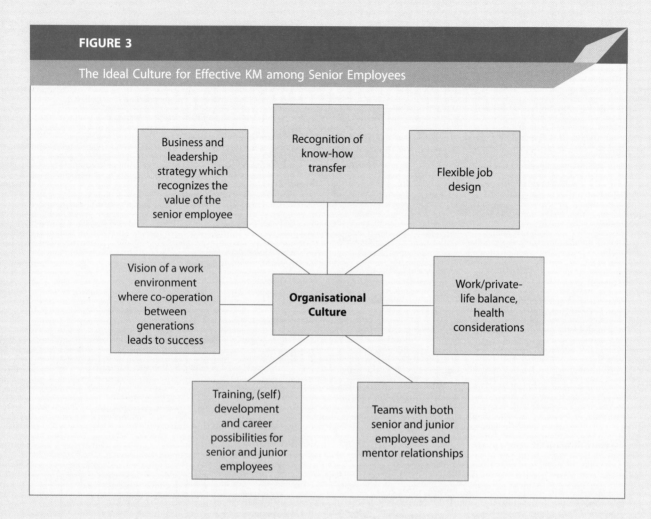

employees and the one's of their customers, like IBM (IBM Consulting Services, 2006). Several other authors address the issue of the ageing workforce and the impact on the knowledge industry (Bradly, 2005). Others stress the factors of how to deal with senior employees in terms of human resource development and training (Rhebergen and Wognum, 1997; Armstrong-Stassen and Templer, 2005).

This article has investigated how KM can take place in an effective way among senior employees, by looking at the CSFs of KM and aligning these CSFs to this particular age group. This first sub-question was: "what are the CSFs of KM?". Different theorists mention different critical success factors of KM, but when looking specifically at the ones that emphasize the human factor, five CSFs come to the fore:

1. Coaching leadership style.
2. Structure, roles, and responsibilities.
3. Emphasis on learning and education.
4. Attention to motivation, trust, reward and recognition.
5. Establishing the right culture.

The last factor comprises a significant part of the other factors; the other factors all have their influence on the organizational culture.

The second sub-question was: "how can these CSFs be aligned to the senior employee?". It appears to be the case that the CSFs of KM can be aligned very successfully to the senior employee. Mainly, because a lot of the critical success factors of KM contain aspects that are valued highly among the senior employee (attention to recognition, trust) or aspects where this age group can benefit by (a coaching leadership style; emphasis on learning, education; and assigning responsibility).

The third sub-question was: "what are the implications for the HR manager?". The most important implication for the HR manager is that they should take a more proactive management style towards the senior employee. They should guide them in their self-development and assist them with deciding on their goals. When this happens, the senior employee experiences the feeling of being appreciated again and than more practical steps that will benefit KM more directly can be taken.

The problem definition of this article that had to be answered was: "which critical success factors of Knowledge Management can be aligned to the senior employee to enhance the effectiveness of this activity? (among this age group)". During the writing of this article the author discovered that there exist a lot of synergetic opportunities between a more proactive management style towards senior employees and effective KM among this group of employees. Therefore, the implications and recommendations for the HR manager point mainly towards an approach that stimulates this leadership style. When this management style is initiated by the HR manager the critical success factors of KM can be very well aligned to the senior employee and the level of effectiveness of KM among this age group will be able to increase significantly. However, further research in this area is recommended, also because the level of impact can differ for each organization.

Furthermore it has become clear that there exist lot of literature that comes to a negative image of the senior employee, but also a lot that comes to a positive image. Mapping out the real situation at micro-level is therefore important.

This article is not extensively based on the direct empirical findings, therefore further research is needed to verify, falsify, specify and complete the recommendations made in this article and the conclusions that can be drawn from it. Undertaking further research in this area is strongly recommended, especially since the significant social relevance of this issue. Further (empirical) research should point out how the effectiveness of KM can be stimulated among senior employees and which theories are relevant to consult in this area. Maybe after more research and bringing the findings into practice HR managers are able to turn the question among senior employees: "How long do you still have to work?" into: "how long do you still can work?" and will it be possible to optimize the effectiveness of KM among this age group.

Recommendations

The implications and conclusions mentioned above point towards a more proactive management style; organizations should face the current developments and start to invest in their senior employees again. But how and where to start?

HR managers should start to map out the current situation in the organization in order to develop a social chart of the organization's personnel file. The company needs to get clear what kind characteristics, based on hard figures, can be assigned to the different age groups present within the organization. Managers need to look at, for example, the age structure of the organization and at retention rates and training participation of employees. When management has fulfilled this task, it should start looking at which trends can be discovered and what the backgrounds of the figures are. Based on trends and backgrounds, the organization can determine if action is needed. By doing this an honest and sincere view of the different groups of employees can be

formed and presumptions that might exist can be eliminated. Management also becomes more conscientious about the situation in their organization.

The next step the HR management should take is to actively involve the employees themselves in the process. This can be done by asking them about the bottlenecks they experience and other experiences they have with regard to the management of personnel, but also by individual interviews between HR manager and senior employee in which self development issues are discussed. In this way the awareness among employees about the issue will increase and management will also demonstrate that it is undertaking some "real" action. This is also a knowledge sharing activity, which positively influences KM.

It will not be easy to establish a complete change in organizational culture. In today's society a lot of prejudices exist about senior employees and a lot of regulations are aimed at resignment of senior employees (although this currently starts to change). It is therefore important that a basis for structural cultural change is created and HR managers should take an active position in this process. They should appoint the value of senior employees, refute the presumptions that exist and change their personnel policy.

When senior employees experience that management is really changing their point of view, their trust in management increases and management can then start to implement activities that facilitate KM, like mentoring relationships and mixed teams. Subsequently, knowledge sharing and transfer can take place and the organizations can begin to work towards effective KM.

Source: Journal of Knowledge Management, 11, (4), 82–96 (2007). Reprinted by permission.

REFERENCES

Abou-Zeid, A. (2002), "A knowledge management reference model", *Journal of Knowledge Management*, Vol. 6 No. 5, pp. 486–99.

Armstrong-Stassen, M. and Templer, A. (2005), "Adapting training for older employees: the Canadian response to an aging workforce", *Journal of Management Development*, Vol. 24 No. 1, pp. 57–67.

Bixler, C.H. (2002), "Applying the four pillars of knowledge management", *KM World*, Vol. 11 No. 11.

Bradly, J. (2005), "The ageing population and knowledge work", *Foresight: The Journal of Future Studies, Strategic Thinking and Policy*, Vol. 7 No. 1, pp. 61–7.

Chourides, P., Longbottom, D., and Murphy, W. (2003), "Excellence in knowledge management: an empirical study to identify critical factors and performance measures", *Measuring Business Excellence*, Vol. 7 No. 2, pp. 29–36.

Diekstra, M.C.W.M. (2003), *Project Arbeidstoekomstverkenning Eindrapportage, ("Project Future Labour Exploration").*

Groff, T.R. and Jones, T.P. (2003), *Introduction to Knowledge Management: KM in Business*, Elsevier, Amsterdam.

Henkens. K. (1998), "Older workers in transition: studies on early retirement decisions in The Netherlands", PhD thesis, Utrecht University, Utrecht.

Heymann, F.V. and Terlien, M.H.D. (2003), *Spelen met je toekomst, 50-plussers op weg naar zingeving, ("Playing with your future, employees who are 50 and above on their way to sensemaking").*

Holowetzki, A. (2002), "The relationship between knowledge management and organizational culture: an examination of cultural factors that support the flow and management of knowledge within an organization", Applied Information Management, University of Oregon, Eugene, OR, available at: http://aim.uoregon.edu/research/pdfs/Holowetzki2002.pdf (accessed 1 June 2005).

IBM Consulting Services (2006), "Addressing the challenges of an aging workforce", available at: www.1.ibm.com/services/us/imc/pdf/g510-3970-aging-workforce-asia.pdf (accessed 16 May 2006).

Kanfer, R. and Ackerman, P.L. (2004), "Aging, adult development and work motivation", *Academy of Management Review*, Vol. 29 No. 3, pp. 440–59.

Keuning, D. (1998), *Management: A Contemporary Approach*, Pitman Publishing, London.

Lyon, P. and Glover, I. (1998), "Divestment or investment? The contradictions of HRM in relation to older companies", *Human Resource Management Journal*, Vol. 8 No. 1, pp. 56–66.

McIntosh, B. (2000), "An employer's guide to older workers: how to win them back and convince them to stay", US Department of Labor, Employment and Training Administration, available at: www.doleta.gov/Seniors/other_docs/EmplGuide.pdf (accessed 20 May 2005).

Maslow, A. (1954), *Motivation and Personality*, Harper & Row, New York, NY.

Metcalf, H. and Thompson, M. (1990), "Older workers: employers' attitudes and practices", Report No. 194, Institute for Manpower Studies, Brighton.

Malhotra, Y. and Galletta, D.F. (2003), "Role of commitment and motivation in KMS implementation: theory, conceptualization, and measurement of antecedents of success", *Proceedings of the 36th Hawaii International Conference on System Sciences.*

Nottingham, A. (1998), "Knowledge management as the next strategic focus", paper no. 42, *Proceedings of the 8th Annual BIT Conference, Manchester Metropolitan University.*

Rastogi, P.N. (2000), "Knowledge management and intellectual capital: the new virtuous reality of competitiveness", *Human Systems Management*, Vol. 19 No. 1, pp. 39–49.

Remery, C., Henkens, K., Schippers, J., and Ekamper, P. (2001). "Managing an ageing workforce and a tight labour market: views held by Dutch employers", *Population Review and Policy Review*, Vol. 22, pp. 21–40.

Rhebergen, B. and Wognum, I. (1997). "Supporting the career development of older employees: an HRD study in a Dutch company", *International Journal of Training and Development*, Vol. 1 No. 3, pp. 191–8.

Sterns. H. and Miklos, S. (1995). "The ageing worker in a changing environment: organizational and individual issues", *Journal of Vocational Behaviour*, Vol. 47 No. 3, pp. 248–68.

Taylor, P. and Walker, A. (1998). "Policies and practices towards older workers: a framework for comparative research". *Human Resource Management Journal*, Vol. 8 No. 3, pp. 61–76.

Wah. L. (1999). "Making knowledge stick", *Management Review*, Vol. 88 No. 5, pp. 24–9.

Zetlin, M. (1992), "Older and wiser: tips to motivate the 50s crowd", *Management Review*, Vol. 81 No. 8, pp. 30–3.

CHAPTER 14

Global Human Resource Management

Global Human Resource Management at Reebok

In 1998, athletic shoe global industry leader Nike was hit by a wave of negative publicity regarding the conditions in many of its overseas factories. Growing reports of strikes, unsafe working conditions, poor wages, worker abuse, and the use of child labor aroused a fury within the United States. Although Nike's market share remained constant, its stock price sagged with each new report of labor abuse in Asia.

Reebok, one of Nike's main competitors and a company with a history of strong support for human rights, acted quickly to ensure that there were no similar problems at overseas sites owned by Reebok or those in which subcontractors produced goods for Reebok. Reebok contracted with a respected nonprofit social research group in Jakarta, Indonesia, for thorough inspections of two of its shoe factories that employed more than 10,000 workers. The researchers interviewed and surveyed workers, performed health and safety tests, and discussed operations with managers. These audits marked the first time that a U.S. company allowed truly independent outsiders with expertise in labor issues to inspect their factories and make their findings public.

The report found a range of problems including poor ventilation, the presence of harmful chemicals, inadequate toilet facilities, and sex bias. Reebok took immediate action but found some cultural challenges in addressing the problems. These problems were largely because of the difficulty of introducing industrialized-world work and culture environments. Workers did not report sexual harassment largely because they did not understand the concept of it. There was also a thriving local market for empty hazardous chemical containers. Reebok's vice president for human rights was relentless in his attempt to force Western values on the reluctant Indonesians. Workers and managers were trained in gender awareness and harassment; requirements were set for the safe disposal of chemical containers; and workers were educated as to the reasons and personal benefits for the protective clothing they were required to wear. Reebok's two Indonesian contractors were forced to spend more than $250,000 to address these issues or lose Reebok's business.

Reebok led the way in ensuring that oppressive sweatshop operations were curtailed. Within days, both Liz Claiborne and Mattel followed suit in having outside independent agencies review their operations and those of their subcontractors. Although these initiatives clearly show good business sense, particularly in light of what happened to Nike, they also show a sensitivity to basic human rights and the ethical treatment of their global labor force.[1]

The strategic business decisions being made by modern organizations increasingly involve some plan to conduct business that was previously conducted domestically in the global arena. In some cases, this may involve a minimal physical presence in another country; in others, it may involve setting up operations that will eventually exceed the size of domestic operations. We no longer live in a domestic economy, as evidenced by diminished trade barriers and regional economic alliances, such as the North American Free Trade Agreement (NAFTA) and the European Union (EU) as well as the acceleration of global financial markets and information networks. Tremendous opportunities exist to market goods and services abroad, particularly in less-developed countries; to participate in joint ventures with foreign organizations; and to outsource operations to other countries as a means of lowering costs. When one considers that less than 10 percent of the world population resides in the United States and that many domestic consumer markets are saturated, it should not be surprising that an increasing number of organizations are developing strategies to expand internationally.

These strategic opportunities are resulting in employers sending an increasing number of employees abroad to start up, manage, and develop their global operations. While a greater percentage of the U.S. workforce is being moved abroad, an increasing number of U.S. domestic workers are natives of other countries. These trends are not just limited to larger organizations as they once were; small- and medium-size employers are taking advantage of international opportunities, and their workforces are becoming more culturally diverse.

An organization might focus on expanding globally for a number of reasons. Foreign countries may present enhanced market opportunities. In addition, expanding the scope and volume of operations to support global initiatives could result in economies of scale in production as well as in the administrative side of the organization. Competitive pressure may require an organization to enter foreign markets to keep pace with industry leaders. Finally, acquisition activity may result in the ownership of a foreign-based organization or subsidiary.

Regardless of the reasons a company may have for expanding operations globally, human resource (HR) management is critical to the success of any global endeavor. If one adopts the perspective that HR strategy must be derived from corporate strategy and that people do determine an organization's success or failure, then the HR function needs to be a key strategic partner in any global undertakings. Ironically, HR is often neglected in the planning and establishment of global operations.

Strategic Global HR at McDonald's

When fast-food king McDonald's initially expanded outside the United States, it followed a very ethnocentric approach to going global. U.S. expatriates were sent abroad to develop the new sites and maintain as much consistency as possible with domestic operations. Locals were "McDonaldized"—taught the specific operations and business plans developed back in the United States. This approach has evolved over the years to one that is now very polycentric. When opening locations outside the United States, expatriates are rarely used and HR professionals at McDonald's partner closely with locals to develop an operation that fits with local culture, customs, and lifestyles. A four-phase approach is used in which HR has a specific and critical role to play at each step. The first phase, development preparation, usually begins 18–24 months prior to the actual opening. During this phase, HR researches issues such as compensation and benefits, considers recruiting strategies, and secures a labor attorney or consultant. The second phase, resources selection, takes place 8–12 months prior to opening. HR takes the information gathered in phase one and begins to develop specific HR programs and plans and determines staffing needs and compensation levels. The third phase, resource development and strategy implementation, takes place 3–8 months prior to opening. HR puts together employee handbooks, considers the effects of local labor laws on operations, and begins to implement its staffing plan by hiring employees. The final phase, preopening preparation, begins 90 days prior to opening.

Here, HR conducts training and lays the groundwork for the performance review system. McDonald's strategy for its global operations includes HR as a key strategic partner, facilitating the implementation of the human and cultural dimension of the operation for maximum success.[2]

How Global HRM Differs From Domestic HRM

Despite the fact that the core principles of strategic HR management also apply to global HR management, global HR presents some unique contingencies. First, managing people in global settings requires HR to address a broader range of functional areas. These areas include clarifying taxation issues; coordinating foreign currencies, exchange rates, and compensation plans; and working directly with the families of employees who may be accepting overseas assignments. Second, it requires more involvement in the employee's personal life. The employee is usually assisted with acquiring housing in the host country; selling or leasing domestic accommodations; locating recreational and cultural opportunities for the employee and family; arranging and paying for school for the employee's children; and locating and securing domestic help for the employee. Third, the organization must often set up different HR management systems for different geographic locations. Fourth, the organization is often forced to deal with more complex external constituencies, including foreign governments and political and religious groups. Finally, global assignments often involve a heightened exposure to risks. These risks include the health and safely of the employee and family; legal issues in the host country; possible terrorism; and the human and financial consequences of mistakes, which may greatly exceed the costs of those made domestically.

The threat of terrorism has added to many of the anxieties employees face when considering and undertaking a global assignment. A recent survey found that expatriates need and want more support from headquarters than they are receiving regarding health and safety concerns; only 20 percent responded that their employers were keeping them sufficiently informed about health and safety issues.[3] Dissatisfied expatriates can be expensive for an organization: The average cost of a three-year assignment abroad is $1.3 million.[4] In addition, concerns about the employee's and/or family safety can diminish productivity and cause stress. Consequently, employers need to communicate with—and provide the needed support for—expatriates about their safety to ensure that the assignment is a success.

The decision to expand globally first involves determining the appropriate strategy for involvement in the host country. For example, the organization may decide to simply export its goods to a foreign country; this might require very limited presence on the part of domestic employees. The organization might also decide to subcontract or license certain goods and services to a foreign partner. On a slightly more involved scale, a joint venture might be undertaken abroad with a foreign partner. Finally, the organization could decide to establish a significant presence abroad by setting up operations in the form of a foreign branch office or subsidiary.

Assessing Culture

Several factors will influence the level of involvement an organization might choose in its foreign operations. Economic, market, social, and political conditions will certainly play a significant role in any decision to go abroad. A larger issue might be the culture of the host country and how it compares to the national culture of the organization's home. National cultures differ on a variety of dimensions, and many global undertakings fail because of a lack of understanding or appreciation of cultural differences.

One of the most popular models of cultural differences among countries was developed by Hofstede, who explained cultural differences along four dimensions.[5] The first dimension is the extent to which a society emphasizes individualism or collectivism. Individualistic societies value the development of and focus on the individual; collectivistic societies value togetherness, harmony, belongingness, and loyalty to others. The second dimension is power distance. This dimension looks at the extent to which a society is hierarchical, with an unequal distribution of power among its members, as opposed to one where there are few distinctions and power is more evenly distributed among individuals. The third dimension is uncertainty avoidance, which refers to the extent to which the society feels comfortable with ambiguity and values and encourages risk taking. The fourth dimension is the extent to which the society displays "masculine" or "feminine" tendencies. A masculine society is one that is more aggressive, assertive, and focused on achievements; the feminine society is one that emphasizes interpersonal relationships and sensitivity toward the welfare and well-being of others. Although many are uncomfortable with the sexist connotations of *masculine* and *feminine* and the stereotypes they encourage, this dimension does significantly explain many differences in cultural behavior in societies. Some researchers who have applied Hofstede's work have substituted *quantity of life* for *masculinity* and *quality of life* for *femininity*. Exhibit 14.1 illustrates how a number of countries fit Hofstede's model of culture.

Another well-known model that explains differences in culture was developed by Hall, who characterized culture by the patterns with which we communicate.[6] His work focused on the more subtle means by which we express and display our culture. These means might not be evident to someone from outside the culture, but they are understood and accepted by insiders. Hall's model describes culture in terms of five silent "languages": time, space, material goods, friendships, and agreement.

The language of time considers how we use time to communicate and how we use it to manage our daily lives. For example, how much do individuals in the culture rely on schedules, appointments, and deadlines? Is it considered appropriate to keep someone waiting for a meeting? Do meetings usually have a timed agenda? Are meetings and appointments scheduled with an ending time or are they open ended?

The language of space considers how we communicate through space and distance. For example, what is considered the appropriate physical distance between two people engaged in a conversation? Friendship, formality, and even intimacy are often communicated by distance. How are spaces in organizations arranged to communicate rank, power, and status? Does an organization have private offices and/or designated parking spaces? Are some offices larger than others?

EXHIBIT 14.1

Examples of Hofstede's Cultural Dimensions

Country	Individualism-Collectivism	Power Distance	Uncertainty Avoidance	Quantity of Life*
Australia	Individual	Small	Moderate	Strong
Canada	Individual	Small	Low	Moderate
England	Individual	Small	Moderate	Strong
France	Individual	Large	High	Weak
Greece	Collective	Large	High	Moderate
Italy	Individual	Moderate	High	Strong
Japan	Collective	Moderate	High	Strong
Mexico	Collective	Large	High	Strong
Singapore	Collective	Large	Low	Moderate
Sweden	Individual	Small	Low	Weak
United States	Individual	Small	Low	Strong
Venezuela	Collective	Large	High	Strong

*A wek quantity-of-life score is equivalent to a high quality-of-life score.

Source: G. Hofstede, "Motivation, Leadership, and Organization: Do American Theories Apply Abroad?" *Organizational Dynamics*, Summer 1980, pp. 42–63.

The language of material goods can be similarly used to signify power, success, and status. In some cultures, these indicators are of critical importance in establishing one's personal and professional identity. In an organizational setting, this language might be communicated through generous perks such as a company car and might be further evidenced by executive salaries that are many times those of lower level workers. Organizations that establish and maintain pay compression plans are attempting to silence this kind of language.

The language of friendships considers how we form interpersonal relationships. For example, are friendships formed and dissolved quickly or are they built on a foundation over a long period of time? Is there a mutual sense of ongoing obligation in interpersonal relationships or are they more transient and maintained only as long as both parties see some benefit? Some cultures communicate status via material goods; other cultures communicate status through one's network of friends and the support this network provides.

The language of agreement considers how consensus is reached among people. For example, are formal, written contracts signed under an oath of law the norm in business negotiations or is a simple handshake sufficient guarantee? Is it acceptable to debate someone with whom you do not agree and, if so, is it acceptable to debate in front of others?

A key issue that impacts an organization's success in the global arena is an awareness of cultural differences and the development of both a business strategy and corresponding HR strategy that is consistent with the culture of the host country. Although it is beyond the scope of this chapter to detail how cultural differences might impact people management systems, a culture in which negotiations are based on trust and friendship that is built over time might pose some difficulty for an American, who might be used to getting down to business and negotiating without developing any kind of interpersonal connection. Also, the candor and outspokenness for which Americans are known could conflict with the styles of those from other cultures. In short, when cultures come together in organizational settings, special consideration must be paid to managing processes such as power dynamics and relationships, norms of participation and decision making, and performance management and compensation systems to prevent misunderstandings.

Much as societies have cultures, organizations also have their own cultures. As a result, decision makers need to examine the interface between the culture of the organization and the culture of the host country in determining whether an appropriate fit exists and, subsequently, in developing an optimal business strategy and appropriate HR management strategies. For example, if the organization strongly values diversity, what will be done when a host country's culture fails to support these values? In many cultures, it is acceptable to discriminate on the basis of gender, race, ethnicity, age, disability, and sexual orientation. Does the organization extend its ban on smoking to all overseas locations? Will it prohibit facial hair on employees or prohibit employees from enjoying a glass of wine with their lunches? What will happen in a culture in which bribes are an accepted and expected means of conducting business?

In going abroad, an organization needs to decide what HR policies will be implemented in the host country and needs to make these decisions prior to arrival. These decisions will force top managers to confront a number of ethical decisions and may test the strength of the organization's culture. Conflict issues will need to be resolved relative to incompatible local and corporate cultures. Decision makers need to understand which values the organization holds so deeply that it will not compromise, even in the face of significant financial consequences. Although these ethical decisions can present difficult choices, they can help to strengthen the organization's mission, strategy, and employment practices.

National culture can have a significant effect on an organization's ability to utilize strategic HR. A culture that is oriented toward tradition, for example, might not understand the logic of, or resist, any kind of planning. Certain cultures have stringent rules regarding staffing and may require the organization to employ individuals assigned to it by a centralized labor bureau. Individuals in some very strict hierarchical cultures would probably not respond well to upward performance feedback programs. In some cultures, it is considered inappropriate for a worker to report to a manager who is younger than the subordinate. The inappropriateness of using direct eye contact in conversation in some cultures might bias the results of the employment interview process.

Where a culture fits on the individualism–collectivism continuum would influence how it defines acceptable performance and appropriate compensation. Consequently, in managing across cultures, it is critical to have a strong sense of cultural self-awareness yet remain aware that oversensitivity to cultural issues can be as detrimental as undersensitivity. Reading 14.1, "In the Eye of the Beholder: Cross-Cultural Lessons in Leadership From Project GLOBE," examines the similarities and differences of the cultures of five major world countries and the implications for both American executives in each of these countries and for the development of effective global leaders. Reading 14.2, "Cross-Cultural Management and Organizational Behavior in Africa," expands this discussion to include Africa.

Strategic HR Issues in Global Assignments

An organization can use several different approaches in managing the process of sending workers abroad. An administrative approach involves merely assisting employees with paperwork and minor logistics—for example, hiring movers, ensuring that taxes are paid, and obtaining a work visa for the employee and travel visas for family members. A tactical approach involves managing the risk or failure factor—for example, handling the administrative paperwork while also providing limited, usually one-day, training for the employee. This approach does only what needs to be done to prevent failure. A strategic approach to global assignments, however, involves much more support and coordination. In addition to those items cited previously, strategically managing such a process would involve adding extensive selection systems; ongoing, integrated training; a specific performance management system; destination services; and a strategized repatriation program at the end of the assignment.

A model that outlines the strategic HR issues in global assignments is presented in Exhibit 14.2. The first step in the strategic management of global assignments is the establishment of a specific purpose for the assignment. There may be numerous reasons for the assignment, including business or market development; the setup, transfer, or integration of information technology; management of an autonomous subsidiary; coordination or integration of foreign with domestic operations; a temporary assignment to a vacant position; or the development of local management talent.

After the purpose of the assignment has been identified, the process of selecting an appropriate employee for the assignment can commence. Much as there is an organizational purpose for the assignment, there should also be an individual purpose for the assignment, as indicated in Exhibit 14.3. An employee could be chosen for and accept an international assignment to prepare that employee for a top management position, develop further technical or interpersonal skills, or allow an employee to follow a dual-career spouse/partner.

Both the organizational and individual purposes for the assignment must be identified and matched. The assignment needs to be conceptualized as a win–win proposition. There should be clear articulated gain for both the organization and the employee as a prerequisite to success on the assignment.

After an appropriate individual has been identified, it is important to assess the adaptability to the host culture of both the employee and any family members who will be accompanying the employee on the assignment. The single greatest reason for failure on an overseas assignment has to do with adaptability skills rather than technical skills and is usually a consequence of the adaptability of the employee's family to the host culture. Individuals and their families should be screened to determine their ability to be comfortable in the host culture. This might include sending the employee and family members to the host country for several weeks to test their adaptability. Among the areas that an organization will need to assess are the technical abilities of the employee; the adaptability, willingness, and motivation to live overseas; tolerance of ambiguity; communication skills; patience and openness to differences in others; and willingness to interact with both the employee and accompanying family members.

EXHIBIT 14.2

Strategic HR Issues in Global Assignments

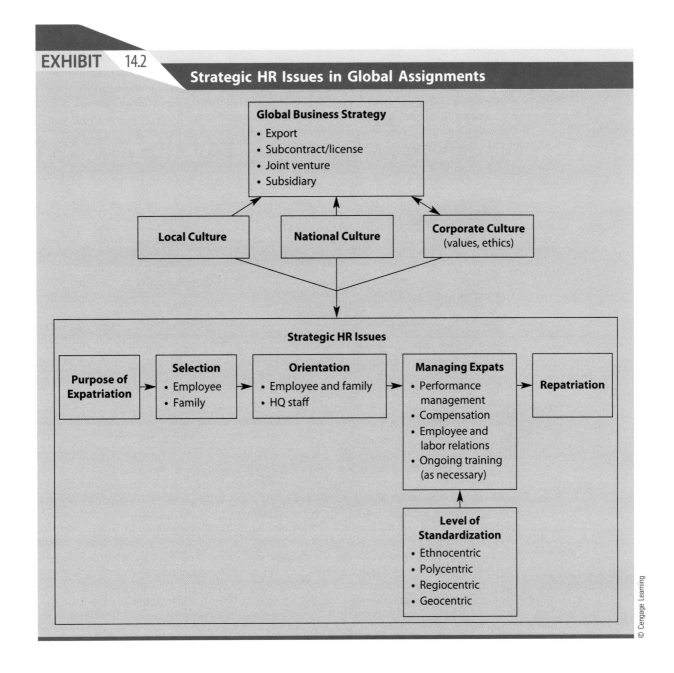

Global Business Strategy
- Export
- Subcontract/license
- Joint venture
- Subsidiary

Local Culture

National Culture

Corporate Culture
(values, ethics)

Strategic HR Issues

Purpose of Expatriation

Selection
- Employee
- Family

Orientation
- Employee and family
- HQ staff

Managing Expats
- Performance management
- Compensation
- Employee and labor relations
- Ongoing training (as necessary)

Repatriation

Level of Standardization
- Ethnocentric
- Polycentric
- Regiocentric
- Geocentric

© Cengage Learning

Expatriate Selection at Kellogg Co.

Given the high cost of most global assignments, it is critical for organizations to get some return on their investment in sending employees abroad. Battle Creek, Michigan–based breakfast cereal manufacturer Kellogg saw its turnover rate among expatriates reach 40 percent. Kellogg viewed the retention problem as being rooted in poor selection of candidates for global assignments. To remedy this problem, Kellogg first implemented a selection strategy for its global assignments, including a pilot program that identified the best candidates based on assessments from managers. HR and senior management partnered to narrow the list down to 16 individuals who were then given assessment tests that examined work styles, habits, values, interests, and lifestyles. Employee spouses were also given the assessment. Key personality traits critical to assignment abroad, such as flexibility, willingness to learn, openness, sense of humor, adaptability, ability to handle ambiguity, and interest in others, were measured. The information was then analyzed and the results given to employees and their spouses to explain potential risks and areas of concern that needed to be addressed prior to any assignment. This new process has had a 100 percent success rate for Kellogg in its expatriate assignments.[7]

EXHIBIT 14.3   Purposes of Expatriation

Organizational	Individual
• Business or market development	• Skill development
• Setup, transfer, or integration of information technology	• Preparation for top management
• Manage autonomous subsidiary	• Follow dual-career partner/spouse
• Coordinate or integrate foreign operation with domestic	
• Fill vacant position temporarily	
• Develop local management talent	

© Cengage Learning

Once an employee has been selected for the overseas assignment, the organization then needs to provide the appropriate training for the employee and family members. The initial training should begin at least six to nine months prior to the start of the assignment. Longer training periods will reflect the need to learn language skills necessary in the host country. Prior to departure, the employee and family, if possible, should be allowed a trial period living overseas (if this was not done as part of the selection process). Although this may involve significant costs, it should be viewed as an investment; the costs incurred for such a trip will be much less than the monetary, political, and reputation-damaging costs of a failed overseas assignment.

Also prior to departure, the employee and family should receive cross-cultural training in the norms and values of the host country, workplace and business practices, language training (as necessary), health and safety issues, and realistic expectations of what day-to-day life in the country will be like. This training should not be considered completed when the employee and family depart for the host country. A critical mistake made by many organizations is the lack of follow-up, once employees have gone abroad, to provide additional support to ensure that there have been no unexpected surprises or consequences.

While the employee and family are being trained, simultaneous training should be conducted for headquarters staff who will be supervising and/or interacting with the employee who is abroad. Clashes between local culture and headquarters are common on overseas assignments, and headquarters personnel should be provided with some sensitivity training. Sensitivity training will (1) help headquarters staff understand how and why local decisions are being made and (2) allow them to give the expatriate employee the necessary support and empathy while keeping the expatriate informed as to what has been happening at headquarters.

After employees have been relocated to the host country, the day-to-day issues in managing expatriates are not dramatically different from those involved in managing domestic employees.

The same principles and practices of general HR management apply with a few additional concerns. First, it is critical to assess the ongoing training needs of the expatriate employee and family after they have arrived at the host country. Particularly if this is the first time an employee of the organization has been assigned to a particular country, it is likely that some unanticipated events that require additional support and training could materialize. Second, performance management will be more of a challenge; the expatriate's functional boss is usually located domestically, and others in the organization may not be aware of how economic, social, and political conditions and everyday living situations impact the expatriate's performance. Third, many aspects of employee and labor relations will be localized. The expatriate may have to manage a local workforce under far more challenging conditions than those presented domestically. The expatriate may also have to manage the dynamics of being a foreign manager of local employees. Finally, compensation for the expatriate will be different. It is costly to send an employee overseas, usually amounting to as much as three times the employee's annual domestic salary. Income tax payments for the employee may be complicated and costly. Benefits such as armed security guards or private schooling for the employee's children may be necessary. Although compensation for expatriates is often outsourced, organizations need to be very careful in this regard; compensation is a key strategic issue not only from a cost perspective but also in impacting the employee family's ability to live in the host country. Outsourcing compensation to a third party who does not fully understand the organization's overall strategy or have a holistic appreciation of all of the organization's HR systems could result in disaster.

There are three traditional approaches to determining expatriate compensation. The first is the balance-sheet method. With this approach, salary is based on home country pay, and additional expenses associated with relocation and the assignment itself are added to arrive at an overall reimbursement and compensation level. These expenses might include the cost of housing in the host country, furniture, household help, a car and driver, or spousal/partner assistance. This approach ensures that the expatriate gains a sense of equity and fairness in the compensation package; however, the local employees, particularly if they are poor, may sense some inequity. This system can be complex to administer, but it is still widely used, particularly for short-term or temporary assignments.

The higher-of-home-or-host approach takes into account the employee's salary at home and adjusts it upward, as necessary, to account for a higher cost of living in the host country. This approach is usually accompanied by standard perquisites for executives in the host country and is used most commonly for intermediate term assignments of indefinite duration.

When the employee is assigned to a host country on a permanent basis, the localization approach is usually used. Here, the employee's salary is converted to the host country equivalent. Depending on the country, salary structures, and the cost of living, this approach can initially result in a salary decrease for the employee. Localization has become an increasing popular approach for organizations now used by upward of 78 percent of employers.[8]

Expatriate selection assignments are some of the most critical decisions that organizations make relative to their global operations. The success or failure of an expatriate assignment can easily determine the fate and success of an organization's entry into a new global market. Much of the focus of expatriation has traditionally been concerned with the selection and training of expatriates and their accompanying family members. However, this focus has been expanding to involve the active and ongoing management of the expatriate assignment after the relocation has taken place.[9]

In establishing general HR policy for the day-to-day management of all employees abroad—locals as well as expatriates—the organization also needs to make a strategic decision as to the level of standardization it desires across locations. Heenan and Perlmutter identified four different approaches an organization can take in setting and enforcing policy: ethnocentric, polycentric, regiocentric, and geocentric, as illustrated in Exhibit 14.4.[10]

An ethnocentric approach involves exporting the organization's home country practices and policies to foreign locations. This strategy is often used by organizations whose competitive strategy is focused on creating an image. An ethnocentric approach can be beneficial in allowing standardization, integration, and efficiency. However, if it is forced on another culture that does not subscribe to the values on which the practices are based, there can be severe problems. Some

EXHIBIT   14.4

EXHIBIT 14.4 — Four Approaches to IHRM

Aspect of the Enterprise	Orientation			
	Ethnocentric	**Polycentric**	**Regiocentric**	**Geocentric**
Standard Setting, Evaluation, and Control	By home country headquarters	By local subsidiary management	Coordination across countries in the region	Global as well as local standards and control
Communication and Coordination	From HQ to local subsidiary	Little among subsidiaries, little between subsidiary and HQ	Little between subsidiary and HQ, medium to high among subsidiaries in region	Totally connected network of subsidiaries and subsidiaries with headquarters
Staffing	Home country managers	Host country managers	Managers may come from nations within region	Best people where they can be best used

Source: Heenan, D. A. and Perlmutter, Howard V., *Multinational Organizational Development,* Addison-Wesley, pp. 18–19 (1979).

turnover can and should be expected and even encouraged when using this approach. It can also help to make expatriate assignments more attractive to the organization's domestic employees.

A polycentric approach involves allowing each location to develop its own practices and policies that are consistent with the local culture and workforce characteristics. Management practices are localized to suit the existing needs of the marketplace, and adaptability to customer tastes is a key strategic initiative facilitated by this approach. Although this approach can be costly, it is also extremely responsive to local market and labor conditions and can help to reduce employee turnover in an acquisition, particularly if there are antiforeign ownership attitudes among locals.

A regiocentric approach involves developing standardized practices and policies by geographic region; therefore, there is some consistency and efficiency within operations. At the same time, there is some variation among regions to support the local markets. This approach commonly involves establishing autonomously managed regional subsidiaries within a geographic region.

A geocentric approach involves developing one set of global practices and policies that are applied at all locations. This approach differs from the ethnocentric approach in that although the ethnocentric approach exports its one set of management systems based on home country culture to all locations, the geocentric approach considers the global workforce in all its areas of operations as well as the numerous local cultures in which it operates and attempts to develop practices and policies that transcend cultural differences. This approach can be very difficult to implement, given different host government policies and regulations and the need to address them simultaneously. Compensation plans and standards of living can be difficult to unify in an equitable way across different cultures.

Repatriation

The final issue in managing international assignments is repatriation of returning employees. This function is probably one of the most neglected areas in global HR management. Ironically, it is the one that has the greatest impact on the return on investment made in employees sent abroad.

Very few companies deal successfully with the issue of repatriation. Retention rates of repatriates during the first year of return are often as low as 50 percent in many companies. This is not surprising in light of the fact that only 27 percent of expatriates are even guaranteed a position upon return from their international assignment.[11] Employers typically make no plans for any post-return assignment, and expatriates are left to fend for themselves in finding a position within or outside the organization upon their return. Despite the fact that expatriates usually undertake international assignments with career development and advancement in mind, only 33 percent of those who return to their employers are promoted. Fifty-eight percent of expatriates remain at the same level of responsibility, and 9 percent end up accepting positions with lesser responsibility.[12]

Organizations need to establish a strategy that allows them to take the valuable experience abroad and (1) integrate it with what is happening at home and (2) allow coworkers to learn of the repatriate's experience to enhance their own performance. As a prerequisite, repatriates need to be considered from an investment perspective. In many cases, the organization has invested a sizable amount of time and money in the global assignment of the employee, during which time the employee has further developed both personally and professionally. If the organization fails to develop career management programs that allow those returning from abroad to share their knowledge and insights—rather than leave the organization and share that knowledge with competitors—then the investment has a negative return. An employee who has worked in another country may be of great value to a competitor who would like to start up overseas operations.

Many repatriates return from overseas assignments and either have no job assignment waiting for them or receive a job that is considered a demotion. Expatriates often have high-ranking autonomous positions overseas and are forced to assume positions that strip them of this autonomy upon their return. It is not surprising that some expatriates choose to move to another expatriate assignment with the same employer or with a different employer rather than return to headquarters.

Any strategy for repatriation has to address the purpose of the expatriation. The process of repatriation can be greatly facilitated if a clear purpose for the assignment was established ahead of time based on the needs of both employer and employee.

A specific repatriation process needs to address several critical career and personal issues, as outlined in Exhibit 14.5. The first career issue is resolving career anxiety by helping the employee returning from abroad find an appropriate place that is connected with a career path for the future. The second career issue is the organization's reaction to the return. Is the repatriate made to feel welcome? Is any value placed on the global experience? Are new skills that have been developed being put to use? The third career issue is the loss of autonomy. In planning repatriation programs, some consideration must be given to the level of autonomy the repatriate enjoyed overseas and the correspondingly appropriate types of responsibilities, work assignments, and supervision for the return assignment. The fourth career issue is adaptation. During the expatriation period, there were probably some significant changes taking place at the home office. The repatriate needs to be provided with assistance in adapting to those changes to facilitate maximum performance in the new assignment.

EXHIBIT 14.5 Issues to be Addressed in a Repatriation Process

Career	Personal
• Career anxiety—current place, future	• Logistics
• Organization's reaction	• Personal re-adjustment
• Loss of autonomy	• Family re-adjustment
• Adaptation to change	

© Cengage Learning

On a personal level, three major issues need to be addressed in repatriation. The first is logistics. Personal savings will need to be transferred, currency converted, personal belongings inventoried and shipped, automobiles and homes possibly purchased and sold, school transfers arranged, and possibly spousal employment assistance arranged. The more logistical details with which the employee has to contend, the more he or she will be distracted from work. The second personal issue is readjustment and integration into the community for the employee. The third personal issue is readjustment and integration into the community for the employee's family. Although it may seem logical that the return home should be a welcome and easy process, experience has shown that it often is not. Much as the workplace has changed, and the community in which the employee's family lives or is moving to may have changed dramatically during the time abroad. Support for such transition for the employee and family can greatly facilitate the repatriation process.

Repatriation at Colgate-Palmolive

One of the biggest problems with the traditional high attrition rate among repatriates is the loss of experience, skills, and knowledge that accompany the employee's departure. To address this, Colgate-Palmolive has established a global succession database. Used primarily for succession planning purposes, the database—available to the organization's management team worldwide—also contains information on experiences and skills related to work abroad in various cultures. Because Colgate-Palmolive operates over a widely dispersed global area, detailed information about local markets is critical to ongoing success. Seventy-five percent of the company's $9.5 billion annual sales comes from outside North America. At any time, approximately 300 expatriate global managers are on assignment. Seventy-five percent of these managers have had two or more global assignments and 40 percent of these managers have had four or more. Because foreign assignments are seen as critical to an individual's career success within Colgate-Palmolive and the necessary track to senior management, global assignments are in demand. By collecting information related to success in a particular location, Colgate-Palmolive is not only able to provide assistance to managers going on a new assignment but also ensures that its investment in skills, knowledge, and experiences stays with the organization, given the longer "shelf life" of cultural information over market data.[13]

The European Union

Employers who choose to do business in the European Union (EU) do not have the option of taking an ethnocentric approach to HR in their operations there. As the world's largest economy with 27 member states, the EU has the challenge of establishing some consistency in and minimum standards across laws across the region while allowing individual member countries flexibility based on culture and values. Laws related to employment are enacted as directives that bind member countries and set minimum standards that must be met. Directives are usually issued as objectives or desired outcomes and allow individual countries to determine how best to meet those objectives. Hence, the actual laws related to employment may vary from one EU country to another, requiring foreign organizations to be particularly astute when setting up European operations. These laws generally provide workers with far more protection than their counterparts in the United States. The common intent of these laws is an employment relationship that is not adversarial or confrontational but one that protects the rights of workers via more collectivist social policy. As an example, Directive 2010/18/EU requires that a minimum of four months parental leave by provided to each parent following the birth or adoption of a child yet individual countries are free to provide more generous leave.

Unlike the United States, the EU does not follow the employment-at-will policy. Terminating an employee can be a very difficult and expensive undertaking, and the laws regulating the ability to terminate, the notification period, and required severance vary from country to country. In The Netherlands, court approval may be needed to terminate an employee; even termination for cause requires very rigid and specific documentation. Germany requires three months' notification before terminations can take effect; Sweden requires up to six months' notice. In Belgium, where terminations are very difficult, employers may be required to pay up to four years' salary to an employee as severance.[14] Spain requires nine weeks of severance pay for each year of service.[15]

Other areas of the employment relationship are also regulated in various EU countries. Most require a minimum of four weeks of paid vacation, but France requires five weeks, with an additional week for employees between 18 and 21 years of age. Maternity leave in France is a minimum of 16 weeks, 10 of which must be taken after the child is born, and can extend up to 26 weeks for a third pregnancy. For any pending layoffs, Germany requires a "social plan," which outlines the specific selection criteria used and performance and education levels of workers. German employers must also report employee ages and the number of dependants, as older workers and those with more dependants enjoy a greater level of job security than others.[16]

One major way in which the employment relationship in the EU differs from that of the United States is the level of worker involvement seen in European organizations. U.S. employers generally have a unilateral right to make decisions that affect employees, but European employers are required to communicate and negotiate many of these decisions with employees as part of the EU's Directive on Information and Consultation. Works councils, composed of employee-elected worker representatives, are required to meet monthly with senior management to discuss all employment policy issues. Works councils operate at individual work sites and in Germany, France, and The Netherlands must approve many of the decisions that employers hope to implement. Employers who do not consult with their works council are subject to fines and possible recision of the decisions implemented. Germany requires works councils in organizations with five or more employees. France requires them in organizations with 50 or more employees. Larger employers, with at least 1,000 employees and at least 150 in each of two member countries, must also form an EU-wide works council. Decisions that affect workers in more than one country must be presented to these groups, which are employer funded. U.S. employers operating in the EU are faced with a dramatically different mandate relative to how they manage their employees than what they are used to domestically. Works councils formalize the employment relationship far more than is seen with a typical collective-bargaining agreement.

Mexico and Canada

Even though Mexico and Canada are border countries with the United States and primary trade partners, HR management in these countries is often carried out in stark difference to HR management in the United States. Employment discrimination that would be illegal in the United States is rampant and ingrained into hiring practices in Mexico. A recent recruiting advertisement in a Mexico City newspaper for retail managers for Office Depot Mexico requested applicants who were no younger than 26 and no older than 38 and preferably married.[17] The ad cautioned that it was useless to apply if one did not meet these requirements. Despite the fact that Mexico's constitution strictly forbids such discrimination, enforcement is lax. Employers frequently mandate that applicants be of a specified age, gender, marital status, height, or satisfy other personal nonwork related criteria. Female applicants are frequently asked to submit photographs as evidence that they possess a "nice appearance." Gender bias in employment runs rampant—consistent with focus on masculinity in the national culture.

On the other hand, Canada is known to vigorously enforce laws that prohibit discrimination in employment and also provide extensive protections for arbitrary or unjust dismissal of employees. While 90 percent of the Canadian population lives within 60 miles of the U.S. border, these individuals receive far more protection in the employment relationship than do their American counterparts. Canada does not subscribe to the doctrine of employment-at-will and requires reasonable notice of termination as well as legally mandated severance pay based on years of service with the employer. The usual standard is one month per year of service of notice from an employer of pending termination. This amount can be higher if a court feels that the termination was not handled fairly. Employees also are entitled to one week's severance pay per year of service. Most Canadian employers must also provide employees up to 52 weeks of parental and maternity leave; employers in Quebec must provide up to 70 weeks. Noncompete clauses for departing employees are frowned upon, as is a former mandatory retirement age of 65. The province of Quebec amended its Labour Standards Act in 2004 to prohibit bullying or "psychological harassment" in the workplace. Within four years, more than 10,000 charges had been filed under this law.[18]

China

With a population of 1.3 billion people and its 2001 accession into the World Trade Organization, which eliminated the requirement that foreign organizations partner with state-owned Chinese partners, China has seen tremendous economic growth, largely through foreign organizations that have set up operations there. Those organizations seeking to take advantage of the rich economic opportunities offered by China have been confronted with significant challenges relative to HR management. Indeed, it has been noted that China's deep historical and cultural heritage mandates an approach to HR management that uniquely fits the Chinese context.[19] While Chinese universities produce nearly 5 million graduates annually, many of these individuals are not suitable for employment in Western-style multinational organizations. In fact, one survey found that only 10 percent of Chinese university graduates were employable in multinational organizations because of deficiencies in language, interpersonal skills, ability to work in teams, and basic literacy.[20] Even more problematic is the lack of middle- and upper-level manager candidates, many of whom were victims of the Chinese Cultural Revolution that stymied the Chinese education system from 1966 to 1976.

The tremendous demand for workers capable of working in a multinational organization—combined with the short supply of such individuals—has created an employment market in which those with sufficient skills can demand high salaries and expect fast upward mobility. Expatriates typically expect very high compensation, yet many remain unaware of the key dimensions of Chinese culture that affect business relations. Recruiting returnees—Chinese citizens who have lived and/or studied abroad—allows an organization the advantage of having employees who are bilingual and bicultural, but many of these individuals have become assimilated to and enjoy Western lifestyle and culture and have no desire to return to China.[21] Even if an employer is successful in hiring qualified applicants, the strong demand for individuals capable of conducting business in China within a multinational organization makes retention of such employees an ongoing challenge.

There are a number of key factors that influence an employer's ability to retain such individuals. The first of these is supervisory relations. Because Chinese society is very hierarchical, shows respect for elders and authority, and is family centered, employees who have good relations with their supervisors and feel that they "belong" in an organization are less prone to risk this dynamic by seeking employment elsewhere.[22] A second factor is employer prestige. Because China has such a brand-conscious culture, 75 percent of Chinese employees prefer to work for a well-known foreign organization rather than a domestic Chinese organization.[23] This brand consciousness extends beyond consumer goods to the workplace. A third factor is development opportunities. A primary component of Chinese culture is learning and growing through one's lifetime. Chinese employees enjoy challenges and the opportunity to discuss what they are learning and projects on which they are working not only with coworkers but also with friends and family members. A fourth factor is compensation. Chinese employees with sought-after skills know their market value and expect to be compensated accordingly. While performance-based bonuses are relatively new to China, employees—particularly younger ones—have been very receptive to incentive-based compensation plans.[24] A fifth factor that can aid in retention is job title. Because the Chinese are very status-conscious, job titles—regardless of associated responsibility—are very meaningful to employees. While Chinese workers do seek opportunities for growth and development, a change in job title can often be a sufficient reward for performance.[25]

India

In some ways similar to China, with a population of 1.5 billion people and a rapidly growing economy, India has become a major player in global economic development and a target of many multinational organizations. However, India presents some significant challenges for employers related to HR management, which distinguish it from its Asian counterpart.

Unlike China, India has a sizable population of citizens who are well equipped to work in a multinational organization. India has more than 22 million university graduates, a third of whom have backgrounds in science and engineering, and produces 2.5 million new graduates annually.[26] Hence, India has been a leader in information technology and business process outsourcing. Despite India's large technically trained workforce, demand for skilled labor exceeds supply. Competition among employers for talent remains intense, and job hopping and poaching of employees are standards of doing business in India.

One of the greatest challenges to doing business in India is the onerous legal system, which involves more than 100 different noncodified and ambiguous laws as well as joint federal and state government oversight of laws related to employment and labor.[27] These laws require employers to maintain registers and provide annual filings to regulatory authorities. Every employee must receive a formal letter of appointment that outlines all terms and conditions of employment and serves as a legally binding contract. Termination of employees in India can be difficult and requires that multiple procedures be followed, which include appropriate cause and notification as well as arbitration. While misconduct is generally accepted as a valid ground for termination, poor performance is not necessarily an acceptable basis. Employers are also required to provide employees with a flexible benefit plan, which accounts for 35 percent of overall compensation. Employers and employees jointly contribute to social security, called the "Provident Fund," whereby each party contributes 12 percent of the employee's wages.[28] The Shops and Establishments Act mandates paid annual leave for all employees, which can be carried forward to subsequent years.

Employment discrimination based on religion, race, caste, sex, or place of birth is specifically banned in the public sector by India's constitution. Gender-based pay disparities are prohibited by the Equal Remuneration Act of 1948, while the Maternity Benefit Act of 1961 provides employees with 12 weeks paid maternity leave. However deeply embedded cultural mores in this male-dominated society have limited the career and general employment-related opportunities for women whose role has largely been tending to the home and family.

Much as in China, retention of skilled workers in India is a challenge because of the demand that exceeds supply. India also has a pronounced shortage of sufficiently experienced and trained middle managers to oversee employees. Because the HR function in most organizations needs to spend an inordinate amount of time on recruiting, compliance, and other associated transactional activities, there is little involvement in strategic issues.

Retention at Prudential Process Management Services

Prudential Process Management Services (PPMS) is a Mumbai, India–based organization that provides customer service for Prudential's financial services customers in the United Kingdom. With 1,200 employees, PPMS had quickly adapted to doing business in India and enjoys a 20 percent annual attrition rate in a customer service industry that has a norm of 45 percent.

PPMS's success can be attributed to its workers in India and its appropriate workplace policies and programs. PPMS hires an average of 25 employees per month but is able to streamline its hiring process so that a candidate can pass through five successive levels of screening in a single day, resulting in an offer of employment letter being extended at the end of the day. Once an employee is hired, training consumes the first 16–20 weeks on the job, where employees learn about the company history, values and culture, industry, and products. Because PPMS hires young entry-level workers with an average age of 23 at the time of hire, opportunities are provided to move laterally and cross-train in other areas of the business. PPMS also offer its own in-house MBA program, developed in partnership with top-rated business schools in India. The workplace is also literally designed to be a family-type environment where friends and family members are invited to visit employees at work. This builds the organization's culture and goodwill in the community as well as affords PPMS with an additional opportunity to recruit employees.[29]

Conclusion

Although the principles and processes of strategic HR management are universal and apply to all organizational settings and cultures, an organization whose strategy involves multinational operations faces some additional challenges in ensuring the success of global assignments. The model for strategically managing global HR presented in this chapter is independent of the larger model for the book for this very reason; it addresses a different set of issues and challenges that present themselves in the global arena. However, the underlying theme of strategic HR management in looking at human assets as investments remains quite apparent when looking at global HR management. Employees on global assignments represent valuable assets who need to be managed more systematically and strategically than they traditionally have been to ensure greater probability of success in global markets.

Critical Thinking

1. How does global HR management differ from domestic HR management?

2. Explain the organizational and individual purposes for expatriation. Why do these need to be incorporated as part of a strategic approach to managing global assignments?

3. Describe the four levels of standardization of global HR practices. For what strategic objectives might each level of standardization be best suited?

4. Explain how each of Hofstede's cultural dimensions might result in specific kinds of HR programs and practices.

5. How can employers be more successful with retention of repatriates?

Reading 14.1

6. What differences need to be taken into account by American managers who oversee employees in Brazil, France, Egypt, and China, and what are the implications for American managers in each of these countries?

Reading 14.2

7. What are the critical social cultural practices that impact business relations in Africa? What specific strategies can be used by American organizations that attempt to conduct business and/or set up operations in Africa?

Exercises

1. Examine the four dimensions of culture presented in Hofstede's framework. What strategies would you recommend in dealing with a different culture that is polar on each of the dimensions? For example, what advice would you give to someone from a culture that stresses individualism when dealing with someone from a collectivist culture?

2. What challenges does doing business in the EU present to an employer? In small groups, have each

member investigate the HR environment in a different EU country and then compare and contrast your findings, making recommendations to U.S. organizations considering doing business there.

3. Apply the concepts presented in the Javidan reading on Project GLOBE across all the countries discussed n the reading (i.e., consider the examples of one manager from Brazil, one from France, one from Egypt,

and one from China operating in each of the other countries, including the United States).

4. You have been asked to design a Web site that would assist expatriates in getting ready for their overseas assignments. What kinds of information would you include on the site? Locate appropriate Internet sites that provide either useful information about culture in general or guidance in how culture affects business relationships with citizens from a particular country.

Chapter References

1. Anonymous. "Business; Best Foot Forward at Reebok," *The Economist*, October 23, 1999, p. 74; Bernstein, A. "Sweatshops: No More Excuses," *Business Week* November 9, 1999, pp. 104–106; Gilley, B. "Sweating It Out," *Far Eastern Economic Review*, December 10, 1998, pp. 66–67.

2. Overman, S. "HR Is Partner in 'McDonaldizing' Employees in New Countries," *HR News*, May 2002, p. 7.

3. Britt, J. "Expatriates Want More Support from Home," *HR Magazine*, July 2002, 47, (7), pp. 21–22.

4. Ibid.

5. Hofstede, G. *Culture's Consequences: International Differences in Work-Related Values*, Beverly Hills: Sage, 1984.

6. Hall, E. T. "The Silent Languages in Overseas Business," *Harvard Business Review*, May-June 1960, 38 (2), pp. 87–96.

7. Poe, A. "Selection Savvy," *HR Magazine*, April 2002, 47, (4), pp. 77–83.

8. Dwyer, T. "Localization's Hidden Costs," *HR Magazine*, 49, (6), June 2004, pp. 135–144.

9. Toh, S. M. and DeNisi, A. S. "A Local Perspective to Expatriate Success," *Academy of Management Executive*, 19, (1), 2005, pp. 132–146.

10. Heenan, D. A. and Perlmutter, H. V. *Multinational Organizational Development*, Reading, MA: Addison-Wesley, Inc., 1979.

11. Tyler, K. "Retaining Repatriates," *HR Magazine*, 51, (3), March, 2006, pp. 97–102.

12. Ibid.

13. Connor, R. "Plug the Expat Knowledge Drain," *HR Magazine*, October 2002, 47, (10), pp. 101–107.

14. Hirschman, C. "When Operating Abroad, Companies Must Adopt European-Style HR," *HR News*, 30, (3), pp. 1, 6.

15. Falcone, P. "Learning From Our Overseas Counterparts," *HR Magazine*, February 2004, 49, (2), pp. 113–116.

16. Ibid.

17. Cox News Services. "In Mexico, Discrimination Is Ingrained," *Baltimore Sun*, 18 July 2004, p. 17A.

18. Hassell, J. and Poysa, S. "Canadian Employment Law: A World Apart from Its U.S. Counterpart," *Society for Human Resource Management*, article 023972, 24 January, 2008. Published at www.shrm.org/hrnes/published/articles/CMS 023972.asp.

19. Liang, X., Marler, J. H. and Cui, Z. "Strategic Human Resource Management in China: East Meets West," *Academy of Management Perspectives*, 26, (2), 2012, pp. 55–70.

20. Fox, A. "China: Land of Opportunity and Challenge," *HR Magazine*, 52, (9), September 2007, pp. 38–44.

21. Gross, A. and Connor, A. "Recruiting, Retention Strategies Can Save HR Managers' 'Face,'" *Society for Human Resource Management*, article 052107, May 2007. Published at www.shrm.org/global/ news/published/XMS 052107.asp.

22. Fox, A. "Developing Managers Key Retention at All Levels," *HR Magazine*, 52, (9), September 2007, p. 41.

23. Fox, A. "China: Land of Opportunity and Challenge," *HR Magazine*, 52, (9), September 2007, pp. 38–44.

24. Gross and Connor, 2007, op. cit.

25. Gross and Connor, 2007, op. cit.

26. Gross, A. and Minot, J. "Workforce Issues in India That HR Needs to Understand," *Society for Human*

Resource Management, article 019786, January, 2007, published atwww.shrm.org/global/news/published/XMS_019786.asp.

27. Iyer, R. and Shroff, V. "Ensuring Compliance with Employment Laws in India," *Society for Human Resource Management*, article 026877, October-November, 2008, published at www.shrm.org/hrresources/lrptpublished/CMS026877.asp.

28. Gross and Minot, 2007, op. cit.

29. Grossman, R. "HR's Rising Star in India," *HR Magazine*, 51, (9), September 2006, pp. 46–52.

READING 14.1

In the Eye of the Beholder: Cross Cultural Lessons in Leadership from Project Globe

Mansour Javidan, Peter W. Dorfman, Mary Sully de Luque, and Robert J. House

Executive Overview

Global leadership has been identified as a critical success factor for large multinational corporations. While there is much writing on the topic, most seems to be either general advice (i.e., being open minded and respectful of other cultures) or very specific information about a particular country based on a limited case study (do not show the soles of your shoes when seated as a guest in an Arab country). Both kinds of information are certainly useful, but limited from both theoretical and practical viewpoints on how to lead in a foreign country. In this paper, findings from the Global Leadership and Organizational Behavior Effectiveness (GLOBE) research program are used to provide a sound basis for conceptualizing worldwide leadership differences. We use a hypothetical case of an American executive in charge of four similar teams in Brazil, France, Egypt, and China to discuss cultural implications for the American executive. Using the hypothetical case involving five different countries allows us to provide in-depth action oriented and context specific advice, congruent with GLOBE findings, for effectively interacting with employees from different cultures. We end the paper with a discussion of the challenges facing global executives and how corporations can develop useful global leadership capabilities.

Impact of Globalization

Almost no American corporation is immune from the impact of globalization. The reality for American corporations is that they must increasingly cope with diverse cross-cultural employees, customers, suppliers, competitors, and creditors, a situation well captured by the following quote.

> *So I was visiting a businessman in downtown Jakarta the other day and I asked for directions to my next appointment. His exact instructions were: Go to the building with the Armani Emporium upstairs—you know, just above the Hard Rock café—and then turn right at McDonalds. "I just looked at him and laughed, "Where am I?"*
>
> Thomas Friedman, New York Times, *July 14, 1997*

Notwithstanding Tom Friedman's astonishment about the global world in Jakarta, the fact is that people are not generally aware of the tremendous impact that national culture has on their vision and interpretation of the world. Because culture colors nearly every aspect of human behavior, a working knowledge of culture and its influences can be useful to executives operating in a multicultural business environment. It is a truism by now that large corporations need executives with global mindsets and cross-cultural leadership abilities. Foreign sales by multinational corporations have exceeded $7 trillion and are growing 20 percent to 30 percent faster than their sales of exports.[1] But while the importance of such business grows, 85 percent of *Fortune* 500 companies have reported a shortage of global managers with the necessary skills.[2] Some experts have argued that most U.S. companies are not positioned to implement global strategies due to a lack of global leadership capabilities.[3]

How can companies best use the available information for executive development and, moreover, what is the validity and value of such information? U.S. and European executives have plenty of general advice available to them on how to perform in foreign settings. During the past few years much has been written about global leadership, inducing several books.[4] Journals are also getting into the global action as seen in *The Human Resource Management Journal* which recently published a special issue on global leadership.[5] Nevertheless, in a recent review of the literature, Morrison concluded that despite the importance of global leadership, "relatively little research has thus far been carried out on global leadership characteristics, competencies, antecedents, and developmental strategies."[6]

Advice to global managers needs to be specific enough to help them understand how to act in different surroundings. For example, managers with an overseas assignment are frequently exhorted to have an open mind and to show respect for other cultures.[7] They may also be told of the importance of cross-cultural relationship management and communication. Some will wrestle with the idea that they need to develop a global perspective while being responsive to local concerns.[8] Or they may wonder if they have the "cognitive complexity" and psychological maturity to handle life and work in a foreign setting. And they are likely to hear or read that they must "walk in the shoes of people from different cultures" in order to be effective.[9] There is nothing wrong with such advice, and the scholars and writers who proffer it have often been pioneers in the field. But it is insufficient for a manager who is likely to assume, mistakenly, that being open minded in Atlanta, Helsinki, and Beijing will be perceived identically, or that walking in someone else's shoes will feel the same in Houston, Jakarta, and Madrid. Because of the lack of scientifically compiled information, businesspeople have not had sufficiently detailed and context-specific suggestions about how to handle these cross-cultural challenges. This is a particular problem for those in leadership positions.

Although there are universal aspects of leadership, information about which will be presented shortly, people in different countries do in fact have different criteria for assessing their leaders.[10] The issue for the American manager is whether the attributes that made him or her successful as a leader in the United States will also lead to success overseas, be of no value or, worst of all, cause harm in the foreign operation. Using the findings from an extensive research effort known as the Global Leadership and Organizational Behavior Effectiveness (GLOBE) project, this article provides a few answers to the questions about the universal and culture specific aspects of leadership. We will present specific information about key cultural differences among nations and connect the "dots" on how these differences influence leadership. This information should help a typical global executive better understand the leadership challenges s/he faces while managing operations outside the United States. It will also provide suggestions on how to more effectively cope with such challenges.

To make the GLOBE findings come alive, we will follow a hypothetical American executive who has been given two years to lead a project based in four different countries: Brazil, France, Egypt, and China. This hypothetical project involves developing a somewhat similar product for the four different markets. The project team in each country is tasked with the marketing of a new technology in the telecommunications industry. The executive will work with local employees in each location. Success will be determined by two criteria: the executive's ability to produce results and to show effective leadership in different cultures and settings.

The four countries represent different continents and very diverse cultures. Brazil is the most populous and economically important South American country. France is the largest, most populous, and most economically developed Latin European country. Egypt is the largest and most populous Arab country. China is the fast growing giant economy with unprecedented growth in its economic and diplomatic power in the world. We chose these countries to provide context specific analysis leading to general recommendations for global executives. Our choice of countries was guided by our efforts to cover a wide range of cultures. Before turning to our hypothetical scenario, we will examine common cultural dimensions that characterize nations and discuss why these dimensions are important for the development of global leaders.

Common Cultural Dimensions

To be open minded and to understand the cultures of the different countries, managers need to be able to compare their own cultures with those of other countries. After a review of the available literature, especially the work of Hofstede, Trompenaars, and Kluckhohn and Strodtbeck,[11] GLOBE conceptualized and developed measures of nine cultural dimensions. These are aspects of a country's culture that distinguish one society from another and have important managerial implications. While a few of these dimensions are similar to the work of other researchers, the manner in which we conceptualized and operationalized them was different.[12] We reconceptualized a few existing dimensions and developed a few new dimensions. In all cases, the scales designed to capture and measure these cultural dimensions passed very rigorous psychometric tests. A brief description of each cultural dimension is provided below along with the basic research design of GLOBE. Further details can be found on GLOBE's website, http://www.thunderbird.edu/wwwfiles/ms/globe/.

It might be noted that the GLOBE Project has been called "the most ambitious study of global leadership."[13] Our worldwide team of scholars proposed and validated an integrated theory of the relationship between culture and societal, organizational, and leadership effectiveness. The 170 researchers worked together for ten years collecting and analyzing data on cultural values and practices and leadership attributes from over 17,000 managers in 62 societal cultures. The participating managers were employed in telecommunications, food, and banking industries. As one output from the project, the 62 cultures were ranked with respect to nine dimensions of their cultures. We studied the effects of these dimensions on expectations of leaders, as well as on organizational practices in each society. The 62 societal cultures were also grouped into a more parsimonious set of ten culture clusters (list provided in the next section). GLOBE studies cultures in terms of their cultural practices (the ways things are) and their cultural values (the way things should be). The nine cultural attributes (hereafter called culture dimensions) are:

Performance Orientation The degree to which a collective encourages and rewards (and should encourage and reward) group members for performance improvement and excellence. In countries like the U.S. and Singapore that score high on this cultural practice, businesses are likely to emphasize training and development; in countries that score low, such as Russia and Greece, family and background count for more.

Assertiveness The degree to which individuals are (and should be) assertive, confrontational, and aggressive in their relationships with others. People in highly assertive countries such as the United States and Austria tend to have can-do attitudes and enjoy competition in business; those in less assertive countries such as Sweden and New Zealand prefer harmony in relationships and emphasize loyalty and solidarity.

Future Orientation The extent to which individuals engage (and should engage) in future-oriented behaviors such as delaying gratification, planning, and investing in the future. Organizations in countries with high future oriented practices like Singapore and Switzerland tend to have longer term horizons and more systematic planning processes, but they tend to be averse to risk taking and opportunistic decision making. In contrast, corporations in the least future oriented countries like Russia and Argentina tend to be less systematic and more opportunistic in their actions.

Humane Orientation The degree to which a collective encourages and rewards (and should encourage and reward) individuals for being fair, altruistic, generous, caring, and kind to others. Countries like Egypt and Malaysia rank very high on this cultural practice and countries like France and Germany rank low.

Institutional Collectivism The degree to which organizational and societal institutional practices encourage and reward (and should encourage and reward) collective distribution of resources and collective action. Organizations in collectivistic countries like Singapore and Sweden tend to emphasize group performance and rewards, whereas those in the more individualistic countries like Greece and Brazil tend to emphasize individual achievement and rewards.

In-Group Collectivism The degree to which individuals express (and should express) pride, loyalty, and cohesiveness in their organizations or families. Societies like Egypt and Russia take pride in their families and also take pride in the organizations that employ them.

Gender Egalitarianism The degree to which a collective minimizes (and should minimize) gender inequality. Not surprisingly, European countries generally had the highest scores on gender egalitarianism practices. Egypt and South Korea were among the most male dominated societies in GLOBE. Organizations operating in gender egalitarian societies tend to encourage tolerance for diversity of ideas and individuals.

Power Distance The degree to which members of a collective expect (and should expect) power to be distributed equally. A high power distance score reflects unequal power distribution in a society. Countries that scored high on this cultural practice are more stratified economically, socially, and politically; those in positions of authority expect, and receive, obedience. Firms in high power distance countries like Thailand, Brazil, and France tend to have hierarchical decision making processes with limited one-way participation and communication.

Uncertainty Avoidance The extent to which a society, organization, or group relies (and should rely) on social norms, rules, and procedures to alleviate unpredictability of future events. The greater the desire to avoid uncertainty, the more people seek orderliness, consistency, structure, formal procedures and laws to cover situations in their daily lives. Organizations in high uncertainty avoidance countries like Singapore and Switzerland tend to establish elaborate processes and procedures and prefer formal detailed strategies. In contrast, firms in low uncertainty avoidance countries like Russia and Greece tend to prefer simple processes and broadly stated strategies. They are also opportunistic and enjoy risk taking.

Regional Clustering of GLOBE Nations

GLOBE was able to empirically verify ten culture clusters from the 62-culture sample. These culture clusters were identified as: Latin America, Anglo, Latin Europe (e.g., Italy), Nordic Europe, Germanic Europe, Confucian Asia, Sub-Saharan Africa, Middle East, Southern Asia, and Eastern Europe. Each culture cluster differs with respect to the nine culture dimensions (e.g., performance orientation). Table 1 shows a summary of how the clusters compare in terms of their scores on cultural practices. The clusters that are relevant to this paper are in bold. For instance, clusters scoring highest in performance orientation were Confucian Asia, Germanic Europe, and Anglo (U.S. and U.K. among other English-speaking countries). Clusters scoring lowest in performance orientation were Latin America and Eastern Europe. The Appendix shows the actual country scores for the six clusters in this paper.

Managing and Leading in Different Countries

Given the differences found in cultures around the globe, what does an effective American manager need to do differently in different countries? Everything, nothing, or only certain things? From a leadership perspective we can ask whether the same attributes that lead to successful leadership in the U.S. lead to success in other countries. Or are they irrelevant or, even worse, dysfunctional? In the following sections, we will answer these questions. We will examine some similarities and differences among cultures regarding management and leadership practices. We then assert that many of the leadership differences found among cultures stem from implicit leadership beliefs held by members of different nations.

Expatriate managers working in multinational companies hardly need to be reminded of the wide variety of *management* practices found around the world. Laurent, and more recently Trompenaars and Briscoe and Shuler,[14] document the astonishing diversity of organizational practices

Table 1

Cultural Clusters Classified on Societal Culture Practices (As Is) Scores

Cultural Dimension	High-Score Clusters	Mid-Score Clusters	Low-Score Clusters	Cluster-Average Range
Performance Orientation	**Confucian Asia**	Southern Asia	**Latin America**	3.73–4.58
	Germanic Europe	Sub-Saharan Africa	Eastern Europe	
	Anglo	**Latin Europe**		
		Nordic Europe		
		Middle East		
Assertiveness	Germanic Europe	Sub-Saharan Africa	Nordic Europe	3.66–4.55
	Eastern Europe	**Latin America**		
		Anglo		
		Middle East		
		Confucian Asia		
		Latin Europe		
		Southern Asia		
Future Orientation	Germanic Europe	**Confucian Asia**	**Middle East**	3.38–4.40
	Nordic Europe	**Anglo**	**Latin America**	
		Southern Asia	Eastern Europe	
		Sub-Saharan Africa		
		Latin Europe		
Humane Orientation	Southern Asia	**Middle East**	**Latin Europe**	3.55–4.71
	Sub-Saharan Africa	**Anglo**	Germanic Europe	
		Nordic Europe		
		Latin America		
		Confucian Asia		
		Eastern Europe		
Institutional Collectivism	Nordic Europe	**Anglo**	Germanic Europe	3.86–4.88
	Confucian Asia	Southern Asia	**Latin Europe**	
		Sub-Saharan Africa	**Latin America**	
		Middle East		
		Eastern Europe		

Table 1

Cultural Clusters Classified on Societal Culture Practices (As Is) Scores *(continued)*

Cultural Dimension	High-Score Clusters	Mid-Score Clusters	Low-Score Clusters	Cluster-Average Range
In-Group Collectivism	Southern Asia	Sub-Saharan Africa	**Anglo**	3.75–5.87
	Middle East	**Latin Europe**	Germanic Europe	
	Eastern Europe		Nordic Europe	
	Latin America			
	Confucian Asia			
Gender Egalitarianism	Eastern Europe	**Latin America**	**Middle East**	2.95–3.64
	Nordic Europe	**Anglo**		
		Latin Europe		
		Sub-Saharan Africa		
		Southern Asia		
		Confucian Asia		
		Germanic Europe		
Power Distance		Southern Asia	Nordic Europe	4.54–5.39
		Latin America		
		Eastern Europe		
		Sub-Saharan Africa		
		Middle East		
		Latin Europe		
		Confucian Asia		
		Anglo		
		Germanic Europe		
Uncertainty Avoidance	Nordic Europe	**Confucian Asia**	**Middle East**	3.56–5.19
	Germanic Europe	**Anglo**	**Latin America**	
		Sub-Saharan Africa	Eastern Europe	
		Latin Europe		
		Southern Asia		

Note: Means of high-score clusters are significantly higher (p < 0.05) than the rest, means of low-score clusters are significantly lower (p < 0.05) than the rest, and means of mid-score clusters are not significantly different from the rest (p > 0.05).

worldwide, many of which are acceptable and considered effective in one country but ineffective in another country. For instance, supervisors are expected to have precise answers to subordinates' questions in Japan, but less so in the United States. As another example, the effectiveness of working alone or in a group is perceived very differently around the world; this would certainly influence the quality, aptitude, and fair evaluation of virtual teams found in multinational organizations.[15] An inescapable conclusion is that acceptable management practices found in one country are hardly guaranteed to work in a different country. Titus Lokananta, for example, is an Indonesian Cantonese holding a German passport, managing a Mexican multinational corporation producing Gummy Bears in the Czech Republic.[16] What management style will he be most comfortable with, and will it be successful with Czech workers and Mexican CEOs? How does he effectively manage if a conflict evolves between managing his workers and satisfying his supervisors?

Should we, however, conclude that cultural differences are so vast that common management practices among countries are the exception rather than the rule and will ever remain so? Not necessarily. Companies are forced to share information, resources, and training in a global economy. The best business schools educate managers from all over the world in the latest management techniques. Using academic jargon, the issue of common versus unique business and management practices is framed using contrasting perspectives embodied in the terms *cultural universals* versus *cultural specifics*. The former are thought to be found from the process of cultural convergence whereas the latter from maintaining cultural divergence. Perhaps not surprisingly, empirical research supports both views. For example, in their event management leadership research program Smith and Peterson found both commonalities and differences across cultures in the manner by which managers handled relatively routine events in their work.[17] All managers preferred to rely on their own experience and training if appointing a new subordinate, relative to other influences such as consultation with others or using formal rules and procedures. However, there were major differences in countries in the degree to which managers used formal company rules and procedures in contrast to more informal networks, and these differences covary with national cultural values.[18] As another example, Hazucha and colleagues[19] found a good deal of similarity among European countries regarding the importance of core management competencies for a Euromanager. Yet there were significant differences among countries in the perceived attainment of these skills. Javidan and Carl have recently shown important similarities and differences among Canadian, Taiwanese, and Iranian managers in terms of their leadership styles.[20]

Should we also expect that leadership processes, like management practices, are similarly influenced by culture? The answer is yes; substantial empirical evidence indicates that leader attributes, behavior, status, and influence vary considerably as a result of culturally unique forces in the countries or regions in which the leaders function.[21] But, as the colloquial saying goes "the devil is in the details," and current cross-cultural theory is inadequate to clarify and expand on the diverse cultural universals and cultural specifics elucidated in cross-cultural research. Some researchers subscribe to the philosophy that the primary impact of culture depends on the level of analysis used in the research program. That is, some view the basic functions of leadership as having universal importance and applicability, but the specific ways in which leadership functions are enacted are strongly affected by cultural variation.[22] Other researchers, including the contributors to this article, question this basic assumption, subscribing more to the viewpoint that cultural specifics are real and woe to the leader who ignores them.

Do Required Leadership Qualities Differ Among Nations?

It has been pointed out that managerial leadership differences (and similarities) among nations may be the result of the citizens' implicit assumptions regarding requisite leadership qualities.[23] According to implicit leadership theory (ILT), individuals hold a set of beliefs about the kinds of attributes, personality characteristics, skills, and behaviors that contribute to or impede outstanding leadership. These belief systems, variously referred to as prototypes, cognitive categories, mental models, schemas, and stereotypes in the broader social cognitive literature, are assumed to affect the extent to which an individual accepts and responds to others as leaders.[24]

GLOBE extended ILT to the cultural level of analysis by arguing that the structure and content of these belief systems will be shared among individuals in common cultures. We refer to this shared cultural level analog of individual implicit leadership theory (ILT) as *culturally endorsed implicit leadership theory (CLT)*. GLOBE empirically identified universally perceived leadership attributes that are contributors to or inhibitors of outstanding leadership. Project GLOBE's leadership questionnaire items consisted of 112 behavioral and attribute descriptors (e.g., "intelligent") that were hypothesized to either facilitate or impede outstanding leadership. Accompanying each item was a short phrase designed to help interpret the item. Items were rated on a 7-point Likert-type scale that ranged from a low of 1 (this behavior or characteristic greatly inhibits a person from being an outstanding leader) to a high of 7 (this behavior or characteristic contributes greatly to a person being an outstanding leader). Project GLOBE also empirically reduced the huge number of leadership attributes into a much more understandable, comprehensive grouping of 21 primary and then 6 global leadership dimensions. The 6 global leadership dimensions differentiate cultural profiles of desired leadership qualities, hereafter referred to as a CLT profile. Convincing evidence from GLOBE research showed that people within cultural groups agree in their beliefs about leadership; these beliefs are represented by a set of *CLT leadership profiles* developed for each national culture and cluster of cultures. For detailed descriptions of the statistical processes used to form the 21 primary and 6 global leadership dimensions and development of CLT profiles see House et al.[25] Using the six country scenarios, in the last half of this paper we will show the range of leadership responses that should be effective in each cultural setting. The six dimensions of the CLT leadership profiles are:

1. **Charismatic/Value-Based.** A broadly defined leadership dimension that reflects the ability to inspire, to motivate, and to expect high performance outcomes from others on the basis of firmly held core beliefs. Charismatic/value-based leadership is generally reported to contribute to outstanding leadership. The highest reported score is in the Anglo cluster (6.05); the lowest score in the Middle East cluster (5.35 out of a 7-point scale).

2. **Team-Oriented.** A leadership dimension that emphasizes effective team building and implementation of a common purpose or goal among team members. Team-oriented leadership is generally reported to contribute to outstanding leadership (Highest score in Latin American cluster (5.96); lowest score in Middle East cluster (5.47)).

3. **Participative.** A leadership dimension that reflects the degree to which managers involve others in making and implementing decisions. Participative leadership is generally reported to contribute to outstanding leadership, although there are meaningful differences among countries and clusters. (Highest score in Germanic Europe cluster (5.86); lowest score in Middle East cluster (4.97)).

4. **Humane-Oriented.** A leadership dimension that reflects supportive and considerate leadership but also includes' compassion and generosity. Humane-oriented leadership is reported to be almost neutral in some societies and to moderately contribute to outstanding leadership in others. (Highest score in Southern Asia cluster (5.38); lowest score in Nordic Europe cluster (4.42)).

5. **Autonomous.** This newly defined leadership dimension, which has not previously appeared in the literature, refers to independent and individualistic leadership. Autonomous leadership is reported to range from impeding outstanding leadership to slightly facilitating outstanding leadership. (Highest score in Eastern Europe cluster (4.20); lowest score in Latin America cluster (3.51)).

6. **Self-Protective.** From a Western perspective, this newly defined leadership dimension focuses on ensuring the safety and security of the individual. It is self-centered and face saving in its approach. Self-protective leadership is generally reported to impede outstanding leadership. (Highest score in Southern Asia cluster (3.83); lowest in Nordic Europe (2.72)).

Table 2 presents CLT scores for all 10 clusters. Analysis of Variance (ANOVA) was used to determine if the cultures and clusters differed with respect to their CLT leadership profiles. Results indicate that cultures (i.e., 62 societal cultures) and clusters (i.e., 10 groups consisting of the 62 societal cultures) differed with respect to all six CLT leadership dimensions (p < .01).

Table 3 presents summary comparisons among culture clusters to indicate which clusters are most likely to endorse or refute the importance of the 6 CLT leadership dimensions. Tables 2 and 3 may be used in combination to provide an overall view of how the different cultural clusters compare on the six culturally implicit leadership dimensions.[26]

Cross-cultural Leadership Is Not Only About Differences

The global and cross-cultural leadership literature is almost exclusively focused on cultural differences and their implications for managers. There is a basic assumption that leaders operating in different countries will be facing drastically different challenges and requirements. GLOBE surveys show that while different countries do have divergent views on many aspects of leadership effectiveness, they also have convergent views on some other aspects. From the larger group of leader behaviors, we found 22 attributes that were universally deemed to be desirable. Being honest, decisive, motivational, and dynamic are examples of attributes that are believed to facilitate outstanding leadership in all GLOBE countries. Furthermore, we found eight leadership attributes that are universally undesirable. Leaders who are loners, irritable, egocentric, and ruthless are deemed ineffective in all GLOBE countries. Table 4 below shows a few examples of universally desirable, universally undesirable, and culturally contingent leadership attributes.

Identifying universally desirable and undesirable leadership attributes is a critical step in effective cross-cultural leadership. It shows managers that while there are differences among countries, there are also similarities. Such similarities give some degree of comfort and ease to leaders and can be used by them as a foundation to build on. Of course, there may still be differences in how leaders enact such attributes. For example, behaviors that embody dynamic leadership in China may be different from those that denote the same attribute in the U.S. Current research currently under way by GLOBE team members is focused on this issue.

Understanding Culturally Contingent Leadership

In this section, we will focus on those attributes of leadership that were found to be culturally contingent. These are attributes that may work effectively in one culture but cause harm in others. To provide an action oriented analysis, we explore differences in effective leadership attributes among the four countries in our hypothetical scenario and discuss specific implications of these differences for our hypothetical American manager. Admittedly, we are being ethnocentric

Table 2

CLT Scores for Societal Clusters

Societal Cluster	CLT Dimensions					
	Charismatic/ Value-Based	Team Oriented	Participative	Humane Oriented	Autonomous	Self-Protective
Eastern Europe	5.74	5.88	5.08	4.76	4.20	3.67
Latin America	5.99	5.96	5.42	4.85	3.51	3.62
Latin Europe	5.78	5.73	5.37	4.45	3.66	3.19
Confucian Asia	5.63	5.61	4.99	5.04	4.04	3.72
Nordic Europe	5.93	5.77	5.75	4.42	3.94	2.72
Anglo	6.05	5.74	5.73	5.08	3.82	3.08
Sub-Sahara Africa	5.79	5.70	5.31	5.16	3.63	3.55
Southern Asia	5.97	5.86	5.06	5.38	3.99	3.83
Germanic Europe	5.93	5.62	5.86	4.71	4.16	3.03
Middle East	5.35	5.47	4.97	4.80	3.68	3.79

Note: CLT leadership scores are absolute scores aggregated to the cluster level.

Table 3

Summary of Comparisons for CLT Leadership Dimensions

Societal Cluster	CLT Leadership Dimensions					
	Charismatic/ Value Based	Team Oriented	Participative	Humane Oriented	Autonomous	Self-Protective
Eastern Europe	M	M	L	M	**H**/H	H
Latin America	H	**H**	M	M	**L**	M/H
Latin Europe	M/H	M	M	L	L	M
Confucian Asia	M	M/H	L	M/H	M	H
Nordic Europe	H	M	H	**L**	M	**L**
Anglo	**H**	M	H	H	M	L
Sub-Sahara Africa	M	M	M	H	L	M
Southern Asia	H	M/**H**	L	**H**	M	**H**/H
Germanic Europe	H	M/L	**H**	M	H/**H**	L
Middle East	**L**	L	L	M	M	H/**H**

Note: For letters separated by a "/", the first letter indicates rank with respect to the absolute score, second letter with respect to a response bias corrected score.

H=high rank; M=medium rank; L=low rank.

H or L (bold) indicates Highest or Lowest cluster score for a specific CLT dimension.

Source: Booysen (1999); Fadiman (1994); Shonhiwa (2008).

Table 4

Cultural Views of Leadership Effectiveness

The following is a partial list of leadership attributes with the corresponding primary leadership dimension in parentheses.

Universal Facilitators of Leadership Effectiveness

- Being trustworthy, just, and honest (integrity)
- Having foresight and planning ahead (charismatic–visionary)
- Being positive, dynamic, encouraging, motivating, and building confidence (charismatic–inspirational)
- Being communicative, informed, a coordinator, and team integrator (team builder)

Universal Impediments to Leadership Effectiveness

- Being a loner and asocial (self-protective)
- Being non-cooperative and irritable (malevolent)
- Being dictatorial (autocratic)

Culturally Contingent Endorsement of Leader Attributes

- Being individualistic (autonomous)
- Being status conscious (status conscious)
- Being a risk taker (charismatic III: self-sacrificial)

using the American manager as the focal person who finds himself/herself managing in a foreign culture. Obviously, expatriate managers are found from virtually all industrialized nations; however, there are over 200,000 U.S. expatriates worldwide.[27] Nevertheless, expatriates from non-American and non-Western countries should be able to identify with cultural differences between their culture and that of the comparison countries. GLOBE cultural data for the five comparison countries can be found in Table 1 and the Appendix. Please note the United States, Brazil, and France are part of the Anglo, Latin American, and Latin European, clusters, respectively. Egypt, and China part of the Middle East, and Confucian Asia clusters respectively.

Each section below begins with a summary of how each culture cluster fares with respect to the CLT profile. We then show how the countries of interest in this paper compare on

specific leadership attributes that are culturally contingent. Next, we examine in detail what these differences mean and what they imply for the hypothetical American executive.

Brazil

Brazil is part of GLOBE's Latin American cluster. Viewing Tables 2 and 3, it is apparent that the CLT leadership dimensions contributing the most to outstanding leadership in this country cluster include Charismatic/Value-Based and Team Oriented leadership, followed by the Participative and Humane Oriented CLT dimensions. Autonomous and Self-Protective leadership are viewed as slightly negative. Table 3 shows that the Latin America cluster receives the highest rank for the Team Oriented dimension, among the highest ranks for Charismatic/Value-Based leadership, and ranks lowest with respect to the Autonomous CLT leadership dimension. It occupies the middle ranks for the remaining CLT dimensions.

Figure 1 below contrasts the U.S. and Brazil on the culturally contingent leadership items. Perhaps due to their high in-group collectivism, Brazilian managers intensely dislike the leaders who are individualistic, autonomous, and independent. A Brazilian sales manager working in the petrochemical industry recently reflected this suggesting, "We do not prefer leaders who take self-governing decisions and act alone without engaging the group. That's part of who we are." While American managers also frown upon these attributes, they do not regard them as negatively as do the Brazilians. An American manager needs to be more cognizant to make sure that his/her actions and decisions are not interpreted as individualistic. He/she needs to ensure that the group or unit feels involved in decision making and that others' views and reactions are taken into consideration.

On the other hand, Brazilian managers expect their leaders to be class- and status-conscious. They want leaders to be aware of status boundaries and to respect them. A manager in a large company in Brazil noted that blue and white-collar workers from the same company rarely socialize together within and outside of work. They expect leaders to treat people according to their social and organizational levels. Perhaps due to their high power distance culture, Brazilians believe that people in positions of authority deserve to be treated with respect and deference. They prefer a formal relationship between the leader and followers. The same petrochemical sales manager told how Brazilian subordinates tend to stay outside of the perceived boundaries of their leaders and respect their own decision-making limitations. He added, "It's clear who has the most power in the work environment in Brazil, but in America this is not always the case." Americans tend to frown on status and class consciousness. Respect, to an American manager, does not necessarily mean deference but mutual respect and open dialogue. Americans tend to see formality as an obstacle to open debate. But what seems an open debate to an American manager may be viewed as

FIGURE 1

USA vs. Brazil

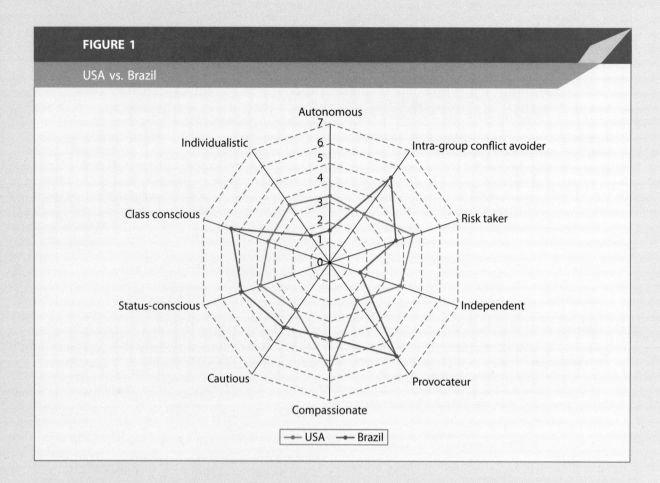

aggressive and unacceptable behavior on the part of the subordinates by a Brazilian manager. So, while Brazilians do not like individualistic leaders, a typical American manager should be cautious using an open style of decision making. While it may be a good idea in an American organization to directly contact anyone with the right information regardless of their level, such behavior may be seen as a sign of disrespect to those in formal positions in a Brazilian organization.

Another important difference is that American managers prefer a less cautious approach and a greater degree of risk taking. In contrast, Brazilian managers prefer a somewhat more cautious and risk averse approach. This is consistent with the finding that U.S. culture is more tolerant of uncertainty than is Brazilian culture. Also, perhaps due to stronger assertiveness and performance orientation in American culture, U.S. managers seem to favor a speedier decision making process and a higher level of action orientation. Brazilians on the other hand, may be more sensitive to group harmony and risk avoidance. A Brazilian account manager leading a four-company consortium working on a $200 million U.S. contract with the Federal Department of

Roads in Brazil realized this when a conflict occurred among the consortium players. He noted,

Since our contract was a long-term relationship, we could not focus only on the particular moment. I had to find a way to motivate and to build a trusting environment. The only way to do so was to promote several meetings with all the consortium members trying to find a way to put all the members back together. By doing this, I assumed this was the best action to produce results, no matter how difficult it was or how much time it required.

Still another difference relates to the strong in-group collectivism dimension of the Brazilian culture. They expect their leaders to avoid conflict within the group to protect its harmony, but at the same time they like their leaders to induce conflict with those outside the group. A particularly successful executive working in Brazil told how Brazilians take pride in membership in small groups, especially families. In business, he said that people who are members of the same group expect special treatment (such as price discounts, exclusivity of contracts, etc.). In fact, without these group affiliations, attracting and conducting business can be difficult. American managers seem to dislike both these attributes, perhaps due to their stronger performance orientation culture. Avoiding internal conflict, simply to maintain group harmony, even at the expense of results, is not a positive attribute to Americans. The typical American view of harmony is reflected in the following quote from the popular book *Execution* by Bossidy and Charan:[28]

Indeed, harmony—sought out by many leaders who wish to offend no one—can be the enemy of truth. It can squelch critical thinking and drive decision making underground. When harmony prevails, here's how things often get settled: after the key players leave the session, they quietly veto decisions they didn't like but didn't debate on the spot. A good motto to observe is: "Truth over harmony."

Last, but not least, an important and counter intuitive finding is that American respondents have a much stronger desire for compassion in their leaders. They want their leaders to be empathetic and merciful. The Brazilian respondents, on the other hand, are quite neutral about this attribute. While this seems to go against the conventional stereotypes of Americans and Brazilians, it seems to be rooted in the fact that Brazil is reported to be a less humane culture than is the U.S. Confirming this finding, one manager stated that this reflects the expectation that people should solve their own problems, relying on help from their family or groups.

When in Brazil ...

Here are a few specific ideas on what our hypothetical American manager needs to do when he starts working with his Brazilian team:

Very early on, he needs to spend time meeting with the key executives in the organization, even those who may not be directly relevant to his project. This is an important step because of high power distance and in-group collectivism in that culture. Being a foreigner and a newcomer, it is crucial to show respect to those in positions of power and to start the process of building personal ties and moving into their in-groups. Further, this step helps make sure that the other stakeholders do not view the manager's team as being insular, something that is likely to happen in high in-group cultures.

While it is important to work with the individual members of the team, it is also critical to spend as much time as possible with the team as a whole, both in formal work related occasions and in informal settings. The families of the team members should also be invited to get together on many occasions. They are an important part of the relationships among team members. The high in-group culture facilitates the group working closely together, and the Brazilians' dislike for independent and individualistic leaders means that the leader is expected to treat the team and their close families as an extended family, spending much time together.

In developing a business strategy for the team's product, it is important to keep in mind Brazil's low scores on performance orientation and future orientation and its high score on power distance. The process of strategy development needs to allow for input from the employees, but the manager needs to be patient and to make an effort to encourage and facilitate the employees' participation. The Brazilian employees will not be as forthcoming with their ideas and input as typical American employees are. At the same time, the manager will need to make the final decision and communicate it. Brazilian employees are not used to strong participation in decision making, but they also do not like leaders who simply dictate things to them. The strategy should not be seen as too risky or ambitious and should not have a long time horizon. Instead, it should consist of explicit short term milestones. It should also focus on delivering short term results to enhance employee understanding and support.

Due to the country's low score on institutional collectivism, employees will not be moved much by grand corporate strategies and visions. Instead, they would be more motivated by their individual and team interests, so the reward system should be based on both individual and team performance, although the team component should have the greater emphasis. The manager should also not be surprised if there are not many clear rules or processes and if the ones in existence are not followed very seriously. These are attributes of a society like Brazil with low levels of rules orientation. Instead, the manager needs to make it very clear early on which rules and procedures are expected to be followed and why.

France

France is part of the Latin Europe GLOBE country cluster. The most desirable CLT dimensions in this cluster are Charismatic/Value-Based and Team Oriented leadership. Participative leadership is viewed positively but is not as important as the first two dimensions. Humane Oriented leadership is viewed as slightly positive, whereas Autonomous leadership is viewed as slightly negative and Self-Protective is viewed negatively. Table 3 shows that the Latin Europe cluster is Medium/High for Charismatic/Value-Based leadership. It is in the middle rank for the remaining CLT leadership dimensions except the Humane Oriented and Autonomous dimensions where it ranks among the lowest scoring clusters.

Figure 2 below shows the contrast between French and American leadership on culturally contingent leadership attributes. The French culture is similar to the U.S. on one cultural dimension, in that they both practice moderate levels of uncertainty avoidance. Although both cultures utilize predictable laws and procedures in business and society, characteristic of uncertainty avoidance cultures, France is much better known for its strong labor unions and bureaucratic formality. There are, however, significant differences between the French and American respondents on other cultural dimensions and leadership attributes. Both groups seem to like sincere and enthusiastic leaders who impart positive energy to their group, although American managers have

FIGURE 2

USA vs. France

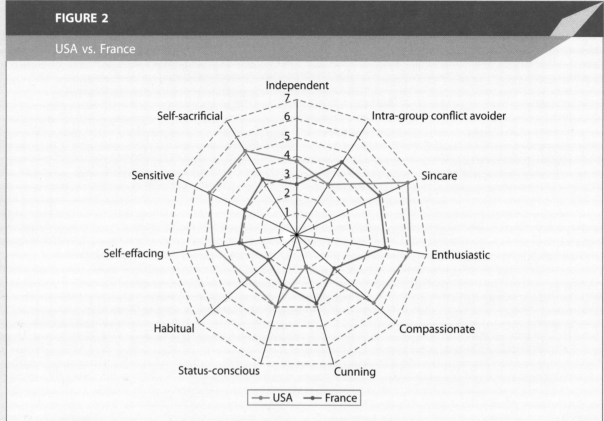

Source: *Adapted from Henson, R. (2002). Culture and the workforce. In K. Beaman, (Ed.), Boundaryless HR: Human capital management in the global economy (pp. 121–141). Austin, TX: Rector Duncan & Associates, Inc.*

much stronger preferences for these attributes. This may be a reflection of the finding that French culture is not as performance oriented as U.S. culture.

Besides their dislike for avoidance of conflict within the group (as discussed earlier) American managers have a clear dislike for cunning and deceitful leaders. The French, on the other hand, are neutral about both attributes. While Americans see these attributes as dysfunctional, the French see them as a part of the job that goes with the position of leadership. Compared to the U.S., in-group collectivism is more noted in French societies in the form of "favoritism" given to people from similar education, family, social, and even regional backgrounds. This is shown in the general tension that is perceived to exist between labor and management, as well and employees and clients.[29]

American managers seem to have a strong preference for compassionate and sensitive leaders who show empathy towards others. In contrast, French managers seem to have a distinctly negative view towards both these attributes. The

CEO of an international audit firm expressed this in a quality audit of a French hotel stating, "The staff had an inability to apologize and empathize. I think that could be construed as typically European, and especially French."[30] These same behaviors would be expected from their leaders. Such a large contrast can perhaps be explained by the fact that the French culture is much less humane oriented and much more power oriented. To French managers, people in positions of leadership should not be expected to be sensitive or empathetic, or to worry about another's status because such attributes would weaken a leader's resolve and impede decision making. Leaders should make decisions without being distracted by other considerations. Indeed, a very successful corporate executive in France noted that a leader should be able to handle change that affects the environment, but at the same time not change his or her characteristics, traits, and skills that put the leader in that position. In other words, they should allow no distractions.

In contrast to Americans, French respondents have a negative view of leaders who are self-sacrificial and self-effacing. They do not like leaders who are modest about their role and forgo their own self-interest. The French executive added, "A leader must be clear about his role and vision. If a leader puts himself in a compromising situation, then doubt will arise in the followers' minds about the leader and that would affect their views of the roles the followers play in the broader picture." To them, the leader has an important role to play and important decisions to make, and s/he should not minimize that. They also do not like leaders who are habitual and tend to routinize everything because that diminishes the importance of their role. They do still prefer their leaders to work with and rely on others to get things done and do not like independent leaders. A French CEO known for his corporate turnaround finesse explained that leaders should not have too much independence from their followers because otherwise this would denote lack of character from the followers. He adds that a leader should guide without having too much power over the followers' thought processes, to ensure diverse thinking critical to conserve several solutions to the leader.

To sum up, a typical American executive taking on a leadership role in a French organization will face a more bureaucratic and formal work environment with higher levels of aggressiveness and lower levels of personal compassion and sensitivity than s/he is used to.

When in France...

The American manager in our scenario will face a very different experience with his or her French team. These managers will experience much more formal and impersonal relationships among the team members. The concept of visionary and charismatic leadership that is popular among American managers may not be as desirable to the French. They do not expect their leaders to play heroic acts and, due to their high power distance, have a more bureaucratic view of leaders. So, the American manager, in contrast to his experience in Brazil, needs to tone down the personal side of relationships and be much more business oriented. The manager also has to be more careful and selective in contacting other executives and stakeholders. Their preference for maintaining high power distance may curb their enthusiasm about meeting with someone if they feel it is a waste of time and of no clear value to them. It is perhaps best for our American manager to make an offer to them and leave it to them to decide. Their low humane orientation culture may mean that they are not particularly interested in being supportive of others, even in the same organization, especially if they are from separate in-groups.

Due to lower levels of future orientation and performance orientation, grand corporate strategies and visions may be of limited value to a French team. Any strong competitive language may be seen as typical American bravado. The manager needs to develop a process for making strategic decisions about the project and get the team members involved, but he needs to keep in mind that French employees may be best motivated by transactional forms of leadership where they see clear individual benefit in implementing the team's plans. The strategy and action plans need to be simple and well planned. So, the content and process of strategy development for the French team may have many similarities with the Brazilian team, even though they are different on many other dimensions.

Egypt

Egypt is part of the Middle East cluster. There are a number of striking differences in comparison to other clusters. While both Charismatic/Value-Based and Team Oriented leadership are viewed as positive, they have the lowest scores and ranks relative to those for all other clusters. Participative leadership is viewed positively, but again scores low compared with other clusters' absolute score and ranks. Humane Oriented leadership is perceived positively, but only about equally to other cluster scores. The Self-Protective CLT dimension is viewed as an almost neutral factor; however, it has the second-highest score and rank of all clusters.

Figure 3 below shows a contrast of leadership styles in the U.S. and Egypt. The Egyptian culture is distinct by its emphasis on in-group and institutional collectivism, power distance, humane orientation, and male domination. In terms of leadership, American managers dislike autocratic leaders who want to make all the decisions themselves and micro-manage their employees. They do not want their leaders to suppress others' ideas, even if they disagree with them. Egyptian managers have a more temperate view of such executives, perhaps due to their strong power distance culture.

A very important difference is the image of leaders in the Egyptian vs. the American mind. Egyptian managers seem to have an elitist, transcendent view of their leaders. They view them as a distinct group and a breed apart. They want their leaders to be unique, superior, status- and class-conscious, individualistic, and better than the others in their group. They show strong reverence and deference toward their leaders. Americans, on the other hand, have a more benign and simplistic view toward their leaders. They do not see them as a breed apart or superhuman. They regard them as successful people but not extraordinary ones.

The country of Egypt has been ruled by dictators dating as far back as the time of the Pharaohs. Leaders were expected to lead by portraying a self-assured image. To maintain power, Egyptian leaders need to continuously be involved in making decisions. In the Arabic culture that is very much influenced by Islam, men do not wish to appear weak.

Despite such high level of respect for leaders, Egyptian employees, perhaps due to their very strong in-group collectivism, prefer their leaders to respect group harmony, avoid group conflict, and take caution in decision making. It is rare to see leaders, especially political leaders, come out publicly

FIGURE 3

USA vs. Egypt

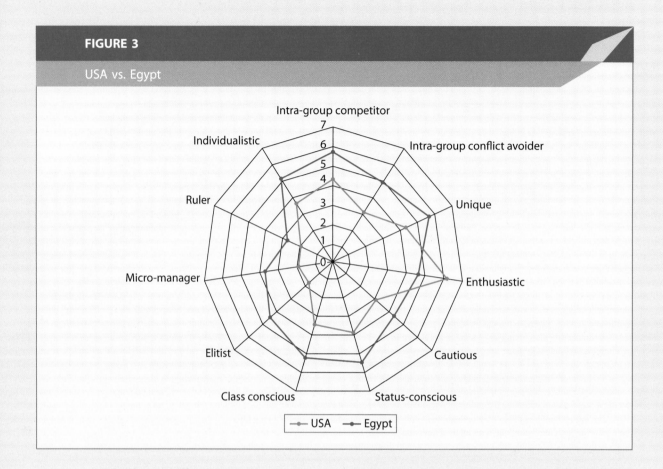

and criticize a popular belief. They tend to avoid a conflict when it is not necessary, and they often use this collectivism to build their influence and popularity.

The importance of kinship as the family is the most significant unit of Egyptian society. An individual's social identity is closely linked to his or her status in the network of kin relations. Kinship is essential to the culture. Describing the tendency toward generosity and caring in their society, an Egyptian manager told of how early Islamic authorities imposed a tax on personal property proportionate to one's wealth and distributed the revenues to the needy. This type of government behavior left a certain culture of doing business in Egypt that has a strong emphasis on harmony with the environment, the industry, and the competition.

When in Egypt...

Our hypothetical American manager will find that his experience in Egypt will have both similarities and differences with his time in France and Brazil. First, what the manager may regard as a normal informal leadership style in the U.S. may be seen as weak and unworthy of a leader. This manager (typically a male) is expected to act and be seen as distinct from the others on the team and present an image of omnipotence. In the minds of his Egyptian team members, he needs to be seen as deserving of his leadership role and status. Addressing his role as a leader, a project manager from Egypt noted that being a leader brought with it great responsibility. He was in charge of disciplining anyone that did not follow the team rules. He noted, "In order to keep the team spirit up and focused on our goals, we can't afford to have individuals deviating from what we have set out to do." This is almost the opposite of his experience in France.

The American manager will also find that due to very strong in-group collectivism, various groups inside and outside the organization tend to show in-group/out-group phenomena in decision making; i.e., strong participation by in-group members, little participation by out-group members; strong communication with in-group members, and little communication with out-group members. The extent to which Egyptians take pride in belonging to certain groups is immensely important. Families have endured through difficult times, requiring many of the members to stay together and work together. Family businesses tend to be passed from father to son without too many exceptions. Maintenance of the in-group is paramount in any decision. Leaders build their legitimacy not necessarily by accomplishing high performance but rather by forging loyalty to the group and group values. Furthermore, as a result of reliance on personal relationships, decision making criteria and processes regarding any aspect of the organization tend to be informal and unclear.

Given such cultural underpinnings, the American manager needs to do even more than he did in Brazil to build and maintain group harmony. Many informal and formal meetings are needed, but there are three important differences compared with the experience in Brazil. First, to Egyptians, the team leader is more than just an executive; he is a paternal figure who will be rather autocratic but benign. He cares about them and their families. The relationship between the boss and employees is much more emotional and personal in Egypt. The Egyptian project manager described how he helped one of his employees who had experienced some personal difficulties. Explaining that the employee's behaviour was unacceptable, the manager added, "At the same time, I tried to understand if there were any personal issues that forced him to behave the way he did. I felt an obligation to try to help him." Secondly, due to very high humane orientation in Egypt, if the family of an employee has a problem, colleagues and the boss will quickly get involved to help. Taking care of friends in need is a major element of the culture and there is very little demarcation between colleagues and friends. Third, it is easier and more acceptable for the boss in Brazil to get to know the family members and spend time with them during social occasions. It is not, however, a good idea for him to try to do the same with Egyptian families. The contact should only be with and through the employee. Egyptian families tend to be more private and inaccessible to outsiders, possibly due to the intense in-group culture. People tend to stay close to their roots and develop a very strong sense of belonging. In short, even though the American manager will spend time building personal ties and maintaining in-group relationships both in Egypt and Brazil, the nature of his behaviour will need to be somewhat different.

Like Brazil, the manager needs to pay his respects and call on the key executives in the Egyptian organization and start the process of building personal relationships. Unlike the French executives, the Egyptian executives will in all likelihood enjoy this approach and respond positively.

In developing a business strategy for the team, several cultural attributes need to be taken into consideration. The team will enjoy providing input but they expect decisions to be made by the leader. Family related activities are always celebrated and employees are often excused from work to

be able to properly plan such occasions. However, leaders also tend to use the friendly environment to maintain their control and build loyalty within their workforce. Egyptian employees expect their leaders to develop and communicate heroic and grand strategies. Due to their high institutional collectivism and performance orientation, it is helpful to design and communicate ambitious strategies and put them into the broader context of the corporation. Employees will resonate to ideas that would help the corporation and the unit achieve prominence in their competitive arenas. They also like strong rhetoric and get excited by the desire to be part of the winning team. In terms of the reward system, individual performance-based financial rewards, while helpful, are not the best motivators. The system should be seen to be humane to all; it should have a strong group based component, and it should consist of a variety of benefits that are not typically offered in the U.S. Such benefits should be focused on the families of employees. For example, tuition assistance to employees' children, paid family vacation, free or subsidized toys or home appliances could be very well received. As with other Middle East countries, although it is important for the individual to be successful, it is the family or group success that is more dominant.

China

China is part of the Confucian Asia cluster. The two CLT dimensions contributing to outstanding leadership are Charismatic/Value-Based and Team Oriented leadership, even though these scores are not particularly high. Humane Oriented leadership is viewed favorably, but it is not as important as the first two CLT dimensions. Although Participative leadership is also viewed positively, it is about equal to the lowest-scoring clusters. Autonomous leadership is viewed neutrally, and Self-Protective leadership is seen as a slight impediment to effective leadership. Table 4 shows that compared to other GLOBE countries, the Confucian Asia cluster is ranked relatively low with respect to Participative and relatively high with respect to Self-Protective leadership dimensions.

As shown in the Appendix, the US and Chinese cultures are similar in terms of their performance orientation, humane orientation, and power distance. The Chinese culture seems to be less future oriented, less assertive, more collectivist, both small group and socially, and more rules oriented.

Figure 4 below shows the comparison of culturally contingent leadership attributes between American and Chinese managers. Both American and Chinese managers like excellence oriented leaders who strive for performance improvement in themselves and their subordinates. This is probably driven by the fact that both cultures share a strong performance orientation, as shown in the Appendix. They also both like leaders who are honest. However, the figure shows that

FIGURE 4

USA vs. China

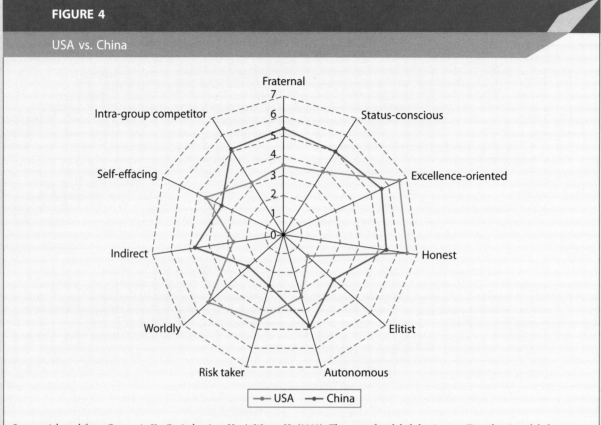

Source: *Adapted from Gupta, A. K., Govindarajan, V., & Wang, H. (2008). The quest for global dominance: Transforming global presence into global competitive advantage, 2nd edition. San Francisco: John Wiley & Sons, Inc*

the US scores on both these attributes are higher that the Chinese scores.

Chinese managers seem to like leaders who are fraternal and friendly with their subordinates and who have an indirect approach to communication, using metaphors and parables to communicate their point. American managers have a neutral view of fraternal leadership and a negative view of indirect leadership. The difference can probably be explained by the fact that the U.S. culture is much more assertive and less in-group oriented than that in China (see appendix). In a less assertive culture like China, people tend to use nuances and a context rich language to communicate. They prefer indirect communication to avoid the possibility of hurting someone. Furthermore, in a highly group oriented culture like China, group harmony is critical and the leader's role is to strengthen group ties. As a result, leaders are expected to be supportive of their subordinates and act as good friends for them. They are expected to build emotional ties with their

groups and their relationships with their subordinates go far beyond what is the norm in a country like the U.S. The leader is seen as a paternal figure who should take care of his subordinates and their families.

American managers are not excited about leaders who are status conscious and are negative towards leaders who are elitist. In contrast, Chinese managers like the former type of leadership and are neutral towards the latter. This is reflective of the importance of hierarchy in the Chinese culture. Confucianism's 'Three Bonds'—emperor rules the minister, father rules the son, and husband rules the wife—serve as the foundation of the Chinese society:

Chinese business structure can be directly linked to the history of patriarchy: the owner or manager plays the father's role, and the subordinates or employees play the son.[31]

Within such a hierarchical structure, the leader tends to be authoritative and expects respect and obedience and tends to make autonomous decisions. That is why Chinese managers do not admire leaders who are self-effacing, because such leaders do not emanate confidence. A group of American managers was recently in China to discuss a possible joint venture with a Chinese company. American managers expected to spend a few days working with their Chinese counterparts to brainstorm ideas and develop action plans. After a few frustrating days, they were told that they needed to find a Chinese agent to help them implement the deal. In conversations with the Chinese agent, they learned that the Chinese counterpart's expectation from the meetings was very different. They learned that the Chinese company wanted to use the meetings to help build personal ties among the Chinese and American managers and was upset that the Americans were asking aggressive questions and were focused solely on business rather than personal matters. They also learned that the top Chinese executive had no interest in sharing decision making with any one. Instead, he wanted to use private lunches and dinners with the head of the American delegation to make serious decisions and reach agreements.

Chinese managers are very negative towards worldly leaders who have a global outlook. In contrast, Americans admire such leaders. This could be explained by the fact that the two cultures are very different in terms of in group collectivism. The Chinese culture is very high on this dimension, which means it is less interested in anything outside of their in-group. Perhaps they view the world as out-group compared to China and view it as less important.

When in China...

The Chinese culture is distinct by its high performance orientation, high institutional orientation, and high in-group collectivism. Building personal ties and relationships is reflected in the Chinese concept of "guan xi" whose loose English translation is networking. It is a manifestation of the fact that one's value and importance is embedded in his/her ties and relationships. As a result:

> In China, the primary qualities expected in a leader or executive is someone who is good at establishing and nurturing personal relationships, who practices benevolence towards his or her subordinates, who is dignified and aloof but sympathetic, and puts the interests of his or her employees above his or her own.[32]

Much of Chinese life and culture is based on Confucian ideas which emphasize the importance of relationships and community. Even the word "self" has a negative connotation.[33] Our hypothetical American manager needs to be careful about how his behavior and manners are perceived by the Chinese. Being polite, considerate, and moral are desirable attributes. At the same time, the American manager can get the Chinese employees excited by engaging their high performance culture. Developing an exciting vision is very effective.

The relative high score on future orientation can also help the new manager get the employees motivated. But perhaps the most critical key success factor is how the manager goes about building personal ties and relationships with a wide network of individuals and groups. His "guan xi" will be the ultimate test of his success. In building guan xi with his employees, he needs to show high respect to the employees' families, keep them in mind when designing work schedules and reward systems, and make sure that employees see him and the organization as a strong supporter of their own guan xi. Perhaps a big challenge to the American executive is how to make sure his natural American assertiveness does not turn his Chinese employees and counterparts off and does not impede his efforts at building strong relationships.

Embarking on a Cross-cultural Leadership Journey

The existing literature on cross-cultural management is more useful at the conceptual level than at the behavioral level. Much of the advice offered to executives tends to be context-free and general such as "understand and respect the other culture." But the problems facing a typical global executive are context-specific; for example, how to understand and respect the Brazilian culture. In behavioral terms, understanding the Brazilian culture may be quite different from understanding and respecting the Egyptian culture because they are very different cultures.

In this paper, we have presented the cultural profiles of four countries based on a rigorous and scientific research project. We have also provided very specific ideas on the managerial implications of the different cultural profiles along with action oriented advice on how an American manager can "put himself in the other culture's shoes" and be adaptable. Besides the culture specific ideas presented earlier, we propose a two-step process for any executive who is embarking on a new assignment in a new country. Regardless of the host country, these two steps help build a positive pathway towards cultural understanding and adaptability.

First, the executive needs to share information about his own as well as the host country's culture. Most of the advice that executives receive is about how they can adapt and adjust to other cultures. We propose a somewhat different approach. When people from different cultures come into contact, they usually have unstated and sometimes false or exaggerated stereotypes about the other side. While it is important that the executive learn about the host culture, it is not sufficient. Executives need to tell the host employees about their own cultures. For example, if these executives are in Egypt, then they should show the employees how the American and Egyptian cultures and leadership attributes compare. They should show both similarities and differences.

In this paper, we showed that there is a set of leadership attributes that are universally desirable and universally undesirable. Similarities represent a fertile ground to build mutual understanding. The informed executive can then use the session to discuss their implications. What does integrity mean to a French manager? Or to a Brazilian manager? The executive can also compare the findings about his or her own culture with their perceptions of American culture to dispel any misunderstandings. This exercise in mapping and surfacing cultural attributes can go a long way to build mutual understanding and trust between the players. For example, our findings show that American culture is reported to be more moderate on many cultural dimensions than it is stereotypically believed to be. One of the unique features of GLOBE is that we have taken several steps to ensure that the reports by country managers are not confounded by such things as methodological problems and represent the true broader culture of their societies.

Second, the global manager needs to think about how to bridge the gap between the two cultures. Much of the advice executives receive seems to suggest, explicitly or implicitly, that the executive needs to become more like them. We do not necessarily subscribe to this viewpoint. While it is important to understand the other culture, it does not necessarily mean that one should automatically apply their approach. For example, leaders are seen as benign autocrats in Egypt. If an American manager does not like this approach, then he should educate the employees on his approach to leadership; why it is not dictatorial, and why he prefers it. Managers need to make sure the employees understand that their approach is not a sign of weakness, but a more effective style for the manager and for the team's and organization's success. It's a judgment call to say it's a "more effective" style than what the team is used to, but it is one that they should employ with the team. The global manager needs to tell the employees what managerial functions they are willing to change and what team functions they would like the employees to change so that the team can work from, and succeed on, common ground incorporating both cultures. The manager then needs to seek their help on both approaches; i.e., each culture making changes to accommodate and strengthen the other. Both approaches can take place at the same time and with respect to both cultures, as long as the manager gets the employees involved in the process. In other words, instead of a solitary learning journey for the executive, managers can create a collective learning journey that can be enriching, educational, and productive for both sides.

Attributes of Global Leaders

The essence of global leadership is the ability to influence people who are not like the leader and come from different cultural backgrounds. To succeed, global leaders need to have a global mindset, tolerate high levels of ambiguity, and show cultural adaptability and flexibility. This paper provides some examples of these attributes. In contrast to a domestic manager, the hypothetical manager discussed in this paper needs a global mindset because s/he needs to understand a variety of cultural and leadership paradigms, and legal, political and economic systems, as well as different competitive frameworks.[34] We used GLOBE findings to provide a scientifically based comparison of cultural and leadership paradigms in the five countries. We showed that countries can be different on some cultural dimensions and similar on others. Brazil and Egypt are both high on in-group collectivism, but different on performance orientation. France and the U.S. are both moderate on uncertainty avoidance but differ on power distance. China and the U.S. are both high on performance orientation but very different on in-group collectivism. Furthermore, there are similarities and differences in the countries' leadership profiles. While a leadership attribute like irritability is universally undesirable, another attribute like compassion is culturally contingent, i.e., it is much more desirable in the U.S. than in France.

Tolerance of ambiguity is another important attribute of a global leader. Every new country that s/he has to work in represents a new paradigm and new ways of doing things. This is typically an uncomfortable position for many people to be in because it requires learning new ideas quickly and letting go of what has already been learned. Of course, in the four scenarios, we showed that there are things in common across cultures and there are portable aspects of cultural learning. But we also showed that there are differences as well. Figuring out which one is which and what to do represents potentially stressful ambiguity to an expatriate manager.

Cultural adaptability refers to a manager's ability to understand other cultures and behave in a way that helps achieve goals and build strong and positive relations with local citizens. In the country scenarios, we showed that while in France the manager should not emphasize grand and ambitious corporate strategies, he can do this in China. Cultural adaptability refers to the mental and psychological ability to move from one situation and country to another. It means the ability to do a good job of developing personal relationships while in Egypt and then doing it very differently in France. The dexterity to adjust one's behavior is a critical requirement. Not everyone can do this; to many people it may bring into question one's own identity. In some ways it is reminiscent of acting but the difference is that the global manager, unlike the actor, lives and works among real people and not other actors, so his task is more complicated.

Developing Global Leaders

As mentioned earlier in this paper, a large majority of *Fortune* 500 corporations report a shortage of global leaders. Devising programs that would develop a global mindset in leaders has been called "the biggest challenge that looms in the new millennium for human resource managers."[35] There are a variety of ways that companies can enhance their pool of global leaders. To start with, they can make a large volume of information on cross-cultural and global issues and country specific reports available to their managers. We have already referred to several books on this topic. In addition to the special issue of the *Human Resource Management Journal* mentioned earlier, there are special issues of other journals.[36] There are also a variety of software packages such as a multimedia package called "Bridging Cultures," a self-training program for those who will be living and working in other cultures. In addition, several services like CultureGrams (www.culturegram.com) provide useful information about many countries. There are also a few Internet sites providing useful information to managers[37] such as www.contactcga.com belonging to the Center for

Global assignments, the CIA World Fact Book at www.odci.gov/cia/publications/factbook/, and Global Dynamics Inc.'s www.globaldynamics.com/expatria.htm.

Formal education and training can also be helpful in developing global leaders. A recent survey showed that a large majority of firms were planning to increase funding for programs that would help globalize their leaders.[38] But despite its prevalence among multinational corporations, there is general consensus among experts that it is not a highly effective source of developing global leaders.[39] It is generally best used as a component of a comprehensive and integrated development program. Work experience and international assignment is by far the most effective source for developing global leadership capabilities.[40] Some experts view long term international assignments as the "single most powerful experience in shaping the perspective and capabilities of effective global leaders."[41] Increasingly, companies like GE, Citigroup, Shell, Siemens, and Nokia are using international assignments of high potential employees as the means to develop their managers' global leadership mindset and competencies.

Appendix Country Scores on Cultural Practices

Performance Orientation	Anglo Cultures	Latin Europe	Middle East Cultures	Confucian Asia	Latin America
	USA 4.49	**France 4.11**	**Egypt 4.27**	**China 4.45**	**Brazil 4.04**
	Canada 4.49	Israel 4.08	Kuwait 3.95	Hong Kong 4.80	Bolivia 3.61
	England 4.08	Italy 3.58	Morocco 3.99	Japan 4.22	Argentina 3.65
	Ireland 4.36	Portugal 3.60	Qatar 3.45	Singapore 4.90	Colombia 3.94
	New Zealand 4.72	Spain 4.01	Turkey 3.83	South Korea 4.55	Costa Rica 4.12
	South Africa (W) 4.11	Swiss (French) 4.25		Taiwan 4.56	Ecuador 4.20
	Australia 4.36				El Salvador 3.72
					Guatemala 3.81
					Mexico 4.10
					Venezuela 3.32
Future Orientation	Anglo Cultures	Latin Europe	Middle East Cultures	Confucian Asia	Latin America
	USA 4.15	**France 3.48**	**Egypt 3.86**	**China 3.75**	**Brazil 3.81**
	Canada 4.44	Israel 3.85	Kuwait 3.26	Hong Kong 4.03	Bolivia 3.61
	England 4.28	Italy 3.25	Morocco 3.26	Japan 4.29	Argentina 3.08

(continued)

	Anglo Cultures	Latin Europe	Middle East Cultures	Confucian Asia	Latin America
	Ireland 3.98	Portugal 3.71	Qatar 3.78	Singapore 5.07	Colombia 3.27
	New Zealand 3.47	Spain 3.51	Turkey 3.74	South Korea 3.97	Costa Rica 3.60
	South Africa (W) 4.13	Swiss (French) 4.27		Taiwan 3.96	Ecuador 3.74
	Australia 4.09				El Salvador 3.80
					Guatemala 3.24
					Mexico 3.87
					Venezuela 3.35
Assertiveness Orientation	Anglo Cultures	Latin Europe	Middle East Cultures	Confucian Asia	Latin America
	USA 4.55	**France 4.13**	**Egypt 3.91**	**China 3.76**	**Brazil 4.20**
	Canada 4.05	Israel 4.23	Kuwait 3.63	Hong Kong 4.67	Bolivia 3.79
	England 4.15	Italy 4.07	Morocco 4.52	Japan 3.59	Argentina 4.22
	Ireland 3.92	Portugal 3.65	Qatar 4.11	Singapore 4.17	Colombia 4.20
	New Zealand 3.42	Spain 4.42	Turkey 4.53	South Korea 4.40	Costa Rica 3.75
	South Africa (W) 4.60	Swiss (French) 3.47		Taiwan 3.92	Ecuador 4.09
	Australia 4.28				El Salvador 4.62
					Guatemala 3.89
					Mexico 4.45
					Venezuela 4.33
Societal Collectivism	Anglo Cultures	Latin Europe	Middle East Cultures	Confucian Asia	Latin America
	USA 4.20	**France 3.93**	**Egypt 4.50**	**China 4.77**	**Brazil 3.83**
	Canada 4.38	Israel 4.46	Kuwait 4.49	Hong Kong 4.13	Bolivia 4.04
	England 4.27	Italy 3.68	Morocco 3.87	Japan 5.19	Argentina 3.66
	Ireland 4.63	Portugal 3.92	Qatar 4.50	Singapore 4.90	Colombia 3.81
	New Zealand 4.81	Spain 3.85	Turkey 4.03	South Korea 5.20	Costa Rica 3.93
	South Africa (W) 4.62	Swiss (French) 4.22		Taiwan 4.59	Ecuador 3.90
	Australia 4.29				El Salvador 3.71
					Guatemala 3.70
					Mexico 4.06
					Venezuela 3.96
In-Group Collectivism	Anglo Cultures	Latin Europe	Middle East Cultures	Confucian Asia	Latin America
	USA 4.25	**France 4.37**	**Egypt 5.64**	**China 5.80**	**Brazil 5.18**
	Canada 4.26	Israel 4.70	Kuwait 5.80	Hong Kong 5.32	Bolivia 5.47

(continued)

Anglo Cultures	Latin Europe	Middle East Cultures	Confucian Asia	Latin America
England 4.08	Italy 4.94	Morocco 5.87	Japan 4.63	Argentina 5.51
Ireland 5.14	Portugal 5.51	Qatar 4.71	Singapore 5.64	Colombia 5.73
New Zealand 3.67	Spain 5.45	Turkey 5.88	South Korea 5.54	Costa Rica 5.32
South Africa (W) 4.50	Swiss (French) 3.85		Taiwan 5.59	Ecuador 5.81
Australia 4.17				El Salvador 5.35
				Guatemala 5.63
				Mexico 5.71
				Venezuela 5.53

Humane Orientation	Anglo Cultures	Latin Europe	Middle East Cultures	Confucian Asia	Latin America
	USA 4.17	**France 3.40**	**Egypt 4.73**	**China 4.36**	**Brazil 3.66**
	Canada 4.49	Israel 4.10	Kuwait 4.52	Hong Kong 3.90	Bolivia 4.05
	England 3.72	Italy 3.63	Morocco 4.19	Japan 4.30	Argentina 3.99
	Ireland 4.96	Portugal 3.91	Qatar 4.42	Singapore 3.49	Colombia 3.72
	New Zealand 4.32	Spain 3.32	Turkey 3.94	South Korea 3.81	Costa Rica 4.39
	South Africa (W) 3.49	Swiss (French) 3.93		Taiwan 4.11	Ecuador 4.65
	Australia 4.28				El Salvador 3.71
					Guatemala 3.89
					Mexico 3.98
					Venezuela 4.25

Power Distance	Anglo Cultures	Latin Europe	Middle East Cultures	Confucian Asia	Latin America
	USA 4.88	**France 5.28**	**Egypt 4.92**	**China 5.04**	**Brazil 5.33**
	Canada 4.82	Israel 4.73	Kuwait 5.12	Hong Kong 4.96	Bolivia 4.51
	England 5.15	Italy 5.43	Morocco 5.80	Japan 5.11	Argentina 5.64
	Ireland 5.15	Portugal 5.44	Qatar 4.73	Singapore 4.99	Colombia 5.56
	New Zealand 4.89	Spain 5.52	Turkey 5.57	South Korea 5.61	Costa Rica 4.74
	South Africa (W) 5.16	Swiss (French) 4.86		Taiwan 5.18	Ecuador 5.60
	Australia 4.74				El Salvador 5.68
					Guatemala 5.60
					Mexico 5.22
					Venezuela 5.40

Gender Egalitarianism	Anglo Cultures	Latin Europe	Middle East Cultures	Confucian Asia	Latin America
	USA 3.34	**France 3.64**	**Egypt 2.81**	**China 3.05**	**Brazil 3.31**
	Canada 3.70	Israel 3.19	Kuwait 2.58	Hong Kong 3.47	Bolivia 3.55

(continued)

	England 3.67	Italy 3.24	Morocco 2.84	Japan 3.19	Argentina 3.49
	Ireland 3.21	Portugal 3.66	Qatar 3.63	Singapore 3.70	Colombia 3.67
	New Zealand 3.22	Spain 3.01	Turkey 2.89	South Korea 2.50	Costa Rica 3.56
	South Africa (W) 3.27	Swiss (French) 3.42		Taiwan 3.18	Ecuador 3.07
	Australia 3.40				El Salvador 3.16
					Guatemala 3.02
					Mexico 3.64
					Venezuela 3.62
Uncertainty Avoidance	**Anglo Cultures**	**Latin Europe**	**Middle East Cultures**	**Confucian Asia**	**Latin America**
	USA 4.15	**France 4.43**	**Egypt 4.06**	**China 4.94**	**Brazil 3.60**
	Canada 4.58	Israel 4.01	Kuwait 4.21	Hong Kong 4.32	Bolivia 3.35
	England 4.65	Italy 3.79	Morocco 3.65	Japan 4.07	Argentina 3.65
	Ireland 4.30	Portugal 3.91	Qatar 3.99	Singapore 5.31	Colombia 3.57
	New Zealand 4.75	Spain 3.97	Turkey 3.63	South Korea 3.55	Costa Rica 3.82
	South Africa (W) 4.09	Swiss (French) 4.98		Taiwan 4.34	Ecuador 3.68
	Australia 4.39				El Salvador 3.62
					Guatemala 3.30
					Mexico 4.18
					Venezuela 3.44

Source: Academy of Management Perspectives, 20, (1), 67–90 (2006). Reprinted by permission.

Source: Javidan, M. et. al. In the Eye of the Beholder: Cross Cultural Lessons in Leadership from Project GLOBE. *Academy of Management Perspectives*, 20, (1), 67-90 (2006). Reprinted by permission of the CCC.

ENDNOTES

1. House, R. J., Hanges, P. J., Ruiz-Quintanilla, S. A., Dorfman, P. W., Javidan, M., Dickson, M., et al. 1999. Cultural influences on leadership and organizations: Project globe. In W. F. Mobley, M. J. Gessner & V. Arnold (Eds.), *Advances in global leadership* (Vol. 1, pp. 171–233). Stamford, CT: JAI Press.

2. Gregersen, H. B., Morrison, A. J., & J. S. Black. 1998. Developing leaders for the global frontier. *Sloan Management Review*, Fall: 21–32.

3. Hollenbeck, G. P. & McCall, M. W. 2003. Competence, not competencies: Making global executive development work. In W. Mobley & P. Dorfman (Eds.), *Advances in global leadership* (Vol. 3). Oxford: JAI Press.

4. Black, J. S., Morrison, A. J., & Gergersen, H. B. 1999. *Global explorers: The next generation of leaders.* New York: Routledge; Rheinsmith, S. H. 1996. *A manager's guide to globalization.* Chicago: Irwin; Osland, J. S. 1995. *The adventure of working abroad: Hero tales from the global frontier.* San Francisco: CA: Jossey-Bass, Inc.; Black, J. S., Gergersen, H. B., Mendenhall, M. E., & Stroh L. K. 1999. *Globalizing people through international assignments.* Reading, MA: Addisson-Wesley; Mobley, W. H. & Dorfman, P. W. 2003. *Advances in global leadership.* In W. H. Mobley & P. W. Dorfman (Eds.), *Advances in global leadership* (Vol. 3). Oxford: JAI Press.

5. Gergerson, H. B., Morrison, A. J., & Mendenhall, M. E. 2000. Guest editors. *Human Resource Management Journal*, 39, 2&3, 113–299.

6. Morrison, A. J. 2000. Developing a global leadership model. *Human Resource Management Journal*, 39, 2&3, 117–131.

7. Kiedel, R. W. 1995. *Seeing organizational patterns: A new theory and language of organizational design*. San Francisco: Berrett-Koehler.

8. Pucik, V. & Saba, T. 1997. Selecting and developing the global versus the expatriate manager: A review of the state of the art. *Human Resource Planning*, 40–54.

9. Wills, S. 2001. *Developing global leaders*. In P. Kirkbride & K. Ward (Eds.), *Globalization: The internal dynamic*. Chicester: Wiley, 259–284.

10. Bass, B. M. 1997. Does the Transactional-Transformational Leadership Paradigm Transcend Organizational and National Boundaries? *American Psychologist*, 52(2), 130–139.

11. Hofstede, G. 1980. Culture's consequences: International differences in work-related values. New Bury Park, CA: Sage; Hofstede, G. 2001 Culture's Consequences: Comparing values, behaviors, institutions, and organizations across nations. 2nd ed. Thousand Oaks, CA: Sage; Trompenaars, F. & Hamden-Turner C. 1998. *Riding the waves of culture*. 2nd ed. New York: McGraw-Hill; Kluckhohn, F. R. & Strodtbeck, F. L. 1961. *Variations in value orientations*. New York: Harper & Row.

12. House, R. J., Hanges, P. J., Javidan, M., Dorfman, P. W., & Gupta, V., & GLOBE Associates. 2004. *Leadership, culture and organizations: The globe study of 62 societies*. Thousand Oaks, CA: Sage Publications, Inc.

13. Morrison, A. J. 2000. Developing a global leadership model. *Human Resource Management Journal*, 39, 2&3, 117–131.

14. Laurent, A. 1983. The cultural diversity of western conceptions of management. *International Studies of Management and Organization*, 13(2), 75–96; Trompenaars, F. 1993. Riding the waves of culture: Understanding cultural diversity in business. London: Breatley; Briscoe, D. R., & Shuler, R. S. 2004. *International human resource management*. 2nd ed. New York: Routledge.

15. Davis, D. D. & Bryant, J. L. 2003. Influence at a distance: Leadership in global virtual teams. In W. H. Mobley & P. W. Dorfman (Eds.), *Advances in global leadership* (Vol. 3, pp. 303–340). Oxford: JAI Press.

16. Millman, J. Trade wins: The world's new tiger on the export scene isn't Asian; it's Mexico. *Wall Street Journal*, p. A1. May 9, 2000.

17. Smith, P. B. & Peterson, M. F. 1988. *Leadership, organizations and culture: An event management model*. London: Sage.

18. Smith, P. B. 2003. Leaders' sources of guidance and the challenge of working across cultures. In W. Mobley & P. Dorfman (Eds.), *Advances in global leadership* (Vol. 3, pp. 167–182). Oxford: JAI Press; Smith, P. B., Dugan, S., & Trompenaars, F. 1996. National culture and the values of organizational employees: A dimensional analysis across 43 nations. *Journal of Cross-Cultural Psychology*, 27(2), 231–264.

19. Hazucha, J. F., Hezlett, S. A., Bontems-Wackens, S., & Ronnqvist. 1999. In search of the Euro-manager: Management competencies in France, Germany, Italy, and the United States. In W. H. Mobley, M. J. Gessner & V. Arnold (Eds.), *Advances in global leadership* (Vol. 1, pp. 267–290). Stamford, CT: JAI Press.

20. Javidan, M. & D. Carl. 2004. East meets West. *Journal of Management Studies*, 41:4, June, 665–691; Javidan, M. & Carl, D. 2005. Leadership across cultures: A study of Canadian and Taiwanese executives, *Management International Review*, 45(1), 23–44.

21. House, R. J., Wright, N. S., & Aditya, R. N. 1997. Cross-cultural research on organizational leadership: A critical analysis and a proposed theory. In P. C. Earley & M. Erez (Eds.), *New perspectives in international industrial/organizational psychology* (pp. 535–625). San Francisco: The New Lexington Press.

22. Chemers, M. M. 1997. An *integrative theory of leadership*. London: Lawrence Erlbaum Associates; Smith, P. B. & Peterson, M. F. 1988. *Leadership, organizations and culture: An event management model*. London: Sage.

23. Shaw, J. B. (1990). A cognitive categorization model for the study of intercultural management. *Academy of Management Review*, 15(4), 626–645.

24. Lord, R. G. & Maher, K. J. 1991. *Leadership and information processing: Linking perceptions and performance* (Vol. 1). Cambridge, MA: Unwin Hyman.

25. House, R. J., Hanges, P. J., Ruiz-Quintanilla, S. A., Dorfman, P. W., Javidan, M., Dickson, M., et al. 1999. Cultural influences on leadership and organizations: Project GLOBE. In W. F. Mobley, M. J. Gessner & V. Arnold (Eds.), *Advances in global leadership* (Vol. 1, pp. 171–233). Stamford, CT: JAI Press.

26. In addition to the aggregated raw (i.e., absolute) scores for CLTs provided in Table 2, we also computed a response bias corrected measure as an integral part of the analysis strategy. We referred to this measure as the relative measure because of a unique property attributed to this procedure. These relative CLT scores indicate the relative importance of each CLT leadership dimension within a person, culture, or culture cluster. This procedure not only removed the cultural response biases, but it also had the advantage of illustrating the differences among the cultures and the clusters. Along with ranking the clusters with absolute CLT scores, we used this relative measure to compare the relative importance of each CLT dimension among cultures. Ranking of clusters using both types of scores are presented in Table 3. We should point out that the correlation between the absolute and relative measures is close to perfect—above .90 for all of the CLT leadership dimensions. Computational procedures for this measure are detailed in House et al. 2004.

27. Cullen, J. B. 2002. *Multinational management. A strategic approach.* (2nd ed.). Cincinnati, OH: South-Western Thomson Learning.

28. Bossidy, L. & Charan, R. 2002. *Execution: The discipline of getting things done.* New York: Crown Business Books. p. 103.

29. Hallowell, R., Bowen, D., & Knoop, C. 2002. Four Seasons goes to Paris, *Academy of Management Executive,* 16(4), 7–24.

30. Hallowell, Ibid.

31. Dayal-Gulati, A. 2004. Kellogg on China: Strategies for success, Northwestern University Press.

32. De Mente, Boye Lafayette. 2000. *The Chinese have a word for it: The complete guide to Chinese thought and culture.* Chicago, IL: Passport Books.

33. Rosen, R. Global *Literacies.* Simon and Schuster, 2000.

34. Black, J. S. & Gergersen, H. B. 2000. High impact training: Forging leaders for the global frontier. *Human Resource Management Journal,* 39 (2&3), 173–184.

35. Oddou, G., Mendenhall, M. E., & Ritchi, J. B. Leveraging travel as a tool for global leadership development. *Human Resource Management Journal,* 39, 2&3, 159–172.

36. Dastmalchian, A. & Kabasakal, H. 2001. Guest editors, special issue on the Middle East, *Applied Psychology: An International Review.* Vol. 50(4); Javidan, M. & House, R. Spring 2002 Guest editors, special Issue on GLOBE. *Journal of World Business,* Vol. 37, No, 1; Peterson, M. F. & Hunt, J. G. 1997. Overview: International and cross-cultural leadership research (Part II). *Leadership Quarterly,* 8(4), 339–342.

37. For more information, see Mendenhall, M. E. & Stahl, G. K. Expatriate training and development: Where do we go from here? *Human Resource Management Journal,* 39, 2&3, 251–265.

38. Black, J. S., Morrison, A. J., & Gergersen, H. B. 1999. *Global explorers: The next generation of leaders.* New York: Routledge.

39. Dodge, B. 1993. Empowerment and the evolution of learning, *Education and Training.* 35(5), 3–10; Sherman, S. 1995. How tomorrow's best leaders are learning their stuff. *Fortune,* 90–106.

40. Conner, J. Developing the global leaders of tomorrow. *Human Resource Management Journal,* 39, 2&3, 147–157.

41. Black, J. S., Gergersen, H. B., Mendenhall, M. E. & Stroh, L. K. 1999. *Globalizing people through international assignments.* Reading, MA: Addisson-Wesley.

READING 14.2

Cross-Cultural Management and Organizational Behavior in Africa

Erika Amoako-Agyei

For Western operations to succeed in Africa, foreign executives must embrace cross-cultural management skills as part of a broad strategic focus. This article examines culture as the crucial dimension to forging strong social, economic, and diplomatic ties between Africa and the Western world. To globalize successfully into the African marketplace, the effective cross-cultural manager must have an in-depth understanding of the African cultural value system. By analyzing African conventions, whose norms differ greatly from Western culture, this article clarifies the key roles that African culture plays in management methods, organizational behavior, and business practices in the sub-Saharan region. © 2009 Wiley Periodicals, Inc.

Introduction

For the Western manager, there are few destinations on earth that present more cultural differences than sub-Saharan Africa. Yet, to be successful in African commercial environments, it is crucial to understand the role culture plays in business development and relationship building. What may be acceptable in Europe or North America may be offensive in Africa. Many of the goals may be the same, but the business styles and ways of communication are likely to differ greatly. For example, questioning a supervisor in Europe or North America may be considered acceptable, demonstrating ambition and intelligence. By contrast, the same behavior in Africa may be viewed as rude and disrespectful. Discerning the difference will come easily to the expatriate manager well grounded in the complexity of core African cultural values and social norms commonly found in local commercial environments.

A Continent of Diversity

To globalize successfully into the African marketplace, Western business leaders must understand what is culturally expected of them. For the effective cross-cultural manager, this includes developing an in-depth understanding of

Published online in Wiley InterScience (www.interscience.wiley.com).
© 2009 Wiley Periodicals, Inc. • DOI: 10.1002/tie.20270

the African cultural value system (Shonhiwa, 2008)—and its direct impact on business practices and organizational behavior. It is of critical importance to note that there is no "one" African culture or society. Africa is vast, comprising 54 independent nations, 900 million people, and 3,000 ethnic groups speaking more than 1,000 indigenous languages—in addition to the six European languages (English, French, Portuguese, German, Spanish, and Italian) carried over from prior colonization.

This article will focus on the behavioral patterns and social customs of the people in the sub-Saharan region, which includes all of Africa except North Africa—Tunisia, Algeria, Morocco, Libya, and Egypt—the five northern nations bordering the Mediterranean. Although these nations are geographically in Africa, their culture and customs have been influenced by the Arab world.

Sub-Saharan Africa is the world's fastest-growing region. It is culturally complex and commonly referred to as "black" Africa. Certainly, sub-Saharan Africans share many cultural elements, but with enormous variations. Ghana is not Angola, and Angola is not Tanzania. Differences exist not only among countries, but within countries as well. In spite of the differences, however, there are some basic cultural understandings and broad principles that have been shared among the people of Africa for centuries. These common beliefs and core cultural values transcend national boundaries, languages, and ethnicities and form a fundamental cultural unit. Building on that common ground, this article adopts cultural generalizations to make cross-cultural comparisons, not to oversimplify or deny the complexity of cultural patterns in Africa but to offer a basic understanding from which Westerners may build business relationships and avoid cultural misunderstandings.[1]

Economic Outlook

Is it possible to think of Africa as the next frontier for major business opportunity? To many Western business leaders, Africa is a poor and unstable region with chronic political hotspots and little to offer. Despite the continent's obvious problems, the development needs of modern Africa provide many opportunities for Western business and volunteer groups. On a global scale, there is a growing recognition of Africa as a major destination with vast stores of untapped opportunity, proven oil reserves, and critically important mineral resources, such as gold, diamonds, chromium, and copper.

Adding to that, prime examples of Africa's promising and positive economic potential lie within the tourism and telecommunications sectors. To the surprise of many, Africa is the fastest-growing market worldwide for international tourism and telecommunications. Led by Kenya, South Africa, and Mozambique, the continent has consistently outperformed the world as a whole in terms of the growth rate of international tourist arrivals, increasing its share from 1.5% in 1970 to a record high of 10.6% in 2006 (Zimmerman, 2008). Furthermore, the continent has the fastest-growing mobile telephone market in the world, making it the first place where mobile phone subscribers have outnumbered fixed-line subscribers (Watson, 2007).

Between the continent's burgeoning trade with China (growing at 40% a year) and its steadily growing economy (above 5%) and multiple stock markets boasting some of the world's highest rates of return, there is an undeniable sense that over the next decade Africa is finally positioned to take its place in the global economy. These figures challenge Western companies and individuals to reassess broad stereotypes and globalization strategies. But for Western operations to work successfully in Africa, foreign executives must embrace cross-cultural management skills as an integral part of a broad strategic focus.

Today more than ever, successful business travel requires cultural awareness and effective cross-cultural communication skills. Yet, many executives, volunteers, and expatriates are often sent into foreign markets with little or no understanding of their host culture. While it's true that travel builds bridges, the only way to effectively communicate across cultural boundaries is by acquiring a thorough understanding of the cultures one encounters. With an increasingly competitive business environment, it is important to develop a tailored approach in working with management teams from new or unfamiliar cultural environments. International managers must recognize that what may be considered unacceptable conduct in one society could be considered normal or even praised in another.

Breaking Into Africa: Developing a Tailored Approach

Of all continents, Africa is the most heterogeneous—linguistically, culturally, and ethnically. Consequently, in the modern business world, identity in Africa can be a complex and sensitive issue. Primarily, identity in Africa still revolves

around ethnic affiliation. In the business office, the expatriate manager will need to tread carefully around personal questions as conversation starters, particularly as they may relate to ethnicity. Such questions should be asked only after mutual trust has been developed. Identity among "black" Africans is based on ethnicity and linguistic and geographic affiliation as opposed to race or nationality (as defined by colonial borders). For example, "ethnically speaking," an African may be (in this order) *Akyem* (ethnic group), *Akan* (linguistic group), Ghanaian (nationality), West African (regional affiliation), and African (ancestral origin) *all at once*.

Awareness of these distinctions is essential in designing strategies for dealing effectively with local counterparts. Throughout much of sub-Saharan Africa, diversity is not about race, especially since well over 90% of the population is black African. Diversity, instead, is based on membership in a variety of ethnic groups. In Ghana, for example, there are five major ethnic groups in the urban south alone, including the *Akan (Fante* and *Ashanti), Ewe,* and *Ga* peoples. And there are well over 50 other smaller ethnic groups dispersed throughout the rest of the country. Southern Ghana is home to the economic center of the country. Subsequently, much of the political power is in the south. Being aware of language differences, status differences, various ethnic perceptions, and stereotypes in the country make a competitive advantage possible when operating in this market. This type of awareness offers deeper insight into a new client base, and cross-cultural training prior to arriving in a country can guide businesspersons toward cultural sensitivity in this environment.

The need to diversify business partners can be a critical task—not just diversity in competency or ability, but, more important, by the various ethnic groups; cultural awareness here can make all the difference. Choosing business partners to represent a company to the general populace is a very sensitive issue. Many business partners of a Western company in Africa are likely to be family-owned enterprises, members of the elite classes, and be operated by members of certain ethnic groups. By putting company representation in the hands of ethnic groups (e.g., *Ewe, Ga, Nzema, Kwahu, Akwapim, Fante,* and *Ashanti*) that cut across the general population, a company might attain more power to influence the buying decisions of companies and consumers in this environment. This strategy can enable a company to capture market share, boost sales, and increase margins.

In the same way that a company should leverage its cultural awareness, it is also possible to leverage the various ethnic backgrounds of the ownerships of local companies. This will diversify the company's presence, expand its commercial reach, and broaden the client base, which, ultimately, increases the bottom line. An expatriate manager, moving among local business partners, a home corporation, and African business and multinational clients, becomes the focal point for ensuring effective communication across all cultural boundaries. This responsibility is as critical as managing daily business activity.

In the same way that a company should leverage its cultural awareness, it is also possible to leverage the various ethnic backgrounds of the ownerships of local companies.

Pointer

As a rule, it is wise to tread cautiously when discussing ethnic-related matters. Since ethnic identity is significant to many Africans, etiquette demands respect for ethnic affiliations and sensitivity to issues surrounding them. Due to complex histories of ethnic strife, Africans themselves may engage in disparaging remarks along ethnic lines. For an expatriate manager, however, careless questioning of ethnic identity—through ignorance or deliberate intention—can be an irreversible breach of etiquette.

Issues in Cross-Cultural Management

Throughout the world, business practices are extensions of culture—and in African society, this is especially true. Africans have an acute sense of solidarity and communal life. A clear perspective of this value will provide deep insights into the principles that drive business practices, behavior patterns, and communication structures. To the surprise of many, Africans have their own distinct systems of commercial management uniquely rooted in their own traditions and ideals. Many African firms are often structured like African families—reflecting the regional history, ethnic origins, linguistic structure, and even the family background of their founders (Fadiman, 1994).

A separate set of distinct principles guides local business managers and leads to specific behavior appropriate to African commercial settings. These same qualities are expected of a nonlocal expatriate manager or supervisor. As a result, knowledge of these principles is not only helpful, but critical, to success in dealing with African organizations.

In South Africa, (black) African scholars often state that central to African management principles is the concept of *Ubuntu*[2] (Mbigi, 1995). *Ubuntu* has been said to form the basis of African management philosophy and is often summarized as "humanity toward others." It is based on the premise that everyone and everything is interconnected. What hurts you hurts me. What heals you heals me. Other management tools used in African commercial environments include paternal leadership, consultation, and cohesive groups—all key to managing people in Africa.

Eight Principles of Modern African Management

For the Western manager of an Africa-based firm to deal effectively across culture lines, the dominant Western management paradigm needs to adapt to, and value, African management strategies as being equally important as those of Western countries. To gain insight into the cultural intricacies of managing in Africa, it is useful to analyze the principles that guide African management methods. Eight key principles have emerged from research that summarizes management tools used in African commercial environments. These are essential to understanding local organizational management (Mthembu, 1996). Hence, effective leadership in the African firm requires the integration of the following eight business principles:

For the Western manager of an Africa-based firm to deal effectively across culture lines, the dominant Western management paradigm needs to adapt to, and value, African management strategies as being equally important as those of Western countries.

1. *Collective Solidarity:* Employee teams work most effectively, achieving cohesiveness and solidarity, by working toward a common purpose (Mbigi, 1995). Thus, African enterprises are often communal, interdependent, family-run, and family-oriented (Fadiman, 1994). Africans are motivated to work in teams and are loyal to their own group.
2. *Group Significance (*Ubuntu*):* *Ubuntu* means that humanity is a shared value in which personhood exists within a group context, only insofar as a person values others. Rooted in that same principle, modern African firms are structured so that every team member is given a meaningful role to play. Concern evolves around team rather than individual interests. Personal achievement is underplayed in favor of group achievement (Booysen, 1999).
3. *Harmony and Social Cohesion:* Emphasis is placed on maintaining peace and keeping conflict to a minimum by promoting internal, communal, and familial harmony (Shonhiwa, 2008). Thus, interconnectedness and communal relationships, dignity, and mutual respect are very highly valued (Lassiter, 1999).
4. *Consensus:* Emphasis is placed on collective decision making. Conformity, collaboration, and cooperation are encouraged (Booysen, 1999). Competition is discouraged, as is individuality.
5. *Consultation:* Group participation is strongly emphasized, as are mutual understanding, joint problem solving, and honoring the collective wisdom of all team members.
6. *Local Time (or "African" Time):* In Africa, time standards are ambiguous, and thus require flexibility on the part of non-African managers. Western time restrictions and deadlines do not apply. An African manager welcoming a business counterpart will take ample time, *before business*, to form a personal connection or relationship. This

may include elaborate evening meals, invitations to social events, and, possibly, even traditional ceremonies. Inquiries will be made about travel to Africa and motives for coming to Africa, about personal interests and background—all in an effort to gain insight into unfamiliar value systems and find compatibility for a mutually trusting, long-term business relationship.

7. *Paternal/Maternal Leadership:* African firms are often structured like African families and, therefore, organizational leaders (managers, supervisors, and owners) tend to behave with paternal (or maternal) responsibility toward their staff members. An African business leader is expected to be more supportive and even somewhat intrusive, providing advice on matters both personal and professional, which would be considered inappropriate in Western business environments. Leaders are also expected to be more parental by nature, working to maintain group harmony, solve employees' personal problems, and generally be considerate and helpful (Booysen, 1999). Leaders will strive to exhibit the capacity to facilitate collective decision making, in addition to exercising strong listening and problem-solving skills. Leaders will also respect and encourage groups' loyalties.

8. *Age and Authority:* It is important for Western business managers to always consider a person's age when doing business in Africa (Fadiman, 1994). Within a business relationship, age is an essential component in Africa. Advanced age is inherently equated with authority, business wisdom, rank, title, and experience. Thus, an older person automatically holds a certain level of superiority, regardless of rank, title, or education.

Pointers

- A wise strategy for Westerners is to make a special effort to acknowledge the elders of their business host. This may include seeking their input first on an issue as a show of respect for their experience and established place within the organization. A subtle show of humility and respect such as this goes a long way in relationship building. Additionally, since rank and authority are highly respected, it is useful to acknowledge the host's authority and recognize company seniority.

- The time invested in building relationships in the beginning will deliver more returns in the long run than technical or industry know-how. Managers should refrain from time-limited, transactional views of African clients, as this will be counterproductive. The goal in initial encounters should be, rather, to build a long-term, mutually supportive, mutually beneficial, and mutually trusting relationship.

These principles can be treated as behavioral ideals, toward which most African business leaders aspire. Thus, they serve as a model against which they actually conduct business. At the same time, they give deeper insight into the traditional value system on which African culture is based.

Dimensions of Culture

To describe some dominant thinking and value systems found in African societies, it is useful to incorporate some of the cultural dimensions developed by Dutch anthropologists Hofstede (2000) and Trompenaars and Hampden-Turner (1998), who both conducted leading studies of cross-cultural management. The dimensions (Table 1) provide a useful framework for comparing African and Western cultural values.

African Collectivism vs. American Individualism

Hofstede contrasted *collectivism* and *individualism*. Is it the goal of individuals to enhance their own position or the advancement of their group (community or corporation)? In the United States, Canada, Western Europe, Australia, and New Zealand, the dominant culture is individualistic, while collectivism predominates in Africa. This is one of the fundamental differences between African and Western cultures—the extent to which members identify with the group rather than themselves as individuals. Individualism refers to cultures in which people see themselves first as individuals and believe that their own interests take priority over those of the groups, while collectivism refers to societies in which individuals identify primarily as members of the group and believe that the group's interests take priority over their own. In collectivist cultures, such as those found in Africa, the group is valued above the individual. People in collectivist societies think naturally in terms of "we" rather than "I." Furthermore, collectivist societies value social relations over individual performance.

In many African business settings, collectivism is reflected in teamwork, discouragement of competition among individuals, encouragement of conformity, collective decision making, cooperation, and collaboration. Group conformity and commitment is maintained at the expense of personal interests. Personal achievement is underplayed (in favor of group achievement). Shame is often used to achieve behavioral goals. Harmony, getting along, and saving face are seen as crucial. Even more, harmony is valued above honesty or truth, and silence more than speech. Overall, success is achieved in groups.

As one Kenyan scholar, John Mbiti, puts it, "Whatever happens to the individual happens to the whole group, and whatever happens to the whole group happens to the individual. The individual can only say: 'I am, because we are; and since we are, therefore I am.' This is a cardinal point in the understanding of the African view of man" (Lassiter, 1999).

Table 2 expands on how these differences impact management styles and business practices. It also supports the

Table 1

Dimensions of Culture: Value Differences Between Western and African Cultures

Western Cultural Values	African Cultural Values
Individualism	Collectivism/Group
Achievement	Ascription/Modesty
Equality/Egalitarianism	Hierarchy
Winning	Collaboration/Harmony
Guilt (internal self-control)	Shame (external control)
Pride	Saving face
Respect for results	Respect for status/Ascription
Respect for competence	Respect for elders
Time is money	Time is life
Action/Doing	Being/Acceptance
Systematic/Mechanic	Humanistic
Tasks	Relationship/Loyalty
Informal	Formal
Directness/Assertiveness	Indirectness
Future/Change	Past/Tradition
Control	Fate
Verbal	Nonverbal
Low power distance	High power distance
Quantity-oriented	Quality-oriented

claim that management philosophies typically evolve in harmony with the cultures within which they function (Hofstede, 2000).

In both personal and professional spheres, Africans have a more communal way of doing things and exhibit a strong preference for joint problem solving. Whereas most Westerners are oriented toward competition and higher profits, Africans are oriented toward cooperation and building long-term relationships. For example, in African firms, new clients, like new employees, represent new relationships. Each new relationship represents an extension of that firm's commercial reach, and thus its economic security. When Americans expand their business, they promote economic security by seeking new sources of long-term profit. When Africans expand their business, they seek new long-term relationships.

In Africa, wealth is counted not only in currency, but in the number of people to whom you are closely linked. The idea is that in times of need there is reliability within your social network—that within networks, members will aid one another on request (Fadiman, 1994).

Where Management Techniques Differ: Performance Reviews

Employee evaluations are a specific area where differences in cultural values have a deep impact on management styles. It is useful to examine the performance evaluation, ubiquitous in Western businesses, to illustrate the differing cultural assumptions in American and African business culture.

In the United States, an individualistic society, performance reviews are periodic, one-on-one interviews, where

Table 2

Collectivism vs. Individualism

African Culture: Collectivism	Western Culture: Individualism
Cooperation, collaboration, and interdependence	Individual rights (privacy), independence
Concern for group interests	Self-interest
Conformity	Self-actualization, self-realization, self-government, and freedom
Personal achievement underplayed (in favor of group achievement)	Motivation based on personal achievement
Cohesive groups, unquestioning loyalty, group consensus	Loose ties, strong private opinions, pursuit of individual goals
Harmony, maintaining social relationships, subdued controversy	Honesty/truth, lack of social relationships, strong privacy rights, personal time, controversial argumentative speech
Mastery of skills, training	Personal challenge, material rewards
Use shame to achieve behavioral goals	Use guilt to achieve behavioral goals
Older, wise, experienced leaders	Youth and action
Encourage teamwork, discourage individual competition	Competition among employees for recognition and reward

the work performance of a subordinate is openly examined and discussed between manager and employee. This process helps to identify an employee's strengths, weaknesses, and opportunities for improvement, as well as to manage career goals. The objective is to let managers and employees openly communicate—to share ideas, opinions, and information. In individualist countries, therefore, the ability to communicate "bad news" and conduct objective performance reviews with subordinates is considered a key skill for a successful manager.

But in collectivist cultures, such as those in sub-Saharan Africa, the expatriate manager has to bear in mind that discussing an employee's performance, weaknesses, shortcomings, or abilities openly with the employee is likely to cause embarrassment and clash head-on with the society's harmony norm. Moreover, this may be felt by the subordinate as an unacceptable loss of face.

African cultures have long endorsed more indirect styles of communication to protect the image of the other and promote trouble-free relationships. This show of concern for a team member continues to serve as a useful management tool in maintaining harmony and preserving significant social

relationships. Since contact with the employee is often through his or her family, African managers are expected to be more paternal and supportive (Booysen, 1999). Aware of their obligations to the community and to the extended family, the African manager will typically not resort to firing an employee, outright, for nonperformance. Socially and financially, the communal consequences may be far greater and longer-lasting than the act itself. This is especially true if the employee was hired based on family obligations (nepotism) or as a favor to a respected community member—an elder, senior political official, or anyone with whom the company has close ties (Fadiman, 1994).

Indeed, team members may go so far as to protect the nonperformer, when necessary, by sharing or dividing his or her responsibilities among themselves (Booysen, 1999). For these reasons, African societies will generally use more subtle, indirect ways of communicating feedback, such as through the withdrawal of a normal favor or verbally through a mutually trusted intermediary. Additionally, the use of shame—reminding the employee of his or her failure to uphold family honor—may be used as another way to guide employee behavior.

Pointer

As a rule, managers should reward teams and not individuals. An effective way to deal with performance evaluations in African collectivist societies is to direct all feedback to team performance rather than individual performance (Booysen, 1999).

High Power Distance vs. Low Power Distance

Power distance describes the degree to which large status differences exist among people in a society and the extent to which these differences in power are accepted. The *high power distance* characterizing African culture shapes the behavior of professionals, elders, subordinates, and youth in important ways. People of lower status show much higher deference toward those of authority or senior status than is typical in the West. High power distance creates a web of social expectation. Traditional upbringing instills from childhood the acceptance of absolute authority on the part of parents, teachers, bosses, or anyone seen as socially superior. Since age and experience are esteemed, it is often considered inappropriate to question or challenge a teacher, supervisor, or any member of the professional elite. This social custom reinforces conformity and carries over to the business world in distinctive ways.

Unlike the Western world, where young executives will openly question their way through the learning curve, young African executives will avoid questioning or even commenting on a decision of their superiors, even if they totally disagree with it. At the same time, most superiors will likely not accept such questioning from subordinates.

As all authority resides in the company's superior, there is very limited, if any, delegation of authority, particularly in smaller firms. Thus, delegation of responsibility normally takes the form of assignment of specific tasks, which are carried out in constant consultation with one's superior. This limits the young executive's responsibility to carrying out instructions. Contrary to young American executives, most African subordinates prefer this approach—especially during their early professional training—as it saves them from making errors and losing face.

job responsibilities. From a local viewpoint, the African may feel unacknowledged by the direct approach—and thus, purposely disregarded—before getting down to what he or she considers "secondary matters." Such an approach is viewed as a direct insult to the African. Take time to greet your colleague first.

American Businesses in Africa

Generally speaking, many businesses and expatriate managers fail on the global market by incorrectly assuming that their ways of conducting business will be easily adaptable the world over, and that issues like time consciousness, negotiation styles, and social formality are simple matters of common sense. However, studies show that roughly 25% of U.S. managers and an estimated 14% of British managers fail in their assignments abroad—notwithstanding their functional business expertise in marketing, accounting, finance, and other areas (Marx, 1999). Accounting for much of their failure is their inability to adapt to new cultural environments.

The question becomes, then, how does an American manager of an Africa-based firm learn to deal effectively across cultural lines? In developing a plan for market entry into Africa, it is good strategy to identify in advance what is culturally expected (Table 3). Conducting business in Africa is complex and tends to be a long process because traditional African culture is based on investing unlimited time in building long-term and mutually trusting relationships. In contemporary African society, this traditional principle is infused in business culture. But once relationships are established, business ties tend to be fruitful and long-lasting. When an American manager is dealing with business practices that differ greatly from those of the home culture, it is useful to consider two questions when designing business and communication strategies to deal effectively with African counterparts:

- Where are the gaps widest between the American cultural framework and that of Africa?
- Where does communication threaten to break down due to cultural differences?

Pointer

An American manager walks into an office and thinks nothing of saying point blank "I need this or that" to an African employee. In American society, this swift approach may be an honest attempt to not waste the other person's time, thereby getting straight to the point. The manager may wonder why the African employee is slow to respond and perhaps appears hostile even though providing assistance may be part of his

Pointer

In America, greetings are generally quite informal. Typically, this is not intended to show a lack of respect, but rather a manifestation of the American belief that everyone is equal. However, an American's easy-going approach can be mistaken as evidence that they do not consider either the interaction or the people they are dealing with to be important. In Africa, greetings are an essential aspect of local culture. Never ask anyone a

Table 3

Business Cultures: African vs. American[a]

African	American
Consensus-driven	Time-driven
Deference to seniority	Glorifies youth
Hierarchical	Individualism
Slow-paced	Fast-paced
Relationships based on rapport, trust, friendship	Relationships based on "bottom line," best deal, best service

[a]In the sub-Saharan region, South Africa may be the one exception here. Due to the country's complex amalgam of several cultures and subcultures, the dominant management practices are, for historical reasons, Western (Booysen, 1999).

Source: Booysen (1999); Fadiman (1994); Shonhiwa (2008).

question without first greeting him. Always start with "good morning," "good afternoon," or "hello" and then proceed. Launching straight into a request is considered rude, as is the failure to greet someone.

Two Corporate Cultures

Consensus-Driven vs. Time-Driven

Throughout Africa, consensus is crucial in decision making. In many African organizations, particularly smaller ones, the entire team must be brought on board and consulted on almost everything before a decision is made. The process can take *as long as required,* without a time limit, to reach decisions that satisfy everyone. This need for reaching consensus is one reason why it may appear so difficult to get things done. In African terms, reaching a decision through consensus has the advantage of taking into account all reasons for concern or disagreement, whereas the Western style of "majority rule" does not (Fadiman, 1994). Thus, the pace of business is much slower, and closing a deal, especially a first transaction, will likely require multiple meetings or trips. This custom of consultation, even though there is a great degree of hierarchy, is a key African value and is summarized in the Ghanaian proverb, "When a king has good counselors, his reign is peaceful."

Harmony Trumps Frankness

In African culture, saving face is highly valued. Direct and frank communication is not the norm in most parts of the sub-Saharan region. Every action and every response is conditioned by the need to avoid offending or hurting the feelings of others. To avoid causing problems, Africans will often use metaphors, analogies, and stories to make a point. Moreover, they may attempt to qualify what they say so that the message is delivered with sensitivity. In general, Africans are uncomfortable with blunt statements. This often leads to evasive replies, incomplete answers, and "white lies." To an American executive trained to interact with directness, openness, and, above all, honesty in business dealings, this seeming lack of transparency can be disconcerting and problematic. Therefore, it is important for the American manager of an Africa-based firm to convey to local subordinates that admitting to a mistake will not cause them to lose face in the eyes of the American boss. Rather, they are more likely to lose that respect and trust by dodging questions and being found out later. Furthermore, American managers may wish to moderate their delivery style and read between the lines to discern what is really being said.

Understanding the African principle of maintaining harmony at almost any cost in interpersonal relationships will serve the Western executive well. An American must understand the degree to which Africans will resist opening up without first being personally close. If the relationship is intimate, the communication style will become more direct. But for newly established and more formal relationships, the use of tact and diplomacy will be of utmost importance—particularly in getting at the truth. Because Africans, generally, are harmony-seeking, many will avoid saying negative things to maintain harmony and save the embarrassment and humiliation of others. In addition, Africans will often not say things as they are, and it is generally accepted that one does not "have" to say everything. The right approach will cement a mutually trusting relationship and avoid alienating African subordinates.

Pointer

American managers should resist outright criticisms. An African subordinate is very likely aware of a mistake, but expressing it explicitly creates shame and is likely to make them withdraw in embarrassment. Rather, American executives may consider turning the tables by admitting to a mistake of their own, thereby showing vulnerability, as this will model the human side of the executive as well as the desired behavior. Additionally, in order to balance the many situations that may require criticisms or corrective behavior, superiors must find reasons to praise subordinates. Praise in African culture, even for small tasks, is highly motivating.

In Conversation, Dissent May Imply Disrespect

One of the most common frustrations American executives experience lies in the question: *"Why do I sometimes get the answer 'yes,' when they really mean 'no'?"* In African business settings, a show of dissent can be interpreted as a show of disrespect. The hierarchical nature of business culture tends to inhibit subordinates from openly disagreeing, challenging the status quo, speaking one's mind, criticizing ideas, giving feedback, and reporting problems. This is especially true when a young executive is facing a superior or a much older person. Thus, people acquiesce to a request, even though they know they won't be able to fulfill it. In a collectivist society, consensus and cooperation are important elements in promoting and maintaining harmony. To avoid disturbing harmony, Africans will often give a positive answer and be reluctant to refuse a request. In African business culture, this is part of an innate sense of loyalty, employee obedience, and courteous and formal behavior.

Pointer

- A question such as "Is this a problem you think you can fix?" will likely be answered "yes," since this is the answer your African host may think will keep you happy—whether true or not. So, avoid "yes" or "no" questions and inquire, through their own explanations, what they find feasible. The key to getting a genuine understanding of your African hosts and their vision is to allow them to do most of the talking.
- Pay special attention to how questions are phrased. Ask open-ended questions—again, those that avoid yes or no answers. For instance, "What do you think the problem is and how do you think it can be fixed?" Then ask "why?" This will aid in getting to the real reasons behind the issue.

- Get all agreements in writing. A verbal "yes" may have been given out of politeness and may not be considered binding. "Maybe" or "we will see" generally means no.

The African practice of yielding to the will of a senior person out of courteous respect can be difficult for the Western businessperson to deal with, as it often stifles progress. In African business settings, exceptionally talented youth often are not taken seriously because youth may be viewed as lacking in business wisdom and knowledge, especially when pitted against less competent seniors. Being aware of this ahead of time will help balance a manager's interactions with all members of the team.

Quality-Oriented, Not Quantity-Oriented

This is an important distinction. Quantity-oriented Americans measure success based on bottom-line figures, which allows an impartial, objective point of view: *How much? How many? What rate? What volume?* These are measurable metrics based on finite terms. In contrast, Africans use a more subjective, quality-oriented approach, which cannot be measured and is usually based on personal experience. This criterion requires a more diffuse and less easily measurable metric: *How will this improve our organizational value? How original is the product? How well is the work performed? How effective is the product?*

Pointer

Many Americans focus on product presentation from the moment they arrive. Their interest lies in closing "the deal" as quickly as possible. Africans, on the other hand, strongly believe that ritual, such as long conversations before business (inquiring about family, health, and personal interests that give further insight to your inner self), nurtures contact and builds trust between teams. As you wait for response to your proposal, return to relationship building. Take the time to market yourself.

Family Ties, Not Organizational Charts, Are the Ties That Bind

In many family-owned businesses, hiring relatives is a common practice. In the extended family firm, the hiring process is based on nepotism (showing favoritism to family members or friends), and succession is viewed as an important factor, and quite unlike American succession planning. Americans tend to hire on the basis of merit (Fadiman, 1994). Thus, company interactions in the African firm are often based on family obligations, rather than the Western commercial supervisor/subordinate relationships. But beyond family, nepotism transcends blood ties to encompass loyal friends and important allies, such as members of other large family firms.

Considering the central role family relationships play in African life, it is unlikely that this traditional value will change anytime soon. For the African, family relationships come first, and foreign executives who expect to be successful in this part of the world must accept and understand this priority. This includes taking their employees' family concerns seriously, listening carefully, and expressing interest and concern about their employees' families.

Pointer

In general, the foreign executive should be alert to the cultural influences family ties will likely have on employee behavior. Effort toward this style of leadership will be reciprocated with long-term employee trust, commitment, and loyalty.

Negotiations and Concessions

In English-speaking African businesses, the hierarchy is generally as follows: the managing director (CEO in the United States), the deputy (corporate vice president to U.S. executives), the divisional officers, the deputy directors, and, finally, the managers. When negotiating with a large company, the final decision maker may not be in the initial meetings. This allows African negotiators to use the top executive as a bargaining tool. Since the top executive did not actively participate in the negotiations, the negotiators may use this person to make concessions later, if necessary. This does not mean one should not negotiate with the original company representatives, but being aware of this tactic makes it possible to anticipate last-minute concessions. It is helpful to clarify decision-making authority early on in negotiations, when possible.

Relationships Precede the Bottom line

In the United States, business relationships are formed between companies based on the "bottom line." In contrast, business in Africa is about friends and colleagues— not solely work-related matters. Personal relations take precedence over business. In order to be successful, it is vital to establish good, personal relationships based on mutual trust and benefit. Africans spend a significant amount of time fostering and developing personal contacts. Thus, time should be allocated for this process, particularly during the first meeting, which is frequently used to simply establish rapport and build trust. Wait patiently for meetings to move beyond preliminary tea

and small talk. Once good, solid relations have been recognized between parties, continuous reinforcement and maintenance is vital. It is not uncommon for Africans to prefer to do mediocre business with a friend than superb business with a stranger.

Pointers

- Since personal relationships are far more important than corporate ones, frequent changes in your company or organization representative can result in setbacks. Each time your company changes its representative, you will virtually be starting from scratch. A new relationship must be built up before business can proceed.
- Your goal is not to market your product but yourself. Take time to nurture a relationship. Show sincerity in your desire to develop rapport and build long-lasting professional friendships. This effort sends symbolic signals that you care for those with whom you hope to deal.
- The exchange of business cards is helpful for initiating introductions. Africans prefer to know the organizational level of the person they are dealing with because of the hierarchical nature of African business culture. It is important to emphasize your title so that the correct authority, status, and rank are established from the beginning.

Source: © 2009 Wiley Periodicals, Inc.

Conclusion

Overall, the ability to recognize, respect, and effectively manage cultural differences in either social or commercial settings will be essential for all Western managers and corporations expecting to find significant returns among African economies. Given Africa's growth and steady integration into the global economy, Western nations can no longer afford to disregard Africa as a viable contributor to the global marketplace. But to succeed and lessen the likelihood of failure in African business environments, Western companies must embrace cross-cultural management skills as an integral part of a broad strategic focus.

ENDNOTES

1. "Africa" and "sub-Saharan Africa" are used interchangeably in this article.

2. Pronounced "oo-boon-too," which means "people are people through other people."

REFERENCES

Booysen, L. (1999). Cultural differences between African black and white managers in South Africa. Retrieved February 20, 2009, from http://74.125.95.132/search?q=cache:B5ClEDxqqaMJ:www.unisa.ac.za/contents/faculties/sbl/PdfDocs/2.4.1.pdf

Fadiman, J. (1994). "Your son is my son"—Black African management principles: An overseas marketers guide. Paper presented at the Annual Eastern Michigan University Conference on Language and Communication for World Business and the Professions. ERIC Microfiche # ED373689.

Hofstede, G. (2000). Culture's consequences: Comparing values, behaviors, institutions, and organizations across nations (2nd ed.). Thousand Oaks, CA: Sage.

Lassiter, J. E. (1999). African culture and personality: Bad social science, effective social activism, or a call to reinvent ethnology? Retrieved March 7, 2008, from http://web.africa.ufl.edu/asq/v3/v3i2a1.htm

Marx, E. (1999). Breaking through culture shock. London: Nicholas Brealey Publishing.

Mbigi, L. (1995). Ubuntu: The spirit of African transformation management. Rosebank, South Africa: Knowledge Resources.

Mthembu, D. (1996). African values: Discovering the indigenous roots of management. Retrieved December 13, 2008, from http://www.barbaranussbaum.com/Book_Sawubona AfricaC11.htm

Shonhiwa, S. (2008). The effective cross-cultural manager: A guide for business leaders in Africa. Cape Town: Zebra Books.

Trompenaars, F., & Hampden-Turner, C. (1998). Riding the waves of culture: Understanding diversity in global business (2nd ed.). New York: McGraw-Hill.

Watson, J. (2007). Africa's mobile explosion. Retrieved December 12, 2008, from http://globaltechforum.wordpress.com/2007/05/19/ africas-mobile-explosion/

Zimmerman, B. (2008). Africa tourism: Growth and opportunity. Retrieved December 12, 2008, from http://www.nuwireinvestor.com/articles/africa-tourism-growth-and-opportunity-51519.aspx

SUBJECT INDEX

NAME INDEX

COMPANY INDEX